Houghton Mifflin Math

Sunshine State Edition

HOUGHTON MIFFLIN BOSTON

Weekly Reader® is a federally registered trademark of Weekly Reader Corp.

Education Place® is a registered trademark of Houghton Mifflin Company.

Printed in the U.S.A.

ISBN-13: 978-0-618-59095-7
ISBN-10: 0-618-59095-1

23456789-DW-09 08 07 06

Program Authors and Consultants

Authors

Dr. Carole Greenes

Professor of Mathematics Education

Boston University
Boston, MA

Dr. Matt Larson

Curriculum Specialist for Mathematics

Lincoln Public Schools
Lincoln, NE

Dr. Miriam A. Leiva

Distinguished Professor of Mathematics Emerita

University of North Carolina
Charlotte, NC

Dr. Jean M. Shaw

Professor Emerita of Curriculum and Instruction

University of Mississippi
Oxford, MS

Dr. Lee Stiff

Professor of Mathematics Education

North Carolina State University
Raleigh, NC

Dr. Bruce R. Vogeli

Clifford Brewster Upton Professor of Mathematics

Teachers College, Columbia University
New York, NY

Dr. Karol Yeatts

Associate Professor

Barry University
Miami, FL

Consultants

Strategic Consultant

Dr. Liping Ma

Senior Scholar

Carnegie Foundation for the Advancement of Teaching
Palo Alto, CA

Language and Vocabulary Consultant

Dr. David Chard

Professor of Reading

University of Oregon
Eugene, OR

Blended Usage Advisor

Houghton Mifflin Math and Math Expressions

Dr. Matt Larson

Curriculum Specialist for Mathematics

Lincoln Public Schools
Lincoln, NE

Reviewers

Grade K

Hilda Kendrick
W E Wilson
Elementary School
Jefferson, IN

Debby Nagel
Assumption
Elementary School
Cincinnati, OH

Jen Payet
Lake Ave. Elementary School
Saratoga Springs, NY

Karen Sue Hinton
Washington Elementary
School
Ponca City, OK

Grade 1

Karen Wood
Clay Elementary School
Clay, AL

Paula Rowland
Bixby North Elementary
School
Bixby, OK

Stephanie McDaniel
B. Everett Jordan
Elementary School
Graham, NC

Juan Melgar
Lowrie Elementary School
Elgin, IL

Sharon O'Brien
Echo Mountain School
Phoenix, AZ

Grade 2

Sally Bales
Akron Elementary School
Akron, IN

Rose Marie Bruno
Mawbey Street Elementary
School
Woodbridge, NJ

Kiesha Doster
Berry Elementary School
Detroit, MI

Marci Galazkiewicz
North Elementary School
Waukegan, IL

Ana Gaspar
Lowrie Elementary School
Elgin, IL

Elana Heinoren
Beechfield Elementary
School
Baltimore, MD

Kim Terry
Woodland Elementary School
West
Gages Lake, IL

Megan Burton
Valley Elementary School
Pelham, AL

Kristy Ford
Eisenhower Elementary
School
Norman, OK

Grade 3

Jenny Chang
North Elementary School
Waukegan, IL

Patricia Heintz
Harry T. Stewart
Elementary School
Corona, NY

Shannon Hopper
White Lick Elementary School
Brownsburg, IN

Allison White
Kingsley Elementary School
Naperville, IL

Amy Simpson
Broadmoore Elementary
School
Moore, OK

Reviewers

Grade 4

Barbara O'Hanlon
Maurice & Everett Haines Elementary School
Medford, NJ

Connie Rapp
Oakland Elementary School
Bloomington, IL

Pam Rettig
Solheim Elementary School
Bismarck, ND

Tracy Smith
Blanche Kelso Bruce Academy
Detroit, MI

Brenda Hancock
Clay Elementary School
Clay, AL

Karen Scroggins
Rock Quarry Elementary School
Tuscaloosa, AL

Lynn Fox
Kendall-Whittier Elementary School
Tulsa, OK

Grade 5

Jim Archer
Maplewood Elementary School
Indianapolis, IN

Maggie Dunning
Horizon Elementary School
Hanover Park, IL

Mike Intoccia
McNichols Plaza
Scranton, PA

Jennifer LaBelle
Washington Elementary School
Waukegan, IL

Anne McDonald
St. Luke The Evangelist School
Glenside, PA

Ellen O'Rourke
Bower Elementary School
Warrenville, IL

Gary Smith
Thomas H. Ford Elementary School
Reading, PA

Linda Carlson
Van Buren Elementary School
Oklahoma City, OK

Grade 6

Robin Akers
Sonoran Sky Elementary School
Scottsdale, AZ

Ellen Greenman
Daniel Webster Middle School
Waukegan, IL

Angela McCray
Abbott Middle School
West Bloomfield, MI

Mary Popovich
Horizon Elementary School
Hanover Park, IL

Debbie Taylor
Sonoran Sky Elementary School
Scottsdale, AZ

Across Grades

Jacqueline Lampley
Hewitt Elementary School
Trussville, AL

Rose Smith
Five Points Elementary School
Orrville, AL

Winnie Tepper
Morgan County Schools
Decatur, AL

Place Value/Addition and Subtraction

1 Place Value of Whole Numbers and Decimals

Algebra Indicates lessons that include algebra instruction.

2 Add and Subtract Whole Numbers

FINISHING THE UNIT

Unit 1
Literature
Connection
he Most Amazing Sights in Nature
pages 638–639

(WR) Indicates WEEKLY WR READER eduplace.com/map

Multiplication, Division, and Algebra

Algebra Indicates lessons that include algebra instruction.

5 Divide by Two-Digit Numbers

FINISHING THE UNIT

Unit 2
Literature
Connection
Ready for Anything
page 640

WR Indicates WEEKLY WR READER eduplace.com/map

Measurement/Data and Graphing

Algebra Indicates lessons that include algebra instruction.

8 Data and Statistics

FINISHING THE UNIT

Unit 3 Literature Connection *Ships of the Desert* page 641

WR Indicates WEEKLY WR READER eduplace.com/map

Addition and Subtraction of Fractions and Decimals

9 Number Theory and Fraction Concepts

10 Add and Subtract Fractions

Algebra Indicates lessons that include algebra instruction.

11 Add and Subtract Decimals

FINISHING THE UNIT

Unit 4
Literature Connection
The Fruitomatic
pages 642–643

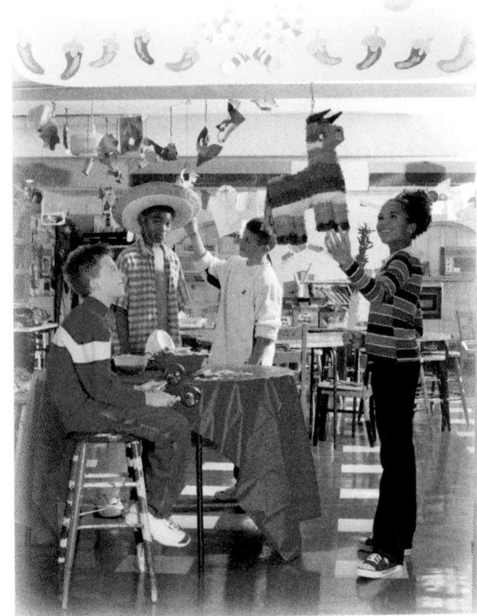

WR Indicates WEEKLY WR READER eduplace.com/map

UNIT 5 Multiplication and Division of Fractions and Decimals

Multiplication and Division of Fractions and Decimals

Algebra Indicates lessons that include algebra instruction.

14 Divide Decimals

FINISHING THE UNIT

Unit 5
Literature Connection
The World's Largest Trees
pages 644–645

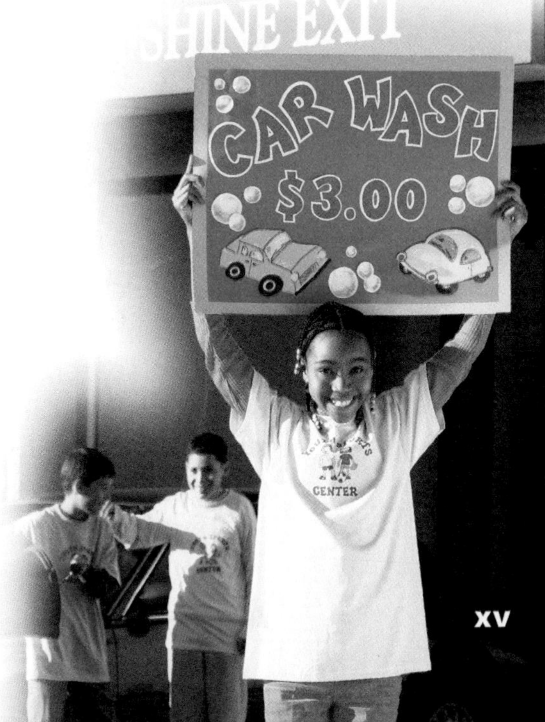

WR Indicates WEEKLY WR READER eduplace.com/map

Geometry and Measurement

15 Plane Figures and Geometric Concepts

16 Perimeter, Area, and Circumference

Algebra Indicates lessons that include algebra instruction.

17 Solid Figures, Surface Area, and Volume

FINISHING THE UNIT

Unit 6
Literature Connection
No Place to Go
page 646

WR Indicates WEEKLY WR READER eduplace.com/map

Ratio, Proportion, Percent, and Probability

Algebra Indicates lessons that include algebra instruction.

20 Probability

FINISHING THE UNIT

Unit 7
Literature Connection
Numbers
page 647

WR Indicates WEEKLY WR READER eduplace.com/map

Algebra, Integers, and Coordinate Graphing

21 Equations and Functions

22 Integers

Algebra Indicates lessons that include algebra instruction.

23 Coordinate Graphing

FINISHING THE UNIT

Unit 8
Literature Connection
Treasure Hunt
pages 648–649

STUDENT RESOURCES

 Indicates 

Welcome!

Scientists, athletes, artists, and health care workers all use math every day—and you will too. This year in math you'll learn about numbers, patterns, shapes, and different ways to measure. You'll use the mathematics you know to solve problems and describe objects and patterns you see. You can get started by finding out about yourself as a mathematician and about the other students in your class.

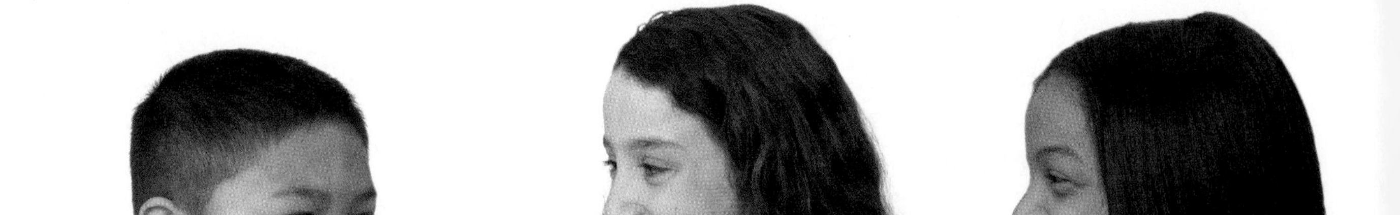

Activity

Real Life Connection

Collecting Data

About Me

Write your math autobiography by answering these questions. You can write about other experiences as well, as long as they tell about you as a math student.

- What do you like best about math class?
- What are you good at in math class?
- How do you use math outside of math class?
- How do you think you might use mathematics in the future?

About My Class

Many of your classmates may like the same things in math that you like. Other classmates may like totally different things.

- Think of one topic you'd like to know your classmates' opinions about.
- Write a survey question for your topic.
- Conduct your survey among your classmates.
- Make a line or bar graph to show your results.
- Write a paragraph, using words and numbers to describe your results. Include predictions about your survey results if you surveyed 100 students.

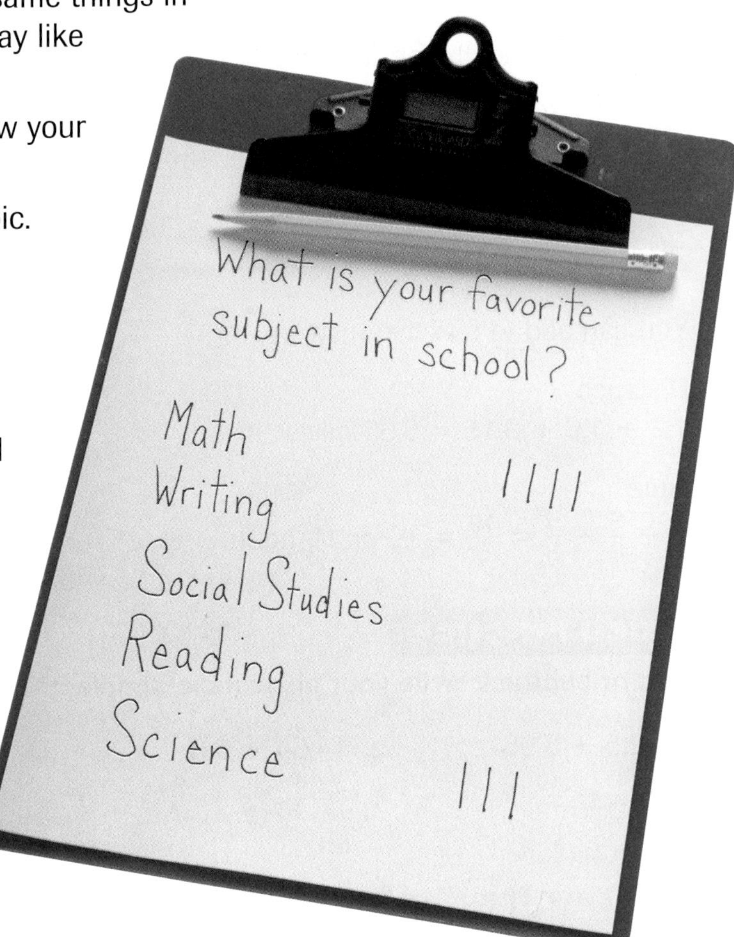

What is your favorite subject in school?
Math
Writing ||||
Social Studies
Reading
Science
|||

Back to School
Lesson

Problem Solving and Numbers

Objective Review basic number and problem solving skills.

Review and Remember

You have worked before with whole numbers, decimals, and fractions. You can use the math you already know to find information about a lot of things.

Josh, Micki, and Jana walked in a walkathon for charity. To raise money, they asked friends and family to pledge an amount of money for each mile they walked.

Josh recorded his times as he completed the walkathon. How far has he walked? How many hours has he walked?

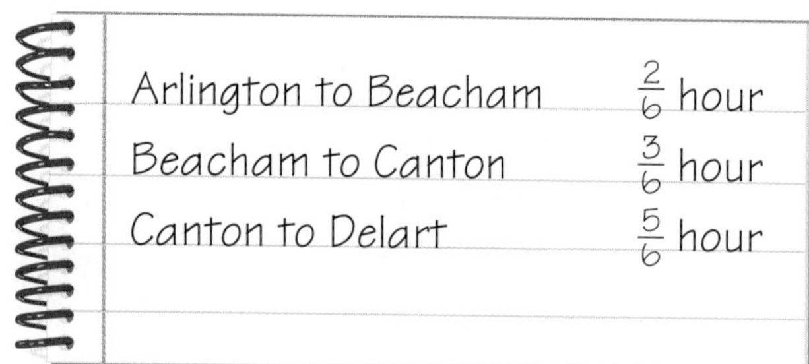

Arlington to Beacham 2/6 hour
Beacham to Canton 3/6 hour
Canton to Delart 5/6 hour

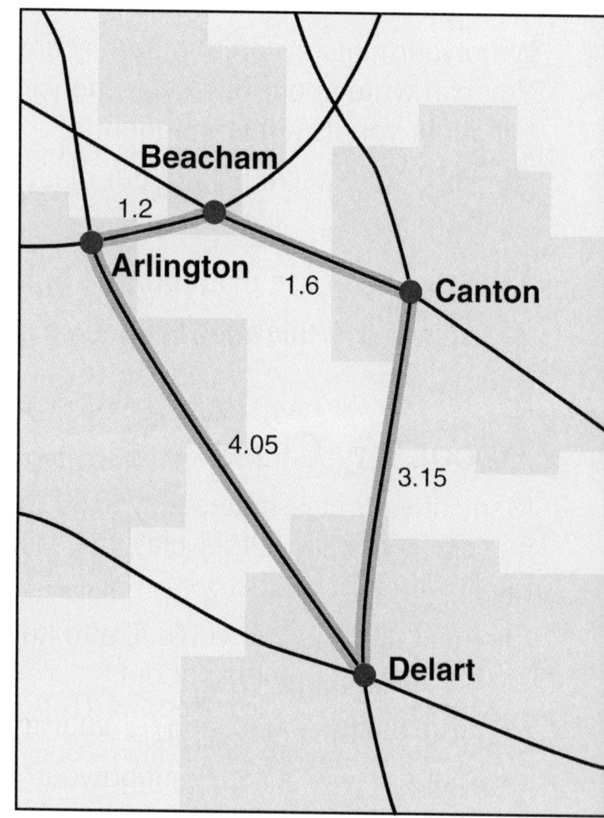

You can add to find the answers.

Distance
$1.2 + 1.6 + 3.15 = 5.95$ miles

Time
$\frac{2}{6} + \frac{3}{6} + \frac{5}{6} = \frac{10}{6} = 1\frac{4}{6}$ or $1\frac{2}{3}$ hours

Guided Practice

Add or subtract. Write your answers in simplest form.

1. $2.5 + 5.95$

2. $14.54 - 6.3$

3. $\frac{11}{12} - \frac{3}{12}$

4. $\frac{7}{10} + \frac{1}{10} + \frac{3}{10}$

Ask Yourself
- Did I align the decimal points?
- Are my answers reasonable?

Explain Your Thinking ▶ How do you know whether a fraction or mixed number is in simplest form?

Practice and Problem Solving

Add or subtract. Write each answer in simplest form.

5. 9.45 − 3.46

6. 5.25 + 4.53 + 2.4 + 0.32

7. 100.3 − 17.67

8. $\frac{5}{6} + \frac{4}{6}$

9. $\frac{9}{10} - \frac{7}{10}$

10. $\frac{3}{8} + \frac{1}{8} + \frac{7}{8} + \frac{5}{8}$

You have learned many problem-solving strategies. Solve each problem. Explain which strategy you used.

11. Look at the map on the previous page. What is the distance of the entire walkathon? How much farther does Josh have to walk?

12. Josh completed the last section in $1\frac{1}{3}$ hours. How long did he take to walk the entire route?

13. Micki and Jana ran for part of the route. Micki ran $\frac{3}{8}$ mile and Jana ran $\frac{5}{8}$ mile. Who ran farther? How much farther?

14. Josh and Jana completed the 10-mile walkathon. Micki had time to walk only 4.75 miles. Which sections of the route did she walk?

15. **Multistep** Josh's mother pledged $2.00 a mile. Jana's uncle pledged $1.50 a mile. How much did they give for Jana's and Josh's walk?

16. **Create and Solve** Write and solve a word problem using the information from the map on page B2. Exchange with a partner.

You Choose

Strategy
- Guess and Check
- Solve a Simpler Problem
- Work Backward
- Write an Equation

Computation Method
- Mental Math
- Estimation
- Paper and Pencil
- Calculator

Mixed Review and Test Prep

Open Response

Multiply or divide. (Grade 4)

17. 14 × 3

18. 27 × 200

19. 98 ÷ 7

20. 2,064 ÷ 2

Multiple Choice

21. Robert ate $\frac{1}{4}$ of the pizza and his brother ate $\frac{1}{4}$. How much was left for their mother? (Grade 4)

A $\frac{1}{4}$ **B** $\frac{1}{2}$ **C** 0 **D** $\frac{2}{8}$

Measurement

Objective Review basic measurement skills needed to start fifth grade.

Materials
12-inch ruler
yardstick

Work Together

You can use math to describe the size of your classroom. (With your teacher, you may decide to describe the size of a smaller, rectangular section of the room.) First, review how to measure length to the nearest foot.

0 1 2 3 4 5 6 7 8 9 10 11 12
inches

0 1 2 3 4 5 6 7 8 9 10 11 12 13 14 15 16 17 18 19 20 21 22 23 24 25 26 27 28 29 30 31 32 33 34 35 36
yardstick

Work with a partner. First, make a chart like this one to record your work.

	My Estimate	Measurement
Length		
Width		
Area		

STEP 1 Estimate the length and width of your classroom in feet. Record your estimate.

STEP 2 Decide whether you will use a yardstick or ruler to measure your classroom. Measure and record the length and width of the room. Round each measurement to the nearest foot.
- How close are your measurements to your estimates?

STEP 3 Estimate the area of your classroom. Then use your measurements to find the area of the classroom.
- How do you find the area of a rectangle?
- How do you label area?
- How close was your estimate to the actual area of your classroom?

Back to School

On Your Own

4. Draw a sketch of your classroom. Use the measurements in your chart to label each side of your sketch.

5. Use your sketch and measurements to find the perimeter of your classroom.

Use centimeter grid paper for Problems 6–9.

6. Copy this rectangle on your paper. Find the perimeter and area of the rectangle.

7. Draw another rectangle with the same area but different length and width. Label the length, width, and perimeter.

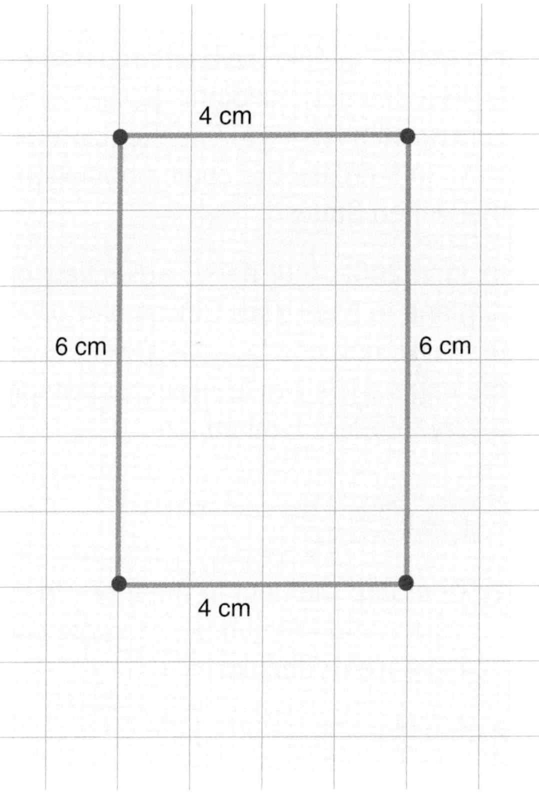

8. What is the area of a rectangle that has twice the length and twice the width of the rectangle at the right?

9. What is the perimeter of a rectangle with the same length and width as the rectangle in Problem 8?

Talk About It • Write About It

10. You are explaining to a younger student how to choose the best measuring instrument for a project. For which types of projects would you use a ruler? A yardstick?

11. Suppose the rectangles you drew for Problems 6 and 7 were models for the floors of two classrooms. Which rectangle do you think is a better shape for a classroom? Tell why you think so. Use the words *length*, *width*, *perimeter*, and *area* in your explanation.

Back to School
Problem Solving

Science Connection
Meet the Eagles

Eagles are large birds that usually build their nests near the tops of tall trees. Many eagle habitats have been destroyed, though, as people have cut down forests to build roads and buildings. Scientists and conservationists have been looking for ways to increase the eagle population in the United States.

In June 2002, four baby eagles flew on an airplane to New York City as part of a brave experiment. Scientists were hoping the eagle pairs would nest and lay eggs in a very different habitat!

Try These

1. Compare the data in the table. In the 1990s, did the number of eagle pairs increase or decrease?

2. Make a line graph of the data, using a grid like this one.

Eagle Pairs in the United States

Year	Number of Eagle Pairs
1990	3,035
1993	4,015
1996	5,094
1999	6,104

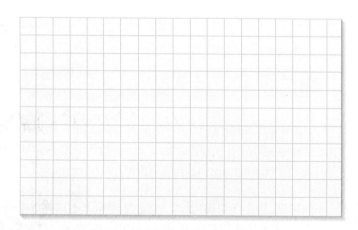

3. When did the number of eagle pairs increase the most? The least?

UNIT 1

Place Value/ Addition and Subtraction

Reading Mathematics

Reviewing Vocabulary

Here are some math vocabulary words that you should know.

place value	the position of a digit in a number that determines the value of the digit
rounding	to find about how many or about how much by expressing a number to the nearest ten, hundred, thousand, and so on
sum	the answer in addition
difference	the answer in subtraction

Reading Words and Symbols

In mathematics, numbers and computation with numbers can be read and written in different ways.

All these statements represent the same number:

- One thousand, two hundred thirty-four
- $(1 \times 1{,}000) + (2 \times 100) + (3 \times 10) + (4 \times 1)$
- 1,234

Different ways to read and write addition:

- The *sum of* 4,385 and 1,729 *is* 6,114.
- 4,385 *plus* 1,729 *equals* 6,114.

Different ways to read and write subtraction:

- The *difference between* 6,025 and 574 *is* 5,451.
- 6,025 *minus* 574 *equals* 5,451.

Write each of the following in a different way.

1. two thousand, eight hundred ninety-six
2. The sum of 3,333 and 197 is 3,530.
3. 26,257
4. $2{,}463 - 1{,}087 = 1{,}376$

Reading Test Questions

Choose the correct answer for each.

5. Which number represents the sum of these sets of blocks?

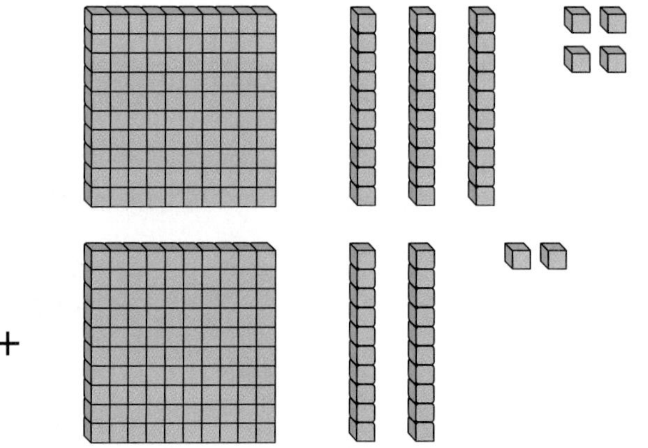

a. 652

b. 625

c. 265

d. 256

Represents means "stands for," or "shows," or "names."

6. Find the approximate difference between 3,867 and 2,124.

a. 5,991

b. 2,000

c. 1,743

d. 1,300

Approximate means to use estimation to find the answer.

7. Calculate the sum of 626 and 321.

a. 305

b. 947

c. 957

d. 1,057

To **calculate** you use a mathematical operation to find an exact answer.

Learning Vocabulary

Watch for these words in this unit. Write their definitions in your journal.

base

exponent

power of ten

variable

expression

evaluate

Education Place

At **eduplace.com/map** see *e*Glossary and *e*Games—Math Lingo.

Literature Connection

Read "The Most Amazing Sights in Nature" on pages 638–639. Then work with a partner to answer questions about the story.

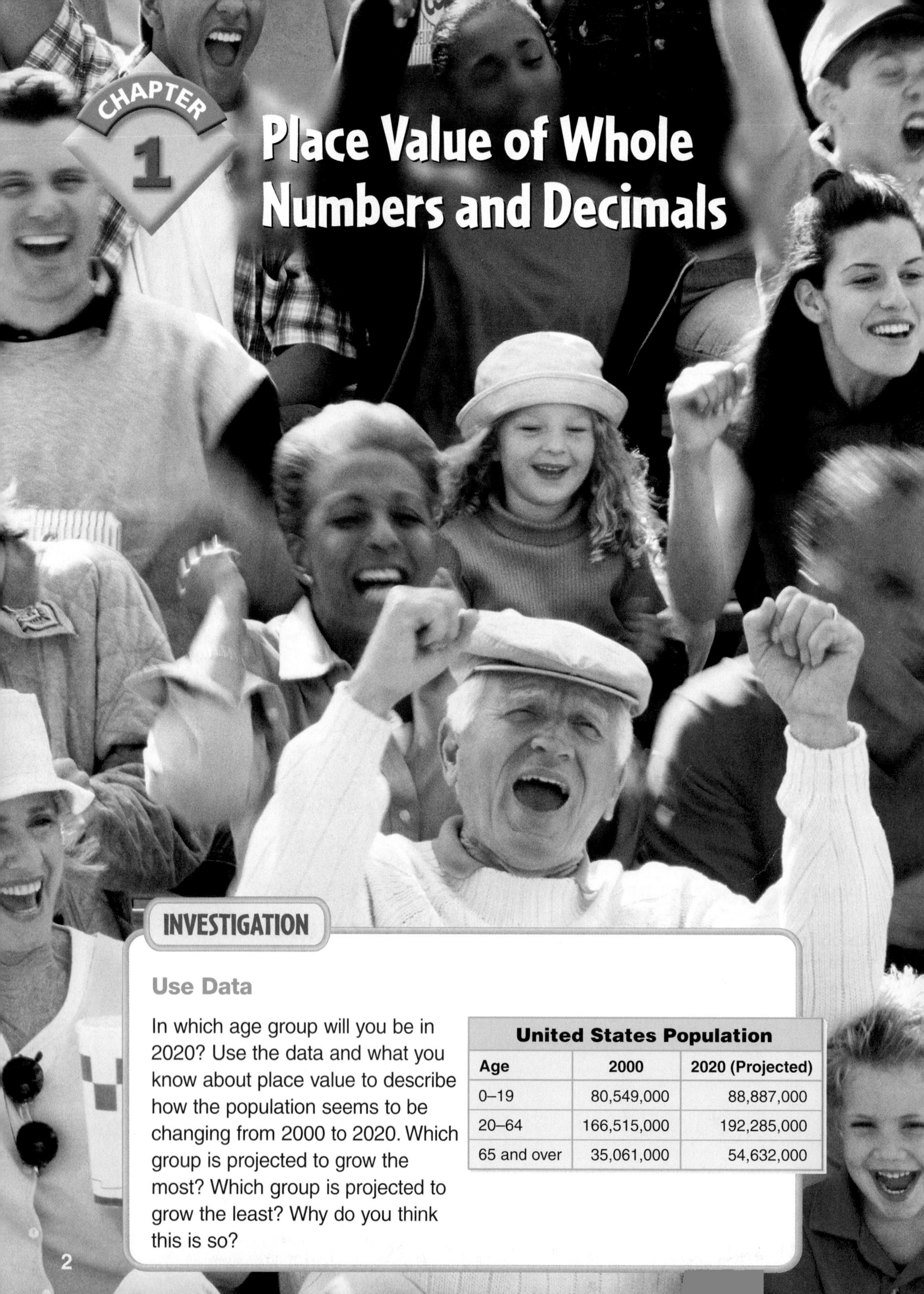

CHAPTER 1 Place Value of Whole Numbers and Decimals

INVESTIGATION

Use Data

In which age group will you be in 2020? Use the data and what you know about place value to describe how the population seems to be changing from 2000 to 2020. Which group is projected to grow the most? Which group is projected to grow the least? Why do you think this is so?

United States Population

Age	2000	2020 (Projected)
0–19	80,549,000	88,887,000
20–64	166,515,000	192,285,000
65 and over	35,061,000	54,632,000

Use What You Know

Use this page to review and remember what you need to know for this chapter.

VOCABULARY

Choose the best word to complete each sentence.

Vocabulary
- decimal
- expanded form
- period
- standard form
- whole number

1. In a number, each group of 3 digits separated by a comma is called a ____.
2. A ____ is a number with one or more digits to the right of a decimal point.
3. The ____ of "two hundred seventeen" is 217.

CONCEPTS AND SKILLS

Write the place value of the 7 in each number.

4. 374,928
5. 32,794
6. 87,312
7. 196,217

Write the number that is 10 more, 1,000 more, and 100,000 more.

8. 88,402
9. 197,651
10. 368,990
11. 71,161

Match each item in Column A with an item in Column B.

Column A	Column B
12. 50,892	a. $(5 \times 10{,}000) + (8 \times 100) + (9 \times 10) + (2 \times 1)$
13. 58,920	b. 58 hundredths
14. 5.89	c. five and eighty-nine hundredths
15. 0.58	d. 58 thousand, 920

Write the number that is greater.

16. 426,719
    426,900
17. 2.20
    0.87
18. 41,997
    41,987
19. 5.51
    5.49

Write About It

20. Why are the zeros important in 206,905?

Facts Practice, See page 658.

Lesson 1

Audio Tutor 1/1 Listen and Understand

Place Value Through Hundred Thousands

Objective Read and write numbers through hundred thousands in standard and expanded form.

Vocabulary
- place value
- period
- standard form
- expanded form

Learn About It

Saint Lucia is located in the Caribbean Sea. In 2001, the population of Saint Lucia was 158,178.

Look at the chart. The value of a digit in a number is determined by its place. For example, the first 8 from the left in 158,178 has a **place value** of 8,000. The second 8 has a place value of 8.

In a number, each group of 3 digits from right to left, called a **period**, is separated by a comma.

Thousands				Ones		
hundreds	tens	ones		hundreds	tens	ones
1	5	8	,	1	7	8

Different Ways to Read and Write Numbers

Way 1 You can use **standard form**.

158,178

Way 2 You can use **expanded form**.

$100,000 + 50,000 + 8,000 + 100 + 70 + 8$
$= (1 \times 100,000) + (5 \times 10,000)$
$+ (8 \times 1,000) + (1 \times 100) + (7 \times 10)$
$+ (8 \times 1)$

Way 3 You can use word form.

one hundred fifty-eight thousand,
one hundred seventy-eight

Way 4 You can use short word form.

158 thousand, 178

Guided Practice

Write each number in standard form.

1. 45 thousand, 79
2. three hundred sixty thousand, nine hundred eight
3. 400,000 + 8,000 + 600 + 20

Ask Yourself
- What is the greatest place value in the number?
- What is the value for each place?

Explain Your Thinking In Exercise 1, how did you decide in which places to write the digits 4 and 5?

Extra Help at eduplace.com/map

Practice and Problem Solving

Write each number in standard form.

4. 8 thousand, 752
5. 240 thousand, 357
6. 872 thousand, 12
7. one hundred forty thousand, four
8. eight hundred thirty thousand, three hundred four
9. 300,000 + 5,000 + 30 + 1
10. 900,000 + 10,000 + 4,000 + 60
11. 60,000 + 5
12. 800,000 + 800 + 8

Write the value of the underlined digit.

13. 2,<u>3</u>46
14. 3<u>4</u>,501
15. 2<u>5</u>7,824
16. <u>6</u>49,192

Data Use the table for Problems 17–21.

17. What was the population of Nauru in 2004? Write the word name for the number.
18. Write the population of San Marino in expanded form. Is this greater or less than 20,000? Use expanded form to explain your answer.
19. Suppose the population of Palau increases by 100. What would be the new population? Use place value to explain your answer.
20. Suppose the population of Palau decreased by 1,000. What would be the new population? Use place value to explain your answer.

Least Populated Countries in 2004

Name	Population
Vatican City	921
Tuvalu	11,468
Nauru	12,809
Palau	20,016
San Marino	28,503

21. **Create and Solve** Write your own problem involving information from the table. Solve your problem. Then have a partner solve the problem.

Mixed Review and Test Prep

Open Response

Multiply or divide. (Grade 4)

22. 7 × 8
23. 48 ÷ 8
24. 54 ÷ 9
25. 12 × 12
26. 6 × 7
27. 63 ÷ 9

Multiple Choice

28. What is the value of the digit 7 in 379,548? (Ch. 1, Lesson 1)

 A 70
 B 7,000
 C 70,000
 D 700,000

Extra Practice See page 25, Set A.

Lesson 2

More About Place Value

Objective Read and write numbers through hundred thousands with exponents.

Vocabulary
- base
- exponent
- power of ten

Learn About It

A short way to write the product $10 \times 10 \times 10 \times 10 \times 10$ is 10^5. To read 10^5, say "ten to the fifth power." The 10 is the base. The small raised 5 is the exponent. The **base** is the factor that is repeated in the product. The **exponent** shows the number of times the base is used as a factor.

Thousands			Ones		
hundreds	tens	ones	hundreds	tens	ones
100,000	10,000	1,000	100	10	1
10×10×10×10×10	10×10×10×10	10×10×10	10×10	10	1
10^5	10^4	10^3	10^2	10^1	10^0

Think

Note the pattern

$1{,}000 = 10^3$

$100 = 10^2$

$10 = 10^1$

$1 = 10^0$

The place-value chart above shows each place as a **power of ten**. You can use powers of ten to write numbers in expanded form.

Different Ways to Write 473,826

Way 1 You can use expanded form.

$(4 \times 100{,}000) + (7 \times 10{,}000) + (3 \times 1{,}000) + (8 \times 100) + (2 \times 10) + (6 \times 1)$

Way 2 You can use expanded form with exponents.

$(4 \times 10^5) + (7 \times 10^4) + (3 \times 10^3) + (8 \times 10^2) + (2 \times 10^1) + (6 \times 10^0)$

Other Examples

A. 2 as the Base

$2^4 = 2 \times 2 \times 2 \times 2$

Read: "two to the fourth power"

Standard form: 16

B. 6 as the Base

$6^3 = 6 \times 6 \times 6$

Read: "six to the third power"

Standard form: 216

Guided Practice

Ask Yourself

- What power of ten represents the greatest place value?

Use exponents to write each number in expanded form.

1. 47,052 **2.** 712,943 **3.** 823,930

Explain Your Thinking ▶ In Exercise 2, how did you decide how to represent the value of the digit 7 in expanded form?

Practice and Problem Solving

Use exponents to write each number in expanded form.

4. 6,507 **5.** 980,062 **6.** 107,914 **7.** 728,050 **8.** 43,207

Write each number in standard form.

9. $(7 \times 10^4) + (5 \times 10^3) + (3 \times 10^2) + (2 \times 10^1) + (8 \times 10^0)$

10. The base is five, and the exponent is two.

11.
$2^5 = 32$
$2^4 = 16$
$2^3 = 8$
$2^2 = 4$
$2^1 = \blacksquare$
$2^0 = \blacksquare$

12.
$3^5 = 243$
$3^4 = 81$
$3^3 = 27$
$3^2 = \blacksquare$
$3^1 = \blacksquare$
$3^0 = \blacksquare$

13.
$4^5 = 1{,}024$
$4^4 = 256$
$4^3 = 64$
$4^2 = \blacksquare$
$4^1 = \blacksquare$
$4^0 = \blacksquare$

14.
$5^5 = 3{,}125$
$5^4 = \blacksquare$
$5^3 = 125$
$5^2 = 25$
$5^1 = \blacksquare$
$5^0 = \blacksquare$

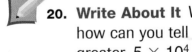

x Algebra • Equations **What is the value of *n* in each equation?**

15. $n = 6 \times 2^3$ **16.** $300 = n \times 10^2$ **17.** $2{,}000 = 2 \times 10^n$ **18.** $50{,}000 = 5 \times 10^n$

Solve.

19. What's Wrong? The paper shows Celine's work. What did Celine do wrong?

Celine

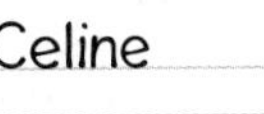

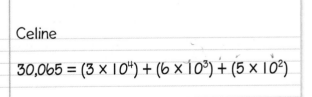

$30{,}065 = (3 \times 10^4) + (6 \times 10^3) + (5 \times 10^2)$

20. Write About It Without calculating, how can you tell which number is greater, 5×10^4 or 7×10^3?

Mixed Review and Test Prep

Open Response

Subtract. (Grade 4)

21. 16 − 9 **22.** 17 − 8 **23.** 15 − 7

24. Use exponents to write the number 406,561 in expanded form. (Ch. 1, Lesson 2)

Extra Practice See page 25, Set B.

Lesson 3

Place Value Through Hundred Billions

Objective Read and write numbers through hundred billions in standard and expanded forms.

Learn About It

In 2001, the population of China reached 1,273,111,290. What are some different ways to write this number?

Billions			Millions			Thousands			Ones		
hundreds	tens	ones	hundreds	tens	ones	hundreds	tens	ones	hundreds	tens	ones
0	0	1,	2	7	3,	1	1	1,	2	9	0

Different Ways to Read and Write Numbers

Way 1 You can use standard form.

1,273,111,290

Way 2 You can use expanded form.

$(1 \times 1{,}000{,}000{,}000) + (2 \times 100{,}000{,}000) + (7 \times 10{,}000{,}000) + (3 \times 1{,}000{,}000) + (1 \times 100{,}000) + (1 \times 10{,}000) + (1 \times 1{,}000) + (2 \times 100) + (9 \times 10)$

Way 3 You can use expanded form with exponents.

$(1 \times 10^9) + (2 \times 10^8) + (7 \times 10^7) + (3 \times 10^6) + (1 \times 10^5) + (1 \times 10^4) + (1 \times 10^3) + (2 \times 10^2) + (9 \times 10^1)$

Way 4 You can use word form.

one billion, two hundred seventy-three million, one hundred eleven thousand, two hundred ninety

Way 5 You can use the short word form.

1 billion, 273 million, 111 thousand, 290

Guided Practice

Write each number in standard form.

1. 8 million, 345 thousand, 752
2. one hundred nine million, three hundred forty-two
3. $(8 \times 10^{10}) + (3 \times 10^{8}) + (4 \times 10^{6}) + (6 \times 10^{5}) + (7 \times 10^{3})$

Ask Yourself

- What place comes before each comma?

Explain Your Thinking ▶ In Exercise 2, how did you decide in which place the digit 9 should be written?

Practice and Problem Solving

Write each number in standard form.

4. 24 million, 79 thousand, 129
5. 392 billion, 34 million, 25
6. three billion, fourteen million, five hundred eighty-nine
7. four hundred two billion, three million, one hundred seventeen
8. $(4 \times 10^{10}) + (6 \times 10^{8}) + (9 \times 10^{7}) + (6 \times 10^{4}) + (1 \times 10^{3}) + (2 \times 10^{0})$

Write the value of the underlined digit in short word form.

9. 45,<u>8</u>76,541
10. 2,<u>3</u>46,780,102
11. 4<u>5</u>6,073,969,208

Write each number in expanded form using exponents.

12. 78,000,000,001
13. 200,000,700
14. 19,600,100

Solve.

15. Russia has a land area of 17,075,400 square kilometers. The United States has a land area of 9 million square kilometers. Write each measurement in expanded form using exponents.
16. In 2000 the population of the United States was two hundred eighty-one million, four hundred twenty-one thousand, nine hundred six. Write that number in standard form.

Mixed Review and Test Prep

Open Response

Add or subtract. (Grade 4)

17. 99 − 96
18. 32 + 45
19. 57 − 32
20. 71 + 28
21. 12 + 23 + 34
22. 96 − 81

Multiple Choice

23. What is the value of the digit 4 in 12,648,067,905? (Ch. 1, Lesson 3)

   A 40,000
   B 400,000
   C 4,000,000
   D 40,000,000

Extra Practice See page 25, Set C.

Lesson 4

Audio Tutor 1/2 Listen and Understand

Compare, Order, and Round Whole Numbers

Objective Compare, order, and round whole numbers through hundred billions.

New York City, U.S.
16,640,000

Tokyo, Japan
26,444,000

Mexico City, Mexico
18,131,000

São Paulo, Brazil
17,755,000

Bombay (Mumbai), India
18,066,000

Learn About It

The map shows the populations of some of the world's largest metropolitan areas in the year 2000. Which metropolitan area had a greater population, Bombay, India or Mexico City, Mexico?

Compare 18,066,000 and 18,131,000.

STEP 1 Line up the numbers by place value.

18,066,000
18,131,000

STEP 2 Start from the left. Compare the digits until they are different.

18,066,000
18,131,000

18,131,000 $>$ 18,066,000

Solution: Mexico City, Mexico had the greater population.

Remember

= is read "is equal to"

$<$ is read "is less than"

$>$ is read "is greater than"

You can use the same method to order three or more numbers.

List the cities—New York City, Tokyo, and São Paulo—in order from greatest population to least population.

STEP 1 Line up the numbers by place value.

16,640,000
26,444,000
17,755,000

STEP 2 Start at the left. Compare digits.

16,640,000
26,444,000 2 $>$ 1
17,755,000

26,444,000 is the greatest number.

STEP 3 Continue comparing.

16,640,000 7 $>$ 6
17,755,000

17,755,000 $>$ 16,640,000

So, 26,444,000 $>$ 17,755,000 $>$ 16,640,000.

Solution: The cities, in order from greatest population to least population, are Tokyo, São Paulo, and New York City.

Round the population of Tokyo to the nearest million.

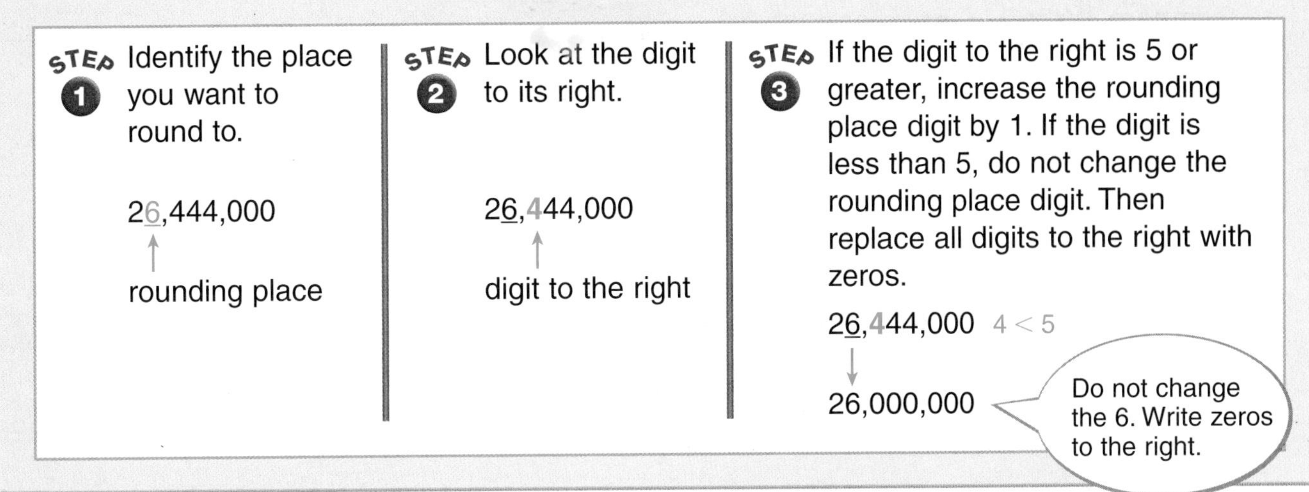

STEP 1 Identify the place you want to round to.
26,444,000
rounding place
STEP 2 Look at the digit to its right.
26,444,000
digit to the right
STEP 3 If the digit to the right is 5 or greater, increase the rounding place digit by 1. If the digit is less than 5, do not change the rounding place digit. Then replace all digits to the right with zeros.
26,444,000 4 < 5
26,000,000
Do not change the 6. Write zeros to the right.

Solution: 26,444,000 rounded to the nearest million is 26,000,000.

Guided Practice

Ask Yourself

- Are the numbers lined up by place value?
- Where are the digits different?
- What is the digit to the right of the place I am rounding to?

Compare. Write >, <, or = for each ●.

1. 25,431 ● 25,661
2. 4,569,102 ● 4,570,000
3. 73,000 ● 9,995
4. 37,329,410 ● 38,000,116

Order each set of numbers from greatest to least.

5. 43,055; 422,007; 42,007
6. 812,661; 82,811,121; 82,935,661

Round to the place indicated by the underlined digit.

7. <u>5</u>45
8. 78<u>3</u>,256
9. 2<u>4</u>,592,124
10. 674,12<u>9</u>,811

Explain Your Thinking ▶ Why is the digit in the hundreds place used to round a number to the nearest thousand?

Go On

Practice and Problem Solving

Compare. Write >, <, or = for each ●.

11. 1,652 ● 1,709 **12.** 38,459 ● 38,459 **13.** 9,302,124 ● 9,298,116

14. 164,275,808 ● 167,001,005 **15.** 90,456,292 ● 89,509,765

Order each set of numbers from greatest to least.

16. 8,714; 8,764; 8,734 **17.** 541,536; 511,394; 601,345

18. 3,906,211; 4,031,232; 4,029,306 **19.** 265,616,845; 99,678,784; 257,724,925

Round to the place indicated by the underlined digit.

20. 5,<u>2</u>61 **21.** 57<u>4</u>,238 **22.** 3,<u>4</u>89,112 **23.** 65<u>9</u>,324,721

Round each number.

24. 28,652 to the nearest thousand **25.** 624,314 to the nearest hundred thousand

26. 421,062,312 to the nearest million **27.** 385,781,521 to the nearest ten million

Write a number for the missing digit that will make the inequality true.

28. 17,7■5 > 17,786 **29.** 32■,494 < 324,210 **30.** 765,789 < 7■5,789

Data Use the table to solve Problems 31–34.

31. Which city is projected to have the greatest population in 2015? Which city will have the least population?

32. Arrange the cities in order from least population to greatest population based on the projected populations in 2015.

33. Which two cities will have populations that round to the same number when rounded to the nearest million?

34. In 2015, which city will have the closest population to 20,000,000? Explain your thinking.

Metropolitan Area	Projected Population for the Year 2015
Bombay	26,138,000
Mexico City	19,180,000
New York City	17,432,000
São Paulo	20,397,000
Tokyo	26,444,000

Extra Practice See page 25, Set D.

Game Activity

Digit Challenge

2 players

What you'll need • two copies of Learning Tool 6, one copy of Learning Tool 29 for each player

How to Play

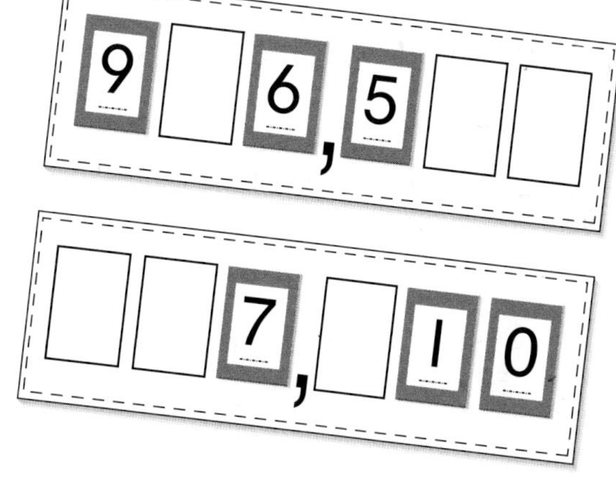

1. Cut out the cards and game board for each player. Shuffle all cards together and place them in a stack.
2. Each player draws a card and places it on his or her game board. Once placed, the card cannot be moved.
3. Repeat Step 2 until each player has placed 6 cards.The player with the greater number scores a point.

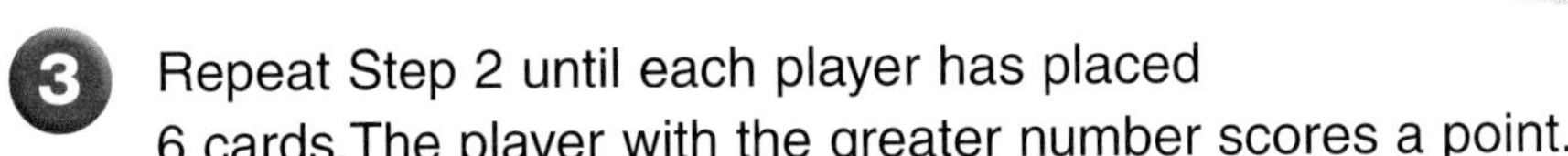

Repeat Steps 2–3. The first player to score a total of 10 points is the winner.

4. Return all cards to the deck and reshuffle.

Quick Check

Check your understanding of Lessons 1–4.

Write each number in standard form. (Lessons 1 and 3)

1. 96 thousand 18

2. 700,000 + 60,000 + 400 + 8

3. two hundred four billion, eight hundred seventy-nine thousand, sixty

Write each number in expanded form with exponents. (Lesson 2)

4. 5,956

5. 734,508

6. 95,096

Order each set of numbers from greatest to least. (Lesson 4)

7. 27,509; 27,590; 29,705

8. 324,678; 315,798; 324,778

Extra Practice at **eduplace.com/map**

Lesson 5

Place Value Through Thousandths

Vocabulary
decimal
decimal point

Objective Read and write decimals through thousandths.

Learn About It

A **decimal** is a number with one or more digits to the right of the **decimal point**. Decimals can be used to compare land areas of the world. The land area of Asia is 0.214 of the land area on Earth.

Express 0.214 in words.

Use the place-value chart to understand decimals.

The value of the digits to the right of the decimal point is less than 1.

Whole Numbers				Decimals		
hundreds	tens	ones		tenths	hundredths	thousandths
		0	.	2	1	4

← decimal point

The last digit after the decimal point tells how to name the decimal parts.

Standard form: 0.214

Word form: two hundred fourteen thousandths

Short word form: 214 thousandths

Another Example

Decimals Greater Than 1

Write 4.035 in word form.

four and thirty-five thousandths

Notice that the decimal point is indicated by the word "and."

Guided Practice

Write each in standard form.

1. five tenths
2. four and sixteen thousandths

Write each decimal in word form.

3. 2.7
4. 0.15
5. 0.094

Ask Yourself

- How can I use the word name to find the last place in the decimal?
- What word do I write for the decimal point?

Explain Your Thinking ▶ How does the value of the last digit help you read a decimal?

Practice and Problem Solving

Write each in standard form.

6. nine hundredths
7. one hundred thirty-eight thousandths
8. twenty-five thousandths
9. five and forty-six hundredths
10. eleven and seven tenths
11. seventy-nine thousandths
12. eighteen and nine thousandths
13. ten and twenty-four hundredths

Write each decimal in words.

14. 0.019
15. 0.3
16. 0.34
17. 25.4
18. 0.789
19. 4.306
20. 0.082
21. 3.17

Write the value of the underlined digit in words.

22. 5.7<u>7</u>
23. 6.<u>2</u>45
24. 7.8<u>8</u>
25. 8.37<u>4</u>
26. 8.10<u>9</u>
27. 4.<u>7</u>3
28. <u>3</u>.99
29. 0.2<u>0</u>4

Data **Use the graph for Problems 30–33.**

30. What part of the Earth's land area does North America cover? Write the decimal in words.
31. Which continent covers one hundred twenty-one thousandths of Earth's land area?
32. Which continent or region covers the smallest part of Earth's land area?
33. Which continents each cover more than two tenths of Earth's land area? Use a place-value chart to explain your answer.

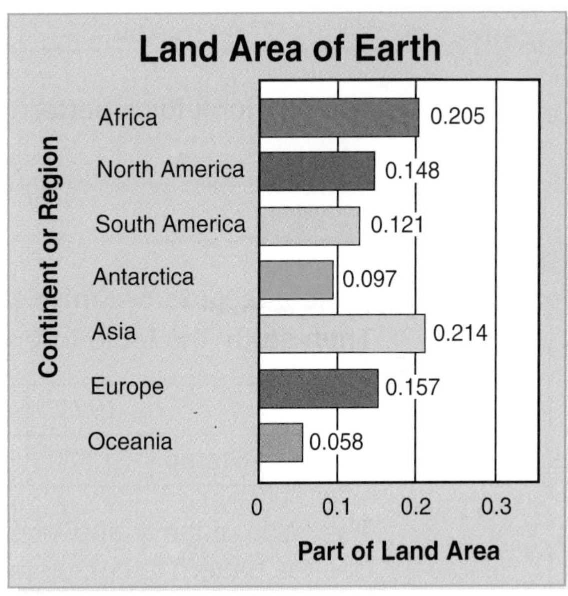

Mixed Review and Test Prep

Open Response

Multiply or divide. (Grade 4)

34. 7×11
35. $36 \div 4$
36. $16 \div 8$
37. 12×4

38. Write the decimal 30.068 in word form and in short word form. (Ch. 1, Lesson 5)

Extra Practice See page 25, Set E.

Lesson 6

Audio Tutor 1/3 Listen and Understand

Problem-Solving Strategy

Find a Pattern

Objective Look for a pattern to solve a problem.

Problem Postage stamps are collected around the world. Some rare stamps are worth over $100,000. In 1980, the 1¢ British Guiana stamp was sold for $935,000.

Lani collects stamps. In 1998, a particular stamp was worth $1,520. The value in 2000 was $1,620. The value in 2002 was $1,720. The value in 2004 was $1,820. If the trend continues, what is the value of the stamp likely to be in 2008?

UNDERSTAND

This is what you know:

- In 1998, a particular stamp was worth $1,520.
- The value in 2000 was $1,620.
- The value in 2002 was $1,720.
- The value in 2004 was $1,820.

PLAN

You can look for a pattern to solve the problem.

SOLVE

Make a table to organize the data.
Then study the table to find a pattern.

Year	1998	2000	2002	2004	2006	2008
Value of Stamp	$1,520	$1,620	$1,720	$1,820	?	?

The value of the stamp increases by $100 every two years.
Use the pattern to complete the table.

$1,820 + 100 = $1,920 $1,920 + 100 = $2,020

Solution: The value of the stamp in 2008 is likely to be $2,020.

LOOK BACK

Look back at the problem. How can I check the answer?

Guided Practice

Use the Ask Yourself questions to help you solve each problem.

1. The value of a rare stamp from Thailand was $130 in 1990, $150 in 1995, $170 in 2000, and $190 in 2005. Predict the value of the stamp in 2010.

2. Michelle writes the following series of numbers.

   0.014, 0.034, __?__, 0.074, 0.094

   What is the missing number in the pattern?

Hint Think about the numbers just before and just after the missing number.

Ask Yourself

- **UNDERSTAND** What facts do I know? Can I find a pattern?
- **PLAN** Did I describe the pattern?
- **SOLVE** Did I continue the pattern?
- **LOOK BACK** Did I solve the problem?

Independent Practice

Find a pattern to solve each problem.

3. People are bidding for a rare stamp from China. The first bid is $120,000. The next three bids are $150,000; $180,000; and $210,000. The seventh bid is the final bid. If the pattern continues, what is the final bid?

4. Carla writes the following series of numbers.

   0.496, 0.796, __?__, 1.396, 1.696

   What is the missing number in the pattern?

5. One city had a population of 18,649 in 1970, 18,446 in 1980, 18,233 in 1990, and 18,021 in 2000. Round each total to the nearest hundred. Then estimate the population of this city in 2010.

6. **Create and Solve** Work with a partner. Make up a pattern of 5 decimal numbers. Rewrite, leaving out one of the numbers in your pattern. Exchange patterns. Explain the patterns and find the missing number.

Go On

Mixed Problem Solving

Solve. Show your work.
Tell what strategy you used.

7. Peter has 7 United States coins worth 53¢. What are the 7 coins?

8. Eileen visits her family in Ireland every year. During one visit, she planted a 3-meter tree. The tree was 3.4 meters tall after one year, 3.8 meters tall after two years, and 4.2 meters tall after three years. How tall will the tree likely be after five years?

9. Kareem received $15 in change from a stamp dealer. The stamps he bought were $6, $8, and $21. How much money did Kareem give the stamp dealer?

You Choose

Strategy
- Find a Pattern
- Guess and Check
- Use Logical Reasoning
- Work Backward
- Write an Equation

Computation Method
- Mental Math
- Estimation
- Paper and Pencil
- Calculator

Data Use the graph to solve Problems 10–13.

The graph shows Blue Globe Air's round-trip airfares for trips between New York City and selected foreign cities.

10. Mr. Tanner goes to Egypt. Including his airfare from New York City to Cairo, Egypt, Mr. Tanner spends a total of $2,500 on his trip. How much does Mr. Tanner spend on expenses other than airfare?

11. Jose buys a round-trip ticket between New York City and Athens, Greece. Helen buys a round-trip ticket to a different city that costs the same amount. To which city is Helen flying?

12. Souvir buys a round-trip ticket between New York City and Bombay, India. Souvir pays $600 towards his ticket. His parents pay the rest. How much do his parents pay?

13. **What's Wrong?** Lisa estimates that round-trip tickets to each city shown on the graph would cost a total of about $5,000. Explain why Lisa's estimate is not reasonable.

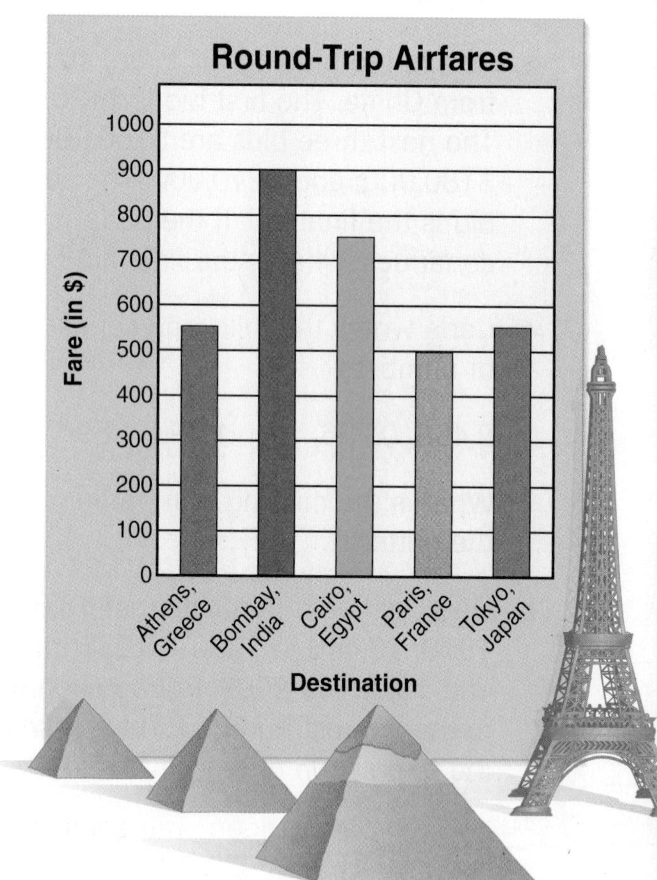

Problem Solving on Tests

Multiple Choice

Choose the letter of the correct answer. If a correct answer is not here, choose NH.

1. Nina bought 8 stamps and gave away 3 stamps. Then she bought 4 more stamps and sold 2 stamps. After buying 3 more stamps, Nina had 47 stamps. How many stamps did Nina start with?

   A 27 **C** 37

   B 32 **D** NH

   (Grade 4)

2. **Measurement** At a museum, a short film starts every 45 minutes. On Saturday the first film starts at 10:00 A.M. What time does the fifth movie start?

   F 10:45 A.M. **H** 1:00 P.M.

   G 12:00 P.M. **J** 1:45 P.M.

   (Grade 4)

Open Response

Solve each problem.

3. How many ▢ will balance △ △ ?

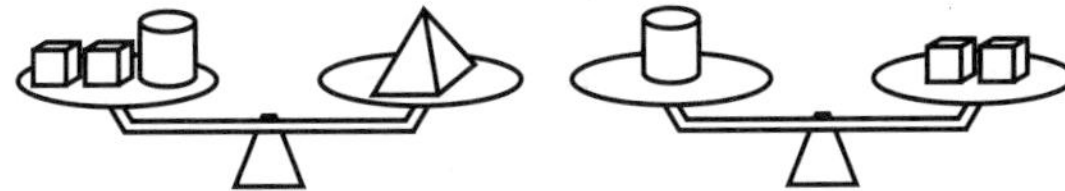

   Explain How can you use logical reasoning to solve the problem?

   (Grade 4)

4. The Drama Club voted to decide which play to produce. One fourth of the club voted for *The Music Man*. The club has 24 members. How many members voted for *The Music Man*?

   Represent Support your solution with a picture. (Grade 4)

Extended Response

5. You are the new head of a movie studio! Your first picture will cost $25,000,000. The director's salary must be less than the combined salaries of all of the actors. Costumes and scenery will cost more than the director's salary but less than the combined salaries of all the actors. You must keep $2,500,000 aside in case of emergencies. You must spend the entire $25,000,000.

   a Decide how much money the actors will make.

   b How much money will the director make?

   c How much will the costumes and scenery cost?

   d After you complete your budget, you learn that the actors want the total of their salaries to be twice the director's salary. Revise your budget to keep the actors happy.

   (Grade 4)

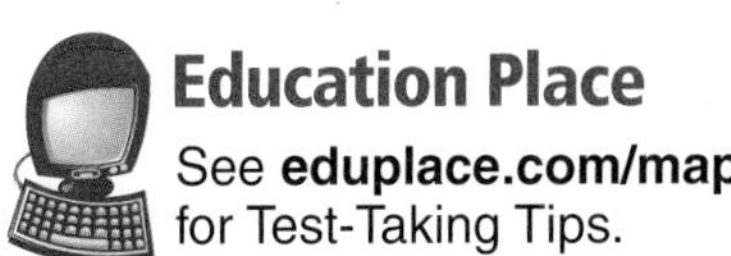

Education Place
See **eduplace.com/map** for Test-Taking Tips.

Lesson 7

Audio Tutor 1/4 Listen and Understand

Compare, Order, and Round Decimals

Objective Compare, order, and round decimals.

0.25

0.5

Learn About It

Which of the numbers at the right is greater?

Compare 0.5 and 0.25.

Different Ways to Compare 0.5 and 0.25

Way 1 You can use a number line.

0.5 is to the right of 0.25, so 0.5 > 0.25.

0.0 0.25 0.5 0.75 1.0

Way 2 You can compare digits.

STEP 1 Align the decimal points.

0.50
0.25

STEP 2 Start from the left. Compare the digits until they are different.

0.50
0.25 Since 5 > 2, 0.5 > 0.25.

Solution: 0.5 is greater than 0.25.

Order 4, 4.32, and 4.317 from greatest to least.

You can use what you know to order three or more decimals.

STEP 1 Align the decimal points. Write zeros if necessary.

4.000
4.320
4.317

STEP 2 Start from the left. Compare the digits.

4.000
4.320
4.317
0 < 3

4.000 is the least number.

STEP 3 Continue comparing.

4.320
4.317
2 > 1

4.320 > 4.317

So, 4.320 > 4.317 > 4.000.

Solution: Ordered from greatest to least, the numbers are 4.32, 4.317, 4.

Round 0.607 to the nearest hundredth.

Different Ways to Round 0.607 to the Nearest Hundredth

Way 1 You can use a number line.

0.607 is closer to 0.61 than to 0.60.

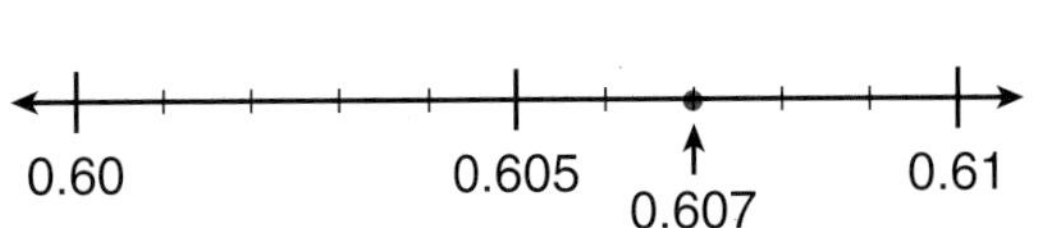

Way 2 You can use rules for rounding decimals.

STEP 1 Identify the place you want to round to.

$0.6\underline{0}7$

↑ rounding place

STEP 2 Look at the digit to its right.

$0.6\underline{0}7$

↑ digit to the right

STEP 3 If that digit is 5 or greater, increase the rounding-place digit by 1. If that digit is less than 5, do not change the rounding-place digit. Then drop all digits to the right.

$0.6\underline{0}7$

↓

0.61

7 > 5, so change 0 to 1.

Solution: 0.607 rounded to the nearest hundredth is 0.61.

Other Examples

A. Round to the Nearest Tenth

$0.\underline{4}18$

1 < 5 0.418 rounds to 0.4.

B. Round to the Nearest Whole Number

$\underline{2}.798$

7 is greater than 5. 2.798 rounds to 3.

Guided Practice

Ask Yourself

- Did I align the decimal points?
- Where are the digits different?
- What is the digit to the right of the rounding place?

Compare. Write >, <, or = for each ●.

1. 0.45 ● 0.88 **2.** 0.6 ● 0.006 **3.** 4.153 ● 4.2

Order the numbers from greatest to least.

4. 0.0825; 0.56; 0.8 **5.** 1.3; 1.52; 2.08

Round to the place of the underlined digit.

6. $0.0\underline{8}5$ **7.** $0.5\underline{7}2$ **8.** $0.1\underline{4}5$ **9.** $\underline{3}.957$

Explain Your Thinking ▶ How does aligning the decimal points help you compare decimals?

Go On

Practice and Problem Solving

Compare. Write >, <, or = for each ●.

10. 0.09 ● 0.11 **11.** 0.945 ● 0.941 **12.** 0.3 ● 0.300 **13.** 0.023 ● 0.23

14. 17 ● 16.882 **15.** 2.454 ● 2.462 **16.** 3.631 ● 3.7 **17.** 9.9 ● 10.1

Order the numbers from greatest to least.

18. 4; 0.425; 4.25 **19.** 0.6; 0.68; 68 **20.** 2.544; 2.545; 25.43

21. 0.34; 0.4; 3 **22.** 3.55; 3.472; 4.14 **23.** 0.72; 7.2; 7

Round to the place of the underlined digit.

24. $0.\underline{4}57$ **25.** $\underline{6}.459$ **26.** $7.5\underline{3}8$ **27.** $28.\underline{7}26$

28. $3.2\underline{1}9$ **29.** $\underline{4}.09$ **30.** $6.\underline{4}63$ **31.** $27.3\underline{5}3$

Algebra • Properties

Compare. Write >, <, or = for each ●, given $a = 0.895$, $b = 0.75$, $c = 0.075$, and $d = 0.1$.

32. b ● c **33.** a ● d **34.** c ● d **35.** b ● a

Find a digit that will make the inequality true.

36. $0.\blacksquare 5 > 0.37$ **37.** $0.4\blacksquare 6 < 0.468$ **38.** $2.396 < 2.39\blacksquare$

Solve.

39. Australia has 2.5 persons per square kilometer, Mongolia has 1.7 persons per square kilometer, and Namibia has 2.2 persons per square kilometer. Order the countries from least to most crowded.

40. Represent Suppose a 10 × 10 grid represents the number 1. Use 10 × 10 grids to represent the numbers 1.24 and 1.05. Explain how you can use the grids to compare the two numbers.

41. Robin weighs a bunch of green grapes and a bunch of red grapes on a digital scale. The green grapes weigh 120.308 grams and the red grapes weigh 120.381 grams. Which bunch of grapes weighs less? Explain.

42. Many libraries use the Dewey Decimal System to classify and order books. Books are shelved from lowest numbers to highest numbers. Three books are numbered 1.971, 1.978, and 1.97. Which book should be first on the shelf?

Extra Practice See page 25, Set F.

Mixed Review and Test Prep

Open Response

Round each number to the place indicated by the underlined digit. (Ch. 1, Lessons 3 and 5)

43. $2{,}04\underline{0}{,}567$ **44.** $0.\underline{6}75$

45. $12\underline{3}.08$ **46.** $15.\underline{7}89$

47. $4{,}\underline{7}82.5$ **48.** $48.\underline{8}00$

Multiple Choice

49. Which set of numbers is ordered from least to greatest? (Ch. 1, Lesson 7)

A 0.378; 0.42; 0.424

B 306.905; 36.999; 306.91

C 3,098; 3,089; 3,088

D 31,333; 31,033; 3,133

Problem Solving

Social Studies Connection

Roman Numerals

Our number system is just one way to write numbers. The Romans created a number system using symbols called Roman numerals.

I (1)
V (5)
X (10)
L (50)
C (100)
D (500)

To read Roman numerals, follow these rules:

- Add the numerals from left to right.

  VI = 5 + 1 = 6 XI = 10 + 1 = 11

  XX = 10 + 10 = 20 DC = 500 + 100 = 600

- If a numeral has a value that is less than the numeral on its right, subtract those numerals. Then continue to add.

  XIV = 10 + (5 − 1) = 14

  CXLV = 100 + (50 − 10) + 5 = 145

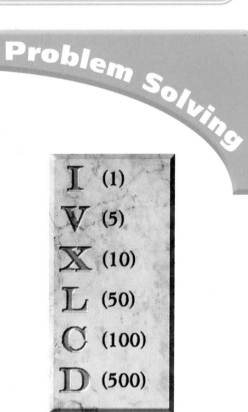

What is each number below?

1. II **2.** XII **3.** LXXIX **4.** DXLIII **5.** DXCVII

6. Explain the similarities and differences between our decimal system and Roman numerals.

WEEKLY WR READER eduplace.com/map

Chapter Review/Test

VOCABULARY

1. In the number 10^5, the 5 tells how many times 10 is used as the factor. It is called the ____.
2. In the number 10^5, the 10 is called the ____.
3. A number written in ____ shows the value of each digit.

Vocabulary
- base
- expanded form
- exponent
- place value
- power of ten

CONCEPTS AND SKILLS

Write each number in standard form. (Lessons 1–3, pp. 4–9, Lesson 5, pp. 14–15)

4. two million, four hundred three thousand, seventy-six
5. $(4 \times 10{,}000{,}000) + (7 \times 1{,}000{,}000) + (9 \times 10{,}000) + (1 \times 1{,}000) + (5 \times 100)$
6. two hundred two and twenty-two hundredths

Use exponents to write each number in expanded form. (Lessons 2–3, pp. 6–9)

7. 70,900,200,408
8. 1,003,080,300
9. 38
10. 3,002

Round each number to the place of the underlined digit. (Lesson 1, pp. 4–5, Lesson 4, pp. 10–13, Lesson 7, pp. 20–23)

11. $12.\underline{0}43$
12. $126{,}\underline{9}53$
13. $12\underline{6}.925$
14. $37.6\underline{2}8$
15. $37\underline{6}.255$

Order the numbers from greatest to least. (Lesson 4, pp. 10–13, Lesson 7, pp. 20–23)

16. 37,483; 37,493; 39,473
17. 0.02; 0.021; 0.201
18. 459,321,002; 49,321,001; 458,399,999
19. 5,034,966; 5,350,955; 5,034,965

PROBLEM SOLVING

Find a pattern to solve the problem. (Lesson 6, pp. 16–18)

20. The membership of the local stamp collectors' club increased steadily in past years. In 2003, there were 21 members; in 2004, 29 members; in 2005, 37 members. How many members is it likely to have in 2008?

Show You Understand

Explain the difference in value of each digit in the number 1,111,111.

Extra Practice

Set A (Lesson 1, pp. 4–5)

Write each number in word form, short word form, and expanded form.

1. 16,362
2. 279,018
3. 36,109
4. 148,300
5. 567,255
6. 100,002

Set B (Lesson 2, pp. 6–7)

Use exponents to write each number in expanded form.

1. 7,094
2. 43,729
3. 309,309
4. 873,209

Set C (Lesson 3, pp. 8–9)

Write each number in standard form.

1. six hundred fifty-three million, seventy-five thousand, one hundred forty-nine
2. $(3 \times 10^9) + (2 \times 10^5) + (9 \times 10^4) + (6 \times 10^3) + (5 \times 10^2) + (5 \times 10^1) + (6 \times 10^0)$

Write each number in short word form.

3. 34,503,598
4. 81,094,389,002
5. 430,398,278,021

Set D (Lesson 4, pp. 10–13)

Order the numbers from greatest to least.

1. 84,392; 804,381; 84,492
2. 2,394,309; 239,410; 2,395,301

Round each number.

3. 108,273 to the nearest ten thousand
4. 489,560,711 to the nearest million

Set E (Lesson 5, pp. 14–15)

Write each decimal in words.

1. 0.069
2. 1.14
3. 0.056
4. 0.049
5. 2.901
6. 0.03

Set F (Lesson 7, pp. 20–23)

Order the numbers from least to greatest.

1. 0.149, 0.073, 0.72
2. 10.002, 0.103, 1.03
3. 0.009, 0.15, 0.8

Round to the place of the underlined digit.

4. $0.\underline{4}7$
5. $\underline{7}.12$
6. $8.5\underline{3}9$
7. $32.\underline{8}09$

Extra Practice at **eduplace.com/map**

Add and Subtract Whole Numbers

INVESTIGATION

Use Data

Using data in the time line below, write 5 word problems about roller coasters. Research roller coasters and report on the data you find.

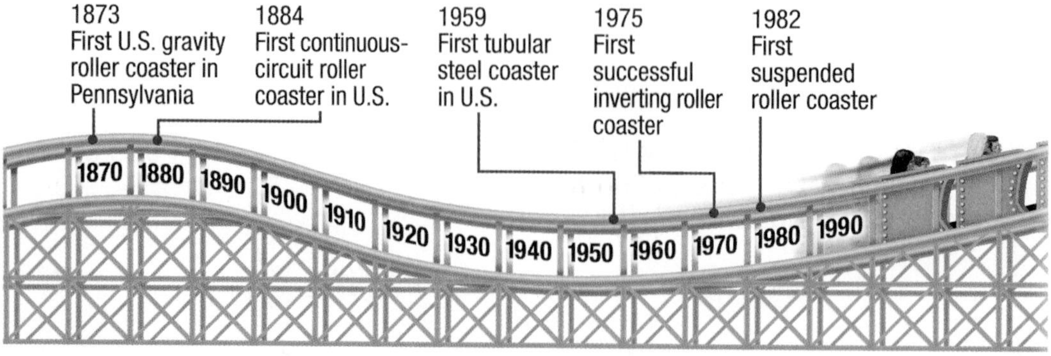

1873
First U.S. gravity roller coaster in Pennsylvania

1884
First continuous-circuit roller coaster in U.S.

1959
First tubular steel coaster in U.S.

1975
First successful inverting roller coaster

1982
First suspended roller coaster

1870 1880 1890 1900 1910 1920 1930 1940 1950 1960 1970 1980 1990

Use this page to review and remember what you need to know for this chapter.

VOCABULARY

Choose the best word to complete each sentence.

Vocabulary
addends
difference
product
sum

1. The answer to a subtraction problem is the ____.
2. A ____ is the answer to an addition problem.
3. Two or more numbers added together are called ____.

CONCEPTS AND SKILLS

Write an expression for each word phrase.

4. 8 reduced by 4
5. 7 more than 6
6. take 12 from 15

Round each number to the greatest place.

7. 46
8. 308
9. 5,555

Use mental math to find the answers.

10. $60 – $20
11. 1,400 – 800
12. 5,000 + 2,000 + 4,000

Regroup.

13. 462 as 3 hundreds, ■ tens, 2 ones
14. 57 as ■ tens and 17 ones
15. 13 hundreds as ■ thousand ■ hundreds
16. 24 tens as 1 ten ■ ones

Substitute a 6 for each ■. Find each expression's value.

17. ■ + ■
18. ■ + 2
19. ■ – 6

Write About It

20. You buy two items. One costs $12, and the other costs $4. Explain how to find how much change you get from a $20 bill.

Facts Practice, See page 659.

Lesson 1

Audio Tutor 1/5 Listen and Understand

Expressions and Addition Properties

Objective Read, write, and evaluate expressions containing variables and apply addition properties.

Vocabulary
- variable
- expression
- evaluate
- Commutative Property
- Associative Property
- Identity Property

Learn About It

Steve has 4 more ride tickets than Lily has. Since you do not know how many tickets Lily has, you can use a **variable**, a letter such as x or n, to stand for the number of tickets Lily has.

You can compare the number of tickets Steve has with the number of tickets Lily has by using a mathematical **expression** that uses a variable. Mathematical expressions that use variables are called algebraic expressions.

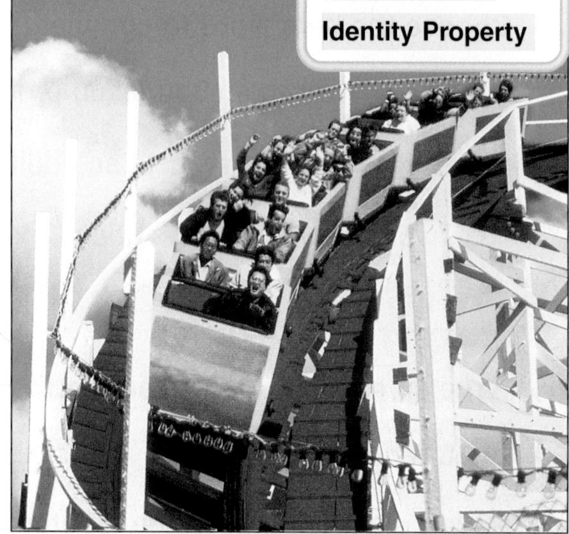

Write an expression.

What if Lily has 1 ticket?	What if Lily has 10 tickets?	What if Lily has n tickets?
Then $1 + 4$ shows how many tickets Steve has.	Then $10 + 4$ shows how many tickets Steve has.	Then $n + 4$ shows how many tickets Steve has.
The expression means 4 more than 1.	The expression means 4 more than 10.	The expression means 4 more than n.

Another Example

Write an Algebraic Expression in Words

Translate $n - 3$ into words.

$n - 3$

some number — subtract — three

The expression $n - 3$ means to subtract three from some number.

Other Possible Answers

Often there is more than one way to write an algebraic expression in words. Other possible ways include:
- three less than some number
- take three away from some number
- a number minus three

Extra Help at eduplace.com/map

Algebraic expressions allow you to replace variables with different numbers.

To **evaluate** an expression, substitute a number for the variable.

Matt has 2 fewer tickets than Lily.

Write the expression for the number of tickets Matt has.	Substitute a number for n.	Simplify.
$n - 2$ ↑ number of tickets Lily has	If Lily has 5 tickets, then $n - 2$ becomes $5 - 2$.	$5 - 2 = 3$

Solution: If Lily has 5 tickets, then Matt has 3 tickets.

The addition properties you know for whole numbers also apply to expressions with variables.

There are three properties that make adding easier.

Addition Properties		
Commutative Property When you add two numbers or variables, you can change the order without changing the sum. Example: $a + 7 = 7 + a$	**Associative Property** When you add numbers or variables, you can group them in different ways without changing the sum. Example: $(y + 4) + 2 = y + (4 + 2)$	**Identity Property** When you add 0 to a number or variable, the result is the same number, variable, or sum. Example: $a + 0 = 0 + a = a$

Guided Practice

Write an algebraic expression for each word phrase.

1. some number plus 6 **2.** 8 less than a number

Translate each algebraic expression into words. Then evaluate when $n = 4$.

3. $n + 9$ **4.** $11 - n$ **5.** $14 + n$ **6.** $n - 4$

Ask Yourself

- Do the words describe an addition expression or a subtraction expression?
- What words did I use for the variables?

Explain Your Thinking ▶ Is the Commutative Property true for subtraction? Why or why not? Use Exercise 2 (or 4) to explain your answer.

Go On

Practice and Problem Solving

Write an algebraic expression for each word phrase.

7. subtract 10 from a number **8.** 9 plus a number **9.** 3 more than a number

10. take 15 from a number **11.** add 5 to a number **12.** 6 is decreased by a number

Translate each algebraic expression into words.

13. $n + 8$ **14.** $8 + n$ **15.** $x - 12$ **16.** $12 - x$ **17.** $a + 0$

18. $k - 5$ **19.** $5 + y$ **20.** $h + 9$ **21.** $16 - t$ **22.** $x - y$

Evaluate each expression when $a = 15$. Then write >, <, or = to compare the expressions.

23. $a + 9$ ● $9 + a$ **24.** $a + 0$ ● $a - 2$

25. $a - 14$ ● $20 - a$ **26.** $(a + 4) + 6$ ● $a + (4 + 6)$

Solve.

27. At 310 feet, the Millennium Force roller coaster once was the tallest coaster in the world. Write an expression to show the height of the current record holder. Explain what the variable represents.

28. To ride on the Millennium Force, passengers must be at least 48 inches tall. Al is taller than that. Write an expression to show how tall Al is. Explain what the variable represents.

29. Draw a diagram and write an expression to show how many are in the group.

A group of friends went on the roller coaster.

- first car: 3 friends
- second car: 4 friends
- third car: ? friends

How many are in the group if 2 friends are in the third car?

30. **What's Wrong?** Alma wrote the associative property this way.

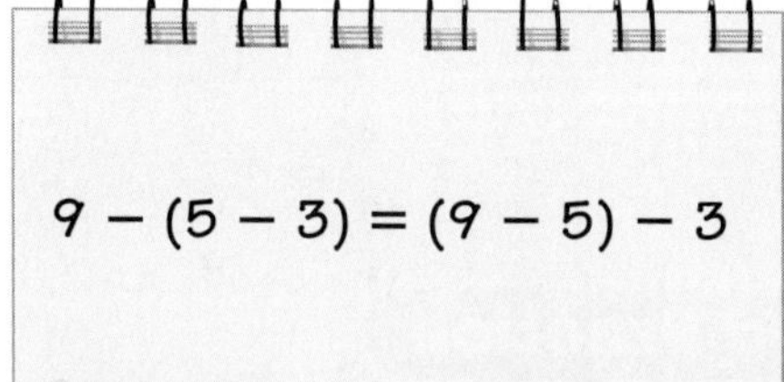

Explain how you know what Alma did wrong.

Mixed Review and Test Prep 

Open Response

Write >, <, or = to compare. (Grade 4)

31. \$3.06 ● 3 dollars + 1 dime

32. \$0.55 ● 1 quarter + 1 nickel

33. 2 dollars ● 8 quarters

Multiple Choice

34. Ben has \$6 less than Emily. If n stands for Emily's money, which expression shows Ben's money? (Ch. 2, Lesson 1)

A $n + \$6$ **B** $\$6 + n$

C $n - \$6$ **D** $\$6 - n$

Extra Practice See page 45, Set A.

Problem Solving

Number Sense
Miniature Numbers

Engineers design larger structures like roller coasters, but they also design extremely small things, too.

A nanoguitar is about the size of 1 blood cell. It measures 10 micrometers long. One micrometer is 1 millionth of a meter. The width of each string on the guitar is about 50 nanometers, which is 50 billionths of a meter; about the size of 100 atoms! The numbers are shown in the place-value chart below.

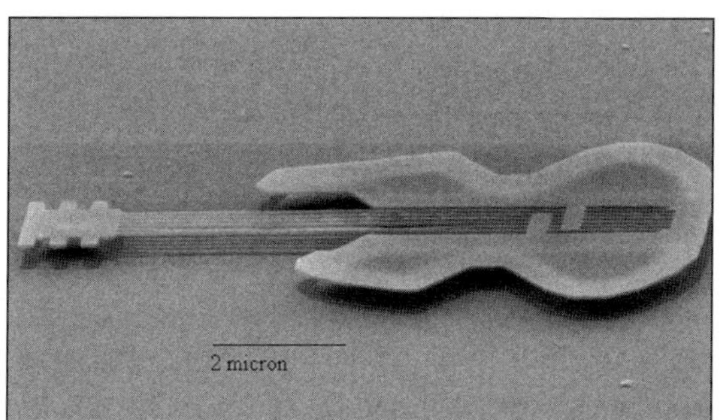

You can round, compare, and order these very small numbers the same way you round, compare, and order other decimals.

Round each number to the nearest millionth.

Then order from *greatest* to *least*.

1. 0.0006723; 0.0010257; 0.0004925
2. 0.0089437; 0.0089586; 0.0089564
3. 0.0000078; 0.0000072; 0.0000086
4. 0.0004624; 0.000480; 0.00046343

ones		tenths	hundredths	thousandths	ten thousandths	hundred thousandths	millionths	ten millionths	hundred millionths	billionths
0	.	0	0	0	0	0	1	0	0	0
0	.	0	0	0	0	0	0	0	5	0

Number Sense
Digit Prices

The price, in cents, of a souvenir pencil at an amusement park is a two-digit number. The ones digit is 3 less than the tens digit. The sum of the digits is 15. How much does a souvenir pencil cost?

Brain Teaser

Use only the digits 0, 1, and 9 to write a decimal in billionths. Use each digit at least once.

Your decimal should be the least possible decimal that rounds up to the nearest millionth.

Education Place

Check out **eduplace.com/map** for more brain teasers.

Lesson 2

Audio Tutor 1/6 Listen and Understand

Estimate Sums and Differences

Objective Estimate sums and differences.

Vocabulary
estimate
round

Learn About It

One flume ride is 3,610 feet long. Another flume ride is 1,315 feet long. About how many feet different are these lengths? An **estimate** is a number close to an exact amount. An estimate tells *about* how much or *about* how many.

You can round to estimate sums or differences.

Different Ways to round

Way 1 **Rounding to the greatest place gives an estimate.**

$$\begin{array}{r} 3{,}610 \\ -\ 1{,}315 \\ \hline \end{array} \rightarrow \begin{array}{r} 4{,}000 \\ -\ 1{,}000 \\ \hline 3{,}000 \end{array}$$

Solution: The difference is about 3,000 ft.

Way 2 **Rounding to a lesser place is more precise. This gives a better estimate.**

$$\begin{array}{r} 3{,}610 \\ -\ 1{,}315 \\ \hline \end{array} \rightarrow \begin{array}{r} 3{,}600 \\ -\ 1{,}300 \\ \hline 2{,}300 \end{array}$$

Solution: The difference is about 2,300 ft.

Way 3 **Rounding both numbers up and down gives an estimated range of answers.**

Round down | Round up

$$\begin{array}{r} 3{,}000 \\ +\ 1{,}000 \\ \hline 4{,}000 \end{array} \leftarrow \begin{array}{r} 3{,}610 \\ +\ 1{,}315 \\ \hline \end{array} \rightarrow \begin{array}{r} 4{,}000 \\ +\ 2{,}000 \\ \hline 6{,}000 \end{array}$$

Solution: The sum of 3,610 and 1,315 is between 4,000 and 6,000.

Other Examples

A. Front-End Estimation

Use the front digits.

$$\begin{array}{r} 3{,}458 \\ +\ 1{,}555 \\ \hline \end{array}$$

$$\begin{array}{r} 3{,}000 \\ +\ 1{,}000 \\ \hline 4{,}000 \end{array}$$

$3{,}458 + 1{,}555 \approx 4{,}000$

B. Clustering

$54 + 49 + 41 + 62 + 39 + 46 = ?$

The numbers *cluster* around 50.
There are 6 numbers.
Use multiplication to estimate the sum.
$6 \times 50 = 300$

$54 + 49 + 41 + 62 + 39 + 46 \approx 300$

Guided Practice

Ask Yourself

- Did I use the rounding rules correctly?
- Did I add or subtract the rounded numbers correctly?

Estimate. Tell which method you used.

1. 746 + 746

2. 30,909 − 18,850

3. 7,749 − 1,654

Explain Your Thinking ▶ If you are estimating a sum and you round both numbers up, will your sum be greater than or less than the actual sum? Explain.

Practice and Problem Solving

Estimate. Tell which method you used.

4. 595 + 820

5. 828 − 371

6. 7,502 + 2,875

7. 3,199 + 2,539

8. 3,392 − 2,800

9. 9,839 + 8,000

10. 3,567 − 2,249

11. 9,003 − 1,654

12. 29,678 − 12,854

13. $29 + $54

14. 3,498 + 2,909 + 2,701

Solve.

15. In one hour, 1,076 riders rode a coaster. In the next hour, 1,423 riders rode the coaster. About how many riders rode the coaster in those two hours?

16. Some coasters can go more than 100 miles per hour. The new X coaster goes 76 miles per hour. About how much less than 100 miles per hour is that?

17. Analyze Each hour 1,834 people can ride one roller coaster. On another coaster, 1,645 people ride per hour. Estimate the difference in the number of riders per hour.

18. Create and Solve Write two problems about roller coasters: one that requires an exact answer and one that requires an estimate. Solve your problems and give to a partner to solve.

Mixed Review and Test Prep

Open Response

Write the value of the underlined digit.
(Ch. 1, Lesson 1)

19. $2\underline{8}1{,}475$

20. $35\underline{5}{,}072$

21. $907{,}3\underline{1}1$

22. $\underline{1}12{,}111$

23. Sandy spent $164 on tickets, $45 on food, and $38 on souvenirs. What is a reasonable estimate of the amount she spent? (Ch. 2, Lesson 2)

Explain.

Extra Practice See page 45, Set B.

Lesson 3

Add and Subtract Whole Numbers

Objective Add and subtract whole numbers with up to five digits.

Learn About It

On Monday 6,395 people rode on a roller coaster. On Tuesday 2,768 people rode. How many people rode the roller coaster on those two days?

Find 6,395 + 2,768.

STEP 1 Add the ones.

Regroup 10 ones as 1 ten whenever possible.

13 ones = 1 ten 3 ones

$$\begin{array}{r} \scriptstyle 1 \\ 6,395 \\ +\ 2,768 \\ \hline 3 \end{array}$$

STEP 2 Add the tens.

Regroup 10 tens as 1 hundred whenever possible.

16 tens = 1 hundred 6 tens

$$\begin{array}{r} \scriptstyle 1\ 1\ \ \\ 6,395 \\ +\ 2,768 \\ \hline 63 \end{array}$$

STEP 3 Add the hundreds.

Regroup 10 hundreds as 1 thousand whenever possible.

11 hundreds = 1 thousand 1 hundred

$$\begin{array}{r} \scriptstyle 1\ \ 1\ 1\ \ \\ 6,395 \\ +\ 2,768 \\ \hline 163 \end{array}$$

STEP 4 Add the thousands.

$$\begin{array}{r} \scriptstyle 1\ \ 1\ 1\ \ \\ 6,395 \\ +\ 2,768 \\ \hline 9,163 \end{array}$$

Solution: The total is 9,163 people.

You should check your work.

Use estimation to check.

6,395	rounds to	6,000
+ 2,768	rounds to	+ 3,000
		9,000

The sum is close to 9,000.

Use subtraction to check.

Addition and subtraction are opposite or inverse operations. Opposite or inverse operations are operations that **undo** and check each other.

Sum	9,163
− Addend	− 2,768
Other Addend	6,395

Solution: The total is 9,163 people.

How many more riders were there on Monday than on Tuesday?

You can draw a model to show the information.

Monday: 6,395 riders	
Tuesday: 2,768 riders	Difference: ? riders

Now you can use the model to solve the problem.

Find 6,395 − 2,768.

STEP 1 Subtract the ones.

Since 8 > 5, you must regroup 1 ten as 10 ones.

```
     8 15
 6, 3 9 5
− 2, 7 6 8
        7
```

STEP 2 Subtract the tens.

```
     8 15
 6, 3 9 5
− 2, 7 6 8
      2 7
```

STEP 3 Subtract the hundreds.

Since 7 > 3, regroup 1 thousand as 10 hundreds.

```
 5 13 8 15
 6, 3 9 5
− 2, 7 6 8
    6 2 7
```

STEP 4 Subtract the thousands.

```
 5 13 8 15
 6, 3 9 5
− 2, 7 6 8
  3, 6 2 7
```

Add to check.

```
   3, 6 2 7
 + 2, 7 6 8
   6, 3 9 5
```

Solution: The difference is 3,627 riders.

You can also use a calculator to check.

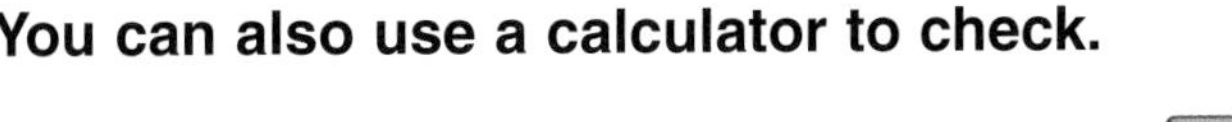

The difference is 3,627.

Another Example

Zeros in Subtraction

30,058 − 17,874 = n

```
 2 9  9 15
 3 0, 0 5 8
− 1 7, 8 7 4
  1 2, 1 8 4
```

← You cannot subtract 7 tens from 5 tens. There are no hundreds or thousands to regroup, so rename 3 ten thousands.

Think
300 hundreds equals 299 hundreds plus 10 tens.

Go On

Guided Practice

Add or subtract. Check that your answer is reasonable.

1. $\begin{array}{r} 457 \\ +\ 285 \\ \hline \end{array}$

2. $\begin{array}{r} 6{,}701 \\ +\ 3{,}495 \\ \hline \end{array}$

3. $\begin{array}{r} 54{,}187 \\ +\ 12{,}579 \\ \hline \end{array}$

4. $\begin{array}{r} 829 \\ -\ 287 \\ \hline \end{array}$

5. $\begin{array}{r} 3{,}402 \\ -\ 1{,}689 \\ \hline \end{array}$

6. $\begin{array}{r} 42{,}317 \\ -\ 19{,}675 \\ \hline \end{array}$

7. 7,814 + 543

8. 34,516 + 478 + 2,347

9. 867 − 328

Ask Yourself

- Do I need to regroup?
- Where should I write the regrouped numbers?

Explain Your Thinking ▶ When subtracting, how do you regroup tens when there is a zero in the hundreds place?

Practice and Problem Solving

Add or subtract. Check that your answer is reasonable.

10. $\begin{array}{r} 746 \\ +\ 459 \\ \hline \end{array}$

11. $\begin{array}{r} 952 \\ +\ 374 \\ \hline \end{array}$

12. $\begin{array}{r} 843 \\ +\ 199 \\ \hline \end{array}$

13. $\begin{array}{r} 587 \\ +\ 96 \\ \hline \end{array}$

14. $\begin{array}{r} 746 \\ -\ 199 \\ \hline \end{array}$

15. $\begin{array}{r} 752 \\ -\ 97 \\ \hline \end{array}$

16. $\begin{array}{r} 500 \\ -\ 354 \\ \hline \end{array}$

17. $\begin{array}{r} 3{,}958 \\ -\ 498 \\ \hline \end{array}$

18. $\begin{array}{r} 3{,}985 \\ +\ 439 \\ \hline \end{array}$

19. $\begin{array}{r} 56{,}583 \\ -\ 9{,}407 \\ \hline \end{array}$

20. $\begin{array}{r} 67{,}109 \\ -\ 15{,}407 \\ \hline \end{array}$

21. $\begin{array}{r} 4{,}782 \\ +\ 561 \\ \hline \end{array}$

22. 567 + 4,986 + 6,998

23. 5,050 − 3,328

24. 7,685 − 3,858

Algebra • Expressions Find each sum or difference when $n = 1{,}000{,}000$ and $s = 499$.

25. $n + 9$

26. $n + 9{,}000$

27. $n + 9{,}000{,}000$

28. $1{,}000 - s$

Data Use the table to solve Problems 29–32.

Roller Coaster	Length (in feet)	Height (in feet)
Flashback	1,876	125
Mr. Freeze™	1,480	238
Shock Wave™	3,500	116
Titan	5,312	255

29. How much longer is Shock Wave™ than Flashback?

30. A mile is 5,280 feet. If you ride Titan twice, how much more or less than 2 miles have you ridden?

31. How much higher is Mr. Freeze™ than Flashback?

32. What is the range of heights of these roller coasters?

Extra Practice See page 45, Set C.

Problem Solving

Social Studies Connection

Time Zones

Each time you cross into a new time zone while traveling from east to west, you need to set your watch 1 hour earlier. Portland, Oregon is located three time zones west of Portland, Maine.

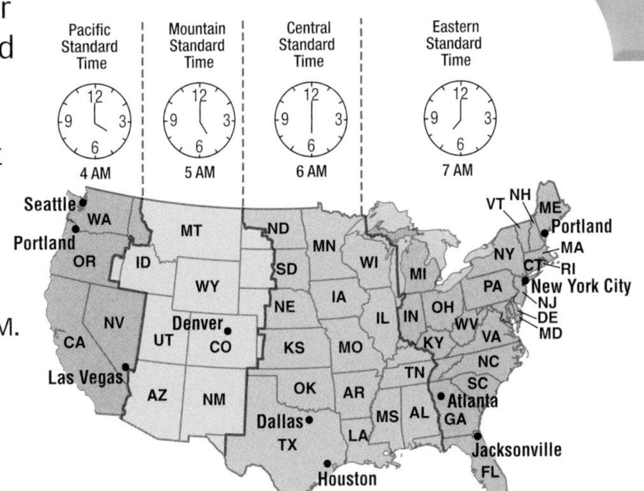

It is 1:30 P.M. in Portland, Maine. What time is it in Portland, Oregon?

Count back 3 hours from 1:30 P.M.

1:30 P.M.   12:30 P.M.   11:30 A.M.   10:30 A.M.

When it is 1:30 P.M. in Portland, Maine, it is 10:30 A.M. in Portland, Oregon.

Identify each missing time.

1. 3:10 P.M. in Atlanta, Georgia is ____ in Houston, Texas.
2. 1:15 P.M. in Dallas, Texas is ____ in Las Vegas, Nevada.
3. 9:00 A.M. in Denver, Colorado is ____ in New York City, New York.
4. 8:30 A.M. in Seattle, Washington is ____ in Jacksonville, Florida.

WEEKLY WR READER eduplace.com/map

Quick Check

Check your understanding of Lessons 1–3.

Evaluate each expression for $n = 8$. (Lesson 1)

1. $n + 14$
2. $12 - n$
3. $n - n$

Estimate each sum or difference. (Lesson 2)

4. 432 + 675
5. 9,240 − 582
6. 647 + 290 + 36

Add or subtract. Check your answer. (Lesson 3)

7. 548 + 397
8. 1,462 − 841
9. 3,290 + 1,876
10. 7,005 − 1,527

Lesson 4

Add and Subtract Greater Numbers

Objective Use mental math, pencil and paper, estimation, or technology to add and subtract greater numbers.

Learn About It

When you add or subtract greater numbers, you need to choose the most appropriate method for solving the problem. You can use mental math, pencil and paper, estimation, a calculator, or a computer.

One amusement park had 2,349,783 visitors in one year. Another park had 2,185,326 visitors. How many visitors did both parks together have that year?

Add. **2,349,783 + 2,185,326 = *n***

Estimate before you add. Round to the greatest place.

$$\begin{array}{r} 2{,}349{,}783 \\ +\ 2{,}185{,}326 \\ \hline \end{array} \rightarrow \begin{array}{r} 2{,}000{,}000 \\ +\ 2{,}000{,}000 \\ \hline 4{,}000{,}000 \end{array}$$

The sum should be about 4,000,000.
Then complete the addition.

STEP 1 Add the digits in the ones period.

$$\begin{array}{r} {\scriptstyle 1\ 1} \quad \\ 2{,}349{,}783 \\ +\ 2{,}185{,}326 \\ \hline 109 \end{array}$$

STEP 2 Add the digits in the thousands period.

$$\begin{array}{r} {\scriptstyle 1\ 1\ 1\ 1} \quad \\ 2{,}349{,}783 \\ +\ 2{,}185{,}326 \\ \hline 535{,}109 \end{array}$$

STEP 3 Add the digits in the millions place.

$$\begin{array}{r} {\scriptstyle 1\ 1\ 1\ 1} \quad \\ 2{,}349{,}783 \\ +\ 2{,}185{,}326 \\ \hline 4{,}535{,}109 \end{array}$$

Solution: The total number of visitors is 4,535,109.

Another Example

You can use a calculator to find the difference in attendance at the two parks.

Subtract. 2,349,783 − 2,185,326

2 3 4 9 7 8 3 − 2 1 8 5 3 2 6 Enter = 164457

Guided Practice

Add or subtract. Tell which method you used.

1. 247,625 + 53,218

2. 746,000 − 156,923

3. 2,386,940 − 1,000,000

Ask Yourself

- Did I regroup in the correct places?
- Did I choose a method that makes sense?

Explain Your Thinking ▶ When is a computer a good choice for adding greater numbers? When is it not a good choice? Explain.

Practice and Problem Solving

Add or subtract. Tell which method you used.

4. 612,956 + 423,890

5. 2,345,976 − 254,500

6. 617,700 + 82,430

7. 5,321,908 + 4,600,000

8. 234,809 − 150,000

9. 7,210,658 − 6,800,321

10. 547,987 − 476,000

11. 475,000 + 125,000

12. 400,000 − 73,300

13. 1,754,867 − 1,235,800

Choose a Computation Method

Mental Math • Estimation • Paper and Pencil • Calculator

Use the table for Problems 14–16.

14. How many fewer than 40,000,000 riders have been on the most popular ride listed in the table?

15. All together, have these four roller coasters had 1 billion riders? How can you tell?

16. How many more than 2,750,000 riders have been on Flight of Fear? Show how you got the answer.

Roller Coaster	Total Number of Riders Since Opened (to 2002)
Flight of Fear	2,768,065
The Beast	32,904,365
The Racer	39,963,282
Top Gun	9,239,507

Mixed Review and Test Prep

Open Response

Multiply. (Grade 4)

17. 2 × 4

18. 5 × 2

19. 4 × 4

20. 9 × 2

21. 5 × 5

22. 7 × 6

Multiple Choice

23. In one week 213,360 people rode on a roller coaster. How many fewer than 250,000 riders is that? (Ch. 2, Lesson 4)

A 36,640 **B** 43,360

C 47,740 **D** 463,360

Extra Practice See page 45, Set D.

Lesson 5

Addition and Subtraction Equations

Vocabulary
equation

Objective Use mental math to solve addition and subtraction equations.

Learn About It

At a rafting ride at the water park, the blue rafts have three more seats than the yellow rafts. The blue rafts have 7 seats. How many seats do the yellow rafts have?

You can make a model of the information.

Blue raft seats: 7	
Yellow raft seats: n	Difference: 3

Use the model to write an equation.

▶ An **equation** is a mathematical statement indicating that the quantities or expressions on either side of the equal sign (=) have the same value.

- Write the equation in words. → yellow raft seats + difference = blue raft seats
- Replace the words with values or variables from the model. → $n + 3 = 7$
- Solve the equation using mental math. → $n + 3 = 7$
  Replace the variable n with 4. $4 + 3 = 7$

What number plus 3 equals 7? Try 4.

Solution: The yellow rafts have 4 seats.

Another Example

Write the equation shown by the model. Use mental math to solve the equation.

46	
n	18

You can write an addition equation.

$$46 = n + 18$$
$$n = 28$$

What number plus 18 equals 46? Try 28.

You can write a subtraction equation.

$$46 - n = 18$$
$$n = 28$$

46 minus what number equals 18? Try 28.

Guided Practice

Ask Yourself

- Does my equation match the information in the model?
- Did I check my solution by substituting it into the equation?

Write the equation shown by the model. Use mental math to solve the equation.

1.

Cars on the first coaster: 15	
Cars on the second coaster: *n*	Difference: 4

2.

12	
8	x

Explain Your Thinking ▶ What model could you draw to show $49 + c = 74$?

Practice and Problem Solving

Write the equation shown by the model. Then solve the equation.

3.

Total minutes: 25	
Time waiting: 23	Time on ride: *a*

4.

18	
n	13

Use mental math to solve the equations. Use models if necessary.

5. $n + 4 = 9$ **6.** $17 - k = 12$ **7.** $50 - n = 20$ **8.** $93 + s = 100$

9. $15 + x = 25$ **10.** $v + 34 = 36$ **11.** $p - 6 = 70$ **12.** $17 - n = 10$

13. $m - 5 = 71$ **14.** $x + 24 = 40$ **15.** $\$2 + n = \$20$ **16.** $x - 87 = 0$

Solve.

17. Henry had 8 rides more than Davey did. If Henry had 15 rides, how many rides did Davey have? Draw a model to represent the problem and solve.

18. Two rides have a 5-mile per hour difference in top speed. The faster ride has a top speed of 21 miles per hour. What is the top speed of the other ride?

19. Measurement Draw a line that is 12 centimeters long. How much longer must you draw the line to make it 20 centimeters long?

20. What If? Suppose the line you drew in Problem 19 were half as long. How much longer must you draw it to be 20 centimeters long?

Mixed Review and Test Prep

Open Response

Identify the value of the underlined digit in each number. (Ch. 1, Lesson 1)

21. $\underline{7}5{,}000{,}000$ **22.** $3{,}7\underline{6}8{,}099$

23. Explain how to find the value of *n* in this equation. (Ch. 2, Lesson 5)

$34 - n = 20$

Extra Practice See page 45, Set E.

Lesson 6

Problem-Solving Decision

Relevant Information

Objective Find the information needed to solve a problem.

When a problem has too much information, you must decide which information is important. When a problem does not give enough information, you must decide what is missing.

Problem At an amusement park 9,576 tickets were sold on Saturday. Ticket sales included adults and senior citizens, and children. There were 3,085 senior citizen tickets sold. There were 1,027 more tickets sold for adults than senior citizens. How many tickets for adults were sold on Saturday?

Ask Yourself

What is the question?

- How many tickets for adults were sold on Saturday?

What do you need to know?

- 3,085 tickets for senior citizens were sold on Saturday.
- 1,027 more tickets for adults were sold on Saturday than for senior citizens.

What do you not need to know?

- 9,576 tickets were sold on Saturday.
- The number of tickets sold for children.

Draw the model to solve.

Total adult tickets: n	
Senior citizen tickets: 3,085	Difference: 1,027

Write an equation to represent the problem. $n = 3,085 + 1,027$ $n = 4,112$

Solution: On Saturday, 4,112 adult tickets were sold.

Try These

Draw a model to solve. If there is not enough information, tell what information is needed.

1. Last week, the park had 10,687 visitors. This week the park had 94,612 visitors. Normally, it has about 85,000 visitors per week. How many visitors less than normal did it have last week?

2. You have to be at least 48 inches tall to ride on most thrill rides. Casey cannot ride the roller coaster because she is too short. By how much does she miss the cut-off height?

Draw a model. If there is not enough information, tell what information is needed.

3. A ride can take up to 1,800 riders each hour. There were 1,143 riders the first hour. There were 1,456 and 1,723 riders the next two hours. How many riders were there in the first 2 hours?

5. Scott was in the amusement park from 12:30 P.M. until 8:15 P.M. Matt was in the park until 6:30 P.M. How much longer was Scott in the park than Matt?

7. Use the following model to write a word problem. Write an equation. Then solve the problem.

20,764 visitors	
Adults: 8,345	Children: *n*

4. You have to be 12 years old to drive a bumper car. Carol is 4 years too young to drive. Sarah is older than Carol. Ben is 2 years older than Sarah. Ben can drive a bumper car. Is Sarah old enough to drive a bumper car? Explain.

6. The roller coaster can carry a maximum of 24 riders. Each car carries 3 people. The carousel can carry a maximum of 56 people. How many more people can the carousel carry?

8. **Create and Solve** Write a problem that contains extra information. Solve your problem. Trade the problem with a friend. Find the extra information in each other's problems and solve.

Activity

Visual Thinking
Cubing Dates

You can make a calendar using three cubes. One cube shows the day of the week. Since a cube has only 6 faces, Saturday and Sunday are on the same face.

This cube calendar shows the date for Monday the 15th.

Arrange the numbers of the faces of the other two cubes. Each face should only have one digit.

Hint Do any numbers need to be on both cubes?

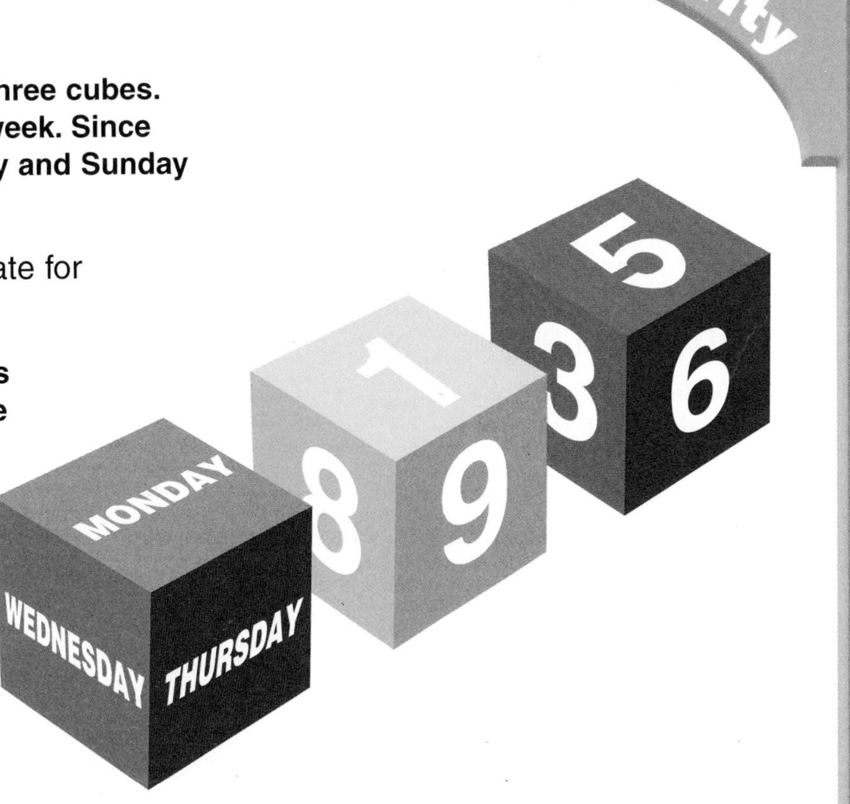

Chapter Review/Test

VOCABULARY

1. The ____ states that the order of addends does not change the sum.

2. A(n) ____ is a letter or symbol that represents a number in an algebraic expression.

3. The ____ states that the sum of any number and 0 is that number.

4. To ____ a mathematical expression is to substitute the value given for each variable and then compute the answer.

Vocabulary

Associative Property

Commutatitve Property

Identity Property

evaluate

variable

CONCEPTS AND SKILLS

Evaluate each expression for $a = 18$. Then write >, <, or = to compare the expressions. (Lesson 1, pp. 28–31)

5. $a + 0$ ⬬ $a - 0$ 6. $(a + 7) + 9$ ⬬ $a + (7 + 9)$ 7. $50 + a$ ⬬ $a + 50$

Estimate. (Lesson 2, pp. 32–33)

8. 679 + 291 9. 423 − 201 10. 63,947 − 12,508 11. 47,031 + 58,098

Add or subtract. (Lessons 3–4, pp. 34–39)

12. 4,608 − 379 13. 28,347 + 16,017 14. 947 + 258 15. 3,694 + 2,613

Use mental math to solve. (Lesson 5, pp. 40–41)

16. $n + 12 = 25$ 17. $81 - p = 80$ 18. $b - 52 = 17$ 19. $75 - t = 70$

PROBLEM SOLVING (Lesson 6, pp. 42–43)

Solve. If there is not enough information, tell what information is needed.

20. The amusement park stops admitting people at 5:00 P.M. Between 5:00 and 5:30, 427 cars left the parking lot. By 6:00, an additional 216 cars had left. How many cars were still parked in the lot at 6:00?

Show You Understand

Look at these examples. Explain how regrouping in addition is different from regrouping in subtraction.

$$\begin{array}{r} 4{,}072 \\ +\,3{,}180 \\ \hline \end{array} \qquad \begin{array}{r} 4{,}072 \\ -\,3{,}180 \\ \hline \end{array}$$

Extra Practice

Set A (Lesson 1, pp. 28–31)

Write an algebraic expression for each word phrase.

1. take 2 from a number
2. 5 increased by a number
3. 20 is reduced by a number

Translate each algebraic expression into words.

4. $n - 25$
5. $17 + a$
6. $100 - c$
7. $k + 12$
8. $m + n$

Evaluate each expression for a = 12. Then write >, <, or =.

9. $a + 1$ ● $a - 1$
10. $100 + a$ ● $a + 100$
11. $a - 5$ ● $18 - a$

Set B (Lesson 2, pp. 32–33)

Estimate. Tell which method you used.

1. $\begin{array}{r} 686 \\ +\ 231 \\ \hline \end{array}$
2. $\begin{array}{r} 346 \\ -\ 188 \\ \hline \end{array}$
3. $\begin{array}{r} 706 \\ +\ 197 \\ \hline \end{array}$
4. $\begin{array}{r} 4{,}673 \\ -\ 3{,}927 \\ \hline \end{array}$
5. $\begin{array}{r} 9{,}706 \\ +\ 3{,}048 \\ \hline \end{array}$
6. $\begin{array}{r} 92{,}545 \\ -\ 36{,}789 \\ \hline \end{array}$

Set C (Lesson 3, pp. 34–37)

Add or subtract. Check that your answer is reasonable.

1. $\begin{array}{r} 276 \\ +\ 412 \\ \hline \end{array}$
2. $\begin{array}{r} 8{,}603 \\ +\ 587 \\ \hline \end{array}$
3. $\begin{array}{r} 9{,}706 \\ -\ 3{,}048 \\ \hline \end{array}$
4. $\begin{array}{r} 5{,}308 \\ -\ 3{,}591 \\ \hline \end{array}$
5. $\begin{array}{r} 72{,}314 \\ +\ 17{,}921 \\ \hline \end{array}$
6. $\begin{array}{r} 95{,}678 \\ -\ 89{,}679 \\ \hline \end{array}$

Set D (Lesson 4, pp. 38–39)

Add or subtract. Tell which method you used.

1. $\begin{array}{r} 342{,}617 \\ +\ 629{,}313 \\ \hline \end{array}$
2. $\begin{array}{r} 580{,}604 \\ -\ 450{,}000 \\ \hline \end{array}$
3. $\begin{array}{r} 628{,}589 \\ +\ 223{,}000 \\ \hline \end{array}$
4. $\begin{array}{r} 781{,}130 \\ -\ 674{,}086 \\ \hline \end{array}$
5. $\begin{array}{r} 4{,}453{,}299 \\ +\ 3{,}958{,}214 \\ \hline \end{array}$
6. $\begin{array}{r} 6{,}624{,}120 \\ -\ 5{,}921{,}532 \\ \hline \end{array}$

Set E (Lesson 5, pp. 40–41)

Use mental math to solve the equations.

1. $4 + z = 10$
2. $14 - g = 8$
3. $5 + p = 12$
4. $d - 17 = 50$
5. $61 + w = 72$
6. $r - \$14 = \$35$
7. $23 - b = 19$
8. $n + \$9 = \$20$

SWARM!

Imagine thousands of bees flying overhead or hundreds of thousands of grasshoppers leaping from one field to another.

Swarming is actually a natural behavior of some animals. When honeybees outgrow their hive, the swarm separates to form a new hive. When ants or grasshoppers need food, large numbers of individuals band together to solve the group's problem. As scientists study this "swarm intelligence," they may find ways to solve human problems, such as traffic congestion and ocean pollution.

Problem Solving

Use the data from the chart about the honeybee swarm to solve Problems 1–3.

Honeybee Swarm		
Type of Bee	**Number**	**Average Length**
Queen	1	1.8 cm
Drone	250	1.55 cm
Worker	12,800	1.2 cm

1. What is the total number of honeybees in this swarm?

2. Compare the lengths of the different types of honeybees. What digit is in the tenths place of each of the lengths?

3. When too many honeybees live in a hive, a swarm of half the bees and one queen look for a new home. If this swarm represents half the original hive, how many more than 25,000 bees were in the original hive?

Education Place
Visit Weekly Reader Connections at **eduplace.com/map** for more on this topic.

Enrichment

Fibonacci Numbers

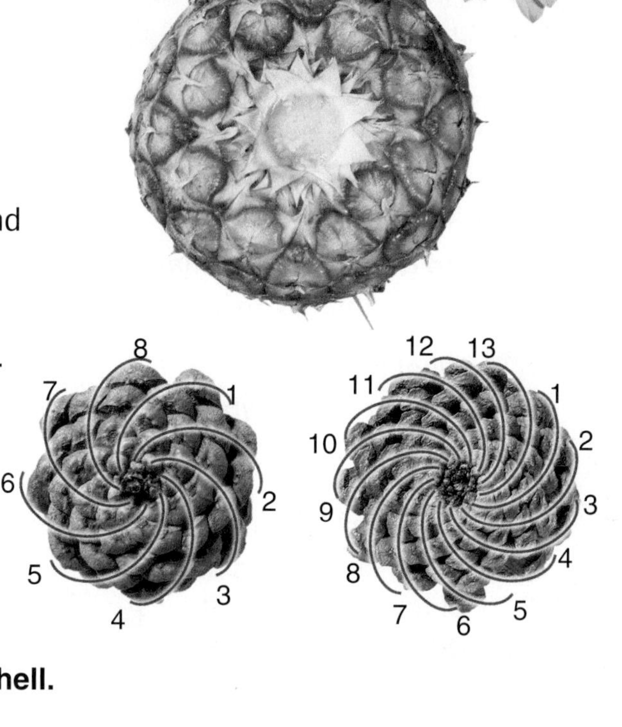

About 800 years ago a mathematician named Leonardo Fibonacci noticed a sequence of numbers that appears throughout nature.

1, 1, 2, 3, 5, 8, 13, 21, 34, 55,...

When Fibonacci analyzed the sequence, he found that each number beginning with 2 is the sum of the two numbers that come before it:

$1 + 1 = 2$, $2 + 1 = 3$, $3 + 2 = 5$, and so on.

Look at this pine cone. It has 8 righthand spirals and 13 lefthand spirals. Both numbers are in the Fibonacci sequence.

Try These!

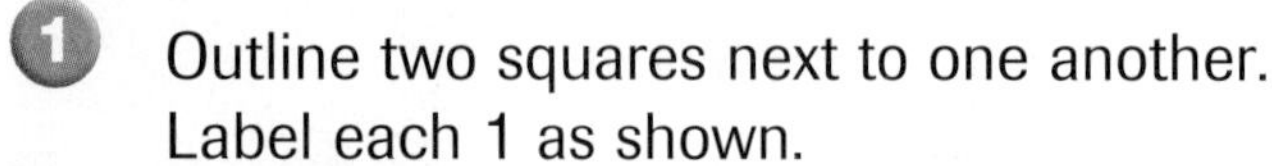

Use grid paper to show how the Fibonacci sequence appears in the spiral of a Nautilus shell.

1. Outline two squares next to one another. Label each 1 as shown.
2. The next square in your drawing must have sides whose length is the sum of the lengths of the first two squares. Outline this square alongside the first two. Label it 2.
3. Continue adding squares. The length of the sides of each new square must be the sum of the lengths of the previous two squares' sides. Label each square. Repeat until you cannot fit any more squares on your paper.
4. If you continued to use this sequence, would you eventually draw a square with sides 1,000 centimeters long? Explain.

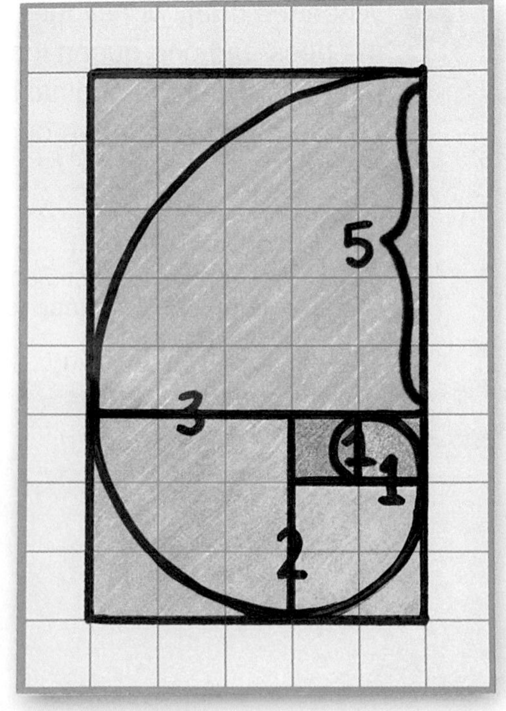

Cross-Calculations

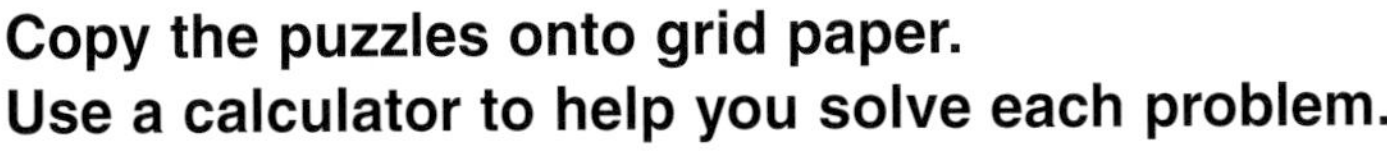

Copy the puzzles onto grid paper.
Use a calculator to help you solve each problem.

Across

Row A: 152,609 + 24,247 = ■

Row B: 975,621 − 102,290 = ■

Row C: 838,620 + ■ = 991,460

Down

Column D: 963,221 − ■ = 205,371

Column E: 900,632 − 57,347 = ■

Column F: ■ − 412,809 = 258,196

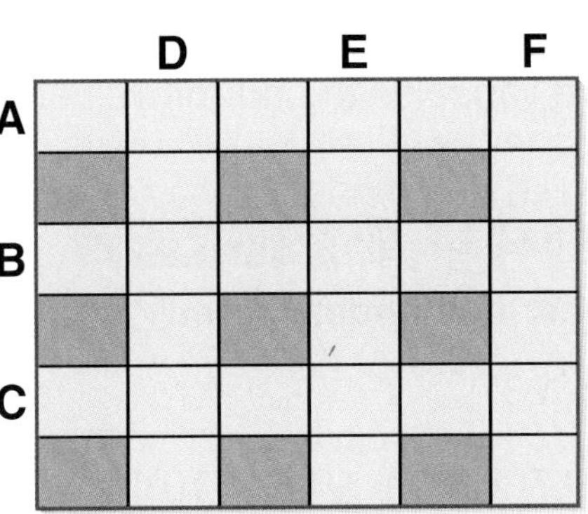

Across

Row G: 546,309 − ■ = 228,453

Row H: 411,256 − 187,388 = ■

Row I: ■ − 175,612 = 61,042

Down

Column J: 685,311 − ■ = 492,381

Column K: 668,321 + 150,139 = ■

Column L: ■ + 334,200 = 962,940

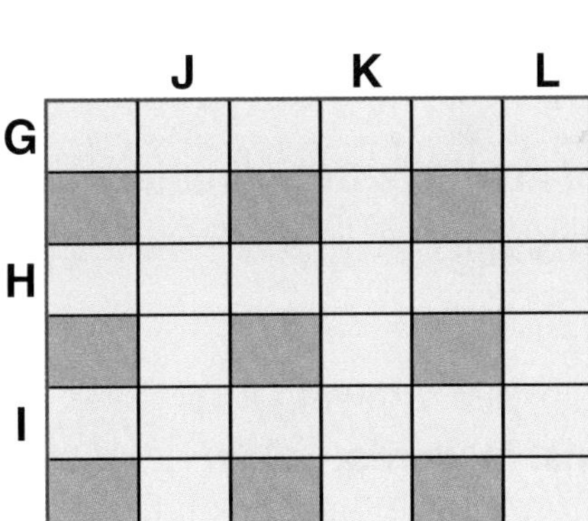

Challenge **Write clues to go along with the cross number puzzle shown at the right.**

		D		E		F
A	3	6	7	2	1	5
		8		1		3
B	7	8	2	1	0	1
		0		8		1
C	3	6	5	7	9	2
		7		1		7

Unit 1 Test

VOCABULARY Open Response

Write *true* or *false* for each statement. If a statement is false, rewrite it to make it true.

1. A variable is a letter that stands for a number.
2. A period shows the number of times a base is used as a factor.
3. You evaluate an expression when you substitute values for the variables to find the value of the expression.

Vocabulary

- base
- period
- variable
- evaluate
- exponent
- expression
- power of ten

CONCEPTS AND SKILLS Open Response

Write each number in standard form. (Chapter 1)

4. 28 thousand, 28
5. 600,000 + 70,000 + 300 + 9
6. $(8 \times 10^9) + (7 \times 10^7) + (7 \times 10^6) + (9 \times 10^5) + (4 \times 10^2) + (1 \times 10^0)$
7. One hundred eight billion, three hundred million, ninety-eight

Write in expanded form using exponents. (Chapter 1)

8. 520,106
9. 1,084,756

Order each set of numbers from greatest to least. (Chapter 1)

10. 9,825; 9,875; 9,845
11. 2,805,110; 3,020,121; 3,022,407
12. 6; 0.625; 6.25
13. 3.655; 3.656; 36.53; 36.35

Write each decimal in words. (Chapter 1)

14. 0.19
15. 0.6
16. 219.042

Round each number. (Chapter 1)

17. 4.328 to the nearest hundredth
18. 3.526 to the nearest tenth

Evaluate each expression for $n = 6$. (Chapter 2)

19. $n + 17$
20. $18 - n$
21. $n + n$

Estimate each sum or difference. (Chapter 2)

22. $523 + 684$
23. $8,140 - 793$
24. $752 + 580 + 39$

Add or subtract. (Chapter 2)

25. $\begin{array}{r} 768{,}923 \\ +\ 14{,}918 \\ \hline \end{array}$

26. $\begin{array}{r} 5{,}428{,}003 \\ -\ 2{,}472{,}460 \\ \hline \end{array}$

27. $\begin{array}{r} 439{,}654 \\ -\ 97{,}835 \\ \hline \end{array}$

Use mental math to solve each equation. (Chapter 2)

28. $n + 19 = 27$

29. $25 - x = 16$

PROBLEM SOLVING Open Response

30. The value of a rare coin was $7,800 in 1998. In 2000 the value rose to $8,300, in 2002 it rose to $8,800, and in 2004 it rose to $9,300. If the pattern continues what is the value of the coin likely to be in 2008?

31. In April, Chris had $1,360 in his bank account. In May, the amount was $1,320, in June it was $1,280, and in July it was $1,240. If the pattern continues, how much will he have in his account in September?

Draw a model to solve. If there is not enough information, tell what information is needed.

32. Last year $12,350 was spent on new math books. This year, $15,690 was spent on math books. Usually $17,000 per year is spent on math books. How much less than usual was spent on math books this year?

33. Tickets for a circus were priced at $18 for adults and $10 for students. At last week's performance, 1,432 student tickets were sold. What was the total number of tickets sold for last week's performance?

Performance Assessment

Constructed Response

Population by Grade Level of Smith County		
Grade 1: 1,296	**Grade 4:** 1,439	**Grade 7:** 1,428
Grade 2: 1,304	**Grade 5:** 1,493	**Grade 8:** 1,387
Grade 3: 1,416	**Grade 6:** 1,471	

Task A symphony orchestra is offering free concerts for students in Smith County.

Use the population figures above and the information to the right. In what combinations should the superintendent of schools send the grades to hear the concerts? How many concerts will be needed? How many students will be at each concert? Explain your thinking.

Information You Need

- The entire population of a grade must attend a concert together.
- The concert hall has 2,900 seats.
- At least 2,750 seats must be filled for each performance.
- Students in Grades 1 and 2 will not go to the concerts.

Cumulative Test Prep

Solve Problems 1–10.

Test-Taking Tip

Sometimes when you take a multiple choice test, you can eliminate answer choices that are clearly wrong.

Look at the example below.

Gary jogged 5 fewer kilometers this week than he jogged last week. If n stands for the distance he jogged last week, which expression shows the distance he jogged this week?

A $n + 5$ **C** $5 - n$

B $5 + n$ **D** $n - 5$

THINK

Look at the first two choices, $n + 5$ and $5 + n$. You know from the Commutative Property of Addition that these two expressions represent the same amount. Therefore, you can eliminate choices A and B.

Multiple Choice

1. There are 12 fewer students in Marie's class than there are in Adele's class. If a stands for the number of students in Adele's class, which expression shows the number of students in Marie's class?

A $a + 12$ **C** $12 - a$

B $a - 12$ **D** $12 + a$

(Chapter 2, Lesson 1)

2. What is the value of n in this equation?

$$46 - n = 20$$

F 66 **H** 26

G 46 **J** 16

(Chapter 2, Lesson 5)

3. What is the value of the digit 3 in 354,968?

A 300 **C** 30,000

B 3,000 **D** 300,000

(Chapter 1, Lesson 1)

4. Tyler spent \$32 on clothing, \$19 on records, and \$28 on food. Which is the best estimate of the total amount he spent?

F \$50 **H** \$90

G \$80 **J** \$170

(Chapter 2, Lesson 2)

For Test-Taking Tips, see page 652.

Open Response

5. What is the value of the underlined digit?

16,<u>2</u>08

(Chapter 1, Lesson 5)

6. A city plans to spend $1,953,631 on schools. What is the digit in the ten thousands place of the number that represents the money spent on schools?

(Chapter 1, Lesson 3)

7. In 1810, the land area of the United States was 1,681,828 square miles. By 1820 the land area was 1,749,462 square miles. By how many square miles had the land area of the United States increased?

(Chapter 2, Lesson 4)

8. Each month, Dale recorded the height of his tomato plant in centimeters. If the heights form a pattern, what is the missing height?

Month	Height (in centimeters)
May	25
June	38
July	?
August	64
September	77

(Chapter 1, Lesson 6)

9. This expression shows the greatest distance from the Earth to the Sun:

$(9 \times 10^7) + (4 \times 10^6) + (5 \times 10^5)$

How many times does the digit 0 appear in this number when written in standard form?

(Chapter 1, Lesson 2)

Extended Response

10. This chart shows the 1990 and 2000 populations of the largest counties in Florida.

County	Population	
	1990	2000
Miami-Dade	1,937,094	2,253,362
Broward	1,255,488	1,623,018
Palm Beach	863,518	1,131,184
Hillsborough	834,054	998,948
Orange	677,491	896,344

A What was the total population of the two largest counties in 2000?

B In 1990, which two counties had a combined population that was about the same as the population of Miami-Dade County?

C Which county had the greatest population growth from 1990 to 2000? Explain how you found your answer.

D In 1990, which county had a population closest to 1 million?

E Suppose the population of Miami-Dade County eventually doubles from the 2000 figure. Write this population figure in expanded form using exponents.

(Chapter 2, Lesson 4)

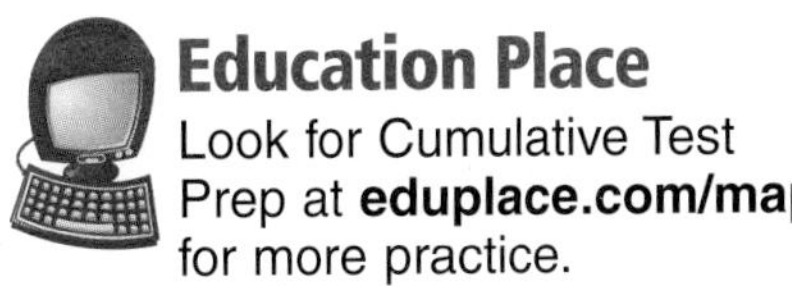

Education Place
Look for Cumulative Test Prep at **eduplace.com/map** for more practice.

Vocabulary Wrap-Up for Unit 1

Look back at the big ideas and vocabulary in this unit.

Big Ideas

A number can be expressed in standard, expanded, word, and short word form.

Compare numbers by aligning them according to place value and, starting from the left, comparing digits until they are different.

You can estimate a sum or difference of whole numbers before you compute to help you judge the reasonableness of a computed sum or difference.

Key Vocabulary

standard form

estimate

place value

expanded form

Math Conversations

Use your new vocabulary to discuss these big ideas.

1. Explain how to write 3,050,710,380 in expanded form with exponents.
2. Explain how to estimate the sum 84,924 + 121,499.
3. Explain how to order these numbers: 8; 0.89; 8.19
4. Explain how you would find the next number in this pattern: 1,283; 1,498; 1,713; ?
5. **Write About It** Every ten years, there is a census in which the people of the United States are counted. Find census information about your state. Has the population been increasing? How many people do you think will live in your state when the next census is taken? Explain your thinking.

I need to compare these two numbers.
Don't forget to line up the numbers according to place value before comparing.

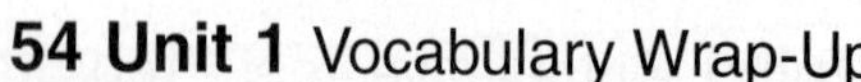

UNIT 2

Multiplication, Division, and Algebra

Reading Mathematics

Reviewing Vocabulary

Here are some math vocabulary words that you should know.

factors	numbers that are multiplied
product	the answer in a multiplication problem
dividend	the number that is divided in division
divisor	the number by which a dividend is being divided
quotient	the answer in division
estimate	a number close to an exact amount that tells about how much or about how many

Reading Words and Symbols

You can use words, symbols, or words and symbols to express multiplication and division in different ways.

All these statements represent the same multiplication problem:

three groups of four

- 3 times 4
- 3×4
- 4×3
- $\begin{array}{r} 4 \\ \times\, 3 \\ \hline \end{array}$

All these statements represent the same division problem:

twelve divided by three

- 12 divided by 3
- $12 \div 3$
- $3\overline{)12}$
- $\frac{12}{3}$

Write whether the symbol *n* represents a factor or a product. Then find the value of *n*.

1. $8 \times n = 40$

2. $n = 8 \times 4$

Tell if the ■ symbol represents the divisor, the dividend, or the quotient. Then find the value of ■.

3. $\begin{array}{r} ■ \\ 4\overline{)36} \end{array}$

4. $35 \div ■ = 5$

5. $■ \div 7 = 8$

Reading Test Questions

Choose the correct answer for each.

6. Which multiplication statement is modeled by the array of dots at the right?

a. $1 \times 24 = 24$

b. $2 \times 12 = 24$

c. $3 \times 8 = 24$

d. $4 \times 6 = 24$

An **array** is an arrangement of objects, pictures, or numbers in columns and rows.

7. Which of these statements about $48 \div 6 = 8$ is false?

a. The dividend is greater than the divisor.

b. The quotient is greater than the divisor.

c. The divisor is greater than the quotient.

d. The quotient is less than the dividend.

False means "wrong" or "not true."

8. Which of the following has a quotient that is at least 7?

a. $48 \div 12$

b. $56 \div 7$

c. $35 \div 7$

d. $30 \div 5$

At least means "equal to or greater than."

Learning Vocabulary

Watch for these words in this unit. Write their definitions in your journal.

compatible numbers

divisible

Distributive Property

front-end estimation

order of operations

partial products

Education Place

At **eduplace.com/map** see *e*Glossary and *e*Games—Math Lingo.

Literature Connection

Read "Ready for Anything" on page 640. Then work with a partner to answer the questions about the story.

Multiply Whole Numbers

INVESTIGATION

Use Data

This tall ship is called the *Christian Radich*. To make all the sails for the *Christian Radich*, you would need a piece of canvas about 79 feet wide and 189 feet long. Estimate the area of the sails. Research other ships and write a problem based on the data you find.

Christian Radich
(approximate measurements)

Hull length overall	about 236 feet
Breadth	32 feet
Draft	15 feet
Sail area	? square feet

Use What You Know

Use this page to review and remember what you need to know for this chapter.

VOCABULARY

Choose the best word to complete each sentence.

Vocabulary
estimate
factor
multiply
product
Identity Property

1. In $5 \times 3 = 15$, the number 15 is called the ■.
2. A(n) ____ can help you tell whether an answer is reasonable.
3. If you know the number of equal sets and the number in each equal set, you can ____ to find the total.
4. An example of the ____ of Addition is $7 + 0 = 7$.

CONCEPTS AND SKILLS

Use basic facts and patterns to find each product.

5. 8×7
   8×70
   8×700
   $8 \times 7{,}000$
6. 6×9
   6×90
   6×900
   $6 \times 9{,}000$
7. 5×7
   5×70
   5×700
   $5 \times 7{,}000$

Find a value for *n* that makes each equation true.

8. $n + 4 = 4 + 5$
9. $(n + 9) + 2 = 6 + (9 + 2)$
10. $8 + n = 8$

Estimate using front-end estimation. Then estimate by rounding.

11. $845 + 656 + 312$
12. $267 + 458 + 522$
13. $789 + 362 + 163$
14. $584 + 471 + 110$
15. $\$30.95 + \$63.20$
16. $\$1.38 + \$5.76$

Estimate by clustering.

17. $32 + 27 + 36 + 29$
18. $76 + 79 + 84 + 81$
19. $302 + 315 + 279$

Write About It

20. How can the Associative Property of Addition help you add mentally?

Facts Practice, See page 660.

Lesson 1

Audio Tutor 1/7 Listen and Understand

Algebra

Expressions and Multiplication Properties

Objective Evaluate algebraic expressions and use the properties of multiplication.

Vocabulary
- Commutative Property
- Associative Property
- Identity Property
- Zero Property

Learn About It

A minivan holds 6 passengers. Write an expression to find the number of passengers that n minivans can hold. Then find how many passengers 5 minivans will hold.

Write and evaluate an algebraic expression.

STEP 1 Write an expression.

2 minivans hold 2×6 passengers.

n minivans hold $n \times 6$ passengers.

STEP 2 Evaluate $n \times 6$ when $n = 5$.

Substitute 5 for n to see how many passengers 5 minivans will hold.

$$n \times 6 = 5 \times 6 = 30$$

Solution: Five minivans will hold 30 passengers.

Different ways to express multiplication.
$n \times 6$ $\quad n \bullet 6$ $\quad n(6)$ $\quad 6n$

You can use multiplication properties to evaluate expressions.

Properties of Multiplication

Commutative Property

Changing the order of factors does not change the product.

$$a \times b = b \times a$$

Example: $5 \times 10 = 10 \times 5$

Associative Property

Changing the grouping of factors does not change the product.

$$a \times (b \times c) = (a \times b) \times c$$

Example: $3 \times (5 \times 4) = (3 \times 5) \times 4$

Identity Property

The product of any number and 1 is that number.

$$m \times 1 = m$$

Example: $72 \times 1 = 72$

Zero Property

The product of any number and 0 is 0.

$$z \times 0 = 0$$

Example: $36 \times 0 = 0$

Guided Practice

Write an expression for each.

1. a number multiplied by 5
2. 7 more than a number

Simplify. Tell which property you used.

3. $27 \times 0 \times 3$
4. $(38)(25)(4)$

Evaluate. Tell which property you used.

5. $20(34 \times p)$, given $p = 5$
6. $a \cdot 15 \cdot 3$, given $a = 1$

Ask Yourself

- What mathematical symbols can I substitute for words?
- Which property can I use to help me simplify the expression?

Explain Your Thinking ▶ How can knowing multiplication properties help you evaluate $(96 \times 20) \times 5$?

Practice and Problem Solving

Write an expression for each.

7. the product of 5 and a number
8. 125 decreased by a number
9. a number divided by 18
10. 96 added to a number

Simplify. Tell which property you used.

11. $1 \times 17 \times 2$
12. $(49 \cdot 500) \cdot 2$
13. $36 \times 0 \times 8$
14. $5 \cdot 27 \cdot 2$

Evaluate each expression, given $n = 4$, $t = 7$, and $v = 5$.

15. $5 \cdot t$
16. $(n \cdot 8) \cdot v$
17. $t \cdot (n + v)$
18. $200 \div v$
19. $n + t + v$

Solve.

20. A plane flies 600 miles per hour. Write an expression for the distance traveled in *m* hours. Then find the number of miles the plane flies in 3 hours.
21. Larry spent \$25 on books and \$32 on CDs. Then Sarah gave him \$10. Larry now has \$31. How much did he have before he bought the books and CDs?
22. **What's Wrong?** Ted says that $2 \times (3 \times d)$ gives twice the sum of 3 and a number *d*. What's wrong?
23. Muriel has \$26. She wants to buy 3 books for \$7 each and 2 magazines for \$3 each. Does she have enough money?

Mixed Review and Test Prep

Open Response

Write in expanded form. (Ch. 1, Lesson 5)

24. 734
25. 8,965
26. 26,421
27. Which property helps you find the product 26×0? (Ch. 3, Lesson 1)

    Explain how you got your answer.

Extra Practice See page 83, Set A.

Audio Tutor 1/8 Listen and Understand

Model the Distributive Property

Objective Use the Distributive Property to multiply.

Vocabulary
Distributive Property
partial products

Materials
grid paper
straightedge
colored pencils

Work Together

You can draw a rectangle to show how to find a product.

A rectangle is 5 units wide and 16 units long. You can use simple multiplication facts to find the area of the rectangle.

Work with a partner to use models to multiply.

STEP 1 With a straightedge, draw a rectangle 5 units wide and 16 units long.

- Would it be easier to find the area of the rectangle if you divided it into two parts? Explain.

Remember
Area = length × width

STEP 2 The diagram shows one way to divide the rectangle. Divide your rectangle. Shade and label each part.

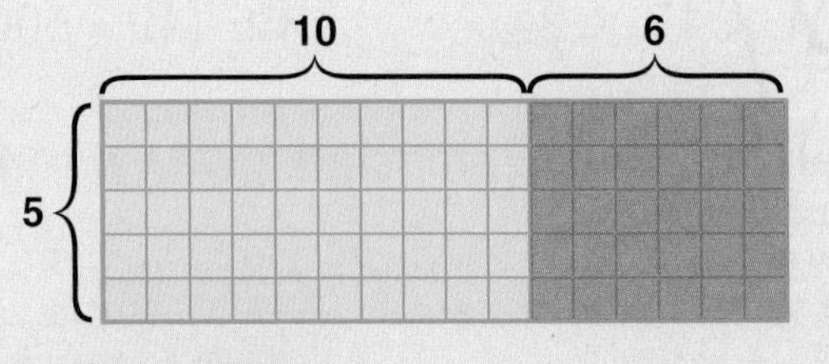

Find the area of the rectangle.

Use the **Distributive Property** to complete the number sentences shown below.

Area = 5 × 16
= 5 × (10 + 6)
= (5 × 10) + (5 × 6)
= ? + ? ← **partial products**
= ?

Distributive Property

When you multiply the sum of two or more addends by a factor, the product is the same as if you multiplied each addend by the factor and then added the products.

$a(b + c) = (a \times b) + (a \times c)$

On Your Own

Use the Distributive Property to multiply. Show the partial products for each and find the sum. Then write a multiplication sentence for each.

1. 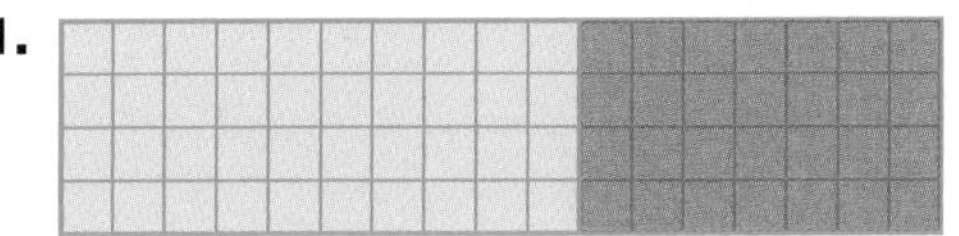

2. 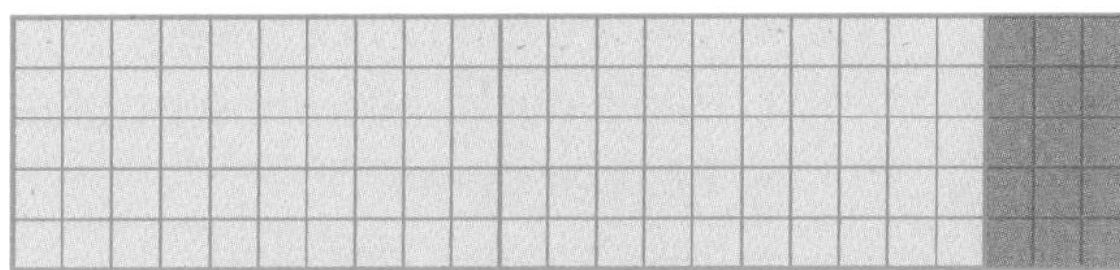

3. 

4. 

Draw and divide a rectangle to show each product. Use the Distributive Property to find the product.

5. 6 × 18
6. 7 × 25
7. 8 × 34
8. 9 × 42
9. 7 × 36
10. 3 × 41
11. 3 × 54
12. 8 × 23

Talk About It • Write About It

You learned how to use the Distributive Property to multiply.

13. Explain how you can use the Distributive Property to find the product of 6 × 27.

14. When you use the Distributive Property to find areas of rectangles, why does it make sense to separate the rectangles so you get groups of 10?

Lesson 3

Problem-Solving Strategy

Use Logical Reasoning

Objective Use logical reasoning to solve problems.

Problem Laura, Rita, Ty, and Mike each have one car. Each car is a different color. Laura's car is not green. Rita's car is not white or blue. Ty's car is red. Mike's car is not blue. What color is each person's car?

UNDERSTAND

This is what you know:

- Each car is a different color.
- Laura's car is not green.
- Rita's car is not white or blue.
- Ty's car is red.
- Mike's car is not blue.

PLAN

You can use logical reasoning to help solve the problem.

SOLVE

- Ty's car is red, so no other car can be red.
- Rita's car is not red, because Ty's car is red. It is also not white or blue. So, Rita's car must be green.
- Since Ty's car is red and Rita's car is green, Mike and Laura must have blue and white cars.
- Mike's car is not blue. So, it must be white.
- Laura's car is blue because that is the only remaining color.

Solution: Ty's car is red, Rita's car is green, Mike's car is white, and Laura's car is blue.

LOOK BACK

Look back at the problem. Does the solution make sense?

Guided Practice

Use the Ask Yourself questions to help you solve each problem.

1. Neil, Karen, and Tonya sit together in an airplane. There are three seats in a row—aisle, middle, and window. Neither Karen nor Tonya sits next to the window. Tonya sits next to Neil. In which seat is each person?

2. Four planes are waiting to take off. They will fly to four cities: Atlanta, Charlotte, Miami, and Houston. The plane to Atlanta is not the first or the last. The plane to Charlotte is second. The plane to Miami is not the first. In what order will the planes take off?

   Hint Start with a list of what you know.

Ask Yourself

UNDERSTAND **What facts do I know?**

PLAN **Did I make a table?**

SOLVE
- **Does my table show all possibilities?**
- **How can I use each fact to write yes or no in the table?**

LOOK BACK **Does the solution make sense?**

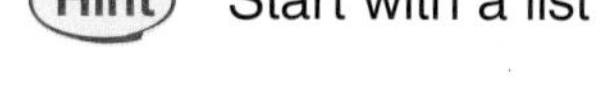

Independent Practice

Use logical reasoning to solve each problem.

3. Ned, Martin, Astrid, and Nasser each arrive on a different flight shown at the right. Astrid arrives after 3:30 P.M. Ned arrives between 3:10 P.M. and 3:50 P.M. Nasser arrives after Astrid. At what time does each person arrive?

Flight Number	Arriving From	Arrival Time	Gate Number
104	Atlanta	3:05 P.M.	E14
078	San Francisco	3:20 P.M.	E22
3456	Portland	3:45 P.M.	E16
7092	Minneapolis	4:00 P.M.	E31

4. Ken, Lisa, and Barry buy a different kind of ticket shown to the right. Barry does not buy the most expensive ticket. Ken's ticket is less expensive than Barry's. Which kind of ticket does each person buy?

Round Trip Boston to San Francisco

Ticket Class	Price
First Class	$1,605
Business	$1,100
Coach	$ 479

5. Fawn, Bill, Celine, and Suki each use a different kind of transportation: boat, car, bus, or airplane. Bill's transportation has no wheels. Fawn flies. Suki does not use a car. Which kind of transportation does each person use?

Mixed Problem Solving

Solve. Show your work. Tell what strategy you used.

6. The price of a car was $16,000 in 2001, $17,500 in 2002, $19,000 in 2003, and $22,000 in 2005. Based on this information, what, most likely, was the price of the car in 2004?

7. Jerry is thinking of two numbers that have a difference of 8 and a product of 48. What are the two numbers?

8. Janelle thinks of a number, doubles it, and then adds 15. The result is 39. Of what number was Janelle thinking?

You Choose

Strategy
- Find a Pattern
- Guess and Check
- Use Logical Reasoning
- Work Backward
- Write an Equation

Computation Method
- Mental Math
- Estimation
- Paper and Pencil
- Calculator

Data Use the advertisement to solve Problems 9–12.

9. Willow buys a three time-zone watch, a computer case, and an appointment book. How much did she spend?

10. Maxwell has $90. He needs to buy a daypack and an insulated water bottle for his trip. He would also like to get a portable disc player. Does he have enough money for all three? Explain why or why not.

11. Kaya is going to buy 4 insulated water bottles and a magnetic chess set. Use b to represent the cost of the water bottles and c to represent the cost of the chess set. What expression could you write to show the cost of all 5 items?

12. **Create and Solve** Write and solve a problem about 3 students going on a hike. Use the data from the advertisement.

GREAT GEAR
Three time-zone watch: $79
Insulated water bottle: $19
Daypack: $32
Magnetic chess set: $25
Computer case: $35
Appointment book: $22
Portable disc player: $40

Problem Solving on Tests

Multiple Choice

Choose the letter of the correct answer. If a correct answer is not here, choose NH.

1. A package holds 12 pencils. Which of the following expressions gives the number of pencils you have if you buy n packages of pencils and 3 single pencils?

   A $n + 12$ **C** $n - 12$

   B $12n$ **D** $n \div 12$

   (Chapter 3, Lesson 1)

2. Joel works a total of 16 hours on Friday, Saturday, and Sunday. He works twice as many hours on Saturday as on Friday. Joel works 4 hours on Sunday. How many hours does Joel work on Saturday?

   F 3 hours **H** 6 hours

   G 4 hours **J** NH

   (Grade 4)

Open Response

Solve each problem.

3. A kitchen is 8 feet long and 10 feet wide. How many tiles would you need to cover the floor with tiles that are 1 foot long and 1 foot wide?

   Represent Support your solution with a picture. (Grade 4)

4. Find the value of each symbol:

   ■, ●, ▲

   ■ + ■ = 80

   ■ + ● = 140

   ● − ▲ = ▲

   Explain How did you find the value of each symbol? (Chapter 2, Lesson 5)

Extended Response

5. You are a ranger at a state park. You have made the list below.

Hiking Trail	Length (in miles)
Grassy Gait	0.75
Fir Mountain	2.60
Rabbit Hill	1.28
Deer Run	2.59
Cliff Challenge	1.78
Rocks and Streams	2.07

   a A park visitor wants to hike a trail that is at least 1.5 miles long. Which trail(s) would you recommend?

   b Another visitor wants to hike a trail that is no longer than 2 miles. Which trail(s) would you recommend?

   c There are plans to mark off a new trail that is longer than Deer Run but shorter than Fir Mountain. What are three possible lengths for the new trail?

   (Chapter 1, Lesson 7)

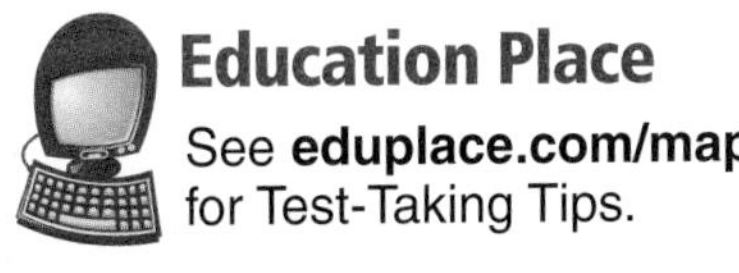

Education Place

See **eduplace.com/map** for Test-Taking Tips.

Lesson 4

Multiply by One-Digit Numbers

Objective Multiply by one-digit numbers.

Learn About It

A plane flies at an average speed of 528 miles an hour. How far does it fly in 6 hours?

Multiply to solve the problem.

Find 6 × 528.

STEP 1 Multiply the ones. Regroup if necessary.

$$\begin{array}{r} {}^{4}\\ 528 \\ \times \quad 6 \\ \hline 8 \end{array}$$

6 × 8 ones = 48 ones
48 ones = 4 tens + 8 ones

STEP 2 Multiply the tens. Add any regrouped tens. Regroup if necessary.

$$\begin{array}{r} {}^{1\,4}\\ 528 \\ \times \quad 6 \\ \hline 68 \end{array}$$

6 × 2 tens = 12 tens
12 tens + 4 tens = 16 tens
16 tens = 1 hundred + 6 tens

STEP 3 Multiply the hundreds. Add any regrouped hundreds.

$$\begin{array}{r} {}^{1\,4}\\ 528 \\ \times \quad 6 \\ \hline 3{,}168 \end{array}$$

6 × 5 hundreds = 30 hundreds
30 hundreds + 1 hundred = 31 hundreds

Solution: In 6 hours, the plane flies 3,168 miles.

To help you understand how multiplication works, you can use the Distributive Property.

Find the value of 6*n*, when *n* = 528.

6×528 ← Substitute 528 for *n*.

$6 \times 528 = 6 \times (500 + 20 + 8)$ ← Write one factor as a sum of numbers.
$= (6 \times 500) + (6 \times 20) + (6 \times 8)$ ← Use the Distributive Property.
$= 3{,}000 + 120 + 48$
$= 3{,}168$

Guided Practice

Ask Yourself

- Do I need to regroup?
- Did I remember to add the regrouped numbers?

Find the product.

1. 51×6
2. 673×4
3. $24{,}087 \times 4$
4. 3×84
5. 809×7
6. $6 \times 4{,}582{,}201$

Explain Your Thinking ▶ How can you use the Distributive Property to find the product in Exercise 5?

Practice and Problem Solving

Find the product.

7. 84×7
8. 38×9
9. 41×5
10. 746×3
11. 314×8
12. 859×4
13. 773×3
14. 246×7
15. $4{,}251 \times 8$
16. $57{,}962 \times 6$
17. $14{,}676 \times 4$
18. $314{,}796 \times 2$
19. $93{,}007 \times 7$
20. $3{,}785{,}092 \times 2$
21. $90{,}608{,}374 \times 3$

x Algebra • Functions **Copy and complete each function table.**

22.

Rule: $y = 5x$				
x	478	392	5,206	1,821
y				

23.

Rule: $y = 10x$				
x	478	392	5,206	1,821
y				

24.

Rule: $y = 3x$				
x	478	392	5,206	1,821
y				

25.

Rule: $y = 6x$				
x	478	392	5,206	1,821
y				

26. Explain how you could use the answers from Exercise 24 to find the answers for Exercise 25.

Use the Distributive Property to rewrite each expression. Then solve.

27. 5×76

28. 902×6

29. $7 \times 8{,}041$

30. $8 \times 82{,}752$

Algebra • Expressions Evaluate each expression, when $a = 3$, $b = 67$, $c = 489$, and $d = 9{,}570$.

31. $7c$

32. $3a \times b$

33. $9(2 \times d)$

34. $a \times d$

Solve.

35. Cleveland, Ohio, is about 2,550 miles from Los Angeles, California. If a train makes 4 round trips from Cleveland to Los Angeles, how far does it travel?

36. Peter averages 5 miles an hour on his scooter. At that rate, how many miles would he travel if he rode the scooter for 24 hours during the week?

37. It is approximately 400 miles from The Everglades in southern Florida to the Florida/Georgia border. If a hot air balloon is traveling 86 mi/h, could it cover that distance in 4 hours? Explain your answer.

38. One train car can carry a maximum of 108 passengers. How many passengers can a train carry with 6 completely full cars? If, in one day, that train makes 8 trips while completely full, how many passengers did it carry that day?

39. Hot air balloons can travel at speeds of up to 200 mi/h. At that rate, how many miles can a hot air balloon travel in 7 hours?

40. Look at the problem below. Find digits that make the multiplication true. Can you find two different answers?

```
  ■ ■,8 ■ 4
×         6
-----------
  ■ 4,■ 2 4
```

Extra Practice See page 83 Set B.

Activity

Algebraic Thinking

Product Patterns

Use a calculator to find the products below.

1. $37 \times 3 = ?$
$37 \times 6 = ?$
$37 \times 9 = ?$

2. $99 \times 11 = ?$
$99 \times 22 = ?$
$99 \times 33 = ?$

3. $143 \times 7 = ?$
$143 \times 14 = ?$
$143 \times 21 = ?$

For each set:

- Describe the pattern in the factors.
- Describe the pattern in the products.
- Predict the next two equations in each set. Use your calculator to check your predictions.

Challenge **Now use your calculator to make your own pattern. Write the first three equations. Then give them to a classmate and have them predict the next two equations.**

Quick Check

Check your understanding of Lessons 1–4.

Evaluate each expression. Tell which property you used. (Lesson 1)

1. $(32 \times n) \times 25$, given $n = 4$

2. $2 \times 20 \times a$, given $a = 1$

Draw and divide a rectangle to show each product.
Use the Distributive Property to find the product. (Lesson 2)

3. 5×13

4. 9×24

5. 3×35

Find the product. (Lesson 4)

6. 69×7

7. 342×9

8. 274×4

Solve. Tell what strategy you used. (Lesson 3)

9. Barbara, Elmo, Zachary, and Alejandro are in line to buy tickets to ride on a hot air balloon. Barbara is third. Zachary is not first or second. Alejandro is not first. In what position is each person?

Lesson 5

Algebra

Patterns in Multiples of 10

Objective Use mental math to multiply a number by a multiple of 10.

Learn About It

Some large ships can carry about 2,000 passengers per trip. About how many passengers could such a ship carry in 8 trips?

Multiply. $8 \times 2{,}000 = n$

Different Ways to Multiply by Multiples of 10

Way 1 You can use patterns.

$8 \times 2 = 16$
$8 \times 20 = 160$
$8 \times 200 = 1{,}600$
$8 \times 2{,}000 = 16{,}000$

Way 2 You can use mental math.

$8 \times 2{,}000 = 8 \times 2 \times 1{,}000$
$= 16 \times 1{,}000$
$= 16{,}000$

Solution: It could carry about 16,000 passengers in 8 trips.

Multiplying 24 × 40 is the same as doing one-digit multiplication and then multiplying by 10.

Find 24 × 40.

Think
$24 \times 40 = 24 \times 4 \times 10$

STEP 1 Find 24 × 4

$$\begin{array}{r} 24 \\ \times\ 4 \\ \hline 96 \end{array}$$

STEP 2 Then multiply the result by 10.

$96 \times 10 = 960$

Other Examples

A. First Product Ends in Zero

Find 6 × 50,000.

$6 \times 5 = 30$
$6 \times 5{,}000 = 30{,}000$
$6 \times 50{,}000 = 300{,}000$

B. Both Factors Are Multiples of 10

Find 8,000 × 4,000.

$8{,}000 \times 4{,}000 = 8 \times 1{,}000 \times 4 \times 1{,}000$
$= 8 \times 4 \times 1{,}000 \times 1{,}000$
$= 32{,}000{,}000$

Guided Practice

Ask Yourself
• How many places in the product will contain zeros?
• Have I multiplied correctly?

Use a pattern or mental math to find each product.

1. 4 × 90 **2.** 7 × 500 **3.** 5 × 700

4. 800 × 50 **5.** 40 × 60 **6.** 60 × 4,000

Multiply.

7. 59 × 10 **8.** 32 × 40 **9.** 265 × 30 **10.** 3,970 × 80

Explain Your Thinking ▶ How many zeros will be in the product of 40 × 3,000? How do you know?

Practice and Problem Solving

Use a pattern or mental math to find each product.

11. 80 × 4 **12.** 50 × 9 **13.** 400 × 3 **14.** 700 × 7

15. 40 × 5 **16.** 60 × 6 **17.** 9,000 × 2 **18.** 7,000 × 8

19. 7,000 × 30 **20.** 6,000 × 30 **21.** 20 × 500 **22.** 70 × 900

Multiply.

23. 28 × 10 **24.** 74 × 30 **25.** 88 × 60 **26.** 42 × 70

27. 376 × 20 **28.** 66 × 60 **29.** 675 × 70 **30.** 812 × 60

Solve.

31. A round-trip plane ticket from Raleigh to Chicago costs $300. How much would it cost a family of 4 to fly round trip from Raleigh to Chicago?

32. Maureen and Sally drove 8 hours a day for 6 days. Their average speed was about 50 miles an hour. How many miles did they drive?

Mixed Review and Test Prep

Open Response

Round to the place of the underlined digit. (Ch. 1, Lesson 4)

33. <u>6</u>7 **34.** 7<u>4</u>,498

35. <u>3</u>52 **36.** <u>8</u>,624

37. How can you use mental math to find the product of 50 × 9,000? (Ch. 3, Lesson 5)

Explain how you got your answer.

Extra Practice See page 83, Set C.

Lesson 6

Audio Tutor 1/9 Listen and Understand

Estimate Products

Objective Estimate products using front-end estimation and rounding.

Vocabulary
front-end estimation

Learn About It

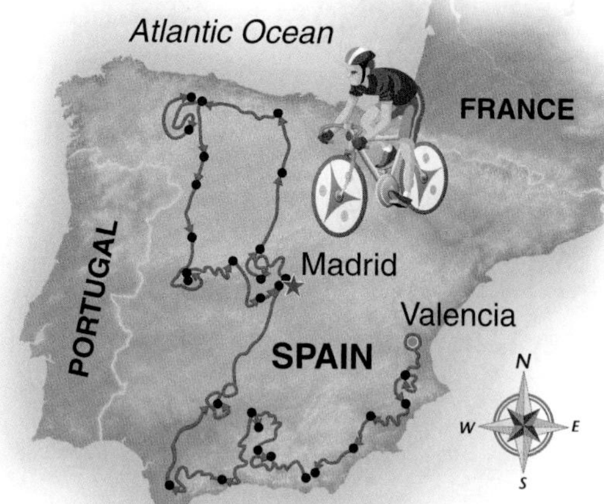

The Tour of Spain bicycle race is held every year. The map shows a recent race course of 3,144 kilometers. If you cycle an average of 75 kilometers a day, can you finish this course in 8 weeks?

8 weeks = 56 days

Since you only need to know if 56 days is enough time to complete the course, use **front-end estimation** .

Estimate: **56 × 75.**

To use front-end estimation, multiply the digits in the greatest place.

$$\begin{array}{r} 75 \\ \times\ 56 \\ \hline \end{array}$$

Front-end estimate: 50 × 70 = 3,500

Since you are rounding both numbers down, a front-end estimate is less than the actual product.

Solution: Yes. Since 3,500 > 3,144, eight weeks is enough time.

If you cycle an average of 75 km a day for 56 days, about how many kilometers can you cycle?

An estimate made by rounding is sometimes less and sometimes greater than the product.

You can use rounding to estimate.

STEP 1 Round each factor.

75 rounds to 80

56 rounds to 60

STEP 2 Multiply the rounded factors.

$$\begin{aligned} 80 \times 60 &= 8 \times 10 \times 6 \times 10 \\ &= (8 \times 6) \times 10 \times 10 \\ &= 48 \times 100 \\ &= 4{,}800 \end{aligned}$$

Solution: You can cycle about 4,800 kilometers.

You can find a range for the actual product by rounding both factors down and rounding both factors up.

Round both down.

$$\begin{array}{r} 70 \\ \times\ 50 \\ \hline 3{,}500 \end{array}$$

Round both up.

$$\begin{array}{r} 80 \\ \times\ 60 \\ \hline 4{,}800 \end{array}$$

Solution: The actual product will fall between 3,500 and 4,800.

Extra Help at **eduplace.com/map**

Guided Practice

Estimate by using front-end estimation. Then estimate by rounding.

1. 48 × 86
2. 73 × 34
3. 62 × 871

Estimate. Give a range for the actual product.

4. 25 × 47
5. 31 × 87
6. 88 × 491

Ask Yourself

- How do I round each number?
- How do I use front-end estimation and rounding to find a range in which the actual product may fall?

Explain Your Thinking ▶ How do you know that the actual product of 69 × 58 is between 3,000 and 4,200?

Practice and Problem Solving

Estimate by using front-end estimation and then by rounding. Then multiply. Circle the estimate that is more accurate.

7. 65 × 84
8. 28 × 67
9. 33 × 54
10. 17 × 96
11. 76 × 521
12. 975 × 76
13. 709 × 71
14. 13 × 555

Estimate. Give a range that includes the actual product.

15. 16 × 39
16. 45 × 22
17. 58 × 67
18. 37 × 51
19. 76 × 473
20. 507 × 45
21. 87 × 712
22. 364 × 39

Solve.

23. Ken cycles an average of 12 kilometers per day. About how many kilometers does Ken cycle in 4 weeks?

24. Nicolas has 16 baseball cards. Each card is worth $21. About how much are his 16 baseball cards worth?

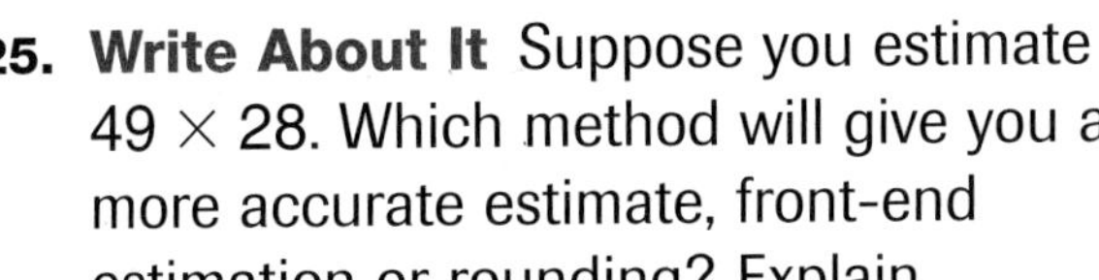

25. **Write About It** Suppose you estimate 49 × 28. Which method will give you a more accurate estimate, front-end estimation or rounding? Explain.

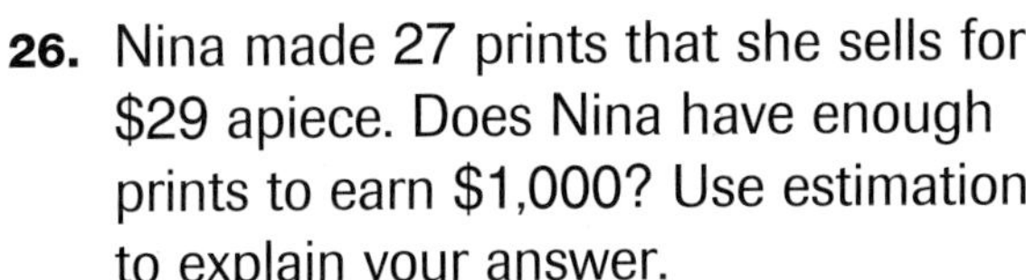

26. Nina made 27 prints that she sells for $29 apiece. Does Nina have enough prints to earn $1,000? Use estimation to explain your answer.

Mixed Review and Test Prep

Open Response

Add. (Ch. 2, Lesson 3)

27. 29 + 5
28. 36 + 8
29. 57 + 7
30. 43 + 4
31. 13 + 3
32. 60 + 9

Multiple Choice

33. Which is the best estimate of 447 × 68? (Ch. 3, Lesson 6)

A 24,000
B 28,000
C 30,000
D 35,000

Extra Practice See page 83, Set D.

Lesson 7

Multiply by Two-Digit Numbers

Objective Multiply by a two-digit number.

Learn About It

One train engineer makes a weekly salary of $986. How much does that train engineer earn in a year?

There are 52 weeks in a year.

Find 986 × 52.

Different Ways to Use the Distributive Property to Find 52 × 986

Way 1 Use an equation.

$$986 \times 52 = n$$
$$\begin{aligned} 986 \times 52 &= 986 \times (50 + 2) \\ &= (986 \times 50) + (986 \times 2) \\ &= 49{,}300 + 1{,}972 \\ &= 51{,}272 \end{aligned}$$

Way 2

STEP 1 Multiply by the ones digit.

```
  11
  986
× 52
 1972  ← 2 × 986
```

STEP 2 Multiply by the tens digit.

```
  43
  11
  986
× 52
 1972
49300  ← 50 × 986
```

STEP 3 Add the partial products.

```
    43
    11
    986
  × 52
   1972
+ 49300
 51,272
```

Solution: The engineer earns $51,272 a year.

Other Examples

A.

```
   2
   5
   47
 × 38
  376  ← 8 × 47
+ 1410 ← 30 × 47
 1,786
```

B.

```
      1
    1 1
    2,231
  ×    54
     8924  ← 4 × 2,231
+  111550  ← 50 × 2,231
   120,474
```

Guided Practice

Ask Yourself

- Did I align the digits correctly to add the partial products?

Find each product. Estimate or use a calculator to check.

1. 57×26

2. 71×34

3. 406×25

4. 236×78

Explain Your Thinking ▶ How can you use the Distributive Property to find the product in Exercise 2?

Practice and Problem Solving

Find each product. Estimate or use a calculator to check.

5. 59×15

6. 36×19

7. 74×24

8. 249×33

9. 82×57

10. 178×16

11. 840×35

12. 98×89

13. 25×98 **14.** 37×85 **15.** 54×73 **16.** 605×52

17. 62×63 **18.** 758×76 **19.** 308×68 **20.** 54×495

Use the Distributive Property to rewrite each expression. Then evaluate.

21. 28×76 **22.** 57×14 **23.** 29×206 **24.** 38×532

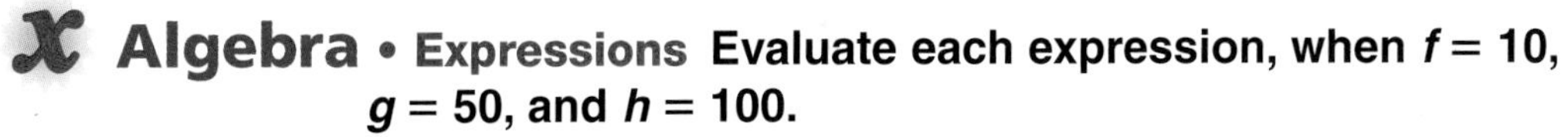

Evaluate each expression, when $f = 10$, $g = 50$, and $h = 100$.

25. $39h$ **26.** $375f$ **27.** $35g$ **28.** $30(f \cdot g)$ **29.** $(7 \cdot h) \cdot 21$

Use a calculator to evaluate each expression.

30. $52m$, when $m = 105$

31. $74 \cdot z$, when $z = 708$

32. $8 \cdot 4 \cdot p$, when $p = 62$

33. $2 \cdot x \cdot y$, when $x = 7$ and $y = 32$

34. $3b \cdot b$, when $b = 17$

35. $(d \cdot e) \cdot f$, when $d = 5$, $e = 29$, and $f = 46$

Go On

Choose a Computation Method

Mental Math • Estimation • Paper and Pencil • Calculator

Data Use the tables to solve Problems 36–40.

Passengers who fly on Europa Air between the cities shown in the Air Distances table earn one frequent flier mile for each mile they fly. They can use frequent flier miles to buy the awards shown in the frequent flier award table.

Frequent Flier Awards	
Award	**Miles Required for Award**
Upgrade ticket from Coach to First-Class, one-way	10,000
Free Round-Trip Coach Ticket	25,000
Free Round-Trip First-Class Ticket	40,000

36. Mr. Himmel flies round trip between Berlin and Rome once a month. How many frequent flier miles does he earn from these trips in a year?

37. Ingrid has enough frequent flier miles to get 10 free round-trip coach tickets. What is the minimum number of frequent flier miles that Ingrid must have?

38. Ms. Nolan makes 21 round trips between Madrid and London and 4 round trips between Madrid and Stockholm. How many miles does she fly?

Air Distances

From \ To	Berlin	Madrid
London	583 mi	785 mi
Moscow	1,006 mi	2,147 mi
Paris	548 mi	655 mi
Rome	737 mi	851 mi
Stockholm	528 mi	1,653 mi

39. Joel makes 10 round trips between Moscow and Madrid. About how many miles does he fly? Does he earn enough frequent flier miles for a free round-trip first-class ticket? Explain your answer.

40. **You Decide** Suppose you are living in Berlin. You have 120,000 frequent flier miles. How would you use your miles? Explain your thinking.

Mixed Review and Test Prep

Open Response

How many minutes and hours are there between these times?
(Grade 4)

41. 3:15 A.M. to 11:05 A.M.

42. 10:20 P.M. to 2:53 A.M.

Multiple Choice

43. A plane carries 425 passengers. How many passengers can the plane carry in 24 trips? (Ch. 3, Lesson 7)

A 1,700 **C** 10,200

B 8,500 **D** 12,000

Extra Practice See page 83, Set F.

Problem Solving

Math Reasoning

"Don't Get Caught Short"

Different situations require different types of estimation.

In a store, you should always round up. Remember that there may be a sales tax on certain items. Depending on the state in which you shop, the average sales tax is 5 to 10 cents for every dollar that you spend.

- Allie has $50. She wants to buy 3 DVDs. Each one costs $16. The total tax is $3. Does she have enough money? Explain how you got your answer.

Math Reasoning

Transportation Estimation

The number of air travelers is expected to triple over the next 20 years. In 1997, Los Angeles International Airport was the fourth busiest in the world, with 60,143,000 passengers. If the number of travelers triples as expected, about how many passengers will use that airport in 2017?

Brain Teaser

What are the next 3 letters in each sequence?

S S M T W __ __ __

O T T F F __ __ __

J F M A M __ __ __

Education Place

Check out **eduplace.com/map** for more Brain Teasers.

Lesson 8

Problem-Solving Decision

Explain Your Solution

Objective Decide whether an exact answer or a range of estimates is needed to explain the solution.

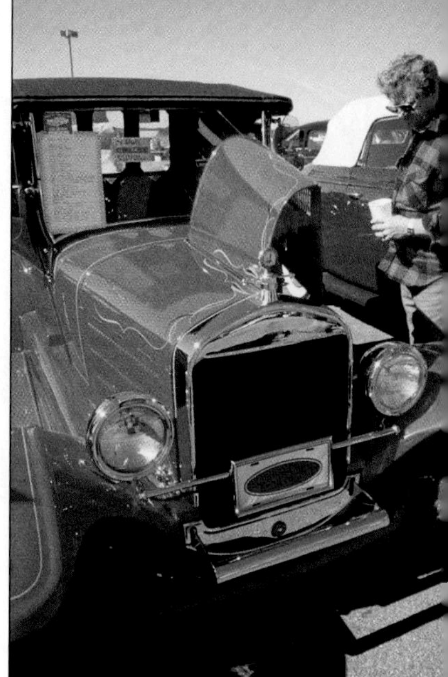

When you solve a problem, you may need an exact computation to explain your solution. At other times, an estimate may be sufficient.

Problem For the past 3 years, the Antique Automobile Club's show has averaged 880 tickets sold per year. Ticket sales are expected to be about the same this year. If the show costs $30,000 to put on, will a ticket price of $35 be enough to cover costs? Explain your answer.

Ask Yourself

- **Do I need an exact answer or is a range of estimates good enough?**

Estimate first.

800 × $30 = $24,000

900 × $40 = $36,000

I can't tell if $35 will work.

Find the exact answer.

880 × $35 = $30,800

Solution: Since $30,800 > $30,000, a ticket price of $35 will be enough to cover costs. In this case an estimate did not give the needed information to solve the problem.

Try These

Solve. Explain your answer.

1. Zida and Sarah are driving from New York to San Francisco. The trip is 2,934 miles. If they travel a maximum of 385 miles per day, will they complete the trip in a week?

2. There are 36 antique cars on display at the antique auto show. A photographer wants to take 16 shots of each car. If he has rolls of film with 24 pictures each, will 24 rolls of film be enough?

3. Alfred bought an antique car for $24,495. Alfred spent $6,000 restoring the car. He sold the car for $60,000. Did Alfred receive double the amount of money he spent buying and restoring the car?

4. **Create and Solve** Write and solve a problem that requires an exact answer. Then, write and solve a problem in which a range of estimates will be sufficient.

Solve. Explain your answer.

5. Tickets for the boat show are $24. The cost of putting on the boat show is $12,000. If 600 people come to the boat show, will this be enough to cover costs?

6. Marni has $125. She spends $49 on pants and $58 on sandals. Does she have enough money to buy a $25 tee shirt?

7. Kim, Karl, and Kris have $20 to pay for lunch. They order 3 sandwiches for $4 each, a large salad to share for $5, and a quart of milk for $2. Will they have enough to give their server a $2 tip?

8. **You Decide** Larry is planning a trip. To travel by car, it would cost $100 for gas each way and $275 for hotels. To travel by plane, it would cost $135 each way and $155 for hotels. Which way would be less expensive for Larry?

Problem Solving

Reading Connection

"In 1,500 Words or Less . . ."

In school, you may be asked to write a book report that is a certain number of words or a certain number of pages in length.

If you double space, you can fit about 250 words on each page.

You can use that estimate, 250 words per page, to determine how many words a paper will be without counting each individual word.

- If you are asked to write a 10-page paper, how many words is that?
- Suppose you are to write an essay in "1,500 words or less." If you use all 1,500 words, how many pages will that be?

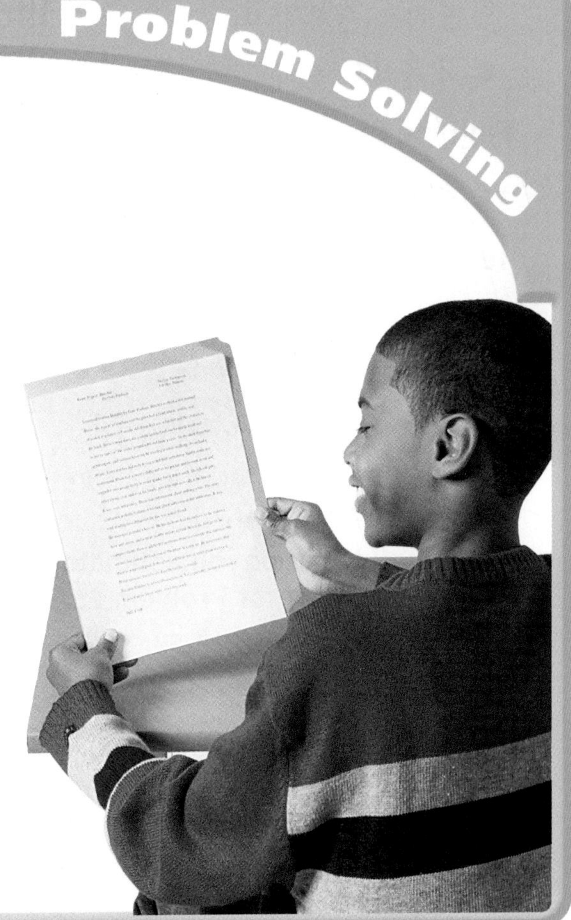

WEEKLY WR READER eduplace.com/map

Chapter Review/Test

VOCABULARY

1. The equation $5 \times 24 = 5 \times 20 + 5 \times 4$ illustrates the ____.
2. The ____ of Multiplication states that the product of any number and 0 is 0.
3. An example of the ____ is $3 \times 4 = 4 \times 3$.
4. $12 \times (2 \times 5) = (12 \times 2) \times 5$ illustrates the ____.

Vocabulary

- Associative Property
- Commutative Property
- Distributive Property
- Identity Property
- Zero Property

CONCEPTS AND SKILLS

Simplify. Tell which property or properties you used.
(Lessons 1–2, pp. 60–63)

5. $2 \times 7 \times 5$
6. 5×15
7. $9 \times 0 \times 8$
8. 2×93
9. $6 \times 1 \times 1$
10. $25 \times 3 \times 4$

Find the product. (Lessons 4–5, 7, pp. 68–70, 72–73, 76–78)

11. 65×9
12. 347×5
13. $21{,}407 \times 4$
14. 5×700
15. 50×900
16. 87×44
17. 571×83
18. 605×76

Estimate using front-end estimation. Then estimate by rounding. (Lesson 6, pp. 74–75)

19. 25×42
20. 91×74
21. 37×629
22. 88×456
23. 75×29

PROBLEM SOLVING

Solve. Tell whether you estimated or found an exact answer for Problem 25.
(Lesson 3, pp. 64–66, Lesson 8, pp. 80–81)

24. Luis, Sy, Dov, and Rey went to music camp for 4, 5, 6, and 8 weeks. Luis did not stay at camp for 4 weeks. Sy was away the longest. Rey was at camp longer than Luis. How much time did each spend at camp?
25. If Amy sells items worth $500 or more during the school fundraiser, she will receive a prize. Amy sells to 47 households at an average price of $11.95 per sale. Will Amy receive a prize?

Show You Understand

How are the identity properties of addition and multiplication alike? How are they different?

Extra Practice

Set A (Lesson 1, pp. 60–61)

Write an expression for each.

1. 12 more than a number **2.** the product of a number and 20 **3.** a number divided by 5

Simplify. Tell which property you used.

4. $(50 \cdot 16) \cdot 2$ **5.** $57 \times 0 \times 9$ **6.** $250 \cdot (9 \cdot 4)$ **7.** $3 \cdot 1 \cdot 9$

Evaluate each expression, given $n = 2$, $t = 12$, $v = 9$.

8. $8 \cdot n$ **9.** $3 \cdot (t - v)$ **10.** $v \cdot (t - n)$ **11.** $50 - v$

Set B (Lesson 4, pp. 68–71)

Find the product.

1. 67×4 **2.** 382×6 **3.** $92{,}093 \times 7$ **4.** $471{,}526 \times 9$ **5.** $1{,}378{,}602 \times 8$

Set C (Lesson 5, pp. 72–73)

Use a pattern or mental math to find each product.

1. 70×5 **2.** 30×9 **3.** 400×5 **4.** $2{,}000 \times 9$

5. 90×50 **6.** 20×80 **7.** $6{,}000 \times 60$ **8.** $70 \times 7{,}000$

Set D (Lesson 6, pp. 74–75)

Estimate by using front-end estimation. Then estimate by rounding.

1. 45×76 **2.** 33×29 **3.** 81×45 **4.** 86×76

5. 37×891 **6.** 495×62 **7.** 98×663 **8.** 278×48

Set E (Lesson 7, pp. 76–79)

Find each product. Estimate to check.

1. 84×29 **2.** 136×23 **3.** 619×97 **4.** 680×72 **5.** 456×25

6. 82×43 **7.** 96×17 **8.** 902×65 **9.** 740×79 **10.** 807×92

Extra Practice at **eduplace.com/map**

CHAPTER 4

Divide by One-Digit Numbers

INVESTIGATION

Use Data

Jennifer has a collection of stamps. She wants to put her stamps in an album. She does not want to mix different categories of stamps. How many stamps should she put on each page? How many pages will she need? Explain your decisions.

Category	Number
President stamps	8
State stamps	24
Animal stamps	20
Flower stamps	44
Foreign stamps	29

Use What You Know

Use this page to review and remember what you need to know for this chapter.

VOCABULARY

Choose the best word to complete each sentence.

Vocabulary
dividend
divisor
factor
quotient
remainder

1. In 16 ÷ 2, 16 is the ____.
2. If the quotient is not a factor of the dividend, there is a ____.
3. In 16 ÷ 2, 2 is the ____.

CONCEPTS AND SKILLS

Write the fact family for each set of numbers.

4. 7, 9, 63
5. 3, 8, 24
6. 6, 7, 42
7. 8, 7, 56
8. 3, 5, 15

Complete.

9. $4\overline{)8\text{ hundreds}}$ with quotient ■ hundreds
10. $5\overline{)15\text{ hundreds}}$ with quotient ■ hundreds
11. $7\overline{)■\text{ hundreds}}$ with quotient 6 hundreds
12. $9\overline{)■\text{ thousands}}$ with quotient 5 thousands

Divide.

13. 640 ÷ 80
14. 484 ÷ 4
15. $4\overline{)73}$
16. $2\overline{)55}$
17. $6\overline{)73}$

Tell whether each statement is true or false. If false, correct the statement to make it true.

18. The quotient and the divisor can sometimes be equal.
19. The dividend and the divisor can never be equal.

20. Why is the remainder always less than the divisor?

Facts Practice, See page 661.

Lesson 1

Audio Tutor 1/11 Listen and Understand

Estimate Quotients

Objective Estimate quotients using basic multiplication facts.

Vocabulary

compatible numbers

Learn About It

Mary wants to organize her 2,340 baseball cards in album pages that each hold 8 cards. About how many pages will she need?

If a dividend is a multiple of a divisor, the dividend and divisor are **compatible numbers.** You can use compatible numbers to estimate a quotient.

Remember

divisor)dividend → quotient

Estimate 2,340 ÷ 8.

STEP 1 Decide where to place the first digit of the quotient. Use a basic fact to find the first digit.

8)2,340 — ? hundreds

Which numbers are compatible with 8?

What value of n makes $8 \times n$ close to 23?

$8 \times 3 = 24$

24 is close to 23, so 3 is the first digit.

STEP 2  Rewrite the dividend so that it is a multiple of the divisor.

8)2,400 — 300

2,400 is close to the dividend.
The estimated quotient is 300.

Check.
Multiplication and division are inverse operations. Use multiplication to check your division.

$8 \times 300 = 2{,}400$

Solution: Mary will need about 300 album pages.

Other Examples

A. Three-Digit Dividend

5)347

$34 \div 5 \approx 35 \div 5$

347 is close to 350.

5)350 — 70

$347 \div 5$ is about 70.

B. Five-Digit Dividend

4)91,654

$9 \div 4 \approx 8 \div 4$

91,654 is close to 80,000.

4)80,000 — 20,000

$91{,}654 \div 4$ is about 20,000.

Guided Practice

Estimate the quotient. Check.

1. $8\overline{)658}$
2. $5\overline{)2,674}$
3. $4\overline{)17,987}$
4. 7,274 ÷ 3
5. 36,149 ÷ 7
6. 563,217 ÷ 9

Ask Yourself

- What multiplication fact will help me find compatible numbers?
- How many digits should be in the estimated quotient?

Explain Your Thinking ▶ Without dividing, how do you know how many digits there will be in a quotient?

Practice and Problem Solving

Estimate the quotient. Check.

7. $7\overline{)223}$
8. $8\overline{)334}$
9. $9\overline{)713}$
10. $5\overline{)4,456}$
11. $7\overline{)1,498}$
12. $8\overline{)4,129}$
13. $9\overline{)45,212}$
14. $9\overline{)42,825}$
15. $8\overline{)39,541}$
16. $6\overline{)162,432}$
17. $9\overline{)342,785}$
18. $4\overline{)294,563}$
19. 248 ÷ 5
20. 813 ÷ 3
21. 2,514 ÷ 6
22. 3,512 ÷ 4
23. 16,945 ÷ 7
24. 46,127 ÷ 8
25. 648,792 ÷ 9
26. 791,342 ÷ 8

Solve.

27. A new box of baseball cards contains 718 cards. If the pages for an album hold 9 cards each, about how many pages are needed to hold all the cards in the set?

28. **You Decide** A box of 50 album pages costs $14.95. Each page holds 6 cards. Album folders with 10 pages, which hold 8 cards each, sell for $12.95. Which would you buy if you had 50 cards? 200 cards? Explain.

29. **Create and Solve** Write your own problem about a baseball card collection. Your problem should require estimating a quotient. Solve your problem, then give it to a partner to solve.

Mixed Review and Test Prep

Open Response

Fill in each ■. (Grade 4)

30. 9 yd = ■ ft
31. 3 yd = ■ in.
32. 6 ft = ■ in.
33. 12 ft = ■ yd
34. 2 mi = ■ ft
35. 36 in. = ■ yd

Multiple Choice

36. Grant put 356 baseball cards in pages that hold 9 cards each. Which is a reasonable estimate of the number of pages he used? (Ch. 4, Lesson 1)

A 4 pages
B 400 pages
C 40 pages
D 3,600 pages

Extra Practice See page 107, Set A.

Lesson 2

One-Digit Divisors

Objective Use compatible numbers and place value to divide.

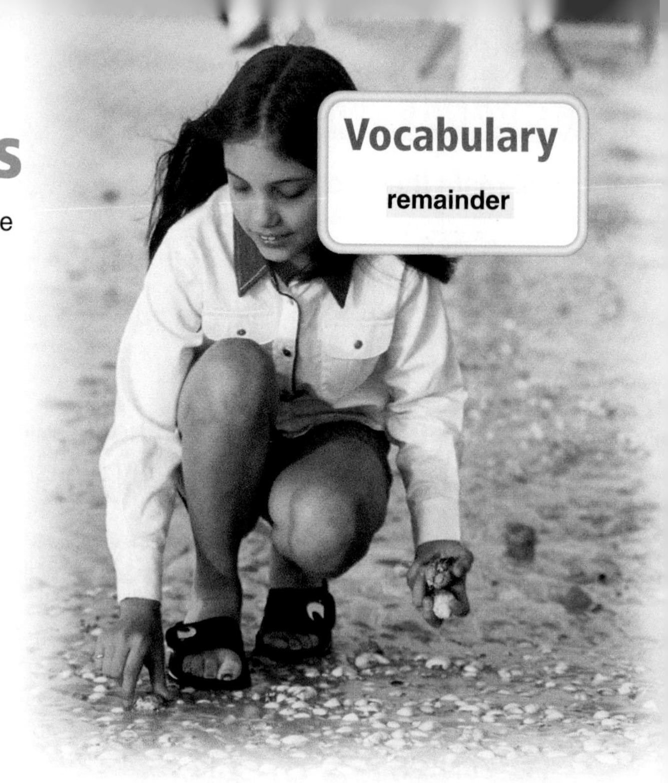

Vocabulary

remainder

Learn About It

A group of fifth-grade students collected 378 seashells. When they got back to class, they put an equal number of shells into 4 piles to study. How many shells are in each pile? How many are left over?

If the divisor is not a factor of the dividend then the answer will include a **remainder**.

Find 378 ÷ 4.

STEP 1 Use basic facts, rounding, and compatible numbers to decide where to place the first digit of the quotient.

$4\overline{)378}$

Think: ? hundreds, $4\overline{)3 \text{ hundreds}}$

3 < 4 There are not enough hundreds to divide. 378 ÷ 4 < 100

37 > 4 Place the first digit in the tens place.

STEP 2 Divide the tens.

Think: ? tens, $4\overline{)37 \text{ tens}}$

```
   9
4)378    Multiply. 9 × 4
 - 36    Subtract. 37 − 36
    1    Compare. 1 < 4
```

STEP 3 Bring down the ones. Divide the ones. Write the **remainder**.

Think: ? ones, $4\overline{)18 \text{ ones}}$

```
   94 R2
4)378
 - 36
   18    Bring down the 8 ones.
 - 16    Multiply. 4 × 4
    2    Subtract. 18 − 16
         Compare. 2 < 4
         The remainder is 2.
```

Check.
Multiply the quotient by the divisor. Then add the remainder. The result should be equal to the dividend.

$(94 \times 4) + 2 = 378$

Solution: There are 94 shells in each group and 2 shells left over.

Guided Practice

Divide and check.

1. $6\overline{)582}$ **2.** $8\overline{)9{,}814}$ **3.** $5\overline{)4{,}217}$

4. $2{,}616 \div 4$ **5.** $8{,}129 \div 7$ **6.** $469{,}642 \div 9$

Ask Yourself

- Can I divide the first digit in the dividend?
- Where should I write the first digit?

Explain Your Thinking ▶ Why must the remainder always be less than the divisor?

Practice and Problem Solving

Divide and check.

7. $6\overline{)556}$ **8.** $5\overline{)285}$ **9.** $3\overline{)732}$ **10.** $7\overline{)6{,}387}$

11. $4\overline{)5{,}824}$ **12.** $8\overline{)5{,}975}$ **13.** $9\overline{)38{,}217}$ **14.** $3\overline{)45{,}849}$

15. $9\overline{)58{,}239}$ **16.** $6\overline{)793{,}481}$ **17.** $9\overline{)867{,}142}$ **18.** $7\overline{)412{,}447}$

19. $894 \div 4$ **20.** $763 \div 2$ **21.** $4{,}873 \div 3$ **22.** $8{,}767 \div 5$

Find the missing divisor or dividend.

23. $\begin{array}{r} 7\text{ R4} \\ n\overline{)39} \end{array}$ **24.** $\begin{array}{r} 123 \\ 5\overline{)n} \end{array}$ **25.** $\begin{array}{r} 156 \\ 9\overline{)n} \end{array}$ **26.** $\begin{array}{r} 4\text{ R2} \\ n\overline{)26} \end{array}$

Solve.

27. A shop sells shadow boxes for displaying shells. If each box holds 8 shells, how many boxes are needed to display 456 shells?

28. Mavis has 512 shells. She has 3 times as many small shells as large shells. How many of each size does she have?

Mixed Review and Test Prep

Open Response

Divide. (Grade 4)

29. $36 \div 3$ **30.** $56 \div 7$

31. $48 \div 8$ **32.** $54 \div 6$

33. $55 \div 5$ **34.** $14 \div 2$

35. Midge arranges her collection of 762 seashells into trays with 8 shells in each tray. Show how to find the number of trays she needs. (Ch. 4, Lesson 2)

Extra Practice See page 107, Set B.

Lesson 3

Problem-Solving Application

Use Operations

Objective Choose operations to solve a problem.

You need to decide which operations to use to solve word problems.

Problem The Ryans have been collecting snowdomes for years. Now they want to organize their collection onto shelves. They will put 8 snowdomes on each shelf.

How many shelves will they need for their entire collection?

OUR SNOWDOMES

KIND	NUMBER
United States	96
World	48
Assorted	72

UNDERSTAND

What is the question?

How many shelves will they need for their entire collection?

What do you know?

- There are 96 snowdomes from the United States, 48 snowdomes from the world, and 72 assorted snowdomes.
- Each shelf will have 8 snowdomes.

PLAN

Add to find the total number of snowdomes.

Then divide by 8 to find the number of shelves needed.

SOLVE

- Find the total number of snowdomes. $96 + 48 + 72 = 216$
- Then divide. $216 \div 8 = 27$

Solution: The Ryans will need 27 shelves.

LOOK BACK

How can I check my answer?

Guided Practice

Use the table on page 90 to solve each problem. Name the operation(s) you used.

1. Suppose the Ryans decide to put 8 snowdomes of only one kind on each shelf. How many shelves will they need for their collection?

   Hint How many shelves do they need for each kind of snowdome?

2. The Ryans bought a box of snowdomes from the United States. They now have 32 shelves of snowdomes with 8 on each shelf and 1 more shelf with 6 snowdomes. How many snowdomes were in the box?

Ask Yourself

What does the question ask me to find?

Did I use the correct information from the table?

- **Did I decide which operation(s) to use?**
- **Did I use the operations in the correct order?**

Did I check my answer?

Independent Practice

Data **Use the table for Problems 3–6. Name the operation(s) you used.**

3. Sue Ann paid $6 each for her Remember the Alamo snowdomes. How much profit will she make if she sells all of her Remember the Alamo snowdomes?

4. Sue Ann put all the snowdomes in layers in a carton. She put 8 snowdomes in a layer. How many layers in the carton did she make with her snowdomes?

5. Since Sue Ann posted her snowdomes on her Web site, she has sold half of her collection. About how much money has she made?

6. Robert spent $19 on 3 snowdomes. He bought The Windy City, Remember the Alamo, and one other. Which other snowdome did he buy? Explain the steps you took to find your answer.

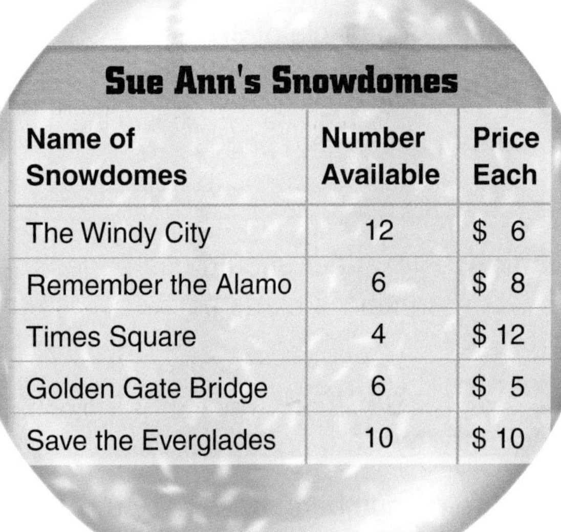

Sue Ann's Snowdomes

Name of Snowdomes	Number Available	Price Each
The Windy City	12	$ 6
Remember the Alamo	6	$ 8
Times Square	4	$ 12
Golden Gate Bridge	6	$ 5
Save the Everglades	10	$ 10

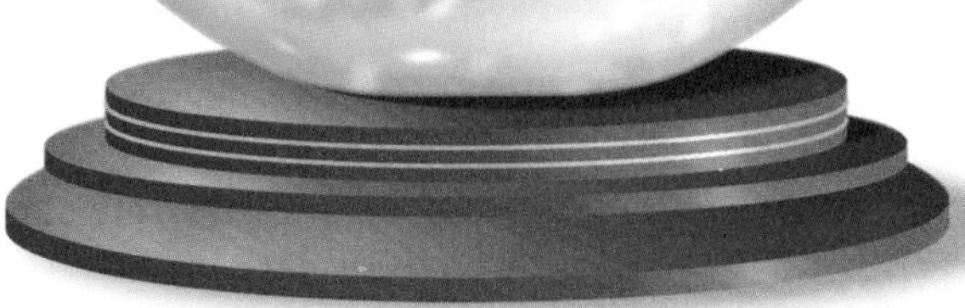

Lesson 4

Audio Tutor 1/12 Listen and Understand

Divisibility

Objective Determine when 2, 3, 4, 5, 6, 9, or 10 is a factor of a number.

Vocabulary

divisible
factor

Learn About It

A number is **divisible** by another number when the quotient is a whole number and there is no remainder. Any **factor** of a given number divides into that number with no remainder.

Alexander has collected 2,032 picture postcards from around the world. He wants to organize the collection into 3-ring binders, and he wants each page filled, with no cards left over. Should he use pages that can contain 3 cards each or 4 cards each?

Is 2,032 divisible by 3 or 4?

Decide whether 2,032 is divisible by 3.

If 2,032 is divisible by 3, then the sum of the digits of 2,032 is equal to a multiple of 3.

$$2 + 0 + 3 + 2 = 7$$

7 is not a multiple of 3.

2,032 is not divisible by 3, so Alexander cannot use 3-card pages.

Decide whether 2,032 is divisible by 4.

If 2,032 is divisible by 4, then the last 2 digits make up a multiple of 4.

The last 2 digits are 3 and 2, and 32 is a multiple of 4.

2,032 is divisible by 4, so Alexander can use 4-card pages.

Solution: Alexander should use pages that can contain 4 cards each.

Another Example

Divisibility by Zero

There are no numbers divisible by 0.

If $5 \div 0 = n$, then $n \times 0 = 5$.

There is no value for n that makes $n \times 0 = 5$ true. This means that the equivalent division sentence, $5 \div 0 = n$, has no solution.

Use divisibility rules to decide which of the numbers at right is divisible by 2, 3, 4, 5, 6, 9, and 10.

725 240 536
360 382 590

Eliminate the numbers that are not divisible by 2, 3, 4, 5, 6, 9, and 10.

STEP 1 Check for divisibility by 2. The number must end with 0, 2, 4, 6, or 8.

~~725~~ 240 536
360 382 590

STEP 2 Check for divisibility by 5. The number must end with 0 or 5.

240 ~~536~~ 360
~~382~~ 590

STEP 3 Check for divisibility by 10. The number must end in 0.

240 360 590

All of the remaining numbers are divisible by 10.

STEP 4 Check for divisibility by 4. The last two digits make up a number divisible by 4.

240 360 ~~590~~

STEP 5 Check for divisibility by 3. The sum of the digits must be divisible by 3.

240 360

Both are divisible by 3.

STEP 6 Check for divisibility by 6. The number must be divisible by both 2 and 3.

240 360

Both are divisible by 6.

STEP 7 Check for divisibility by 9. The sum of the digits must be divisible by 9.

~~240~~ 360

Think
$2 + 4 + 0 = 6$
$3 + 6 + 0 = 9$

Solution: The number 360 is divisible by 2, 3, 4, 5, 6, 9, and 10.

Guided Practice

Tell whether each number is divisible by 2, 3, 4, 5, 6, 9, or 10.

1. 325 **2.** 540 **3.** 393 **4.** 632

5. 315 **6.** 990 **7.** 323 **8.** 3,012

Ask Yourself

- Did I check the final digits for divisibility by 2, 4, 5, and 10?
- Did I check for divisibility by 3, 6, and 9?

Explain Your Thinking ▶ If a number is divisible by 9, must it be divisible by 3? Explain why or why not.

Go On

Practice and Problem Solving

Tell whether each number is divisible by 2, 3, 4, 5, 6, 9, or 10.

9. 110 **10.** 29 **11.** 177 **12.** 531 **13.** 455

14. 7,100 **15.** 1,278 **16.** 1,123 **17.** 6,765 **18.** 1,107

Algebra • Expressions Find a value of n that makes the expression divisible by 2, 3, and 5.

19. $18n$ **20.** $n + 7$ **21.** $10n$ **22.** $20 + n$

23. $9n + 3$ **24.** $n - 5$ **25.** $5n$ **26.** $2n - 4$

Data The table below shows the number of stamps in various stamp sets. Use the table for Problems 27–30.

Stamp Sets

Country	Number Per Set
Mexico	245
Canada	144
Brazil	270
United States	210

27. Dwayne bought a set of stamps whose number of stamps is divisible by 2, 3, 5, 6, 9, and 10. Which set is it?

28. One set of stamps is divisible only by 5. Which set is it? How can you tell?

29. Berta puts all the stamps from a set in an album. She puts 9 stamps on each page because that is the greatest number by which the number of stamps is divisible. Which set did Berta use?

30. Shelly bought one of each set. Use divisibility rules to see if 2, 3, 4, 5, 6, 9, or 10 stamps will fit on a page so that the same number of stamps are on each page.

31. Is a multiple of 2 always a multiple of 4? Is a multiple of 4 always a multiple of 2? Explain why or why not.

32. Write About It Tony says that if a number is divisible by 3 and 9, it must also be divisible by 6. Using examples, explain whether or not his rule works.

Extra Practice See page 107, Set C.

Activity

Algebraic Thinking

Finding Patterns

You can use your calculator to find division patterns.

STEP 1 Enter 1 followed by as many zeros as your display will show.

STEP 2 Now divide by 9. Drop the numbers after the decimal point.

100000000 ÷ 9 → 11111111

STEP 3 Repeat Steps 1 and 2 but enter a 2 first in Step 1.

200000000 ÷ 9 → 22222222

What do you predict you will see when you divide 300000000 by 9? Try it. What pattern do you notice? Use the pattern to predict what you will see when you divide 800000000 by 9.

Use the same steps as above but this time divide by 99. How is the pattern the same? How is it different?

Quick Check

Check your understanding of Lessons 1–4.

Estimate each quotient. Then divide. (Lessons 1–2)

1. 634 ÷ 8 **2.** 8,256 ÷ 7 **3.** 523 ÷ 6 **4.** 7,294 ÷ 3

Tell whether each number is divisible by 2, 3, 4, 5, 6, 9, or 10. (Lesson 4)

5. 332 **6.** 540 **7.** 945

Solve. Name the operation(s) you used. (Lesson 3)

8. Aunt Karen bought one set of 236 stamps and another set of 149 stamps. She gave the same number of stamps to each of her 5 nieces. How many stamps did each girl get?

Lesson 5

Zeros in the Quotient

Objective Determine when to put zeros in the quotient.

Learn About It

Ramón has 2,515 marbles. He has bought 5 plastic boxes for storing his marbles. If Ramón puts the same number of marbles in each box, how many marbles will be in each box?

Solve 2,515 ÷ 5 = *n*.

STEP 1 Decide where to place the first digit of the quotient. Then divide.

Think $5\overline{)2 \text{ thousands}}$? thousands

There are not enough thousands to divide.

Think $5\overline{)25 \text{ hundreds}}$? hundreds

```
   5
5)2515    Multiply 5 × 5
 - 25 ←   Subtract. 25 − 25
    0     ← Compare. 0 < 5
```

STEP 2 Bring down the tens. Divide the tens.

Think $5\overline{)1 \text{ ten}}$? ten

There are not enough tens to divide.

```
   50 ← Write 0 in the tens
5)2515   place to show that
 -25↓    the quotient has 0
   01    tens.
```

STEP 3 Bring down the ones. Divide the ones.

Think $5\overline{)15 \text{ ones}}$? ones

```
   503
5)2,515
 - 25 ↓
    015      Multiply. 3 × 5
   - 15  ←   Subtract. 15 − 15
      0      There is no
             remainder.
```

Check.
Multiply.
503 × 5 = 2,515

Solution: There will be 503 marbles in each of the 5 boxes.

Other Examples

A. Zero In The Dividend

```
  2,265 R3
4)9,063
 - 8↓
   10 ←  Bring down the zero from
  - 8    the hundreds place.
   26
  - 24
    23
   - 20
     3
```

B. More Than One Zero

```
   700 R4
7)4,904
 - 49
    00 ←  The result is 0, but there
   - 0    are more places to divide.
    04    Write 0 in the quotient,
   - 0    because 0 tens ÷ 7 = 0
     4    tens. Then continue.
```

Guided Practice

Divide and check.

1. 7)284 **2.** 4)3,602 **3.** 8)34,421

4. 301 ÷ 5 **5.** 2,801 ÷ 3 **6.** 240,120 ÷ 6

Ask Yourself

- Where do I write the first digit?
- How do I know when the division is done?

Explain Your Thinking ▶ In Exercise 5, what would happen if you did not bring down the zero?

Practice and Problem Solving

Divide and check.

7. 7)568 **8.** 3)624 **9.** 2)801 **10.** 8)5,632

11. 4)3,603 **12.** 5)43,004 **13.** 6)300,056 **14.** 2)121,481

15. 613 ÷ 3 **16.** 5,522 ÷ 6 **17.** 8,208 ÷ 8 **18.** 18,006 ÷ 5

19. 70,200 ÷ 9 **20.** 63,564 ÷ 7 **21.** 627,153 ÷ 3 **22.** 457,287 ÷ 9

Solve.

23. A company made 52,250 of one kind of marble in 5 days. Each day, it made the same number of marbles. How many marbles are made each day?

24. Fill in the missing numbers in the division.

```
      5■28
  6)■■,16■
   −■■
     01
    −■■
      ■■
     −12
       ■■
      −■■
         0
```

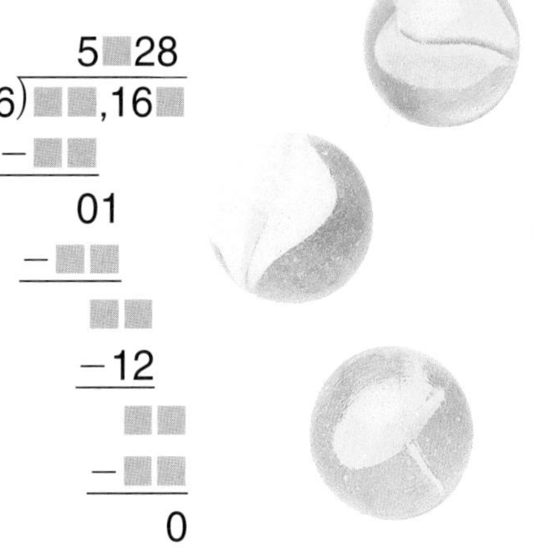

25. A toy show ran for two days. Tickets cost $3. On the first day, ticket sales were $3,213. On the second day, sales were $2,949. How many tickets were sold?

26. A collector of antique marbles paid $1,000 for 4 marbles. What is the average price paid per marble?

Mixed Review and Test Prep

Open Response

Round each number to the underlined place. (Ch. 1, Lessons 4 and 7)

27. 1.06$\underline{7}$4 **28.** $\underline{2}$45,324,936,316

29. 2.$\underline{5}$4 **30.** 22$\underline{4}$,809,302

31. 0.0$\underline{3}$5 **32.** 71$\underline{9}$,805

Multiple Choice

33. A marble collector has 1,230 marbles. If she displays them in trays that hold 6 marbles each, how many trays does she need? (Ch. 4, Lesson 5)

A 25 trays **B** 200 trays

C 205 trays **D** 230 trays

Extra Practice See page 107, Set D.

Lesson 6

Problem-Solving Strategy

Guess and Check

Objective Use guess and check to solve a problem.

Problem Glen collects 3 different kinds of salt and pepper shakers. The number of his sets with food is 3 times the number that show characters. The number of sets that show animals is divisible by 2 and 3. Glen has 24 sets. How many of each kind does he have?

UNDERSTAND

This is what you know:

- Glen has 24 sets of salt and pepper shakers.
- The number of food sets is 3 times the number of character sets.
- The number of animal sets is divisible by 2 and 3.

PLAN

You can use a Guess-and-Check strategy to solve the problem.

SOLVE

Use what you know. Organize your guesses in a table.

3 times C = F

A is divisible by 2 and 3.

F + C + A = 24

Continue guessing and checking until you know you have the correct answer.

Solution: Glen has 3 character, 12 animal, and 9 food sets.

Characters (C)	Food (F)	Animals (A)	Correct?
Think: If C is 1, then F must be 3 and A is 24 − (1 + 3), or 20.			
1	3	20	No. 20 is not divisible by 3.
2	6	16	No.
3	9	12	Yes.
4	12	8	No.
5	15	4	No.
6	18	0	No. He has 3 kinds of shakers.

LOOK BACK

Look back at the problem.

Is my answer reasonable? How do I know?

Guided Practice

Use the Ask Yourself questions to help you solve each problem.

1. Ella has 18 cuckoo clocks. Each clock is made of wood or plastic. She has twice as many wood cuckoo clocks as plastic ones. How many of each kind does she have?

2. Gene spent $25 for an unusual set of salt and pepper shakers. He paid for the set using $10, $5, and $1 bills. If he gave the clerk 8 bills in all, how many of each bill did he use?

   Hint What is the maximum number of $10 bills he could have used?

Ask Yourself

What facts do I know?

PLAN **Can I use Guess and Check?**

SOLVE

- **Did I make a reasonable first guess?**
- **Did I use the results from the guess to make a better guess?**

LOOK BACK **Did I solve the problem?**

Independent Practice

Use Guess and Check to solve each problem.

3. The fifth grade made $25 on a hobby show. They received only $5 and $1 bills and collected a total of 9 bills. What combination of bills did they receive?

4. Claudio has 6 more trees in his front yard than Flora. If they have 20 trees together, how many trees does each person have?

5. Scott has 13 music boxes that play either patriotic songs or holiday tunes. He has 5 more music boxes that play patriotic tunes than music boxes that play holiday tunes. How many of each kind does he have?

6. Ashley has 9 lawn ornaments. She has cat, dog, and bird lawn ornaments. If there are 30 legs in all on her lawn ornaments, how many bird ornaments does she have?

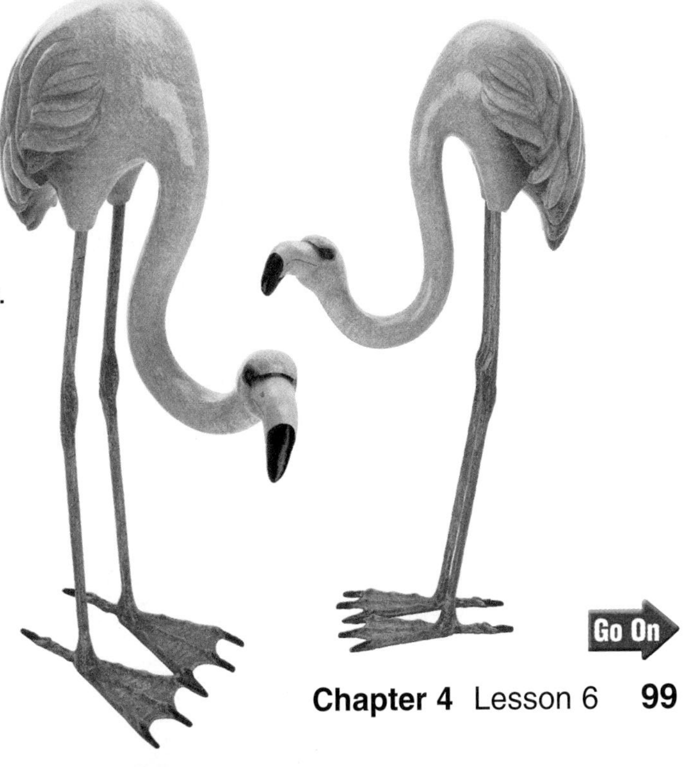

Go On

Mixed Problem Solving

Solve. Show your work. Tell what strategy you used.

7. At the first stop, 3 people got off and 7 people got on a bus. At the next stop, 8 people got off and 12 got on. Now the bus has 30 passengers. How many people did the bus have on it in the beginning of its route?

8. Pranee bought three shirts: one white, one blue, and one yellow. She bought a pair of tan shorts and a pair of green slacks. How many outfits can she make with these clothes?

9. **Measurement** Draw a rectangle whose length is 2 centimeters less than twice its width of 10 centimeters.

You Choose

Strategy
- Draw a Picture
- Make an Organized List
- Use Logical Reasoning
- Work Backward
- Write an Equation

Computation Method
- Mental Math
- Estimation
- Paper and Pencil
- Calculator

Data Use the graph to solve Problems 10–14.

Angie has an auction Web site for collectors of dolls and action figures. The graph shows the number of bids she got on her Web site at four times during one day.

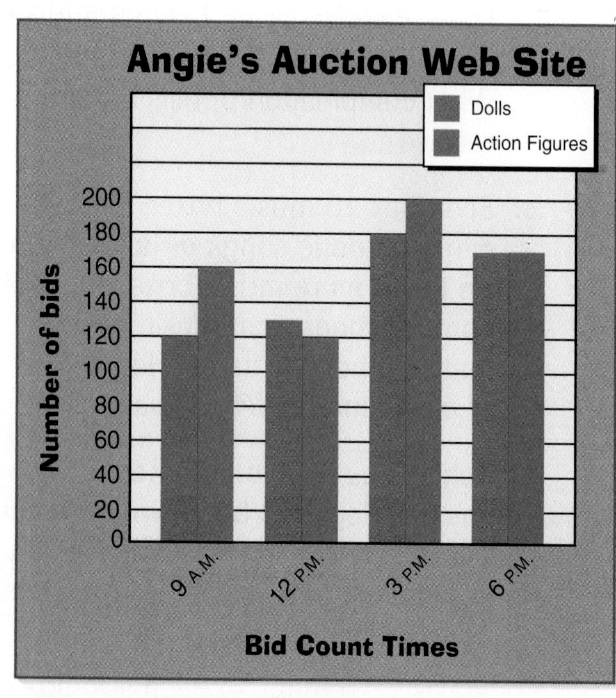

10. At 9:00 P.M., the number of bids on dolls was double the number at 9:00 A.M. How many bids on dolls were there at 9:00 P.M.?

11. Of the total number of bids, were more bids placed on dolls or action figures? How many more?

12. How many more bids for dolls came in at 3:00 P.M. and 6:00 P.M. than at 9:00 A.M. and 12:00 P.M.?

13. At which time was the combined number of bids on dolls and action figures between 300 and 350?

14. **Create and Solve** From the information given in the graph above, write your own problem and solve it.

Problem Solving on Tests

Multiple Choice

Choose the letter of the correct answer.

1. Alex, Sue, and Jo sold tickets for a show. Alex sold 52 tickets. Sue sold 10 more than Alex. Jo sold 10 more than Sue. How many tickets did Alex, Sue, and Jo sell in all?

   A 32 tickets **C** 124 tickets

   B 72 tickets **D** 186 tickets

   (Chapter 2, Lesson 6)

2. You exercise 10 minutes each day of Week 1. Each week you double your daily exercise time from the week before. How many minutes per day will you exercise in Week 5?

   F 50 minutes **H** 160 minutes

   G 80 minutes **J** 320 minutes

   (Chapter 1, Lesson 6)

Open Response

Solve each problem.

3. Which point on the number line represents a number that is divisible by both 2 and 6?

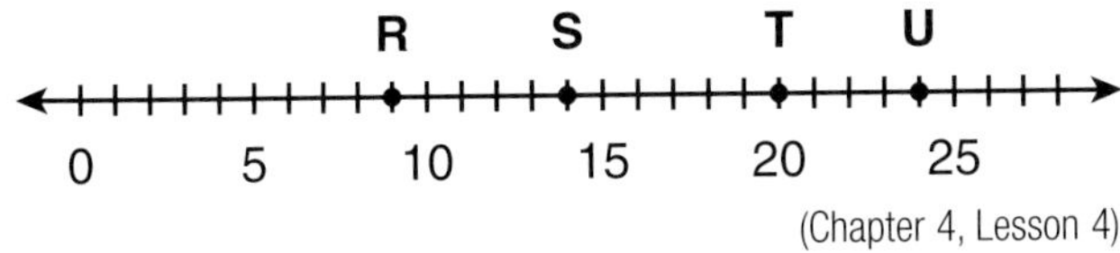

   (Chapter 4, Lesson 4)

4. Manny packed 8 boxes. The small boxes contain 4 bowls each, and the big boxes have 6 bowls each. If Manny packed 40 bowls, how many of each size box did he pack?

   Represent Support your solution by drawing a picture or making a table.

   (Chapter 4, Lesson 6)

Constructed Response

5. You decide to give away your collection of 1,800 marbles. Your friends Lena and Mel have agreed to help you. You divide the marbles equally among the three of you.

   a You give away your share to the 24 students in your class. Each classmate gets an equal number. How many marbles will each classmate get?

   b Lena gives away her share to the 30 students in her class. How many marbles will each person get if she divides her share evenly?

   c Mel decides to keep half the marbles you gave him. He gives away the other half. He wants to give fewer than 100 marbles to each person. Find three different numbers of friends who could get an equal number of marbles from Mel.

   (Chapter 5)

Education Place

See **eduplace.com/map** for Test-Taking Tips.

Lesson 7

Audio Tutor 1/13 Listen and Understand

Algebra

Solve Equations

Objective Use mental math to solve multiplication and division equations.

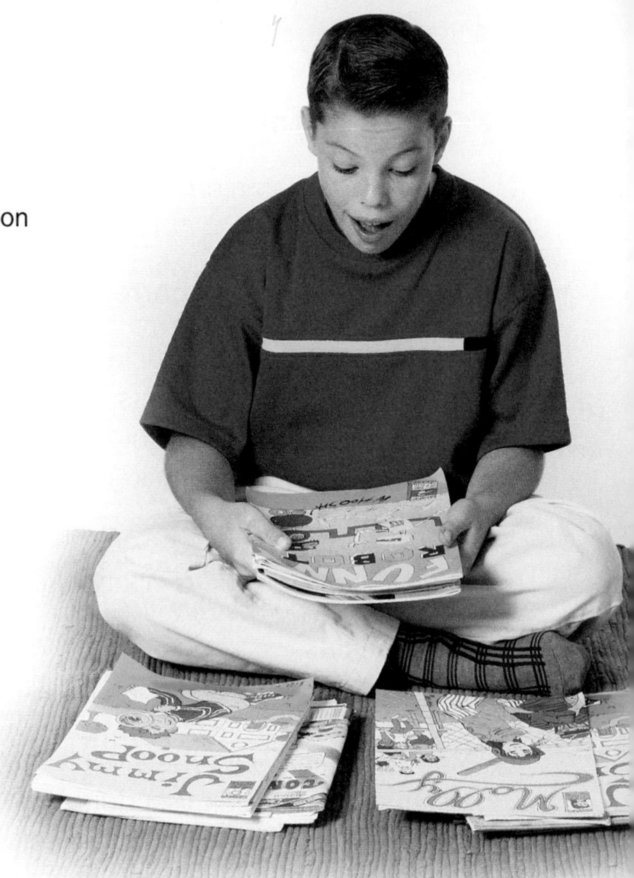

Learn About It

Alvin brought his comic book collection to school to show the class. He gave n comic books to each of 4 small groups. If he had 12 comic books, how many did each group get?

You can make a model of the information and write an equation.

Total number of comic books: 12			
n	n	n	n

Solve $4n = 12$.

Remember
$4n$ means $4 \times n$

You can use mental math to solve the equation.

$4n = 12$
$n = 3$

What number times 4 equals 12? Try 3.

Solution: Each group got 3 comic books.

Other Examples

A. Use a Division Equation.

$28 \div n = 7$

28						
n	n	n	n	n	n	n

$28 \div 4 = 7$

$n = 4$

What number times 7 equals 28? Try 4.

B. Find the Unknown Dividend.

$n \div 7 = 9$

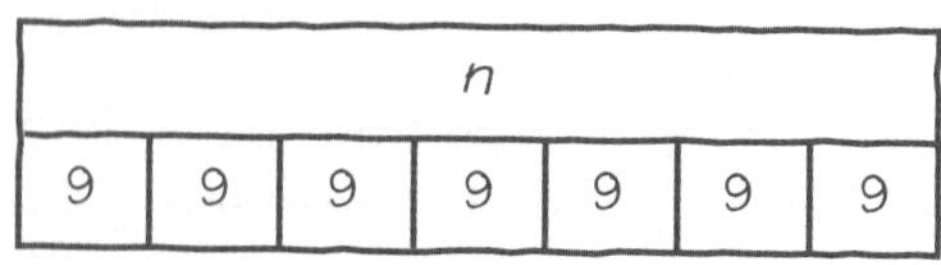

$63 \div 7 = 9$

$n = 63$

Since $n \div 7 = 9$, $n = 7 \times 9$. Try 63.

Guided Practice

Ask Yourself

- What multiplication or division fact can help me solve this equation?
- Did I check my solution?

Solve each problem.

1. Jonah has 30 comic books. He wants to read them over the next 5 days. If he reads the same number each day, how many will he read a day?

   Solve $5n = 30$.

Total number of comic books: 30				
n each day	n each day	n each day	n each day	n each day

2. Marion gave each of her 7 friends 7 comic books. How many comic books did she give out?

   Solve $7 \times 7 = n$.

Total number of comic books: n						
7 to each friend	7 to each friend	7 to each friend	7 to each friend	7 to each friend	7 to each friend	7 to each friend

Explain Your Thinking ▶ How does knowing multiplication and division facts help you solve equations mentally?

Practice and Problem Solving

Solve each problem.

3. Sharon has 36 comic books. She has 4 of each type of comic book. How many different types does she have?

   Solve $4n = 36$.

36			
n	n	n	n

4. At the comic book convention, Nelson sold comic books for $3 apiece. He sold $27 worth. How many did he sell?

   Solve $27 \div n = 3$.

27		
n	n	n

Make a model of the information; write and solve an equation.

5. Seven issues of a certain comic book cost $42. How much does one issue cost?

42						
n	n	n	n	n	n	n

6. Five friends shared some comic books. Each friend got 8 comic books. How many did they share?

n				
8	8	8	8	8

Go On

Use mental math to solve the equations.

7. $6n = 48$
8. $4x = 8$
9. $9y = 81$
10. $5s = 20$
11. $18 \div y = 6$
12. $49 \div n = 7$
13. $45 \div n = 5$
14. $12 \div n = 2$
15. $8t = 32$
16. $18 \div s = 9$
17. $36 \div n = 6$
18. $7t = 21$
19. $4y = 24$
20. $n \div 4 = 5$
21. $72 \div x = 8$
22. $t \div 4 = 8$

Algebra • Equations **Replace *n* with 4. Is the equation true? Write *yes* or *no*.**

23. $3n = 12$
24. $n \div 4 = 8$
25. $8 \div n = 2$
26. $6n = 24$
27. $20 \div n = 5$
28. $7n = 74$
29. $n \div 2 = 2$
30. $n \times n = 16$

Use the function rule to find each value of *y*.

31.

Rule: $y = 3x$				
x	2	4	6	8
y				

32.

Rule: $x = 36 \div y$				
x	3	4	6	9
y				

Solve.

33. Savannah organizes her collection of 28 comic books in bags. If she puts *n* books in each of 7 bags, how many books are in each bag? Explain.

34. Draw a model or use algebra tiles to show $6n = 24$. Solve the equation and explain how your model helped you.

35. Debbie saves $5 each week for *n* weeks from her babysitting money. If she spends $18 of her savings on comic books and has $2 left, how many weeks did she save her money?

36. Kevin has 3 times as many comic books as Jen. Serena has twice as many comic books as Jen. If Serena has 6 comic books, how many comic books do the three friends have in all?

37. **What If?** Look back at Problem 36. What if Serena had 30 comic books? How many comic books would Kevin, Serena, and Jen have in all?

38. **Create and Solve** Choose an equation. Then write a word problem for it and solve it.

$5x = 35$ $\quad r \div 4 = 9$ $\quad 12y = 3$

39. **Write About It** Write a fact family for $3n = 18$. How can writing a fact family help you solve this equation?

40. **What's Wrong?** Jason said that to solve $6n = 12$, you multiply 6 and 12. What is wrong with Jason's answer?

Extra Practice See page 107, Set E.

Mixed Review and Test Prep 

Open Response

Divide. (Ch. 4, Lesson 5)

41. 432 ÷ 4

42. 1,134 ÷ 9

43. 2,346 ÷ 6

44. 9,045 ÷ 7

45. Jared collects paintings. He has 11 rooms in his house where he can put his paintings. He has 121 paintings. How many paintings can he put in each room? Make a model and explain. (Ch. 4, Lesson 7)

Activity

Math Reasoning

Patterns on a Hundred Chart

You can use a hundred chart to find divisibility patterns.

This pattern shows the numbers that are divisible by 10.

If you draw a triangle around each number that is divisible by 5, how will that pattern be the same or different from the pattern for divisibility by 10?

Copy the hundred chart on another sheet of paper.

1. Draw an X on each number in the chart that is divisible by 2. What pattern do you notice?
2. If you draw a square around all the numbers that are divisible by 4 and put a star on the numbers that are divisible by 8, what patterns do you notice?
3. Use a different color to draw a horizontal line through the numbers that are divisible by 3. Next, draw a vertical line through numbers that are divisible by 6. What new patterns do you notice?

1	2	3	4	5	6	7	8	9	10
11	12	13	14	15	16	17	18	19	20
21	22	23	24	25	26	27	28	29	30
31	32	33	34	35	36	37	38	39	40
41	42	43	44	45	46	47	48	49	50
51	52	53	54	55	56	57	58	59	60
61	62	63	64	65	66	67	68	69	70
71	72	73	74	75	76	77	78	79	80
81	82	83	84	85	86	87	88	89	90
91	92	93	94	95	96	97	98	99	100

Chapter Review/Test

VOCABULARY

1. A number is ____ by another number if the quotient has no remainder.

2. A ____ of a number divides into that number with no remainder.

3. If a dividend is a multiple of a divisor, the dividend and the divisor are ____.

Vocabulary

compatible numbers
divisible
factor
quotient
remainder

CONCEPTS AND SKILLS

Estimate the quotient. (Lesson 1, pp. 86–87)

4. 598 ÷ 3
5. 18,320 ÷ 9
6. 173,462 ÷ 4
7. 21,568 ÷ 7

Divide. (Lesson 2, pp. 88–89, Lesson 5, pp. 96–97)

8. 2,014 ÷ 6
9. 672,461 ÷ 7
10. 16,715 ÷ 5
11. $9\overline{)18{,}207}$
12. $7\overline{)2{,}906}$
13. $7\overline{)49{,}079}$

Test each number to see whether it is divisible by 2, 3, 4, 5, 6, 9, or 10. (Lesson 4, pp. 92–95)

14. 315
15. 600
16. 720
17. 317

Use mental math to solve each equation. (Lesson 7, 102–105)

18. $8b = 64$
19. $16 \div c = 4$
20. $c \div 7 = 7$
21. $9b = 18$
22. $72 \div n = 24$
23. $6y = 54$

PROBLEM SOLVING

Name the operation(s) you used to solve the problem. (Lesson 3, pp. 90–91)

24. Ralph buys a used collection of 105 snowdomes for $50. If only 8 can ship in a box, how many boxes will he receive?

Solve. (Lesson 6, pp. 98–101)

25. Toni has a collection of 24 angel figurines. She has 5 times the number of crystal angels as hand-painted ones. How many of each kind does she have?

Write About It

Show You Understand

If a number is divisible by 6, what other numbers is it divisible by? Explain.

Extra Practice

Set A (Lesson 1, pp. 86–87)

Estimate the quotient.

1. $9\overline{)355}$
2. $4\overline{)118}$
3. $7\overline{)2,906}$
4. $6\overline{)5,280}$
5. 42,426 ÷ 8
6. 290,000 ÷ 9
7. 322,164 ÷ 8
8. 375,166 ÷ 4

Set B (Lesson 2, pp. 88–89)

Divide.

1. $6\overline{)547}$
2. $9\overline{)6,642}$
3. $5\overline{)70,655}$
4. $8\overline{)490,826}$
5. 160 ÷ 7
6. 6,444 ÷ 4
7. 57,699 ÷ 9
8. 684,996 ÷ 7

Set C (Lesson 4, pp. 92–95)

Tell whether each number is divisible by 2, 3, 4, 5, 6, 9, or 10.

1. 174
2. 630
3. 725
4. 164
5. 279
6. 204
7. 432
8. 1,080
9. 4,096
10. 1,188

Set D (Lesson 5, pp. 96–97)

Divide.

1. $8\overline{)810}$
2. $5\overline{)7,050}$
3. $6\overline{)36,094}$
4. $9\overline{)630,728}$
5. 413 ÷ 4
6. 15,514 ÷ 3
7. 60,432 ÷ 6
8. 738,264 ÷ 7

Set E (Lesson 7, pp. 102–105)

Solve each problem.

1. Laura has collected 81 stamps. If 9 stamps fit on one page of her album, how many pages will she need?
2. There are 54 people waiting in line for a roller coaster ride. If each car holds 6 people, how many cars will be needed?

Use mental math to solve the equations.

3. $5x = 25$
4. $64 = 8k$
5. $72 = 9p$
6. $10g = 110$
7. $4x = 48$
8. $w \div 3 = 9$
9. $21 \div z = 7$
10. $42b = 84$

CHAPTER 5

Divide by Two-Digit Numbers

INVESTIGATION

Use Data

Amelia Earhart's first solo flight across the Atlantic lasted about 15 hours. She flew about 2,025 miles. Find her average speed in miles per hour. Prepare a report on one of the other fliers on the time line.

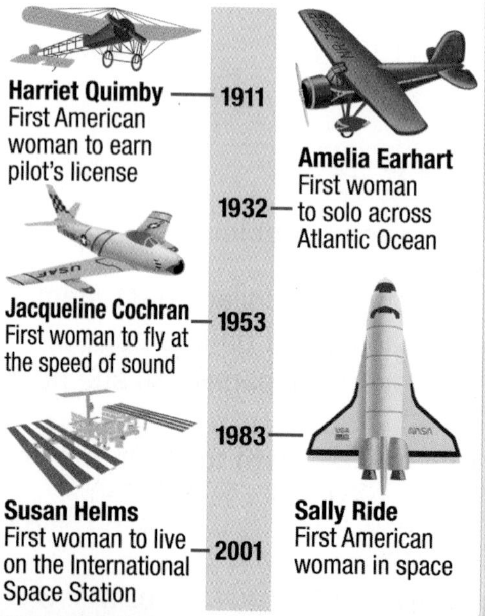

Harriet Quimby — 1911
First American woman to earn pilot's license

Amelia Earhart — 1932
First woman to solo across Atlantic Ocean

Jacqueline Cochran — 1953
First woman to fly at the speed of sound

Sally Ride — 1983
First American woman in space

Susan Helms — 2001
First woman to live on the International Space Station

Use What You Know

Use this page to review and remember what you need to know for this chapter.

VOCABULARY

Choose the best word to complete each sentence.

Vocabulary
dividend
divisible
divisor
multiply
multiple

1. If one number can be evenly divided by another, the first number is ____ by the second number.
2. To check division, ____ the divisor by the quotient.
3. The number to be divided in division is called the ____.
4. The ____ is the number by which another number is to be divided.

CONCEPTS AND SKILLS

Multiply.

5. 4×71
6. 8×34
7. 7×216
8. 9×147
9. 131×5
10. 10×13
11. 911×6
12. 3×222

Tell whether each number is divisible by 2, 3, 4, 5, 6, 9, or 10.

13. 432
14. 3,000
15. 735
16. 690
17. 582
18. 600

Divide. Then check.

19. $2\overline{)83}$
20. $9\overline{)724}$
21. $6\overline{)468}$
22. $75 \div 8$
23. $127 \div 5$
24. $549 \div 7$

Write About It

25. Explain or demonstrate why there are no numbers divisible by 0.

Facts Practice, See page 662.

Lesson 1

Audio Tutor 1/14 Listen and Understand

Divide by Multiples of 10, 100, and 1,000

Objective Use patterns and mental math to divide by multiples of 10, 100, and 1,000.

Learn About It

In 1998, John Glenn was the oldest astronaut to orbit Earth. As the first American to orbit Earth in 1962, part of his orbit was 99 miles above Earth. It is about 240,000 miles to the Moon. About how many times farther would a trip to the Moon be than the height of Glenn's orbit?

Estimate. $240{,}000 \div 99 \approx 240{,}000 \div 100$

Find 240,000 ÷ 100.

$240{,}000 \div 1 = 240{,}000$
$240{,}000 \div 10 = 24{,}000$
$\mathbf{240{,}000 \div 100 = 2{,}400}$
$240{,}000 \div 1{,}000 = 240$

What do you notice about the pattern?

Solution: The distance to the Moon is about 2,400 times farther.

Other Examples

A. Use Basic Facts

Find 16,000 ÷ 8.

$16 \div 8 = 2$
$160 \div 8 = 20$
$1{,}600 \div 8 = 200$
$16{,}000 \div 8 = 2{,}000$

B. Use Multiples of 10

Find 28,000 ÷ 7,000.

$28 \div 7 = 4$
$280 \div 70 = 4$
$2{,}800 \div 700 = 4$
$28{,}000 \div 7{,}000 = 4$

C. Use Compatible Numbers

Estimate 26,000 ÷ 400.

$28 \div 4 = 7$;
$28{,}000 \div 400 = 70$

$24 \div 4 = 6$;
$24{,}000 \div 400 = 60$

The quotient is between 60 and 70.

Guided Practice

Divide. Use patterns, basic facts, or multiples of 10.

1. $800 \div 4$ **2.** $6{,}000 \div 20$ **3.** $4{,}000 \div 500$

4. $80\overline{)6{,}400}$ **5.** $900\overline{)36{,}000}$ **6.** $4{,}000\overline{)200{,}000}$

Ask Yourself

- Which basic division fact should I use?
- Did I write the correct number of zeros?

Explain Your Thinking ▶ What pattern do you notice in the quotients when you divide multiples of 10 by multiples of 10?

Extra Help at eduplace.com/map

Practice and Problem Solving

Divide. Use patterns, basic facts, or multiples of 10.

7. 280 ÷ 7 **8.** 540 ÷ 90 **9.** 18,000 ÷ 600

10. 4,800 ÷ 800 **11.** 24,000 ÷ 8,000 **12.** 32,000 ÷ 40

13. 180,000 ÷ 2,000 **14.** 56,000 ÷ 8,000 **15.** 36,000 ÷ 600

16. $80\overline{)64,000}$ **17.** $300\overline{)900,000}$ **18.** $1,000\overline{)700,000}$

19. $700\overline{)140,000}$ **20.** $50\overline{)25,000}$ **21.** $4,000\overline{)120,000}$

Use compatible numbers and multiples of 10 to estimate each quotient.

22. 7,240 ÷ 80 **23.** 8,500 ÷ 40 **24.** 624,000 ÷ 900

25. 23,900 ÷ 46 **26.** 623,000 ÷ 270 **27.** 938,000 ÷ 526

Data Use the table to solve Problems 28–32.

28. How long did one orbit last?

29. About how many miles did Glenn travel each minute in orbit?

30. At what time did John Glenn's flight end?

31. What was the difference between Glenn's closest and farthest points from Earth during his orbits?

32. Create and Solve Use the data in the table to write and solve your own problem.

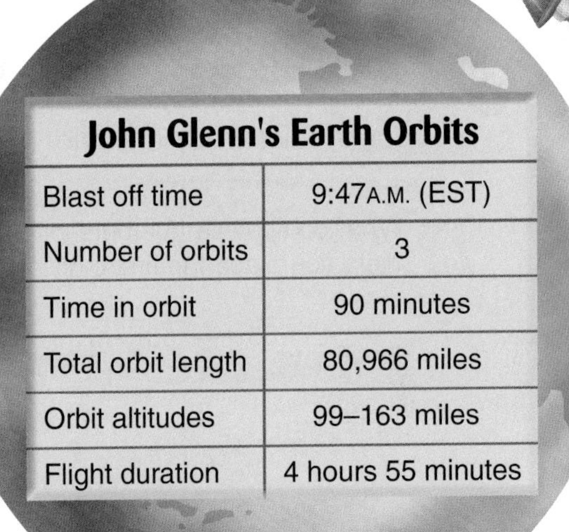

John Glenn's Earth Orbits	
Blast off time	9:47 A.M. (EST)
Number of orbits	3
Time in orbit	90 minutes
Total orbit length	80,966 miles
Orbit altitudes	99–163 miles
Flight duration	4 hours 55 minutes

Mixed Review and Test Prep

Open Response

Fill in each blank. (Grade 4)

33. 3,000 centimeters = ■ meters

34. 8,000 milliliters = ■ liters

35. 56,000 grams = ■ kilograms

36. 227,000 meters = ■ kilometers

37. 49,000 millimeters = ■ meters

Multiple Choice

38. The distance from Earth to the Moon is about 240,000 miles. The *Ulysses* spacecraft can travel about 30,000 miles in one hour. How long would it take *Ulysses* to travel 240,000 miles? (Ch. 5, Lesson 1)

A 8 hours **C** 800 hours

B 80 hours **D** 8,000 hours

Extra Practice See page 133, Set A.

Lesson 2

Audio Tutor 1/15 Listen and Understand

Two-Digit Divisors

Objective Divide by a two-digit divisor and estimate to place the first digit in the quotient.

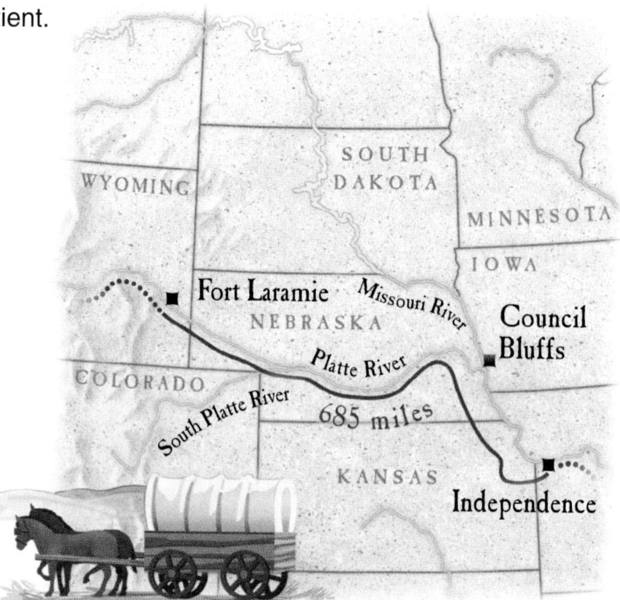

Learn About It

From 1841 to 1866, more than a half million people moved west. The Oregon Trail was a popular route for wagon trains to take. A wagon train left Independence and arrived in Fort Laramie 45 days later. About how many miles did the wagon train travel daily?

Find 685 ÷ 45.

STEP 1 Use an estimate to predict the first digit in the quotient. Test your prediction by dividing.

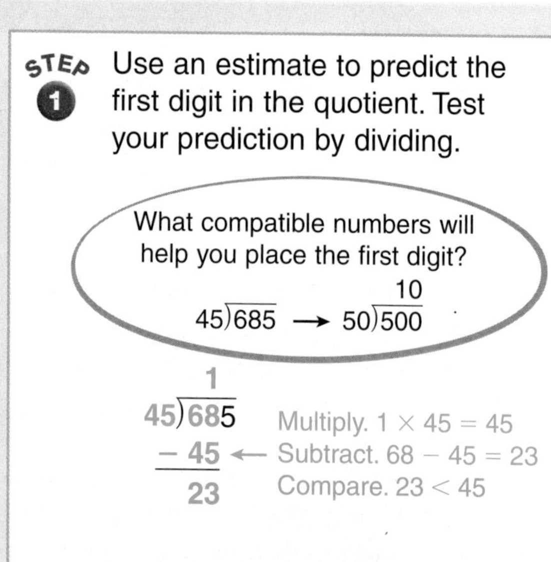

What compatible numbers will help you place the first digit?
45)685 → 50)500 (10)
1
45)685
− 45 ← Subtract. 68 − 45 = 23
23
Multiply. 1 × 45 = 45
Compare. 23 < 45

STEP 2 Bring down the ones. Divide and record the remainder.

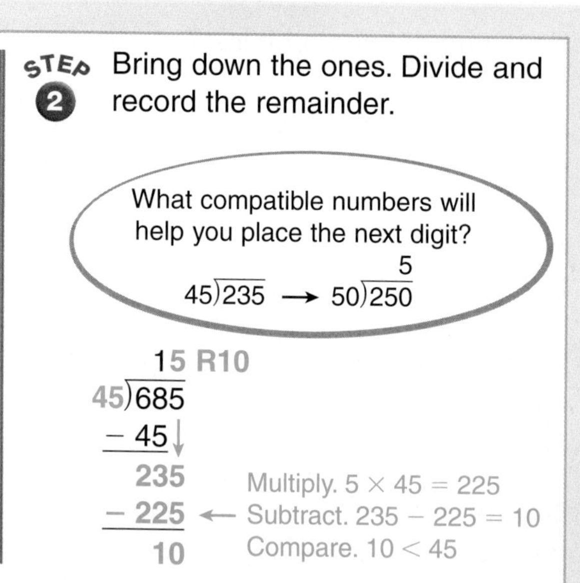

What compatible numbers will help you place the next digit?
45)235 → 50)250 (5)
15 R10
45)685
− 45
235
− 225 ← Subtract. 235 − 225 = 10
10
Multiply. 5 × 45 = 225
Compare. 10 < 45

Solution: The wagon train traveled about 15 miles daily.

Check.
Multiply the quotient by the divisor and add the remainder.

(15 × 45) + 10 = 685

The result equals the dividend, so the quotient is correct.

Another Example

Zeros in the Quotient

Find 852 ÷ 42.

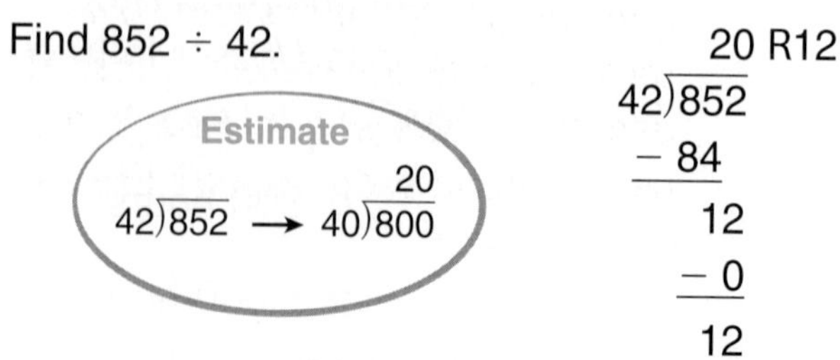


```
     20 R12
42)852
   - 84
     12
    - 0
     12
```

Guided Practice

Divide. Check your answer.

1. $11\overline{)89}$ **2.** $45\overline{)905}$ **3.** $19\overline{)798}$

4. $91 \div 27$ **5.** $68 \div 31$ **6.** $663 \div 82$

Ask Yourself

- What basic fact can I use to estimate the first digit of the quotient?

Explain Your Thinking ▶ In Exercise 6, how did you know where to place the first digit in the quotient?

Practice and Problem Solving

Divide. Check your answer.

7. $20\overline{)87}$ **8.** $26\overline{)84}$ **9.** $31\overline{)93}$

10. $32\overline{)74}$ **11.** $43\overline{)86}$ **12.** $21\overline{)66}$

13. $31\overline{)930}$ **14.** $15\overline{)724}$ **15.** $41\overline{)825}$

16. $11\overline{)568}$ **17.** $61\overline{)860}$ **18.** $42\overline{)882}$

19. $47 \div 22$ **20.** $88 \div 44$ **21.** $99 \div 32$

22. $390 \div 75$ **23.** $544 \div 32$ **24.** $378 \div 62$

Solve.

25. A family spent $260 for oxen to pull their wagon along the Oregon Trail. If each ox cost $65, how many oxen did they buy?

26. A family saved the same amount each month for two years to get $792 they needed for oxen and supplies for their trip west. How much did they save each month?

27. A wagon train left Missouri on April 15. It arrived in Oregon 138 days later. On what date did it arrive?

28. **What If?** Suppose the family in Problem 26 only had 18 months to save the money they needed. How much money would they need to save each month?

Mixed Review and Test Prep

Open Response

Evaluate each expression. Write >, <, or = for each ●. (Ch. 2, Lesson 1; Ch. 3, Lesson 1)

29. $(24 - 8) \times (82 - 82)$ ● $77 - 13$

30. $(9 \times 8) \times 1$ ● $(4 \times 5) \times 2$

31. 32×6 ● $240 \div 10$

32. A wagon train with 90 wagons uses 8 wagons for supplies. The remaining wagons contain 574 travelers with the same number of people in each wagon. How many people are in each wagon? Explain. (Ch. 5, Lesson 2)

Extra Practice See page 133, Set B.

Lesson 3

Audio Tutor 1/16 Listen and Understand

Problem-Solving Strategy

Work Backward

Objective Solve problems by working backward.

Problem One fourth of the total number of signers of the Declaration of Independence were from Pennsylvania and Massachusetts. There were 4 fewer signers from Massachusetts than from Pennsylvania. If there were 9 signers from Pennsylvania, how many signers were there in all?

UNDERSTAND

This is what you know:

- One fourth of the total number of signers were from Massachusetts and Pennsylvania.
- Four fewer signers were from Massachusetts than from Pennsylvania.
- Nine signers were from Pennsylvania.

PLAN

You can use Work Backward to solve the problem.

You can draw a model.

Total number of signers			
PA + *MA*	*PA* + *MA*	*PA* + *MA*	*PA* + *MA*

Think
$PA = 9$;
$MA = 9 - 4$;
$PA + MA = 9 + (9 - 4)$

SOLVE

Start at the end of the problem with facts you know and work backward through the problem. $PA = 9$

- Find the number of signers from Massachusetts. $9 - 4 = 5$ $MA = 5$
- Find the number of signers from Massachusetts and Pennsylvania. $9 + 5 = 14$ $PA + MA = 14$
- Find the total number of signers. $14 \times 4 = 56$

Solution: There were 56 signers of the Declaration of Independence.

LOOK BACK

Look back at the problem.

Does the answer seem reasonable and make sense?

Guided Practice

Use the Ask Yourself questions to help you solve each problem.

1. Thomas Jefferson, the third President of the United States, was in office for 8 years. He began his term 25 years after he drafted the Declaration of Independence in 1776. During what years was Thomas Jefferson President?

   Hint Should you start with the number of years he was in office or the year he drafted the Declaration of Independence?

2. Most delegates signed the Declaration of Independence 1 month and 1 day after the Continental Congress first met to discuss it. They began discussing it 3 days before adopting it on July 4, 1776. When was it signed?

Ask Yourself

UNDERSTAND **What facts do I know?**

PLAN **Did I plan the operations to use at each step by drawing a model?**

SOLVE
- **Did I start with facts I learned from the end of the problem?**
- **Which operations did I need to use?**
- **Did I work backward through the facts in the problem?**

LOOK BACK **Did I solve the problem?**

Independent Practice

Work backward to solve each problem.

3. To find out how old John Adams was when he signed the Declaration of Independence, divide the sum of 24 and the year he signed it by 45. How old was John Adams, our second President, in 1776 when he signed?

4. Ben Franklin was the oldest signer of the Declaration of Independence. To find his age when he signed it, divide the product of 50 and Franklin's age when he died by 60. Franklin died at age 84. How old was he when he signed?

5. Of all the signers of the Declaration of Independence, Carter Braxton had the most children. He had twice as many children as Arthur Middleton, who had 3 times as many as Ben Franklin. Franklin had 3 children. How many did Braxton have?

6. Samuel Adams, cousin of John Adams, was a delegate to the Continental Congress for 7 years. He became Massachusetts' governor 13 years after that. His 3 years as governor ended in 1797. When did Samuel Adams begin work in the Continental Congress?

IN CONGRESS, JULY 4, 1776.

The unanimous Declaration of the thirteen united States of America,

Go On

Mixed Problem Solving

Solve. Show your work.
Tell what strategy you used.

7. Of the 56 signers of the Declaration of Independence, only William Ellery was a lawyer and a merchant. Of the rest, 39 were either lawyers or merchants. There were 9 more lawyers than merchants. The product of the numbers of these careers is 360. How many lawyers were there?

8. When Dr. Benjamin Rush signed the Declaration of Independence, he was half as old as his fellow delegate George Taylor, who was seven years older than Samuel Adams at the time. If Samuel Adams was fifty-three, how old was Dr. Rush?

You Choose

Strategy

- Guess and Check
- Solve a Simpler Problem
- Use Logical Reasoning
- Work Backward
- Write an Equation

Computation Method

- Mental Math
- Estimation
- Paper and Pencil
- Calculator

Data Use the table to solve Problems 9–14.

District 12 Middle School Students

Grade	Number of Students
5	336
6	312
7	288
8	306

9. One middle school grade orders buses for their field trip to the National Archives. If the buses each seat 48 students, and this grade just fits in 7 buses, which grade is it?

10. Three of the 10 classes in one grade have 2 more students than the other classes have. If this is eighth grade, how many students are in each of the other classes?

11. Of the students in the spring play, 1 less than half have speaking parts. A third of all the fifth-graders in the school are involved in the play. How many fifth-graders have speaking parts?

12. All of the students in two grades went on a ski trip for the weekend. There was one adult for every 10 students. There were exactly 60 adults. Which two grades went on the ski trip?

13. For a school assembly, Mr. Lang sets up chairs with 24 chairs per row. How many rows will each grade need?

14. **Create and Solve** Write a division problem using data from the chart. Solve your problem.

Problem Solving on Tests

Multiple Choice

Choose the letter of the correct answer.

1. Which of these expressions has the *greatest* value?

   A 2^5 **B** 3^4 **C** 4^3 **D** 5^2

   (Chapter 1, Lesson 2)

2. This decimal model shows 0.06. Which of these statements about 0.06 is true?

   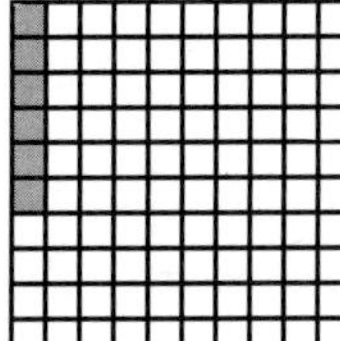

   F $0.06 > 0.0$ **H** 0.06 rounds to 1.0

   G $0.06 = 0.6$ **J** $0.06 < 0.01$

   (Chapter 1, Lesson 7)

Open Response

Solve each problem.

3. By which of the following numbers is 4,680 divisible?

   2, 3, 4, 5, 6, 9, 10

   Explain Use divisibility rules to explain how to find the answer.

   (Chapter 4, Lesson 4)

4. This year's field trip to Washington, D.C., costs each student \$5.50 for the bus, \$18.75 for food, and \$29.95 for the hotel room. Last year the trip cost \$49.65 per student. By how much has the trip's price increased?

   Represent Draw a model to show how to find the answer.

   (Grade 4)

Extended Response

5. You are the producer of a variety show. The table gives the cost of hiring different types of performers.

Performers	Fee each
Dancers	\$125
Actors	\$ 90
Singers	\$145
Magicians	\$110

   a If you want to hire 5 of each kind of performer, how much will you pay in all?

   b Suppose you hire the same number of singers and dancers and pay \$160 more for the singers. How many singers and dancers did you hire?

   c Your budget for performers is \$4,400. You want to spend at least \$4,200, and must have at least 2 of each kind of performer. How many of each kind could you hire?

   (Chapter 3)

Education Place

See **eduplace.com/map** for Test-Taking Tips.

Lesson 4

Audio Tutor 1/17 Listen and Understand

Adjusting Quotients

Objective Adjust the estimate of the quotient.

Learn About It

Henry Ford invented a way to make automobiles quickly. By 1927, the assembly line completed one Model T automobile every 24 seconds. How many Model T's could the assembly line complete in 15 minutes (900 seconds)?

Find 24)900. Estimate first. 24)900 → 800 ÷ 20 = 40

Estimate Too Large

STEP 1 Place the first digit in the quotient. Try 4.

4
24)900
− 96

96 > 90
4 is too large.

STEP 2 Adjust. Try 3.

3
24)900
− 72
18

18 < 24
3 is correct.

STEP 3 Try 8.

38
24)900
− 72↓
180
− 192

192 > 180
8 is too large.

STEP 4 Adjust.

37 R 12
24)900
− 72↓
180
− 168
12

12 < 24
7 is correct.

Solution: They could make 37 Model T's in 15 minutes.

Remember
In division the remainder must be less than the divisor.

Find 16)849. Estimate first. 16)849 → 800 ÷ 20 = 40

Estimate Too Small

STEP 1 Place the first digit. Try 4.

4
16)849
− 64
20

20 > 16
4 is too small.

STEP 2 Adjust. Try 5.

5
16)849
− 80
4

4 < 16
5 is correct.

STEP 3 Try 2.

52
16)849
− 80↓
49
− 32
17

17 > 16
2 is too small.

STEP 4 Adjust. Try 3.

53 R1
16)849
− 80↓
49
− 48
1

1 < 16
3 is correct.

Solution: 849 ÷ 16 ➡ 53 R1.

Guided Practice

Ask Yourself

- Did I estimate the first digit of the quotient?
- Is the remainder less than the divisor?

Divide. Check your answers.

1. $64\overline{)558}$ **2.** $64\overline{)316}$ **3.** $27\overline{)139}$

4. $420 \div 46$ **5.** $782 \div 16$ **6.** $650 \div 24$

Explain Your Thinking ▶ What should you do if your estimated quotient is too large? too small?

Practice and Problem Solving

Divide. Check your answers.

7. $45\overline{)230}$ **8.** $75\overline{)626}$ **9.** $23\overline{)823}$ **10.** $24\overline{)620}$

11. $64\overline{)439}$ **12.** $18\overline{)176}$ **13.** $73\overline{)431}$ **14.** $67\overline{)408}$

15. $16\overline{)120}$ **16.** $93\overline{)362}$ **17.** $29\overline{)203}$ **18.** $43\overline{)808}$

19. $618 \div 32$ **20.** $314 \div 63$ **21.** $816 \div 27$ **22.** $629 \div 17$

x Algebra • Functions Copy and complete.

23. Rule: Divide by 12.

Input	Output
24	■
48	■
144	■
192	■

24. Rule: Divide by 25.

Input	Output
50	■
■	3
■	5
200	■

25. Rule: ■

Input	Output
200	10
240	12
360	18
480	24

Solve.

26. A Model T could travel at a maximum speed of 45 miles per hour. At that rate, how long would it take for a Model T to travel a distance of 315 miles?

27. Ford's 1914 assembly line could turn out a Model T in 93 minutes. About how many times faster than the normal 728 minutes is that?

Mixed Review and Test Prep

Open Response

Name the place value of the digit 6 in each number. (Ch. 1, Lesson 5)

28. 2.067 **29.** 0.624

30. 1.376 **31.** 0.6

32. 6.041 **33.** 0.060

Multiple Choice

34. A Model T could go 19 miles on a gallon of gas. How much gas would it use to go 475 miles? (Ch. 5, Lesson 2)

A 25 gallons **C** 35 gallons

B 26 gallons **D** 250 gallons

Extra Practice See page 133, Set C.

Lesson 5

Division With Greater Numbers

Objective Divide a two-digit number into a dividend with up to six digits.

Learn About It

In the 1850s, stagecoaches delivered letters and packages out West. Suppose a stagecoach traveled from Missouri to California and back in 42 days. If it traveled 5,416 miles, about how many miles did the stagecoach travel each day?

Find 5,416 ÷ 42.

STEP 1 Estimate the first digit of the quotient. Then divide the hundreds.

Try 1 hundred.

$$\begin{array}{r} 1 \\ 42\overline{)5{,}416} \\ -\,4\,2 \\ \hline 1\,2 \end{array}$$

Multiply. 1 × 42
Subtract. 54 − 42
Compare. 12 < 42

Think: $40\overline{)4{,}000}$ = 100

STEP 2 Bring down the tens. Divide the tens.

Try 3 tens.

$$\begin{array}{r} 13 \\ 42\overline{)5{,}416} \\ -\,4\,2 \\ \hline 1\,21 \\ -\,1\,26 \\ \hline \end{array}$$

Estimate is too large. Try 2 tens.

$$\begin{array}{r} 12 \\ 42\overline{)5{,}416} \\ -\,4\,2 \\ \hline 121 \\ -\,84 \\ \hline 37 \end{array}$$

Multiply. 2 × 42
Subtract. 121 − 84
Compare. 37 < 42

Think: $40\overline{)1{,}200}$ = 30

STEP 3 Bring down the ones. Divide the ones.

Try 9 ones.

$$\begin{array}{r} 129 \\ 42\overline{)5{,}416} \\ -\,4\,2 \\ \hline 1\,21 \\ -\,84 \\ \hline 376 \\ -\,378 \\ \hline \end{array}$$

Estimate is too large. Try 8 ones.

$$\begin{array}{r} 128 \text{ R40} \\ 42\overline{)5{,}416} \\ -\,4\,2 \\ \hline 121 \\ -\,84 \\ \hline 376 \\ -\,336 \\ \hline 40 \end{array}$$

Multiply. 8 × 42
Subtract. 376 − 336
Compare. 40 < 42

Think: $40\overline{)360}$ = 9

Solution: The stagecoach traveled between 128 and 129 miles each day.

Other Examples

A. Zeros in the Quotient

Find 72,096 ÷ 24.

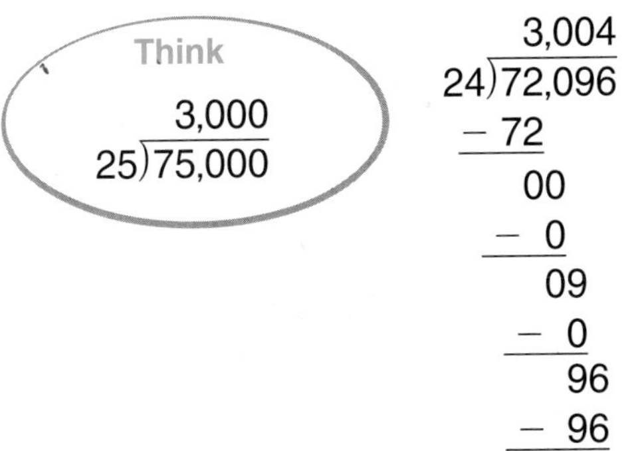

B. Three-Digit Divisor

Find 74,530 ÷ 256.

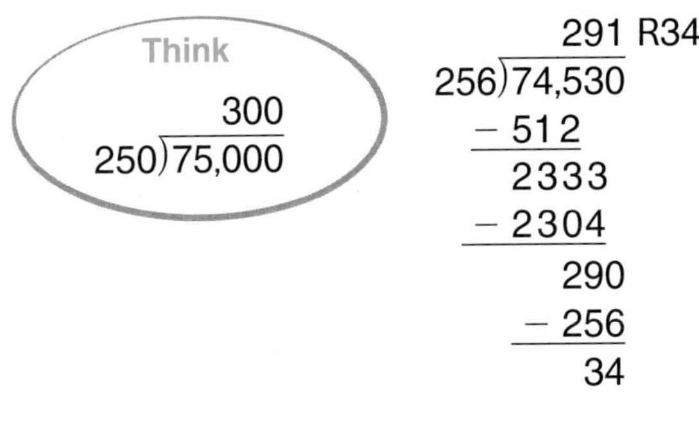

Guided Practice

Ask Yourself

- Where should I place the first digit?
- Is the estimated digit too large or too small?

Divide. Check.

1. 14)5,634
2. 42)5,425
3. 29,622 ÷ 12
4. 91,233 ÷ 731

Explain Your Thinking ▶ Explain how to use multiplication and addition to check your answer in Exercise 4.

Practice and Problem Solving

Divide. Check.

5. 17)5,185
6. 48)2,400
7. 73)7,408
8. 35)11,144
9. 59)35,424
10. 91)27,636
11. 9,427 ÷ 31
12. 9,454 ÷ 47
13. 7,664 ÷ 58
14. 493,438 ÷ 16
15. 682,675 ÷ 25
16. 75,223 ÷ 729

Algebra • Equations **If q is the quotient and r is the remainder, write and solve a division problem for each equation.**

17. $20q + r = 3{,}221$
18. $35q + r = 7{,}805$
19. $29q + r = 16{,}258$
20. $52q + r = 89{,}162$
21. $11q + r = 1{,}090$
22. $15q + r = 3{,}333$

Go On

Extra Practice See page 133, Set D.

Solve.

23. June wants to place a border along the top of her bedroom. She needs 576 inches. How many packages will she need to buy if each package contains 10 feet of border?

24. The variables *a*, *b*, and *c* in the division problem shown below represent 3 different digits. The division has been started for you. Complete the division.

$$\begin{array}{r} a \\ ab\,\overline{)\,a,ccb} \\ -\,ab \\ \hline a \end{array}$$

25. What is the maximum number of digits there could be in the quotient of a five-digit dividend divided by a three-digit divisor? Give examples to show your reasoning.

Choose a Computation Method

Mental Math • Estimation • Paper and Pencil • Calculator

Data **The table shows information about the Butterfield Overland Stage Company. Use the table for Problems 26–28. Then explain which method you chose.**

26. If each of the stations on the route was the same distance apart, about how far is the distance between stations?

27. If the fare is based on the length of a trip, about how much would it cost to travel 700 miles?

28. When the Pony Express began delivering mail in 1860, its riders took an average of 12 days to cover 1,866 miles. On average, who covered more miles in a day, Pony Express riders or stagecoach drivers? How did you decide?

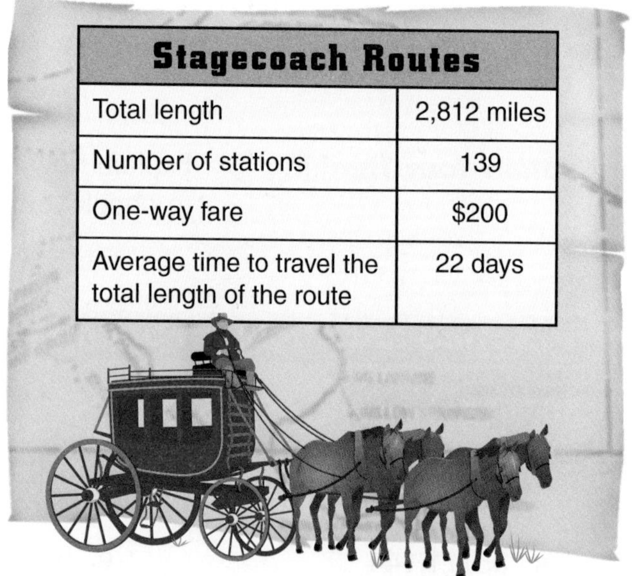

Stagecoach Routes	
Total length	2,812 miles
Number of stations	139
One-way fare	$200
Average time to travel the total length of the route	22 days

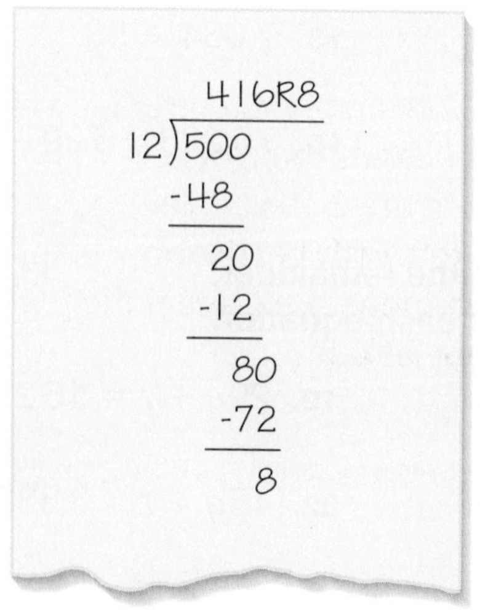

29. **What's Wrong?** Stagecoach horses might be changed every 12 miles. To find the number of changes made in 500 miles, Jared divided 500 by 12. Jared's work is shown at the left. What did he do wrong?

30. **Create and Solve** Do some research about transportation in the 1800s. Write a problem based on your research. Trade problems with a classmate and solve.

Game

Activity

Quotient Quest

2 Players

What You'll Need • four sets of number cards (Learning Tool 6)
• division frames (Learning Tool 30)

How to Play

1. Shuffle the cards and give five cards to each player.
2. Arrange your cards in a division frame so the quotient will be the least possible one you can make.
3. Divide to find your quotient and compare with the other player's quotient. The smaller quotient gets 1 point.

Take turns dealing the cards, repeating Steps 1 to 3. The first player to get a total of 10 points wins.

Quick Check

Check your understanding for Lessons 1–5.

Divide. Check your answer. (Lessons 1, 2, 4, and 5)

1. $600 \div 60$
2. $25{,}000 \div 500$
3. $420{,}000 \div 7{,}000$
4. $32\overline{)672}$
5. $15\overline{)107}$
6. $34\overline{)884}$
7. $4{,}290 \div 56$
8. $36{,}247 \div 29$

Work backward to solve each problem. (Lesson 3)

9. Maggie rides her horse 3 more miles than Tasha. Emmaline rides 5 more miles than Tasha. Catherine rides 2 fewer miles than Emmaline. Emmaline rides 6 miles. How many miles does each girl ride?

10. At one shop, there are 2 fewer jackets with beads than jackets with fringe. There are 3 fewer plain jackets than jackets with beads. How many jackets with fringe are there if there are 15 plain jackets?

Lesson 6

Audio Tutor 1/18 Listen and Understand

Algebra

Order of Operations

Objective Use the order of operations to simplify expressions.

Vocabulary

order of operations

simplify

Learn About It

Simplify. 8 + (4 × 24) ÷ 32

To **simplify** an expression when there are more than two operations in the expression, you must use a set of rules called the **order of operations**. The order of operations tells you in which order to perform the operations when simplifying.

Some people use this sentence as a memory device to help them remember the order of operations: Please excuse my dear Aunt Sally.

Order of Operations

1. Simplify the terms within **parentheses**.
2. Simplify the terms with **exponents**.
3. **Multiply** and **divide** from left to right.
4. **Add** and **subtract** from left to right.

Find 8 + (4 × 24) ÷ 32.

STEP 1 Simplify within the parentheses.

(4 × 24)

$$\begin{array}{r} 24 \\ \times\ 4 \\ \hline 96 \end{array}$$

STEP 2 Divide 96 by 32.

$$\begin{array}{r} 3 \\ 32\overline{)96} \\ -\ 96 \\ \hline 0 \end{array}$$

STEP 3 Add 8.

$$\begin{array}{r} 3 \\ +\ 8 \\ \hline 11 \end{array}$$

Solution: 8 + (4 × 24) ÷ 32 = 11

Using the order of operations to simplify an expression ensures that the expression has the same value.

Here are the ways two students simplified 14 − (5 + 2) × 2.

Problem: Who used the order of operations correctly?

Solution: Delia used the correct order of operations. After simplifying the terms within the parentheses, she multiplied 7 and 2 before subtracting.

Janet

14 − (5 + 2) X 2
= 14 − 7 X 2
= 7 X 2
= 14

Delia

14 − (5 + 2) X 2
= 14 − 7 X 2
= 14 − 14
= 0

Another Example

Parentheses and Exponents

$(12 \div 4)^2 \times (4 \times 5) - (8 - 4) + 5^2$

$= 3^2 \times 20 - 4 + 5^2$ ← Simplify within parentheses.

$= 9 \times 20 - 4 + 25$ ← Simplify exponents.

$= 180 - 4 + 25$ ← Multiply.

$= 176 + 25 = 201$ ← Add and subtract from left to right.

Guided Practice

Simplify.

1. $5 + (8 - 6)$

2. $(14 \div 2) \times 5$

3. $25 + (2 + 20) - 40$

4. $(12 + 13) \times (8 \div 4)$

Ask Yourself

- Which operation should I start with?
- Have I simplified the expression completely?

Explain Your Thinking ▶ How would you solve Exercise 2 if you did not have parentheses to show which operations go together?

Practice and Problem Solving

Simplify.

5. $(12 + 6) - 3$

6. $9 + (18 \div 9) \times 6$

7. $(8 \times 2) \div 4^2$

8. $(27 - 2) - (20 \div 5)^2$

9. $(21 - 3) \div (4 + 5) + (3 \times 5)$

10. $(8^2 + 6) \div (10 - 3)$

11. $5 + (124 - 2) + 32$

12. $1{,}295 - (49 - 42) \times 14$

13. $(65 \div 5) + 4^2$

Write >, <, or = for each ●.

14. $11 + (32 - 7)$ ● $(11 + 32) - 7$

15. $26 - (18 \div 6)$ ● $(24 \div 3) + 2^2$

16. $(36 \div 3^2) \times 8$ ● $(24 \times 2) - 42$

17. $1{,}822 - (153 + 22)$ ● $(1{,}822 - 153) + 22$

Mental Math Use mental math to simplify.

18. $(7 + 2) - 9 + 8$

19. $(4 + 2) + (3 + 3) + (7 - 1)$

20. $(5 \times 5) \times 2 \times (2 \times 2)$

21. $(4 \div 4) \times 4 \div (2 \times 2)$

Algebra • Expressions Evaluate the expression, given $x = 2$ and $y = 6$.

22. $x^2 + (y - x)$

23. $(y^2 - 4) \div x$

24. $3x + y^2$

25. $2(x + y) - x^2$

26. $(x \cdot y)^2$

27. $(4x + 3) - y$

Go On

Solve.

28. A steamboat has 112 passengers. At one stop, 2 groups of 8 passengers get off the boat to sightsee and 24 more passengers go shopping. How many passengers are left on the boat?

29. Use parentheses to write two different expressions with equal values.

30. **What's Wrong?** When Alexander simplified the expression $5^2 + 8 \times 3 - 4$, he said the result was 95. Did he follow the order of operations? If he did not, which rule did he fail to follow, and what should the result have been?

31. **You Decide** Copy this expression on paper and decide where you want the parentheses to go. Simplify.

$4 \times 5 + 6 - 8 \div 2 + 2^2$

Tell a partner the value of your expression. Have your partner find where the parentheses belong.

32. Use parentheses to make the sentence true.
$5 \times 8 + 4 \div 2 = 30$

33. Use the numbers 3, 4, 6, and 8 to make each sentence true.
a. $\blacksquare \times (\blacksquare - \blacksquare) + \blacksquare = 20$
b. $(\blacksquare - \blacksquare) \times (\blacksquare \times \blacksquare) = 120$

Mixed Review and Test Prep

Open Response

Add or subtract. (Ch. 2, Lesson 3)

34. 34,229 + 6,183

35. 72,405 + 8,924 + 16,308

36. 2,419 − 1,728

37. Explain the steps you would take to simplify this expression. Then simplify. Show your work.
(Ch. 5, Lesson 6)

$(4 + 3) \times 8 - (18 \div 2) + 3^2$

Extra Practice See page 133, Set E.

Activity

Number Sense
Other Ways to Divide

There is more than one way to solve most problems. Two other ways to find a quotient are **short division** and **repeated subtraction**.

Way 1 Short Division

Find 7,473 ÷ 8.

STEP 1 Divide 74 hundreds by 8. Write the remainder in the dividend.

Think: 74 ÷ 8 ➡ 9 R2

Write: $8\overline{)74^{2}73}$ with quotient 9

STEP 2 Divide 27 tens by 8. Write the remainder in the dividend.

Think: 27 ÷ 8 ➡ 3 R3

Write: $8\overline{)74^{2}7^{3}3}$ with quotient 9 3

STEP 3 Divide 33 by 8. Write the last remainder in the quotient.

Think: 33 ÷ 8 ➡ 4 R1

Write: $8\overline{)74^{2}7^{3}3}$ with quotient 9 3 4 R1

Way 2 Repeated Subtraction

Find 224 ÷ 56.

STEP 1 Start with 224. Subtract 56 repeatedly.

Think: How many groups of 56 are there in 224?

$$\begin{array}{r} 224 \\ -\ 56 \\ \hline 168 \\ -\ 56 \\ \hline 112 \\ -\ 56 \\ \hline 56 \\ -\ 56 \\ \hline 0 \end{array}$$

STEP 2 Count how many times you subtracted 56.

You subtracted 56 four times, so there are 4 groups of 56 in 224.

$$56 + 56 + 56 + 56 = 224$$
$$4 \times 56 = 224$$
$$224 \div 56 = 4$$

Divide. Show your work. Use short division or repeated subtraction.

1. 5,622 ÷ 9 **2.** $7\overline{)23{,}401}$ **3.** $28\overline{)224}$ **4.** 5,103 ÷ 567

5. 10,251 ÷ 3 **6.** $8\overline{)25{,}082}$ **7.** $27\overline{)162}$ **8.** 2,808 ÷ 351

9. When is it easier to use short division?
When is it easier to use repeated subtraction?
Explain.

Lesson 7

Problem-Solving Application

Interpret Remainders

Objective Solve problems involving remainders.

When you solve a problem with a remainder, you need to decide how to interpret the remainder.

Problem One summer 103 hikers signed up to hike part of Lewis and Clark's route. If a maximum of 8 people could be in a group, how many groups were there?

UNDERSTAND

What is the question?

How many groups of hikers were there?

What do you know?

- There were 103 hikers.
- A maximum of 8 people were in a group.

PLAN

Divide 103 by 8. Decide how you will interpret the remainder.

- **Will you increase the quotient?** Increase the quotient when you must include the remainder.
- **Will you drop the remainder?** Drop the remainder when you do not need to include it.
- **Will your remainder be the answer?** Use the remainder as the answer when you want to know how many are left over.

SOLVE

- Find the number of full groups of hikers.
- Decide how to use the remainder.

$$8\overline{)103}\quad 12\text{ R}7$$

The 7 remaining people made their own group.
Add 1 more group to your answer. $12 + 1 = 13$

Solution: There were 13 groups on the hike.

LOOK BACK

Look back at the problem.

Does the answer make sense?

Guided Practice

Use the Ask Yourself questions to help you solve each problem.

1. To keep hikers away from delicate plants on the Lewis and Clark trail, park rangers set up rope barriers. If they cut rope into 7-foot strips, how many strips of rope can they make from 85 feet of rope?

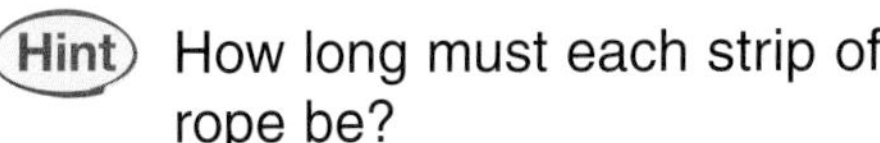

Hint How long must each strip of rope be?

2. A group of 300 hikers will stay in cabins. Each cabin, except one, holds 8 hikers. How many hikers are in the smaller cabin?

Ask Yourself

What facts do I know?

What question must I answer?

- **Did I use the remainder to add to the quotient?**
- **Did I drop the remainder?**
- **Did I use the remainder as the answer?**

LOOK BACK

Did I interpret the remainder correctly so that the answer makes sense?

Independent Practice

Solve. Explain how you decided to interpret each remainder.

3. From April 8 to April 11, 1805, suppose the Lewis and Clark expedition traveled 93 miles up the Missouri River. Captain Lewis hoped to average 23 miles per day. Did he reach his goal?

4. A white-water rafting company gets 57 life jackets ready for a trip along a river where Lewis and Clark explored. Each raft must have 8 life jackets. How many spare life jackets are there?

5. After hiking all day, a group of tourists ordered pizzas for dinner. If they ate 309 slices of pizza and each pizza was cut into 6 slices, how many whole pizzas did they eat?

6. A group of 39 people go on a rafting trip. If 7 people can go on each raft, how many rafts must they rent?

2003–2006 marks the 200-year anniversary of the Lewis and Clark expedition. Lewis and Clark with their Shoshone guide, Sacagawea, mapped the West for then-President Thomas Jefferson.

Go On

Mixed Problem Solving

Solve. Show your work.
Tell what strategy you used.

7. Janell took 71 photographs. She wants to put them in an album. If each page holds 6 pictures, how many pages will Janell need for her photographs?

8. Miguel made 40 sandwiches for his hiking group. He made half as many with peanut butter as with jam. The rest are cheese sandwiches. If he made 10 cheese sandwiches, how many peanut butter sandwiches did he make?

9. Don bought shirts for the Lewis and Clark bicentennial. Sweatshirts cost \$16, and T-shirts cost \$10. If he spent \$46, how many of each did Don buy?

You Choose

Strategy
- Draw a Diagram
- Guess and Check
- Use Logical Reasoning
- Work Backward
- Write an Equation

Computation Method
- Mental Math
- Estimation
- Paper and Pencil
- Calculator

Data The Water Sports Center on the river has many different kinds of boats to rent. Use the table to solve Problems 10–13.

10. The Water Sports Center has reservations for 4 groups of 4 and 1 group of 8 people who want to go kayaking. If they only rent 2-person kayaks, how many are left for others?

11. A group of 40 students wants to go kayaking. Are there enough kayaks for them? If so, what is the fewest number they can rent?

12. What is the greatest number of people that can be in the Water Sports Company's boats at the same time?

13. Create and Solve Use the data in the table to write your own problem. Solve it and give it to a partner to solve.

Water Sports Center Rentals

Type of Boat	Number Available
2-person kayak	16
1-person kayak	12
3-person canoe	8
4-person row-boat	8
10-person raft	8
6-person raft	8

Problem Solving

Calculator Connection

Order of Operations

Not all calculators have the algebraic logic required to perform the order of operations. Try entering $3 + (4 \times 6) - 8$ into your calculator in order from left to right.

If your answer is 19, then your calculator does order of operations for you. If your answer is 34, then your calculator doesn't use order of operations. *You* have to enter the keys in the correct order according to the order of operations.

Press:        

You need to press the equals sign after each operation in order to get the correct result.

Your calculator may have a key that looks like "^" or "y^x." Either one of these keys indicate that the next number entered is an exponent. You can use these keys to simplify expressions that contain exponents.

For example,

$(6 - 4)^3 + 9 - 4^2$

Press:       

$3 + 5^4 - (10 - 3)^3$

Press: 

If your calculator does not have either of these keys, you will have to do a repeated multiplication when an exponent is shown.

For example: $4^3 + 15^2$

Press:

Use your calculator to find each value.

1. $7 \times (8 - 3) + 12$

2. $(16 \times 4) \div (2 + 6)$

3. $(15 - 8) \times (4 + 7)$

4. 3^5

5. $10^3 - 99 + (14 - 10)^2$

6. $12^3 + 13^4 - (20 - 13)^2$

Chapter Review/Test

VOCABULARY

1. The ____ is a set of rules that tells the order in which you perform the operations when simplifying.

2. A ____ is the product of a given number and any other number.

Vocabulary
- estimate
- multiple
- order of operations
- quotient

CONCEPTS AND SKILLS

Divide. Check your answer. (Lessons 1–2, pp. 110–113, Lesson 4, pp. 118–119, Lesson 5, pp. 120–122)

3. $20\overline{)4{,}000}$
4. $27\overline{)198}$
5. $81\overline{)476}$
6. $785 \div 12$
7. $928 \div 32$
8. $596 \div 34$
9. $19\overline{)2{,}834}$
10. $80\overline{)8{,}000}$
11. $87\overline{)21{,}484}$
12. $45\overline{)30{,}655}$
13. $55\overline{)55{,}055}$
14. $34\overline{)12{,}062}$

Simplify. (Lesson 6, pp. 124–127)

15. $(76 - 14) - (48 \div 8)^2$
16. $(63 - 7) \div (7 - 5)^3 + 8$
17. $(24 + 6) \div (30 \div 6)$
18. $(6 \times 9) \div 3^3$
19. $2{,}000 - (95 - 45) \times 20$
20. $72 + 24 - 16$
21. $12 + 11 \times 7 - 20$
22. $121 \div 11 + 3^2$
23. $44 + (63 \div 9) \times 8$

PROBLEM SOLVING

Solve. (Lesson 3, pp. 114–116, Lesson 7, pp. 128–130)

24. At the age of 54, Hattie Caraway became the first woman elected to the United States Senate. She served in the Senate until 1945, thirteen years after she was elected. In what year was Hattie Caraway born?

25. Park rangers are cutting 9-foot lengths of rope. How many lengths can they make from 78 feet of rope?

Show You Understand

When dividing, as the divisor becomes greater why does the quotient become less?

Extra Practice

Set A (Lesson 1, pp. 110–111)

Divide. Use mental math.

1. $240 \div 4$
2. $560 \div 80$
3. $9{,}000 \div 10$
4. $2{,}100 \div 30$
5. $16{,}000 \div 200$
6. $64{,}000 \div 800$
7. $720{,}000 \div 800$
8. $450{,}000 \div 500$
9. $49{,}000 \div 7{,}000$

Set B (Lesson 2, pp. 112–113)

Divide. Check your answer.

1. $22\overline{)53}$
2. $32\overline{)98}$
3. $24\overline{)72}$
4. $41\overline{)89}$
5. $840 \div 42$
6. $727 \div 42$
7. $496 \div 61$
8. $245 \div 22$

Set C (Lesson 4, pp. 118–119)

Divide. Check your answer.

1. $68\overline{)201}$
2. $74\overline{)294}$
3. $47\overline{)338}$
4. $89\overline{)566}$
5. $58\overline{)264}$
6. $38\overline{)183}$
7. $22\overline{)433}$
8. $39\overline{)707}$
9. $26\overline{)514}$
10. $42\overline{)803}$
11. $27\overline{)628}$
12. $29\overline{)415}$

Set D (Lesson 5, pp. 120–121)

Divide.

1. $24\overline{)7{,}252}$
2. $46\overline{)1{,}286}$
3. $62\overline{)1{,}406}$
4. $19\overline{)7{,}365}$
5. $63\overline{)25{,}864}$
6. $26\overline{)14{,}610}$
7. $82\overline{)46{,}613}$
8. $65\overline{)23{,}486}$

Set E (Lesson 6, pp. 124–126)

Simplify.

1. $(15 + 6) - 8$
2. $7 + (24 \div 6) \times 8$
3. $(7 \times 4) \div 2^2$
4. $(72 - 3) - (16 \div 4)^3$
5. $(36 - 9) - (9 - 4)^2 + (6 \times 7)$
6. $(3^2 + 7) \div (20 \div 5)$
7. $8 + (11 - 7) + 42$
8. $2{,}550 - (69 - 64) \times 500$
9. $(108 \div 12) + 3^3$

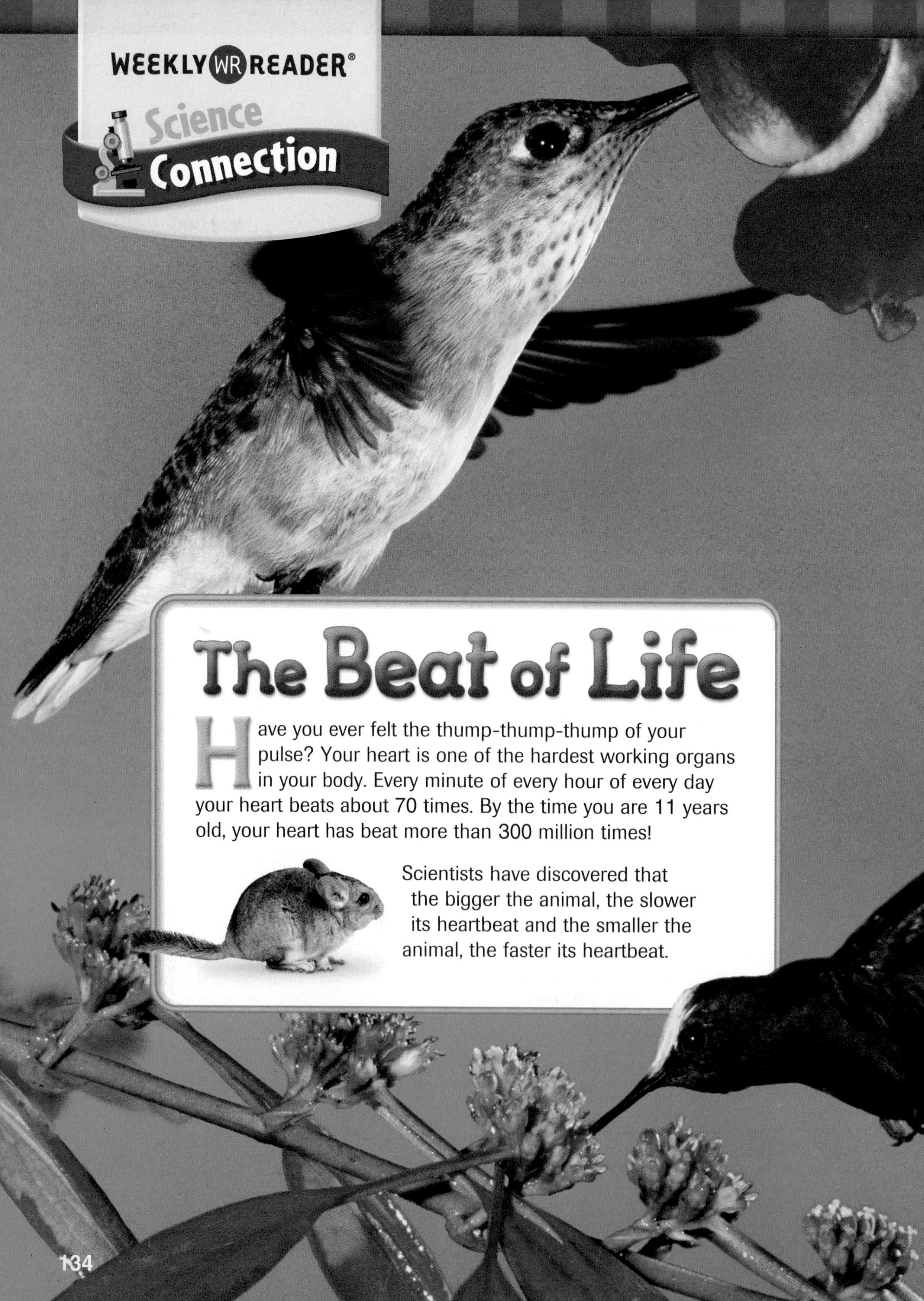

The Beat of Life

Have you ever felt the thump-thump-thump of your pulse? Your heart is one of the hardest working organs in your body. Every minute of every hour of every day your heart beats about 70 times. By the time you are 11 years old, your heart has beat more than 300 million times!

Scientists have discovered that the bigger the animal, the slower its heartbeat and the smaller the animal, the faster its heartbeat.

Heartbeats per Minute (at rest)			
Whale	8	Ground Squirrel	150
Polar Bear	46	Hummingbird	480
Human	70	Mouse	650

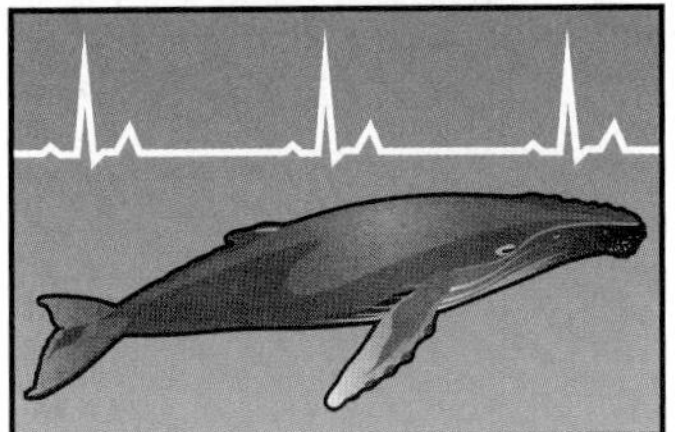

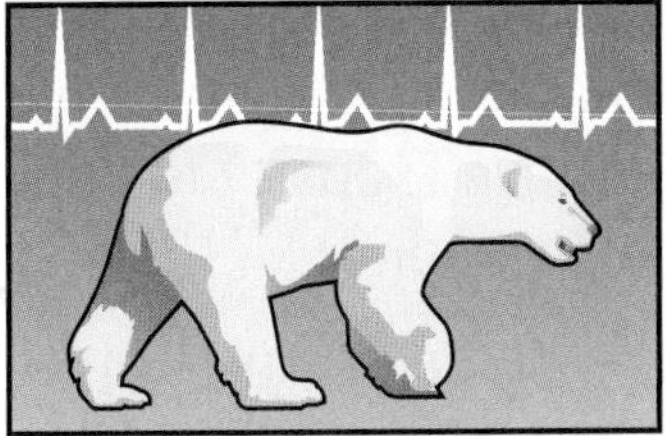

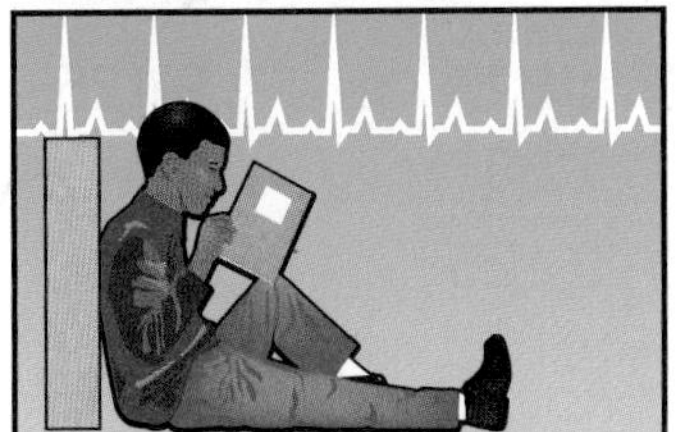

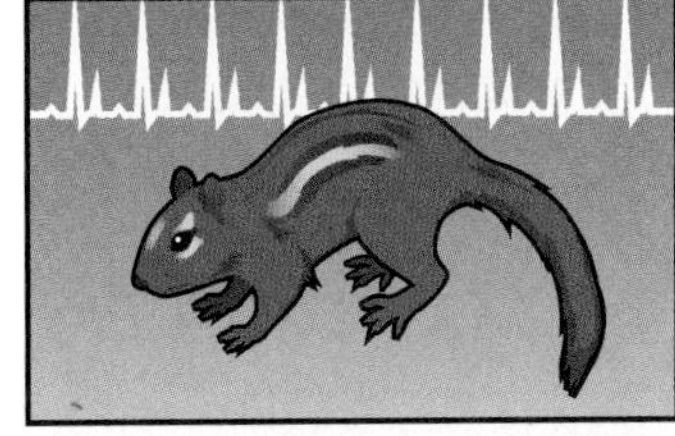

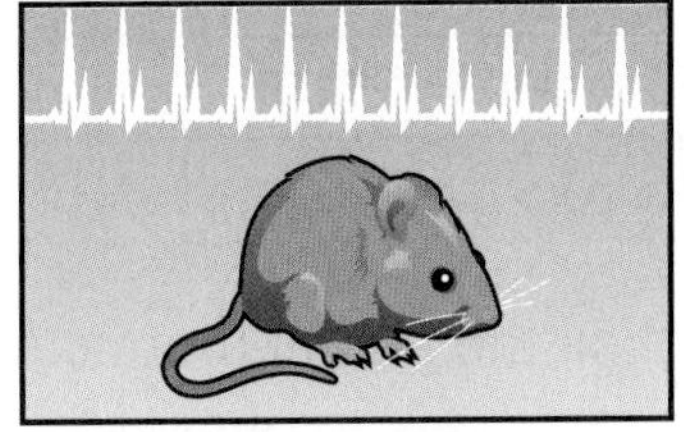

Problem Solving

Use the data in the chart to solve Problems 1–5.

1. How many times does a ground squirrel's heart beat in 1 hour? (Hint: 60 minutes = 1 hour)

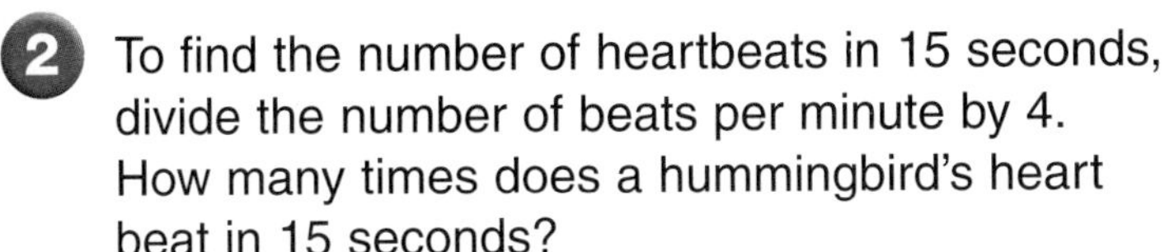

2. To find the number of heartbeats in 15 seconds, divide the number of beats per minute by 4. How many times does a hummingbird's heart beat in 15 seconds?

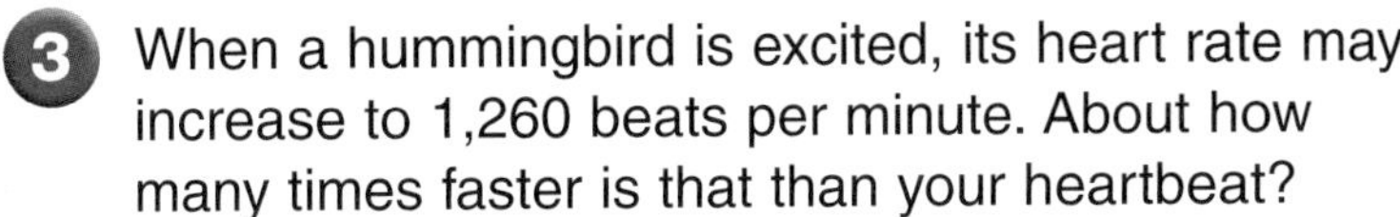

3. When a hummingbird is excited, its heart rate may increase to 1,260 beats per minute. About how many times faster is that than your heartbeat?

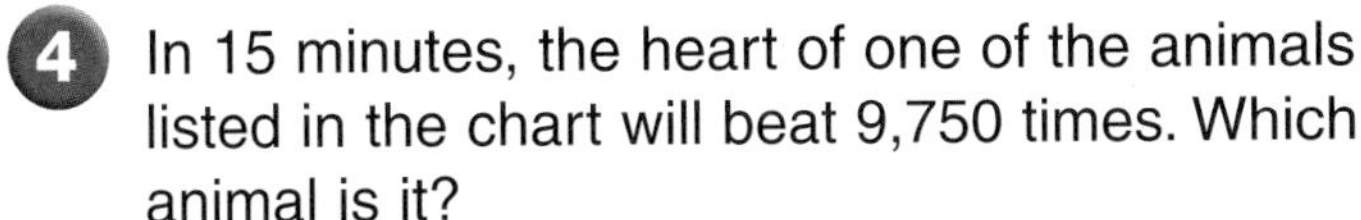

4. In 15 minutes, the heart of one of the animals listed in the chart will beat 9,750 times. Which animal is it?

5. A scientist used special equipment to monitor a polar bear's resting heart rate. The equipment registered 1,150 heartbeats. For how long did the scientist monitor the polar bear's heart rate?

Education Place

Visit Weekly Reader Connections at **eduplace.com/map** for more on this topic.

Enrichment

Your school is celebrating its 25th anniversary. Using 365 days per year, you find that 9,131 days have passed since your school first opened. How can you use the Distributive Property to check your multiplication?

$$\begin{array}{r} 365 \\ \times\ 25 \\ \hline 1\,825 \\ 7\,30 \\ \hline 9{,}125 \end{array}$$

There have been 6 leap years, so add 6 days.

$$\begin{array}{r} 9{,}125 \\ +\quad 6 \\ \hline 9{,}131 \end{array}$$

You can use a special table, called a diagram.

Write each factor in expanded form and multiply:

$25 \times 365 = (20 + 5) \times (300 + 60 + 5).$

	300	60	5	
20	20 × 300 = 6,000	20 × 60 = 1,200	20 × 5 = 100	
5	5 × 300 = 1,500	5 × 60 = 300	5 × 5 = 25	

Now add all the partial products.

	300	60	5	
20	20 × 300 = 6,000	20 × 60 = 1,200	20 × 5 = 100	7,300
5	5 × 300 = 1,500	5 × 60 = 300	5 × 5 = 25	+ 1,825
	7,500 +	1,500 +	125 =	**9,125**

Notice that by adding across and then down you get the same sum as when you add down and then across.

Show how to use the Distributive Property to solve each problem.

1. Daniel's father earns $28 per hour. He works 35 hours each week. Find how much Daniel's father earns in one week.

2. Heather's mother is 38 years old. Find how many days old she is. There have been 9 leap years since she was born.

Tic-Tac-Toe

Work with a partner and try to be the first to get 4 in a row!

How to Play:

1. Copy the game board shown below.

Multiplication Tic-Tac-Toe				
	29	51	12	68
327				
479				
512				
716				

2. Decide who will be X's and who will be O's.
3. The first player chooses a number from the top and a number from the side and estimates their product. The player then finds the actual product using a calculator.
4. If the difference between the estimate and the actual product is less than 500, the first player marks their letter in the box where the column and row meet. If the difference is greater than 500, the second player marks their letter in the box.
5. Players take turns until one player gets 4 in a row horizontally, vertically, or diagonally.

Now, try Division Tic-Tac-Toe. Estimate the quotient, then use the Int÷ key to check.

Division Tic-Tac-Toe				
	39,502	52,438	88,692	69,730
22				
39				
32				
11				

Unit 2 Test

VOCABULARY Open Response

1. When you multiply 25×28, you get the ■ 200 and 500, which you then add to find the product.
2. If one number divides into another with a remainder of 0, the numbers are called ■.
3. You use ■ to simplify expressions with more than one operation.

Vocabulary

- compatible numbers
- Distributive Property
- front-end estimation
- order of operations
- partial products

CONCEPTS AND SKILLS Open Response

Evaluate. Tell which property you used. (Chapter 3)

4. $(57 \times n) \times 25$, given $n = 4$
5. $4 \times 40 \times a$, given $a = 1$
6. Show how to use the Distributive Property to find the product 8×53. Show your work.

Find the product. (Chapter 3)

7. 432×7
8. 86×67

Estimate. (Chapters 3–4)

9. 69×83
10. 79×318
11. $705 \div 9$
12. $1{,}452 \div 7$

Use mental math to solve each equation. (Chapter 4)

13. $7n = 56$
14. $64 \div n = 8$

Divide. Check your answer. (Chapters 4–5)

15. $1{,}705 \div 3$
16. $1{,}080 \div 16$

Divide. Use mental math. (Chapter 5)

17. $4{,}900 \div 70$
18. $64{,}000 \div 800$

Simplify. (Chapter 5)

19. $9 \times 9 - 6 \div 2 + 1$
20. $(7 \times 5) - 4^2 - (11 + 8)$
21. $(3 + 4)^2 - (4 + 3)$

PROBLEM SOLVING **Open Response**

22. Eric, Fran, Greg, and Hannah each have a different color pencil: red, yellow, gray, or brown. Fran's pencil is not red or yellow. Greg's pencil is brown. Hannah's pencil is not yellow. What color is each student's pencil?

23. Theresa spent $45 on refreshments for the fifth-grade class party. She paid for the refreshments using $10, $5, and $1 bills. She received no change. If Theresa gave the cashier 10 bills in all, how many of each bill did she use?

24. A group of 59 students signed up to go on a field trip. Each minivan holds 1 driver and 7 student passengers. How many minivans will be needed?

25. A shipment of 300 math books came in boxes. Each box, except one, held 24 books. How many books were in the carton that did not hold 24 books?

Performance Assessment

Extended Response

Task Mitchell has saved $400. He would like to use some of the money to buy clothes while they are on sale.

Use the advertisement above and the information at the right. What can Mitchell buy? Explain your thinking.

Information You Need

- Mitchell wants to spend only half of the money he's saved at the clothing sale.
- He wants to buy at least one of each type of clothing that is on sale.
- He wants no more than $5 in change for the entire purchase.

Cumulative Test Prep

Solve Problems 1–10.

Test-Taking Tip

Some answer choices are word statements. Translate the word statements into number statements to help you decide whether the statements are *true* or *false*.

Look at the example below.

Which of the following statements is false?

A The product of two different even counting numbers is always greater than either of the factors.

B If the dividend is greater than the divisor, then the quotient of two counting numbers is always less than the dividend.

C The product of two counting numbers is always greater than either of the factors.

D If the product of two counting numbers is odd, then the factors are both odd.

THINK

Translate Statement **A** to $2 \times 4 = 8$.
Translate Statement **B** to $12 \div 6 = 2$.
Translate Statement **C** to $1 \times 2 = 2$.
Translate Statement **D** to $15 = 3 \times 5$.
Because of the Identity Property of multiplication, you know that if a factor is 1, the product is equal to the other factor. So Statement **C** is false.

Multiple Choice

1. Which of the following statements is true?

A A number divisible by 6 is also divisible by 3.

B A number divisible by 3 is also divisible by 9.

C A number divisible by 5 is also divisible by 10.

D A number divisible by 3 is also divisible by 6.

(Chapter 4, Lesson 4)

2. Which of the following statements is true about whole numbers?

F The third place from the right is the thousands place.

G The tens place is to the left of the hundreds place.

H The ones place is to the right of the tens place.

J The hundreds place is to the right of the tens place.

(Chapter 1, Lesson 1)

3. Which of the following statements is false?

A The hundredths place is to the right of the tenths place.

B The tenths place is to the right of the hundredths place.

C The ones place is to the left of the tenths place.

D The hundredths place is to the left of the thousandths place.

(Chapter 1, Lesson 7)

For Test-Taking Tips, see page 652.

Open Response

4. The population of the city where Matt lives increased from 126,780 to 135,017. How much did the population increase?

(Chapter 2, Lesson 4)

5. Tyler consumed an average of 620 calories for breakfast each day for two weeks. How many total calories did he consume for all breakfasts during those two weeks?

(Chapter 3, Lesson 7)

6. Carrie jogs every day. Last week she jogged a total of 105 kilometers. On average, how many kilometers did she jog each day?

(Chapter 4, Lesson 2)

7. A can of paint covers 500 square feet. How many cans of paint will Ellen need to buy to cover 3,000 square feet?

(Chapter 5, Lesson 1)

8. During a 32-day recycling campaign, a group of fifth-graders collected 3,360 pounds of newspaper. On average, how many pounds did they collect per day?

(Chapter 5, Lesson 5)

9.

VACATION PACKAGE SPECIALS	
Adults	$349
Senior Citizens	$289
Children	$250

What would the total cost be for a group of 8 adults, 4 senior citizens, and 12 children?

(Chapter 3, Lesson 7)

Extended Response

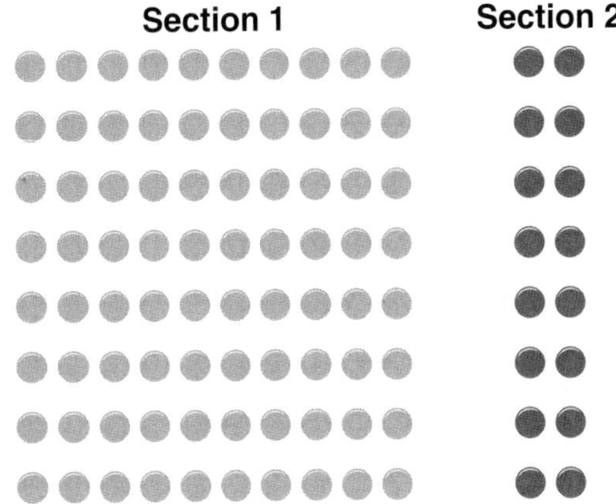

10. This diagram represents a marching band. There is a section with 8 rows of 10 marchers and a section of 8 rows of 2 marchers.

A How many marchers are in each section? How many marchers are there in all? How do you know?

B Suppose 1 row of marchers were added to each section. How many marchers would be in each section? How many would there be in all?

C Suppose one more row per section were added to the original formation and then one more marcher in each row. How many marchers would be in each section? How many marchers would there be in all? Make a drawing to explain your answer.

(Chapter 5, Lesson 2)

Education Place
Look for Cumulative Test Prep at **eduplace.com/map** for more practice.

Vocabulary Wrap-Up for Unit 2

Look back at the big ideas and vocabulary in this unit.

Big Ideas

You can estimate a product to help you decide if a computed product is reasonable.

When you simplify expressions, use the order of operations: parentheses, exponents, multiplication, division, addition, subtraction.

Key Vocabulary

order of operations
simplify
expression

Math Conversations

Use your new vocabulary to discuss these big ideas.

1. Explain how you evaluate the following expression.
   $3 \times (5 - 1)^2 + (28 \div 4)$
2. Explain how you can tell that 75,834 is divisible by 6 without doing the division.
3. Explain how to find the product mentally.
   $80{,}000 \times 9{,}000$
4. Explain how to find the quotient of $6{,}553 \div 47$.
5. **Write About It** Find data on how much money is spent on schools in your area. How could you estimate the amount spent on the fifth grade? How could you estimate the amount spent on each student?

I multiplied 19 by 62 and got 1,178. Is that reasonable?
Try multiplying 20 by 60 to check.

UNIT 3

Measurement/ Data and Graphing

Reading Mathematics

Reviewing Vocabulary

Here are some math vocabulary words that you should know.

mass	a measure of the amount of matter in an object
metric system	a system of measures in which all units are formed by multiplying or dividing a standard unit by a power of 10.
meter	the standard unit of length in the metric system
liter	the standard unit of capacity in the metric system
gram	the standard unit of mass in the metric system

Reading Words and Symbols

Units of measure are often abbreviated to save space.

Examples: *3 in.* is read as *three inches.*
12 cm is read as *twelve centimeters.*

In the table below, write the word or abbreviation for each ■.

Customary Units of Measure	Metric Units of Measure
1. 1 yard (yd) = 3 feet (■)	**4.** 1 kilometer (■) = 1,000 ■ (m)
2. 1 ■ (qt) = 2 pints (■)	**5.** 1 ■ (L) = 1,000 ■ (mL)
3. 1 pound (■) = 16 ■ (oz)	**6.** 1 ■ (kg) = 1,000 grams (■)

Reading Test Questions

Choose the correct answer for each.

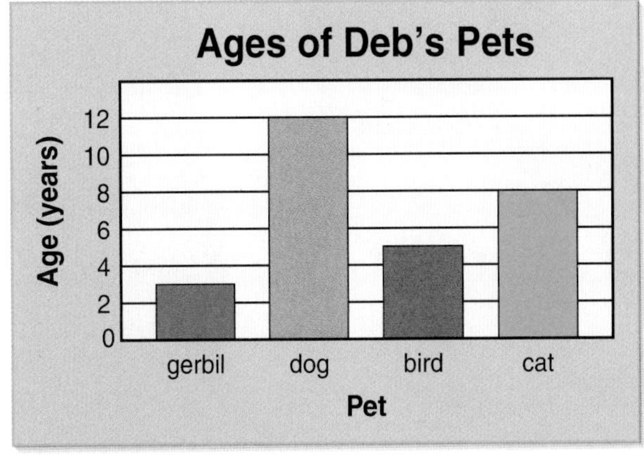

7. Which unit would you use to measure the ages of Deb's pets?

   a. inches **c.** years

   b. gallons **d.** miles

A unit is any standard amount that is used to measure something.

8. Which interval is used on the graph to show the pets' ages?

   a. 2 years

   b. 4 years

   c. 5 years

   d. 12 years

Intervals are the equal spaces between marks on the numerical scale of a graph. Intervals show how the data are measured.

9. Based on the data in the graph, which of these statements is **not** true?

   a. The bird is older than the gerbil.

   b. The cat is less than 10 years old.

   c. The dog is 12 years old.

   d. The cat is younger than the bird.

Data are pieces of information.

Learning Vocabulary

Watch for these words in this unit. Write their definitions in your journal.

metric ton

milligram

double bar graph

histogram

double line graph

stem-and-leaf plot

Education Place

At **eduplace.com/map** see *e*Glossary and *e*Games—Math Lingo.

Literature Connection

Read "Ships of the Desert" on page 641. Then work with a partner to answer the questions about the story.

CHAPTER 6

Units of Measure

INVESTIGATION

Use Data

This black-browed albatross chick will grow to be a large bird that lives most of its life at sea. The table shows some information about this kind of albatross. Find your height and your arm span in centimeters. The head and body length, and the wingspan, of the albatross are the maximum lengths. Write ratios in simplest terms for the albatross' wingspan: head and body length, and for your arm span: your height. How do the ratios compare? Explain.

$$\frac{\text{albatross wingspan}}{\text{head and body length}}$$

$$\frac{\text{your arm span}}{\text{your height}}$$

Size Range for Adult Black-Browed Albatross

Mass	3–5 kg
Head and Body Length	80–95 cm
Wingspan	210–250 cm

Use What You Know

Use this page to review and remember what you need to know for this chapter.

VOCABULARY

Choose the best word to complete each sentence.

Vocabulary
divide
feet
inches
multiply

1. There are three ____ in a yard.
2. If the wheels on a bicycle are 26 ____ wide, they would be a little wider than 2 feet.
3. To find the number of inches in 2 feet, you would ____ 2 by 12.

CONCEPTS AND SKILLS

Which unit would you use to measure each? Write *inch, foot, yard,* or *mile*.

4. a pencil
5. the distance from school to your home

Choose the most reasonable measure for each.

6. width of a lion's cage
   4 cm   4 m   4 km
7. weight of a zebra
   270 mg   270 g   270 kg

Compute.

8. $5{,}280 \times 3 + 4$
9. $4{,}004 \div 2$

10. Which would serve more people at a party, 1 gallon of ice cream or 7 pints of ice cream? Use pictures, symbols, or words to explain your answer.

Facts Practice, See page 663.

Measurement Concepts

Objective Measure to a given degree of precision using appropriate tools and units of measure.

Vocabulary
precision

Materials
tape measure
ruler
Learning Tool 31

Work Together

The **precision** of a measurement is determined by the unit of measure that you use. A smaller unit produces a more precise measurement than a larger unit.

To the nearest inch, this paper clip is 2 inches long. To the nearest eighth inch, the paper clip is $1\frac{7}{8}$ inches long. The measurement $1\frac{7}{8}$ inches is a more precise measurement than 2 inches.

0 1 2
inches

Work with a partner to estimate and measure lengths to the nearest yard, foot, inch, half inch, and eighth inch.

STEP 1 Estimate the length of your classroom in yards. Record your estimate.

Measure and record the length to the nearest yard, the nearest foot, and the nearest inch.

Measurement and Precision

Object	Estimate	Measurements
Length of room		

STEP 2 Estimate the width of your desk in feet. Record your estimate.

Measure and record the width to the nearest foot, the nearest inch, and the nearest half inch.

STEP 3 Estimate the width of your hand in inches. Record your estimate.

Measure and record the width to the nearest inch, the nearest half inch, and the nearest eighth inch.

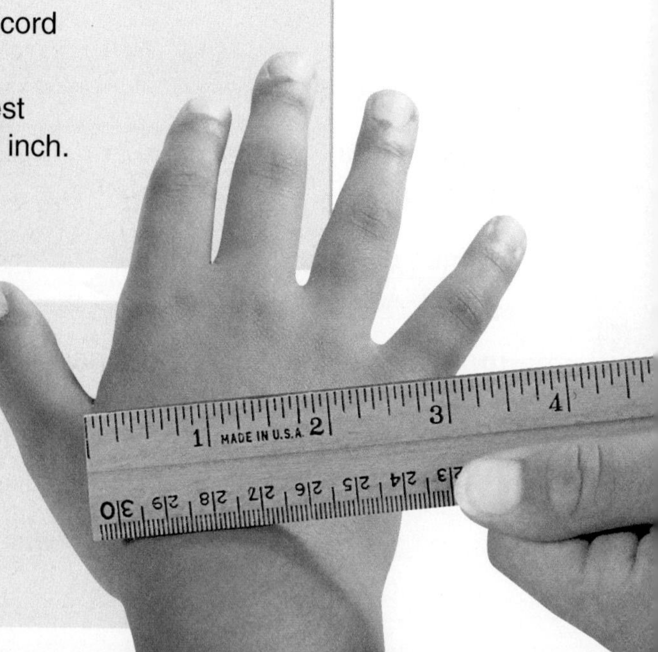

On Your Own

Decide what unit of measure to use. Then measure each item.

1. the length of the chalkboard
2. the length of a pencil
3. the height of your desk
4. the width of an eraser
5. the width of your foot
6. the length of your arm

Tell whether a precise measurement is needed or if an estimate is sufficient. Explain your answer.

7. finding the length and width of a picture that you want to frame
8. finding the distance between Chicago, Illinois, and Jacksonville, Florida
9. finding the height of a twenty-five-story building
10. finding the lengths of wood boards for a bookcase

Make a list of 3 objects that you think have about the given measurement. Check your estimates and record the actual measurement of each object.

11. 1 inch
12. 6 inches
13. 1 foot
14. 1 yard

Choose an object that is between one foot and one yard long. Measure its length to the nearest

15. foot
16. yard
17. inch
18. half inch

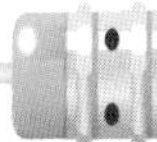

Talk About It • Write About It

You learned how to estimate and measure using different customary units of length.

19. When you measure an object, can you ever get an exact measurement? Explain your answer.
20. How do you choose which measuring tool to use for an object? For what objects would you use the least precise units of measure?
21. The length of a pencil measured to the nearest inch, half inch, and quarter inch is 2 inches. Use a drawing to explain how this is possible.

Lesson 2

Customary Units of Length

Objective Estimate, compare, and convert customary units of length.

Vocabulary
unit lengths

Learn About It

The system of measurement used in the United States is called the customary system of measurement. Standard **unit lengths** in this system include mile (mi), yard (yd), foot (ft), and inch (in.).

The snake shown at the right is an anaconda. Anaconda snakes are some of the largest snakes in the world and can be up to 360 inches long. How many feet is this?

360 in. = ■ ft

Changing Customary Units of Length

STEP 1 Use the table to find the relationship between inches and feet.

STEP 2 Divide by 12 to find the number of feet.

360 ÷ 12 = 30

360 in. = 30 ft

Customary Units of Length
12 inches (in.) = 1 foot (ft)
3 feet = 1 yard (yd)
5,280 feet = 1 mile (mi)
1,760 yards = 1 mile

Solution: Since 360 inches is equal to 30 feet, an anaconda can be up to 30 feet long.

Other Examples

A. Feet and Inches

54 in. = ■ ft ■ in.

Since 12 in. = 1 ft, divide 54 by 12.

54 ÷ 12 = 4 R6

54 in. = 4 ft 6 in.

B. Yards and Feet

5 yd 2 ft = ■ ft

Since 1 yd = 3 ft, multiply 5 by 3.

5 × 3 = 15; then add the 2 feet.

15 ft + 2 ft = 17 ft

5 yd 2 ft = 17 ft

Guided Practice

Complete.

1. 2 mi = ■ ft
2. 70 in. = ■ ft ■ in.
3. 3 ft = ■ in.
4. 12 yd 2 ft = ■ ft

Ask Yourself

- How do I decide whether to multiply or divide to change units?

Explain Your Thinking ▶ Do you multiply or divide to change from a smaller unit to a larger unit? Explain your choice.

Practice and Problem Solving

Complete.

5. 7 ft = ■ in.
6. ■ ft = 3 yd 1 ft
7. ■ in. = 2 ft 6 in.
8. 125 in. = ■ ft ■ in.
9. 5 mi = ■ yd
10. 6,000 ft = ■ mi ■ ft

Compare. Write >, <, or = for each ●.

11. 4 ft ● 46 in.
12. 6 yd 2 ft ● 20 ft
13. 4 mi ● 24,000 ft
14. 200 in. ● 20 ft
15. 5 mi ● 10,000 yd
16. 3 yd 2 ft ● 100 in.

Which unit would you use to measure each? Write *inch, foot, yard,* or *mile*.

17. the height of a giraffe
18. the width of a monkey's foot
19. the distance a migrating bird travels
20. the length of an alligator

Solve.

21. One elephant seal is 21 feet long. A ringed seal is 48 inches long. How many feet longer is the elephant seal?
22. One fully grown lion is 107 inches long, and another is 8 feet 2 inches long. Which lion is longer? Explain.

23. **Write About It** Explain how to change 112 inches to feet and inches, then to yards, feet, and inches.
24. About how many inches are there in a mile? Explain how you got your estimate.

Mixed Review and Test Prep

Open Response

Use mental math to solve the equation.
(Ch. 2, Lesson 5)

25. $m + 3 = 12$
26. $16 - n = 2$
27. $p - 3 = 15$
28. $b + 5 = 5$

Multiple Choice

29. Choose the best unit of measure to find the distance from Utah to Texas.
(Ch. 6, Lesson 2)
   - **A** inch
   - **B** foot
   - **C** yard
   - **D** mile

Extra Practice See page 169, Set A.

Lesson 3

Customary Units of Weight and Capacity

Objective Change one customary unit of weight or capacity to another.

Vocabulary

capacity

Learn About It

An African elephant weighs about 14,000 pounds. What is the weight of an African elephant in tons?

14,000 lb = ■ T

Changing Customary Units of Weight

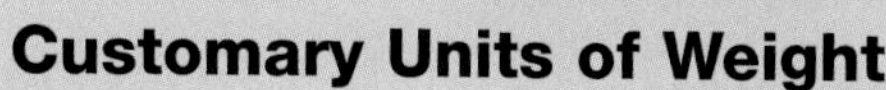

- Use the table to find the relationship between pounds and tons.
- Divide by 2,000 to find the number of tons.

14,000 ÷ 2,000 = 7
14,000 lb = 7 T

Customary Units of Weight
16 ounces (oz) = 1 pound (lb)
2,000 pounds = 1 ton (T)

Solution: An African elephant weighs about 7 tons.

▶ **Capacity** is the amount that a container can hold. Gallons, quarts, and pints are all units of capacity.

An African elephant can take $1\frac{1}{2}$ gallons of water into its trunk for a drink. How many quarts are in $1\frac{1}{2}$ gallons?

$1\frac{1}{2}$ gal = ■ qt

Changing Customary Units of Capacity

- Use the table to find the relationship between gallons and quarts.
- Each gallon is 4 quarts. So $\frac{1}{2}$ gallon is 2 quarts.

$1\frac{1}{2}$ gal = 4 qt + 2 qt = 6 qt

Customary Units of Capacity
8 fluid ounces (fl oz) = 1 cup (c)
2 cups = 1 pint (pt)
2 pints = 1 quart (qt)
4 quarts = 1 gal (gal)

Solution: There are 6 quarts in $1\frac{1}{2}$ gallons.

Guided Practice

Ask Yourself

- Do I multiply or divide to change units?

Complete.

1. 32 oz = ■ lb
2. ■ lb = 2 T
3. ■ c = 2 pt
4. 8 qt = ■ gal
5. 6 pt = ■ qt
6. ■ pt = 64 fl oz

Explain Your Thinking ▶ How many fluid ounces are in $1\frac{1}{2}$ pints? How do you know?

Practice and Problem Solving

Complete.

7. 5 T = ■ lb
8. ■ lb = 48 oz
9. 19 pt = ■ qt ■ pt
10. $16\frac{1}{2}$ T = ■ lb
11. 80 oz = ■ lb
12. 17,500 lb = ■ T ■ lb
13. 12 c = ■ pt
14. ■ gal = 24 pt
15. $8\frac{1}{2}$ gal = ■ qt
16. 15 pt = ■ c
17. ■ oz = 7 lb
18. 26 qt = ■ gal ■ qt

Compare. Write >, <, or = for each ●.

19. 52 oz ● 3 lb
20. 2 lb 3 oz ● 35 oz
21. 4,200 lb ● 2 T 300 lb
22. 13 c ● 7 pt
23. 6 gal 3 qt ● 27 qt
24. 62 pt ● 7 gal 2 qt

Which unit would you use to measure each?
Write *oz, lb, T, fl oz, c, pt, qt,* or *gal.*

25. A gorilla weighs about 220 ■.
26. A dozen apples weigh about 5 ■.
27. A swimming pool holds 10,000 ■ of water.
28. The capacity of a drinking glass is about 10 ■.
29. A single-serving container of yogurt has a capacity of 8 ■.
30. A car's fuel tank can hold about 20 ■ of gasoline.
31. A picture postcard from your favorite state weighs about $\frac{1}{2}$ ■.
32. The heaviest turtle in the world weighs about $\frac{3}{4}$ ■.

Go On

Data **The table at the right shows the weights of some sea creatures. Use the table for Problems 33–37.**

33. About how many pounds does an Olive Ridley turtle weigh?

34. What is the weight of a Baird's whale in tons?

35. Alexander said that 25,990 lb was the difference in weight between the heaviest and the lightest sea creatures. What error did he make? What answer should he have given?

36. List the sea creatures in order from lightest to heaviest.

37. Draw a bar graph that compares the weights of the 3 heaviest sea creatures.

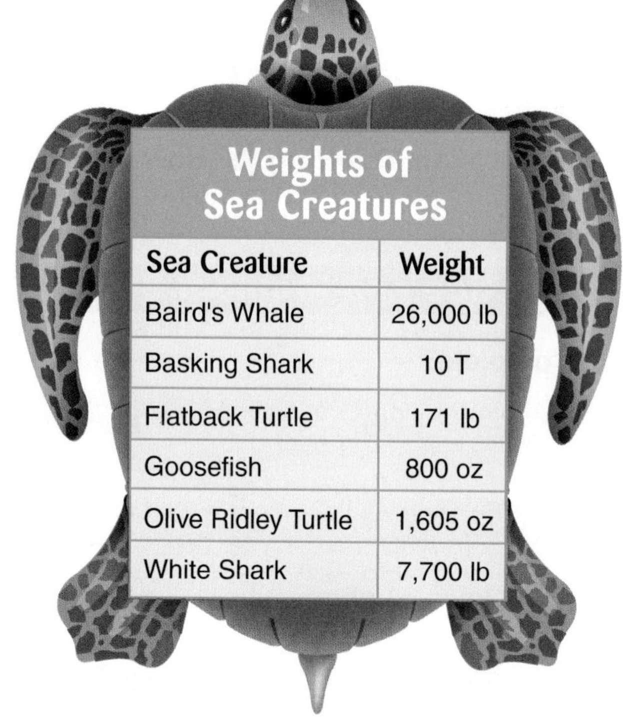

Weights of Sea Creatures

Sea Creature	Weight
Baird's Whale	26,000 lb
Basking Shark	10 T
Flatback Turtle	171 lb
Goosefish	800 oz
Olive Ridley Turtle	1,605 oz
White Shark	7,700 lb

38. A baby African elephant can weigh as much as 3,600 ounces at birth. Is that more than or less than one-half ton? Explain how you found your answer.

39. **What's Wrong?** Look at the notebook below. It shows how Kyle changed fluid ounces to pints. Explain what Kyle did wrong. Then show how to complete the problem correctly.

32 fl oz = ? pt

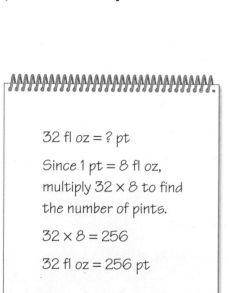

Since 1 pt = 8 fl oz, multiply 32 × 8 to find the number of pints.

32 × 8 = 256

32 fl oz = 256 pt

40. Sandra bought 2 gallons of orange juice for a party. The juice came in quart containers. The total cost of the juice was $24. What was the cost of each quart?

41. There are 240 people weighing an average of 150 pounds each on a plane. What is the weight, in tons, of the people on that plane?

42. Marla took 168 pictures in a rainforest. She took 3 times as many pictures of plants as pictures of animals. How many pictures of plants did she take?

43. **Create and Solve** Write your own problem about animals. Draw a picture to go with your problem. Then solve.

Extra Practice See page 169, Set B.

Activity

Measurement Sense

How Tall Is It?

Materials: tape measure or yardstick, ruler

Work with your partner to find the height of your classroom.

To find a way to solve this problem, discuss the following questions with your partner.

- Is the classroom wall made of cinderblocks? If so, find the height of a cinderblock. How can you use this measurement to estimate the height of the classroom?
- Choose an object with a height that is easy to measure. How can you use the height of this object to help you estimate the height of the classroom?

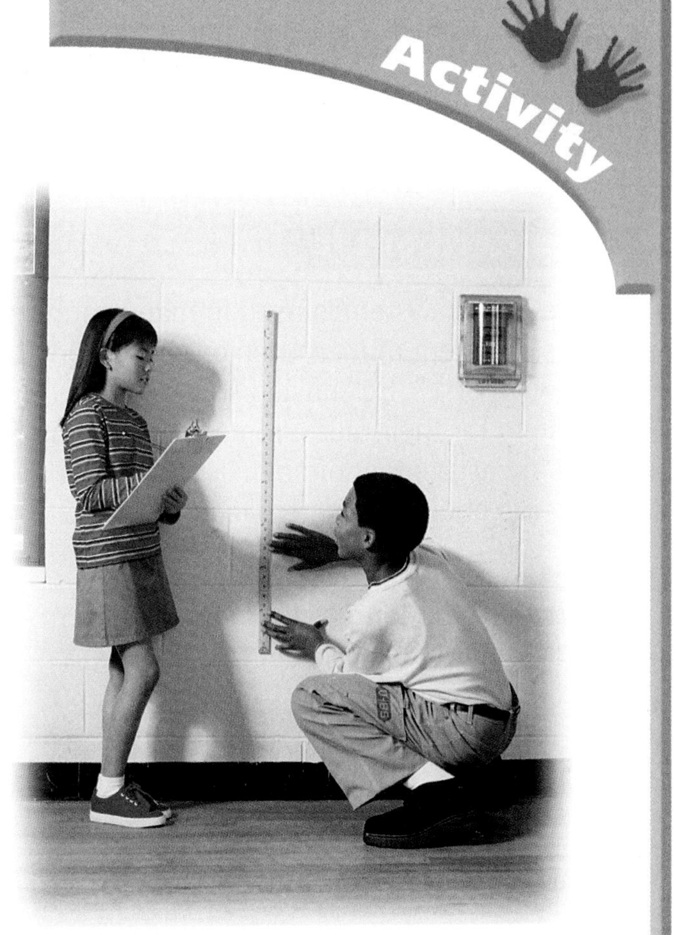

Quick Check

Check your understanding of Lessons 1–3.

Decide what unit of measure to use. Then measure each item. (Lesson 1)

1. the width of your chair
2. the length of your thumb

Which unit would you use to measure each? Write *c, ft, gal, lb, mi,* or *T*. (Lessons 2–3)

3. A bowling ball weighs about 10 ■.
4. A door is about 3 ■ wide.
5. At breakfast, you might drink 2 ■ of milk.
6. A beluga whale might weigh about 2 ■.

Complete. (Lessons 2–3)

7. 48 in. = ■ ft
8. 3 lb = ■ oz
9. ■ qt = 16 pt
10. 84 in. = ■ yd ■ ft

Lesson 4

Metric Units of Length

Objective Measure lengths in metric units and change from one unit of metric length to another.

Vocabulary
decimeter (dm)
centimeter (cm)
millimeter (mm)

Learn About It

The metric system is used in many countries. It is a system of measurement based on powers of 10. Scientists use the metric system for their measurements, including the measurement of animals. This Siberian tiger is about 3.3 meters long.

Measure the length of the line segment below using metric units.

Measuring With Metric Units of Length

Measure the length to the nearest decimeter.

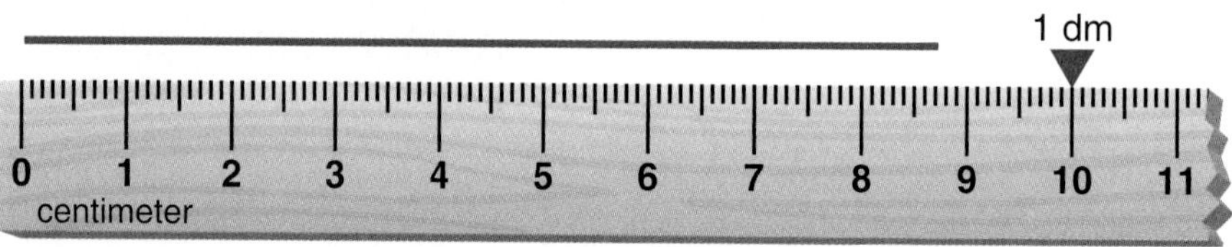

- 1 **decimeter** (1 dm) = 10 **centimeters** (cm)
- Between which two decimeter marks is the end of the purple line segment?
- What is the length of the segment to the nearest decimeter?

Measure the length to the nearest centimeter.

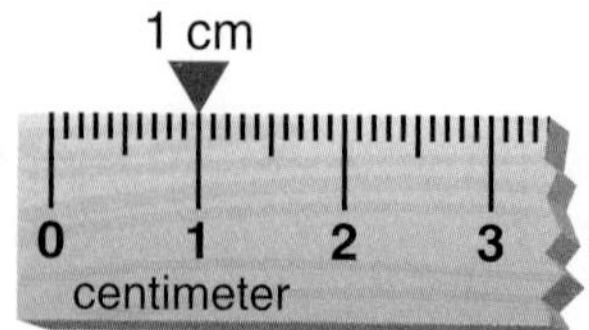

- Is the length of the purple line segment closer to 8 cm or to 9 cm? How can you tell?
- What is the length of that segment to the nearest centimeter?

Measure the length to the nearest millimeter.

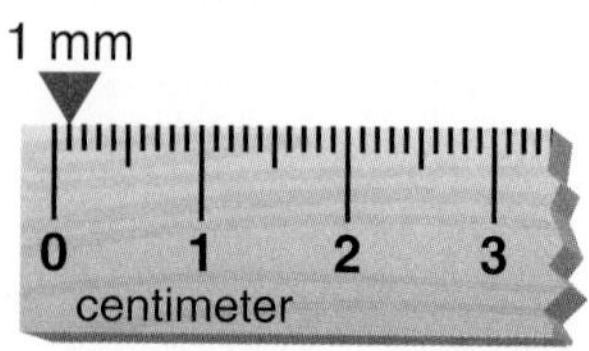

- 1 **millimeter** (mm) = 0.1 cm
- How many millimeters are in 1 cm?
- What is the length of the purple line segment to the nearest millimeter?

Changing Metric Units of Length

To change from one metric unit of length to another, multiply or divide by a power of 10. Powers of 10 include 10, 100, and 1,000.

Metric Units of Length
10 millimeters (mm) = 1 centimeter (cm)
10 centimeters = 1 decimeter (dm)
10 decimeters = 1 meter (m)
1,000 meters = 1 kilometer (km)

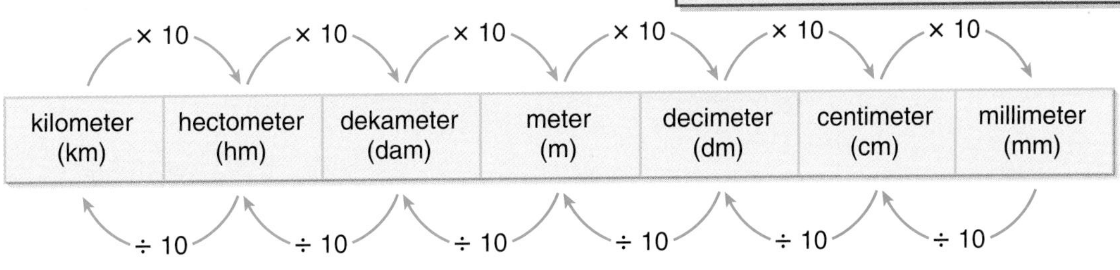

1 kilometer 1,000 m	1 hectometer 100 m	1 dekameter 10 m	1 meter 1 m	1 decimeter 0.1 m	1 centimeter 0.01 m	1 millimeter 0.001 m

Multiply to change from a larger unit to a smaller unit.

2 cm = ■ mm

2 × 10 = 20

2 cm = 20 mm

Think
1 cm = 10 mm

Divide to change from a smaller unit to a larger unit.

5,000 m = ■ km

5,000 ÷ 1,000 = 5

5,000 m = 5 km

Think
1,000 m = 1 km

Guided Practice

Use a ruler. Measure each line segment to the nearest decimeter, centimeter, and millimeter.

1. ———

2. ————————————————

3. ——————————————————————————————————

Ask Yourself

- Which unit of measure am I using?
- Which marks on the ruler show that unit of measure?

Complete.

4. 3 km = ■ m **5.** ■ m = 20 dm **6.** 120 mm = ■ cm

Explain Your Thinking ▶ What is the relationship between multiplying and dividing by powers of 10 and moving the decimal point? Use an example to explain your answer.

Go On

Practice and Problem Solving

Grass and twigs are part of an African elephant's diet. Measure each twig below to the nearest decimeter, centimeter, and millimeter.

7.

8.

9.

10.

11. Draw a blade of grass that is 2 decimeters long. How many millimeters long is your blade of grass?

12. What is the length of the longest blade of grass you can draw on your paper? It must be a single straight blade.

Complete.

13. 3 m = ■ cm

14. ■ dm = 10 m

15. 600 mm = ■ dm

16. 3,000 cm = ■ m

17. 500 cm = ■ dm

18. ■ mm = 25 cm

19. 2 km = ■ m

20. 750 dm = ■ cm

21. 30 m = ■ dm

Compare. Write >, <, or = for each ●.

22. 300 cm ● 30 m

23. 250 mm ● 25 cm

24. 5 dm ● 60 cm

25. 7 km ● 700 m

26. 3,600 cm ● 4 m

27. 9,000 mm ● 10 m

28. 410 cm ● 4 m

29. 8,400 mm ● 84 dm

30. 95 m ● 906 dm

For Exercises 31–34, write the metric unit of length that is reasonable.

31. 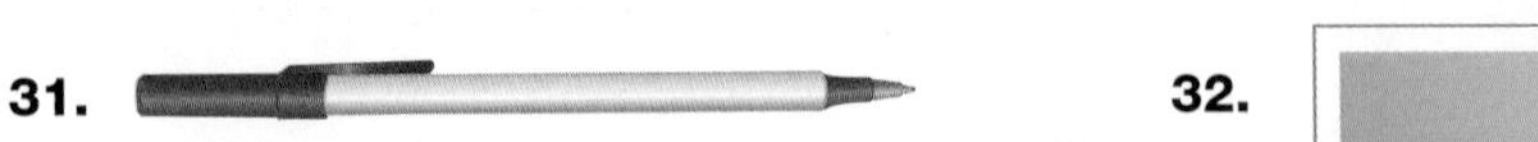

32. 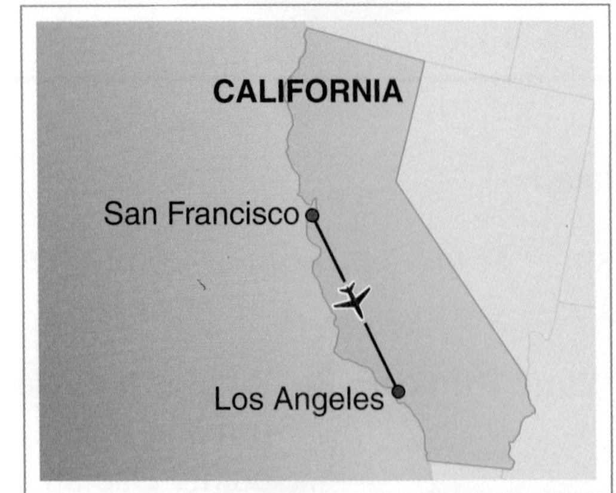

33. 

34. 

Solve.

35. An Arabian camel is 35 decimeters long. A hippopotamus is 4 meters long. Which animal has the greater length?

36. The Brookfield Zoo is 27,000 meters from the Lincoln Park Zoo. How many kilometers apart are the two zoos?

37. Robert has $27 in his wallet. He has $10, $5, and $1 bills. Robert has 10 bills in all. How many of each bill does he have?

38. Will a book that is 278 millimeters stand up straight in a bookcase with shelves that are 27 centimeters apart? Explain.

39. Look at the giraffe at the right. Which is a better estimate of its height in meters, 5 meters or 6 meters? Explain.

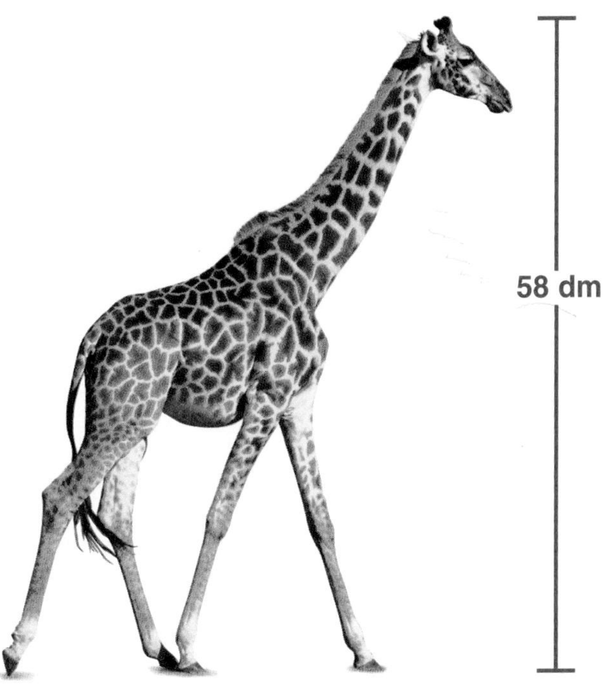

40. How is changing from one metric unit to another like changing from one customary unit to another? How is it different?

41. In the line for the dolphin show, Josh was ahead of Anne, and Barbara was ahead of David. Mary was in the middle. Anne was second. Tell the order of the 5 people in line.

42. **Write About It** Choose an object from your classroom and measure its length to the nearest millimeter, centimeter, and decimeter. Which measure best describes the object's length? Tell why.

Mixed Review and Test Prep

Open Response

Multiply. (Ch.3, Lesson 5)

43. 223×20

44. 17×300

45. 9×40

46. 24×600

47. 158×200

48. 460×600

49. 999×900

50. Use the data in the table to find how many decimeters taller Francisco is than Bethany. (Ch. 6, Lesson 4)

Name	Height
Andrew	100 cm
Bethany	120 cm
Danita	140 cm
Francisco	160 cm

Extra Practice See page 169, Set C.

Lesson 5

Metric Units of Mass and Capacity

Objective Change from one metric unit of mass or capacity to another.

Vocabulary
- **kilogram**
- **liter**
- **metric ton (t)**

Learn About It

The basic metric unit of mass is the **kilogram**. The kilogram was intended to be the mass of a cube of water one-tenth of a meter (1 dm) on a side.

There are 1,000 kilograms in 1 **metric ton (t)**.

The basic metric unit of capacity is the **liter**. A liter is the amount (capacity) of a cube of water with one-tenth of a meter (1 dm) on a side.

1dm

1dm

1dm

1cm

1cm

1cm

The official standard of the kilogram is a cylindrical piece of platinum-iridium alloy kept in a secure location in France.

One milliliter (mL) of water will fill one cubic centimeter (cc).

So, 1 mL = 1 cc.

1 cc can also be written as 1cm

2,000 kg = ■ t

Changing Metric Units of Mass

STEP 1 Use the table to find the relationship between kilograms and metric tons. 1,000 kg = 1 t

STEP 2 Divide by 1,000 to find the number of metric tons. 2,000 ÷ 1,000 = 2
2,000 kg = 2 t

Metric Units of Mass
1,000 milligrams (mg) = 1 gram (g)
1,000 grams = 1 kilogram (kg)
1,000 kilograms = 1 metric ton (t)

Solution: 2,000 kg = 2 t

There are 35 liters of water in a bucket. How many milliliters of water are in the bucket?

35 L = ■ mL

Changing Metric Units of Capacity

STEP 1 Use the table to find the relationship between liters and milliliters.

1 L = 1,000 mL

STEP 2 Multiply by 1,000 to find the number of milliliters.

$35 \times 1,000 = 35,000$
35 L = 35,000 mL

Metric Units of Capacity
1,000 milliliters (mL) = 1 liter (L)
10 deciliters (dL) = 1 liter (L)

Solution: There are 35,000 milliliters of water in the bucket.

Guided Practice

Ask Yourself

- Which power of 10 do I use?
- Do I multiply or divide?

Complete.

1. 2 L = ■ mL
2. 3,000 dL = ■ L
3. 8,000 kg = ■ t
4. 6 g = ■ mg
5. 31,000 mg = ■ g
6. 5 t = ■ kg

Explain Your Thinking ▶ What power of 10 would you use to change liters to milliliters? Would you multiply or would you divide?

Practice and Problem Solving

Complete.

7. 4 kg = ■ g
8. 7 L = ■ mL
9. 7,000 g = ■ kg
10. 10 t = ■ kg
11. 2 L = ■ dL
12. 13 g = ■ mg
13. 5,000 kg = ■ t
14. 25,000 mg = ■ g
15. 250 dL = ■ L

For Exercises 16–19, tell which metric unit you would use to measure each. Explain your choice.

16. the amount of water in a glass
17. the amount of medicine in an eye dropper
18. the mass of a hummingbird
19. the mass of an elephant

Go On

Practice and Problem Solving

Choose the most reasonable measure for each.

20. 

- **a.** 65 g
- **b.** 65 mg
- **c.** 6 kg

21. 

- **a.** 3 mL
- **b.** 35 mL
- **c.** 350 mL

22. 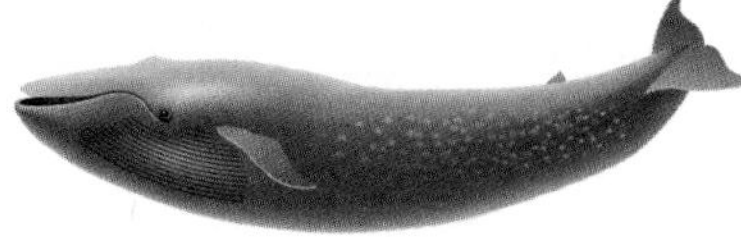

- **a.** 120 t
- **b.** 120 kg
- **c.** 1,200 g

Compare. Write >, <, or = for each ●.

23. 2 t ● 20,000 kg

24. 2,000 g ● 3 kg

25. 12 kg ● 10,000 g

26. 4,000 mL ● 40 L

27. 8,000 cm^3 ● 8,000 mL

28. 400 kg ● 4 t

29. 5,000 mL ● 5 cm^3

30. 9,005 g ● 9 kg

31. 50 t ● 5,100 kg

32. 500 dL ● 50 L

Solve.

33. A penny has a mass of 2,500 milligrams. What is the mass, in grams, of a roll of 50 pennies?

34. A sink holds 1,500 deciliters of water. Explain how you can find its capacity in liters.

35. A moose has a mass of about 550 kg. An American bison has a mass of one metric ton. The mass of a bison is how many kilograms greater than the mass of a moose?

36. Are there less than one million, exactly one million, or more than one million milligrams in one kilogram?

Mixed Review and Test Prep

Open Response

Estimate the product. (Ch. 3, Lesson 6)

37. 22×387

38. $38 \times 4,224$

39. 94×671

40. $39 \times 7,003$

41. 27×875

42. $31 \times 8,661$

Multiple Choice

43. Hector drank 2 liters of water. Tanya drank 2,500 milliliters of water. How much more water did Tanya drink than Hector? (Ch. 6, Lesson 5)

- **A** 2,500 mL
- **B** 2,000 mL
- **C** 1,500 mL
- **D** 500 mL

Extra Practice See page 169, Set D.

Estimating Measures

Game

Activity

2–4 Players

What You'll Need
- customary measurement tools (inch ruler, yardstick, tape measure, measuring cups, scale)
- metric measurement tools (centimeter ruler, meter stick, tape measure, measuring cups, scale)
- Learning Tool 32

How to Play

1. Pick one player to be the "measure master." This player thinks of a distance or an object that can be measured with the tools provided. This player also chooses the type of measurement (length, capacity, or weight/mass) to be made.

2. In a table like the one shown, each player records what will be measured and the kind of measurement that will be made. Players then estimate the measurement in both customary and metric units and record the estimates.

3. The "measure master" uses a customary tool to make the measurement. He or she then uses a metric tool to make the measurement.

4. Players compare their estimates to the actual measurement. The player who has the estimate that is closest to the actual measurement is the "measure master" for the next round.

Learning Tool 32

Name ____________________

Estimating Measures

Object	Type of Measure (circle one.)	Tool	Customary Units		Metric Units	
			Estimate	Measurement	Estimate	Measurement
	Length Capacity Weight Mass					
	Length Capacity Weight Mass					
	Length Capacity Weight Mass					
	Length Capacity Weight Mass					
	Length Capacity Weight Mass					
	Length Capacity Weight Mass					

Learning Tool 32

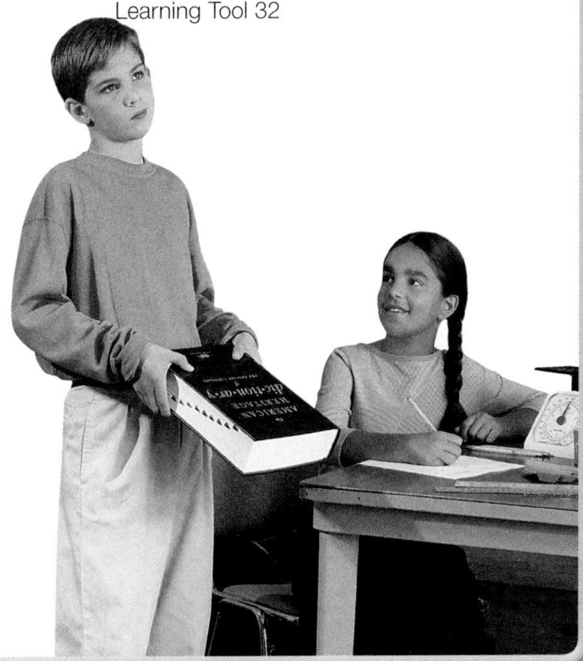

Lesson 6

Audio Tutor 1/19 Listen and Understand

Add and Subtract Measurements

Objective Add and subtract measurements.

Learn About It

The picture shows a giraffe that is 13 feet 3 inches tall and a boy who is 4 feet 8 inches tall. How much taller is the giraffe than the boy?

Find 13 ft 3 in. – 4 ft 8 in.

STEP 1 Subtract inches. Since 3 < 8, regroup 1 ft as 12 in.

```
   12    15
  1̸3 ft 3̸ in.
 –  4 ft 8 in.
 ------------
         7 in.
```

Think
1 ft = 12 in.
3 + 12 = 15; so
13 ft 3 in. = 12 ft 15 in.

STEP 2 Subtract feet.

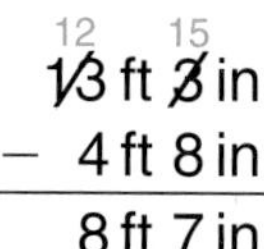

```
   12    15
  1̸3 ft 3̸ in.
 –  4 ft 8 in.
 ------------
    8 ft 7 in.
```

Solution: The giraffe is 8 feet 7 inches taller than the boy.

Other Examples

A. Metric Units

1 m – 35 cm = 65 cm

1 m = 100 cm
100 – 35 = 65

B. Time

```
   3 h 35 min
 + 5 h 46 min
 ------------
   8 h 81 min = 8 h + 1 h + 21 min
              = 9 h 21 min
```

81 min = 60 min + 21 min

Guided Practice

Add or subtract.

1. 6 ft 7 in. + 4 ft 9 in.

2. 7 h 12 min – 4 h 32 min

3. 5 m 7 dm + 1 m 3 dm

Ask Yourself
- Are the units the same?
- Do I need to regroup or simplify?

Explain Your Thinking ▶ When you add or subtract feet and inches, when do inches need to be regrouped as feet?

Extra Help at eduplace.com/map

Practice and Problem Solving

Add or subtract.

4. 7 ft 3 in. − 4 ft 2 in.

5. 3 lb 5 oz + 2 lb 14 oz

6. 12 h 29 min + 6 h 43 min

7. 5 yd 1 ft + 1 yd 2 ft

8. 5 T 112 lb + 2 T 400 lb

9. 9 gal 1 qt − 5 gal 2 qt

10. 9 g 600 mg + 8 g 900 mg

11. 8 km 500 m − 1 km 900 m

12. 4 L 5 dL + 5 L 7 dL

13. 9 t 900 kg + 5 t 300 kg

14. 10 yd 1 ft − 4 yd 2 ft

15. 5 h 18 min − 2 h 39 min

16. 9 ft − 7 in.

17. 5 h 15 min + 51 min

18. 1 gal − 1 pt

19. 3 m + 42 cm

20. 9 kg − 240 g

21. 4 L − 49 mL

22. 59 cm − 122 mm

23. 1 L − 17 mL

24. 3 m − 41 cm

Algebra • Equations Find the height represented by *h*.

25. 7 ft − *h* = 6 ft 4 in.

26. *h* − 34 mm = 66 mm

27. 4 yd − *h* = 3 yd 1 ft

28. *h* − 3 cm = 1 dm 7 cm

Solve.

29. A gorilla weighs 192 pounds 4 ounces. Another gorilla weighs 186 pounds 9 ounces. How much more does the heavier gorilla weigh?

30. Chef Jourdan put a 13-pound turkey in the oven at 11:20 A.M. He removed it from the oven at 4:30 P.M. How long did the turkey cook?

31. Joel bought a computer for $978. This price included a tax of $28 and a discount of $139. Find the original price before the tax and discount.

32. **Create and Solve** Write a problem in which a unit of measure must be regrouped in order to solve the problem. Then solve your problem.

Mixed Review and Test Prep

Open Response

Find the product. (Ch. 3, Lesson 7)

33. 66 × 34

34. 82 × 50

35. 76 × 24

36. 89 × 43

37. Subtract. (Ch. 6, Lesson 6)

6 lb 4 oz − 2 lb 10 oz

Extra Practice See page 169, Set E.

Lesson 7

Problem-Solving Strategy

Multistep Problems

Objective Decide how to solve elapsed time problems that involve more than one step.

To solve some problems, you need to complete more than one step.

Problem Ellen takes Train 409 from Summit to Center Station. She needs about 15 minutes to drive from her house to Summit Station. About how long does it take Ellen to get from her house to Center Station?

Train Number	409	545	1008
Station	**A.M.**	**A.M.**	**A.M.**
Summit	**6:38**	**7:05**	**7:35**
Smoke Rise	....	7:12	....
Melrose	....	7:22	....
Newburgh	....	7:31	....
Steen's Mountain	**7:00**	**7:39**	**7:58**
Oakwood	....	7:50	8:09
Great Hills	....	8:01	8:21
Fort Tyron	....	8:13	8:34
Ithaca	**7:26**	**8:22**	**8:43**
Center Station	**7:51**	**8:50**	**9:09**

RXR

Ask Yourself

What data do I need to use to solve the problem?

- 15 minutes to drive
- Train 409 from Summit to Center Station takes from 6:38 to 7:51.

Which operation or operations do I need to use to solve the problem?

- Subtract to find how long the train trip is.
- Add 15 min to find how long the total trip is.

How do I find the solution?

$$\begin{array}{r} 7{:}51 \\ -\ 6{:}38 \\ \hline 1{:}13 \end{array} \qquad \begin{array}{r} 1\text{ hr }13\text{ min} \\ +\quad 15\text{ min} \\ \hline 1\text{ hr }28\text{ min} \end{array}$$

Solution: It takes Ellen about 1 hour 28 minutes to get from her house to Center Station.

Try These

Use the schedule to solve. Show all your steps.

1. Mr. Parker gets on Train 1008 at Steen's Mountain. The train reaches Center Station 12 minutes late. How long does it take Mr. Parker to get from Steen's Mountain to Center Station?

2. Judy takes Train 545 from Melrose to Fort Tyron. She needs about 10 minutes to drive from her house to Melrose. About how long does it take Judy to get from her house to Fort Tyron?

3. Lucy takes Train 409 from Steen's Mountain to Ithaca. Eric takes Train 545 from Oakwood to Ithaca. Whose trip takes less time? How much less?

4. Charles takes Train 1008 from Great Hills to Center Station. Linda takes Train 545 from Newburgh to Center Station. Whose trip takes longer? How much longer?

Solve. Show all your steps.

5. **Create and Solve** Write a multistep problem that involves time. Solve the problem and exchange it with a partner.

6. If there are 8 commercials shown during a 30-minute television show, how many commercials might be shown in 90 minutes?

7. Jacob plans to spend 2 hours shopping for dinner and then 2 hours 15 minutes to make dinner. He is planning to serve dinner at 7:15 P.M. What time should he start shopping for dinner?

8. There is a 20 minute break between showings of a movie. A movie has showings of 1:35 P.M. and 3:35 P.M. How long is the movie? What time should the next showing be?

Problem Solving

Science Connection

Time and Tide

The gravitational pull of the moon and the sun cause the high and low tides of the oceans on earth. Because the moon is closer to the earth, its gravitational pull has more than twice the effect of the pull of the sun on the tides. In most places, two high tides and two low tides occur in a 24 hour and 50 minute period.

The table below shows the times of high tides for 5 days at a beach. Use the table to answer these questions.

- How much time is there between high tides each day?
- How much time is there between high tides from one day to the next (Sunday evening to Monday morning, for example)?
- Is the amount of time between high tides always the same?
- About what times would you predict for high tides on Friday of this same week?

High Tides at Sea Shell Beach		
Sunday	5:58 A.M.	8:14 P.M.
Monday	7:23 A.M.	9:08 P.M.
Tuesday	8:44 A.M.	9:53 P.M.
Wednesday	9:57 A.M.	10:32 P.M.
Thursday	11:01 A.M.	11:09 P.M.

Chapter Review/Test

VOCABULARY

1. A(n) ____ is the smallest metric unit typically used to measure length.
2. A liter is a measure of ____.
3. A(n) ____ is a metric unit of mass.

Vocabulary
- capacity
- centimeter (cm)
- milligram (mg)
- millimeter (mm)
- precision

CONCEPTS AND SKILLS

Complete. (Lessons 1–5, pp. 148–162)

4. 22 in. = ■ ft ■ in.
5. 2 T 826 lb = ■ lb
6. 250 dm = ■ cm
7. 3,680 mL = ■ L ■ mL
8. 14,000 mg = ■ g
9. 38 qt = ■ gal ■ qt

Compare. Write >, <, or = for each ●. (Lessons 1–5, pp. 148–162)

10. 40 ft ● 400 in.
11. 3 lb 7 oz ● 56 oz
12. 17 fl oz ● 2 c
13. 2 yd 2 ft ● 96 in.
14. 22 L ● 2,200 mL
15. 3 km ● 3,000 m

Add or subtract. (Lesson 6, p. 166)

16. 4 lb 8 oz + 3 lb 9 oz
17. 6 ft 4 in. − 3 ft 8 in.
18. 3 L 6 dL + 9 L 7 dL

PROBLEM SOLVING

Solve. (Lesson 7, p. 166)

19. Paul's train ride takes 56 minutes. From there he has a 20-minute walk to his office. If he allows himself $1\frac{1}{2}$ hours from the time he gets on the train, how much extra time is left when he reaches the office?

20. Sandra buys $1\frac{1}{2}$ pounds of grated cheese. She uses 13 ounces of it for a recipe. How much more cheese does she need to make another dish that calls for 14 ounces of cheese?

Write About It

Show You Understand

Sheree wants to make a paper cover for her math book. Does she need an exact measurement of how large a sheet of paper she needs, or can she use an estimate? Explain.

Extra Practice

Set A (Lesson 2, pp. 150–151)

Complete.

1. ■ in. = 10 ft
2. 2 mi = ■ yd
3. 8 ft = ■ in.

Compare. Write >, <, or = for each ●.

4. 1 mi ● 5,000 ft
5. 2 yd 2 ft ● 10 ft
6. 9 yd ● 28 ft

Set B (Lesson 3, pp. 152–155)

Complete.

1. 9 c = ■ fl oz
2. 20 oz = ■ lb
3. 5,280 lb = ■ T ■ lb

Compare. Write >, <, or = for each ●.

4. 30 fl oz ● 2 pt
5. 4 lb ● 64 oz
6. 2 pt 7 fl oz ● 40 fl oz

Set C (Lesson 4, pp. 156–159)

Complete.

1. 92 km = ■ m
2. 860 cm = ■ dm
3. 40 m = ■ dm
4. ■ cm = 420 dm
5. ■ cm = 780 mm
6. 400 mm = ■ dm

Compare. Write >, <, or = for each ●.

7. 45 km ● 4,500 m
8. 33 cm ● 330 mm
9. 550 m ● 5 dm

Set D (Lesson 5, pp. 160–163)

Complete.

1. 400 kg = ■ g
2. ■ g = 6,000 mg
3. 20 dL = ■ mL
4. ■ t = 1,500 kg
5. ■ mL = 25 L
6. ■ L = 1,250 dL

Compare. Write >, <, or = for each ●.

7. 89 g ● 89,000 mg
8. 70 L ● 67,000 mL
9. 10,001 g ● 10 kg

Set E (Lesson 6, pp. 164–165)

Find each sum or difference.

1. 6 ft 2 in. − 3 ft 8 in.
2. 6 lb 3 oz + 3 lb 13 oz
3. 8 gal 2 qt − 6 gal 3 qt
4. 6 h 20 min + 45 min
5. 5 L − 839 mL
6. 8 kg − 160 g

CHAPTER 7

Graph Data

INVESTIGATION

Use Data

This giant panda will spend about 12 hours today eating its favorite food, bamboo. Look at the line graph below. About how many pounds of bamboo had the panda already eaten by 10 A.M.?

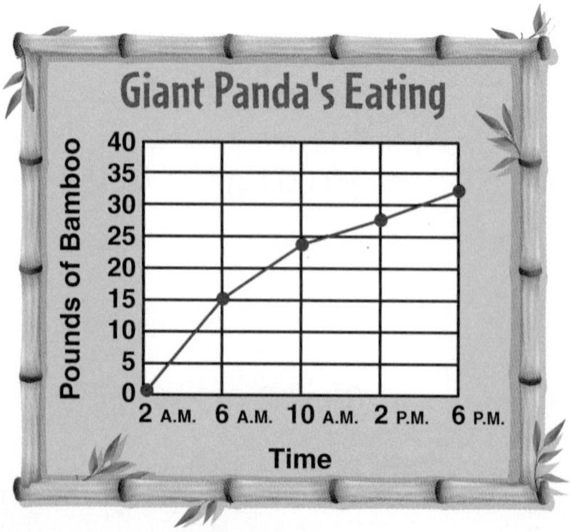

Giant Panda's Eating

Pounds of Bamboo: 0, 5, 10, 15, 20, 25, 30, 35, 40

Time: 2 A.M., 6 A.M., 10 A.M., 2 P.M., 6 P.M.

Use What You Know

Use this page to review and remember what you need to know for this chapter.

VOCABULARY

Choose the best word to complete each sentence.

Vocabulary
- bar graph
- circle graph
- data
- line graph

1. A ____ would be the best graph to show how many inches of rain fell on five different days.
2. When you collect information, you have ____ that you can use to make a graph.

CONCEPTS AND SKILLS

Copy and complete the frequency table to tally how many times each letter occurs in the data set.

A	C	D	C	Q	A
D	A	A	A	C	D
Q	C	D	C	C	C

	Letter	Tally Marks	Frequency
3.	A		
4.	C		
5.	D		
6.	Q		

Use the bar graph for Problems 7–10.

7. On which three days were more vegetarian meals sold than on Wednesday?
8. On which day were the most vegetarian meals sold?
9. How many more meals were sold on Tuesday than on Monday?

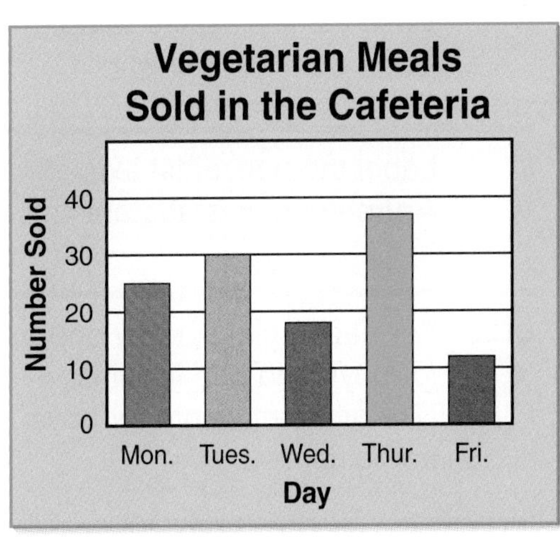

Write About It

10. Look at the bar graph. Tell how many vegetarian meals were sold during the week shown on the graph. Explain how you found your answer.

Facts Practice, See page 664.

Double Bar Graphs

Objective Use a double bar graph to compare sets of data.

Vocabulary
double bar graph

Materials
Learning Tools 33 and 34.
grid paper
10 pennies
ruler

Learn About It

Linda took a survey to find out which wild animals the boys and girls in her class liked the most. She recorded the girls' and the boys' responses separately.

You can follow the steps below to make a **double bar graph** in order to visually compare the two sets of data.

Favorite Wild Animals

Animal	Boys	Girls
Giraffe	8	24
Cheetah	6	6
Tiger	36	10
Gorilla	6	2

Making a Double Bar Graph

STEP 1 Draw the axes.

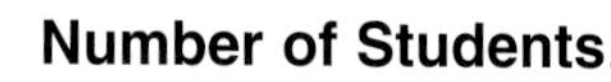

STEP 2
- Label the vertical axis **Number of Students**.
- Choose an appropriate scale and mark equal intervals.
- For this double bar graph, use a scale from 0 to 36. Use equal intervals of 4.

STEP 3 Label the horizontal axis **Animals** and list the animals.

STEP 4 For each animal, draw one bar for boys and one for girls. Use different colors for boys and girls.

STEP 5 Make a key to show what each color represents. Then give the graph a title.

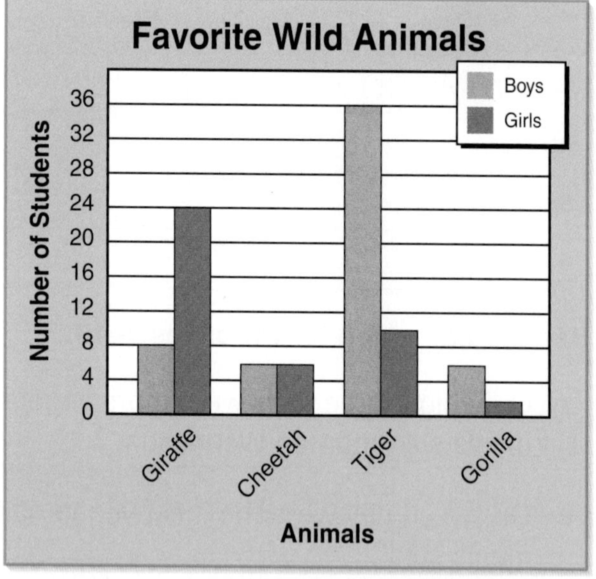

Try this activity with a partner to compare two sets of data by using a double bar graph.

STEP 1 Make a target like the one shown or use Learning Tool 33.

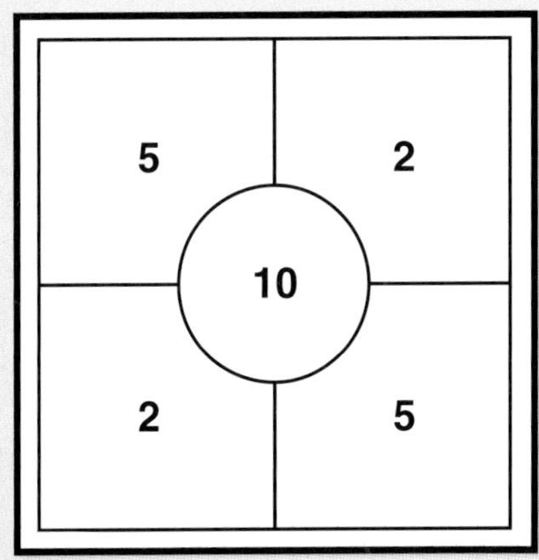

Learning Tool 33

STEP 2 Players take turns dropping 5 pennies onto the target. The score for each turn is determined by where the penny lands. A penny landing on the border of two regions scores the lesser of the two values.

STEP 3 Repeat Step 2 four more times. Use Learning Tool 34 to record the scores.

STEP 4 Use a ruler and grid paper to make a double bar graph to compare your score in each round with your partner's score in each round.

- What scale should you use? What equal intervals should you use?
- How will you label the horizontal axis? the vertical axis?
- What title will you choose for the graph?

Round Number	Round Score	Total Score

Learning Tool 34

Guided Practice

Use the graph on page 172 for Problems 1–3.

1. How many more girls than boys liked giraffes the most?
2. For which wild animal is there the greatest difference between boys and girls?
3. Which animal was chosen equally by boys and girls?

Ask Yourself

- Do I need to see the numbers survey or could I answer by looking at the bar lengths?
- Did I read the graph correctly?

Explain Your Thinking Why is it important to choose an appropriate scale for a graph? Use an example to support your thinking.

Go On

Practice and Problem Solving

Use the graph for Problems 4–7.

Five hundred zoologists were surveyed in 1992 and 2002 about which animals they thought were at risk of extinction.

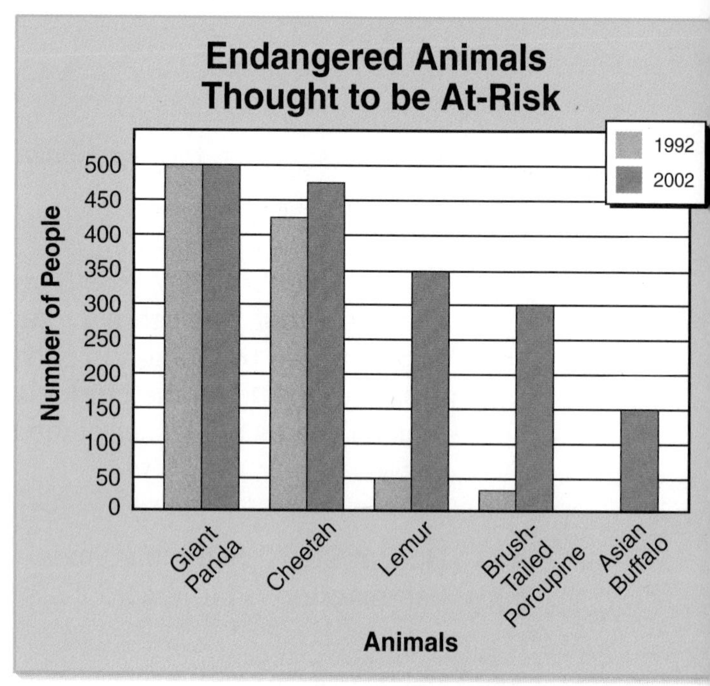

4. Which endangered animal did most zoologists think was at risk in both 1992 and 2002?

5. How many more zoologists thought the lemur was at risk in 2002 than in 1992?

6. Why is there no bar to represent the Asian Buffalo in 1992?

7. If only 500 zoologists were surveyed, how could 500 zoologists choose Giant Panda and 300 zoologists choose Brush-Tailed Porcupine in 2002?

Choices of T-Shirt Colors for the Ecology Club

	Purple	Orange	Blue	Green	Red
Like	12	6	18	14	10
Dislike	6	16	6	10	4

8. Use the table of students' T-shirt color preferences to make a double bar graph.

9. **Write About It** If you were designing a T-shirt for other students, which color would you choose? Explain your thinking.

10. Make up your own survey about T-shirt color preferences. Give your survey to your classmates. Present your results in a tally chart.

11. Use your results in Exercise 10 to create a double bar graph.

12. **Create and Solve** Write a problem based on the graph in Exercise 11. Exchange problems with a classmate and solve.

Use the double bar graph for Problems 13–17.

Time Spent at Ecology Club

Waneta | Laurence

Minutes: 0, 10, 20, 30, 40, 50, 60, 70, 80, 90, 100

Week: 1, 2, 3, 4

13. During which week did Laurence spend more time at the Ecology Club than Waneta?

14. During which week did Waneta and Laurence together spend the least amount of time at the Ecology Club?

15. During week 4, about how much longer did Waneta spend at the Ecology Club than Laurence spent?

16. About how many hours total did Laurence spend at the Ecology Club that month?

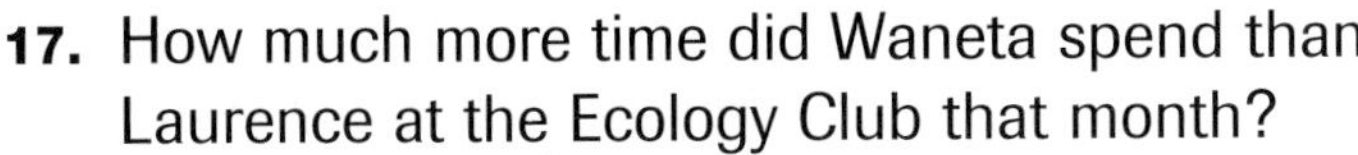

17. How much more time did Waneta spend than Laurence at the Ecology Club that month?

18. Five teachers surveyed their students to see how many went to the Wildlife Zoo. Make a double bar graph showing the data from the table.

Did You Visit the Wildlife Zoo?					
Class	Mrs. Smith	Mr. Kaufman	Mr. Ross	Ms. Brown	Ms. Cruz
Yes	12	10	9	20	5
No	12	15	14	4	19

Mixed Review and Test Prep

Open Response

1 foot = 12 inches
1 yard = 3 feet
1 mile = 5,280 feet
1 mile = 1,760 yards

Complete. (Ch. 6, Lesson 2)

19. 16 inches = ■ feet ■ inches

20. 2 miles = ■ feet

21. 6 yards 2 feet = ■ inches

22. 110 inches = ■ yards ■ inches

23. How many more boys than girls want to work in forestry? (Ch. 7, Lesson 1)

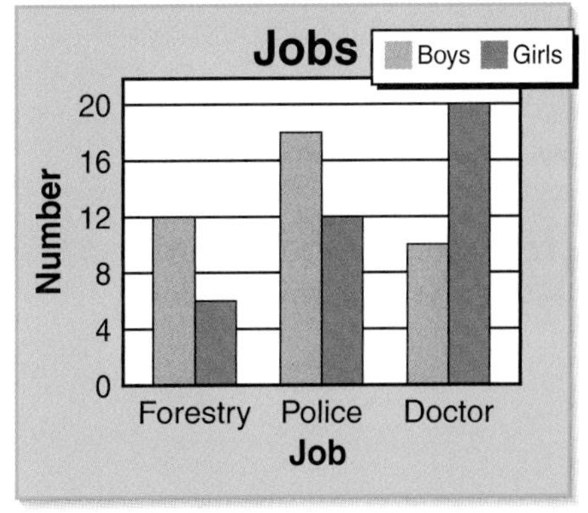

A 24 **B** 16 **C** 14 **D** 6

Extra Practice See page 189, Set A.

Lesson 2

Histograms

Objective Make and use a histogram and understand the differences between bar graphs and histograms.

Vocabulary
histogram
frequency table

Learn About It

The data below show the ages of whales that scientists tracked and studied for one year.

10	11	35	36	55	28	32	46	57
69	58	14	8	9	10	11	7	12
8	13	11	12	25	19	45	52	35
42	62	27	31	29	15	17	16	18
20	19	22	34	29	30	20	25	13
14	15	16	15	17				

How did the number of whales in the 20–29 age group compare with that in the 10–19 age group?

You can use a histogram to display and compare the data. A **histogram** is a bar graph that displays how frequently data occur within equal intervals.

Follow these steps to make a histogram. Start by making a **frequency table** to organize the data in equal intervals.

Making a Frequency Table

STEP 1 Look at the data to decide what intervals to use.

STEP 2 Use tally marks to record the frequency.

STEP 3 Count the tally marks and write the frequency.

Intervals	Tally Marks	Frequency
0–9	||||	4
10–19	~~||||~~ ~~||||~~ ~~||||~~ ~~||||~~ |	21
20–29	~~||||~~ ||||	9
30–39	~~||||~~ ||	7
40–49	|||	3
50–59	||||	4
60–69	||	2

Then use the frequency table to make a histogram.

Making a Histogram

STEP 1 Draw the axes. Label the vertical axis. Choose an appropriate scale and mark equal intervals.

STEP 2 Label the horizontal axis and list the age intervals.

STEP 3 Draw a bar for each age interval. Do not leave spaces between the bars.

STEP 4 Give the graph a title.

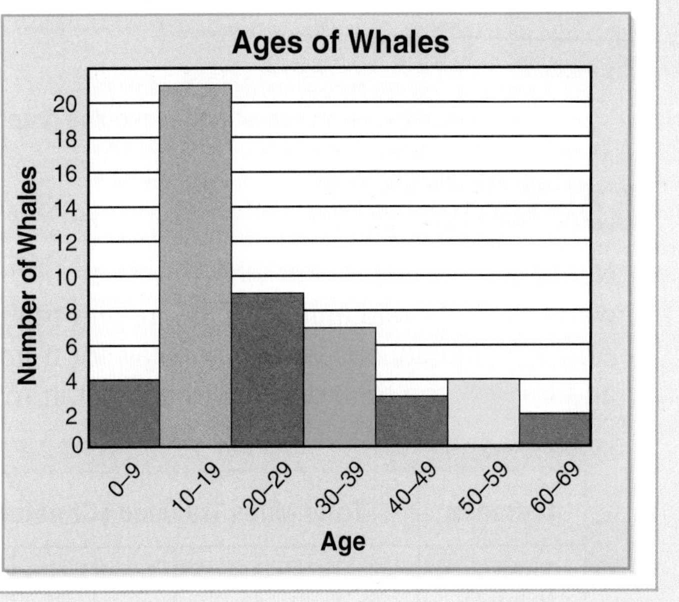

Solution: There were more than twice as many whales in the 10–19 age group as there were in the 20–29 age group.

Guided Practice

Use the histogram above for Problems 1–2.

1. How many whales were in the 20–29 age group?
2. How many more whales were there in the 20–29 age group than in the 50–59 age group?

Ask Yourself

- Do I need to know the exact number the bar shows?

Explain Your Thinking ▶ When would you use a histogram instead of a bar graph to display data? Explain your thinking.

Practice and Problem Solving

Use the histogram at the right for Problems 3 and 4.

3. How many whales have been studied from 4 to 15 years?
4. How many more whales have been studied from 8 to 11 years than from 0 to 3 years?

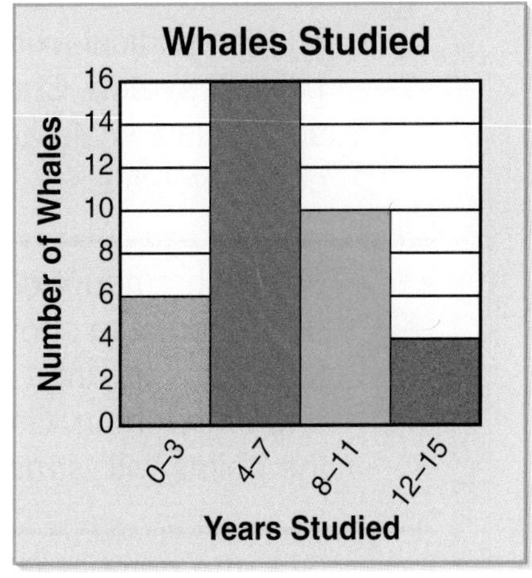

Mixed Review and Test Prep

Open Response

Estimate. (Ch. 3, Lesson 6)

5. 299 × 8
6. 2,763 × 5
7. 708 × 9
8. 8,950 × 6

9. What intervals would you use to graph these data? (Ch. 7, Lesson 2)

7, 9, 12, 10, 7, 8, 15, 7, 11

Extra Practice See page 189, Set B.

Lesson 3

Line and Double Line Graphs

Objective Interpret and make line graphs and double line graphs.

Vocabulary
ordered pair
double line graph

Learn About It

Nathaniel is a researcher who travels around the world to study wild animals. On a recent trip to Africa, Nathaniel observed a cheetah for 6 hours and tracked the total distance the cheetah roamed.

Distance	Total Miles Traveled (Cheetah)					
Time (hours)	1	2	3	4	5	6
Total Miles	30	42	48	71	94	127

Make a line graph to show the data Nathaniel collected.

Making a Line Graph

STEP 1 Draw the axes. Label the horizontal axis **Time (hours)** and the vertical axis **Total Miles Traveled**. Choose an appropriate scale and mark equal intervals.

STEP 2 For each amount of time, draw a point to show the total miles traveled at the end of that hour. Connect the points with straight lines.

STEP 3 Give the graph a title.

The point on the grid that corresponds to 1 hour on the horizontal axis and 30 miles on the vertical axis is represented by the **ordered pair** (1, 30).

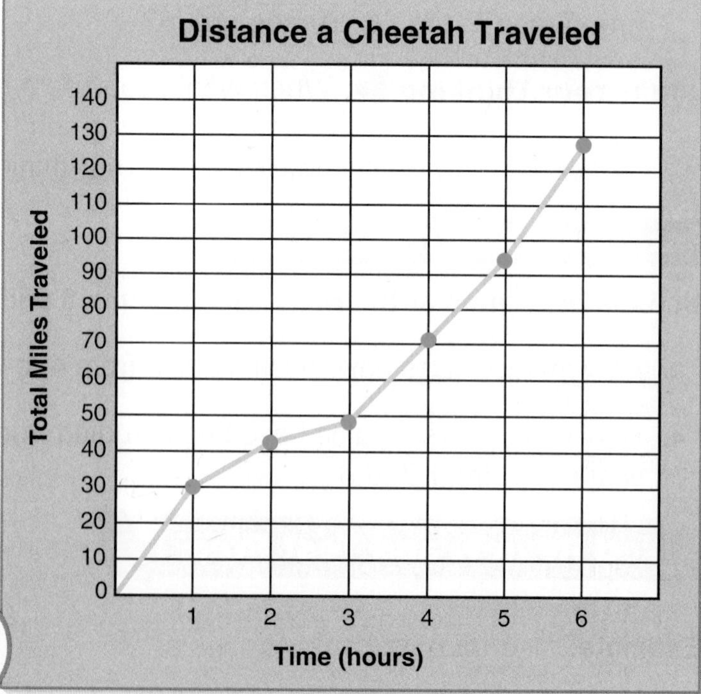

While on a trip to India, Nathaniel also observed how far a tiger roamed in 6 hours. Make a **double line graph** to compare the data for the cheetah and the tiger.

Distance	Total Miles Traveled (Tiger)					
Time (hours)	1	2	3	4	5	6
Total Miles	6	21	27	33	42	49

Note: The table at the left gives the *total* miles traveled. During the first hour, the tiger traveled 6 miles. During the second hour, the tiger traveled 15 miles.

Making a Double Line Graph

STEP 1 Draw the axes. Label the horizontal axis **Time (hours)** and the vertical axis **Total Miles Traveled**. Choose an appropriate scale and mark equal intervals.

STEP 2 Plot the ordered pairs and draw the line graph for the cheetah data.

STEP 3 Repeat Step 2 for the tiger data. Use a different color for the points and the line.

STEP 4 Make a key to show what each line represents. Then write a title for the graph.

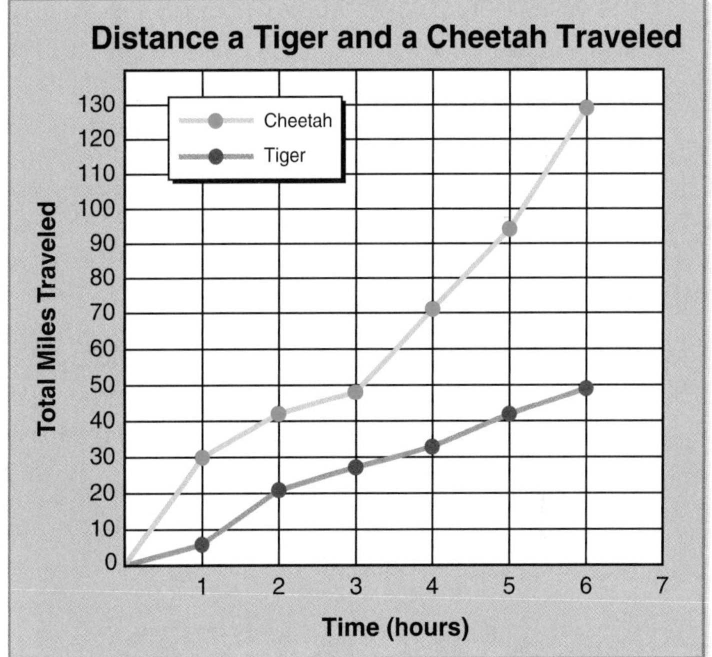

Guided Practice

Use the graph above for Problems 1 and 2.

1. How much farther had the cheetah traveled than the tiger at the end of 6 hours?
2. Between which two hours did the cheetah travel the farthest? the least?

Ask Yourself

- What scale is used?
- What does the key tell me?
- Is the information I need on the horizontal or the vertical axis?

Explain Your Thinking ▶ Why are line graphs useful for showing data over time?

Practice and Problem Solving

Use the graph at the right for Exercises 3–7.

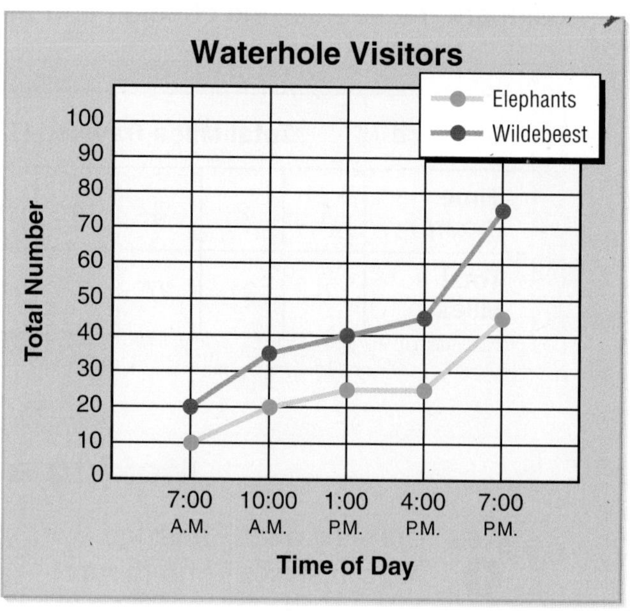

3. As of 10 A.M., how many more wildebeest than elephants had visited the waterhole?

4. During which 3-hour time period did no elephants visit the waterhole?

5. During which 3-hour time period did the most animals visit the waterhole?

6. **Predict** If the graph shows the results for a typical day at the waterhole, how many elephants would you expect to visit the waterhole in one week between 7 A.M. and 7 P.M.?

7. **Create and Solve** Write a problem that can be solved using the graph.

The bar graph shows the number of visitors entering Safari Fun Land one weekend.

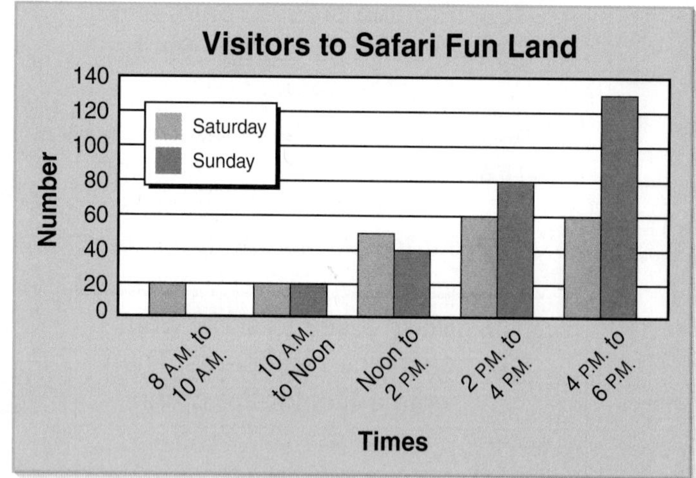

8. Use the data in the bar graph to complete the table below to show the total number of visitors to Safari Fun Land that weekend.

   Hint: The total number of visitors at noon is equal to the number of visitors at 10 A.M. plus the number of visitors at noon.

Total Number of Visitors to Safari Fun Land

	10 A.M.	Noon	2 P.M.	4 P.M.	6 P.M.
Sat.	20	40			
Sun.					

9. Use the data in your table from Exercise 8 to make a double line graph.

10. **You Decide** Describe a situation in which you could use a double line graph to display data.

Extra Practice See page 189, Set C.

Problem Solving

Math Challenge

Without Numbers

Even though the graph at the right has no numbers, you can still find information from it.

1. Was it colder at the start of the day or at the end of the day?

2. Estimate the time of day when the highest temperature occurred.

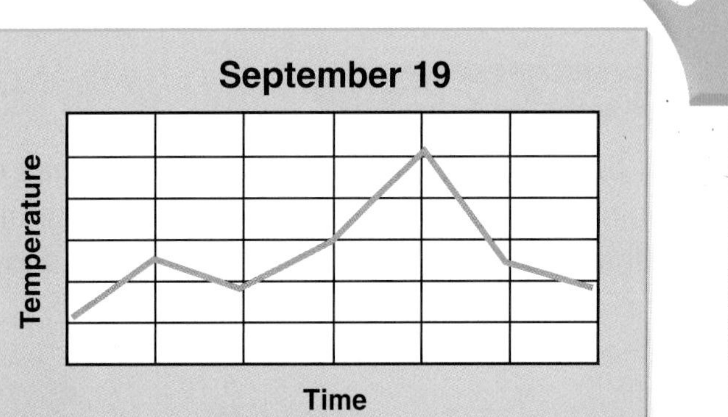

Quick Check

Check your understanding of Lessons 1–3.

Use the double bar graph for Questions 1–4.
(Lessons 1 and 2)

1. How many more ospreys were seen by grade 5 students than by grade 4 students?

2. How many of these four kinds of birds did the grade 5 students see?

3. For which bird is there the greatest difference in the number seen between the two grades?

4. Overall, which bird did the students see the least? How many of these birds did they see?

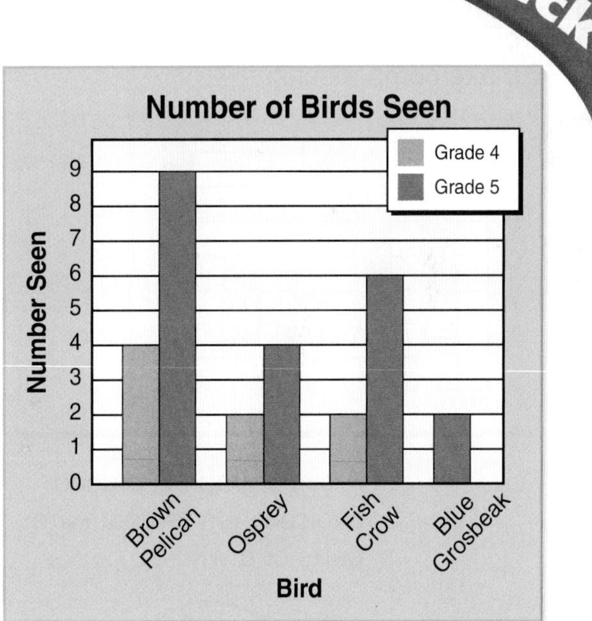

5. Create a double line graph of the information in the table. (Lesson 3)

Blue Whales Seen

	June	July	Aug.	Sept.	Oct.
Ahab Tours	60	35	35	25	20
Blue Whale Watch Co.	35	30	30	25	25

Lesson 4

Audio Tutor 1/20 Listen and Understand

Choose an Appropriate Graph

Objective Choose an appropriate graph to display data.

Learn About It

In the United States, nearly 1,000 species of animals and plants are in danger of extinction. Which type of graph would you use to show the data given in the table?

Endangered Species

Group	Number of Species
Mammals	61
Birds	74
Reptiles	14
Amphibians	9
Fish	69
Total	227

Different Types of Graphs

A bar graph is a good choice when the data can be counted and you want to make comparisons.

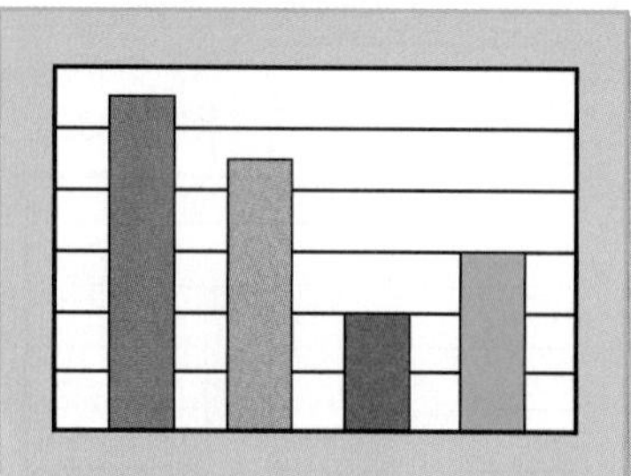

A line graph is appropriate when you want to show change over time.

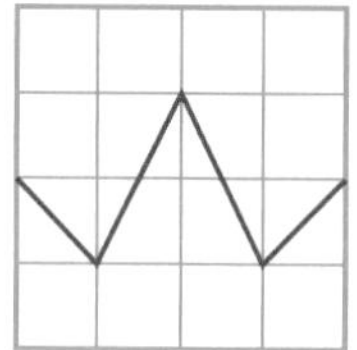

A pictograph is a good choice when the data are multiples of a number.

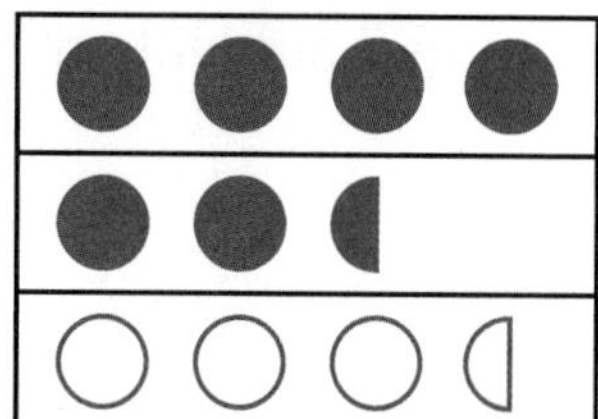

A circle graph is a good choice when the data are parts of a whole.

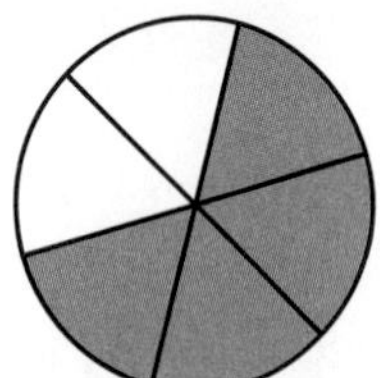

A histogram is a good choice to show how frequently data occur within equal intervals.

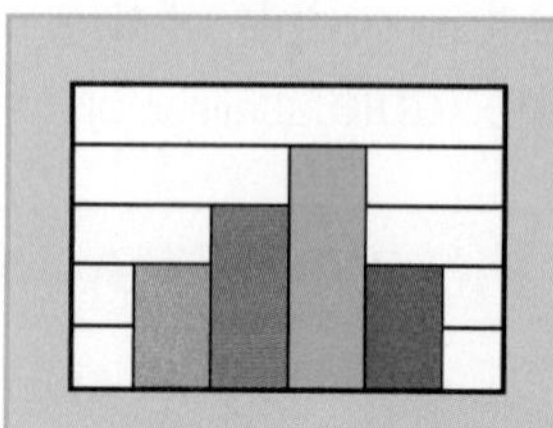

Solution: A bar graph or circle graph would be an appropriate choice.

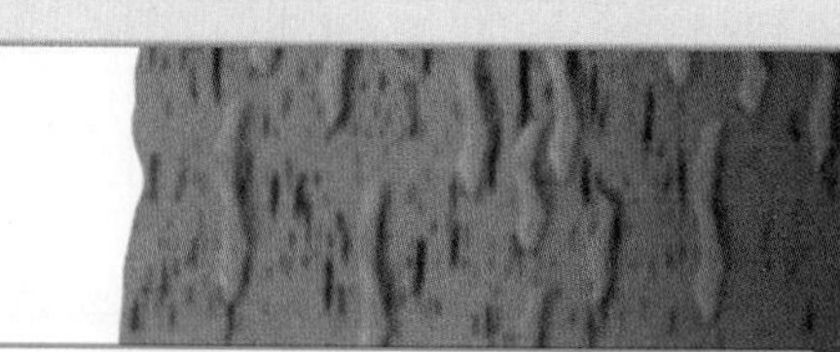

Extra Practice at **eduplace.com/map**

Guided Practice

Ask Yourself

- Do I arrange the data in intervals?
- Do I show separate data, parts of a whole, or change over time?

Choose an appropriate graph for the data described.

1. Wingspans of these endangered or threatened birds: bobwhite, California condor, Mariana mallard, whooping crane, and Hawaiian hawk.
2. The number of species of birds sighted, organized in the intervals 0–2, 3–5, 6–8, 9–11, and 12–14.

Explain Your Thinking ▶ Give an example of data that could be shown in a line graph.

Practice and Problem Solving

Choose and make an appropriate graph for the data.

3.

Amount Collected to Save the Manatees	
Day	**Amount ($)**
Monday	200
Tuesday	250
Wednesday	300
Thursday	225
Friday	450

4.

Life Expectancy of Endangered Animals	
Animal	**Average (years)**
Bison	15
Chimpanzee	20
Kangaroo	7
Zebra	15
Leopard	12

5.

Fish Hatchery Weight Check	
Weight (oz)	**Fish**
0–3.99	6
4–7.99	3
8–11.99	2
12–15.99	3
16–19.99	2

Data Use the table at the right for Problems 6 and 7.

6. By about how many pairs did the bald eagle population increase from 1981 to 1998?
7. What type of graph would be appropriate to represent the data? Explain. Draw and label the graph you chose.

Bald Eagle Population	
Year	**Adult Pairs**
1981	1,188
1986	1,875
1990	3,020
1998	5,748

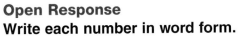

Mixed Review and Test Prep

Open Response

Write each number in word form.
(Ch. 1, Lesson 1)

8. 6,780
9. 48,309
10. 586,147
11. 2,346
12. 34,501
13. 257,824

Multiple Choice

14. Which would be the best choice to display data about the mass of an owl from birth to 18 months?
(Ch. 7, Lesson 4)

A circle graph
B line graph
C pictograph
D histogram

Extra Practice See page 189, Set D.

Lesson 5

Audio Tutor 1/21 Listen and Understand

Misleading Graphs

Objective Recognize when and explain why data on graphs are displayed in misleading ways.

Learn About It

The two line graphs at the right both show the number of visitors to the Wildlife Zoo for 4 months. What differences do you notice?

Look at the scale on each graph. The intervals you choose for a scale can affect the appearance of the graph.

Which graph would you use if you wanted to say that this zoo's popularity has not changed much in six months?

- The scale on Graph A shows equal intervals of 1,000. The scale also does not begin intervals at zero. The scale gives the appearance that the number of visitors to the Wildlife Zoo increased greatly between May and August.
- The scale on Graph B shows equal intervals of 6,000. What appearance does the scale give to Graph B?

Graph A

Graph B

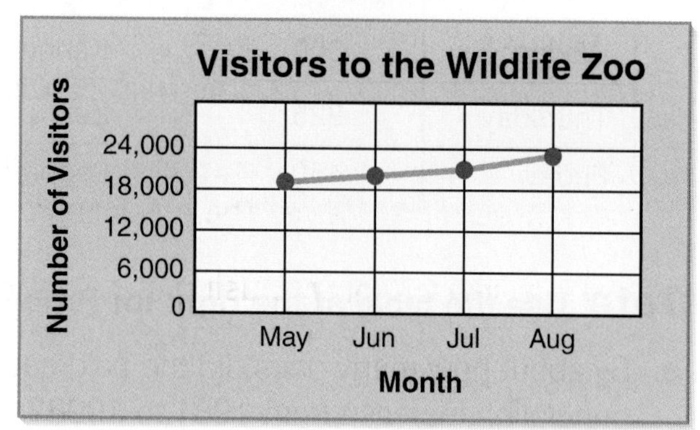

Another Example

Many newspapers show data in circle graphs. One way to make these graphs misleading is to tilt the graph. Which graph looks like it shows more foreign visitors?

Visitors to the State Capital

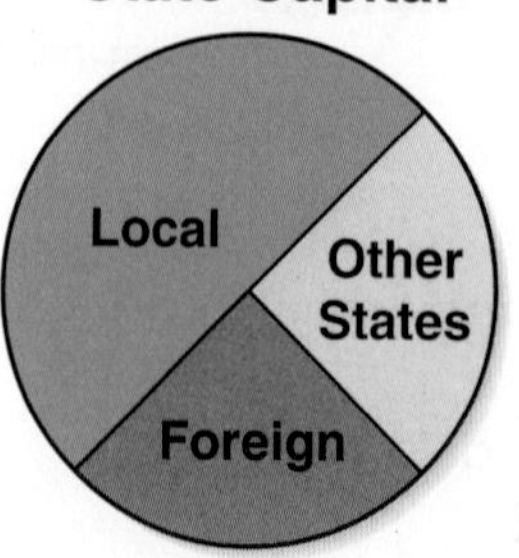

Visitors to the State Capital

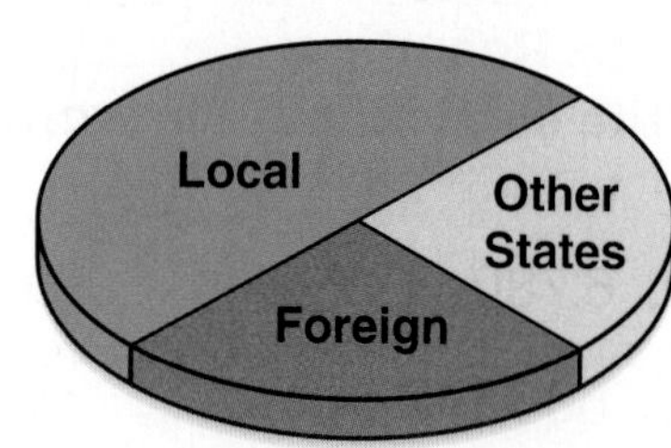

Guided Practice

Use the graph below for Exercises 1–3.

1. What was the zoo attendance in 2005?
2. What was the zoo attendance in 2000?
3. What is misleading about the graph?

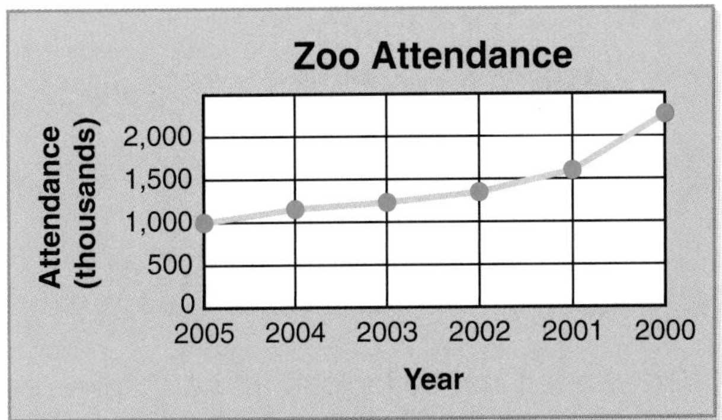

Ask Yourself

- Did I read the graph carefully?

Explain Your Thinking ▶ How does a change in the scale affect the appearance of a graph?

Practice and Problem Solving

Use the graph at the right for Problems 4–5.

4. Tell why it seems as if the walrus is more than two times as popular as the polar bear.
5. Make a new bar graph, using a scale that represents the data on the graph more accurately.
6. **What's Wrong?** Suppose Jack graphed the the data from a survey and used the following scale intervals for the vertical axis of the bar graph: 10, 15, 19, 25, 27, 29, and 30. What would be wrong with his graph?

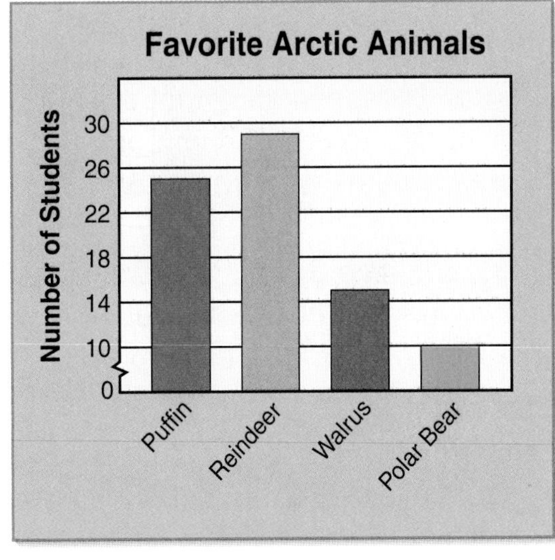

Mixed Review and Test Prep

Open Response

Evaluate. (Ch. 5, Lesson 6)

7. $5 \times 3 - 12 \div 4$
8. $4 \times 6 - 8 \div 2$
9. $3 + 6 \div 3 + 8$
10. $5 \times 5 \div 5 + 7$

11. A graph used intervals of 0, 100, 200, 700, 800, 1,000. Explain how the graph is misleading. (Ch. 7, Lesson 5)

Extra Practice See page 189, Set E.

Lesson 6

Problem-Solving Decision

Relevant Information

Objective Decide which information on a graph is relevant.

Problem The students in grades 5 and 6 were given their choice of animals to research for a project. The results of their choices are organized in the double bar graph. Which topic was the most popular? Which was the least popular?

When you look at the information on a graph, you need to determine what information is relevant.

To find the most popular topic, use the scale to find the totals for each topic.

You can tell just by looking at the graph that the least popular topic was Elephants.

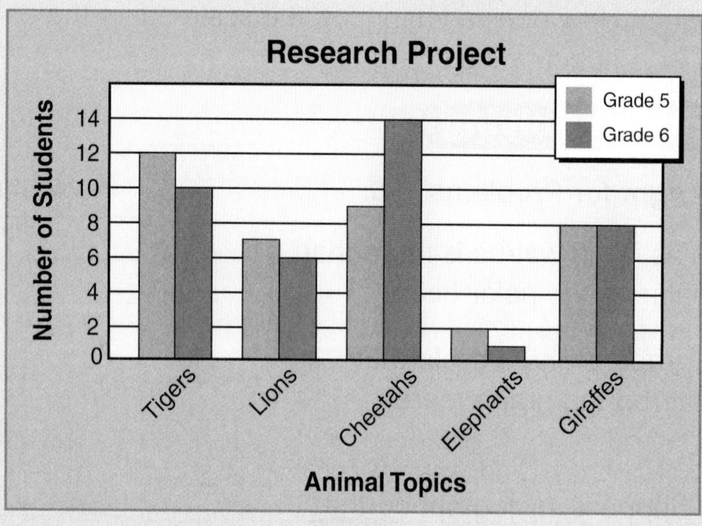

Solution: The most popular topic was Cheetahs.
The least popular topic was Elephants.

Try These

Use the relevant information in the graph above to solve.

1. The number of students who chose Lions and Elephants is equal to the number of students who chose what other topic?
2. For which topic is there the greatest difference in popularity between fifth-graders and sixth-graders? What is this difference?
3. Which grade has the greater number of students–grade 5 or grade 6? Explain how you know.
4. Six times as many fifth-graders chose this topic over another. What topics were they?

Use the relevant information in the graph to the right to solve.

5. Each point represents two pieces of information. What two pieces of information does the first point on the graph represent? The last point?
6. By what time were 125 slices sold?
7. Does the graph show an increase or a decrease in the number of slices sold?
8. Between which two hours were the greatest number of slices sold?
9. How many more pieces of pie were sold by 5:00 P.M. than by 4:00 P.M.?
10. Between which two hours were no slices sold?
11. Would you use a line graph to show different types of pie sold? Explain.

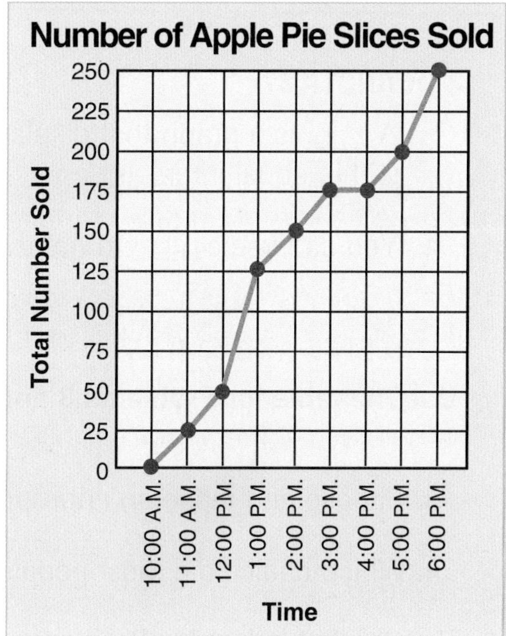

Activity

Technology Connection

Graph It

You can use a spreadsheet like the one below to create a graph.

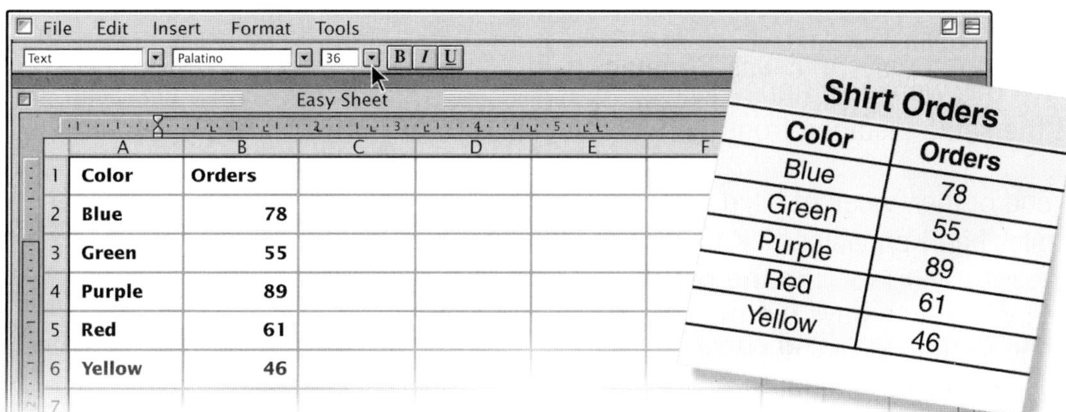

	A	B	C	D	E	F
1	Color	Orders				
2	Blue	78				
3	Green	55				
4	Purple	89				
5	Red	61				
6	Yellow	46				
7						

Shirt Orders

Color	Orders
Blue	78
Green	55
Purple	89
Red	61
Yellow	46

1. Enter the data shown in a spreadsheet program.
2. Use the help menu from the spreadsheet program to create a bar graph that displays the data.

Chapter Review/Test

VOCABULARY

Vocabulary
double line graph
frequency table
histogram

1. A ____ is a graph that displays how often data occur within equal intervals.

2. You can use a ____ to help you count and organize data.

CONCEPTS AND SKILLS

Use the table for Problems 3 and 4.
(Lesson 1, pp. 172–175; Lesson 4, pp. 182–183)

3. Choose and make an appropriate graph for the data.

4. Which choice did most people like? dislike?

Transportation Choice		
	Like	Dislike
Car	16	6
Bus	7	15
Train	18	3
Plane	14	9

Use the list below for Problems 5 and 6.
(Lesson 2, pp. 176–177; Lesson 6, pp. 186–187)

5. Make a histogram of the data. Use intervals of 0–4, 5–9, 10–14, and 15–19.

6. Did most of the students read more than or fewer than 10 books during the summer?

Number of Books Read											
5	10	2	7	3	9	8	10	3	0	5	19
11	7	15	6	10	12	9	13	8	17	12	7

PROBLEM SOLVING

Use the line graph for Problems 7–9.
(Lesson 3, pp. 178–180; Lesson 6, p. 186)

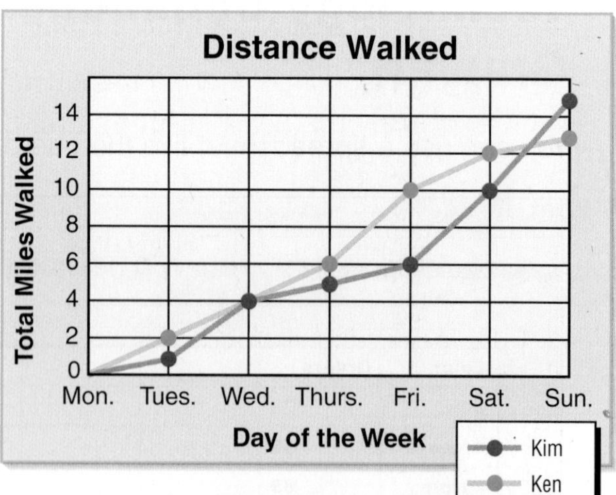

7. On which day were Ken and Kim at the same distance from the start?

8. By the end of their week of hiking, how many miles had Ken walked? Kim?

9. Between which two days did the distance walked by each increase the most?

10. Describe one way in which a graph can be misleading. (Lesson 5, pp. 184–185)

Write About It

Show You Understand

Why is it important to look at the scale when interpreting a graph?

Extra Practice

Set A (Lesson 1, pp. 172–175)

Use the graph for Problems 1–2.

1. Which activity was more popular with girls than boys?
2. How many times more do boys use computers for games than for Web searches?

How Computers Are Used

Number of Students

36, 32, 28, 24, 20, 16, 12, 8, 4, 0

Boys

Girls

E-mail, Web Search, Games, Word Processing

Computer Use

Set B (Lesson 2, pp. 176–177)

The data show the distances of bright stars from the Earth in light-years.

1. Make a histogram of the data using intervals of 100 light-years.
2. How many more stars are between 0 and 99 light-years away than are between 100 and 199 light-years away?

396, 428, 623, 39, 54, 215, 73, 77, 39, 678, 245, 67, 30, 80, 135, 164

Set C (Lesson 3, pp. 178–181)

The tables show the use of gas and electric power for heating in new homes from 1970 to 2000.

1. Make a double line graph to compare the data.
2. In 1990, how many new homes out of 100 were heated with electricity? with natural gas?

Number of New Homes Out of 100

Electricity			
1970	1980	1990	2000
30	50	30	25

Natural Gas			
1970	1980	1990	2000
60	40	60	70

Set D (Lesson 4, pp. 182–183)

Choose an appropriate graph for the data.

1. the parts in 100 of nitrogen, oxygen, water vapor, and other gases in air
2. the amounts of snow in two cities, over a one-year span
3. the weight of a baby from birth to 18 months

Set E (Lesson 5, pp. 184–185)

Use the graph at the right for the following questions.

1. Explain what is misleading in the graph at the right.
2. Draw a graph that is not misleading.

Extra Practice at **eduplace.com/map**

CHAPTER 8 Data and Statistics

INVESTIGATION

Use Data

In order to improve his shooting skills, William practiced every day for two weeks. He took 25 shots during each practice. The results are shown on the line plot. What was the typical number of shots William made?

Use What You Know

Use this page to review and remember what you need to know for this chapter.

VOCABULARY

Choose the best word to complete each sentence.

1. The _____ of an item of data is the number of times it occurs.

2. The _____ of a set of data is sometimes called the average.

Vocabulary

- data
- frequency
- mean
- median

CONCEPTS AND SKILLS

Order these numbers from least to greatest.

3. 4, 9, 7, 7, 5, 6, 8, 2, 3

4. 36, 48, 16, 93, 21, 73, 4

Match each definition with a word.

5. The number that occurs most often in a data set
6. The middle number in a set of numbers ordered from least to greatest
7. The difference between the greatest number and the least number in a set of data

a. mean
b. median
c. mode
d. range

Decide whether each statement is always, sometimes, or never true.

8. A set of data has a mode.

9. A line plot uses bars to represent data.

Write About It

10. A survey is done to find out your class's favorite snacks. What graph would best display the results? Explain your choice.

Facts Practice, See page 665.

Collect and Organize Data

Objective Collect, organize, and interpret data from a survey.

Vocabulary
survey
frequency

Materials
Learning Tool 35

Work Together

A **survey** is a method of collecting information about a group of people.

Work with a partner to conduct a survey and interpret the results.

STEP 1 Make up a survey question such as "What is your favorite sport?" or "What is your favorite color?" Write your question on the record sheet.

Survey Results	
Survey Question: What is your favorite sport?	
Answer Choice	**Tally Marks**

STEP 2 List five or six likely answer choices for the survey question on the record sheet.

Survey Results	
Survey Question: What is your favorite sport?	
Answer Choice	**Tally Marks**
Baseball	
Basketball	
Football	
Soccer	
Tennis	
Other	

STEP 3 Ask each of your classmates the survey question.

- Use a tally mark to record each answer.
- Count the tally marks for each answer and write the number in the Frequency column. The **frequency** of each answer is the number of times it is chosen.

Survey Results		
Survey Question: What is your favorite sport?		
Answer Choice	**Tally Marks**	**Frequency**
Baseball	卌	5
Basketball	卌 I	6
Football	卌	5
Soccer	卌 III	8
Tennis	II	2
Other	III	3

Discuss your results.

- Which choice was the most popular? the least popular?
- Was that choice picked by less than one half, one half, or more than one half of the class?
- Use the information you collected to write a short summary of your survey results.

On Your Own

Data The table shows the results of a survey of a fifth-grade class. Use the table for Problems 1–4.

Number of Brothers and Sisters	Tally	Frequency
0	𝍷	
1	𝍷𝍷𝍷	
2	𝍸	
3	𝍷𝍷𝍷𝍷	
4	𝍷𝍷𝍷	
More than 4	𝍷𝍷	

1. Copy and complete the table.
2. How many of those surveyed had 2 brothers and sisters?
3. How many students were in the survey?
4. Can you tell how many students surveyed had 5 brothers and sisters? Explain your answer.

Follow Steps 1–3 on page 192 to survey your classmates about their favorite kinds of music. Then use your results for Problems 5–8.

5. Which answer choice was the most popular? Which answer choice was the least popular?
6. Did any of your answer choices have the same frequency? Which ones?
7. What is the difference in frequency between the most popular choice and the least popular choice?
8. Write a short summary of your survey results. Did any of your results surprise you? Explain.

Talk About It • Write About It

You learned how to conduct a survey and interpret the results.

9. Look at your results from the activity on pages 192–193. Do you think your results would be different if you surveyed adults? Explain why or why not.
10. How might a store owner use a survey to decide what games to sell in the store?

Lesson 2

Audio Tutor 1/22 Listen and Understand

Mean, Median, Mode, and Range

Objective Make and use a line plot to find the mean, median, mode, and range of a set of data.

Vocabulary
- line plot
- cluster
- gap
- mean
- median
- mode
- range

Learn About It

Kenny's class had a bowling party. Their scores in the first game are shown at the right.

▶ You can organize the data in a **line plot** to make the data easier to describe.

10th Frame
Final Score
3 4 84
84
1 8 72
72
8 1 83
83
7 - 84
84
X 2 4 92
92
6 3 85
85
9 - 80
80
7 1 83
83
6 / 4 84
84

Make a line plot.

STEP 1 List the data in order.
72, 80, 83, 83, 84, 84, 84, 85, 92

STEP 2 Create a number line that covers all the numbers in your list.

STEP 3 Put an *X* above each number as many times as the number appears in the list. For example, the score 84 appears 3 times in the list, so put 3 *X*'s above 84.

A **cluster** is an isolated group of data. There is a cluster from 83 to 85.

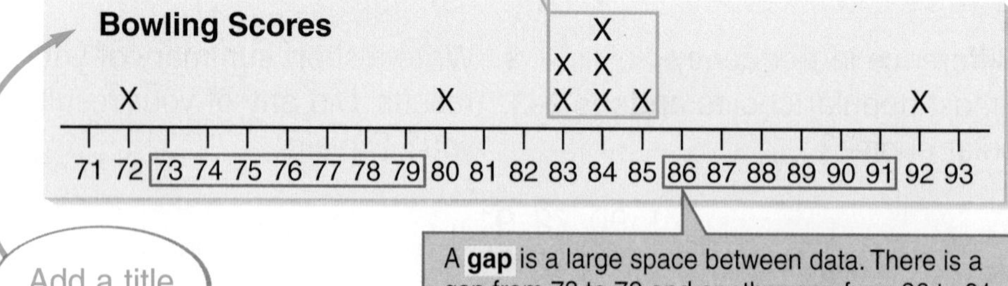

Add a title.

A **gap** is a large space between data. There is a gap from 73 to 79 and another gap from 86 to 91.

- Can you tell just by looking at the line plot what the typical scores of the group were? Were there any scores that were not typical?
- How do the gaps and clusters help you see this?

To describe a set of data, you can use the mean, median, and mode. You can use the range to tell how far the data are spread out.

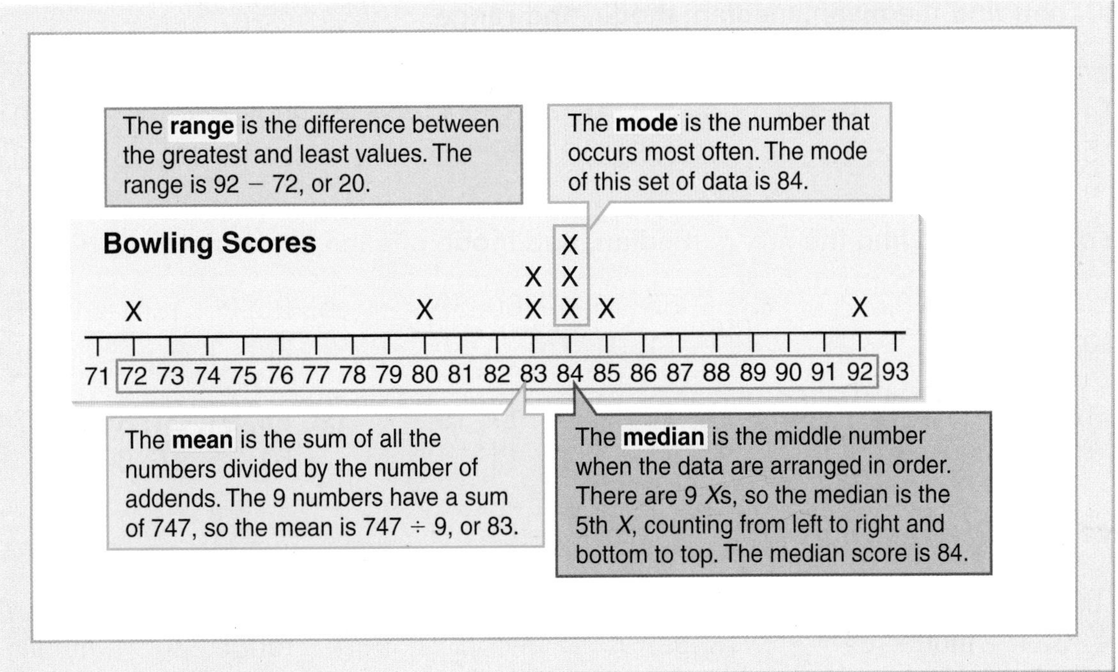

The **range** is the difference between the greatest and least values. The range is 92 − 72, or 20.
The **mode** is the number that occurs most often. The mode of this set of data is 84.
Bowling Scores
X X X X X X X X X
71 72 73 74 75 76 77 78 79 80 81 82 83 84 85 86 87 88 89 90 91 92 93
The **mean** is the sum of all the numbers divided by the number of addends. The 9 numbers have a sum of 747, so the mean is 747 ÷ 9, or 83.
The **median** is the middle number when the data are arranged in order. There are 9 *X*s, so the median is the 5th *X*, counting from left to right and bottom to top. The median score is 84.

Other Examples

A. Even Number of Data

For an even number of data, the median is the average of the middle two numbers.

Find the median of 6, 10, 11, 13, 13, and 13.

$\frac{11 + 13}{2} = 12$ The median is 12.

B. More Than One Mode

Find the mode of 1, 1, 2, 2, 2, 3, 3, 4, 4, 4, and 7.

1 1 2 2 2 3 3 4 4 4 7

The numbers 2 and 4 both occur three times, so both numbers are modes.

Guided Practice

Make a line plot for the data in Exercise 1. Then use the line plot to complete Exercises 2–3.

1. Miniature golf scores
   69, 72, 74, 73, 73, 72, 75, 73, 70, 71, 90, 72, 91
2. Describe the data. Where do these data cluster? Are there any gaps? Where?
3. Find the mean, median, mode, and range of the data.

Ask Yourself

- Did I arrange the numbers in order?
- Did I include all the data on the line plot?

Explain Your Thinking ▶ Why is it helpful to describe the miniature golf scores above by using the mean, median, mode, and range?

Go On

Practice and Problem Solving

Make a line plot for each set of data. Identify clusters and gaps. Then find the mean, median, mode, and range.

4. number of miles biked
15, 14, 8, 27, 15, 20, 19, 13, 19, 15, 20, 14, 15, 13, 13

5. trips to the zoo
2, 4, 5, 16, 4, 5, 5, 11, 0, 2, 1, 5, 2, 3, 1, 2, 0

6. dollars in bank account
28, 32, 36, 22, 12, 40, 32, 46, 42, 18, 42, 32, 28, 24

Use a calculator to find the mean, median, and mode of each set of data.

7. 13, 2, 3, 6, 9, 8, 4, 8, 10, 10, 6, 5

8. 66, 55, 15, 49, 60, 59, 59, 11, 91, 75

9. 25, 26, 1, 4, 4, 6, 11, 4, 2, 8, 1, 4

10. 103, 104, 101, 102, 75, 100, 100, 89, 90

11. 16, 15, 10, 43, 17, 19, 31, 31, 14, 13, 11

12. 86, 91, 21, 86, 83, 74, 61, 75, 76, 80, 81

Algebra • Equations Find *n*.

13. 3, 4, 8, 8, 10, 12, 16, *n*
range: 32 mode: 8
median: 9 mean: 12

14. 5, 6, 7, 9, 12, *n*
range: 7 mode: 9
median: 8 mean: 8

15. 4, 8, 10, 16, 20, 38, *n*
range: 34 mode: *n*
median: *n* mean: *n*

Data Use the line plot below for Problems 16–19.

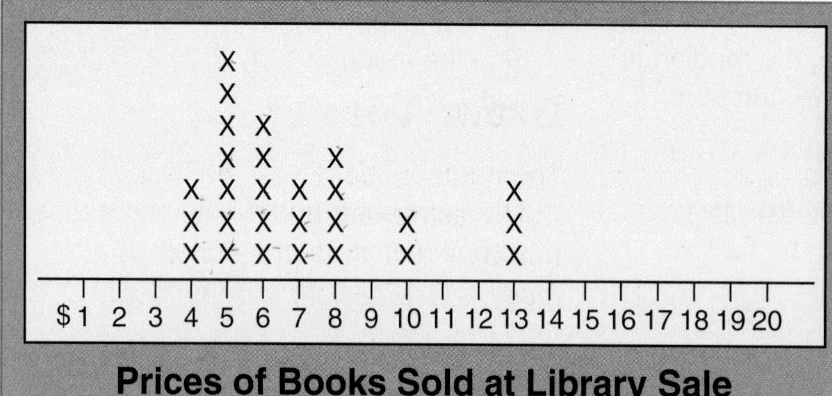

Prices of Books Sold at Library Sale

16. How many books are represented in the line plot?

17. Find the range, mean, median, and mode of the data.

18. Write About It Use your results from Problem 17 to write a short summary of the data.

19. How many books cost less than $7? How many books cost more than $7?

Mixed Review and Test Prep

Open Response

Complete. (Ch. 6, Lessons 4–5)

20. 5 m = ■ cm

21. 7,000 mg = ■ g

22. 96 dm = ■ m

23. 3,500 mL = ■ L

Multiple Choice

24. Nathan's math grades are 85, 70, 84, 91, 88, and 92. Find the mean of his grades. (Ch. 8, Lesson 2)

A 85 **B** 87 **C** 88 **D** 90

Extra Practice See page 209, Set A.

Quick Check

Quick Check

Check your understanding of Lessons 1–2.

Use the table to complete Problems 1–3.
(Lessons 1 and 2)

1. Make a tally sheet for the data in the table. Write the frequency for each answer choice.
2. Make a line plot for the data in the table.
3. Find the mean, median, mode, and range.

Number of Years Each Student Has Lived in Town									
4	10	4	7	8	8	9	10	9	8
6	8	10	10	9	8	6	7	9	10
5	6	9	9	10	9	7	8	8	9

Use the line plot to complete Problems 4–5.
(Lesson 2)

4. Identify any clusters and gaps in the data.
5. How many students took the spelling quiz?
6. Find the mean, median, mode, and range.

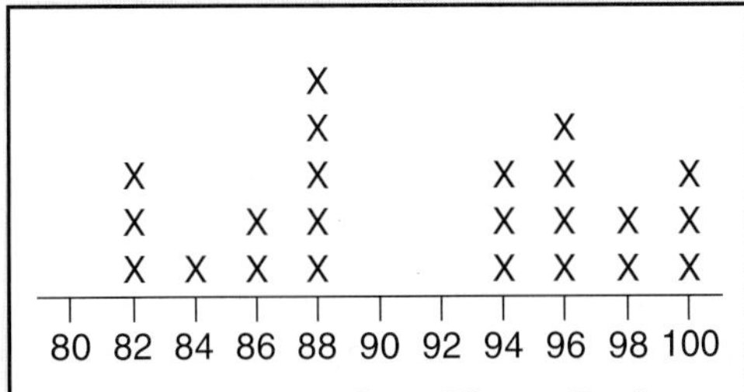

Scores on Spelling Quiz

Activity

Number Sense

Raise It Up

You have a mean of 78 for five quizzes. Each quiz has a possible score of 100.

- Can you raise your mean to 80 after six quizzes?
- Can you raise your mean to 82 after six quizzes?
- If there will be 10 quizzes in all, can you ever raise your mean to 90?

Explain each of your answers.

Education Place
Check out **eduplace.com/map** for more Brain Teasers.

Brain Teaser

The numbers below are ordered from least to greatest. The mean of the numbers is 5, the median is 6, and the mode is 2. What are the numbers?

Lesson 3

Make and Use a Stem-and-Leaf Plot

Objective Use a stem-and-leaf plot to display data.

Vocabulary
stem-and-leaf plot
stem
leaf

Learn About It

Have you ever ridden on an inverted roller coaster, where your feet hang free? The list below shows the speeds, in miles per hour, of some inverted roller coasters.

25, 45, 46, 50, 50, 50, 55, 55, 55, 55,
55, 57, 58, 58, 60, 60, 62, 65, 67, 72

One way to display these data is to make a **stem-and-leaf plot.**

Making a Stem-and-Leaf Plot

STEP 1 Write a title.

STEP 2 Write the tens digits needed to represent the data in order from least to greatest. Each of these numbers is a **stem.**

STEP 3 For each piece of data, write the ones digit, or **leaf,** next to its tens digit. Arrange the leaves in order from least to greatest. Write a key.

Roller Coaster Speeds (miles per hour)

Stem	Leaf
2	5
3	
4	5 6
5	0 0 0 5 5 5 5 5 7 8 8
6	0 0 2 5 7
7	2

7 | 2 means 72.

Guided Practice

Use the stem-and-leaf plot above for Problems 1–4.

1. What does 4 | 6 mean in the stem-and-leaf plot above?
2. How many roller coasters are represented in the data?
3. How many of the inverted roller coasters reach speeds of more than 55 miles per hour?
4. Find the mean, median, mode, and range of the data.

Ask Yourself
- What do the stems represent?
- What do the leaves represent?

Explain Your Thinking ▶ How did you use the stem-and-leaf plot to find the mean, median, mode, and range of the data?

Practice and Problem Solving

Use the stem-and-leaf plot for Problems 5–8.

Number of Amusement Parks in Different Countries

Stem	Leaf
0	2 2 3 4 4 4 5 6 7
1	1 1 1 1 3 4 5 8
2	
3	8
4	7
5	
6	
7	4

7 | 4 means 74.

5. What does 0 | 7 mean in this line plot?
6. How many countries are represented in the data?
7. **Write About It** Identify any clusters and gaps you see. What do these tell you about the data?
8. Find the mean, median, mode, and range of the data.
9. Suppose you had these scores on a computer game: 123, 123, 123, 123, 123. What is true about the mean score, the median score, and the mode?

Make a stem-and-leaf plot for the data at the right. Each "ring" of a peg scores 2 points. Then solve Problems 10–15.

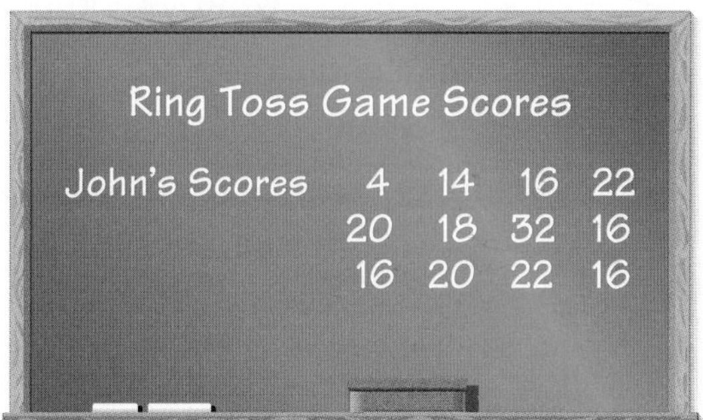

10. How many times did John play the game?
11. What was John's highest score?
12. What was John's lowest score?
13. Find the mean, median, mode, and range of the data.
14. **What's Wrong?** Ana and John will compete in the Ring Toss Game. Ana says that she needs to score about 10 points to have a good chance of beating John's score. What's wrong with Ana's prediction?
15. Tell why the median of John's scores is not the best statistic to use to describe John's typical score. Explain your thinking.

Mixed Review and Test Prep

Open Response

Evaluate each expression when $n = 7$.
(Ch. 2, Lesson 3)

16. $n + 3$
17. $4 + n$
18. $2 + n - 5$
19. $13 - n$
20. $25 - (n + 5)$
21. $(n + n) - 1$

22. List the data below in order from greatest to least. (Ch. 8, Lesson 3)

Stem	Leaf
1	0 1 1 2
2	2
3	4 4 5 7 9

3 | 4 means 34.

Extra Practice See page 209, Set B.

Lesson 4

Audio Tutor 1/23 Listen and Understand

Problem-Solving Strategy

Make a Table

Objective Make a table to solve problems.

Problem Fifth-grade students conducted a survey about how many hours they spend watching TV each week. The results are shown below. Do most of the students watch TV 0–4 hours, 5–9 hours, 10–14 hours, or 15–19 hours each week?

Survey Results

0	5	7	11	13	10
5	3	9	1	15	7
16	8	0	9	4	8
13	4	8	2	15	5

UNDERSTAND

This is what you know:

The number of hours each student watches TV each week.

PLAN

You can make a table to help you solve the problem.

SOLVE

- Make a table with the intervals stated in the problem: 0–4 hours, 5–9 hours, 10–14 hours, and 15–19 hours.
- Write a tally mark next to the correct interval for each number in the list. Then count the tally marks and write the frequencies.
- Compare the frequencies.

$10 > 7 > 4 > 3$

Hours	Tally	Frequency
0–4	𝍸 ||	7
5–9	𝍸 𝍸	10
10–14	||||	4
15–19	|||	3

Solution: Most of the students surveyed watch TV 5–9 hours each week.

LOOK BACK

Look back at the problem. Is your answer reasonable? How can you check the answer?

Extra Help at **eduplace.com/map**

Guided Practice

Use the Ask Yourself questions to help you solve each problem.

1. Kami and Brady played a word game. The scores for each word are shown below. Are most of the scores from 1–10, 11–20, 21–30, or over 30 points?

   12, 17, 42, 16, 22, 14, 22, 38, 9, 14, 20, 8, 7, 27, 19, 13, 18, 25, 6, 29, 17, 24, 7, 18, 16, 50, 9, 22, 27, 18, 15, 42, 6, 12, 30, 8, 4

2. Use the data above. Are more of the scores from 11–15 points or 16–20 points?

   Hint Make a new table. The sum of these frequencies should equal the frequency for 11–20 above.

Ask Yourself

What facts do I know?

Did I make a table with the correct headings and intervals?

- **Did I tally the data?**
- **Did I find the frequency for each interval?**

Did I check my answer?

Independent Practice

Make a table to solve each problem.

3. The students in Shayna's class recorded the number of minutes they spent on the Internet during one night. The results are shown at the right. Did most of the students spend 0–20 minutes, 21–41 minutes, 42–62 minutes, 63–83 minutes, or over 83 minutes?

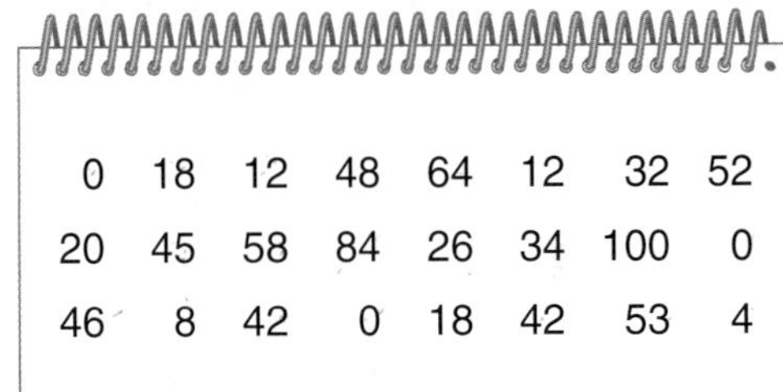

0	18	12	48	64	12	32	52
20	45	58	84	26	34	100	0
46	8	42	0	18	42	53	4

4. Use the data above. How many students in Shayna's class spent 0–10 minutes on the Internet? How many spent 11–20 minutes?

5. Taylor collects coins. The dates of the coins are shown at the right. Are most of Taylor's coins from before 1940, between 1940 and 1960, or after 1960?

1944	1957	1955	1953	1960
1931	1949	1985	1966	1943
1982	1947	1922	1978	1964
1970	1974	1941	1976	1980
1936	1952	1980	1932	1995

6. **Create and Solve** Find out in which month each of your classmates was born. Were most of them born from January–March, April–June, July–September, or October–December? Make a table to solve the problem.

7. Could you solve Problem 6 by using a line plot? Explain.

Go On

Mixed Problem Solving

Solve. Show your work. Tell what strategy you used.

8. Brett bought a T-shirt and a baseball cap for $40. The T-shirt was $8 less than the baseball cap. What was the cost of the T-shirt? What was the cost of the baseball cap?

9. In a basketball game, Amber scored 5 more points than Tonya and 4 fewer points than Juanita. Juanita scored 22 points. How many points did Tonya score?

10. The price for two people to play a round of miniature golf was $11 in 2000, $13 in 2002, $15 in 2004, and $17 in 2006. If the pattern continues, what will the price be in 2010?

11. Paige is thinking of two numbers that have a product of 180 and a difference of 3. What are the two numbers?

You Choose

Strategy
- Find a Pattern
- Guess and Check
- Make a Table
- Use Logical Reasoning
- Work Backward

Computation Method
- Mental Math
- Estimation
- Paper and Pencil
- Calculator

Data Use the graph to solve Problems 12–15.

Ed and Sal earn money by giving tennis lessons to younger children. The graph shows how much money Ed and Sal earned in three months.

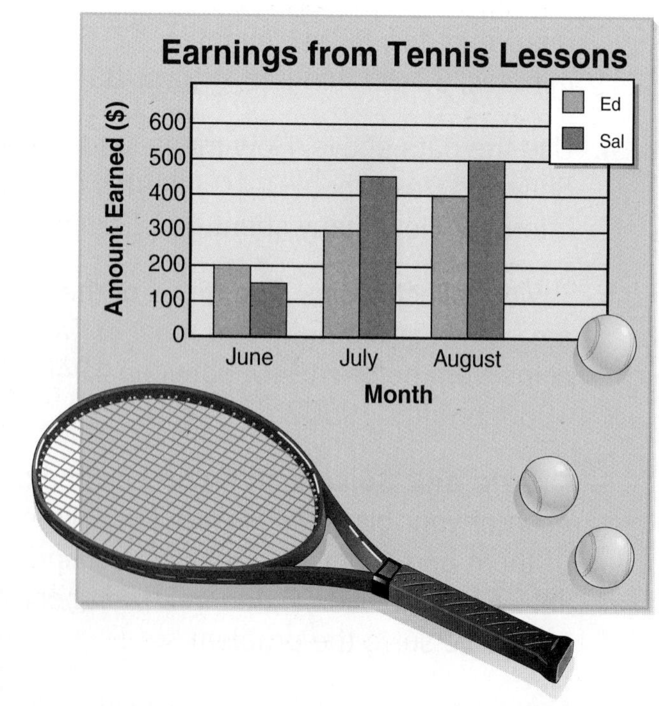

12. In which month was the difference between Ed and Sal's earnings the greatest?

13. Who has more total earnings over the three months shown on the graph? About how much more?

14. Sal saves half of his total earnings. About how much money did he save from June to August?

15. **Create and Solve** Write and solve a problem that uses data from the graph.

Problem Solving on Tests

Multiple Choice

Choose the letter of the correct answer.

1. Look at the histogram. How many people surveyed saw fewer than 11 plays this year?

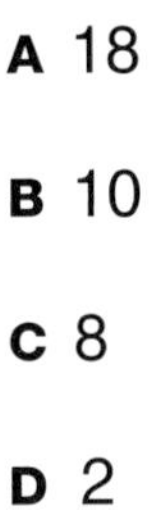

A 18

B 10

C 8

D 2

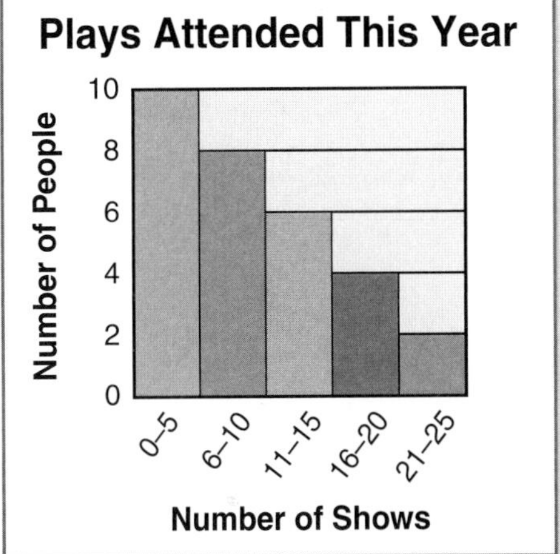

(Chapter 7, Lesson 2)

2. **Measurement** Norbert brought 3 quarts and 2 cups of water on a hike. How many cups of water did he bring?

F 8 cups **H** 14 cups

G 12 cups **J** 26 cups

(Chapter 6, Lesson 3)

Open Response

Solve each problem

3. Seventy people buy tickets to a dinner. They will sit at tables with 6 seats each. How can they be seated at these tables with an equal number of people at each table?

Explain How did you solve this problem?

(Chapter 4, Lesson 6)

4. Allen made model cars and motorcycles. He made 12 models that used a total of 40 wheels. How many model motorcycles did Allen make?

Represent Support your solution with a picture or a table.

(Chapter 1, Lesson 6)

Extended Response

5. The list shows the results of a survey about how many minutes it takes students to get to school in the morning. In order to draw conclusions about the data, organize it into a line plot.

20, 25, 30, 30, 15, 20, 10, 5, 35, 50, 30, 25, 20, 15, 20, 30, 25, 30, 30, 15

a Create a number line that shows the range of the times in the data set.

b Complete the line plot by putting an X above each number as many times as that number appears in the list.

c Find the mode, median, and mean of the data.

d Is there an outlier? If so, identify it.

Explain How did you find your answer?

(Chapter 8)

Education Place

See **eduplace.com/map** for Test-Taking Tips.

Lesson 5

Audio Tutor 1/24 Listen and Understand

Draw Conclusions and Make Predictions

Objective Draw conclusions based on data and make predictions based on those conclusions.

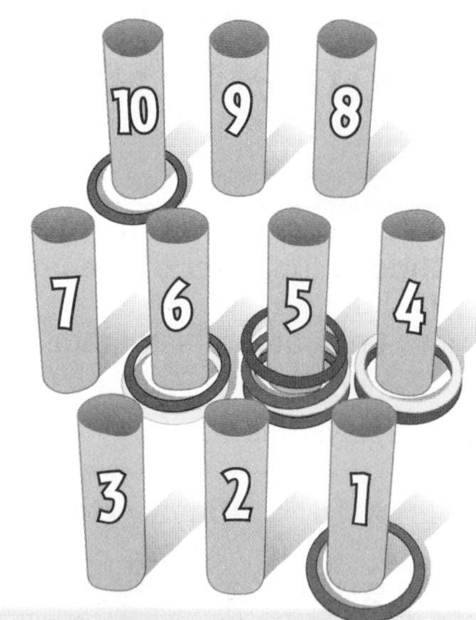

Learn About It

Chase, Kimiko, and Jared each threw 10 rings in a ring-toss game. The line plots below show their scores.

You can use the mean, median, and mode to describe each student's typical score.

Jared

Mean = **5.1**
Median = **5**
Mode = **5**

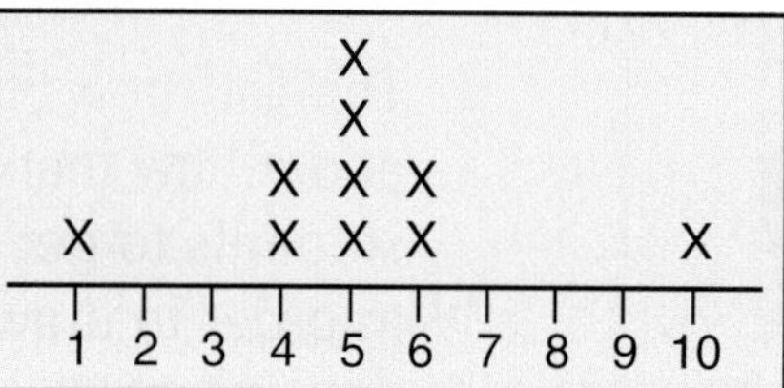

Since the mean, median, and mode are all about 5, Jared's typical score is 5.

Kimiko

Mean = **8**
Median = **9.5**
Mode = **10**

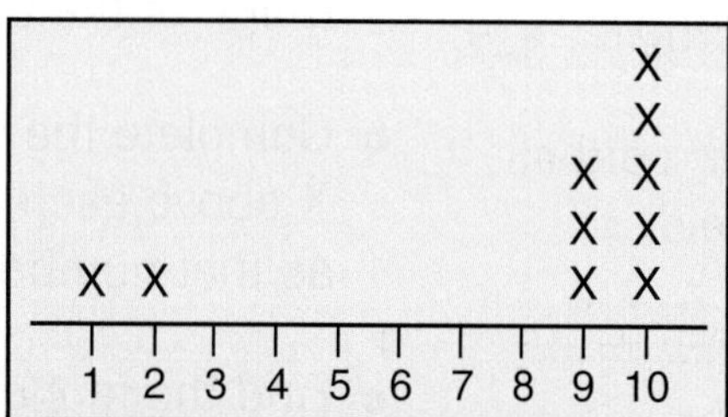

The two low scores "pull" the mean away from the rest of the data. Use the median and the mode. Kimoko's typical score is 9 or 10.

Chase

Mean = **4**
Median = **3**
Mode = **1**

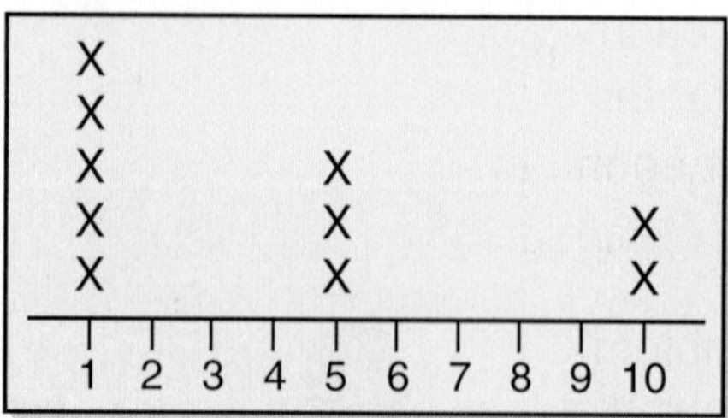

These data do not center around any score. So the score that occurs most often, the mode, best describes Chase's typical score.

Guided Practice

> **Ask Yourself**
> - Do most of the data center around one or a few numbers?
> - Is the mean "pulled" away from the rest of the data?

The line plot shows the ticket prices for movie theaters in Metropole. Use the line plot below for Problems 1–4.

1. Find the mean, median, and mode of the data.
2. Suppose you are going to a movie in Metropole. How much money should you expect to pay for a ticket? Use the mean, median, and mode to explain your answer.

Ticket Prices (Dollars)

For the summer, the two movie theaters with the lowest-priced tickets doubled their ticket prices. Two of the movie theaters with $10 ticket prices cut their ticket prices in half.

3. Make a new line plot to show the summer ticket prices for the ten theaters.
4. Using the new data, how much would you expect to pay for a theater ticket? Explain your reasoning.

Explain Your Thinking ▶ When looking at data, why is it important to know all three statistics—the mean, median, and mode?

Practice and Problem Solving

Use the data from the line plot for Problems 5–7.

The line plot shows attendance at seven softball games that were played at the home field.

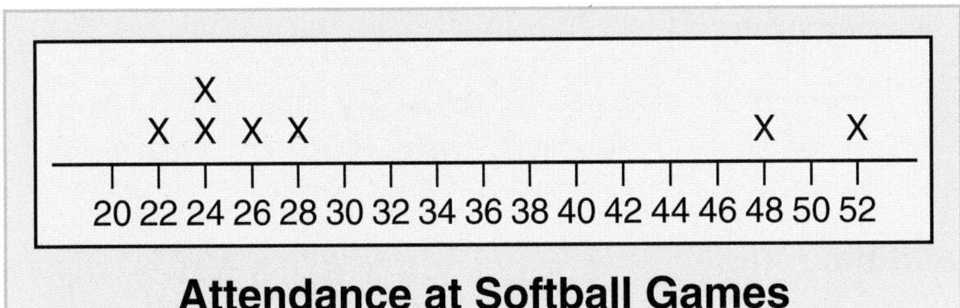

Attendance at Softball Games

5. Find the mean, median, and mode of the data.
6. Use the mean, median, or mode to describe the typical number of people who attended the games. Explain your answer.
7. Suppose the eighth, ninth, and tenth home games get crowds of 52 each. How would that affect your answers in Problem 5? Explain your thinking.

Go On

Data Use the stem-and-leaf plot for Problems 8–13.

High Temperatures (°F) at Ocean Bay, January 1–14

Stem	Leaf
7	9
8	0 0 0 3 6 8
9	0 0 1 1 3 3 4

9 | 0 means 90.

8. What are the highest and lowest temperatures shown in the plot?

9. What is the range of the data?

10. Find the mean of the data.

11. What was the median high temperature at Ocean Bay from January 1–14?

12. Find the mode of the data.

13. What was the typical high temperature for Ocean Bay during the first two weeks of January? Explain how you used the mean, median, or mode to answer the question.

14. The page to the right is from a travel brochure for Ocean Bay. Do you think the brochure's description of Ocean Bay's weather is accurate? How do you think the brochure's writer used the data to create the description?

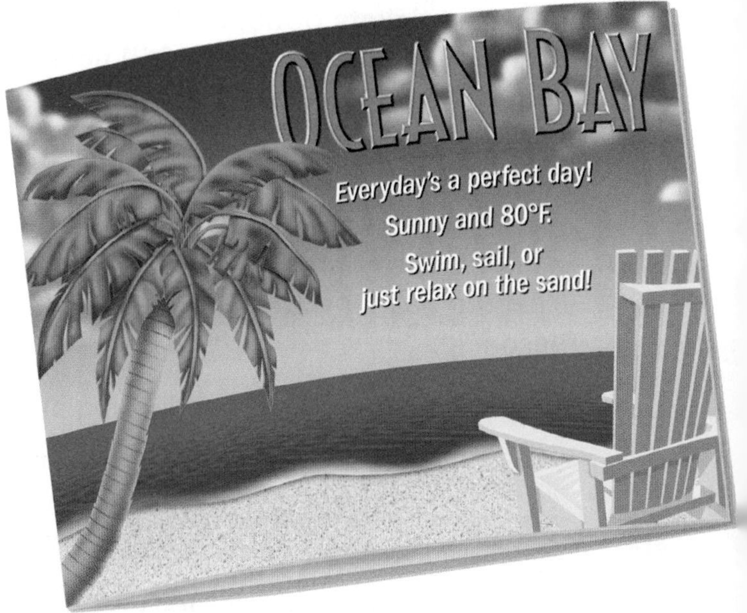

The table shows the goals scored by a field hockey team in thirteen regular-season games. Use the data from the table for Problems 15–19.

Goals Scored by the Crimson Crowd Field Hockey Team
3 5 0 1 2 5 1 6 1 5 4 4 2

15. Show the data on a line plot.

16. Find the mean of the data.

17. Find the median, mode and range of the data.

18. Write About It Which would you use to best describe the typical number of goals scored by the team—the mean, median, or mode? Explain why you chose this statistic.

19. The team scored the same number of goals in the next two games and brought their mean goals up to 3.4. How many goals did they score in their next two games?

Extra Practice See page 209, Set C.

Mixed Review and Test Prep

Open Response

Compare. Write $>$, $<$, = for each ●.
(Ch. 6, Lesson 5)

20. 17 kg ● 1,700 g

21. 50 t ● 50,000 kg

22. 300 mL ● 3,000 cm^3

23. 250 dL ● 25 L

24. 35 L ● 3,500 mL

25. 1,500 g ● 150 mg

26. Suppose you want to describe Randi's typical quiz score. Which statistic would be the better one to use, the mean or the median? Explain. (Ch. 8, Lesson 5)

Randi's Quiz Scores

Stem	Leaf
6	1
7	9
8	1 2 2

8 | 1 means 81.

Problem Solving

Social Studies Connection

Slippery Samples

Surveys were conducted at a water park to find which water slide was the most popular. Group 1 surveyed students between the ages of 6 and 10. Group 2 randomly surveyed adults and children at the park. Why are their results different?

To collect data about a large group of people, researchers must choose a **representative sample** of the group. Group 2 chose a representative sample because they randomly interviewed children and adults at the water park.

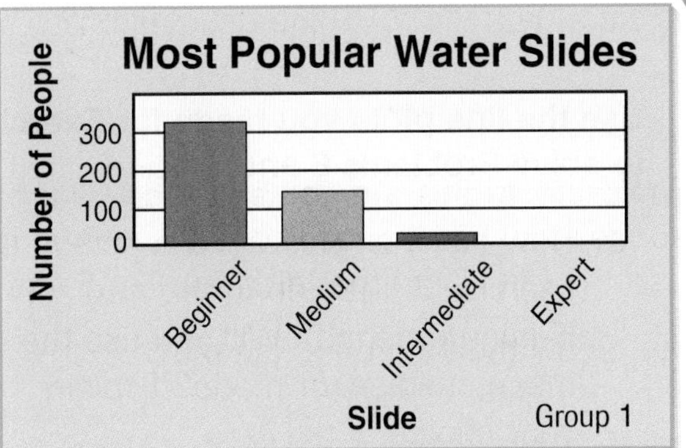

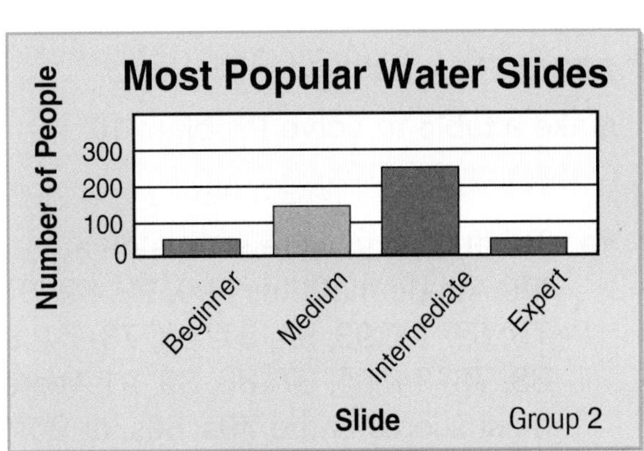

Discuss how you would choose a representative sample to answer each question.

1. Which sport do the students at your school like the most?
2. Which type of music is the most popular in your state?

WEEKLY WR READER eduplace.com/map

Chapter Review/Test

VOCABULARY

1. In a data display, a large space between data is called a ____.
2. A ____ is a group of data that are close together.

Vocabulary
- cluster
- gap
- line plot
- stem-and-leaf plot
- survey

CONCEPTS AND SKILLS

Make a line plot for each set of data. Identify any clusters or gaps. Then find the mean, median, mode, and range.
(Lessons 1–2, pp. 192–196)

3. number of sit-ups in 5 minutes: 35, 31, 40, 35, 35, 35, 35, 34, 35, 31
4. number of points scored: 59, 60, 60, 59, 51, 60, 59, 52, 53, 60

Use the stem-and-leaf plot at the right for Problems 5–7. (Lesson 3, pp. 198–199)

5. What were the highest and lowest admission charges?
6. How many admission charges were higher than $25?
7. Find the mean, median, mode, and range of the data.

Admission Charges

Stem	Leaf
5	0
4	5 2 2 2 0
3	9 7 6 0
2	9 8 4 0

4 | 5 means $45.

Use the line plots you made for Exercises 3 and 4 to solve Problems 8 and 9. (Lesson 5, pp. 204–206)

8. How many sit-ups will the person in Exercise 3 likely do in the next 5-minute period? Will you use the mean, median, or mode? Explain your choice.
9. How many points will the person in Exercise 4 likely score in the next turn? Will you use the mean, median, or mode? Explain your choice.

PROBLEM SOLVING

Make a table to solve Problem 10.
(Lesson 4, pp. 200–202)

10. The following were scores on a fifth-grade math test: 99, 98, 89, 87, 75, 69, 94, 93, 94, 97, 83, 73, 74, 84, 83, 73, 84, 85, 87, 88, 89, 91. Were most scores in the 70s, 80s, or 90s?

Show You Understand

How does a line plot make it easier to find the mode and median?

Extra Practice

Set A (Lesson 2, pp. 194–197)

Make a line plot for each set of data. Identify any clusters or gaps. Then find the mean, median, mode, and range.

1. number of CD's owned
   15, 22, 5, 10, 23, 18, 24, 14, 19, 4, 22
2. class attendance
   28, 24, 23, 26, 14, 29, 20, 18, 25, 29, 26, 14
3. test scores
   101, 98, 100, 97, 100, 87, 103, 98, 99, 100

Find the mean, median, and mode of each set of data.

4. 45, 46, 39, 47, 49, 42, 38, 46, 49, 43
5. 68, 59, 67, 66, 54, 67, 68, 70, 63, 66, 61
6. 120, 118, 117, 107, 123, 121, 119, 120, 120, 118

Set B (Lesson 3, pp. 198–199)

Use the stem-and-leaf plot for Problems 1–4.

1. How many amusement parks are represented in the data?
2. How many parks had fewer than 20 rides?
3. What is the greatest number of rides at any amusement park?
4. Find the mean, median, mode, and range of the data.

Kinds of Rides in Amusement Parks

Stem	Leaf
0	9
1	2 4 5 5 6 8 9
2	0 0 0 1 2 4 4 5 5 6 6 7 7 8 8 9
3	0

1 | 2 means 12 rides.

Set C (Lesson 5, pp. 204–209)

Use the data from the line plot for Problems 1–5.

1. How many days had a low temperature below 5°?
2. How many days are represented in the line plot?
3. Which low temperatures occurred more than once?
4. Find the mean, median, mode, and range of the data.
5. Use the mean, median, or mode to predict the normal low temperature for Green Bay in February. Explain your answer.

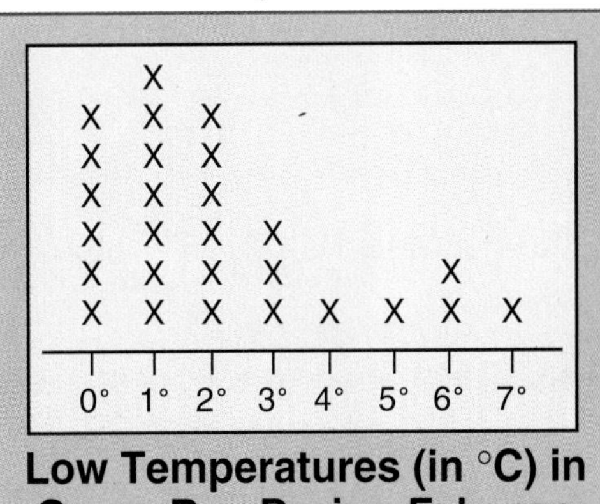

Low Temperatures (in °C) in Green Bay During February

WEEKLY WR READER®

Real World Connection

What a Kick!

The largest international soccer tournament is the World Cup. Thirty-two countries from 6 different continents send their national teams to compete once every four years.

The first World Cup soccer tournament was held in Uruguay in 1930. Over the next 60 years the tournament was played only by men's teams. In 1991, however, the first Women's World Cup was held in China. The U.S. women's team achieved stardom by winning the World Cup in 1999.

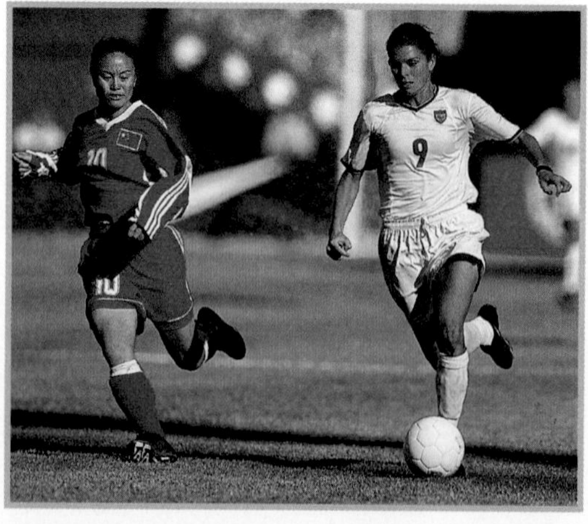

Problem Solving

1 The men's World Cup trophy is made of solid gold and a green semi-precious mineral called malachite. The trophy has a mass of 5,000 grams and stands 0.36 meter tall. What is the trophy's mass in kilograms? What is its height in centimeters?

2 Nearly 1,400,000 people attended the 1999 Women's World Cup games. The mean for the number of people attending these games was 40,000. How many games were played?

Use the bar graph for Problems 3–5.

3 If you combined the number of goals scored by the men's and women's World Cup teams for each country, which country would have the most goals?

4 Find the range of the number of goals scored by the men's and women's teams.

5 Find the difference between the median number of goals for the men's and women's teams.

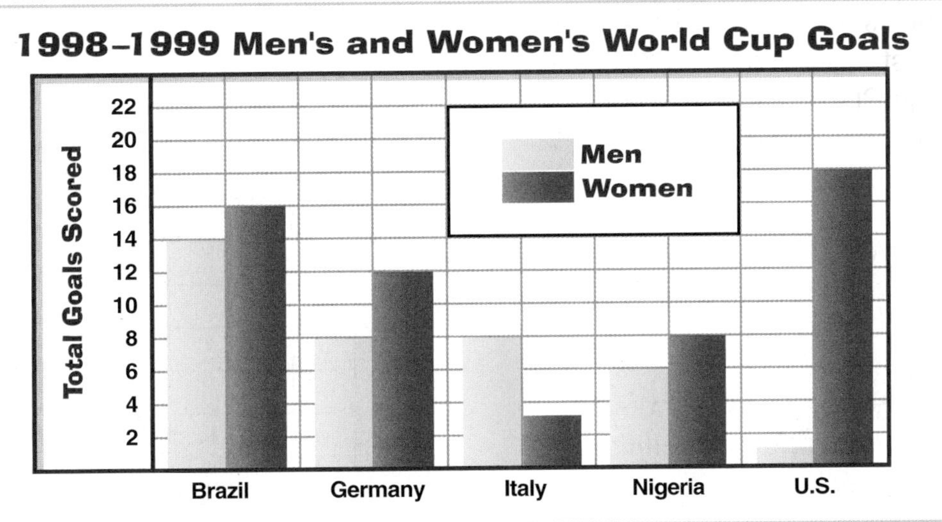

Education Place

Visit Weekly Reader Connections at **eduplace.com/map** for more on this topic.

Enrichment: Graphs in Everyday Life

Whether you are watching TV, reading a newspaper or magazine, or doing your homework, you will find graphs to read and interpret. Why? Because a picture is worth a thousand words.

The graph at the right supports the headline that says that from 2001 to 2002, gas prices dropped.

You can read specific data from this graph. For example, notice how, even before the decrease in prices, the $1.380 cost of gas per gallon in Texas was less than the other states' 2002 prices.

Gas Prices Drop!

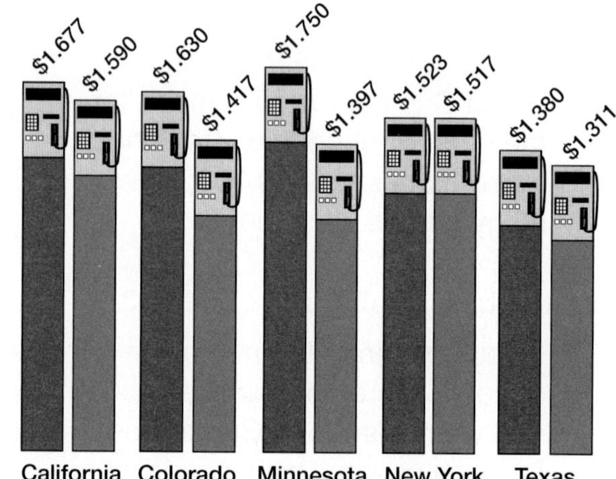

Try These!

Use the graph at the right for Problems 1–4.

1. In 1970, the Clean Air Act required the reduction of lead in gasoline. About how many fewer tons of lead were emitted in 1980 than in 1970?

2. During which five-year period did lead emissions drop the most between 1970 and 1990?

3. In 1990, lead emissions were 1,197,000 tons. By 1999, the amount of lead emitted was 661,000 tons less than 1990. How many tons of lead were put into the air in 1999?

4. Explain why it would be hard to show data for years after 1990 on the graph.

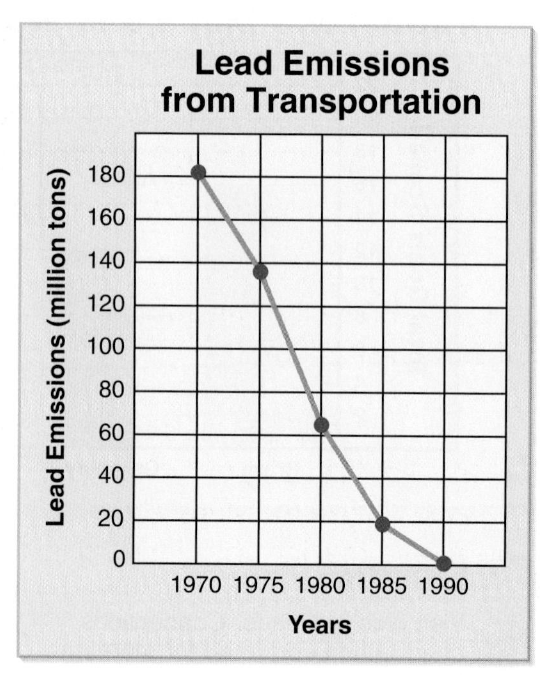

What's It All Mean?

How much does a pair of sneakers cost? Use the Internet to find the prices of 8 different pairs of sneakers. Then use a spreadsheet program to graph your data and find the mean and median.

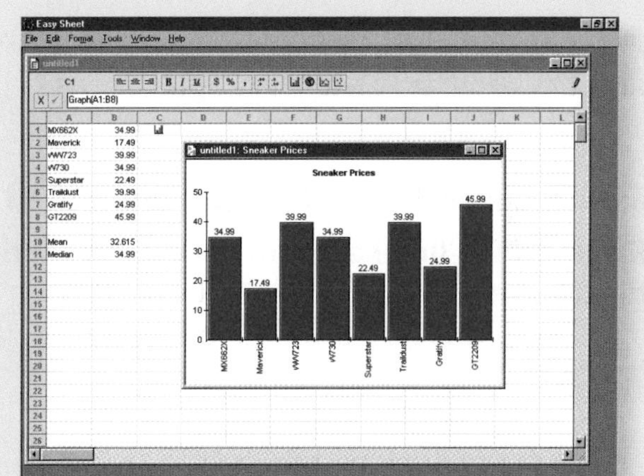

- Enter the shoe names in Column A.
- Enter the shoe prices in Column B. Do not include dollar signs.
- Click on cell A1 and drag to cell B8 to highlight the data.
- Click [chart button]. Double click on the graph.
- Click on the tab marked **Labels**. Enter a title for your graph. Click the box next to **Label Data**. Click **OK**.
- Type "Mean" in cell A10 and "Median" in A11.
- Click **Window**. Choose **Function List**.
- Click on cell B10. Double click **Avg(range)**. Click on cell B1 and drag to cell B8. Press **Enter**. Click on cell B11. Double click **Median(range).** Click on cell B1 and drag to cell B8. Press **Enter**.

Solve.

1. What are the mean and median of the sneaker prices?
2. How can you use the graph to find the mode and range of the data?
3. **Challenge** Add 1 more sneaker price to your graph. Predict how your mean and median will change. Follow the steps above to find the new mean and median, this time dragging from cell B1 to cell B9. How do your new mean and median compare to your predictions?

Unit 3 Test

VOCABULARY Open Response

Match the definitions below with the correct vocabulary word.

Vocabulary
- mean
- mode
- median
- capacity
- histogram
- stem-and-leaf plot

1. A way to display data in which the size of the bars shows how frequently the data occur in equal intervals.
2. The amount a container can hold.
3. The number found by dividing the sum of a group of addends by the number of addends.
4. A display that uses place value to show frequencies of data.

CONCEPTS AND SKILLS Open Response

Measure the line segment according to the directions given below. (Chapter 6)

5. to the nearest eighth inch
6. to the nearest decimeter
7. to the nearest centimeter

Compare. Write >, <, or = . (Chapter 6)

8. 1 g ● 750 mg
9. 1,000 mL ● 1 L
10. 3 qts ● 7 pts

Use the graph to answer Problems 11–12. (Chapter 7)

11. Tyrell collected some data and made the graph at the right. What kind of graph did he make? What does the graph show?
12. What was the temperature at 3 P.M.?

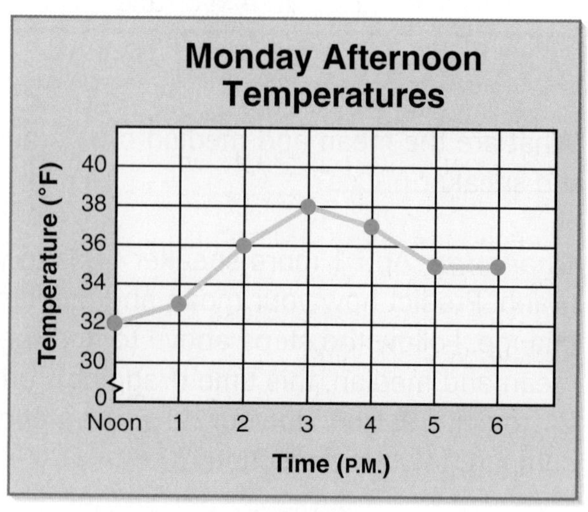

Use the line plot for Exercises 13–16. (Chapter 8)

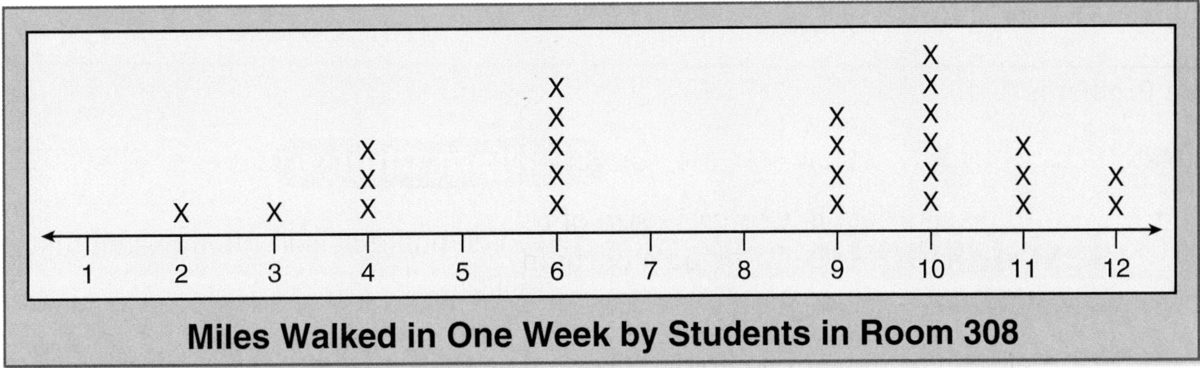

Miles Walked in One Week by Students in Room 308

13. mean

14. median

15. mode

16. range

PROBLEM SOLVING Open Response

Use the line graph on page 214 to solve Problems 17–18.

17. Between which two times did the temperature change the most? not change at all?

18. Tina says that Tyrell's graph is misleading. Is she correct? Explain your answer.

19. Suppose you survey 50 people who can respond *yes*, *no*, or *not sure*. Decide whether the data are best displayed in a line graph, a bar graph, or a histogram. Explain your choice.

20. You are to make a line plot showing the sizes of shoes worn by students in your class. Describe how to make the line plot and how to find the mean, median, and mode.

Performance Assessment

Constructed Response

Task Four students were in a race. The chart at the right shows the results of the race.

Choose the best way to display the data. Consider a bar graph, line graph, pictograph, circle graph, or histogram. Make a graph to display the data. What affected the type of graph you chose? Explain your thinking.

Race Results

Student	Time (minutes)
1	7.98
2	6.23
3	7.35
4	7.01

Cumulative Test Prep

Solve Problems 1–10.

Test-Taking Tip

If you get stuck on a problem, skip it and go on. Then go back to it, if you have time, and try again to work the problem.

Look at the example below.

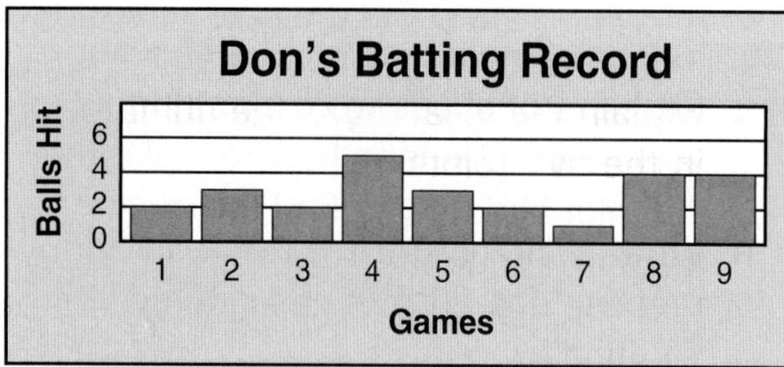

What is the median of the number of balls Don hit in 9 games?

A 1 **B** 2 **C** 3 **D** 4

THINK

If you are not as good at reading graphs as doing computation, skip it and go on. After working other problems, make a table or different kind of graph from the given data.

The middle value for the data on the graph is 3, so the answer is **C**.

Multiple Choice

1. Which numeral is in the thousandths place?

40,321.978

A 0 **C** 7

B 4 **D** 8

(Chapter 1, Lesson 5)

2. Which distance traveled by fifth-grade students last summer is the greatest?

F 7×10^3 miles **H** 5 hundred miles

G 8.432 miles **J** 900 + 50 miles

(Chapter 1, Lesson 4)

3. Marty has kept track of how he has spent his money during the past year. He wants to display the data on a graph. Which type of graph is the best choice?

A circle graph **C** double line graph

B double bar graph **D** frequency table

(Chapter 7, Lesson 1)

4. Sally wants to make a graph that shows how much her grades have improved over the past few months. Which kind of graph is her best choice?

F circle graph **H** line graph

G bar graph **J** histogram

(Chapter 7, Lesson 3)

For Test-Taking Tips, see page 652.

Open Response

5. Exactly 5,092 fans came to the school's first football game. There are 4,887 fans at the second game. How many fewer fans came to the second game than the first game?

(Chapter 2, Lesson 3)

6. Otis and Ellen mixed batter for a pancake breakfast. If they mixed 20 batches and each batch makes 12 pancakes, how many pancakes can they make in all?

(Chapter 3, Lesson 6)

7. Sarah has $135.75, and she wants to buy 5 outfits that are about the same price for school. Find out how much she can spend on each outfit to the nearest dollar.

(Chapter 4, Lesson 1)

8. Bala and her sisters used 3,000 beads to make 150 necklaces. Each necklace has the same number of beads. How many beads are in each necklace?

(Chapter 5, Lesson 1)

9. A mini-bus can carry a maximum weight of one ton. The average weight of each of the 27 students going on a field trip is 105 pounds. The bus driver weighs 150 pounds. What is the greatest number of students who can ride the bus? (Hint: 1 ton = 2,000 pounds)

(Chapter 6, Lesson 3)

Extended Response

Ring Toss Results

Stem	Leaf
0	9 9
1	0 0 1 3 4 4 5 8
2	2 3 3 7
3	0

Key: 3 | 0 means 30.

10. The stem-and-leaf plot above shows how many times 15 ring toss players were able to ring a bottle in 50 tries.

A Explain the meaning of the numbers in the two columns.

B What is the greatest cluster you find in these data? What gaps, if any, do you find?

C Explain why a stem-and-leaf plot is a good way to organize this kind of data.

(Chapter 8, Lesson 3)

Education Place

Look for Cumulative Test Prep at **eduplace.com/map** for more practice.

Vocabulary Wrap-Up for Unit 3

Look back at the big ideas and vocabulary in this unit.

Big Ideas

Measurements can be added and subtracted. First, write the measurements to the same unit of measure.

Double bar graphs and double line graphs compare two sets of data. Predictions can be made from data displays.

Key Vocabulary

measurement
data
prediction

Math Conversations

Use your new vocabulary to discuss these big ideas.

1. Explain the relationship between decimeters and centimeters.
2. Explain how you can change a measurement of 7 yards into feet.
3. Explain how to read a double bar graph.
4. Explain how to make a line plot.
5. **Write About It** Search for graphs in books, newspapers, and magazines. List the kinds of graphs you find and tell what you can learn from the way the data are displayed.

Let's compare how many inches we have grown in the last year.
That's 2 sets of data. We should use a double line graph to compare.

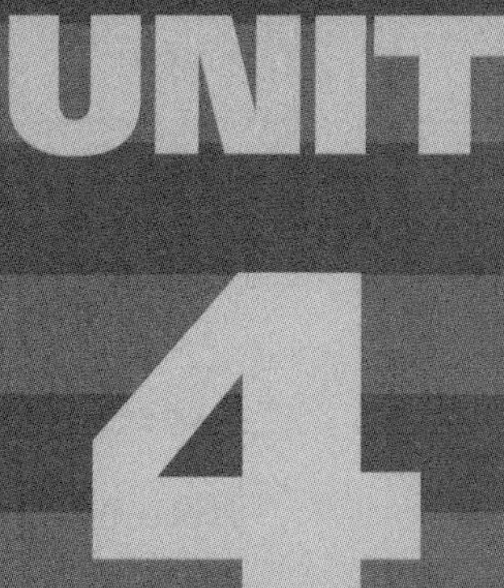

Addition and Subtraction of Fractions and Decimals

Reading Mathematics

Reviewing Vocabulary

Here are some math vocabulary words that you should know.

fraction	a number that describes part of a whole or part of a group
numerator	the number above the bar in a fraction that tells how many equal parts of the whole have been counted
denominator	the number below the bar in a fraction that tells how many equal parts are in the whole
decimal	a number with one or more digits to the right of a decimal point
decimal point	a symbol used to separate the ones and tenths places in a decimal

Reading Words and Symbols

Sometimes the same number can be expressed in more than one way. Here is an example:

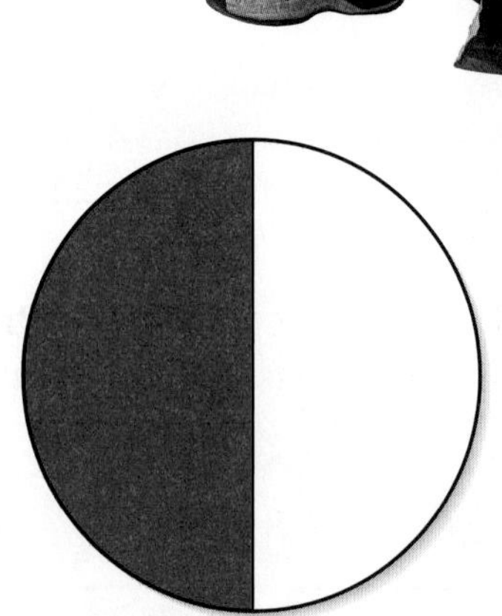

Write in words: one half

Write as a fraction: $\frac{1}{2}$

Write as a decimal: 0.5

Write as a division expression: $1 \div 2$

Use words and symbols to answer the questions.

1. In the fraction $\frac{4}{8}$, which number is the denominator? What does the number mean?
2. How do you express the decimal 0.5 in words?

Reading Test Questions

Use the diagram at the right for Exercises 3–5. Choose the correct answer for each.

3. Which of these statements is unreasonable?

a. Part of the rectangle is red.

b. Most of the rectangle is red.

c. Some of the rectangle is red.

d. Some of the rectangle is blue.

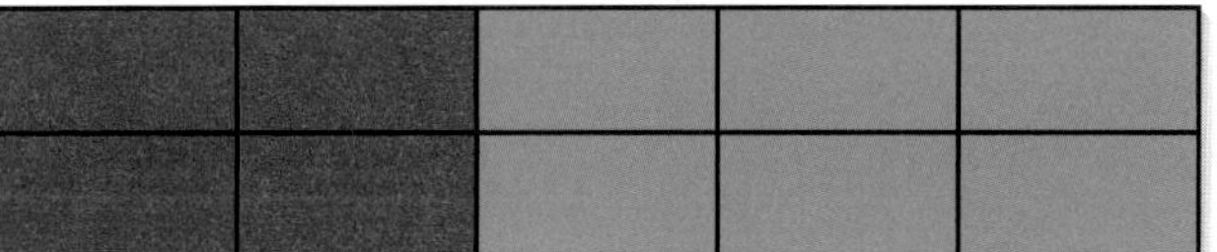

Unreasonable means not reasonable or not possible.

4. Which fraction represents the red part of the rectangle?

a. $\frac{1}{5}$ **c.** $\frac{2}{4}$

b. $\frac{1}{4}$ **d.** $\frac{2}{5}$

Represents means stands for, or shows, or names.

5. Which decimal represents the blue part of the model?

a. 0.3 **c.** 0.5

b. 0.4 **d.** 0.6

A **model** is something that represents, or shows, an idea.

Learning Vocabulary

Watch for these words in this unit. Write their definitions in your journal.

prime number

composite number

prime factorization

greatest common factor (GCF)

least common multiple (LCM)

least common denominator (LCD)

Literature Connection

Read "The Fruitomatic" on pages 642–643. Then work with a partner to answer the questions about the story.

Education Place

At **eduplace.com/map** see *e*Glossary and *e*Games—Math Lingo.

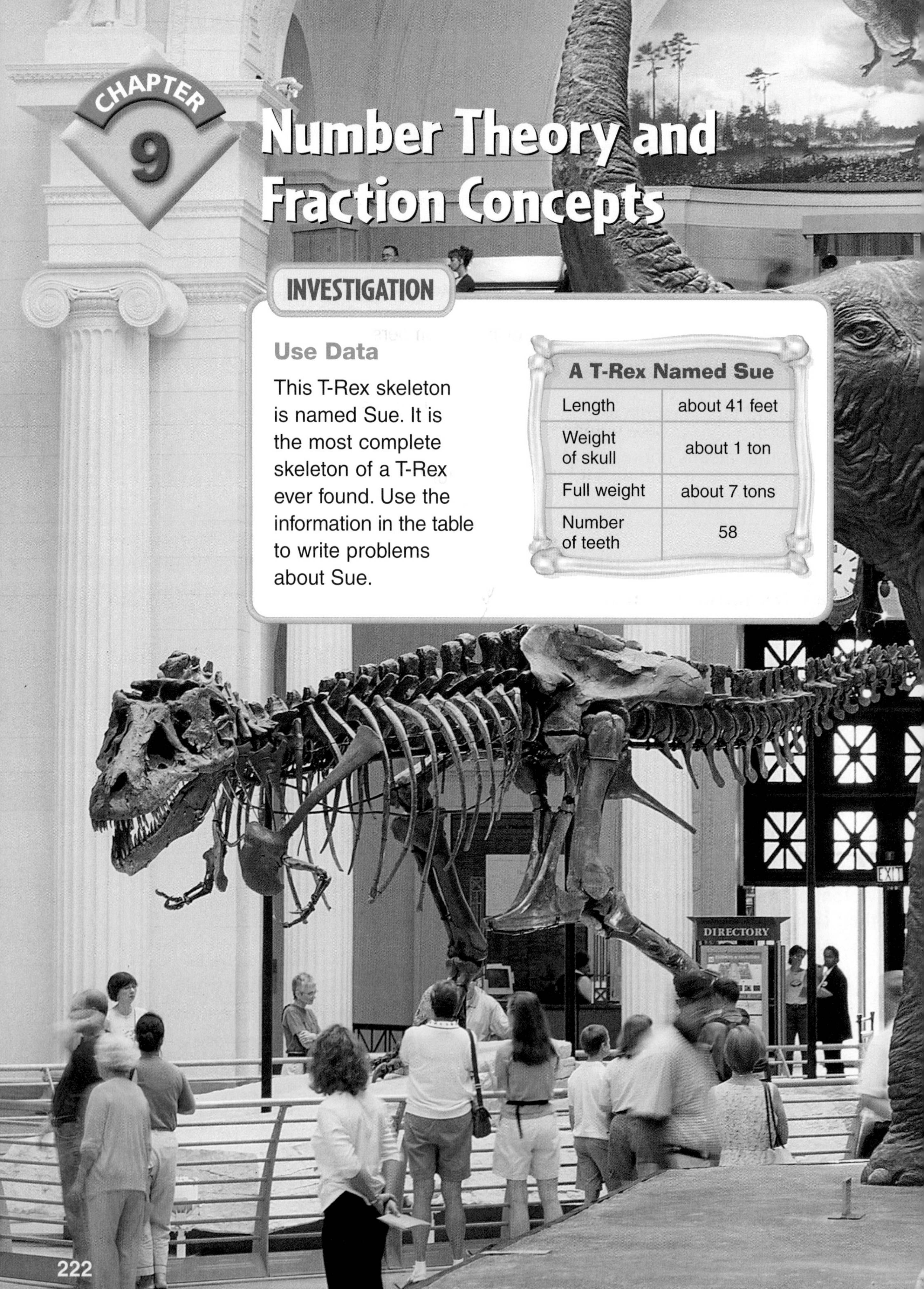

CHAPTER 9

Number Theory and Fraction Concepts

INVESTIGATION

Use Data

This T-Rex skeleton is named Sue. It is the most complete skeleton of a T-Rex ever found. Use the information in the table to write problems about Sue.

A T-Rex Named Sue	
Length	about 41 feet
Weight of skull	about 1 ton
Full weight	about 7 tons
Number of teeth	58

 Use What You Know

Use this page to review and remember what you need to know for this chapter.

VOCABULARY

Choose the best word to complete each sentence.

1. A number that is a factor of two or more numbers is a(n) ____ of those numbers.
2. A number that is a multiple of two or more numbers is a(n) ____ of those numbers.
3. A(n) ____ is a fraction that has a numerator that is greater than or equal to its denominator.

Vocabulary

- common factor
- common multiple
- improper fraction
- mixed number

CONCEPTS AND SKILLS

Write the factors of each number. Then list the first three multiples of each.

4. 2   5. 4   6. 10   7. 20

8. 12   9. 21   10. 11   11. 30

Draw a picture to represent each fraction or mixed number.

12. $\frac{1}{4}$ 13. $\frac{3}{7}$ 14. $\frac{5}{5}$ 15. $1\frac{1}{2}$ 16. $2\frac{1}{4}$

Order the decimals from least to greatest.

17. 0.4, 0.20, 0.02   18. 1.54, 5.51, 5.45   19. 1.0, 0.100, 0.01

20. Do pictures A and B below show the same fraction? Explain.

A. 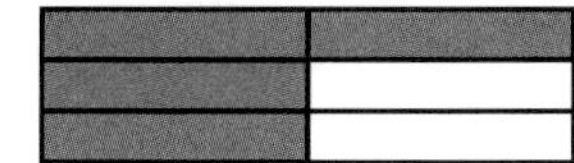

B.      

Facts Practice, See page 663.

Prime and Composite Numbers

Objective Identify prime and composite numbers.

Vocabulary
factors
prime number
composite number

Materials
grid paper

Work Together

Henry is arranging 8 photographs for a museum exhibit. He has been told that each row must contain the same number of photographs. Henry sketched two possible arrangements by drawing squares on grid paper.

How many ways can he arrange the photographs in equal rows?

Work with a partner to solve the problem.

STEP 1 Copy the table below.

Number of Photographs	Arrangements Possible	Factors
1	1 × 1	1
2	1 × 2, 2 × 1	1, 2
3	■	■
4	■	■
5	■	■
6	1 × 6, 6 × 1, 2 × 3, 3 × 2	1, 2, 3, 6
7	■	■
8	■	■

When a number is written as a product of counting numbers, those counting numbers are called **factors**.

STEP 2 Draw squares on grid paper to help you complete the table.

Solution: Henry can arrange the photographs 4 different ways: 1 row of 8, 8 rows of 1, 2 rows of 4, or 4 rows of 2.

A **prime number** is a counting number greater than 1 with exactly two different factors–1 and the number itself.

Which of the numbers from 1 to 8 are prime numbers?

A **composite number** is a counting number that has more than two different factors.

Which of the numbers from 1 to 8 are composite numbers?

On Your Own

Write all the factors of each number. Then identify the number as prime or composite.

1. 17 **2.** 18 **3.** 20 **4.** 23 **5.** 24

6. 26 **7.** 27 **8.** 28 **9.** 29 **10.** 30

Solve.

11. At a science museum, visitors were handed numbered tickets. Tickets with prime numbers won free posters. Which tickets at the right would win posters?

13 75 15 2
52 37 19 7

12. Look back at page 224. How many different ways could Henry have arranged 20 photographs? Use factors to explain your answer.

13. Melina has 45 photographs. She wants to arrange them in equal rows. In how many ways can she arrange them?

14. The science museum has 80 stones available for display in equal rows. How many different arrangements of these stones can be made if each row must contain at least 8 stones?

15. The director of the art museum has between 45 and 55 paintings to display. She wishes to display an equal number on each of two walls. How many paintings could the museum display? Give as many answers as possible.

Talk About It • Write About It

16. Use the definitions of *prime number* and *composite number* above to explain why the number 1 is neither prime nor composite.

17. There is only one prime number that is not an odd number. Which number is it? Tell how you know.

18. Explain how you can use the rules for divisibility to find factors of a number.

Lesson 2

Audio Tutor 1/25 Listen and Understand

Prime Factorization

Objective Write the prime factorization of a number.

Vocabulary
prime factorization

Learn About It

$10 = 2 \times 5$

10 ↑ composite; 2 ↑ prime; 5 ↑ prime

Any composite number can be written as a product of prime numbers. An expression written as a product of prime factors is called the **prime factorization** of the number.

You can use a factor tree to find the prime factorization of a number.

Write the prime factorization of 45.

STEP 1 Write 45 as the product of two numbers.

45

5 × 9

STEP 2 Write each composite factor as a product of two numbers until only prime numbers are obtained.

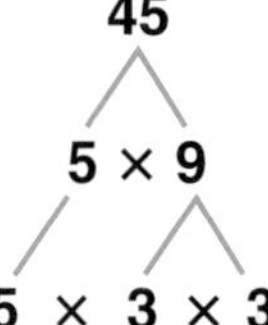

STEP 3 Write the prime factors from the bottom row of the factor tree in order. Use exponents to write the prime factorization.

$45 = 3 \times 3 \times 5$

$= 3^2 \times 5$

Solution: The prime factorization of 45 is $3^2 \times 5$.

Guided Practice

Complete each factor tree. Then write the prime factorization. Use exponents if possible.

1. 10

2 × ■

2.

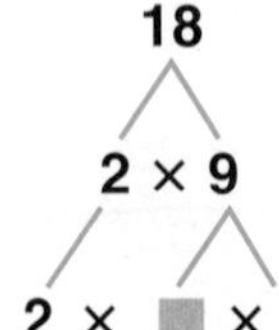

3.

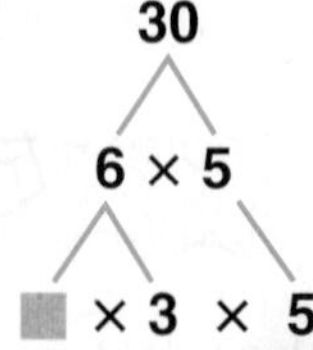

Ask Yourself

- What basic multiplication fact do I use?
- Can I use exponents to write the prime factorization?

Explain Your Thinking ▶ Look back at Exercise 2. If you used 3 and 6 for the first factor pair, would the prime factorization be the same? Why or why not?

Practice and Problem Solving

Complete the factor tree. Then write the prime factorization.

4. 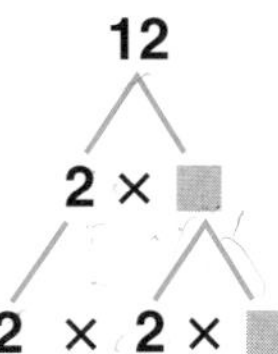

5. 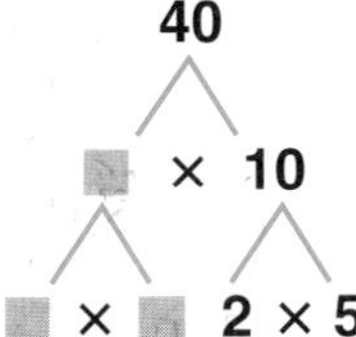

6. 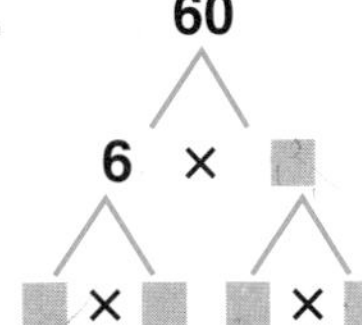

Write the prime factorization of each number. Use exponents if possible. If the number is prime, write *prime*.

7. 2 **8.** 3 **9.** 4 **10.** 5 **11.** 6 **12.** 7

13. 8 **14.** 9 **15.** 10 **16.** 11 **17.** 12 **18.** 13

19. 14 **20.** 15 **21.** 16 **22.** 17 **23.** 18 **24.** 19

 **Algebra • Expressions** **The variable *p* stands for a prime number. Make a factor tree. Then write the prime factorization without exponents for each expression.**

25. $6p$ **26.** $50p$ **27.** p^2 **28.** $2p^2$ **29.** $13p^2$ **30.** $12p^3$

Solve.

31. You are told that the prime factorization of a number is $2 \times 3^2 \times 5 \times 7 \times 13$. What is the number?

32. For any composite number, why does the last row of its factor tree contain only prime numbers?

33. The price of a painting was $12,000 in 1980, $36,000 in 1990, and $108,000 in 2000. If the pattern continues, what is the price likely to be in 2010?

34. Each of two composite numbers has 2, 3, and 5 in its prime factorization, but one of the numbers is twice as large as the other. What might the numbers be?

35. Write About It What does the factor tree of a prime number look like? Use an example to explain.

36. Takala designs a box for paint cans. The box is 2 cans high, 6 cans long, and 3 cans wide. How many cans fit in the box?

Mixed Review and Test Prep

Open Response

Write each number in expanded form with exponents. (Ch. 1, Lesson 2)

37. 36,519 **38.** 602,708 **39.** 562,412

40. Write the prime factorization of 140. (Ch. 9, Lesson 2)

Show how you got your answer.

Extra Practice See page 253, Set A.

Lesson 3

Audio Tutor 1/26 Listen and Understand

Greatest Common Factor

Objective Find common factors and the greatest common factor of two numbers.

Vocabulary

common factor

greatest common factor (GCF)

greatest common divisor (GCD)

Learn About It

If a number is a factor of two or more counting numbers, it is called a **common factor** of those numbers. The **greatest common factor (GCF)** of two or more numbers is the common factor that is greater than any other common factor.

You are to arrange 32 Egyptian statues and 40 Chinese statues in groups. Each group must have the same number of statues, and all be from one country. What is the greatest number of statues you can put in each group?

Since 32 = 2 × 16 and 40 = 2 × 20, I could put 2 statues in each group. Can the groups be larger?

Find the greatest common factor of 32 and 40.

Different Ways to Find the GCF of 32 and 40

Think about factor pairs.
32 = 1 × 32
32 = 2 × 16
32 = 4 × 8

Way 1 You can make a list.

STEP 1	List all the factors of each number.	Factors of 32: 1, 2, 4, 8, 16, 32 Factors of 40: 1, 2, 4, 5, 8, 10, 20, 40
STEP 2	Identify common factors.	The common factors are 1, 2, 4, and 8.
STEP 3	Compare to find the greatest common factor.	The greatest common factor of 32 and 40 is 8.

Way 2 You can use prime factorization.

STEP 1 Make factor trees for 32 and 40.

STEP 2 Identify all the common prime factors.

STEP 3 The product of the common prime factors is the GCF. The GCF is 8.

32
4 × 8
2 × 2 × 4 × 2
2 × 2 × 2 × 2 × 2

40
2 × 20
2 × 2 × 10
2 × 2 × 2 × 5

32 = (2) × (2) × (2) × 2 × 2
40 = (2) × (2) × (2) × 5

The GCF is $2 \times 2 \times 2 = 2^3 = 8$.

Solution: You can put 8 statues at most in each group.

Since each common factor of two or more numbers is a divisor of each number, the GCF often is called the **greatest common divisor (GCD)**.

Other Examples

A. GCF of Greater Numbers

Find the GCF of 160 and 200.

Write each prime factorization.

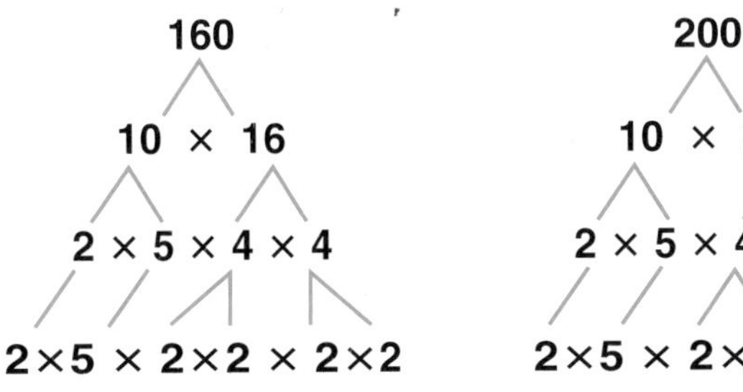

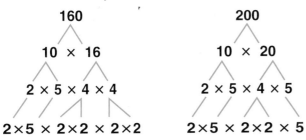

Ring common factors

$160 = 2 \times 2 \times 2 \times 2 \times 2 \times 5$
$200 = 2 \times 2 \times 2 \times 5 \times 5$

The GCF of 160 and 200 is $2^3 \times 5$, or 40.

B. GCF is 1

Find the GCF of 21 and 26.

List the factors of each number.

Factors of 21: 1, 3, 7, 21
Factors of 26: 1, 2, 13, 26

1 is the only common factor.

The GCF is 1.

Guided Practice

List the factors of each number. Then find the greatest common factor (GCF) of the numbers.

1. 9, 27 **2.** 15, 22 **3.** 20, 28

Write the prime factorization of each number using exponents. Then find the greatest common factor (GCF) of the numbers.

4. 10, 45 **5.** 45, 100 **6.** 16, 100

Ask Yourself

- What are the factors of each number?
- Did I find all the common factors?

Explain Your Thinking ▶ Why is the prime factorization a good way to find the GCF of two large numbers?

Practice and Problem Solving

List the factors of each number. Then find the GCF of the numbers.

7. 14, 22 **8.** 30, 55 **9.** 10, 12 **10.** 9, 25 **11.** 15, 17

12. 20, 38 **13.** 26, 34 **14.** 13, 19 **15.** 12, 24 **16.** 36, 45

Go On

Write the prime factorization of each number using exponents. Then find the GCF of the numbers.

17. 10, 24 **18.** 6, 15 **19.** 9, 28 **20.** 10, 55 **21.** 12, 42

22. 75, 120 **23.** 20, 125 **24.** 35, 105 **25.** 10, 240 **26.** 30, 150

x Algebra • Variables Give three possible values for *n*.

	Numbers	GCF
27.	9, n	3
28.	16, n	4
29.	20, n	5

	Numbers	GCF
30.	36, n	12
31.	50, n	10
32.	72, n	18

Solve.

33. A display shows five paintings. "Red River" is immediately to the right of "Blue Bayou." "Green Grass" is not first. "Pink Plateaus" is in the middle. "Orange Outback" is at the far right. List the paintings in order from left to right.

35. Measurement Computers in the research room of the history museum are 30 inches wide, 30 inches apart, and, at either end of a row, 30 inches from the wall. How many computers can fit across a room that is 25 feet wide?

37. The GCF of an odd number and an even number is 17. The greater number is 51. Find the other number.

38. Write About It If two numbers are prime, is their GCF always 1? Support your answer with examples.

34. An artist had 45 pieces of turquoise and 60 cat's eye marbles. Each sculpture she made contained the same number of each kind of stone and more than one of each. What is the greatest number of sculptures she could have made?

36. The museum is arranging 42 plates from the 1800s and 64 plates from the 1900s in equal groups. All plates in each group must be from the same century. What is the greatest number of plates they can put in each group?

Mixed Review and Test Prep

Open Response

Divide. (Ch. 5, Lesson 5)

39. 6,229 ÷ 27 **40.** 54,907 ÷ 69

41. 39,524 ÷ 82 **42.** 62,424 ÷ 47

Multiple Choice

43. Find the GCF of 24 and 36.
(Ch. 9, Lesson 3)

A 6 **C** 12

B 8 **D** 18

Extra Practice See page 253, Set B.

Number Sense

The Sieve of Eratosthenes

In the third century B.C., Eratosthenes, a Greek mathematician, developed a method for finding prime numbers.

Follow these steps to find the prime numbers from 1 to 100.

- Copy the table at the right.
- Cross out 1, since 1 is not a prime.
- Circle 2 because 2 is a prime. Cross out all the multiples of 2.
- Go to the next number that is not crossed out. Circle it. Then cross out its multiples.
- Repeat the previous step until all the numbers are either circled or crossed out.

Explain how you know that the circled numbers are prime numbers.

Sieve of Eratosthenes

1	2	3	4	5	6	7	8	9	10
11	12	13	14	15	16	17	18	19	20
21	22	23	24	25	26	27	28	29	30
31	32	33	34	35	36	37	38	39	40
41	42	43	44	45	46	47	48	49	50
51	52	53	54	55	56	57	58	59	60
61	62	63	64	65	66	67	68	69	70
71	72	73	74	75	76	77	78	79	80
81	82	83	84	85	86	87	88	89	90
91	92	93	94	95	96	97	98	99	100

Number Sense

Twin Primes

Prime numbers with a difference of 2 are called twin primes. The numbers 3 and 5 are twin primes. List all pairs of twin primes between 1 and 99.

Brain Teaser

A three-digit number greater than 500 has five consecutive numbers among its factors. What could the three-digit number be?

Education Place

Check out **eduplace.com/map** for more Brain Teasers.

Lesson 4

Least Common Multiple

Objective Find common multiples and the least common multiple of two or more numbers.

Vocabulary
multiple
common multiple
least common multiple (LCM)

Learn About It

A **multiple** of a number is the product of the number and any counting number. If a number is a multiple of two or more numbers, it is called a **common multiple** of the numbers.

The **least common multiple (LCM)** of two or more numbers is the common multiple that is less than all other common multiples.

In a museum, the sculpture garden has a new show every 9 months. The sculpture gallery has a new show every 12 months. Suppose the garden and the gallery have new shows that begin today. How long will it be until they have new shows that begin on the same day again?

Find the LCM of 9 and 12.

When do new shows begin in the sculpture garden?
List some multiples of 9. — 9: 9, 18, 27, 36, 45, 54, 63, 72

When do new shows begin in the sculpture gallery?
List some multiples of 12. — 12: 12, 24, 36, 48, 60, 72

When do new shows begin in both sculpture areas?
List the common multiples. — 36, 72

How long will it be until both sculpture areas have new shows on the same day again? — The LCM is 36.

Solution: The sculpture garden and the sculpture gallery will have new shows begin on the same day in 36 months.

Other Examples

A. LCM is One of the Numbers Itself

Find the LCM of 2 and 6.

Multiples of 2: 2, 4, **6,** 8, 10, **12,** 14,...

Multiples of 6: **6, 12,** 18, 24, 30...

The LCM of 2 and 6 is 6.

B. LCM of Greater Numbers

Find the LCM of 10 and 25.

Multiples of 10: 10, 20, 30, 40, **50,**...

Multiples of 25: 25, **50,** 75, **100,**...

The LCM of 10 and 25 is 50.

You can use prime factorization to find the LCM.

Find the LCM of 45 and 55.

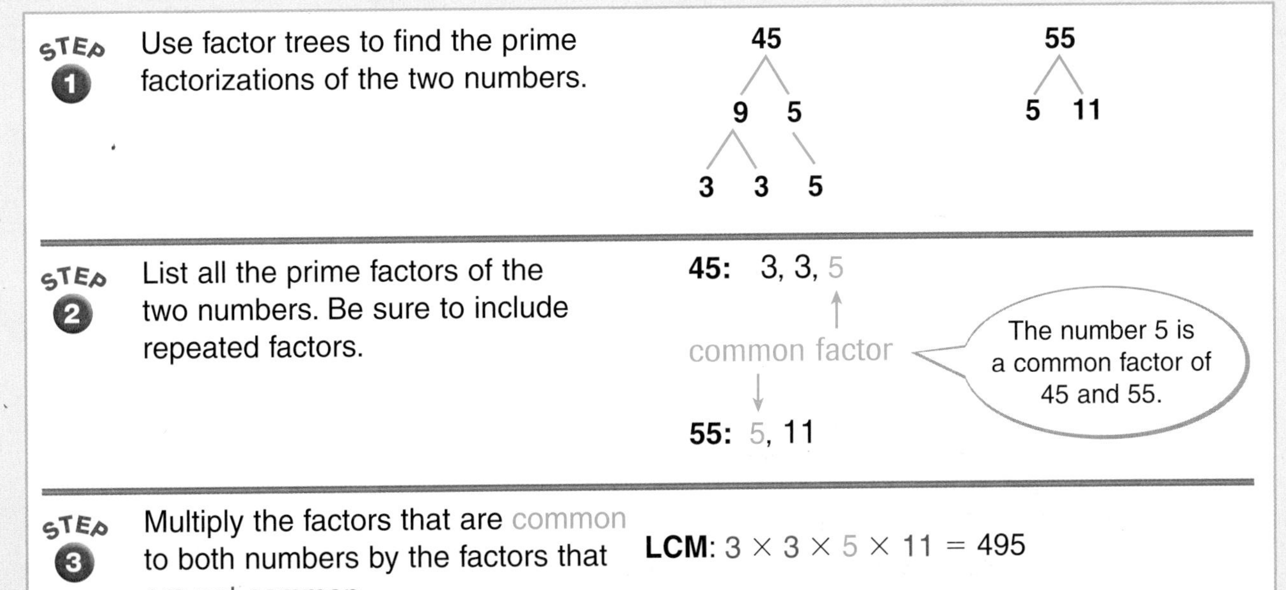

STEP 1
Use factor trees to find the prime factorizations of the two numbers.
45
9 5
3 3 5
55
5 11
STEP 2
List all the prime factors of the two numbers. Be sure to include repeated factors.
45: 3, 3, 5
common factor
55: 5, 11
The number 5 is a common factor of 45 and 55.
STEP 3
Multiply the factors that are common to both numbers by the factors that are not common.
LCM: 3 × 3 × 5 × 11 = 495

Solution: The LCM of 45 and 55 is 495.

Other Examples

A. No Common Prime Factors

Find the LCM of 6 and 49.

Prime factors of 6: 2, 3

Prime factors of 49: 7, 7

LCM $= 2 \times 3 \times 7 \times 7 = 294$

The LCM of 6 and 49 is 294.

B. LCM of Greater Numbers

Find the LCM of 84 and 120.

$84 = 2 \times 2 \times 3 \times 7$

$120 = 2 \times 2 \times 2 \times 3 \times 5$

LCM $= 2 \times 2 \times 2 \times 3 \times 5 \times 7 = 840$

The LCM of 84 and 120 is 840.

Guided Practice

Ask Yourself

- Did I list enough multiples of both numbers?
- Is my answer a multiple of both numbers?

List multiples to find the LCM.

1. 5, 20 **2.** 18, 24

3. 12, 30 **4.** 21, 28

Use prime factorization to find the LCM.

5. 20, 25 **6.** 17, 51

7. 100, 288 **8.** 30, 45

Explain Your Thinking ▶ How can you use division to check if a number is a common multiple of two numbers?

Go On

Practice and Problem Solving

Write the first five multiples of each number.

9. 8	**10.** 14	**11.** 7	**12.** 25	**13.** 15
14. 12	**15.** 11	**16.** 30	**17.** 18	**18.** 24

Write the prime factorization of each number.

19. 9	**20.** 6	**21.** 4	**22.** 8	**23.** 10
24. 15	**25.** 20	**26.** 12	**27.** 25	**28.** 16

Find the LCM of the numbers in each pair.

29. 5, 9	**30.** 4, 10	**31.** 2, 11	**32.** 3, 15	**33.** 10, 12
34. 15, 20	**35.** 16, 32	**36.** 12, 18	**37.** 18, 27	**38.** 7, 13
39. 16, 18	**40.** 24, 72	**41.** 36, 48	**42.** 16, 80	**43.** 40, 50

Solve.

44. The museum has tours every 75 minutes. A video about mobiles begins every 45 minutes. The tour and the video both start at 10:00 A.M. When will they start at the same time again?

45. A sculpture has a gong that strikes every 6 minutes, a whistle that blows every 8 minutes, and a bell that rings every 12 minutes. How often will you hear all three sounds at the same time?

Use the following information to solve Problems 46–48.

A museum is building a brick wall on one side of an exhibit. The wall is made of 8-inch and 10-inch bricks. Whenever the ends of the bricks align, a vertical decorative divider is placed in the wall.

46. There is a decorative divider used at the beginning of the wall. How far from that first divider will the next divider be placed?

47. The brick part of the wall is 10 feet long. There is a decorative divider at the beginning and at the end of the wall. How many decorative dividers will be used in all?

48. Suppose 8-inch, 10-inch, and 12-inch bricks are used as shown at the right. Then how far from that first divider will the next divider be?

Extra Practice See page 253, Set C.

Open Response

Write each number in standard form.
(Ch. 1, Lesson 2)

49. $(5 \times 10^4) + (2 \times 10^3) + (8 \times 10^1)$

50. $(7 \times 10^5) + (4 \times 10^2) + (9 \times 10^0)$

51. Mai says the LCM of 20 and 30 is 10. José says it is 60. Who is correct? Why? (Ch. 9, Lesson 4)

Activity

Math Challenge

Riddle Me This

What is the easiest way to make a bandstand?

Copy the table at the right. Find the least common multiple for each pair of numbers. Then use the key to decode the puzzle. Read down the last column to find the answer to the riddle.

Decoding Key:

LCM	Letter
8	R
10	I
12	Y
15	K
16	W
18	T
20	E

LCM	Letter
22	D
24	A
26	S
28	X
30	H
40	C
48	M

Numbers	LCM	Letter
6, 9	18	T
12, 8	■	■
3, 5	■	■
4, 10	■	■
3, 18	■	■
2, 15	■	■
5, 4	■	■
10, 8	■	■
6, 10	■	■
24, 4	■	■
5, 2	■	■
8, 4	■	■
13, 2	■	■
6, 8	■	■
16, 4	■	■
8, 24	■	■
6, 4	■	■

Lesson 5

Fractions and Mixed Numbers

Objective Write fractions and mixed numbers.

Vocabulary
unit fraction
improper fraction
mixed number

Learn About It

Some museums and other historic buildings have beautiful stained glass windows.

A fraction can represent part of a set.

$\frac{1}{3}$ of the glass panels are blue.

A fraction can represent part of a whole.

$\frac{3}{4}$ of the center panel is orange.

A unit fraction has a numerator of 1.

$\frac{1}{3}$ is a unit fraction. $\frac{3}{4}$ is not a unit fraction.

Any fraction can be thought of as a division problem. For example, when 2 units are separated into 3 equal parts, each is $\frac{2}{3}$ of 1 unit.

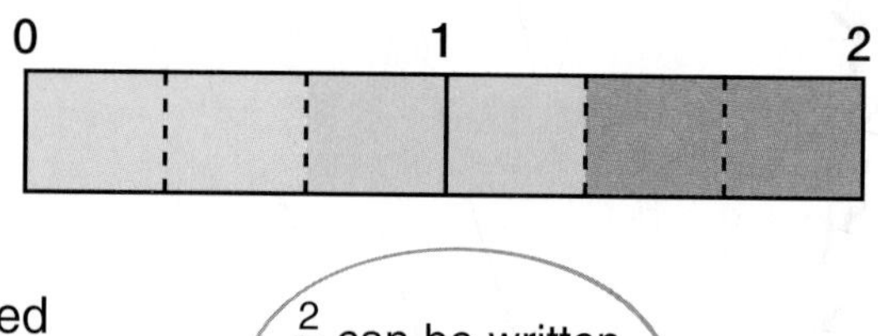

$\frac{2}{3}$ can be written as $2 \div 3$ or $3\overline{)2}$

You can represent fractions on a number line.

If intervals of length 1 on the number line are separated into 3 equal pieces, the length of any one of the pieces represents $\frac{1}{3}$.

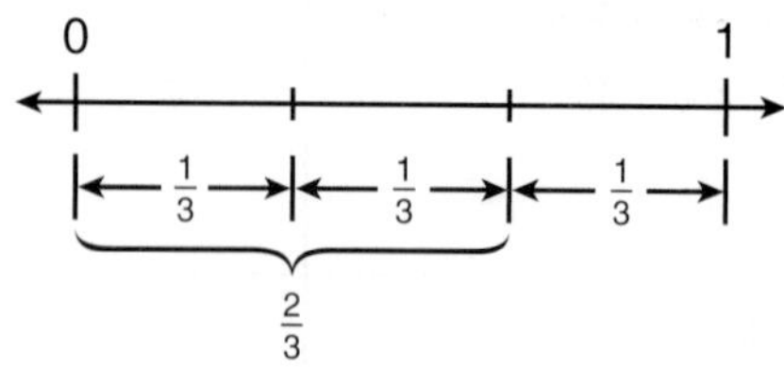

A fraction is written $\frac{a}{b}$ where a and b are whole numbers and $b \neq 0$. The fraction $\frac{2}{3}$ means 2 unit fractions of $\frac{1}{3}$.

Fractions can be used to label many points on a number line.

This number line is labeled with $\frac{0}{3}, \frac{1}{3}, \frac{2}{3}, \ldots$

The number line shows that $\frac{0}{3} = 0$, $\frac{3}{3} = 1$, $\frac{6}{3} = 2$, and $\frac{9}{3} = 3$.

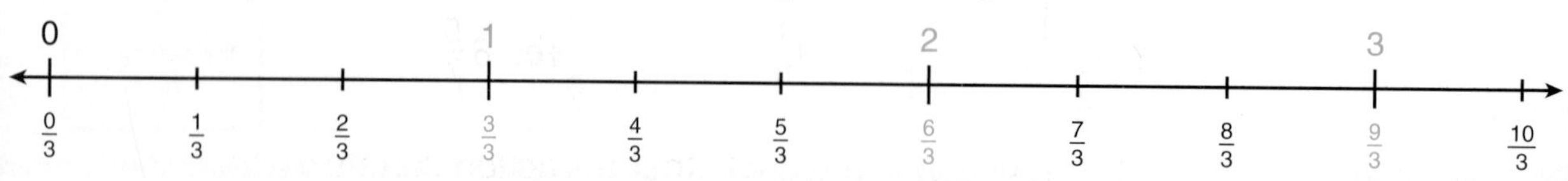

An **improper fraction** has a numerator that is greater than or equal to its denominator. Numbers like $\frac{3}{3}$ and $\frac{4}{3}$ are improper fractions.

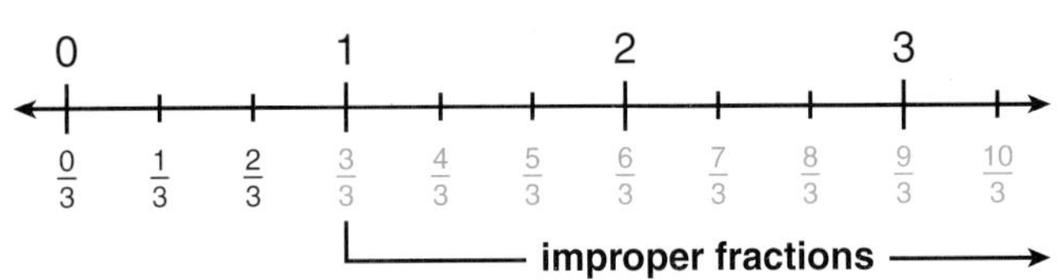

Improper fractions can be written as whole numbers or **mixed numbers**. A mixed number is the sum of a whole number and a fraction.

Here's how to change from one to another.

To change an improper fraction to a mixed number, you can divide.

The fraction bar stands for "divided by." So $\frac{9}{4}$ means "9 divided by 4."

$$\begin{array}{r} 2 \\ 4\overline{)9} \\ -8 \\ \hline 1 \end{array}$$

2 ← number of wholes

1 ← number of fourths

So $\frac{9}{4}$ is equal to $2\frac{1}{4}$.

To change a mixed number to an improper fraction, you can multiply and add.

$$2\frac{1}{4} = \frac{9}{4}$$

+ ×

← $(4 \times 2) + 1$

← denominator stays the same

The shortcut shows $2\frac{1}{4}$ means $2 + \frac{1}{4} = \frac{8}{4} + \frac{1}{4} = \frac{9}{4}$. So $2\frac{1}{4} = \frac{9}{4}$.

Guided Practice

Ask Yourself

- How can I use division to find or check my answers?

1. Study the number line below. Write each missing fraction. Then draw a picture to represent each missing fraction.

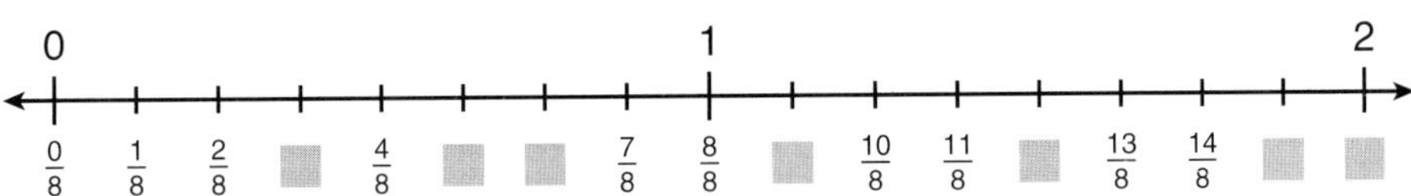

Write each improper fraction as a mixed number or a whole number.

2. $\frac{7}{2}$ **3.** $\frac{3}{2}$ **4.** $\frac{8}{2}$ **5.** $\frac{5}{2}$ **6.** $\frac{10}{2}$

Write each mixed number as an improper fraction.

7. $4\frac{1}{2}$ **8.** $7\frac{1}{2}$ **9.** $3\frac{1}{8}$ **10.** $6\frac{5}{7}$ **11.** $4\frac{2}{3}$

Explain Your Thinking ▶ How can you tell whether a fraction can be written as a mixed number or a whole number?

Go On

Practice and Problem Solving

12. Study the number line below. Write each missing fraction. Then draw different models to represent each fraction you wrote.

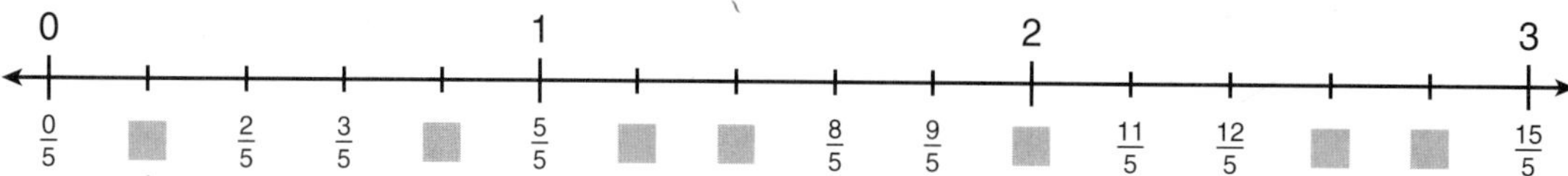

Write each improper fraction as a mixed number or a whole number.

13. $\frac{10}{5}$ **14.** $\frac{8}{5}$ **15.** $\frac{15}{7}$ **16.** $\frac{9}{4}$ **17.** $\frac{12}{5}$

Write each mixed number as an improper fraction.

18. $2\frac{3}{4}$ **19.** $2\frac{3}{5}$ **20.** $5\frac{2}{3}$ **21.** $4\frac{2}{7}$ **22.** $6\frac{1}{6}$

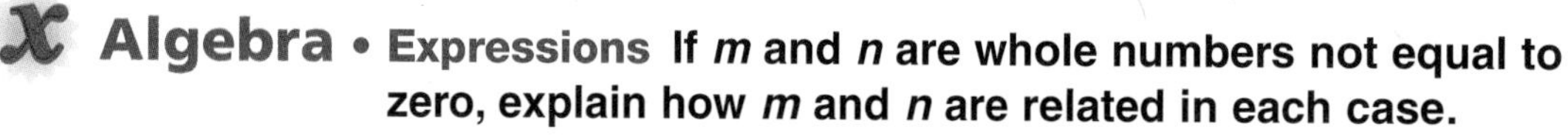

Algebra • Expressions If *m* and *n* are whole numbers not equal to zero, explain how *m* and *n* are related in each case.

23. $\frac{m}{n}$ is a fraction between 0 and 1.

24. $\frac{m}{n}$ is a fraction between 1 and 2.

25. $\frac{m}{n}$ is equal to a whole number.

Solve.

26. A totem pole is made of 8 equal sections. Three sections have been painted. Write a fraction to show the part of the totem pole that is not painted.

27. The total value of paintings by Pablo Picasso sold at auctions is over 1.3 billion dollars. Is this number an exact figure or an estimate? How do you know?

28. What division expression is equivalent to the fraction $\frac{37}{4}$? How can you use this expression to write a mixed number for $\frac{37}{4}$?

29. Show each mixed number on the same number line. Then write each as an improper fraction.

a. $2\frac{2}{3}$ **b.** $4\frac{1}{3}$ **c.** $1\frac{2}{3}$

30. Measurement Roberto has had his newspaper route for $3\frac{3}{4}$ years. Write $3\frac{3}{4}$ as an improper fraction. How many months is this?

31. Create and Solve Write a problem that uses mixed numbers and improper fractions. Solve your problem. Then give it to a partner to solve.

Extra Practice See page 253, Set D.

Problem Solving

Visual Thinking

Are Halves Always the Same?

The pictures show three pizzas.

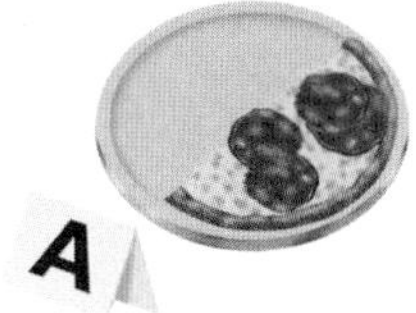

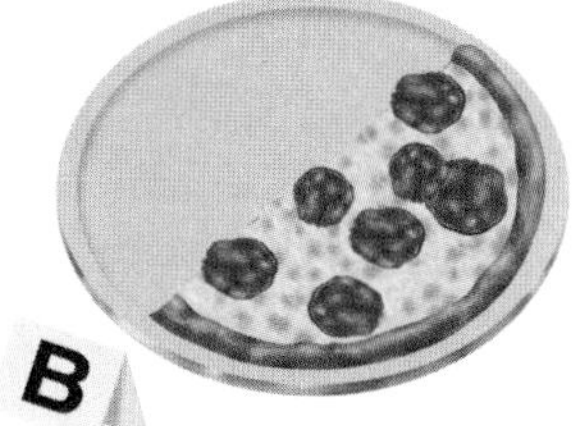

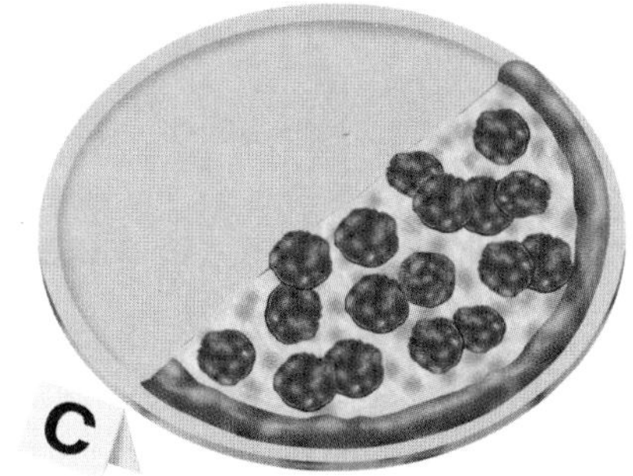

1. What fraction of each pizza is left?
2. Compare the amount of pizza that is left in each pan. Is $\frac{1}{2}$ of pizza A the same amount as $\frac{1}{2}$ of pizza C? Explain.
3. How does the value of a fraction depend on the size of the region or set that it describes?

Quick Check

Check your understanding of Lessons 1–5.

Write all the factors of each number. Then identify the number as prime or composite. (Lesson 1)

1. 19
2. 48
3. 41

Write the prime factorization of each number. Then find the greatest common factor (GCF) of the numbers. (Lessons 2–3)

4. 20, 32
5. 21, 24
6. 36, 54

Find the LCM of the numbers. (Lesson 4)

7. 18, 30
8. 12, 16
9. 15, 60

Use the number line for Exercise 10. (Lesson 5)

10. Write each missing fraction.

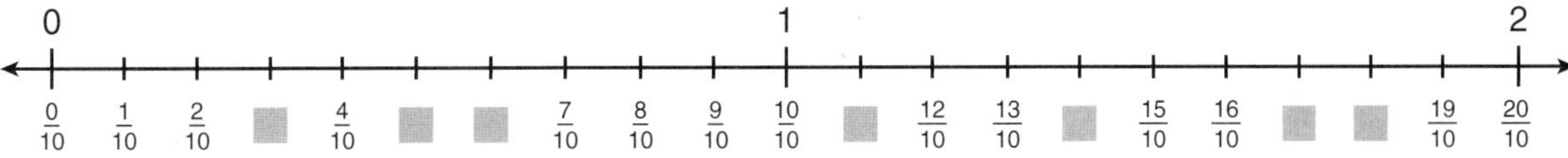

Lesson 6

Audio Tutor 1/27 Listen and Understand

Equivalent Fractions and Simplest Form

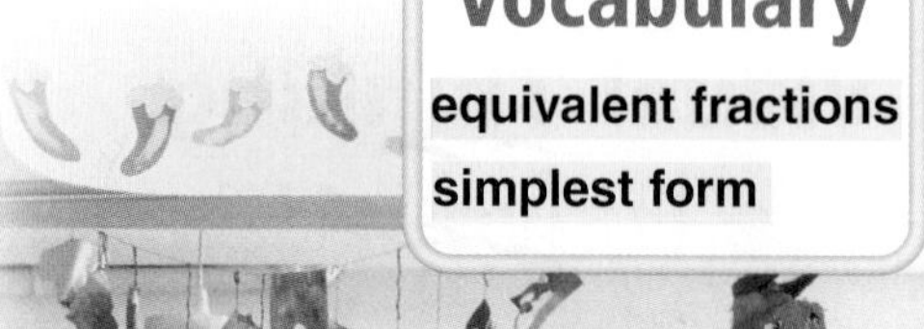

Vocabulary

equivalent fractions

simplest form

Objective Find equivalent fractions and write fractions in simplest form.

Learn About It

Equivalent fractions are fractions that name the same number.

Four sixths of the 12 art club members helped decorate for a Cinco de Mayo party. Did two thirds of the members help?

Find two equivalent fractions for $\frac{2}{3}$.

Different Ways to Find Equivalent Fractions

Way 1 You can use number lines.

$\frac{4}{6}$, $\frac{8}{12}$, and $\frac{2}{3}$ are equivalent fractions.

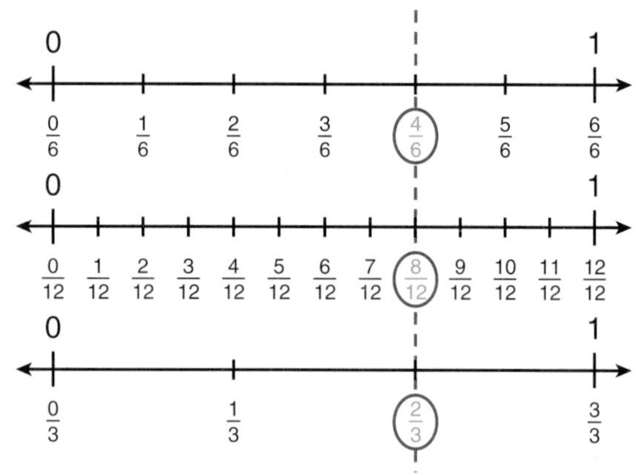

Way 2 You can multiply.

Find the number to multiply the denominator by to obtain the new denominator. Multiply by that number.

$$\frac{4 \times 2}{6 \times 2} = \frac{8}{12}$$

$\frac{4}{6}$ and $\frac{8}{12}$ are equivalent fractions.

Way 3 You can divide.

Find the number to divide the denominator by to obtain the new denominator. Divide by that number.

$$\frac{4 \div 2}{6 \div 2} = \frac{2}{3}$$

$\frac{4}{6}$ and $\frac{2}{3}$ are equivalent fractions.

Solution: Two thirds of the art club (eight members) volunteered to decorate the cafeteria.

Extra Help at eduplace.com/map

▶ A fraction is in **simplest form** when the GCF of its numerator and denominator is 1.

Different Ways to Find Simplest Form

Way 1 **You can divide the numerator and the denominator by the GCF of the numbers.**

$12 = 2 \times 2 \times 3$
$18 = 2 \times 3 \times 3$

The GCF of 12 and 18 is 2×3, or 6.

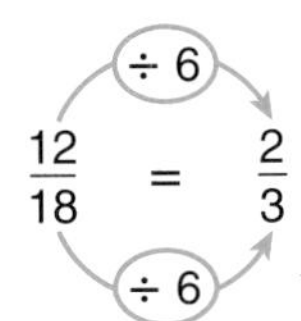

$\frac{12}{18} = \frac{2}{3}$ (÷ 6)

Way 2 **You can cancel common factors.**

Write the prime factorization of the numerator and the denominator. Then cancel common factors.

$\frac{12}{18} = \frac{\cancel{2} \times 2 \times \cancel{3}}{\cancel{2} \times \cancel{3} \times 3} = \frac{2}{3}$

Think $\frac{2}{2} = 1$, $\frac{3}{3} = 1$

Guided Practice

Complete.

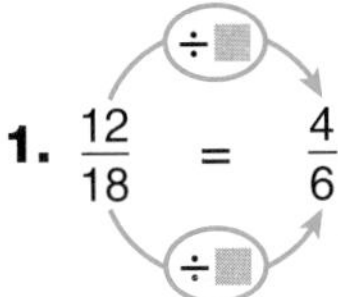

1. $\frac{12}{18} = \frac{4}{6}$ (÷ ■)

2. $\frac{21}{12} = \frac{■}{4}$ (÷ ■)

3. $\frac{4}{9} = \frac{■}{54}$

Ask Yourself

- Did I multiply or divide the numerator and denominator by the same number?

Explain Your Thinking ▶ In Exercise 3, how did you decide whether to multiply or divide to find the missing numerator?

Practice and Problem Solving

Complete.

4. $\frac{1}{3} = \frac{■}{9}$
5. $\frac{15}{35} = \frac{■}{7}$
6. $\frac{3}{10} = \frac{9}{■}$
7. $1\frac{3}{12} = \frac{■}{4}$
8. $4 = \frac{■}{6}$

Simplify each fraction.

9. $\frac{5}{10}$
10. $\frac{39}{15}$
11. $\frac{15}{18}$
12. $\frac{26}{18}$
13. $\frac{28}{42}$
14. $\frac{22}{30}$

15. **Write About It** How many equivalent fractions can be written for any given fraction? Explain.

16. The art club has 6 girls. If $\frac{3}{5}$ of the members are girls, how many members does the club have? Explain.

Mixed Review and Test Prep

Open Response

Find the mean, median, mode, and range.
(Ch. 8, Lesson 2)

17. 24, 28, 24, 32
18. 8, 20, 6, 20, 101

Multiple Choice

19. Simplify $\frac{30}{42}$. (Ch. 9, Lesson 6)

A $\frac{5}{8}$ **B** $\frac{5}{7}$ **C** $\frac{3}{4}$ **D** $\frac{6}{7}$

Extra Practice See page 253, Set E.

Lesson 7

Audio Tutor 1/28 Listen and Understand

Problem-Solving Strategy

Use Logical Reasoning

Objective Use logical reasoning and Venn diagrams to solve a problem.

Problem The LCM of two numbers, *x* and *y*, is 210. Their GCF is 3. The numbers differ by 9. What are the numbers?

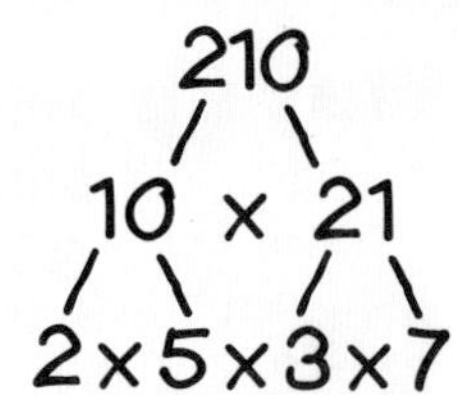

UNDERSTAND

This is what you know:

- The LCM is 210.
- The GCF is 3.
- The numbers differ by 9.

Remember The GCF must be a factor of both numbers. The LCM must contain all the prime factors of both numbers.

PLAN

You can use logic to analyze the information you have.

SOLVE

Make a Venn diagram to represent the factors of the two numbers, *x* and *y*.

- Write the common factor 3 in both circles.

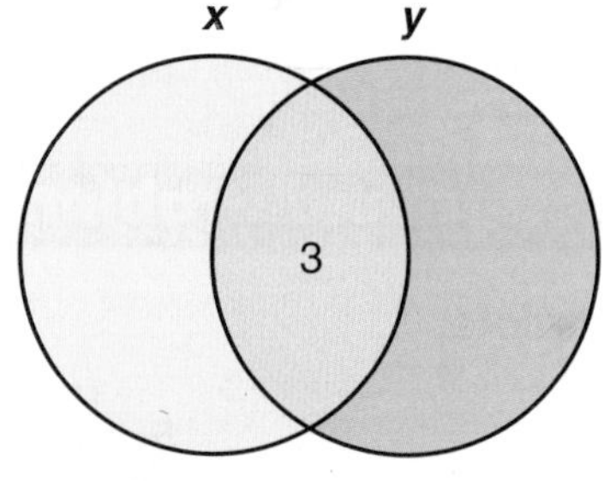

- Factor the LCM to find all the factors of both numbers, *x* and *y*.

$$210 = 2 \times 3 \times 5 \times 7$$

If 3 is the GCF, then 2, 5, and 7 cannot be common factors.

- Try different arrangements of factors.

Look for the pair of numbers with a difference of 9.

Solution: The numbers are 21 and 30.

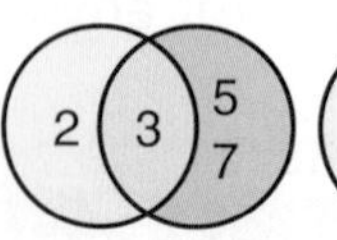

6 and 105

5 | 3 | 2, 7

15 and 42

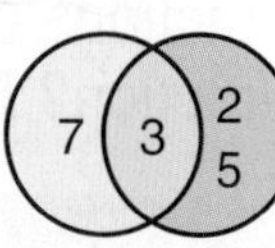

21 and 30

LOOK BACK

Look back at the problem. Does your answer meet all the given conditions?

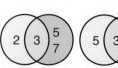

Guided Practice

Use the Ask Yourself questions to help you solve each problem.

1. The LCM of two numbers is 60. One of the numbers is 20. The other number is even and has only two prime factors. What is the other number?

2. The GCF of two numbers is 12. Both of these numbers are greater than 12 and both are less than 40. What are the numbers?

   Hint Think about how you can use the GCF to find possible answers. Check those answers to see if they fit with the other information in the problem.

Ask Yourself

UNDERSTAND **What facts do I know?**

PLAN **How can I organize what I know so that I can use logical thinking?**

SOLVE
- **Can I draw a Venn diagram?**
- **Did I label the parts of my diagram?**
- **Did I find the factors of the two numbers?**

How can I check the answer?

Independent Practice

Use logical reasoning to solve each problem.

3. The LCM of two numbers is 120. The GCF of the same two numbers is 4. The sum of the numbers is 44. What are the numbers?

4. The LCM of two numbers is 360. The GCF of two numbers is 8. The numbers differ by 32. What are the numbers?

5. A number is called "perfect" if it equals the sum all of its factors except the number itself. Factors of 6: 1, 2, 3, 6; $1 + 2 + 3 = 6$. Find all the perfect numbers greater than 0 and less than 40.

6. For fraction $\frac{a}{b}$, $b - a = 9$ and $a \times b = 90$. Find the fraction. Explain how you can use a factor tree and a Venn diagram to help you solve the problem.

7. Fraction $\frac{c}{d}$ is equivalent to $\frac{4}{14}$, and $c + d = 27$. Find fraction $\frac{c}{d}$.

8. Fraction $\frac{e}{f}$ is equivalent to $\frac{5}{6}$, and $f - e = 7$. Find fraction $\frac{e}{f}$.

9. **Write About It** The GCF of two numbers is 30. The LCM is 420. One of the numbers is 210. What is the other number? Tell how you found your answer.

10. Numbers are relatively prime if their GCF is 1. Find a pair of composite numbers greater than 1 and less than 10 that are relatively prime.

Go On

Mixed Problem Solving

Solve. Show your work. Tell what strategy you used.

11. In his first month at an art gallery, Ken sells $10,000 worth of art. Ken's goal is to increase his sales by $1,500 each month. If Ken meets his goal, what will his sales be in the sixth month?

12. Mr. Sammler bought a group of 12 prints for his collection. Then Mr. Sammler sold 3 prints. Mr. Sammler now has 38 prints. How many prints did Mr. Sammler have before he bought the group of 12 prints?

13. Marina bought a set of paintbrushes and a set of oil paints for $90. The oil paints cost $42 more than the paintbrushes. What was the cost of the oil paints? What was the cost of the paintbrushes?

You Choose

Strategy

- Draw a Diagram
- Find a Pattern
- Use Logical Reasoning
- Work Backward
- Write an Equation

Computation Method

- Mental Math
- Estimation
- Paper and Pencil
- Calculator

Data Use the stem-and-leaf plot to solve Problems 14–17.

Paul is selling photos at an art fair. The stem-and-leaf plot shows the sale prices for the photos that Paul has sold so far.

Sale Prices of Paul's Photos

Stem	Leaf
0	
1	9
2	5 9
3	0 5 5
4	9 9 9 9
5	0 0 5 5
6	
7	
8	8 9 9 9 9 9
9	8

9 | 8 means $98.

14. How many photos has Paul sold so far?

15. Find the mean, median, mode, and range of the data. Round your answers to the nearest cent.

16. Would you use the mean or the median to describe the typical sale price? Explain your choice.

17. The next photo Paul sells raises the mean sale price of his photos to $59. What is the sale price of the photo?

18. In Clare's painting of a farm, there are 36 sheep and geese. She has painted all of their 118 legs. How many of each kind of animal are in Clare's painting?

Problem Solving on Tests

Multiple Choice

Choose the letter of the correct answer.

1. You want to find out how many minutes per day students use computers. Which of the following choices would best represent the entire school?

A Survey the entire computer club.

B Survey 30 students in each grade.

C Survey the advanced math classes.

D Survey 75 fifth graders.

(Chapter 8, Lesson 1)

2. Jerry thinks of a number. He then doubles the number and adds 5. The result is 39. Which equation could you use to find Jerry's number?

F $2 \times n = 39$

G $2 \times (n + 5) = 39$

H $(2 \times n) + 5 = 39$

J $2 \times (n - 5) = 39$

(Chapter 5, Lesson 6)

Open Response

Solve each problem.

3. Forty-five students and 12 adults are going on a trip. They are traveling in minivans that hold 8 students and 2 adults. How many minivans will be needed for the trip?

Represent Support your solution with a picture or a table.

(Chapter 5, Lesson 7)

4. Maria has test scores of 75, 76, 81, and 84. What score does Maria need on her fifth test in order to raise her mean to 80?

Explain how you found your answer.

(Chapter 8, Lesson 2)

Extended Response

5. Imagine that you could tape 12 meter sticks together to form a cube.

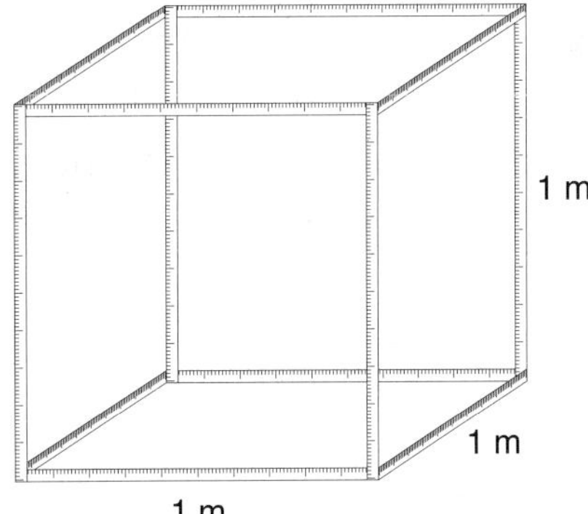

a How many centimeter cubes would it take to cover the floor of your meter cube? **Explain** how you know.

b How many layers of centimeter cubes could you fit inside the cube? **Explain** how you know.

c How many centimeter cubes would it take to fill your meter cube? **Explain** how you know.

d How many meter cubes would you need to hold 1 billion centimeter cubes? **Explain** your answer.

(Chapter 6)

Education Place

See **eduplace.com/map** for Test-Taking Tips.

Relate Fractions, Mixed Numbers, and Decimals

Objective Change decimals to fractions and mixed numbers, and change mixed numbers and fractions to decimals.

Materials
fraction strips

Work Together

A survey found that 0.2 of the visitors to an art museum stopped at the gift store. A survey five years later finds that $\frac{2}{5}$ of the museum's visitors go to the gift store. Did the two surveys produce the same result?

Work with a partner to decide whether 0.2 and $\frac{2}{5}$ represent the same number.

Way 1 **Write the decimal as a fraction in simplest form.**

$$0.2 = \frac{2}{10} = \frac{1}{5}$$

Locate the fractions on a number line.

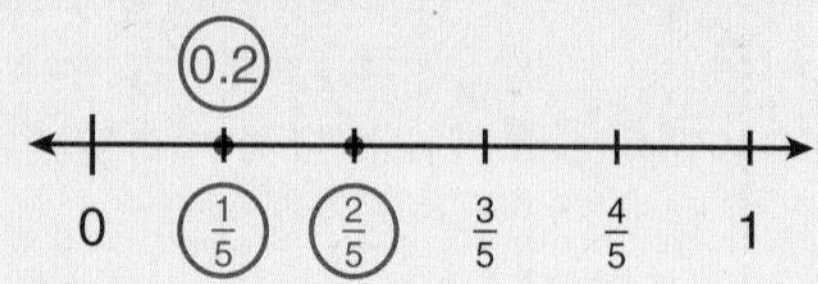

- Are the results the same?

Way 2 **Write the fraction as a decimal.**

$$\frac{2}{5} = \frac{4}{10}$$

$$\frac{4}{10} = 0.4$$

Think
To write a fraction as a decimal, the denominator needs to be a power of 10.

Locate the decimals on a number line.

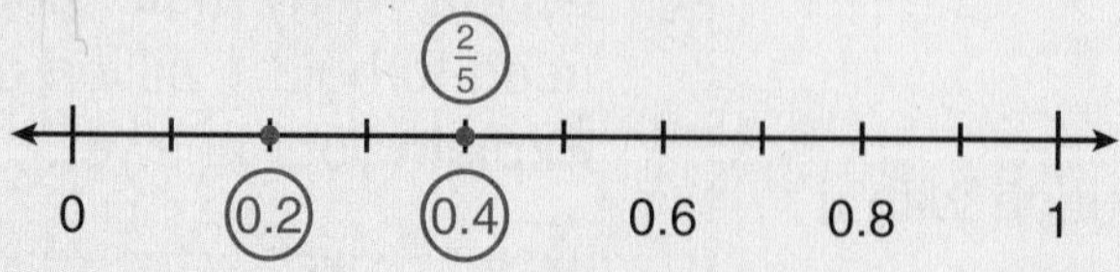

- Are the results the same?

Now decide whether 1.25 and $1\frac{1}{4}$ represent the same number.

STEP 1 Write the decimal as a mixed number in simplest form.

$1.25 = 1\frac{25}{100} = 1\frac{1}{4}$

$1.25 = 1\frac{1}{4}$

STEP 2 Write the mixed number as a decimal.

$1\frac{1}{4} = 1\frac{25}{100}$

$\frac{1}{4} = \frac{?}{100}$

$1\frac{25}{100} = 1.25$

$1\frac{1}{4} = 1.25$

On Your Own

Write each decimal as a fraction or mixed number in simplest form.

1. 0.8 **2.** 0.13 **3.** 0.75 **4.** 3.6 **5.** 4.5 **6.** 7.25

Write each fraction or mixed number as a decimal.

7. $\frac{1}{5}$ **8.** $\frac{7}{10}$ **9.** $\frac{3}{25}$ **10.** $2\frac{7}{10}$ **11.** $3\frac{3}{4}$ **12.** $5\frac{3}{100}$

Use the number line to complete Exercises 13–16.

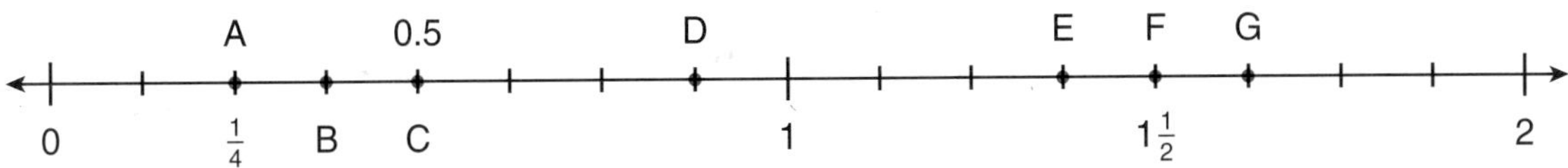

13. Write the decimal represented by point *A*.

14. Write the fraction represented by point *C*.

15. Write the fraction and the decimal represented by point *D*.

16. Which point represents 1.375? Explain your answer.

17. What's Wrong? Each flat represents one whole. Marnie says the shaded parts of the flats show that $2.3 = 2\frac{3}{100}$. Do you agree? Explain your reasoning.

Talk About It • Write About It

18. When you write a decimal in the form of an equivalent fraction, why is it important to use a denominator that is a power of 10?

19. How do you know what power of 10 to use as a denominator, when writing a decimal as an equivalent fraction?

Hands On Lesson 9

Audio Tutor 1/29 Listen and Understand

Compare and Order Fractions and Decimals

Objective Compare and order fractions and decimals.

Vocabulary
common denominator

Learn About It

Jeff made a clay animal that is $\frac{3}{8}$ foot tall. Andrea made a clay animal that is $\frac{5}{8}$ foot tall. Who made the taller animal?

Two fractions with the same, or like, denominators are said to have a **common denominator**. You can compare them by comparing the numerators.

$5 > 3$, so $\frac{5}{8} > \frac{3}{8}$. Andrea made the taller animal.

Fractions with different, or unlike, denominators can also be compared.

Compare $\frac{5}{6}$ and $\frac{5}{8}$.

Different Ways to Compare $\frac{5}{6}$ and $\frac{5}{8}$

Way 1 You can find equivalent fractions with a common denominator.

STEP 1 Find the LCM of the denominators of the fractions.

Multiples of 6: 6, 12, 18, 24, 30, ...

Multiples of 8: 8, 16, 24, 32, ...

The LCM of 6 and 8 is 24. So, use 24 as the common denominator.

STEP 2 Use the common denominator to find equivalent fractions.

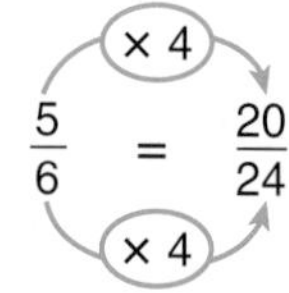

$\frac{5}{6} = \frac{20}{24}$ (× 4)

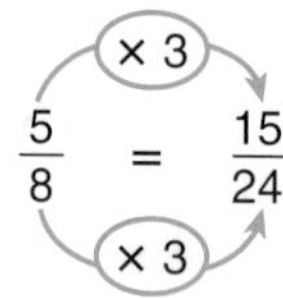

$\frac{5}{8} = \frac{15}{24}$ (× 3)

STEP 3 To compare the fractions, compare the numerators.

Since $20 > 15$, $\frac{20}{24} > \frac{15}{24}$.

So, $\frac{5}{6} > \frac{5}{8}$.

Way 2 You can think about distance on a number line.

When the numerators are the same, the fraction with the greater denominator is less than the other fraction.

$\frac{5}{6} > \frac{5}{8}$

Way 3 You can relate fractions to benchmarks.

$\frac{5}{6}$ is close to 1 on the number line.

$\frac{5}{8}$ is closer to $\frac{1}{2}$ than it is to 1.

$1 > \frac{1}{2}$, so $\frac{5}{6} > \frac{5}{8}$.

Solution: $\frac{5}{6} > \frac{5}{8}$

You can use what you know about comparing fractions to order fractions and decimals.

To order fractions, you can find equivalent fractions, then compare.

Order $\frac{3}{5}$, $\frac{3}{4}$, and $\frac{7}{10}$ from least to greatest.

- Use the LCM of the denominators to find a common denominator.
- Find equivalent fractions with that common denominator.

$\frac{3}{5} = \frac{12}{20}$ (× 4) $\quad \frac{3}{4} = \frac{15}{20}$ (× 5) $\quad \frac{7}{10} = \frac{14}{20}$ (× 2)

- Order the fractions.

$\frac{12}{20} < \frac{14}{20} < \frac{15}{20}$, so the order from least to greatest is $\frac{3}{5}$, $\frac{7}{10}$, $\frac{3}{4}$.

To order fractions and decimals, write them in the same form.

Order 1.5, $1\frac{9}{20}$, and 1.42 from greatest to least.

- Write the mixed number as a decimal.

$$1\frac{9}{20} = 1 + \frac{9}{20}$$
$$= 1 + \frac{45}{100}$$
$$= 1.45$$

Think
$\frac{9}{20} = \frac{45}{100}$

- Order the numbers.

$1.5 > 1.45 > 1.42$,

so $1.5 > 1\frac{9}{20} > 1.42$.

The order from greatest to least is 1.5, $1\frac{9}{20}$, 1.42.

Work with a partner.

Complete the steps to order decimals and fractions.

STEP 1 Write the following numbers on a sheet of paper: 0.6, $\frac{3}{8}$, and $\frac{2}{3}$.

- Guess the order of the values, from least to greatest.
- Discuss your guess with your partner.

STEP 2 Use fraction strips to show each of the three numbers. Line up the fraction strips so that they align on one end.

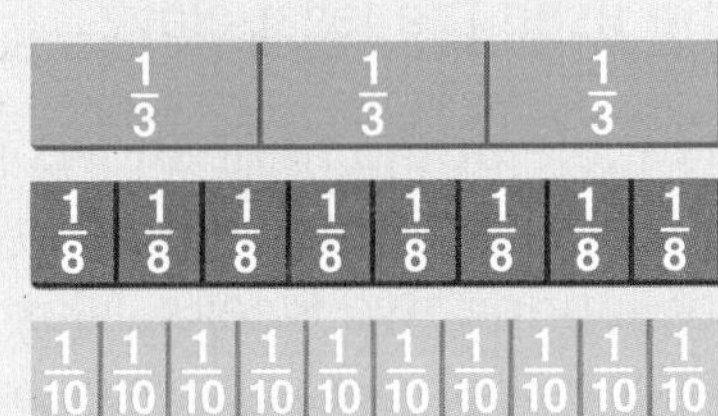

- Order the numbers from least to greatest.
- Is the order the same as your guesses?

STEP 3 Use equivalent fractions to check your answer.

Go On

Guided Practice

Compare. Write >, <, or = for each ●.

1. $\frac{7}{9}$ ● $\frac{5}{9}$
2. $\frac{5}{9}$ ● $\frac{5}{8}$
3. $\frac{2}{3}$ ● $\frac{7}{12}$
4. $3\frac{1}{4}$ ● $3\frac{2}{5}$
5. 0.25 ● $\frac{1}{5}$
6. $1\frac{1}{2}$ ● 1.5

Ask Yourself

- Did I find a common denominator?
- Did I write the numbers in the same form to compare them?

Explain Your Thinking ▶ How can you compare $\frac{4}{9}$ and $\frac{4}{11}$ without using a common denominator?

Practice and Problem Solving

Compare. Write >, <, or = for each ●.

7. $\frac{3}{8}$ ● $\frac{5}{12}$
8. $\frac{9}{10}$ ● $\frac{5}{6}$
9. $3\frac{8}{15}$ ● $3\frac{3}{5}$
10. $2\frac{3}{10}$ ● $2\frac{1}{3}$
11. $\frac{5}{8}$ ● 0.6
12. 0.75 ● $\frac{3}{4}$
13. 1.4 ● $1\frac{2}{5}$
14. $4\frac{1}{8}$ ● 4.2

Order each set of numbers from least to greatest.

15. $\frac{17}{24}$, $\frac{7}{12}$, $\frac{5}{8}$
16. $2\frac{17}{20}$, 2.75, $2\frac{4}{5}$, 0.9
17. $\frac{7}{20}$, $1\frac{1}{8}$, $\frac{11}{15}$, 0.5

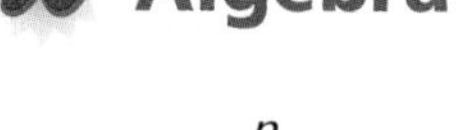

Algebra • Equations and Inequalities For each expression, write a whole number for n that will make the expression true.

18. $\frac{n}{4} = 0.25$
19. $0.3 = \frac{n}{10}$
20. $\frac{5}{6} < \frac{n}{7}$
21. $\frac{1}{2} > \frac{n}{10}$

Solve.

22. Some students made clay sculptures. Juan used $\frac{3}{4}$ pound of clay. Arleta used $\frac{1}{2}$ pound of clay. Maureen used $\frac{5}{6}$ pound of clay. Who used the most clay? Who used the least clay?

23. Penny cuts three lengths of ribbons. The ribbons are $1\frac{3}{4}$ ft, $1\frac{7}{12}$ ft, and 1.5 ft. Show all three of these lengths on a number line. Then list the lengths from shortest to longest.

24. The table at the right shows prices of train tickets from Eastport to Central City. During two weeks, Max makes 8 round trips between the towns. He spends \$71. Does he make the same number of trips each week? Explain.

25. **You Decide** During the month of January, you make the round trip between Eastport and Central City 3 times per week. What tickets would you buy? Explain your thinking.

Type of Ticket	Price
Single Trip	\$6.50
Round Trip	\$11.00
10-Trip Pass	\$55.00
Weekly Pass	\$60.00
Monthly Pass	\$225.00

Extra Practice See page 253, Set F.

Mixed Review and Test Prep

Open Response

Simplify each of the following. (Ch. 5, Lesson 6)

26. $23 + (7 + 4) \times 5$

27. $35 - 3 \times (21 - 12)$

28. $(4 \times 6) + 8 \div 4$

29. $4^2 + 3^2 - 6$

30. $(3 - 1)^2 \times 9$

31. $(4 + 6)^2 - 8^2 + 2$

32. To make paste, Janna uses $\frac{7}{8}$ pound of flour. She also uses $\frac{7}{12}$ pound of salt. Does she use more salt or more flour to make paste? Explain. (Ch. 9, Lesson 9)

Problem Solving

Social Studies Connection

Mangled Money

Each day the United States Bureau of Engraving and Printing produces **thirty-seven million** pieces of paper money. This money has a face value of approximately **six hundred ninety-six million dollars**.

If a piece of paper money is torn apart and more than half of it remains, the U.S. Treasury Department will issue a check for the face value of the bill. The U.S. Treasury handles about **thirty thousand** claims every year for torn or mutilated currency, worth over **thirty million dollars**.

1. Write the four numbers shown above in bold print in standard form.

Write *yes* or *no* to indicate if the U.S. Treasury would issue a check for that part of the dollar bill.

2. $\frac{2}{3}$ **3.** $\frac{3}{8}$ **4.** $\frac{5}{12}$ **5.** $\frac{5}{10}$

WEEKLY WR READER eduplace.com/map

Chapter Review/Test

VOCABULARY

Vocabulary
- composite number
- greatest common factor (GCF)
- least common multiple (LCM)
- prime factorization
- prime number

1. A ____ is a number greater than 1 with exactly two different factors–itself and 1.

2. A ____ is the greatest whole number that is a common factor of two or more numbers.

3. A whole number that has more than two factors is called a ____.

CONCEPTS AND SKILLS

Write the prime factorization of each number. Use exponents if possible. If the number is prime, write *prime*. (Lessons 1–2, pp. 224–227)

4. 7 5. 12 6. 19 7. 20 8. 16 9. 30

Find the GCF of the numbers. (Lesson 3, pp. 228–230)

10. 36, 81 11. 18, 45 12. 35, 77 13. 24, 96

Find the LCM of the numbers. (Lesson 4, pp. 232–235)

14. 6, 18 15. 20, 48 16. 15, 55 17. 12, 32

Simplify if possible. Then write each as a decimal.
(Lessons 5–6, pp. 236–241; Lesson 8, pp. 246–247)

18. $\frac{18}{36}$ 19. $\frac{3}{2}$ 20. $\frac{4}{10}$ 21. $\frac{32}{20}$ 22. $\frac{15}{4}$

23. $\frac{3}{10}$ 24. $\frac{2}{5}$ 25. $2\frac{23}{100}$ 26. $\frac{11}{50}$ 27. $1\frac{3}{25}$

Compare. Write >, <, or = for each ⬬.
(Lesson 9, pp. 248–251)

28. $\frac{5}{7}$ ⬬ $\frac{5}{8}$ 29. 1.2 ⬬ $1\frac{2}{5}$ 30. $\frac{3}{25}$ ⬬ 0.12 31. $\frac{3}{10}$ ⬬ 0.15 32. 3.25 ⬬ $\frac{7}{2}$

PROBLEM SOLVING

Solve. (Lesson 7, pp. 242–245)

33. The LCM of two numbers is 200. The GCF is 10. The sum of the numbers is 90. What are the numbers?

Write About It

Show You Understand

How does knowing that $\frac{1}{9} < \frac{1}{8}$ help you know that $\frac{7}{8} < \frac{8}{9}$ without using a common denominator?

Extra Practice

Set A (Lesson 2, pp. 226–227)

Write the prime factorization of each number. Use exponents if possible. If the number is prime, write *prime*.

1. 23 **2.** 41 **3.** 48 **4.** 50 **5.** 51

Set B (Lesson 3, pp. 228–231)

Find the greatest common factor of the numbers.

1. 16, 36 **2.** 27, 54 **3.** 48, 72 **4.** 56, 120 **5.** 99, 121

6. 24, 56 **7.** 12, 48 **8.** 39, 51 **9.** 15, 60 **10.** 36, 54

Set C (Lesson 4, pp. 232–234)

Find the least common multiple of the numbers.

1. 7, 42 **2.** 16, 36 **3.** 13, 52 **4.** 8, 28 **5.** 12, 32

6. 9, 45 **7.** 6, 20 **8.** 20, 30 **9.** 7, 9 **10.** 12, 40

Set D (Lesson 5, pp. 236–239)

Write each improper fraction as a mixed number or a whole number. Write each mixed number as an improper fraction.

1. $\frac{11}{3}$ **2.** $\frac{16}{5}$ **3.** $\frac{12}{6}$ **4.** $\frac{17}{8}$ **5.** $\frac{30}{7}$

6. $5\frac{1}{7}$ **7.** $7\frac{1}{3}$ **8.** $3\frac{5}{8}$ **9.** $10\frac{2}{3}$ **10.** $6\frac{3}{10}$

Set E (Lesson 6, pp. 240–241)

Simplify each fraction.

1. $\frac{16}{36}$ **2.** $\frac{33}{54}$ **3.** $\frac{6}{27}$ **4.** $\frac{18}{48}$ **5.** $\frac{55}{77}$

Set F (Lesson 9, pp. 248–251)

Compare. Write >, <, or = for each ●.

1. $\frac{3}{14}$ ● $\frac{3}{28}$ **2.** $2\frac{5}{6}$ ● $2\frac{1}{12}$ **3.** 5.2 ● $5\frac{5}{25}$ **4.** 1.8 ● $1\frac{23}{25}$

5. $\frac{1}{5}$ ● 0.08 **6.** $\frac{1}{4}$ ● 0.25 **7.** $\frac{11}{12}$ ● $\frac{5}{12}$ **8.** 1.75 ● $1\frac{3}{4}$

Extra Practice at eduplace.com/map

Add and Subtract Fractions

INVESTIGATION

Use Data

In-line skating is a good way to keep fit. For a 120-pound skater, how does the number of calories burned change as he or she goes faster? How does the weight of the skater affect calories burned?

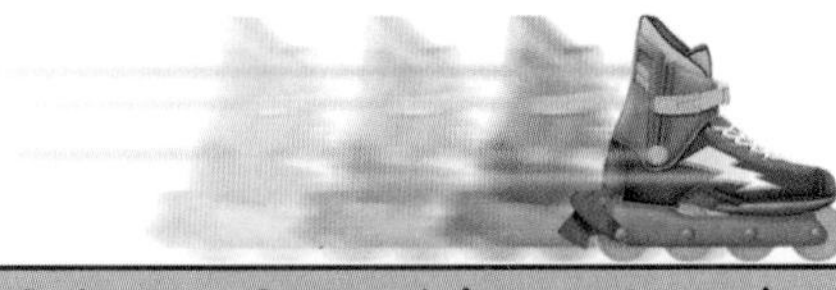

Calories Burned (per minute) In-Line Skating					
Skater's Weight (pounds)	Speed of Skater (miles per hour)				
	8	9	10	11	12
120	$4\frac{1}{5}$	$5\frac{4}{5}$	$7\frac{2}{5}$	$8\frac{9}{10}$	$10\frac{1}{2}$
150	$5\frac{3}{5}$	$7\frac{1}{5}$	$8\frac{4}{5}$	$10\frac{2}{5}$	$11\frac{9}{10}$

Use What You Know

Use this page to review and remember what you need to know for this chapter.

VOCABULARY

Choose the best term to complete each sentence.

1. The fractions $\frac{1}{3}$ and $\frac{1}{4}$ have ____.
2. The fractions $\frac{2}{5}$ and $\frac{3}{5}$ have ____.
3. Fractions that represent the same number are called ____.

Vocabulary

- equivalent fractions
- like denominators
- unlike denominators

CONCEPTS AND SKILLS

Write each fraction in simplest form.

4. $\frac{2}{6}$
5. $\frac{8}{10}$
6. $\frac{3}{12}$
7. $\frac{3}{18}$

Write each improper fraction as a mixed number or whole number.

8. $\frac{25}{8}$
9. $\frac{18}{3}$
10. $\frac{19}{5}$
11. $\frac{4}{4}$

Complete.

12. $\frac{1}{3} = \frac{3}{■}$
13. $\frac{5}{20} = \frac{■}{4}$
14. $1\frac{1}{5} = \frac{■}{5} = \frac{■}{10}$
15. $4\frac{2}{3} = \frac{■}{3} = \frac{■}{6}$

Find the least common multiple of these numbers.

16. 6, 36
17. 4, 10
18. 3, 11
19. 3, 25

Write About It

20. Is $\frac{3}{8}$ closer to 0, $\frac{1}{2}$, or 1? Use a number line or words to explain your thinking.

Facts Practice, See page 661.

Lesson 1 Estimate With Fractions

Objective Estimate fraction sums and differences.

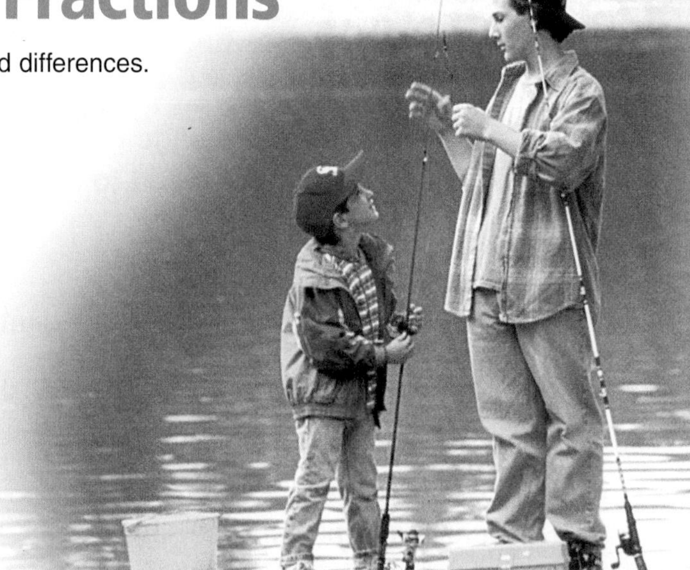

Learn About It

Dan is $53\frac{1}{8}$ inches tall. His older brother is $72\frac{3}{4}$ inches tall. About how many more inches would Dan need to grow to match his brother's height?

Estimate the difference $72\frac{3}{4} - 53\frac{1}{8}$.

You can use front-end estimation.

STEP 1 Identify the greatest place in each number.

$$\begin{array}{r} 72\frac{3}{4} \\ -\ 53\frac{1}{8} \\ \hline \end{array}$$

STEP 2 Subtract. Write zeros in the other whole-number places.

$$\begin{array}{r} 72\frac{3}{4} \\ -\ 53\frac{1}{8} \\ \hline \end{array} \Rightarrow \begin{array}{r} 70 \\ -\ 50 \\ \hline 20 \end{array}$$

Solution: Dan would need to grow about 20 inches to match his brother's height.

You can also use rounding to estimate with fractions.

Estimate the sum $\frac{5}{6} + \frac{7}{12} + \frac{1}{6}$.

You can round fractions to 0, $\frac{1}{2}$, or 1 in order to estimate.

STEP 1 Decide if each fraction is closest to 0, $\frac{1}{2}$, or 1. A number line can help you decide.

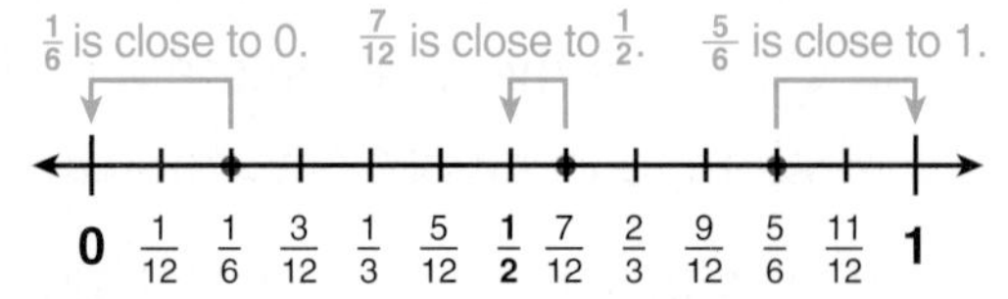

STEP 2 Round up or down. Then add the rounded numbers.

$$\frac{5}{6} + \frac{7}{12} + \frac{1}{6}$$

$$\downarrow \quad \downarrow \quad \downarrow$$

$$1 + \frac{1}{2} + 0 \approx 1\frac{1}{2}$$

$\approx$ means "is approximately equal to."

Solution: The sum of $\frac{5}{6}$, $\frac{7}{12}$, and $\frac{1}{6}$ is about $1\frac{1}{2}$.

Guided Practice

Estimate the sum or difference. Name the method you used to estimate.

1. $\frac{5}{8} - \frac{3}{8}$
2. $15\frac{3}{4} + 12\frac{7}{8}$
3. $\frac{7}{8} + \frac{1}{12}$
4. $22\frac{9}{10} - 18\frac{2}{5}$

Ask Yourself

- Is the fraction close to 0, $\frac{1}{2}$, or 1?
- Can I use front-end estimation?

Explain Your Thinking ▶ Explain how you could use rounding to find the difference in Exercise 4 above.

Practice and Problem Solving

Estimate the sum or difference.
Name the method you used to estimate.

5. $\frac{1}{4} + \frac{7}{10}$
6. $\frac{3}{5} + \frac{2}{3}$
7. $16\frac{1}{8} + 12\frac{1}{12}$
8. $\frac{4}{5} + \frac{1}{8} + \frac{3}{4} + \frac{1}{2}$
9. $\frac{7}{8} - \frac{1}{12}$
10. $\frac{5}{8} - \frac{1}{10}$
11. $9\frac{1}{8} - 3\frac{3}{4}$
12. $19\frac{5}{12} + 14\frac{1}{2}$
13. $\frac{4}{5} - \frac{1}{6}$
14. $\frac{1}{2} - \frac{3}{8}$
15. $37\frac{5}{8} + 26\frac{3}{5}$
16. $87\frac{1}{3} - 24\frac{4}{5}$
17. $16\frac{2}{3} - \frac{7}{8}$
18. $58 - 46\frac{1}{3}$
19. $6\frac{7}{8} + \frac{2}{3} + 4\frac{9}{10} + 5\frac{1}{10} + \frac{4}{5}$

Solve.

20. Show why this statement is true: $1\frac{1}{8} - \frac{3}{4} \approx 0$. Use a number line or draw a picture to explain your reasoning.

21. Melba is $60\frac{3}{4}$ inches tall. When she puts on her new shoes, she grows $3\frac{1}{2}$ inches. About how tall is Melba in her new shoes?

Mixed Review and Test Prep

Open Response

Complete. (Grade 4)

22. 3 hours = ■ seconds
23. 300 minutes = ■ hours
24. 1 day = ■ minutes
25. 2 years = ■ days

Multiple Choice

26. Last year Robin was $50\frac{1}{4}$ inches tall. Now Robin is $54\frac{7}{8}$ inches tall. Which is the best estimate of the change in height? (Ch. 10, Lesson 1)

A 1 inch
B 2 inches
C 3 inches
D 5 inches

Extra Practice See page 279, Set A.

Lesson 2

Add With Like Denominators

Objective Add fractions and mixed numbers with like denominators.

TRAIL MIX

$\frac{1}{4}$ cup yogurt-covered peanuts

$\frac{1}{4}$ cup mini–chocolate chips

$\frac{2}{4}$ cup dried cherries

$\frac{3}{4}$ cup granola

$\frac{3}{4}$ cup dried apricots

Learn About It

Delia chooses foods that will help keep her body healthy. At the right is her recipe for trail mix.

How much fruit is in the trail mix?

Add. $\frac{2}{4} + \frac{3}{4} = n$

The sum of 2 unit fractions of $\frac{1}{4}$ and 3 unit fractions of $\frac{1}{4}$ is 5 unit fractions of $\frac{1}{4}$.

Add. Then simplify the sum.

$\frac{2}{4} + \frac{3}{4} = \frac{5}{4} = \frac{4}{4} + \frac{1}{4} = 1\frac{1}{4}$

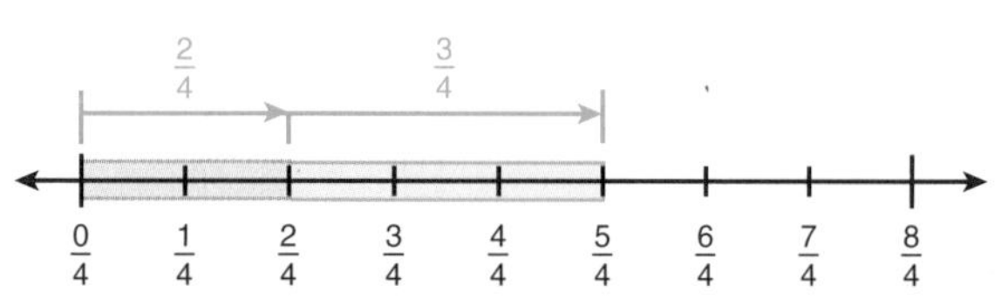

To add fractions with like denominators, add the numerators and keep the same denominator.

Solution: The trail mix has $1\frac{1}{4}$ cups of fruit.

Mike also likes to make healthy snacks. His recipe mixes $1\frac{5}{8}$ cups of mini-pretzels with $1\frac{7}{8}$ cups of yogurt-covered cranberries. How much snack does this recipe make?

Find $1\frac{5}{8} + 1\frac{7}{8}$.

STEP 1 Add the fractions.

$$\begin{array}{r} 1\frac{5}{8} \\ +\ 1\frac{7}{8} \\ \hline \frac{12}{8} \end{array}$$

STEP 2 Add the whole numbers.

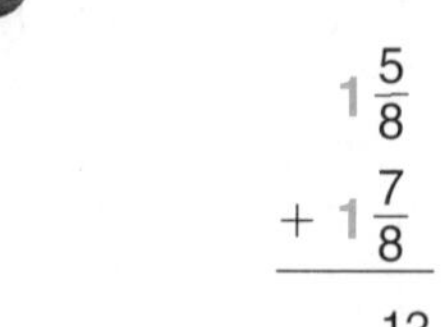

STEP 3 Simplify the sum, if possible.

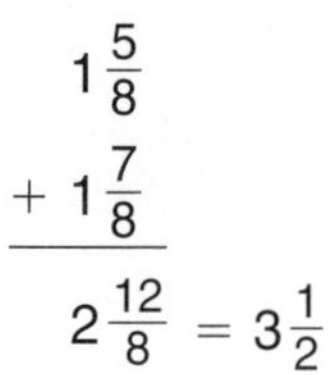

Think

$\frac{12}{8} = 1\frac{4}{8} = 1\frac{1}{2}$

$2 + 1\frac{1}{2} = 3\frac{1}{2}$

Solution: Mike's recipe makes $3\frac{1}{2}$ cups of his healthy snack.

Guided Practice

Add. Write each sum in simplest form.

1. $\frac{2}{5} + \frac{2}{5}$
2. $\frac{5}{6} + \frac{1}{6}$
3. $\frac{3}{4} + \frac{2}{4}$
4. $2\frac{4}{5} + 4\frac{3}{5}$
5. $3\frac{2}{3} + 3\frac{2}{3}$
6. $1\frac{5}{8} + \frac{7}{8}$

Ask Yourself

- Did I add the numerators?
- Did I add the whole numbers?
- Is the sum in simplest form?

Explain Your Thinking ▶ When you add fractions with like denominators, why do you only add the numerators?

Practice and Problem Solving

Add. Write each sum in simplest form.

7. $\frac{3}{10} + \frac{4}{10}$
8. $\frac{5}{8} + \frac{7}{8}$
9. $2\frac{5}{12} + 1\frac{1}{12}$
10. $3\frac{2}{3} + 4\frac{1}{3}$
11. $\frac{2}{6} + \frac{2}{6}$
12. $\frac{4}{9} + \frac{3}{9}$
13. $3\frac{5}{6} + 1\frac{1}{6}$
14. $2\frac{5}{6} + 3\frac{5}{6}$
15. $6\frac{7}{10} + 3\frac{9}{10}$

Mental Math **Use mental math to add. Write each sum in simplest form.**

16. $\frac{7}{16} + \frac{9}{16}$
17. $\frac{3}{8} + \frac{5}{8}$
18. $2\frac{3}{4} + \frac{1}{4}$
19. $1\frac{1}{2} + 4\frac{1}{2}$

Solve.

20. To stay healthy, about $\frac{1}{5}$ of the foods that you eat should be vegetables, and about $\frac{2}{5}$ should be grains. What fraction of the foods that you eat should be vegetables and grains?

21. Sonja and Adam need $1\frac{3}{4}$ cups of cucumbers, $\frac{1}{4}$ cup of onions, and $\frac{1}{2}$ cup of cheese to make a snack. Find how many cups of vegetables they need to make their snack.

Mixed Review and Test Prep

Open Response

Add or subtract. (Ch. 2, Lesson 3)

22. $362 + 517$
23. $1{,}376 - 429$
24. $24{,}522 - 7{,}165$

25. For a punch recipe, Brian uses $2\frac{2}{5}$ cups of fruit juice and $4\frac{1}{5}$ cups of ginger ale. How much punch is he making? (Ch. 10, Lesson 2)

Extra Practice See page 279, Set B.

Lesson 3

Audio Tutor 1/30 Listen and Understand

Add Fractions With Unlike Denominators

Objective Add fractions with unlike denominators.

Vocabulary
equivalent fractions
least common denominator (LCD)

Learn About It

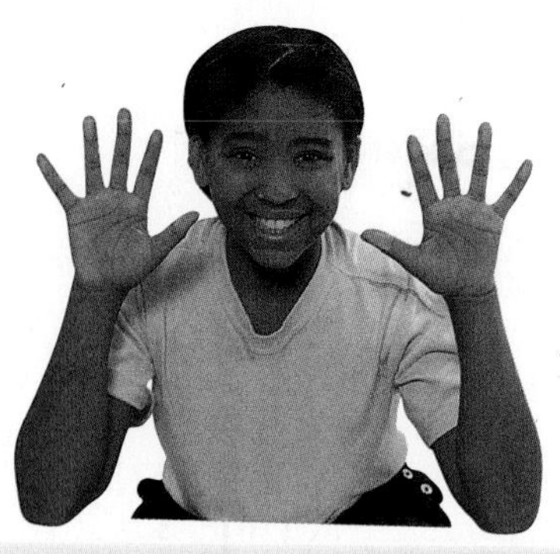

About $\frac{1}{5}$ of the bones in your body are in your hands and $\frac{1}{4}$ of your bones are in your feet. What fraction of the bones in your body are in your hands and feet?

Add. $\frac{1}{5} + \frac{1}{4} = n$

STEP 1 To add the fractions, you need to find a common denominator.

Use the product of the denominators to write **equivalent fractions** with like denominators.

$5 \times 4 = 20$ ← common denominator

$\frac{1}{5} = \frac{1 \times 4}{5 \times 4} = \frac{4}{20}$ $\frac{1}{4} = \frac{1 \times 5}{4 \times 5} = \frac{5}{20}$

STEP 2 Rewrite the problem. Then add.

$\frac{1}{5} + \frac{1}{4} = \frac{4}{20} + \frac{5}{20}$

$= \frac{9}{20}$

Solution: About $\frac{9}{20}$ of the bones in your body are in your hands and feet.

To add fractions, find the **least common denominator (LCD)**.

Find $\frac{7}{8} + \frac{5}{12}$.

STEP 1 Find the least common multiple (LCM) of the denominators. This is the LCD.

8: 8, 16, **24**, 32

12: 12, **24**, 36

The LCD of the fractions is 24.

STEP 2 Use the LCD to find equivalent fractions.

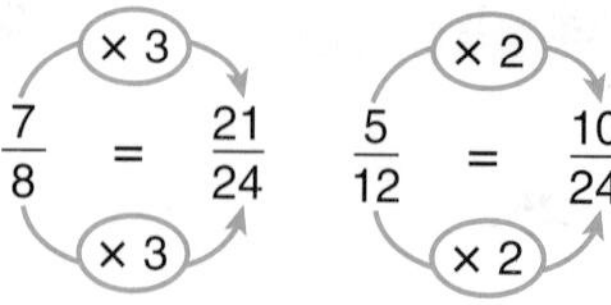

$\frac{7}{8} = \frac{7 \times 3}{8 \times 3} = \frac{21}{24}$ $\frac{5}{12} = \frac{5 \times 2}{12 \times 2} = \frac{10}{24}$

STEP 3 Add the fractions. Write the sum in simplest form.

$\frac{21}{24} + \frac{10}{24} = \frac{31}{24}$

$\frac{31}{24} = \frac{24}{24} + \frac{7}{24} = 1\frac{7}{24}$

Solution: $\frac{7}{8} + \frac{5}{12} = 1\frac{7}{24}$

Extra Help at **eduplace.com/map**

Guided Practice

Ask Yourself

- Did I use equivalent fractions?
- Is each sum in simplest form?

Add. Write each sum in simplest form.

1. $\frac{1}{6} + \frac{1}{3}$
2. $\frac{2}{3} + \frac{5}{6}$
3. $\frac{1}{8} + \frac{1}{4}$
4. $\frac{1}{3} + \frac{2}{5}$
5. $\frac{2}{3} + \frac{5}{9}$
6. $\frac{7}{8} + \frac{1}{12}$
7. $\frac{2}{5} + \frac{1}{10}$
8. $\frac{5}{6} + \frac{5}{8}$

Explain Your Thinking ▶ Show how to use fraction strips to add $\frac{1}{2}$ and $\frac{3}{8}$.

Practice and Problem Solving

Add. Write each sum in simplest form.

9. $\frac{1}{6} + \frac{1}{4}$
10. $\frac{1}{10} + \frac{3}{4}$
11. $\frac{2}{3} + \frac{3}{4}$
12. $\frac{9}{16} + \frac{1}{12}$
13. $\frac{1}{2} + \frac{9}{10}$
14. $\frac{1}{2} + \frac{1}{4}$
15. $\frac{3}{8} + \frac{9}{16}$
16. $\frac{11}{12} + \frac{5}{6}$
17. $\frac{7}{16} + \frac{7}{8}$
18. $\frac{5}{8} + \frac{7}{12}$

Solve.

19. Anna mixed $\frac{3}{4}$ cup peanuts with $\frac{3}{8}$ cup almonds. How many cups of nuts did she have?

20. Rob added $\frac{5}{8}$ cup of water to $\frac{1}{3}$ cup of juice concentrate. About how much juice did Rob make?

21. **Write About It** Without adding, decide if each sum is greater than or less than $\frac{1}{2}$. Explain your decision.

    a. $\frac{1}{3} + \frac{1}{4}$
    b. $\frac{3}{8} + \frac{1}{5}$

22. **What's Wrong?** Rob found that 9 was the LCD of $\frac{1}{3}$ and $\frac{1}{6}$ this way:

    $\frac{1}{3} + \frac{1}{6} \quad 3 \times 6 = 18 \quad 18 \div 2 = 9$

    Explain why Rob's way is wrong.

Mixed Review and Test Prep

Open Response

Write *prime* or *composite* to classify each number. (Ch. 9, Lesson 1)

23. 10
24. 7
25. 4
26. 9
27. 15
28. 5
29. 13
30. 21
31. 12

Multiple Choice

32. In simplest form, what is the sum of $\frac{3}{4}$ and $\frac{5}{8}$? (Ch. 10, Lesson 3)

    A $\frac{2}{3}$
    B $1\frac{1}{8}$
    C $1\frac{3}{8}$
    D 2

Extra Practice See page 279, Set C.

Audio Tutor 1/31 Listen and Understand

Lesson 4 Add Mixed Numbers With Unlike Denominators

Objective Add mixed numbers with unlike denominators.

Learn About It

As you walk, swim, or bike, your heart pumps oxygen-rich blood through your circulatory system.

Evelyn walks each day to keep her heart healthy. Her journal shows the number of miles she walked on Monday and Tuesday. How far did she walk in those two days?

Walking Journal	
Monday	$3\frac{1}{2}$
Tuesday	$2\frac{4}{5}$

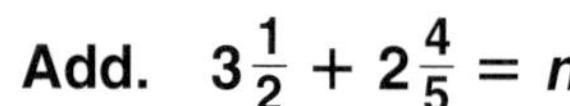

Add. $3\frac{1}{2} + 2\frac{4}{5} = n$

STEP 1 Write equivalent fractions for $\frac{1}{2}$ and $\frac{4}{5}$ by using the LCD, which is 10.

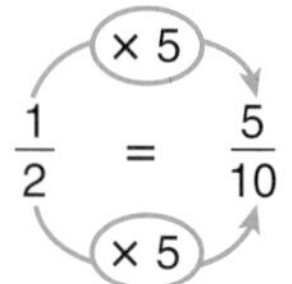

$\frac{1}{2} = \frac{5}{10}$ (× 5) $\frac{4}{5} = \frac{8}{10}$ (× 2)

STEP 2 Add. Simplify the sum if possible.

$$\begin{array}{rcr} 3\frac{1}{2} & = & 3\frac{5}{10} \\ +\,2\frac{4}{5} & = & +\,2\frac{8}{10} \\ \hline & & 5\frac{13}{10} \end{array}$$

$$5\frac{13}{10} = 5 + 1 + \frac{3}{10}$$
$$= 6\frac{3}{10}$$

$\frac{13}{10} = \frac{10}{10} + \frac{3}{10}$

Solution: Evelyn walked $6\frac{3}{10}$ miles on Monday and Tuesday.

Check your work.

Estimate to check that your answer is reasonable.

Round $\frac{1}{2}$ and $\frac{4}{5}$ to 0, $\frac{1}{2}$, or 1. $3\frac{1}{2} = 3\frac{1}{2}$ $2\frac{4}{5} \approx 3$

Add the rounded numbers. $3\frac{1}{2} + 3 = 6\frac{1}{2}$

$6\frac{1}{2} \approx 6\frac{3}{10}$

Guided Practice

Add. Write each sum in simplest form.

1. $1\frac{1}{2} + 1\frac{1}{4}$

2. $2\frac{1}{4} + 3\frac{1}{6}$

3. $2\frac{4}{5} + 4\frac{1}{2}$

4. $3\frac{5}{12} + 7\frac{5}{6}$

5. $8\frac{9}{16} + 5\frac{1}{2}$

6. $1\frac{3}{4} + 6\frac{1}{3}$

7. Jeremiah jogged $3\frac{1}{4}$ miles on Saturday and $4\frac{2}{5}$ miles on Sunday. Find the total distance he jogged on those two days.

Ask Yourself

- Did I write equivalent fractions?
- Is each sum in simplest form?

Explain Your Thinking ▶ Why is it easy to find the LCD when one denominator is a multiple of the other?

Practice and Problem Solving

Add. Write each sum in simplest form.

8. $3\frac{5}{6} + 1\frac{1}{6}$

9. $2\frac{1}{4} + 8\frac{3}{8}$

10. $1\frac{1}{2} + 2\frac{3}{4}$

11. $4\frac{3}{5} + 5\frac{7}{10}$

12. $4\frac{3}{5} + 2\frac{1}{2}$

13. $3\frac{1}{3} + 7\frac{5}{6}$

14. $9\frac{11}{12} + 6\frac{2}{3}$

15. $2\frac{5}{8} + 6\frac{2}{3}$

16. $8\frac{1}{2} + 9\frac{3}{5}$

17. $10\frac{7}{8} + 2\frac{3}{4}$

18. $4\frac{1}{6} + 7\frac{1}{12}$

19. $6\frac{2}{5} + 3\frac{1}{6}$

20. $7\frac{1}{3} + 4\frac{7}{12}$

21. $5\frac{3}{10} + 2\frac{1}{2}$

22. $8\frac{2}{3} + 10\frac{11}{16}$

23. $2\frac{9}{16} + 12\frac{1}{4}$

24. $2\frac{2}{5} + 2\frac{5}{6}$

Algebra • Expressions **Evaluate. Let $x = \frac{1}{2}$, $y = 3\frac{1}{3}$, and $z = 1\frac{3}{4}$.**

25. $y + z$

26. $z + x$

27. $y + x$

28. $z + z$

Go On

Add. Write each sum in simplest form.

29. $\begin{array}{r} 1\frac{3}{8} \\ 2\frac{5}{6} \\ +\ 1\frac{1}{6} \\ \hline \end{array}$

30. $\begin{array}{r} 2\frac{1}{10} \\ 1\frac{3}{4} \\ +\ 4\frac{7}{10} \\ \hline \end{array}$

31. $\begin{array}{r} 5\frac{1}{2} \\ 2\frac{1}{2} \\ +\ 6\frac{3}{4} \\ \hline \end{array}$

32. $\begin{array}{r} 8\frac{1}{10} \\ 5\frac{7}{8} \\ +\ 2\frac{1}{8} \\ \hline \end{array}$

33. $\begin{array}{r} 1\frac{1}{3} \\ 3\frac{5}{6} \\ +\ 4\frac{1}{6} \\ \hline \end{array}$

Solve.

34. Manuel runs the same route each day. It's $1\frac{3}{4}$ miles on River Road, $1\frac{7}{10}$ miles on Back Street, and $2\frac{1}{4}$ miles on Elm Street. How far does Manuel run each day?

35. Lily practices for a swim meet by warming up for $\frac{1}{4}$ hour, swimming slow laps for $1\frac{2}{3}$ hours, and doing sprints for $\frac{1}{6}$ hour. How long is her practice?

36. Show how to use fraction strips to add $\frac{3}{4}$ and $\frac{5}{6}$.

37. What mixed number, when added to itself three times, equals 10?

$$n + n + n = 10$$

Data Use the table for Problems 38–43.

38. On Saturday, Jerome played basketball for the same amount of time he exercised on Monday and Tuesday. How long did he play basketball?

39. Jeff's goal was to exercise at least 5 hours by the end of the day on Wednesday. Did he reach his goal? Explain.

40. What pattern do you notice in the amount of time Jerome exercised during the week?

41. On which day did Jerome and Jeff together spend exactly 4 hours exercising?

42. How many hours did each athlete spend exercising this week?

43. **Create and Solve** Write your own problem that uses data from the table. Solve your problem.

Hours of Exercise

Day	Jerome's Hours	Jeff's Hours
Monday	$1\frac{1}{4}$	$1\frac{2}{3}$
Tuesday	$1\frac{1}{2}$	$1\frac{1}{4}$
Wednesday	$1\frac{3}{4}$	$2\frac{1}{4}$
Thursday	2	$2\frac{3}{4}$
Friday	$2\frac{1}{4}$	$1\frac{1}{4}$

Extra Practice See page 279, Set D.

Activity

Number Sense
Magic Squares

In a magic square, each row, column, and diagonal has the same sum.

In the magic square at the right, each row, column, and diagonal should have a sum of $1\frac{1}{2}$, and each missing numerator is a different number from 1 to 9.

Copy and complete this fraction magic square.

Can you find another way to complete the fraction magic square?

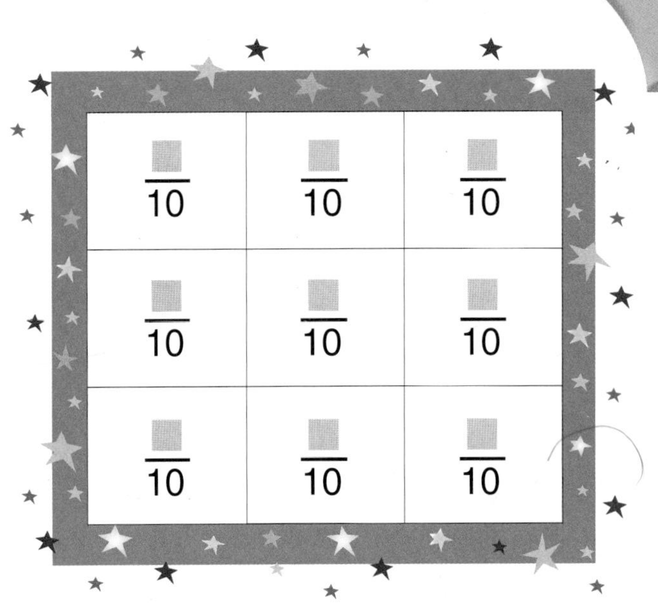

Quick Check

Check your understanding of Lessons 1–4.

Estimate the sum or difference. (Lesson 1)

1. $\frac{1}{10} + \frac{1}{16}$ **2.** $14\frac{7}{8} + 10\frac{3}{5}$ **3.** $\frac{9}{10} - \frac{5}{8}$ **4.** $83\frac{4}{8} - 12\frac{5}{6}$

Add. Write each sum in simplest form. (Lessons 2–4)

5. $\frac{5}{8} + \frac{7}{8}$ **6.** $\frac{2}{3} + \frac{1}{2}$ **7.** $\frac{9}{10} + \frac{4}{5}$

8. $4\frac{5}{6} + 2\frac{1}{6}$ **9.** $7\frac{3}{4} + 4\frac{5}{8}$ **10.** $3\frac{1}{5} + 4\frac{1}{2}$

Lesson 5

Subtract With Like Denominators

Objective Subtract fractions and mixed numbers with like denominators.

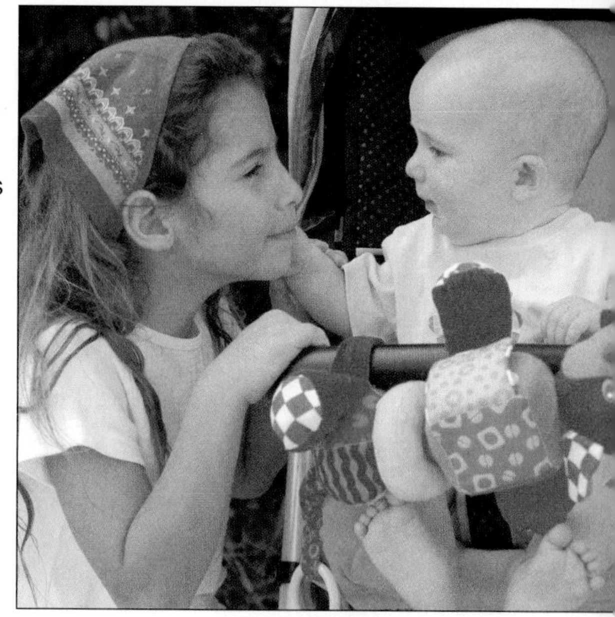

Learn About It

Did you know that your brain grows? When you were born, your brain's mass was about $\frac{4}{10}$ kilogram. By age $1\frac{1}{2}$ its mass was about $\frac{7}{10}$ kilogram. How much mass does your brain gain in those $1\frac{1}{2}$ years?

Subtract. $\frac{7}{10} - \frac{4}{10} = n$

To subtract fractions with like denominators subtract the numerators and keep the same denominator.

The difference between 7 unit fractions of $\frac{1}{10}$ and 4 unit fractions of $\frac{1}{10}$ is 3 unit fractions of $\frac{1}{10}$.

$\frac{7}{10} - \frac{4}{10} = \frac{3}{10}$

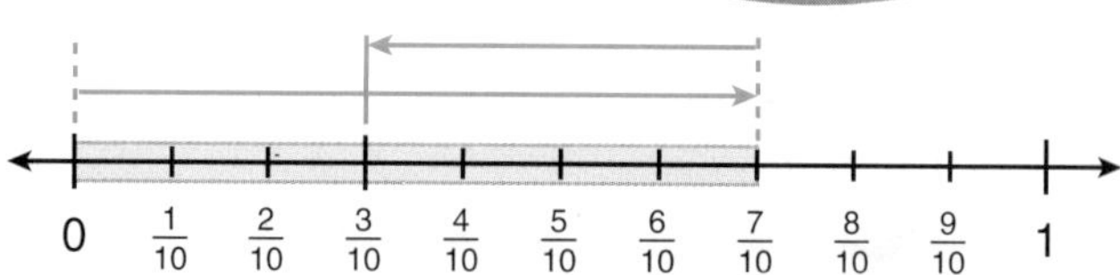

Add to check.
$\frac{3}{10} + \frac{4}{10} = \frac{7}{10}$

Solution: In the first $1\frac{1}{2}$ years, your brain gains about $\frac{3}{10}$ kilogram.

Any fraction with the same numerator and denominator is equivalent to 1.

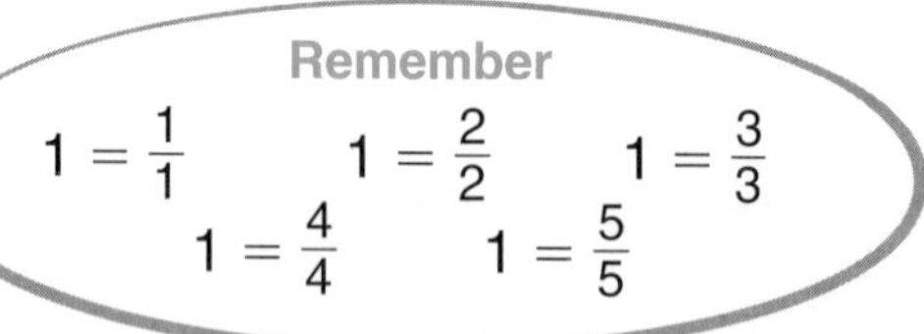

Remember
1 = 1/1
1 = 2/2
1 = 3/3
1 = 4/4
1 = 5/5

Find $5 - 1\frac{2}{3}$.

STEP 1 Rename 5 as 4 + 1. Then rename 1, using 3 for the denominator.

$5 = 4 + 1$

$4 + \frac{3}{3} = 4\frac{3}{3}$

STEP 2 Subtract the fractions.

$$\begin{array}{rcr} 5 & = & 4\frac{3}{3} \\ -1\frac{2}{3} & = & -1\frac{2}{3} \\ \hline & & \frac{1}{3} \end{array}$$

STEP 3 Subtract the whole numbers.

$$\begin{array}{rcr} 5 & = & 4\frac{3}{3} \\ -1\frac{2}{3} & = & -1\frac{2}{3} \\ \hline & & 3\frac{1}{3} \end{array}$$

Solution: $5 - 1\frac{2}{3} = 3\frac{1}{3}$

Find $7\frac{1}{4} - 1\frac{3}{4}$.

STEP 1 Rename $7\frac{1}{4}$.

$7\frac{1}{4} = 7 + \frac{1}{4}$

$= 6 + \frac{4}{4} + \frac{1}{4}$

$= 6 + \frac{5}{4} = 6\frac{5}{4}$

STEP 2 Subtract the fractions.

$$\begin{array}{rcr} 7\frac{1}{4} & = & 6\frac{5}{4} \\ -1\frac{3}{4} & = & -1\frac{3}{4} \\ \hline & & \frac{2}{4} \end{array}$$

STEP 3 Subtract the whole numbers. Simplify.

$$\begin{array}{rcr} 7\frac{1}{4} & = & 6\frac{5}{4} \\ -1\frac{3}{4} & = & -1\frac{3}{4} \\ \hline & & 5\frac{2}{4} = 5\frac{1}{2} \end{array}$$

Solution: $7\frac{1}{4} - 1\frac{3}{4} = 5\frac{1}{2}$

Guided Practice

Ask Yourself

- Do I need to rename?
- Did I simplify my answer?
- Did I check my work?

Subtract. Write each difference in simplest form.

1. $\frac{3}{10} - \frac{1}{10}$ **2.** $2 - 1\frac{1}{3}$ **3.** $10\frac{1}{9} - 9\frac{4}{9}$

Explain Your Thinking ▶ Show how to check your answer in Exercise 3.

Practice and Problem Solving

Subtract. Write each answer in simplest form.

4. $\frac{11}{12} - \frac{5}{12}$ **5.** $2 - 1\frac{5}{8}$ **6.** $8 - 4\frac{1}{5}$ **7.** $5\frac{2}{9} - 3\frac{8}{9}$

8. $\frac{8}{9} - \frac{5}{9}$ **9.** $\frac{3}{4} - \frac{1}{4}$ **10.** $3 - 2\frac{4}{6}$ **11.** $27 - 11\frac{3}{10}$

12. $14\frac{5}{9} - 12\frac{7}{9}$ **13.** $32\frac{1}{5} - 21\frac{4}{5}$ **14.** $2\frac{2}{8} - 1\frac{5}{8}$ **15.** $2\frac{1}{6} - 1\frac{5}{6}$

16. At birth, a person's brain weighs about $\frac{9}{10}$ pound. An adult's brain weighs about 3 pounds. By how much does the weight of your brain increase from birth to adulthood?

Mixed Review and Test Prep

Open Response

Write the LCM of the numbers.

(Ch. 9, Lessons 3–4)

17. 15, 18 **18.** 12, 30 **19.** 10, 12

20. Find $2\frac{5}{8} - 1\frac{7}{8}$. Be sure to write your answer in simplest form.

(Ch. 10, Lesson 5)

Extra Practice See page 279, Set E.

Lesson 6

Audio Tutor 1/32 Listen and Understand

Subtract With Unlike Denominators

Objective Subtract fractions with unlike denominators.

Vocabulary
common denominator
simplest form

Learn About It

When you are in a dark room, the pupil of your eye opens to let in as much light as possible. The diameter of your pupil then may be $\frac{3}{10}$ inch.

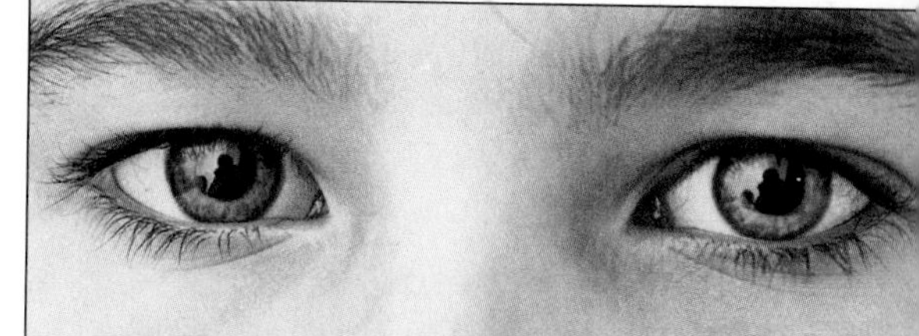

When in bright light, your pupil will contract or get smaller to let in less light. If the diameter of your pupil contracts to $\frac{3}{20}$ inch, how much does it contract?

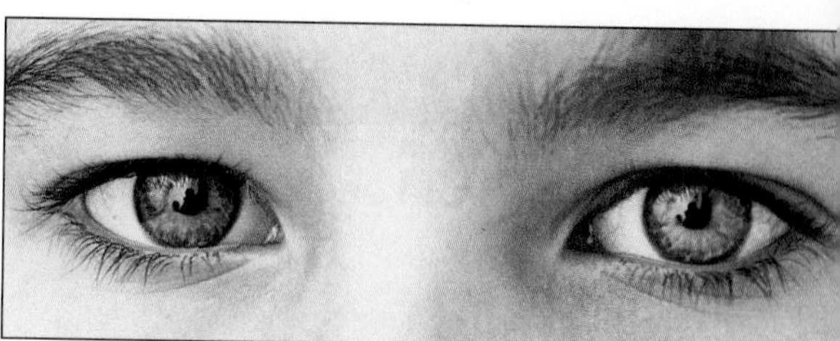

Subtract. $\frac{3}{10} - \frac{3}{20} = n$

Different Ways to Find $\frac{3}{10} - \frac{3}{20}$

Way 1 You can use any **common denominator**.

The product of the denominators, 10×20, can be used to write equivalent fractions with a common denominator.

$$\frac{3 \times 20}{10 \times 20} = \frac{60}{200} \qquad \frac{3 \times 10}{20 \times 10} = \frac{30}{200}$$

$$\frac{60}{200} - \frac{30}{200} = \frac{30}{200}$$

$\frac{30}{200} = \frac{3}{20}$ in **simplest form**.

Way 2 You can use the least common denominator.

The LCM of 10 and 20 is 20.
So the LCD of the fractions is 20.

$$\frac{3 \times 2}{10 \times 2} = \frac{6}{20} \qquad \frac{3 \times 1}{20 \times 1} = \frac{3}{20}$$

$$\frac{6}{20} - \frac{3}{20} = \frac{3}{20}$$

The difference already is in simplest form.

Check your answer.
Use addition.

$$\frac{3}{20} + \frac{3}{20} = \frac{6}{20}$$

$\frac{6}{20} = \frac{3}{10}$ in **simplest form**.

Solution: Your pupil contracts $\frac{3}{20}$ inch.

Guided Practice

Ask Yourself

- Can I find the LCD?
- Is my answer in simplest form?

Subtract. Write the difference in simplest form.

1. $\begin{array}{r} \frac{1}{2} \\ -\frac{1}{6} \\ \hline \end{array}$
2. $\begin{array}{r} \frac{2}{3} \\ -\frac{1}{9} \\ \hline \end{array}$
3. $\begin{array}{r} \frac{2}{3} \\ -\frac{1}{6} \\ \hline \end{array}$
4. $\frac{5}{12} - \frac{3}{8}$
5. $\frac{4}{5} - \frac{1}{4}$
6. $\frac{1}{2} - \frac{2}{5}$

Explain Your Thinking ▶ Why does multiplying the numerator and the denominator of a fraction by the same number produce an equivalent fraction?

Practice and Problem Solving

Subtract. Write the difference in simplest form.

7. $\begin{array}{r} \frac{7}{8} \\ -\frac{1}{2} \\ \hline \end{array}$
8. $\begin{array}{r} \frac{3}{4} \\ -\frac{1}{2} \\ \hline \end{array}$
9. $\begin{array}{r} \frac{11}{12} \\ -\frac{1}{3} \\ \hline \end{array}$
10. $\begin{array}{r} \frac{7}{10} \\ -\frac{2}{5} \\ \hline \end{array}$
11. $\begin{array}{r} \frac{11}{12} \\ -\frac{2}{3} \\ \hline \end{array}$
12. $\begin{array}{r} \frac{1}{2} \\ -\frac{2}{5} \\ \hline \end{array}$
13. $\frac{1}{3} - \frac{1}{8}$
14. $\frac{3}{4} - \frac{2}{5}$
15. $\frac{2}{3} - \frac{2}{10}$
16. $\frac{1}{4} - \frac{1}{10}$
17. $\frac{4}{5} - \frac{3}{4}$
18. $\frac{9}{18} - \frac{3}{6}$
19. $\frac{3}{4} - \frac{1}{10}$
20. $\frac{3}{8} - \frac{1}{16}$

Solve.

21. In soft light, your pupil contracts from about $\frac{3}{10}$ inch to about $\frac{1}{5}$ inch. How much does your pupil contract in soft light?

22. **Predict** Write the three fractions that will likely come next in the pattern below. Explain your answer.

$\frac{1}{2}$ $\frac{2}{3}$ $\frac{3}{4}$ $\frac{4}{5}$ ■ ■ ■

23. **Model** Show how to use fraction strips to subtract $\frac{1}{3}$ from $\frac{3}{4}$.

Mixed Review and Test Prep

Open Response

Multiply or divide.
(Ch. 3, Lesson 4; Ch. 4, Lesson 2)

24. 673×4
25. $894 \div 4$
26. 202×3
27. $612 \div 9$

Multiple Choice

28. If you spend \$50, you can win a discount of $\frac{1}{5}$ off or $\frac{1}{2}$ off. What is the difference in the two discounts?
(Ch. 10, Lesson 6)

A $\frac{1}{3}$ **B** $\frac{1}{7}$ **C** $\frac{3}{5}$ **D** $\frac{3}{10}$

Extra Practice See page 279, Set F.

Lesson 7

Problem-Solving Strategy

Draw a Diagram

Objective Use a diagram to solve problems.

Problem Miguel and Heather are building a model of human lungs for the science fair. Together they have worked $\frac{3}{4}$ hour. Miguel has worked twice as long as Heather has. How long has each student worked?

UNDERSTAND

This is what you know:

- Together they worked $\frac{3}{4}$ hour.
- Miguel has worked twice as long as Heather has.

PLAN

You can draw a diagram to help you solve the problem.

SOLVE

- Draw 2 strips. Make one strip twice the length of the other.

Miguel	▭▭
Heather	▭

Together: $\frac{3}{4}$ hour

- There are 3 small strips that make $\frac{3}{4}$. So each small strip is $\frac{1}{4}$, because 3 unit fractions of $\frac{1}{4}$ make $\frac{3}{4}$.
- Miguel has worked 2 unit fractions of $\frac{1}{4}$, or $\frac{1}{2}$ hour.

$$\frac{1}{4} + \frac{1}{4} = \frac{2}{4} = \frac{1}{2}$$

- Heather has worked 1 unit fraction of $\frac{1}{4}$, or $\frac{1}{4}$ hour.

Miguel has worked $\frac{1}{2}$ hour, and Heather has worked $\frac{1}{4}$ hour.

LOOK BACK

Look back at the problem. Is the answer reasonable? How do you know?

Guided Practice

Use the Ask Yourself questions to help you solve the problem.

1. Josh worked $\frac{3}{4}$ hour on a science fair project. That's three times as long as Chester worked. How many hours did they work in all?

   Hint Think about the fraction each rectangle represents.

   Josh

   Chester

Ask Yourself

UNDERSTAND What facts do I know?

PLAN Did I draw a diagram?

SOLVE
- Did I make the right number of strips?
- Did I label the strips?
- Did I find the number that each strip represents?

LOOK BACK Did I solve the problem?

2. Sarah and Flora won the science fair. Sarah worked $2\frac{1}{3}$ hours on their project, and Flora worked $\frac{1}{2}$ hour more than Sarah. How much time did they work altogether?

   Sarah $2\frac{1}{3}$ hours

   Flora $\frac{1}{2}$ hour

Independent Practice

Draw a diagram to solve each problem.

3. Three fifths of Miss Kwon's and Mr. Taylor's students are boys. Miss Kwon's class has twice as many boys as Mr. Taylor's class. If the classes have the same number of students, what part of each class is boys?

4. Catherine and Alexandria studied together for a history test for $1\frac{1}{2}$ hours. Afterwards Catherine studied for $\frac{2}{3}$ of that time by herself. Alexandria studied for $\frac{1}{2}$ of the time they studied together. How much time did each girl study?

5. A total of 135 students entered the science fair. There were 15 more girls than boys who entered. How many boys and how many girls entered the science fair?

6. A school has 40 classrooms allotted for grades 4–6. Three times as many classrooms are used for grades 4 and 5 together as for grade 6 alone. How many classrooms does grade 6 use?

Mixed Problem Solving

Solve. Show your work. Tell what strategy you used.

7. When Ken turned 11, he was 48 inches tall. A month later, he was $49\frac{1}{4}$ inches tall. Ken thinks he'll grow that much every month. How tall might Ken be when he turns 12?

8. If you subtract $\frac{3}{4}$ from a number and then add $1\frac{6}{8}$, you'll end up with the number 5. What is the mystery number?

9. Use your inch ruler. Measure each line segment to the nearest eighth of an inch. What will the length of the tenth line segment likely be?

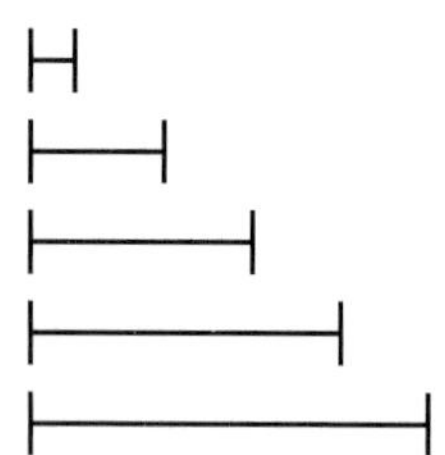

You Choose

Strategy
- Draw a Diagram
- Find a Pattern
- Make a Table
- Work Backward

Computation Method
- Mental Math
- Estimation
- Paper and Pencil
- Calculator

Data Use the graph to solve Problems 10–13.

The graph shows survey results about breakfasts of fifth-grade students.

10. How many fifth-grade students responded to the survey?

11. How many more fifth-graders ate cold cereal than hot cereal on Saturday?

12. What fraction of the students surveyed ate a cold cereal on Saturday?

13. What fraction of the students surveyed did not eat hot cereal on Saturday?

Problem Solving On Tests

Multiple Choice

Choose the letter of the correct answer. If the correct answer is not here, choose NH.

1. A recipe calls for $1\frac{1}{2}$ cups of flour. You set $\frac{1}{4}$ cup aside and put the rest in a bowl. How much do you put in the bowl? (Chapter 10, Lesson 6)

   A $1\frac{1}{4}$ cups **C** $1\frac{1}{2}$ cups

   B $1\frac{1}{3}$ cups **D** $1\frac{3}{4}$ cups

2. What is the least possible whole number you can make that uses the digits 9, 6, 8, and 3 only once and has a 9 in the tens place? (Chapter 9, Lesson 7)

   F 3,896 **G** 3,986 **H** 3,698 **J** NH

Open Response

Solve each problem.

3. This Venn diagram shows factors of 24 and 36.

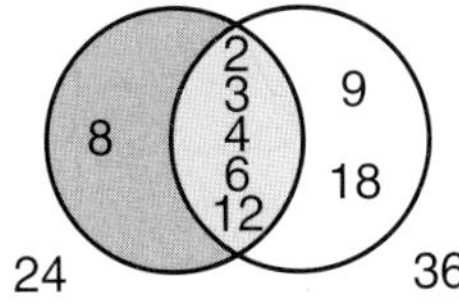

   What is the GCF of 24 and 36?

   Explain How does a Venn diagram help you identify the GCF? (Chapter 9, Lesson 3)

4. Sal has a collection of stamps. He has 30 stamps in all. For every stamp from another country, Sal has two from the United States. How many United States stamps does Sal have? (Chapter 10, Lesson 7)

   Represent Support your solution with a diagram.

Constructed Response

5. You and two classmates want to make a classroom flag the same size as last year's flag. Your two partners have measured the length and width of last year's flag. (Chapters 9–10)

Susan's measurement	ßBen's measurement
Length $17\frac{1}{4}$ inches	Length 17.25 inches
Width $12\frac{1}{2}$ inches	Width 12.5 inches

   a Did both of your partners find the same measurements? Check by writing the decimals as mixed numbers in simplest form.

   b You have a piece of cloth that is $24\frac{1}{8}$ inches long and $12\frac{1}{2}$ inches wide. How much should you cut off the length and width to make a flag with the same dimensions as last year's?

   c Design a new flag that is wider but shorter in length. Using mixed numbers, tell the dimensions of your new flag. Remember to use fractions of an inch that can be measured on a ruler.

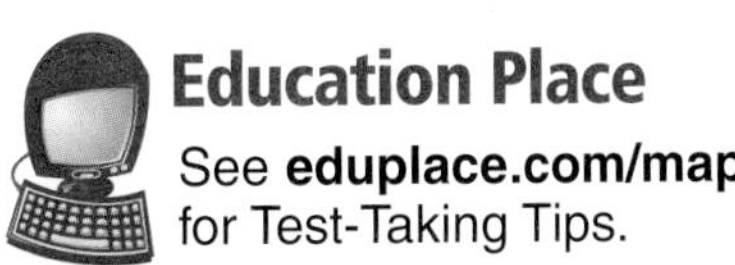

Education Place
See **eduplace.com/map** for Test-Taking Tips.

Lesson 8

Audio Tutor 1/33 Listen and Understand

Subtract Mixed Numbers With Unlike Denominators

Objective Subtract mixed numbers with unlike denominators.

Learn About It

Last night, Tyler slept $8\frac{1}{2}$ hours, and Vanessa slept $9\frac{1}{4}$ hours. How much longer did Vanessa sleep than Tyler?

Subtract. $9\frac{1}{4} - 8\frac{1}{2} = n$

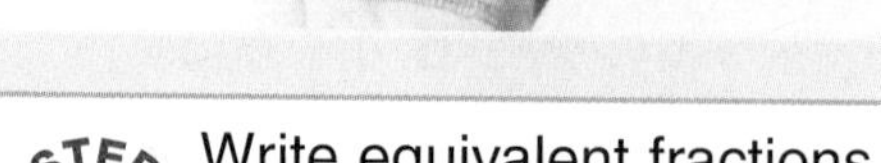

STEP 1 Find the LCD of the fractions.

$$\begin{array}{rcr} 9\frac{1}{4} & = & 9\frac{\blacksquare}{4} \\ -\ 8\frac{1}{2} & = & -\ 8\frac{\blacksquare}{4} \\ \hline \end{array}$$

← LCD

STEP 2 Write equivalent fractions.

$$\begin{array}{rcr} 9\frac{1}{4} & = & 9\frac{1}{4} \\ -\ 8\frac{1}{2} & = & -\ 8\frac{2}{4} \\ \hline \end{array}$$

STEP 3 Rename mixed numbers if necessary.

$$\begin{array}{rcr} 9\frac{1}{4} & = & 8\frac{5}{4} \\ -\ 8\frac{2}{4} & = & -\ 8\frac{2}{4} \\ \hline \end{array}$$

STEP 4 Subtract and simplify.

$$\begin{array}{rcr} 9\frac{1}{4} & = & 8\frac{5}{4} \\ -\ 8\frac{2}{4} & = & -\ 8\frac{2}{4} \\ \hline & & \frac{3}{4} \end{array}$$

Solution: Vanessa slept $\frac{3}{4}$ hour longer than Tyler.

Guided Practice

Subtract. Write each difference in simplest form.

1. $\begin{array}{r} 4\frac{1}{3} \\ -\ 2\frac{1}{5} \\ \hline \end{array}$

2. $\begin{array}{r} 9\frac{9}{10} \\ -\ 4\frac{2}{5} \\ \hline \end{array}$

3. $\begin{array}{r} 4\frac{1}{2} \\ -\ 2\frac{7}{10} \\ \hline \end{array}$

4. $\begin{array}{r} 8\frac{5}{12} \\ -\ 6\frac{7}{8} \\ \hline \end{array}$

Ask Yourself

- Did I rename when necessary?
- Did I simplify each difference?

Explain Your Thinking ▶ The value of a number does not change when it is renamed correctly. Explain why.

Practice and Problem Solving

Subtract. Write each difference in simplest form.

5. $9\frac{6}{8} - 2\frac{1}{2}$

6. $7\frac{1}{2} - 3$

7. $7\frac{3}{16} - 6\frac{1}{8}$

8. $3\frac{1}{5} - 1\frac{4}{20}$

9. $4\frac{1}{5} - 3\frac{3}{10}$

10. $4\frac{7}{10} - 1\frac{7}{15}$

11. $2\frac{1}{2} - 1\frac{2}{3}$

12. $4\frac{1}{3} - 1\frac{3}{4}$

13. $6\frac{3}{4} - 3\frac{5}{8}$

14. $9\frac{1}{4} - 6\frac{5}{6}$

15. $2\frac{5}{12} - 1\frac{4}{5}$

Write >, <, or = for each ⬤.

16. $3\frac{3}{8} - 1\frac{1}{4}$ ⬤ $4 - 2\frac{2}{3}$

17. $8\frac{1}{4} - 3\frac{1}{2}$ ⬤ $6\frac{3}{4} - 2$

18. $6\frac{1}{3} - 2\frac{4}{5}$ ⬤ $9\frac{1}{8} - 4\frac{5}{12}$

19. $6\frac{1}{4} - 4\frac{5}{8}$ ⬤ $10 - 7\frac{1}{8}$

Mental Math **Use mental math to subtract.**

20. $5\frac{5}{8} - 3\frac{5}{8}$

21. $9\frac{2}{3} - 1\frac{1}{3}$

22. $6\frac{3}{4} - 4$

23. $1\frac{1}{2} - 1\frac{1}{2}$

24. $15 - 7\frac{1}{2}$

25. $10\frac{1}{11} - 9$

Algebra • Expressions **Evaluate each expression, when $a = 3\frac{3}{4}$, $b = 5\frac{1}{8}$, and $c = 1\frac{2}{3}$.**

26. $a - c$

27. $b - a$

28. $b - c$

29. $(a + c) - b$

Copy and complete each function table.

30.

Rule: $y = x - 2$	
x	y
$3\frac{1}{4}$	■
$5\frac{7}{8}$	■
$9\frac{3}{5}$	■

31.

Rule: $y = x + 1\frac{1}{2}$	
x	y
$1\frac{2}{3}$	■
$4\frac{1}{2}$	■
$6\frac{5}{8}$	■

32.

Rule: $y = x - 1\frac{3}{4}$	
x	y
4	■
$5\frac{3}{4}$	■
$7\frac{1}{4}$	■

Go On

Solve.

33. On Friday night, Lim slept for $10\frac{1}{3}$ hours. That was $2\frac{1}{2}$ hours more than he slept the night before. How many hours did Lim sleep on Thursday night?

34. Frances used to get 8 hours sleep each night. Now she takes a $1\frac{1}{2}$ hour nap and sleeps 5 hours at night. How much has her total sleep time changed?

35. Leon's goal is to sleep at least $8\frac{1}{2}$ hours each night. He goes to bed at 10:30 and wakes up at 6:45. Does Leon get the sleep he wants? If not, by how much does he miss his goal?

36. An infant sleeps about 16 hours each day. On Tuesday, her longest nap was $2\frac{2}{3}$ hours long, and her shortest nap was $\frac{3}{10}$ of an hour long. What is the range of her nap times?

37. Measurement With your math book closed, measure the length and width of its pages to the nearest eighth of an inch. What is the difference in these measures?

38. You Decide Teenagers should get $9\frac{1}{4}$ hours sleep each night. A middle school starts at 7:30 A.M. What do you think might be a better starting time? Explain your reasoning.

Choose a Computation Method

Mental Math • Estimation • Paper and Pencil • Calculator

Data **Use the table for Problems 39–43. Then explain which method you chose.**

39. How much more time does Judy spend getting ready for school than Rob does?

40. On which activity does Judy spend $\frac{1}{4}$ hour more than Rob does?

41. From the time he leaves school to the time he goes to bed, how much time does Rob spend on homework and other activities?

42. How much time is Judy awake during the day?

43. Create and Solve Write your own problem that uses data from the table. Solve your problem. Then give your problem to a partner to solve.

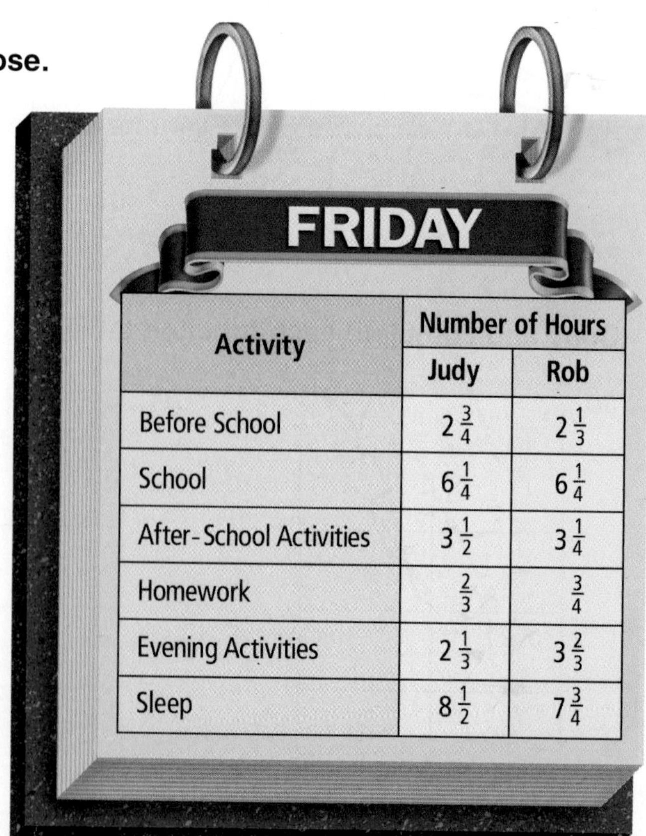

FRIDAY

Activity	Number of Hours	
	Judy	Rob
Before School	$2\frac{3}{4}$	$2\frac{1}{3}$
School	$6\frac{1}{4}$	$6\frac{1}{4}$
After-School Activities	$3\frac{1}{2}$	$3\frac{1}{4}$
Homework	$\frac{2}{3}$	$\frac{3}{4}$
Evening Activities	$2\frac{1}{3}$	$3\frac{2}{3}$
Sleep	$8\frac{1}{2}$	$7\frac{3}{4}$

Extra Practice See page 279, Set G.

Mixed Review and Test Prep

Open Response

Use mental math to solve each equation.
(Ch. 4, Lesson 7)

44. $3y = 12$

45. $m \div 7 = 5$

46. $36 \div x = 3$

47. $6w = 42$

48. $56 \div a = 7$

49. $8b = 24$

50. On Saturday and Sunday, John jogged for a total of $4\frac{1}{2}$ hours. On Saturday, he jogged twice as long as on Sunday. How long did he jog each day? Draw a diagram to explain. (Ch. 10, Lesson 8)

Problem Solving

Calculator Connection

What's the Rule?

You can use your calculator to show fractions as decimals by dividing the numerator by the denominator.

For each exercise, complete the following:

- Describe the pattern in the numerators and denominators.
- Use your calculator to convert the fractions to decimals.
- Describe the pattern in the decimals.
- Predict the next 2 fractions and decimals in the pattern.

1. $\frac{1}{50}$ $\frac{2}{50}$ $\frac{3}{50}$ $\frac{4}{50}$

2. $\frac{2}{5}$ $\frac{2}{10}$ $\frac{2}{20}$ $\frac{2}{40}$

3. $\frac{1}{25}$ $\frac{2}{50}$ $\frac{3}{75}$

Chapter Review/Test

VOCABULARY

1. The ____ of two or more denominators is the least common denominator.

2. $\frac{3}{4}$ and $\frac{6}{8}$ are ____.

3. The ____ of $\frac{7}{8}$ and $\frac{3}{4}$ is 8.

Vocabulary

- equivalent fractions
- least common denominator
- least common multiple
- simplest form

CONCEPTS AND SKILLS

Estimate each sum or difference.
Name the method you used to estimate. (Lesson 1, pp. 256–257)

4. $\frac{7}{8} - \frac{1}{6}$
5. $3\frac{3}{4} + \frac{5}{8}$
6. $23\frac{1}{8} + 14\frac{1}{4}$
7. $\frac{7}{9} - \frac{9}{16}$
8. $\frac{5}{8} - \frac{11}{20}$
9. $\frac{3}{8} + \frac{5}{6}$

Add. Write each sum in simplest form. (Lessons 2–4, pp. 258–265)

10. $\frac{7}{8} + \frac{5}{12}$
11. $\frac{2}{5} + \frac{2}{3}$
12. $4\frac{1}{2} + 8\frac{3}{8}$
13. $3\frac{3}{4} + 6\frac{3}{8}$
14. $\frac{5}{16} + \frac{7}{8}$
15. $\frac{5}{11} + \frac{7}{11}$
16. $6\frac{2}{5} + 9\frac{4}{5}$
17. $3\frac{1}{5} + 5\frac{1}{2}$

Subtract. Write each answer in simplest form. (Lessons 5–6, pp. 266–269; Lesson 8, pp. 274–277)

18. $\frac{6}{7} - \frac{2}{7}$
19. $21\frac{1}{8} - 18\frac{6}{8}$
20. $13\frac{2}{5} - 4\frac{1}{4}$
21. $\frac{13}{15} - \frac{2}{3}$
22. $\frac{2}{3} - \frac{3}{8}$
23. $10 - 4\frac{3}{4}$

PROBLEM SOLVING

Draw a diagram to solve each problem.
(Lesson 7, pp. 270–273)

24. Roger walks $6\frac{1}{2}$ blocks to school. Juanita walks $2\frac{3}{4}$ blocks to school. How much farther does Roger walk than Juanita?

25. Jorge worked $2\frac{1}{3}$ hours on his exhibit for the science fair. Juan worked $\frac{3}{4}$ hour more than Jorge. How long did the boys work altogether?

Show You Understand

Mandy added $\frac{3}{5}$ and $\frac{12}{15}$. Did she do it correctly? If not, explain.

$$\frac{3}{5} + \frac{12}{15} = \frac{3 + 12}{5 + 15} = \frac{15}{20} = \frac{3}{4}$$

Extra Practice

Set A (Lesson 1, pp. 256–257)

Estimate each sum or difference. Name the method you used to estimate.

1. $\frac{5}{6} + \frac{7}{8}$
2. $75\frac{1}{4} - 36\frac{1}{8}$
3. $7\frac{9}{10} - \frac{5}{8}$
4. $43\frac{2}{3} + 22\frac{5}{8}$
5. $3\frac{3}{4} - \frac{4}{7}$
6. $\frac{1}{9} + \frac{4}{5} + \frac{1}{3} + \frac{1}{15}$
7. $\frac{1}{5} + 1\frac{2}{3} + 2\frac{1}{3} + 3\frac{1}{6} + \frac{2}{10}$

Set B (Lesson 2, pp. 258–259)

Add. Write each sum in simplest form.

1. $2\frac{1}{5} + 3\frac{2}{5}$
2. $3\frac{5}{8} + 2\frac{3}{8}$
3. $4\frac{3}{4} + 5\frac{3}{4}$
4. $2\frac{1}{6} + 3\frac{1}{6}$

Set C (Lesson 3, pp. 260–261)

Add. Write each sum in simplest form.

1. $\frac{1}{4} + \frac{1}{8}$
2. $\frac{2}{3} + \frac{2}{9}$
3. $\frac{3}{5} + \frac{3}{10}$
4. $\frac{1}{5} + \frac{3}{10}$
5. $\frac{5}{12} + \frac{1}{3}$
6. $\frac{7}{8} + \frac{1}{16}$
7. $\frac{11}{12} + \frac{2}{3}$
8. $\frac{3}{8} + \frac{7}{12}$
9. $\frac{1}{4} + \frac{2}{5}$
10. $\frac{1}{6} + \frac{2}{3}$

Set D (Lesson 4, pp. 262–265)

Add. Write each sum in simplest form.

1. $4\frac{2}{3} + 5\frac{3}{4}$
2. $4\frac{1}{2} + 3\frac{3}{4}$
3. $3\frac{3}{4} + 3\frac{7}{8}$
4. $6\frac{3}{4} + 7\frac{5}{6}$
5. $2\frac{1}{2} + 3\frac{3}{4}$
6. $8\frac{1}{16} + 9\frac{1}{3}$
7. $6\frac{5}{12} + 3\frac{2}{3}$
8. $5\frac{1}{5} + 3\frac{1}{2}$

Set E (Lesson 5, pp. 266–267)

Subtract. Write each difference in simplest form.

1. $\frac{7}{8} - \frac{5}{8}$
2. $\frac{4}{5} - \frac{1}{5}$
3. $\frac{9}{10} - \frac{3}{10}$
4. $\frac{6}{7} - \frac{3}{7}$
5. $7 - 3\frac{1}{6}$

Set F (Lesson 6, pp. 268–269)

Subtract. Write each difference in simplest form.

1. $\frac{3}{4} - \frac{1}{8}$
2. $\frac{5}{12} - \frac{1}{6}$
3. $\frac{11}{12} - \frac{5}{8}$
4. $\frac{5}{6} - \frac{1}{2}$
5. $\frac{3}{4} - \frac{3}{5}$
6. $\frac{6}{8} - \frac{5}{16}$
7. $\frac{19}{24} - \frac{1}{6}$
8. $\frac{9}{10} - \frac{2}{5}$

Set G (Lesson 8, pp. 274–277)

Subtract. Write each answer in simplest form.

1. $3\frac{3}{4} - 2\frac{2}{3}$
2. $8\frac{1}{2} - 4\frac{3}{4}$
3. $6\frac{5}{6} - 3\frac{2}{3}$
4. $2\frac{3}{8} - 1\frac{1}{4}$
5. $4\frac{3}{12} - 2\frac{3}{4}$
6. $9\frac{1}{4} - 6\frac{3}{8}$
7. $7 - 1\frac{4}{5}$
8. $5\frac{1}{6} - 2\frac{1}{4}$

Extra Practice at eduplace.com/map

Add and Subtract Decimals

INVESTIGATION

Use Data

The table shows the average speed of Indy 500 winners. What trends do you notice? Do research to find why this is true and write a brief report.

Indy 500 Winning Average Speed

Year	Speed
1988	114.809
1992	134.477
1996	147.956
2000	167.607
2004	138.518

Use What You Know

Use this page to review and remember what you need to know for this chapter.

VOCABULARY

Choose the best word to complete each sentence.

1. In the number 3.25, the 2 is in the ____ place.
2. The decimals 5.6 and 5.60 are ____.
3. When comparing numbers, you compare the ____ that have the same place values.
4. In the number 5.20, the 0 is in the ____ place.

Vocabulary

- digits
- equal
- hundredths
- tenths
- thousandths

CONCEPTS AND SKILLS

Write a fraction and a decimal for the shaded part.

5. 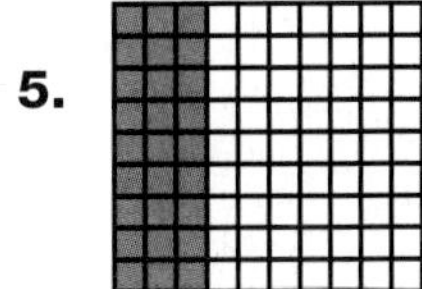

6. 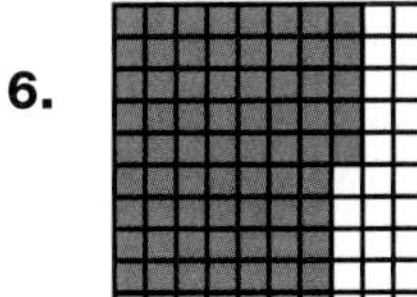

7. 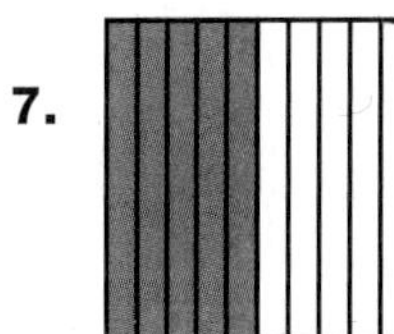

Order the numbers from greatest to least.

8. 4.06, 3.14, 3.7, 4.08
9. 235.03, 194.3, 235.3, 194.03
10. 11.52, 12.07, 12.8, 12.5
11. 4.05, 4.5, 4.005, 45
12. 2.2, 22.02, 2.22, 2.02
13. 0.3, 0.081, 0.2, 0.02

Round to the place of the underlined digit.

14. 2.<u>3</u>24
15. 3.<u>2</u>59
16. 0.2<u>6</u>5
17. 8<u>3</u>.351
18. 0.<u>6</u>72
19. 1<u>3</u>.559

Write About It

20. The Rivoli Theater sold 12,217 tickets, and the Capital Theater sold 2,250. About how many more tickets did the Rivoli sell? Explain how you found your answer.

Facts Practice, See page 662.

Lesson 1

Explore Addition and Subtraction With Decimals

Objective Add and subtract decimals.

Learn About It

A car dealer sells used sports cars. Of all the cars she has on her lot, 0.89 are red. Only 0.03 are green. What part of the cars on her lot are red or green?

Solve 0.89 + 0.03 = *n*.

You can use models and what you know about fractions to find 0.89 + 0.03. Try changing the decimals to fractions and then modeling the addition.

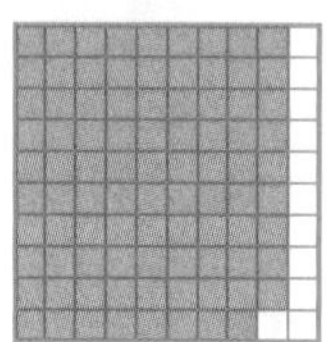
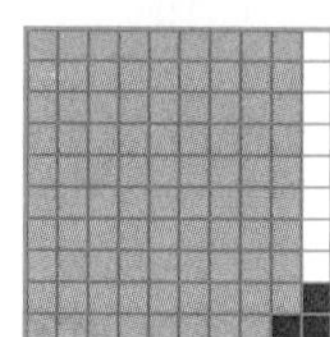

- What fractions are equivalent to 0.89 and 0.03? $0.89 = \frac{89}{100}$ $0.03 = \frac{3}{100}$
- How can you model $\frac{89}{100}$?
- How can you show $\frac{3}{100}$ more than $\frac{89}{100}$?
- Think about what you are to find.

  How much is 0.89 + 0.03?

  How much is $\frac{89}{100}$ plus $\frac{3}{100}$?
- How do you add fractions with like denominators? $\frac{89}{100} + \frac{3}{100} = \frac{92}{100}$
- How can you write your answer as a decimal? $\frac{92}{100} = 0.92$

Solution: Of the cars on the dealer's lot, 0.92 are red or green.

Another Example

Subtract Decimals

Subtract. 2.14 − 1.12 = *n*

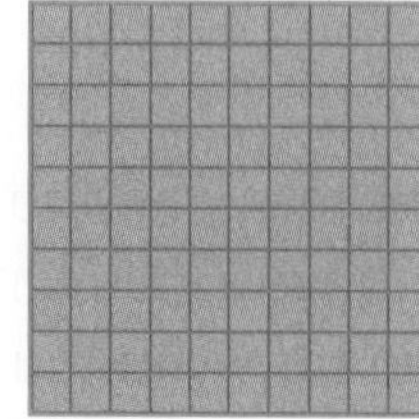
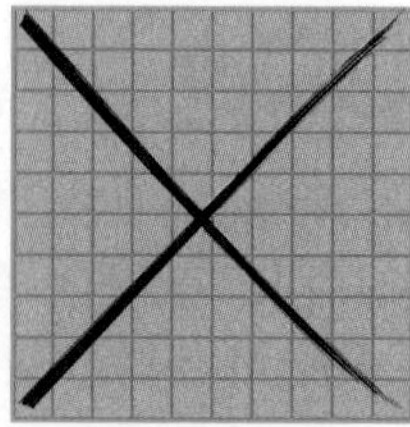
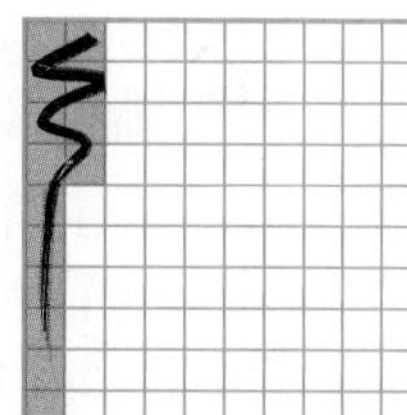

$2.14 = 2\frac{14}{100}$ $1.12 = 1\frac{12}{100}$

$2\frac{14}{100} - 1\frac{12}{100} = 1\frac{2}{100}$

So 2.14 − 1.12 = 1.02

Guided Practice

Change each decimal to a fraction. Model each addition and subtraction. Write each sum as a decimal.

1. 0.3 + 0.5
2. 0.25 + 0.15
3. 1.2 + 1.8
4. 0.9 − 0.1
5. 0.67 − 0.22
6. 2.08 − 1.15

Ask Yourself

- Did I change the decimals to fractions?
- Did I write my answer as a decimal?

Explain Your Thinking ▶ Why is it easy to change a decimal to a fraction and then change it back again? Give examples to support your thinking.

Practice and Problem Solving

Change each decimal to a fraction. Model each addition and subtraction. Write each sum as a decimal.

7. 0.7 + 0.7
8. 0.76 + 0.15
9. 0.34 + 0.98
10. 1.25 + 2.37
11. 0.4 − 0.3
12. 0.25 − 0.12
13. 1.26 − 1.05
14. 2.8 − 1.4
15. 0.56 + 0.3
16. 0.92 + 0.8
17. 0.93 − 0.5
18. 0.6 − 0.15

Solve.

19. Of the cars the dealer sold two years ago, 0.4 were blue. Last year 0.09 of the cars she sold were blue. In which year did she sell a greater fraction of blue cars? Draw a model to explain.

20. A car dealer noted that an older sports car model was 167.3 inches long and a newer model was 12.4 inches longer than that. How long was the newer model?

21. Jenna filled the gas tank of her car with 14.3 gallons of gas. She used 8.2 gallons driving to work over 5 days. How much gas is left in her tank?

22. Of the 3,460 sports cars sold this year, only 4 were gold. Is that about 0.1, 0.01, or 0.001 of the sports cars? Explain how you know.

Mixed Review and Test Prep

Open Response

Draw the next two figures in each pattern. (Grade 4)

23. 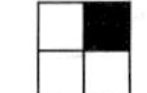   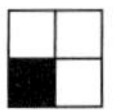 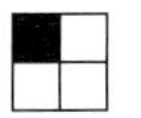 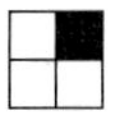 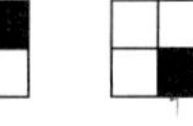

24.      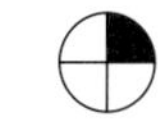 

25. Dave spent 4.5 hours cleaning his car. He spent 3.5 hours polishing it. Write a fraction equation and draw a model to show how much longer it took Dave to clean his car than to polish it. (Ch. 11, Lesson 1)

Extra Practice See page 295, Set A.

Lesson 2

Audio Tutor 1/34 Listen and Understand

Add Decimals

Objective Add decimals through thousandths.

Vocabulary
hundredths
thousandths

Learn About It

Add. 0.07 + 2.8 + 0.5 = *n*

STEP 1 Align the digits in the addends. Use the decimal points as guides. Then add the **hundredths**.

```
  0.07
  2.80    Write zeros as
+ 0.50    needed.
     7
```

STEP 2 Add the tenths.

```
  1
  0.07
  2.80
+ 0.50
    37
```

STEP 3 Add the ones.

```
  1
  0.07    Align the
  2.80    decimal point in
+ 0.50    the sum with the
  3.37    decimal point in
          the addends.
```

Use a calculator to check.

0 . 0 7 + 2 . 8 + 0 . 5 Enter =

Solution: $n = 3.37$

Another Example

Add Decimals Through Thousandths

Add.

124.057 + 45.8 + 77.345 = *n*

```
 1 1 1  1 1
 124.057
  45.800
+ 77.345
 247.202
```

Guided Practice

Add. Use a calculator to check.

1. 4.517 + 2.824

2. $57.99 + 4.23

3. 54.1 + 8.376 + 12

4. 78.94 + 5.57

5. 19.07 + 1.23

6. 8 + 4.794 + 2.3

Ask Yourself

- Did I line up the digits in the addends?
- Did I remember to write the decimal point in the answer?

Explain Your Thinking ▶ Why is it important to align the decimal points in the addends?

Practice and Problem Solving

Add. Use a calculator to check.

7. $\$8.49 + 4.59$
8. $9.527 + 3.75$
9. $178.03 + 8.4$
10. $1.699 + 90.5$
11. $\$10.00 + 8.05$
12. $\$51.70 + 83.62$
13. $78.427 + 27.309$
14. $85.076 + 7.925$
15. $5.76 + 28.569$
16. $41.75 + 9.863$
17. $31.85 + 5.8 + 53.85$
18. $\$8.03 + 9.80 + 24.57$
19. $7.9 + 5.662 + 14.038$
20. $4.887 + 46.2 + 7.09$
21. $4.47 + 4.46 + 6.592$

22. 28.5 + 85.7 **23.** 2.06 + 46.99 **24.** 0.007 + 0.925 **25.** 7.48 + 0.351

26. 11.2 + 16.801 **27.** 5.05 + 1.3 **28.** 2.089 + 5 + 4.8 **29.** 20.49 + 17.5

Data Use the log book below to solve Problems 30–33.

Juanita is a bicycle messenger in Washington, D.C. The log book is a record of distances she rides in doing her job.

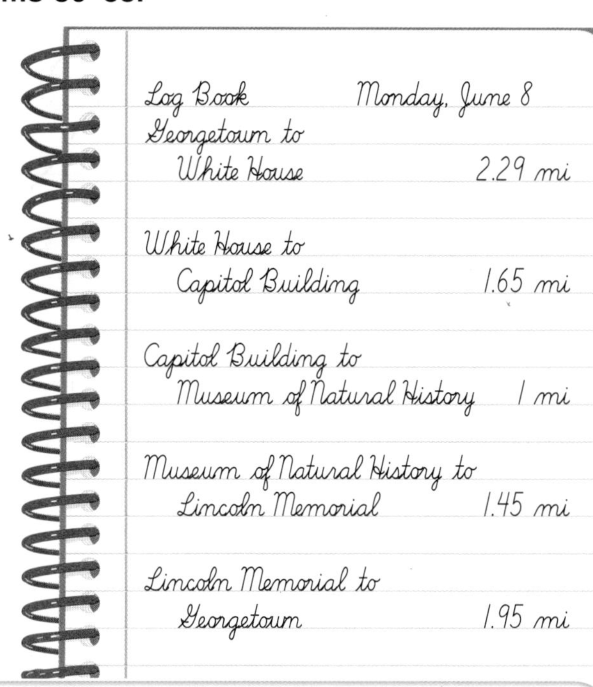

Log Book Monday, June 8
Georgetown to White House 2.29 mi
White House to Capitol Building 1.65 mi
Capitol Building to Museum of Natural History 1 mi
Museum of Natural History to Lincoln Memorial 1.45 mi
Lincoln Memorial to Georgetown 1.95 mi

30. How far is it from the White House to the Capitol to the museum?

31. How far was the trip from the museum to Georgetown?

32. Juanita's odometer read 168.8 when she left one place and 170.25 at her next stop. Where did she go?

33. **Create Your Own** Write an addition word problem using information from the log book.

Mixed Review and Test Prep

Open Response

Estimate the sums and differences.
(Ch. 2, Lesson 4)

34. 324 + 456 + 535 **35.** 9,220 + 984

36. 13,562 − 9,480 **37.** 10,100 − 750

38. A car emitted 0.750 grams more of a pollutant than the 0.09 grams allowed. How many grams of this pollutant did the car emit? Explain how you found your answer.
(Ch. 11, Lesson 2)

Extra Practice See page 295, Set B.

Lesson 3

Audio Tutor 1/35 Listen and Understand

Subtract Decimals

Objective Subtract decimals through thousandths with and without regrouping.

Learn About It

On the highway, John's car can travel 31.42 miles on one gallon of gas. When he is driving in the city, his car gets 26.98 miles per gallon. How many more miles per gallon does John's car get on the highway than in the city?

You can draw a model to help you solve the problem.

Highway miles per gallon	
City miles per gallon	Difference: ?

Highway: 31.42 miles per gallon	
City: 26.98 miles per gallon	Difference: ?

Subtract. $31.42 - 26.98 = n$

STEP 1 Write the addends so the digits are aligned. Subtract the hundredths.

$$\begin{array}{r} \overset{3\ 12}{31.\cancel{4}\cancel{2}} \\ -\ 26.98 \\ \hline 4 \end{array}$$

STEP 2 Subtract the tenths.

$$\begin{array}{r} \overset{0\ 13\ 12}{3\cancel{1}.\cancel{4}\cancel{2}} \\ -\ 26.98 \\ \hline 44 \end{array}$$

STEP 3 Subtract the ones. Write the decimal point in the answer.

$$\begin{array}{r} \overset{2\ 10\ 13\ 12}{\cancel{3}\cancel{1}.\cancel{4}\cancel{2}} \\ -\ 26.98 \\ \hline 4.44 \end{array}$$

STEP 4 Subtract the tens.

$$\begin{array}{r} \overset{2\ 10\ 13\ 12}{\cancel{3}\cancel{1}.\cancel{4}\cancel{2}} \\ -\ 26.98 \\ \hline 4.44 \end{array}$$

Add to check.

$$\begin{array}{r} \overset{1\ 1\ \ 1}{26.98} \\ +\ \ 4.44 \\ \hline 31.42 \end{array}$$

Solution: John's car gets 4.44 more miles per gallon on the highway than in the city.

Extra Help at eduplace.com/map

Other Examples

A. Zeros as Placeholders

Find 27.5 − 2.71.

```
    6  14 10
 2 7 . 5 0
-  2 . 7 1
 2 4 . 7 9
```

B. Money

Find $28 − $9.76.

```
     17  9
   1 18 1010
 $ 2 8 . 0 0
 -   9 . 7 6
 $ 1 8 . 2 4
```

Guided Practice

Ask Yourself

- Have I aligned the digits correctly?
- Do I need to write zeros to help me subtract?

Subtract. Add or use a calculator to check your answer.

1. $4.5 - 3.7$
2. $7.0 - 4.37$
3. $4.18 − $2.99
4. 7.514 − 5.439
5. 2 − 0.065
6. $84.01 − $47.86

Use the model to solve the problem.

7. A car gets 4.6 more miles per gallon on the highway than it does in the city. If the car gets 26.25 miles per gallon on the highway, how many miles per gallon does it get in the city?

Highway: 26.25 miles per gallon	
City: ?	Difference: 4.6 miles per gallon

Explain Your Thinking ▶ How is subtraction with decimals like subtraction with whole numbers? How is it different?

Practice and Problem Solving

Subtract. Add or use a calculator to check your answer.

8. $5.6 - 4.9$
9. $9.2 - 3.7$
10. $12.5 - 9.8$
11. $28.09 − $17.99
12. $3.45 − $0.79
13. $72.325 - 5.61$
14. $57.681 - 24.925$
15. $8.42 - 3.693$
16. 6.74 − 5.89
17. $34.56 − $13.67
18. 65.23 − 37.68
19. 4.056 − 2.345
20. 29.547 − 18.918
21. 0.523 − 0.097

Go On

Mental Math **Add or subtract using mental math.**

22. 0.8 + 0.1

23. 4.5 + 1.5

24. 0.9 − 0.2

25. 0.006 + 0.027

26. 0.09 + 0.01

27. 0.5 − 0.3

28. 0.042 − 0.03

29. 9.08 − 9.03

30. $5.85 + $1.15

31. 0.004 + 0.076

32. 4.34 − 0.28

33. $7.05 + $2.15

Algebra • Equations **Find the value of *x*.**

34. $x + 1.4 = 2$

35. $x - 1.4 = 2$

36. $2.8 - x = 2.3$

37. $0.5 + x = 1.0$

38. $3.2 + x = 4.3$

39. $2.65 - x = 2.5$

Data **Use the table below to solve Problems 40–42.**

Roberta drives her car to her job. The table shows her gas log for the month of April.

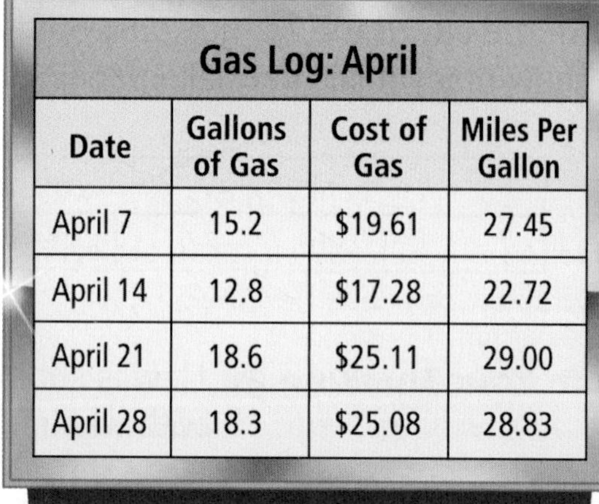

Gas Log: April			
Date	Gallons of Gas	Cost of Gas	Miles Per Gallon
April 7	15.2	$19.61	27.45
April 14	12.8	$17.28	22.72
April 21	18.6	$25.11	29.00
April 28	18.3	$25.08	28.83

40. What is the range for the gas mileage (miles per gallon) that Roberta gets with her car?

41. Roberta budgets $100 per month for gasoline for her job. How much over or under her budget was Roberta during April?

42. In May, Roberta bought 56.8 gallons of gas. How many more or fewer gallons of gas did Roberta buy during April?

43. Write the missing digits.

```
  4.■3■
− ■.684
  2.5■1
```

44. **Measurement** Draw a rectangle 6.8 centimeters long with a width 2.25 centimeters shorter than its length.

45. The sum of two numbers is 16.4. Their difference is 0.8. What are the two numbers?

Extra Practice See page 295, Set C.

Quick Check

Check your understanding for Lessons 1–3.

Add or subtract. (Lessons 1–3)

1. 0.9 − 0.2
2. \$53.24 + \$16.82
3. 4.9 + 3.75 + 0.84
4. 9 − 0.87
5. 0.025 − 0.006
6. \$20 − \$5.29
7. 0.206 + 0.324 + 0.74
8. 1.732 − 0.585

Solve. (Lesson 3)

9. A car gets 38.6 miles per gallon on the highway. It gets 5.75 miles per gallon less when it is in the city. How many miles per gallon does the car get in the city?

Problem Solving

Math Challenge

Zero Sum-thing

If you subtract 2 − 2, you know the answer is zero. If you add 4 and then subtract 1 and then subtract 3, the answer is also zero. These are zero sums. Adding and subtracting the same amount is the same as adding 0. Do you think this also works with decimals? Check It Out.

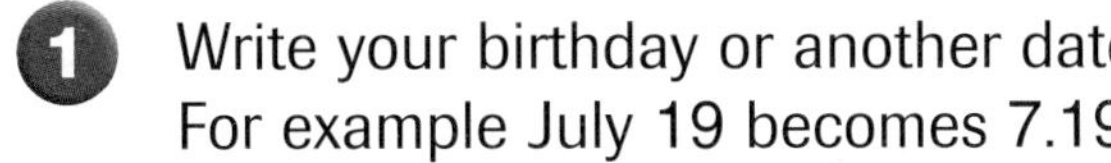

1. Write your birthday or another date as a decimal. For example July 19 becomes 7.19.
   - Add 2.06.
   - Subtract 1.32.
   - Subtract 0.08.
   - Add 3.5.
   - Subtract 2.16.
   - Subtract 2.

$$\begin{array}{r} 7.19 \\ +\ 2.06 \\ \hline 9.25 \\ -\ 1.32 \\ \hline 7.93 \\ -\ 0.08 \\ \hline 7.85 \\ +\ 3.5 \\ \hline 11.35 \\ -\ 2.16 \\ \hline 9.19 \\ -\ 2.00 \\ \hline 7.19 \end{array}$$

2. What do you notice about your answer?
3. Why did this work?
4. Use decimals to make up your own zero sum challenge for a friend to try.

Lesson 4

Estimate Decimal Sums and Differences

Objective Estimate decimal sums and differences.

Learn About It

In a race, the second-place finisher was about 0.038 seconds behind the winner. The third-place car was about 0.139 seconds behind the winner. About how many seconds behind the second-place car was the third-place car?

Estimate 0.139 – 0.038.

You can use what you know about rounding decimals to estimate the difference. For decimals less than one, round to the nearest tenth. For decimals greater than 1, round to the nearest whole number.

STEP 1 Round each number to the nearest tenth.

$0.139 \approx 0.1$

3 < 5, so round down.

$0.038 \approx 0.0$

3 < 5, so round down.

STEP 2 Subtract.

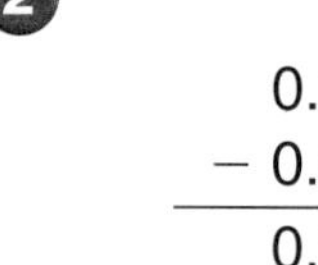

$$\begin{array}{r} 0.1 \\ -\ 0.0 \\ \hline 0.1 \end{array}$$

Solution: The third-place car was about 0.1 second behind the second-place car.

Other Examples

A. Nearest Whole Number

Estimate 23.27 – 15.64.

Round each decimal to the nearest whole number.

$23.27 \approx 23$
$15.64 \approx 16$

$23 - 16 = 7$
$23.27 - 15.64 \approx 7$

B. Front-End Estimation

Estimate 4.14 + 5.22.

Add the leading digits.

$4.14 \rightarrow 4$
$5.22 \rightarrow 5$

$4 + 5 = 9$
$4.14 + 5.22 \approx 9$

Since both decimals are rounded down, the estimated sum will be a little less than the actual sum.

C. Clustering

Estimate.

0.46 ⎤ about 1 whole
0.54 ⎦
0.76 ⎤ about 1 whole
+ 0.28 ⎦

The sum is about 2.

Guided Practice

Ask Yourself

- Did I follow the rounding rules?
- Did I estimate to the given place?
- Is my estimate reasonable?

Estimate each sum or difference to the place indicated.

1. $0.45 + 0.37$ (tenths)
2. $0.389 - 0.258$ (tenths)
3. $24.346 + 36.789$ (ones)
4. $75.44 - 32.98$ (ones)

Explain Your Thinking ▶ Why wouldn't rounding to the nearest tenth make sense if you want to estimate the sum of 14,302.85 and 9,394.83?

Practice and Problem Solving

Estimate each sum or difference to the nearest tenth.

5. $0.237 + 0.129$
6. $0.545 + 0.435$
7. $0.321 + 0.434$
8. $0.854 + 0.649$
9. $0.298 - 0.154$
10. $0.934 - 0.856$
11. $0.487 - 0.265$
12. $0.912 - 0.544$

Estimate each sum or difference to the nearest whole number.

13. $1.56 + 4.58$
14. $12.87 + 6.7$
15. $64.97 + 31.9$
16. $43.983 + 8.6$
17. $76.84 - 52.19$
18. $27.8 - 15.99$
19. $87.4 - 74.18$
20. $7.824 - 0.516$

Solve.

21. The average winning speed at the first Indy 500 was 74.602 miles per hour. The 2002 average winning speed was 166.499 miles per hour. Estimate the difference in those two speeds.

22. **Create and Solve** Write a problem about racing times and speeds that requires estimating a decimal sum or difference. Solve your problem and give it to a partner to solve.

23. The track for the Indy 500 has two straightaways. Each is 0.625 mile long. Together, about how long are the straightaways?

24. **What's Wrong?** Gina estimated the sum of 0.925 and 0.674 as 0.16. Why is Gina's estimate unreasonable? What did she do wrong?

Mixed Review and Test Prep

Open Response

Write the numbers in order from least to greatest. (Ch. 1, Lessons 4 and 7)

25.	19	18.76	18.903	19.09
26.	5.609	5.702	5.92	5.6
27.	7.04	7.082	7	7.45

28. During one pit-stop, the first-place car took 8.555 seconds. The second-place car took 1.5 to 2 seconds more than that. What is a reasonable estimate of the second-place car's time? Explain. (Ch. 11, Lesson 4)

Extra Practice See page 295, Set D.

Lesson 5

Problem-Solving Decision

Choose a Method

Objective Choose a computation method to solve a problem.

Before you solve a problem with decimals, you need to decide what is the best computation method to use.

Problem Last year at the Auto Show, a car company rented a booth that covered 453.75 square meters of floor space. This year they are cutting back to a booth that is 378.5 square meters. How much less floor space do they have this year than last year?

Ask Yourself

Should I use mental math?

Think

453.75 − 378.5 = 75.25

Do I need to use pencil and paper?

Does it make sense to use a calculator?

Which method would you choose?

Solution: This year's booth is 75.25 square meters smaller than last year's booth.

Try These

Solve. Explain which method you chose.

1. Ben worked at the Auto Show for 3.5 hours on Friday and 8.25 hours on Saturday. How many more hours did he work on Saturday than Friday?
2. During the show, Deanna sold two cars. One sold for $22,156.94 and the other sold for $19,209.38. What is the total of her two sales?
3. A speaker gave a 1.5-hour presentation followed by a 2.5-hour documentary film on experimental electric cars. How long were the two presentations?
4. Jill's car averages 18.65 miles per gallon of gasoline. The car she likes at the Auto Show averages 22 miles per gallon. How much better mileage does the new car get?

Solve. Explain which method you chose.

5. Marilyn has to work 7.75 hours at the auto show. She earns $8.95 per hour. She has already worked 6.25 hours. How much longer does she have to work?

6. Tickets for the auto show were $12 for adults and $5 for children. The Williams family paid $39 to get into the show. If both parents went, how many children went to the auto show?

7. Aidan saw some seat covers at the auto show that he wants for his car. He has $73.89. He needs another $44.21 to buy the seat covers. How much do the seat covers cost?

8. At the auto show, Karl sold two cars. He sold the first car for $23,789.21 and the other for $7,342.78 less than the first car. How much did the second car sell for?

Game

Activity

Estimation Destination

2 players

What You'll Need • a number cube labeled 1 to 6 • pennies • 4 sets of number cards labeled 0 to 9 or Learning Tool 6.

How to Play

1. One player tosses the number cube twice and writes the numbers rolled in order. The other player uses a penny as a decimal point and places it before, after, or between the numbers. This is the target number.

2. Each player then draws 4 number cards. Players use the cards to make two decimal numbers, whose sum or difference is as close as possible to the target number.

3. The sum or difference closest to the target number scores two points. Repeat. The first player with 10 points wins.

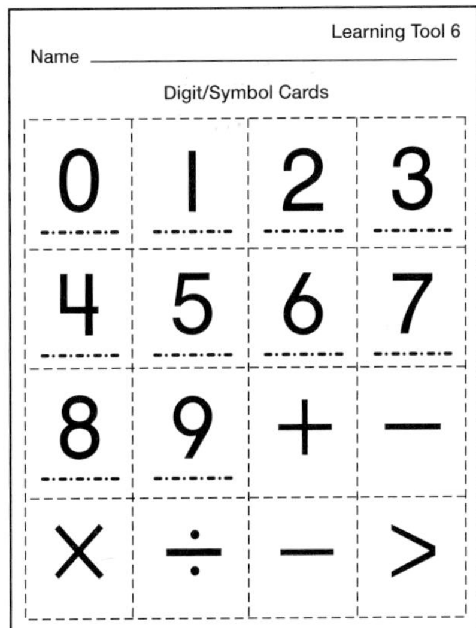

Learning Tool 6

Chapter Review/Test

VOCABULARY

1. The ____ separates the ones and tenths places in a decimal.
2. The decimal 0.04 is read as "four ____."
3. The 6 in the decimal 2.416 is in the ____ place.
4. Any decimal can be written as a ____ or mixed number.

Vocabulary

decimal point
fraction
hundredths
tenths
thousandths

CONCEPTS AND SKILLS

Change each decimal to a fraction. Write each sum or difference as a decimal. (Lesson 1, pp. 282–283)

5. 0.6 + 0.5
6. 0.46 + 3.76
7. 2.3 + 1.2
8. 0.82 + 1.19

Add or subtract. (Lessons 2–3, pp. 284–289)

9. 8.3 + 4.73 + 38.407
10. \$37.05 + 95.89 + 6.81
11. 3.668 + 52.75 + 5.14
12. 4.076 + 7 + 5.3
13. 5.7 − 3.9
14. \$95.09 − 67.57
15. 16.08 − 7.657
16. 0.8 − 0.059

Estimate each sum or difference to the nearest tenth.
(Lesson 4, pp. 290–291)

17. 0.539 + 0.283
18. 0.679 − 0.261
19. 0.935 + 0.364
20. 0.825 − 0.177

Estimate each sum or difference to the nearest whole number. (Lesson 4, pp. 290–291)

21. 4.068 − 0.375
22. 77.26 − 41.82
23. 34.612 + 8.09
24. 7.159 + 3.123

PROBLEM SOLVING

Solve. Write the computation method you used. (Lesson 5, pp. 292–293)

25. Mustafa worked at a store for 4.5 hours on Monday and 1.75 hours on Tuesday. How many more hours did he work on Monday?

Show You Understand

Antonio estimated the sum of 0.825 and 0.415 as 12. Was his estimate reasonable? Explain.

Extra Practice

Set A (Lesson 1, pp. 282–283)

Change each decimal to a fraction. Write each answer as a decimal.

1. 0.3 + 0.5
2. 5.3 + 6.4
3. 0.31 + 0.52
4. 0.12 + 0.63
5. 0.83 − 0.6
6. 0.65 − 0.27
7. 1.82 − 1.36
8. 1.91 − 0.04
9. 0.85 + 0.9
10. 0.7 + 0.23
11. 2.1 − 0.06
12. 1.76 − 0.17

Set B (Lesson 2, pp. 284–285)

Add.

1. 7.42 + 22.58
2. 2.09 + 56.43
3. \$ 8.65 + 40.25
4. \$27.45 + 53.75
5. 46.3 + 5 + 3.821
6. 18.07 + 7.3 + 5.682
7. 93.14 + 5.78 + 235.309
8. 23.06 + 15.7 + 3.28 + 71.697
9. 51.6 + 3.7 + 5
10. 27.06 + 0.97 + 0.002
11. 5.825 + 3.45
12. 17.067 + 5.643

Set C (Lesson 3, pp. 286–289)

Subtract. Add to check your answer.

1. 4.4 − 3.5
2. 7.3 − 5.6
3. 5.87 − 1.09
4. \$47.75 − 12.99
5. 43.634 − 10.81
6. 5.650 − 0.789
7. 66.9 − 36.782
8. 47.0 − 46.071
9. 5.038 − 1.429
10. 92.745 − 81.819
11. 78.49 − 57.565
12. 24.63 − 15.44

Set D (Lesson 4, pp. 290–291)

Estimate each sum or difference to the nearest tenth.

1. 0.623 + 0.192
2. 0.924 + 0.817
3. 0.869 + 0.032
4. 0.524 + 0.238
5. 0.843 − 0.316
6. 0.549 − 0.273
7. 0.741 − 0.692
8. 0.485 − 0.214

Speed Story

The roller coaster craze probably began in Russia where giant ice slides over 27 meters high were built in the 1600s. Riders would climb all the way to the top, then speed down the icy slope on sleds at 50 miles per hour. It took only a few seconds to cover several city blocks but, oh, what a ride!

Over the centuries, inventors have improved upon the idea of these Russian "Flying Mountains." They have added wheels to the sleds, tracks for the cars, and cables to pull riders to the top of each hill. Today roller coasters all over the world give riders a thrill.

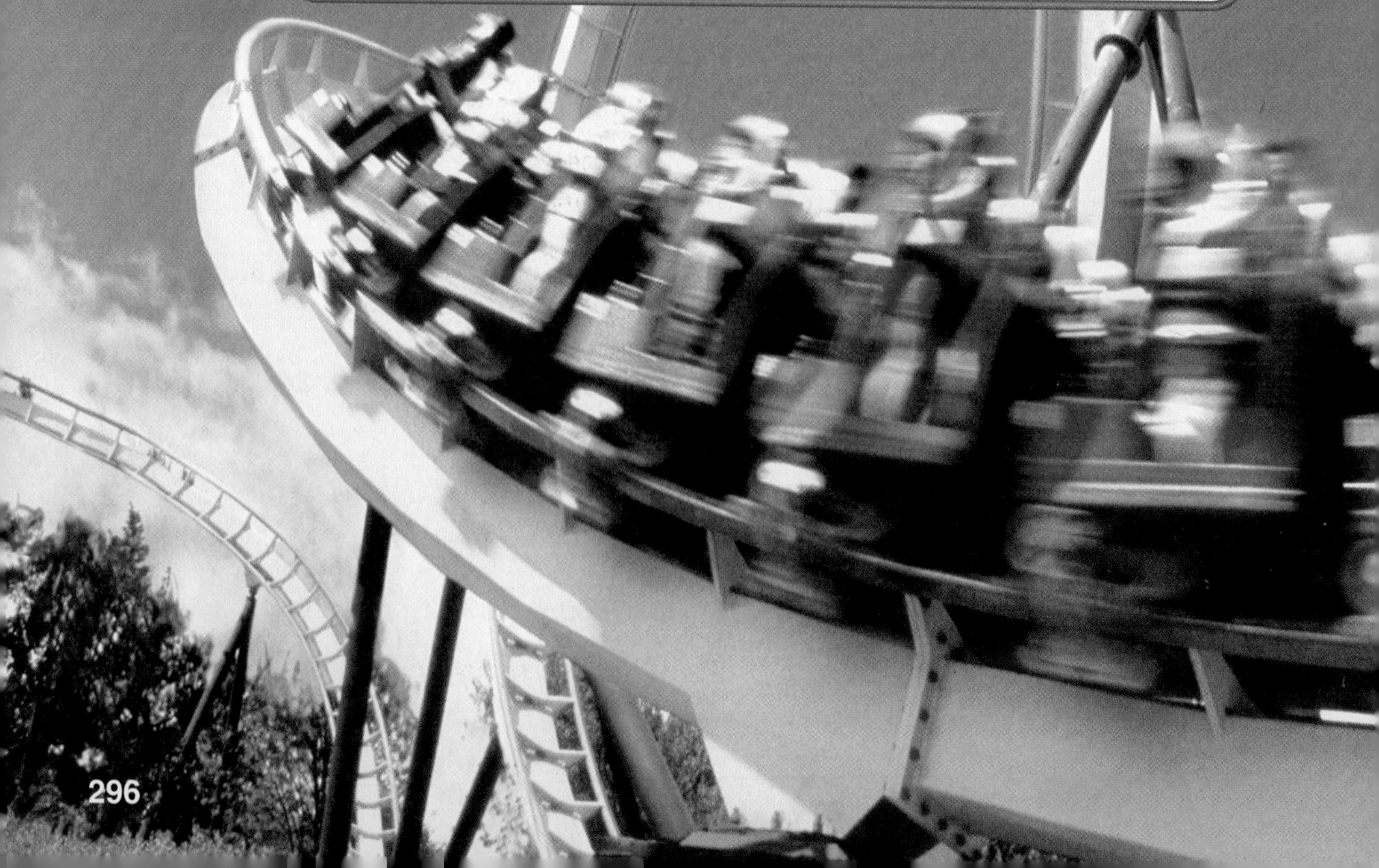

Problem Solving

Many wooden roller coasters built in the 1920s and 1930s are still in operation. Use the data in the graph to solve Problems 1–4.

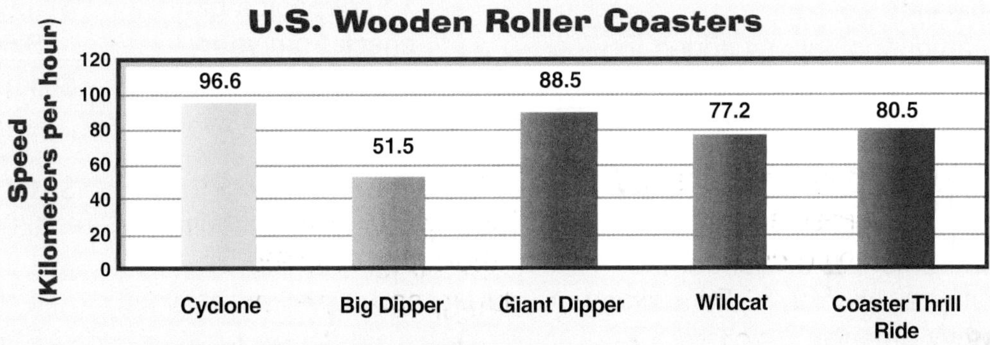

1. How much faster is the fastest coaster shown than the second fastest?

2. What is the range of speeds of the coasters shown?

3. The fastest wooden roller coaster in 2002 had a top speed of 29.6 kilometers per hour faster than the Cyclone. How fast was that?

4. A ride on the Wildcat is $\frac{1}{2}$ minute shorter than a ride on the Big Dipper. A ride on the Cyclone is $\frac{1}{12}$ minute longer than the Big Dipper's ride. The ride on the Wildcat is $1\frac{1}{4}$ minutes long. How long does a ride on the Cyclone last?

5. The Mauch Chunk Switchback Railway was the earliest U.S. roller coaster ride. This coal train ride down a mountain was 29 kilometers long. Today's longest wooden coaster is 2,255.5 meters long. How many meters longer was the Mauch Chunk Railway?

Education Place

Visit Weekly Reader Connections at **eduplace.com/map** for more on this topic.

Enrichment: Adding and Subtracting Decimals

Keeping a Checkbook

You can use a checkbook to keep a record of how much money you put into and take out of a bank account. See how each of the following transactions are recorded in a checkbook register.

Recording a Deposit

A deposit is an amount of money added to the account. Enter the amount in the deposit column and add it to the previous balance.

You deposit a gift check from your aunt.

$$\begin{array}{r} \$75.65 \\ +\ 15.50 \\ \hline \$91.15 \end{array}$$

Recording a Withdrawal

A withdrawal is an amount of money subtracted from the account. Enter the amount of the money in the withdrawal column and subtract it from the previous balance.

You withdraw $10.00 from your account.

$$\begin{array}{r} \$91.15 \\ -\ 10.00 \\ \hline \$81.15 \end{array}$$

Fees

Some banks charge a fee if you use an ATM card. Be sure to record these fees, so your checkbook balance is accurate. Other banks may charge a monthly fee for maintaining your account.

You get $20.00 from the ATM. There is a fee of $1.50.

$$\begin{array}{r} \$81.15 \\ -\ 20.00 \\ \hline \$61.15 \\ -\ 1.50 \\ \hline \$59.65 \end{array}$$

NUMBER	DATE	TRANSACTION	DEPOSIT	FEE	WITHDRAWAL	BALANCE
	1/4	Balance from last page				$75 65
	1/15	Check from Aunt Joan	15 50			91 15
919	1/17	Lincoln School/Lunch			10 00	81 15
	1/24	ATM – Money for shopping		1.50	20 00	59 65

If you write a check, the number goes here.

It is always a good idea to check your computations.

Try These!

Make your own checkbook record sheet. Use the current date for all transactions.

1. Start with the balance of $59.65 as shown above.
2. You deposit $18.50 from dog walking in your checking account.
3. You write a check, numbered 920, for $8.75 for a hat.
4. You withdraw $30.00 at the ATM. There is a $1.50 fee.

Fraction Finesse

You can add and subtract fractions on your calculator.

Find the sum of $3\frac{5}{6}$ and $2\frac{1}{2}$.

• Enter the first addend.	3 Unit 5 n 6 d	$3\frac{5}{6}$ ◄
• Enter the operation, the second addend and the equals sign.	+ 2 Unit 1 n 2 d Enter =	$3\frac{5}{6}+2\frac{1}{2}=$ $6\frac{2}{6}$
• Change the answer to simplest form.	Simp Enter =	$6\frac{2}{6}$ ▸S $6\frac{1}{3}$

Use a calculator. Write each sum or difference in simplest form. Then match the answers to a letter to solve the riddle below.

1. $1\frac{3}{4} + \frac{1}{5}$

2. $3\frac{6}{8} - 1\frac{1}{4}$

3. $8\frac{1}{4} - 3\frac{5}{6}$

4. $6\frac{6}{16} - 3\frac{1}{5}$

5. $2\frac{4}{7} + 3\frac{2}{8}$

6. $5\frac{3}{9} - 2\frac{1}{3}$

7. $4\frac{3}{6} + \frac{2}{5}$

8. $1\frac{9}{15} - 1\frac{1}{4}$

9. $3\frac{8}{12} + 4\frac{2}{4}$

10. $3\frac{1}{8} + 5\frac{1}{6}$

11. $2\frac{6}{9} - 1\frac{1}{3}$

12. $4\frac{12}{13} - 3\frac{1}{7}$

RIDDLE: **What do you get when you cross a dog with a calculator?**

___   ___ ___ ___ ___ ___ ___   ___ ___ ___
8   2 3 6 12 4 1   10 7 9

___ ___ ___   ___ ___ ___ ___ ___   ___ ___!
11 8 4   11 7 9 4 5   7 4

KEY:

$\frac{7}{20}$	$1\frac{1}{3}$	$1\frac{19}{20}$	$1\frac{71}{91}$	$2\frac{1}{2}$	$2\frac{2}{3}$	3	$3\frac{7}{40}$	$4\frac{9}{10}$	$4\frac{5}{12}$	$4\frac{19}{20}$	$5\frac{23}{28}$	$8\frac{1}{6}$	$8\frac{7}{24}$
A	C	D	E	F	G	I	N	O	R	S	T	U	Y

Unit 4 Test

VOCABULARY Open Response

Write *true* or *false* for each statement. Rewrite each false sentence to make it true.

1. A prime number is a counting number greater than 1 whose only factors are 1 and the number itself.
2. The greatest common factor of two or more numbers is the common factor that is less than any other common factor.
3. A fraction with a 1 in the denominator is called a unit fraction.

Vocabulary

- equivalent fractions
- unit fraction
- prime number
- least common multiple
- greatest common factor

CONCEPTS AND SKILLS Open Response

Identify each number as *prime* or *composite*. If composite, write the prime factorization, using exponents if possible. (Chapter 9)

4. 9
5. 17
6. 20

Find the greatest common factor (GCF) and the least common multiple (LCM) of each pair. (Chapter 9)

7. 6 and 15
8. 2 and 3

Write each as a whole number or mixed number in simplest form. (Chapter 9)

9. 4.2
10. $\frac{24}{12}$
11. $\frac{17}{6}$
12. 25.75

Compare. Write >, <, or =. (Chapter 9)

13. $\frac{1}{3}$ ● $\frac{1}{2}$
14. 2 ● $\frac{6}{3}$
15. $\frac{7}{3}$ ● $2\frac{3}{4}$

Estimate. Then add or subtract. Write your answers in simplest form. (Chapter 10)

16. $\frac{5}{8} + \frac{1}{16}$
17. $3\frac{1}{2} + 2\frac{2}{3}$
18. $\frac{7}{10} - \frac{3}{5}$
19. $7\frac{1}{4} - 3\frac{5}{6}$

Estimate. Then add or subtract. (Chapter 11)

20. $\begin{array}{r} 3.479 \\ -\ 2.581 \\ \hline \end{array}$
21. $\begin{array}{r} 68.2 \\ 345.301 \\ +\ 18 \\ \hline \end{array}$
22. $\begin{array}{r} \$2.68 \\ -\ 0.81 \\ \hline \end{array}$

PROBLEM SOLVING Open Response

23. Connie is making a 9-foot long path through her garden. If each square stone is $\frac{3}{4}$ foot long, how many stones should she buy?

24. Hong is planting a garden. In one row he plants $4\frac{1}{2}$ feet of lettuce and $5\frac{3}{4}$ feet of carrots. How long is that row of lettuce and carrots?

25. At his father's vegetable stand, Abdul made a list of his sales for three days. What was the value of the vegetables he sold on all three days? Tell which computation method you used and why.

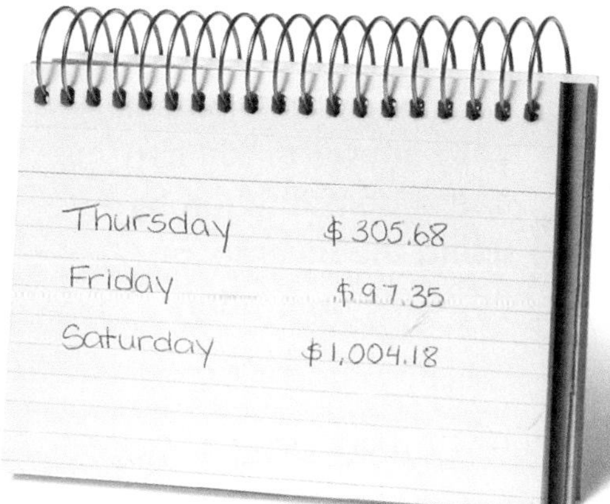

Performance Assessment

Constructed Response

Task David and Angie have only 2 hours to ride their bicycles in the park. They bike at a speed of 8 miles per hour.

Plan a route for David and Angie that will allow them to bike as many of the trails as possible and yet get them back to the park entrance within 2 hours. Explain why your route is the best route for them to take.

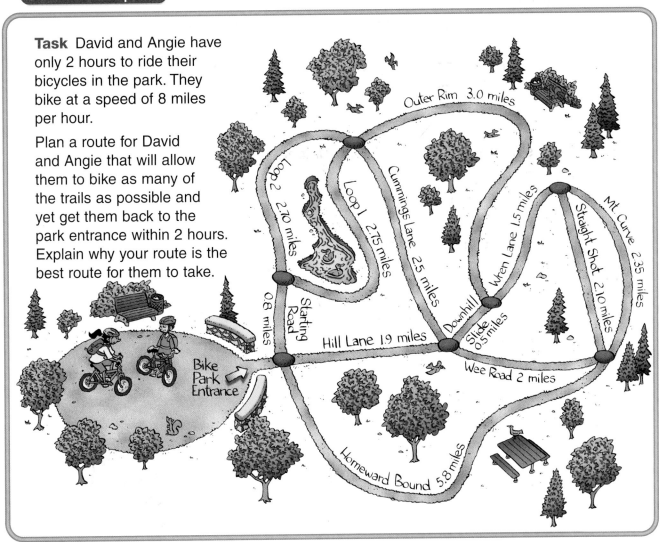

Outer Rim 3.0 miles
Loop 2 2.70 miles
Loop 1 2.75 miles
Cummings Lane 2.5 miles
Wren Lane 1.5 miles
Mt. Curve 2.35 miles
Straight Shot 2.10 miles
Starting Road 0.8 miles
Downhill
Slide 0.5 miles
Hill Lane 1.9 miles
Wee Road 2 miles
Bike Park Entrance
Homeward Bound 5.8 miles

Cumulative Test Prep

Solve Problems 1–10.

Test-Taking Tip

As time permits, check your answers. You can check computation by using the inverse, or opposite, operation.

Look at the example below.

Sheldon wants to buy a 3-piece snorkel set for $17.88. He has $9.89. How much more money does Sheldon need?

A $7.99 **C** $12.01

B $8.01 **D** $25.77

THINK

When computing with decimals, remember to align the decimal points.

Use the inverse operation, addition, to check subtraction.

$17.88		$ 7.99	
− 9.89	same	+ 9.89	
$ 7.99		$17.88	It checks.

Since the answer checks, mark **A** as the answer.

Multiple Choice

1. Florida has an area of 65,755 square miles. Texas has an area of 268,581 square miles. How many square miles greater is the area of Texas than the area of Florida?

A 202,826 **C** 212,213

B 208,213 **D** 325,555

(Chapter 2, Lesson 3)

2. String cheese costs $2.99 per package. If Selma buys 15 packages, how much will she spend altogether?

F $42.45 **H** $44.45

G $42.85 **J** $44.85

(Chapter 3, Lesson 7)

3. Which is the prime factorization of 24?

A 2×3 **C** $2^2 \times 3$

B 2×4 **D** $2^3 \times 3$

(Chapter 9, Lesson 2)

4. Brian is making a friendship bracelet. On Tuesday it was $3\frac{3}{8}$ inches long. He added $4\frac{1}{4}$ inches on Wednesday. How much more must he add for the bracelet to be 8 inches long?

F $\frac{1}{4}$ inch **H** $\frac{1}{2}$ inch

G $\frac{3}{8}$ inch **J** 1 inch

(Chapter 10, Lesson 4)

For Test-Taking Tips, see page 652.

Open Response

5. Write the names of the states in the chart in order from the greatest to the least area.

State	Area (square miles)
Nebraska	77,358
North Dakota	70,704
South Dakota	77,121
Washington	71,300

(Chapter 1, Lesson 4)

6. Mr. Broeker purchased three mountain bikes for his daughters at a total cost of $357. If each bike costs the same amount, how much did each bike cost?

(Chapter 5, Lesson 2)

7. The Kendalls' car broke down $\frac{1}{3}$ mile from home. How many feet from home did the car break down? (Hint: 1 mi = 5,280 ft)

(Chapter 6, Lesson 2)

8. Karin wants to glue a $4\frac{1}{2}$-inch piece of ribbon onto her hat. The ribbon she has is $8\frac{5}{8}$ inches long. How much of the ribbon should she cut off?

(Chapter 10, Lesson 8)

9. A January snowstorm left 12.2 inches of snow on Rapid City, South Dakota, and 6.5 inches on Minneapolis, Minnesota. How much more snow did Rapid City get?

(Chapter 11, Lesson 3)

Extended Response

Activity	Time (minutes)
Swimming	45
Reading	35
Lunch	30
Crafts	45
Canoeing	55
Bow and arrow	45
Camping skills	60
Cooking	55

10. The chart above shows the amount of time that each summer camp activity takes.

A Make a line plot of the amounts of time the activitives take.

B What is the range of the data?

C Find the mode, median, and mean of the data.

D Which of the activities would you say take an average amount of time? Explain your thinking.

(Chapter 8, Lesson 2)

Education Place
Look for Cumulative Test Prep at **eduplace.com/map** for more practice.

Vocabulary Wrap-Up for Unit 4

Look back at the big ideas and vocabulary in this unit.

Big Ideas

A factor tree can be used to find the prime factorization of a number.

You can estimate sums and differences of fractions by rounding to 0, $\frac{1}{2}$, or 1.

Key Vocabulary

factor
prime
composite

Math Conversations

Use your new vocabulary to discuss these big ideas.

1. Explain how you can decide whether a number is prime or composite.
2. Explain how to write decimals as fractions and fractions as decimals.
3. Explain how to write answers in simplest form.
4. Explain how to subtract \$5.17 from \$10.00.
5. **Write About It** Measuring cups and measuring spoons are used to measure ingredients when cooking or baking. Describe different ways you might go about measuring these ingredients: $5\frac{1}{3}$ cups flour; $2\frac{2}{3}$ cups milk; $1\frac{3}{4}$ teaspoons baking powder.

15 is divisible by 5 and 3, so it can't be prime.
Is 15 a prime number?

UNIT 5

Multiplication and Division of Fractions and Decimals

Reading Mathematics

Reviewing Vocabulary

Here are some math vocabulary words that you should know.

factor	one of two or more numbers that are multiplied to give a product
common factor	a factor of two or more numbers
prime factor	a prime number that is a factor of a composite number
unit fraction	a fraction that has 1 as the numerator
simplest form	a fraction whose numerator and denominator have 1 as their only common factor

Reading Words and Symbols

Sometimes a model can be used to illustrate more than one idea in mathematics.

The model at the right can be used to show that each of the following statements is true:

Words and Symbols	Symbols Only
The sum of $\frac{3}{4}$ and $\frac{1}{4}$ is 1.	$\frac{3}{4} + \frac{1}{4} = 1$
Subtracting $\frac{3}{4}$ from 1 leaves $\frac{1}{4}$.	$1 - \frac{3}{4} = \frac{1}{4}$

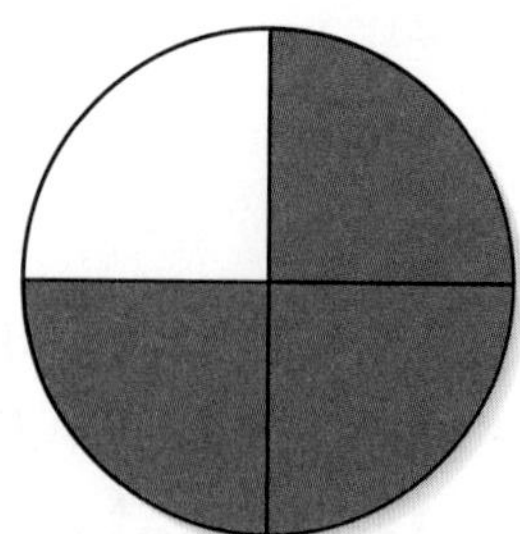

Use words and symbols to answer the questions.

1. How many equal sections are in the model above? What fraction represents each section?
2. What decimal represents the purple portion of the model? What decimal represents $\frac{1}{3}$ of the purple portion?

Reading Test Questions

Choose the correct answer for each.

3. Using the fraction strips, find the number of eighths there are in $\frac{3}{4}$.

a. 5 **c.** 7

b. 6 **d.** 8

$\frac{1}{4}$	$\frac{1}{4}$	$\frac{1}{4}$	$\frac{1}{4}$

$\frac{1}{8}$	$\frac{1}{8}$	$\frac{1}{8}$	$\frac{1}{8}$	$\frac{1}{8}$	$\frac{1}{8}$	$\frac{1}{8}$	$\frac{1}{8}$

Fraction strips are models used to show fraction equivalents. These are sometimes called fraction bars.

4. What is the sum of $\frac{5}{8}$ and $\frac{1}{8}$? Express your answer in lowest terms.

a. $\frac{6}{16}$ **c.** $\frac{6}{8}$

b. $\frac{4}{8}$ **d.** $\frac{3}{4}$

When you express a fraction in **lowest terms**, you express it in simplest form.

5. Find $\frac{7}{8} - \frac{5}{8}$. Be sure to reduce your answer.

a. $\frac{1}{4}$ **c.** $1\frac{1}{2}$

b. $\frac{2}{8}$ **d.** 2

To **reduce** an answer means to express it in lowest terms or in simplest form.

Learning Vocabulary

Watch for these words in this unit. Write their definitions in your journal.

- **reciprocal**
- **compatible numbers**
- **power of 10**
- **repeating decimal**

Education Place

At **eduplace.com/map** see *e*Glossary and *e*Games—Math Lingo.

Literature Connection

Read "The World's Largest Trees" on pages 644–645. Then work with a partner to answer the questions about the story.

CHAPTER 12

Multiply and Divide Fractions

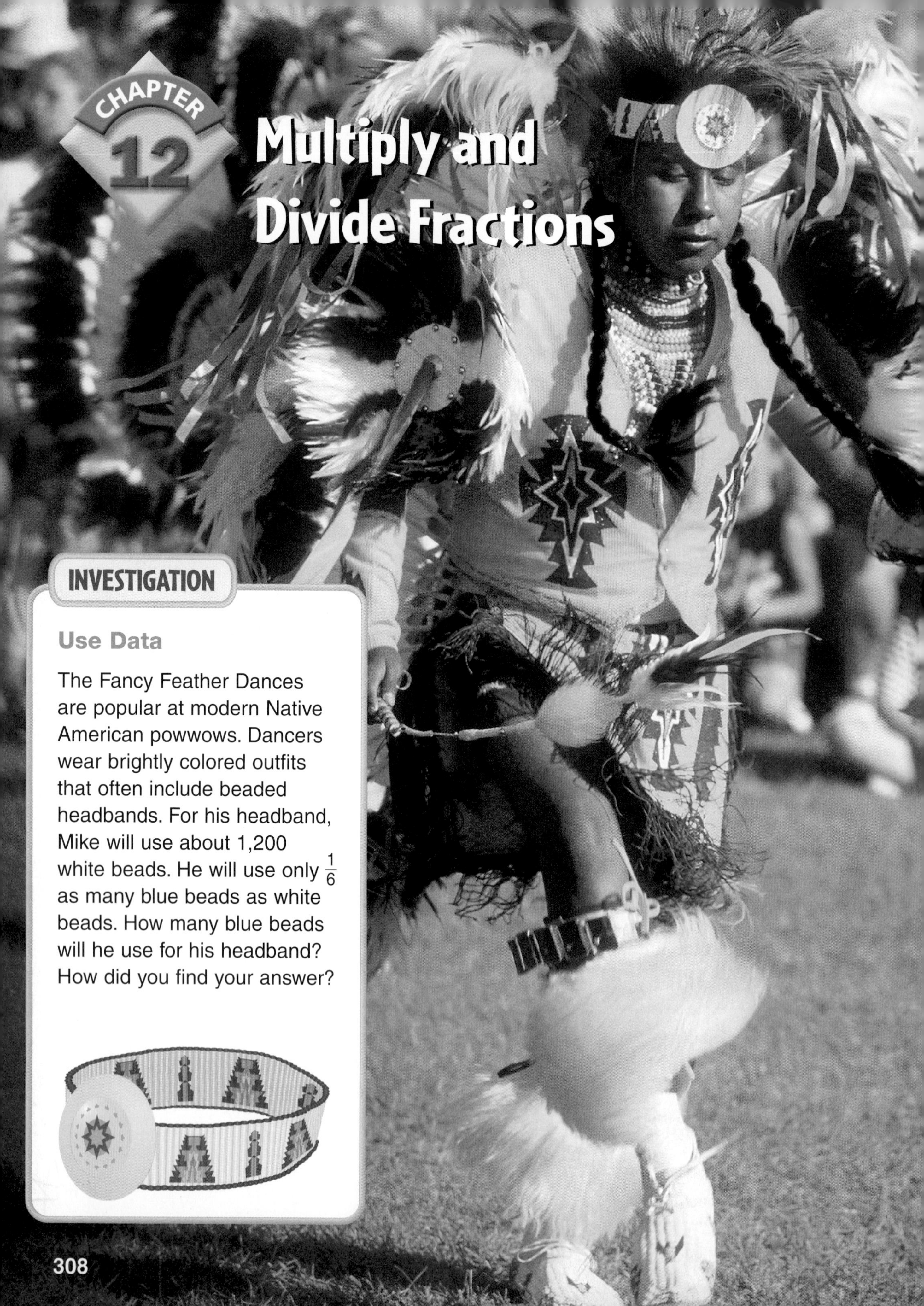

INVESTIGATION

Use Data

The Fancy Feather Dances are popular at modern Native American powwows. Dancers wear brightly colored outfits that often include beaded headbands. For his headband, Mike will use about 1,200 white beads. He will use only $\frac{1}{6}$ as many blue beads as white beads. How many blue beads will he use for his headband? How did you find your answer?

Use What You Know

Use this page to review and remember what you need to know for this chapter.

VOCABULARY

Choose the best term to complete each sentence.

1. You can always rename a mixed number as a(n) ____.
2. A(n) ____ is the largest number that divides evenly into two or more numbers.
3. You can use the greatest common factor of the numerator and denominator to find the ____ of a fraction.

Vocabulary

- greatest common factor
- improper fraction
- least common denominator
- simplest form

CONCEPTS AND SKILLS

Use the numbers listed to answer each question.

$\frac{1}{3}$ $\frac{4}{2}$ 2 $\frac{1}{6}$ $\frac{4}{10}$

4. Which two name the same number?
5. Which two fractions have an LCD of 6?
6. Which fractions are not in simplest form?
7. Which is a counting number?

Rename each mixed number as an improper fraction.

8. $6\frac{2}{9}$
9. $11\frac{4}{5}$
10. $4\frac{3}{7}$

Rename each improper fraction as a mixed number.

11. $\frac{301}{3}$
12. $\frac{23}{8}$
13. $\frac{38}{5}$

Find the GCF of each pair.

14. 15, 27
15. 12, 32
16. 10, 25
17. 14, 35
18. 72, 144
19. 81, 108

Write About It

20. How can you use multiplication to find an equivalent fraction for $\frac{2}{5}$?

Facts Practice, See page 658.

Model Multiplication

Objective Use area to find the product of two fractions.

Work Together

You can use an area model to multiply two fractions.

Find $\frac{2}{3} \times \frac{4}{5}$.

STEP 1 Draw a 5×3 square.

Use horizontal lines to separate the square into thirds. Label each third.

Use vertical lines to separate the square into fifths. Label each fifth.

- How many rectangles have you separated the large square into?
- What fraction of the square does each rectangle represent?

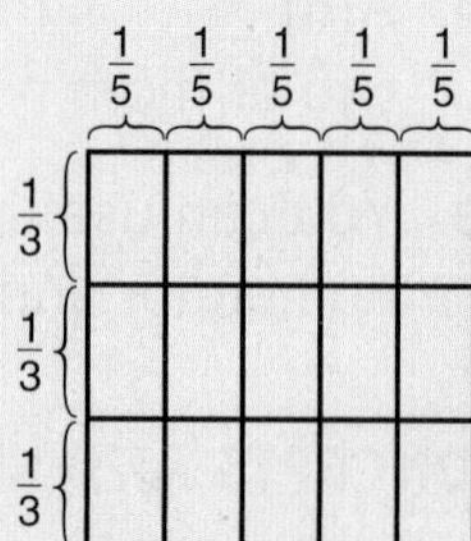

STEP 2 Shade part of the square to show $\frac{2}{3} \times \frac{4}{5}$ by doing the following:

Shade $\frac{2}{3}$ of the square red.

Shade $\frac{4}{5}$ of the square blue.

- Identify the part that is shaded twice. That part shows $\frac{2}{3} \times \frac{4}{5}$.

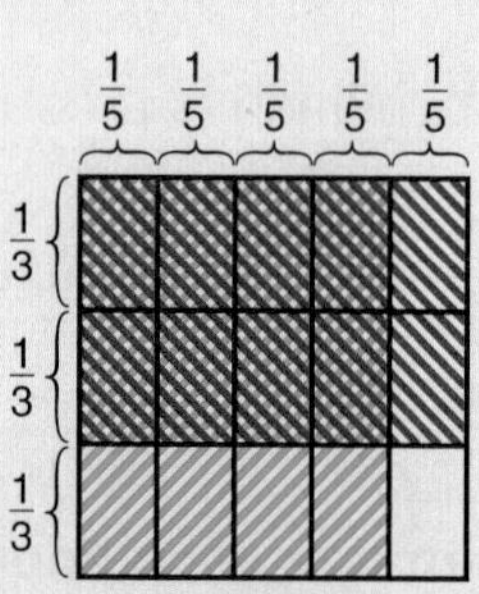

- Complete: $\frac{2}{3} \times \frac{4}{5} = \frac{■}{■}$ ← number of rectangles shaded twice ← total number of rectangles

Check your answer.

You are multiplying $\frac{2}{3}$ and $\frac{4}{5}$.

You know that you can multiply any number by 1 to get the same number again.

$\frac{2}{3} \times 1 = \frac{2}{3}$, so $\frac{2}{3} \times \frac{4}{5} < \frac{2}{3}$ and $\frac{4}{5} \times \frac{2}{3} < \frac{4}{5}$.

Is your answer less than either factor?

You can use models to multiply a fraction and a counting number.

Find $2 \times \frac{3}{4}$.

STEP 1 Draw two squares.

Shade the two squares blue.

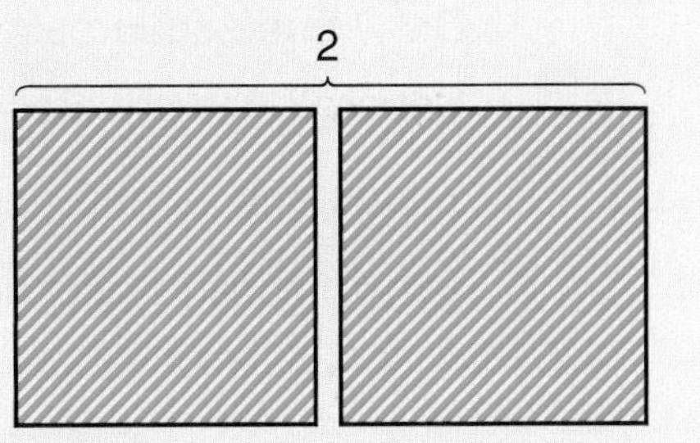

STEP 2 Separate both squares into fourths.

Shade $\frac{3}{4}$ of each square red.

- How many fourths are shaded twice?

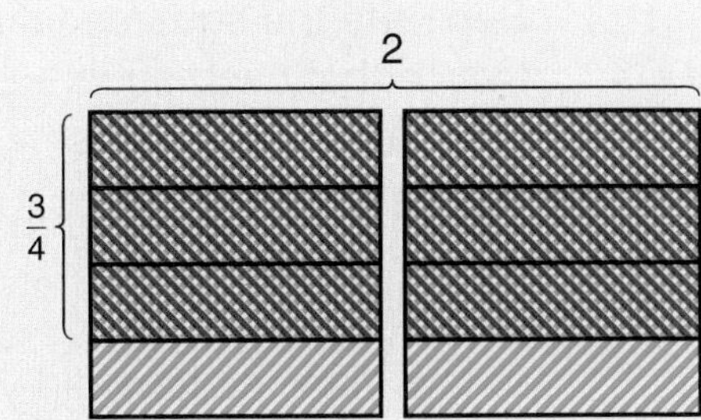

- Complete: $2 \times \frac{3}{4} = \frac{\blacksquare}{4}$ ← number of fourths shaded twice / ← number of fourths in 1 square
- Write your answer in simplest form.

Check your answer.

You are multiplying 2 and $\frac{3}{4}$. You know that if you multiply any number *n* by 1, the product is that number.

$2 \times 1 = 2$, so $2 \times \frac{3}{4} < 2$.

Is your answer less than the counting number?

Go On

You can use models to multiply with mixed numbers.

Find $\frac{1}{2} \times 2\frac{1}{4}$.

STEP 1 Draw three squares.

Separate the squares into fourths.

Shade and label $2\frac{1}{4}$ of the three squares.

- How many fourths are in $2\frac{1}{4}$?

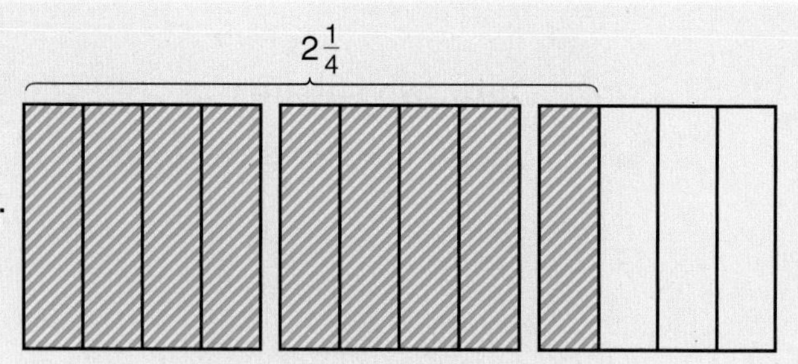

STEP 2 Separate the squares into halves. Notice that each square is now separated into eighths.

- Shade and label $\frac{1}{2}$ of the three squares.
- How many eighths did you shade twice?
- Complete: $\frac{1}{2} \times 2\frac{1}{4} = \frac{■}{8}$ ← number of eighths shaded twice / ← number of eighths in 1 square
- Write your answer in simplest form.

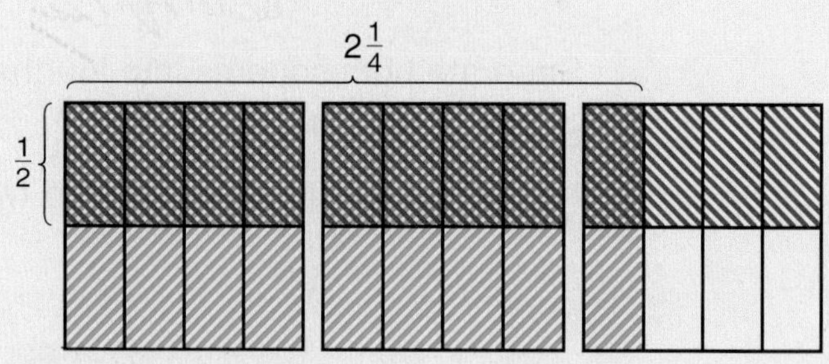

Check your answer.
Another way to estimate products is to round fractions to 0, $\frac{1}{2}$, or 1.
$\frac{1}{2}$ rounds to $\frac{1}{2}$ and $2\frac{1}{4}$ rounds to 2.

$\frac{1}{2} \times 2\frac{1}{4} \approx \frac{1}{2} \times 2$
$\frac{1}{2} \times 2 = 1$

The product of $\frac{1}{2}$ and $2\frac{1}{4}$ is about 1.

On Your Own

1. Use area to model multiplication of $\frac{2}{5}$ and $\frac{3}{4}$. Draw a unit square. Use horizontal lines to separate the square into fifths. Use vertical lines to separate the square into fourths.

   a. What fraction of the square does each small rectangle represent?

   b. Shade and label $\frac{2}{5} \times \frac{3}{4}$.

   c. Write your answer in simplest form. $\frac{2}{5} \times \frac{3}{4} = ■$

Complete the equation represented by each model. Write each answer in simplest form.

2. 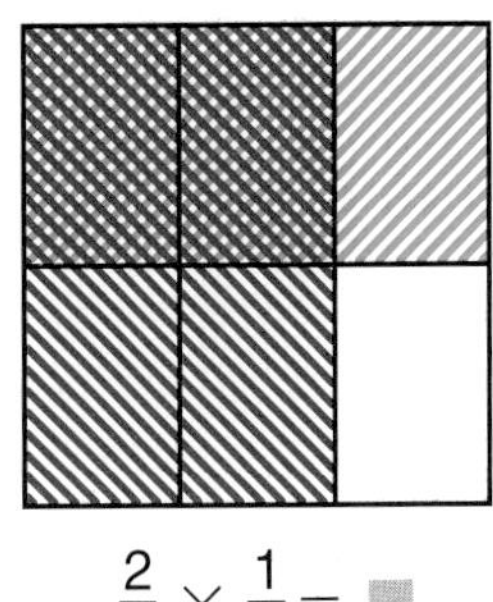

$\frac{2}{3} \times \frac{1}{2} = \blacksquare$

3. 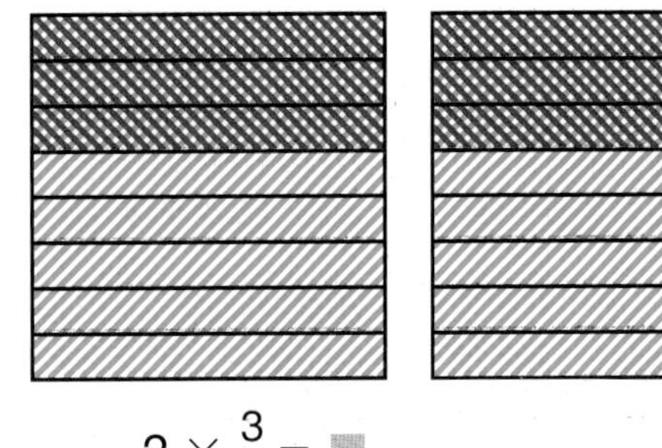

$2 \times \frac{3}{8} = \blacksquare$

4. 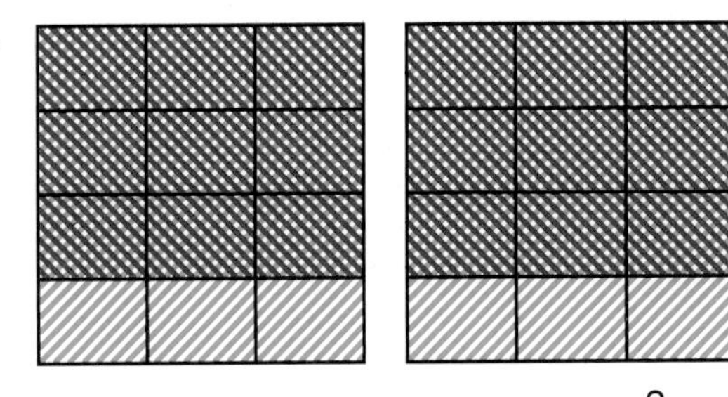 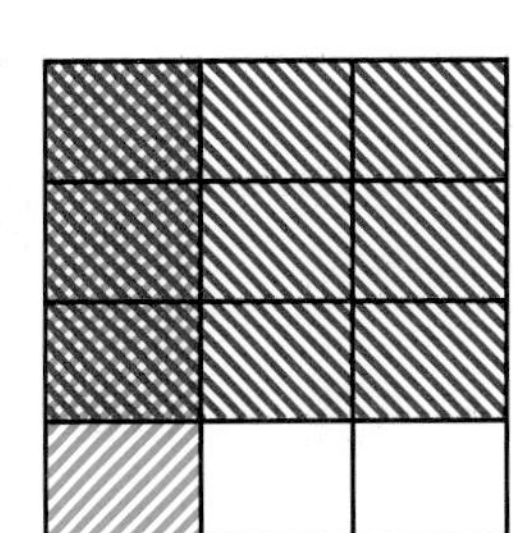

$\frac{3}{4} \times 3\frac{1}{3} = \blacksquare$

Use models to find each product. Write each product in simplest form.

5. $\frac{1}{2} \times \frac{1}{3} = \blacksquare$ **6.** $\frac{1}{3} \times \frac{3}{4} = \blacksquare$ **7.** $4 \times \frac{1}{2} = \blacksquare$ **8.** $\frac{3}{4} \times \frac{4}{5} = \blacksquare$

9. $3 \times \frac{2}{3} = \blacksquare$ **10.** $5 \times \frac{3}{5} = \blacksquare$ **11.** $\frac{3}{4} \times 4\frac{1}{2} = \blacksquare$ **12.** $1\frac{2}{5} \times 2\frac{1}{2} = \blacksquare$

13. $2 \times \frac{1}{6} = \blacksquare$ **14.** $\frac{1}{4} \times \frac{3}{5} = \blacksquare$ **15.** $\frac{2}{3} \times 1\frac{2}{3} = \blacksquare$ **16.** $3\frac{1}{3} \times 2\frac{1}{8} = \blacksquare$

Talk About It • Write About It

You have learned how to use models to multiply with fractions and mixed numbers.

17. When you multiply two fractions that are both less than one, will the product be less than or greater than either factor? Use words, pictures, and numbers to justify your answer.

18. When you multiply a counting number by a fraction less than one, will the product be a counting number all of the time, some of the time, or none of the time? Explain how you know.

Lesson 2

Multiply Fractions

Objective Find the product of two fractions.

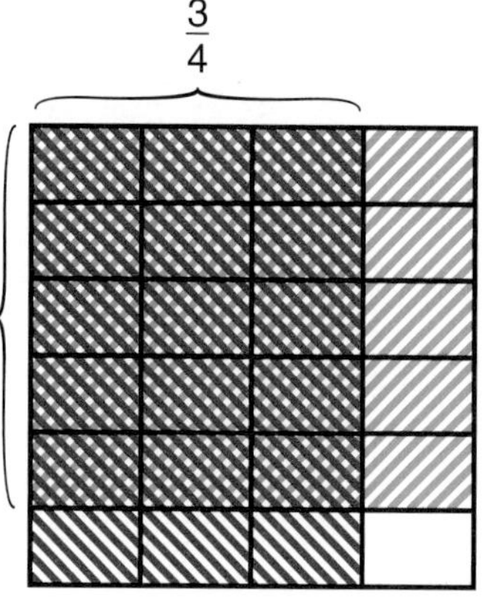

Learn About It

To find a fraction of a fraction, you need to find the product of the fractions. You know how to use models to multiply fractions. Here are some other ways to find products of fractions.

Find $\frac{5}{6}$ of $\frac{3}{4}$.

Different Ways to Find $\frac{5}{6}$ of $\frac{3}{4}$

Way 1 You can multiply first, then simplify.

STEP 1 Multiply the numerators. Multiply the denominators.

$$\frac{5}{6} \times \frac{3}{4} = \frac{5 \times 3}{6 \times 4} = \frac{15}{24}$$

STEP 2 Simplify the product if necessary.

$$\frac{15}{24} \overset{\div 3}{=} \frac{5}{8}$$

Way 2 You can simplify first, then multiply.

STEP 1 Rewrite using factors.

$$\frac{5}{6} \times \frac{3}{4} = \frac{5 \times 3}{2 \times 3 \times 4}$$

STEP 2 Divide by common factors.

$$\frac{5}{6} \times \frac{3}{4} = \frac{5 \times \cancel{3}^{1}}{2 \times \cancel{3}_{1} \times 4}$$

STEP 3 Multiply.

$$\frac{5 \times 1}{1 \times 2 \times 4} = \frac{5}{8}$$

Solution: $\frac{5}{6}$ of $\frac{3}{4}$ is $\frac{5}{8}$.

Other Examples

A. Prime Factorization

$$\frac{9}{10} \times \frac{2}{3} = \frac{9 \times 2}{10 \times 3}$$

$$= \frac{3 \times 3 \times 2}{2 \times 5 \times 3}$$

$$= \frac{3}{5} \times \frac{3}{3} \times \frac{2}{2}$$

$$= \frac{3}{5}$$

Notice that $\frac{2}{2} = 1$ and $\frac{3}{3} = 1$. The product of 1 and any number is that number.

B. Fraction and Whole Number

$$\frac{1}{5} \times 4 = \frac{1}{5} \times \frac{4}{1}$$

$$= \frac{1 \times 4}{5 \times 1}$$

$$= \frac{4}{5}$$

Guided Practice

Multiply. Write your answer in simplest form.

1. $\frac{2}{3} \times \frac{3}{5}$ **2.** $\frac{3}{8} \times \frac{4}{5}$ **3.** $\frac{5}{6} \times \frac{3}{10}$

4. $8 \times \frac{3}{4}$ **5.** $6 \times \frac{2}{5}$ **6.** $\frac{4}{7} \times 4$

Ask Yourself

- Can I use prime factorization?
- Did I write my answer in simplest form?

Explain Your Thinking ▶ Why can you divide by common factors in the numerator and denominator to simplify a fraction?

Practice and Problem Solving

Multiply. Write your answer in simplest form.

7. $\frac{1}{5} \times \frac{5}{8}$ **8.** $\frac{2}{5} \times \frac{5}{8}$ **9.** $\frac{3}{5} \times \frac{5}{9}$ **10.** $\frac{4}{5} \times \frac{5}{12}$ **11.** $\frac{1}{6} \times \frac{2}{3}$

12. $\frac{1}{8} \times 6$ **13.** $\frac{3}{8} \times 4$ **14.** $9 \times \frac{5}{8}$ **15.** $8 \times \frac{1}{6}$ **16.** $2 \times \frac{3}{4}$

x Algebra • Expressions **Multiply. Write each answer in simplest form.**

17. $\frac{a}{6} \cdot \frac{2}{b}$ **18.** $2 \cdot \frac{2}{n}$ **19.** $\frac{p}{q} \cdot \frac{q}{p}$

20. $3 \cdot \frac{6}{y}$ **21.** $\frac{x}{8} \cdot \frac{2}{y}$ **22.** $\frac{a}{x} \cdot \frac{b}{y}$

The multiplication dot is used to avoid confusion between the multiplication symbol (×) and the variable *x*.

Solve.

23. Two fifths of a class is in the drama club. $\frac{1}{4}$ of them have roles in a play. What fraction of that class has roles?

24. The middle school has 135 students. Two thirds of them are girls. How many of the students are girls?

25. Write About It How could you use two-color counters or coins to model $\frac{3}{4} \times \frac{1}{2}$?

26. A bottle of water contains $\frac{7}{8}$ liter. Annette buys 12 bottles. How many liters does she buy? Explain.

Mixed Review and Test Prep

Open Response

Find the product. (Ch. 3, Lesson 7)

27. 24 × 32 **28.** 18 × 43

29. 15 × 16 **30.** 92 × 87

31. 42 × 27 **32.** 83 × 13

Multiple Choice

33. John memorized $\frac{2}{3}$ of his lines for the school play. Then he memorized $\frac{1}{3}$ of what was left on Sunday. What fraction of his lines did he memorize on Sunday? (Ch.12, Lesson 2)

A $\frac{1}{9}$ **B** $\frac{1}{3}$ **C** $\frac{1}{2}$ **D** 1

Extra Practice See page 331, Set A.

Audio Tutor 2/1 Listen and Understand

Lesson 3 Multiply With Mixed Numbers

Vocabulary
mixed number
improper fraction

Objective Find products of fractions and mixed numbers.

Learn About It

You can multiply with a **mixed number**, like $2\frac{3}{4}$, or an **improper fraction**, like $\frac{11}{4}$.

Max is a clown who juggles and does yo-yo tricks for parties. He has been hired for a party that will last $1\frac{3}{4}$ hours. Max plans to spend $\frac{2}{3}$ of that time juggling. How long will Max's juggling last?

Multiply. $\frac{2}{3} \times 1\frac{3}{4} = n$

You can write the mixed number as an improper fraction and multiply.

STEP 1 Write the mixed number as an improper fraction.

$1\frac{3}{4} = \frac{4}{4} + \frac{3}{4} = \frac{7}{4}$

$\frac{2}{3} \times 1\frac{3}{4} = \frac{2}{3} \times \frac{7}{4}$

STEP 2 Use common factors to simplify. Then multiply.

$\frac{2}{3} \times \frac{7}{4} = \frac{\overset{1}{\cancel{2}} \times 7}{3 \times 2 \times \underset{1}{\cancel{2}}}$

$= \frac{1 \times 7}{3 \times 2}$

$= \frac{7}{6}$

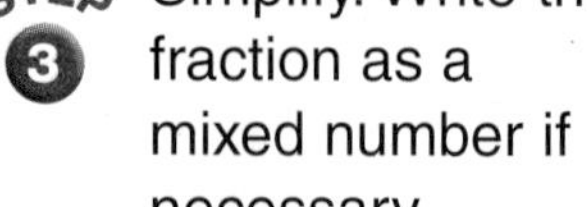

STEP 3 Simplify. Write the fraction as a mixed number if necessary.

$\frac{7}{6} = \frac{6}{6} + \frac{1}{6} = 1\frac{1}{6}$

$\frac{2}{3} \times 1\frac{3}{4} = 1\frac{1}{6}$

Solution: Max will juggle for $1\frac{1}{6}$ hours.

Other Examples

A. Two Mixed Numbers

$1\frac{2}{3} \times 3\frac{1}{4} = \frac{5}{3} \times \frac{13}{4}$

$= \frac{5 \times 13}{3 \times 4}$

$= \frac{65}{12}$ (65 ÷ 12 = ■)

$= 5\frac{5}{12}$

B. Mixed Number and Whole Number

$2\frac{1}{8} \times 4 = \frac{17}{8} \times \frac{4}{1}$

$= \frac{17 \times \overset{1}{\cancel{2}} \times \overset{1}{\cancel{2}}}{2 \times \underset{1}{\cancel{2}} \times \underset{1}{\cancel{2}}}$

$= \frac{17}{2}$ (17 ÷ 2 = ■)

$= 8\frac{1}{2}$

Guided Practice

Multiply. Write each product in simplest form.

1. $\frac{4}{5} \times 1\frac{2}{3}$ **2.** $2\frac{3}{4} \times 1\frac{1}{2}$ **3.** $1\frac{3}{8} \times 4$

4. $6 \times 2\frac{3}{4}$ **5.** $1\frac{2}{3} \times \frac{2}{5}$ **6.** $1\frac{1}{4} \times 3\frac{2}{5}$

Ask Yourself

- Did I use improper fractions?
- Did I write my answer in simplest form?

Explain Your Thinking ▶ How is multiplying with mixed numbers similar to multiplying with fractions?

Practice and Problem Solving

Multiply. Write each product in simplest form.

7. $1\frac{5}{6} \times \frac{1}{3}$ **8.** $\frac{3}{4} \times 2\frac{1}{3}$ **9.** $1\frac{7}{9} \times 2$ **10.** $5 \times 4\frac{1}{5}$

11. $2\frac{1}{3} \times 3\frac{3}{4}$ **12.** $3\frac{1}{2} \times \frac{2}{5}$ **13.** $3 \times 4\frac{1}{6}$ **14.** $2\frac{5}{6} \times 2\frac{1}{4}$

15. $\frac{3}{8} \times 1\frac{1}{4}$ **16.** $3\frac{5}{8} \times 2\frac{1}{2}$ **17.** $1\frac{7}{9} \times \frac{1}{12}$ **18.** $2\frac{3}{4} \times \frac{5}{6}$

19. $3\frac{1}{8} \times 4$ **20.** $2\frac{1}{5} \times \frac{2}{3}$ **21.** $3 \times 2\frac{2}{3}$ **22.** $4\frac{5}{8} \times 2\frac{2}{3}$

23. $9 \times 2\frac{1}{3}$ **24.** $\frac{5}{8} \times 1\frac{3}{5}$ **25.** $2\frac{1}{4} \times 3\frac{1}{9}$ **26.** $3\frac{5}{6} \times 2\frac{3}{8}$

Complete each multiplication equation.

27. $\frac{1}{6} \times ■ = \frac{5}{6}$ **28.** $■ \times 32 = 8$ **29.** $■ \times 4 = 3$ **30.** $\frac{2}{3} \times ■ = 10$

31. $\frac{3}{4} \times ■ = 6$ **32.** $■ \times 24 = 3$ **33.** $■ \times \frac{6}{7} = 36$ **34.** $45 \times ■ = 10$

Algebra • Functions

Complete each function table. Write each answer in simplest form.

35.

Rule: $y = \frac{1}{4}x$				
x	$2\frac{1}{8}$	$2\frac{1}{4}$	$2\frac{3}{8}$	$2\frac{1}{2}$
y				

36.

Rule: $y = 8x$				
x	$3\frac{3}{4}$	4	$4\frac{1}{4}$	$4\frac{1}{2}$
y				

37.

Rule: $y = 1\frac{1}{4}x$				
x	$\frac{4}{5}$	$1\frac{3}{5}$	$3\frac{1}{3}$	$6\frac{2}{3}$
y				

38.

Rule: $y = 3\frac{1}{3}x$				
x	$1\frac{1}{8}$	$2\frac{1}{8}$	$3\frac{1}{8}$	$4\frac{1}{8}$
y				

Go On

Solve.

39. For the yo-yo trick "Rock the Baby," Max places his fingers halfway down the string. The string is $2\frac{3}{4}$ feet long. How long is each half?

40. Vicki bought a yo-yo with a string that was $\frac{5}{8}$ of her height. How long was the string on Vicki's yo-yo?

41. For the trick "Tidal Wave," Max placed a finger under the yo-yo string about 4 inches from the end of its $2\frac{3}{4}$-foot length. How long is the rest of the string?

42. For one job, Max earned $8 for each hour he worked. How much did he earn if he worked $1\frac{1}{2}$ hours?

43. Of the 40 jobs Max has worked so far this year, $\frac{5}{8}$ of them were from repeat customers. How many of his jobs were from new customers?

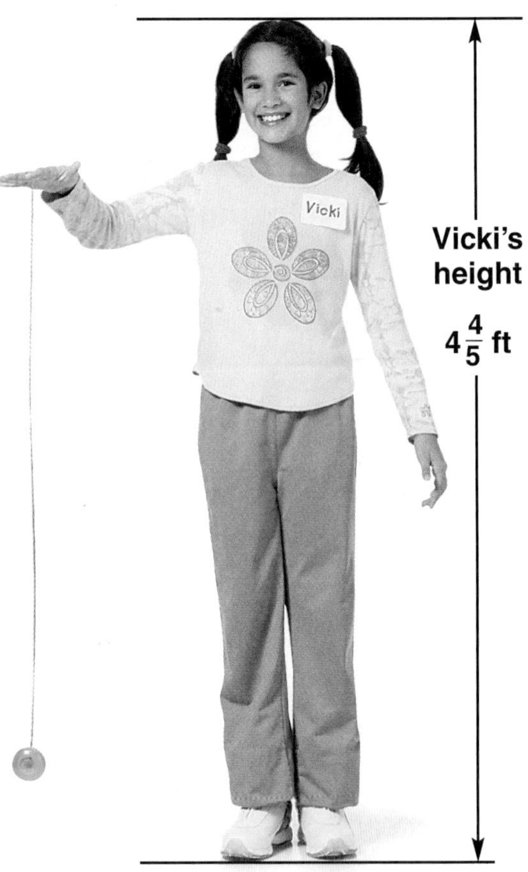

Data Use the table for Problems 44–47.

The table shows the number of hours Max worked at various jobs this week and the amount he was paid for each job.

Jobs		
Event	**Hours Worked**	**Amount Earned**
Mall Opening	$6\frac{1}{2}$	$65
Rosa's Party	$3\frac{3}{4}$	$40
Graduation	$1\frac{1}{3}$	$15
Josh's Party	$2\frac{1}{4}$	$20
Town Picnic	$5\frac{2}{3}$	$60

44. Max sets aside $\frac{1}{4}$ of his earnings to put into savings. How much did he save from the five jobs shown in the table?

45. Max spent half of his time at Rosa's party putting on a magic show. How long was the magic show?

46. Find the mean, median, mode, and range of the amounts Max earned at his jobs this week.

47. **Create and Solve** Write your own problem that uses data from the table. Solve your problem.

Extra Practice See page 331, Set B.

Science Connection

How Hot Is It?

Activity

If a recipe shows a temperature in °C, you can convert that temperature to °F using this formula: $F = \frac{9}{5}C + 32$.

Here's how to change 200°C to °F.

 Substitute values in the formula.

$$F = \frac{9}{5}C + 32$$
$$= \left(\frac{9}{5} \times 200\right) + 32$$

 Multiply first.

$$F = \left(\frac{9}{5} \times 200\right) + 32$$
$$= \left(\frac{9}{\cancel{5}_1} \times \frac{\cancel{200}^{40}}{1}\right) + 32$$
$$= 360 + 32$$

 Then add.

$$F = 360 + 32$$
$$F = 392$$

The temperature 200°C is the same as the temperature 392°F.

Change these temperatures to °F.

1. 190°C **2.** 150°C **3.** 235°C **4.** 100°C

WEEKLY WR READER eduplace.com/map

Quick Check

Check your understanding for Lessons 1–3.

Multiply. Write your answer in simplest form. (Lessons 1 and 2)

1.

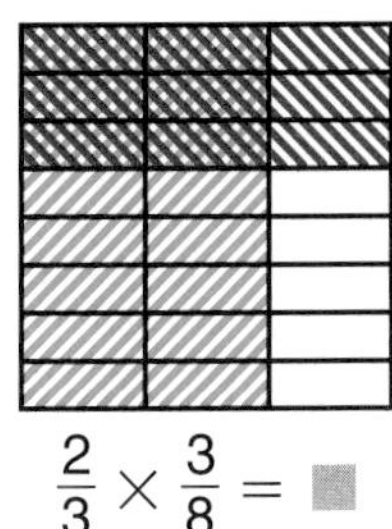

$\frac{2}{3} \times \frac{3}{8} = ■$

2.

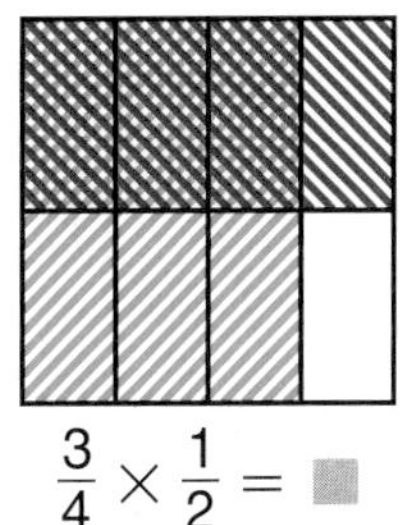

$\frac{3}{4} \times \frac{1}{2} = ■$

3. $\frac{4}{5} \times \frac{5}{6}$ **4.** $\frac{1}{3} \times \frac{5}{8}$ **5.** $\frac{7}{8} \times 6$ **6.** $8 \times \frac{3}{4}$

Multiply. Write each product in simplest form. (Lesson 3)

7. $2\frac{7}{8} \times 8$ **8.** $1\frac{3}{5} \times 2\frac{1}{2}$ **9.** $4 \times 5\frac{3}{4}$ **10.** $2\frac{1}{3} \times 5\frac{1}{7}$

Model Division

Objective Use models to divide with fractions.

Vocabulary
unit fraction

Materials
grid paper
fraction strips

Work Together

A **unit fraction** is a fraction in which the numerator is 1. You can use models to divide a counting number by a unit fraction.

Work with a partner to find $6 \div \frac{1}{2}$.

Draw 6 whole circles.

Separate each circle into halves.

Dividing 6 by $\frac{1}{2}$ is the same as finding how many halves are in 6.

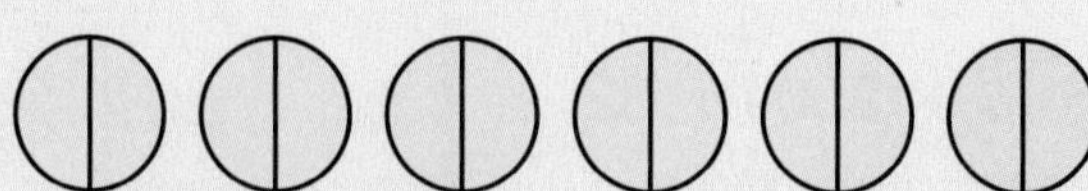

Count to find how many halves are in 6 circles.

- What is $6 \div \frac{1}{2}$?

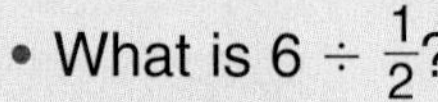

There are 12 halves in 6 circles, so $6 \div \frac{1}{2} = 12$.

11 12

Check your answer using multiplication.

$12 \times \frac{1}{2} = 6$

You can use models to divide a fraction by a fraction.

Work with a partner to find $\frac{4}{5} \div \frac{2}{5}$.

Model $\frac{4}{5}$.

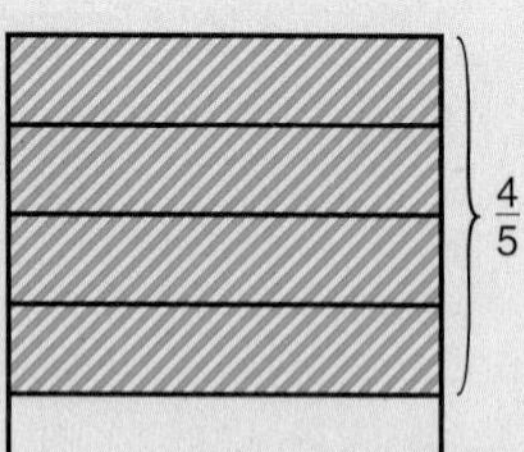

STEP 2

Find how many 2 fifths are in 4 fifths.

- What is $\frac{4}{5} \div \frac{2}{5}$?

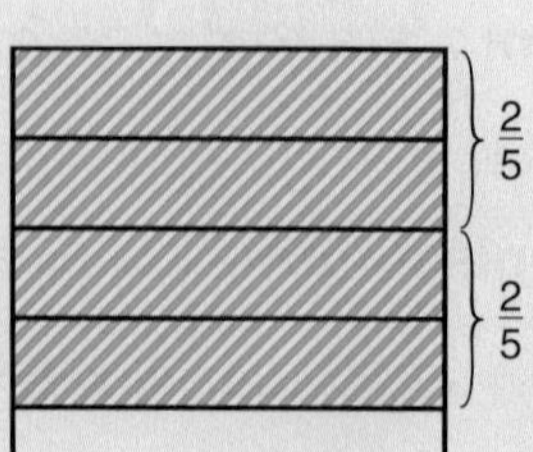

Check.

$2 \times \frac{2}{5} = \frac{4}{5}$

On Your Own

Match each question with the correct model. Then complete the division sentence.

1. What is 3 divided by $\frac{1}{4}$?
   $3 \div \frac{1}{4} = \blacksquare$

A

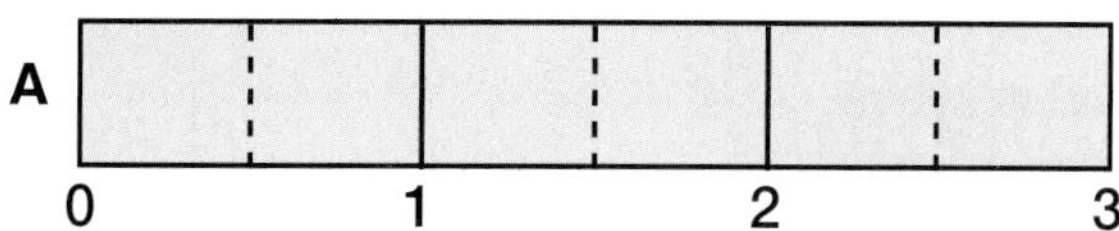

2. What is 3 divided by $\frac{1}{2}$?
   $3 \div \frac{1}{2} = \blacksquare$

B

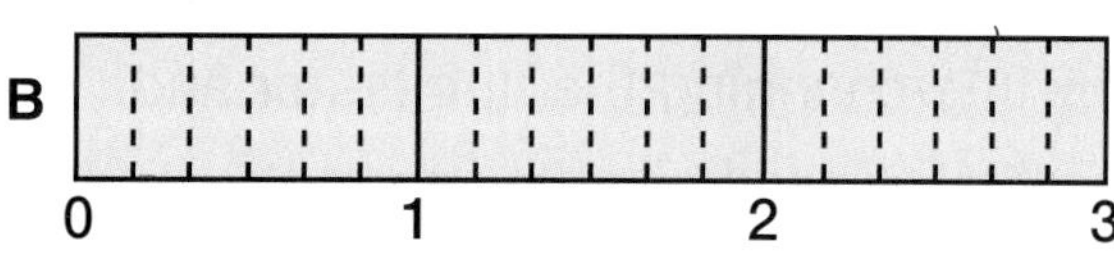

3. What is 3 divided by $\frac{1}{6}$?
   $3 \div \frac{1}{6} = \blacksquare$

C

0 1 2 3

Complete each division and multiplication to find *a* and *b*. Use fraction strips or grid paper for help.

4. $4 \div \frac{1}{2} = a \quad 4 \times 2 = b$
5. $5 \div \frac{1}{3} = a \quad 5 \times 3 = b$
6. $6 \div \frac{1}{5} = a \quad 6 \times 5 = b$
7. $9 \div \frac{1}{2} = a \quad 9 \times 2 = b$

Use your answers from Exercises 4–7 to answer Exercises 8–9.

8. What is true about *a* and *b* in each exercise?
9. To divide a whole number by a unit fraction, by what can you multiply the whole number?

Divide. Check your answers.

10. $\frac{3}{4} \div \frac{1}{4}$
11. $\frac{2}{3} \div \frac{1}{3}$
12. $\frac{4}{5} \div \frac{1}{5}$
13. $\frac{4}{9} \div \frac{2}{9}$
14. $\frac{6}{8} \div \frac{2}{8}$
15. $\frac{9}{12} \div \frac{3}{12}$
16. $\frac{8}{10} \div \frac{2}{10}$
17. $\frac{4}{6} \div \frac{2}{6}$

Talk About It • Write About It

You have learned how to use models to divide fractions.

18. How would you explain to another student how to divide a fraction by a unit fraction?
19. Explain how you found the answers to Exercises 16 and 17.

Audio Tutor 2/2 Listen and Understand

Lesson 5 Divide Fractions

Objective Use the reciprocal to divide fractions.

Vocabulary
reciprocal

Learn About It

If a fraction is not equal to 0, then its **reciprocal** is obtained by interchanging the numerator and the denominator. For example, the fraction $\frac{4}{3}$ is the reciprocal of $\frac{3}{4}$. If neither a nor b is zero, then the fraction $\frac{b}{a}$ is the reciprocal of $\frac{a}{b}$.

The product of a fraction and its reciprocal is always 1.

$$\frac{3}{4} \times \frac{4}{3} = \frac{\overset{1}{\cancel{3}} \times \overset{1}{\cancel{4}}}{\underset{1}{\cancel{4}} \times \underset{1}{\cancel{3}}} = \frac{a}{b} \times \frac{b}{a} = 1$$

A concert lasted for 4 hours. The concert was divided into acts. Each act was different and lasted $\frac{2}{5}$ hour. How many acts performed at the concert?

Find $4 \div \frac{2}{5}$.

STEP 1 Rewrite the division as a multiplication by the **reciprocal** of the divisor.

$$4 \div \frac{2}{5} = \frac{4}{1} \times \frac{5}{2}$$

STEP 2 Look for common factors to cancel.

$$= \frac{\overset{2}{\cancel{4}} \times 5}{1 \times \underset{1}{\cancel{2}}} = 10$$

Check your work.

$$10 \times \frac{2}{5} = \frac{\overset{2}{\cancel{10}} \times 2}{\underset{1}{\cancel{5}}} = 2 \times 2 = 4$$

Solution: Ten acts performed.

Other Examples

A. Divide by Counting Number

Find $\frac{9}{10} \div 3$.

$$\frac{9}{10} \div 3 = \frac{9}{10} \times \frac{1}{3}$$
$$= \frac{9}{30}$$
$$= \frac{3}{10}$$

B. Divide Counting Numbers

Find $3 \div 6$.

$$3 \div 6 = 3 \times \frac{1}{6}$$
$$= \frac{3}{6}$$
$$= \frac{1}{2}$$

C. Divide Fractions

Find $\frac{3}{4} \div \frac{5}{8}$.

$$\frac{3}{4} \div \frac{5}{8} = \frac{3}{4} \times \frac{8}{5}$$
$$= \frac{3 \times \overset{2}{\cancel{8}}}{\underset{1}{\cancel{4}} \times 5} = \frac{6}{5}$$
$$= 1\frac{1}{5}$$

Guided Practice

Divide. Write each answer in simplest form. Check.

1. $3 \div \frac{1}{2}$ **2.** $\frac{1}{2} \div \frac{7}{12}$ **3.** $\frac{1}{2} \div 7$

4. $6 \div 8$ **5.** $\frac{2}{3} \div 12$ **6.** $\frac{5}{12} \div \frac{1}{4}$

> **Ask Yourself**
> - Did I multiply by the reciprocal of the divisor?
> - Did I divide by common factors to simplify?

Explain Your Thinking ▶ Why does dividing by $\frac{1}{2}$ give the same result as multiplying by 2?

Practice and Problem Solving

Divide. Write each answer in simplest form. Check.

7. $8 \div \frac{1}{4}$ **8.** $\frac{4}{5} \div 8$ **9.** $\frac{1}{4} \div \frac{2}{3}$ **10.** $\frac{5}{6} \div \frac{5}{12}$ **11.** $12 \div \frac{2}{3}$

12. $\frac{3}{4} \div \frac{1}{3}$ **13.** $\frac{3}{8} \div 2$ **14.** $\frac{1}{3} \div 6$ **15.** $5 \div 15$ **16.** $\frac{4}{7} \div 2$

17. $9 \div 12$ **18.** $12 \div 9$ **19.** $\frac{9}{10} \div \frac{7}{10}$ **20.** $\frac{7}{8} \div \frac{3}{4}$ **21.** $\frac{3}{10} \div \frac{4}{5}$

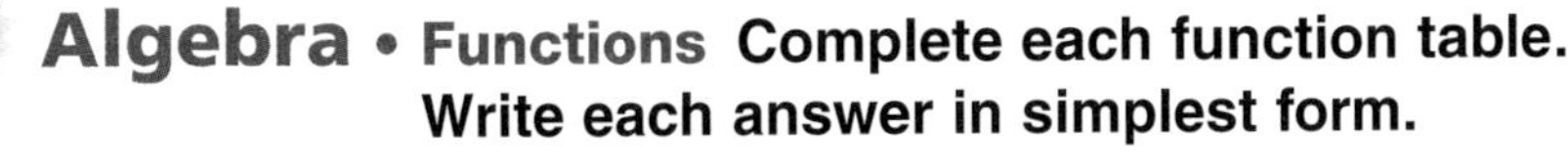

Algebra • Functions **Complete each function table. Write each answer in simplest form.**

22.

Rule: $y = x \div 8$				
x	$1\frac{1}{4}$	2	$2\frac{3}{4}$	$3\frac{1}{2}$
y				

23.

Rule: $y = x \div \frac{4}{5}$				
x	$\frac{4}{5}$	$1\frac{3}{5}$	$2\frac{2}{5}$	$3\frac{1}{5}$
y				

Solve.

24. A band played for $\frac{1}{2}$ hour on stage. Each song lasted $\frac{1}{10}$ hour. How many songs did they perform?

25. One band played 4 audience requests in 15 minutes. What was the average length of each song they played?

26. A band took 3 breaks during a 4-hour concert. Each break was $\frac{1}{6}$ hour. How many minutes of breaks were there?

27. During a $\frac{1}{4}$-hour act, the band performs 3 songs. Each song is the same length. How long is each song?

Mixed Review and Test Prep

Open Response

Divide. (Ch. 4, Lesson 2)

28. $674 \div 3$ **29.** $984 \div 8$

30. $742 \div 9$ **31.** $102 \div 5$

32. During a 2 hour meeting, each person spoke for $\frac{1}{6}$ hour. How many speakers were there? Explain how you got your answer. (Ch. 12, Lesson 5)

Extra Practice See page 331, Set C.

Lesson 6

Audio Tutor 2/3 Listen and Understand

Divide Mixed Numbers

Objective Divide with mixed numbers.

Vocabulary
mixed number

Learn About It

A dance teacher has scheduled $3\frac{1}{2}$ hours of practice before the spring recital. Today's practice lasted $1\frac{1}{4}$ hours. What fraction of the practice time is that? You can write each **mixed number** as an improper fraction to divide.

Divide. $1\frac{1}{4} \div 3\frac{1}{2} = n$

STEP 1 Write the mixed numbers as improper fractions.

$$1\frac{1}{4} \div 3\frac{1}{2} = \frac{5}{4} \div \frac{7}{2}$$

STEP 2 Rewrite as a multiplication problem using the reciprocal of the divisor.

$$\frac{5}{4} \div \frac{7}{2} = \frac{5}{4} \times \frac{2}{7}$$

STEP 3 Look for common factors.

$$\frac{5}{4} \times \frac{2}{7} = \frac{5 \times 2}{4 \times 7}$$

$$= \frac{5 \times \cancel{2}^{1}}{2 \times \cancel{2}_{1} \times 7}$$

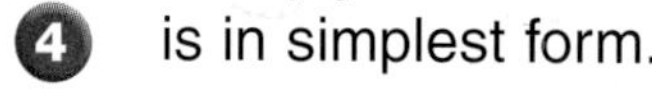

STEP 4 Multiply. Be sure the answer is in simplest form.

$$\frac{5 \times 1}{2 \times 1 \times 7} = \frac{5}{14}$$

Check your work.

$$\frac{5}{14} \times 3\frac{1}{2} = \frac{5}{14} \times \frac{7}{2}$$

$$= \frac{5 \times \cancel{7}^{1}}{2 \times \cancel{7}_{1} \times 2}$$

$$= \frac{5}{4}, \text{ or } 1\frac{1}{4}$$

Solution: $1\frac{1}{4} \div 3\frac{1}{2} = \frac{5}{14}$

$1\frac{1}{4}$ hours is $\frac{5}{14}$ of the total practice time.

Other Examples

A. Dividend is Counting Number

Find $9 \div 2\frac{1}{4}$.

$$9 \div 2\frac{1}{4} = \frac{9}{1} \div \frac{9}{4}$$

$$= \frac{9}{1} \times \frac{4}{9}$$

$$= \frac{\cancel{9}^{1} \times 4}{1 \times \cancel{9}_{1}}$$

$$= \frac{4}{1} = 4$$

B. Divisor is Fraction

Find $2\frac{1}{4} \div \frac{3}{4}$.

$$2\frac{1}{4} \div \frac{3}{4} = 2\frac{1}{4} \times \frac{4}{3}$$

$$= \frac{9}{4} \times \frac{4}{3}$$

$$= \frac{\cancel{9}^{3} \times \cancel{4}^{1}}{\cancel{4}_{1} \times \cancel{3}_{1}}$$

$$= \frac{3}{1} = 3$$

C. Dividend is Fraction

Find $\frac{5}{8} \div 1\frac{2}{3}$.

$$\frac{5}{8} \div 1\frac{2}{3} = \frac{5}{8} \div \frac{5}{3}$$

$$= \frac{5}{8} \times \frac{3}{5}$$

$$= \frac{\cancel{5}^{1} \times 3}{8 \times \cancel{5}_{1}}$$

$$= \frac{3}{8}$$

Guided Practice

Ask Yourself

- Did I invert the divisor to form the reciprocal?
- Did I cancel common factors?
- Did I write the quotient in simplest form?

Rewrite each division as a multiplication. Write all mixed numbers as improper fractions.

1. $\frac{2}{3} \div 4\frac{2}{5}$ **2.** $11 \div 1\frac{1}{2}$ **3.** $8\frac{2}{3} \div 12\frac{1}{2}$

4. $2\frac{1}{3} \div 4$ **5.** $1\frac{3}{4} \div \frac{1}{2}$ **6.** $5\frac{3}{8} \div 1\frac{3}{4}$

Write each quotient in simplest form. Multiply to check.

7. $\frac{1}{4} \div 1\frac{1}{4}$ **8.** $4\frac{7}{8} \div 2$ **9.** $8\frac{5}{8} \div 2\frac{7}{8}$ **10.** $6 \div 1\frac{1}{2}$

Explain Your Thinking ▶ How are the reciprocals of unit fractions and counting numbers related?

Practice and Problem Solving

Rewrite each each division as a multiplication.

11. $\frac{3}{4} \div 1\frac{2}{3}$ **12.** $10 \div 3\frac{1}{5}$ **13.** $7\frac{3}{4} \div 4$ **14.** $1\frac{1}{5} \div 3\frac{7}{8}$

Write each quotient in simplest form. Multiply to check.

15. $\frac{4}{5} \div 1\frac{1}{2}$ **16.** $4\frac{1}{4} \div 3$ **17.** $\frac{2}{3} \div 1\frac{1}{3}$ **18.** $3\frac{2}{3} \div \frac{1}{3}$

19. $2\frac{1}{8} \div \frac{1}{2}$ **20.** $4\frac{1}{2} \div \frac{3}{8}$ **21.** $3 \div 1\frac{1}{2}$ **22.** $6 \div 3\frac{1}{3}$

23. $6 \div 1\frac{3}{4}$ **24.** $6\frac{1}{2} \div \frac{3}{4}$ **25.** $5\frac{1}{8} \div 3$ **26.** $\frac{2}{3} \div 2\frac{2}{3}$

Algebra • Expressions **Rewrite each expression as a fraction in simplest form. No variable equals 0.**

27. $n \div 2$ **28.** $2 \div n$ **29.** $b \div a$ **30.** $3n \div 3m$

Compare **Write >, <, or = for each ●.**

31. $6\frac{3}{4} \div 2\frac{1}{4}$ ● $6\frac{1}{3} \div 2$ **32.** $5 \div 1\frac{1}{2}$ ● $2 \div \frac{1}{2}$

33. $\frac{1}{2} \div \frac{1}{3}$ ● $\frac{5}{8} \div \frac{2}{3}$ **34.** $3\frac{3}{4} \div \frac{1}{2}$ ● $1\frac{7}{8} \div \frac{1}{4}$

Go On

Choose a Computation Method

Data **Use the schedule for Problems 35–38.**

Beth is studying at a ballet school. The schedule at the right shows her Monday classes and their times.

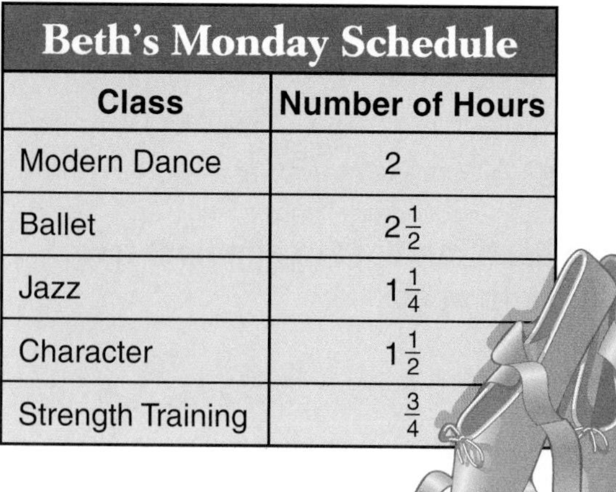

Beth's Monday Schedule	
Class	**Number of Hours**
Modern Dance	2
Ballet	$2\frac{1}{2}$
Jazz	$1\frac{1}{4}$
Character	$1\frac{1}{2}$
Strength Training	$\frac{3}{4}$

35. What fraction of Beth's Monday class schedule does ballet represent?

36. Last Monday, Beth was late for her Jazz class. She missed $\frac{1}{3}$ of the class. How much time is that?

37. One of Beth's teachers divides each hour of class into thirds. She uses those six sessions to work with different groups. Which class is this?

38. Beth's Tuesday schedule is like Monday's, except ballet class is half as long, and jazz class is twice as long. Does her total time change?

39. Measurement Draw a line segment that is $3\frac{1}{8}$ inches long. If you divide the line segment into five equal lengths, how long will each piece be? Show it on your line.

40. Glennis drew a line segment that was $9\frac{3}{5}$ inches long. Then she divided it into line segments that were each $1\frac{1}{5}$ inches long. How many line segments did she make?

Mixed Review and Test Prep

Open Response

Write the prime factorization. Use exponents if possible. (Ch. 9, Lesson 2)

41. 36

42. 42

43. 56

44. 72

45. 90

46. 144

Multiple Choice

47. Lance did homework for $2\frac{1}{4}$ hours. He spent the same amount of time on each of 3 subjects. How long did he spend on each subject?
(Ch. 12, Lesson 6)

A $\frac{1}{4}$ hour

B $\frac{3}{4}$ hour

C $1\frac{1}{3}$ hours

D $6\frac{3}{4}$ hours

Extra Practice See page 331, Set D.

Game

Activity

Division Scramble

2 players

What You'll Need • two copies of Learning Tool 42 or 2 game boards; 4 sets of number cards, numbered 1 to 10

How to Play

1. Shuffle the number cards and place them on the table facedown in a stack. Give each player a game board. The goal of the game is to create a division example that will have a greater quotient than your opponent's example has.
2. In turn each player takes one card from the stack and places that card face up on his or her game board. Once placed, a card cannot be moved.
3. The game continues until each player has four cards showing on his or her game board.
4. Each player then divides the fractions displayed on the game board. The player whose example has the greater quotient wins.
5. Shuffle the number cards and play again. This time the player whose example has the lesser quotient wins.

Lesson 7

Problem-Solving Decision

Choose the Operation

Objective Review how to choose the operation that will help you solve a problem.

When solving problems you must decide which operation to use.

Problem The area of the gym floor is 610 square feet. Five eighths of the floor will be used as the stage for a "battle of the bands" concert. The stage will be separated equally into four sections–one for each of the four bands. How much space is given to each band?

Find the area of the gym floor to be used as the stage.	Find how much of the stage each band will have.
Multiply to find a fraction of a number.	**Divide to separate a number equally.**
$610 \times \frac{5}{8} = 381\frac{1}{4}$	$381\frac{1}{4} \div 4 = 95\frac{5}{16}$

Solution: Each band is given $95\frac{5}{16}$ square feet of space.

Try These

Solve.

1. Look back at the problem above. The remaining $\frac{3}{8}$ of the gym floor was separated equally into 5 sections for seating. How large was each section?

2. Tickets for the concert cost $5.00 at the door. Students could buy tickets in advance for $\frac{3}{4}$ of the door price. How much did advance tickets cost?

3. The drummer needs $29\frac{1}{4}$ square feet. The bassist needs $10\frac{1}{2}$ square feet of space. How much more space does the drummer need? How much space do they need combined?

4. The 320 people in the audience each cast one vote for their favorite band. If $\frac{5}{16}$ of the audience voted for Band 1, $\frac{1}{8}$ for Band 2, $\frac{3}{16}$ for Band 3, and $\frac{3}{8}$ for Band 4, how many votes did each band get?

Solve. Tell what operation you used.

5. A recipe makes two and one half dozen cookies. How many dozen cookies can Sarah make if she used three times the original recipe?

6. Rachel's garden has 134 square feet. She wants to separate the space equally into 6 parts. What will be the size of each part?

7. A full-grown male otter can weigh as much as 92 lb. A full-grown female otter weighs about $\frac{3}{4}$ the weight of a full-grown male. About how much does a full-grown female weigh?

8. Male sea otters have body length, not including their tail, that is about $\frac{4}{5}$ of their total length. Suppose a male sea otter is 45 inches long from the tip of his head to the tip of his tail. About how long is the sea otter's body?

9. The full-grown male sea lion is about 20 times heavier than a full-grown male sea otter who weighs 92 lb. About how heavy is a full-grown male sea lion?

10. The total length of a grown sea otter (head to tail) is only about $\frac{1}{3}$ the length of a sea lion. If a sea otter is 45 inches long, about how long is a grown sea lion?

Problem Solving

Social Studies Connection

United States Congress

The United States Congress is made up of the House of Representatives and the Senate. The House of Representatives has 435 members and the Senate has 100 members. To pass a bill, a majority of the members (one half of the members plus 1) of each house must vote to pass the bill.

Problem To pass a bill, how many members of the Senate must vote for the bill?

Now solve the problem. Look back. Does your answer make sense?

1. How many members of the House of Representatives are needed for a majority?

2. It takes $\frac{2}{3}$ of the House of Representatives and $\frac{2}{3}$ of the Senate to vote to override a veto. How many members of each house is that?

WEEKLY WR READER eduplace.com/map

Chapter Review/Test

VOCABULARY

1. The product of a number and its ____ is always 1.

2. A(n) ____ is a fraction in which the numerator is 1.

3. A(n) ____ has a numerator that is greater than or equal to the denominator.

Vocabulary

improper fraction
mixed number
reciprocal
unit fraction

CONCEPTS AND SKILLS

Draw a model to show how you find each product. Write your answer in simplest form. (Lesson 1, pp. 310–313)

4. $\frac{1}{2} \times \frac{2}{3}$

5. $\frac{1}{6} \times 3$

Multiply. Write your answers in simplest form. (Lessons 2–3, pp. 314–319)

6. $\frac{3}{7} \times 21$

7. $\frac{5}{8} \times \frac{1}{3}$

8. $\frac{5}{8} \times \frac{4}{25}$

9. $6 \times 2\frac{5}{6}$

10. $\frac{3}{8} \times \frac{4}{7}$

11. $2\frac{3}{5} \times 5$

12. $9\frac{1}{5} \times 1\frac{1}{2}$

13. $2\frac{1}{4} \times 3\frac{1}{3}$

Use the models to divide. Write each answer in simplest form. (Lesson 4, pp. 320–321)

14. 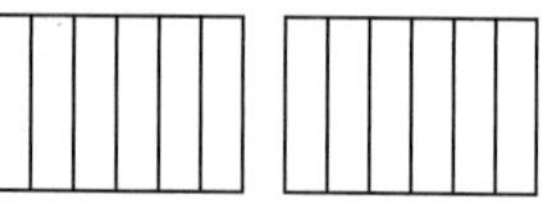 $2 \div \frac{1}{6} = ■$

15. 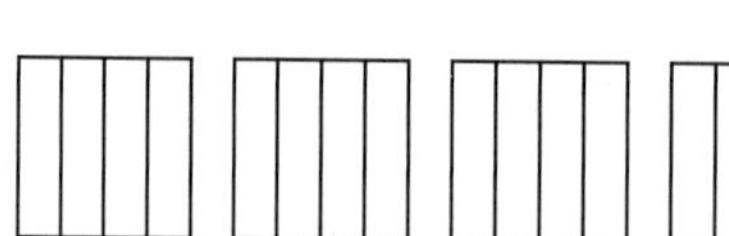 $4 \div \frac{1}{4} = ■$

Divide. Write each answer in simplest form. (Lessons 5–6, pp. 322–327)

16. $\frac{3}{4} \div \frac{1}{2}$

17. $\frac{7}{9} \div \frac{2}{3}$

18. $\frac{5}{8} \div \frac{5}{6}$

19. $8 \div 20$

20. $\frac{3}{5} \div 9$

21. $9 \div \frac{3}{5}$

22. $2\frac{1}{4} \div 1\frac{1}{2}$

23. $3\frac{3}{5} \div 1\frac{2}{7}$

PROBLEM SOLVING

Solve and name the operation(s) you chose. (Lesson 7, pp. 328–329)

24. The string section is $\frac{3}{5}$ of the school orchestra. 50 students are in the orchestra. How many of them are string players?

25. Marianne practices her violin $7\frac{1}{2}$ hours each week. If she practices $1\frac{1}{4}$ hours each day, how many days does she practice each week?

Show You Understand

Why is $3 \div 6$ equal to $\frac{1}{2}$ and not 2? Explain, using pictures, symbols, or words.

Extra Practice

Set A (Lessons 1–2, pp. 310–315)

Multiply. Write your answer in simplest form.

1. $\frac{1}{3} \times \frac{1}{6}$ **2.** $8 \times \frac{3}{5}$ **3.** $\frac{5}{9} \times \frac{2}{3}$ **4.** $\frac{3}{4} \times 4$

5. $\frac{2}{5} \times 3$ **6.** $\frac{5}{8} \times \frac{1}{3}$ **7.** $5 \times \frac{3}{4}$ **8.** $\frac{5}{6} \times 6$

9. $\frac{1}{4} \times \frac{8}{9}$ **10.** $\frac{7}{8} \times \frac{6}{7}$ **11.** $\frac{5}{6} \times \frac{9}{10}$ **12.** $\frac{4}{7} \times \frac{5}{2}$

13. $\frac{2}{3} \times \frac{1}{12}$ **14.** $\frac{10}{13} \times \frac{1}{10}$ **15.** $\frac{3}{10} \times \frac{7}{9}$ **16.** $\frac{1}{5} \times \frac{10}{11}$

Set B (Lesson 3, pp. 316–319)

Multiply. Write each product in simplest form.

1. $1\frac{4}{5} \times \frac{5}{6}$ **2.** $\frac{1}{3} \times 1\frac{1}{3}$ **3.** $3\frac{1}{4} \times \frac{4}{9}$ **4.** $\frac{4}{9} \times 1\frac{3}{4}$

5. $1\frac{1}{8} \times \frac{4}{7}$ **6.** $2\frac{2}{5} \times \frac{5}{7}$ **7.** $2\frac{1}{4} \times \frac{8}{9}$ **8.** $4 \times 3\frac{1}{8}$

9. $1\frac{2}{3} \times 3\frac{6}{7}$ **10.** $2\frac{7}{8} \times 2$ **11.** $1\frac{12}{13} \times \frac{1}{5}$ **12.** $2\frac{4}{7} \times \frac{5}{9}$

13. $3\frac{3}{8} \times \frac{7}{9}$ **14.** $\frac{3}{4} \times 4\frac{3}{5}$ **15.** $3\frac{1}{5} \times 2\frac{5}{8}$ **16.** $2\frac{1}{2} \times 1\frac{3}{5}$

Set C (Lessons 4–5, pp. 320–323)

Divide. Write each answer in simplest form.

1. $4 \div \frac{1}{5}$ **2.** $\frac{5}{6} \div \frac{3}{4}$ **3.** $\frac{1}{6} \div 2$ **4.** $10 \div \frac{1}{10}$

5. $3 \div \frac{1}{4}$ **6.** $\frac{4}{5} \div \frac{2}{3}$ **7.** $4 \div 6$ **8.** $\frac{1}{2} \div 16$

9. $\frac{1}{4} \div \frac{7}{8}$ **10.** $5 \div \frac{1}{3}$ **11.** $\frac{1}{6} \div \frac{1}{2}$ **12.** $\frac{2}{5} \div 10$

13. $\frac{7}{8} \div \frac{5}{9}$ **14.** $12 \div 8$ **15.** $\frac{5}{7} \div \frac{1}{4}$ **16.** $\frac{6}{7} \div \frac{1}{4}$

Set D (Lesson 6, pp. 324–327)

Write each quotient in simplest form.

1. $\frac{2}{5} \div 1\frac{1}{5}$ **2.** $\frac{2}{3} \div 6$ **3.** $2\frac{1}{4} \div \frac{3}{8}$ **4.** $\frac{3}{4} \div 2\frac{5}{8}$

5. $2\frac{5}{6} \div 1\frac{7}{9}$ **6.** $\frac{5}{9} \div 3$ **7.** $\frac{5}{8} \div 2\frac{3}{4}$ **8.** $1\frac{3}{4} \div \frac{1}{8}$

9. $10 \div 3\frac{1}{5}$ **10.** $2\frac{4}{5} \div 1\frac{2}{3}$ **11.** $1\frac{3}{4} \div 1\frac{3}{8}$ **12.** $\frac{2}{5} \div 1\frac{3}{5}$

13. $4 \div 2\frac{1}{4}$ **14.** $11 \div 3\frac{2}{3}$ **15.** $1\frac{1}{8} \div 4$ **16.** $3\frac{1}{3} \div \frac{2}{9}$

Extra Practice at eduplace.com/map

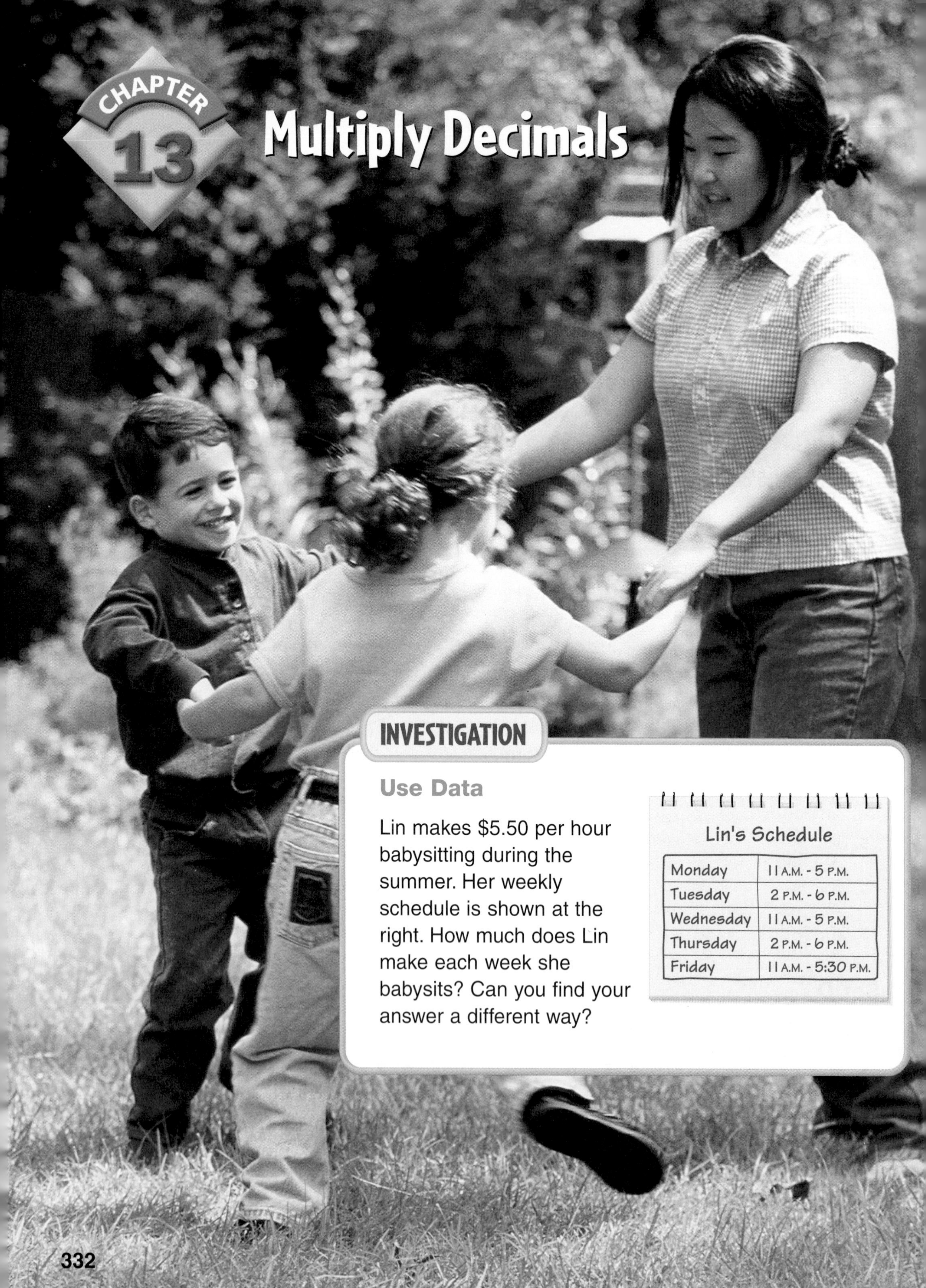

CHAPTER 13 Multiply Decimals

INVESTIGATION

Use Data

Lin makes $5.50 per hour babysitting during the summer. Her weekly schedule is shown at the right. How much does Lin make each week she babysits? Can you find your answer a different way?

Lin's Schedule

Monday	11 A.M. - 5 P.M.
Tuesday	2 P.M. - 6 P.M.
Wednesday	11 A.M. - 5 P.M.
Thursday	2 P.M. - 6 P.M.
Friday	11 A.M. - 5:30 P.M.

Use What You Know

Use this page to review and remember what you need to know for this chapter.

VOCABULARY

Choose the best word to complete each sentence.

Vocabulary
hundred
hundredths
ten
tenths
thousandths

1. In the decimal 0.095, the 9 is in the ____ place.
2. The six in the decimal 0.62 is in the ____ place.
3. The decimal 0.002 is read as "two ____."
4. The decimal 10.02 is read as ____ and two hundredths.

CONCEPTS AND SKILLS

Write each fraction as a decimal.

5. $\frac{8}{10}$ 6. $\frac{32}{100}$ 7. $\frac{1}{4}$ 8. $\frac{1}{2}$

Write these numbers from least to greatest.

9. 60.05, 6.5, 6.005
10. 74.3, 79.02, 54.85, 54.58
11. 1.1, 9.11, 3.4, 1.101

Write >, <, or = for each ●.

12. 27.1 ● 27.01
13. 6.102 ● 6.021
14. 13.20 ● 13.2

Multiply.

15. 31×23
16. 49×17
17. 52×36
18. 22×45
19. 93×90

Write About It

20. Adventure videos cost $7.49, and comedies are on sale at 3 for $20. If you could afford to buy three videos, which kind of movie would cost you less? Explain.

Facts Practice, See page 662.

Lesson 1

Explore Multiplication

Objective Use models to explore multiplication with decimals.

Materials
grid paper
Decimal/Percent Models

Learn About It

How many more liters of juice does the larger container of Just Juice hold?

You need to find $\frac{1}{5}$ of 1.5.

Different Ways to Find $\frac{1}{5}$ of 1.5

Way 1 You can use models to find $\frac{1}{5}$ of 1.5.

STEP 1 Use 10 × 10 grids. Shade 1.5 in blue.

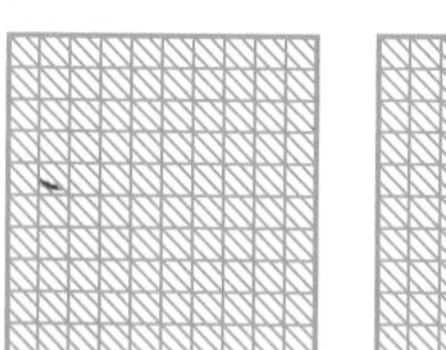
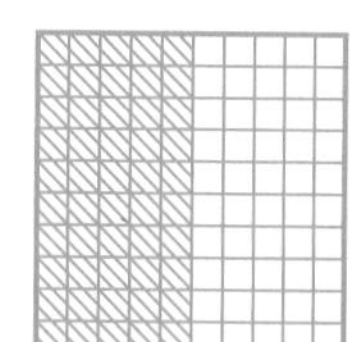

STEP 2 Shade $\frac{1}{5}$ of 1.5 in red.

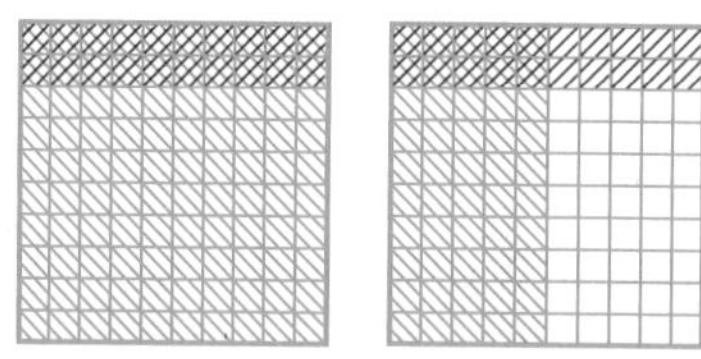

STEP 3 Count the purple squares.

$\frac{1}{5}$ of 1.5 is $\frac{30}{100}$, or 0.30, or 0.3.

Way 2 You can use what you know about multiplication of fractions and mixed numbers to find $\frac{1}{5}$ of 1.5.

STEP 1 Change 1.5 to a mixed number.

$1.5 = 1\frac{5}{10}$, or $1\frac{1}{2}$

STEP 2 Multiply.

$$1\frac{1}{2} \times \frac{1}{5} = \frac{3}{2} \times \frac{1}{5}$$
$$= \frac{3}{10}, \text{ or } 0.3$$

Solution: The larger container of Just Juice holds 0.3 liter more.

Another Example **Find 0.18 × 3.**

Use fractions.

$$\frac{18}{100} \times \frac{3}{1} = \frac{54}{100}$$
$$= 0.54$$

Use models.

54 of 100 squares, or 0.54 is shaded.

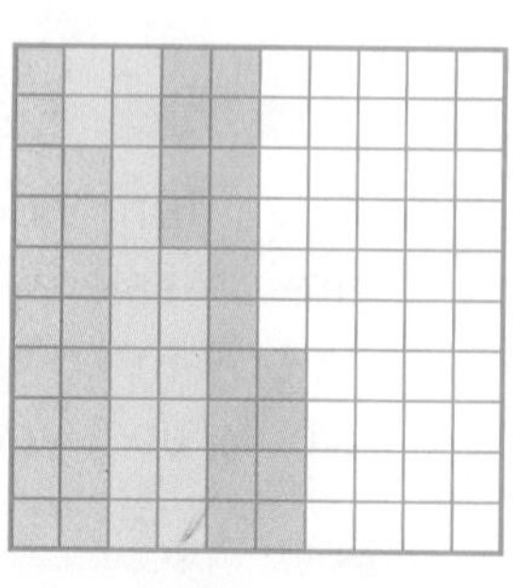

$$\frac{18}{100} + \frac{18}{100} + \frac{18}{100} = \frac{54}{100}$$

Guided Practice

Use models or fractions to multiply. Write each product as a decimal.

1. 0.6 × 0.2 **2.** 0.5 × 0.8 **3.** 0.7 × 2.6

4. 1.5 × 0.4 **5.** 0.8 × 0.9 **6.** 0.6 × 1.4

Ask Yourself

- Did I model the multiplication correctly?
- Did I multiply correctly?
- Did I write the product as a decimal?

Explain Your Thinking ▶ Is $\frac{1}{2} \times 0.4$ equal to $\frac{2}{5} \times 0.5$? Explain why or why not.

Practice and Problem Solving

Use models or fractions to multiply. Write each product as a decimal.

7. 0.6 × 0.5 **8.** 0.4 × 0.8 **9.** 1.5 × 0.5 **10.** 0.5 × 2.8 **11.** 2.1 × 0.5

12. 1.7 × 0.3 **13.** 0.9 × 0.9 **14.** 0.3 × 0.3 **15.** 1.3 × 0.8 **16.** 1.2 × 0.2

Solve.

17. Miguel works at a juice bar 8.5 hours each week. Kim works half as many hours. How many hours does Kim work in a week?

18. A manufacturer puts a bonus coupon on 0.1 of its juice bottles. In a case with 20 bottles, how many juice bottles would you expect to have the coupon?

19. **Create and Solve** Write a problem that can be solved using the model at the right. Solve your problem. Then give it to a partner to solve.

20. Look back at page 334. Suppose the advertisement read, "New size holds 0.2 liter more!" How many liters would the new container hold?

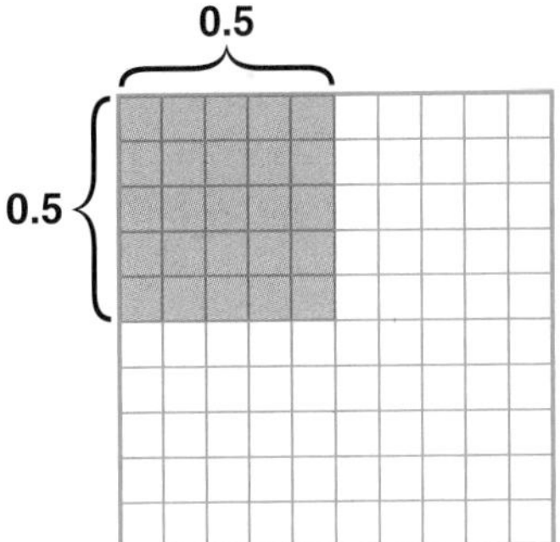

Mixed Review and Test Prep

Open Response

Subtract. (Ch. 11, Lesson 3)

21. 23.2 − 7.5 **22.** 107.26 − 27.05

23. 222.22 − 78.51 **24.** 79.305 − 12.047

Multiple Choice

25. Use models or fractions to find $\frac{2}{3}$ of 0.6. (Ch. 13, Lesson 1)

A 0.2 **C** 0.4

B 0.5 **D** 0.9

Extra Practice See page 349, Set A.

Lesson 2

Multiply Whole Numbers and Decimals

Objective Find the product of a whole number and a decimal.

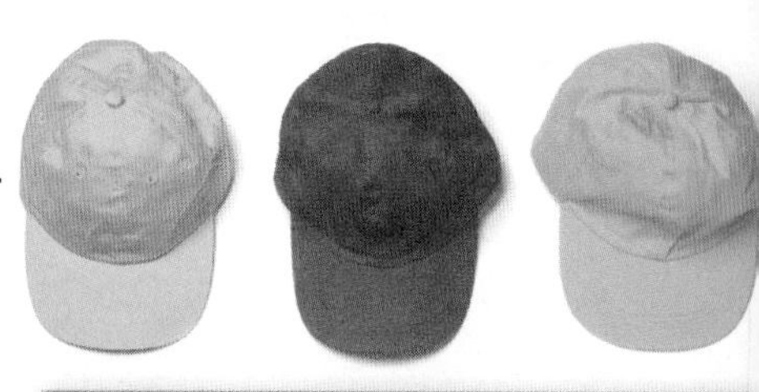

Learn About It

Lian bought 3 caps that were on sale. How much did Lian pay for the caps?

CAPS ON SALE!
$5.68 each

Multiply. $3 \times \$5.68 = c$

STEP 1 Estimate before solving by rounding to the nearest whole number.

$3 \times \$6 = \$18$

Your answer should be close to $18.

STEP 2 Multiply. Ignore the decimal point.

$$\begin{array}{r} 568 \\ \times \quad 3 \\ \hline 1704 \end{array}$$

STEP 3 Place the decimal point in the product.

The number of decimal places in the product must equal the total number of decimal places in the factors.

5.68	←	2 decimal places
× 3	←	+ 0 decimal places
17.04	←	2 decimal places

Compare your answer with your estimate.

$18 is close to $17.04.

An answer of $17.04 is a reasonable answer.

Solution: Lian paid $17.04 for the caps.

Another Example

Find 14 × 0.45.

0.45	←	2 decimal places
× 14	←	+ 0 decimal places
180		
450		
6.30	←	2 decimal places

Guided Practice

Find each product.

1. 4×1.3
2. 2.6×5
3. 0.59×8
4. 6×1.82
5. 3.25×16
6. 0.515×7

Ask Yourself

- Did I estimate first?
- Did I use the correct number of decimal places in my answer?

Explain Your Thinking ▶ Why does it help to estimate before you find the exact answer?

Practice and Problem Solving

Find each product.

7. 6 × 2.4 **8.** 3.8 × 2 **9.** 9.6 × 8 **10.** 9 × 5.6 **11.** 0.13 × 5

12. 3 × 3.4 **13.** 9 × 0.18 **14.** 0.1 × 13 **15.** 8 × 10.8 **16.** 3 × 31.44

17. 7 × 7.7 **18.** 20.5 × 4 **19.** 0.9 × 11 **20.** 50.2 × 6 **21.** 4.412 × 8

22. 6 × 9.8 **23.** 12 × 0.56 **24.** 23 × 2.1 **25.** 16 × 9.5 **26.** 35 × 0.86

x Algebra • Expressions Find one value of *n* so that each statement is true.

27. 13 × *n* is between 55 and 65.

28. *n* × 138 is between 200 and 250.

29. *n* × 11 is between 135 and 140.

30. *n* × 25 is between 40 and 45.

Solve.

31. Kayla works 8 hours one week and earns $48. If 0.08 of that amount is for taxes, how much money does Kayla have to spend that week?

32. John's cost for a sweater is $21 after his discount of 0.7 off the original price. Is the price of the sweater before the discount more or less than $42? Explain.

33. Sierra worked 3.5 hours on Saturday morning and 2.5 hours on Sunday afternoon. If Sierra earns $9.80 per hour, how much did she earn on Saturday and Sunday?

34. Because his father works at the store, Gavin pays only 0.7 of the marked price on clothing. Wayne has a coupon for $5 off any jacket. Who will pay the least for the jacket at the right? Explain how you decided.

Mixed Review and Test Prep

Open Response

Add. (Ch. 11, Lesson 2)

35. 1.8 + 3.246 **36.** 4.01 + 5.07

37. 3.02 + 4.08 **38.** 5.02 + 2.88

39. 8.6 + 3.4 **40.** 3.21 + 3.22

41. 6.90 + 1.1 **42.** 0.35 + 0.07

43. Grant's purchases at the grocery store come to $130. He saves 0.2 of this by using coupons. How much does Grant pay after using the coupons?

Explain how you got your answer.
(Ch. 13, Lesson 2)

Extra Practice See page 349, Set B.

Lesson 3

Estimate Products

Objective Use rounding to estimate products of decimals.

Learn About It

When Isaac's father makes a call on his cell phone, it costs 11 cents for each minute the call lasts. About how much did it cost Isaac to talk on his father's cell phone for 86 minutes after school?

Estimate the product. 86 × $0.11

You can use fractions and a number line to estimate.

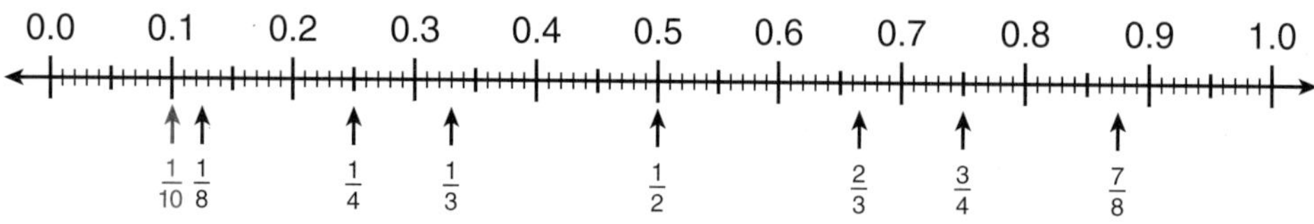

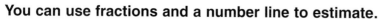

STEP 1 Round the numbers.

86 rounds to 90.

0.11 is about $\frac{1}{10}$.

STEP 2 Multiply.

$90 \times \frac{1}{10} = \frac{90}{10}$, or 9

Solution: It cost about $9 for Isaac's phone call.

Different Ways to Estimate 328 × 0.62

Way 1 **To find a low estimate, round 328 down to 300 and 0.62 to 0.6.**

$$\begin{array}{rcr} 328 & \rightarrow & 300 \\ \times 0.62 & \rightarrow & \times 0.6 \\ \hline & \rightarrow & 180 \end{array}$$

Since both factors were rounded to a lesser number, the actual product must be greater than 180.

Way 2 **To find a high estimate, round 328 up to 350 and 0.62 to 0.7.**

$$\begin{array}{rcr} 328 & \rightarrow & 350 \\ \times 0.62 & \rightarrow & \times 0.7 \\ \hline & \rightarrow & 245 \end{array}$$

Since both factors were rounded to a greater number, the actual product must be less than 245.

So, the actual product of 328 × 0.62 is between 180 and 245.

Guided Practice

Ask Yourself
- How can I round each number?
- Can I easily use fractions?

Estimate each product.

1. 6.572 × 18
2. 122 × 0.24
3. 532 × 1.7
4. 87 × 3.12
5. 32 × 0.48
6. 2.5 × 351

Explain Your Thinking ▶ How does your estimated product in Exercise 6 compare with the actual product? Explain.

Practice and Problem Solving

Estimate each product.

7. 0.23 × 41
8. 8 × 0.119
9. 12.7 × 32
10. 209 × 0.467
11. 6.6 × 27
12. 0.45 × 80
13. 3.5 × 58
14. 25 × 7.92

Data **Use the table to solve Problems 15–19.**

The table shows the current cellular phone plan Mr. Henry uses and two alternate plans to which he may consider switching.

Plan	Peak Minute Cost	Off-Peak Minute Cost
Current Plan	\$0.350	\$0.055
Alternate 1	\$0.700	Free
Alternate 2	\$0.125	\$0.125

15. Last month, Mr. Henry's cellular phone bill included 135 peak minutes and 240 off-peak minutes. About how much was this bill?

16. If a person uses 100 peak and 100 off-peak minutes each month, which plan is least expensive to use?

17. Which calling plan has the greatest difference between peak and off-peak charges? How much is the difference?

18. A customer with Alternate 1 plan has a bill of \$35. The customer used the same number of peak and off-peak minutes. How many minutes each was that?

19. Mr. Henry's average bill includes 98 peak minutes and 516 off-peak minutes. Should he switch plans or stay with the one he has? Explain your reasoning.

Mixed Review and Test Prep

Open Response

Write each sum or difference in simplest form. (Ch. 10, Lessons 2 and 5)

20. $\frac{1}{4} + \frac{1}{4}$
21. $\frac{3}{7} + \frac{2}{7}$
22. $\frac{7}{8} - \frac{3}{8}$
23. $\frac{5}{9} - \frac{2}{9}$
24. $\frac{3}{5} + \frac{7}{5}$
25. $\frac{6}{3} - \frac{3}{3}$

Multiple Choice

26. A box of crackers costs \$0.296 per ounce. Which is a reasonable estimate for the cost of a 12-ounce box of those crackers? (Ch. 13, Lesson 3)

A \$2.00 **C** \$4.00

B \$6.00 **D** \$12.00

Extra Practice See page 349, Set C.

Audio Tutor 2/4 Listen and Understand

Lesson 4 Multiply Decimals

Objective Find the product of two decimals.

Learn About It

The parking lot at the shopping mall covers 0.9 acre. Three tenths of the parking lot is reserved for compact cars. How large is the area reserved for compact cars?

You can multiply 0.9 and 0.3 to solve the problem.

Before you multiply, estimate to get a sense of where the decimal point belongs in your answer.

$0.9 \approx 1$

$1 \times 0.3 = 0.3$

Remember $\approx$ means "about equal to."

The answer should be a little less than 0.3.

Multiply. $\mathbf{0.9 \times 0.3 = n}$

Multiply and then place the decimal point.

STEP 1 Multiply. Ignore the decimal points.

$$\begin{array}{r} 3 \\ \times\ 9 \\ \hline 27 \end{array}$$

STEP 2 Place the decimal point in the product.

0.3	←	1 decimal place
× 0.9	←	+ 1 decimal place
0.27	←	2 decimal places

Use fractions to check.

$$\frac{3}{10} \times \frac{9}{10} = \frac{3 \times 9}{10 \times 10} = \frac{27}{100}, \text{ or } 0.27$$

Solution: In the parking lot, 0.27 acre is reserved for compact cars.

Other Examples

A. Factor in Hundredths

0.71	←	2 decimal places
× 0.9	←	+ 1 decimal place
0.639	←	3 decimal places

B. Factors Greater Than 1

1.43	←	2 decimal places
× 3.2	←	+ 1 decimal place
286		
4290		
4.576	←	3 decimal places

Extra Help at eduplace.com/map

Guided Practice

Multiply.

1. $\begin{array}{r} 0.6 \\ \times\ 0.4 \\ \hline \end{array}$

2. $\begin{array}{r} 0.6 \\ \times\ \ 5 \\ \hline \end{array}$

3. $\begin{array}{r} 0.46 \\ \times\ \ \ 2 \\ \hline \end{array}$

4. 0.8×0.34

5. 4.28×1.2

6. 0.23×0.7

Ask Yourself

- Did I count the number of decimal places in the product correctly?

Explain Your Thinking ▶ Look back at Exercise 1. Why would 24 be an unreasonable answer to 0.6×0.4?

Practice and Problem Solving

Multiply.

7. $\begin{array}{r} 0.5 \\ \times\ 0.5 \\ \hline \end{array}$

8. $\begin{array}{r} 0.9 \\ \times\ 0.2 \\ \hline \end{array}$

9. $\begin{array}{r} 0.4 \\ \times\ 0.7 \\ \hline \end{array}$

10. $\begin{array}{r} 0.7 \\ \times\ 0.3 \\ \hline \end{array}$

11. $\begin{array}{r} 1.6 \\ \times\ 0.8 \\ \hline \end{array}$

12. $\begin{array}{r} 4.5 \\ \times\ 0.7 \\ \hline \end{array}$

13. $\begin{array}{r} 0.47 \\ \times\ \ 0.3 \\ \hline \end{array}$

14. $\begin{array}{r} 1.34 \\ \times\ \ 0.2 \\ \hline \end{array}$

15. 0.8×0.22

16. 0.68×0.5

17. 8.34×4.7

18. 12.3×5.4

Algebra • Equations **Choose the value for the variable that makes each equation true. A value may be used more than once.**

19. $n \times 4 = 0.08$

20. $n \times 0.1 = 0.2$

21. $16 \times n = 35.2$

22. $n^2 = 4.84$

Compare **Write >, <, or = for each ●.**

23. 0.4×0.5 ● 0.2×0.6

24. 0.8×0.4 ● 0.7×0.5

25. 4×0.9 ● 6×0.6

26. 0.2×7 ● 0.7×2

Go On

Solve.

27. A new parking lot at the city swimming pool will cover 0.7 acre. The planners want to use two tenths of the parking lot for handicapped parking. How large is the handicapped parking area?

28. At a bookstore, *The World Almanac for Kids* costs $11.95. If you bought that book at the school book sale, you would pay 0.4 of that amount. How much does the book cost at the book sale?

29. Shane walks 1.2 miles to school. Michael's home is 0.6 of the way between Shane's home and school. How far has Shane walked when he reaches Michael's on the way to school?

30. Look back at Problem 29. Emma's home is 0.4 of the way between Shane's home and Michael's home. How far is Emma's from Shane's? How far is Emma's from school?

Choose a Computation Method

Mental Math • Estimation • Paper and Pencil • Calculator

Data **Use the table to solve Problems 31–34.**

31. Last year, Ursula's allowance was $10 a week. The table shows how she spent her money. How much did she spend each week on clothing?

32. Ursula earned $24.50 from doing yard work. According to her budget, how much of that should she save?

Ursula is keeping the same budget this year. Her allowance is now $17.50 a week.

33. This year, how much should Ursula save in 4 weeks?

34. How much more will she spend each week on clothes than on food?

Ursula's Budget From Last Year	
Food	$\frac{2}{10}$
Entertainment	$\frac{4}{10}$
Savings	$\frac{1}{10}$
Clothing	$\frac{3}{10}$

35. Measurement Draw a line that is 8.6 cm long. Draw a second line that is 0.5 of that length. Draw a third line that is 0.5 the length of the second line. How long is the third line?

36. Write About It Jennifer multiplied two decimals less than one and got an answer greater than one. Explain to Jennifer why her answer cannot be correct. Use words, examples, and drawings to explain.

Extra Practice See page 349, Set D.

Problem Solving

Number Sense
Far, Far Away

You can use scientific notation to write very large numbers. The mean distance from the Sun to Pluto is about 5 billion, 900 million km.

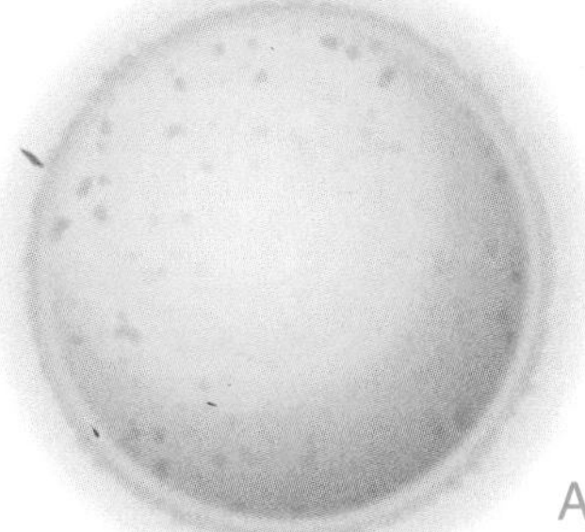

Pluto

5,900,000,000 km

In scientific notation: 5.9×10^9

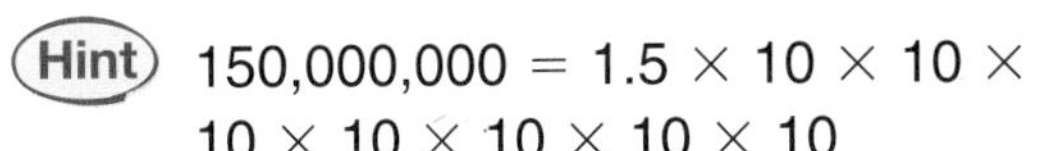

A number between 1 and 10 — A power of 10

Earth is only about 150,000,000 km from the Sun. Try writing that number in scientific notation.

Hint $150{,}000{,}000 = 1.5 \times 10 \times 10 \times 10 \times 10 \times 10 \times 10 \times 10 \times 10$

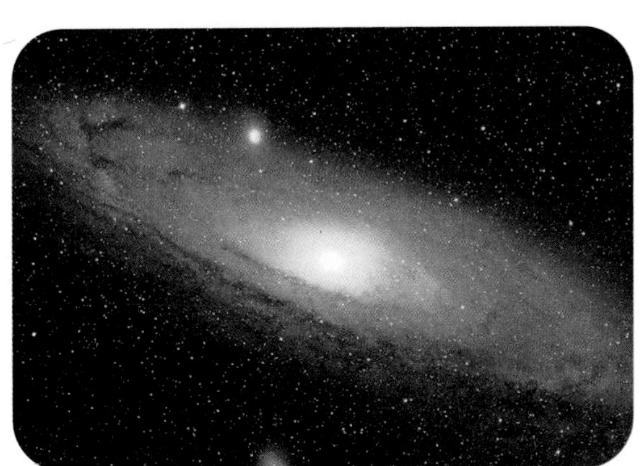

The Andromeda Galaxy is the nearest spiral galaxy to our own galaxy. It is about 21 quintillion km away. That is 21,000,000,000,000,000,000 km. How would you write that distance in scientific notation?

Quick Check

Check your understanding of Lessons 1–4.

Use models or fractions to multiply. Write each product as a decimal. (Lesson 1)

1. 0.5×0.8 **2.** 0.2×0.3

Estimate each product. (Lesson 3)

3. 0.83×6 **4.** 5.22×4.79

Find each product. (Lessons 2 and 4)

5. 7×0.2 **6.** 0.4×5 **7.** 5.28×7

8. 1.6×0.05 **9.** 0.9×0.6 **10.** 0.7×0.7

Lesson 5

Zeros in the Product

Objective Decide when to write zeros in the products of decimal factors.

Learn About It

Sylvia bought a pencil for $0.40. Where Sylvia lives, a sales tax of $0.05 for every dollar spent is added to all purchases. How much will the sales tax be on the pencil Sylvia bought?

Find 0.4 × 0.05.

STEP 1 Multiply as you would with whole numbers. Ignore the decimal points.

$$\begin{array}{r} 5 \\ \times\ 4 \\ \hline 20 \end{array}$$

STEP 2 Count the number of decimal places needed for the product.

$$\begin{array}{rl} 0.05 & \leftarrow \text{2 decimal places} \\ \times\ 0.4 & \leftarrow + \underline{\text{1 decimal place}} \\ \hline 20 & \leftarrow \text{3 decimal places} \end{array}$$

STEP 3 Write zeros in front of the whole number to place the decimal point correctly.

$$\begin{array}{r} 0.05 \\ \times\ 0.4 \\ \hline 0.020 \end{array}$$

Solution: The sales tax on the pencil will be $0.02.

Other Examples

A. Factors in Tenths and Hundredths

$$\begin{array}{rl} 0.17 & \leftarrow \text{2 decimal places} \\ \times\ 0.5 & \leftarrow + \underline{\text{1 decimal place}} \\ \hline 0.085 & \leftarrow \text{3 decimal places} \end{array}$$

B. Factor in Thousandths

$$\begin{array}{rl} 0.001 & \leftarrow \text{3 decimal places} \\ \times\ \ \ \ 9 & \leftarrow + \underline{\text{0 decimal places}} \\ \hline 0.009 & \leftarrow \text{3 decimal places} \end{array}$$

Guided Practice

Multiply.

1. $\begin{array}{r} 0.1 \\ \times\ 0.7 \\ \hline \end{array}$

2. $\begin{array}{r} 0.04 \\ \times\ 2 \\ \hline \end{array}$

3. $\begin{array}{r} 0.34 \\ \times\ 0.1 \\ \hline \end{array}$

4. 0.06 × 1.3

5. 0.3 × 0.02

6. 0.004 × 3

Ask Yourself

- Did I multiply the factors as if they were whole numbers?
- Do I have the correct number of decimal places in my answer?

Explain Your Thinking ▶ Why can 0.020 be written as 0.02?

Practice and Problem Solving

Multiply.

7. $\begin{array}{r} 3 \\ \times 0.3 \\ \hline \end{array}$

8. $\begin{array}{r} 0.3 \\ \times 0.3 \\ \hline \end{array}$

9. $\begin{array}{r} 0.03 \\ \times 0.3 \\ \hline \end{array}$

10. $\begin{array}{r} 0.03 \\ \times 3 \\ \hline \end{array}$

11. $\begin{array}{r} 7 \\ \times 0.2 \\ \hline \end{array}$

12. $\begin{array}{r} 0.7 \\ \times 0.2 \\ \hline \end{array}$

13. $\begin{array}{r} 0.7 \\ \times 0.02 \\ \hline \end{array}$

14. $\begin{array}{r} 0.07 \\ \times 0.2 \\ \hline \end{array}$

15. $\begin{array}{r} 0.2 \\ \times 0.06 \\ \hline \end{array}$

16. $\begin{array}{r} 0.5 \\ \times 0.06 \\ \hline \end{array}$

17. 0.04×0.6 **18.** 0.6×0.25 **19.** 0.8×0.1 **20.** 0.03×0.7

21. 0.5×0.3 **22.** 0.01×0.9 **23.** 0.09×0.5 **24.** 0.7×0.06

25. 0.02×0.4 **26.** 0.04×0.4 **27.** 0.05×0.8 **28.** 0.002×6

Data Use the table to solve Problems 29–34.

The table shows sales tax per dollar for some states in 2002.

State	Sales Tax per Dollar (2002)
Texas	0.0625
New Jersey	0.06
Maryland	0.05
Georgia	0.04
Colorado	0.029

29. A shirt is priced at \$11.95. With sales tax, what will that shirt cost in Colorado? in Texas?

30. A jacket costs \$25. How much will the sales tax be on this jacket if it is sold in Maryland?

31. You are in Georgia and you buy items that cost \$4.79, \$5.99, and \$9 before tax. All you have in your wallet is \$20. Do you have enough money? Explain.

32. Suppose a city government in Maryland decides to add on a local sales tax that is 0.5 of the state sales tax. What would the combined sales tax be in that city?

33. What is the mean, median, and range of the sales taxes for the states listed in the table?

34. **Create and Solve** Use the information in the table to write and solve a problem.

Mixed Review and Test Prep

Open Response

Find the mean, median, mode, and range of each set of data. (Ch. 8, Lesson 2)

35. 78°F, 74°F, 75°F, 68°F, 75°F

36. 6°C, 8°C, 8°C, 8°C, 4°C, 6°C, 7°C, 9°C

37. 85, 85, 85, 80, 84, 85

38. What is the sales tax on \$5, if a state charges 6.5¢ sales tax on every dollar you spend? Explain how you found your answer. (Ch. 13, Lesson 5)

Extra Practice See page 349, Set E.

Lesson 6

Audio Tutor 2/5 Listen and Understand

Problem-Solving Decision

Reasonable Answers

Objective Review how to decide if the answer to a problem is reasonable.

After you have solved a problem, look back at the problem and decide if the answer is reasonable.

Problem Ishana's dad tells her she must save 0.6 of the money she earns. Ishana earns $15 one week. She figures that her savings must be $6. Is this reasonable?

Here are the responses from three students:

Hannah

No, Ishana's answer should be $15.60.

$15 + $0.60 is $15.60

The problem may be misinterpreted.

To find the amount Ishana must save, you have to multiply, not add.

$0.6 \times \$15$

Antonio

No, Ishana's answer should be $15.

$0.6 \approx 1 \quad 1 \times \$15 = \$15$

An answer may not make sense.

$15 is the total amount Ishana earned. She is only saving part of her money, not all of it.

Sora

No, Ishana needs to multiply.

$0.6 \times \$15 = \$0.90$

The calculations may be incorrect.

Check that you have the correct number of decimal places in the product.

$$\begin{array}{rl} 15 & \leftarrow \text{ 0 decimal places} \\ \times\ 0.6 & \leftarrow +\text{1 decimal place} \\ \hline 9.0 & \leftarrow \text{ 1 decimal place} \end{array}$$

Solution: Ishana's answer is not reasonable. Ishana should save 0.6 × $15, or $9.

Try These

Solve. Explain why the answer is reasonable or unreasonable.

1. Each month Dan's savings account pays 0.03 of the balance as interest. Dan says that the interest on his $200 will be $0.03. Is he correct?
2. Ella's credit card balance is $325. Interest charges are 0.06 of the balance. Ella thinks the interest would be $1.95. Is Ella correct?
3. Linda earns $40. She plans to put 0.5 of that money into savings and 0.5 of what is left toward a new bike. She says she'll have $10 left. Is she correct?
4. Clarice has $2 and she wants to buy a fruit drink for $1.80. The sales tax on the drink is $0.05 per dollar spent. Clarice says she has enough money. Is she right?

Solve. Explain why the answer is reasonable or unreasonable.

5. Jason plans to save 0.25 of his earnings for a gift for his mom. He earns $50 this week. He puts $25 of that money away toward his mom's gift. Is this the correct amount?

6. Shawna's mom keeps 0.25 of the profits from sales in her store. The store's profits for this month are $2,350. Shawna thinks that her mom should keep $58.75. Is Shawna correct?

7. Andrew's room is 0.19 the size of his entire house. His entire house has 1,750 ft^2. Andrew says his room has 332.5 ft^2. Is he correct?

8. Three sisters share some grapes. Carla eats 0.5 of them, Inez eats 0.5 of them, and Nella eats 0.5 of them. Is this reasonable?

9. Jacqueline has 10 square yards of material to make some shirts. She needs 0.2 of the material to make 1 shirt. She thinks she could make at least 500 shirts from the material. Is she correct?

10. Han must make some cookies for a bake sale. He will make 72 cookies. He thinks that this is 0.75 of the total needed for the sale. If the bake sale needs 96 cookies, is Han correct?

Math Reasoning

Activity

It Goes On and On and On — or Does It?

Start with a sheet of paper that is 10 inches by 10 inches. Think about folding the paper exactly in half. Then folding it in half again and then again.

1. **Calculator** Copy and complete the table to show mathematically what will happen to the area that the folded paper covers. Round answers to the nearest tenth.

2. Try the experiment. Measure to check your results with your table. What happened?

3. Try the experiment again with a piece of paper that is 2 or 4 times as big as the 10 by 10 square. What happened this time?

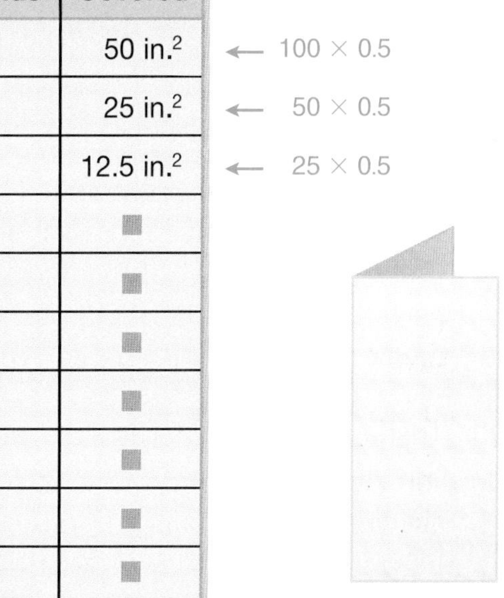

Number of Folds	Area Covered	
1	50 in.^{2}	← 100 × 0.5
2	25 in.^{2}	← 50 × 0.5
3	12.5 in.^{2}	← 25 × 0.5
4	■	
5	■	
6	■	
7	■	
8	■	
9	■	
10	■	

Chapter Review/Test

VOCABULARY

1. To ____ is to find an approximate rather than an exact answer.

2. When you ____ a number, you express it to the nearest hundredth, tenth, and so on.

3. A ____ is made up of a whole number and a fraction.

Vocabulary

estimate
factor
mixed number
product
round

CONCEPTS AND SKILLS

Use models or fractions to multiply. Write each product as a decimal. (Lesson 1, pp. 334–335)

4. 0.9×0.5
5. 0.3×1.7
6. 0.2×2.4
7. 1.9×0.6

Estimate each product. (Lesson 3, pp. 338–339)

8. 0.85×7
9. 3.82×5
10. 8.36×61
11. 4.72×4.9

Multiply. (Lessons 2, 4, pp. 336–337, 340–343)

12. 7×6.2
13. 7.25×0.4
14. 8.3×6.5
15. 2.6×4
16. 9.12×4.7
17. 0.96×0.8
18. 3.15×7.4
19. 0.7×0.77

Multiply. Write zeros in front of the whole number to place the decimal point correctly. (Lesson 5, pp. 344–345)

20. 0.8×0.007
21. 0.4×0.012
22. 0.06×0.4
23. 4×0.0008

PROBLEM SOLVING

Solve. (Lesson 6, pp. 346–347)

24. At Franklin Middle School, 0.24 of the students are involved in a school sport. Of these students, 0.4 of them are girls. Janet says this means about 0.1 of girls are involved in sports. Is she correct?

25. Trisha makes $65 dollars a month babysitting. She makes $40 of this babysitting for Mrs. Ramirez. She thinks this is about 0.33 of her income. Is this reasonable?

Write About It

Show You Understand

Look at how Sasha multiplied.

$$\begin{array}{r} 0.2 \\ \times\ 0.007 \\ \hline 0.014 \end{array}$$

Explain what Sasha did wrong.

Extra Practice

Set A (Lesson 1, pp. 334–335)

Use models or fractions to multiply. Write each product as a decimal.

1. 0.7×0.3
2. 0.6×0.9
3. 0.4×1.3
4. 0.3×0.6
5. 1.7×0.5
6. 0.5×1.8
7. 0.9×2.1
8. 1.2×0.8
9. 0.7×0.9
10. 3.2×0.2

Set B (Lesson 2, pp. 336–337)

Find each product.

1. 6×0.2
2. 9×0.5
3. 8×0.61
4. 5×0.82
5. 2×5.47
6. 8×4.17
7. 6×7.08
8. 3×4.98
9. 6.5×4.2
10. 7.4×17

Set C (Lesson 3, pp. 338–339)

Estimate each product.

1. 0.17×4
2. 3.97×6
3. 7.22×7
4. 11.79×3
5. 82×0.58
6. 21×4.07
7. 48×9.39
8. 4×10.77
9. 0.42×300
10. 4.25×6

Set D (Lesson 4, pp. 340–343)

Multiply.

1. 0.6×0.3
2. 0.5×0.7
3. 0.8×0.8
4. 0.5×0.8
5. 0.18×0.8
6. 5.75×0.5
7. 3.6×1.3
8. 6.14×3.5
9. 0.83×0.7
10. 5.16×6.1

Compare. Write >, <, or =.

11. 0.3×0.5 ⬤ 0.4×0.4
12. 0.9×0.3 ⬤ 0.7×0.4
13. 0.7×0.7 ⬤ 0.6×0.8

Set E (Lesson 5, pp. 344–345)

Multiply. Write zeros in front of the whole number to place the decimal point correctly.

1. $\begin{array}{r} 0.6 \\ \times\ 4 \\ \hline \end{array}$
2. $\begin{array}{r} 0.4 \\ \times\ 0.6 \\ \hline \end{array}$
3. $\begin{array}{r} 0.4 \\ \times\ 0.06 \\ \hline \end{array}$
4. $\begin{array}{r} 0.9 \\ \times\ 0.09 \\ \hline \end{array}$
5. $\begin{array}{r} 0.09 \\ \times\ 0.08 \\ \hline \end{array}$
6. 0.5×7
7. 0.5×0.7
8. 0.5×0.07
9. 0.05×0.07
10. 0.5×0.04

Extra Practice at **eduplace.com/map**

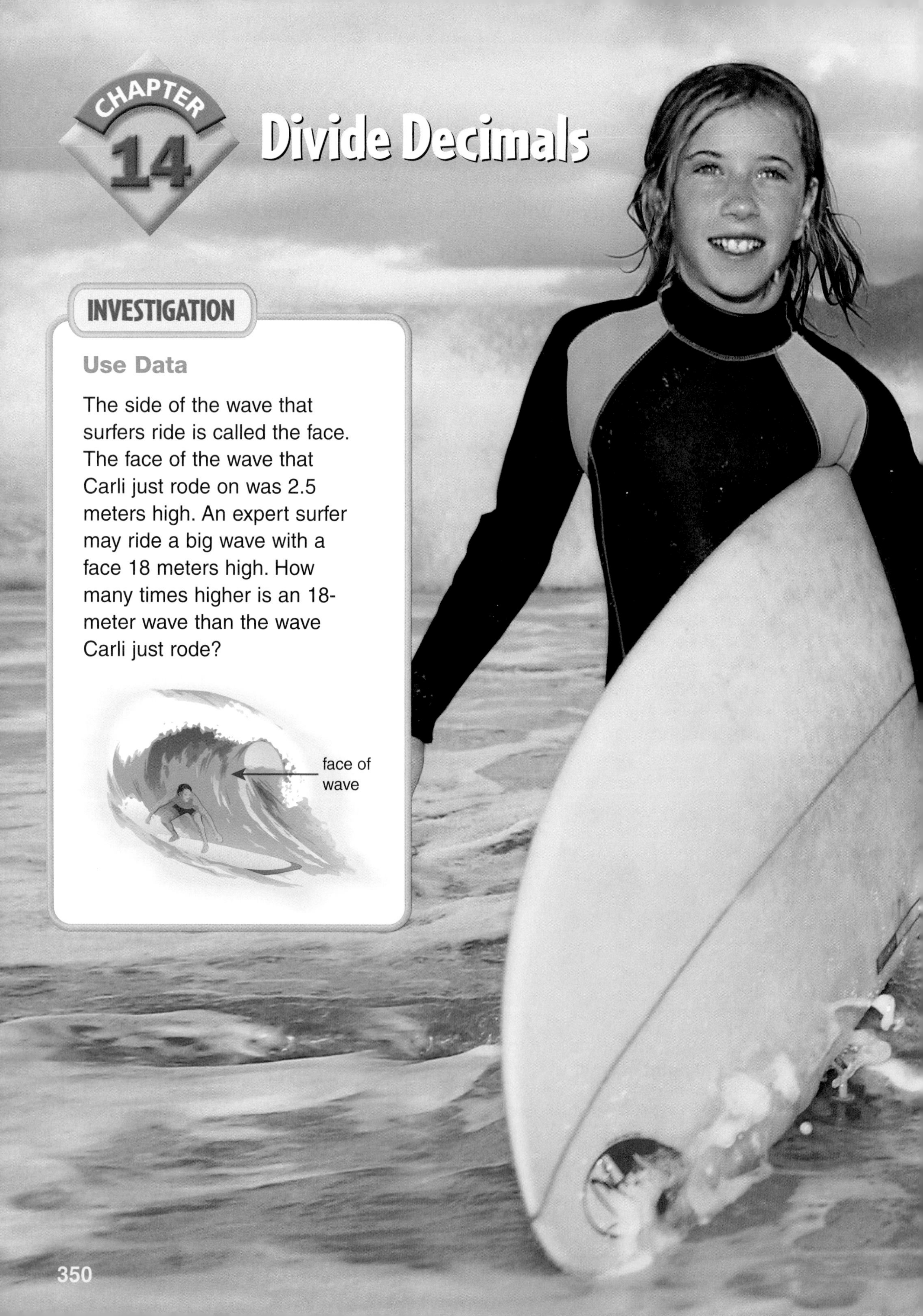

Divide Decimals

INVESTIGATION

Use Data

The side of the wave that surfers ride is called the face. The face of the wave that Carli just rode on was 2.5 meters high. An expert surfer may ride a big wave with a face 18 meters high. How many times higher is an 18-meter wave than the wave Carli just rode?

Use What You Know

Use this page to review and remember what you need to know for this chapter.

VOCABULARY

Choose the best word to complete each sentence.

1. The ____ is the result of dividing one number by another.
2. In the expression 24 ÷ 6, 24 is the ____.
3. In the expression 63 ÷ 9, the ____ is 9.

Vocabulary

- decimal
- dividend
- divisor
- quotient
- remainder

CONCEPTS AND SKILLS

Write a fraction in simplest form for each decimal.

4. 0.2
5. 0.5
6. 0.75
7. 0.6

Estimate using compatible numbers.

8. 92 ÷ 28
9. 403 ÷ 17
10. 2,361 ÷ 74
11. 589 ÷ 28

Multiply.

12. $\frac{8}{10} \times \frac{1}{6}$
13. $\frac{45}{10} \times \frac{1}{5}$
14. $\frac{36}{10} \times \frac{1}{4}$
15. $\frac{16}{10} \times \frac{1}{9}$

Divide.

16. $22\overline{)451}$
17. 738 ÷ 17
18. $65 ÷ 13
19. 9,802 ÷ 34

Write About It

20. Amelia computed 237 ÷ 18 and got a quotient of 13 R3. Explain how you could check to see whether her answer is correct.

Facts Practice, See page 659.

Explore Division With Decimals

Objective Use models to show the relationship between dividing fractions and decimals.

Learn About It

Melissa is training for a 5-kilometer race. Her coach has separated the course into 0.5-kilometer sections. How many sections is that for a 5-kilometer course?

Solve $5 \div 0.5 = n$.

You can use models and what you know about fractions to find $5 \div 0.5$. Try changing the decimals to fractions and then modeling the division.

STEP 1 Write 5 and 0.5 as fractions.

$5 = \frac{5}{1}$

$0.5 = \frac{5}{10} = \frac{1}{2}$

STEP 2 Model 5 wholes.

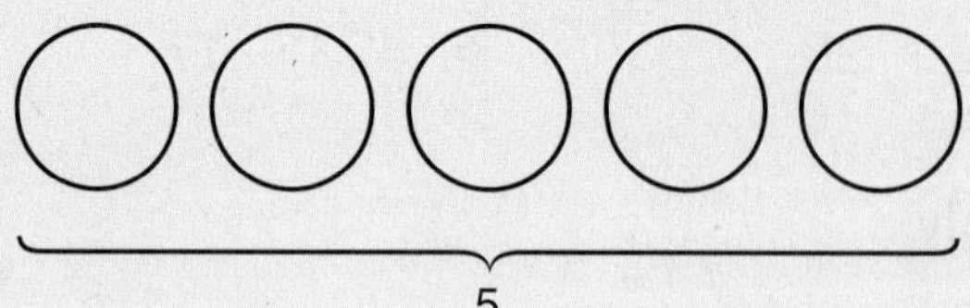

STEP 3 Separate the 5 wholes into halves.

STEP 4 Think about what you are asked to find.

- How many 0.5s are in 5?
- How many $\frac{1}{2}$s are in 5?

STEP 5 Count to find the number of $\frac{1}{2}$s in 5.

There are 10 halves in 5 wholes.

Write a multiplication sentence that shows the answer to $5 \div \frac{1}{2}$.

$5 \div \frac{1}{2} = 5 \times 2 = 10.$

There are two $\frac{1}{2}$s in each whole. Multiplying 2 times 5 shows that there are 10 halves in 5 wholes.

Solution: Since $5 \div \frac{1}{2} = 10$, then $5 \div 0.5 = 10$.

Other Examples

A. Use a Model

Find $2 \div 0.4$.

You can use models to show how many groups of 4 tenths there are in 2.

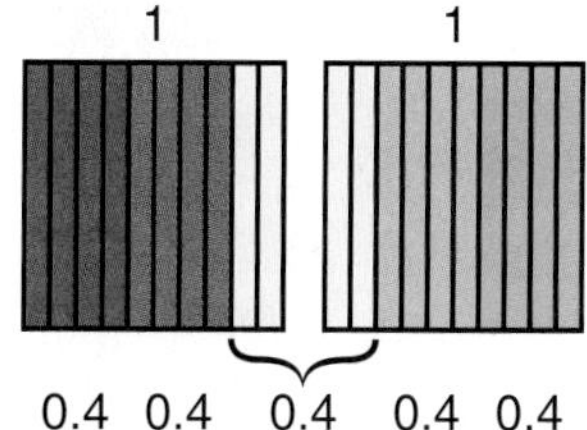

There are 5 groups of 4 tenths in 2, $2 \div 0.4 = 5$.

B. Use Number Sense

Find $6 \div 0.2$.

> **Think**
> Since $0.2 = \frac{1}{5}$, then there are 5 fifths in each whole.

So, in 6 wholes, there are 6×5, or 30 fifths.

$6 \div 0.2 = 30$

Guided Practice

Model the division. Write the quotient in decimal form.

1. $6 \div 0.5$ **2.** $4 \div 0.4$ **3.** $12 \div 0.25$

4. $10 \div 0.25$ **5.** $8 \div 0.5$ **6.** $9 \div 0.2$

Ask Yourself

- Did I change the decimal to a fraction?
- Did I think about the number of parts in each whole?

Explain Your Thinking ▶ Explain how you could use number sense to find the quotient for Exercise 6.

Practice and Problem Solving

Model the division and write the quotient in decimal form.

7. $3 \div 0.5$ **8.** $4 \div 0.5$ **9.** $8 \div 0.4$ **10.** $2 \div 0.25$ **11.** $3 \div 0.25$

12. $4 \div 0.25$ **13.** $3 \div 0.6$ **14.** $4 \div 0.8$ **15.** $5 \div 0.2$ **16.** $10 \div 0.2$

17. As Melita trains, she checks her heart rate every 0.25 kilometer. How many times does she check it in 1 kilometer?

18. Cameron speed walks 2 miles in 0.5 hour. At this pace, how far can he speed walk in 1 hour? Draw a model to show your solution.

Mixed Review and Test Prep

Open Response

Compare. Write $<$, $>$, or $=$ for each ⬭.
(Ch. 9, Lessons 8 and 9)

19. 0.5 ⬭ $\frac{1}{3}$ **20.** $1\frac{3}{4}$ ⬭ 1.6

21. 2.6 ⬭ $2\frac{3}{5}$ **22.** 0.125 ⬭ $\frac{1}{8}$

Multiple Choice

23. Each runner's number bib uses 0.2 meter of cloth. How many bibs can be made from 3 meters of cloth?
(Ch. 14, Lesson 1)

A 0.2 **C** 6

B 1.5 **D** 15

Extra Practice See page 375, Set A.

Audio Tutor 2/6 Listen and Understand

Lesson 2 Estimate Quotients

Objective Estimate decimal quotients using compatible numbers.

Vocabulary
compatible numbers

Learn About It

During its history, one team's win ratio has been 0.23. They have won 38 games. To find about how many games they have played in all, divide 38 by 0.23.

You can use fractions, rounded decimals, and **compatible numbers** to estimate a quotient. Using equivalent unit fractions for decimals makes estimation easier.

$0.1 = \frac{1}{10}$	$0.25 = \frac{1}{4}$
$0.125 = \frac{1}{8}$	$0.33... = \frac{1}{3}$
$0.2 = \frac{1}{5}$	$0.5 = \frac{1}{2}$

Estimate. $38 \div 0.23 = n$

STEP 1 Change the decimal to an equivalent unit fraction.

$0.23 \approx 0.25$

$0.25 = \frac{1}{4}$

STEP 2 Change the dividend to a compatible number.

$38 \approx 40$

40 is easy to work with.

STEP 3 Estimate the number of fourths in 40.

There are 160 fourths in 40.
The quotient will be about 160.

$38 \div 0.23 \approx 160$

Think
There are 4 fourths in 1. 40 has 4×40 fourths, or 160 fourths.

Solution: The team has played about 160 games.

Another Example

Dividend and Divisor Are Decimals

Estimate. $54.8 \div 0.13 = n$

$54.8 \approx 50$, $0.13 \approx 0.125$ and $0.125 = \frac{1}{8}$

$54.8 \div 0.13 \approx 50 \div \frac{1}{8}$

$54.8 \div 0.13 \approx 400$

Think
There are 8 eighths in 1, so there are 50×8 eighths, or 400 eighths, in 50.

Guided Practice

Estimate each quotient.

1. 127 ÷ 0.19
2. 57 ÷ 0.32
3. 190 ÷ 0.49
4. 17.6 ÷ 0.09
5. 48.4 ÷ 0.27
6. 57.6 ÷ 0.11

Ask Yourself

- Did I change the decimal to an equivalent unit fraction?
- Is my new dividend easy to work with?

Explain Your Thinking ▶ Explain how you chose the numbers you used to estimate the quotient in Exercise 1.

Practice and Problem Solving

Estimate each quotient.

7. 47 ÷ 0.53
8. 152 ÷ 0.29
9. 408 ÷ 0.18
10. 36 ÷ 0.54
11. 8 ÷ 0.236
12. 19 ÷ 0.179
13. 5 ÷ 0.475
14. 47 ÷ 0.345
15. 8.38 ÷ 0.24
16. 6.97 ÷ 0.341
17. 52.1 ÷ 0.18
18. 17.6 ÷ 0.26

Solve.

19. A newspaper finds the field hockey team's winning ratio by dividing the number of games won by the number of games played. The team has won 6 games and has a winning ratio of 0.33. About how many games has the team played?

Field Hockey Team Gets 6TH Win

In the last ten minutes of hectic play and two turn-arounds, our team surprised the fans with the final goal against the Panthers.

The Rockets are becoming dominant in local girls field hockey as they defeated the Panthers for their sixth consecutive win.

The Rock Falls Rockets started the season as defending state champion. The team has bounced back from a loss in the opening game of the season with a 4-2 victory last night over the Afton Panthers.

Rockets' coach Jill Williams knows it may be a challenge for the team to maintain the focus, but she also has the benefit of experienced on-field leadership. Seven starters from the team were on last year's state championship team.

"We have clear leaders who lead by example and are very supportive other players," said coach Williams.

"We're excited to get out there and prove we can win it all again," senior Glenda Bruns said.

20. **You Decide** Decide on a win ratio for a team and the number of games it has won. Use the data you create to figure out the number of games the team has lost.

21. **Write About It** How does thinking about an equivalent fraction for a decimal help you estimate quotients?

22. In field hockey the goal cage takes up $\frac{1}{5}$ of the 60-foot goal line. How many feet long is the goal cage?

Mixed Review and Test Prep

Open Response

Add or subtract. Write your answer in simplest form. (Ch. 10, Lessons 4 and 8)

23. $2\frac{3}{5} + 1\frac{7}{10}$
24. $5\frac{3}{4} + 2\frac{1}{3}$
25. $4\frac{2}{3} - 3\frac{5}{6}$
26. $7\frac{1}{8} - \frac{9}{10}$

27. For fifth-graders, field hockey games last an average of 0.55 hour. About how many games can be played on one field during a 4-hour tournament? (Ch. 14, Lesson 2)

Extra Practice See page 375, Set B.

Lesson 3

Multiply and Divide by Powers of 10

Objective Use patterns to multiply and divide by powers of 10.

Vocabulary
power of 10
exponent

Learn About It

When you multiply a number by 10^n, or a **power of 10**, you are using 10 as a factor n times. In 10^n, n is called the **exponent.**

A researcher might need to examine blood cells. The diameter of a red blood cell is 0.008 millimeter. Microscopes can make objects appear 10^1 times, 10^2 times, or 10^3 times larger.

How large would a red blood cell appear at each magnification level?

Remember
Multiplying a number by 10 moves the decimal point one place to the right.

Multiply 0.008 mm by 10^1, 10^2, and 10^3.

10^1 level	10^2 level	10^3 level
0.008×10^1	0.008×10^2	0.008×10^3
$\begin{array}{r} 0.008 \\ \times\ 10 \\ \hline 0.080 \end{array}$ or 0.08	$\begin{array}{r} 0.008 \\ \times\ 100 \\ \hline 0.800 \end{array}$ or 0.8	$\begin{array}{r} 0.008 \\ \times\ 1{,}000 \\ \hline 8.000 \end{array}$ or 8
The diameter of the cell appears to be 0.08 mm.	The diameter of the cell appears to be 0.8 mm.	The diameter of the cell appears to be 8 mm.

Solution: A red blood cell can be enlarged so its diameter appears to be 0.08 millimeter, 0.8 millimeter, or 8 millimeters.

Other Examples

Remember
Dividing a number by 10 moves the decimal point one place to the left.

A. Use Patterns

$6.5 \div 10^1 = 0.65$

The decimal point moves one place to the left.

B. Divide by 10^2

$6.5 \div 10^2 = 0.065$

The decimal point moves two places to the left.

Guided Practice

Ask Yourself

- Do I move the decimal point to the right or to the left?

Multiply or divide by using patterns.

1. 0.5×10^2 **2.** $0.2 \div 10$ **3.** 3.8×100

4. $159 \div 10^3$ **5.** 0.04×10^3 **6.** $6.1 \div 10^2$

Explain Your Thinking ▶ Why is the expression 4.2×10^3 equal to the expression 42×10^2?

Practice and Problem Solving

Multiply or divide by using patterns.

7. 5.34×10^1 **8.** 5.34×10^2 **9.** $5.34 \div 10^1$ **10.** $5.34 \div 10^2$

11. 2.0×10^3 **12.** $75 \div 10^2$ **13.** 0.68×10^3 **14.** $4.72 \div 10^1$

Algebra • Equations **Solve for *a*.**

15. $100 = 10^a$ **16.** $1{,}000 = 10^a$ **17.** $10 = 10^a$ **18.** $10{,}000 = 10^a$

19. $0.01a = 12$ **20.** $0.001a = 12$ **21.** $\frac{a}{10} = 15$ **22.** $\frac{a}{100} = 15$

Solve.

23. One type of cell is 0.005 mm across. It is put under a microscope so it appears to be 10^3 larger. How large would that cell seem under that microscope?

24. Draw a line segment to show how large the cell in Problem 23 would appear under the microscope.

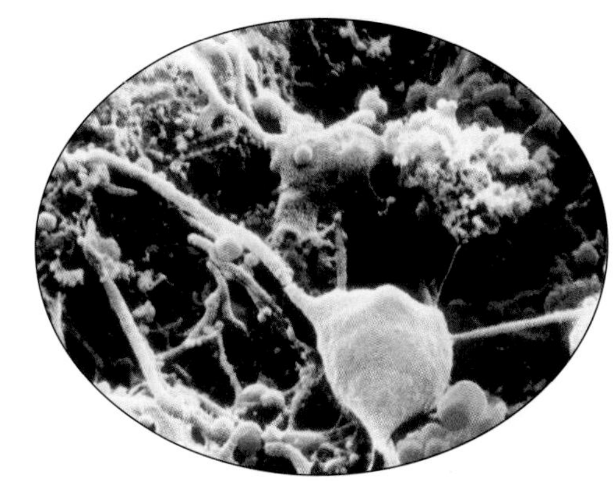

Mixed Review and Test Prep

Open Response

Multiply. Write each product in simplest form. (Ch. 12, Lessons 2 and 3)

25. $\frac{4}{5} \times \frac{1}{3}$ **26.** $3\frac{1}{2} \times \frac{5}{7}$

27. $\frac{3}{4} \times 1\frac{5}{9}$ **28.** $5\frac{1}{3} \times 1\frac{1}{2}$

Multiple Choice

29. A sports photographer's telephoto lens keeps the shutter open for only $1.0 \div 10^3$ seconds. Which fraction shows how long that is? (Ch. 14, Lesson 3)

A $\frac{10}{1}$ **B** $\frac{1}{10}$ **C** $\frac{1}{100}$ **D** $\frac{1}{1{,}000}$

Extra Practice See page 375, Set C.

Lesson 4

Divide a Decimal by a Whole Number

Objective Divide a decimal by a whole number.

Learn About It

The starting section for a BMX race is 7.2 meters wide. It is divided into equal-width lanes for 8 riders. How wide is each rider's lane?

Divide. $7.2 \div 8 = n$

Different Ways to Divide 7.2 by 8

Way 1 You can use fractions.

STEP 1 Write the dividend and the divisor as fractions.

$$\frac{72}{10} \div \frac{8}{1}$$

$$7.2 = 7\frac{2}{10} = \frac{72}{10}$$

STEP 2 Multiply the dividend by the reciprocal of the divisor.

$$\frac{72}{10} \times \frac{1}{8} = \frac{72}{80}$$

STEP 3 Write the quotient as a decimal.

$$\frac{72}{80} = \frac{9}{10} = 0.9$$

Way 2 You can divide and place the decimal point in the quotient.

STEP 1 Divide as though the dividend were a whole number.

$$\begin{array}{r} 9 \\ 8\overline{)72} \\ -72 \\ \hline 0 \end{array}$$

STEP 2 Place a decimal point in the quotient directly above the decimal point in the dividend.

$$\begin{array}{r} 0.9 \\ 8\overline{)7.2} \\ -7\,2 \\ \hline 0 \end{array}$$

Estimate to check.

Since 7.2 m is a little less than 8 m, each of the 8 lanes would be a little less than 1 m wide. So 0.9 m is a reasonable answer.

Solution: Each lane is 0.9 meter wide.

Other Examples

A. Quotient Less Than 1

$$\begin{array}{r} 0.92 \\ 7\overline{)6.44} \\ -6\,3 \\ \hline 14 \\ -14 \\ \hline 0 \end{array}$$

Estimate to check.

$6.44 \approx 7$
$7 \div 7 = 1$
$0.92 \approx 1$

B. Quotient Is in Dollars and Cents

$$\begin{array}{r} \$0.15 \\ 5\overline{)\$0.75} \\ -5\downarrow \\ \hline 25 \\ -25 \\ \hline 0 \end{array}$$

Multiply to check.

$$\begin{array}{r} \$0.15 \\ \times 5 \\ \hline \$0.75 \end{array}$$

Guided Practice

Divide and check.

1. $2\overline{)16.2}$ **2.** $5\overline{)9.75}$ **3.** $6\overline{)5.4}$

4. $22.8 \div 4$ **5.** $58.1 \div 7$ **6.** $0.03 \div 3$

Ask Yourself

- Would it help me to use fractions?
- Did I place the decimal point correctly?

Explain Your Thinking ▶ Why is it important to align the quotient and the dividend correctly when you divide with decimals?

Practice and Problem Solving

Divide and check.

7. $6\overline{)7.2}$ **8.** $7\overline{)41.3}$ **9.** $3\overline{)16.2}$ **10.** $7\overline{)11.9}$

11. $5.5 \div 5$ **12.** $8.4 \div 4$ **13.** $0.8 \div 2$ **14.** $20.7 \div 3$

15. $8\overline{)2.80}$ **16.** $2\overline{)3.46}$ **17.** $6\overline{)1.44}$ **18.** $7\overline{)26.25}$

19. $42.8 \div 4$ **20.** $3.87 \div 9$ **21.** $9.75 \div 3$ **22.** $6.32 \div 8$

Insert a decimal point in each dividend to make each quotient correct.

23. $24 \div 6 = 0.4$ **24.** $35 \div 7 = 0.5$ **25.** $129 \div 3 = 0.43$

26. $196 \div 4 = 4.9$ **27.** $3252 \div 4 = 0.813$ **28.** $5327 \div 7 = 7.61$

Algebra • Expressions **Evaluate each expression for $a = 3.2$, $b = 0.08$, $c = 2$, and $d = 8$.**

29. $a \div c$ **30.** $\frac{b}{c}$ **31.** $a \div d$ **32.** $b \div d$

Go On

Write the missing values in each table.

33.

Rule: $b = a \div 3$				
a	0.96	1.29	6.33	6.78
b				

34.

Rule: $b = a \div 6$				
a	0.72			0.90
b		0.13	0.14	

Solve.

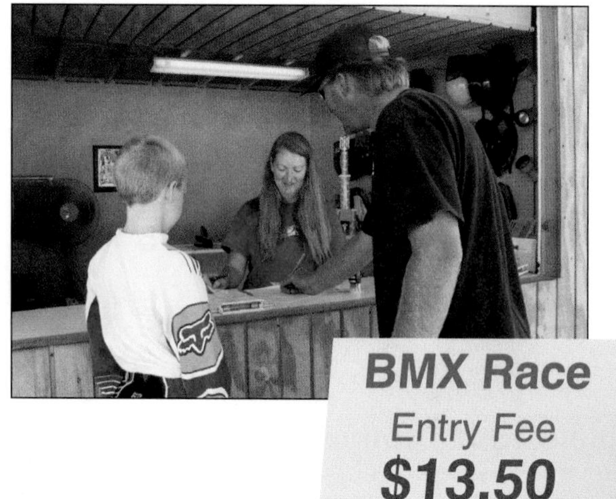

35. One third of the entry fee for each rider in the BMX race shown at the right goes to pay taxes and other fees. If 150 riders enter a race, how much goes for taxes and other fees?

36. A BMX track is made up of 0.8 part clay and 0.2 part sand for every 1 part of soil. There are 3,500 cubic yards of soil on the track. How many cubic yards of clay are there? of sand?

37. The maximum length of a BMX track is 454 meters. The minimum length is 0.66 of that. Estimate the minimum length.

38. Tony and Jan are training for a bike race. Tony rode his bike 4.5 km in 9 minutes. Jan rode her bike 3.6 km in 6 minutes. Who rides farther in 1 minute? How much farther?

39. Which will be greater: the quotient $6.56 \div 8$, or the quotient $656 \div 80$? Explain how you can tell without dividing.

40. A city bought a 20-acre section of land for recreational use. The land was split into 0.5-acre pieces. Draw a model to show the number of 0.5-acre pieces that can be made from that 20 acres.

41. **What's Wrong?** Darlene divided 1.2 by 6. Her work is shown below. Explain why Darlene's method is not correct.

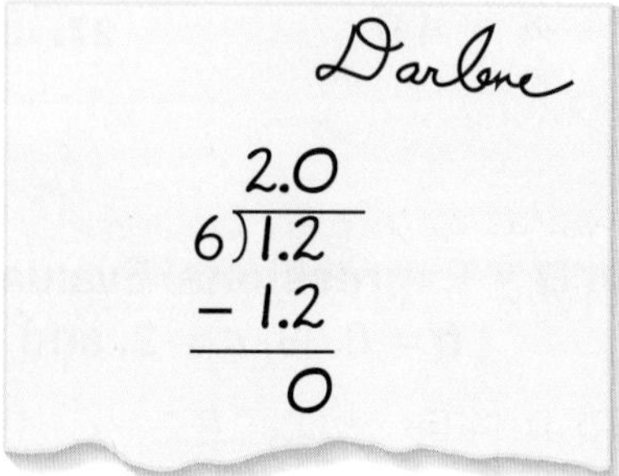

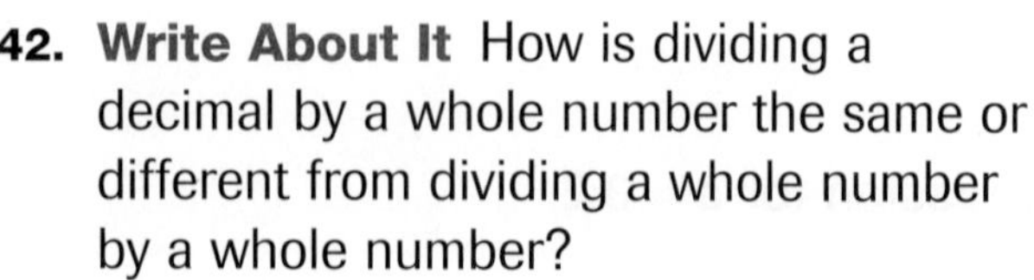

42. **Write About It** How is dividing a decimal by a whole number the same or different from dividing a whole number by a whole number?

Extra Practice See page 375, Set D.

Problem Solving

Math Challenge

Use Knowledge

You know how to divide whole numbers with two-digit divisors. You also know how to divide decimals with one-digit divisors. You can use what you know to divide decimals by two-digit divisors.

STEP 1 Divide the dividend by the divisor as if both are whole numbers.

```
      604
24)14.496
 - 14 4↓↓
     096
   -  96
       0
```

STEP 2 Place a decimal point in the quotient directly above the decimal point in the dividend.

```
    0.604
24)14.496
 - 14 4↓↓
     096
   -  96
       0
```

Divide. Show your work.

1. $37.5 \div 15$ 2. $157.44 \div 32$ 3. $64.05 \div 21$ 4. $0.406 \div 14$

Quick Check

Check your understanding of Lessons 1–4.

Use models to divide. Write the quotients. (Lesson 1)

1.
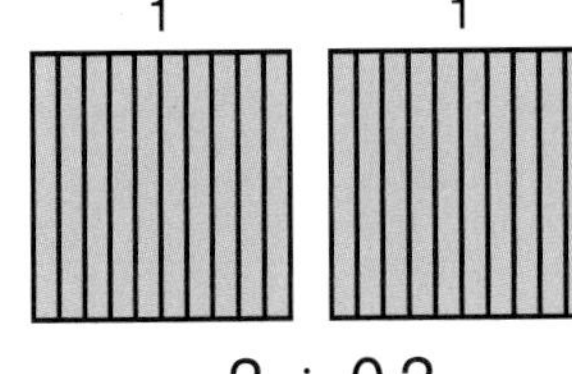

$2 \div 0.2$

2.
1 1 1
$3 \div 0.5$

3. $5 \div 0.2$ 4. $2 \div 0.5$

Estimate each quotient. (Lesson 2)

5. $28 \div 0.34$ 6. $57.9 \div 0.46$

Multiply or divide. (Lessons 3 and 4)

7. 52.3×10^2 8. $53.2 \div 10^2$ 9. $0.84 \div 7$ 10. $16.05 \div 3$

Audio Tutor 2/7 Listen and Understand

Lesson 5 Write Zeros in the Dividend

Objective Write one or more zeros in the dividend to help solve division problems.

Learn About It

Billie's first long jump was 4.5 meters. Her second long jump was 6 meters. What part of her second long jump was Billie's first attempt?

Divide. $4.5 \div 6 = n$

Different Ways to Divide 4.5 by 6

Way 1 You can use the pencil-and-paper method.

STEP 1 Divide as though the dividend were a whole number.

$$\begin{array}{r} 7 \\ 6\overline{)4.5} \\ -4\,2 \\ \hline 3 \end{array}$$

Think: 45 ÷ 6 is about 7.

STEP 2 To continue, write a 0 in the hundredths place.

$$\begin{array}{r} 75 \\ 6\overline{)4.50} \\ -4\,2\downarrow \\ \hline 30 \\ -30 \\ \hline 0 \end{array}$$

Bring down the 0. Continue dividing.

STEP 3 Place the decimal point in the quotient above the decimal point in the dividend.

$$\begin{array}{r} 0.75 \\ 6\overline{)4.50} \\ -4\,2\downarrow \\ \hline 30 \\ -30 \\ \hline 0 \end{array}$$

Write 0 in the ones place.

Way 2 You can divide decimals using a calculator.

Press the calculator keys to enter the division.
Press the equals sign to calculate the quotient.

0.75

Solution: Billie's first long jump was 0.75 of her second long jump.

Check that the quotient is reasonable.

Think How many 6s are in 4.5?

$6 \times 1 = 6$

There is less than one 6 in 4.5.

0.75 is a reasonable answer.

Another Example

Divide Whole Numbers

When dividing whole numbers, you can add zeros after the decimal point to get a decimal answer.

Find 42 ÷ 8.

```
    5.25
 8)42.00
 - 40
     20
   - 16
     40
   - 40
      0
```

Guided Practice

Divide. Check using a calculator or estimation.

1. $5\overline{)2.7}$
2. $5\overline{)24}$
3. $4\overline{)3.5}$
4. $6\overline{)0.75}$
5. $8\overline{)51}$
6. $2\overline{)39.77}$
7. 6.11 ÷ 2
8. 9.6 ÷ 5
9. 2.7 ÷ 4

Ask Yourself

- Did I place the first digit of the quotient correctly?
- Did I write zeros in the dividend until there was no remainder?

Explain Your Thinking ▶ Why does writing zeros to the right of the least-place digit in a decimal not change the value of that number?

Practice and Problem Solving

Divide. Check using a calculator or estimation.

10. $2\overline{)9}$
11. $8\overline{)5.2}$
12. $4\overline{)19}$
13. $16\overline{)12.4}$
14. $46\overline{)16.1}$
15. $10\overline{)6.24}$
16. $5\overline{)24.72}$
17. $6\overline{)106.5}$
18. $8\overline{)19}$
19. $24\overline{)15}$
20. $12\overline{)4.2}$
21. $6\overline{)8.67}$
22. 33 ÷ 22
23. 9 ÷ 5
24. 15 ÷ 8
25. 32.6 ÷ 4

Compare. Write >, <, or = for each ●.

26. 2.5 ÷ 4 ● 5 ÷ 8
27. 3.6 ÷ 8 ● 1 ÷ 4
28. 12 ÷ 5 ● 9 ÷ 4
29. 3.2 ÷ 8 ● 8 ÷ 2
30. 0.4 ÷ 4 ● 0.2 ÷ 2
31. 5.25 ÷ 3 ● 14 ÷ 8

Go On

 **Algebra • Equations Find each missing value for *n*.**

32. $19 \div n = 4.75$ **33.** $n \div 4 = 0.525$ **34.** $n \div 5 = 3.44$ **35.** $15 \div n = 7.5$

 **Data Use the chart below to solve Problems 36–40.**

The chart shows two jumps each member of a track team made during a recent meet.

36. What part of her second jump is Sarah's first jump?

37. What is the mean of the distances of Lita's jumps? Remember, to find the mean, you divide the sum of the distances by the number of jumps.

38. What is the mean distance of the jumps made by this team?

39. Which team member had the greatest range in her jumps? How much difference was there between her longest and shortest jumps?

40. To convert from meters to feet, multiply the number of meters by 3.281. Who had a first jump of about 15 feet?

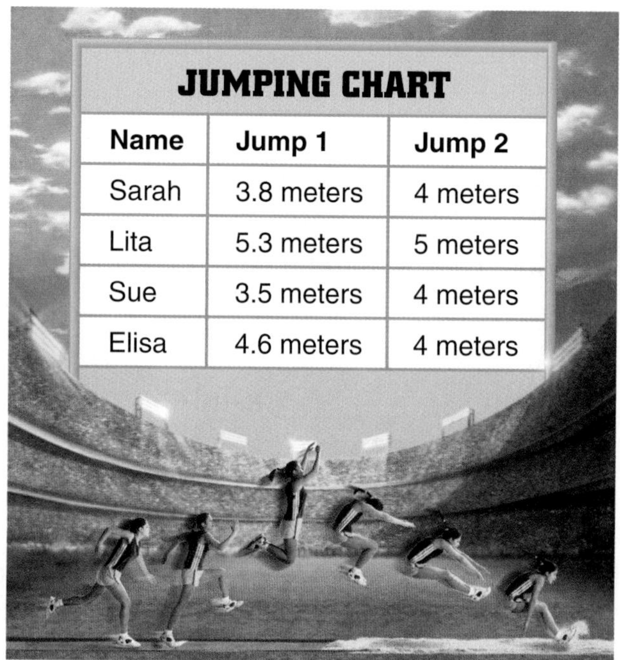

JUMPING CHART

Name	Jump 1	Jump 2
Sarah	3.8 meters	4 meters
Lita	5.3 meters	5 meters
Sue	3.5 meters	4 meters
Elisa	4.6 meters	4 meters

 **41. Write About It** When you are dividing 63 by 4, how can you tell whether or not you need to write zeros in the dividend?

42. In the 2000 Olympics, second place in the long jump was a jump of 6.92 m. The winning jump was 7 cm longer. How long was the winning jump?

Mixed Review and Test Prep 

Open Response

Multiply. Write your answer in simplest form. (Ch. 12, Lessons 2 and 3)

43. $\frac{2}{3} \times \frac{3}{5}$

44. $\frac{3}{4} \times \frac{8}{9}$

45. $1\frac{5}{6} \times 2\frac{3}{4}$

46. $4\frac{2}{5} \times 3\frac{1}{4}$

47. The following temperatures were recorded in Antarctica: 27.2°F, 24.6°F, 29°F, 22.1°F, and 28.1°F. What was the mean daily temperature for these five days? (Ch. 14, Lesson 5)

Explain your thinking.

Extra Practice See page 375, Set E.

Problem Solving

Measurement
Flying Measures

In the 1920s, the Frisbie Baking Company sold pies to students at Yale University. The students discovered that the empty pie tins made great flying discs. Adding a spin to their toss kept the pie tins aloft for great distances.

In 1948, a California building inspector and carpenter made the first plastic flying disc. Since that time, these discs have gained in popularity.

Four results for outdoor distance throwing are shown below. Convert the results to feet using 1 m $\approx$ 3.281 ft. Round your answer to the nearest hundredth.

1. Boys under 11: 82.3 m
2. Girls under 11: 70.2 m
3. Boys under 12: 101.5 m
4. Girls under 12: 97.74 m

Number Sense
Money Power

Businesses circulate coupons on the Internet. One Web site offers a coupon worth $3.25. If the value of the coupons that have been downloaded so far totals $32,500, how many coupons have been downloaded so far?

Brain Teaser

1 2 3 4 5

Use each of these digits once to create a decimal division expression whose quotient is about 2.

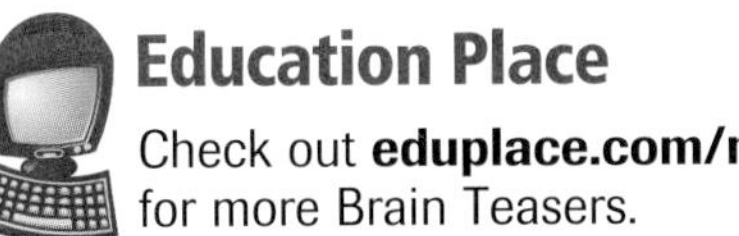

Education Place
Check out eduplace.com/map for more Brain Teasers.

Lesson 6

Repeating Decimals

Objective Change a fraction to a decimal using division.

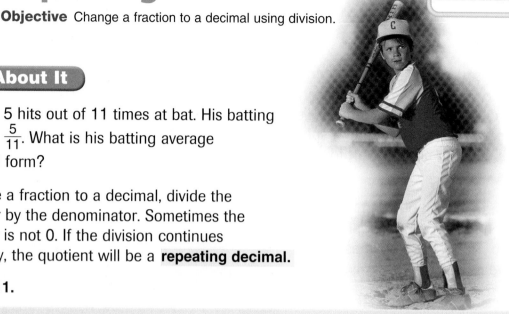

Vocabulary
repeating decimal

Learn About It

Mack had 5 hits out of 11 times at bat. His batting average is $\frac{5}{11}$. What is his batting average in decimal form?

To change a fraction to a decimal, divide the numerator by the denominator. Sometimes the remainder is not 0. If the division continues indefinitely, the quotient will be a **repeating decimal.**

Find 5 ÷ 11.

STEP 1 Divide until the quotient ends or repeats.

```
    0.4545
11)5.0000...
  - 4 4
     60
   - 55
     50   <- The division pattern begins to repeat each time the remainder is 5.
   - 44
      60
    - 55
       5
```

The three dots (...) means that pattern continues.

STEP 2 Write a bar over the part of the quotient that repeats.

$$11\overline{)5.0000\ldots} = 0.45\overline{45}$$

```
  - 4 4
     60
   - 55
     50
   - 44
      60
    - 55
       5
```

The bar over the digits 4 and 5 show that they are the digits that repeat.

Solution: Mack's batting average is $0.\overline{45}$.

Other Examples

A. Single Repeating Digit

Change $\frac{1}{3}$ to decimal form.

```
  0.33...
3)1.0...
 - 9
   10
  - 9
    1
```

The decimal form of $\frac{1}{3}$ is $0.\overline{3}$.

B. Calculator

Some calculators round the last digit of a repeating decimal. Check how your calculator displays repeating decimals.

5 ÷ 9 =
0.5555555556

Guided Practice

Change each fraction to decimal form.

1. $\frac{1}{6}$ **2.** $\frac{2}{6}$ **3.** $\frac{5}{6}$

4. $\frac{7}{15}$ **5.** $\frac{4}{9}$ **6.** $\frac{1}{11}$

Ask Yourself

- Does the decimal terminate or not?
- Do one or more digits repeat?

Explain Your Thinking ▶ If you know the decimal for $\frac{1}{3}$, how can you find the decimal for $\frac{2}{3}$?

Practice and Problem Solving

Change each fraction to decimal form.

7. $\frac{1}{12}$ **8.** $\frac{2}{12}$ **9.** $\frac{3}{12}$ **10.** $\frac{4}{12}$ **11.** $\frac{5}{12}$

12. $\frac{2}{11}$ **13.** $\frac{3}{11}$ **14.** $\frac{4}{11}$ **15.** $\frac{5}{11}$ **16.** $\frac{6}{11}$

17. $\frac{10}{4}$ **18.** $\frac{10}{11}$ **19.** $\frac{1}{5}$ **20.** $\frac{1}{15}$ **21.** $\frac{1}{30}$

Solve.

22. Compare the quotients of $\frac{8}{7}$ and $\frac{22}{7}$. How are they alike? How are they different?

23. Ed has had 5 hits in his last 8 at bats. How much more or less than a 0.500 batting average does he have?

24. Look at the denominators of the fractions below. Which denominators always result in a repeating decimal? Give examples.

$\frac{\blacksquare}{5}$ $\frac{\blacksquare}{6}$ $\frac{\blacksquare}{9}$ $\frac{\blacksquare}{10}$ $\frac{\blacksquare}{11}$

25. Look at the decimal values for the fractions below.

$\frac{1}{9} = 0.\overline{1}$ $\frac{2}{9} = 0.\overline{2}$ $\frac{3}{9} = 0.\overline{3}$

Without dividing, predict the quotients of $\frac{5}{9}$, $\frac{7}{9}$, and $\frac{8}{9}$.

Mixed Review and Test Prep

Open Response

Write each pair of numbers as fractions with common denominators. Then write >, <, or = for each ⬬. (Ch. 9, Lessons 8 and 9)

26. $\frac{8}{5}$ ⬬ 1.3 **27.** $\frac{16}{7}$ ⬬ $\frac{7}{3}$

28. $5\frac{1}{4}$ ⬬ 5.25 **29.** 3.02 ⬬ $\frac{16}{5}$

Multiple Choice

30. Lionel's batting average is $\frac{7}{11}$. Which of the following best represents his batting average in decimal form? (Ch. 14, Lesson 6)

A 0.6 **C** $0.6\overline{3}$

B 0.63 **D** 0.636

Extra Practice See page 375, Set F.

Lesson 7

Audio Tutor 2/8 Listen and Understand

Divide a Decimal by a Decimal

Objective Divide one decimal by another.

Learn About It

In a triathlon, athletes swim 1.5 km, bike for 40 km, and then run 10 km. A winning triathlete completed the swimming portion of a race in 0.4 hour. How fast did he swim in kilometers per hour?

Divide. $1.5 \div 0.4 = n$

STEP 1 Multiply the divisor and dividend by the same power of 10.

$0.4\overline{)1.5}$

$$\frac{1.5}{0.4} \xrightarrow{\times 10} \frac{15}{4}$$

When dividing by a decimal, use multiplication to change the divisor to a whole number. Remember to multiply the dividend by the same number.

STEP 2 Write a decimal point and zeros after the final digit to continue dividing.

$$\begin{array}{r} 3\;75 \\ 4\overline{)15.00} \\ -12 \\ \hline 30 \\ -28 \\ \hline 20 \\ -20 \\ \hline 0 \end{array}$$

STEP 3 Place a decimal point in the quotient over the decimal point in the dividend.

$$\begin{array}{r} 3.75 \\ 4\overline{)15.00} \\ -12 \\ \hline 30 \\ -28 \\ \hline 20 \\ -20 \\ \hline 0 \end{array}$$

Solution: The triathlete swam at an average speed of 3.75 kilometers per hour.

Estimate to check.
$0.4 \approx 0.5$ and $1.5 \approx 2$.

$2 \div 0.5 = 4$

A quotient of 3.75 is reasonable.

Another Example

Divide to a Specified Place

Divide $1.5 \div 0.45$ to the nearest hundredth.

To find a quotient to the nearest hundredth, divide to the nearest thousandth and round the quotient to the nearest hundredth.

$$\begin{array}{r} 3.333 \\ 0.45\overline{)1.50000} \\ -1\;35 \\ \hline 150 \\ -135 \\ \hline 150 \\ -135 \\ \hline 150 \\ -135 \\ \hline 15 \end{array}$$

3 < 5 so round down.
$1.5 \div 0.45 = 3.33$ to the nearest hundredth

Extra Help at **eduplace.com/map**

Guided Practice

Ask Yourself

- Do I need to write any zeros after the dividend?
- Did I place the decimal point correctly?

Divide. Check that your answer is reasonable.

1. $0.8\overline{)1.6}$
2. $0.4\overline{)1.84}$
3. $0.2\overline{)0.101}$
4. $9 \div 0.8$
5. $30 \div 1.5$
6. $1.44 \div 1.2$

Explain Your Thinking ▶ How do you decide which power of 10 to use for multiplying when simplifying division by a decimal?

Practice and Problem Solving

Divide. Round to the nearest hundredth if necessary. Check that your answer is reasonable.

7. $0.3\overline{)1.8}$
8. $0.3\overline{)0.18}$
9. $0.5\overline{)38.5}$
10. $0.5\overline{)3.85}$
11. $0.05\overline{)0.385}$
12. $6.1\overline{)32}$
13. $3.5\overline{)17.5}$
14. $0.35\overline{)17.5}$
15. $0.8\overline{)1.12}$
16. $0.08\overline{)11.2}$
17. $0.7\overline{)42}$
18. $4.5\overline{)387}$
19. $0.23\overline{)54.3}$
20. $0.04\overline{)4.3}$
21. $1.4\overline{)0.342}$

Solve.

22. A triathlete averaged 33.3 kilometers per hour for a 40-kilometer portion of a bike race. To the nearest tenth, how long did this portion of the race take?

23. You know that $4 \div 8 = 0.5$. Use patterns below to explain how to complete divisions involving small numbers. Then complete the next division problem in each pattern.

a.
$4 \div 8 = 0.5$
$4 \div 0.8 = 5$
$4 \div 0.08 = 50$
$4 \div 0.008 =$ ■

b.
$4 \div 8 = 0.5$
$0.4 \div 8 = 0.05$
$0.04 \div 8 = 0.005$
$0.004 \div 8 =$ ■

24. Catherine ran the 10-kilometer race portion of a triathlon in 0.91 hour. To the nearest tenth, what was her average speed in kilometers per hour?

Mixed Review and Test Prep

Open Response

Add or subtract. Write your answers in simplest form. (Ch. 10, Lessons 4 and 8)

25. $3\frac{3}{4} + 2\frac{5}{8}$
26. $7\frac{1}{6} + 1\frac{1}{5}$
27. $4\frac{3}{4} - 2\frac{1}{8}$
28. $6\frac{1}{4} - 4\frac{2}{3}$

29. A triathlete swims the 1.5-kilometer course in 0.5 hour. What is the athlete's average speed in kilometers per hour? (Ch. 14, Lesson 7)

Extra Practice See page 375, Set G.

Lesson 8

Problem-Solving Application

Decide How to Write the Quotient

Objective Decide how to write the quotient to solve a problem.

Learn About It

When you solve a division problem, sometimes you need to decide how to interpret the remainder.

Sometimes you use the remainder to decide on the answer.

A store received boxes containing 19 jackets. Only 5 jackets fit in each box. How many boxes did they receive?

$$\begin{array}{r} 3 \text{ R4} \\ 5\overline{)19} \\ -\,15 \\ \hline 4 \end{array}$$

There are 3 full boxes. Another box is needed for the extra 4 jackets.

Solution: They received 4 boxes in all.

Sometimes you write the remainder as a fraction.

A group makes sweatshirts. They use 18 feet of material to make 4 sweatshirts. How much material does each sweatshirt require?

$$\begin{array}{r} 4 \text{ R2} = 4\frac{2}{4} = 4\frac{1}{2} \\ 4\overline{)18} \\ -\,16 \\ \hline 2 \end{array}$$

Solution: Each sweatshirt requires $4\frac{1}{2}$ feet of material.

Sometimes you write the quotient as a decimal.

Liang buys 8 identical T-shirts at the sports center store. If he spends $30 in all, how much does each shirt cost?

$$\begin{array}{r} 3.75 \\ 8\overline{)30.00} \\ -\,24 \\ \hline 60 \\ -\,56 \\ \hline 40 \\ -\,40 \\ \hline 0 \end{array}$$

Solution: Each T-shirt costs $3.75.

Look Back How does thinking about the question in each situation help you decide what to do with the remainder?

Guided Practice

Use the Ask Yourself questions to help you solve each problem.

Ask Yourself

- What does the question ask me to find?
- What does the remainder represent?
- Does my answer make sense?

1. Each pair of sweatpants requires 2 yards of fabric. How many pairs of sweatpants can be made with 7 yards of fabric?

   Hint Can you make part of a pair of sweatpants?

2. It cost 8 runners a total of $42.00 to enter a local race. How much was each runner's entry fee?

Independent Practice

Solve. Explain how you used each remainder.

3. During a parade, 46 award winners from the Youth Sports Center rode in automobiles. If only 6 winners could fit in each automobile, how many automobiles did they need for all the winners?

4. At the car wash shown in the picture below, $434 was raised for the Youth Sports Center. Of that, $107 was from donations. The rest was from washing cars. How many cars did they wash?

5. Pedro is making a 7-foot banner for Awards Night. Pedro needs to find the center of the banner so he can space the lettering correctly. How far from the end of the banner is its center?

6. The Youth Sports Center will have pizzas at their Awards Night. Each pizza is cut into 8 slices. If 150 people plan to attend and each eats 3 slices of pizza, what is the fewest number of pizzas they should order?

7. **Write Your Own** Write a word problem in which the quotient must be used to decide the answer.

8. **Create and Solve** Write a word problem in which the quotient must be written as a decimal.

Go On

Choose a Computation Method

Mental Math • Estimation • Paper and Pencil • Calculator

Solve each problem. Name the computation method you used.

9. The room for the Youth Sports Center's Awards Night has tables that seat 4 people. If 146 people attend the Awards Night, how many tables are needed?

10. Val donated four times as much money to the equipment fund as Gary did. Together they donated $150. How much did each person donate?

11. The board at the Youth Sports Center got an estimate of $15,450 to redo the basketball courts. They've raised $\frac{2}{3}$ of the amount they need. About how much do they still have to raise?

12. To decorate for a party, a youth group needed 750 feet of ribbon. The ribbon is sold on rolls of 8 yards each. No partial rolls are sold. How many rolls of ribbon will they need?

13. The sports club members made refrigerator magnets for a fundraiser. On Monday they made 20 magnets, 2 more than on Sunday. On Sunday they made 4 fewer than on Saturday. On Saturday they made twice as many as on Friday. How many did they make in all?

Data **Use the table for Problems 14–17.**

Program	Number of Participants
Basketball	128
Soccer	142
Swimming	95
Tennis	48
Weightlifting	18

14. Each soccer team has 11 players. What is the greatest number of soccer games that these players could have going on at the same time?

15. About 0.6 of the people who participate in swimming also take part in another sport at the Sports Center. About how many people is that?

16. Each morning at 8:00 A.M. all the people signed up for weightlifting show up. They each sign up for a $\frac{1}{2}$-hour session on one of the four weight benches. At what time does the last of those people finish?

17. It costs the Youth Sports Center $250 to rent each 48-person bus. If they hire enough buses to take all the people signed up for basketball to a local tournament, how much do they spend on buses?

Calculator Connection

Garden Math

Activity

What kind of flower do you get if you plant a crazy pickle?

Copy the chart at the right.

Use a calculator to find each quotient. Then use the key to decode the puzzle. Read down the last column to find the answer to the riddle.

Problem	Quotient	Letter
0.192 ÷ 0.8	▒	▒
0.9 ÷ 2.5	▒	▒
0.84 ÷ 3.5	▒	▒
0.232 ÷ 0.4	▒	▒
5.394 ÷ 9.3	▒	▒
0.665 ÷ 0.38	▒	▒
0.09 ÷ 0.25	▒	▒
0.656 ÷ 0.8	▒	▒
4.275 ÷ 4.5	▒	▒
0.931 ÷ 0.98	▒	▒

Key

Quotient	0.24	0.36	0.58	0.71	0.82	0.95	1.26	1.32	1.67	1.75
Letter	A	D	F	G	I	L	N	O	T	Y

Chapter Review/Test

VOCABULARY

1. In the expression 83×10^r, 10^r is a(n) ____.
2. ____ can be used to estimate a quotient.
3. When a denominator does not divide into a numerator without a remainder, the result may be a(n) ____.

Vocabulary

- compatible numbers
- exponent
- power of 10
- repeating decimal

CONCEPTS AND SKILLS

Model the division and write the quotient in decimal form. (Lesson 1, pp. 352–353)

4. $7 \div 0.5$
5. $9 \div 0.9$
6. $9 \div 0.3$
7. $6 \div 0.4$
8. $8 \div 0.25$

Estimate each quotient. (Lesson 2, pp. 354–355)

9. $4 \div 0.19$
10. $82 \div 0.26$
11. $16 \div 0.147$

Divide. (Lessons 4–5, pp. 358–364)

12. $0.8 \div 10^1$
13. $4.2 \div 7$
14. $4\overline{)6.5}$
15. $1{,}593.65 \div 10^3$
16. $8.8 \div 5$
17. $8\overline{)56.36}$

Change each fraction to decimal form. (Lesson 6, pp. 366–367)

18. $\frac{3}{5}$
19. $\frac{7}{12}$
20. $\frac{2}{9}$

Divide. Round to the nearest hundredth if necessary. Check that your answer is reasonable. (Lesson 7, pp. 368–369)

21. $0.4\overline{)6.4}$
22. $6.2\overline{)31.62}$
23. $4.1\overline{)33.62}$

PROBLEM SOLVING

Solve. Explain how you used each remainder. (Lesson 8, pp. 370–372)

24. Each pep squad uniform requires 2.5 yards of fabric. How many uniforms can be made from 22 yards of fabric?
25. There are 27 people going to a soccer game. If each car can hold 5 people, how many cars will be needed?

Write About It

Show You Understand

Josh divides these two decimals incorrectly. Explain what he did wrong. Show how to find the correct quotient.

```
      5.45
0.5)27.25
   -25
     2.2
    -20
      25
     -25
       0
```

Extra Practice

Set A (Lesson 1, pp. 352–353)

Model the division and write the quotient in decimal form.

1. $6 \div 0.2$
2. $9 \div 0.5$
3. $5 \div 0.25$
4. $12 \div 0.6$

Set B (Lesson 2, pp. 354–355)

Estimate each quotient.

1. $79 \div 0.77$
2. $309 \div 0.33$
3. $26 \div 0.492$
4. $54.7 \div 0.89$
5. $5.63 \div 0.621$
6. $9 \div 0.258$
7. $16.2 \div 0.41$
8. $22 \div 0.108$

Set C (Lesson 3, pp. 356–357)

Multiply or divide by using patterns.

1. 6.12×10^1
2. 8.34×10^2
3. $2{,}745.64 \div 10^2$
4. $7.25 \div 10^1$
5. $8.67 \div 10^2$
6. $6.534 \div 10^3$
7. 0.054×10^2
8. 0.19×10^3

Set D (Lesson 4, pp. 358–361)

Divide and check.

1. $6\overline{)4.8}$
2. $2\overline{)2.36}$
3. $4\overline{)21.84}$
4. $7\overline{)\$61.95}$
5. $7.2 \div 6$
6. $\$24.75 \div 3$
7. $1.44 \div 6$
8. $0.87 \div 3$

Set E (Lesson 5, pp. 362–365)

Divide and check using estimation.

1. $4\overline{)4.2}$
2. $5\overline{)6.7}$
3. $10\overline{)7.74}$
4. $8\overline{)24.6}$
5. $8\overline{)4}$
6. $4\overline{)15}$
7. $63 \div 15$
8. $36.8 \div 5$

Set F (Lesson 6, pp. 366–367)

Change each fraction to decimal form.

1. $\frac{1}{15}$
2. $\frac{7}{12}$
3. $\frac{7}{11}$
4. $\frac{4}{15}$
5. $\frac{15}{4}$
6. $\frac{5}{9}$

Set G (Lesson 7, pp. 368–369)

**Divide. Round to the nearest hundredth if necessary.
Check that your answer is reasonable.**

1. $0.5\overline{)1.5}$
2. $0.15\overline{)55.5}$
3. $0.6\overline{)3.6}$
4. $0.52\overline{)13}$
5. $0.8\overline{)5.84}$
6. $3.7\overline{)22.2}$
7. $0.9\overline{)5.04}$
8. $0.8\overline{)0.584}$

WEEKLY WR READER®

Social Studies Connection

Philatelic Fun

Are you a philatelist? If you collect or study postage stamps, you are. Some people collect stamps for the pure pleasure of it. Others collect stamps because some historic stamps are worth a lot of money.

The very first postage stamps were used on May 6, 1840, in England. The "1 Penny Black" and "2 Pence Blue" were so named because of their purchase price and color. Before long, most countries in the world were using postage stamps.

New stamps are being issued all the time. Recently, the U.S. Postal Service even released a series of stamps called *Stampin' the Future* that used drawings made by children between the ages of 8 and 12.

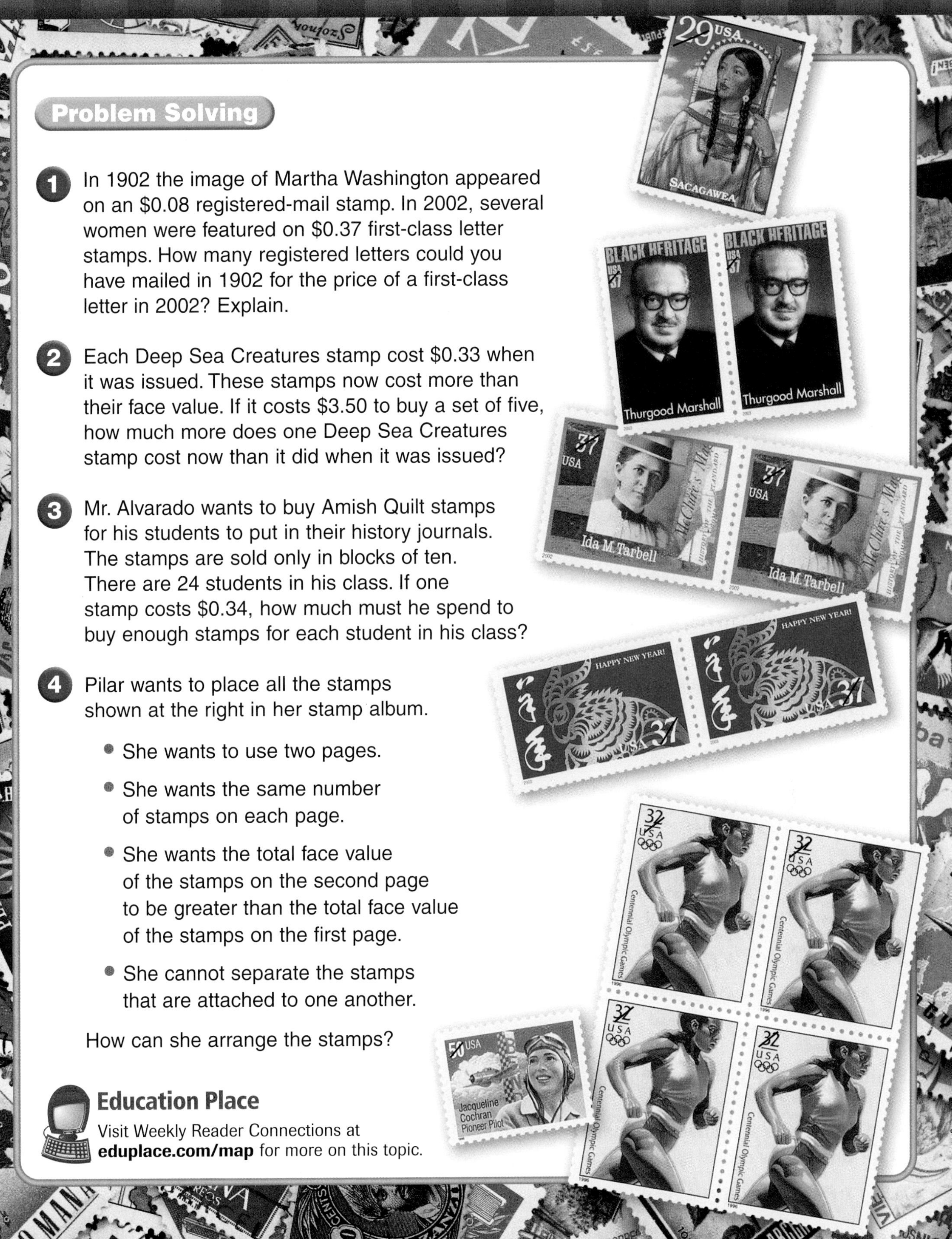

Problem Solving

1. In 1902 the image of Martha Washington appeared on an $0.08 registered-mail stamp. In 2002, several women were featured on $0.37 first-class letter stamps. How many registered letters could you have mailed in 1902 for the price of a first-class letter in 2002? Explain.

2. Each Deep Sea Creatures stamp cost $0.33 when it was issued. These stamps now cost more than their face value. If it costs $3.50 to buy a set of five, how much more does one Deep Sea Creatures stamp cost now than it did when it was issued?

3. Mr. Alvarado wants to buy Amish Quilt stamps for his students to put in their history journals. The stamps are sold only in blocks of ten. There are 24 students in his class. If one stamp costs $0.34, how much must he spend to buy enough stamps for each student in his class?

4. Pilar wants to place all the stamps shown at the right in her stamp album.
   - She wants to use two pages.
   - She wants the same number of stamps on each page.
   - She wants the total face value of the stamps on the second page to be greater than the total face value of the stamps on the first page.
   - She cannot separate the stamps that are attached to one another.

   How can she arrange the stamps?

Education Place
Visit Weekly Reader Connections at **eduplace.com/map** for more on this topic.

Enrichment: Estimating With Mixed Numbers

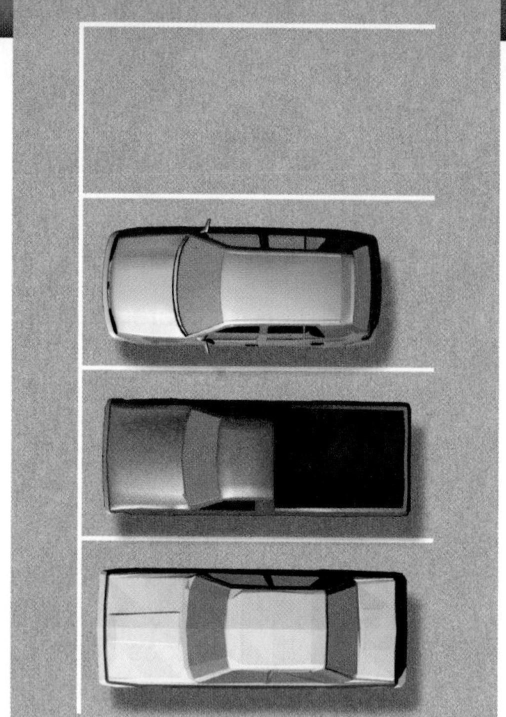

The width of a parking lot is $78\frac{1}{3}$ feet, and each space is to be the same width. For compact cars, each parking space must be at least $7\frac{3}{4}$ feet wide. What is the greatest number of compact-car parking spaces that will fit in one row? How wide will each space be?

First, you need to estimate how many parking spaces will fit. Then you can divide to find how wide to make each parking space.

Rules for Rounding Mixed Numbers

To estimate with mixed numbers, round to the nearest whole number:

- If the fraction part of the mixed number is equal to $\frac{1}{2}$ or greater, round up.
- If the fraction part of the mixed number is less than $\frac{1}{2}$, round down.

Estimate: $78\frac{1}{3} \div 7\frac{3}{4} = ?$

Round down for fractions less than $\frac{1}{2}$. $78\frac{1}{3} \rightarrow 78$

Round up for fractions $\frac{1}{2}$ or greater. $7\frac{3}{4} \rightarrow 8$

$78 \div 8 = 9$ R6 or $9\frac{3}{4}$.

There will be 9 or 10 parking spaces in the lot.

Solve: Check whether 9 spaces will fit. $78\frac{1}{3} \div 9 \approx 9$; 9 feet is too wide.

Check whether 10 spaces will fit. $78\frac{1}{3} \div 10 = 7\frac{5}{6}$

$\frac{5}{6} > \frac{3}{4}$, so $7\frac{5}{6}$ feet wide works.

Solution: There will be 10 spaces, each $7\frac{5}{6}$ feet wide.

Find the greatest number of spaces that will fit in one row. Then find the width of each space.

1. The width of a compact-car parking lot is $47\frac{1}{4}$ feet. Each parking space must be at least $7\frac{3}{4}$ feet wide. Each space is to be the same width.

2. The width of a full-size car parking lot is 70 feet. Each parking space must be at least $8\frac{1}{2}$ feet wide. Each space is to be the same width.

It's A-maze-ing!

How does a bumblebee get to school?

To find out:

- Enter the maze at the bumblebee.
- Copy the first problem. Estimate the answer and then use a calculator to find the exact answer.
- Find the answer in the maze and write the letter found below it.
- Follow the correct answer to the next problem.
- Continue until you reach the schoolhouse at the end of the maze and have found the answer to the riddle.

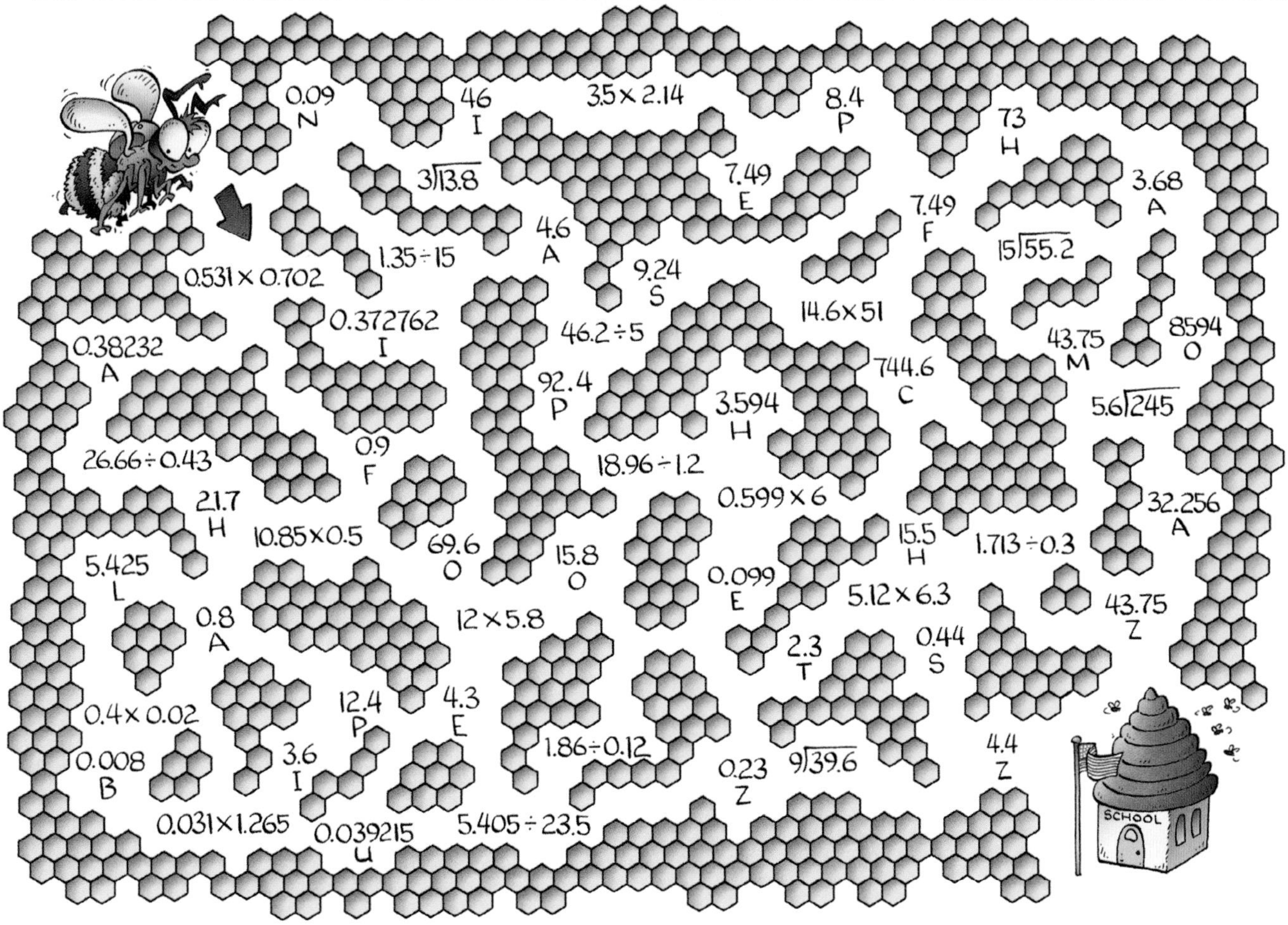

0.09 N
46 I
3.5 × 2.14
8.4 P
73 H
3)13.8
7.49 E
3.68 A
7.49 F
4.6 A
1.35 ÷ 15
15)55.2
0.531 × 0.702
9.24 S
0.372762 I
46.2 ÷ 5
14.6 × 51
43.75 M
8594 O
0.38232 A
744.6 C
92.4 P
3.594 H
5.6)245
26.66 ÷ 0.43
0.9 F
18.96 ÷ 1.2
0.599 × 6
32.256 A
21.7 H
10.85 × 0.5
69.6 O
15.8 O
15.5 H
1.713 ÷ 0.3
5.425 L
0.099 E
5.12 × 6.3
0.8 A
12 × 5.8
43.75 Z
2.3 T
0.44 S
0.4 × 0.02
12.4 P
4.3 E
0.008 B
3.6 I
1.86 ÷ 0.12
0.23 Z
9)39.6
4.4 Z
0.031 × 1.265
0.039215 U
5.405 ÷ 23.5
SCHOOL

Unit 5 Test

VOCABULARY Open Response

1. The product of a number and its ■ is 1.
2. A(n) ■ is a quotient that repeats digits an unlimited number of times.
3. A(n) ■ is a number that tells how many times the base is used as a factor.

Vocabulary
- exponent
- reciprocal
- compatible numbers
- mixed number
- repeating decimal

CONCEPTS AND SKILLS Open Response

Write a multiplication sentence for each model. (Chapter 12)

4. 

5. 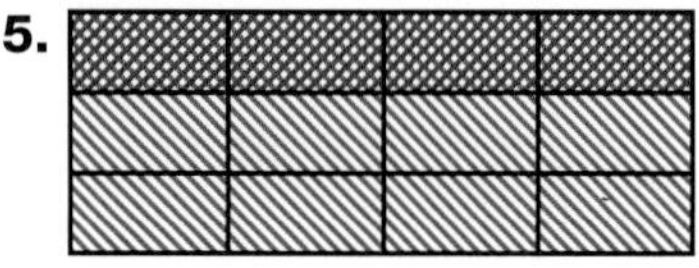 

Multiply or divide. Write your answer in simplest form. (Chapter 12)

6. $\frac{2}{3} \times \frac{3}{9}$
7. $5\frac{1}{6} \times \frac{2}{7}$
8. $7 \times \frac{1}{3}$
9. $2 \div \frac{5}{6}$
10. $2\frac{3}{4} \div \frac{5}{8}$
11. $3\frac{1}{6} \times 1\frac{1}{3}$
12. $\frac{3}{4} \div 2\frac{1}{2}$
13. $4\frac{1}{3} \div \frac{1}{2}$

Estimate. Then multiply. (Chapter 13)

14. 7×6.2
15. 1.02×0.6
16. 204×7.81
17. 17.24×52

Multiply or divide by using patterns. (Chapter 14)

18. 6.23×10^3
19. $8.6 \div 10^1$
20. 5.348×10^2
21. $267.9 \div 10^3$

Estimate. Then find each quotient and check your answer. (Chapter 14)

22. $8\overline{)20.8}$
23. $4\overline{)5.3}$
24. $426 \div 0.8$
25. $50.84 \div 6.2$

Write each as a decimal. (Chapter 14)

26. $\frac{3}{10}$
27. $\frac{2}{3}$
28. $\frac{4}{11}$
29. $\frac{1}{7}$

PROBLEM SOLVING Open Response

30. The Reading-For-All group raised \$308 for new library books. Each book costs \$5. How many new library books can they buy?

31. The temperature during the day on Mercury is 450°C. What is Mercury's temperature during the day in degrees Fahrenheit? Hint: $F = \frac{9}{5}C + 32$.

32. Earth makes a complete revolution around the sun in about 365 days. Mercury revolves around the sun in 0.24 of an Earth year. How many days does it take for Mercury to revolve around the sun?

33. Lil deposited \$1 in her savings account after the first week of summer, \$2.50 after the second week, \$4 after the third week, and \$5.50 after the fourth week. If she continues this pattern, how much will Lil deposit after the tenth week?

Performance Assessment

Constructed Response

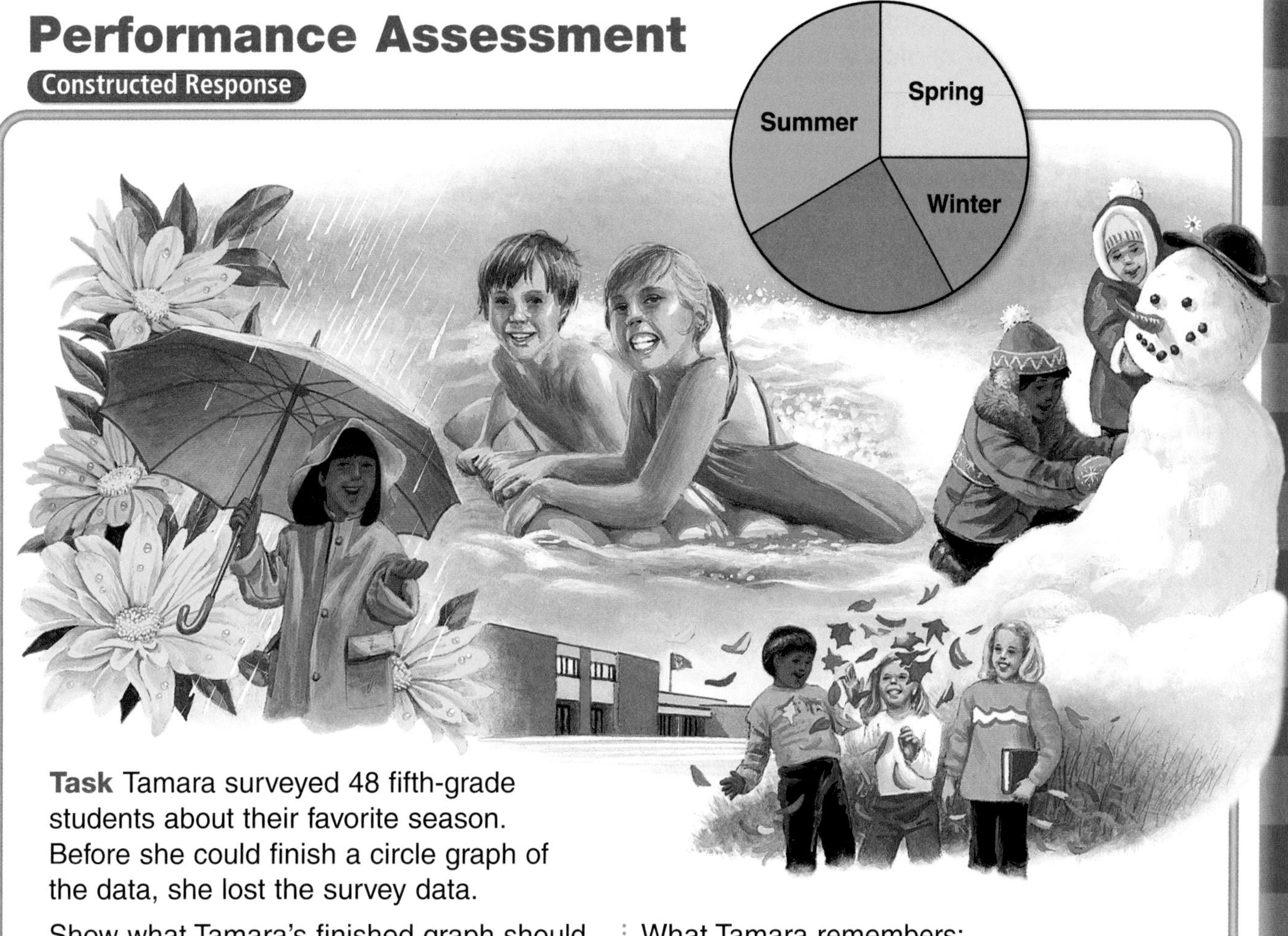

Task Tamara surveyed 48 fifth-grade students about their favorite season. Before she could finish a circle graph of the data, she lost the survey data.

Show what Tamara's finished graph should look like. Find how many students said they prefer each of the seasons. Explain how you found your answers. Show the fraction for each of the seasons on the completed circle graph of the data.

What Tamara remembers:

- One third of the students prefer summer, and half that many prefer winter.
- Spring and fall are preferred by the same number of students.

Cumulative Test Prep

Solve Problems 1–10.

Test-Taking Tip

Compute the answer *before* you read the answer choices. Then check whether your answer is reasonable. If you find an answer choice that matches your answer, you will feel more confident that your answer choice is correct.

Look at the example below.

It rained $\frac{3}{4}$ inch on Saturday and $1\frac{3}{4}$ inches on Sunday. How much did it rain over the weekend?

A $2\frac{1}{4}$ **C** $2\frac{3}{4}$

B $2\frac{1}{2}$ **D** 3

THINK

I must add the fractions to get the answer and show the answer in simplified form:

$$\frac{3}{4} + 1\frac{3}{4} = 1\frac{6}{4} = 1 + \frac{4}{4} + \frac{2}{4} = 2\frac{1}{2}$$

My answer, $2\frac{1}{2}$, is answer choice **B**.

Multiple Choice

1. Subtract $\frac{1}{5}$ from $\frac{3}{4}$.

A $\frac{7}{20}$ **B** $\frac{7}{10}$ **C** $\frac{11}{20}$ **D** $\frac{11}{10}$

(Chapter 10, Lesson 6)

2. Mario wants to extend a shelf that is 7 feet 10 inches long by 2 feet 3 inches. What is the length of the new shelf?

F 5 feet 7 inches **H** 10 feet 1 inch

G 9 feet 7 inches **J** 10 feet 3 inches

(Chapter 6, Lesson 2)

3. In May, Roberto was $59\frac{7}{8}$ inches tall. By the end of October, he had grown $\frac{3}{4}$ inch. How tall was Roberto at the end of October?

A $59\frac{1}{8}$ inches **C** $60\frac{5}{8}$ inches

B $59\frac{1}{4}$ inches **D** $60\frac{8}{13}$ inches

(Chapter 10, Lesson 3)

4. On a camping trip, $5\frac{1}{2}$ cups of oatmeal were made for breakfast. The oatmeal is divided equally among 4 campers. How much does each camper get?

F $1\frac{3}{8}$ cups **H** $1\frac{5}{6}$ cups

G $1\frac{1}{2}$ cups **J** $2\frac{1}{3}$ cups

(Chapter 12, Lesson 5)

For Test-Taking Tips, see page 652.

Open Response

5. Every Monday for 3 weeks, a truck brought 1.5 tons of crushed stone to a construction site. How many tons of stone did the truck bring in all?

(Chapter 13, Lesson 2)

6.

Metric Units of Capacity
1,000 milliliters (mL) = 1 liter (L)
10 deciliters (dL) = 1 liter (L)

Hamid wants to pour equal amounts from a pitcher holding 2 liters of apple juice into several glasses. How many deciliters should he pour into each of 5 glasses?

(Chapter 6, Lesson 5)

7. The school board budget is $7,000,000. What is the largest exponent you would use to write this number in expanded form?

(Chapter 1, Lesson 2)

8. A city school district has 1,701 students in 9 elementary schools. If the same number of students go to each school, how many students are in each school?

(Chapter 4, Lesson 5)

9. A hummingbird flaps its wings once every 0.074 second. How much time does it take a hummingbird to flap its wings 12 times?

(Chapter 13, Lesson 4)

Extended Response

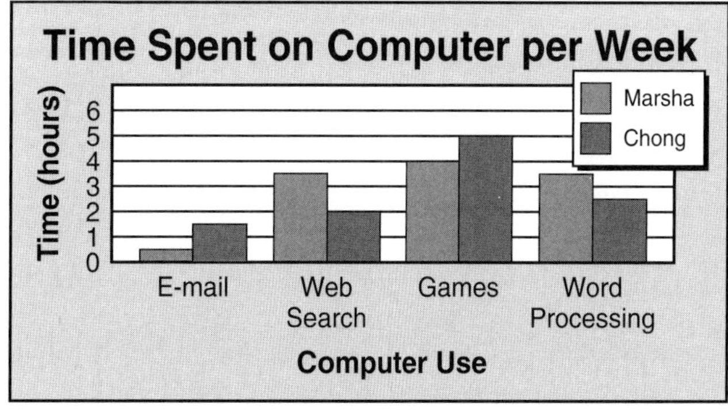

10. The double bar graph shows how many hours Chong and Marsha spend on different computer activities each week.

A On which computer activity does each student spend the most time?

B Who spends more time using a word processing application?

C What is the total time that Marsha spends using a computer each week? Chong?

D How much more time does Chong spend playing computer games than Marsha?

E Write two to three sentences to compare Chong and Marsha's computer use.

(Chapter 7, Lesson 1)

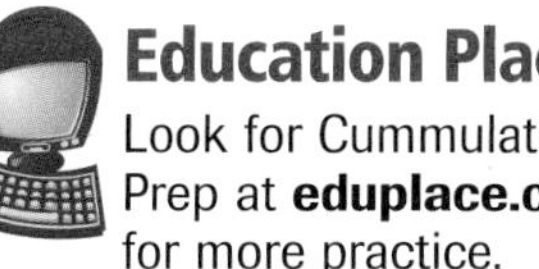

Education Place
Look for Cummulative Test Prep at **eduplace.com/map** for more practice.

Vocabulary Wrap-Up for Unit 5

Look back at the big ideas and vocabulary in this unit.

Big Ideas

To divide a fraction by a fraction, multiply by the reciprocal of the divisor.

The product of two decimals will have the same number of decimal places as the sum of the number of decimal places in each factor.

Key Vocabulary

reciprocal
product
quotient

Math Conversations

Use your new vocabulary to discuss these big ideas.

1. Explain what the written form of this decimal means: $1.\overline{2}$
2. Explain how the numbers $\frac{3}{5}$, $\frac{6}{10}$, and 0.6 are related.
3. Explain how you would locate the decimal point in this product.

   $$0.02 \times 0.4 = 0008$$

   Why are zeros used in the answer?
4. **Write About It** Meteorologists often write daily amounts of rainfall in decimal form, even when the rainfall is measured in inches. With a partner, discuss and then explain in writing some reasons why scientists might use decimals instead of fractions when measuring rainfall.

To find the reciprocal of a fraction, I exchange the numerator and denominator.
Right. So the reciprocal of $\frac{1}{10}$ is $\frac{10}{1}$.

UNIT 6

Geometry and Measurement

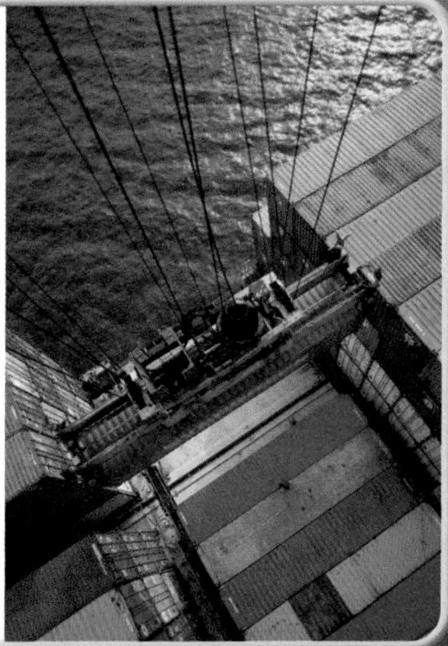

Reading Mathematics

Reviewing Vocabulary

Here are some math vocabulary words that you should know.

ray	part of a line that begins at an endpoint and goes on forever in one direction
angle	a figure formed by two rays with the same endpoint
line segment	part of a line that has two endpoints
polygon	a simple closed plane figure made up of three or more line segments
circle	a closed figure in which every point is the same distance from a given point called the center

Reading Words and Symbols

The two rays that make up the angle have a common endpoint, which is called the vertex.

One way you can name angles is to name three points on the angle–a point on each ray and the vertex. The vertex must always be in the middle.

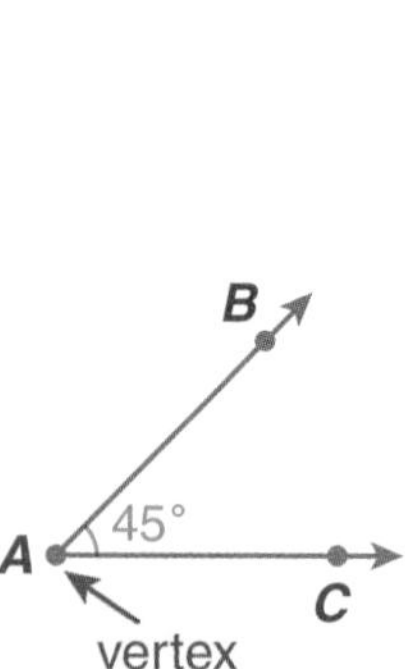

Another way you can name angles is by using only the vertex letter. In $\angle BAC$, A is the vertex. For $\angle BAC$ (read "angle *BAC*") you can also write $\angle A$ (read "angle *A*").

The measure of angles is given in degrees. The symbol for degrees is °. This angle has a measure of forty-five degrees or 45°.

Use words and symbols to answer these questions.

1. What are two other names for $\angle BAC$? Explain.
2. What is the measure of an angle that has twice the measure of $\angle BAC$? three times the measure of $\angle BAC$?

Reading Test Questions

Choose the correct answer for each.

3. Which figure is shown on the grid paper?

   a. square

   b. rectangle

   c. parallelogram

   d. all of the above

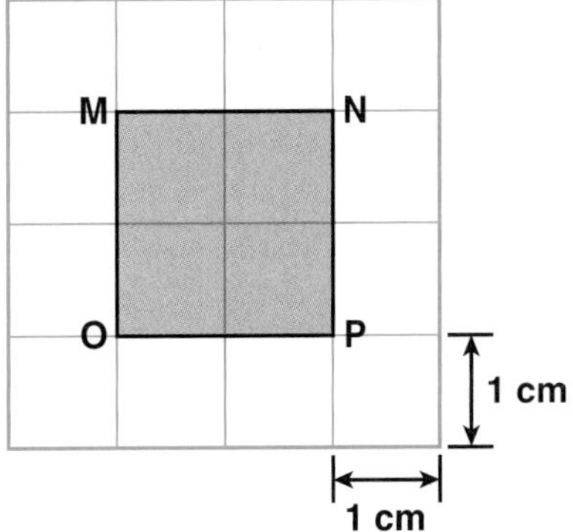

A **grid** is an arrangement of lines intersecting at right angles and dividing a plane into congruent squares.

4. As part of which group would you classify the figure?

   a. circles
   b. quadrilaterals
   c. triangles
   d. pentagons

To **classify** in geometry means to identify the type of figure.

5. How many square centimeters do you count inside the figure?

   a. 4
   b. 8
   c. 12
   d. 16

A **square centimeter** is a metric unit used for measuring the area of a figure. The symbol for square centimeter is cm^2. Each cm^2 has a measure of 1 cm $\times$ 1 cm.

Learning Vocabulary

Watch for these words in this unit. Write their definitions in your journal.

diagonal

transformation

tessellation

circumference

π (pi)

net

Literature Connection

Read "No Place to Go" on page 646. Then work with a partner to answer the questions about the story.

Education Place

At **eduplace.com/map** see *e*Glossary and *e*Games—Math Lingo.

CHAPTER 15

Plane Figures and Geometric Concepts

INVESTIGATION

Use Data

A geodesic dome is a type of structure that uses triangles to approximate the shape of a sphere. Richard Buckminster Fuller (1895–1983) created the geodesic dome in the early 1950s.

Can you find these shapes in the picture?

a rectangle

a parallelogram

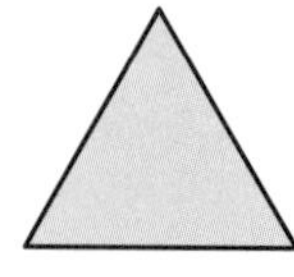
an equilateral triangle

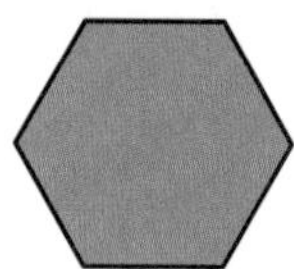
a hexagon

Use What You Know

Use this page to review and remember what you need to know for this chapter.

VOCABULARY

Choose the best word to complete each sentence.

1. A _____ is a closed, flat figure made up of line segments.
2. A _____ is a figure made up of points that are all the same distance from the center point.

Vocabulary
- circle
- flip
- polygon

CONCEPTS AND SKILLS

Is each figure a polygon? Write *yes* or *no*.

3. 
4. 
5. 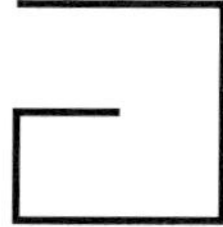

Match. Write the letter of the figure with the same size and shape.

6. 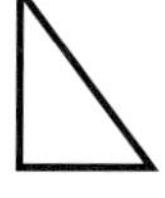

a. 

7. 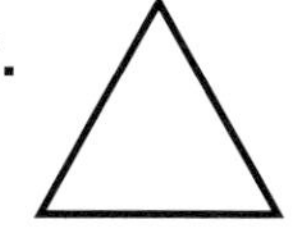

b. 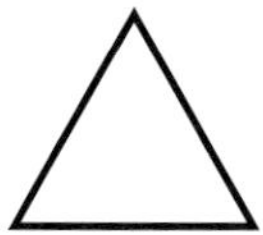

8. 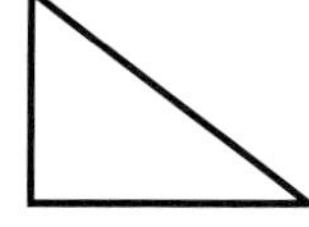

c. 

9. 

d. 

Write About It

10. Is a circle a polygon? Explain your answer.

Facts Practice, see page 665.

Lesson 1

Points, Lines, and Rays

Objective Identify and label points, lines, line segments, and rays.

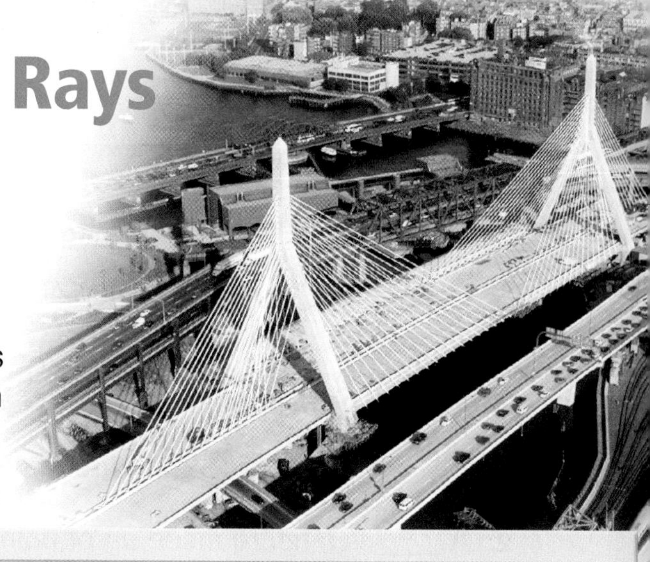

Learn About It

The widest cable-stayed bridge in the world spans the Charles River in Boston. In the picture you can identify many geometric features.

Leonard P. Zakim Bunker Hill Bridge

- A **point** is an exact location in space. **Read:** point *C* **Write:** *C*

- A **line** is an endless straight path made up of a continuous collection of points.

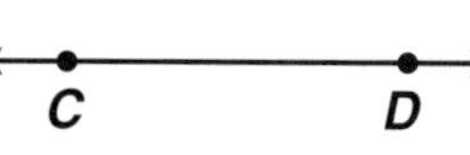

Read: line *CD* or line *DC*
Write: $\overleftrightarrow{CD}$ or $\overleftrightarrow{DC}$

- A **line segment** is a part of a line and has two endpoints.

Read: line segment *CD* or line segment *DC*
Write: $\overline{CD}$ or $\overline{DC}$

- A **ray** has one endpoint and extends without end in one direction.

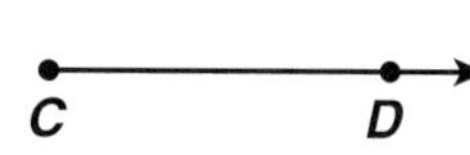

Read: ray *CD*
Write: $\overrightarrow{CD}$ (The endpoint is always the first letter.)

- A **plane** is a collection of points that forms a flat, continuous, and unending surface.

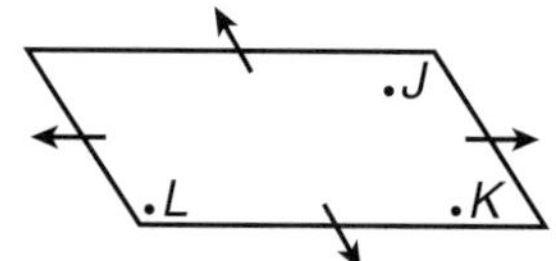

Read: plane *JKL*
(The 3 letters can be in any order.)

- **Intersecting lines** have one point in common.

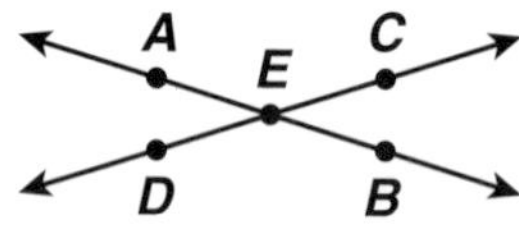

Read: Line *AB* intersects line *CD* at point *E*.

- **Perpendicular lines** intersect at right angles.

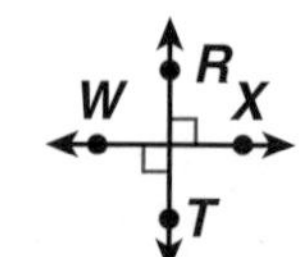

Read: Line *RT* is perpendicular to line *WX*.
Write: $\overleftrightarrow{RT} \perp \overleftrightarrow{WX}$

- **Parallel lines** lie in the same plane and do not intersect.

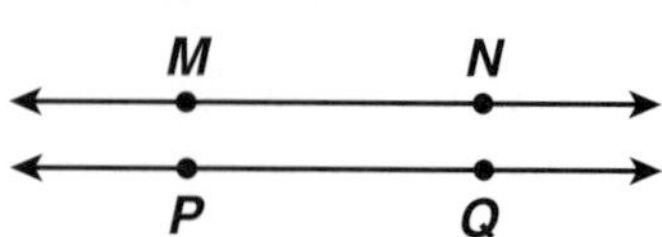

Read: Line *MN* is parallel to line *PQ*.
Write: $\overleftrightarrow{MN} \parallel \overleftrightarrow{PQ}$

Guided Practice

Ask Yourself

- Which letters do I use to name each figure?
- Do I need to write the letters in a certain order?

Name each figure.

1. • T

2. F E

3. S T

4. C M

Explain Your Thinking ▶ Why do $\overrightarrow{CD}$ and $\overrightarrow{DC}$ name different rays?

Practice and Problem Solving

Name each figure.

5. Y Z

6. 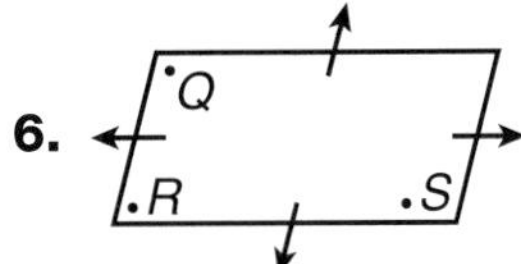

7. 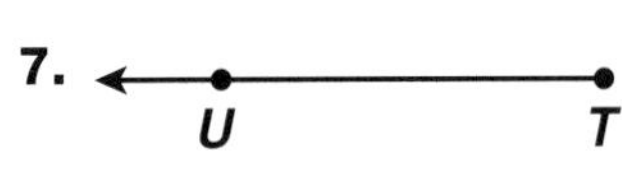

Describe each pair of lines. Use symbols if possible.

8. 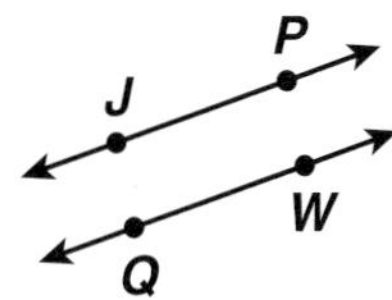

9. 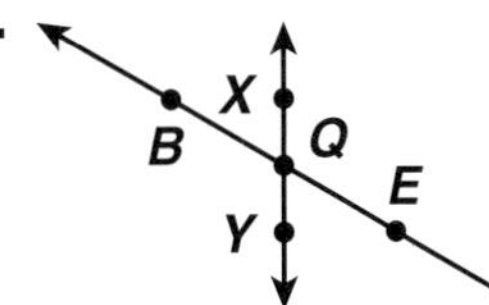

10. 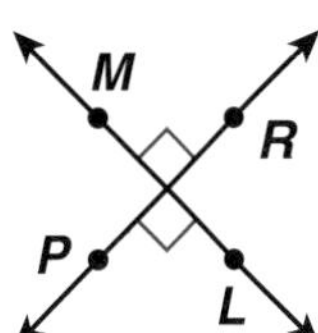

Draw and label each figure.

11. $\overrightarrow{DR}$ 12. $\overleftrightarrow{DF} \perp \overleftrightarrow{LN}$ 13. $\overleftrightarrow{CQ} \parallel \overleftrightarrow{DX}$ 14. plane *EBT*

Solve.

15. Four parallel lines are perpendicular to two other lines. At how many points do the lines intersect?

16. Which of these–a line, a line segment, or a ray–can contain the other two?

17. **Write About It** Explain how perpendicular lines are one special case of intersecting lines.

18. How many lines can intersect at a point? Use a diagram to explain your thinking.

Mixed Review and Test Prep

Open Response

For each exercise, write the fractions that are equivalent. Then circle the fraction in the pair that is in simplest form. (Ch. 9, Lesson 6)

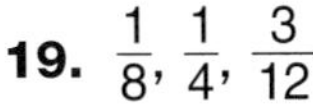

19. $\frac{1}{8}, \frac{1}{4}, \frac{3}{12}$

20. $\frac{1}{8}, \frac{8}{16}, \frac{2}{16}$

21. $\frac{9}{18}, \frac{2}{6}, \frac{1}{2}$

22. $\frac{1}{6}, \frac{1}{3}, \frac{5}{15}$

Multiple Choice

23. Identify this figure. (Ch. 15, Lesson 1)

A line *MN* **C** plane *MN*

B point *MN* **D** ray *MN*

Extra Practice See page 419, Set A.

Hands On Lesson 2

Audio Tutor 2/9 Listen and Understand

Measure, Draw, and Classify Angles

Objective Measure, draw, and classify angles.

Vocabulary
- degrees
- right angle
- acute angle
- obtuse angle
- straight angle

Materials
protractor or Learning Tool 12

Work Together

Angles are formed by two rays with a common endpoint. The common endpoint of the rays is called the vertex of the angle. A small arc is used to identify the inside, or interior, of an angle.

To name an angle, you can name three points on the angle–a point on each ray and the vertex in the middle. You can also name an angle just by naming its vertex if no other angles share that vertex.

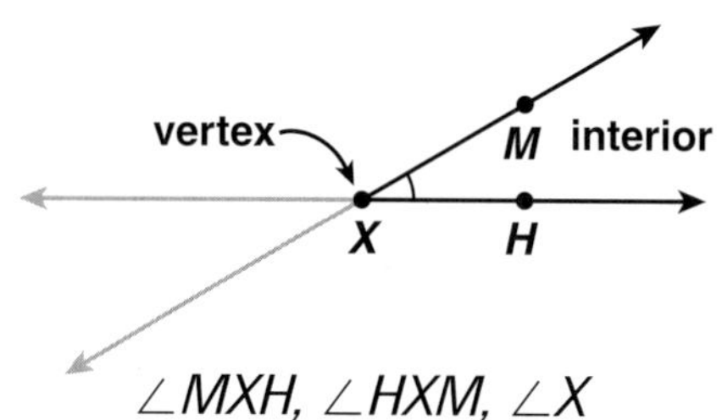

$\angle MXH$, $\angle HXM$, $\angle X$

The symbol $\angle$ is used to identify an angle.

A protractor is a tool used to measure angles in **degrees** (°).

Follow the steps below to measure $\angle FDE$ and $\angle BDC$.

Measuring Angles

STEP 1 Place the center mark of the protractor on the vertex, *D*. Align the 0° mark of one of the protractor scales with one ray of the angle.

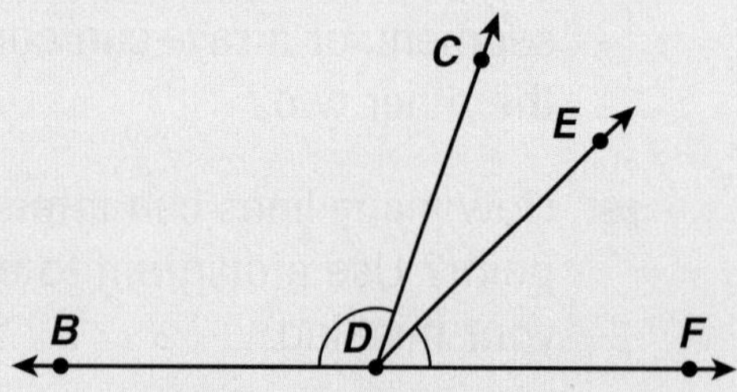

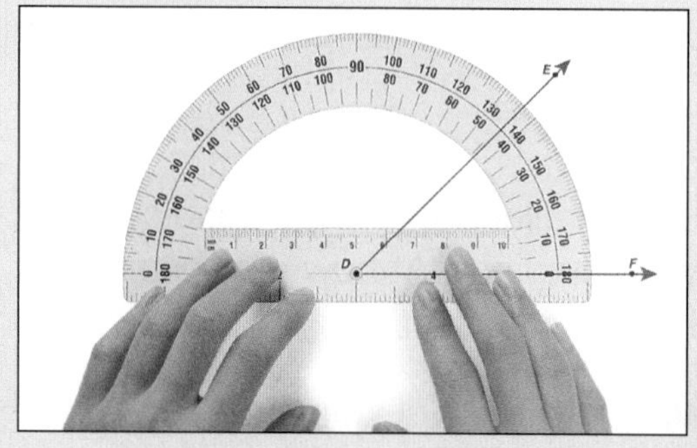

STEP 2 Find where the other ray passes through the same scale. Read the measure of the angle on that scale.

- What is the measure of $\angle FDE$? $\angle BDC$?
- How can you tell when to use the inside scale and when to use the outside scale of the protractor?

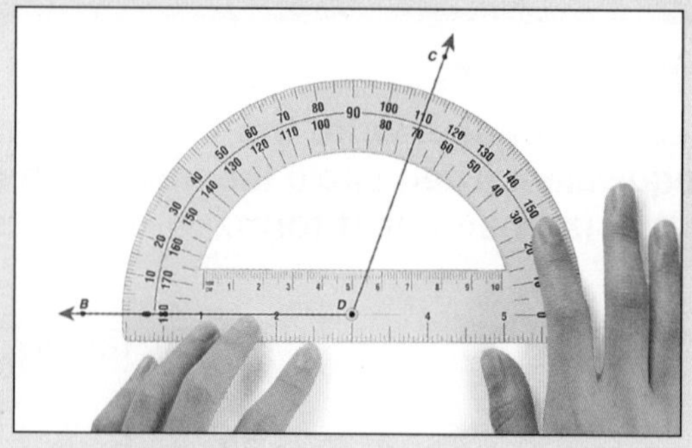

You can also use a protractor to draw an angle of a given measure.

Draw an angle that measures 75°.

Drawing Angles

STEP 1 On a sheet of paper, draw and label a ray.

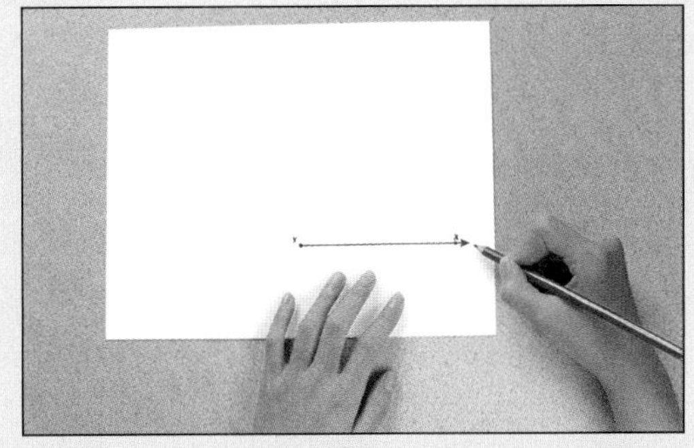

STEP 2 Place the center mark of the protractor on the endpoint of the ray. Align the ray with the 0° mark of one of the protractor scales. The endpoint of the ray will be the vertex of the angle.

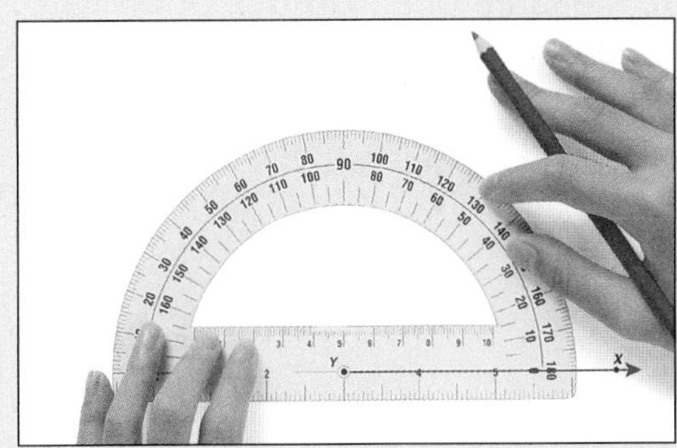

STEP 3 Using the scale on which the ray aligns with 0°, mark the point at 75°. Label the point.

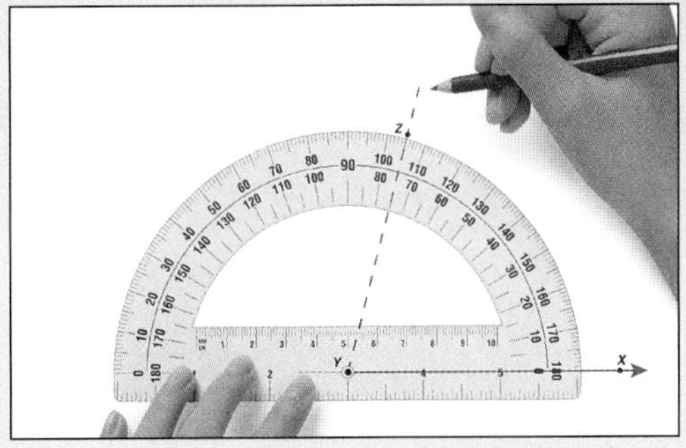

STEP 4 Draw a ray from the vertex through the point you labeled. Write the name of the angle.

- What is the measure of the angle?
- Which point is the vertex of the angle?

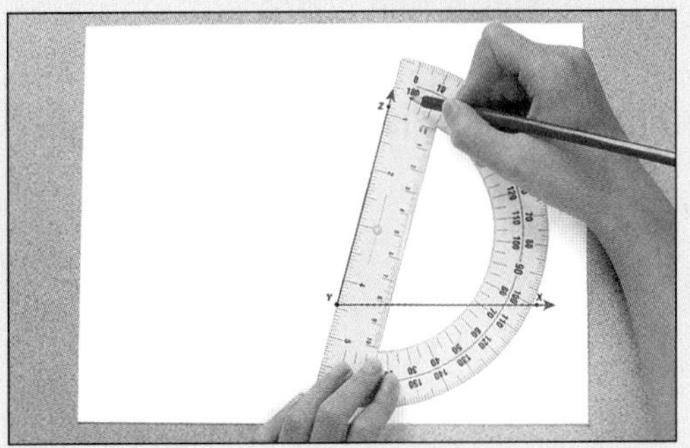

Go On

You can classify an angle by its measure.

Classifying Angles

The measure of a **right angle** is equal to 90°.

A small square is often used to identify a right angle.

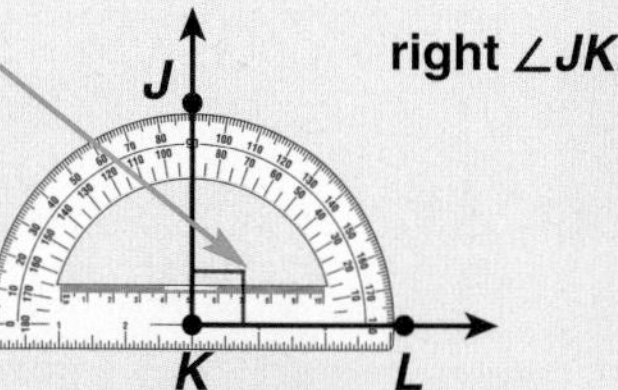

right ∠JKL

The measure of an **acute angle** is greater than 0° and less than 90°.

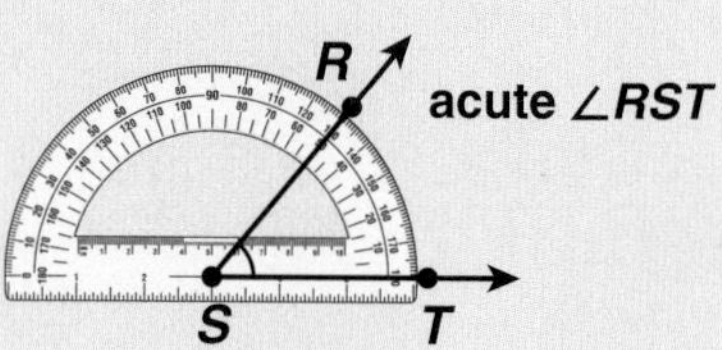

The measure of an **obtuse angle** is greater than 90° and less than 180°.

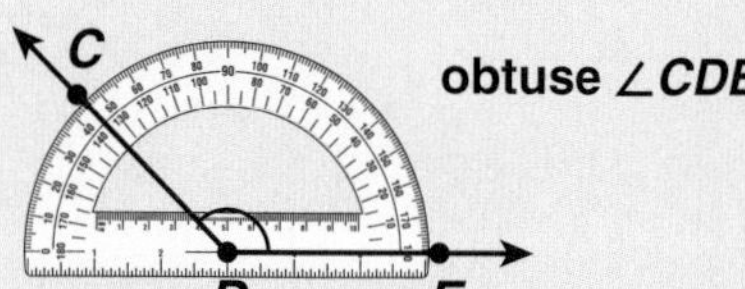

obtuse ∠CDE

The measure of a **straight angle** is equal to 180°.

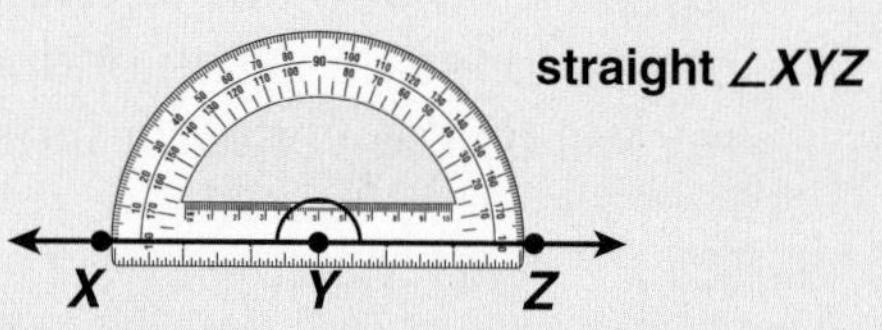

straight ∠XYZ

On Your Own

In Exercises 1–4, use symbols to name each angle three different ways.

1. 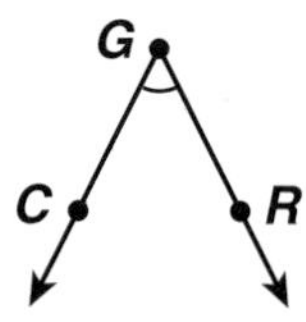

2. 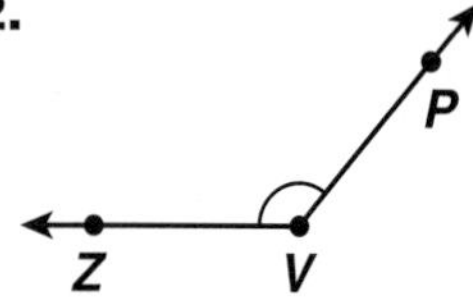

3. 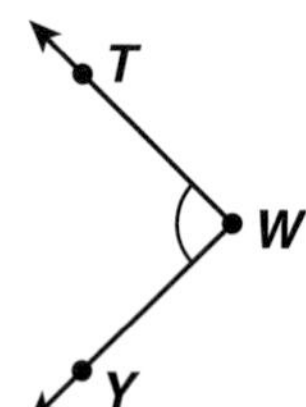

4. 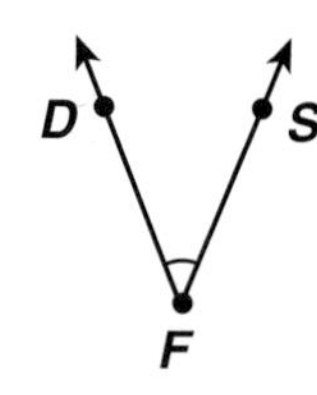

5. Which angle has a greater measure, ∠*CGR* or ∠*ZVP*?

Classify each angle as acute, obtuse, straight, or right.

6. 

7. 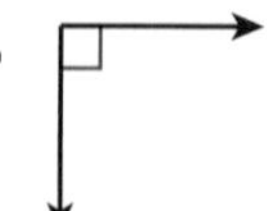

8. 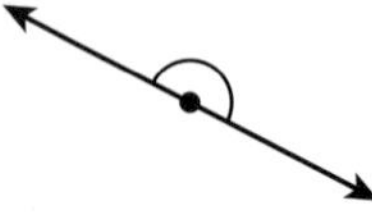

9. 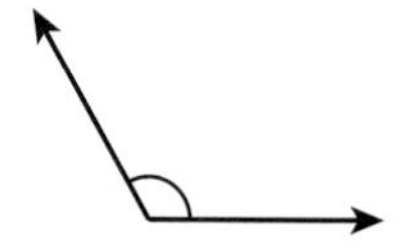

10. 

11. 

12. 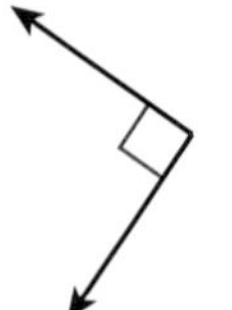

13. 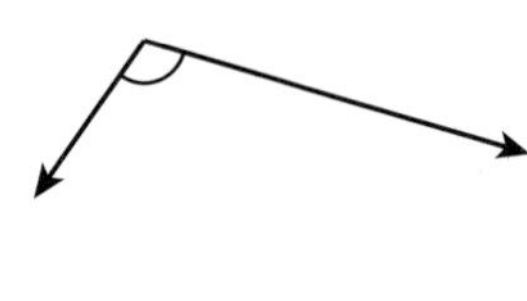

Use a protractor to draw an angle having each measure. Classify each angle as right, acute, obtuse, or straight.

14. 165°
15. 90°
16. 20°
17. 85°

18. 50°
19. 115°
20. 10°
21. 135°

Talk About It • Write About It

You have learned how to classify, draw, and measure angles.

22. Is the sum of the measures of two acute angles always less than 90°? Explain why or why not.

23. How could you list the kinds of angles you know–right, straight, acute, and obtuse–in order from least to greatest measure? Explain.

Activity

Visual Thinking
Construct Perpendicular Lines

You can use a compass and a straightedge to construct perpendicular lines.

Follow these steps to construct perpendicular lines.

STEP 1 Draw line *c* and point *W* as shown at the right. Put the compass point on *W*. Draw an arc that intersects line *c* at two points. Label these points *X* and *Y*.

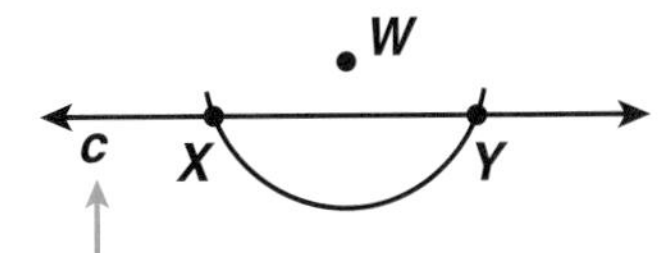

Lines can be named using lowercase letters.

STEP 2 Place the point of the compass at *X* and draw an arc below line *c*. From point *Y*, use the same compass measure and draw an arc below line *c*. Label the intersection point *V*.

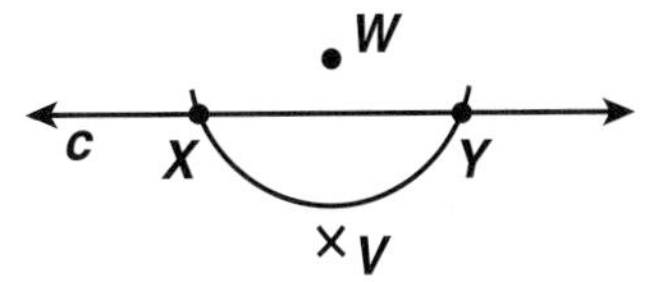

STEP 3 Draw line *WV* and label it *d*. Line *d* is perpendicular to line *c*.

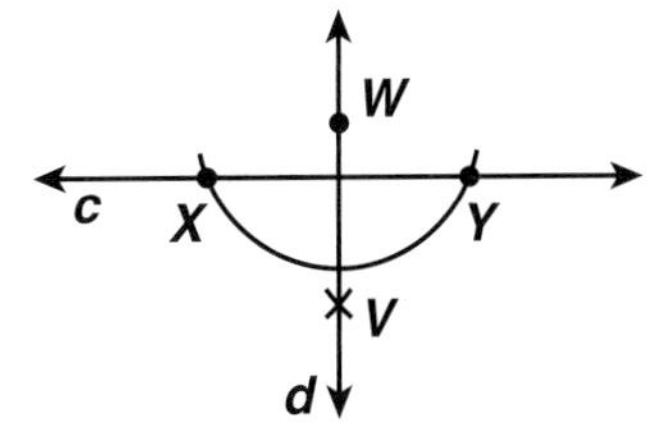

Triangles

Objective Classify triangles and find missing angle measures.

Vocabulary

equilateral
isosceles
scalene

Materials
straightedge

Learn About It

A triangle is made up of 3 line segments called sides. Each pair of sides has a common endpoint, or vertex, and forms an angle.

You can classify triangles by the lengths of their sides.

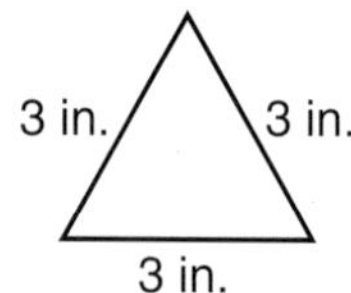

equilateral triangle
All sides are the same length.

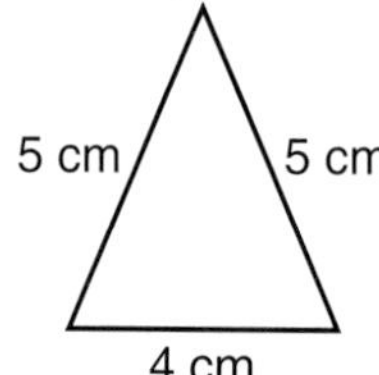

isosceles triangle
At least two sides are the same length.

2 ft 4 ft
5 ft

scalene triangle
No sides are the same length.

You can also classify triangles by their angle measures.

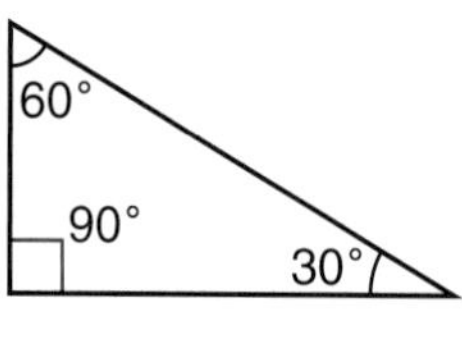

right triangle
one right angle

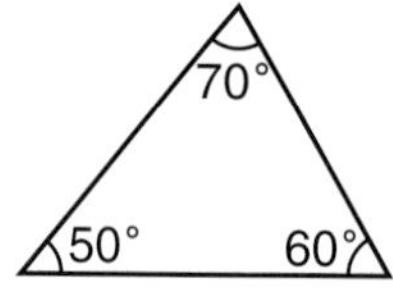

acute triangle
all acute angles

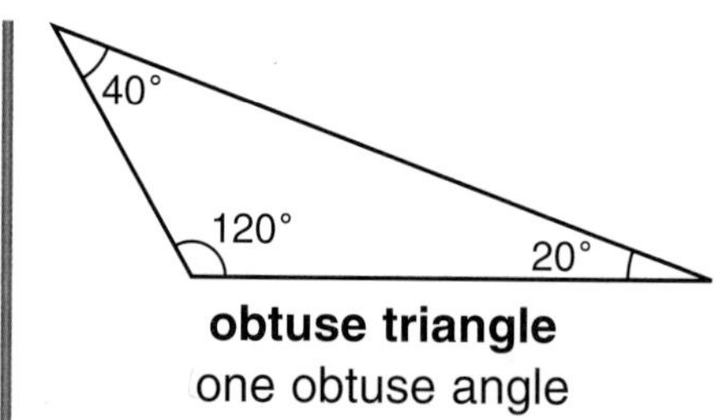

obtuse triangle
one obtuse angle

Try this activity with a partner to learn about angle measures in a triangle.

STEP 1 Use a straightedge to draw a triangle. Cut it out. Label the angles *a*, *b*, and *c*.

b
a *c*

STEP 2 Tear off the three angles of the triangle.

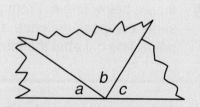

STEP 3 Arrange the angles to make a straight angle.

- What is the measure of a straight angle?
- What is the sum of the angle measures in a triangle?
- Does this work for any triangle? Explain.

Guided Practice

Classify each triangle in two ways. Then find the missing angle measures.

1.

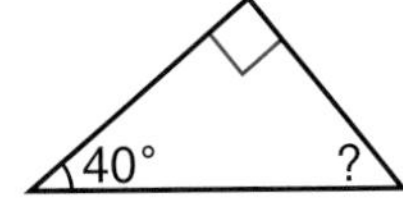

2.

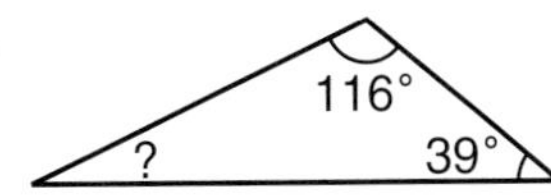
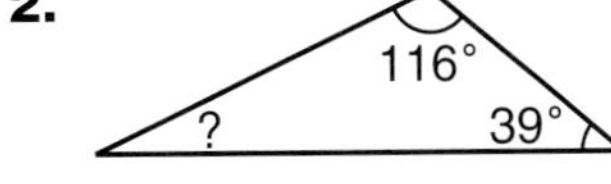

Ask Yourself

- Are the angles acute? obtuse? right?
- What is the sum of the angle measures in a triangle?

Explain Your Thinking ▶ Is an equilateral triangle also an isosceles triangle? Explain why or why not.

Practice and Problem Solving

Classify each triangle in two ways.

3.

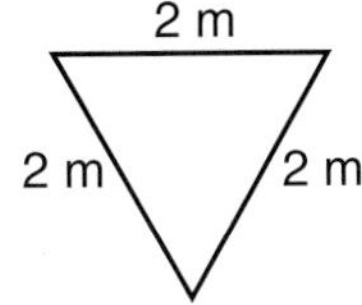

4.

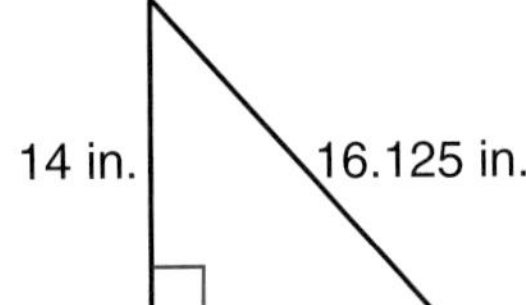

5.

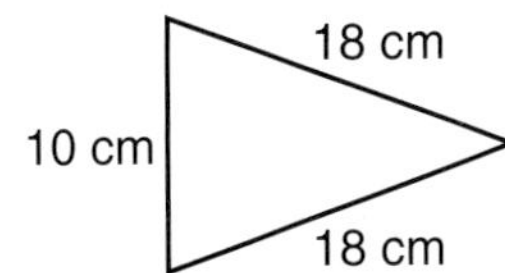

6.

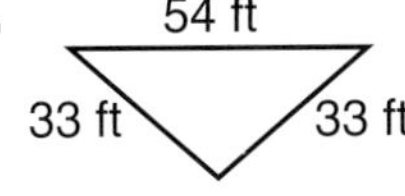

Algebra • Expressions **Write an expression to represent *a*. Then find the value of *a*.**

7.

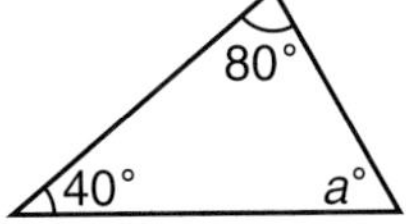

8.

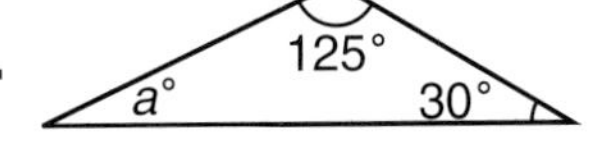

9.

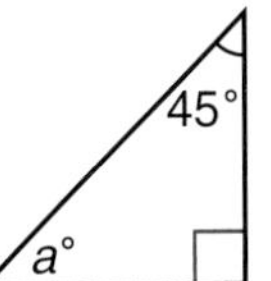

10.

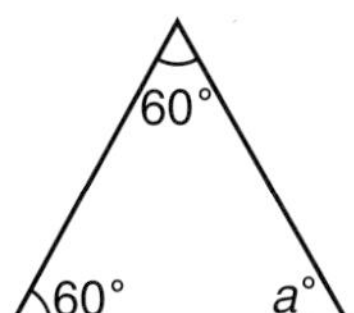

Use a straightedge and protractor for Problems 11 and 12.

11. **What's Wrong?** Ari says that an isosceles triangle can also be obtuse. Is Ari right or wrong? Draw triangles to help you explain.

12. Try to draw each of the following. If a figure cannot be drawn, explain why.

- a scalene acute triangle
- an equilateral right triangle
- a scalene right triangle

13. **Create and Solve** Use the sum of the angle measures in a triangle to write and solve your own triangle problem.

Mixed Review and Test Prep

Open Response

Multiply. Write each product in simplest form. (Ch. 12, Lesson 2)

14. $\frac{2}{3} \times \frac{3}{5}$

15. $\frac{3}{8} \times \frac{4}{5}$

16. $\frac{5}{6} \times \frac{3}{10}$

17. $\frac{4}{9} \times \frac{3}{4}$

18. $\frac{2}{25} \times \frac{2}{5}$

19. $\frac{3}{8} \times \frac{4}{11}$

20. Find *p*. Explain how you found your answer. (Ch. 15, Lesson 3)

p°
p°

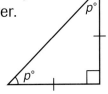

Extra Practice See page 419, Set B.

Lesson 4

Congruence

Objective Identify congruent figures and congruent parts of figures.

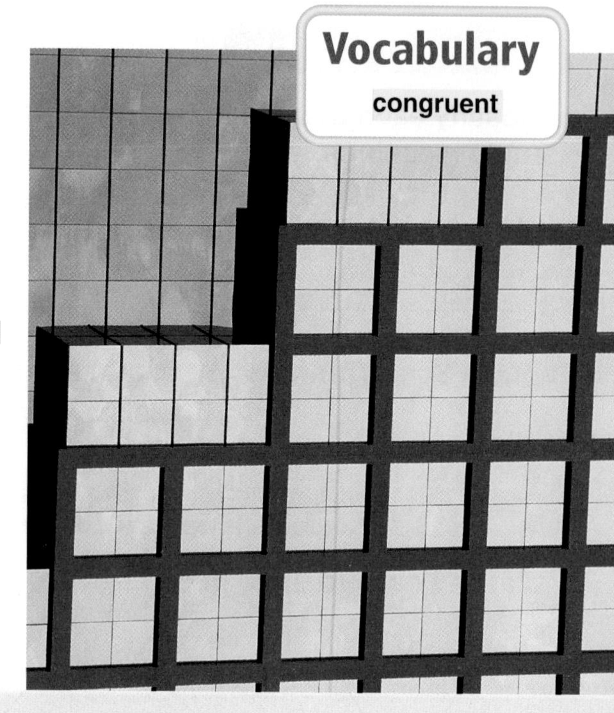

Vocabulary
congruent

Learn About It

Figures that are the same size and shape are called **congruent** figures. The symbol $\cong$ is used to indicate congruence. Corresponding parts of congruent figures are congruent.

Which figures in the photograph appear to be congruent?

Different Ways to Check for Congruence

Way 1 You can use tracing.

If you trace triangle *ABC* and place the tracing on top of triangle *DEF*, you will find that the triangles are congruent.

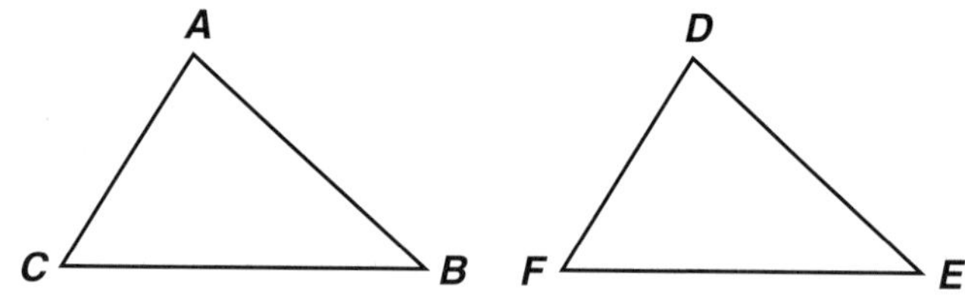

The symbol $\triangle$ is used to identify a triangle.

$\triangle ABC \cong \triangle DEF$

So, $\overline{AB} \cong \overline{DE}$, $\overline{BC} \cong \overline{EF}$, $\overline{CA} \cong \overline{FD}$.

Also, $\angle A \cong \angle D$, $\angle B \cong \angle E$, and $\angle C \cong \angle F$.

Way 2 You can use a ruler and a protractor.

In an equilateral triangle, the three sides are congruent and the three angles are congruent. Small lines indicate congruent sides and congruent angles.

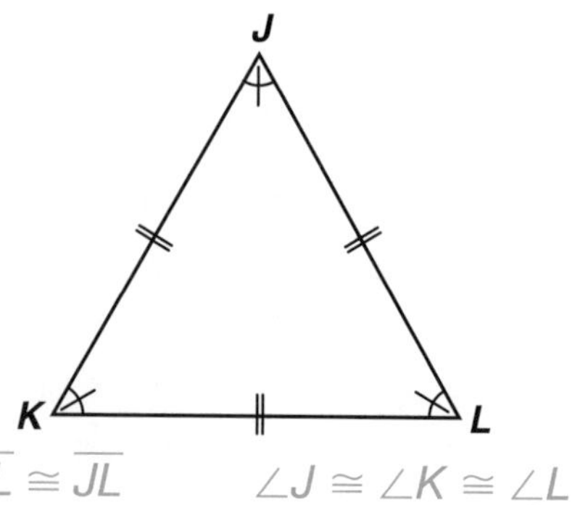

$\overline{JK} \cong \overline{KL} \cong \overline{JL}$ $\angle J \cong \angle K \cong \angle L$

Another Example

Squares

These squares are not congruent. They have the same shape, but they are not the same size.

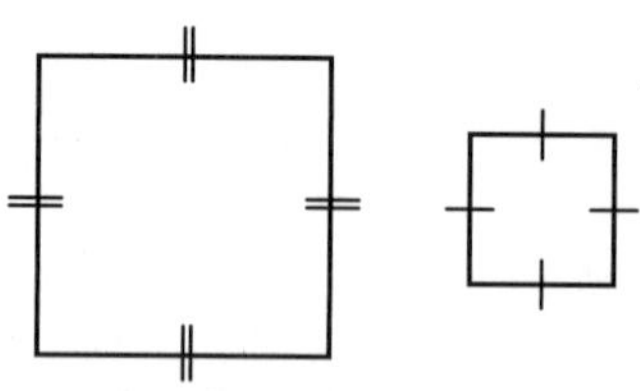

Guided Practice

Ask Yourself

- Which sides are the same length?
- Which angles have the same measure?

Trace each figure. Mark the congruent sides and the congruent angles.

1. 

2. 

Explain Your Thinking ▶ Draw three squares on a piece of paper. Can you divide each square differently into four congruent parts? Show your work.

Practice and Problem Solving

Trace each figure. Use a ruler to measure the sides and a protractor to measure the angles of each figure. Mark the congruent sides and angles.

3. 

4. 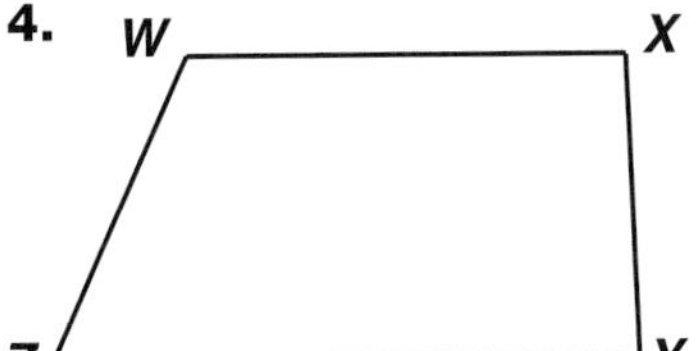

5. 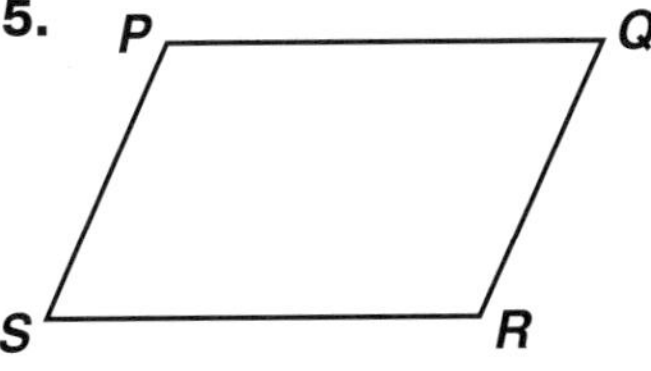

Use the diagram to answer the questions. Explain your reasoning.

6. What is the length of $\overline{DE}$?

7. What is the measure of $\angle A$?

8. What is the measure of $\angle F$?

9. What is the length of $\overline{DF}$?

10. What is the measure of $\angle D$?

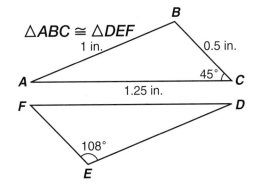

$\triangle ABC \cong \triangle DEF$

B, 1 in., 0.5 in., A, 45°, C, 1.25 in., F, D, 108°, E

Mixed Review and Test Prep

Open Response

Find each statistic for the data below.
(Ch. 8, Lesson 2)

90, 75, 80, 80, 80

11. mean

12. range

13. mode

14. median

Multiple Choice

15. Which of the following statements is true? (Ch. 15, Lesson 4)

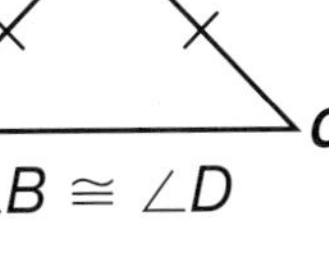

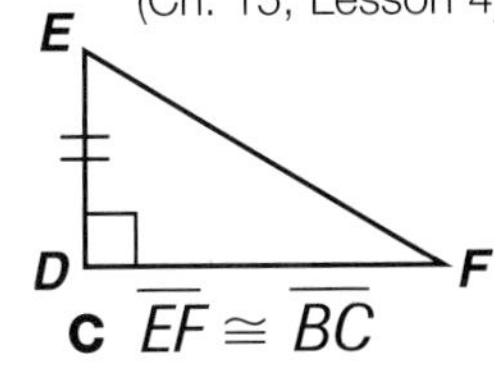

A $\angle B \cong \angle D$

B $\overline{AC} \cong \overline{DF}$

C $\overline{EF} \cong \overline{BC}$

D $\angle A \cong \angle D$

Extra Practice See page 419, Set C.

Lesson 5

Quadrilaterals and Other Polygons

Objective Identify, classify, and compare polygons.

Vocabulary
- quadrilateral
- polygon
- regular polygon
- diagonal

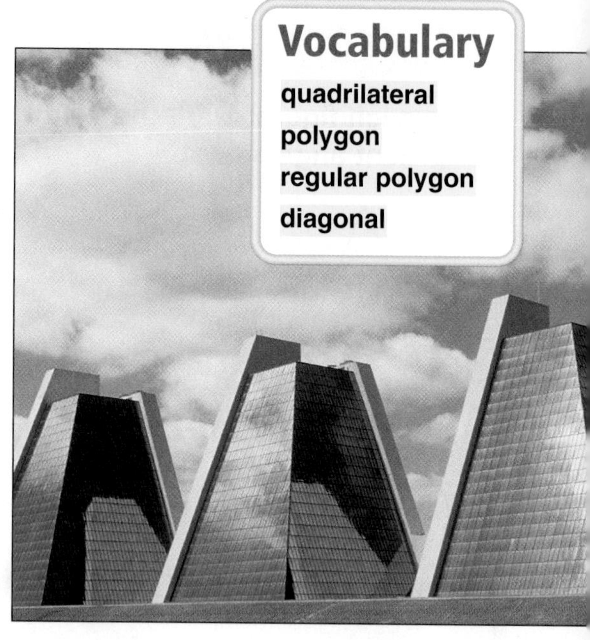

Learn About It

A **quadrilateral** is a four-sided figure. The sum of the angle measures in any quadrilateral is 360°. In a city you will see many things that are like quadrilaterals.

There are many different kinds of quadrilaterals. You can use sides and angles to classify them.

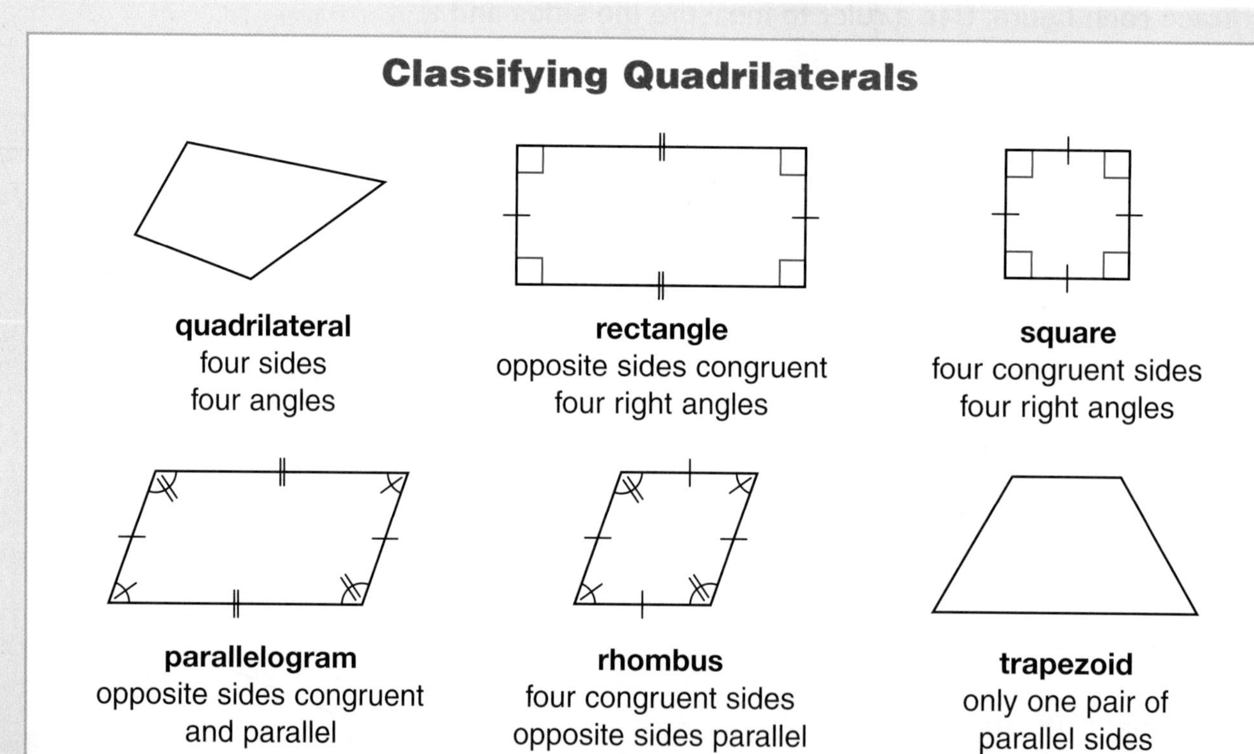

A quadrilateral is one type of **polygon**. A polygon is a closed figure that has three or more sides. Each side is a line segment, and the sides meet only at their endpoints.

Polygons

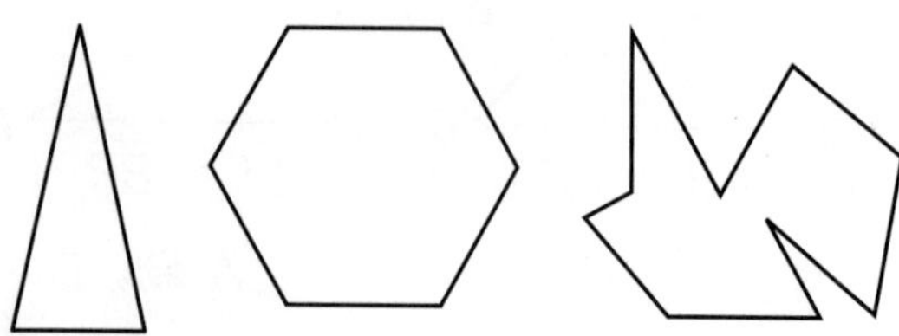

Not Polygons

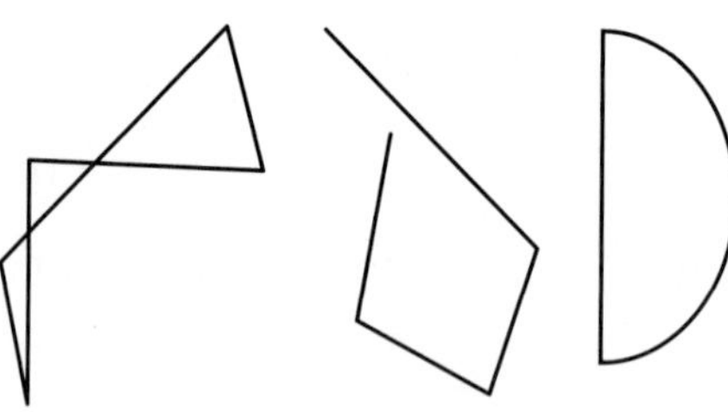

A **regular polygon** is a polygon with all sides congruent and all angles congruent.

Polygons			
Name	**Examples**	**Name**	**Examples**
Triangle 3 sides		**Octagon** 8 sides	
Quadrilateral 4 sides		**Nonagon** 9 sides	
Pentagon 5 sides		**Decagon** 10 sides	
Hexagon 6 sides		**Undecagon** 11 sides	
Heptagon 7 sides		**Dodecagon** 12 sides	

A **diagonal** of a polygon is a segment that joins two vertices of a polygon but is not a side.

$\overline{AD}$ and $\overline{BE}$ are two diagonals of this hexagon.

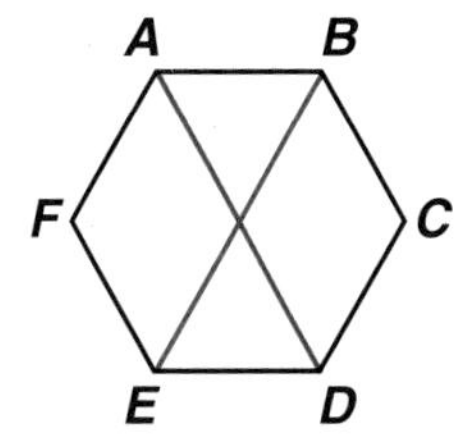

Guided Practice

Ask Yourself

- How many sides does the polygon have?
- Are any sides parallel?
- Are any sides congruent?
- Are any angles congruent?

Classify each polygon in as many ways as you can.

1. 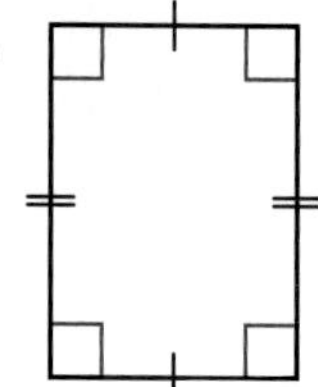

2. 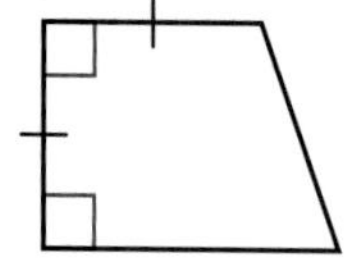

3. 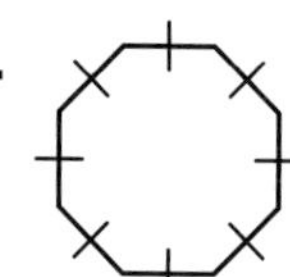

Explain Your Thinking ▶ Use the drawing at the right to explain why the sum of the angle measures in a quadrilateral is 360°.

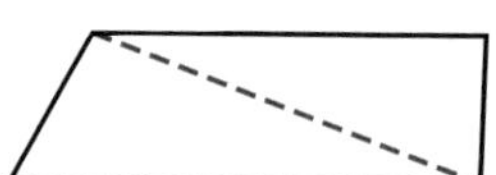

Practice and Problem Solving

Classify each polygon in as many ways as you can.

4. 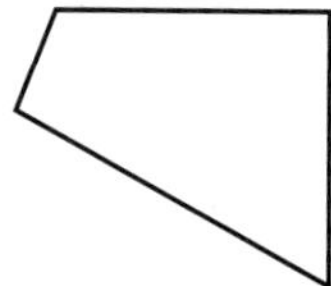

5. 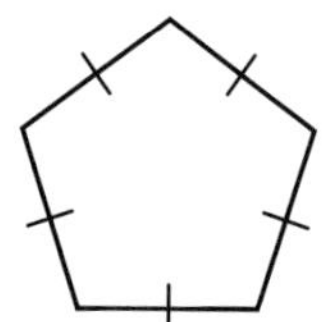

6. 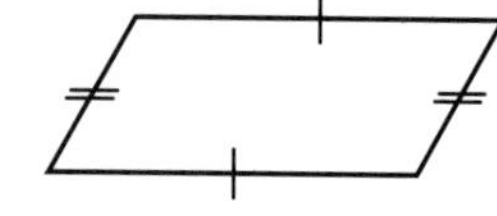

7. 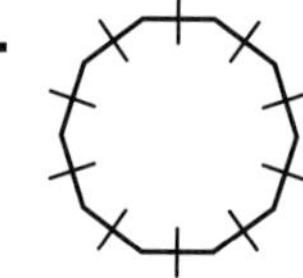

Write *polygon* or *not a polygon* to classify each figure. If possible, find the measure of each missing angle.

8. 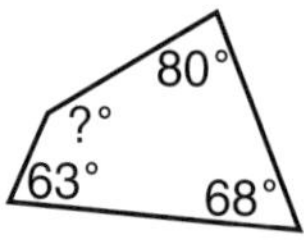

9. 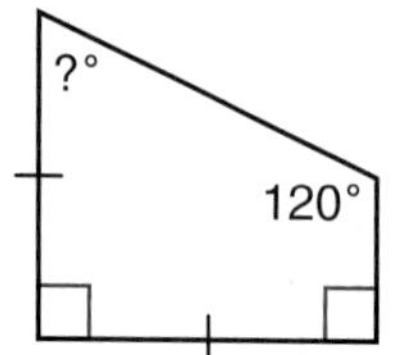

10. 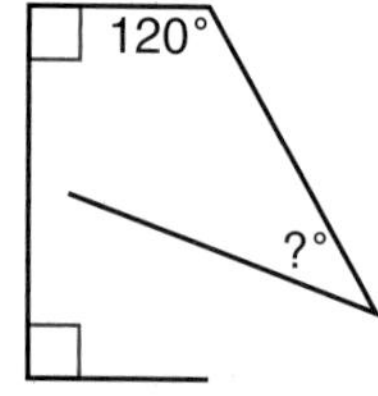

11. 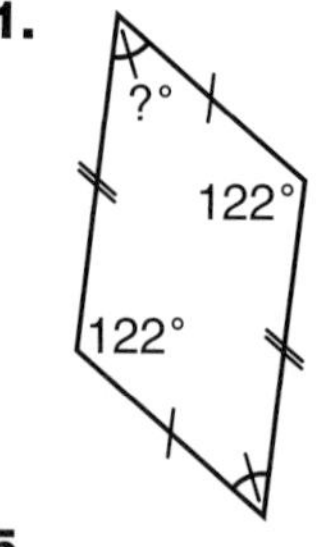

12. 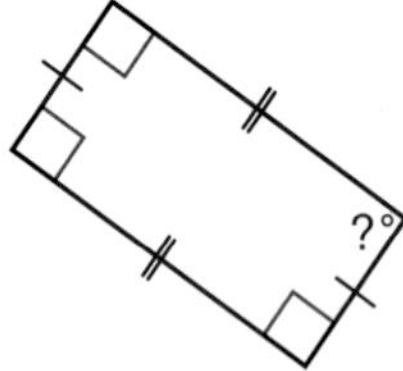

13. 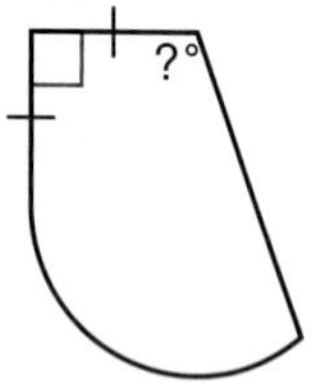

14. 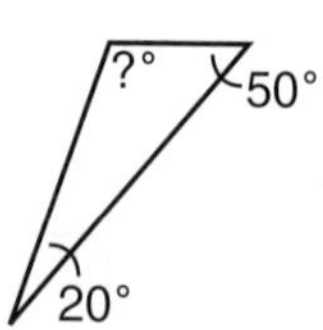

15. 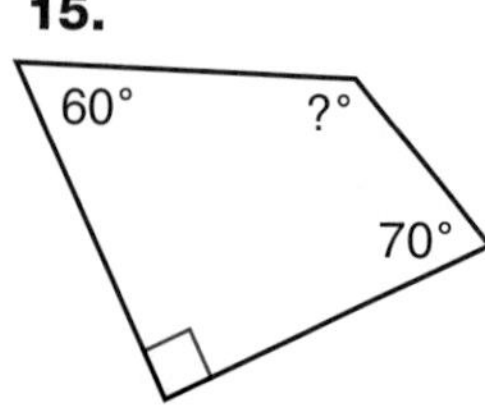

Solve.

16. Draw a quadrilateral that is not a parallelogram and has two pairs of congruent sides.

17. Draw several parallelograms, including special cases—squares, rectangles, and rhombi. For each figure draw the diagonals. In which kind of parallelogram are the diagonals perpendicular? congruent?

18. Is every square a rhombus? Is every rhombus a square? Explain.

Extra Practice See page 419, Set D.

Math Reasoning

Sum It Up

Activity

The sum of the angle measures of a triangle is 180°. You can use that fact to find the sum of the angle measures of any polygon.

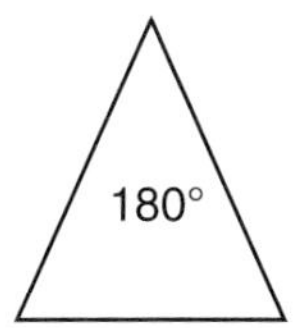

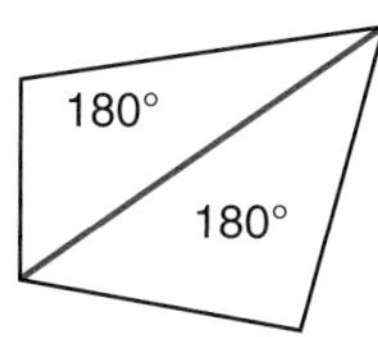

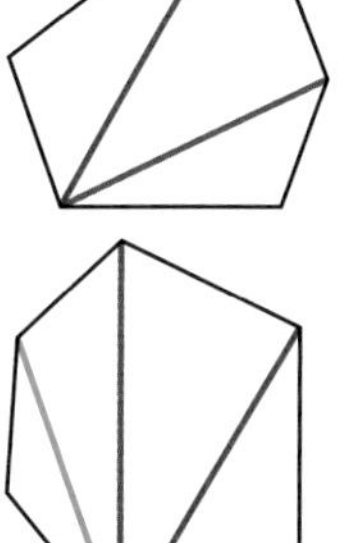

Complete the table below. Then answer these questions.

1. What pattern do you see between the number of sides of the polygon and the number of interior triangles?
2. Write a formula for finding the sum of the angle measures in any polygon.
3. Use your formula to find the number of degrees in an octagon.

Number of Sides	Number of Interior Triangles	Sum of Angles	180° × ?
3	1	180°	180° ×
4	2	360°	180° ×
5	3	540°	180° ×
6	4		180° ×

Quick Check

Check your understanding of Lessons 1–5.

Classify each figure in as many ways as possible. (Lessons 1–2)

1. 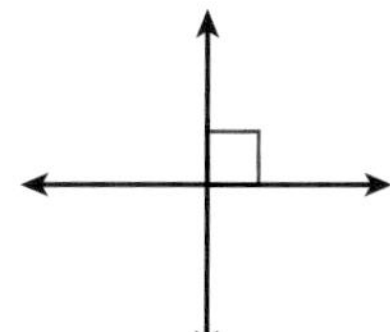

2. 

3. 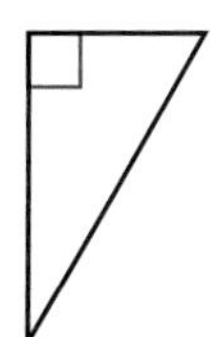

4. 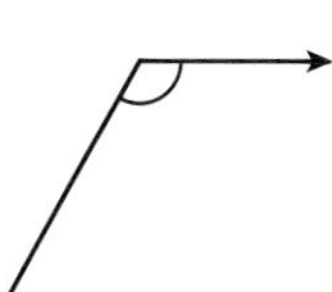

5. 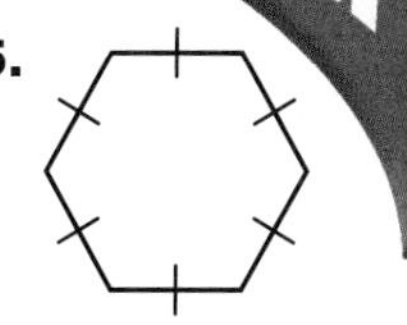

Find the missing angle measures. (Lessons 3–4)

6. 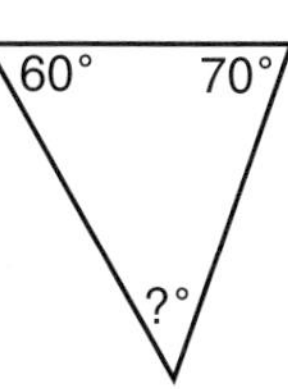

7. 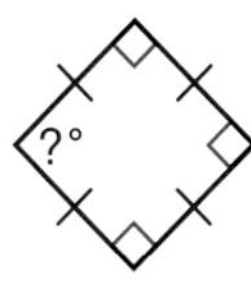

8. 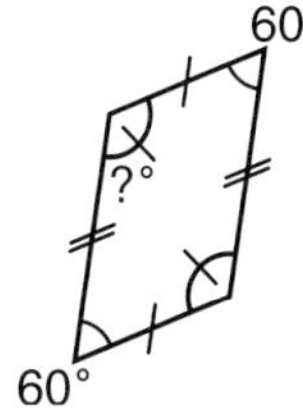

9. 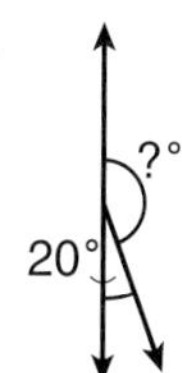

10. Are the figures in Exercises 2 and 8 congruent? Explain how you know. (Lesson 5)

Hands On Lesson 6

Audio Tutor 2/10 Listen and Understand

Rotations, Reflections, and Translations

Objective Identify and model translations, rotations, and reflections.

Vocabulary
- transformation
- reflection
- rotation
- translation

Work Together

Materials
grid paper
ruler

A **transformation** changes the position, but not the shape, of a plane figure. Reflections, rotations, and translations are three kinds of transformations.

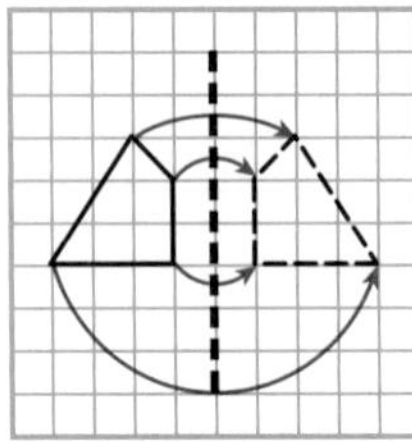

reflection
figure flips over a line

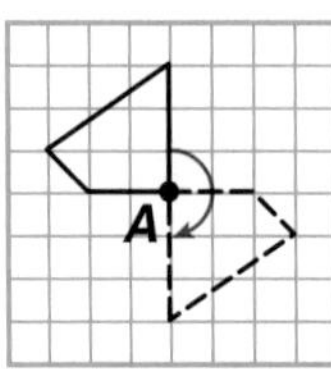

rotation
figure turns about a point

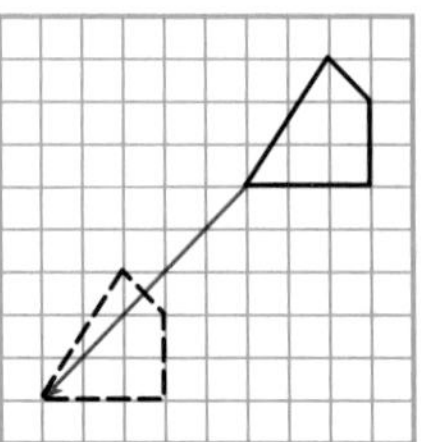

translation
figure slides a given distance in a given direction

You can describe a rotation using the 360° of a circle.

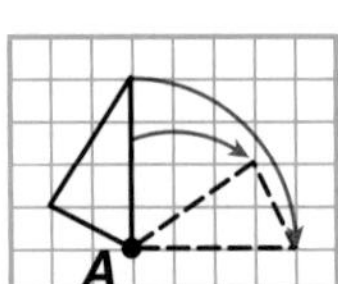

90°
a quarter turn clockwise about point *A*

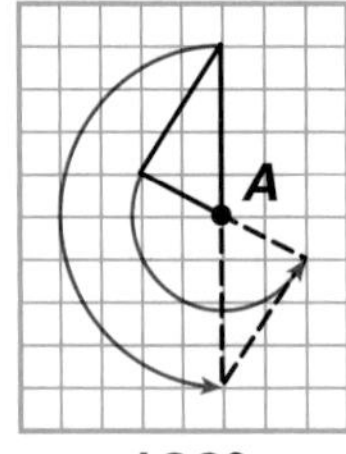

180°
a half turn counterclockwise about point *A*

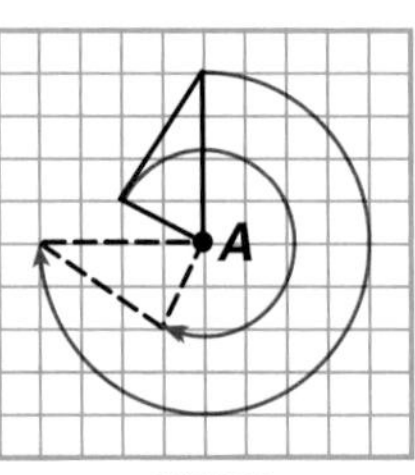

270°
a three-quarter turn clockwise about point *A*

Work with a partner to model transformations.

STEP 1 Use a ruler to draw a right triangle on grid paper. Shade and cut out the triangle.

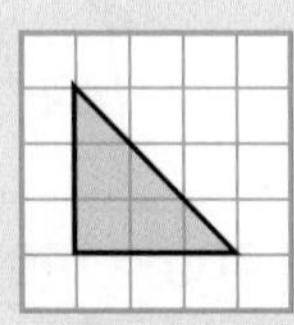

STEP 2 Outline the cut-out triangle on a new sheet of grid paper. Label the triangle with *A*. Then draw and label point *O* on the grid paper as shown.

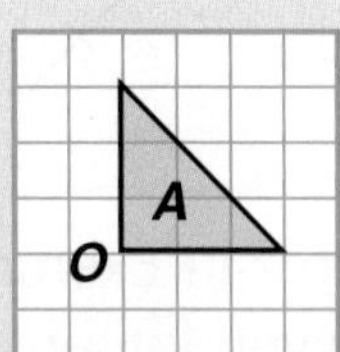

Rotate triangle A a half turn counterclockwise about point O. Outline the triangle. Label the triangle with B.

- What transformation did you perform?
- How many degrees did you rotate the triangle?

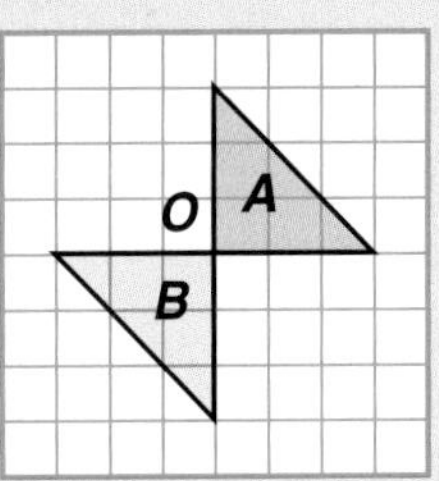

Now reflect triangle B across a vertical line through point O. Outline the triangle. Label the triangle with C.

- What transformation did you perform?

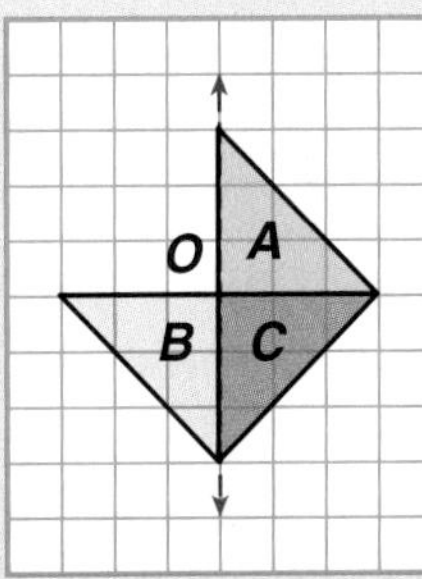

Rotate triangle C a half turn clockwise about point O as shown. Outline the triangle. Label the triangle with D.

- Is triangle D congruent to triangle A? Use a transformation to find out.
- Show another way to use reflections, rotations, or translations to transform triangle A into triangle D.

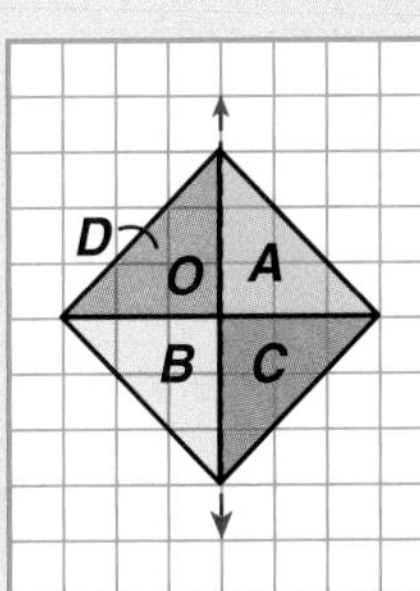

On Your Own

Tell whether each figure shows a translation, reflection, or rotation. If a figure shows a rotation, name the number of degrees of rotation.

1.

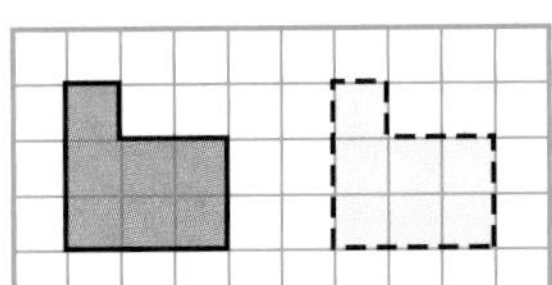

2.

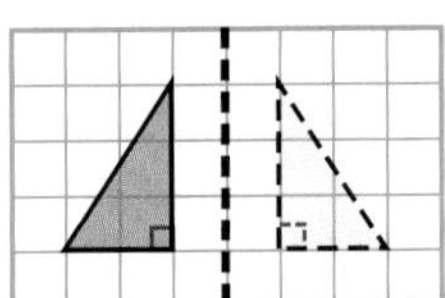

3.

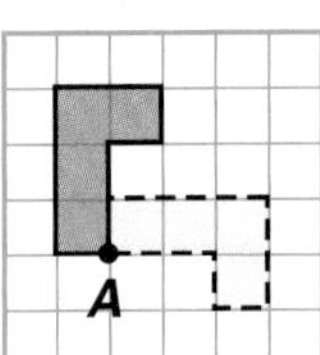

Copy each figure onto grid paper. Then complete the given transformation.

4.

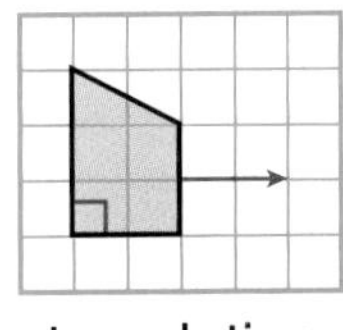

translation

5.

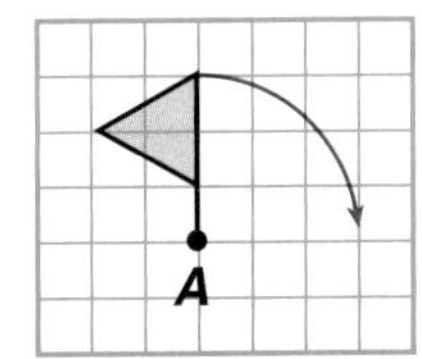

rotation of 90° clockwise

6.

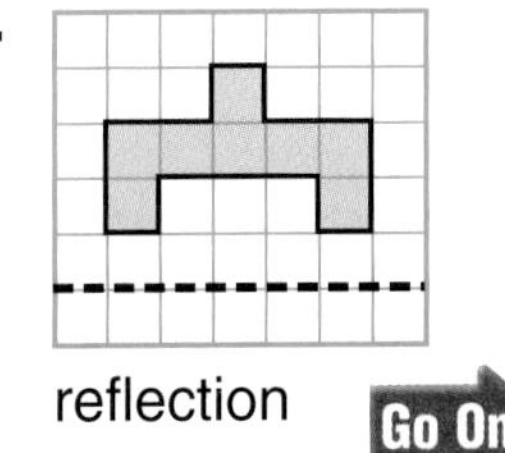

reflection

On grid paper, copy triangle *A*. Label point *O*. Draw and label the figure in each new position for Exercises 7–11.

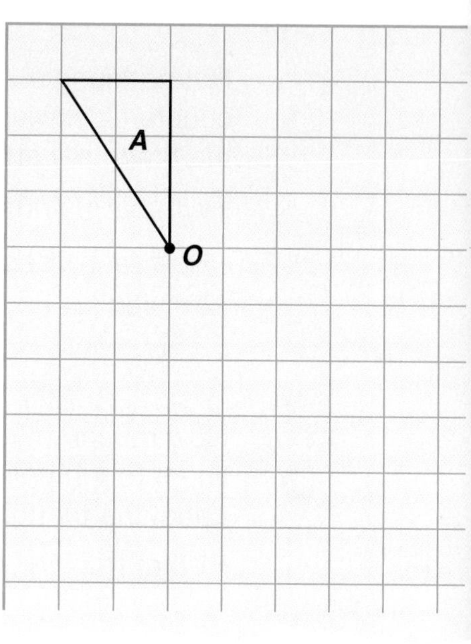

7. Translate triangle *A* 2 units to the right. Label the new triangle *B*.

8. Translate triangle *A* 5 units down. Label the new triangle *C*.

9. Rotate triangle *A* 90° counterclockwise about point *O*. Label the new triangle *D*.

10. Reflect triangle D across a vertical line through point *O*. Label the new triangle *E*.

11. What one transformation can be used to move triangle *A* to the position shown by triangle *E*?

12. Which picture shows a reflection of the shaded figure?

a. 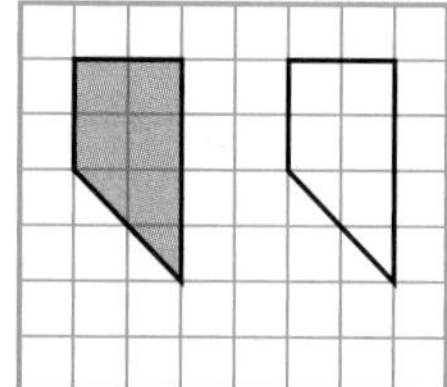

b. 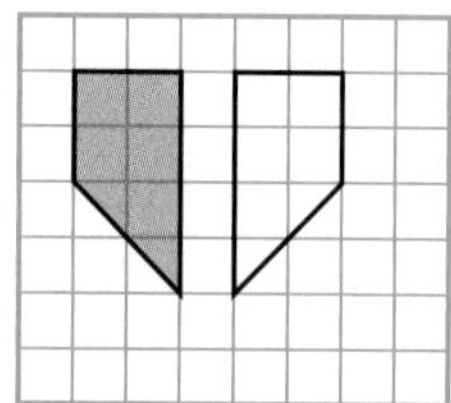

c. 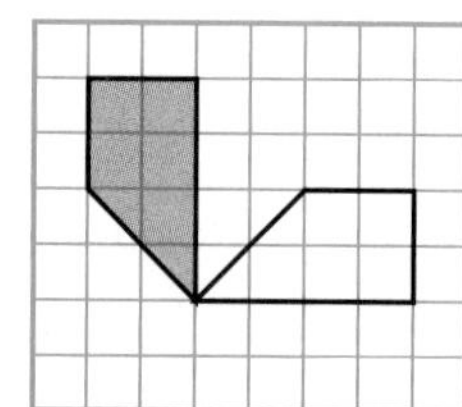

d. 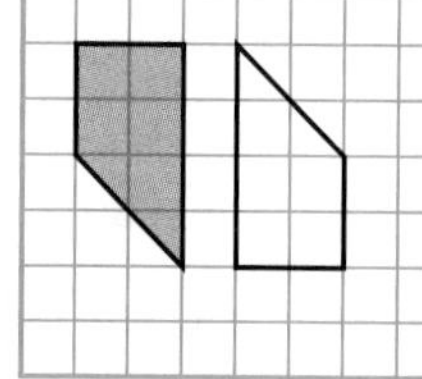

13. Which picture shows a rotation of the shaded figure?

a. 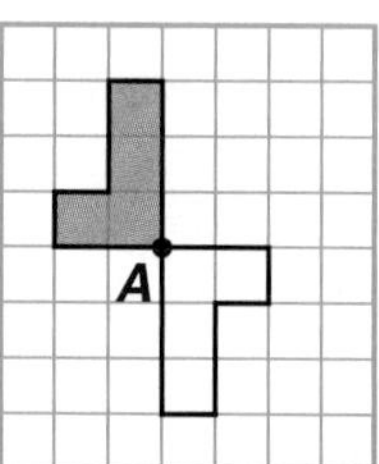

b. 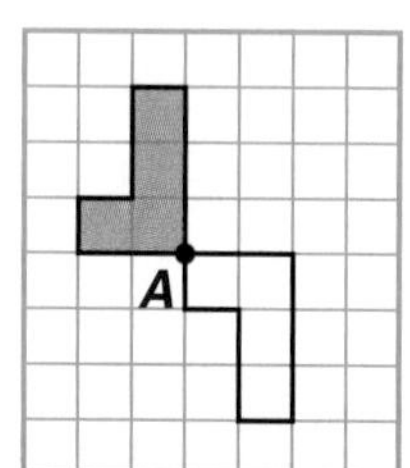

c. 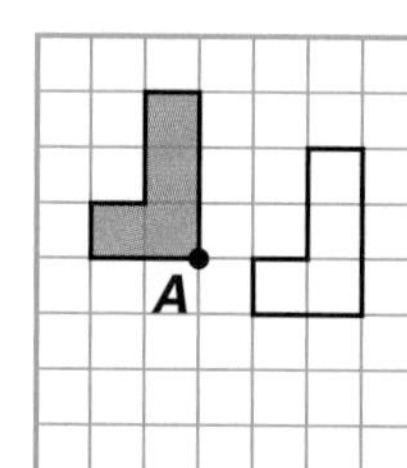

d. 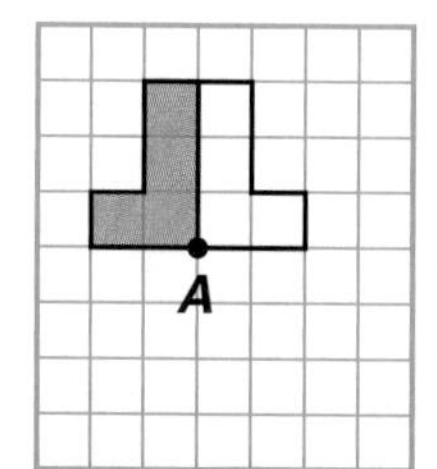

14. Which picture shows a translation of the shaded figure?

a. 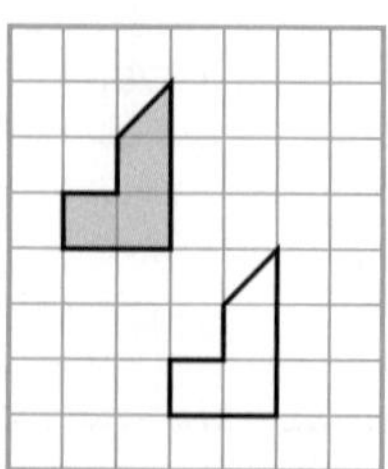

b. 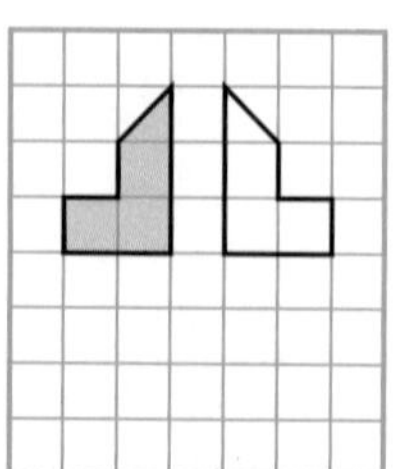

c. 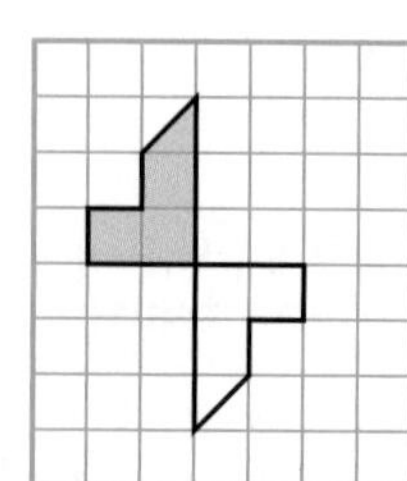

d. 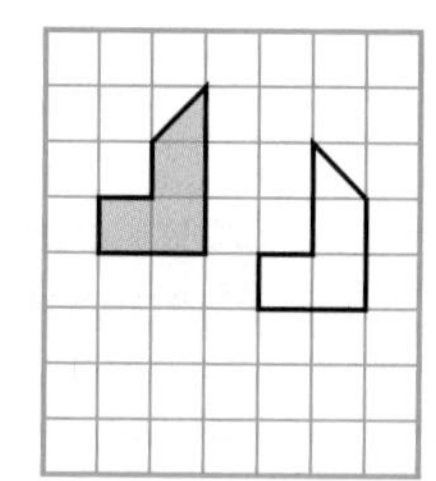

15. Donya says that reflecting a right triangle across its base is the same as rotating it 180° about its right angle. Is she right? Draw a diagram to explain.

16. **Create and Solve** Draw a design on grid paper. Write steps to change the design using rotations, reflections, and translations. Draw the solution.

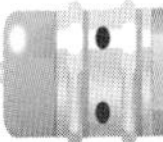

Talk About It • Write About It

You learned how to identify and model reflections, rotations, and translations.

17. Explain how reflections and rotations are alike and different. Use words or a diagram.

18. Explain how rotations, reflections, and translations can help you decide if two figures are congruent.

Game

Activity

Tangrams

2 players

What You'll Need • Learning Tool 52 or a set of tangram pieces like the ones shown.

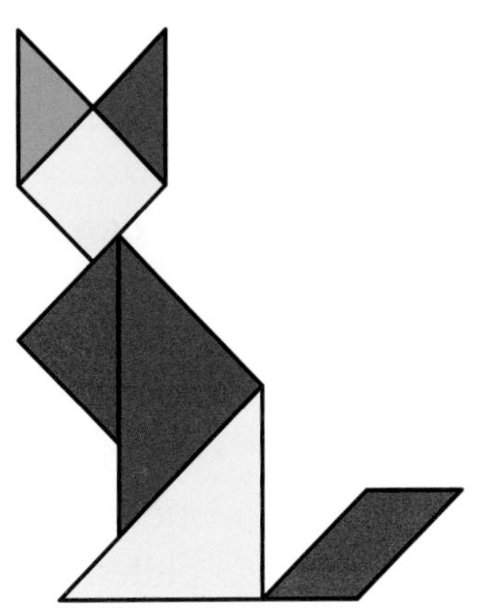

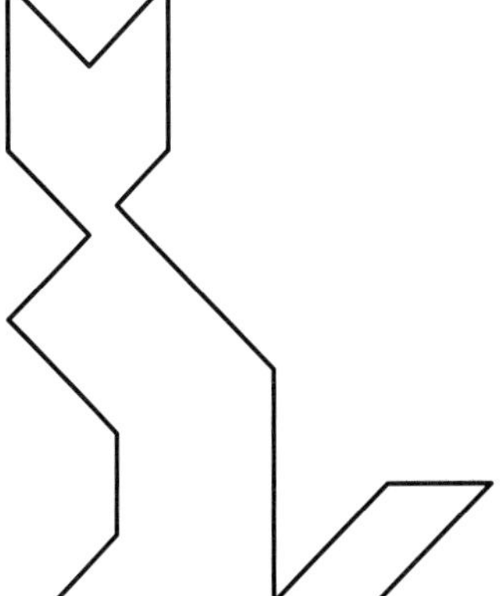

How to Play

1. If you don't have tangrams or Learning Tool 52, you can make your own pieces by tracing the ones on this page and cutting them out.

2. The first player makes a shape with the tangram pieces and traces its outline. The pieces should not overlap. At least some of them should be placed edge to edge.

3. The pieces are removed and mixed up. The second player must decide how to arrange the pieces within the outline, without any overlapping pieces.

4. Take turns repeating Steps 2 and 3.

You may want to make a sketch of your design to help you remember it if your partner can't solve the puzzle.

Lesson 7

Audio Tutor 2/11 Listen and Understand

Problem-Solving Strategy

Make a Model

Objective Make models to solve tiling or tessellation problems.

Problem In social studies class, Vi and her classmates have been studying tessellation patterns from a dome on a building. A tessellation is a repeating pattern that covers a plane without gaps or overlaps. Vi made a tile using four trapezoid pattern blocks. Will Vi's pattern tessellate?

UNDERSTAND

This is what you know:

- A tessellation or tiling is a repeating pattern that covers a plane without gaps or overlaps.
- There are four trapezoids in the pattern.

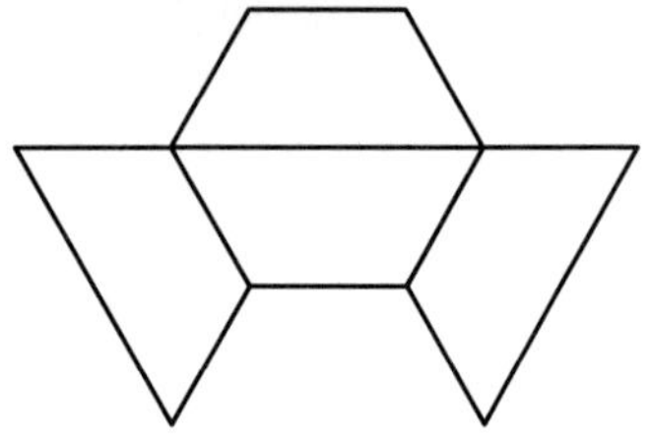

PLAN

You can make a model to help you solve the problem.

SOLVE

- Use pattern blocks to make a model of Vi's pattern. Trace the pattern and cut it out.
- You know that a translation moves a figure a given distance in a given direction. So you can translate the pattern to begin the tessellation.
- You know that you can rotate figures 180°. So use rotation to fill in the gaps.

Solution: Vi's pattern tessellates.

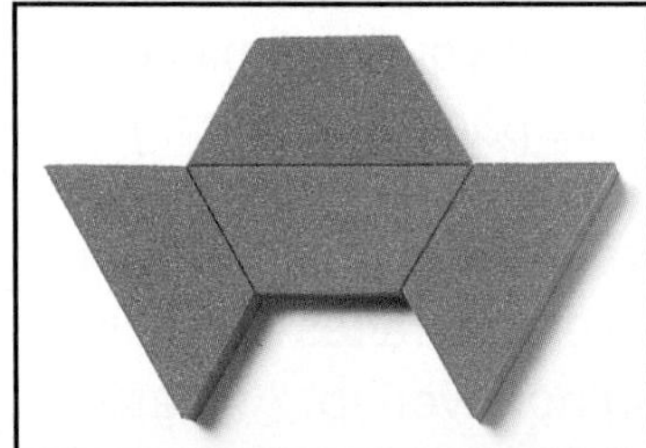

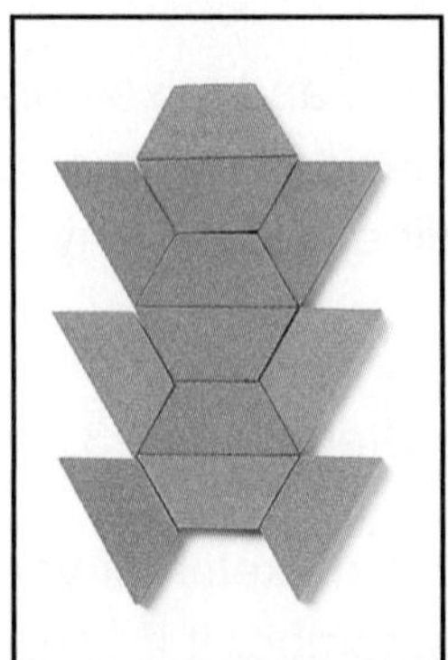

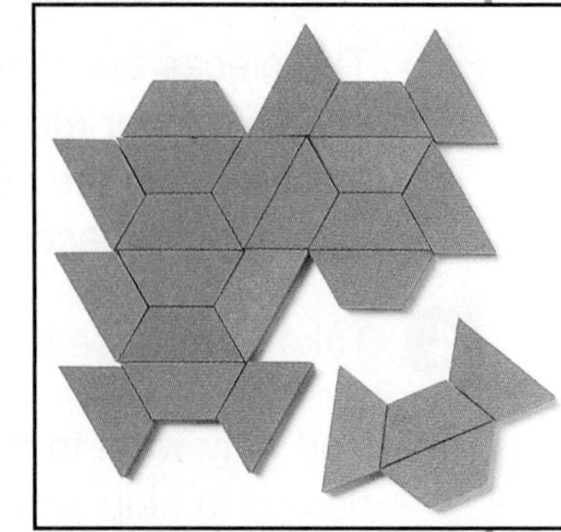

LOOK BACK

Look back at the problem. Can you use a different strategy to check the answer?

Guided Practice

Use the Ask Yourself questions to help you solve each problem.

1. Hamid cut a small square from one side of a large square and translated it to the other side of the square. Will Hamid's pattern tessellate?

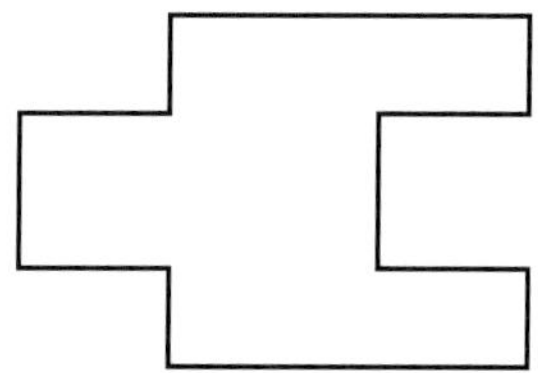

2. Jan cut out two pentagons. Only one pentagon tessellates. Which one is it?

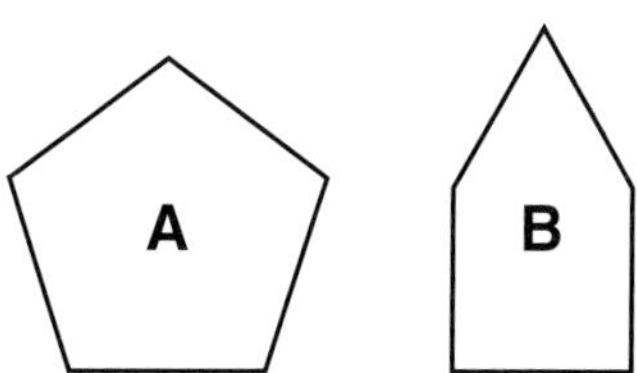

Hint: To tessellate, the sum of the angles that meet must be 360°.

Ask Yourself

UNDERSTAND What facts do I know?

PLAN Did I make a model?

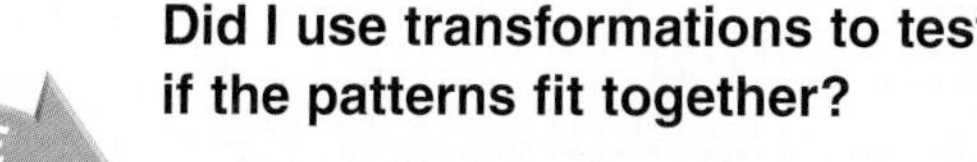

SOLVE Did I use transformations to test if the patterns fit together?

- Did I repeat the pattern enough so I could see if it tessellated?
- Did I tile the plane without gaps or overlaps?

LOOK BACK Did I solve the problem?

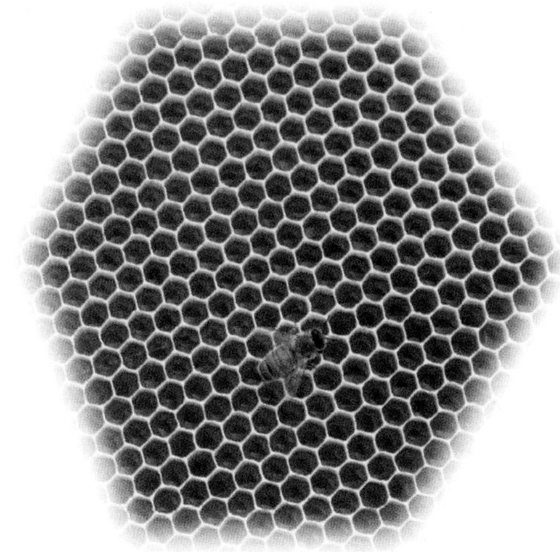

Independent Practice

Make a model to solve each problem.

3. Brittany designed this pattern. Will it tessellate? Explain why or why not.

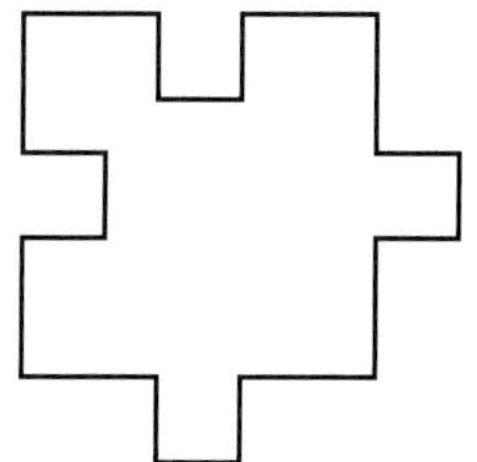

4. **What's Wrong?** Ricky said that a regular octagon will tessellate. Is he right or wrong? How do you know?

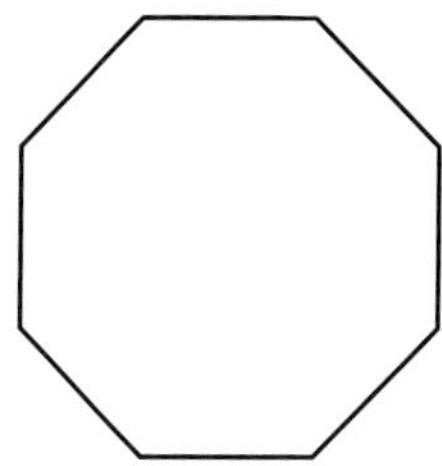

5. **Create and Solve** Start with a rectangle. Create a pattern that will tessellate. Then create a different pattern that will not tessellate. Trade patterns with a classmate. Then tell which of the two patterns will tessellate.

Mixed Problem Solving

Solve. Show your work. Tell what strategy you used.

6. A panel of 5 architects sit in a row. Juan is to the right of Mike. Mavis is to the left of Tara. Mike is on Yuki's right. Juan is on one end. Name their order from left to right.

7. A building has 264 windows. There are three times as many rectangular windows as circular windows. How many of each kind of window are there?

8. Lita uses cubes to design a building. For the top four layers she uses 1, 2, 4, and 8 cubes. If she continues this way, which layer will use more than 100 cubes?

You Choose

Strategy
- Draw a Diagram
- Find a Pattern
- Make an Organized List
- Use Logical Reasoning
- Write an Equation

Computation Method
- Mental Math
- Estimation
- Paper and Pencil
- Calculator

Data **The graph at the right shows the tolls to be paid for crossing the George Washington Bridge going into New York. Use the graph for Problems 9–12.**

9. Sue drives her car into New York each Saturday afternoon. How much will she save in 4 weeks if she gets an E-Z Pass instead of paying cash?

10. Bena just got her E-Z Pass bill. She made 5 trips into the city for a cost of $21. How many peak and off-peak trips was that?

11. A car with an E-Z pass has 4 passengers. They travel into New York during peak hours 5 weekdays each week. If they share the cost of the tolls equally, how much do they each pay at the end of each week?

12. Max does not have an E-Z Pass for his 2-axle dual rear-wheel truck, but he does have one for his car. He went to New York twice in off-peak hours with each vehicle. How much more did it cost to drive the truck in?

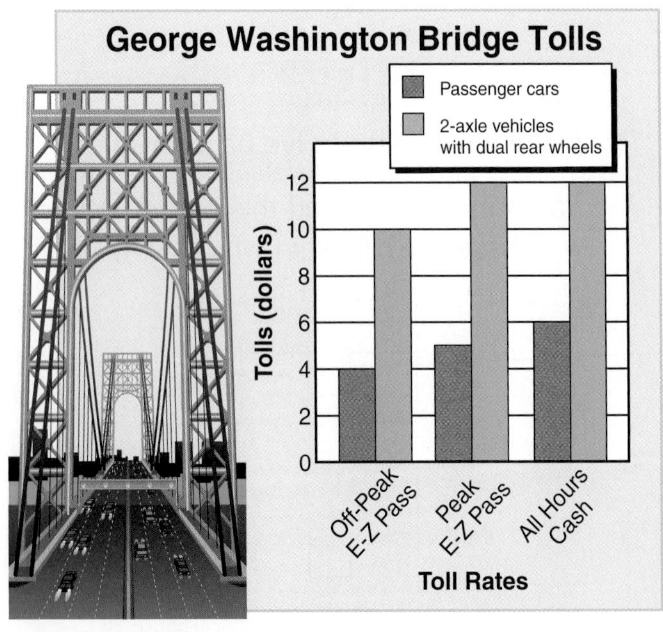

Peak hours: 6–9 A.M. and 4–7 P.M. on weekdays; 12 P.M.–8 P.M. on weekends

Problem Solving on Tests

Multiple Choice

Choose the letter of the correct answer. If a correct answer is not here, choose NH.

1. Use your ruler to measure the length of the segment to the nearest centimeter. How many centimeters less than a meter is this?

A 1 centimeter **C** 94 centimeters

B 6 centimeters **D** NH

(Chapter 6, Lesson 4)

2. In a skyscraper, the first floor is 20 feet tall. All the other floors are 12.5 feet. On which floor is the ceiling 70 feet off the ground?

F 3rd **G** 4th **H** 5th **J** 6th

(Chapter 1, Lesson 6)

Open Response

Solve each problem.

3. The greatest common factor of two numbers is 4. Their least common multiple is 120. Their sum is 52. What are the numbers?

(Chapter 9, Lesson 7)

4. Angie said that all quadrilaterals tessellate. She drew these quadrilaterals to prove she is correct.

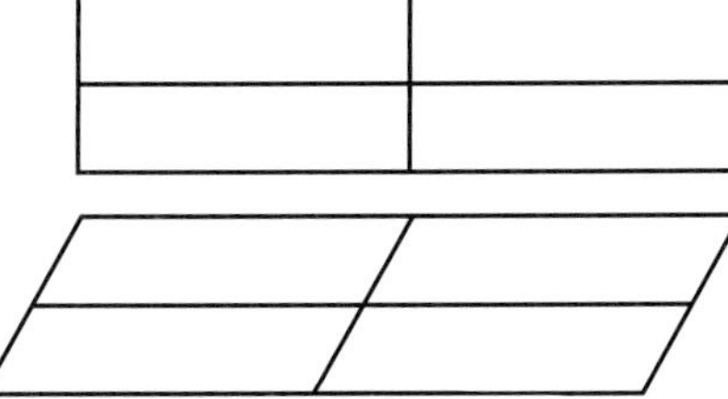

Is Angie correct?

Represent Support your solution by making a model or drawing a picture.

(Chapter 15, Lesson 7)

Extended Response

5. You are shopping for school clothes.

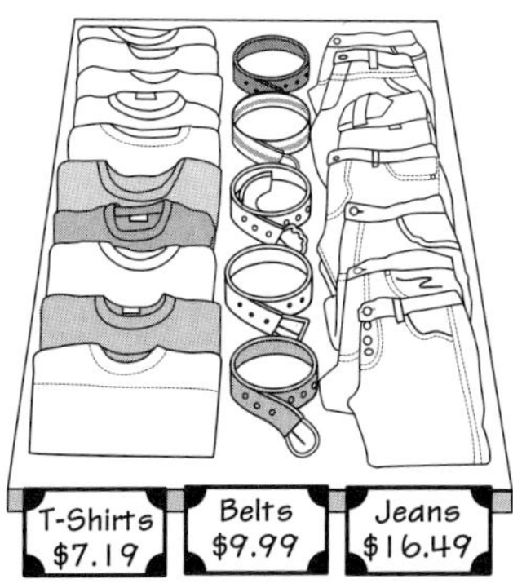

a Decide how to combine the items on sale to create about a week's worth of outfits. How many T-Shirts, belts, and jeans will you buy? Buy at least two of each item.

b Multiply to find the total cost of each type of item. Then find the total cost of your purchase.

c Suppose you bought the same number of each item. If you spent a total of $134.68, how many of each item did you buy?

(Chapter 13, 14)

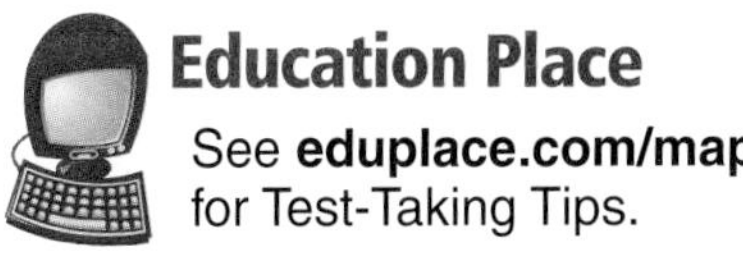

Education Place

See **eduplace.com/map** for Test-Taking Tips.

Circles

Objective Draw circles and construct and identify parts of a circle.

Vocabulary
- center
- radius
- diameter
- chord
- central angle

Materials
safe drawing compass
straightedge

Work Together

A circle is the set of all points in a plane that are the same distance from a given point called the **center**. A safe drawing compass and straightedge can be used to draw a circle and the parts of that circle.

Follow these steps to draw a circle with center *A* and identify parts of a circle.

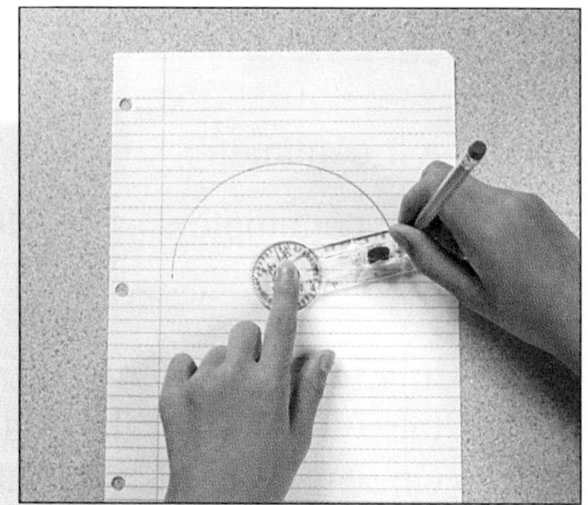

STEP 1
- Draw a point and label it *A*. This is the center of the circle.
- Place the pivot point of your compass on point *A* and move the slider to any measure.
- Insert your pencil in one of the holes in the slider and draw a circle.

STEP 2 A **radius** is a segment that connects the center of a circle to any point on the circle. To draw a radius,
- Label point *B* on the circle.
- Connect *A* and *B* to draw radius $\overline{AB}$.

The plural of *radius* is *radii.* How many radii can a circle have?

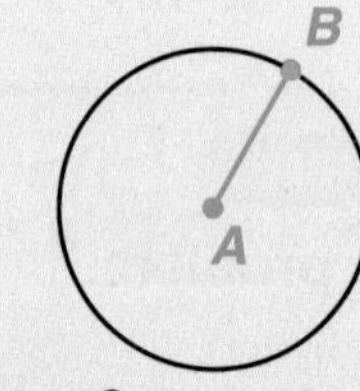

STEP 3 A **diameter** is a segment that connects two points on the circle and passes through the center of the circle. To draw a diameter,
- Draw point *C*. Connect *C* to *A* and extend the segment until it intersects the circle. Label that point *D*.
- $\overline{CD}$ is a diameter.

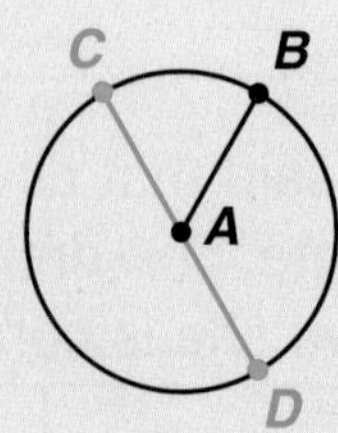

STEP 4 A **chord** is any segment that connects two points on the circle. To draw a chord,
- Draw points *E* and *F* on the circle.
- Draw chord $\overline{EF}$.

Is a diameter of a circle also a chord of that circle?

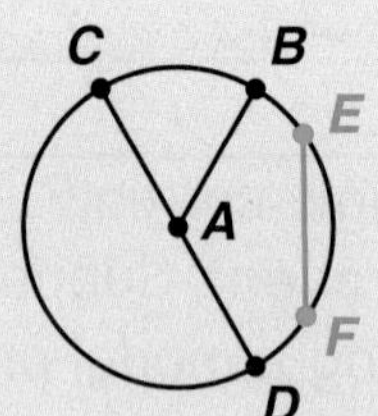

A **central angle** is an angle with its vertex at the center of the circle. To identify a central angle,

- Look for an angle whose vertex is the center point of the circle.
- $\angle CAB$ is a central angle.

Name another central angle of the circle.

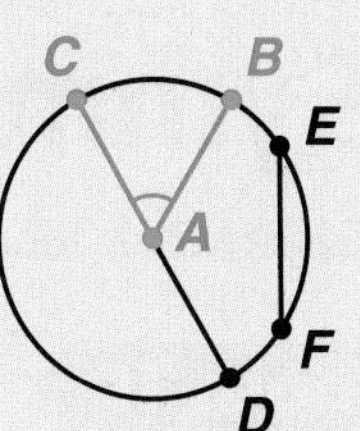

On Your Own

Use symbols to identify the following parts of this circle.

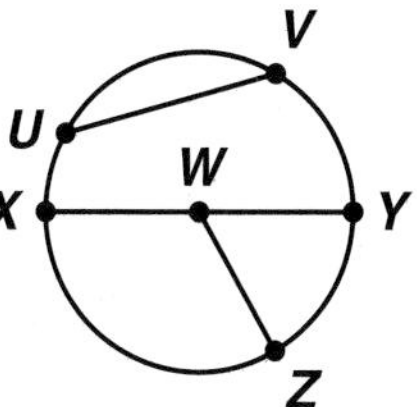

1. radii
2. chords
3. diameter
4. central angles

Classify each figure as a radius, diameter, chord, or central angle. Indicate if more than one term applies.

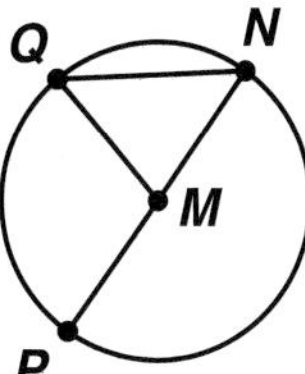

5. $\overline{MP}$
6. $\overline{MQ}$
7. $\angle NMQ$
8. $\overline{QN}$
9. $\overline{NP}$
10. $\angle QMP$

On a separate sheet of paper, construct a circle that contains all of the following.

11. center B
12. radius $\overline{BC}$
13. diameter $\overline{RL}$
14. central angle RBH
15. chord $\overline{CL}$
16. chord $\overline{RH}$
17. For the circle at the right, write a number sentence that can be used to find the missing angle measures. Then solve.

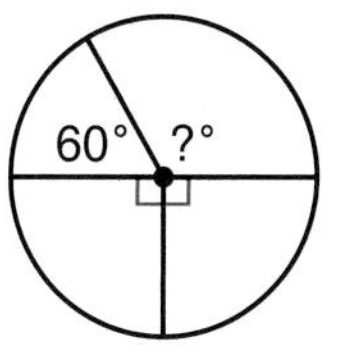

Talk About It • Write About It

18. How are a radius and a diameter of a circle related?
19. A diameter forms two central angles of a circle. What is the sum of the measures of these central angles?

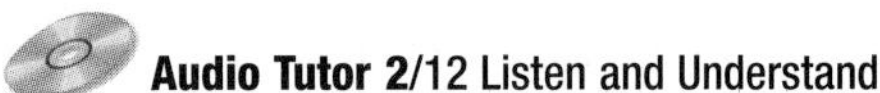

Symmetry

Objective Identify rotational and line symmetry.

Vocabulary

rotational symmetry

line symmetry

Learn About It

Suppose the blades of this windmill make a half turn (180°). How will the appearance of the windmill compare to the way it looks in this picture?

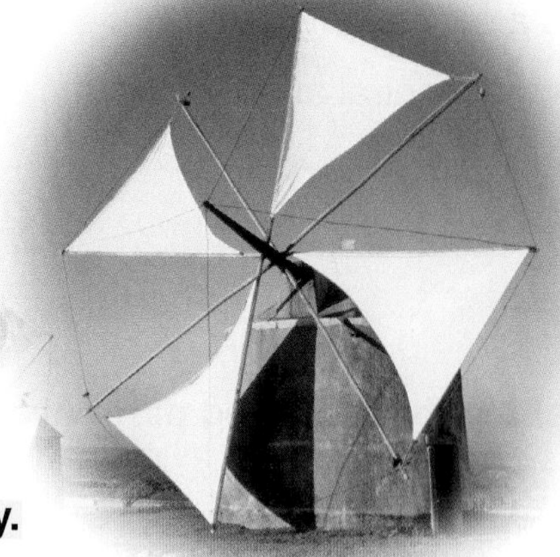

If you can turn a figure less than a full turn about a fixed point and the figure looks exactly the way it did before the turn, that figure has **rotational symmetry.**

Materials
ruler
unlined paper
compass
scissors

Try this activity to explore rotational symmetry.

Remember
full turn = 360°
$\frac{1}{2}$ turn = 180°
$\frac{1}{4}$ turn = 90°

STEP 1 Trace the hexagon at the right and cut it out.

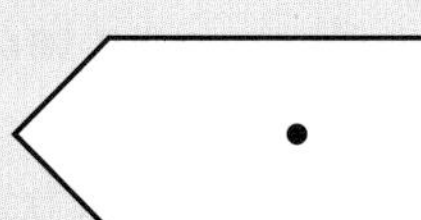

STEP 2 Use a ruler and a compass to draw a circle as shown at the right. Label the circle as shown.

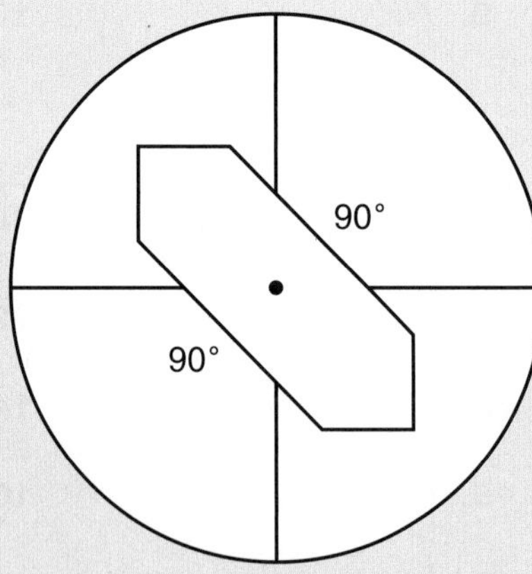

STEP 3 Place the point in the hexagon on the center of the circle. With the point of your pencil, hold the figure at the center point. With your other hand, slowly rotate the figure.

STEP 4 Continue turning until the figure matches the original image.

- What kind of turn resulted in a figure that matched the original image? How many degrees is this?
- Does the hexagon have rotational symmetry?

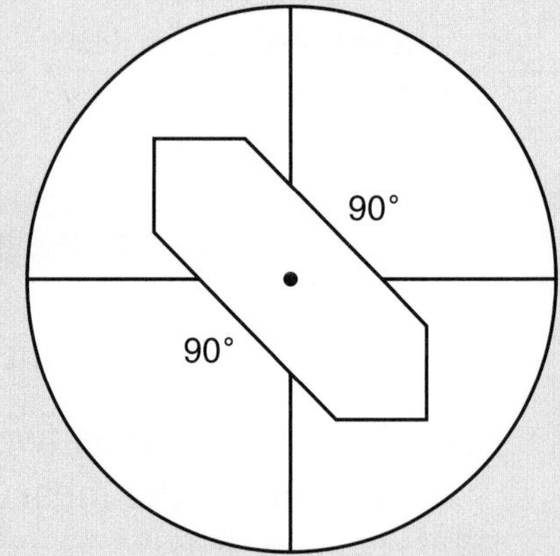

Extra Help at **eduplace.com/map**

If a figure can be folded in half, and the two halves are congruent, the figure has **line symmetry**. The fold is called a line of symmetry.

Try this activity to explore line symmetry.

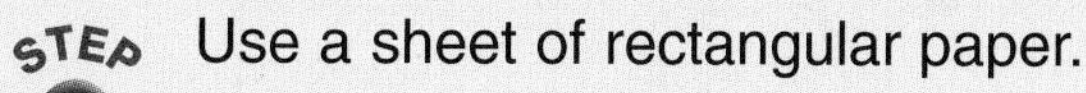

STEP 1 Use a sheet of rectangular paper.

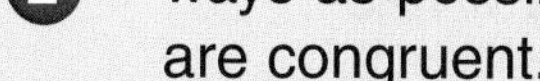

STEP 2 Try to fold the rectangle in as many ways as possible so that both halves are congruent.

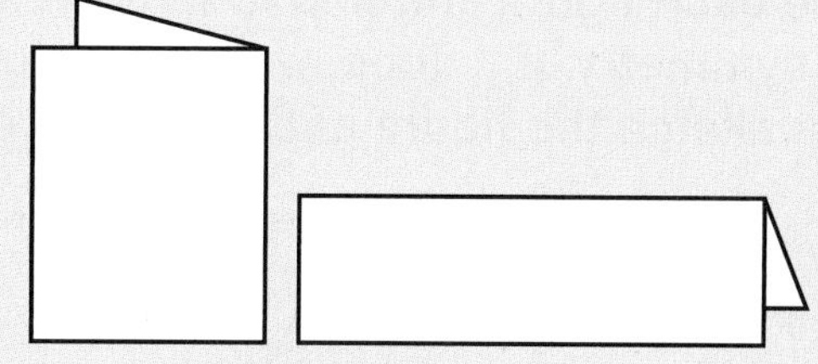

Your rectangle has two lines of symmetry. Draw dashed lines to show the lines of symmetry.

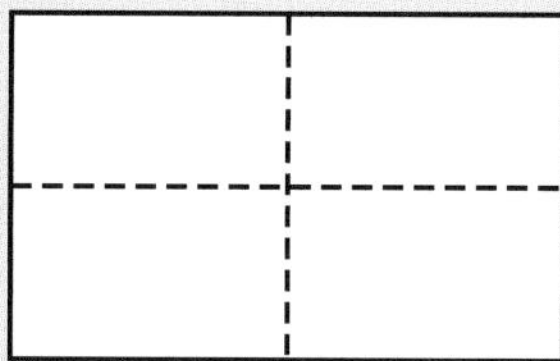

- Can a figure have more than one line of symmetry?
- Try this activity with a square. How many lines of symmetry does a square have?

Guided Practice

Ask Yourself

- Does this figure look exactly the way it did before the turn?
- How many degrees are in a full turn? a half turn? a quarter turn?

Trace each figure and turn it. Write *yes* or *no* to tell if it has rotational symmetry. If it does, tell how many degrees you turned it.

1. 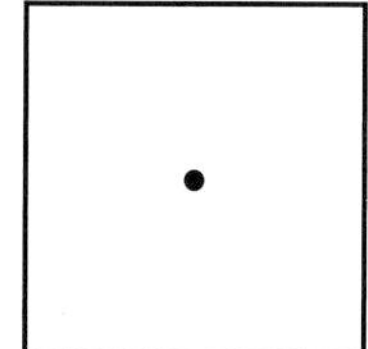

2. 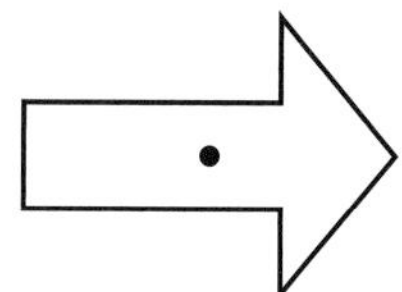

Trace each figure and fold it. Write *yes* or *no* to tell if it has line symmetry. If it does, write the number of lines of symmetry it has.

3. 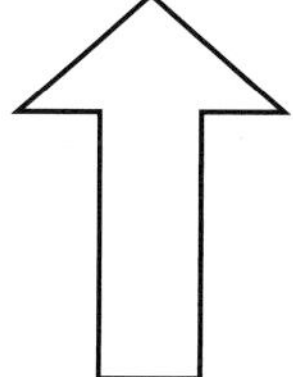

4. 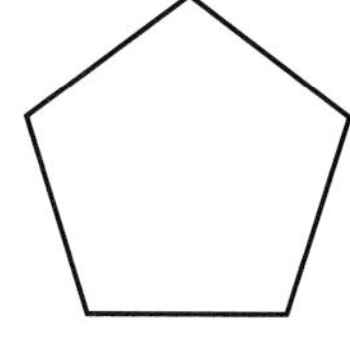

5. 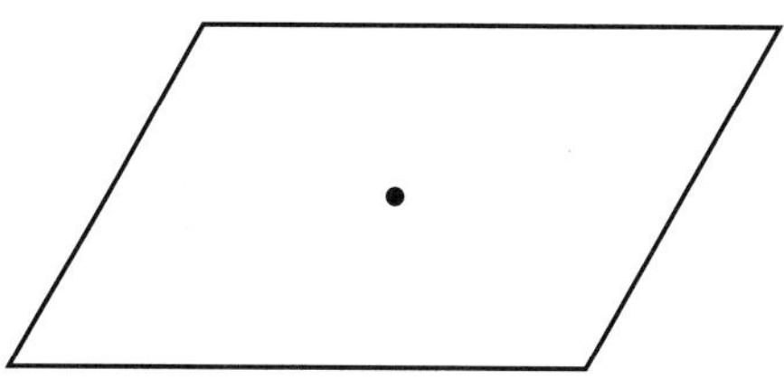

Explain Your Thinking ▶ Can a figure have both line and rotational symmetry? Give an example to support your thinking.

Practice and Problem Solving

Trace each figure and turn it. Write *yes* or *no* to tell if it has rotational symmetry. If it does, tell how many degrees you turned it.

6. 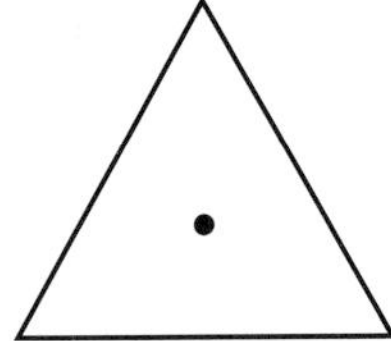

7. 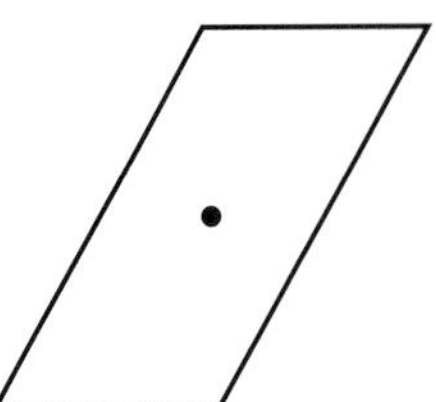

8. 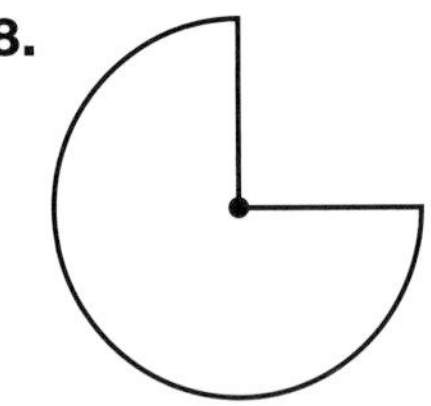

9. 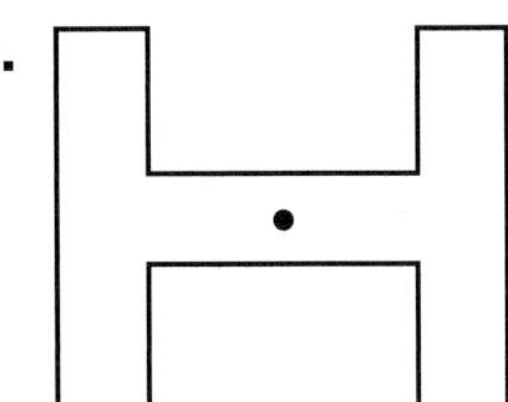

Trace each figure and fold it. Write *yes* or *no* to tell if it has line symmetry. If it does, write the number of lines of symmetry it has. Then sketch the figure and its line(s) of symmetry.

10. 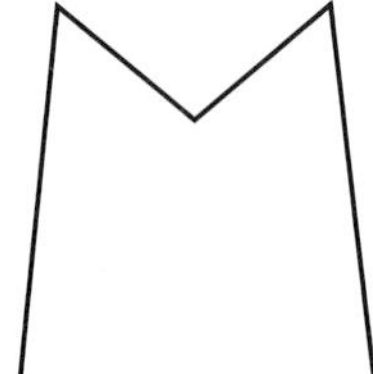

11. 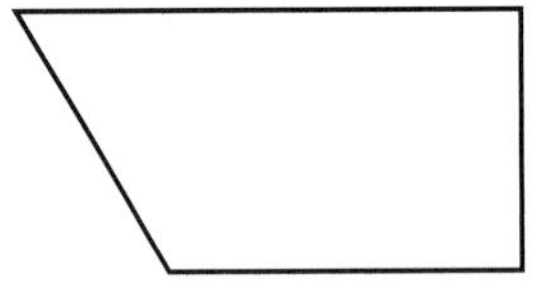

12. 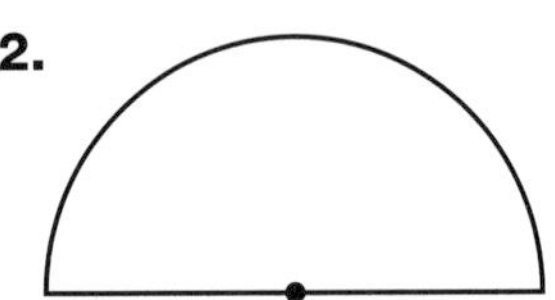

13. 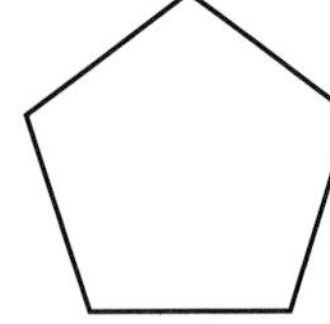

14. 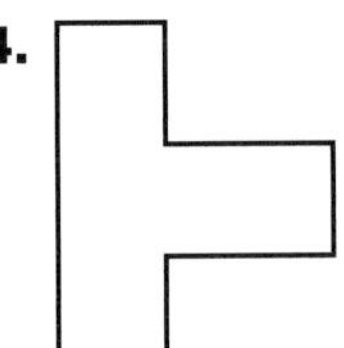

15. 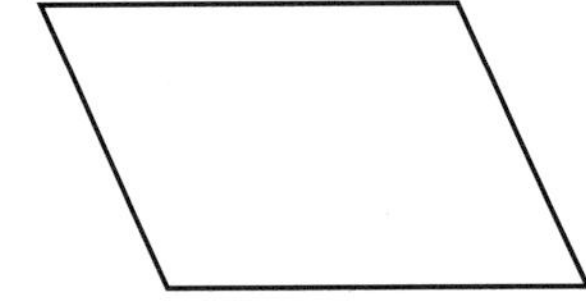

16. 

17. 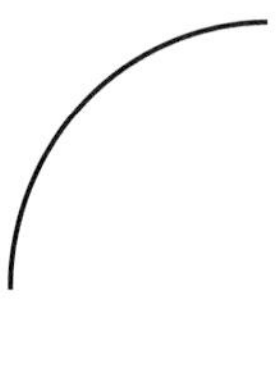

Use a compass and a protractor to draw these figures.

18. a figure that has line symmetry but not rotational symmetry

19. a figure that has rotational symmetry but not line symmetry

Use the photograph at the right for Problems 20–22.

20. Make a list of the geometric shapes you see.

21. Write About It Write a paragraph about the kinds of symmetry you see.

22. You Decide Windows can be squares, rectangles, circles, or semicircles. Draw the front or side of a house that has at least one line of symmetry. Decide on the shape of the house and its windows. Explain how you made it symmetrical.

Mixed Review and Test Prep 

Open Response

Change each fraction to decimal form.
(Ch. 14, Lesson 6)

23. $\frac{4}{11}$

24. $\frac{1}{15}$

25. $\frac{2}{12}$

26. $\frac{7}{9}$

27. Using a straightedge and a compass draw a regular hexagon. Does this hexagon have line symmetry? Does it have rotational symmetry? Explain. (Ch. 15, Lesson 9)

Art Connection

Escher-esque

Activity

M. C. Escher was a famous Dutch artist who used transformations to make unusual tiling or tessellation patterns.

Use what you learned about tessellations in Lesson 7 to make an Escher-like tessellation of your own.

1. To get started draw a square.
2. Draw another figure coming out from the square and then draw a similar figure from the opposite side *inside* the square.
3. Cut out the altered square. This is the stencil.
4. Trace the stencil. Place the stencil so you can trace it again so there are no spaces between the figures.
5. Repeat this process several times, flip the stencil to make another row, and fill in the figures with colors, as you wish.

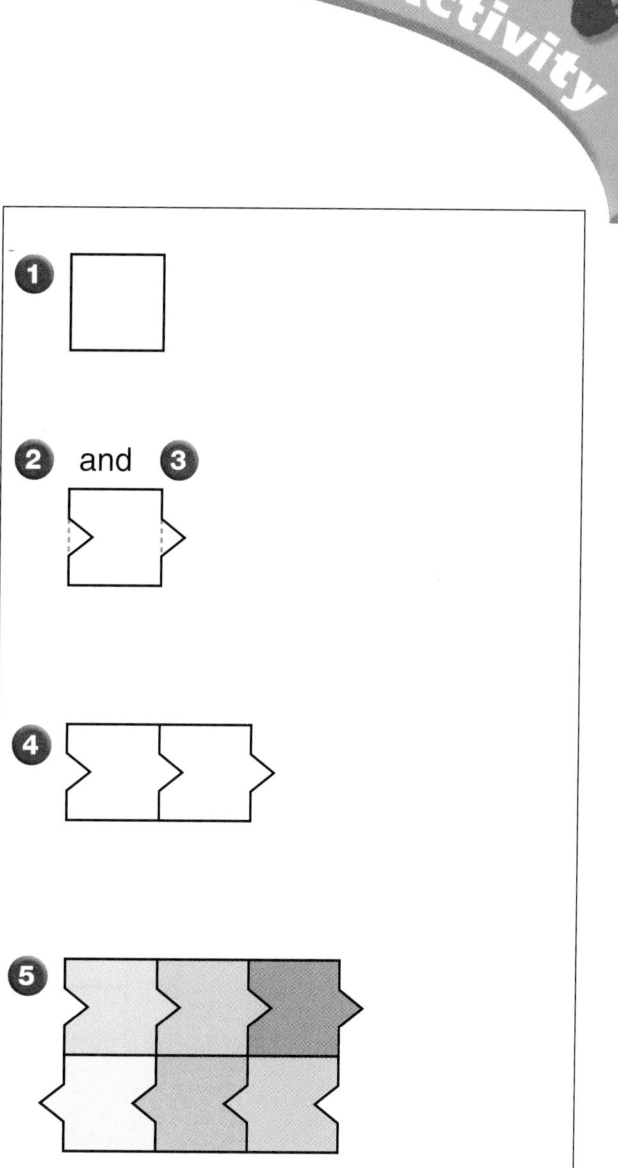

Extra Practice See page 419, Set E.

Chapter Review/Test

VOCABULARY

Vocabulary
- diagonal
- perpendicular
- reflection
- rotation

1. Two lines that intersect at right angles are said to be ____.

2. A ____ occurs when you flip a figure over a line.

CONCEPTS AND SKILLS

3. Identify this figure. Q B

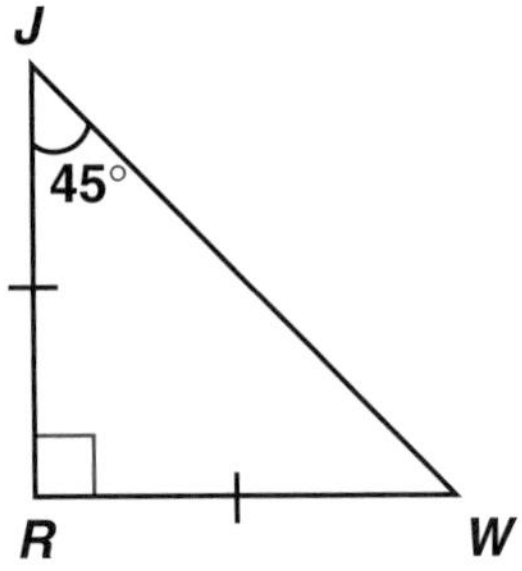

4. Find the missing angle measure in $\triangle RJW$. Then classify the triangle in two ways. (Lessons 2–3, pp. 292–297)

5. Trace each figure. Use a ruler to measure the sides of each figure to the nearest $\frac{1}{16}$ inch. Mark congruent sides. (Lesson 4, pp. 398–399)

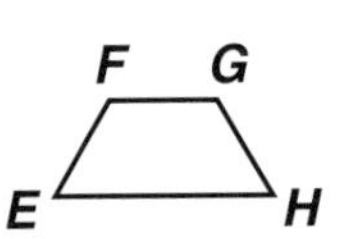

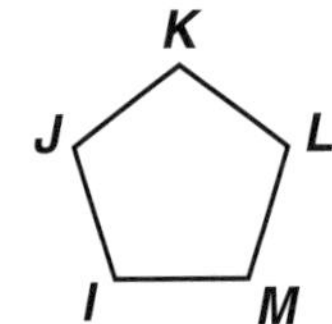

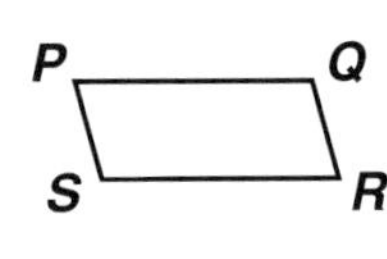

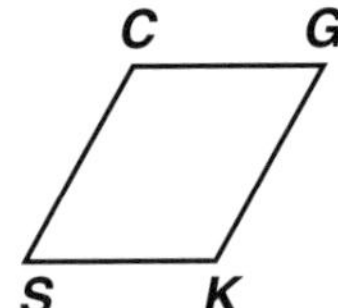

6. Classify *CGKS* in as many ways as possible. (Lesson 5, pp. 400–402)

7. Tell whether *CGKS* has rotational and/or line symmetry. (Lesson 9, pp. 414–417)

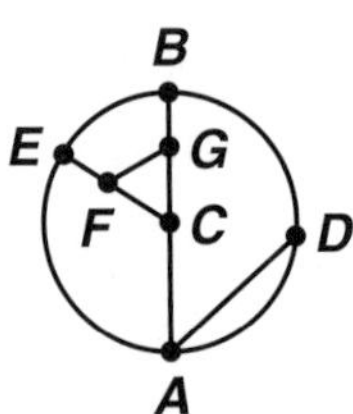

8. Sketch a triangle and its reflection. (Lesson 6, pp. 404–407)

9. In the circle at the right, name each of the following: a radius, a diameter, and a chord. (Lesson 8, pp. 412–413)

PROBLEM SOLVING

Make a model to solve. (Lesson 7, pp. 408–411)

10. Does the figure to the right tessellate? Explain why or why not.

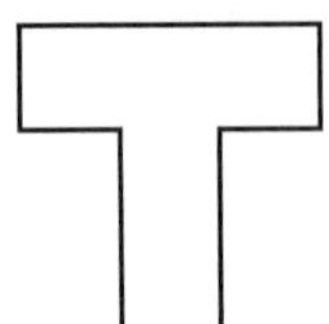

Write About It

Show You Understand

You know that $\triangle JBW$ has line symmetry. Can $\triangle JBW$ be a scalene triangle? Explain how you know.

Extra Practice

Set A (Lesson 1, pp. 390–391)

Name each figure.

2. S L

3. H G

Set B (Lesson 3, pp. 396–397)

Classify each triangle in two ways. Then find the missing angle measures.

1. 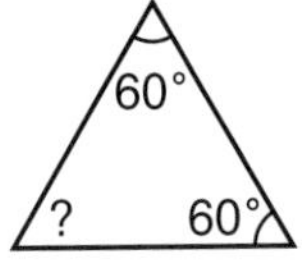

2. 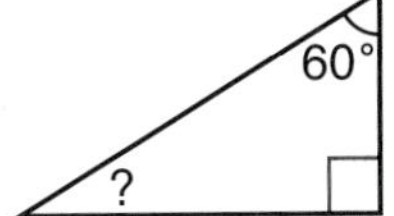

3. 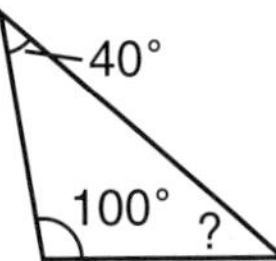

4. 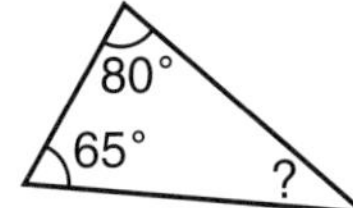

Set C (Lesson 4, pp. 398–399)

Trace each figure. Mark the congruent sides and congruent angles.

1. 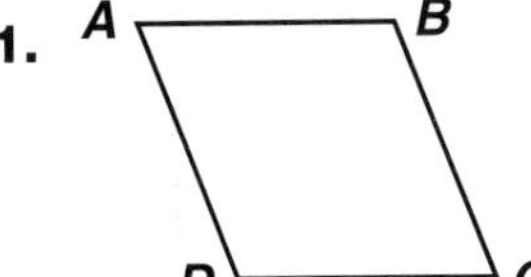

2. 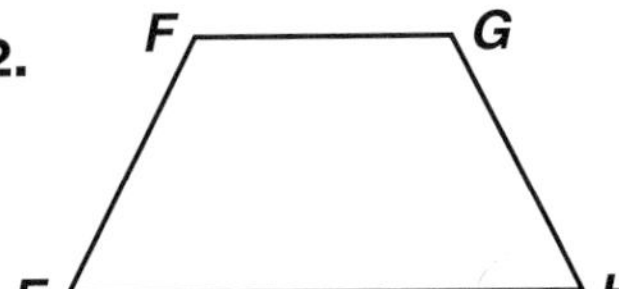

3. 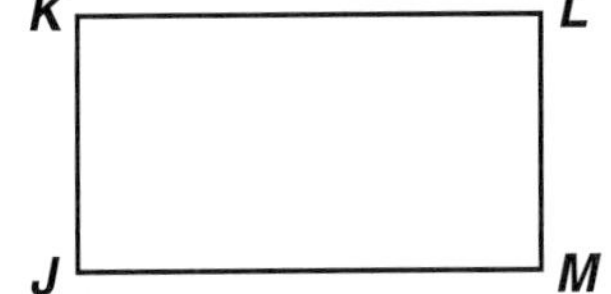

Set D (Lesson 5, pp. 400–403)

Classify each polygon in as many ways as possible.

1. 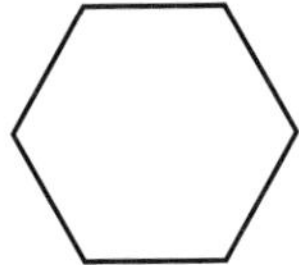

2. 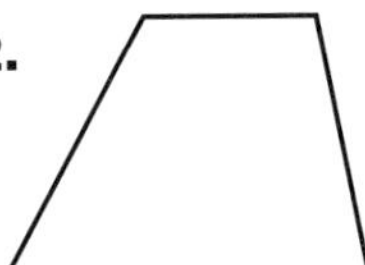

3. 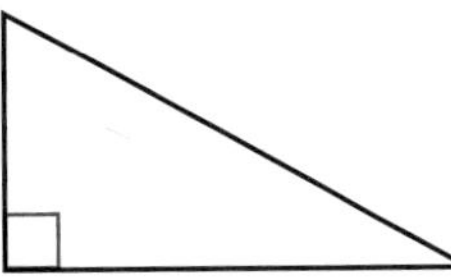

4. 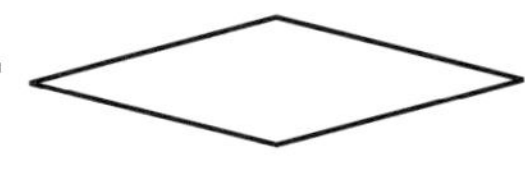

Set E (Lesson 9, pp. 414–417)

Tell whether each figure has rotational symmetry and/or line symmetry.

1. 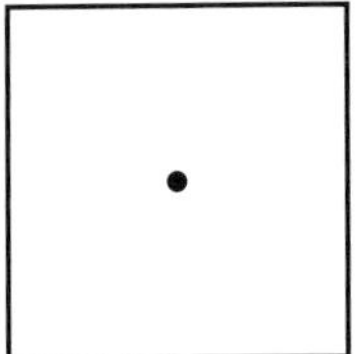

2. 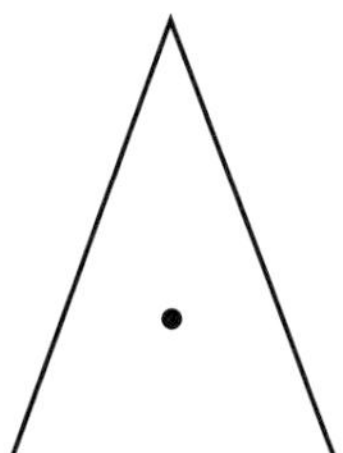

3. 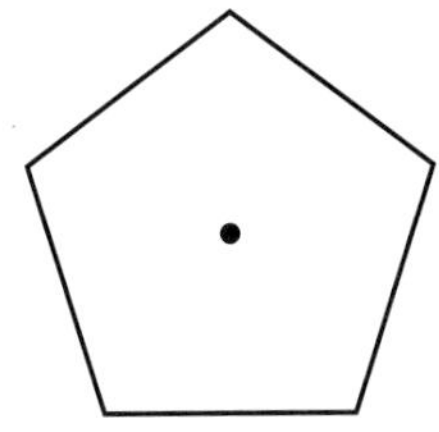

Extra Practice at **eduplace.com/map**

CHAPTER 16

Perimeter, Area, and Circumference

INVESTIGATION

Use Data

Marcy is making a quilt for her bed. It will be 21 inches wider than her bed and 9 inches longer. Find the perimeter and area of her bed and of the quilt she plans to make. How much larger is the quilt than the bed in perimeter and in area?

Marcy's Bed

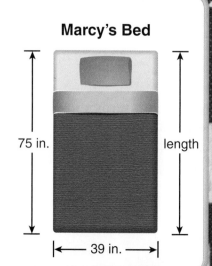

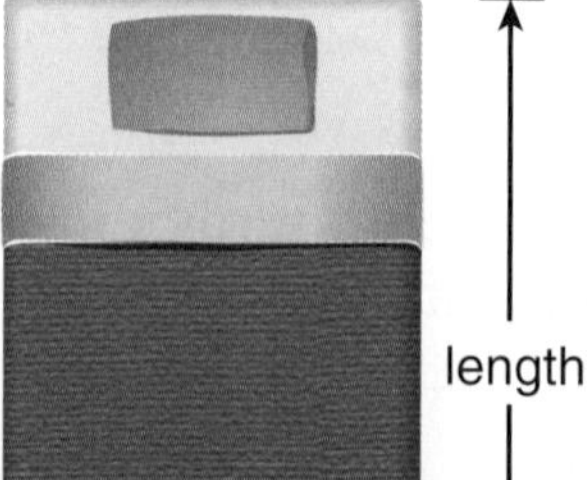

Use What You Know

Use this page to review and remember what you need to know for this chapter.

VOCABULARY

Choose the best word to complete each sentence.

Vocabulary
- right
- square
- triangle
- vertex

1. Two sides of a polygon meet at a point called the ____.

2. A polygon made up of three line segments is called a ____.

3. A quadrilateral with four right angles and four congruent sides is a ____.

CONCEPTS AND SKILLS

Add.

4. $7 + 3\frac{1}{2} + 4\frac{1}{2} + 10$

5. $2.45 + 6.7 + 8.05$

6. $6.2 + 3.91 + 3.91 + 6.2$

7. $3\frac{1}{4} + 5\frac{1}{2} + 1\frac{1}{2} + 6\frac{1}{4}$

Multiply.

8. $3\frac{1}{2} \times 6$

9. 3.14×25

Write About It

10. Copy the figures shown below. Then explain how to separate each figure into one rectangle and two triangles.

Facts Practice, see page 664.

Hands On Lesson 1

Audio Tutor 2/13 Listen and Understand

Perimeter

Objective Find the perimeter of plane figures.

Vocabulary
perimeter

Materials
centimeter grid paper

Learn About It

Lance is putting braid around a picture that is 16 inches long and 14 inches wide for a gift. He needs to find the perimeter of the picture.

Perimeter is the distance around a plane figure. You can measure the perimeter of a plane figure by finding the sum of the lengths of its sides.

STEP 1 On a piece of centimeter grid paper, draw this rectangle.

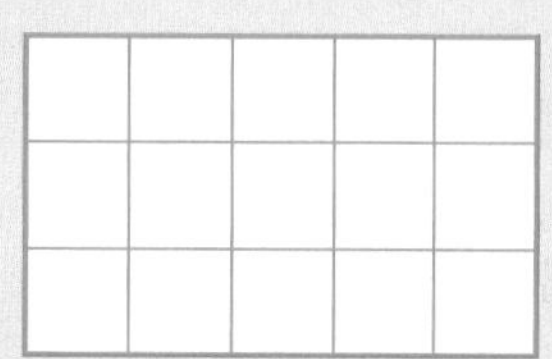

STEP 2 Copy and complete the addition sentence to find the perimeter of the rectangle.

$5 + 3 + \blacksquare + \blacksquare = \_\_\_\_$

You can also use a formula to find the perimeter of a rectangle. If P represents perimeter, l represents length, and w represents width, then:

$$P = l + w + l + w$$
$$= 2 \times l + 2 \times w$$
or
$$2l + 2w$$

You can use formulas to find the perimeter of any square or rectangle.

Using Formulas for Perimeter

Perimeter of a rectangle.

Length is 8 ft and width is 5 ft.

$P = 2l + 2w$

$= (2 \times 8) + (2 \times 5)$

$= 16 + 10$

$= 26$

The perimeter is 26 ft.

8 ft

5 ft

Perimeter of a square.

Each side is 5 mm long.

$P = 4s$

$= 4(5)$

$= 20$

The perimeter is 20 mm.

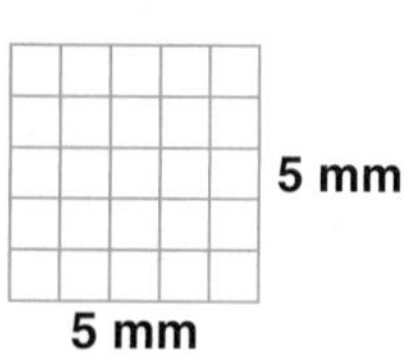

Guided Practice

Ask Yourself

- Can I use $P = 2l + 2w$?
- Can I use $P = 4s$?

Find the perimeter of each figure.

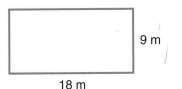

1. 3 in., 4 in.

2. 5 ft, 5 ft

Explain Your Thinking ▶ How much braid does Lance need for the picture shown on page 422? Explain how you know.

Practice and Problem Solving

Find the perimeter or the missing measurement for each rectangle.

3. 9 m, 18 m

4.

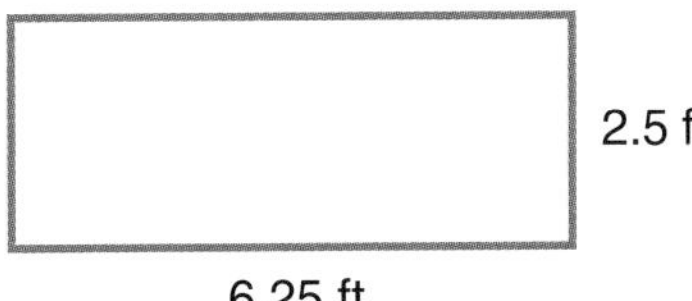

2.5 ft, 6.25 ft

5.

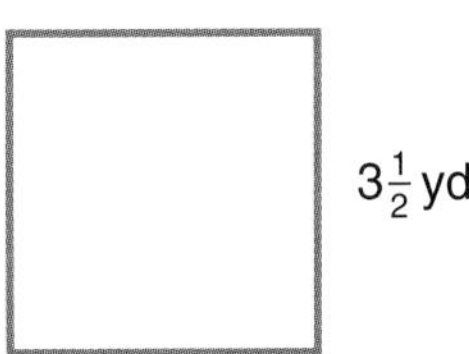

$3\frac{1}{2}$ yd, $3\frac{1}{2}$ yd

6.

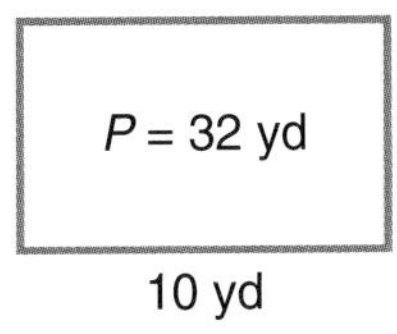

$P = 32$ yd, 10 yd

7. $P = 80$ ft, 20 ft

8. $P = 21.6$ m, 4.1 m

Copy and complete the chart below. Each figure in the chart is a regular figure with sides of 3 centimeters.

	Regular Figure	Addition Expression	Multiplication Expression	Perimeter
9.	pentagon	3 + 3 + 3 + 3 + 3	5 × 3	
10.	hexagon			
11.	octagon			

Solve.

12. A border will be put at the top of the walls in a 12 ft by 16 ft room. What is the maximum length of border that should be bought? Why might less be needed?

13. A rectangular room has sides of 15 feet and 18 feet. You want to use the formula $P = 2l + 2w$. What values would you use for l and w? Does it matter if you switch the values? Explain.

Mixed Review and Test Prep

Open Response

Complete. (Ch. 6, Lessons 2–3)

14. 3 T = ■ lb

15. 6 ft = ■ in.

16. 2 gal = ■ qt

17. 3 lb = ■ oz

18. Find the perimeter of a rectangle with a length of 6 cm and width of 8 cm. (Ch. 16, Lesson 1)

Extra Practice See page 443, Set A.

Lesson 2

Problem-Solving Strategy

Find a Pattern

Objective Use a pattern to solve a problem.

Problem Jenny uses triangular tiles to make the shapes on the right. If the pattern continues, how many tiles will be in the sixth figure in the pattern?

UNDERSTAND

This is what you know:

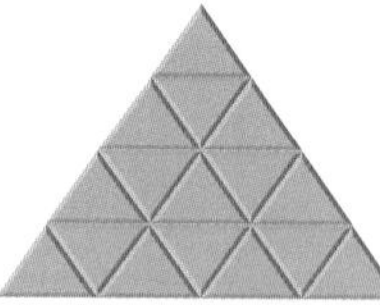

1 tile 4 tiles 9 tiles 16 tiles

PLAN

You can find a pattern to solve the problem.

SOLVE

Make a table to organize the data. Then study the table to find a pattern.

Shape in Pattern	1st	2nd	3rd	4th	5th	6th
Tiles	1	4	9	16	?	?

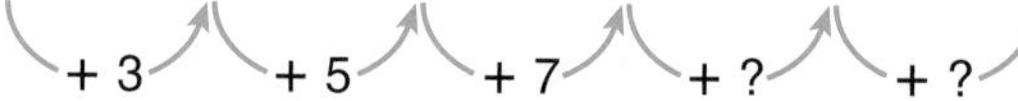

One Pattern

The number of additional tiles needed to make the next figure increases by 2 each time. Use the pattern to complete the table.

$16 + 9 = 25$

$25 + 11 = 36$

Another Pattern

The table shows square numbers:

$1 = 1 \times 1$ $4 = 2 \times 2$

$9 = 3 \times 3$ $16 = 4 \times 4$

Find the next two square numbers:

$5 \times 5 = 25$ $6 \times 6 = 36$

Solution: There will be 36 tiles in the sixth figure.

LOOK BACK

Look back at the problem.
How can I check the answer?

Guided Practice

Use the Ask Yourself questions to help you solve each problem.

1. Look at the figures below. If the pattern continues, how many small squares will be in the fifth figure?

2. Find the seventh figure in the pattern shown below.

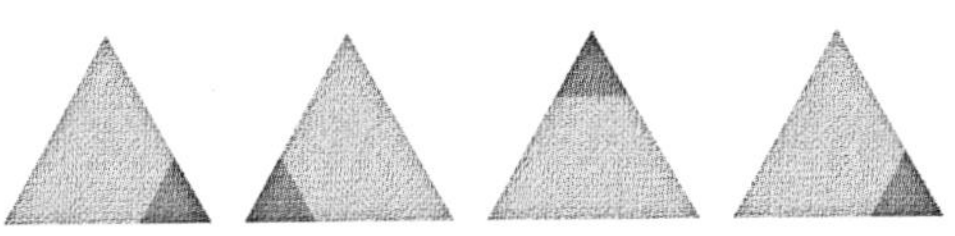

(Hint) Think about how the shape moves.

Ask Yourself

What facts do I know?

What kinds of patterns can I look for?

SOLVE

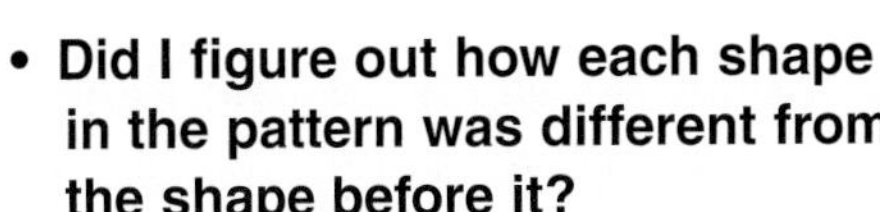

- **Did I figure out how each shape in the pattern was different from the shape before it?**
- **Did I describe the pattern?**
- **Did I continue the pattern?**

LOOK BACK

How can I check the answer?

Independent Practice

Find a pattern to solve each problem.

3. Howard uses triangular tiles to make the figure at the right. If the finished figure has 7 rows, and the pattern continues, how many white tiles are in the figure?

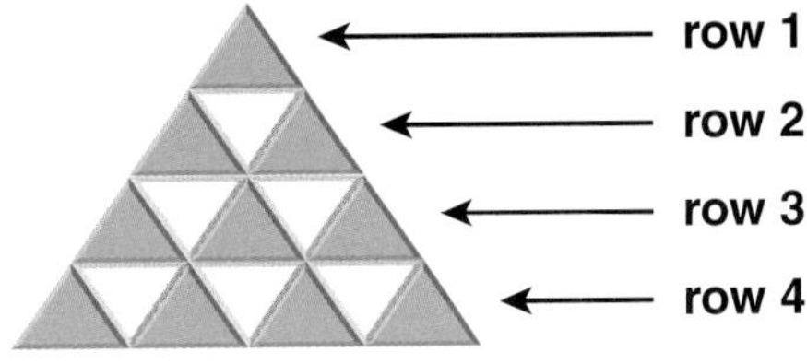

4. Look at these grids. How many squares of any size are there in a 5×5 grid?

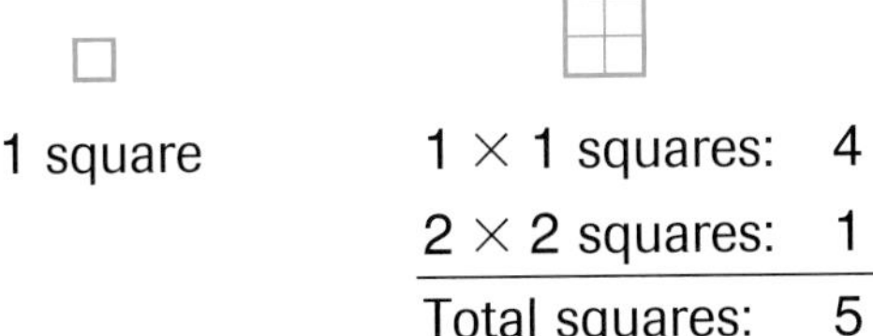

1 square

1×1 squares: 4
2×2 squares: 1
Total squares: 5

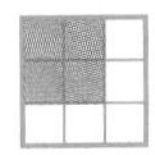

1×1 squares: 9
2×2 squares: 4
3×3 squares: 1
Total squares: ?

5. Find the next three times in the pattern that the shaded triangle will be in the same position as it was in the first shape in the pattern. Explain.

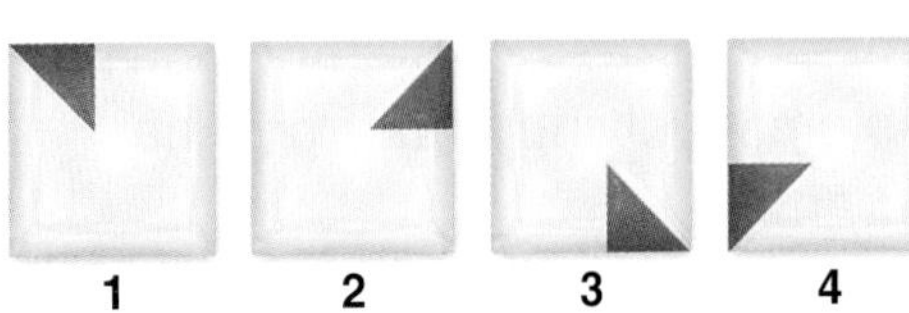

Go On

Mixed Problem Solving

Solve. Show your work. Tell what strategy you used.

6. Emma cleans her couch. She finds 8 coins worth a total of 58¢. What coins does Emma find?

7. Ken cuts a 10-foot long speaker wire into two pieces. The first piece is three times as long as the second piece. How long is each piece of speaker wire?

8. Yossi used blocks to build a pattern. How many blocks will be in the next figure in the pattern?

You Choose

Strategy
- Draw a Diagram
- Find a Pattern
- Guess and Check
- Work Backward
- Write an Equation

Computation Method
- Mental Math
- Estimation
- Paper and Pencil
- Calculator

Data **Use the histogram to solve Problems 9–14.**

The histogram shows how old the houses on Wyoming Avenue were in the year 2000.

9. How many houses are on Wyoming Avenue?

10. How many houses were built more than 30 years before 2000?

11. How many houses were built less than 30 years before 2000?

12. How many houses were built within 10 years before 2000?

13. What years are represented by Age (years) labeled 21–30?

14. **Create and Solve** Write and solve a problem involving data from the histogram.

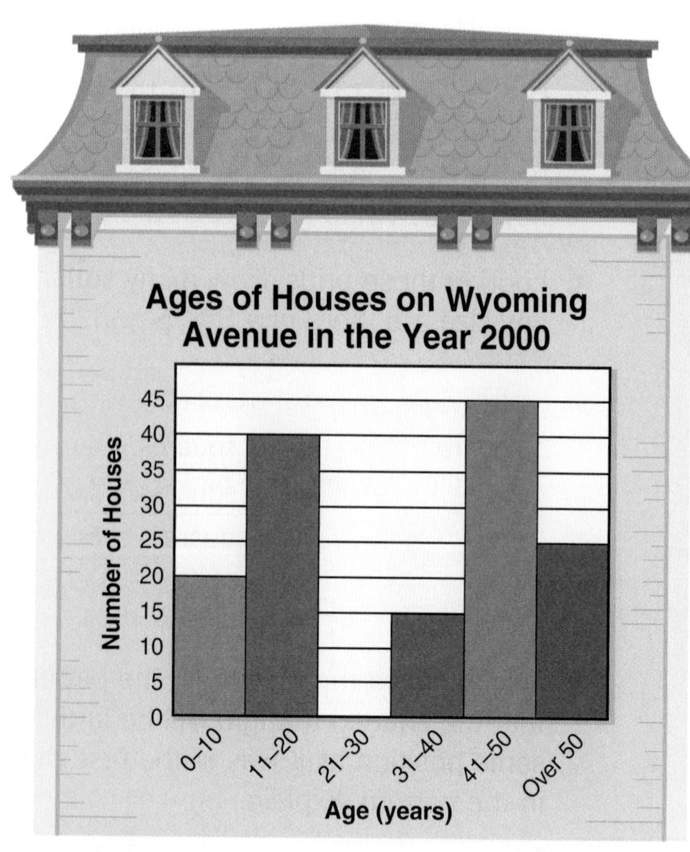

Problem Solving on Tests

Multiple Choice

Choose the letter of the correct answer. If a correct answer is not here, choose NH.

1. Helen is packing her collection of 250 books. Each carton can hold 75 books. How many cartons does Helen need?

   A 2 **B** 3 **C** 4 **D** NH

   (Chapter 14, Lesson 8)

2. What angle measure is missing?

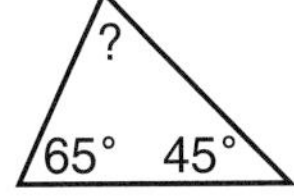

   F 45° **G** 70° **H** 115° **J** NH

   (Chapter 15, Lesson 3)

Open Response

Solve each problem.

3. Two fifths of Mr. Wilson's class of 20 students are in after-school clubs. One third of Mr. Judd's class of 24 students are in after-school clubs. In which class are more students in after-school clubs?

   (Chapter 12, Lesson 2)

4. The table shows the population growth of Marion Falls. If the pattern continues, what will be the population in 2010?

Marion Falls Population			
Year	**1980**	**1990**	**2000**
Population	**4,500**	**4,150**	**3,800**

   Explain How did you find the pattern? How did you use the pattern to solve the problem?

   (Chapter 1, Lesson 6)

Extended Response

`5. You want to make a diagram of a baseball diamond.

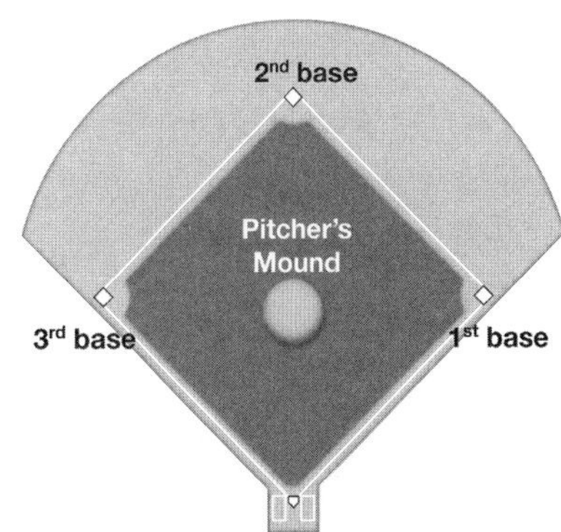

   a Use grid paper. Choose the length of the line segment you will draw to represent the baseline between home plate and first base.

   b Draw a line segment of the same length to represent the baseline between first base and second base. What is the measure of the angle whose vertex is first base?

   c To complete the diamond, draw a reflection of the angle formed by the two line segments. Label the bases and mark the location of the pitcher's mound with a circle.

   d Give the perimeter and area of your baseball diamond. Show how you found your answers.

   (Chapters 15, 16)

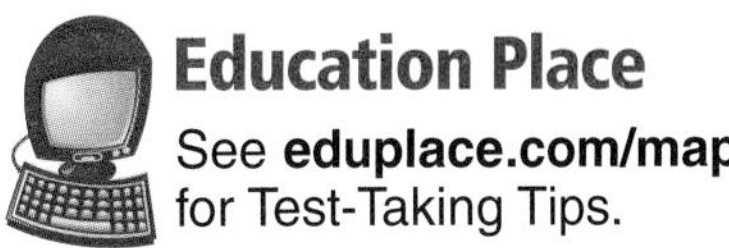

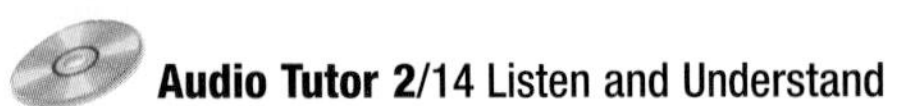

Area of a Parallelogram

Objective Use a formula for the area of parallelograms.

Vocabulary

square unit

area

Materials

centimeter grid paper

ruler

scissors

Learn About It

A hallway is 9 feet × 5 feet. How much carpeting do you need to cover the floor in the hallway completely?

To solve the problem, you need to find the area of the hallway.

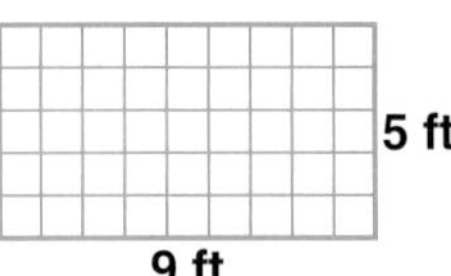

A **square unit** is a square with sides one unit long. You can measure **area** (A) by finding the number of square units that cover a surface with no overlap.

To find the area of a rectangle, you can count square units, or you can multiply its length by its width.

$$A \text{ (rectangle)} = l \times w$$
$$= 9 \times 5$$
$$= 45$$

Remember

Area is expressed in square units. For example, if the length and width are measured in feet, the area will be in square feet, or ft^2.

Solution: You need 45 square feet of carpeting.

Since the length and width of a square are the same, you can write the formula for area of a square as $A = s \times s$, or $A = s^2$.

$A = s^2$

$A = 3^2$

$A = 9$ The area is 9 square meters, or 9 m^2.

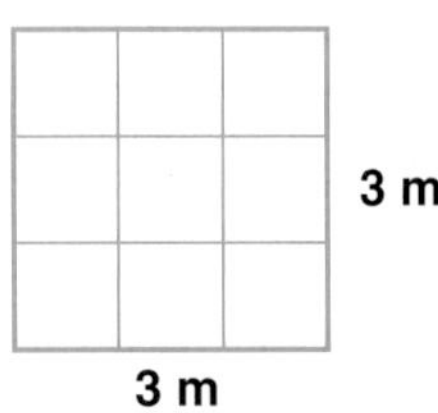

You can use what you know about the area of a rectangle to find the formula for the area of any parallelogram.

STEP 1 On a sheet of centimeter grid paper, copy the parallelogram shown at the right. The red dotted line is perpendicular to the base, b, and represents the height, h.

STEP 2 Cut along the red dotted line. Move the right triangle to the other side of the parallelogram to form a rectangle.

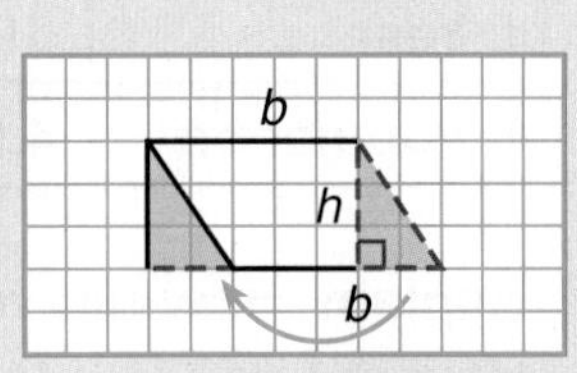

Write a multiplication sentence for the area of the rectangle. You can also use the formula for the area of a rectangle to find the formula for the area of a parallelogram.

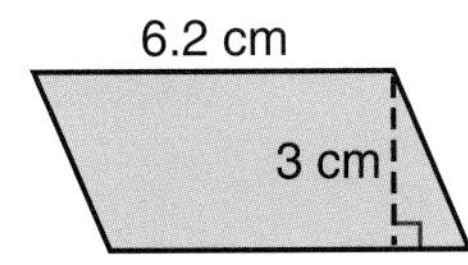

You can use a formula to find the area of any parallelogram.

Using the Formula for Area of a Parallelogram

$A = bh$

$= 6.2 \times 3$

$= 18.6$

The area is 18.6 square centimeters, or 18.6 cm^2.

$A = bh$

$= 7 \times 5\frac{1}{2}$

$= 38\frac{1}{2}$

The area is $38\frac{1}{2}$ square inches, or $38\frac{1}{2}$ $in.^2$.

Guided Practice

Find the area of each figure.

1.

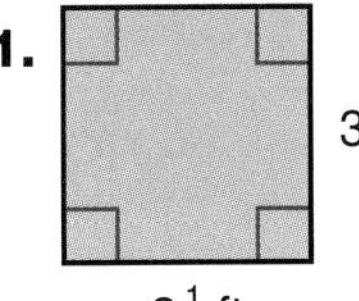

2.

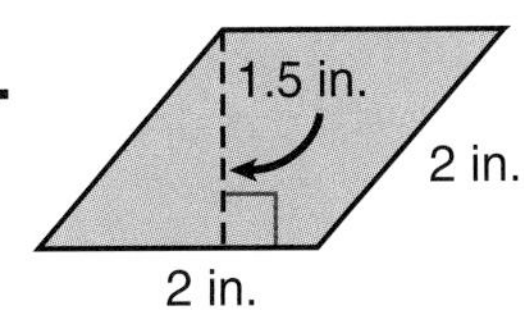

Ask Yourself

- Which measure is the height?
- Which measures do I multiply?

Explain Your Thinking ▶ Can the formula $A = bh$ be used to find the area of any rectangle? Explain.

Practice and Problem Solving

Find the area of each figure.

3.

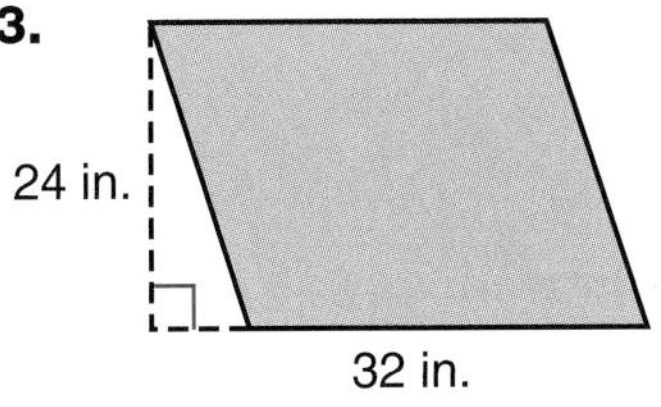

4.

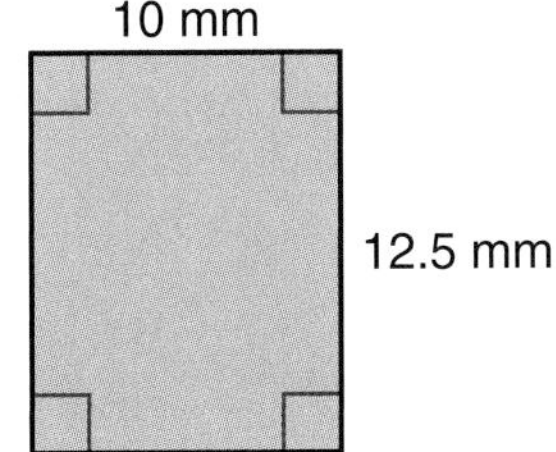

5.

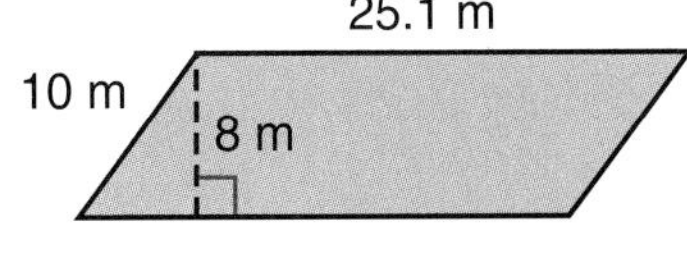

6.

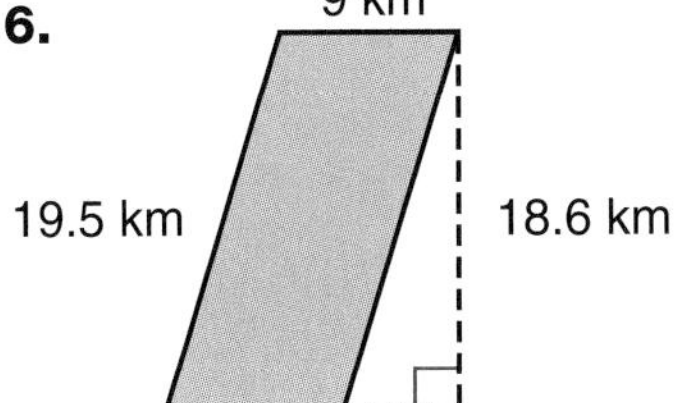

7.

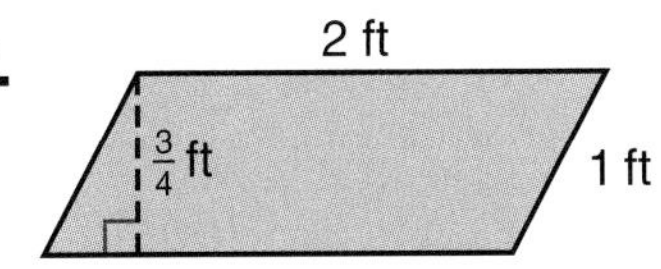

8.

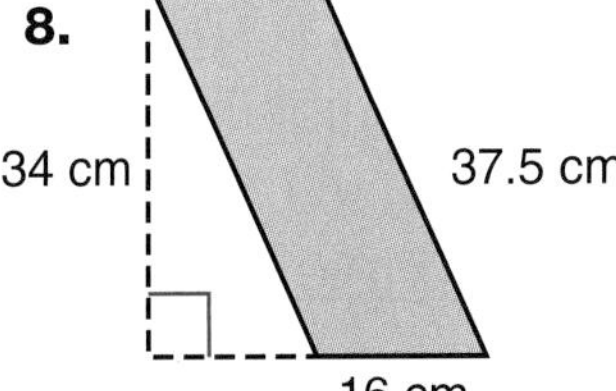

Go On

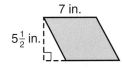

Practice and Problem Solving

Use Figures A, B, and C for Exercises 9–14.

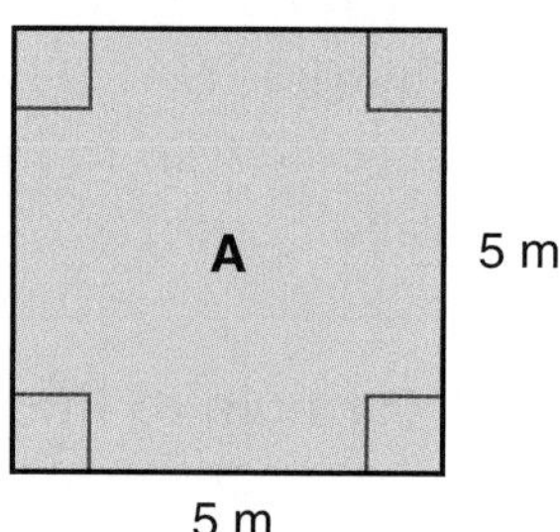

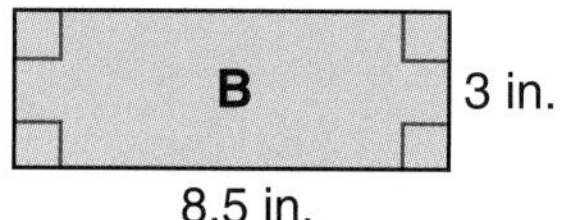

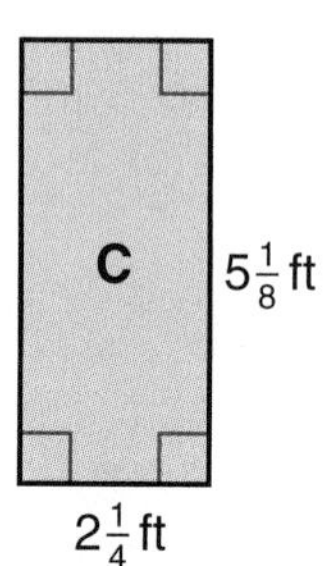

9. Find the perimeter of each figure.

10. Find the perimeter of a rectangle that has twice the length and twice the width as Figure A. Repeat for Figure B and Figure C.

11. What is the relationship between the perimeter of a figure and the perimeter of a figure when the length and width are doubled?

12. Find the area of each figure.

13. Find the area of a rectangle that has twice the length and twice the width as the Figure A. Repeat for Figure B and Figure C.

14. What is the relationship between the area of a figure and the area of a figure with twice the length and width?

Data **Copy and complete the table so that it shows the length, width, and perimeter for different rectangles with an area of 36 square inches.**

	Area of Rectangle	Length	Width	Perimeter
15.	36 in.^{2}	1 in.		
16.	36 in.^{2}	2 in.		
17.	36 in.^{2}	3 in.		
18.	36 in.^{2}	4 in.		
19.	36 in.^{2}	6 in.		

20. Look at the results of Exercises 15–19. What is the relationship between the length and the width of rectangles with the same area? How does that relationship affect the perimeter?

21. Joe drew a parallelogram with a height of 2 centimeters and an area of 14.7 square centimeters. Draw Joe's parallelogram. How long is its base?

22. Nan used 64 feet of fencing to make a rectangular space for her dog. Find the dimensions of the space if she made the largest possible area for the dog.

23. Write About It A square and a non-square rhombus each have sides 3 cm long. Which has the greater area? Use a diagram to explain.

24. A garden is planted in the shape of a rhombus and fenced with 40 feet of fencing. The height of the rhombus is 8 feet. What is the area of the garden?

Extra Practice See page 443, Set B.

Problem Solving

Social Studies Connection

On The Farm

1 square inch (in.²)

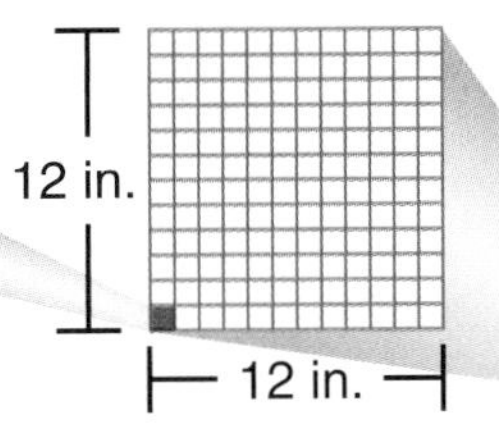

1 square foot (ft²)

144 square inches

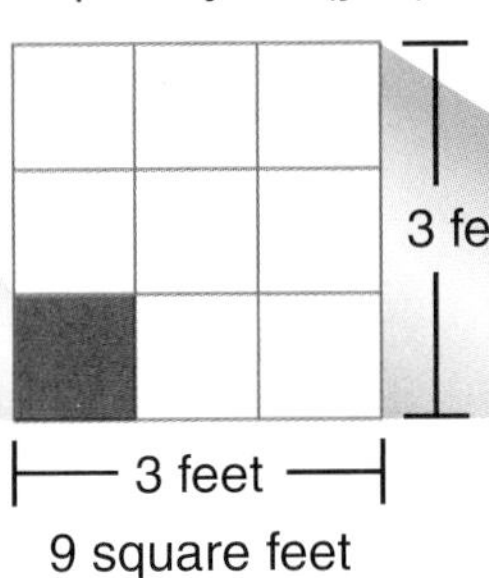

1 square yard (yd²)

9 square feet

1 acre

43,560 square feet

The area of a farm is measured in acres.

1. How large is an acre in square yards?

2. **Calculator** How many square feet are in 1 square mile?
3. **Calculator** How many acres are there in 1 square mile?
4. A rectangular piece of land is almost a square, and is 2 acres in area. Find its dimensions in feet, rounded to the nearest ten feet.

WEEKLY WR READER eduplace.com/map

Quick Check

Check your understanding of Lessons 1–3.

Find the perimeter and area. (Lessons 1 and 3)

1. 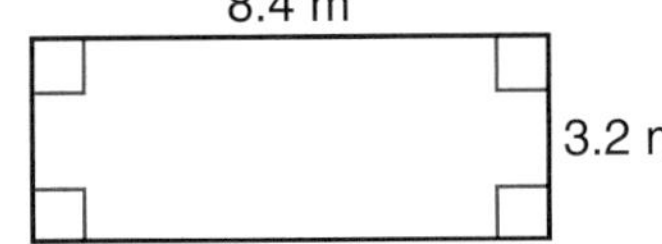

2. 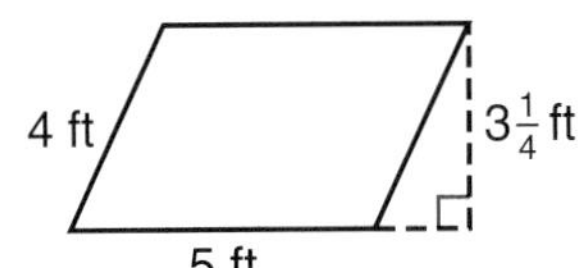

3. 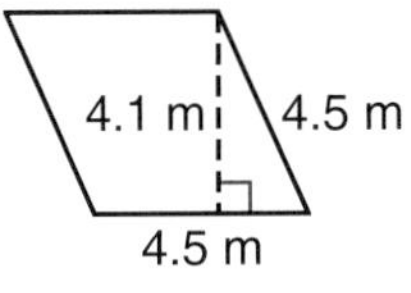

Solve. (Lesson 2)

4. Look at the figures below. If the pattern continues, how many small squares will be in the fifth figure?

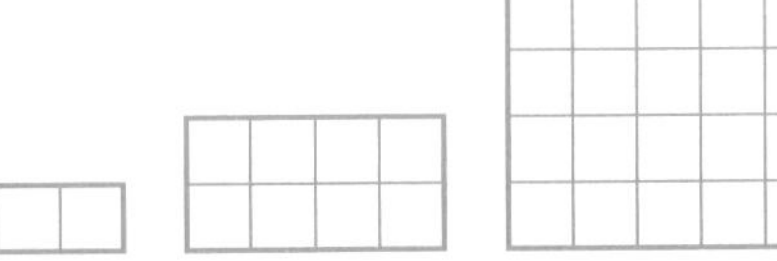

5. The first four figures in a pattern are shown below. When will the dot be in the same position as it was in the first figure in the pattern?

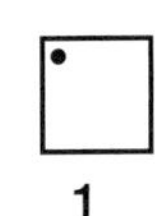
1

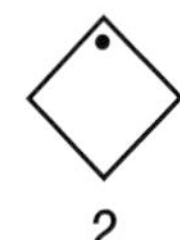
2

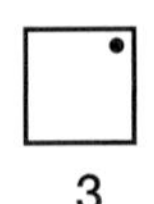
3

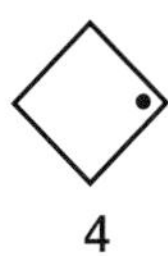
4

Lesson 4

Area of a Triangle

Objective Find and use the formula to find the area of a triangle.

Learn About It

A surveyor lays out building lots along a river. Some lots are parallelograms and some are triangles. How can the surveyor find the area of a triangular lot?

Use what you know about the formula for the area of a parallelogram to write a formula for the area of a triangle.

STEP 1 Trace and cut out this triangle.

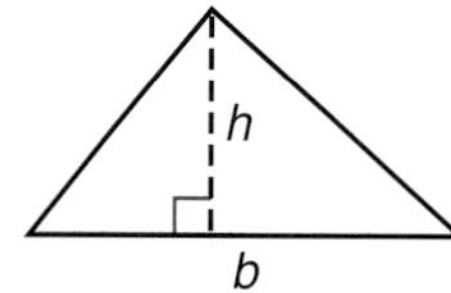

STEP 2 Place the triangle you traced next to the one shown to make the parallelogram.

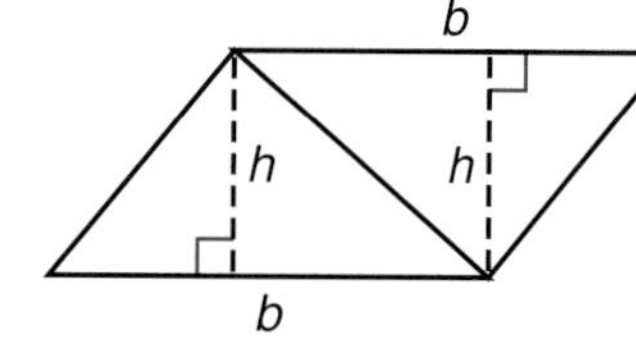

Remember
The formula for the area of a parallelogram is $b \times h$.

STEP 3

- The triangles are congruent so each triangle represents one half of the area of the parallelogram.
- The area of the triangle is $\frac{1}{2} \times b \times h$.

  So, $A = \frac{1}{2} \times b \times h$ or $A = \frac{1}{2}bh$

- In the building lot, $b = 20$ yd and $h = 15$ yd. $A = \frac{1}{2} \times 20 \text{ yd} \times 15 \text{ yd} = 150 \text{ yd}^2$

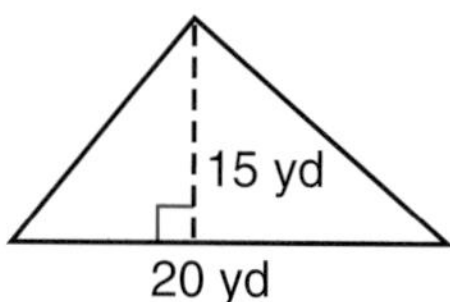

Solution: The area of the building lot is 150 yd².

Guided Practice

Find the area of each triangle.

1.

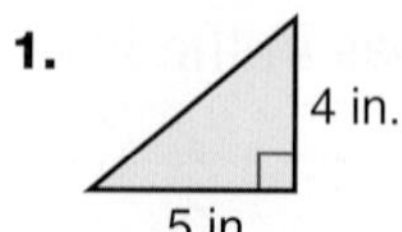

2.

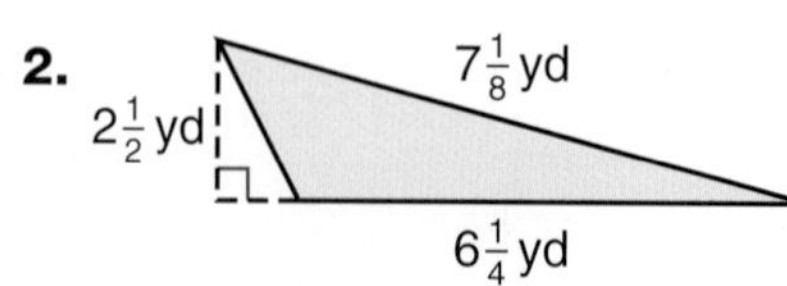

Ask Yourself

- What formula do I use?
- Did I use the right numbers?

Explain Your Thinking ▶ If you know the lengths of the sides of a right triangle, can you find its area? Use a diagram to explain.

Practice and Problem Solving

Find the area of each triangle.

3. 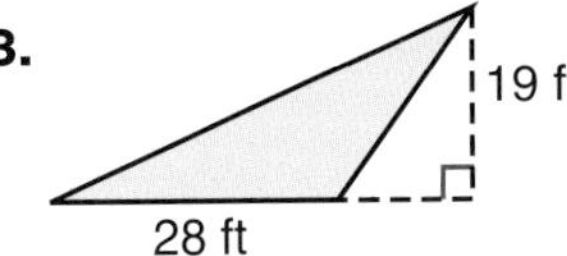

4. 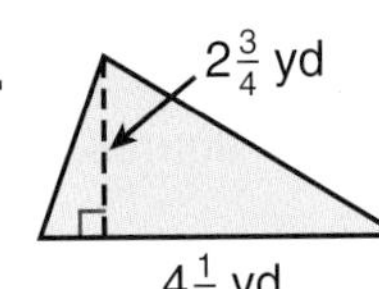

5.  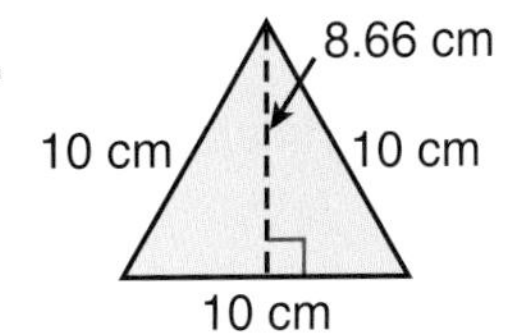

6.  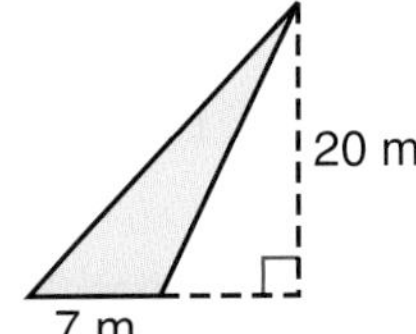

Solve.

7. The corners of the yellow pane of glass at the right meet at the midpoints of each side of the window. What is the area of each purple pane? What is the area of the yellow pane? (Hint: The midpoint of a side is the center point, or middle of that side.)

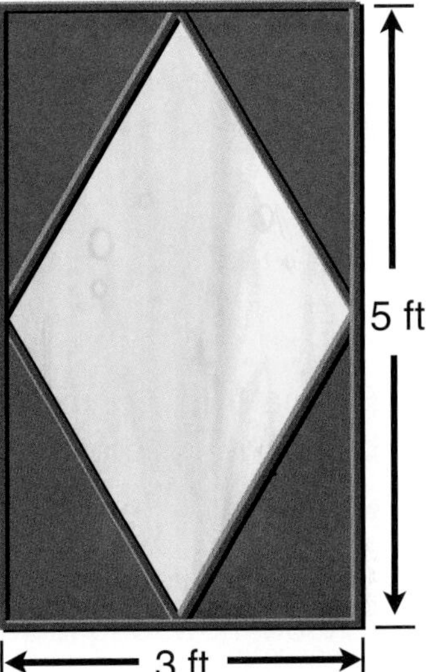

8. A triangle has a height of 6 inches and an area of 24 in.^{2}. What is the length of the base of that triangle?

9. A triangle has a base of 4.5 cm and an area of 27 cm^2. Find its height.

10. A triangle has a height of m inches and a base of p inches. Write an expression to represent the area of that triangle.

11. **What's Wrong?** The notebook at the right shows how Alan found the area of a triangle. Explain what Alan did wrong.

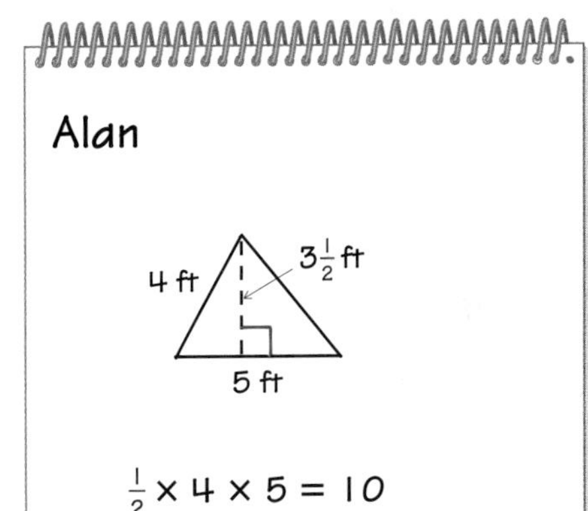

12. **You Decide** You need $1\frac{1}{2}$ pounds of peanuts to make trail mix. A 6-oz jar of peanuts costs \$1.99. A 10-oz can of peanuts costs \$2.89. How will you buy the peanuts? Explain.

Mixed Review and Test Prep

Open Response

For each figure, name the number of lines of symmetry it has. (Ch. 15, Lesson 9)

13. 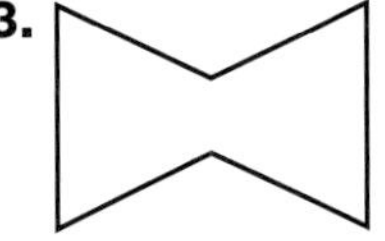

14. 

Multiple Choice

15. Find the area of a triangle with a height of 8 inches and base of $6\frac{1}{4}$ inches. (Ch. 16, Lesson 4)

A $14\frac{1}{4}$ in.^{2} **C** $28\frac{1}{2}$ in.^{2}

B 25 in.^{2} **D** 52 in.^{2}

Extra Practice See page 443, Set C.

Hands On Lesson 5

Audio Tutor 2/15 Listen and Understand

Perimeter and Area of Irregular Figures

Materials
centimeter grid paper
inch grid paper
(Learning Tool 13)
(Learning Tool 15)

Objective Find the perimeters and areas of irregular figures.

Work Together

Some figures are irregular and have curved sides. You can estimate the perimeter and area of these figures.

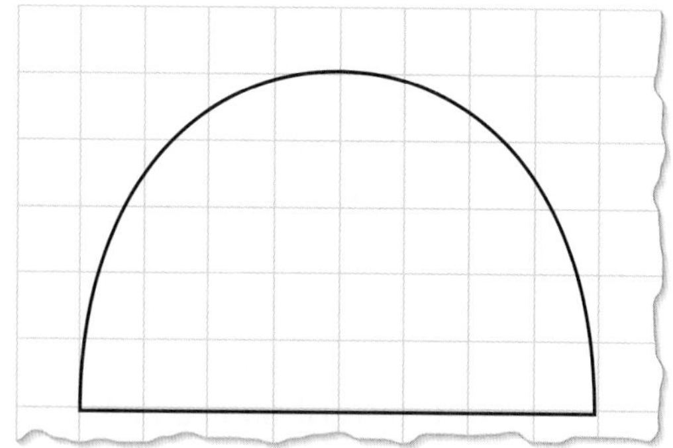

STEP 1 Estimate the perimeter of the figure above by answering these questions.

- What is the length of each straight line in the figure?
- How can you estimate the length of the curved side? About how long is the curved side?
- What is the sum of the sides?
- What is your estimate of the perimeter?

STEP 2 Estimate the area by answering these questions.

- How many whole squares are in the figure?
- How many partial squares are in the figure?
- What is your estimate of the area?

STEP 3 Now trace the same figure on a piece of grid paper that has squares of a smaller size. Estimate the perimeter and area.

- How does changing the size of the squares affect the perimeter and the area of the figure?

Some shapes are complex figures that are made of smaller polygons. You can use what you know about finding the perimeter and area of simple figures to find the perimeter and area of these shapes.

STEP 1 Find any missing lengths.

15 ft − 6 ft = 9 ft

18 ft − 9 ft = 9 ft

Add the lengths of the sides to find the perimeter of the figure.

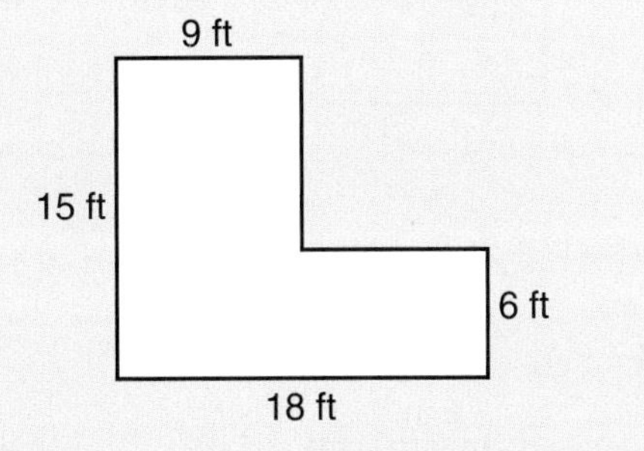

STEP 2 Find the area by separating the figure into simple figures.

Draw a line that separates the figure into a square and a rectangle.

Use formulas to find the area of each figure.

- What is the area of the square?
- What is the area of the rectangle?
- What is the sum of the areas?
- Can you think of another way to find the area of this figure?

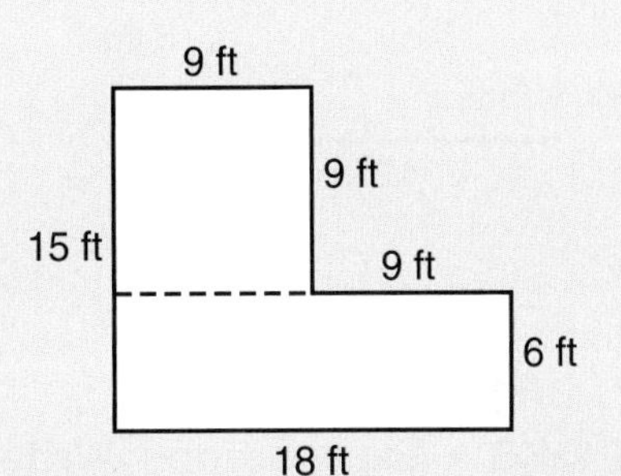

Hint
Think of the figure as a large rectangle with a small rectangle cut from one corner.

On Your Own

Estimate the perimeter and area of each figure. Each square is 1 cm^2.

1. 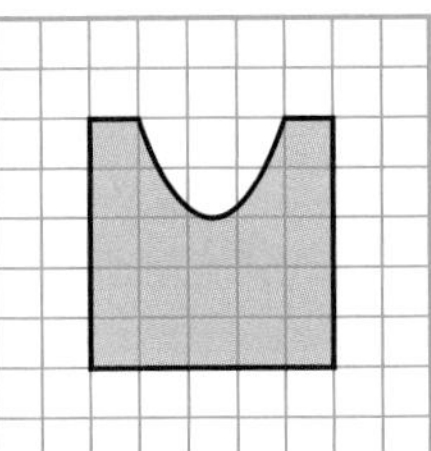

2. 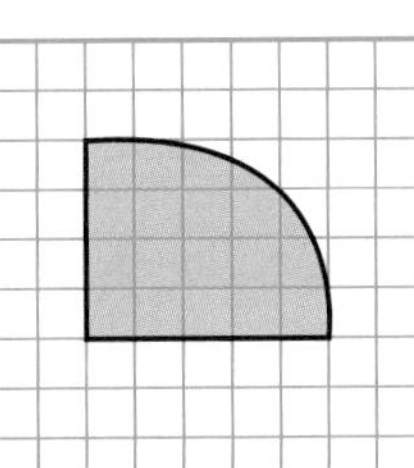

3. 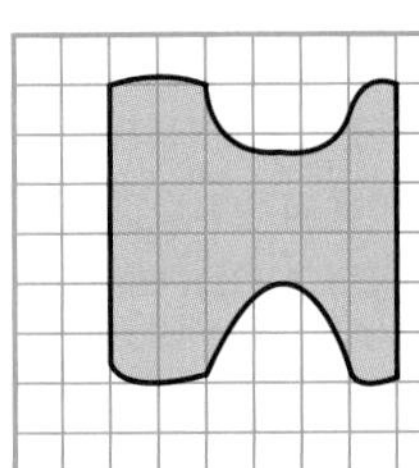

4. 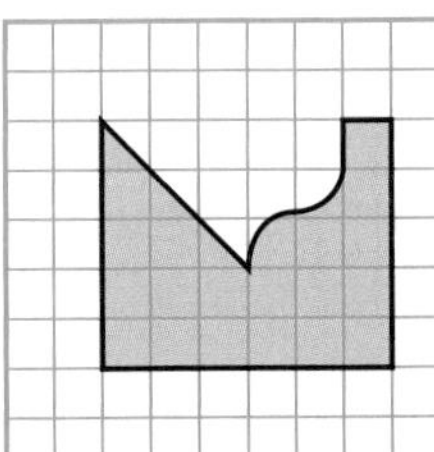

5. 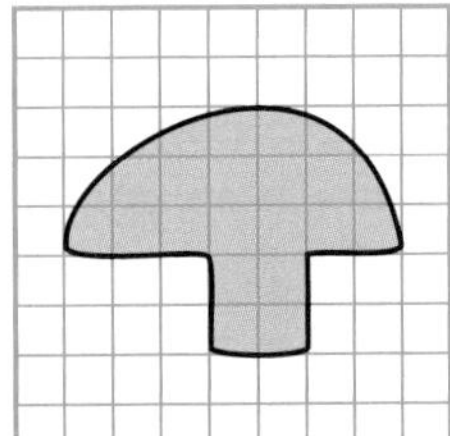

6. 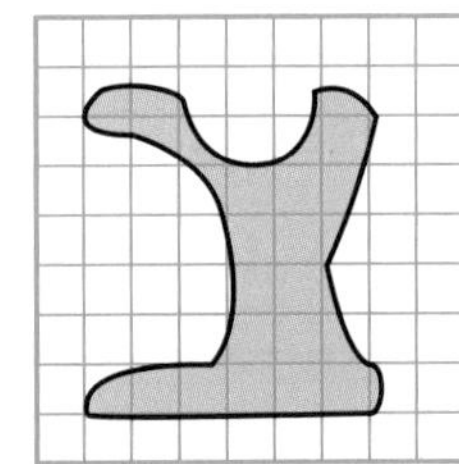

Go On

Find the perimeter and area of each figure. All intersecting sides meet at right angles.

7. 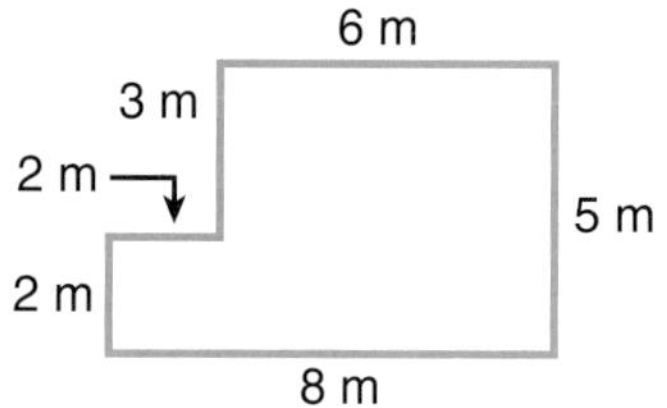

8. 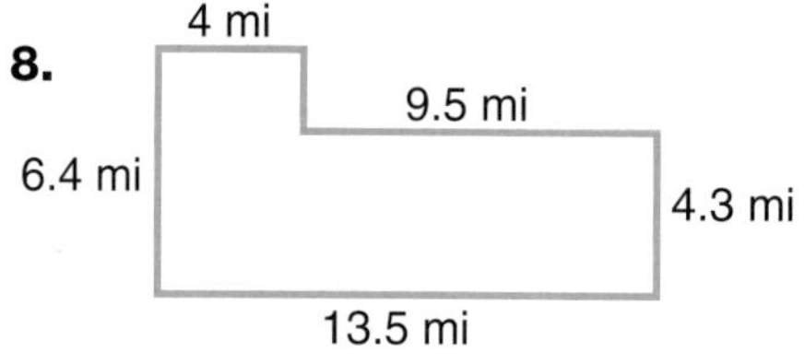

9. 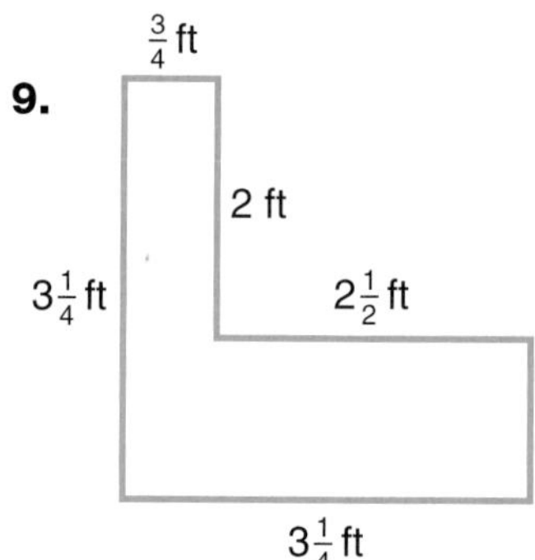

10. 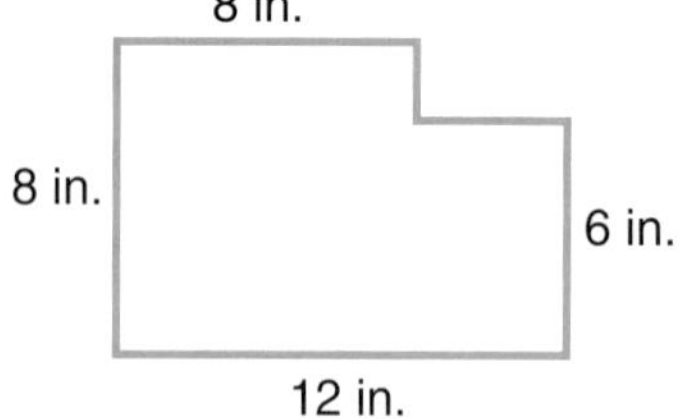

11. 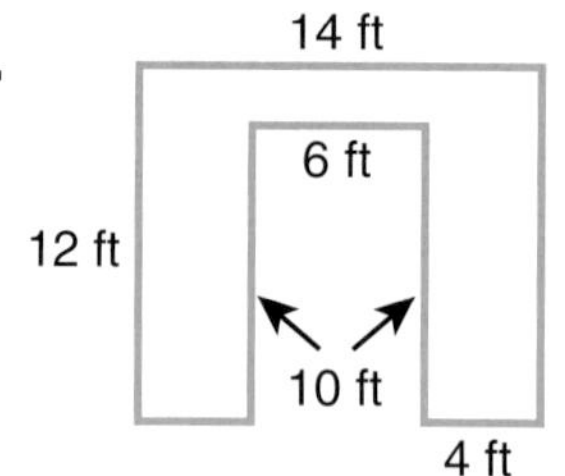

12. 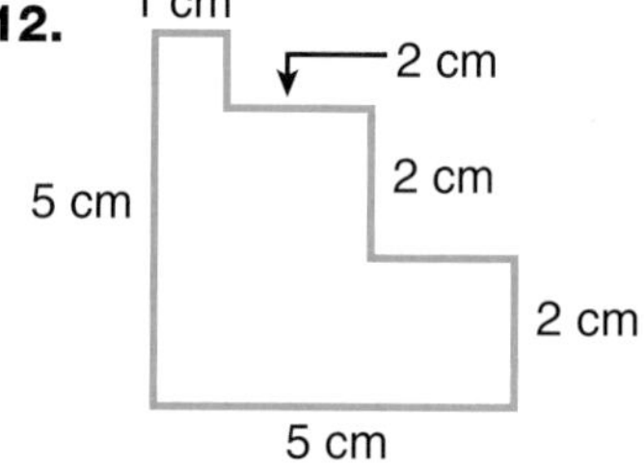

Algebra • Expressions

Write an expression to represent the perimeter of each figure. Then write an expression to represent the area of each figure.

13. 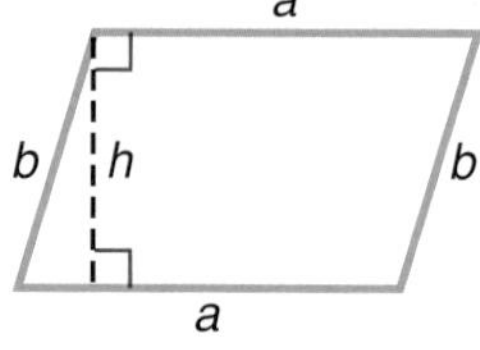

14. 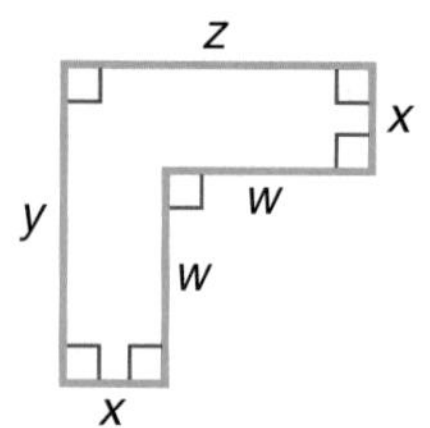

15. 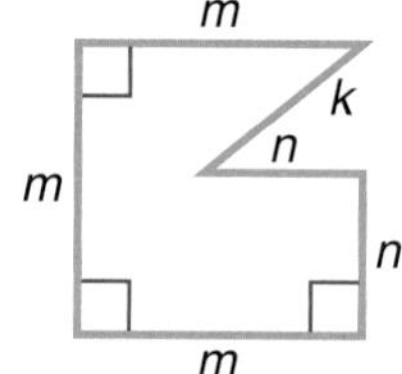

Talk About It • Write About It

You learned how to estimate and find the area and perimeter of irregular and complex figures.

16. Explain how to estimate the perimeter and area of Shape A.

17. Explain how to find the area of Shape B.

A

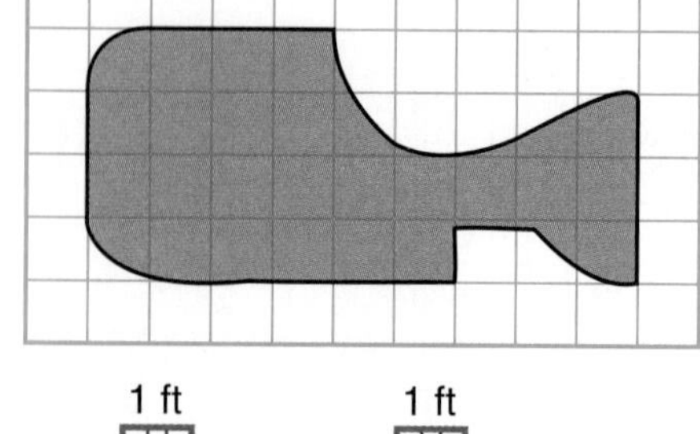

B

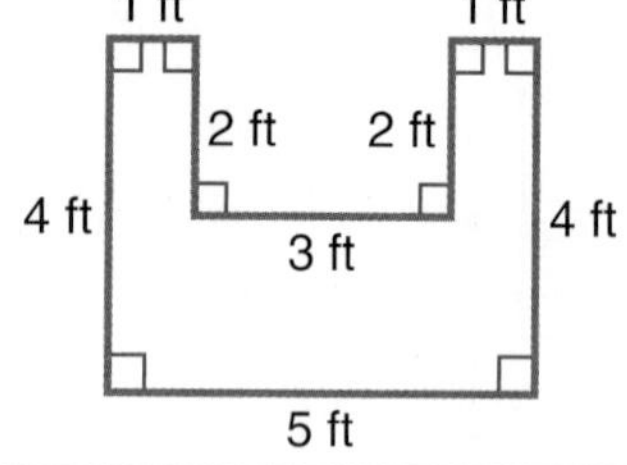

Measurement Sense

Historical Blueprints

Thomas Jefferson was an author of the Declaration of Independence and was the third President of the United States (1801–1809). Jefferson was also one of the leading architects of his time.

Besides designing the Virginia Capitol and the University of Virginia, Jefferson designed his home, called Monticello. The diagram at the right shows floor plans for the tea room and the dining room in Monticello.

Study the floor plan.

- Estimate the area of the tea room. You may wish to trace the diagram on a piece of grid paper to help you.
- About how much smaller is the tea room than the dining room?
- About how much of the tea room's area does the large table in the center cover?
- Would the rug from the dining room fit in the tea room? Explain.

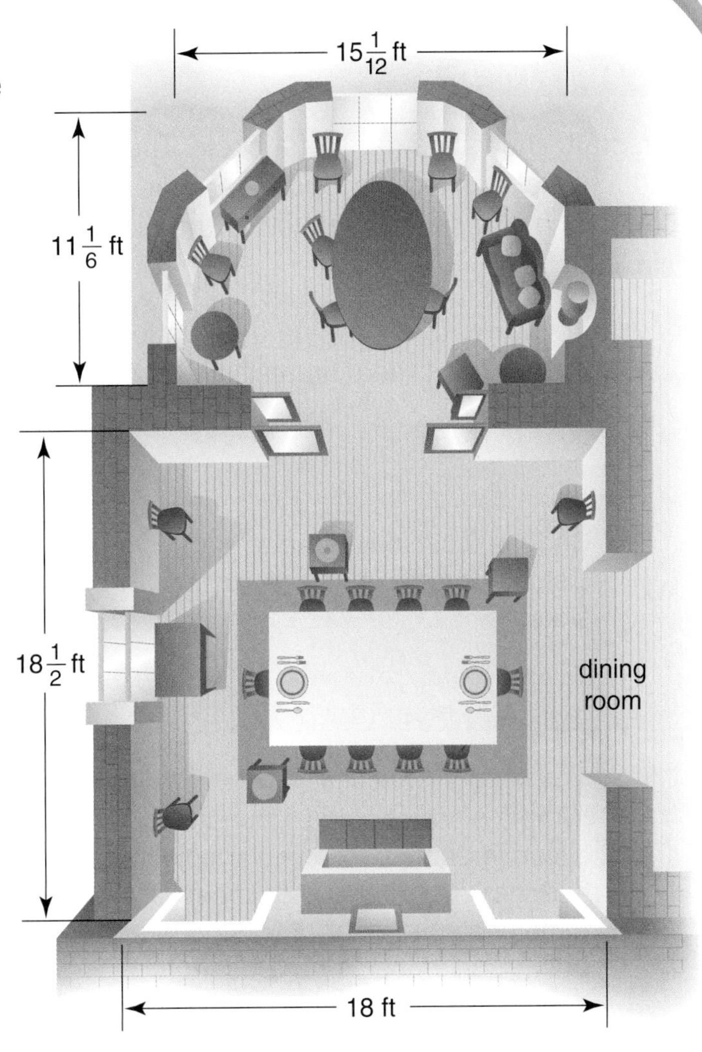

Visual Thinking

Tetrominoes

A tetromino is a design made of 4 squares. Each square has at least one side in common with another.

Two tetrominoes are shown. How many different tetrominoes can you make?

Brain Teaser

Square Deal

The area of one square is 16 times the area of another square. How are the side lengths of the two squares related? How are the perimeters of the two squares related?

Education Place

Check out **eduplace.com/map** for more Brain Teasers.

Circumference of a Circle

Objective Find and use the formula to find the circumference of a circle.

Vocabulary
circumference
pi (π)

Materials
Learning Tool 53
string
circular objects
calculator
ruler or meter stick

Work Together

The diagram shows the parts of a circle. The distance around a circle is called the **circumference** *(C)*. The circumference of a circle is related to the diameter of the circle.

Work with a partner to determine the relationship of the circumference and the diameter of a circle.

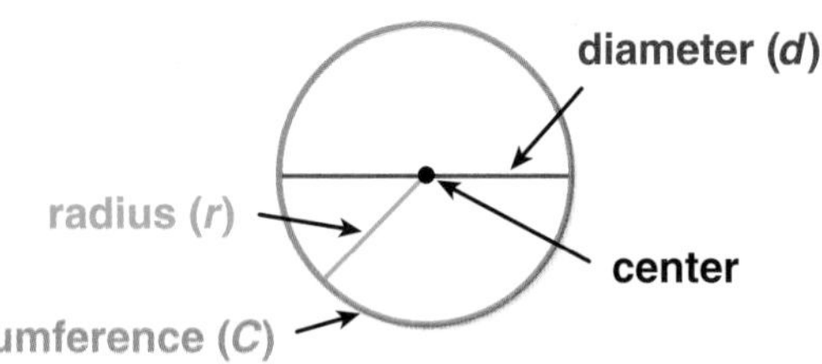

STEP 1 Choose 3 circular objects. List the objects on the recording sheet.

Circumference and Diameter			
Object	Circumference (C)	Diameter (d)	$C \div d$
Can			

STEP 2 Wrap a piece of string around the circumference of the circular object and mark where the ends meet. Use a meter stick or ruler to find the length of this part of the string. Record this measurement.

STEP 3 Measure the diameter of the circular object. Record this measurement.

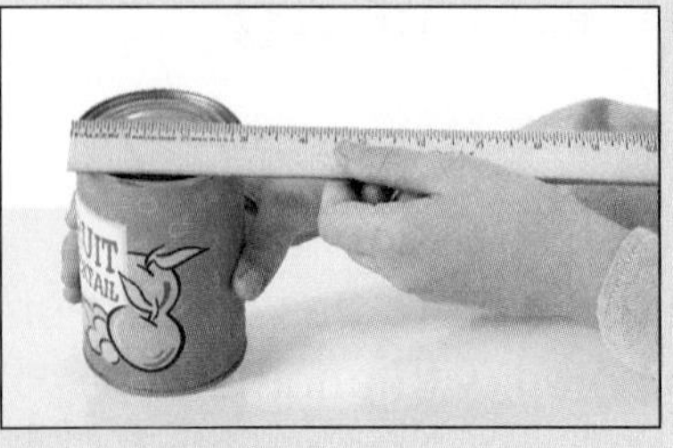

STEP 4 Use a calculator to complete the last column of the recording sheet. Round each quotient ($C \div d$) to the nearest hundredth.

- What patterns do you see?
- How is the circumference of a circle related to its diameter?

In the activity, you found that the circumference of a circle is always a little more than three times its diameter. The quotient for $C \div d$ is represented by the Greek letter π. The name for that letter is **pi**.

As a decimal, $\pi \approx 3.14$
As a fraction, $\pi \approx \frac{22}{7}$

$\approx$ means "is approximately equal to"

If you know the diameter of a circle, you can use π to find the circumference.

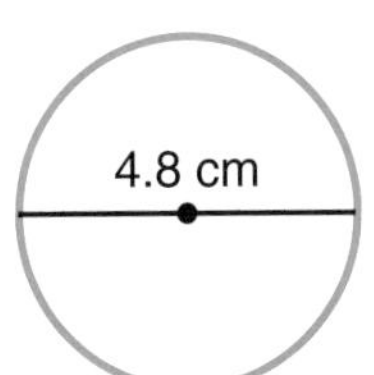

$C = \pi d$
$\approx 3.14 \times 4.8$
≈ 15.072

Rounded to the nearest tenth of a centimeter, the circumference is about 15.1 centimeters.

The diameter of a circle is twice as long as the radius, $d = 2r$. If you know the radius of a circle, you can use π to find the circumference.

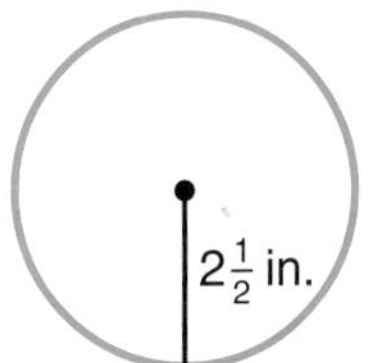

$C = 2\pi r$
$\approx 2 \times \frac{22}{7} \times 2\frac{1}{2}$
$\approx 15\frac{5}{7}$

The circumference of the circle is about $15\frac{5}{7}$ inches.

You can check your answer by using the value of π rounded to a whole number, 3.
$C \approx 2 \times 3 \times 2\frac{1}{2}$
≈ 15

Sometimes you should round your answers when working with measurements.

You can use the π key to find the circumference of the circle at the right.

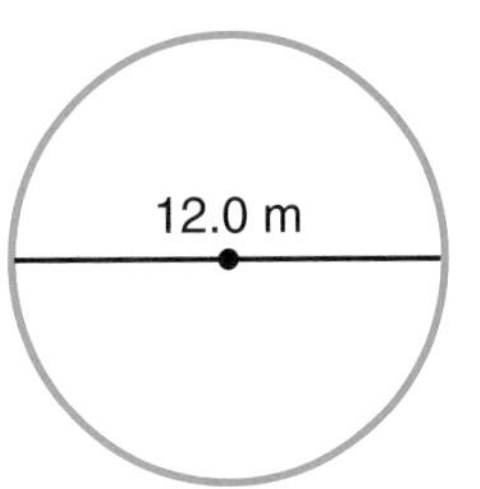

The result will be:

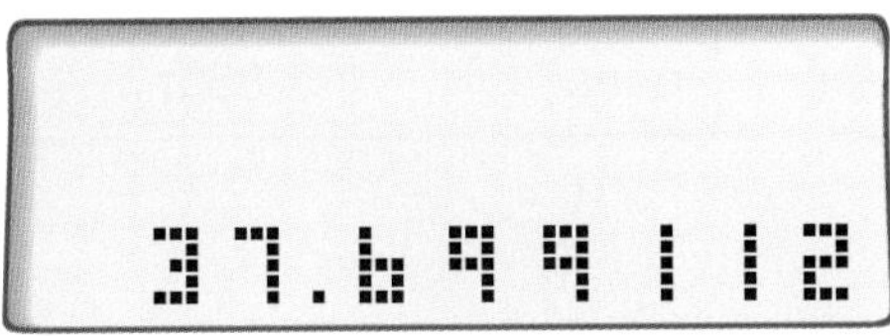

An answer of 37.699112 meters indicates that the answer is accurate to six decimal places. A more sensible answer would be 37.7 meters. The diameter of the circle is given in tenths, so the answer should also be given in tenths.

When working with measurements, round the answer to the same degree of precision as the least precise of the measurements in the problem.

The circumference of the circle is 37.7 m.

Go On

On Your Own

Find the circumference. Use 3.14 for π. Round your answer to the same degree of precision as given in the diameter or radius.

1. 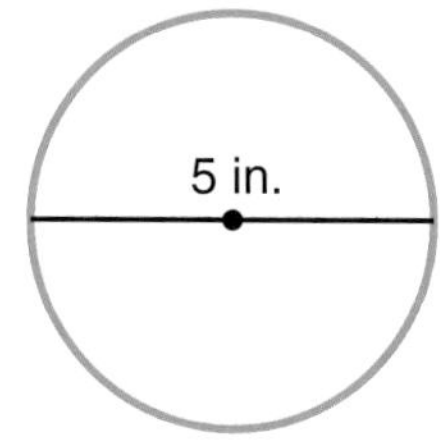

2. 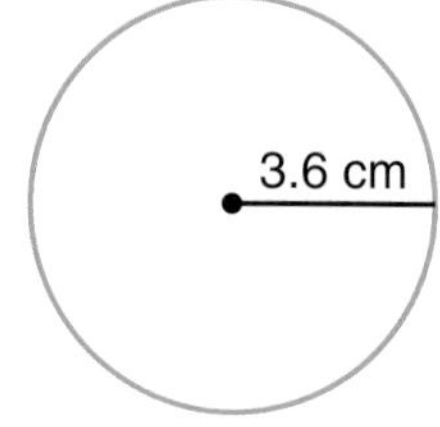

3. 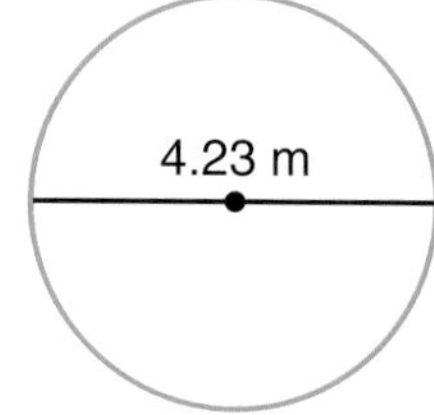

4. diameter = 10 yd

5. radius = 10 m

6. diameter = 24.362 m

Express each circumference as a fraction or mixed number in simplest form. Use $\frac{22}{7}$ for π.

7. 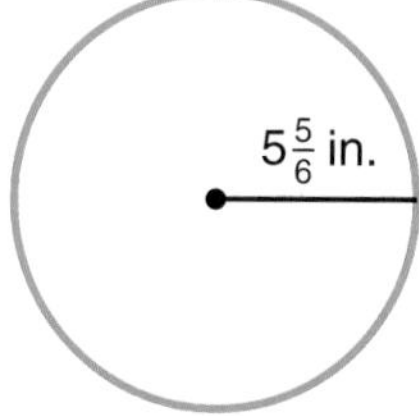

8. 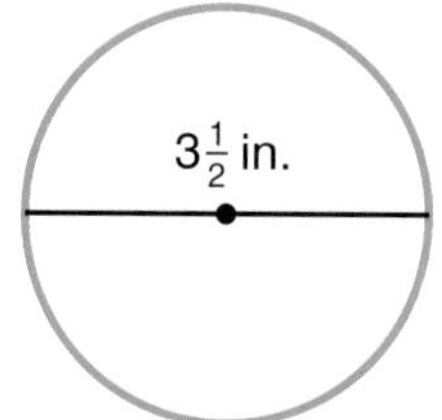

9. 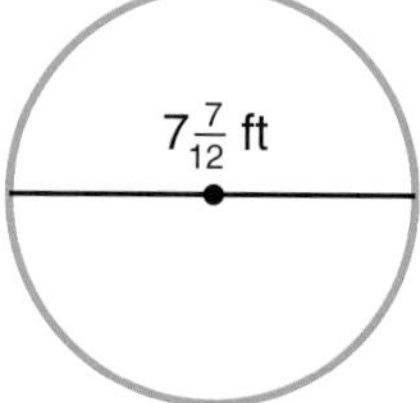

10. diameter = 7 ft

11. radius = 7 in.

12. diameter = $22\frac{3}{4}$ ft

Data Use the table to solve Problems 13–15.

13. Calculate the length of the label around each can. Use 3.14 for π.

14. If the height of the label of the tomato can is 11 cm, what is the approximate area of the label?

15. Suppose the cans of fruit cocktail and peas are both 10 cm tall. Find the difference between the areas of the labels.

Can	Diameter
tomatoes	10 cm
fruit cocktail	7.5 cm
soup	2.5 in.
peas	85 mm

Talk About It • Write About It

You learned how to use a formula to find the circumference of a circle, and how to round your answer.

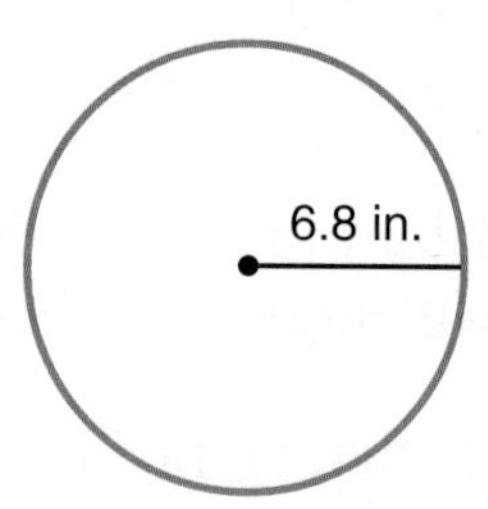

16. Explain how you can find the circumference of the circle at the right.

17. To which digit should you round your answer? Explain.

Math Reasoning

Thinking In Circles

Materials: paper plate, scissors

Use this activity to find the formula for the area of a circle.

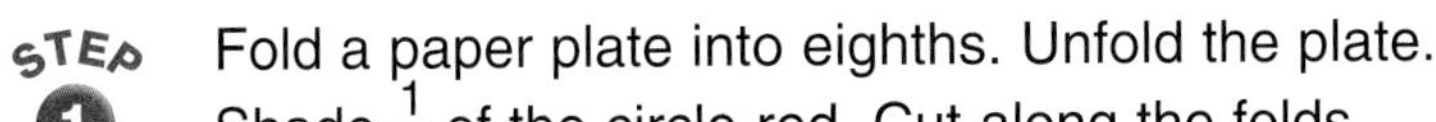

STEP 1 Fold a paper plate into eighths. Unfold the plate. Shade $\frac{1}{2}$ of the circle red. Cut along the folds.

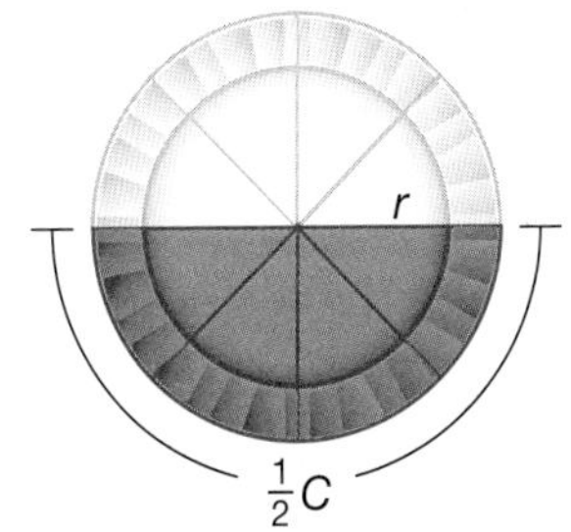

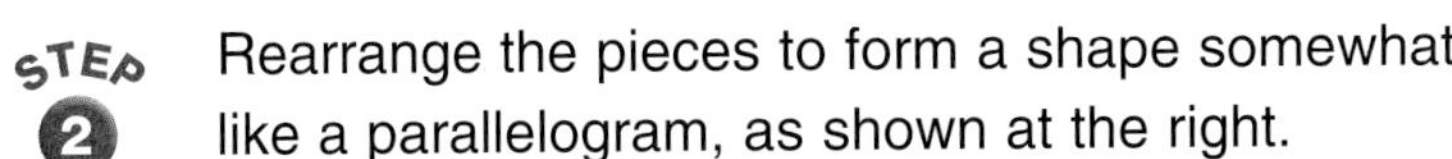

STEP 2 Rearrange the pieces to form a shape somewhat like a parallelogram, as shown at the right.

- What part of the circle could be used as the height of the "parallelogram?"
- How is the circumference of the circle related to the base of the parallelogram?
- How would you find the approximate area of the parallelogram? Express your answer using parts of the circle.

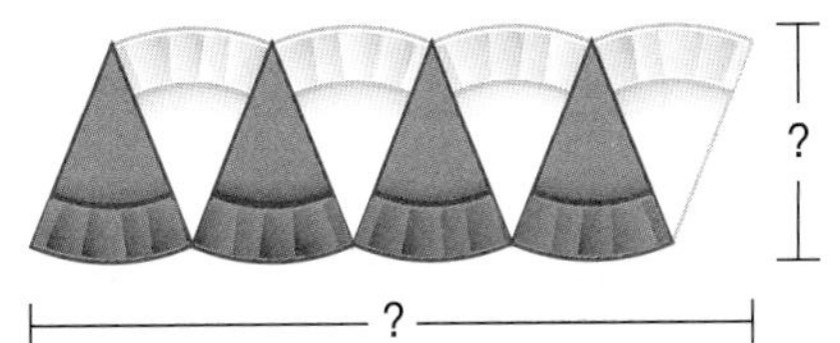

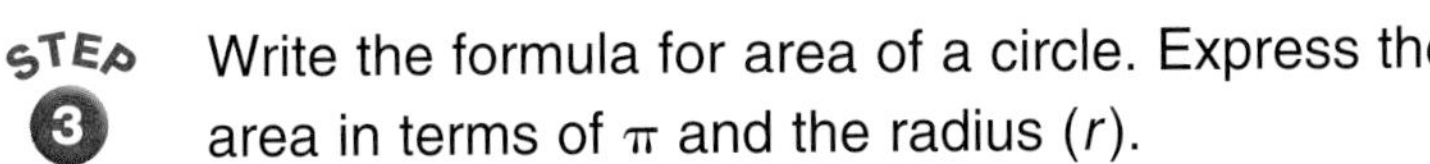

STEP 3 Write the formula for area of a circle. Express the area in terms of π and the radius (r).

Suppose you cut each sector in half again and arranged the new sectors in the shape of a parallelogram, how would you expect the shape of the parallelogram to be affected? How would it affect the approximate area of the parallelogram? Explain.

Use the formula to find the area of each circle to the nearest whole number. Use 3.14 for π.

1. radius = 4 cm

2. diameter = 6 m

3. radius = 8 in.

Use the formula to find the area of a circle to the nearest whole number. Use $\frac{22}{7}$ for π.

4. radius = 7 in.

5. diameter = 14 ft

6. radius = 2 cm

7. Why do we use "≈" symbol when writing the area of a circle if we are using 3.14 or $\frac{22}{7}$ for π?

Chapter Review/Test

VOCABULARY

1. The distance around a circle is called the ____.
2. The quotient of $C \div d$ is called ____.
3. ____ is the number of square units needed to cover a region.

Vocabulary

- area
- circumference
- perimeter
- pi
- square units

CONCEPTS AND SKILLS

Find the perimeter and area of each figure. (Lessons 1, 3, 4; pp. 422–423, 428–433)

4.

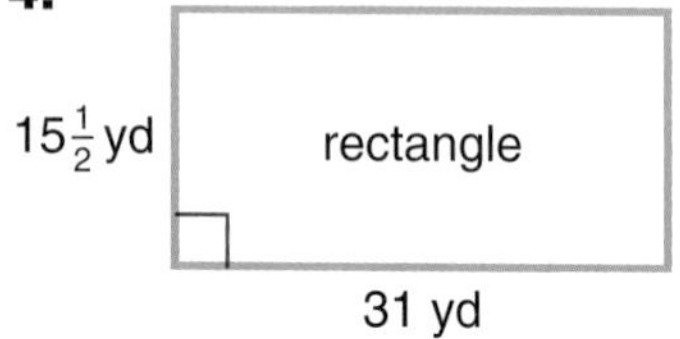

5.

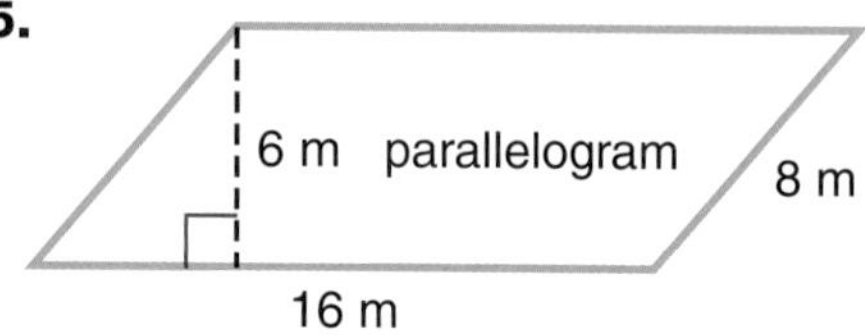

6.

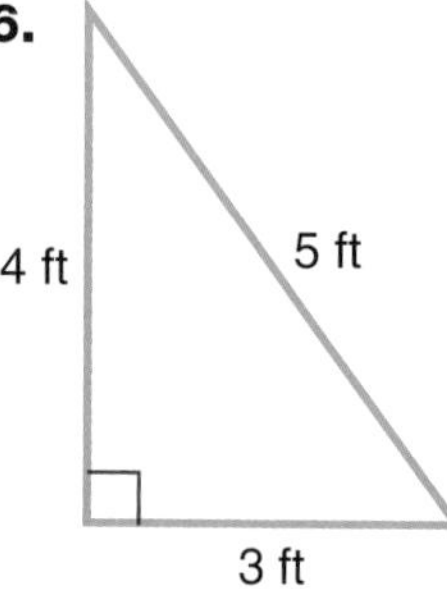

Estimate the area of each figure. Then find the area and perimeter of the figures. (Lesson 5, 434–437)

7.

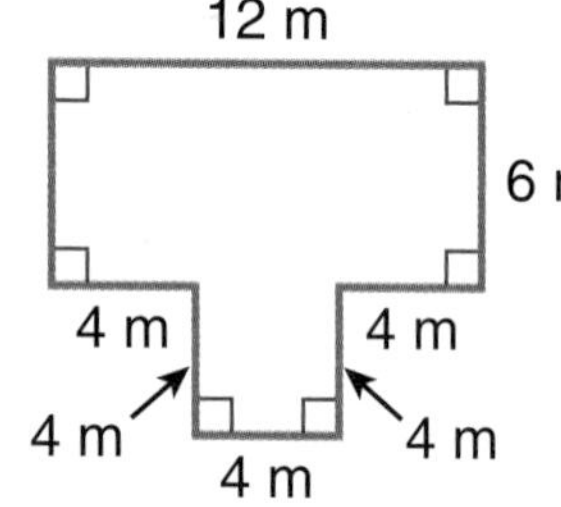

8.

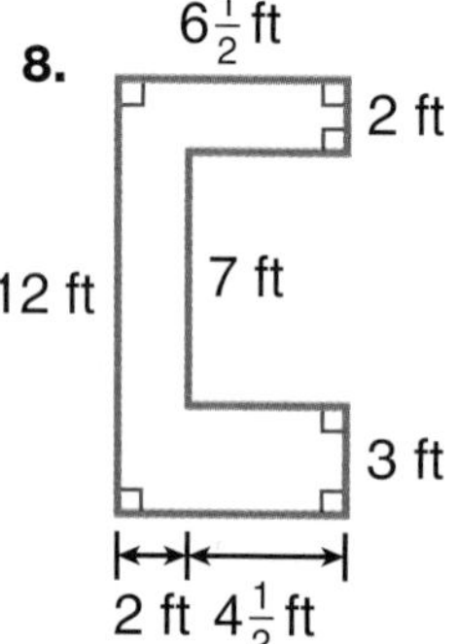

9. Find the circumference of the circle at the right to the nearest tenth. Use 3.14 for π. (Lesson 6, pp. 438–441)

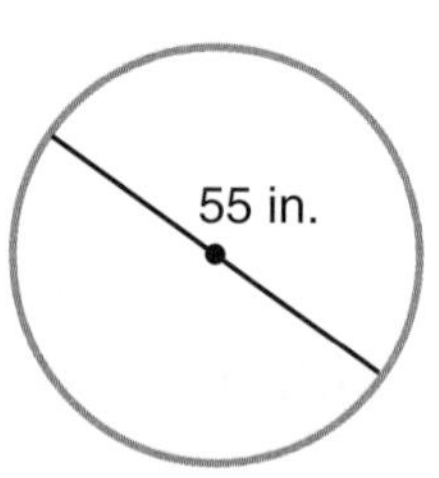

PROBLEM SOLVING

Find a pattern to solve. (Lesson 2, pp. 424–427)

10. If the pattern continues, draw the ninth figure.

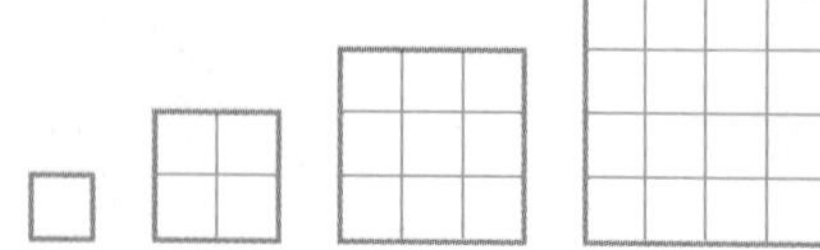

Write About It

Show You Understand

How are perimeter and circumference alike? How are they different?

Extra Practice

Set A (Lesson 1, pp. 422–423)

Find the perimeter or missing length for each rectangle.

1. 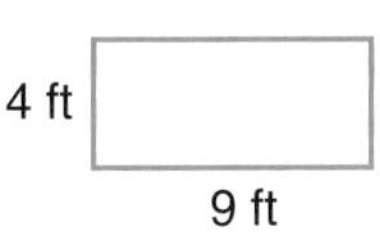

2. 11 yd 11 yd

3. 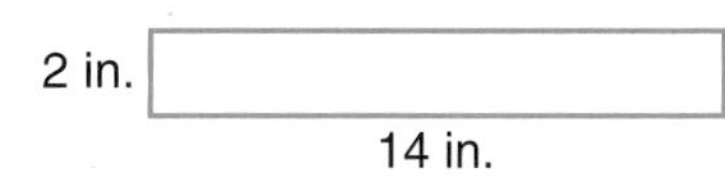

4. 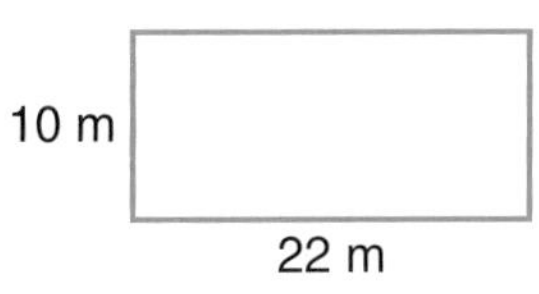

5. 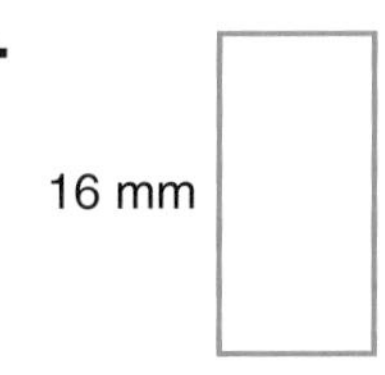

$P = 48$ mm

6. 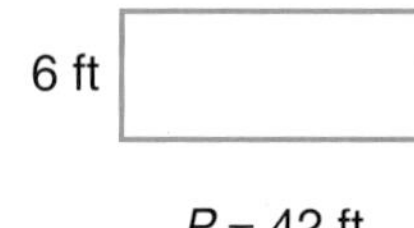

$P = 42$ ft

Set B (Lesson 3, pp. 428–431)

Find the area of each figure.

1. 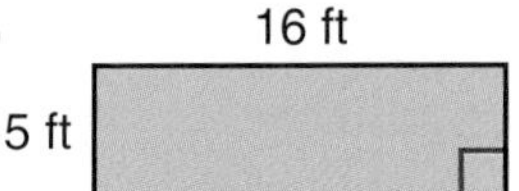

2. 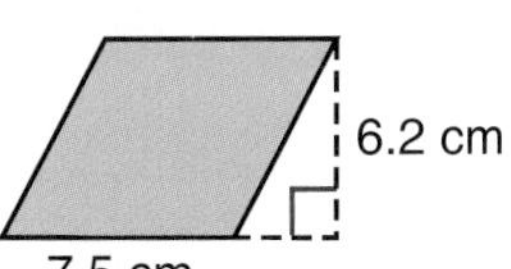

3. 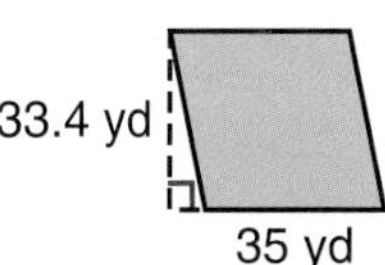

4. 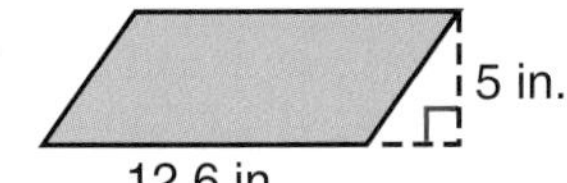

5. 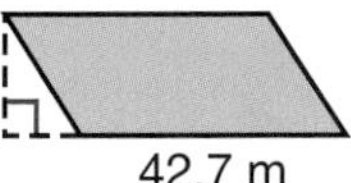

6. 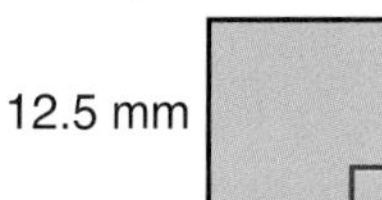

Set C (Lesson 4, pp. 432–433)

Find the area of each triangle.

1. 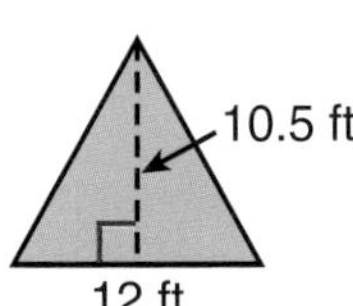

2. 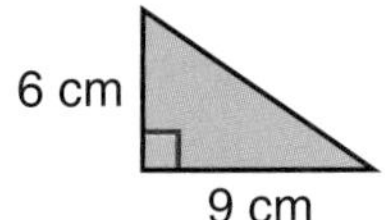

3. 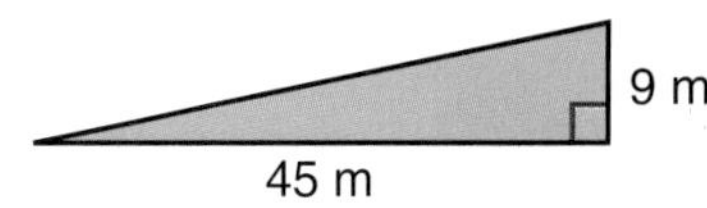

4. 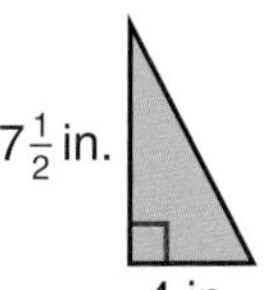

5. 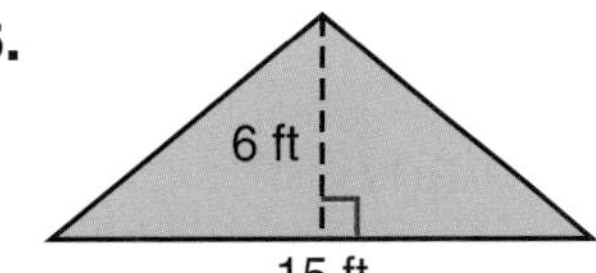

6. 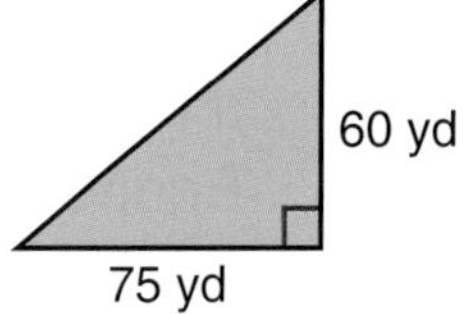

CHAPTER 17

Solid Figures, Surface Area, and Volume

INVESTIGATION

Use Data

Container ships carry thousands of boxes, all the same sizes. At the right is a drawing of a twenty-foot container that holds 1 TEU. The abbreviation TEU means Twenty-feet Equivalent Units. How many boxes like the one shown will fit into 1 container?

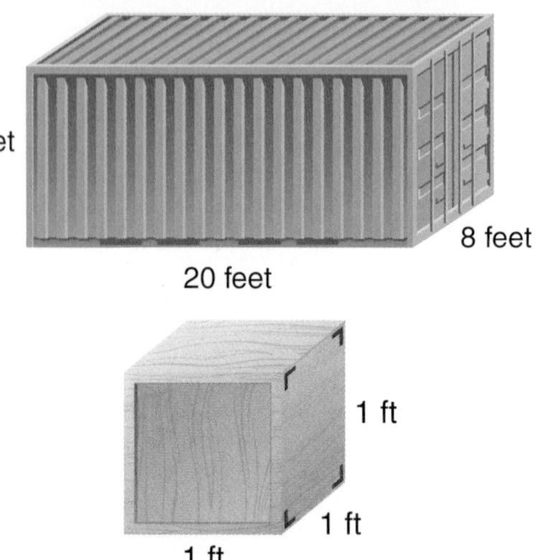

Use What You Know

Use this page to review and remember what you need to know for this chapter.

VOCABULARY

Choose the best word to complete each sentence.

Vocabulary
- **area**
- **polygon**
- **rectangle**
- **volume**

1. A ____ is a simple closed plane figure made up of three or more line segments.
2. The ____ of a solid figure is the number of cubic units that make up a solid figure.
3. The number of square units in a region is called the ____ of the region.

CONCEPTS AND SKILLS

Identify each figure.

4. 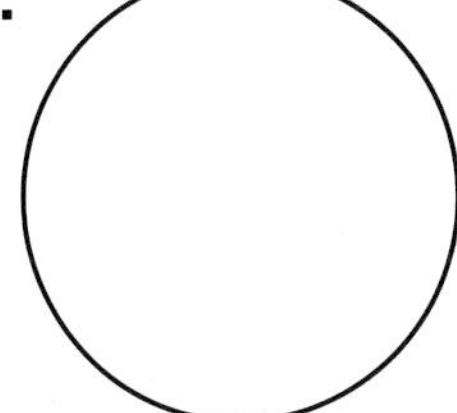

5. 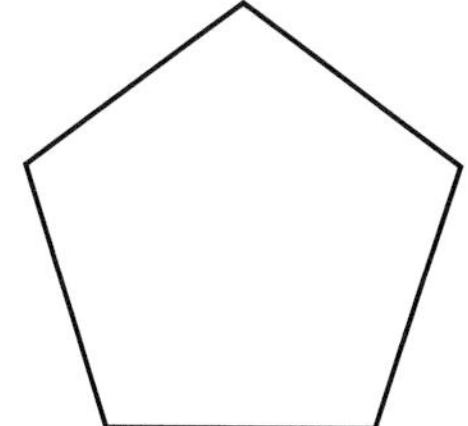

6. 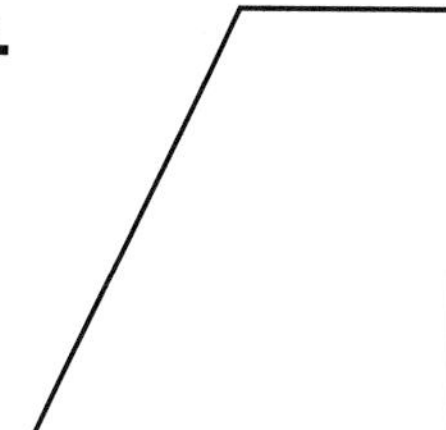

Find the perimeter and area of each figure.

7. 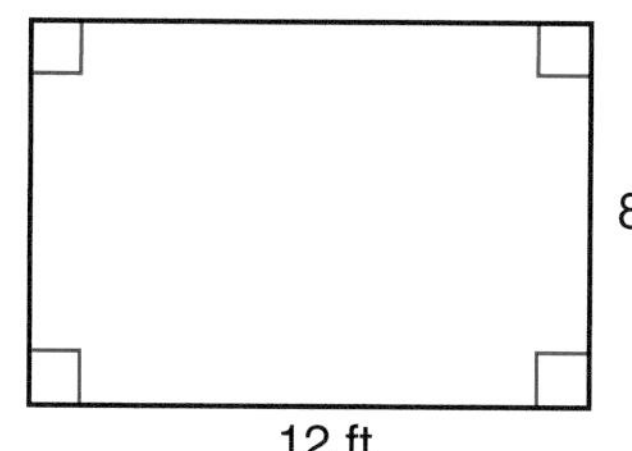

8. 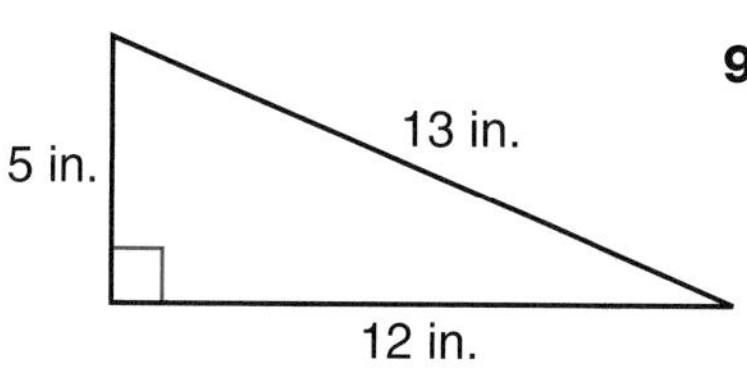

9. 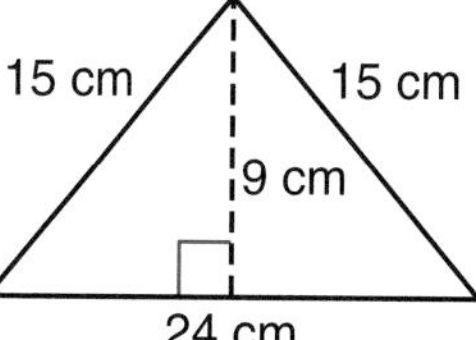

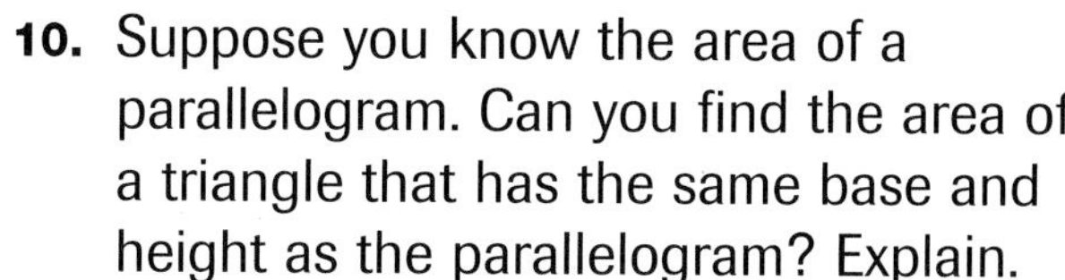

10. Suppose you know the area of a parallelogram. Can you find the area of a triangle that has the same base and height as the parallelogram? Explain.

Facts Practice, See page 663.

Lesson 1

Audio Tutor 2/16 Listen and Understand

Solid Figures

Objective Identify solid figures.

Vocabulary
- solid figure
- face
- edge
- vertex
- base
- prism
- pyramid
- cylinder

Learn About It

Most of the objects that you see every day are solid figures. Boxes, cups, cans, and other containers are all examples of solid figures.

▶ A **solid figure** has length, width, height, and takes up space.

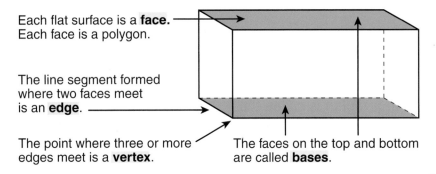

Each flat surface is a **face.** Each face is a polygon.

The line segment formed where two faces meet is an **edge**.

The point where three or more edges meet is a **vertex**.

The faces on the top and bottom are called **bases**.

▶ A **prism** is a solid figure that has two parallel congruent bases joined by rectangular faces. Each prism is named by the shape of its base. The pasta box to the right is a rectangular prism since its bases are rectangles.

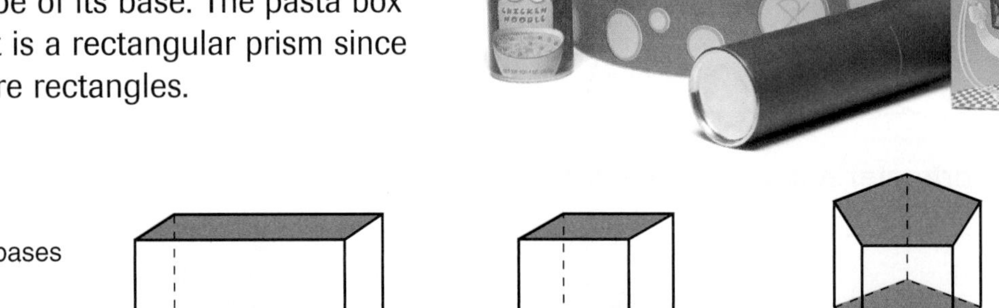

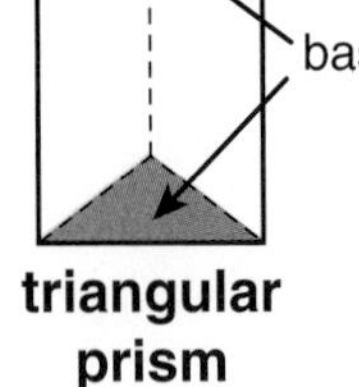

triangular prism

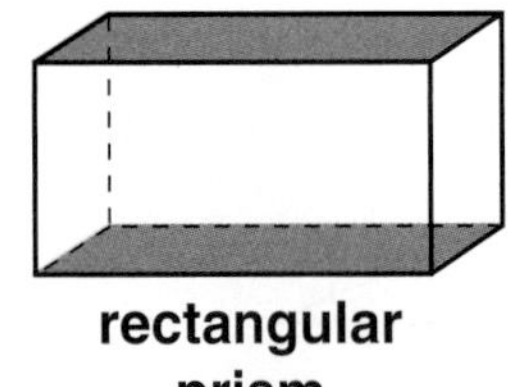
rectangular prism

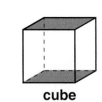

cube (all faces are congruent)

pentagonal prism

▶ A **pyramid** has one base that can be any polygon. All of the other faces are triangles that share a vertex.

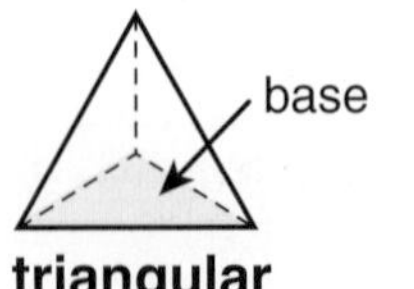

triangular pyramid

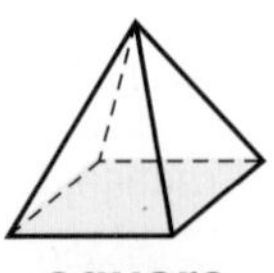
square pyramid

pentagonal pyramid

Some solid figures have curved surfaces.

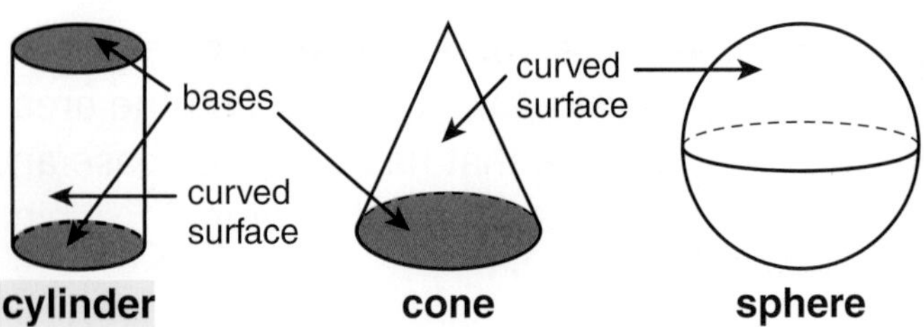

cylinder **cone** **sphere**

Extra Help at eduplace.com/map

Guided Practice

Classify each solid figure. Then write the number of faces, vertices, and edges.

1. 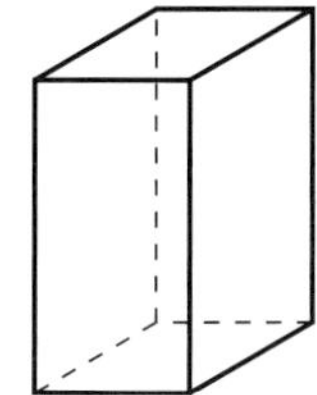

2. 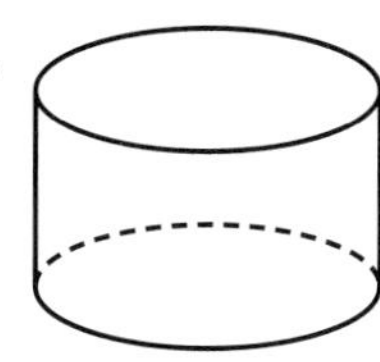

3. 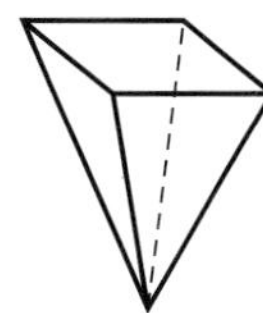

Ask Yourself

- How many bases are there?
- What shape is the base?

Explain Your Thinking ▶ What is the difference between a rectangular pyramid and a rectangular prism?

Practice and Problem Solving

Name each solid figure. Then write the number of faces, vertices, and edges.

4. 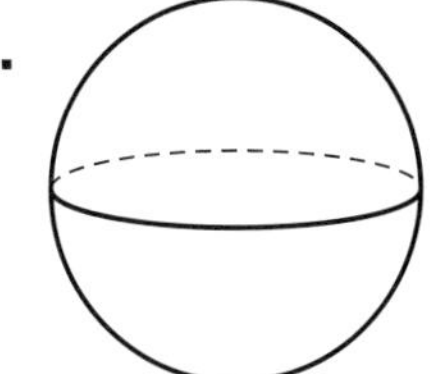

5. 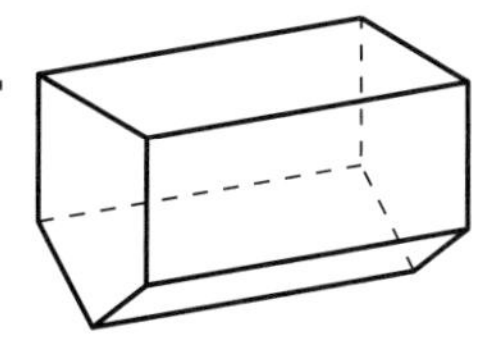

6. 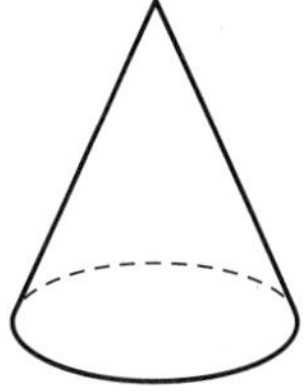

7. 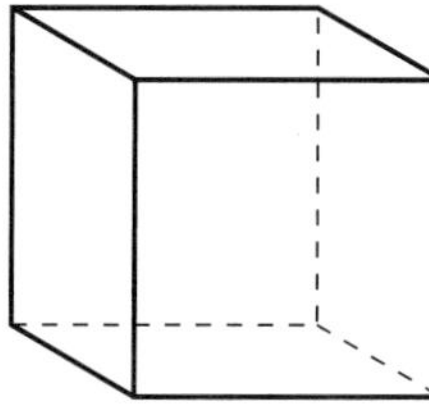

8. 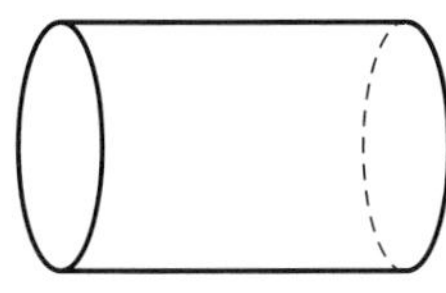

9. 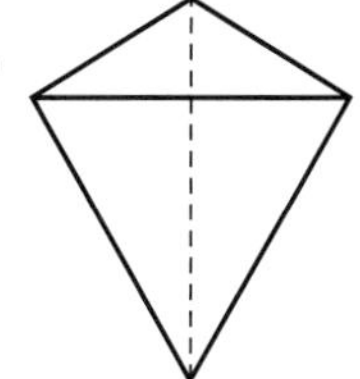

10. 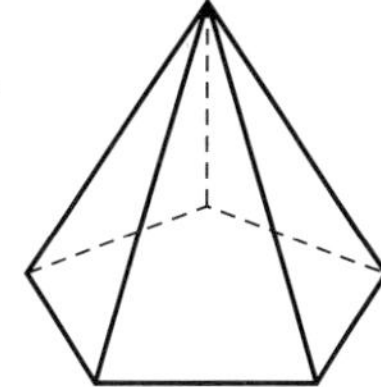

11. 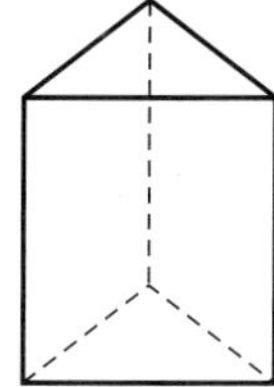

Solve.

12. Use 24 cubes to build a rectangular prism. Then sketch it on a sheet of graph paper.

13. Sketch a figure with one square base and four triangular faces. Then name the figure.

14. Write About It What solid figure can you make if you combine two congruent cubes? Explain.

15. A pyramid has six faces, including the base. What type of pyramid must it be? Explain.

Mixed Review and Test Prep

Open Response

Estimate. Then add or subtract.
(Ch. 11, Lessons 2–3)

16. $4.73 + 6.8$

17. $23.81 - 5.64$

18. $0.69 + 0.45$

19. $0.9 - 0.44$

Multiple Choice

20. Which solid figure has exactly one circular base? (Ch. 17, Lesson 1)

A cone

B cylinder

C pyramid

D sphere

Extra Practice See page 469, Set A.

Two-Dimensional Views of Solid Figures

Materials
cubes
grid paper
(Learning Tool 14)
triangular dot paper
(Learning Tool 17)

Objective Identify different two-dimensional views of a solid figure.

Work Together

To make a two-dimensional drawing of the solid figure, you can use triangular dot paper and grid paper as shown at the right. You can also use two-dimensional drawings to show what solid figures look like from different views.

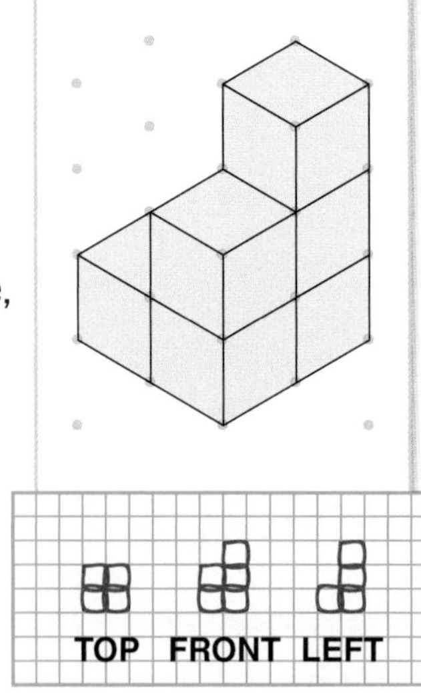
TOP FRONT LEFT

Try this activity to identify different two-dimensional views of the figure shown below.

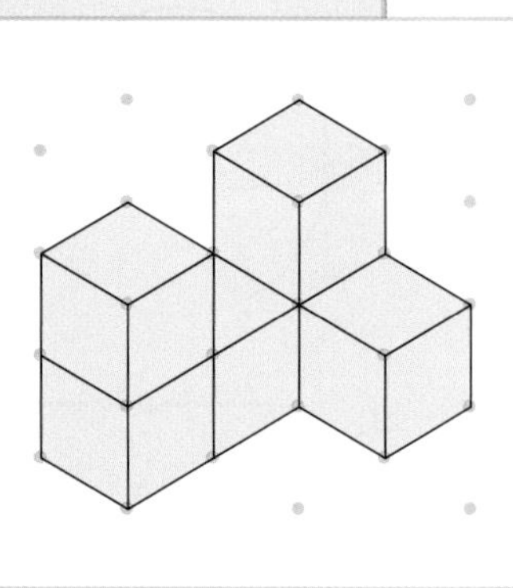

STEP 1 Use cubes to build the figure.

STEP 2 Draw these views on grid paper:
- the top view
- the view from the right side
- the front view

You can use two-dimensional views to build and draw a three-dimensional figure.

Try this activty to create a solid figure that looks like this:

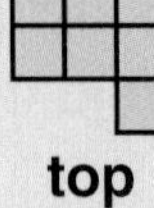
top

right side

front

STEP 1 Look at the top view. What can you say about the bottom of the figure? Use cubes to build the bottom layer of the figure.

STEP 2 Use the side and front views to visualize the middle layer and then the top layer of the figure. Build each layer.

STEP 3 Draw the figure on triangular dot paper. Could you draw another figure? Explain.

On Your Own

Use cubes to build each figure. On graph paper, draw each figure from the top, from the side, and from the front.

1. 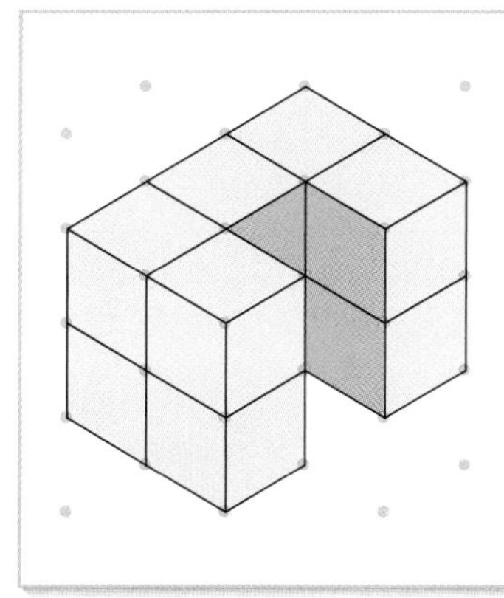

2. 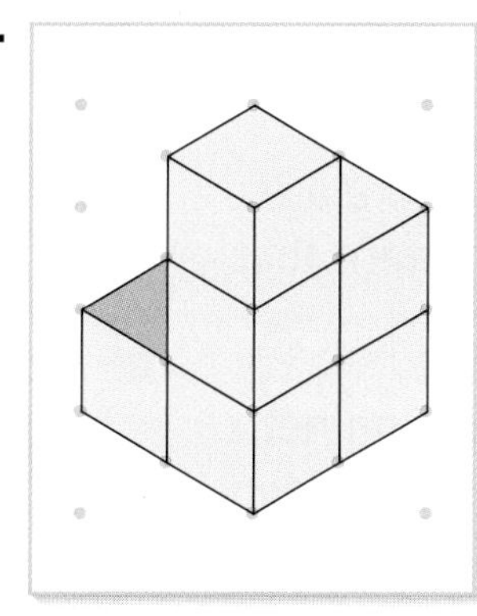

3. 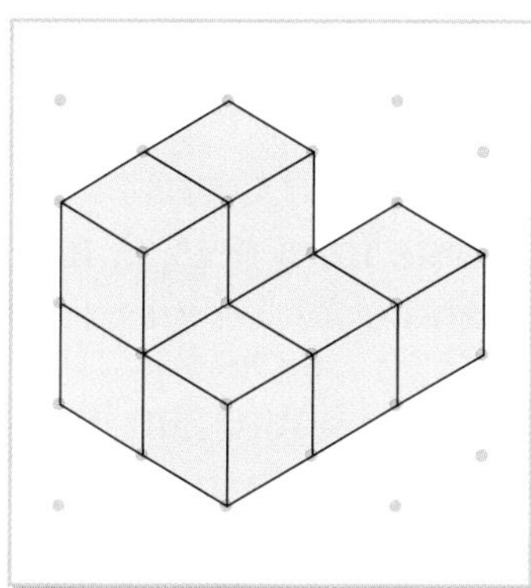

Use cubes to build a three-dimensional figure with these views. Then draw the figure on triangular dot paper.

4. 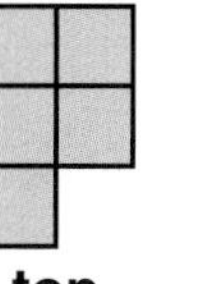

top

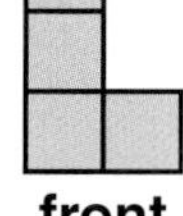

side

front

5. 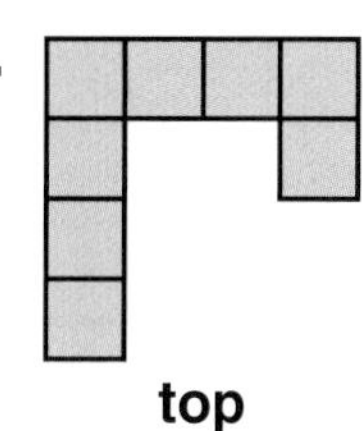

top

side

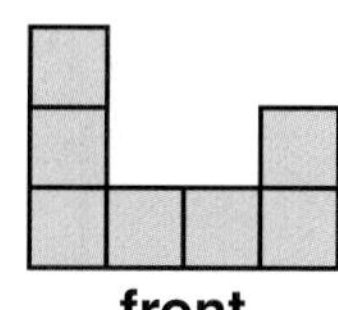

front

6. Could the three views shown below be views of a rectangular prism? Explain.

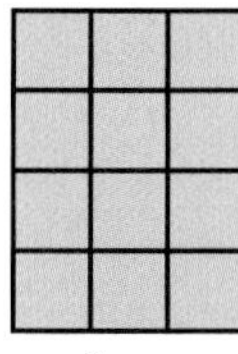

top

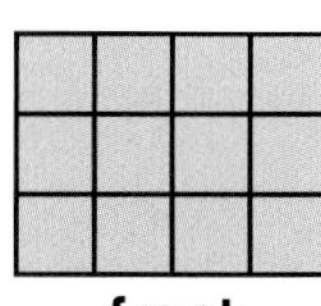

side

front

7. Name a solid figure that is a triangle from the top view and has congruent rectangles from the side views.

8. Sketch the top, side, and front views of each solid figure.

   a. cube **b.** cylinder

   c. cone **d.** sphere

Talk About It • Write About It

Use what you have learned about modeling and drawing solid figures to answer these questions.

9. Why does the top view tell you how the bottom layer of cubes must be arranged?

10. A figure has a top view and side view that are identical. What type of solid figure might this be? Explain how you know.

Nets

Objective Identify the nets of solid figures.

Vocabulary

net

Materials
inch grid paper (Learning Tool 15)
scissors
tape

Learn About It

Cardboard boxes and other containers are made from nets. A **net** is a flat pattern that can be folded into a solid figure.

A solid figure can have more than one net. For example, both nets below can be folded to make a triangular prism.

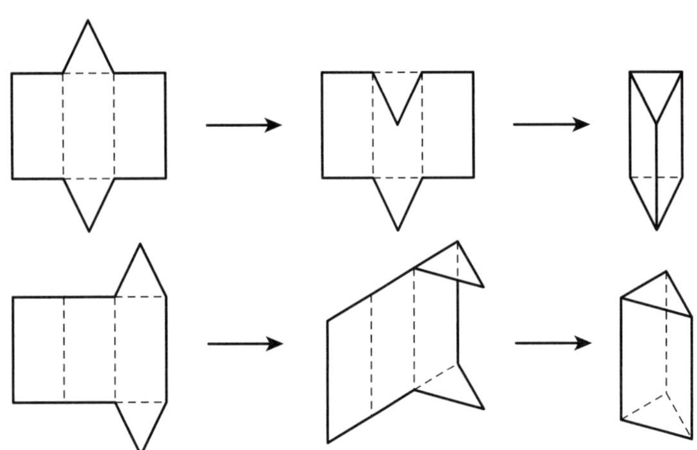

When making a net, you may need to add "flaps" in order to secure the net. However, the "flaps" are not part of a geometric net.

Try this activity to make nets.

STEP 1 On a sheet of grid paper, draw the net shown at the right. Then cut it out.

- Predict what solid figure the net will make.

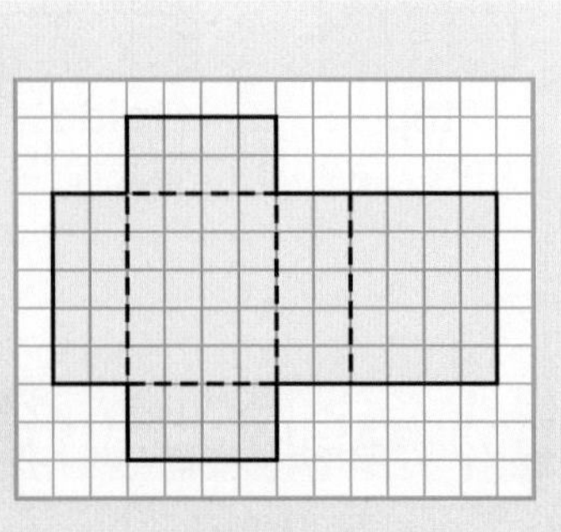

STEP 2 Fold the net on the dotted lines. Tape the edges together.

- Was your prediction correct?

STEP 3 Repeat Step 1 and Step 2 using the net at the right.

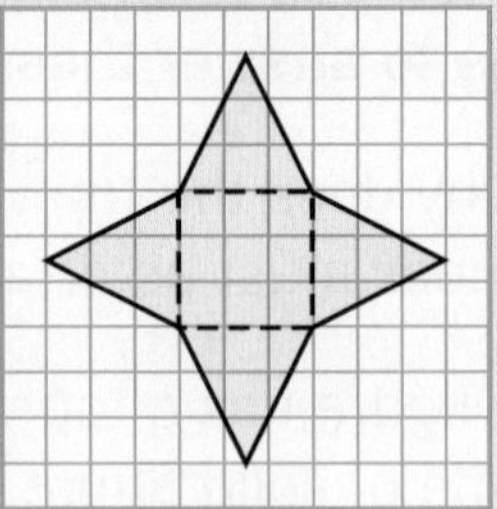

Guided Practice

Predict what shape each net will make.

1.  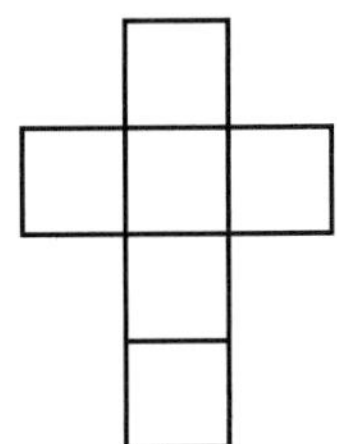

2. 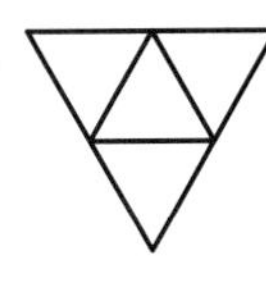

3. 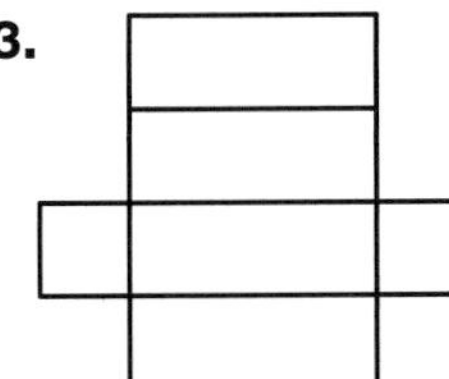

> **Ask Yourself**
> - Which side of the net is the base? What shape does it have?
> - How many faces will the shape have?

Explain Your Thinking ▶ How did you make your prediction for Exercise 2?

Practice and Problem Solving

Predict what shape each net will make.

4. 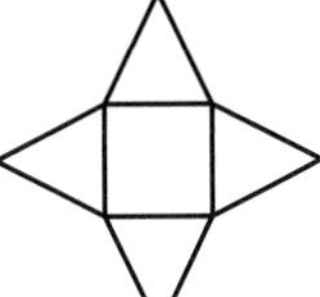

5. 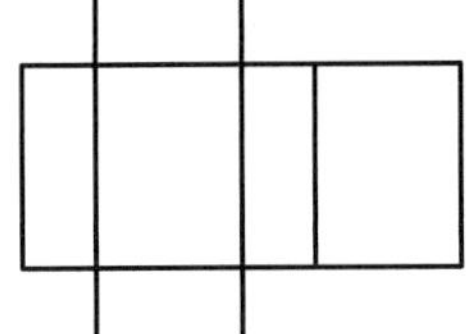

6. 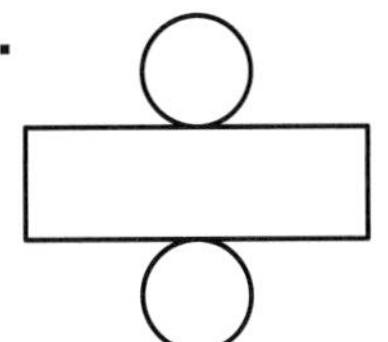

7. 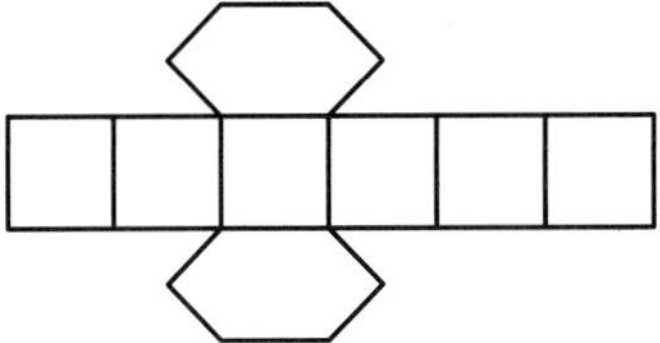

Draw a net for each solid figure.

8. 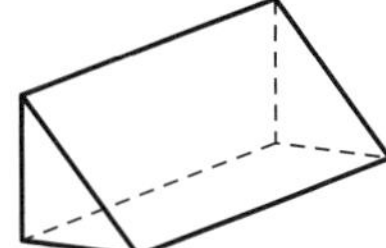

9. 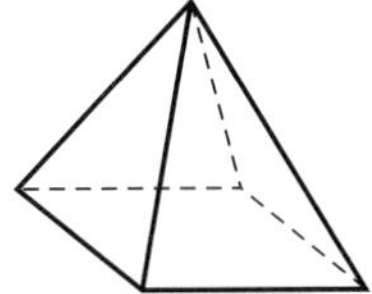

10. 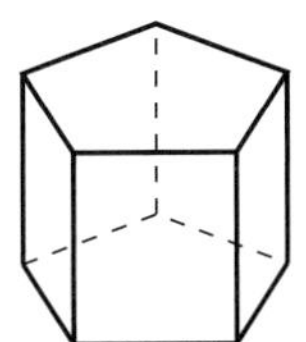

11. 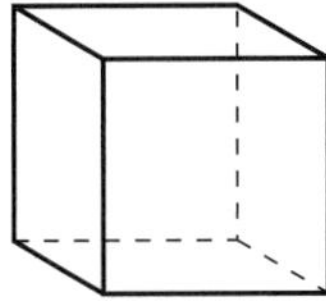

Solve.

12. **Predict** Which of the nets to the right will not form a cube? Explain your answer.

13. Draw another net that will form a cube.

14. A rectangular room is 15 feet by 17 feet. How much will it cost to cover the floor with carpet that costs $8.99 per square foot?

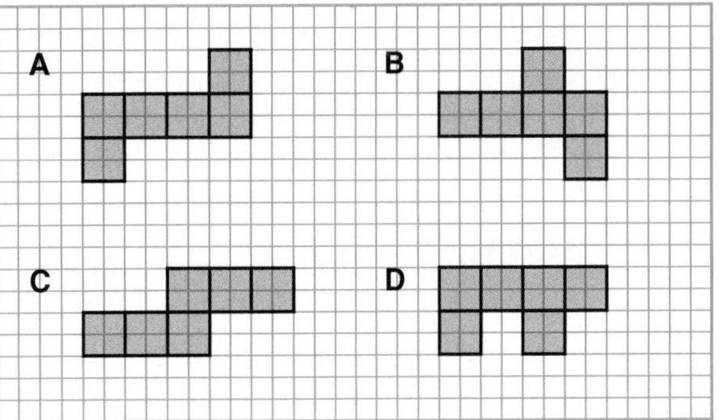

Mixed Review and Test Prep

Open Response

Find the area. (Ch. 16, Lessons 3–4)

15. 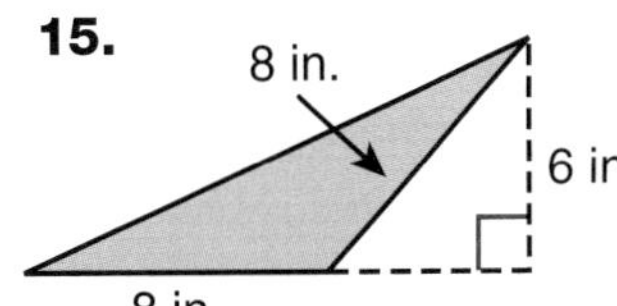

16. 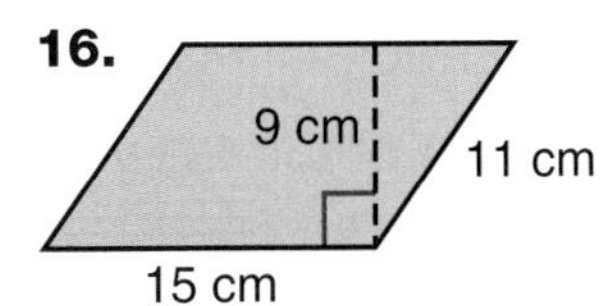

17. Describe the solid that could be made from this net. Explain your thinking. (Ch. 17, Lesson 3)

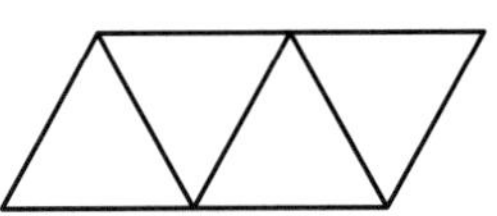

Extra Practice See page 469, Set B.

Lesson 4

Audio Tutor 2/17 Listen and Understand

Surface Area

Objective Use nets to find the surface area of solid figures.

Vocabulary
surface area

Learn About It

A department store stocks wrapping paper that can be folded to wrap shirt boxes. What is the least amount of wrapping paper you need to cover this shirt box?

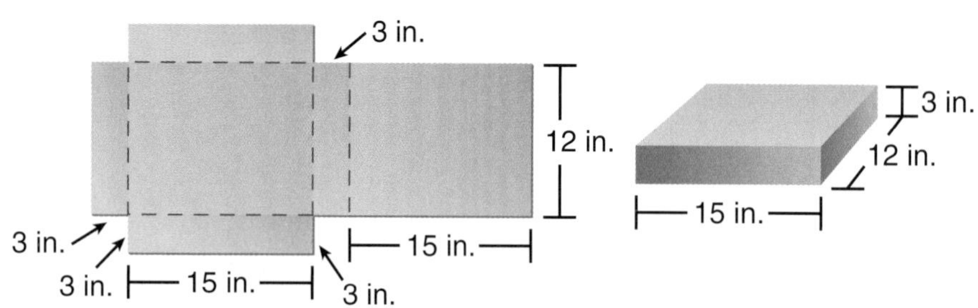

To solve the problem, find the surface area of the box. The **surface area** of a solid figure is the sum of the areas of all its faces and is measured in square units.

You can use a table to list the area of each face.

Face	Length	Width	Area
top	15 in.	12 in.	180 in.^{2}
bottom	15 in.	12 in.	180 in.^{2}
front	3 in.	12 in.	36 in.^{2}
back	3 in.	12 in.	36 in.^{2}
left side	3 in.	15 in.	45 in.^{2}
right side	3 in.	15 in.	45 in.^{2}
		sum:	522 in.^{2}

Solution: You need at least 522 in.^{2} of wrapping paper to cover the shirt box.

Think
However, you will probably need more paper, because the paper will have to overlap.

Since rectangular prisms have opposite faces that are congruent, you can compute the areas of opposite faces to find surface area.

Determine the surface area of the solid figure.

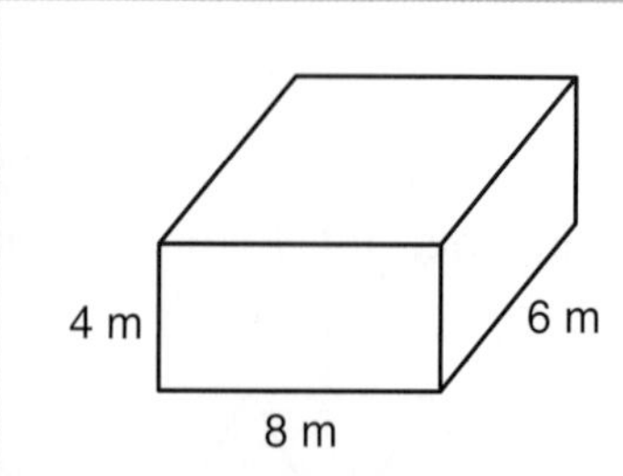

Area of Faces:

top and bottom: $2 \times (8 \times 6) = 96$
front and back: $2 \times (8 \times 4) = 64$
right and left sides: $2 \times (6 \times 4) = 48$

The sum of the areas is: $96 + 64 + 48 = 208$

Solution: The surface area is 208 m^2.

Another Example

Surface Area of a Triangular Prism

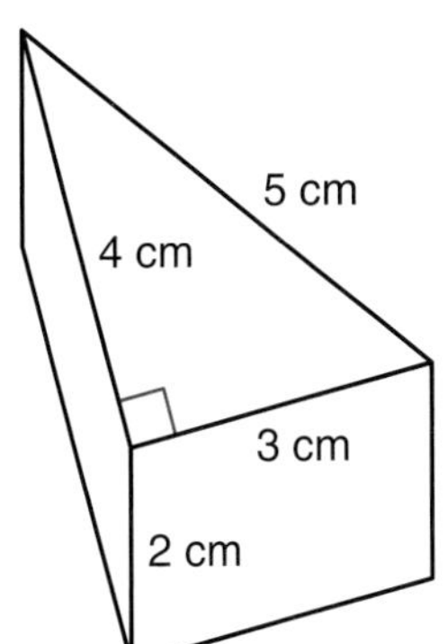

Think
The top and the bottom are congruent triangles. The front, left side, and right side are rectangles that are not congruent.

Area of Faces:

top and bottom: $2 \times (\frac{1}{2} \times 3 \times 4) = 12$

front: $3 \times 2 = 6$

left side: $2 \times 4 = 8$

right side: $2 \times 5 = 10$

The sum of the areas is: $12 + 6 + 8 + 10 = 36$

Solution: The surface area is 36 cm^2.

Guided Practice

Ask Yourself
- Which numbers do I multiply to find the surface area of each face?
- Which numbers do I add to find the surface area of the solid?

Predict what solid each net will make. Then determine the surface area of the solid figure. Each square is 1 cm^2.

1. 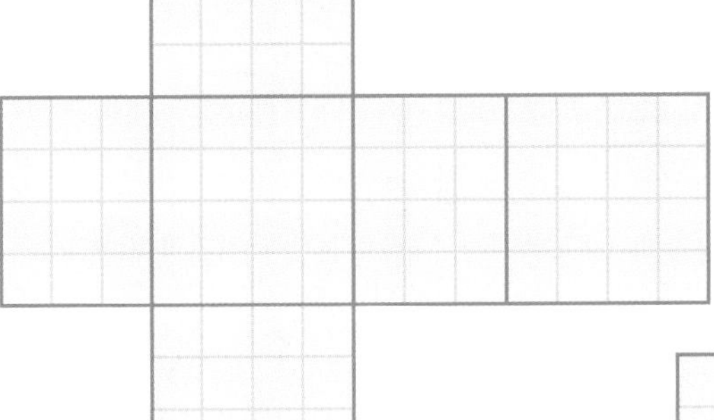

2. 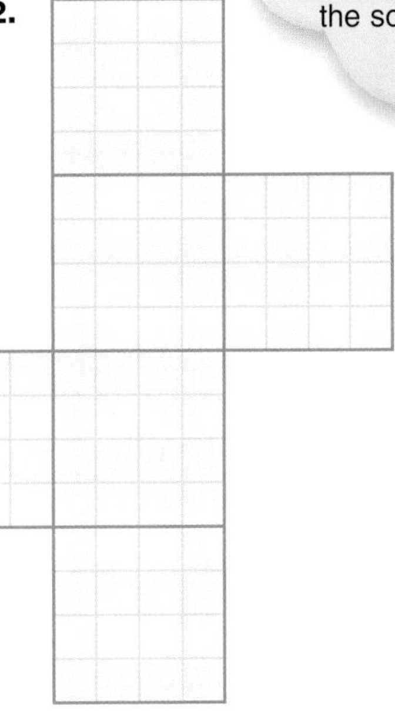

Determine the surface area of each solid figure.

3. 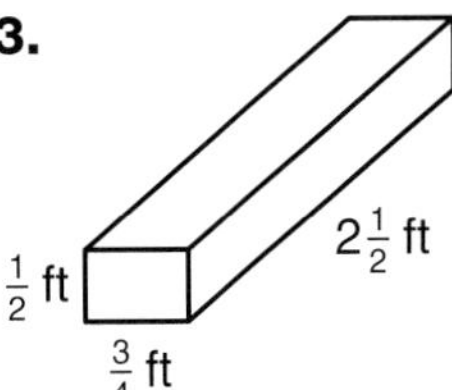

4. 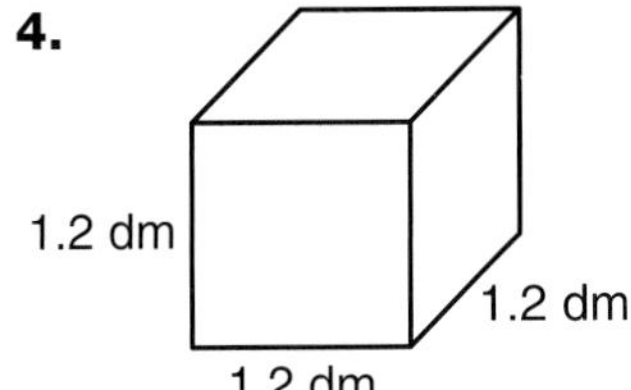

5. 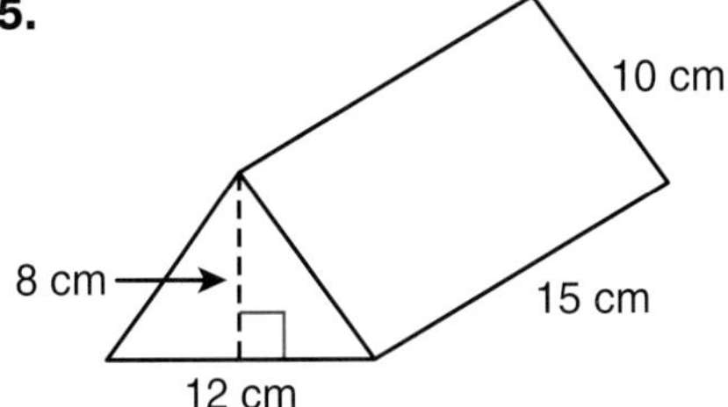

Explain Your Thinking ▶ Explain how you found the surface area in Exercise 5.

Practice and Problem Solving

Determine the surface area of each solid figure.

6. 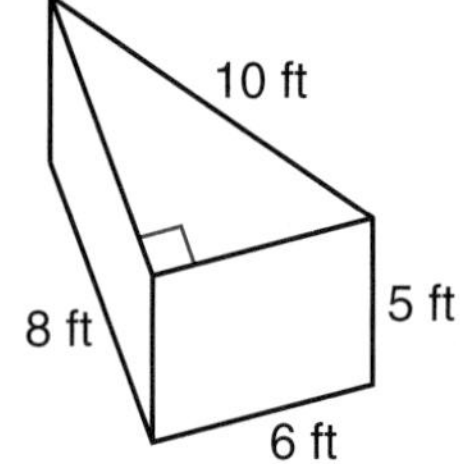

7. 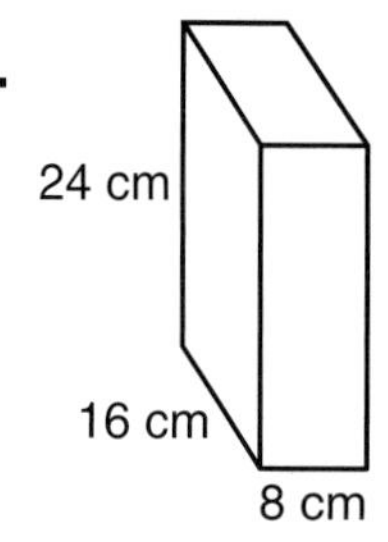

8. 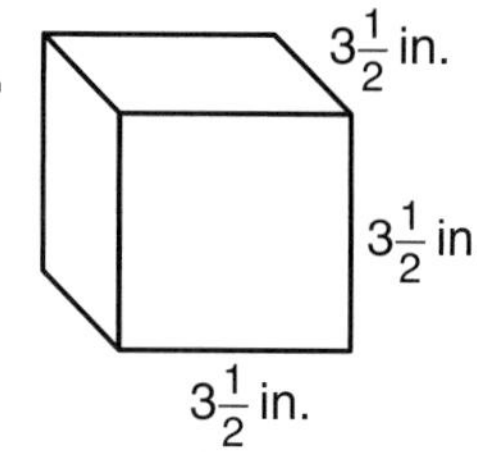

Copy and complete the table.

	Length of One Side (*s*) of Cube	Area of One Face (*f*)	Surface Area of Cube (*SA*)
9.	3 cm		
10.	4 cm		
11.	15 cm		
12.	6 cm		
13.	7 cm		
14.	8 cm		

Solve.

15. Study your results from Exercises 9–14. Write a formula that uses the length of a side (*s*) to find the surface area of a cube (*SA*).

16. What is the minimum amount of wrapping paper needed to wrap a box that has a length of 6 inches, a height of 4 inches, and a width of 5 inches?

17. The Graysons are sending 140 holiday cards. The cards come in boxes of 25. How many boxes of cards do the Graysons need?

18. **Predict** A box that is 10 inches long, 3 inches deep, and 4 inches high holds 6 pounds of snack mix. What size box will hold 12 pounds?

19. A fish tank is $2\frac{2}{3}$ feet long, $1\frac{1}{3}$ feet wide, and $1\frac{1}{2}$ feet high. The tank is open on top. How many square feet of glass were used to make the tank?

20. What is the minimum amount of wrapping paper needed to cover a box 5.2 cm high, 10.2 cm long, and 8.4 cm wide?

21. **Write About It** How does the surface area of a box change if you double each dimension of the box? Give examples to support your conclusion.

22. A box is 10 cm long, 12 cm wide, and 14 cm high. Does doubling the height double the surface area of the figure? Explain.

Extra Practice See page 469, Set C.

Problem Solving

Math Reasoning

Wrap It Up

Find the approximate length and width of a single rectangular sheet of wrapping paper that will completely wrap each gift below. Explain how you found your answers.

Remember when you wrap a gift, some of the paper usually overlaps. Note the overlap allowed for each.

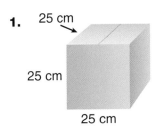

1. 25 cm, 25 cm, 25 cm

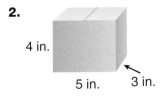

2. 4 in., 5 in., 3 in.

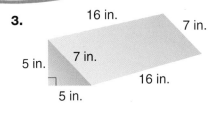

3. 16 in., 7 in., 5 in., 7 in., 16 in., 5 in.

Quick Check

Check your understanding of Lessons 1–4.

Name each solid figure. Then write the number of faces, vertices, and edges. (Lesson 1)

1.

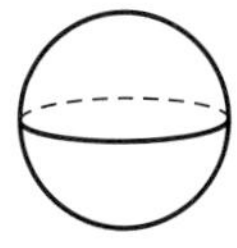

2.

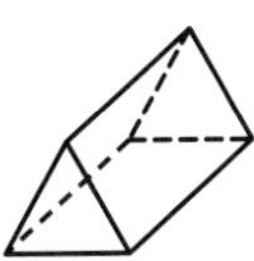

Predict what solid figure the net will make. Then determine the surface area. Each square is 1 cm^2. (Lessons 3–4)

3.

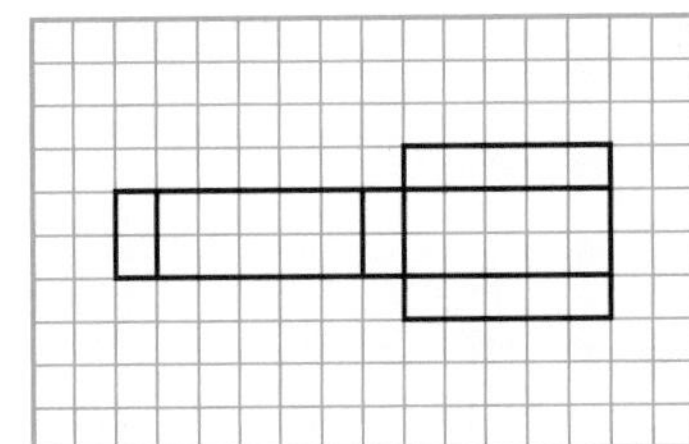

Use cubes to build each figure. Then draw the top view, the side view, and the front view of each figure. (Lesson 2)

4.

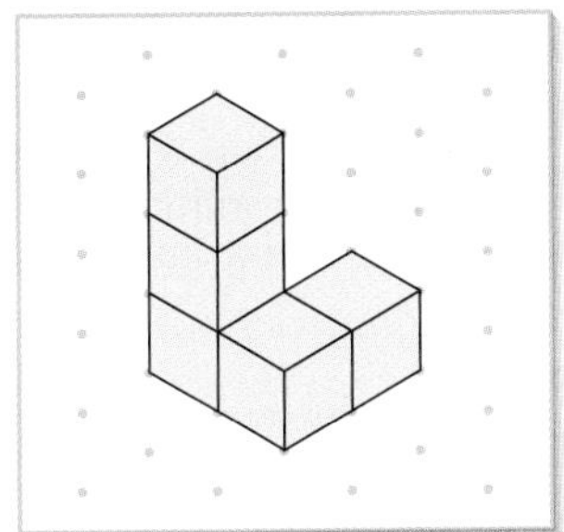

5.

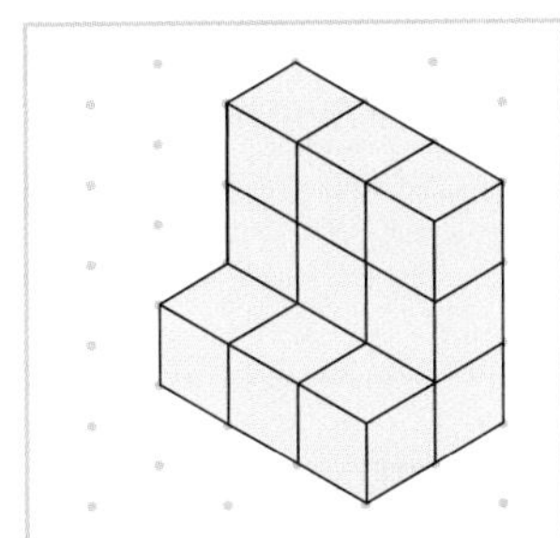

Lesson 5

Problem-Solving Strategy

Solve a Simpler Problem

Objective Solve problems by first solving simpler problems.

Problem José makes a solid figure that is 6 cubes long, 6 cubes high, and 6 cubes wide. José paints the outside of the figure orange. Suppose José takes the figure apart. How many of the cubes will have no orange paint on them?

UNDERSTAND

This is what you know:

- The large cube is made of $6 \times 6 \times 6$ small cubes.
- The outside faces of the small cubes are painted orange.

PLAN

You can solve a simpler problem.

SOLVE

Use models to represent the problem for smaller solid figures.

- Build a large cube that is 2 cubes long, 2 cubes wide, and 2 cubes high.
- Put a sticker or small piece of tape on the outside of each small cube.
- Take the large cube apart. Count the number of cubes with no stickers. Record that number in a table.
- Repeat the steps above, adding one cube to each dimension.
- Look for a pattern in your results. Use the pattern to find the answer.

Dimensions of Large Cube	Cubes With No Orange Paint	Pattern
$2 \times 2 \times 2$	0	0^3
$3 \times 3 \times 3$	1	1^3
$4 \times 4 \times 4$	8	2^3
$5 \times 5 \times 5$	27	3^3
$6 \times 6 \times 6$	?	?

Visualize the cubes without paint as a solid figure within the larger cube. What are the dimensions of the figure without paint?

Solution: The pattern shows that there will be 4^3, or 64 cubes with no orange paint.

LOOK BACK

Look back at the problem. Does the solution answer the question? Is the answer reasonable?

Guided Practice

Use the Ask Yourself questions to help you solve each problem.

1. Suppose 7 friends meet for dinner. Each friend shakes hands with every other friend. How many handshakes will there be?

 Draw pictures of simpler problems with fewer handshakes.

 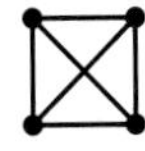

2 friends 1 handshake	3 friends 3 handshakes	4 friends 6 handshakes

2. Pilar makes a figure 6 cubes long, 6 cubes high, and 6 cubes wide. She paints the outside of the figure red. How many of the cubes have 2 or more red faces?

Ask Yourself

UNDERSTAND What facts do I know?

PLAN Did I use all the needed information?

SOLVE Did I solve a simpler problem first?

- Did I find the pattern?
- Did I continue the pattern to find the number of handshakes for 7 friends?

LOOK BACK Did I solve the problem?

Independent Practice

Solve each problem by solving a simpler problem.

3. A warehouse has 10 security guards. A team of 2 guards must be present at any given time. How many different teams of 2 guards are possible?

4. Mark builds a brick wall that is 10 bricks long and 3 bricks high. He paints the front, back, top, and sides of the wall. How many of the sides of individual bricks are painted? Explain the pattern you used to find the answer.

5. Janelle's Restaurant has 12 square tables. Each table can seat one person on each side. If the tables are pushed together to make one long table, how many people can sit at the long table?

6. An industrial park has 8 storage centers. Each storage center has a direct road to each of the other storage centers. How many roads are in the industrial park?

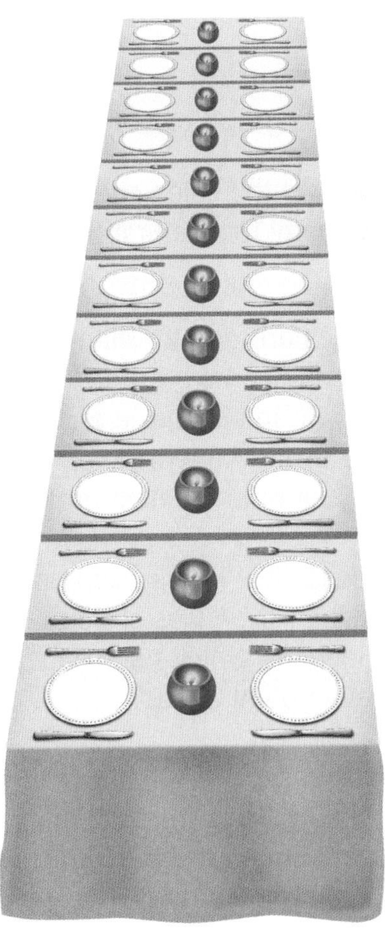

Go On

Mixed Problem Solving

Solve each problem. Tell what strategy you used.

7. Find the seventh figure in the pattern shown below.

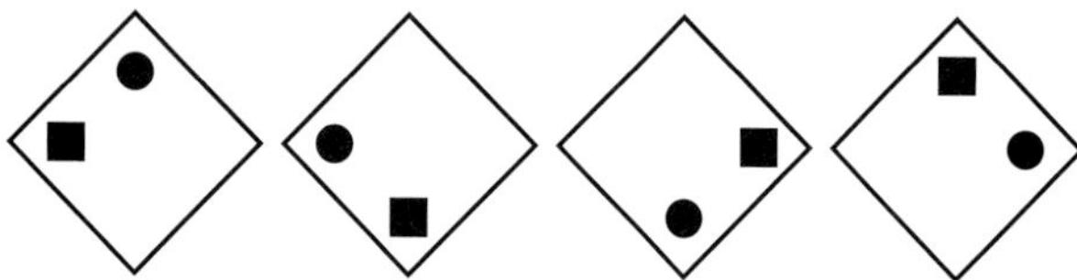

8. The LCM of two numbers is 60. The GCF of the same two numbers is 4. The sum of the numbers is 32. What are the numbers?

9. A solid figure is made up of blue cubes and white cubes. It is 4 cubes wide, 4 cubes long, and 4 cubes high. There are 3 times as many blue cubes as white cubes. How many blue cubes are there?

You Choose

Strategy
- Draw a Diagram
- Find a Pattern
- Guess and Check
- Solve a Simpler Problem
- Use Models

Computation Method
- Mental Math
- Estimation
- Paper and Pencil
- Calculator

Data Use the graph to solve Problems 10–13.

The graph shows the sales and expenses for a toy company for the first five years in business.

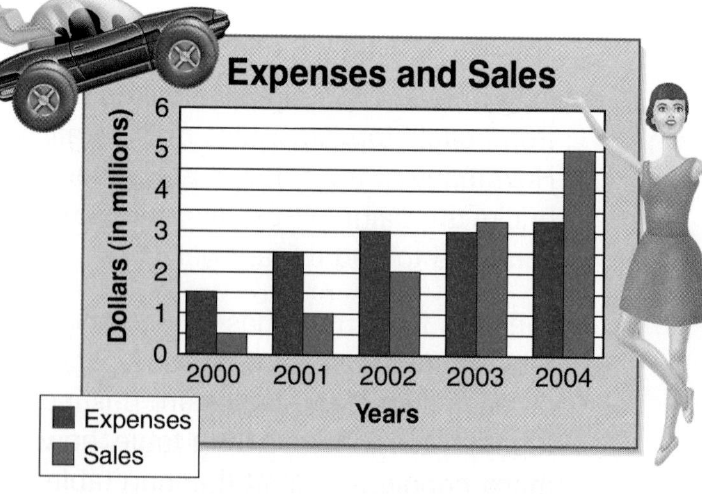

10. When sales are greater than expenses, the company earns a profit. What was the first year in which the toy company earned a profit? In which year did the company earn its greatest profit?

11. In business, the "break-even point" occurs when expenses are equal to sales. Between which two years did the break-even point occur?

12. When expenses are greater than sales, the company has a loss. During which years was there a loss? In which year did the company have its greatest loss?

13. **Predict** Do you think the company will have a profit or loss in 2005? About how great do you think that profit or loss will be? Explain your answer.

Problem Solving on Tests

Multiple Choice

Choose the letter of the correct answer. If a correct answer is not here, choose NH.

1. **Measurement** Gracie feeds her dog an average of 8 ounces of dog food per day. About how many pounds of dog food does Gracie feed her dog per month?

A 15 lb **C** 60 lb

B 20 lb **D** NH

(Chapter 6, Lesson 3)

2. The area of the triangle is 30 square centimeters. What is the measure of side *A*?

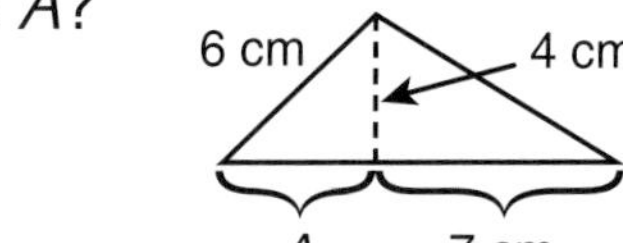

F 3 cm **H** 8 cm

G 7.5 cm **J** 15 cm

(Chapter 16, Lesson 4)

Open Response

Solve each problem.

3. Melanie uses 6-inch blocks to build a tower that is 24 inches high. Jack uses 8-inch blocks to build a tower of the same height. Who uses more blocks? How many more?

Represent Support your solution with a picture. (Chapter 10, Lesson 7)

4. In the first six games of a seven-game tournament, a basketball player has these point totals: 18, 24, 22, 12, 15, and 24. The player's score in the seventh game does not change her median score. What does the player score in the seventh game?
Explain How did you find your answer? (Chapter 8, Lesson 2)

Constructed Response

5. Annie has moved into a new house. She is planning to decorate her bedroom. Annie made a drawing on grid paper.

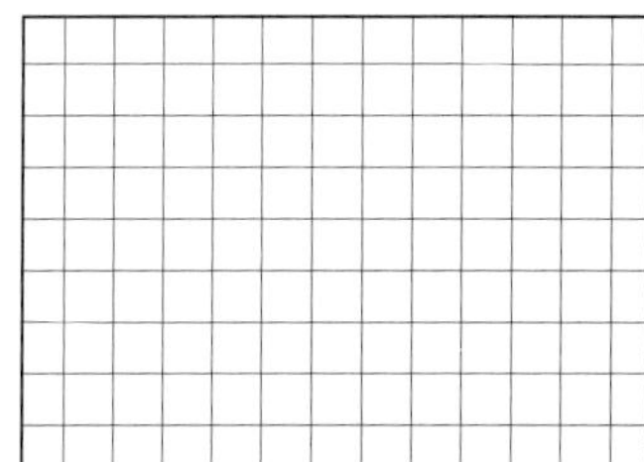

Information you need

- The ceiling is 8 ft high. The length of the room is 14 ft and the width is 10 ft.
- The room has two doors, one is for the entrance, the other for the closet. Each door measures 36 inches by 84 inches.
- Annie plans to put shutters on the two windows in the room. The windows each measure 2 ft by 5 ft.

a What is the volume of Annie's room? How do you know?

b Annie plans to put tiles on the floor. The tiles are 6 in. square. How many tiles will she need? Explain.

c The paint salesman said that 1 gallon of paint is enough to paint up to 400 square feet. Will 1 gallon be enough to paint Annie's bedroom walls? How many square feet of wall space does Annie have?

(Chapter 17)

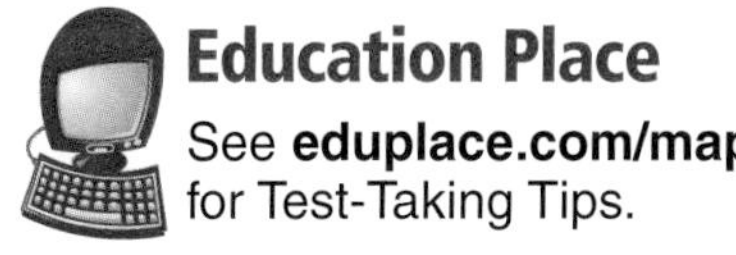

Education Place
See **eduplace.com/map** for Test-Taking Tips.

Hands On Lesson 6

Audio Tutor 2/18 Listen and Understand

Volume

Objective Use a formula to find the volume of a cube, a rectangular prism, and a triangular prism.

Vocabulary
volume
cubic unit

Materials
cubes

Learn About It

Cedric's collection of CDs is growing. Each case is a rectangular prism, and when he stacks the cases, they form an even larger prism. Soon the "prism" of CDs will be too large for Cedric's shelf!

The **volume** of a solid figure is the amount of space the figure occupies. Volume is measured using **cubic units**. A cube measuring 1 unit on each edge has a volume of 1 cubic unit.

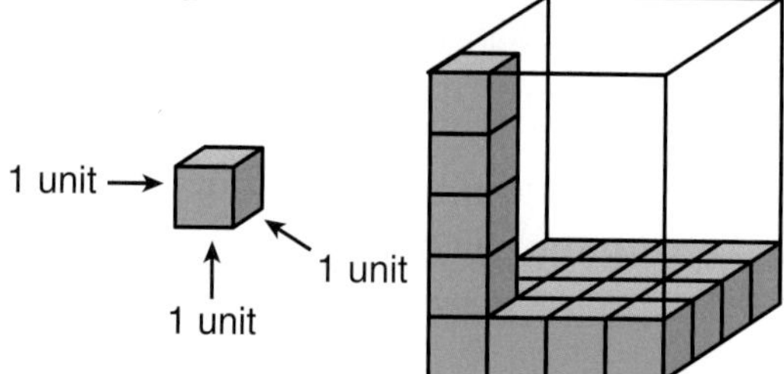

Try this activity to find the volume of a solid figure.

STEP 1 Create a rectangular prism that is 2 cubes long, 3 cubes wide, and 1 cube high. Count the number of cubes. Record the data on the recording sheet.

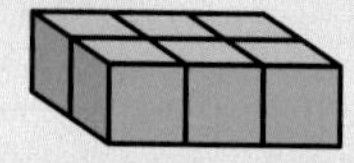

STEP 2 Add a second layer of cubes on top of the figure. Record the data.

STEP 3 Add a third layer of cubes on top of the figure. Record the data.

STEP 4 Write a multiplication sentence that shows how to find the volume of each of the following:

a. one layer of cubes

b. two layers of cubes

c. three layers of cubes

What multiplication equation could you use to find the volume (V) of any rectangular prism with length l, width w, and height h? Explain.

In a cube, the length, width, and height are equal and are represented by the variable s. What equation could you use to find the volume of any cube?

You can use a formula to find the volume of any prism.

Using Formulas for Volume

Volume of a Cube

$V = s^3$

$= 4 \times 4 \times 4$

$= 64$

The volume is 64 cubic units.

Volume of a Rectangular Prism

$V = l \times w \times h$

$= 3 \times 5 \times 8$

$= 120$

The volume is 120 in.^{3}.

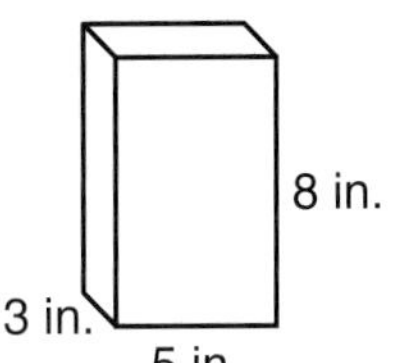

Volume of a Triangular Prism

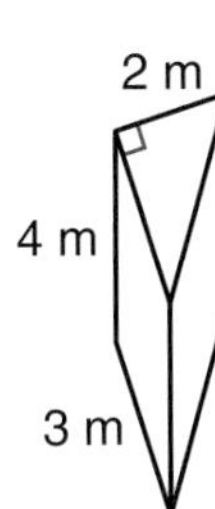

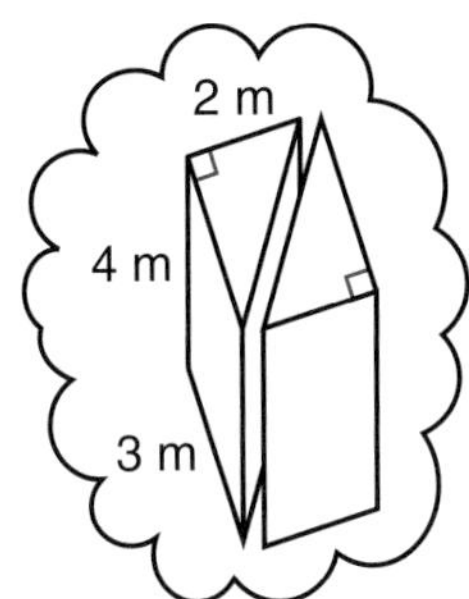

Think
The volume of the triangular prism at the left is one half of the volume of a rectangular prism with the same length, width, and height.

$V = B \times h$

$= \frac{1}{2} \times l \times w \times h$

$= \frac{1}{2} \times 3 \times 2 \times 4$

$= 12$

The volume is 12 m^3.

B means "area of base"
Area of base $= \frac{1}{2}lw$

Remember
how to write abbreviations
cubic inches: in.^{3}
cubic centimeters: cm^3
cubic meters: m^3

Some solid figures are complex figures that are made of smaller prisms. You can use what you know about finding the volume of prisms to find the volume for these figures.

Determine the volume of the solid figure.

STEP 1 Separate the figure into simpler solid figures. Find the volume of each figure. A cube is 1 cm on each side.

Volume of A $= 1 \times 3 \times 2$

$= 6$

The volume of A is 6 cm^3.

Volume of B $= 2 \times 3 \times 3$

$= 18$

The volume of B is 18 cm^3.

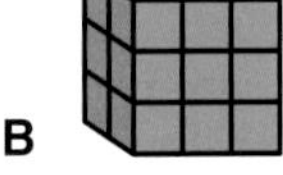

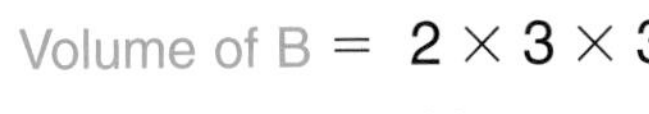

STEP 2 Add the volumes of the simpler solid figures to find the volume of the complex solid.

$V = 6 \text{ cm}^3 + 18 \text{ cm}^3$

$= 24 \text{ cm}^3$

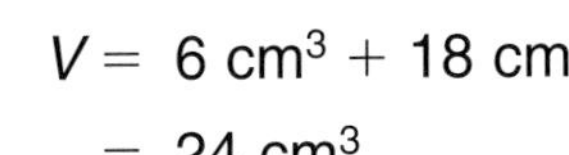

Solution: The volume of the solid figure is 24 cm^3.

Guided Practice

Ask Yourself

- Which numbers do I multiply?
- Which unit symbol do I use?
- Is the answer in cubic units?

Determine the volume of each solid figure.

1. 

2. 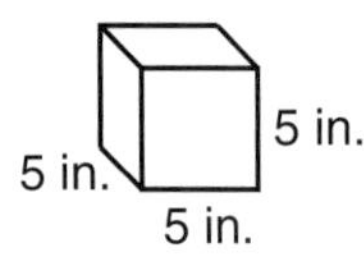

3. 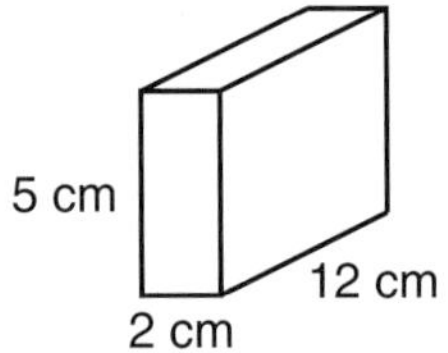

4. 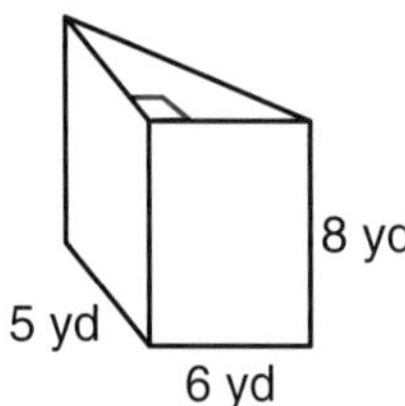

5. 

Explain Your Thinking ▶ How can you use multiplication and addition to find the volume of the figure in Exercise 5?

Practice and Problem Solving

Determine the volume of each solid figure.

6. 

7. 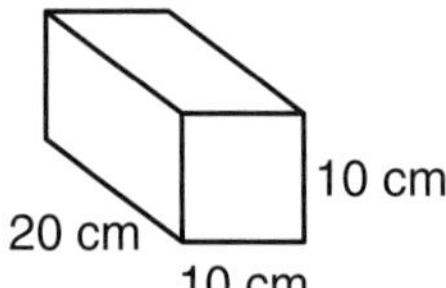

8. 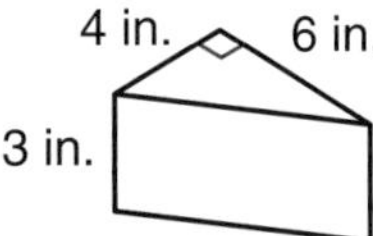

9. 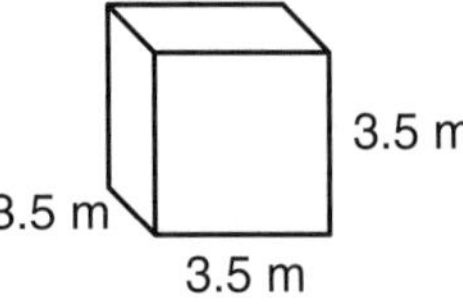

10. 

11. 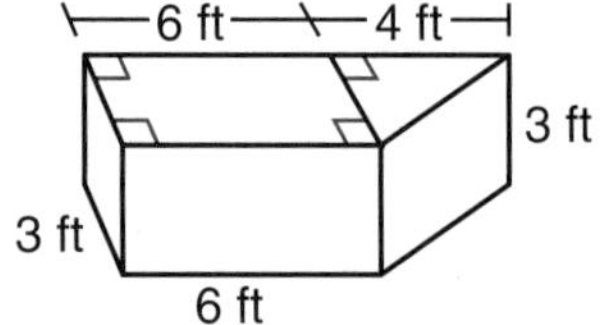

Copy and complete the chart below.

	Measurements of Rectangular Prisms					
	length	width	height	perimeter of base	area of base	volume
12.	3 cm	5 cm		16 cm	15 cm^2	30 cm^3
13.	4 cm	5 cm	2 cm			
14.	5 cm		4 cm	20 cm	25 cm^2	
15.	8 cm	3 cm				72 cm^3
16.		6 cm	10 cm			180 cm^3
17.	7 cm		4 cm	30 cm	56 cm^2	

Choose the most appropriate measure.
Write *perimeter, area,* or *volume*.

18. the distance around a baseball diamond

19. the amount of sand needed to fill a box

20. the amount of carpeting to cover a floor

21. the amount of space in a car's trunk

22. the amount of fencing to enclose a rectangular garden

23. the amount of wall space one gallon of paint will cover

Data Use the picture to solve Problems 24–28.

Cynthia builds the cedar chest shown on the right. The bottom and each side is 1 inch thick.

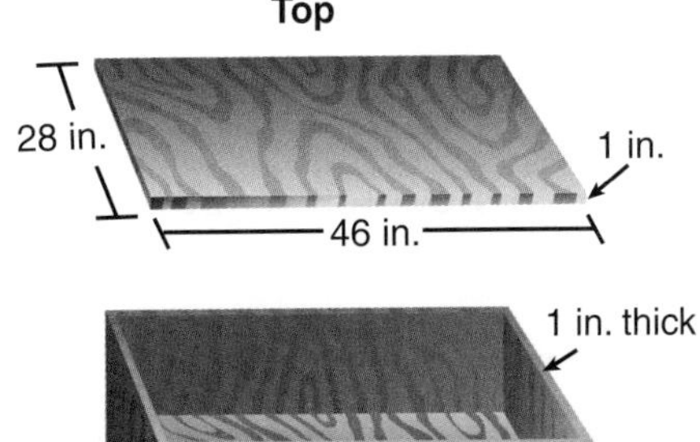

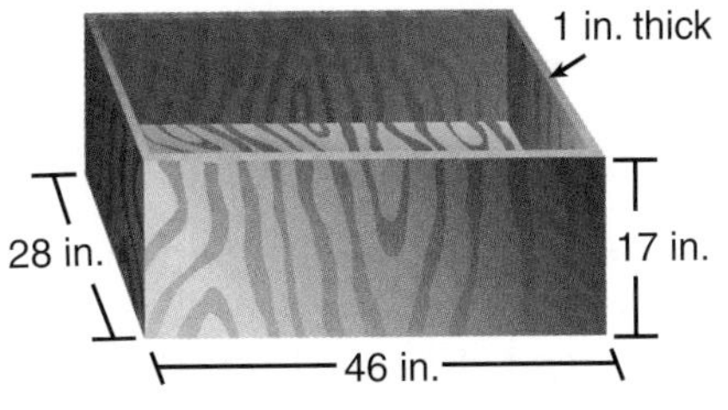

24. She lines the bottom of the inside with felt. How much felt does she need? Explain how you found your answer.

25. Cynthia puts a strip of copper around the top of the chest. How much copper does she need?

26. What is the volume of the cedar chest? Explain how you decided what dimensions should be used to find the volume. [*Hint:* The volume is not 21,896 $in.^3$.]

27. Cynthia packs the chest with sweater bags that are 12 inches wide, 13 inches long, and 2 inches high. How many sweater bags can Cynthia fit in the chest?

28. **What If?** Suppose that Cynthia increases the height of the chest by 2 inches. How would that increased height change the volume of the chest? How many more sweater bags would Cynthia be able to put in the chest?

29. **You Decide** Think of something you might need to store, such as books or clothing. Design a container for storing that item. Include the dimensions and an explanation of why that container would be suited for storing that item.

Mixed Review and Test Prep

Open Response

Divide (Ch. 5, Lesson 1)

30. 10,000 ÷ 2

31. 18,000 ÷ 600

32. 2,500 ÷ 50

33. 81,000 ÷ 900

34. $80\overline{)64,000}$

35. $1,000\overline{)70,000}$

36. $60\overline{)540,000}$

37. $50\overline{)600,000}$

38. The box below has a volume of 80 cm^3. Find the height of the box. Explain how you got your answer.
(Ch. 17, Lesson 6)

Extra Practice See page 469, Set D.

Lesson 7

Problem-Solving Application

Use Formulas

Objective Use a formula to solve a problem.

You can use formulas to solve problems.

Problem The manager of a warehouse wants to know how much space he will need to stack a shipment of boxes. Each edge of each box is 3 feet long. The total shipment will take up 3,240 cubic feet of space. If the boxes are stacked 6 high and 4 deep, how many feet wide will the stack of boxes be?

UNDERSTAND

What is the question?

- How many feet wide will the stack of boxes be?

What do you know?

- Each edge of each box is 3 feet long.
- The entire shipment is 3,240 cubic feet.
- The boxes are to be stacked 6 high and 4 deep.

PLAN

Find the height of 6 boxes and the length of 4 boxes. Then divide the volume by the product of the height and length.

Volume of a rectangular prism = length × width × height = $l \times w \times h$

SOLVE

- Find the height of 6 boxes.

  $h = 3 \text{ ft} \times 6 = 18 \text{ ft}$

- Find the length of 4 boxes.

  $l = 3 \text{ ft} \times 4 = 12 \text{ ft}$

- Multiply $l \times h$.

  $18 \times 12 = 216$

- Then divide.

  $3{,}240 \div 216 = 15$

Solution: The stack of boxes will be 15 ft wide.

LOOK BACK

Look back at the problem.
Does the solution make sense?

Guided Practice

Use the formulas for area and volume to solve Problems 1 and 2.

1. Warren builds a flower planter that is 4 feet long, 3 feet wide, and 2 feet high. He paints the outside of the planter, but not the bottom. What area did Warren paint?

2. A tank is 5 meters long and 3 meters wide. The tank holds 30 cubic meters of water. How deep is the tank?

   Hint What measurements do you know? What measurement do you need to find?

Ask Yourself

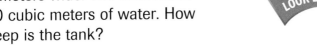

UNDERSTAND **What does the question ask me to find?**

PLAN **Which formulas do I need to use?**

SOLVE
- **Did I choose the correct formulas?**
- **Did I substitute the correct numbers for the variables?**

Is the answer reasonable?

Independent Practice

Use the formulas for perimeter, area, and volume to solve Problems 3–7.

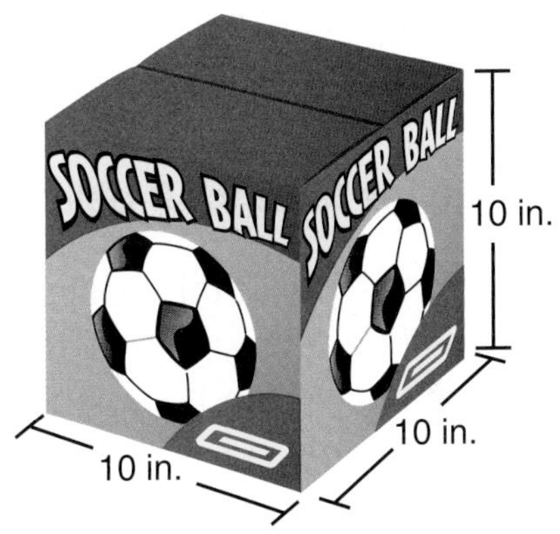

3. A manufacturer packages soccer balls in 10-inch cubes. How many boxes of soccer balls can fit in a cardboard container that is 30 in. by 40 in. by 20 in.?

4. What is the minimum amount of cardboard that is needed to make one soccer-ball box as shown at the right?

5. Kevin covers the rectangular floor of his room with 240 square feet of carpet. The length of the room is 20 feet. What is the width of the room? What is the perimeter of the room?

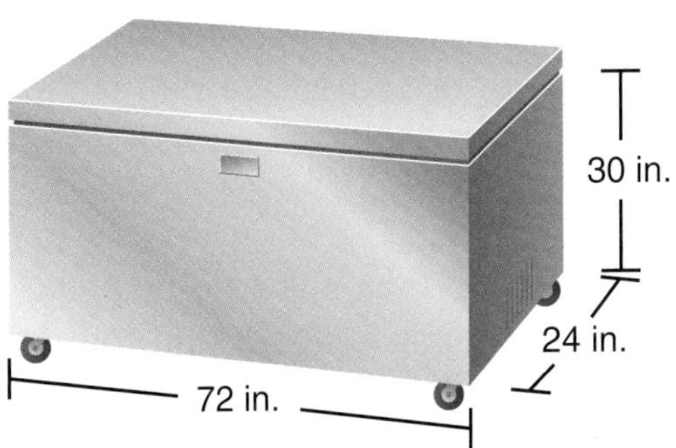

6. A restaurant buys the freezer shown at the right. What is the volume of the freezer in cubic inches?

7. There are 1,728 cubic inches in one cubic foot. What is a reasonable estimate for the volume of the freezer in cubic feet? Explain how you made your estimate.

Go On

Mixed Problem Solving

Solve. Show your work. Tell what strategy you used.

8. Three containers have a combined volume of 144 cubic feet. The larger container has two times the volume of each of the other two containers. What is the volume of each container?

9. At the end of its first month, a health club had 240 members. The manager's goal is to sign up at least 25 new members per month. If the manager meets her goal, how many members will there be at the end of the first year?

10. Sarah, Michael, Fred, and Tawana are waiting in line. Neither Sarah nor Michael is first. Tawana is behind Sarah. Fred is ahead of Michael. The two girls are not next to each other. In what order are the four friends?

You Choose

Strategy

- Draw a Diagram
- Solve a Simpler Problem
- Use Logical Reasoning
- Use Models
- Write an Equation

Computation Method

- Mental Math
- Estimation
- Paper and Pencil
- Calculator

Data Use the table for Problems 11–15.

11. The backpack with the least volume is recommended for kindergartners and first-graders. Which backpack is this? What is the volume of this backpack?

12. Suppose the company makes a wheeled version of the Alpha Backpack that is 2 inches wider than the version without wheels. What will be the change in volume?

13. What's Wrong? Martin says that the volume of the Gym Bag is 1,000 cubic inches. What mistake did Martin make? What is the correct answer?

14. Donna has a Mars Backpack. The backpack is about half full. About how many cubic inches of it are filled?

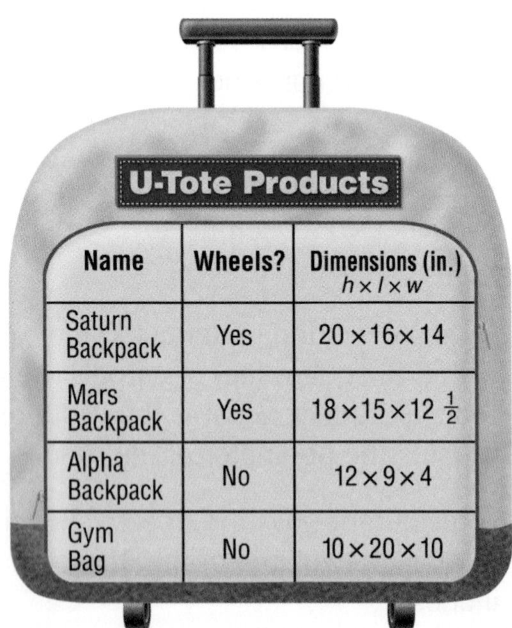

U-Tote Products

Name	Wheels?	Dimensions (in.) $h \times l \times w$
Saturn Backpack	Yes	$20 \times 16 \times 14$
Mars Backpack	Yes	$18 \times 15 \times 12\frac{1}{2}$
Alpha Backpack	No	$12 \times 9 \times 4$
Gym Bag	No	$10 \times 20 \times 10$

15. Create and Solve Use the data from the table to create and solve your own problem.

Solve. Show your work.

16. Eleven friends play in a chess match. After the match, each player shakes hands with every other player. How many handshakes will there be?

17. A small rectangular playground is 2,250 square feet. The width of the playground is 45 feet. What is the length of the playground?

18. A cereal box has a width of 6 cm, a length of 36 cm, and a height of 45 cm. What is the volume of the cereal box?

Problem Solving

Science Connection

Fish for an Aquarium

To choose fish for an aquarium, you need to know the size of the aquarium and the size of the fish.

1. Find the volume of the aquarium at the right.

2. The volume of 1 gallon of water is about 231 cubic inches. About how many gallons will the aquarium hold?

3. Many aquarium owners follow this rule: 1 inch of fish per gallon of tank space. According to this rule, about how many 2-inch fish can fit in the aquarium?

4. **You Decide** Suppose you stock your aquarium with the fish shown in the table. How many of each type of fish will you put in your tank?

Fish	Length (in inches)
Neon Tetra	1.5
Tiger Barb	2.75
Marble Angelfish	6
Goldfish	5

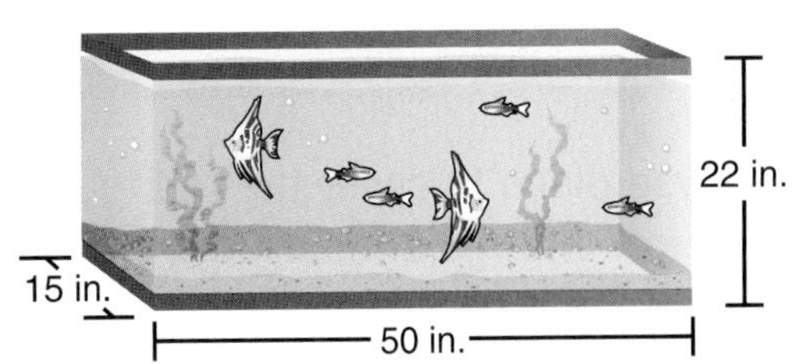

WEEKLY WR READER eduplace.com/map

Chapter Review/Test

VOCABULARY

Vocabulary
- cylinder
- prism
- pyramid

1. A ____ is a solid figure that has two parallel congruent bases and rectangles and parallelograms for faces.

2. A solid figure whose base can be a polygon and whose faces are triangles is called a ____.

CONCEPTS AND SKILLS

Use Figures A, B, and C for Exercises 3–8.

Figure A

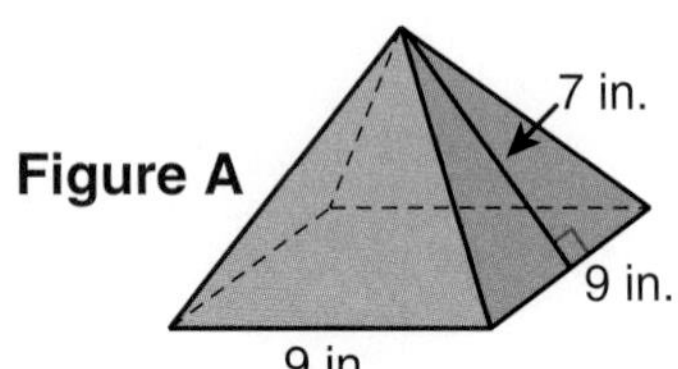

Figure B

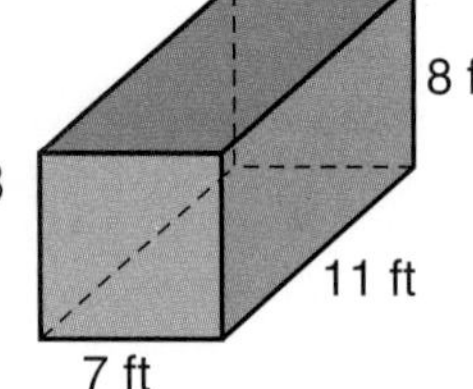

Figure C

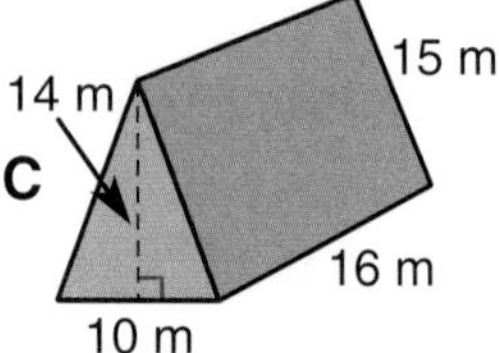

3. Name each solid figure. (Lesson 1, pp. 446–447)

4. Determine the number of faces, vertices, and edges for each figure. (Lesson 1, pp. 446–447)

5. Draw a net for Figure A. (Lessons 2–3, pp. 448–451)

6. Determine the surface area for each figure. (Lesson 4, pp. 452–455)

7. Find the volume for Figure B. (Lesson 6, pp. 460–463)

8. Find the volume for Figure C. (Lesson 6, pp. 460–463)

PROBLEM SOLVING

Solve. (Lessons 5, 7, pp. 456–458, 464–466)

9. Elyse plans to cover the triangular prism below with gold foil. How much gold foil will she need?

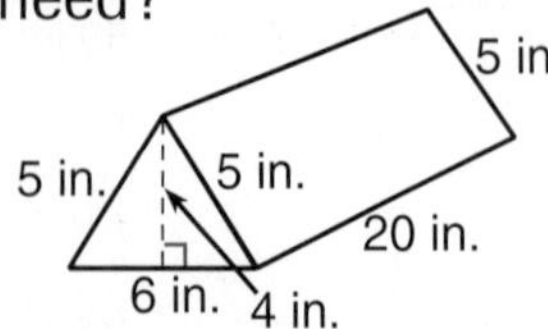

10. A box shaped like a rectangular prism is 24 cm wide and 8 cm high. Its volume is 1,920 cm^3. How long is the box?

Show You Understand

If you know the number of sides of the base of a pyramid, can you determine the number of its faces and vertices without counting? Explain.

Extra Practice

Set A (Lesson 1, pp. 446–447)

Name each solid figure. Then write the number of faces, vertices, and edges.

1. 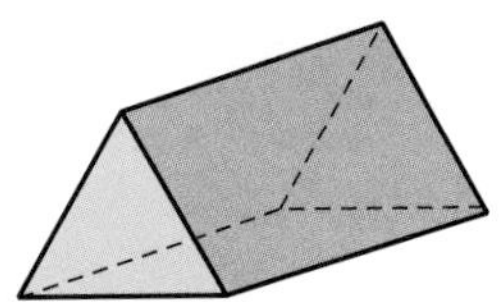

2. 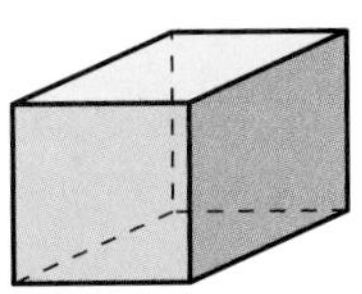

3. 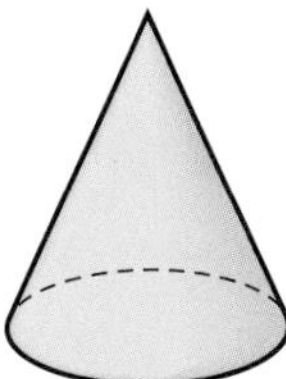

4. 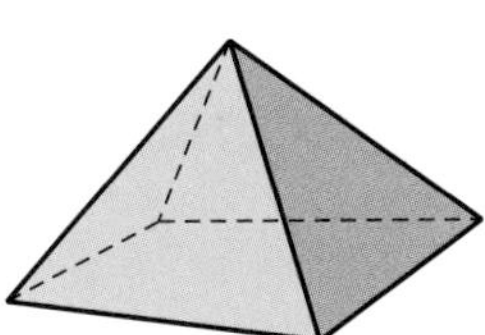

Set B (Lesson 3, pp. 450–451)

Draw a net for each solid figure.

1. 

2. 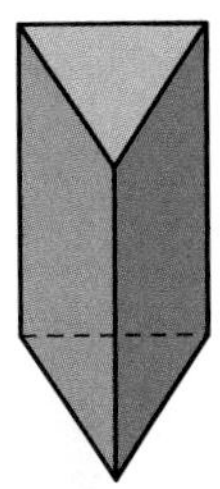

Set C (Lesson 4, pp. 452–455)

Determine the surface area of each solid figure.

1. 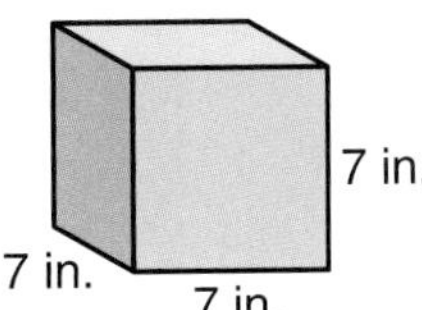

2. 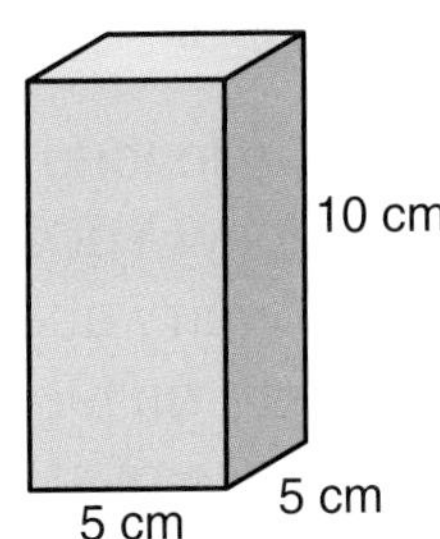

3. 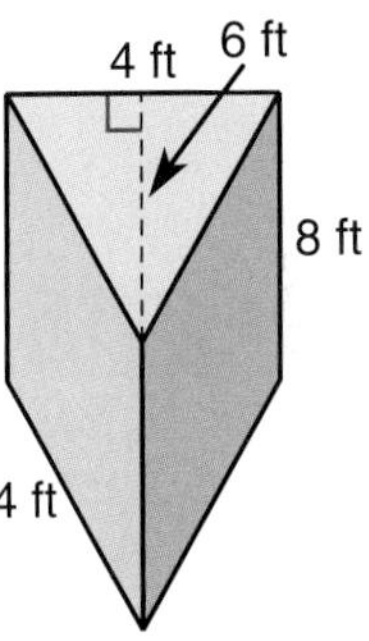

Set D (Lesson 6, pp. 460–463)

Determine the volume of each solid figure.

1. 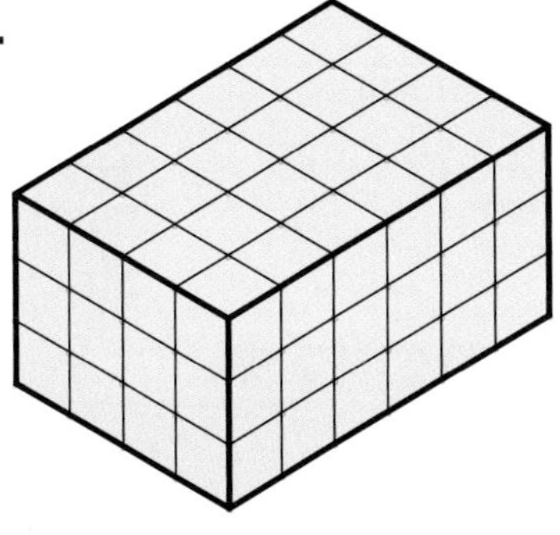

2. 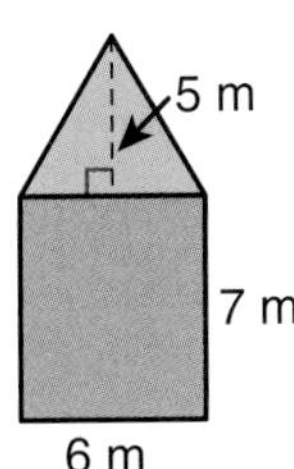

3. 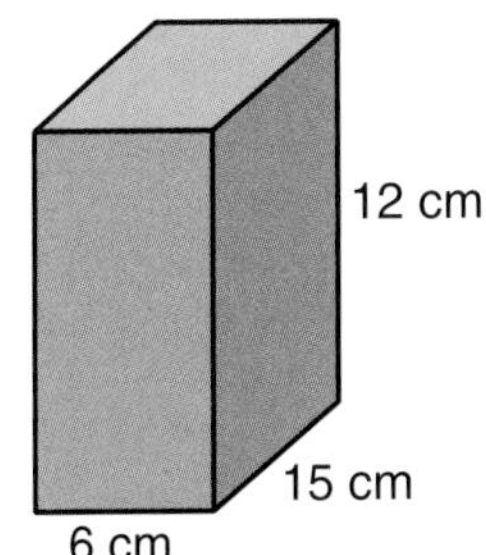

WEEKLY WR READER®

Art Connection

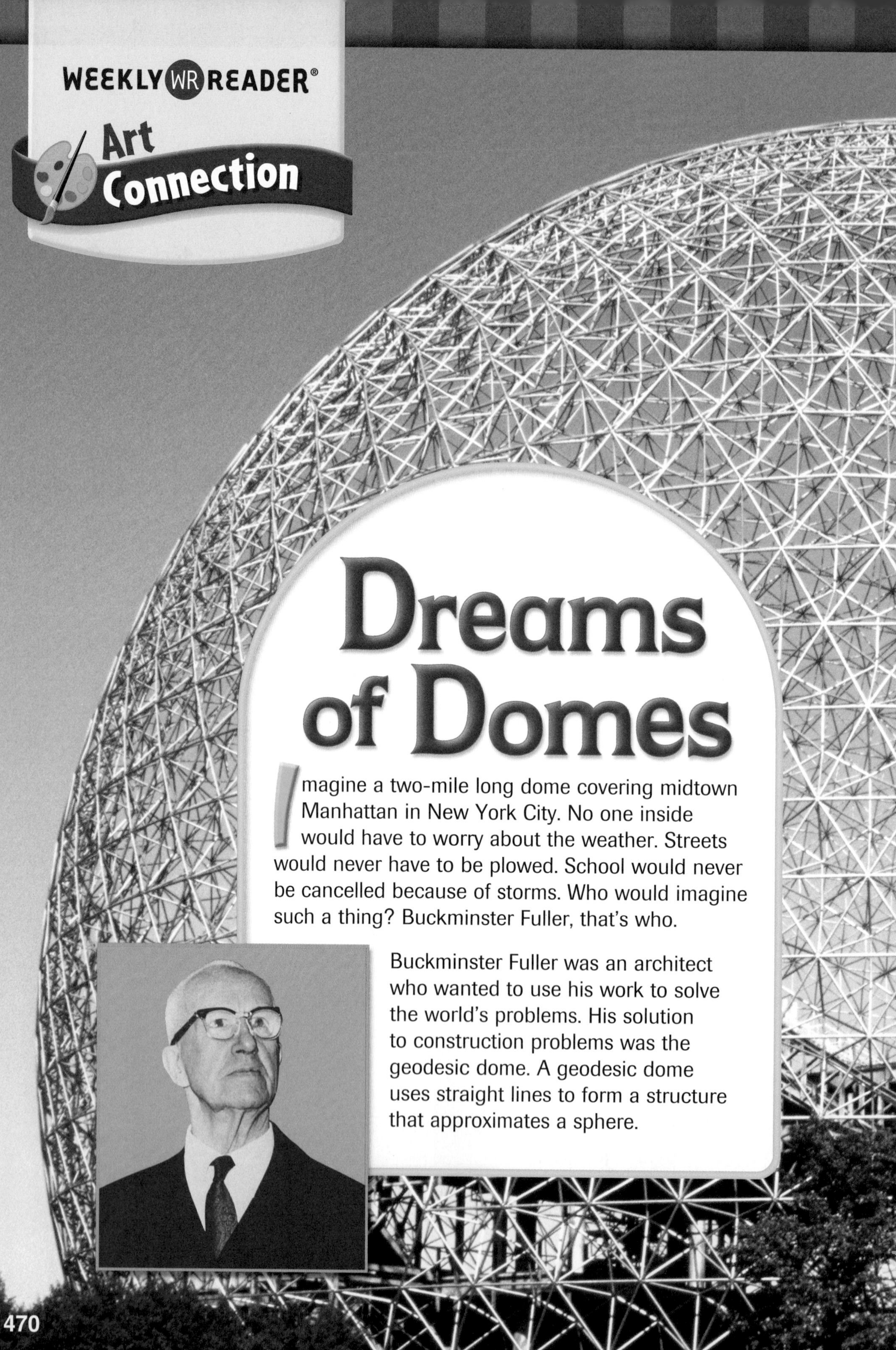

Dreams of Domes

Imagine a two-mile long dome covering midtown Manhattan in New York City. No one inside would have to worry about the weather. Streets would never have to be plowed. School would never be cancelled because of storms. Who would imagine such a thing? Buckminster Fuller, that's who.

Buckminster Fuller was an architect who wanted to use his work to solve the world's problems. His solution to construction problems was the geodesic dome. A geodesic dome uses straight lines to form a structure that approximates a sphere.

Problem Solving

Use the data in the chart to solve Problems 1–6. Use $\pi \approx 3.14$.

U.S. Pavilion	
Height	206 ft
Diameter of outer dome	250 ft
Side length of outer dome triangle	8 ft
Side length of inner dome hexagon	5 ft

1. Classify the kind of triangle Fuller used to make the outer part of the dome. Explain how you decided.

2. If the height of an outer dome triangle of the U.S. pavilion is about 7 feet, estimate the area of a hexagon made from six of these triangles.

Since a geodesic dome approximates a sphere, you can use the formula for the circumference of a circle to find the circumference of the dome.

3. What is the circumference of the outer dome of the U.S. Pavilion?

4. The outer dome of the U.S. Pavilion is made of triangles, and the inner dome is made of hexagons. If the surface of the inner dome is 3 feet inside the outer dome, what is the circumference of the inner dome? Explain your thinking.

5. What about the triangles and hexagons that Fuller used make them excellent choices for building the geodesic dome?

6. The U.S. Pavilion is not a complete sphere. Draw a top and front view of the dome. How are the views different?

Education Place
Visit Weekly Reader Connections at **eduplace.com/kids/map** for more about this topic.

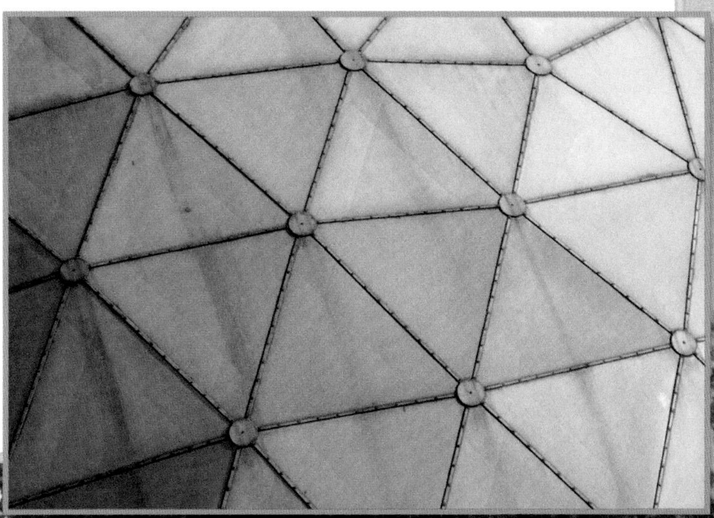

Enrichment: Fractals

INFINITE SIMILARITY

Have you ever noticed that each small piece of broccoli is similar to the shape of the whole head? This type of pattern occurs often in nature and is called **self-similarity**. In mathematics, self-similar patterns are called **fractals**.

You can make a self-similar pattern using an equilateral triangle. This pattern was invented by the mathematician Waclaw Sierpinski. It is called the Sierpinski Triangle.

STEP 1 Draw a large equilateral triangle. **Remember:** Each angle of an equilateral triangle measures 60°.

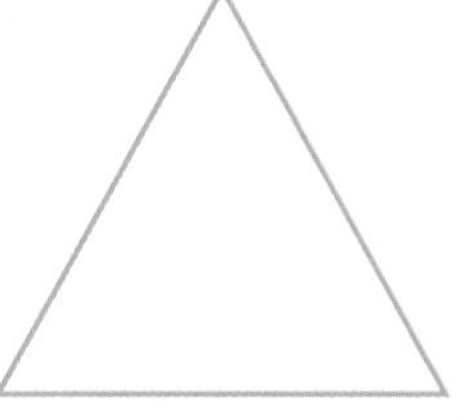

Stage 0

STEP 2 Find the midpoint of each side, and connect them to form 4 similar triangles. "Remove" the middle triangle by shading it.

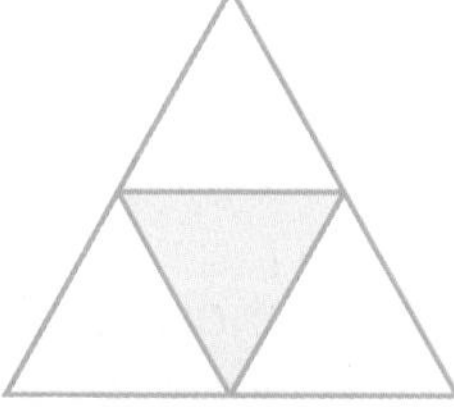

Stage 1

STEP 3 Connect the midpoints to make more similar triangles. Shade the middle triangle in each to continue the pattern.

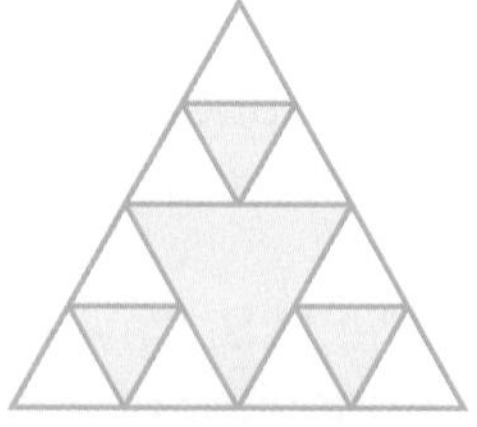

Stage 2

Try These!

Use the Sierpinski Triangle above for Problems 1–2.

1. Draw Stage 3 of the Sierpinski Triangle. How many shaded triangles are in your drawing?

2. If you continue the Sierpinski Triangle from Problem 1, how many stages are possible? Explain how you decided.

3. At the right is Stage 1 of a fractal pattern that divides each side of the triangle into thirds. Draw Stage 2.

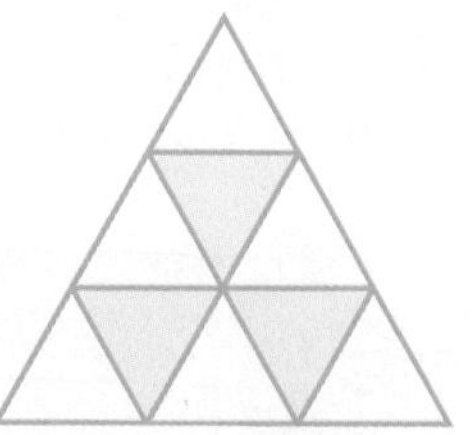

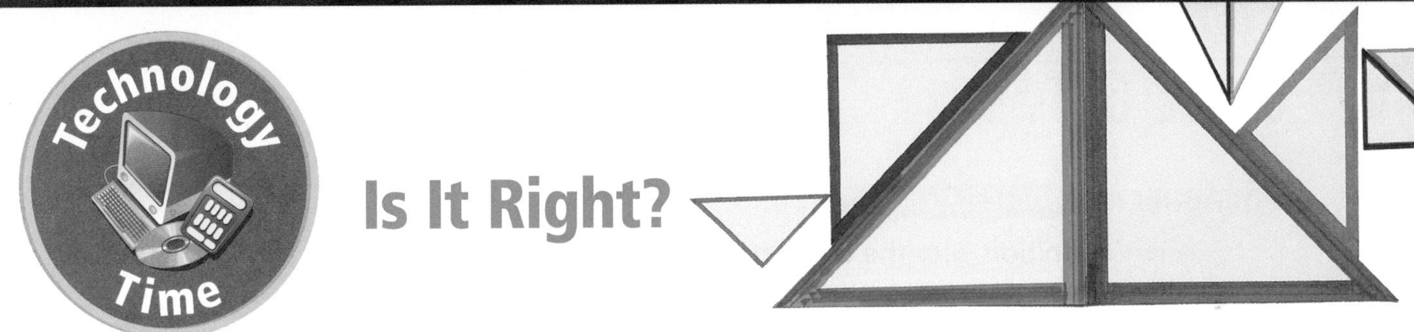

Is It Right?

The Pythagorean Theorem states that, in a right triangle, if the lengths of the two shorter sides are squared then added, the sum equals the square of the longest side. The equation $a^2 + b^2 = c^2$ is used to represent the Pythagorean Theorem.

In the equation $a^2 + b^2 = c^2$:

- a and b are always the lengths of the shorter sides
- c is always the length of the longest side

The ^ key on a calculator is the exponent key.

For 3^2, enter:

3 ^ 2 Enter/=

For 12^2, enter:

1 2 ^ 2 Enter/=

$3^2 + 4^2 = 5^2$

3 cm, 5 cm, 4 cm

A right triangle

Press: 3 ^ 2 + 4 ^ 2 Enter/= → 25

Press: 5 ^ 2 Enter/= → 25

25 is equal to 25

$7^2 + 12^2 \neq 13^2$

7 cm, 12 cm, 13 cm

Not a right triangle

Press: 7 ^ 2 + 1 2 ^ 2 Enter/= → 193

Press: 1 3 ^ 2 Enter/= → 169

193 is not equal to 169

Use your calculator to determine if the lengths of sides given below form a right triangle.

1. 28, 45, and 53

2. 16, 18, and 28

3. 20, 21, and 29

4. 20, 25, and 36

5. 23, 264, and 265

6. 15, 112, and 113

7. 8, 12, and 12

8. 16, 63, and 65

9. 62, 67, and 114

Unit 6 Test

VOCABULARY Open Response

Match each definition with the correct vocabulary word.

Vocabulary
pi
net
radius
diameter
circumference
obtuse angle

1. The distance around a circle is called its ■.
2. A(n) ■ is a flat pattern that can be folded to represent a solid figure.
3. A segment that connects the center of a circle to any point on the circle is called a(n) ■.
4. A(n) ■ has a measure greater than that of a right angle and less than 180°.

CONCEPTS AND SKILLS Open Response

Classify each polygon in as many ways as you can. (Chapter 15)

5. 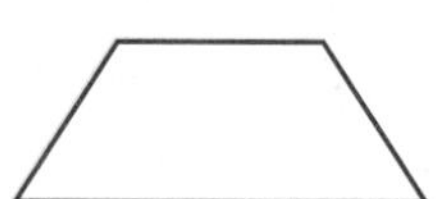

6. 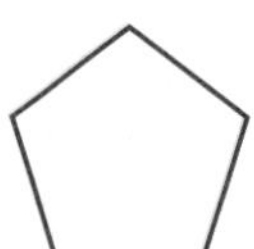

7. 

8. 

Identify each transformation. (Chapter 15)

9. 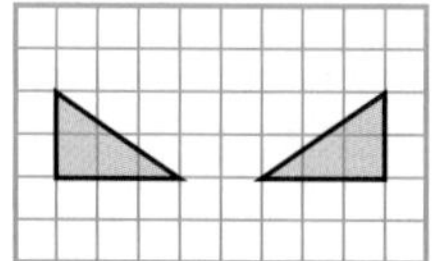

10. 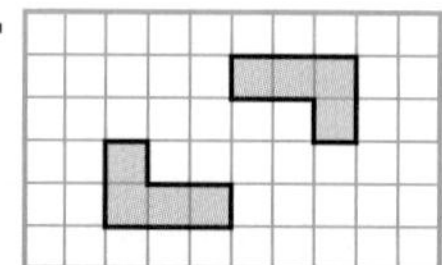

11. 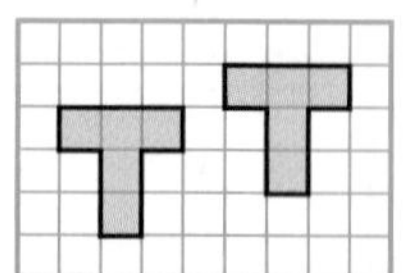

Find the perimeter and area of each figure. (Chapter 16)

12. 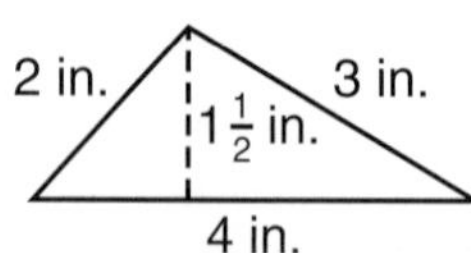

13. 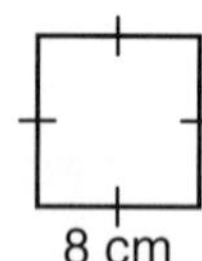

14. 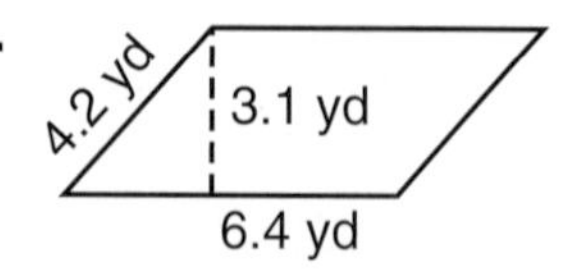

15. 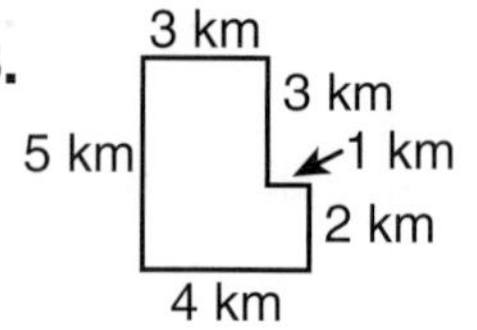

Name the figure. Then find the information for each. (Chapter 17)

16. 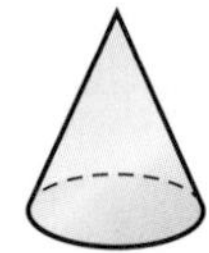

2-dimensional view of base: ■

17. 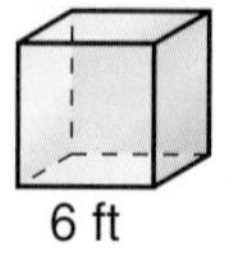

surface area: ■

18. 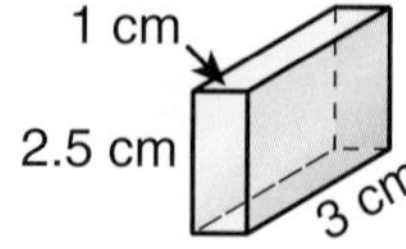

volume: ■

19. 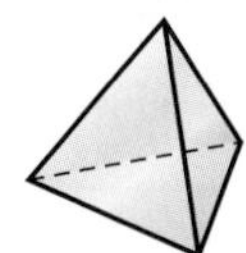

number of faces: ■

PROBLEM SOLVING Open Response

20. Gaby is designing a tessellation using a right triangle that measures 3 inches by 4 inches by 5 inches. To fill in an area that is 8 inches by 9 inches, how many triangles must she use?

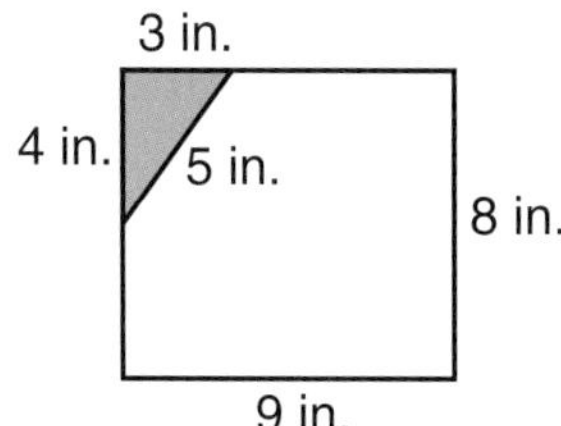

21. Jennifer is tracing pattern blocks to draw a five-pointed star like the one below. Will she be able to use the same triangle pattern block to draw the entire star? Explain.

22. Sandra is measuring the angles in a parallelogram. One of the angles has a measure of 60°. What are the measures of the other three angles?

23. Hamid builds a sandbox that is 4 feet long, 2 feet wide, and 1.5 feet high. How many cubic feet of sand does he need to fill it completely?

24. Robert draws a rectangle that is 8 inches long and 5 inches wide. If he decides to double the dimensions, what will the area of the new rectangle be?

25. Franklin is digging a circular flower bed. He wants to place flexible edging around the entire bed. If the radius is 5 feet, how many feet of edging will he need? (Use $\pi \approx 3.14$.)

Performance Assessment

Constructed Response

The students in Mrs. Pierce's art class are painting a mural on the wall near the cafeteria. The mural will show various school activities. Copy the diagram of the wall at the right to plan your mural. You may use grid paper or dot paper to help you. Find the wall's perimeter and area. Decide how much of the area you will use for each image of an activity. Explain your thinking.

Information You Need

- You can't paint on the doors.
- Activities to show include: after-school sports, chorus, school clean-up day, science fair, art fair, local history day.

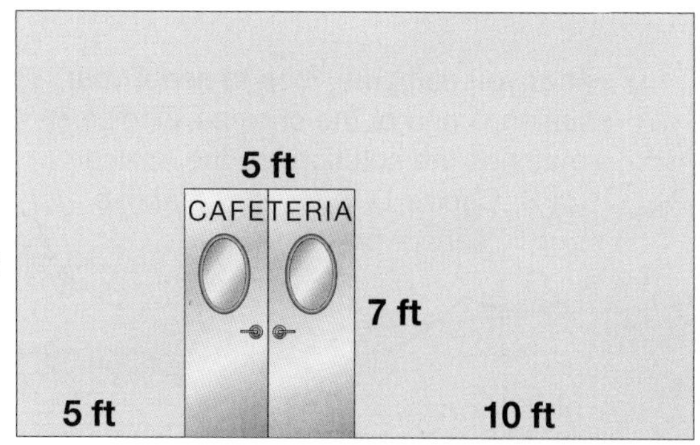

Cumulative Test Prep

Solve Problems 1–10.

Test-Taking Tip

If one of the answer choices is *none of the above*, compute to see if your solution is one of the other choices.

Look at the example below.

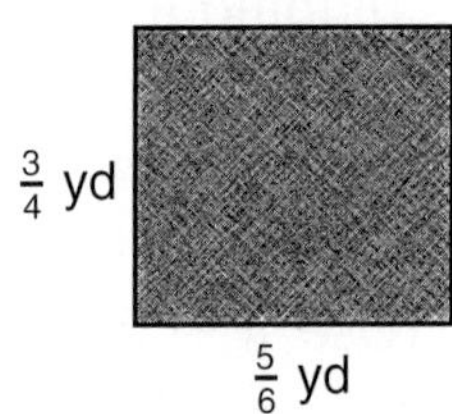

If a cloth measures $\frac{5}{6}$ yard by $\frac{3}{4}$ yard, how many square yards of fabric do you have?

A $\frac{3}{8}$ square yard **C** $1\frac{1}{8}$ square yards

B $\frac{5}{8}$ square yard **D** none of the above

THINK

First solve the problem.

$$\frac{5}{6} \times \frac{3}{4} = \frac{5}{\cancel{6}_2} \times \frac{\cancel{3}^1}{4} = \frac{5}{8}$$

After you compute, look to see if your solution is one of the choices. Choice B matches the solution, so the answer is **B**. Choice D, *none of the above*, cannot be the answer.

Multiple Choice

1. About 60,000 people live in Albertville. How would you express this estimate using expanded form with exponents?

A 6×10^3 **C** 6×10^5

B 6×10^4 **D** none of the above

(Chapter 1, Lesson 2)

2. Millie takes 2,000 milligrams of Vitamin C each day. How many grams of Vitamin C does she take?

F 1 gram **H** 5 grams

G 2 grams **J** none of the above

(Chapter 6, Lesson 5)

3. One fourth of the students in Mr. Roger's class were absent on Wednesday. If there are 24 students in the class, how many were present on Wednesday?

A 16 **C** 22

B 20 **D** none of the above

(Chapter 12, Lesson 3)

4. Name the figure.

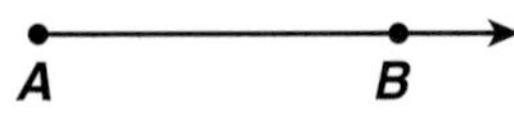

F ray **H** line segment

G line **J** none of the above

(Chapter 15, Lesson 1)

For Test-Taking Tips, see page 652.

Open Response

5. A stadium can seat 52,320 people. If there are 24 seating sections of equal capacity, how many people does each section seat?

(Chapter 5, Lesson 2)

6. Katrina made this stem-and-leaf plot to show scores for a card game. What is the mean of the scores?

Card Game Scores

Stem	Leaf
0	7 8
1	2 4 9
2	0 1 6 6

Key: 2|0 means 20.

(Chapter 8, Lesson 3)

7. Ms. Johnson ordered 5 jumbo pizzas for a class party. If each pizza cost $14.59, how much did she pay for the pizzas?

(Chapter 13, Lesson 3)

8. This net is for a prism. What is the volume of the prism in cubic centimeters?

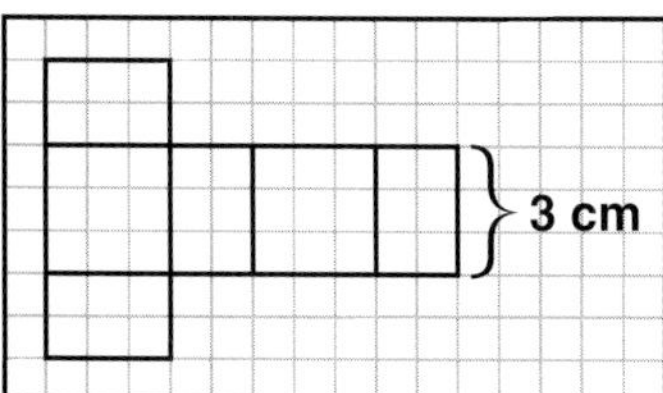

(Chapter 17, Lesson 1)

Extended Response

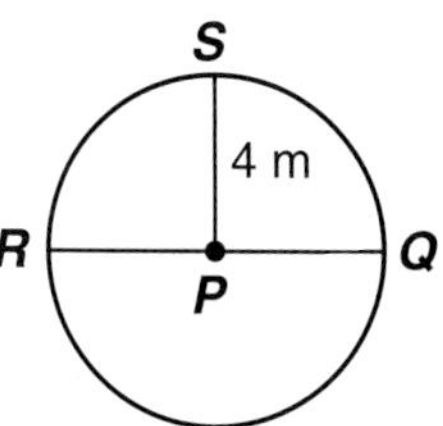

9. In the circle above, $\overline{RQ}$ passes through the center, P.

A You have a friend visiting from a foreign country. Use the proper vocabulary to talk about the line segments in circle P. Assume your friend knows about circles, but does not know the English words to name each line segment.

B If $\overline{SP}$ is perpendicular to $\overline{RQ}$, what are each of the measures of $\angle RPS$ and $\angle SPQ$?

(Chapter 15, Lesson 8)

10. You can use a formula to find the circumference of circle P.

A Use the formula $C = \pi d$ to find the circumference of circle P. Round your answer to the nearest whole number. (Use $\pi \approx 3.14$)

B The radius of the circle is given in meters. If the radius had been given in centimeters, would your computation of the circle's circumference be more exact? Explain.

(Chapter 16, Lesson 6)

Education Place

Look for Cumulative Test Prep at **eduplace.com/map** for more practice.

Vocabulary Wrap-Up for Unit 6

Look back at the big ideas and vocabulary in this unit.

Big Ideas

A geometric figure may have line symmetry or rotational symmetry, or both.

You can use formulas to find the area of a polygon, the circumference of a circle, and the volume of a solid figure.

Key Vocabulary

symmetry

area

circumference

volume

Math Conversations

Use your new vocabulary to discuss these big ideas.

1. Explain how these pairs of lines are similar and different: intersecting lines, perpendicular lines, and parallel lines.
2. Explain how congruent figures are used to determine whether or not a figure has symmetry.
3. Explain how you find the perimeter of a regular polygon. Then explain how circumference is related to perimeter and tell how to find the circumference of a circle.
4. **Write About It** Look around to find examples of geometric figures in buildings, bridges, furniture, and other objects. Describe how some of these figures serve a particular purpose.

How can I find the volume of a box?
Use the formula length × width × height.

UNIT 7

Ratio, Proportion, Percent, and Probability

Reading Mathematics

Reviewing Vocabulary

Here are some math vocabulary words that you should know.

fraction	a number that describes part of a whole or part of a group
unit fraction	a fraction in which the numerator is 1, such as $\frac{1}{3}$
decimal	a number with one or more digits to the right of a decimal point
circle graph	a graph in the shape of a circle that shows data as part of a whole

Reading Words and Symbols

A fraction or a decimal can represent parts of a whole or part of a group. Statements about parts of a whole or part of a group can be written with words, a combination of words and symbols, or only symbols.

All these statements represent the same situation:

- Three out of the ten crayons are yellow.
- The part of the group that is yellow is three tenths.
- $\frac{3}{10}$ of the crayons are yellow.
- 0.3 of the crayons are yellow.
- 30% of the crayons are yellow.

Use the picture of the crayons. Write a statement for each situation. Use words, words and symbols, or just symbols.

1. The part of the crayons that is green
2. The part of the crayons that is red

Use the picture of the crayons. For each fraction or decimal, write a word statement.

3. 0.2 **4.** $\frac{1}{10}$ **5.** 0.4

Reading Test Questions

Choose the correct answer for each.

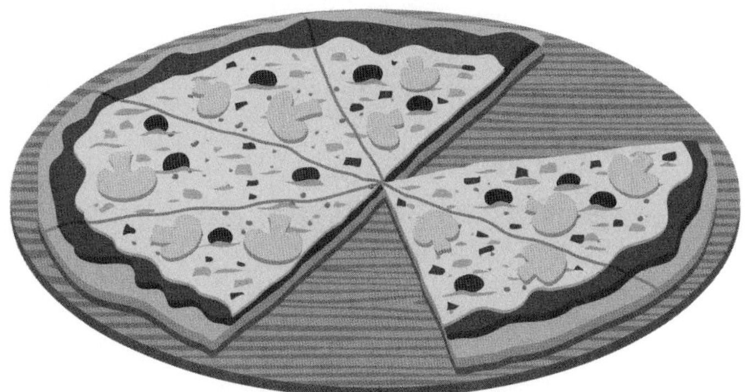

6. Write a fraction to tell how much of the pizza has been eaten. Then write an equivalent fraction.

a. $\frac{2}{6}$; $\frac{1}{4}$ **c.** $\frac{2}{8}$; $\frac{1}{5}$

b. $\frac{2}{6}$; $\frac{1}{3}$ **d.** $\frac{2}{8}$; $\frac{1}{4}$

Equivalent means "the same value" or "equal to."

7. Nancy has \$100 in savings. Petra has saved one quarter of that amount. How much does Petra have in savings?

a. \$4 **c.** \$40

b. \$25 **d.** \$2,500

One quarter in this problem means $\frac{1}{4}$. So to find one quarter of an amount, you multiply by $\frac{1}{4}$ or divide by 4. Find $\frac{1}{4} \times 100$.

8. Martha should leave for school at quarter to eight. At which time should she leave for school?

a. 8:45 **c.** 8:15

b. 8:25 **d.** 7:45

Quarter to in this problem refers to $\frac{1}{4}$ hour before eight. Since 1 hour = 60 minutes, find one fourth of 60. $\frac{1}{4} \times 60 = 15$.

Learning Vocabulary

Watch for these words in this unit. Write their definitions in your journal.

ratio

rate

proportion

similar figures

percent

probability

Education Place

At **eduplace.com/map** see *e*Glossary and *e*Games—Math Lingo.

Literature Connection

Read "Numbers" on page 647. Then work with a partner to answer the questions about this story.

CHAPTER 18

Ratio and Proportion

INVESTIGATION

Use Data

Ray collects marbles. He's noticed that there are always fewer of the red marbles, his favorite color. In sets of 25 marbles, only 5 are red. How many sets will he need to buy to get 10 red marbles? 25? 50?

✓ Use What You Know

Use this page to review and remember what you need to know for this chapter.

VOCABULARY

Choose the best word to complete each sentence.

1. When the numerator and denominator have 1 as their only common factor, the fraction is in ____.

2. ____ are two or more fractions that have the same value.

3. The fractions $\frac{2}{4}$ and $\frac{3}{4}$ have a(n) ____.

Vocabulary

- common denominator
- equivalent fractions
- estimate
- simplest form

CONCEPTS AND SKILLS

Write three equivalent fractions for each.

4. 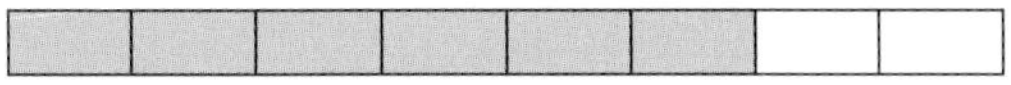

5. 

6. 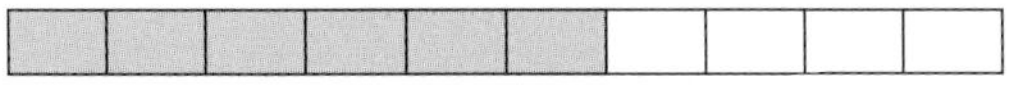

7. 

Write each fraction in simplest form.

8. $\frac{8}{10}$ **9.** $\frac{32}{36}$ **10.** $\frac{75}{100}$ **11.** $\frac{56}{84}$

Complete.

12. $\frac{1}{2} = \frac{\blacksquare}{10}$ **13.** $\frac{2}{3} = \frac{\blacksquare}{24}$ **14.** $\frac{8}{48} = \frac{1}{\blacksquare}$ **15.** $\frac{20}{55} = \frac{\blacksquare}{11}$

16. $\frac{\blacksquare}{8} = \frac{24}{32}$ **17.** $\frac{3}{\blacksquare} = \frac{18}{24}$ **18.** $\frac{7}{100} = \frac{\blacksquare}{900}$ **19.** $\frac{\blacksquare}{5} = \frac{48}{60}$

Write About It

20. Are the fractions $\frac{3}{5}$ and $\frac{60}{100}$ equivalent? Explain how you know.

Facts Practice, See page 663.

Lesson 1

Audio Tutor 2/19 Listen and Understand

Ratios

Objective Read, write, and simplify ratios.

Vocabulary
terms
ratio

Learn About It

Olga finds 7 wooden tangram pieces in a box. Two shapes are quadrilaterals and 5 are triangles. One way to compare the number of quadrilaterals with the number of triangles is to write a ratio.

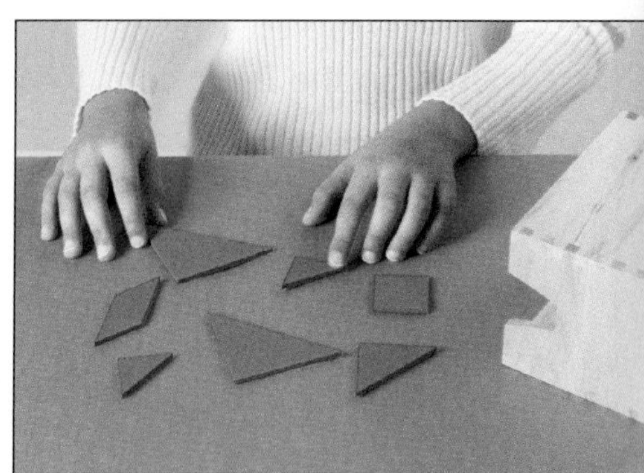

The **terms** of a ratio are the numbers you are comparing. You can write a **ratio** in fraction form, with the first term above the bar and the second term below the bar.

What is the ratio of quadrilaterals to triangles?

STEP 1 Identify the terms of the ratio.

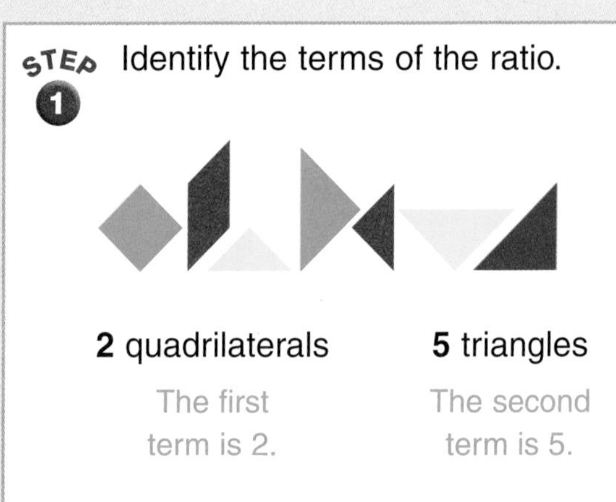

2 quadrilaterals — The first term is 2.

5 triangles — The second term is 5.

STEP 2 Write the ratio of quadrilaterals to triangles.

The ratio can be written 3 ways.

Word form: **2 to 5**

Ratio form: **2:5**

Fraction form: $\frac{2}{5}$

To read all three forms, say, "2 to 5."

Solution: The ratio of quadrilaterals to triangles is 2 to 5, 2:5, or $\frac{2}{5}$.

Guided Practice

Write each ratio three different ways.

1. 5 cars to 6 trucks

2. 16 cats to 3 dogs

3. 2 balls to 3 bats

4. 4 caps to 5 coats

5. 7 squares to 2 triangles

6. 9 paints to 4 brushes

Ask Yourself

- Did I write the terms in the correct order?
- Did I write each ratio three different ways?

Explain Your Thinking In Exercise 6, if you write the ratio of brushes to paints, would you write 4:9 instead of 9:4?

Practice and Problem Solving

Use the triangles, squares, and circles below to write each ratio three different ways.

7. squares to triangles
8. circles to squares
9. circles to triangles
10. squares to circles
11. triangles to squares
12. triangles to circles
13. circles to all figures
14. triangles to squares and circles

Data **Use the table and the completed tangram to answer Problems 15–19.**

Tangram Pieces	Number of Each Shape
triangles	15
squares	3
parallelograms	3

15. Olivia emptied a box of wooden tangram pieces onto the desk. She counted the number of each shape and organized her findings in a table. What is the ratio of triangles to squares?

16. A tangram is made from 5 triangles, 1 square, and 1 parallelogram. If all the pieces are the right size, how many complete tangrams can be made from the shapes Olivia has?

17. Write the ratio of the number of yellow pieces to the number of purple pieces.

18. Write the ratio of the number of purple pieces to the number of yellow pieces.

19. **Write About It** Explain why the answers to Problems 17 and 18 are not the same.

Mixed Review and Test Prep

Open Response

Write two equivalent fractions. Use multiplication and division. (Ch. 9, Lesson 6)

20. $\frac{4}{6}$
21. $\frac{5}{20}$
22. $\frac{7}{14}$
23. $\frac{8}{20}$

24. Write the ratio of triangles to figures that are not triangles. Explain. (Ch. 18, Lesson 1)

Extra Practice See page 503, Set A.

Lesson 2

Audio Tutor 2/20 Listen and Understand

Equivalent Ratios

Objective Use multiplication and division to find equivalent ratios.

Vocabulary
- equivalent ratio
- simplest form

Learn About It

Melinda wants to paint her little sister's dollhouse. She has chosen a color that requires 4 parts of red for every 12 parts of yellow. The ratio of red to yellow is $\frac{4}{12}$.

If Melinda uses 8 parts of red, how many parts of yellow will she need? If Melinda uses 2 parts of red, how many parts of yellow will she need?

You can find an **equivalent ratio** for $\frac{4}{12}$ that has 8 as its first term. Then you can find an equivalent ratio for $\frac{4}{12}$ that has 2 as its first term.

Different Ways to Find Equivalent Ratios

Way 1 Multiply each term by the same number.

Think:

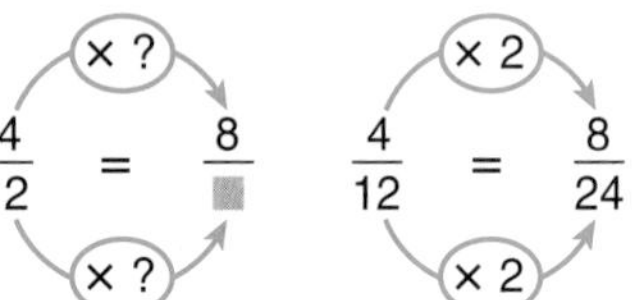

$\frac{4}{12} = \frac{8}{■}$ (× ?) $\qquad \frac{4}{12} = \frac{8}{24}$ (× 2)

Way 2 Divide each term by the same number.

Think:

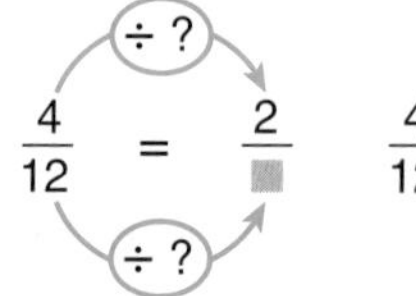

$\frac{4}{12} = \frac{2}{■}$ (÷ ?) $\qquad \frac{4}{12} = \frac{2}{6}$ (÷ 2)

Solution: If Melinda uses 8 units of red, she will need 24 units of yellow.
If Melinda uses 2 units of red, she will need 6 units of yellow.

▶ A ratio is in **simplest form** when the GCF of the terms is 1. To write a ratio in simplest form, divide each term by its greatest common factor (GCF).

Write $\frac{12}{16}$ in simplest form.

$\frac{12}{16} = \frac{3}{4}$ (÷ 4)

Think
$12 = (2 \times 2) \times 3$
$16 = (2 \times 2) \times 2 \times 2$
2×2, or 4, is the GCF.

The simplest form of $\frac{12}{16}$ is $\frac{3}{4}$.

Extra Help at **eduplace.com/map**

Complete the equivalent ratio: $\frac{4}{6} = \frac{\blacksquare}{9}$.

STEP 1 Write the ratio in simplest form.

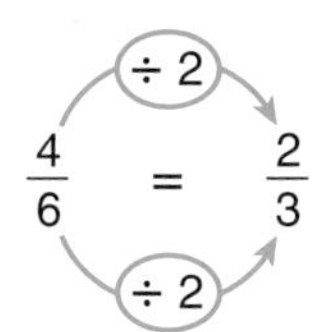

STEP 2 Multiply by a number so 9 is the new second term.

$\frac{2}{3} = \frac{\blacksquare}{9}$

× ?

STEP 3 Multiply each term by the same number.

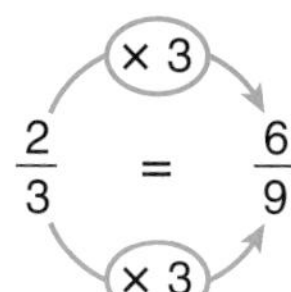

Solution: $\frac{4}{6} = \frac{6}{9}$.

Guided Practice

Write four equivalent ratios for each.

1. $\frac{4}{8}$ **2.** 8 to 12 **3.** 6:15 **4.** $\frac{20}{25}$

Ask Yourself

- Did I multiply or divide both terms by the same number?

Explain Your Thinking ▶ How would you write 6:15 in simplest form? How did you get your answer?

Practice and Problem Solving

Write four equivalent ratios for each.

5. $\frac{1}{3}$ **6.** 5 to 6 **7.** 1:5 **8.** 10 to 4 **9.** 10:16 **10.** $\frac{6}{3}$

Write each ratio in simplest form.

11. $\frac{10}{40}$ **12.** 6:18 **13.** 24 to 42 **14.** 12:60 **15.** $\frac{16}{36}$ **16.** 28:32

Algebra • Equations **Complete each set of equivalent ratios.**

17. $\frac{1}{4} = \frac{\blacksquare}{12}$ **18.** $\frac{8}{24} = \frac{\blacksquare}{6}$ **19.** $\frac{15}{25} = \frac{9}{\blacksquare}$ **20.** $\frac{6}{9} = \frac{\blacksquare}{12}$

Mixed Review and Test Prep

Open Response

Multiply. (Ch. 13, Lessons 4–5)

21. 0.09×0.8 **22.** 3.2×0.6

23. 0.21×0.9 **24.** 8.34×4.7

25. 0.002×0.6 **26.** 0.03×0.03

Multiple Choice

27. Complete the equivalent ratio: $\frac{20}{24} = \frac{\blacksquare}{6}$. (Ch. 18, Lesson 2)

A 4 **C** 80

B 5 **D** 120

Extra Practice See page 503, Set B.

Lesson 3 Rates

Objective Compare two quantities with different units.

Vocabulary
- rate
- unit rate
- per
- speed

Learn About It

A **rate** is a ratio that compares numbers expressed in different units. A rate in which the second term is 1 is called a **unit rate**.

A toy factory produces 120 robots in 5 days. At this rate, how many robots will it produce in 20 days?

Different Ways to Solve Problems With Rates

Way 1 Use equivalent ratios.

$$\frac{120 \text{ robots}}{5 \text{ days}} = \frac{\blacksquare \text{ robots}}{20 \text{ days}}$$

$5 \times ? = 20$

$$\frac{120}{5} = \frac{\blacksquare}{20} \quad (\times ?)$$

$$\frac{120}{5} = \frac{480}{20} \quad (\times 4)$$

Way 2 Find the unit rate and multiply.

STEP 1 Divide to find the unit rate in robots per day. **Per** means "for each."

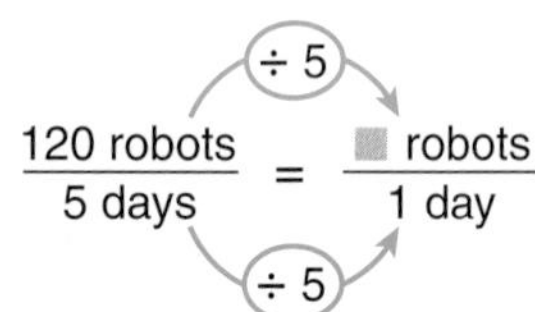

$$\frac{120 \text{ robots}}{5 \text{ days}} = \frac{\blacksquare \text{ robots}}{1 \text{ day}} \quad (\div 5)$$

The rate is 24 robots per day.

STEP 2 Multiply by the number of days.

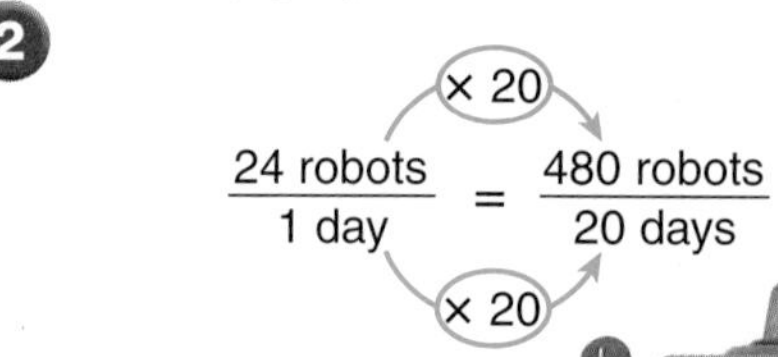

$$\frac{24 \text{ robots}}{1 \text{ day}} = \frac{480 \text{ robots}}{20 \text{ days}} \quad (\times 20)$$

Solution: The factory will produce 480 robots in 20 days.

Other Examples

A. Speed as a Unit Rate

A car travels 220 miles in 4 hours. Find the unit rate in miles per hour.

$$\frac{220 \text{ mi}}{4 \text{ h}} = \frac{55 \text{ mi}}{1 \text{ h}} \quad (\div 4)$$

A rate that shows distance per unit of time is called **speed**. A slash, /, is often used for the word *per*.

The rate is 55 miles per hour, or 55 mi/h.

B. Use Speed to Find Time

How long will it take to travel 450 km at a rate of 90 km/h?

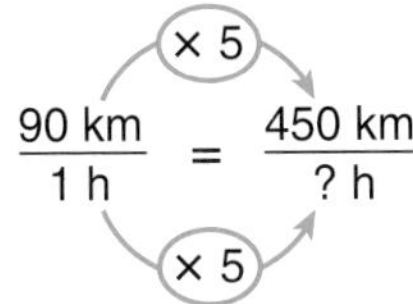

It will take 5 hours.

C. Rates With Money

A worker receives $75 for 6 hours of work. What is the rate of pay per hour?

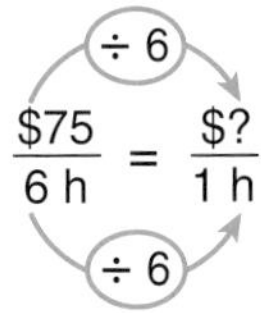

The rate is $12.50 per hour.

Guided Practice

Find the unit rate.

1. 30 toys in 10 days
2. $20 in 4 hours
3. 60 meters in 5 seconds
4. $1,000 in 5 days
5. 100 miles in 4 hours
6. 50 km in 5 hours

Ask Yourself

- Did I write the units?
- Is my answer reasonable?

Explain Your Thinking ▶ How can you use division to find any unit rate?

Practice and Problem Solving

Find the unit rate.

7. 80 miles in 16 min
8. 72 ft in 9 seconds
9. 108 meters in 18 min
10. 160 pages in 8 days
11. $100 in 5 hours
12. $56 in 7 hours

Complete the unit rate.

13. 400 mi:16 gal = ■ mi:1 gal
14. 84¢:12 copies = ■ ¢:1 copy
15. $6:2 oz = $■:1 oz
16. 437 mi:23 gal = ■ mi:1 gal
17. 1,394 people:34 square miles = ■ people:1 square mile
18. 288 photos:12 rolls of film = ■ photos:1 roll of film

Find the distance traveled in the given amount of time.

19. 5 hours at 50 mi/h
20. 2.5 hours at 40 km/h
21. 12 seconds at 16 ft/s
22. 0.5 hour at 30 mi/h
23. 7 days at 25 mi/day
24. 3 min at 9 m/min

Go On

Find the length of time for each trip.

25. 200 mi at 50 mi/h
26. 75 km at 25 km/h
27. 1,500 ft at 30 ft/s
28. 225 mi at 45 mi/h
29. 252 ft at 12 ft/sec
30. 175 m at 35 m/min

Algebra • Variables

Use the rate of 140 toy robots produced in 5 days to complete each rate.

31. *n* robots in 8 days
32. *n* robots in 2 days
33. *n* robots in 0.5 day
34. 420 robots in *n* days
35. 350 robots in *n* days
36. 490 robots in *n* days

Data Use the advertisement for Problems 37–40.

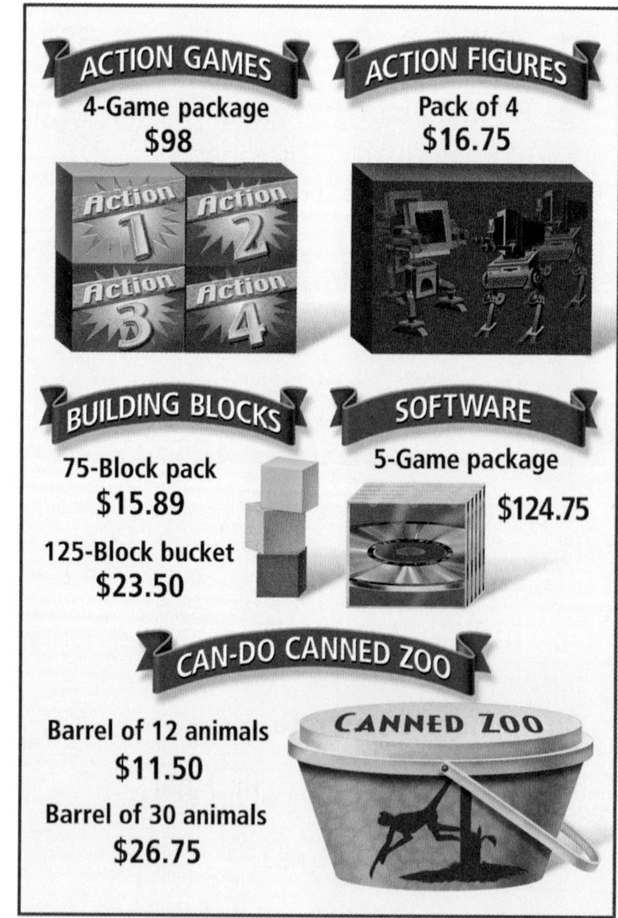

37. To the nearest cent, what is the unit price of an action figure?

38. Which has a greater price per game, the Action Games package or the Software 5-Game package? What is the difference between the two unit prices?

39. Which package of building blocks has a greater price per block, the 75-block pack or the 125-block bucket? To the nearest cent, what is the difference between the two unit prices?

40. **You Decide** Suppose you play a game in which you need at least 50 Can-Do Canned Zoo animals. How would you buy the animals? To the nearest cent, what is the unit rate per animal?

41. **What's Wrong?** Hal's car travels 450 miles on 15 gallons of gas. Hal calculated that he would need 63,000 gallons for a 2,100-mile trip. What did Hal do wrong?

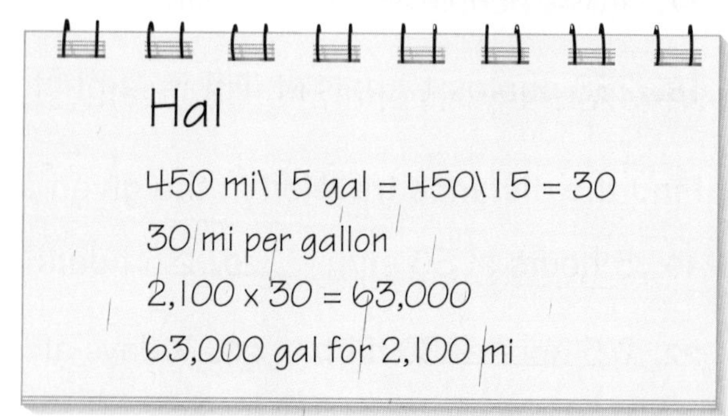

Hal
450 mi\15 gal = 450\15 = 30
30 mi per gallon
2,100 x 30 = 63,000
63,000 gal for 2,100 mi

Extra Practice See page 503, Set C.

Activity

Math Challenge

Heart Smart

Complete the following activity in order to determine your heart rate for a minute, an hour, a day, and a week.

The easiest place to find your pulse is on the side of your neck.

STEP 1 Make the following table.

Time	10 seconds	1 minute	1 hour	1 day	1 week
Number of ♥ beats at rest					
Number of ♥ beats after exercise					

STEP 2 Take your pulse for 10 seconds. Based on your 10-second heart rate, fill in the first row of your table.

STEP 3 *Let's exercise!* Do as many jumping jacks as you can in 1 minute.

STEP 4 Take your pulse for 10 seconds. Based on your 10-second heart rate after exercising, fill in the second row of your table.

Quick Check

Check your understanding for Lessons 1–3.

Write each ratio three different ways. (Lesson 1)

1. circles to rectangles
2. rectangles to circles
3. pentagons to circles
4. pentagons to other shapes

Write four equivalent ratios for each. (Lesson 2)

5. $\frac{2}{7}$
6. 8 to 10
7. 6:2
8. 12 to 9

Complete the unit rate. (Lesson 3)

9. 252 mi:9 gal = ■ mi:1 gal
10. \$3.48:6 cans = \$■:1 can

Lesson 4

Audio Tutor 2/21 Listen and Understand

Proportions

Objective Learn what a proportion is and how to find cross products.

Vocabulary
proportion
cross product

Learn About It

Martin and Tina are playing a word game. In Martin's group of tiles, the ratio of vowel tiles to his total tiles is 5 to 9. This is the same as the ratio of vowel tiles to the total tiles in the game. The game has a total of 81 tiles. How many vowel tiles does the game have?

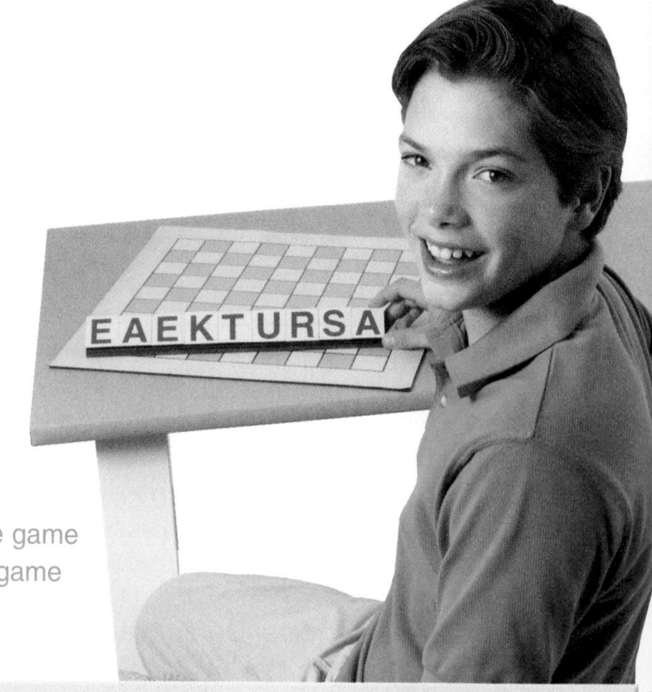

To solve the problem, you can write a proportion. A **proportion** is a statement that two ratios are equivalent.

Martin's vowel tiles → $\frac{5}{9} = \frac{n}{81}$ ← vowel tiles in the game
Martin's total tiles → ← total tiles in the game

Solve for *n*. $\frac{5}{9} = \frac{n}{81}$

Different Ways to Solve $\frac{5}{9} = \frac{n}{81}$

Way 1 Use equivalent ratios.

$\frac{5}{9} = \frac{■}{81}$

$9 \times ? = 81$

$\frac{5}{9} = \frac{■}{81}$ (× ? top and bottom)

$\frac{5}{9} = \frac{45}{81}$ (× 9 top and bottom)

Way 2 Use cross products.

STEP 1 Write the proportion.

$\frac{5}{9} = \frac{n}{81}$

STEP 2 Identify the terms to be multiplied. These are the **cross products.**

$\frac{5}{9} \times \frac{n}{81}$ → $9 \times n$, 5×81

STEP 3 Write an equation that shows cross products are equal. Solve for *n*.

$5 \times 81 = 9 \times n$

$\frac{405}{9} = \frac{9 \times n}{9}$

$45 = n$

Solution: The game has 45 vowel tiles.

Dina says that you can use $\frac{18}{48}$ and $\frac{3}{8}$ to form a proportion. Is she correct? You can use cross multiplication to find out if two ratios form a proportion.

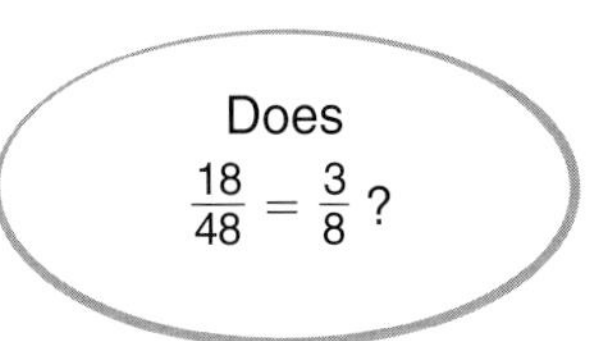

Do $\frac{18}{48}$ and $\frac{3}{8}$ form a proportion?

STEP 1 Write the two ratios.

$$\frac{18}{48} \stackrel{?}{=} \frac{3}{8}$$

STEP 2 Write the cross products.

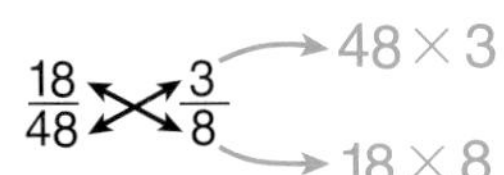

$$48 \times 3 \stackrel{?}{=} 18 \times 8$$

STEP 3 Whenever the cross products are equal, the ratios are equivalent.

$$144 = 144$$

The cross products are equal.

Solution: Since the cross products are equal, the ratios are equivalent, and therefore, form a proportion.

Another Example

Find Another Term

$\frac{15}{18} = \frac{10}{t}$ Cross multiply. $\frac{15}{18} \times \frac{10}{t}$ → 18×10, $15 \times t$

Cross products are equal. $15 \times t = 180$

Solve for t. $\frac{15 \times t}{15} = \frac{180}{15}$ $t = 12$

Guided Practice

Solve each proportion.

1. $\frac{18}{24} = \frac{a}{8}$
2. $\frac{t}{20} = \frac{9}{15}$
3. $\frac{6}{30} = \frac{2}{b}$

Write the cross products for each pair of ratios. Do the two ratios form a proportion? Write *yes* or *no*.

4. $\frac{3}{8}; \frac{12}{40}$
5. $\frac{12}{8}; \frac{3}{2}$
6. $\frac{5}{6}; \frac{10}{18}$

Ask Yourself

- Did I write the cross products correctly?
- Are the cross products equal?

Explain Your Thinking ▶ How can you tell if the ratios $\frac{6}{9}$ and $\frac{8}{12}$ form a proportion?

Go On

Practice and Problem Solving

Solve each proportion.

7. $\frac{5}{15} = \frac{h}{3}$
8. $\frac{4}{9} = \frac{12}{n}$
9. $\frac{k}{16} = \frac{4}{8}$
10. $\frac{12}{j} = \frac{6}{2}$
11. $\frac{32}{24} = \frac{8}{f}$
12. $\frac{w}{7} = \frac{8}{8}$
13. $\frac{14}{20} = \frac{a}{30}$
14. $\frac{16}{y} = \frac{14}{35}$
15. $\frac{9}{20} = \frac{m}{100}$
16. $\frac{36}{48} = \frac{21}{v}$
17. $\frac{q}{12} = \frac{14}{24}$
18. $\frac{s}{90} = \frac{16}{60}$

Write the cross products for each pair of ratios.
Do the two ratios form a proportion? Write *yes* or *no*.

19. $\frac{3}{5}; \frac{9}{15}$
20. $\frac{6}{18}; \frac{1}{3}$
21. $\frac{3}{8}; \frac{9}{32}$
22. $\frac{15}{20}; \frac{3}{5}$
23. $\frac{8}{24}; \frac{3}{9}$
24. $\frac{10}{12}; \frac{24}{30}$
25. $\frac{3}{12}; \frac{9}{36}$
26. $\frac{12}{3}; \frac{6}{2}$
27. $\frac{32}{40}; \frac{6}{10}$
28. $\frac{15}{27}; \frac{25}{45}$
29. $\frac{42}{28}; \frac{12}{8}$
30. $\frac{4}{7}; \frac{16}{21}$
31. $\frac{20}{5}; \frac{16}{4}$
32. $\frac{40}{48}; \frac{12}{16}$
33. $\frac{9}{6}; \frac{15}{10}$
34. $\frac{10}{8}; \frac{25}{16}$

Data **Use the table for Problems 35–37.**

At the right are the results of a survey of two fifth grade classes. Six students did not respond to the survey.

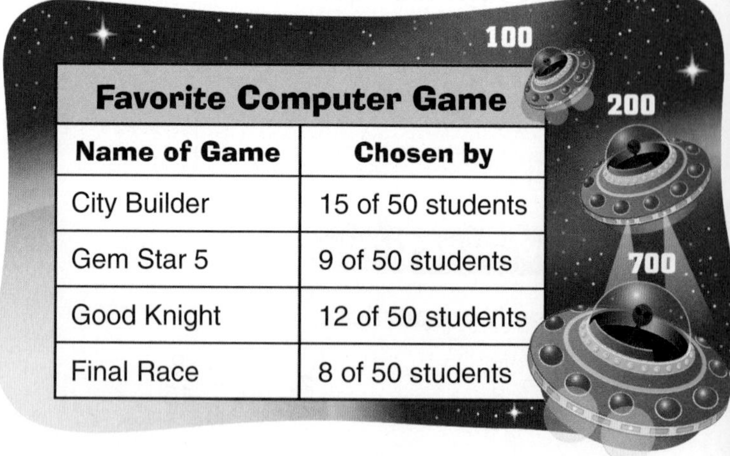

Favorite Computer Game

Name of Game	Chosen by
City Builder	15 of 50 students
Gem Star 5	9 of 50 students
Good Knight	12 of 50 students
Final Race	8 of 50 students

35. **Predict** Suppose 350 students are in your school. Based on the survey, about how many of those students would you expect to choose Gem Star 5?

36. Suppose there are 500 students in a school. Predict how many more students would choose Good Knight than Final Race.

37. **Create and Solve** Write and solve a problem in which the data from the survey and proportions are used.

38. A survey of 239 voters shows that 148 people plan to vote for McAllen for Mayor. About 10,000 people are expected to vote. About how many do you think will vote for McAllen?

39. Nick draws 4 green squares and 5 red squares. Draw a group of 27 squares in which the ratio of green squares to red squares is equivalent to the ratio shown in Nick's drawing.

Extra Practice See page 503, Set D.

Mixed Review and Test Prep

Open Response

Estimate. Then add or subtract. (Ch. 10, Lessons 1, 4, and 8)

40. $12\frac{7}{8} - 5\frac{1}{8}$

41. $9\frac{1}{2} + 8\frac{3}{10}$

42. $20\frac{1}{10} - 7\frac{4}{5}$

43. $6\frac{3}{4} + 9\frac{7}{8}$

Multiple Choice

44. Find the value of x to make a proportion. $\frac{6}{8} = \frac{x}{32}$ (Ch. 18, Lesson 4)

A $x = 18$

B $x = 20$

C $x = 22$

D $x = 24$

Game

Activity

Proportion Pushups

Practice making proportions by playing this game with a partner or several friends. Two to six can play. Try to be the first person to score 10 points.

2 Players

What You'll Need • 2 proportion cards (Learning Tool 55) • 4 sets of number cards, numbered 1–9 (Learning Tool 6)

Here's What to Do

1. Shuffle the number cards. Deal 4 cards facedown to each player. Place the next two cards faceup on the Proportion Card (Learning Tool 55).

2. Each player, in turn, tries to use 2 cards to make a proportion.
   - If a correct proportion is made, that player scores 2 points.
   - If an incorrect proportion is made, the other players score 1 point.
   - If no proportion is made, the player scores 0 points.

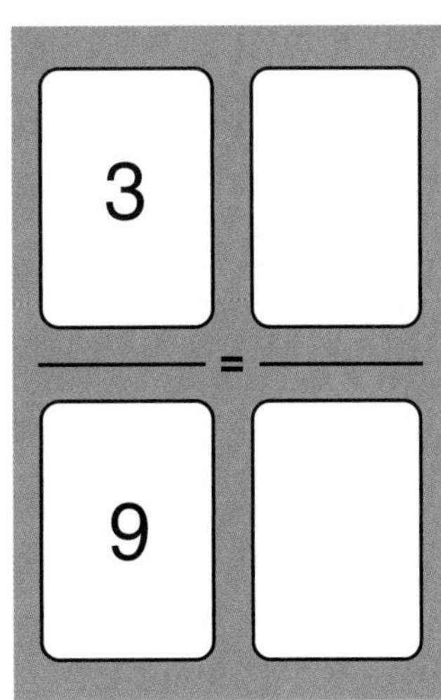

Reshuffle all cards and repeat Steps 1 and 2. The first player to score 10 points wins.

Lesson 5

Similar Figures and Scale Drawings

Objective Use equivalent ratios to interpret scale drawings.

Vocabulary
- scale
- scale drawing
- similar figures

Learn About It

A **scale** is a ratio of the measurements in a drawing of an object to the corresponding measurements of the actual object. When a drawing is created using a scale, it is called a **scale drawing.**

You can create a scale drawing by enlarging or reducing all of the actual measurements by the same factor.

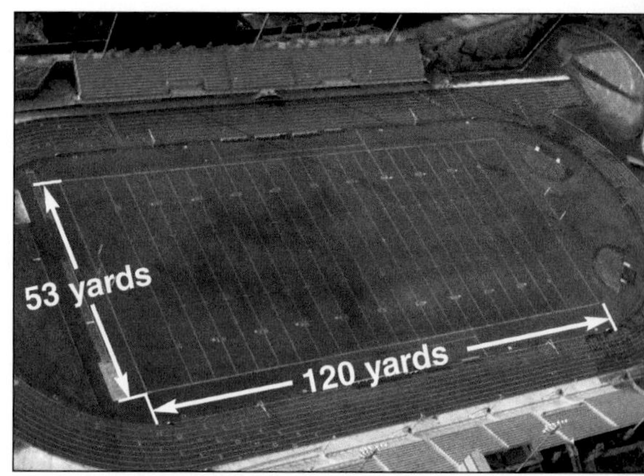

Make a scale drawing of a football field using the scale 1 cm:10 yd.

STEP 1 Write the scale as the first half of a proportion.

length in drawing / actual length → $\frac{1 \text{ cm}}{10 \text{ yd}}$

STEP 2 Write and solve a proportion that shows the scale is equivalent to the length of the field in the drawing to the actual length.

$$\frac{1 \text{ cm}}{10 \text{ yd}} = \frac{■ \text{ cm}}{120 \text{ yd}} \quad (\times 12)$$

(length in drawing / actual length on each side)

scale length = 12 cm

STEP 3 Repeat these steps to find the scale width of the field.

$$\frac{1 \text{ cm}}{10 \text{ yd}} = \frac{■ \text{ cm}}{53 \text{ yd}} \quad (\times 5.3)$$

scale width = 5.3 cm

STEP 4 Use the answers you found in Steps 2 and 3 to create your scale drawing.

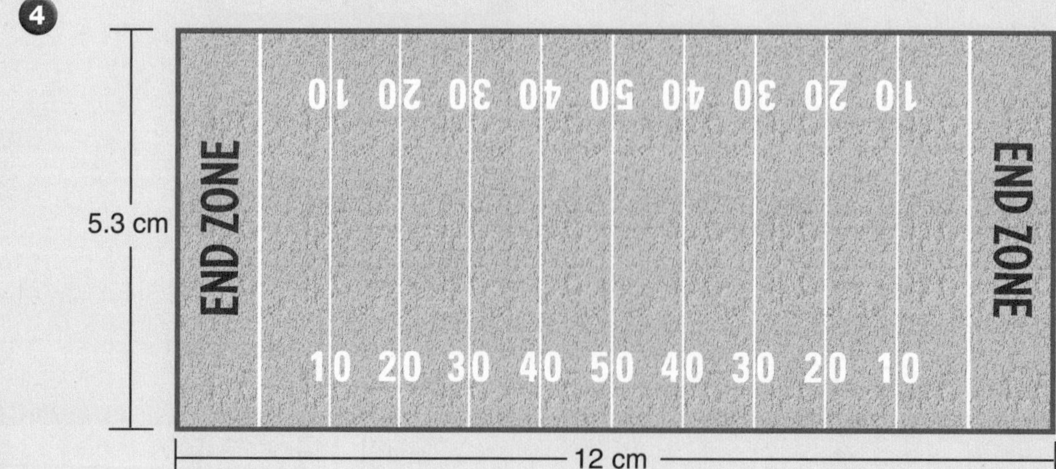

Scale drawings and the actual figures they represent are similar figures. **Similar figures** have the same shape, but they do not have to be the same size.

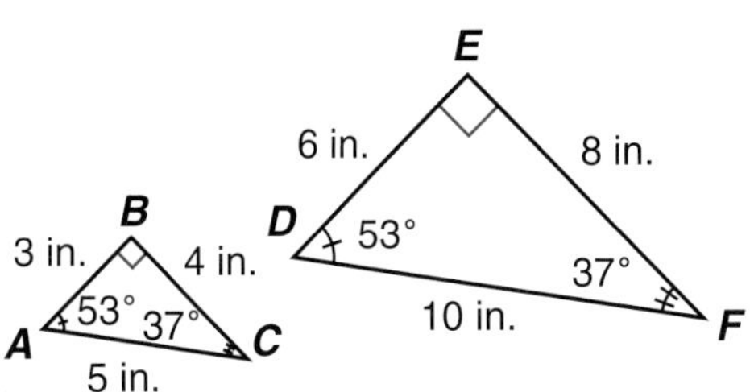

If figures are similar, the lengths of their corresponding sides are proportional and the measures of their corresponding angles are equal.

The symbol ~ is read as "is similar to."

Determine whether or not the given triangles are similar.

STEP 1 Make sure all corresponding angles have equal measures.

$\angle A \cong \angle D$

$\angle B \cong \angle E$

$\angle C \cong \angle F$

STEP 2 Write a proportion to represent the relationship between the pairs of corresponding sides.

$\frac{3}{6} = \frac{4}{8} = \frac{5}{10}$

STEP 3 Write each ratio in simplest form. If they are equivalent, the figures are similar.

$\frac{3}{6} = \frac{4}{8} = \frac{5}{10}$

$\frac{1}{2} = \frac{1}{2} = \frac{1}{2}$

Solution: $\triangle ABC \sim \triangle DEF$

Guided Practice

Use the scale 1 in.:5 ft to find *n*.

1. 4 in. in the drawing represents *n* ft.

   Hint: in drawing → $\frac{1 \text{ in.}}{5 \text{ ft}} = \frac{4 \text{ in.}}{n \text{ ft}}$ ← in drawing; actual → (bottom) ← actual

2. 6 in. in the drawing represents *n* ft.

3. *n* in. in the drawing represents 45 ft.

Ask Yourself

- Did I write a proportion?
- Did I use the correct units in my answers?

Use the figures to the right to answer each question.

In the triangles, $\angle J \cong \angle P$ and $\angle K \cong \angle Q$. The measure of $\angle J$ is 53°.

4. What is the measure of $\angle P$?

5. What is the measure of $\angle K$?

6. What is the measure of $\angle Q$?

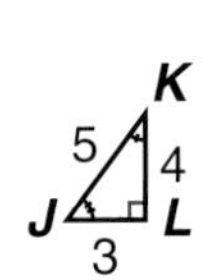

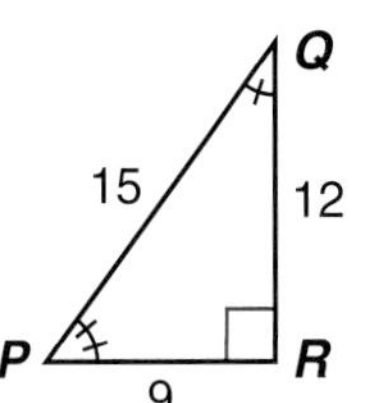

7. Write a proportion to represent the relationship between the pairs of corresponding sides. Are the ratios equivalent? Explain how you know.

8. Are the two triangles similar? How do you know?

Explain Your Thinking ▶ Can you determine if two figures are similar just by looking at them? Explain why or why not.

Go On

Practice and Problem Solving

Use the scale 1 cm:4 m to find *n*.

9. 2 cm in the drawing represents *n* m.

10. 7 cm in the drawing represents *n* m.

11. *n* cm in the drawing represents 100 m.

12. *n* cm in the drawing represents 60 m.

13. 6 cm in the drawing represents *n* m.

14. *n* cm in the drawing represents 80 m.

A blueprint is made with a scale of $\frac{1}{8}$ in.:1 ft. Find *n*.

15. *n* in. represents 5 ft.

16. $\frac{1}{4}$ in. represents *n* ft.

17. $\frac{3}{4}$ in. represents *n* ft.

18. *n* in. represents 12 ft.

19. *n* in. represents 1.5 ft.

20. $\frac{5}{16}$ in. represents *n* ft.

Tell whether the rectangles in each pair are similar. Explain your answers.

21. rectangle *ABCD* and rectangle *EFGH*

22. rectangle *EFGH* and rectangle *WXYZ*

23. rectangle *STUV* and rectangle *ABCD*

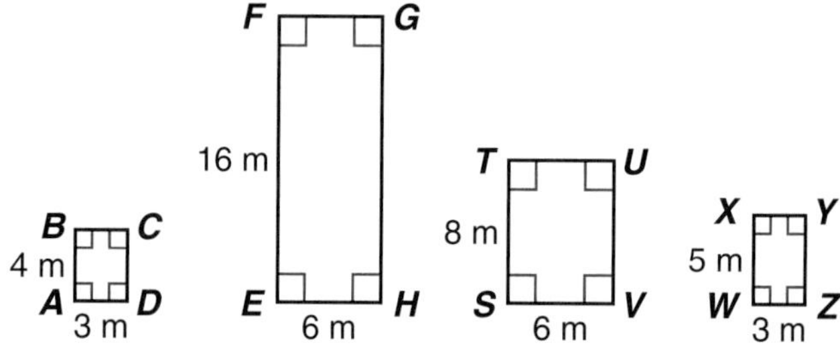

Solve.

24. An architect is making a scale drawing of a room that is 12 ft by 18 ft. He is using a scale of 1 in.:2 ft. What are the measurements of the drawing?

25. An architect's drawing of a room has a scale of 1 in.:2 ft. What are the measurements of the actual room if it is 30 in. by 16 in. in the drawing?

26. Name something that would require a scale enlargement in order for the human eye to see what the actual object looks like.

27. The official measurements of an NBA basketball court are 94 ft by 50 ft. Make a scale drawing of an NBA basketball court using the scale 1cm:10 ft.

Mixed Review and Test Prep

Open Response

Write each quotient in simplest form.
(Ch.12, Lessons 5–6)

28. $6 \div 1\frac{1}{5}$

29. $1\frac{1}{3} \div 3$

30. $\frac{5}{8} \div 1\frac{1}{4}$

31. $2\frac{3}{4} \div 3$

32. $\frac{5}{6} \div 3\frac{2}{3}$

33. $2\frac{1}{4} \div 1\frac{3}{4}$

34. Are these two triangles similar? Explain. (Ch.18, Lesson 5)

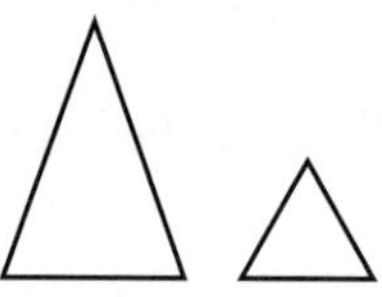

Extra Practice See page 503, Set E.

Activity

Social Studies Connection

Map Skills

A standard orienteering course consists of a start, a series of control sites marked on the map, and a finish. The person who visits all of the control sites in the fastest time wins.

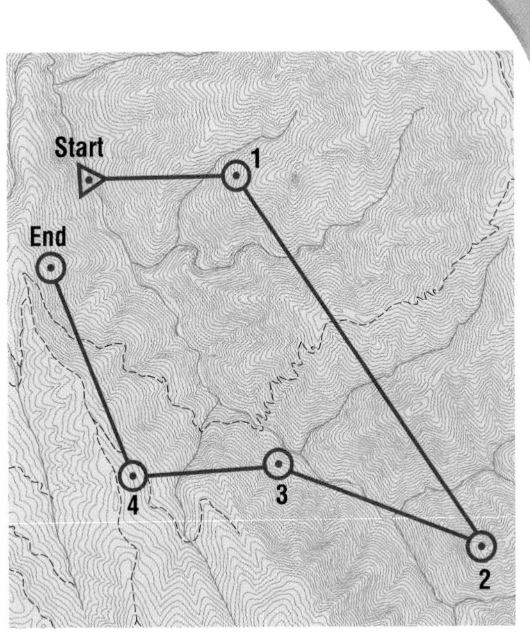

At the right, there is an example of an orienteering map. The standard scale on an orienteering map is 1 cm:15,000 cm, which is the same as 1 cm:150 m.

The map's scale is used to compare the distance on the map with the actual distance.

On the map, the distance between the start of the course and the first control site is 2 cm. What is the actual distance? Use the scale 1 cm:150 m.

STEP 1 Write the scale as the first half of a proportion.

distance on map → $\frac{1 \text{ cm}}{150 \text{ m}}$ ← actual distance

STEP 2 Write and solve a proportion that shows the scale is equivalent to the ratio of the distance on the map to the actual distance.

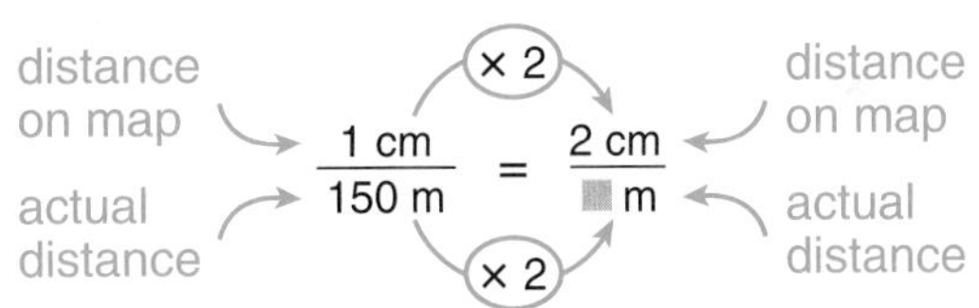

Solution: The actual distance between the start of the course and the first control site is 300 meters.

Use the map above and a centimeter ruler to answer each question.

1. What is the distance between control site 2 and control site 3?
2. What is the distance along the course from control site 3 to the end of the course?
3. How much longer is it from site 4 to the end of the course than it is from the beginning of the course to site 1?
4. **Create and Solve** Create your own problem based on the map above. Ask a partner to solve your problem.

Lesson 6

Problem-Solving Decision
Estimate or Exact Answer?

Objective Decide when to estimate or calculate an exact answer.

When you solve a problem, you can sometimes use an estimate. An estimate is often easier. At other times, you need an exact answer. An exact answer gives you more precise information.

Problem Look at the ads for table tennis balls shown at the right. Which is the better buy?

Ask Yourself

Can I use an estimate?

If I use compatible numbers to estimate the unit prices:

$\frac{\$4.49}{5} \approx \frac{\$4.50}{5} = \$0.90$

$\frac{\$7.09}{8} \approx \frac{\$7.20}{8} = \$0.90$

$\$0.90 = \$0.90$

The estimated unit prices are equal.

Do I need to find the exact answer?

$\frac{\$4.49}{5} = \$0.898 \approx \$0.90$

$\frac{\$7.09}{8} = \$0.886 \approx \$0.89$

$\$0.89 < \$0.90$

The exact unit prices are slightly different.

Solution: The exact answer shows that $7.09 for 8 table tennis balls is a better buy than $4.49 for 5 table tennis balls. The estimate did not show a difference. Therefore, I would need an exact answer.

Try These

Solve. Tell whether you used an estimate or an exact answer, and explain why.

1. At Ted's Toys, a bag of 20 marbles costs $3.99. At Toy Club, a bag of 30 marbles costs $7.49. Which is the better buy?
2. A package of 6 miniature flags costs $11.95. A package of 10 miniature flags costs $19.79. Which is the better buy?
3. The Balloon Stop sells 200 balloons for $99. The Fun Factory sells 500 balloons for $299. Which is the better buy?
4. A barrel of 50 Tough Tiles costs $15.99. A barrel of 75 Tough Tiles costs $22.49. Which is the better buy?

Solve. Tell whether you used an estimate or an exact answer, and explain why.

5. In Edwards Pharmacy a 6-oz tube of toothpaste costs $2.98. In the discount store a 10-oz tube of toothpaste costs $3.99. Which one is the better buy?

6. At Mel's Office supplies, a package of 6 pens costs $4.09. At Office King, a package of 8 pens costs $5.55. Which is the better buy?

7. A pint of cream costs $1.19. A quart of cream costs $2.29. Which is the better buy? (Hint: How many pints in a quart?)

8. Alan's yogurt is 8 cups for $1.89. Carol's yogurt is 10 cups for $2.29. Which is the better buy?

Real World Connection
Model Railroads

Model railroad designs have many of the features of an actual railroad system. They include such items as trains, stations, signals, and bridges.

Model railroad cars are exact scale replicas of real trains. Many model trains use the HO scale, which is 1 in.:87 in. Another popular scale is the *N* scale, which is 1 in.:160 in.

1. The length of a model boxcar done in HO scale is 6.07 in. What is the actual length of the boxcar in inches?

2. The length of a model engine done in *N* scale is 4.8 in. What is the actual length of the engine in inches?

WEEKLY WR READER eduplace.com/map

Chapter Review/Test

Vocabulary

proportion
rate
ratio
scale
similar

VOCABULARY

1. Two figures that have the same shape but are not the same size are ____.
2. A ratio that compares different units is called a ____.
3. A ____ is a ratio of the measurements in a scale drawing of an object to the corresponding measurements of the actual object.
4. A statement that two ratios are equivalent is a ____.

CONCEPTS AND SKILLS

Write each ratio three different ways. (Lesson 1, pp. 484–485)

5. 7 drums to 14 drumsticks
6. 11 forks to 8 knives

Write 4 equivalent ratios for each. (Lesson 2, pp. 486–487)

7. $\frac{2}{3}$
8. 1 to 7
9. 12:9
10. $\frac{10}{6}$

Find the rate per unit of time. (Lesson 3, pp. 488–491)

11. $240 in 6 days
12. 455 km in 7 h
13. 360 beats in 5 min

Do the two ratios form a proportion? Write *yes* or *no*. (Lesson 4, pp. 492–495)

14. $\frac{3}{4}$ $\frac{39}{52}$
15. $\frac{5}{6}$ $\frac{4}{5}$
16. $\frac{77}{132}$ $\frac{7}{12}$

Use the scale $\frac{1}{2}$ in.:5 mi to find *n*. (Lesson 5, pp. 496–499)

17. *n* in. represents 20 mi
18. 3 in. represents *n* mi
19. *n* in. represents 45 mi

PROBLEM SOLVING

Solve. Tell whether you used an estimate or an exact answer, and explain why.
(Lesson 6, pp. 500–501)

20. A box of 30 diskettes costs $15.99. A box of 50 diskettes costs $26.00. Which is the better buy?

Show You Understand

Alan says that the ratios $\frac{3}{5}$ and $\frac{4}{6}$ form a proportion. Is he correct? Explain your thinking.

Extra Practice

Set A (Lesson 1, pp. 484–485)

Write each ratio three different ways.

1. 5 cups to 8 saucers
2. 3 windows to 2 doors
3. 6 girls to 7 boys
4. 9 red to 4 blue
5. 1 car to 5 buses
6. 13 horses to 6 sheep

Set B (Lesson 2, pp. 486–487)

Write each ratio in simplest form.

1. 6 to 10
2. 9:24
3. $\frac{25}{100}$
4. 14:56
5. $\frac{8}{12}$
6. 30:72

Write four equivalent ratios for each.

7. $\frac{1}{3}$
8. $\frac{2}{5}$
9. $\frac{3}{7}$
10. $\frac{1}{2}$
11. $\frac{1}{4}$
12. $\frac{5}{6}$

Set C (Lesson 3, pp. 488–491)

Find the rate per unit of time.

1. 96 meters in 12 seconds
2. 360 words in 3 min
3. $420 in 35 hours

Complete the unit rate.

4. $4:5 lb = $■:1 lb
5. 275 mi:11 gal = ■ mi:1 gal

Set D (Lesson 4, pp. 492–495)

Solve each proportion.

1. $\frac{6}{30} = \frac{u}{5}$
2. $\frac{5}{75} = \frac{1}{v}$
3. $\frac{24}{w} = \frac{8}{2}$
4. $\frac{x}{100} = \frac{4}{25}$

Do the ratios form a proportion? Write *yes* or *no*.

5. $\frac{2}{3}$ $\frac{9}{12}$
6. $\frac{5}{8}$ $\frac{30}{48}$
7. $\frac{32}{80}$ $\frac{2}{5}$
8. $\frac{10}{4}$ $\frac{15}{5}$

Set E (Lesson 5, pp. 496–499)

Use the scale $\frac{1}{4}$ in.:1 ft to find *n*.

1. *n* in. represents 8 ft
2. 3 in. represents *n* ft

Use the figure at the right to answer each question.

3. What is the measure of $\angle G$?
4. Are the triangles similar? How do you know?

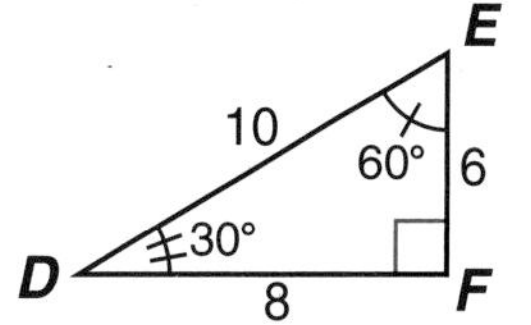

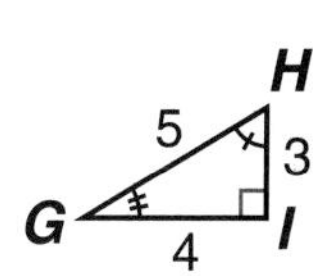

Extra Practice at eduplace.com/map

CHAPTER 19

Percent

INVESTIGATION

Use Data

The Wishnok family budget circle is at the right. Decide how much money the Wishnok family of four would need for food for a month. Then using that number and the percents in the circle graph, find how much the family income, transportation, savings, insurance and taxes, housing, and other would be.

Wishnok Family Budget

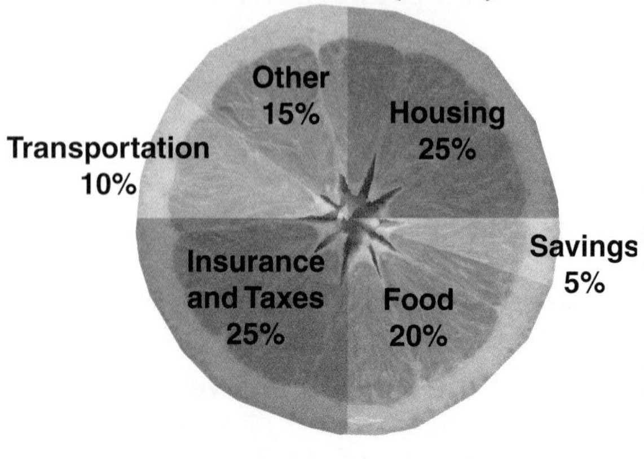

Use What You Know

Use this page to review and remember what you need to know for this chapter.

VOCABULARY

Choose the best word to complete each sentence.

Vocabulary
decimal point
denominator
hundredths
numerator
tenths

1. In the decimal 3.45, the 5 is in the ____ place.
2. The ____ of a fraction tells the number of equal parts in the whole.
3. In writing money amounts, the dollars and cents are separated by a ____ .

CONCEPTS AND SKILLS

Write a decimal and a fraction to represent the shaded part of each model.

4. 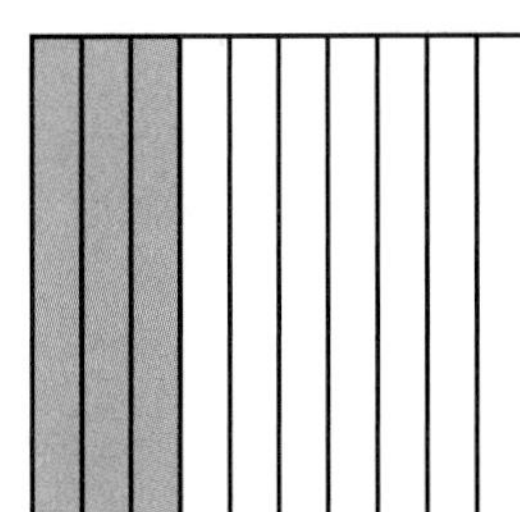

5. 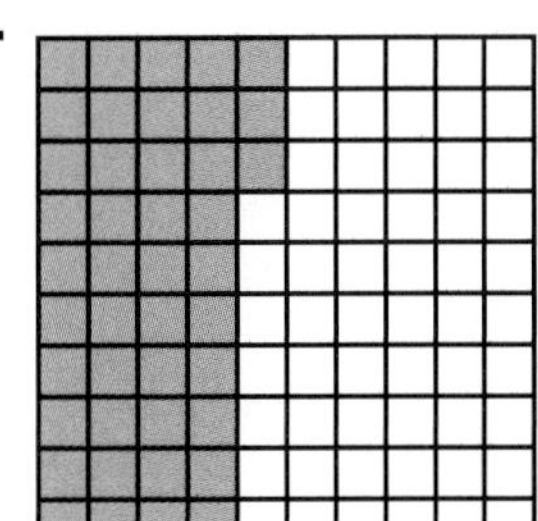

6. 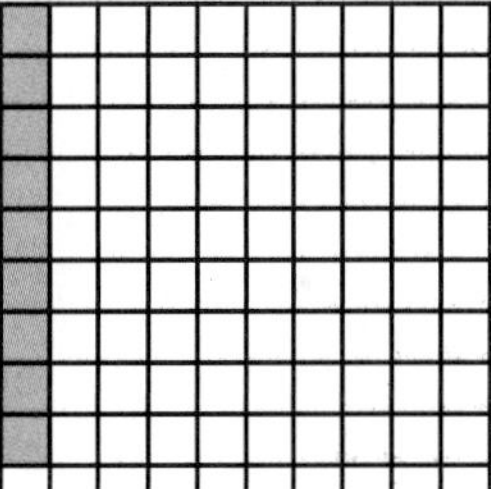

Write each decimal as a fraction in simplest form.

7. 0.4
8. 0.75
9. 0.35
10. 0.66

Find each product.

11. 0.5×21
12. 0.26×300
13. 0.34×192
14. 0.62×475
15. $\frac{3}{4} \times 80$
16. $\frac{1}{2} \times 644$
17. $\frac{4}{5}$ of 135
18. $\frac{3}{8}$ of 96
19. $\frac{1}{5}$ of 200

Write About It

20. Would you prefer to multiply 0.25×84 or $\frac{1}{4} \times 84$? Explain.

Facts Practice, See page 664.

Hands On Lesson 1

Understand Percent

Objective Understand percents as ratios.

Vocabulary
percent

Materials
grid paper
ruler
colored pencils

Work Together

Work with a partner to write percents.

A **percent** is a ratio that compares a number to 100. The word *percent* means "per hundred." So *fifty percent* means "fifty per hundred," or "fifty out of 100." Percents can also be written in fraction or decimal form.

The symbol for percent is %.

Fifty percent is written 50%.

$50\% = 50{:}100 = \frac{50}{100} = 0.50$ or 0.5

STEP 1 On a sheet of grid paper, use a ruler to outline an area that measures 10 units by 10 units.

- How many square units are in the figure?

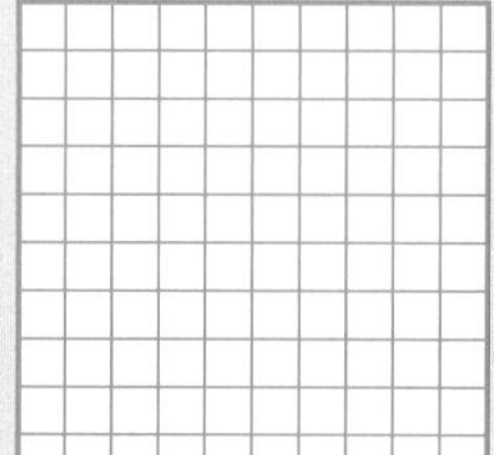

STEP 2 Shade 40 square units blue, 25 square units yellow, and 15 square units green.

- What is the ratio of blue squares to the total number of squares?
- What is the ratio of yellow squares to the total number of squares?
- What is the ratio of shaded squares to the total number of squares?

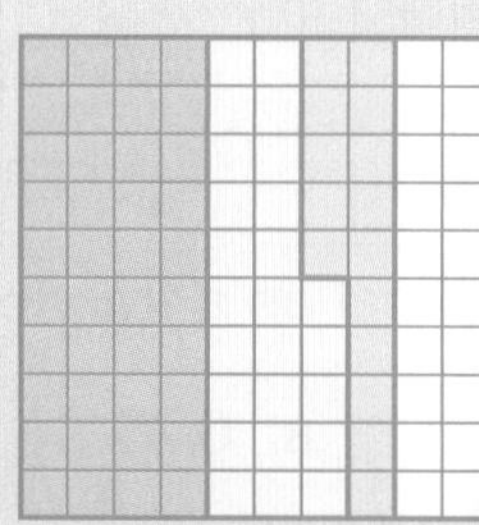

STEP 3 Use the percent symbol to write each percent. What percent of the figure is

- blue?
- yellow?
- green?
- shaded?
- unshaded?

On Your Own

Write the percent of each grid that is shaded.

1. 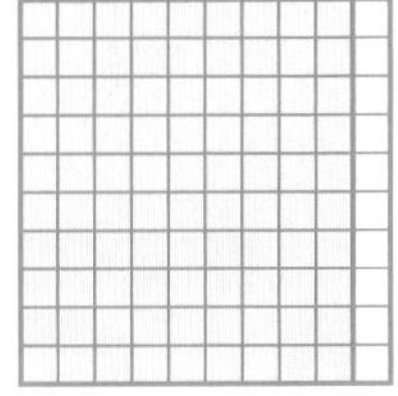

2. 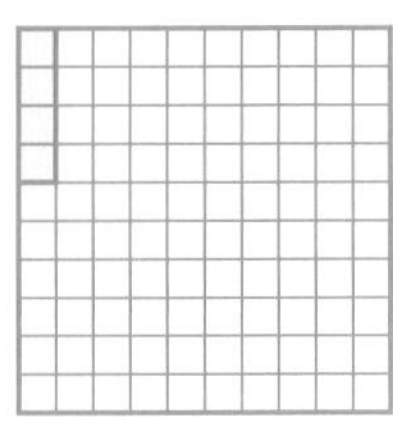

3. 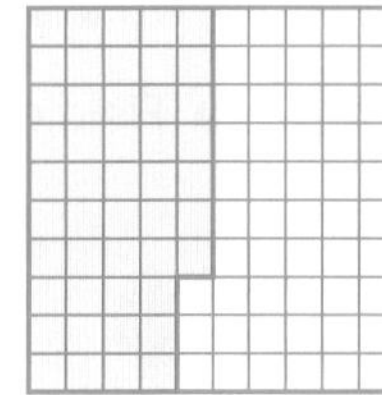

4. 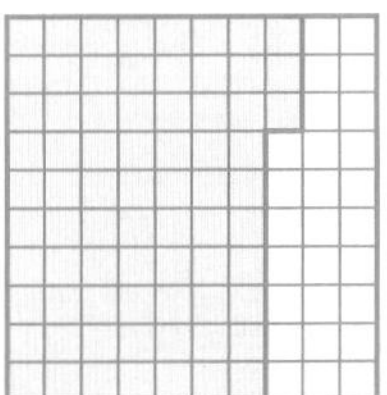

5. 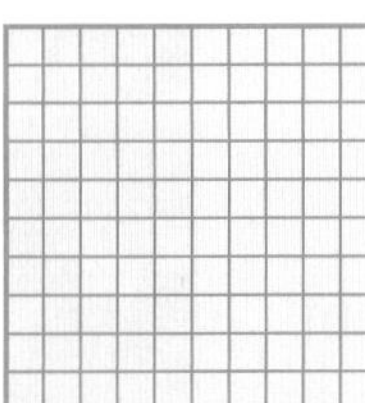

6. 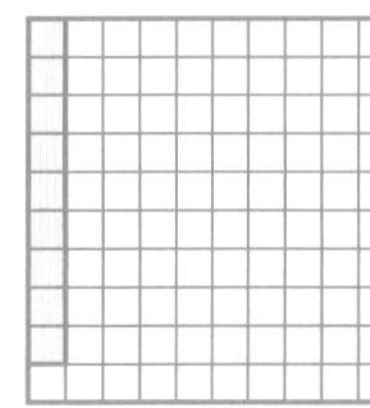

Write each ratio as a percent.

7. $\frac{55}{100}$
8. $\frac{2}{100}$
9. $\frac{31}{100}$
10. $\frac{79}{100}$
11. $\frac{90}{100}$
12. 48:100
13. 16:100
14. 91:100
15. 63:100
16. 8:100
17. 35 parts out of 100
18. 6 parts out of 100
19. 15 parts out of 100
20. 1 part out of 100
21. 0 parts out of 100
22. 50 parts out of 100

Write each percent as a ratio in simplest form.

23. 10%
24. 28%
25. 81%
26. 12%
27. 39%
28. 53%
29. 62%
30. 98%
31. 70%
32. 23%
33. 40%
34. 75%
35. 65%
36. 17%
37. 99%
38. 100%

Talk About It • Write About It

You learned about percents as ratios and how to write percents.

39. How would you show 10% on a 10 × 10 grid? How would you show 100%?

40. Use models to show how 9% and 90% are different. Which model shows the decimal 0.9? Which model shows the decimal 0.09?

Relate Fractions, Decimals, and Percents

Materials
grid paper
ruler
colored pencils

Objective Relate fractions, decimals, and percents.

Learn About It

On Saturday, 50% of the people who visited a department store bought only one item and one out of four people bought more than one item. The rest of the people did not buy anything. What decimal represents the percent of people who bought nothing?

You can write percents in fraction form or in decimal form.

Try this activity to relate fractions, decimals, and percents.

STEP 1 Fifty percent of the people bought only one item. Outline a 10 × 10 grid on grid paper. Shade 50% of the grid red.

- How many square units do you need to shade?
- What decimal can you write for 50%?
- What fraction of the grid is shaded?

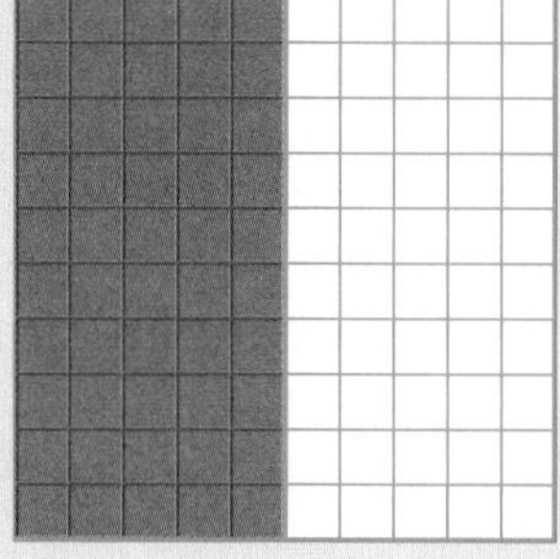

STEP 2 One out of four people who visited the store bought more than one item. Shade $\frac{1}{4}$ of the grid blue.

- How many square units did you shade blue?
- What percent of the grid is shaded blue?
- What decimal can you write for that percent?

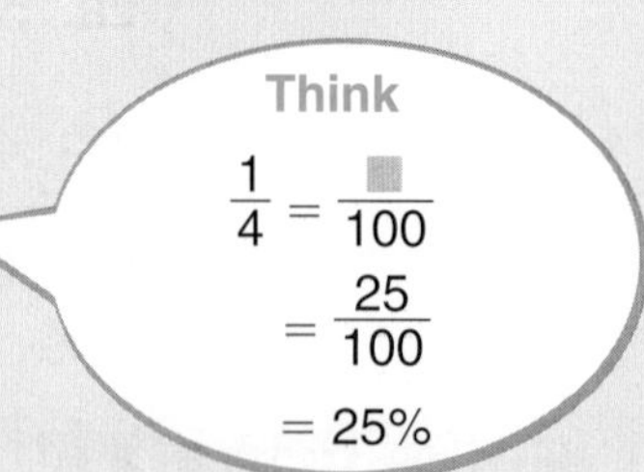

STEP 3 The part of the grid that is unshaded represents the percent of the people who bought nothing on Saturday.

- What percent of the grid is unshaded?
- What decimal can you write for that percent?

Solution: 25% of the people bought nothing at the store on Saturday. The decimal form of this percent is 0.25.

Guided Practice

Copy and complete the table. Write each fraction in simplest form.

	Fraction Form	Decimal Form	Percent
1.	$\frac{1}{10}$	■	10%
2.	■	0.2	■
3.	■	■	65%

Ask Yourself

- Did I write each percent or decimal as a ratio with a second term of 100?
- Did I write each fraction in simplest form?

Explain Your Thinking ▶ Explain why $\frac{5}{100}$ and 5% represent the same ratio.

Practice and Problem Solving

Copy and complete the table. Write each fraction in simplest form.

	Fraction Form	Decimal Form	Percent
4.	■	■	50%
5.	■	0.6	■
6.	$\frac{3}{4}$	■	■

	Fraction Form	Decimal Form	Percent
7.	■	■	80%
8.	■	0.9	■
9.	■	0.4	■

Algebra • Equations **Solve each equation for *n*.**

10. $\frac{25}{100} = \frac{1}{n}$ **11.** $\frac{36}{n} = \frac{9}{25}$ **12.** $12\% = \frac{n}{25}$ **13.** $18\% = \frac{36}{n}$

14. $n\% = \frac{7}{20}$ **15.** $n\% = \frac{23}{50}$ **16.** $0.94 = n\%$ **17.** $0.72 = n\%$

Solve.

18. Three fifths of the items in a grocery store are marked down from their original prices. What percent of the items in the store are marked down?

19. There are 25 students practicing soccer. Nine of them are girls. What percent of the students are girls? Explain.

Mixed Review and Test Prep

Open Response

Estimate. Then add or subtract. (Ch. 11, Lessons 2–4)

20. 5.691 + 0.78 **21.** 0.932 − 0.64

22. A goalie blocked 95% of the shots during a soccer game. How many shots out of 20 did the goalie block? Explain. (Ch. 19, Lesson 2)

Extra Practice See page 525, Set A.

Hands On Lesson 3

Audio Tutor 2/22 Listen and Understand

Compare Fractions, Decimals, and Percents

Materials
grid paper
ruler
colored pencils

Objective Use fractions, decimals, and percents to compare numbers.

Learn About It

On the first of the month, The Beach Shop received a shipment of shorts in 3 colors–red, blue, and green. There were equal numbers of each color.

By the end of the month, $\frac{2}{5}$ of the red shorts, 78% of the blue shorts, and 0.55 of the green shorts had been sold. Which color of shorts was the most popular that month?

Try this activity to represent and compare $\frac{2}{5}$, 78%, and 0.55.

STEP 1 Outline a 10 × 10 grid on grid paper. Shade 2 of every 5 squares red.

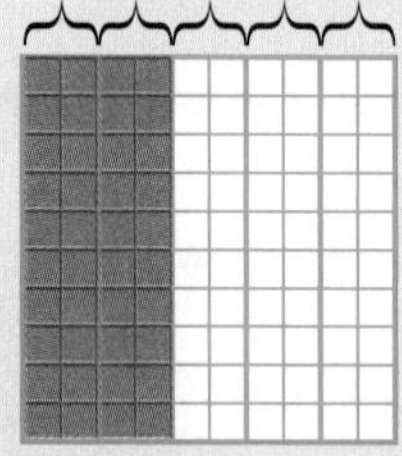

- How did you find $\frac{2}{5}$ of the grid?
- What decimal does the grid show?

STEP 2 Outline another 10 × 10 grid and shade 78% blue.

- How did you know how to show 78%?
- What decimal does the grid show?

STEP 3 Outline a third 10 × 10 grid and shade 0.55 green.

- How did you know how to show 0.55?

STEP 4 Compare the three grids.

- Which color had the greatest number of squares shaded? Which percent is greatest?

Solution: Blue shorts were the most popular that month.

Extra Help at **eduplace.com/map**

Compare $\frac{4}{5}$, 27%, and 0.7.

Different Ways to Compare $\frac{4}{5}$, 27%, and 0.7

Way 1 You can use a number line.

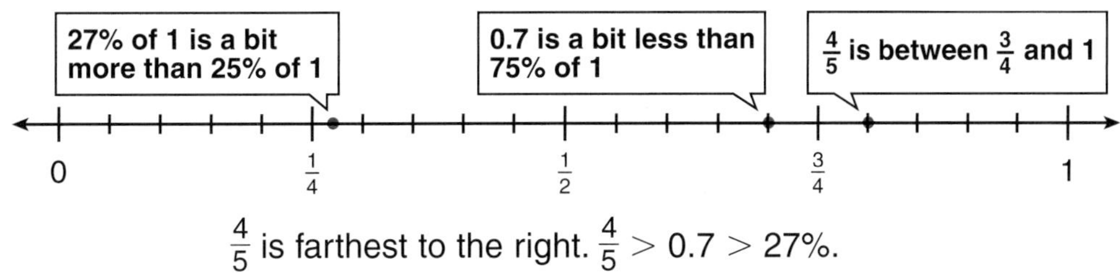

27% of 1 is a bit more than 25% of 1
0.7 is a bit less than 75% of 1
$\frac{4}{5}$ is between $\frac{3}{4}$ and 1
0
$\frac{1}{4}$
$\frac{1}{2}$
$\frac{3}{4}$
1

$\frac{4}{5}$ is farthest to the right. $\frac{4}{5} > 0.7 > 27\%$.

Way 2 You can rewrite each in decimal form.

Step 1 To rewrite the fraction, divide the numerator by the denominator.

$$\begin{array}{r} 0.8 \\ 5\overline{)4.0} \\ \underline{4\,0} \\ 0 \end{array} \quad \frac{4}{5} = 0.8$$

Step 2 Think of the percent as a number of hundredths.

$$27\% = \frac{27}{100} = 0.27$$

Step 3 Compare 0.8, 0.27, and 0.7.

$$0.8 > 0.7 > 0.27$$

So, $\frac{4}{5} > 0.7 > 27\%$.

Solution: $\frac{4}{5}$ is greater than 0.7 and 0.7 is greater than 27%.

Another Example

Order $\frac{9}{25}$, 38%, and 0.313 from the greatest to the least.

$9 \div 25 = 0.36$, so $\frac{9}{25} = 0.36$. 38% can be written in decimal form as 0.38.

$0.38 > 0.36 > 0.313$, so $38\% > \frac{9}{25} > 0.313$.

Guided Practice

Which is greatest?

1. 0.4 $\frac{1}{2}$ 30%

2. $\frac{1}{5}$ 30% 0.25

3. $\frac{1}{8}$ 0.2 40%

4. $\frac{9}{20}$ 44% $\frac{3}{8}$

Ask Yourself

- Did I write the numbers in the same form?
- Did I check the order to see if it's reasonable?

Explain Your Thinking ▶ How could you write $\frac{9}{20}$ in decimal form by first writing it as a percent in ratio form?

Go On

Practice and Problem Solving

Which is greatest?

5. $\frac{3}{5}$ 59% 0.62

6. $\frac{3}{8}$ 9% 0.8

7. $\frac{11}{25}$ 0.4 43%

8. $\frac{5}{8}$ 0.56 59%

9. $\frac{17}{25}$ 70% 0.69

10. $\frac{1}{10}$ 8% 0.09

Which is least?

11. $\frac{4}{5}$ 0.2 60%

12. $\frac{3}{5}$ 0.4 80%

13. $\frac{4}{5}$ 0.9 85%

14. $\frac{1}{5}$ 0.1 25%

15. $\frac{3}{20}$ 4% 0.06

16. $\frac{7}{10}$ 0.6 30%

Order each set from greatest to least.

17. $\frac{3}{10}$ 0.25 20%

18. $\frac{9}{10}$ 0.75 80%

19. $\frac{7}{20}$ 0.3 40%

20. $\frac{12}{25}$ 0.3 50%

21. $\frac{13}{20}$ 0.7 67%

22. $\frac{3}{50}$ 0.6 3%

Order each set from least to greatest.

23. $\frac{19}{20}$ 0.99 98%

24. $\frac{1}{3}$ 0.25 30%

25. $\frac{3}{8}$ 0.43 52%

Algebra • Inequalities **Write a number that will make the number sentence true.**

26. $\frac{2}{5} < ■ < 45\%$

27. $62\% < ■ < \frac{2}{3}$

28. $\frac{12}{25} < ■ < 50\%$

29. $0.82 < ■\% < \frac{17}{20}$

30. $\frac{5}{8} < ■ < 63\%$

31. $0.03 < ■\% < \frac{1}{16}$

Solve.

32. In Ben's Books, 0.3 of the shelves have adult fiction, 25% have adult nonfiction, and $\frac{9}{20}$ of the shelves have children's books. Which kinds of books take up the most shelves in the bookstore?

33. What's Wrong? Sam ordered the numbers $\frac{7}{20}$, 4%, and 0.34 from least to greatest. What did Sam do wrong?

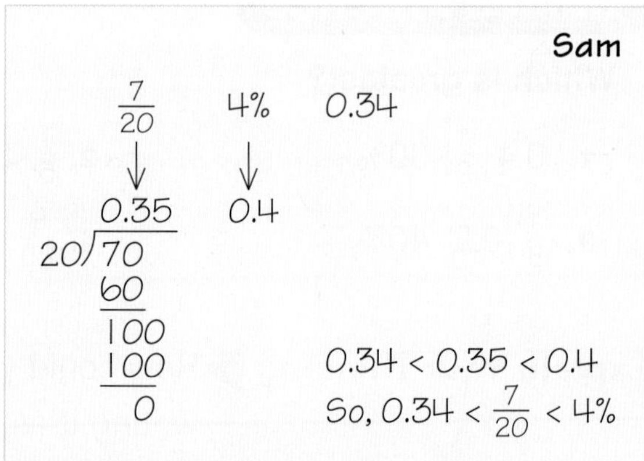

34. Orange juice and lemonade were sold during a concert intermission. Three fifths of the sales were orange juice and 40% were lemonade. Which drink was less popular?

Extra Practice See page 525, Set B.

Activity

Real World Connection

Looking Around

You have learned about percent.

Look around your school, your home, and your shopping mall. Make a display of all the places where you see percents!

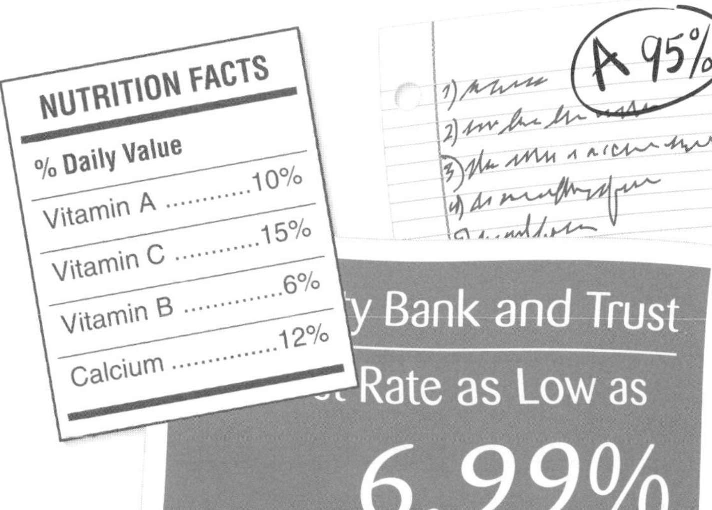

WEEKLY WR READER eduplace.com/map

Quick Check

Check your understanding of Lessons 1–3.

Write each ratio as a percent. (Lesson 1)

1. $\frac{27}{100}$ **2.** 6:100 **3.** 41 out of 100

Write a decimal, a percent, and a fraction in simplest form for each ratio. (Lesson 2)

4. $\frac{12}{50}$ **5.** $\frac{29}{100}$ **6.** $\frac{40}{100}$ **7.** $\frac{112}{200}$

Order each set from the greatest to the least. (Lesson 3)

8. $\frac{13}{40}$ 0.3 25% **9.** 0.65 $\frac{21}{25}$ 70% **10.** 5% 0.1 $\frac{1}{8}$

Lesson 4

Find 10% of a Number

Objective Use mental math to find 10% and multiples of 10% of a number.

Learn About It

A skateboard regularly sells for $60. The skateboard is on sale for 10% off the regular price. How much money would you save if you bought the skateboard on sale?

10% of 60 = n

Different Ways to Find 10% of 60

Way 1 You can use a model.

To find n, divide $60 by 10.

$60 \div 10 = 6$

100% of $60 = $60

10%

n

Way 2 You can multiply by $\frac{1}{10}$.

Finding 10% of a number is the same as finding $\frac{1}{10}$ of that number.

$$10\% \times 60 = \frac{1}{10} \times 60$$

$$\frac{1}{10} \times \frac{60}{1} = \frac{60}{10} = 6$$

Way 3 You can divide by 10 by moving the decimal point to the left.

An easy way to find 10% of any number is to move the decimal point one place to the left to divide the number by 10.

$60 \div 10 = 6.0$

Solution: You would save $6.

Other Examples

A. Find 20% of a Number

Find 20% of 42.

20% of $42 = 42 \div 5$

$= 8.4$

100% of 42 = 42

20%	20%	20%	20%	20%

20% of 42

B. Estimate a Percent of a Number

Estimate 11% of 47.

11% of 47 is about 10% of 50

$10\% \times 50 = \frac{1}{10} \times 50 = 5$

11% of 47 $\approx$ 5

Guided Practice

Ask Yourself

- Did I move the decimal point one place to the left to find 10%?

Find 10% of each number.

1. 75 **2.** 19 **3.** 3.8 **4.** 0.4

Find 20% of each number.

5. 40 **6.** 120 **7.** 26 **8.** 8.2

Explain Your Thinking ▶ What decimal would you multiply by to find 10% of a number? Explain.

Practice and Problem Solving

Find 10% of each number.

9. 42 **10.** 25 **11.** 9 **12.** 3 **13.** 1

14. 783 **15.** 4,012 **16.** 7.8 **17.** 100.5 **18.** 4.41

Find 20% of each number.

19. 20 **20.** 46 **21.** 1,020 **22.** 8.4 **23.** 0.6

Estimate each percent of a number.

24. 12% of 73 **25.** 48% of 69 **26.** 18% of 503 **27.** 9% of 397

Find the number.

28. 10% of a number is 32.

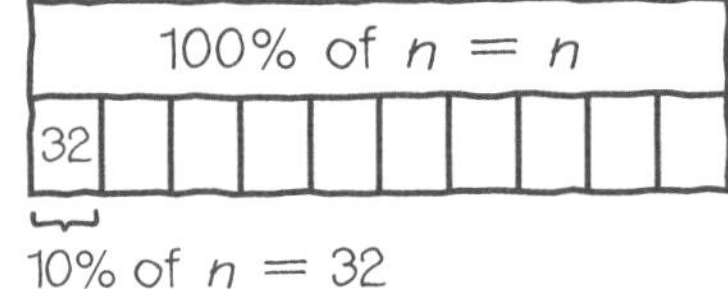

29. 20% of a number is 27.

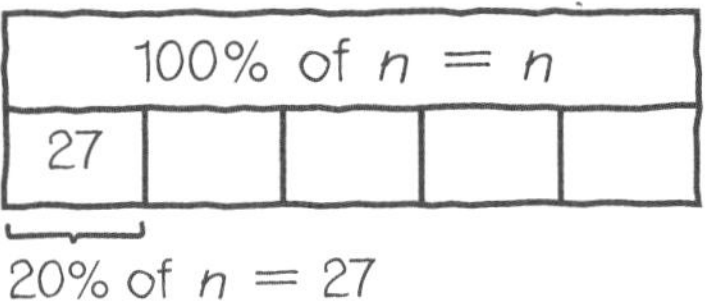

Solve.

30. Mel's bill comes to $31. He leaves 20% of the bill as a tip. How much is the tip?

31. The sum of two numbers is 17. Their product is 60. Find the two numbers.

32. **What's Wrong?** Monique says that 13% of 152 is about 50. Is her estimate reasonable? Tell how you know.

33. How can you find 50% of a number? How can you find 100% of a number?

Mixed Review and Test Prep

Open Response

Divide. (Ch. 14, Lessons 4–5)

34. 2.1 ÷ 6 **35.** 28.63 ÷ 7

Multiple Choice

36. Find 20% of 140. (Ch. 19, Lesson 4)

A 28 **B** 14 **C** 7 **D** 1.4

Extra Practice See page 525, Set C.

Lesson 5

Audio Tutor 2/23 Listen and Understand

Algebra

Percent of a Number

Objective Use different ways to find a percent of a number.

Learn About It

On display in a store window are 20 kites. If 75 percent of the kites are red, how many kites are red?

75% of 20 = n

Different Ways to Find 75% of 20

Way 1 You can use a model.

To find n, divide 20 by 4. Then multiply by 3.

$20 \div 4 = 5 \qquad 5 \times 3 = 15$

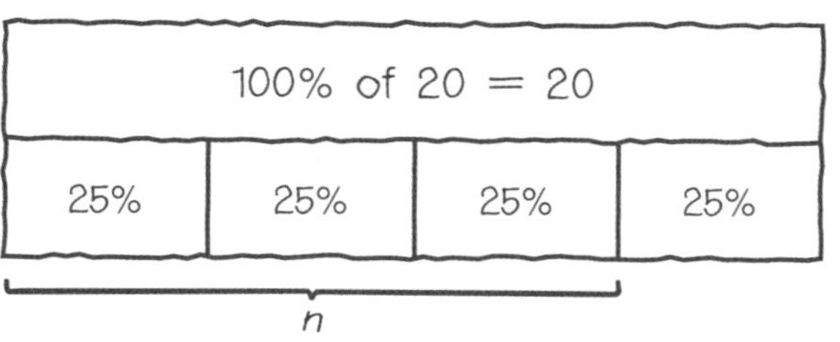

Way 2 You can write the percent as a fraction and multiply.

STEP 1 Write the percent as a ratio.

$$75\% = \frac{75}{100} = \frac{3}{4}$$

STEP 2 Multiply.

$$\frac{3}{4} \times \frac{20}{1} = \frac{60}{4} = 15$$

Way 3 You can write the percent in decimal form and multiply.

STEP 1 Write the percent in decimal form.

75% = 75 hundredths
= 0.75

STEP 2 Multiply.

$$\begin{array}{r} 20 \\ \times\ 0.75 \\ \hline 1\ 00 \\ 14\ 00 \\ \hline 15.00 \end{array}$$

$\times$ 0.75 ← 2 decimal places in the factors

15.00 ← 2 decimal places in the product

Solution: There are 15 red kites.

Guided Practice

Solve by using a model.

1. 50% of 80
2. 75% of 28

Solve by writing the percent as a fraction.

3. 70% of 90
4. 5% of 80

Solve by writing the percent as a decimal.

5. 16% of 40
6. 80% of 150

Ask Yourself

- Do I write the percent as a fraction?
- Do I write the percent as a decimal?

Explain Your Thinking ▶ Which method would you use to find 28% of 66? Why?

Practice and Problem Solving

Solve by writing the percent as a fraction.

7. 90% of 30
8. 35% of 300
9. 20% of 45
10. 40% of 25
11. 75% of 80
12. 15% of 40
13. 50% of 36
14. 30% of 1,000

Solve by writing the percent as a decimal.

15. 25% of 44
16. 33% of 30
17. 16% of 15
18. 90% of 50
19. 7% of 20
20. 60% of 12
21. 37% of 20
22. 14% of 300

Solve. Use any method.

23. 25% of 232
24. 20% of 20
25. 1% of 100
26. 65% of 40
27. 7% of 30
28. 19% of 200
29. 75% of 4
30. 49% of 300

Algebra • Functions **Use the rule to complete each function table.**

31. $y = x\%$ of 200

x	y
5	■
10	■
15	■
20	■

32. $y = 25\%$ of x

x	y
10	■
20	■
30	■
40	■

33. $y = x\%$ of 200

x	y
■	50
■	100
■	150
■	200

Go On

Choose a Computation Method

Mental Math • Estimation • Paper and Pencil • Calculator

Data **Use the table for Problems 34–36.**

34. A *discount* is the amount of money deducted from the price of an item. Use a calculator to find the price of a box kite after the discount indicated in the table has been subtracted.

35. Elena has saved \$15. Does she have enough money to buy a dragon kite after the discount? Explain how you know.

36. **You Decide** You are in charge of buying kites for the kite club. You have \$100 to spend, and want to buy a few different kinds of kites. Which kites will you buy? What is the total cost?

37. At the Flying Kite Festival, 7,958 children's tickets were sold. The total number of tickets sold was about 20,608. About what percent were children's tickets?

38. **Create and Solve** A newspaper reported that the attendance at this year's kite festival was 20% less than the year before. This year's attendance was 12,000. Use this information to write your own problem. Then solve the problem.

Kite	Price	Discount
Parafoil	\$50.00	10%
Dragon	\$25.00	20%
Box	\$20.00	30%
Delta	\$40.00	50%

Mixed Review and Test Prep

Open Response

Find the area and perimeter.
(Ch. 16, Lessons 1 and 3)

39.

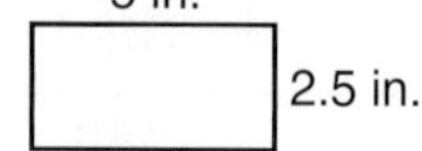

40.

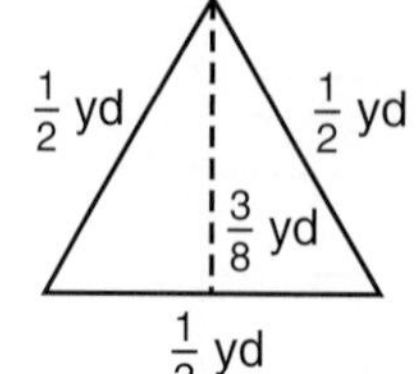

41. Helena has \$25. She wants to buy a disc player that has a regular price of \$39. The player is on sale with a 30% discount. Does Helena have enough money? Explain how you found your answer. (Ch. 19, Lesson 5)

Extra Practice See page 525, Set D.

Problem Solving

Number Sense

Ratios and Percents

You buy a sweatshirt that is on sale. How much will you save? When you estimate or calculate a percent of a number, it helps to think of ratios and their related percents. Here are some relationships you should know.

Ratio	$\frac{1}{20}$	$\frac{1}{10}$	$\frac{1}{8}$	$\frac{1}{6}$	$\frac{1}{5}$	$\frac{1}{4}$	$\frac{1}{3}$	$\frac{1}{2}$
Percent	5%	10%	12.5%	$16\frac{2}{3}\%$	20%	25%	$33\frac{1}{3}\%$	50%

Estimate 35% of 48.

If you only need an estimate, you can find a ratio that converts to a percent close to 35%.

Estimate

$33\frac{1}{3}\% = \frac{1}{3}$, so 35% of 48 is about $\frac{1}{3}$ of 48.

$48 \div 3 = 16$

So 35% of 48 must be slightly more than 16.

You will save about $16.

Find 35% of 48.

If you need an exact calculation, you can find ratios whose corresponding percents have a sum or difference of 35%.

Think: Add 25% of 48 and 10% of 48 to get 35% of 48.

$25\% + 10\% = 35\%$

$25\% \text{ of } 48 = \frac{1}{4} \text{ of } 48 = 48 \div 4 = 12$

$10\% \text{ of } 48 = \frac{1}{10} \text{ of } 48 = 48 \div 10 = 4.8$

So, $35\% \text{ of } 48 = 12 + 4.8 = 16.8$.

You will save $16.80.

1. Why are ratios and their related percents helpful if you want to find the percent of a number using mental math?
2. How could you use ratios to find 20% of 60? to find 45% of 90?

Lesson 6

Problem-Solving Application

Use Circle Graphs

Objective Interpret data to make circle graphs to solve problems.

Making a circle graph is a good way to display data expressed as percents.

Problem The table at the right shows the results of a survey of 240 customers at a department store. How can you show the data from the table as percents in a circle graph?

PAYMENT FOR PURCHASES

Method of Payment	Number of Customers
Cash	60
Check	30
Credit Card	120
Debit Card	30

UNDERSTAND

What is the question?

How can you show the data from the table as percents in a circle graph?

What do you know?

- 60 customers used cash.
- 120 customers used credit cards.
- 240 customers were in the survey.
- 30 customers used checks.
- 30 customers used debit cards.

PLAN

Find the ratio of the data represented by each method of payment to total sales. Write each ratio as a percent. Then divide a circle so that it shows the percent.

SOLVE

- Find the ratio for each method.
- Write the ratio in simplest form and as a percent.

Cash $= \frac{60}{240} = \frac{1}{4} = 25\%$

Check $= \frac{30}{240} = \frac{1}{8} = 12.5\%$

Credit card $= \frac{120}{240} = \frac{1}{2} = 50\%$

Debit card $= \frac{30}{240} = \frac{1}{8} = 12.5\%$

- Use the ratios to make a circle graph.
- Label each section.

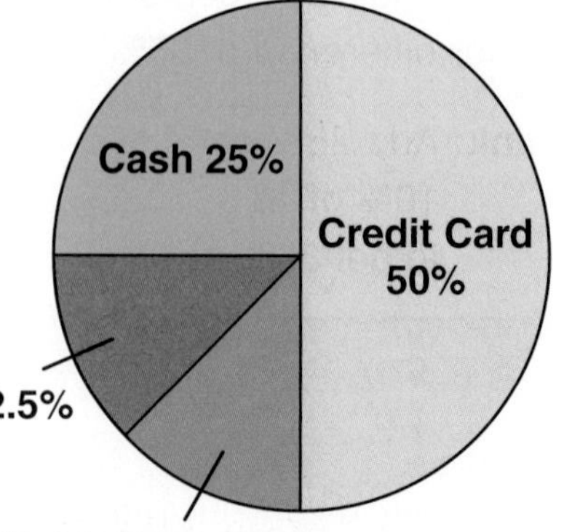

LOOK BACK

Look back at the data. Does the graph seem reasonable?

Guided Practice

Use the circle graph on page 520 to solve each problem.

1. Predict the number of customers out of 1,000 that would use a method other than cash.

   Hint What part of the circle represents other payment methods?

2. Suppose 120 more customers are surveyed. Of these customers, 60 use credit cards, 30 use checks, and 30 use debit cards. If that data is added to the existing data, how will the circle graph change?

Ask Yourself

What does the question ask me to find?

Did I use the data to find the ratio?

SOLVE

Did I write each ratio as a percent?

LOOK BACK

Does my answer make sense?

Independent Practice

Use the circle graph for Problems 3 and 4.

3. The circle graph at the right shows how Ted budgets his money. If his total budget is $3,000, how much money does Ted spend on his rent?

4. **You Decide** Ted wants to increase his savings to $600 per month. Suggest a way that Ted can change his spending to increase his savings.

Ted's Budget

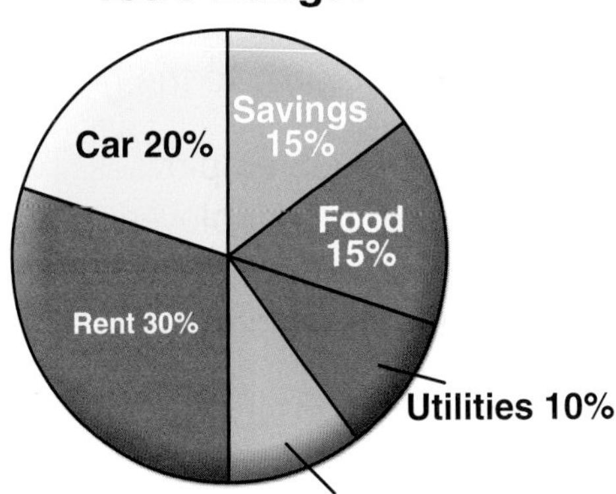

 **Data** **Use the table at the right for Problems 5–7.**

5. The table at the right shows the results of a survey of 560 people who bought sneakers at 4 kinds of stores. Make a circle graph to display the data as percents.

6. Use the circle graph that you made in Problem 5. What percent of the people bought their sneakers in a store other than a sneaker store?

7. **Predict** Based on the survey results, how many people out of 1,600 would you expect to buy sneakers from a sneaker store?

Buying Sneakers

Type of Store	Number of People
Sporting Goods	140
Department or Discount	280
Sneaker	70
Other	70

Go On

Mixed Problem Solving

Solve. Show your work. Tell what strategy you used.

8. **Measurement** A rectangle has a perimeter of 26 cm and an area of 36 cm^2. What are the dimensions of the rectangle?

9. The Drama Club spends $600 on sets and props, $500 on costumes, $250 on tickets and programs, and $200 on a cast party. After spending this money, the club is left with $325. How much did the club start with?

10. The monthly rent on an apartment was $1,000 in 2004, $1,050 in 2005, and $1,103 in 2006. What was the rent increase each year? What percent is each increase? Predict the rent in 2007, to the nearest dollar.

11. A store has 36 employees. Twenty-five percent of the employees are managers. How many managers does the store have? Draw a picture that supports your solution.

You Choose

Strategy
- Draw a Diagram
- Find a Pattern
- Guess and Check
- Work Backward
- Write an Equation

Computation Method
- Mental Math
- Estimation
- Paper and Pencil
- Calculator

Data Use the diagram for Problems 12–14.

The diagram shows the floor plan of a home supplies store. The labels show the different departments within the store.

12. **Measurement** How many square feet of space does the store have?

13. Find the percent of each department's space in the store. Round your answers to the nearest tenth of a percent.

14. The store has total sales of $10,000,000. The ratio of the Kitchen Wares Department's sales to total sales is equal to the ratio of its floor area to the total floor area. Find the Kitchen Wares Department's sales.

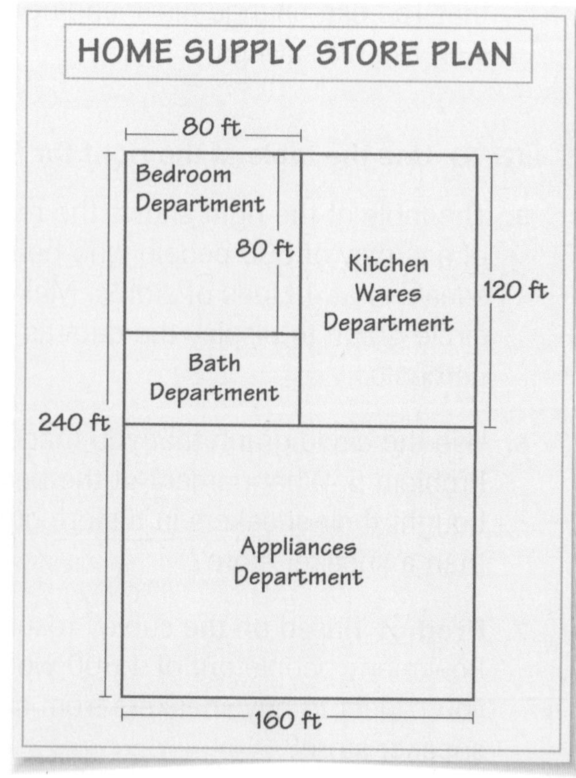

Calculator Connection

Ratios, Percents, and Calculators

Activity

You can use a calculator to convert ratios and percents to decimal form.

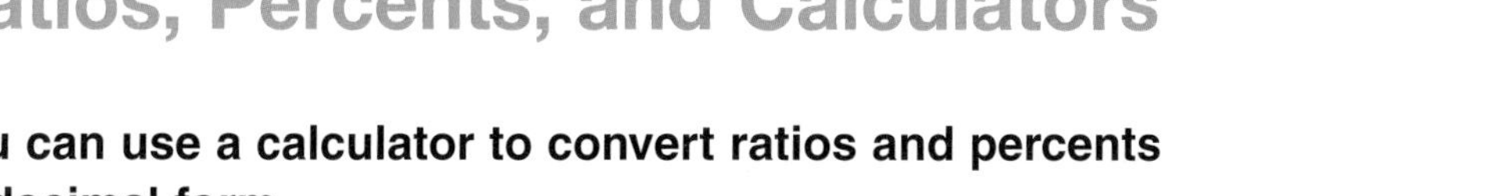

To find the decimal equivalent for $\frac{4}{5}$
press: 4 ÷ 5 Enter =
To find the decimal equivalent for 75%
press: 7 5 ÷ 1 0 0 Enter =

Use a calculator to rewrite each set in order from least to greatest. Then match each one to a word to solve the riddles below.

Riddle: Why didn't the fraction slurp his soup?

1. $\frac{3}{20}$ 0.2 18%

____ ____ ____

2. $\frac{5}{7}$ 0.688 74%

____ ____ ____

3. $\frac{7}{16}$ 45% 0.4499

____ ____ ____

Key:

$\frac{3}{20}$	$\frac{7}{16}$	$\frac{5}{7}$	0.2	0.4499	0.688	18%	45%	74%
He	he	would	afraid	was	someone	was	improper	think

Riddle: What did the termites do to the wooden ship?

4. $\frac{3}{7}$ 0.24 23%

____ ____ ____

5. $\frac{5}{9}$ 0.47 50%

____ ____ ____

6. $\frac{8}{11}$ 0.75 85%

____ ____ ____

Key:

0.24	0.47	23%	85%	$\frac{5}{9}$	$\frac{3}{7}$	$\frac{8}{11}$	0.75	50%
ate	much	They	decagon	the	so	ship	the	of

Chapter Review/Test

VOCABULARY

1. A ____ is a ratio of a number to 100.
2. You can show how parts of a whole are related in a ____.
3. A ____ is a number that shows tenths, hundredths, thousandths, and so on.

Vocabulary

- circle graph
- decimal
- fraction
- percent
- ratio

CONCEPTS AND SKILLS

Copy and complete each table. Write each fraction in simplest form. (Lessons 1–2, pp. 506–509)

	Fraction	Decimal	Percent
4.	$\frac{1}{2}$	■	■
5.	■	0.08	■

	Fraction	Decimal	Percent
6.	$\frac{1}{5}$	■	■
7.	■	■	15%

Order each set from greatest to least. (Lesson 3, pp. 510–513)

8. $\frac{17}{40}$ 35% 0.4
9. $\frac{7}{20}$ 68% 0.37
10. $\frac{8}{10}$ 75% 0.95

Find 10% of each number. Then find 20% of each number. (Lesson 4, pp. 514–515)

11. 95
12. 3,780
13. 54.7
14. 0.14

Solve. Use any method. (Lesson 5, pp. 516–519)

15. 25% of 96
16. 70% of 120
17. 60% of 60
18. 30% of 40

PROBLEM SOLVING

Use the circle graph to solve.
(Lesson 6, pp. 520–523)

19. How many students play soccer and baseball?
20. What fraction of the students surveyed play football?

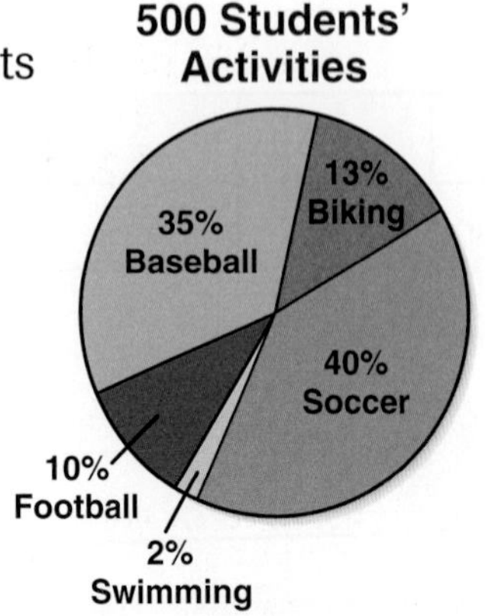

Write About It

Show You Understand

Sue says that $\frac{15}{20}$ is equal to 60%. Is this reasonable? Explain.

Extra Practice

Set A (Lesson 2, pp. 508–509)

Copy and complete each table. Write each fraction in simplest form.

	Fraction	Decimal	Percent
1.	$\frac{3}{10}$	0.3	■
3.	$\frac{7}{10}$	■	■
5.	■	0.09	■
7.	■	0.45	■

	Fraction	Decimal	Percent
2.	$\frac{21}{100}$	■	■
4.	■	■	40%
6.	■	■	84%
8.	$\frac{3}{5}$	■	■

Set B (Lesson 3, pp. 510–513)

Order each set from greatest to least.

1. $\frac{7}{10}$ 0.5 80%

2. $\frac{2}{5}$ 0.35 27%

3. $\frac{13}{20}$ 0.92 30%

4. $\frac{5}{8}$ 50% 0.61

5. $\frac{12}{25}$ 78% 0.4

6. $\frac{7}{8}$ $\frac{37}{50}$ 86%

7. 0.47 $\frac{3}{8}$ 39%

8. 28% 0.27 $\frac{7}{20}$

9. 0.6 59% $\frac{8}{10}$

Set C (Lesson 4, pp. 514–515)

Find 10% of each number. Then find 20% of each number.

1. 72 **2.** 2,410 **3.** 5 **4.** 700 **5.** 12,305

6. 39.5 **7.** 8.31 **8.** 2 **9.** 514.74 **10.** 6.3502

Set D (Lesson 5, pp. 516–519)

Solve by writing the percent as a fraction.

1. 30% of 70 **2.** 75% of 96 **3.** 60% of 85 **4.** 50% of 64

5. 25% of 40 **6.** 20% of 10 **7.** 45% of 200 **8.** 55% of 800

Solve by writing the percent as a decimal.

9. 25% of 88 **10.** 37% of 90 **11.** 15% of 70 **12.** 85% of 200

13. 40% of 20 **14.** 75% of 400 **15.** 8% of 64 **16.** 1% of 6

Extra Practice at **eduplace.com/map**

CHAPTER 20

Probability

INVESTIGATION

Use Data

These athletes have come from all over the world to compete for a medal in table tennis. The table shows the games currently being played. If each of these 8 athletes plays each other athlete once, how many games will be played? What if there were twice as many athletes?

Table Tennis Tournament

(Round 2)
Player versus Player
H ←→ C
D ←→ A
F ←→ E
B ←→ G

Use What You Know

Use this page to review and remember what you need to know for this chapter.

VOCABULARY

Choose the best word to complete each sentence.

Vocabulary
- equally likely
- frequency
- outcome
- tally marks

1. Groups of five ____ help you keep a running count of how often an object appears or something occurs.
2. A(n) ____ is a possible result of a probability experiment.
3. In a table, the number that tells how often something happens is called the ____.

CONCEPTS AND SKILLS

Write the fraction for the shaded part in simplest form.

4. 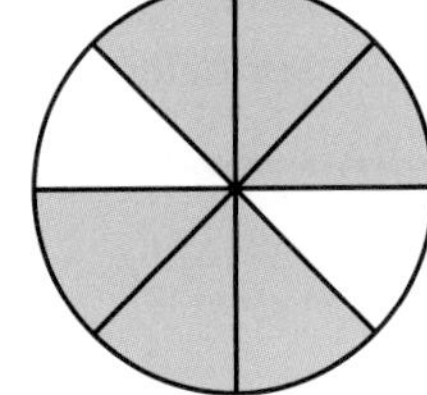

5. 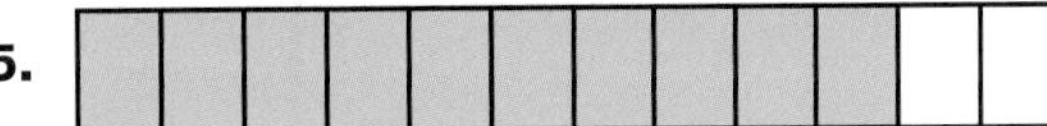

Write each ratio in simplest form.

6. 2 to 6
7. $\frac{4}{10}$
8. 30:72
9. $\frac{8}{48}$

10. How do you write a fraction in simplest form?

Facts Practice, See page 665.

Lesson 1

Make Choices

Objective Use organized lists, tree diagrams, and multiplication to find all the possible combinations of given items.

Vocabulary
organized list
tree diagram

Learn About It

At the school fair frozen yogurt is sold in two flavors—vanilla and peach. You can choose one of three toppings for your yogurt—fruit, nuts, or sprinkles. How many different ways can you choose one flavor and one topping?

Different Ways to Find the Number of Choices

Way 1 **You can make an organized list.**

peach, fruit
peach, nuts
peach, sprinkles
vanilla, fruit
vanilla, nuts
vanilla, sprinkles

Way 2 **You can make a tree diagram.**

Yogurt **Toppings**

Desserts
- peach: fruit, nuts, sprinkles
- vanilla: fruit, nuts, sprinkles

Way 3 **You can multiply to find the number of possible choices.**

flavor choices × topping choices = number of choices
↓ ↓ ↓
2 × 3 = 6

Solution: You can choose one flavor and one topping in 6 different ways.

Guided Practice

You have one choice from each category.
Make an organized list to show all the possible choices.

1. 3 flavors, 4 toppings

2. 4 styles, 5 colors

3. 7 colors, 3 designs

Ask Yourself
- How do I organize the list so I don't miss any choices?

Explain Your Thinking How can you be sure that an organized list of choices is complete?

Practice and Problem Solving

You have one choice from each column. Make an organized list and a tree diagram to show all the possible choices.

4.

T-Shirts	
Style	**Color**
V-neck	blue
crew neck	yellow
sleeveless	black
	red

5.

School Ring	
Metal	**Stone**
silver	turquoise
gold	amber
	agate
	lapis

6.

Games	
3:00 Game	**3:45 Game**
Ring Toss	Frisbee Golf
Darts	Sack Race
Spelling	Brain Teasers
Horseshoes	Extreme Math

You have one choice from each category. Multiply to find the number of choices possible.

7. 5 styles, 3 sizes
8. 4 colors, 12 designs
9. 8 flavors, 4 toppings
10. 7 cars, 4 colors
11. 8 dinners, 7 desserts
12. 3 drinks, 1 flavor

Data **Use the menu to solve Problems 13–15.**

13. How many choices are there if you want to order a hot sandwich and a large drink?

14. How many choices are there if you want to order a salad and a small drink?

15. How could you find the number of choices for a hot sandwich, a salad, and a small drink?

School Fair Menu
Hot Sandwiches $5.25
• Grilled Chicken
• Roast Beef
• Roast Turkey
• Hamburger
• Grilled Tuna
Salads $3.25
• Caesar
• Oriental
Drinks
Small 75¢
Medium $1.00
Large $1.50
• Lemonade
• Orange Juice
• Apple Juice
• Sparkling Water

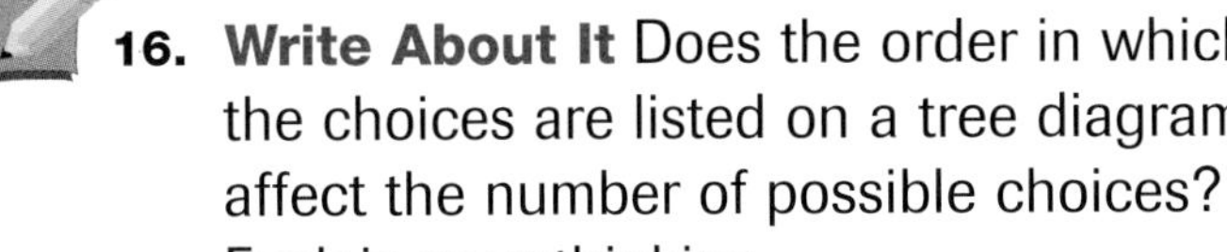

16. **Write About It** Does the order in which the choices are listed on a tree diagram affect the number of possible choices? Explain your thinking.

Mixed Review and Test Prep

Open Response

Name each shape. (Ch. 15, Lesson 5)

17. [pentagon figure] **18.** [hexagon figure] **19.** [parallelogram figure]

20. Nell packs blue pants, white pants, a striped shirt, a gray shirt, and a yellow shirt. How many different ways can she choose a pair of pants and a shirt?

Explain how you got your answer.
(Ch. 20, Lesson 1)

Extra Practice See page 551, Set A.

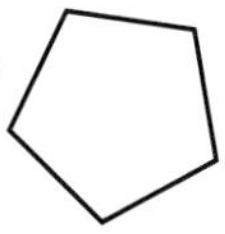

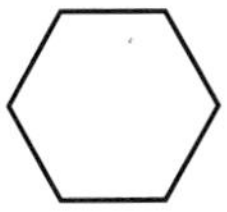

Lesson 2

Audio Tutor 2/24 Listen and Understand

Probability Concepts

Objective Describe the probability of an event.

Vocabulary
- probability
- event
- impossible event
- certain event

Learn About It

Look at this game spinner. It has four congruent sectors.

- If the spinner lands on green, Player *A* wins.
- If the spinner lands on purple, Player *B* wins.
- If the spinner lands on yellow, no one wins.

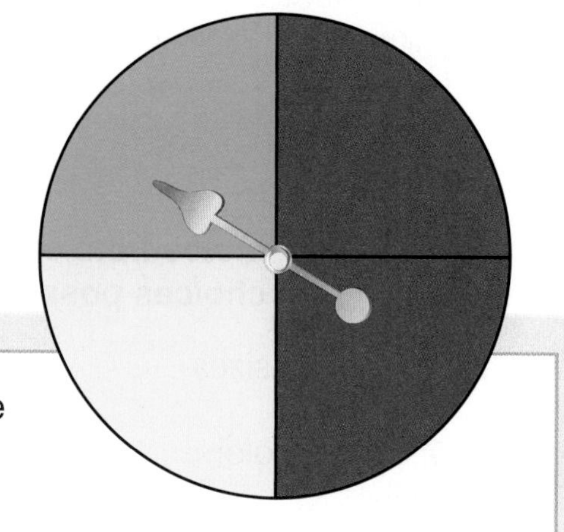

Is this a fair game?

When a player spins the spinner, there are three possible results, or outcomes. The spinner can land on a green, yellow, or purple sector. Why is the spinner more likely to land on purple than on green or yellow?

Solution: There are more purple sectors than green sectors. The game is not fair, because Player *B* has a greater chance of winning than Player *A*.

The **probability** of an **event** describes the likelihood that the event will occur. When an event has a probability of 0, it is called an **impossible event**. An event that has a probability of 1 is a **certain event**. The sum of all the probabilities of an event must equal 1.

less likely ← - - - - → more likely

impossible	0 ———— 1	certain
The probability of spinning red is 0.		The probability of landing on a colored section is 1.

Look at the diagram above. As the probability of an event gets closer to 1, it becomes more likely. As it gets closer to 0, the event becomes less likely.

If Event *A* is more likely than Event *B*, Event *A* has a greater probability than Event *B*. If Event *A* is less likely than Event *B*, Event *A* has a lesser probability than Event *B*. In the spinner at the top of the page, having the spinner land on purple is more likely than it landing on yellow.

Extra Help at eduplace.com/map

Guided Practice

You spin once on a spinner that has six congruent sectors labeled 2, 2, 3, 4, 5, and 5. Tell which event is more likely. If possible, describe an event that is impossible or certain.

Ask Yourself

- How many sectors of the spinner are labeled with each number?

1. a 2 or a 6
2. a 3 or a 5
3. a composite number or a prime number
4. a number greater than 5 or a number less than 5

Explain Your Thinking ▶ Why is the second event in Exercise 2 more likely?

Practice and Problem Solving

You spin once on the spinner at the right. Tell which event is less likely. If possible, describe an event as impossible or certain.

5. yellow or green
6. orange or green
7. green or blue
8. red or blue
9. purple or any other color on the spinner

Use the spinner at the right for Problems 10 and 11.

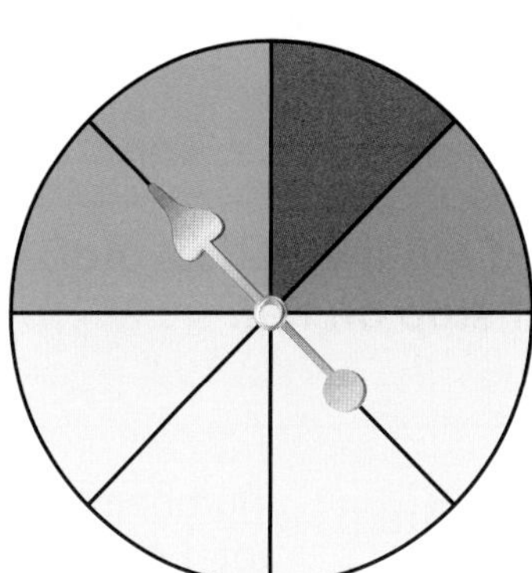

10. Shari and Sam play a game. If the spinner lands on red or blue, Shari wins. If the spinner lands on green, Sam wins. Is the game fair? Explain.
11. **Create and Solve** Use the spinner to create a fair game and an unfair game that are different from the game in Problem 10. Explain why each game is fair or unfair.
12. Survey your classmates to find out what board games they play. If you chose someone from your class at random, which games would he or she be likely to play?

Mixed Review and Test Prep

Open Response

Write 4 equivalent ratios for each.
(Ch. 18, Lesson 2)

13. 1 to 4
14. 10 to 12
15. 2:3
16. 20 to 25
17. 3:8
18. 6:10
19. 5 to 1
20. 14:6

Multiple Choice

21. A spinner has congruent sectors labeled 1, 3, 5, 7, 9, and 11. What is the probability of spinning an odd number? (Ch. 20, Lesson 2)

A 0 **C** $\frac{1}{2}$

B $\frac{1}{6}$ **D** 1

Extra Practice See page 551, Set B.

Lesson 3

Audio Tutor 2/25 Listen and Understand

Theoretical Probability

Objective Use fractions to find theoretical probability.

Vocabulary
- outcome
- theoretical probability
- equally likely

Learn About It

If the wheel stops on a red sector, Tamara wins a prize. What is the probability that the wheel will stop on red?

Since the wheel has 16 sectors of equal size, there are 16 possible **outcomes.**

To solve the problem, you want to find out how likely it is that the wheel will stop on a red sector. Stopping on red is called a favorable outcome.

The **theoretical probability** of an event can be found by comparing the number of favorable outcomes with the number of possible outcomes.

Find the theoretical probability that the wheel will stop on red.

$$P(\text{red}) = \frac{\text{number of red sectors}}{\text{total number of sectors}}$$

$$= \frac{8}{16}$$

$$= \frac{1}{2}$$

There are 8 red sectors and 8 other sectors. It is **equally likely** that the wheel will stop on red as on a different colored sector.

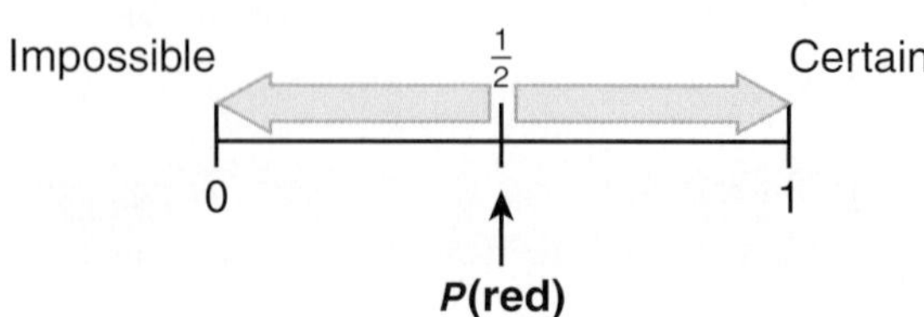

When you express probability as a fraction, write the fraction in simplest form.

Solution: The theoretical probability that the wheel will stop on red is $\frac{1}{2}$.

Guided Practice

Look at the wheel on page 532. Express the theoretical probability of each event as a fraction in simplest form.

Ask Yourself
- How many outcomes are there?
- How many outcomes are favorable?

1. yellow **2.** green **3.** blue

4. not yellow **5.** orange **6.** blue or yellow

Explain Your Thinking  In Exercise 6, how did you find the theoretical probability?

Practice and Problem Solving

Use the spinner for Problems 7–14. Express the theoretical probability of each event as a fraction in simplest form.

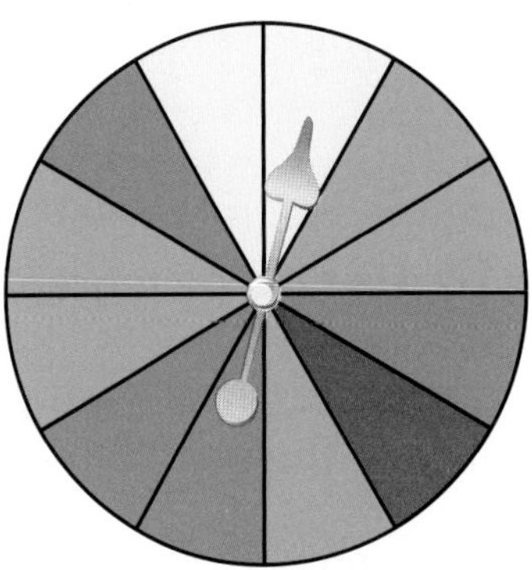

7. yellow **8.** red

9. green **10.** blue

11. blue or yellow **12.** not red

13. not yellow **14.** not green or blue

Use the bag of marbles for Problems 15–26. You pick one marble from the bag without looking. Find the theoretical probability of each event. Express the probability as a fraction in simplest form.

15. a black marble **16.** a marble that is not black

17. a yellow marble **18.** a marble that is not yellow

19. a green marble **20.** a marble that is not green

21. a purple marble **22.** a marble that is not purple

23. a red or black marble **24.** a white marble

25. a marble that is not green or red or black **26.** a marble that is green or yellow

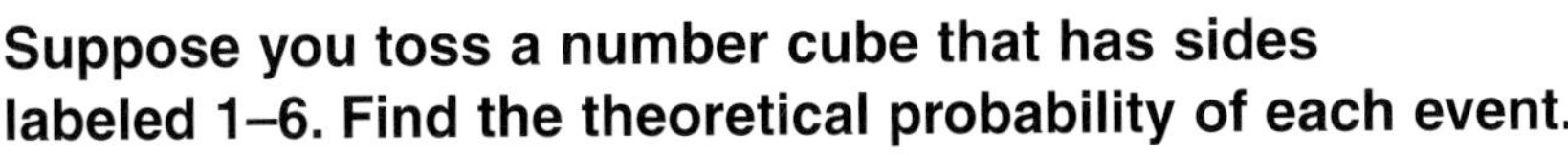

Suppose you toss a number cube that has sides labeled 1–6. Find the theoretical probability of each event.

27. a 6 **28.** an even number

29. a number that is not 2 or 4 **30.** a number greater than 1 and less than 6

Go On

Use the bag of cubes for Problems 31–35.

The bag of cubes is used for a game in which you pick one cube without looking. Tell how you would add or remove cubes in order to create the given situation.

31. The probability of picking a red cube is $\frac{1}{3}$.

32. The chances of picking any color cube are equally likely.

33. The chance of picking a black cube is 1 out of 10.

34. The probability of picking a blue cube is $\frac{1}{6}$.

35. The chance of picking a purple cube is 1 out of 4.

Data Use the pictograph for Problems 36–40.

Toy ducks are picked without looking and replaced in the pond after each pick.

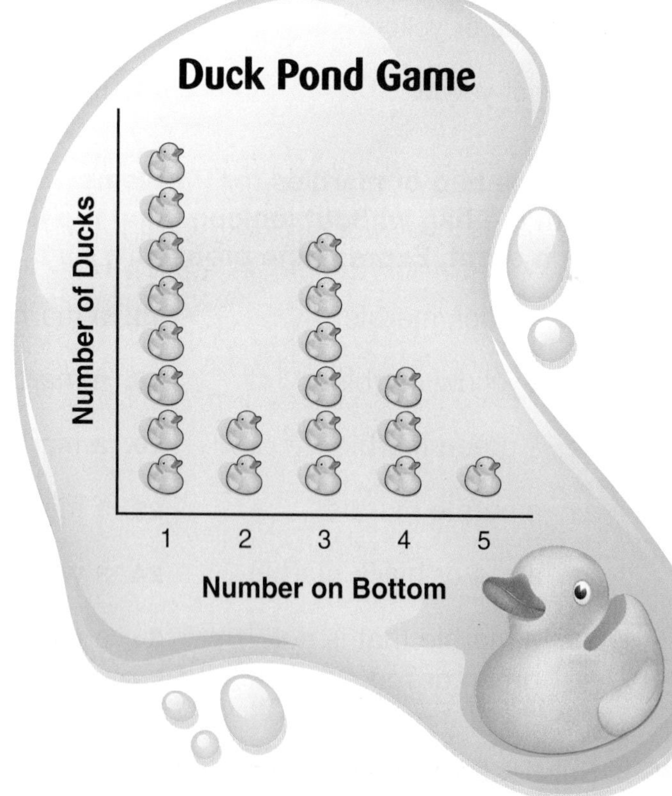

36. How many ducks are in the pond if each duck symbol represents 1 duck?

37. What is the probability of picking a yellow duck with a number 5 on the bottom?

38. Which two numbers are the most likely to be picked?

39. The probability of picking a duck with one of two numbers is $\frac{9}{20}$. What could those two numbers be?

40. Suppose each duck symbol represented 3 ducks instead of 1 duck. Would the probability of picking each number change? Explain.

41. Write About It If the theoretical probability of winning a game is $\frac{1}{2}$, does this mean that if you play that game twice, you are certain to win one of the games? Explain your reasoning.

Extra Practice See page 551, Set C.

Problem Solving

Logical Thinking
NOT a Chance

Look at the spinner. The probability of spinning blue is $\frac{5}{12}$. What is the probability of NOT spinning blue? To find the probability of NOT spinning blue, you can subtract $\frac{5}{12}$ from 1.

$$1 - \frac{5}{12} = \frac{12}{12} - \frac{5}{12} = \frac{7}{12}$$

Solution: The probability of NOT spinning blue is $\frac{7}{12}$.

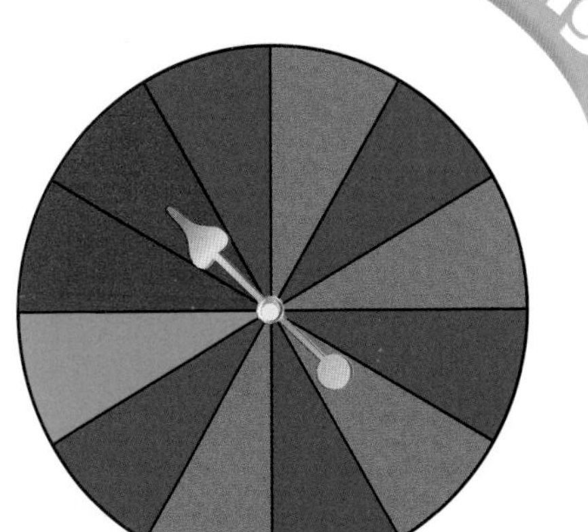

Use the spinner above. Subtract to find each probability.

1. not spinning green
2. not spinning red
3. not spinning purple
4. **Explain** Use what you know about probability to explain why this method works.

Quick Check

Check your understanding of Lessons 1–3.

Make an organized list and a tree diagram to show all the possible choices. Then multiply to find the number of possible choices. (Lesson 1)

1.

Footwear	Color
sneakers	brown
slippers	red
boots	black
	white

2.

Snack	Size
peanuts	small
cashews	large
walnuts	
almonds	

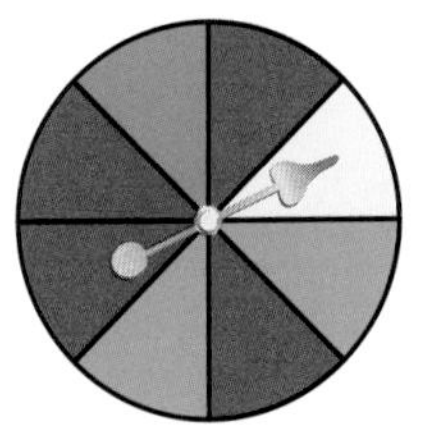

Use the spinner for Problems 3–6. Tell which event is more likely. If possible, describe an event as impossible or certain. (Lesson 2)

3. yellow or blue
4. red or green
5. blue or green
6. red or orange

Suppose you toss a number cube that has sides labeled 2, 2, 2, 4, 8, and 10. Find the theoretical probability of each event. (Lesson 3)

7. a 4
8. an even number
9. a number that is not a 2

Extra Practice at eduplace.com/map

Lesson 4

Audio Tutor 2/26 Listen and Understand

Problem-Solving Strategy
Make an Organized List

Objective Solve a problem by making an organized list.

There is room for one more team of 2 players in the three-legged race. Sal, Ed, Juan, and Mia are willing to be on the team. How many different ways can you choose a team of 2 players from these 4 children?

UNDERSTAND

This is what you know:

Sal, Ed, Juan, and Mia are willing to be on the team.

Each team has 2 players.

PLAN

You can make an organized list to show all of the possible ways to select the team.

SOLVE

Make an organized list. Use letters to stand for each player's name.

- List all teams of 2 that include Sal (S).
- List all teams of 2 that include Ed (E).
- List all teams of 2 that include Juan (J).
- List all teams of 2 that include Mia (M).
- Ring teams with the same 2 players. Then count the rings. The order of the players does not matter. The team of Sal and Ed is the same as the team of Ed and Sal.

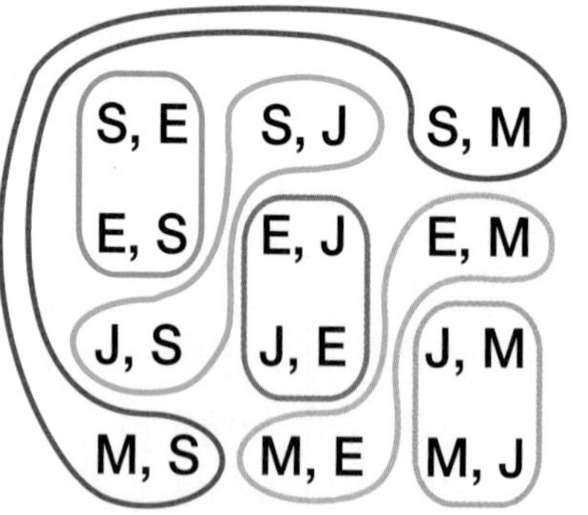

Solution: There are 6 different ways to choose a team of 2 players.

LOOK BACK

Look back at the problem.

Does the solution make sense?

Guided Practice

Use the Ask Yourself questions to help you solve each problem.

1. Billy wins enough points to choose 3 prizes. The available prizes are a puzzle, a goldfish, a pack of cards, a toy monkey, and a model car. How many different ways can Billy choose 3 different prizes?

2. Benjamin, Erin, Chun, Julia, Amanda, and Elizabeth are in a race. First place receives a gold medal and second place receives a silver medal. How many different ways can the medals be given out?

   Hint: Since the order of the racers matters, there are no duplicates in a list of possible first and second place winners.

UNDERSTAND What facts do I know?

Did I make an organized list?

Does the order of the possibilities matter?

- **How can I show all of the possibilities?**
- **Do I need to cross out duplicates?**

Did I solve the problem?

Independent Practice

Make an organized list to solve each problem.

3. A team of 4 players is needed for tug of war. How many different teams of 4 players can be chosen from a group of 5 children?

4. The 4 finalists in a history quiz game are Jessica, Brian, Evan, and Grace. The top 2 finalists win first prize and second prize. In how many different ways can these prizes be given out to the 4 finalists?

5. The school fair has a hall of mirrors, a carousel, a horse ride, and a maze. You buy a ticket that allows you to do 3 of these activities. In how many different ways can you go to 3 of these activities?

6. Shawn, Scott, Rip, Trish, and Yoshi are finalists in a drawing for a trip to Water World. Two winners will be picked at random. How many different pairs could go to Water World?

Mixed Problem Solving

Solve. Show your work. Tell what strategy you used.

7. Wendy, Barbara, Howard, and Marvin are the top four finishers in a race. Barbara is not first or second. Marvin finishes after Barbara. Howard finishes before Wendy. Who is in each of the top four places?

8. Number cards for the numbers 3, 4, 5, 6, 7, 8, 9, and 10 are placed facedown on a table. Suppose you turn up two cards. How many different pairs of numbers are possible?

9. Mr. Willard has 8 bills in his wallet. The bills are \$10, \$5, and \$1. If Mr. Willard has \$29, what bills does he have in his wallet?

You Choose

Strategy
- Guess and Check
- Make an Organized List
- Use Logical Reasoning
- Work Backward

Computation Method
- Mental Math
- Estimation
- Paper and Pencil
- Calculator

Data Use the graph to solve Problems 10–13.

The graph shows the number of game tickets that each of four students sold.

10. How many more tickets did Daisy sell than Evan?

11. A game ticket sells for \$2.95. About how many dollars worth of game tickets did Myra sell?

12. How many game tickets did the four students sell in all? How many dollars worth of tickets is this?

13. Last year, George's ticket sales were 20% greater than his total shown in the graph. How many tickets did George sell last year?

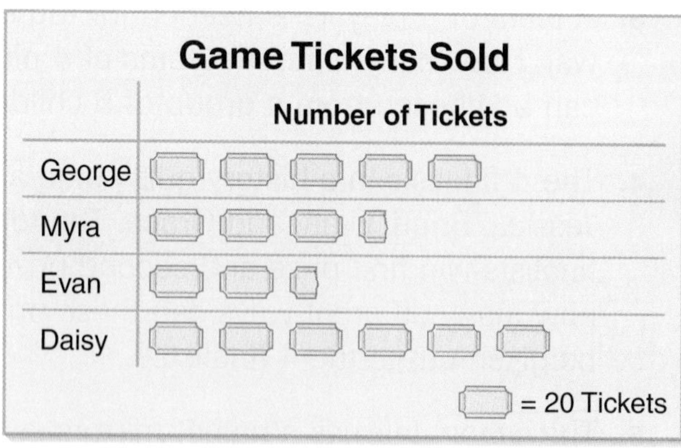

14. Sierra, Gavin, Kayla, Jacob, and Amanda can tutor some third-grade students in math. Only 2 tutors are needed. How many different pairs of tutors can there be? Explain how you found your answer.

Problem Solving on Tests

Multiple Choice

Choose the letter of the correct answer. If a correct answer is not here, choose NH.

1. What is the missing angle measure?

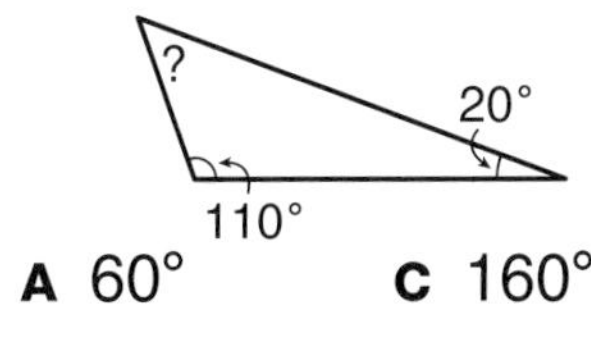

A 60° **C** 160°

B 70° **D** NH

(Chapter 15, Lesson 3)

2. In a survey of 200 students at Warren High School, 88 say they favor year-round schools. Warren High School has a total of 950 students. Based on the survey, how many students are likely to favor year-round schools?

F 418 **H** 880

G 440 **J** 936

(Chapter 18, Lesson 4)

Open Response

Solve each problem.

3. A restaurant has 3 tables. Each table can seat 1 person on each end and 3 people along each of the other sides. The ends of the tables are pushed together to make one long table. How many people can sit at the long table?

Represent Support your solution with a picture.

(Chapter 10, Lesson 7)

4. **Measurement** A rug that measures 2 yards by 3 yards costs $540. Another rug that measures 5 feet by 8 feet costs $360. Which rug has a higher price per square foot of area?

Explain How did you find your answer?

(Chapter 16, Lesson 3)

Extended Response

5. You are using the plan below to design a garden. Use an inch ruler to measure the scale drawing and help you complete this task.

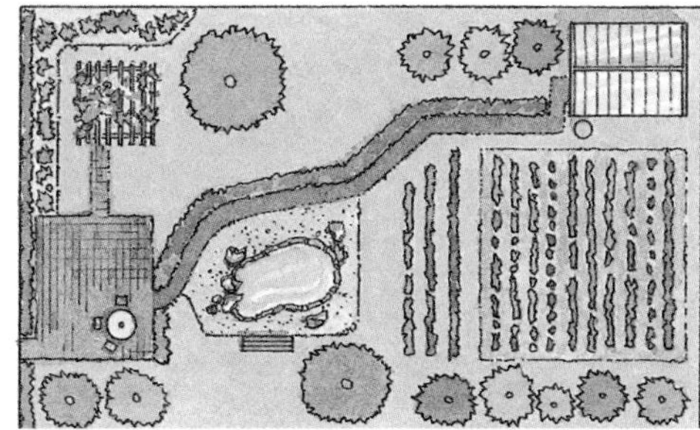

Scale: $\frac{1}{4}$ inch = 10 feet

a What are the actual dimensions of the garden?

b You need to include a square planting area whose actual sides measure 30 feet. What will be the dimensions of the square in the drawing?

c Suppose you have to design a new garden whose dimensions are 75% of the length and 75% of the width of the garden pictured. What will be the actual dimensions of the new garden?

d Will the polygon defining the shape of the new garden (in part **c**) and that of the original garden be similar? Explain.

(Chapters 18, 19)

Education Place

See **eduplace.com/map** for Test-Taking Tips.

Hands On Lesson 5

Experimental Probability

Objective Determine the experimental probability for a given set of data.

Vocabulary

experimental probability

Materials

number cube
Learning Tool 56
red, blue, and yellow connecting cubes

Work Together

When you perform an experiment, you may get results that differ from the results predicted by theoretical probability.

To find the **experimental probability** of an event, compare the number of favorable outcomes with the total number of completed trials or experiments.

Work with a partner to find experimental probability of tossing each number on a number cube.

STEP 1 On the recording sheet, list all the possible outcomes for tossing a number cube once. Then write the theoretical probability for each outcome.

- How many possible outcomes are there?
- How can you find the theoretical probability of each outcome?

Event	Theoretical Probability	Prediction ? times in ? trials
1	$\frac{1}{6}$	$\frac{1}{6} = \frac{x}{30}$
2		
3		

STEP 2 Use theoretical probability to predict the number of times each outcome should occur in an experiment with 30 trials. Write your predictions on the recording sheet.

- How did you make your predictions?

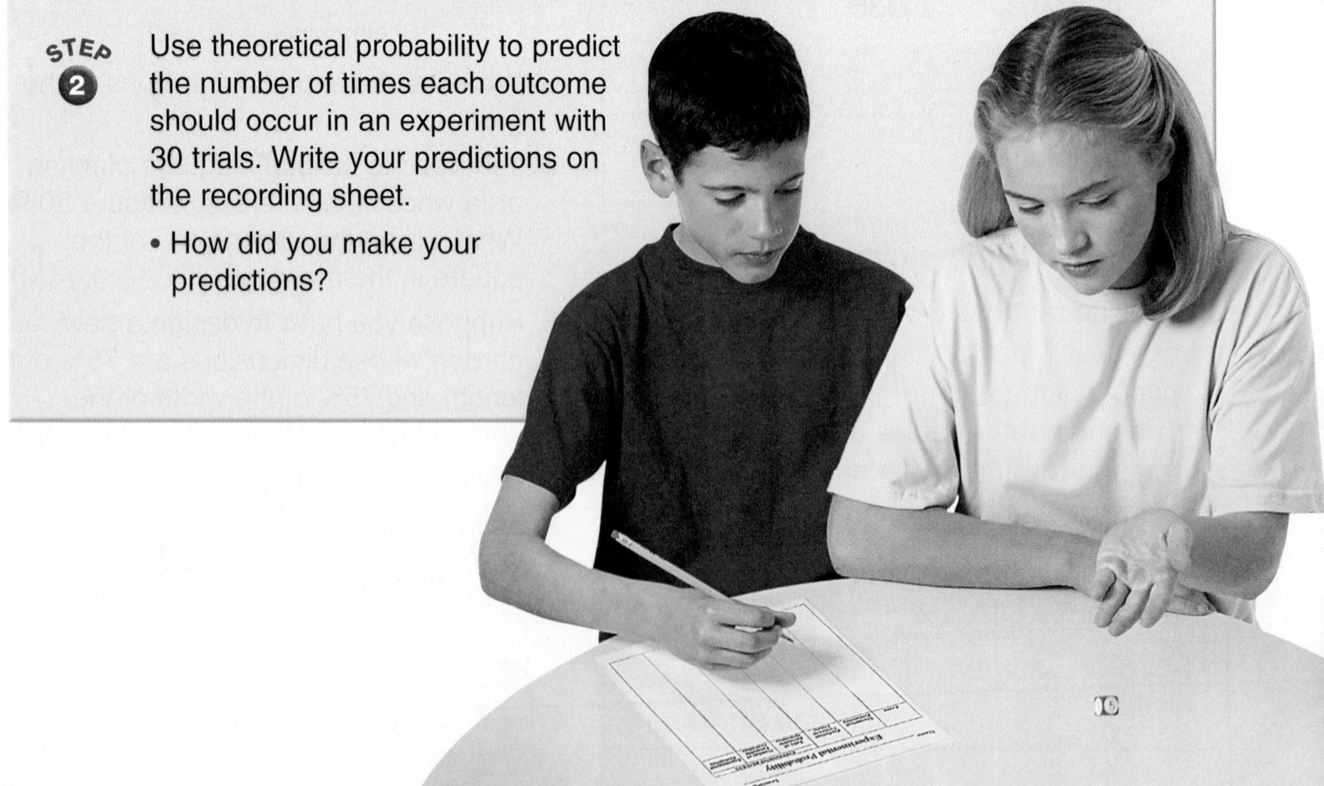

Perform the experiment. Toss the number cube 30 times. Record each outcome. Then find the total number of times each outcome occurred.

- Find the experimental probability of each outcome and record it in the last column on the sheet.
- How close are the experimental probabilities to the theoretical probabilities?

Event	RIMENT RESULTS	
	Number of Favorable Outcomes	Experimental Probability
1	7	$\frac{7}{30}$
2	5	$\frac{5}{30} = \frac{1}{6}$
3	4	$\frac{4}{30} = \frac{2}{15}$
4	5	$\frac{5}{30} = \frac{1}{6}$
5	4	$\frac{4}{30} = \frac{2}{15}$
6	5	$\frac{5}{30} = \frac{1}{6}$

Repeat the experiment. Toss the cube another 30 times. Combine your results with the results of the original experiment.

- How did including the additional 30 trials affect the results of the entire experiment?

On Your Own

Use the recording sheet to complete each probability experiment. Record each probability as a fraction in simplest form.

1. Toss a number cube and get an even number. Complete 20 tosses.

Event	Theoretical Probability	Prediction ? times in ? trials	EXPERIMENT RESULTS		
			Tally of Favorable Outcomes	Number of Favorable Outcomes	Experimental Probability
Even (2, 4, 6)	$\frac{3}{6} = \frac{1}{2}$	$\frac{1}{2} = \frac{x}{20}$			

Go On

For Problems 2–5, select 2 blue cubes, 5 yellow cubes, and 3 red cubes—a total of 10 cubes. Place them in a bag. Then use the recording sheet to complete each probability experiment.

2. Find the theoretical probability of selecting a blue cube. Then pick a cube, tally the result, and return the cube to the bag. Repeat 20 times. Then find the experimental probablility.

3. Find the theoretical probability of selecting a yellow cube. Then pick a cube, tally the result, and return the cube to the bag. Repeat 20 times. Then find the experimental probablility.

4. Find the theoretical probability of selecting a red cube. Then pick a cube, tally the result, and return the cube to the bag. Repeat 20 times. Then find the experimental probablility.

5. Do the experiment in Problem 4 of selecting a red cube, but repeat 50 times. Then find the experimental probablility.

			EXPERIMENT RESULTS		
Event	**Theoretical Probability**	**Prediction ? times in ? trials**	**Tally of Favorable Outcomes**	**Number of Favorable Outcomes**	**Experimental Probability**
Blue	$\frac{2}{10} = \frac{1}{5}$	$\frac{1}{5} = \frac{X}{20}$			
Yellow					$\frac{?}{20}$
Red					

Talk About It • Write About It

You learned the difference between experimental probability and theoretical probability.

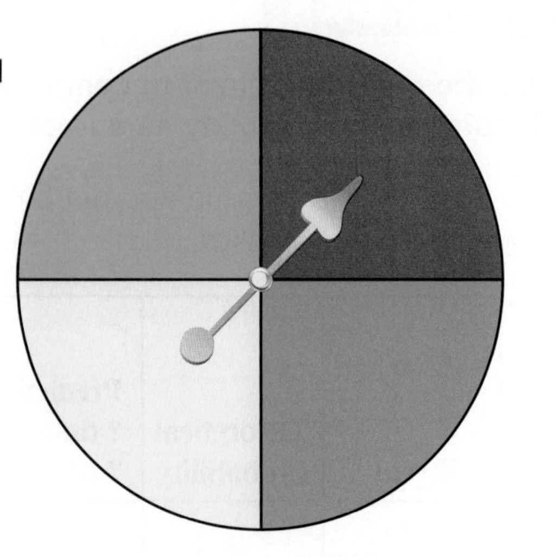

6. Suppose you spin this spinner 20 times and find the experimental probability of spinning red is $\frac{1}{5}$. Is this close to what you would have predicted? Explain.

7. Use your results from Problems 4 and 5. Does the experimental probability get closer to or farther from the theoretical probability as the number of trials increases?

Problem Solving

Number Sense

The 50 States

Suppose you choose one of the 50 states at random.

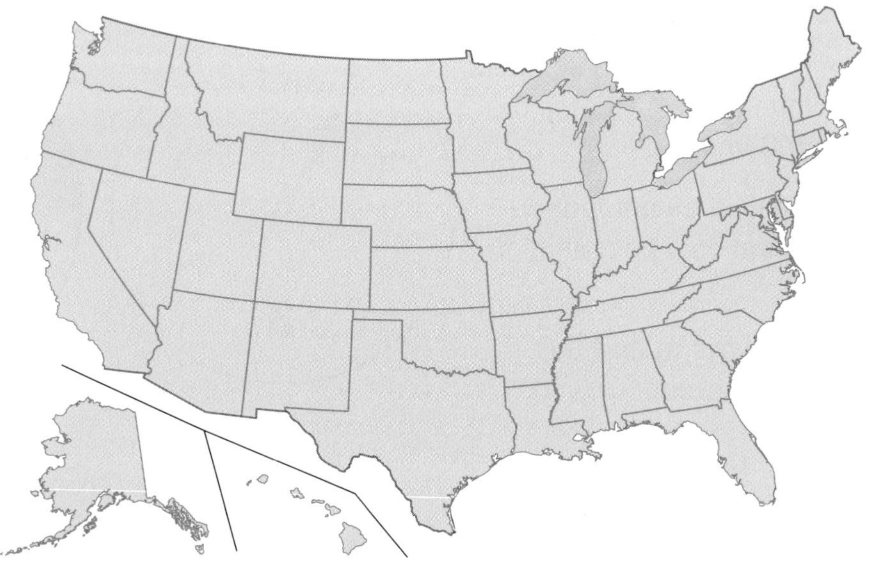

1. What is the probability of choosing a state name that begins with the letter F? the letter N?

2. Is there a greater chance of choosing a state east of the Mississippi River or west of it? Explain.

3. Write 5 probability problems about the 50 states. Solve your problems and then give them to a partner to solve.

Logical Thinking

Common Sense

Describe each event as *likely, unlikely, impossible,* or *certain.*

- It will snow tomorrow.
- You will read a book today.
- Your school will grow legs and walk.
- The sun will set tonight.
- You will finish reading this sentence.

Brain Teaser

The cards shown are numbered 1 to 4. One card has been set aside. What is the probability that the next card is a 2?

Ask Yourself
What is the probability if 3 cards are set aside?

Education Place

See **eduplace.com/map** for more Brain Teasers.

Audio Tutor 2/27 Listen and Understand

Lesson 6 Compound Events

Objective Find the probability of compound events.

Vocabulary
compound event

Learn About It

Lara and Will play a game using two spinners. If Lara spins both spinners once, what is the probability of spinning 3 and red?

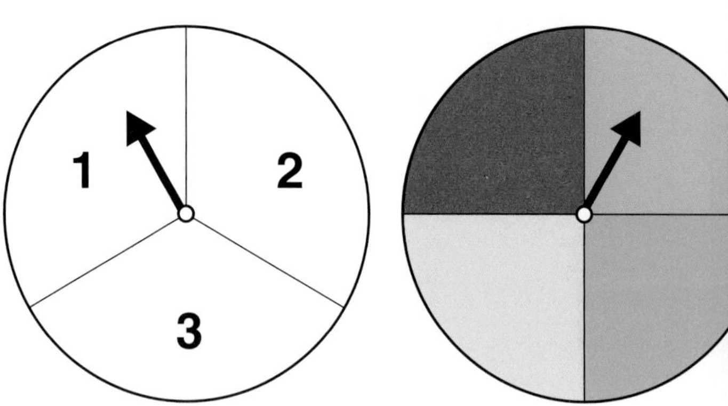

Spinning 3 and red is called a compound event. A **compound event** is a combination of two or more events.

Here are some different ways to find the probability of a compound event.

Different Ways to Find the Probability of a Compound Event

Way 1 You can make a tree diagram.

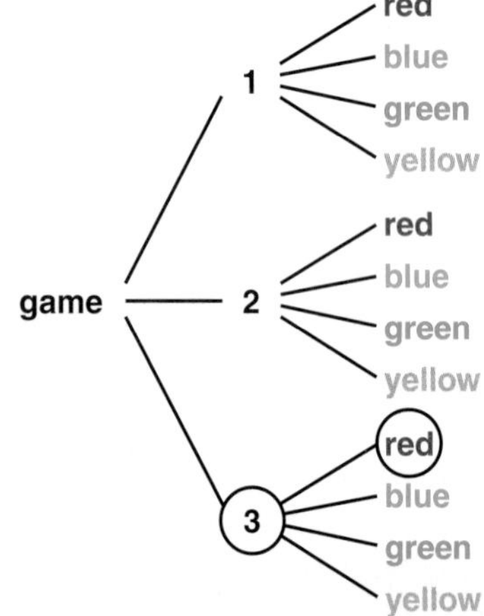

There are 12 possible outcomes and 1 favorable outcome.

Way 2 You can make an organized list.

1 red	2 red	3 red
1 blue	2 blue	3 blue
1 green	2 green	3 green
1 yellow	2 yellow	3 yellow

There are 12 possible outcomes and 1 favorable outcome.

Solution: The probability of spinning red and 3 can be expressed as $\frac{1}{12}$.

Guided Practice

Suppose you toss a nickel and roll a number cube labeled 1–6. Find the probability of each compound event.

1. heads and 3
2. tails and an odd number

Ask Yourself
- Did I find all of the possible outcomes?
- What is the favorable outcome?

Explain Your Thinking In Exercise 2, how did you find the probability?

Practice and Problem Solving

Suppose you spin each spinner once. Find the probability of each compound event.

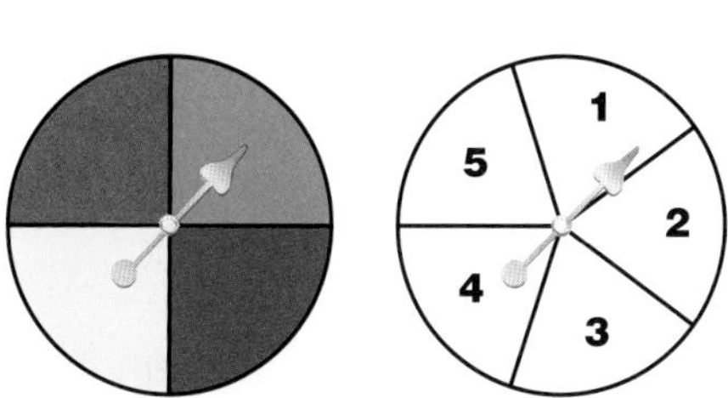

3. purple and 5
4. yellow and 3
5. red and even
6. yellow and odd
7. blue or purple, and 4
8. purple, and 2 or 3
9. red or purple, and even
10. yellow or red, and odd

Use a penny and the spinners to solve Problems 11–16.

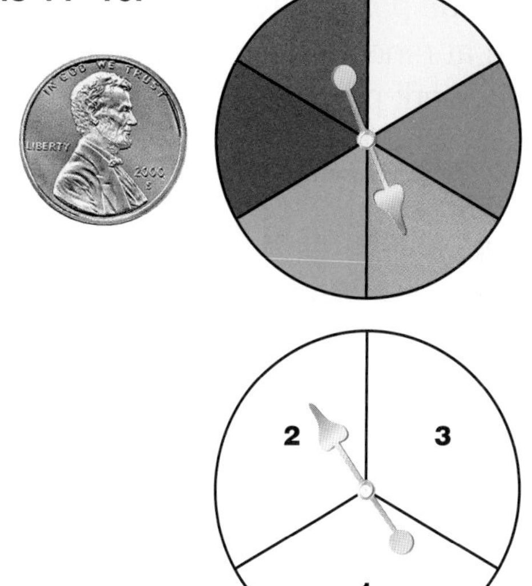

11. Use a tree diagram to show all the possible outcomes of the compound event of tossing a penny and spinning the color spinner. Then find the probability of tossing tails and spinning green.

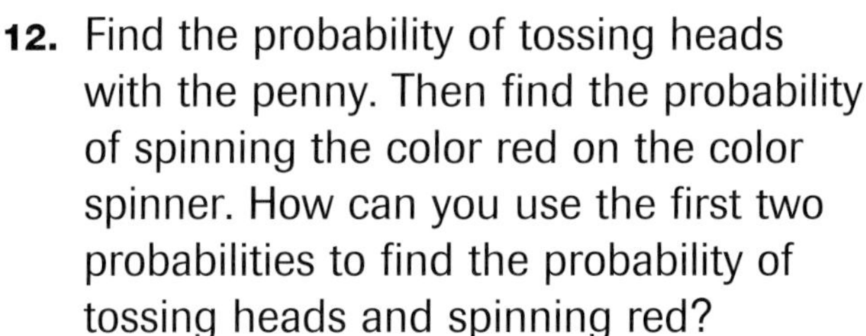

12. Find the probability of tossing heads with the penny. Then find the probability of spinning the color red on the color spinner. How can you use the first two probabilities to find the probability of tossing heads and spinning red?

13. Make an organized list to show all the possible outcomes of spinning the number and color spinners. What is the probability of spinning 2 and purple?

14. Decide which is more likely: to spin red and toss heads or to spin purple and 2? Explain how you made your decision.

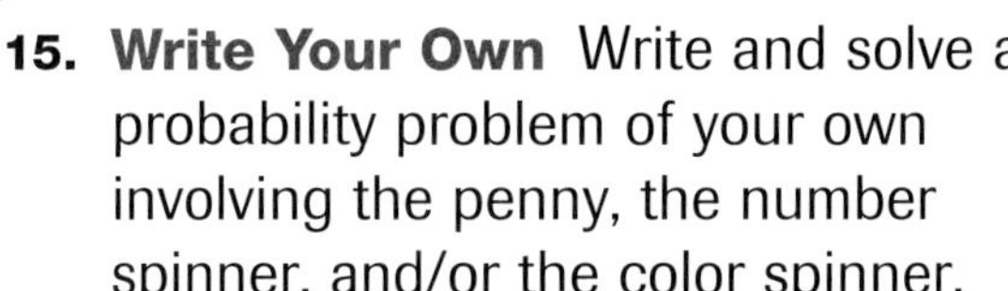

15. **Write Your Own** Write and solve a probability problem of your own involving the penny, the number spinner, and/or the color spinner.

16. Suppose you toss the penny and spin both spinners above. What is the probability of getting heads, the number 2, and red?

Mixed Review and Test Prep

Open Response

Find the product. (Ch. 13, Lessons 3–5)

17. 0.7 × 0.4
18. 5 × 1.49
19. 0.68 × 0.3
20. 0.9 × 0.2
21. 1.63 × 2.5
22. 4.29 × 1.3

23. You toss a coin and roll a number cube labeled 1–6. Find the probability of getting heads and an even number.

Explain how you got your answer. (Ch. 20, Lesson 6)

Extra Practice See page 551, Set D.

Lesson 7

Problem-Solving Application

Make Predictions

Objective Use data to make predictions.

Sometimes you can use data to make predictions about outcomes.

Problem At the Tuscan Middle School Fair some students conducted a homework survey. The table shows the results.

What is the probability that a student chosen at random does 15 or more hours of homework per week?

Homework Survey Results

Hours of Home Work per Week	Tally of Students	Frequency
0 – 4.9	|||	3
5 – 9.9	~~||||~~ |||	8
10 – 14.9	~~||||~~ ~~||||~~ ~~||||~~ ~~||||~~ ||	22
15 – 19.9	~~||||~~ |	6
20 – 24.9	|	1

UNDERSTAND

What is the question?

- What is the probability that a student chosen at random does 15 or more hours of homework per week?

What do you know?

- A total of 40 students were surveyed.
- 6 students did between 15 and 19.9 hours of homework.
- 1 student did between 20 and 24.9 hours of homework.

PLAN

Use the formula for probability. $P = \frac{\text{number of favorable outcomes}}{\text{number of possible outcomes}}$

SOLVE

- Use the number of students who were surveyed as the number of possible outcomes.
- Use the number of students who did 15 or more hours of homework per week as the number of favorable outcomes.

$P = \frac{6+1}{40} = \frac{7}{40}$

Solution: The probability that a randomly chosen student does 15 or more hours of homework per week is $\frac{7}{40}$.

LOOK BACK

Look back at the problem.

Is the answer reasonable?

Guided Practice

Use the table on page 546 to solve each problem.

1. What is the probability of a student doing less than 10 hours of homework per week?

2. Tuscan Middle School has 600 students. How many students would you expect to do between 5 and 15 hours of homework per week?

   Hint What part of the students surveyed did between 5 and 15 hours of homework per week?

Ask Yourself

UNDERSTAND **What does the question ask me to find?**

Did I use the formula for probability?

- **Did I use the correct information from the table?**
- **Did I find the probability of the event?**
- **Did I use the probability to make a prediction?**

Does my answer make sense?

Independent Practice

Use the table to solve Problems 3–7.

Each ticket to the Tuscan Middle School Fair gives you a chance to win a prize. The table shows the prizes won by the first 50 people who came to the fair.

Prizes Won at Middle School Fair

Prize Won	Number of Ticket Holders
No prize	38
Flashlight	6
School cap	4
Pizza party	2

3. What is the probability of winning no prize?

4. Suppose 400 people come to the fair. How many people would you expect to win a prize?

5. Suppose 500 people come to the fair. About how many more people would you expect to win flashlights than school caps?

6. **What's Wrong?** Marina found the probability of winning a school cap. What did Marina do wrong?

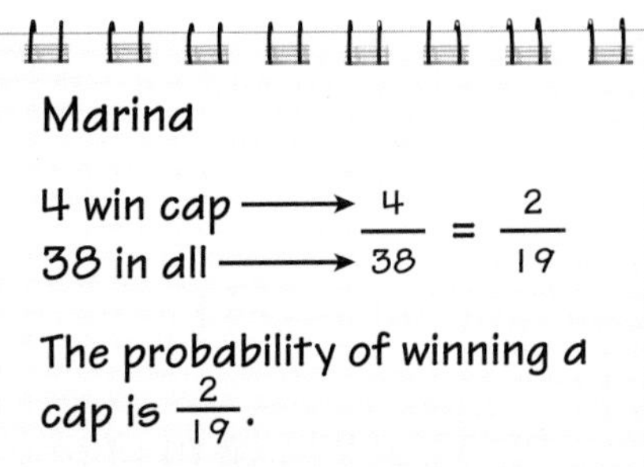

Marina

4 win cap → $\frac{4}{38} = \frac{2}{19}$
38 in all →

The probability of winning a cap is $\frac{2}{19}$.

7. Of 800 tickets, 8 have a code that shows that the owner wins a pizza party. Is the number of winners in the first 50 tickets less than, greater than, or the same as you would expect? Explain your answer.

Go On

Mixed Problem Solving

Solve. Show your work. Tell what strategy you used.

8. Norma spends $7 on playing games, $5.95 on a sandwich, $2.50 on drinks, and $19.95 on a sweatshirt. She has $25 left. How much money did she start with?

9. Two numbers have a sum of 54 and a quotient of 5. What are the numbers?

10. Sabrina, Paul, Nina, Fred, and Tyrone are the last players left in the Math Challenge contest. The last two players will win first prize and second prize. How many different ways can the prizes be given out?

You Choose

Strategy
- Draw a Diagram
- Guess and Check
- Use Models
- Work Backward
- Write an Equation

Computation Method
- Mental Math
- Estimation
- Paper and Pencil
- Calculator

Data **Use the histogram to solve Problems 11–14. Then explain which method you chose.**

A hardware store donated flashlights with new batteries to the Tuscan Middle School Fair. The flashlights were given out as prizes. The histogram shows the results of the number of hours that the flashlight batteries last.

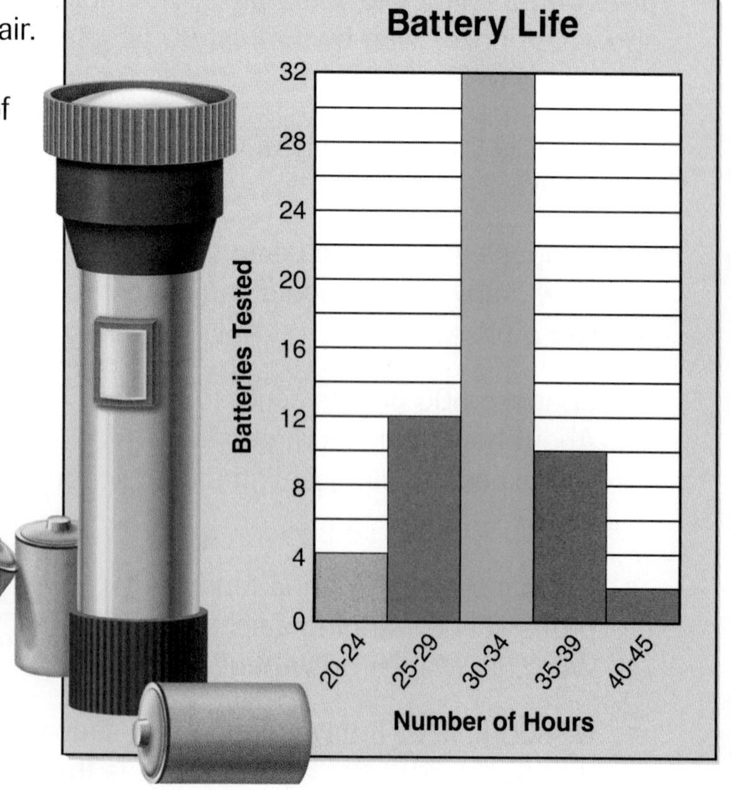

11. About what percent of flashlight batteries last between 30 and 34 hours?

12. Is it reasonable to expect one of these flashlights to last 35 hours or more? Use probability to explain your answer.

13. A hardware store receives a case of 120 flashlights with batteries. Predict the number that will last fewer than 30 hours.

14. **Create and Solve** Use the data from the histogram to create and solve your own problem.

Activity

Math Reasoning

Fair or Foul

Use what you know about probability as you play the following game.

1. Play Math Roll a few times. Is it fair? Why or why not?

2. Play the game again but instead of subtracting, multiply the two numbers. Use the product to tell whether the even player or the odd player wins a point. Is this version fair? Explain.

Math Roll

Materials:
2 cubes labeled 1–6

1. One player is "even"; the other is "odd."
2. Take turns rolling two number cubes. Subtract the smaller number from the greater number.
3. If the difference is an even number, the even player wins a point. (Zero counts as even.)
4. If the difference is an odd number, the odd player scores.
5. The first player to get ten points wins.

Activity

Reading Connection

Likely Letters

The letter E is the most frequently occurring letter in the English language. When you read, you probably will see the letter E more often than any other letter.

Count 100 letters in a newspaper, magazine, or a favorite book. Record how many times each of the letters on the right occurs.

- Use your data to predict how many times out of 500 letters you will see each letter in the list. Then test your predictions.
- Repeat this activity for other letters of the alphabet.

Chapter Review/Test

VOCABULARY

Vocabulary
certain event
impossible event
outcome
probability

1. The chance that an event will occur is called the ____ of the event.
2. Tossing a 9 on a 1–6 number cube is a(n) ____.
3. If there are 12 different letters on each equal section of a spinner, each letter is a(n) ____.

CONCEPTS AND SKILLS

You have one choice from each category. Multiply to find the number of choices possible. (Lesson 1, pp. 528–529)

4. 3 sizes, 5 flavors
5. 6 colors, 5 styles
6. 4 salads, 9 soups

Use the bag of balls to tell which event is more likely. Then find the probability of that event. (Lessons 2–3, pp. 530–535)

7. 0 or 5
8. 3 or 4
9. 1 or 3
10. 1 or 5
11. 2 or 3
12. not 4 or not 5

Suppose you toss a 1–6 number cube and spin the spinner once. Find the probability of each compound event. (Lessons 5–6, pp. 540–545)

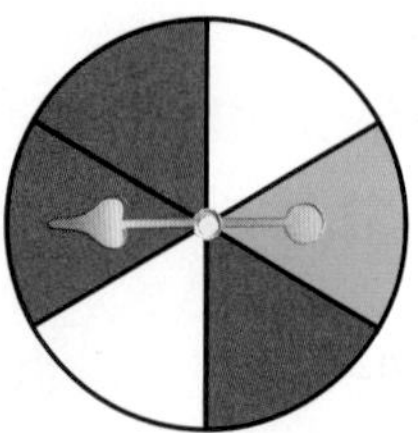

13. 1 and white
14. 6 and blue
15. 4 or 5 and white
16. 5 and red
17. odd and red
18. even and white

PROBLEM SOLVING

Solve. (Lessons 4, 7, pp. 536–537, 547–549)

19. Shannon wants to enter 3 different kinds of pies in the 4-H fair. The pie categories are apple, squash, pecan, lemon meringue, and banana cream. How many different sets of 3 pies can she bake?
20. A wheel is divided into 20 equal sections. Each section is labeled differently. Suppose you spin 100 times. How many times would you expect to land on any one of the sections?

Show You Understand

What is the difference between theoretical probability and experimental probability?

Describe a situation for each to show this difference.

Extra Practice

Set A (Lesson 1, pp. 528–529)

You have one choice from each column. Make an organized list and a tree diagram to show all the possible choices.

1. Sweaters

Style	Color
crew neck	red
V-neck	blue
	black
	yellow

2. Pizzas

Size	Topping
small	green peppers
medium	mushrooms
large	onions

3. Book Reports

Type	Subject
fiction	people
non-fiction	animals
	places

Set B (Lesson 2, pp. 530–531)

You spin once on the spinner at the right. Tell which event is more likely. If possible, describe an event as impossible or certain.

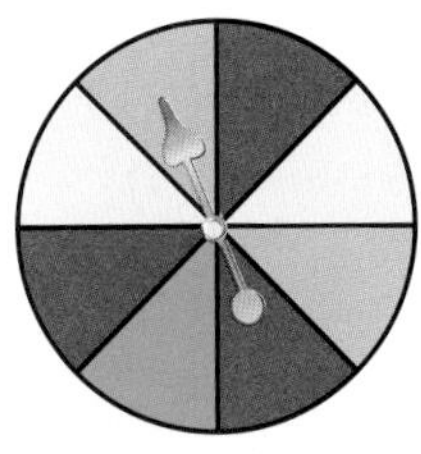

1. red or blue
2. green or yellow
3. blue or green
4. green or red
5. black or red
6. yellow or red

Set C (Lesson 3, pp. 532–535)

Use the spinner at the right. Express the probability of each event as a fraction in simplest form.

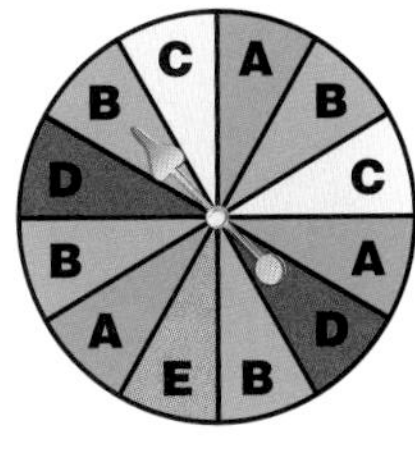

1. A
2. C
3. D
4. B
5. A or B
6. A or C
7. D or E
8. not F
9. not E
10. not A or C
11. not D or E
12. not A or E

Set D (Lesson 6, pp. 544–545)

Suppose you spin each spinner once. Find the probability of each compound event.

1. A and 3
2. C and odd
3. B and 1
4. A and even
5. C or B, and 3
6. A or C, and 4
7. not B, and 3
8. B or C, and not 4

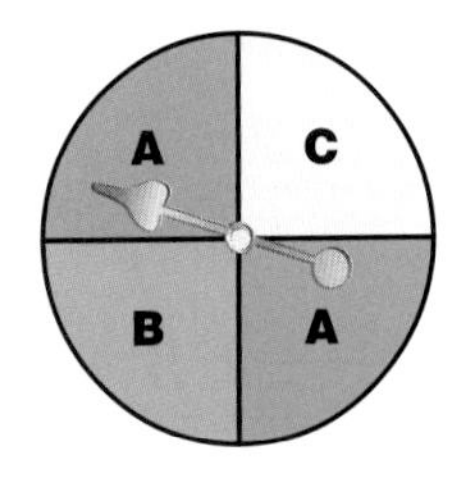

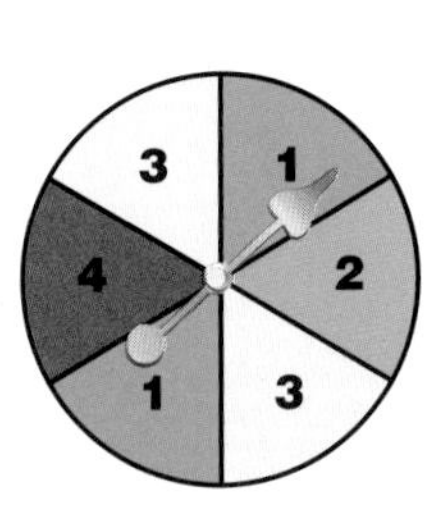

Extra Practice at eduplace.com/map

WEEKLY WR READER®

Science Connection

All in the Family

When a family is about to have a baby, everyone wonders, "Will the baby be a boy or a girl?" In humans and other mammals, the X- and Y-chromosomes determine a baby's gender. Babies who get two X-chromosomes are female. Babies getting one X-chromosome and one Y-chromosome are male.

Scientists can use special tests to determine whether a baby will be male or female, but many people still rely on probability. Since there are only two outcomes, it is equally likely that a couple will have a boy or a girl. In probability notation, $P(\text{boy}) = \frac{1}{2}$ and $P(\text{girl}) = \frac{1}{2}$.

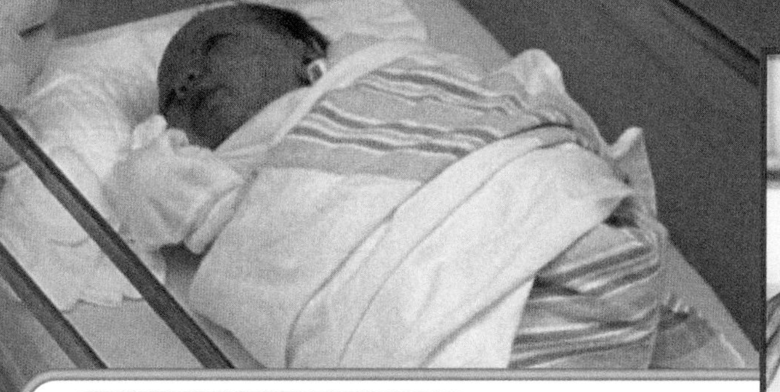

Problem Solving

A couple wants to have 4 children. They hope to have 2 boys and 2 girls. To find the probability that the couple will get their wish, work with a partner to solve the problems.

1. Find the theoretical probability that the 4 children will be 2 boys and 2 girls. Draw a tree diagram as your sample space.

2. Create a simulation to find the experimental probability.
   - Use a coin or a two-color counter. Decide which side of the coin or counter stands for girls and which side stands for boys.
   - Flip the coin 4 times to simulate the birth of each of the 4 children in one family.
   - Repeat the experiment until you have completed 24 trials. Record the results on a recording sheet to show the number of girls and the number of boys in each "family."
   - Use your results to find the experimental probability *P*(2 girls and 2 boys).

3. Compare the results of your experiment with the theoretical probability. Describe any differences.

4. Conduct a survey with a large number of students in your school. Ask for the number of boys and girls in each family, and record each as a trial in a probability experiment. Compare the survey results with results from your coin-tossing experiment.

***P* (2 girls and 2 boys)**		
Trial "Family"	**Girls**	**Boys**
1		
2		
3		

Education Place

Visit Weekly Reader Connections at **eduplace.com/map** for more on this topic.

Enrichment: Circle Graphs and Percents

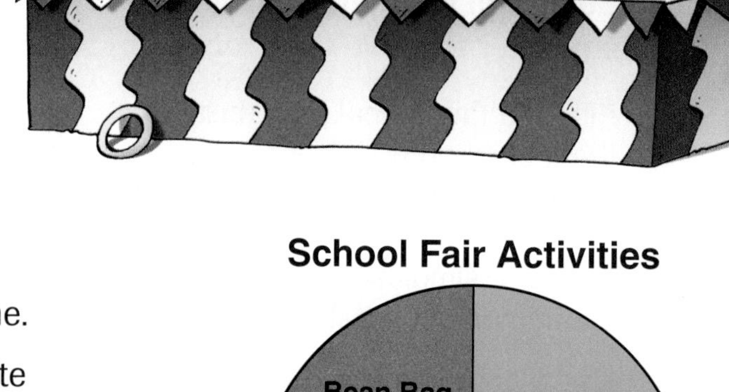

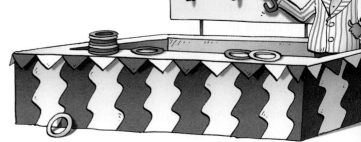

The 20 students in a fifth-grade class wanted to decide on the kind of booth they would have at the school fair. The sections of the circle graph show the percent of the class that voted for each kind of booth.

The graph shows that 25% of the students voted for the Balloon-Dart Game. The figure 25% means $\frac{25}{100}$. You can write 25% as a fraction or as a decimal.

$$25\% = \frac{25}{100} = \frac{1}{4}$$

$$25\% = 0.25$$

School Fair Activities

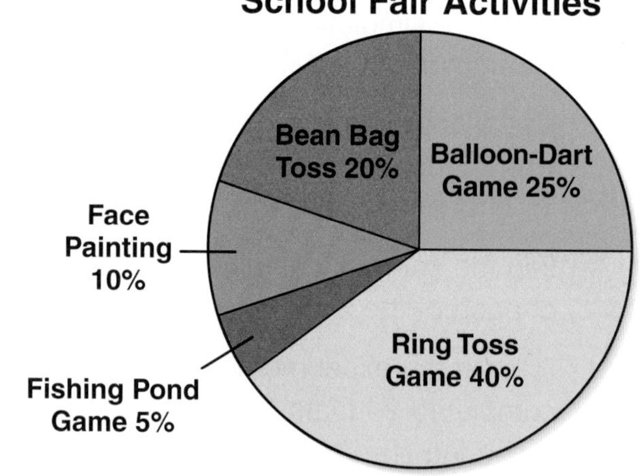

Try These!

Use the circle graph to solve the problems.

1. Write a fraction for the part of the class that voted for the Ring-Toss Game. How many students does that represent?
2. Write a decimal for the part of the class that voted for the Face Painting booth. How many students does that represent?
3. Which activity received 4 votes? Explain how you found your answer.
4. Arrange all the games in order from greatest to least number of votes.
5. Find the number of students who voted for the Fishing Pond Game. Explain how you found your answer.
6. **Write Your Own** Create and solve a problem using the data in the graph. The problem should involve working with percents.

It Takes Time!

How do you spend your time each day? Estimate the number of minutes you spend in one day on each of the following categories: school, homework, sports and hobbies, reading, watching TV, sleeping, and other. Make sure you have a total of 24 hours.

You can make a circle graph of your data using a spreadsheet program.

- Enter the categories in column A.
- Enter the number of minutes you spend on each category in column B.
- Click on cell A1 and drag to cell B7 to highlight all the cells with data.
- Click .
- Double click anywhere on the graph.
- Click on the tab marked **Labels**. Enter a title. Click the box next to **Label Data**. Click **OK**.

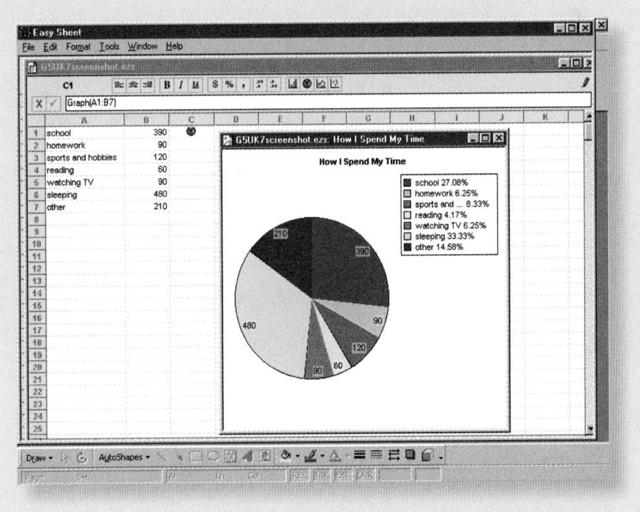

Use the graph you created to answer Problems 1–5.

1. On which activity do you spend the most amount of time? the least amount of time?
2. What percentage of your day is spent on things other than school and homework?
3. Suppose you added eating as another category. How would it affect your graph?
4. Look at the legend. Round each percent to the nearest whole number and then write as a ratio in simplest form.
5. Write the ratio of the number of minutes spent on each activity to 1,440, the number of minutes in a day. Use a calculator to simplify each ratio. Do these ratios match the ones from Problem 4?

Unit 7 Test

VOCABULARY Open Response

Write *true* or *false* for each. Rewrite each false statement to make it true.

1. A rate is a ratio that compares different units.
2. A probability shows that two ratios are equal.
3. Similar figures have the same shape.
4. An event that has a probability of 0 is a certain event.

Vocabulary

ratio
rate
percent
proportion
probability
certain event
similar figures
impossible event

CONCEPTS AND SKILLS Open Response

Write each ratio three different ways. (Chapter 18)

5. 2 trucks to 5 cars
6. 9 rectangles to 5 triangles

Find the unit rate. (Chapter 18)

7. 90 miles in 15 minutes
8. $105 in 7 hours

Find the missing term in each proportion. (Chapter 18)

9. $\frac{n}{5} = \frac{6}{30}$
10. $\frac{4}{6} = \frac{6}{n}$
11. $\frac{10}{8} = \frac{n}{12}$

A blueprint has a scale of $\frac{1}{4}$ inch:1 foot. Find *n*. (Chapter 18)

12. n inches represent 7 feet
13. $\frac{1}{2}$ inch represents n feet

Copy and complete the table. Write each fraction in simplest form. (Chapter 19)

	Fraction	Decimal	Percent
14.	■	■	30%
15.	■	0.8	■
16.	$\frac{9}{20}$	■	■

Order each set from greatest to least. (Chapter 19)

17. $\frac{1}{3}$, 0.25, 13%
18. $\frac{5}{8}$, 0.65, 63%

Estimate each percent of a number. (Chapter 19)

19. 11% of 59
20. 48% of 81

Solve by writing each percent as a fraction or as a decimal. (Chapter 19)

21. 15% of 80
22. 75% of 64
23. 2% of 300

You have one choice from each category. Find the total number of possible combinations. (Chapter 20)

24. 3 styles, 4 colors **25.** 7 flavors, 3 toppings

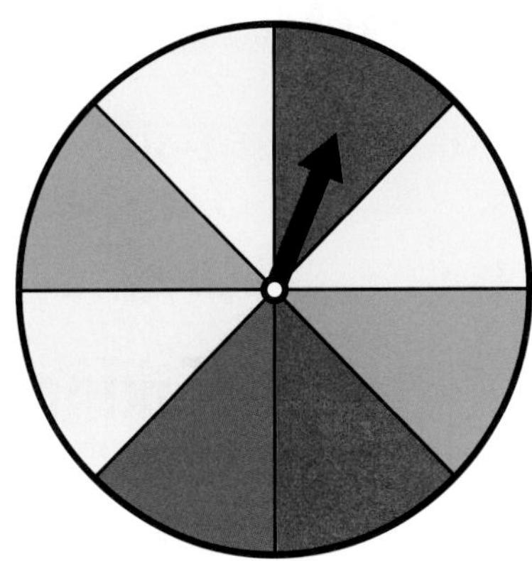

Use the spinner. Express the probability of each event in simplest form. (Chapter 20)

26. red **27.** not yellow or green

Suppose you flip a penny and toss a 1–6 number cube. Find the probability of each compound event. (Chapter 20)

28. heads and 5 **29.** tails and an even number

PROBLEM SOLVING Open Response

30. At Produce Patch market, a bag of 20 large green apples sells for \$5.99. At Fruit Fresh market a bag of 30 large green apples sells for \$7.59. Which is the better buy?

31. Tad wants to buy 3 T-shirts in different colors. The available colors are blue, red, yellow, brown, and black. How many different ways can he choose 3 different colors of T-shirts?

32. The school cafeteria surveyed 160 students about favorite lunches. There were 40 votes for salad, 80 votes for pizza, and 40 votes for sandwiches. Create a circle graph to display these data as percents.

33. Use the data from Problem 32. Suppose you interviewed a student from the school in which the favorite lunch survey was conducted. What is the probability that the student prefers sandwiches for lunch?

Performance Assessment

Extended Response

Which sport is most important in our school sports program?
Please check only one choice.

☐ Baseball ☐ Basketball ☐ Volleyball ☐ Soccer ☐ Football

Task Students used the survey form above to collect data. They plan to present the results to the school athletic committee.

Use the information at the right. Arrange the sports in order from first to last choice. Explain your thinking.

Information You Need

- $\frac{1}{5}$ chose baseball.
- The probability that a student voted for basketball was $\frac{1}{8}$.
- 0.12 chose football.
- 18% chose volleyball.
- The remaining students chose soccer.

Cumulative Test Prep

Solve Problems 1–10.

Test-Taking Tip

When a test question involves an equation with variables, you can check your answer by substituting answer choices for the variable in the given equation.

Look at the example below.

Last week, Ivan worked 21 hours and Jeff worked 34 hours. In this equation, h represents the difference in the number of hours they worked.

$$34 - h = 21$$

What is the value of h?

A 3 **C** 17

B 13 **D** 23

THINK

Substitute each value in the left side of the equation:

A $34 - 3$
B $34 - 13$
C $34 - 17$
D $34 - 23$

Then simplify, and compare the result with 21. The difference between 34 and 13 is 21, so the answer is **B**.

Multiple Choice

1. Kendra earned $40 and Lenny earned $19. In this equation, n represents the number of dollars more than Lenny that Kendra earned.

$$19 + n = 40$$

What is the value of n?

A 11 **B** 21 **C** 31 **D** 59

(Chapter 2, Lesson 5)

2. Twenty-four ride tickets were shared equally by some students. Each student received 4 tickets. In this equation, s represents the number of students.

$$24 \div s = 4$$

What is the value of s?

F 2 **G** 6 **H** 20 **J** 28

(Chapter 4, Lesson 7)

3. Mona drove 120 miles at a speed of 40 miles per hour. In this equation, t represents the number of hours she drove.

$$120 = 40 \times t$$

What is the value of t?

A 3 **B** 30 **C** 80 **D** 160

(Chapter 4, Lesson 7)

4. Nina completed 12 more laps than Otis. Otis completed 9 laps. In this equation, n represents the number of laps Nina completed.

$$n - 12 = 9$$

What is the value of n?

F 3 **G** 21 **H** 31 **J** 41

(Chapter 2, Lesson 5)

For Test-Taking Tips, see page 652.

Open Response

5. Tracey collected these data on the number of calories consumed by classmates at lunch.

640, 570, 710, 640, 720, 690, 700

What is the median of her data?

(Chapter 8, Lesson 2)

6. Stuart has a piece of wood that is 135 inches long. How many blocks, each 1.5 inches long, can he cut from the wood?

(Chapter 14, Lesson 7)

7. Paolo wants to fence in a square patch of basil plants. The patch measures 500 centimeters on a side. How many meters of fencing will he need?

(Chapter 16, Lesson 1)

8. Rosa wants to cover this gift box with wrapping paper. What is the least number of square inches of wrapping paper she'll need?

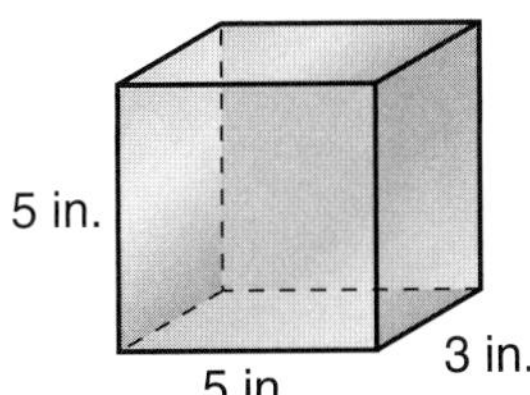

(Chapter 17, Lesson 4)

9. The original price of a DVD was $50. Hugo bought the DVD on sale and paid 75% of the original price. How much did Hugo pay for the DVD?

(Chapter 19, Lesson 5)

Extended Response

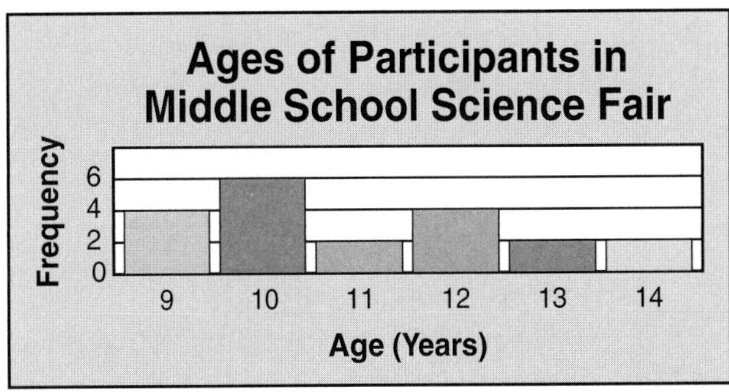

10. Use the bar graph above to answer the following questions.

A How many students were at least 11 years old?

B How many students were under 12 years old?

C What is the mode of the data?

D What is the median of the data? Explain how you found the answer.

E Find the mean of the data to the nearest whole number. Explain how you found the answer.

(Chapter 7, Lesson 2 and Chapter 8, Lesson 2)

Education Place

Look for Cumulative Test Prep at **eduplace.com/map** for more practice.

Vocabulary Wrap-Up for Unit 7

Look back at the big ideas and vocabulary in this unit.

Big Ideas

You can use equivalent fractions or cross products to find the missing term in a proportion.

The theoretical probability of an event is the ratio of the number of favorable outcomes to the total number of outcomes.

Key Vocabulary

proportion

ratio

probability

Math Conversations

Use your new vocabulary to discuss these big ideas.

1. Explain what it means when an event has a probability of 1.
2. Explain how to find 25% of 60 in two different ways.
3. Explain how to find the missing term in this proportion. $\frac{10}{n} = \frac{15}{9}$.
4. Explain how to find the probability of this compound event: tails when tossing a coin and tossing a number less than 5 on a 1–6 number cube.
5. **Write About It** Look for examples of percents in newspapers, magazines, and on television. Make a list of the kinds of articles that use percents. Tell why percents are used in these articles.

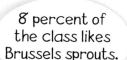

8 percent of the class likes Brussels sprouts.
You can also write that as $\frac{8}{100}$ or 0.08

UNIT 8

Algebra, Integers, and Coordinate Graphing

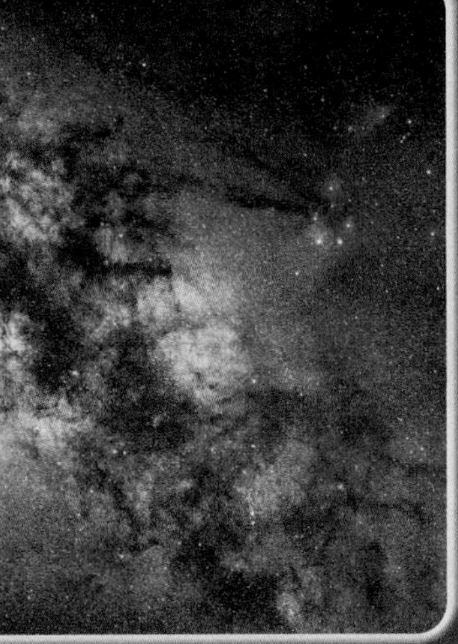

Reading Mathematics

Reviewing Vocabulary

Here are some math vocabulary words that you should know.

function	a rule that pairs each input value x with exactly one output value y
function table	a table that shows the x and corresponding y values for a function rule
equation	a mathematical sentence with an equals sign
negative number	a number that is less than zero
inverse operations	a pair of operations that have opposite effects, such as addition and subtraction or multiplication and division
ordered pair	a pair of numbers in which one number is considered to be first and the other number second

Reading Words and Symbols

You can use words, a combination of words and symbols, or symbols to describe relationships between numbers.

Words: Carola, who is fifteen, is three times as old as Donald.

Words and symbols: Carola's age $=$ 3 $\times$ Donald's age

Symbols: $15 = 3 \times d$ (with d representing Donald's age)

Use words and symbols or only symbols to describe each situation.

1. Eddie saved seventeen dollars, which is four dollars more than Frieda saved.
2. Ginny completed twelve laps, which is five fewer laps than Hal completed.
3. Thirty-six apples were divided into equal shares. There were four apples in each share.

Reading Test Questions

Choose the correct answer for each.

4. Which ordered pair shows the location of the library?

a. (2, 3)

b. (3, 2)

c. (2, 5)

d. (3, 5)

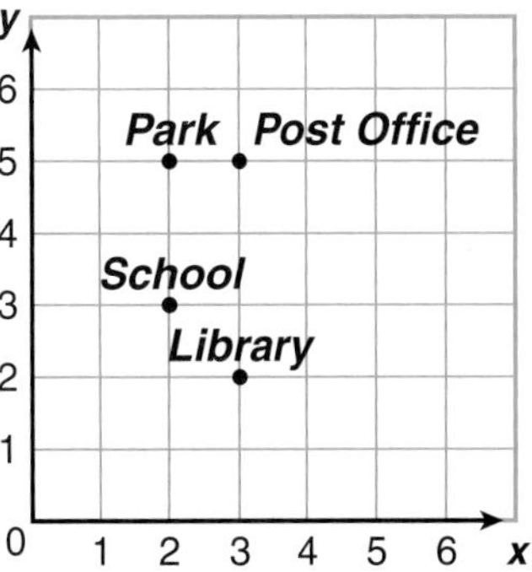

Location means "position" or "place."

5. Which number is the solution of this equation?

$$m - 34 = 19$$

a. 15 **c.** 45

b. 43 **d.** 53

To find the **solution** of an equation means to find "a number that can be substituted for the variable to make the equation true."

6. Al, Ben, Cara, and Donna scored $^{-}4$, 3, 2, and $^{-}3$ points, respectively. Who scored the fewest points?

a. Al **c.** Cara

b. Ben **d.** Donna

Respectively means the scores are in the same order as the names. So, Al scored $^{-}4$, Ben scored 3, Cara scored 2, and Donna scored $^{-}3$.

Learning Vocabulary

Watch for these words in this unit. Write their definitions in your journal.

absolute value

integers

coordinates

origin

rational numbers

square number

Education Place

At **eduplace.com/map** see *e*Glossary and *e*Games—Math Lingo.

Literature Connection

Read "Treasure Hunt" on pages 648–649. Then work with a partner to answer the questions about the story.

CHAPTER 21 Equations and Functions

INVESTIGATION

Use Data

Artists often use scale drawings and grids to plan large pieces of art. This scaled drawing is a plan for one of the stained-glass pieces in the picture. To enlarge the drawing to full size, use 1 in. × 1 in. graph paper and reproduce the picture, square by square.

 Use What You Know

Use this page to review and remember what you need to know for this chapter.

VOCABULARY

Choose the best word to complete each sentence.

1. In the expression $4 + x = 5$, the 4 is a(n) ____.
2. The equation $36 \div 9 = 4$ asks that you ____ 36 by 9.
3. To check division, you ____ the quotient and the divisor.

Vocabulary

- addend
- divide
- factor
- multiply
- number sentence

CONCEPTS AND SKILLS

Find the missing addend.

4. $5 + \blacksquare = 13$
5. $\blacksquare + 11 = 31$
6. $22 + \blacksquare = 61$
7. $\blacksquare + 49 = 74$

Find the missing factor.

8. $7 \times \blacksquare = 42$
9. $\blacksquare \times 9 = 99$
10. $\blacksquare \times 8 = 56$
11. $\blacksquare \times 15 = 60$

Match. Write the letter of the correct missing number.

12. $42 - \blacksquare = 33$ — **a.** 8
13. $\blacksquare \div 9 = 7$ — **b.** 9
14. $\blacksquare - 16 = 40$ — **c.** 56
15. $96 \div \blacksquare = 12$ — **d.** 63

Write the next two numbers in each pattern.

16. 2, 9, 16, 23, 30, ...
17. 2, 10, 18, 26, 34, ...
18. 5, 20, 35, 50, 65, ...
19. 79, 67, 55, 43, 31, ...

Write About It

20. Describe this pattern in words. Then name the next two numbers.

    79, 85, 75, 81, 71

Facts Practice, See page 661.

Model Equations

Objective Determine what happens when you perform the same operation on both sides of an equation.

Vocabulary

equation

Materials

counters
variable cards
plus sign cards
equal sign cards

Work Together

An **equation** is a mathematical sentence showing that two mathematical expressions are equal. You can use counters to model equations.

The blue variable card represents the number of hidden counters. How many counters are hidden?

$x + 3 = 7$

What number plus 3 equals 7? Since $4 + 3 = 7$, $x = 4$. There are 4 hidden counters.

Work with a partner to see what happens when you perform the same operation on both sides of an equation.

STEP 1 Use the variable card, counters, and an equal sign card to model the equation $x + 3 = 7$.

- Add 2 counters to each side of the equal sign. What equation does your model represent now?
- How many counters does the blue card represent? Did adding 2 counters to each side change the value of x?

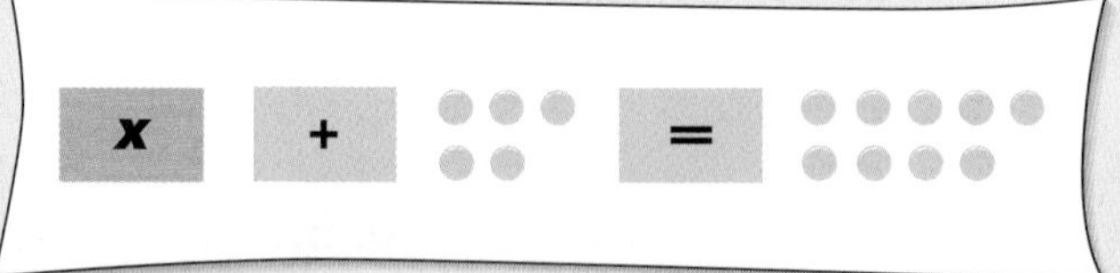

STEP 2 Model the equation $x + 3 = 7$ again.

- Subtract 2 counters from each side of the equal sign. What equation does your model represent now?
- How many counters does the blue card represent? Did taking away 2 counters from each side change the value of x?

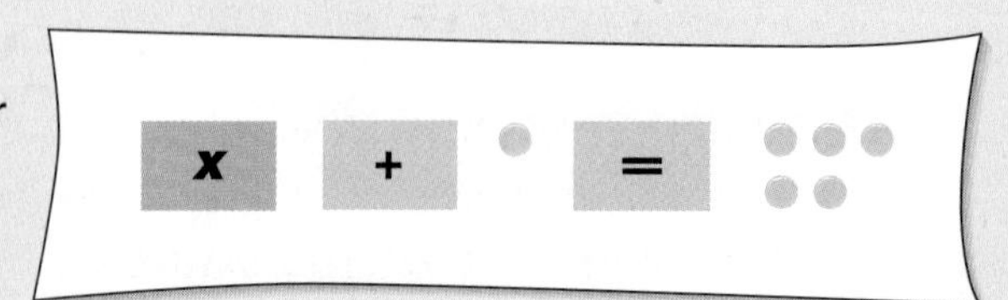

STEP 3 Model the equation $x = 2$ with 1 variable card and 2 counters.

- Use variable cards and counters to show multiplying both sides of the equation by 5. What equation does your model represent now?
- How many counters does the blue card represent? Did multiplying each side by 5 change the value of x?

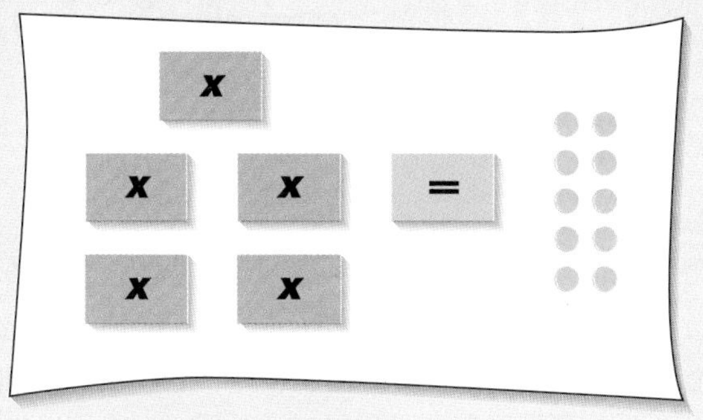

On Your Own

1. In $x + 3 = 5$, what value does x represent?
2. Add 2 to both sides of $x + 3 = 5$. What value does x represent?

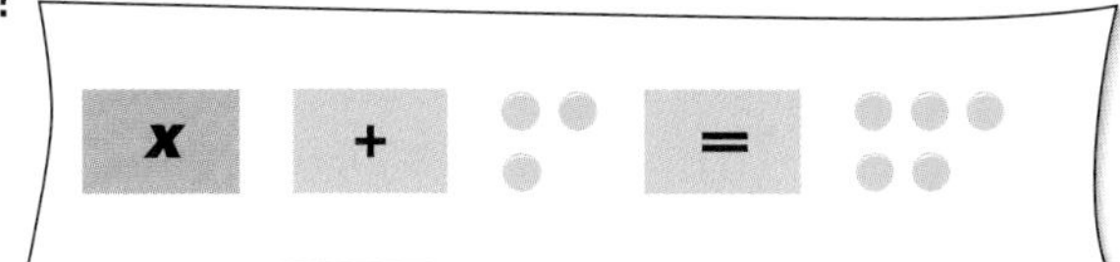

3. Subtract 1 from both sides of $x + 3 = 5$. What value does x represent?
4. In $4x = 12$, what value does x represent?
5. Multiply both sides of $4x = 12$ by 2. What value does x represent?
6. Divide both sides of $4x = 12$ by 2. What value does x represent?

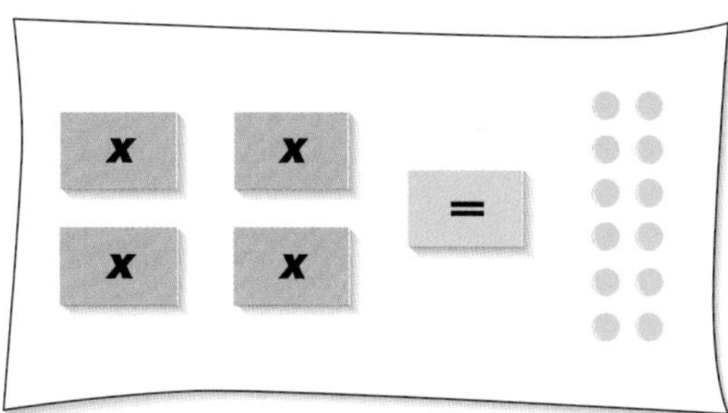

Talk About It • Write About It

You learned that the two sides of an equation are always balanced.

7. What happens to the value of the variable when you add or subtract the same number from both sides of the equation?
8. What happens to the value of the variable when you multiply or divide both sides of the equation by the same counting number?

Lesson 2

Audio Tutor 2/28 Listen and Understand

Write and Solve Equations

Objective Write and solve equations.

Vocabulary
inverse operations

Learn About It

Wayne and his friends are answering telephones at a 24-hour telethon to raise money for local youth programs. There are 18 hours left in the telethon. How many hours has the telethon been on?

Write and solve an equation to solve the problem.

Let n represent the number of hours the telethon has been on.

Equation: $n + 18 = 24$ ← total number of hours in telethon

hours telethon has been on (n); number of hours left (18)

▶ You can use inverse operations to solve equations. **Inverse operations** are two operations that have opposite effects.

Inverse Operations	
addition ⟷ subtraction	
multiplication ⟷ division	

Addition and subtraction are inverse operations.

Solve Addition and Subtraction Equations

Solve: $n + 18 = 24$

$n + 18 = 24$

$n + 18 - 18 = 24 - 18$

$n + 0 = 6$

$n = 6$

Think
18 is added to n.
Addition and subtraction are inverse operations. So subtract 18 from both sides.

Solve: $x - 8 = 27$

$x - 8 = 27$

$x - 8 + 8 = 27 + 8$

$x + 0 = 35$

$x = 35$

Think
8 is subtracted from x.
Addition and subtraction are inverse operations. So add 8 to both sides.

Extra Help at eduplace.com/map

Multiplication and division are inverse operations.

Multiplication and Division Equations

Solve: $4m = 36$

$$4m = 36$$
$$4m \div 4 = 36 \div 4$$
$$1 \cdot m = 9$$
$$m = 9$$

Think
m is multiplied by 4. Multiplication and division are inverses. So divide by 4 on both sides.

Remember
$4m$ means $4 \bullet m$, or four times m. The multiplication sign, $\times$, is not used to avoid confusion with the variable x.

Solve: $t \div 6 = 12$

$$t \div 6 = 12$$
$$(t \div 6) \cdot 6 = 12 \cdot 6$$
$$t \div 1 = 72$$
$$t = 72$$

Think
t is divided by 6. Multiplication and division are inverse operations. So multiply by 6 on both sides.

Guided Practice

Solve using inverse operations.

1. $7d = 28$ **2.** $c \div 9 = 3$ **3.** $h + 26.5 = 51.3$

4. $j - 14 = 13$ **5.** $f \div 8 = 12$ **6.** $y - 48.2 = 98.6$

Use words to describe each equation.

7. $15 + x = 20$ **8.** $3c = 16$ **9.** $y \div 6 = 8$

Ask Yourself

- Which operation can I use to undo the operation in the equation?

Explain Your Thinking ▶ Describe how you can write and solve an equation that shows increasing the number of hours worked by 7 hours equals 32 hours in all.

Practice and Problem Solving

Solve using inverse operations.

10. $6k = 42$ **11.** $c + 108 = 242$ **12.** $g \div 6 = 90$

13. $a - 174 = 308$ **14.** $r \div 8 = 18$ **15.** $u \div 12 = 70$

Use words to describe each equation.

16. $m + 14 = 20$ **17.** $p \div 3 = 12$ **18.** $w - 6 = 18$

Go On

In Problems 19–22, write and solve an equation for each problem.

19. Matt raised \$18 on Saturday morning. He raised more money Saturday afternoon. In all, he raised \$43 on Saturday. How much did he raise Saturday afternoon?

20. Marcus had 28 ride tickets. Each ride took the same number of tickets. Marcus rode 7 rides and used all his tickets. How many tickets did it take for each ride?

21. Margarita had some money. She spent \$28 on jewelry. Then she had \$29. How much did she have before buying jewelry?

22. Each floor of a hotel has an equal number of rooms. The total number of rooms on 12 floors is 240 rooms. How many rooms are on each floor?

23. What's Wrong? Jonah solved the equation $n \div 6 = 18$. What did Jonah do wrong? What is the value of n?

Jonah

$n \div 6 = 18$

$(n \div 6) \div 6 = 18 \div 6$

$n = 3$

24. Create and Solve Write a problem that could be described by the equation $5r = 125$. Then solve the problem.

Quick Check

Check your understanding of Lessons 1–2.

Solve. (Lesson 1)

1. $5t = 80$ **2.** $j - 7 = 46$ **3.** $a \div 4 = 32$ **4.** $v + 84 = 152$

5. $s - 8 = 51$ **6.** $12a = 48$ **7.** $x \div 7 = 35$ **8.** $b + 120 = 235$

Write an equation and solve. (Lesson 2)

9. In a crew of 32 workers, each member works the same number of hours. They work a total of 1,600 hours in a week. Write the equation for this situation.

10. Juan bought 8 tickets to a soccer game. He paid a total of \$96. How much did each ticket cost?

Extra Practice See page 583, Set A.

Number Sense

Square Numbers and Exponents

You can use your calculator to work with square numbers and exponents. The product of a number multiplied by itself is a **square number**. For example, 9 is a square number because it is the product of 3×3.

To show that a number has been squared, write the number and then the exponent 2.

3^2 ← exponent
↑
base

The exponent tells you how many times the base is a factor in the product. So, $3^2 = 3 \times 3$.

To find the square of 3, press 3 ^ 2 Enter = 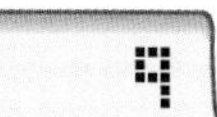

Sometimes you need to multiply a number by itself more than once. This means you are raising it to a power greater than 2.

To show $5 \times 5 \times 5$, write 5^3. The exponent 3 tells you that the base, 5, is a factor 3 times. So, $5 \times 5 \times 5 = 5^3$.

To find 5^3 on your calculator, press    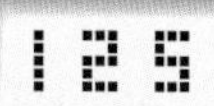

1. **a.** Multiply to square the numbers 1 through 8.
   b. Write an equation in the form of $a^2 = a \times a$ to represent each square number.
   c. Complete the table at the right. Describe the patterns you notice.

1	1
2	4
3	9
4	
5	
6	
7	49
8	

Use the ^ key to simplify the expressions below.

2. $4^3 + 5^2 - 2^2$ **3.** $5^3 - 3 \times 2^4$ **4.** $6^2 \div 3^2 + 5^3$

5. $30 \times (40 - 3^2)$ **6.** $a^2 + 9$, if $a = 5$ **7.** $b^3 - b^2 \times 2$, if $b = 3$

Audio Tutor 2/29 Listen and Understand

Lesson 3

Problem-Solving Strategy

Write an Equation

Objective Write an equation to solve a problem.

You can often use an equation to help you find an unknown amount.

Problem Nate is paid by the hour. He works 6 hours and earns $48. How much does Nate earn each hour?

UNDERSTAND

This is what you know:

- Nate is paid by the hour.
- He works 6 hours and earns $48.

PLAN

You can write an equation to describe the situation. First you have to decide which operation to use. Then you can write and solve the equation.

SOLVE

Think Why write a multiplication equation?

- Write the equation.

  Let d represent the amount that Nate is paid each hour.

  6 hours times d dollars per hour equals $48.

- Solve the equation using inverse operations.

$$6d = 48$$

$$6d \div 6 = 48 \div 6$$

$$d = 8$$

Solution: Nate earns $8 per hour.

LOOK BACK

Look back at the problem.

How can you check your answer?

Guided Practice

Use the Ask Yourself questions to help you solve each problem.

1. Last week, Terri worked 9.5 hours. This was 3.5 hours less than the number of hours that Brad worked. How many hours did Brad work?

2. A company has 160 employees. This is 4 times the number of employees that it had ten years ago. How many employees did the company have ten years ago?

Hint: What will the variable represent?

Ask Yourself

UNDERSTAND **What facts do I know?**

PLAN **Did I write an equation?**

SOLVE
- **Did I use a variable to represent what I need to know?**
- **Did I use the correct operation to solve the equation?**

LOOK BACK **Does my answer make sense?**

Independent Practice

Write an equation to solve each problem.

3. Benita gets a raise of \$315 per month. Her new monthly salary is \$3,425. What was Benita's monthly salary before she got a raise?

4. In one restaurant, the waiter gives the dishwasher $\frac{1}{4}$ of his tips. On Friday night, the waiter receives \$88 in tips. How much does the waiter give to the dishwasher?

5. **You Decide** Find how much each job listed to the right pays per hour. Decide which job you would prefer. Give reasons for your decision.

Summer Jobs at Cameron Park
Painting $180 per week
Work 15 hours per week.
Working hours: 7 A.M.—10 A.M.
Cleaning $200 per week
Work 16 hours per week.
Working hours: 7 P.M.—11 P.M.
Tour Guide $120 per week
Work 12 hours per week.
Working hours: 1 P.M.— 4 P.M.

6. Tom has a weekly salary of \$750. This is \$95 less than Carol's weekly salary. What is Carol's weekly salary?

7. One department has 4 employees. Each employee works the same number of hours per week. The employees in that department worked a total of 150 hours in one week. How many hours did each employee work?

Mixed Problem Solving

Solve. Show your work. Tell what strategy you used.

8. In a blizzard, a technician monitors the snowfall each hour. The total snowfall is 2.8 cm after 2 hours, 4.2 cm after 3 hours, and 5.6 cm after 4 hours. If the pattern continues, what will be the total snowfall after 5 hours?

9. Fran makes a set of 49 prints. If all 49 prints sell for a total of $9,800, how much does Fran charge for one print?

10. A jewelry store has 7 clerks. Two clerks must be working at the store at any time that it is open. How many different combinations of 2 clerks are possible?

11. Julianna earned $344 last week working at a local print shop. She earned $8 per hour. How many hours did Julianna work last week at the print shop?

You Choose

Strategy
- Find a Pattern
- Make a Table
- Solve a Simpler Problem
- Use Models
- Write an Equation

Computation Method
- Mental Math
- Estimation
- Paper and Pencil
- Calculator

Data Use the table to solve Problems 12–15.

The Dog Bone Inn offers the services to dog owners shown in the table.

12. Mari's dog, Jiffy, weighs 32 lbs. How much will it be to board and feed Jiffy for two days at the Dog Bone Inn?

13. Ms. Owens has two small dogs, one large dog, and two giant dogs to groom at the Doggie Spa. What is the total amount she will charge the owners of the dogs?

14. Calculator Which will cost less: day care for a large dog for 5 days with a field trip to the beach or boarding a medium dog for 6 days with 3 field trips to the lake, and a grooming at the Doggie Spa? How much less?

15. Create and Solve Use the data from the table to create and solve a problem.

DOG BONE INN

Daily Charges				
	Small	Medium	Large	Giant
Day Care	$11	$14	$17	$30
Boarding	$16	$22	$27	$50
Doggie Spa	$15	$20	$35	$60
Feeding	$1.75	$3.50	$3.50	$3.50

Field Trips To:	
Tail-wagging Bakery	$15
Lake	$25
Beach	$100

Small dogs: Up to 25 pounds **Large dogs:** 61 to 110 pounds
Medium dogs: 26 to 60 pounds **Giant dogs:** Over 110 pounds

Problem Solving on Tests

Multiple Choice

Choose the letter of the correct answer.

1. A sound system is on sale for 10% off list price. Including a sales tax of $9, Jeremy pays $189 for the sound system. Which equation could you use to find the list price (p)?

A $0.9p = 189$

B $0.9p - 9 = 189$

C $0.9p + 9 = 189$

D $0.1p - 9 = 189$

(Chapter 19, Lesson 5)

2. Which set has numbers that are all equivalent?

F $\frac{1}{3}$, 0.3, 3%

G $\frac{1}{5}$, 0.25, 25%

H $\frac{3}{10}$, 0.03, 3%

J $\frac{3}{5}$, 0.6, 60%

(Chapter 19, Lesson 3)

Open Response

Solve each problem.

3. A park has 6 entrance gates. A direct path connects each gate to every other gate. How many paths are there in all?

Represent Support your solution with a picture.

(Chapter 17, Lesson 5)

4. Bill has twice as many stickers as Amy. Together they have 24 stickers. Let a represent the number of stickers that Amy has. Write an equation that you can use to find how many stickers Amy has.

Explain How does your equation represent the situation?

(Chapter 21, Lesson 3)

Extended Response

5. The fifth-graders at Stony Point School planned an international dinner to raise money for a class trip to Philadelphia. Parents offered to cook favorite ethnic foods for the event.

a Three hundred eighty-five tickets were sold for $12.50 each. How much money was collected from the sale of tickets to the dinner?

b Forty percent of the people chose Italian food. How many people chose Italian food? Show your work.

c Seventy-seven people chose Mexican food. What percent is that of all the people who bought tickets? Explain how you know.

d Each table at the dinner could seat 12 people. How many tables did the fifth-graders need? Were all of the tables filled? How might they have seated people?

(Chapter 19)

Education Place

See **eduplace.com/map** for Test-Taking Tips.

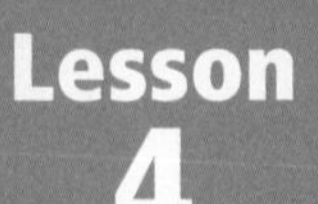

Audio Tutor 2/30 Listen and Understand

Lesson 4

Variables and Functions

Objective Use a function table to solve equations.

Vocabulary
function
function table

Learn About It

A **function** is a rule that relates pairs of variables, such as x and y. For each value of x, there is exactly one related value of y. A function is often written as an equation.

Look at the pattern. How many squares will there be in Shape 10?

1 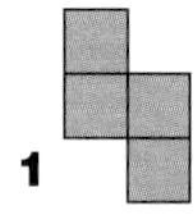 2 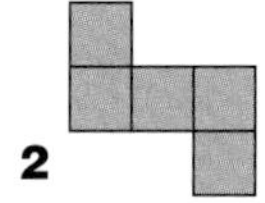 3 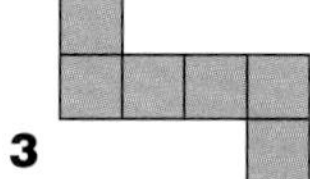 4 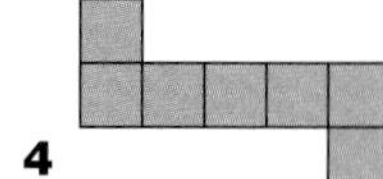

STEP 1 Organize the information in a table. Write the shape number in the first column. Write the number of squares in the second column.

The table of values is called a **function table** because there is exactly one entry in the second column for each shape number.

Shape Number	Number of Squares
1	4
2	5
3	6
4	7

STEP 2 Write the equation that describes the relationship between x and y.

The number of squares is always equal to 3 more than the shape number.

$$y = x + 3$$

(y: number of squares; x: shape number)

STEP 3 To find the number of squares in Shape 10, substitute 10 for x and simplify.

$$y = x + 3$$
$$y = 10 + 3$$
$$y = 13$$

Solution: There will be 13 squares in Shape 10.

Another Example

Find the Value

The rule $y = 9x$ describes a function. What is the value of y when $x = 4$?

$y = 9x$ Substitute 4 for x in the equation.
$y = 9(4)$
$y = 36$

Guided Practice

Copy and complete each function table.

1. $y = 5 + x$

x	y
4	
3	
2	

2. $y = x - 5$

x	y
10	
7	
6	

3. $y = 7x$

x	y
12	
	14
8	

Ask Yourself

- What value did I use for x?
- How did I get the value of y?
- Did a pattern help me find the missing values?

Explain Your Thinking ▶ What are some other pairs of values that would fit in the function table in Exercise 2?

Practice and Problem Solving

Copy and complete each function table.

4. $y = 12 \div x$

x	y
1	
2	
3	

5. $y = 4 - x$

x	y
0	
3	
4	

6. $y = 1 + x$

x	y
0	
6	
9	

7. $y = 9x$

x	y
0	
	9
2	

Use the figures for Problems 8–10.

8. Make a function table to show how the number of circles in each figure is related to the figure number.

Figure 1

9. Make a function table to show how the number of triangles in each figure is related to the figure number.

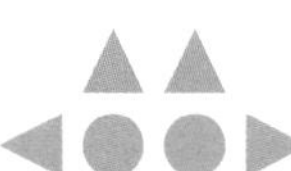

Figure 2

10. Write an expression for the number of circles and for the number of triangles in the nth figure. Use the expressions to find how many circles and triangles are in the nth figure.

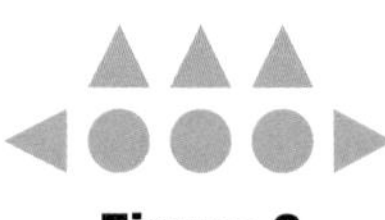

Figure 3

Mixed Review and Test Prep

Open Response

Find the missing term.
(Ch. 18, Lesson 4)

11. $\frac{6}{9} = \frac{g}{3}$ **12.** $\frac{8}{10} = \frac{20}{a}$ **13.** $\frac{3}{z} = \frac{9}{21}$

14. Ron's earnings (y) for a number of hours (x) are given by the rule $y = 10x$. Make a function table for five values of x. (Ch. 21, Lesson 4)

Extra Practice See page 583, Set B.

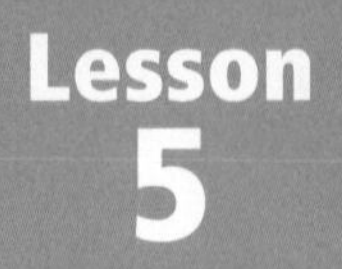

Lesson 5

Audio Tutor 2/31 Listen and Understand

Patterns and Functions

Objective Use function tables and equations to describe and extend patterns.

Learn About It

Some functions involve more than one operation.

Theo opened a savings account at the local bank with a deposit of $250. Theo intends to deposit $5 each week. How much will Theo have in his savings account after 7 weeks?

Different Ways to Represent Functions

Way 1 You can use a function table.

The function table for the first $250 shows that each week after the first deposit adds $5 to the bank account.

Use that pattern to extend the function table so that it shows the amount for 7 weeks.

Number of weeks (x)	Amount in Savings (y)
0	$250
1	$255
2	$260
3	$265
4	$270
5	$275
6	$280
7	$285

Way 2 You can use an equation that represents the values in the function table.

STEP 1 Write an equation that represents the relationship between x and y.

The function table shows that the initial deposit is $250 and each week adds $5 to the account.

amount deposited each week (→ 5)

$$y = 250 + 5x$$

number of weeks (→ x); total amount (→ y); beginning deposit (→ 250)

STEP 2 To find the amount, substitute the number of weeks after the initial deposit for x and simplify.

Think
7 weeks in all.
$x = 7$

$y = 250 + 5(7)$

$y = 250 + 35$

$y = 285$

Solution: Theo will have $285 in his bank account in 7 weeks.

Guided Practice

Copy and complete each function table.

1. $y = 2x - 3$

x	y
3	■
4	■
5	■

2. $y = 5 + 5x$

x	y
1	■
2	■
3	■

3. $y = (x \div 2) - 4$

x	y
26	■
24	■
22	■

Ask Yourself

- What pattern does the function table show?

Use the function table. Find the value of *y* for the given value of *x*.

4. If $x = 6$, $y = $ ■.

x	y
0	4
1	7
2	10
3	13

5. If $x = 8$, $y = $ ■.

x	y
0	5
1	10
2	15
3	20

6. If $x = 10$, $y = $ ■.

x	y
0	7
1	11
2	15
3	19

7. If $x = 25$, $y = $ ■.

x	y
3	8
5	14
7	20
9	26

Explain Your Thinking ▶ What equation describes the relationship between *x* and *y* in Exercise 6?

Practice and Problem Solving

Copy and complete each function table.

8. $y = 10x + 2$

x	y
0	■
1	■
2	■

9. $y = 65 + 2x$

x	y
0	■
3	■
6	■

10. $y = 20 - 4x$

x	y
0	■
2	■
■	8

11. $y = 9 + 4x$

x	y
0	■
■	13
■	25

Use the function table. Find the value of *y* for the given value of *x*. Then write the equation for the function.

12. If $x = 5$, $y = $ ■.

x	y
0	1
1	7
2	13
3	19

13. If $x = 9$, $y = $ ■.

x	y
0	9
3	12
5	14
7	16

14. If $x = 8$, $y = $ ■.

x	y
0	8
2	18
4	28
6	38

15. If $x = 6$, $y = $ ■.

x	y
0	10
1	14
2	18
3	22

Go On

Data **Julio's grandfather designed the gardens shown. Use the diagram for Problems 16–20.**

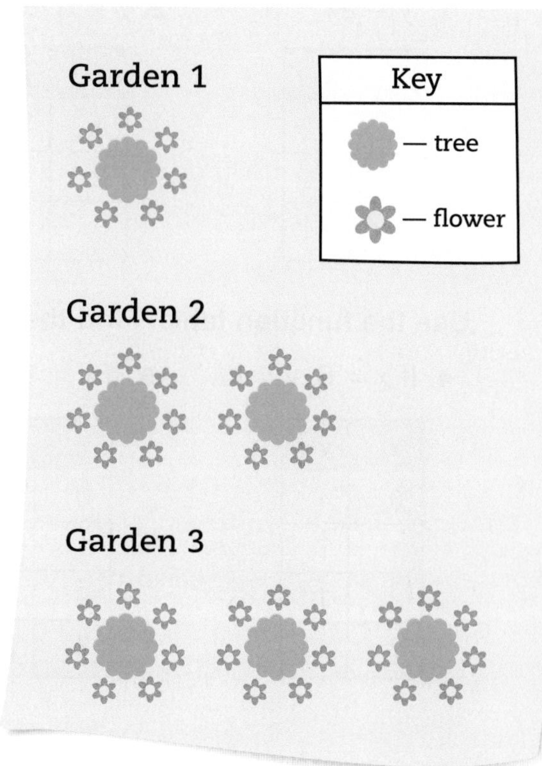

16. Look at the trees and flowers of the gardens. What patterns do you see?

17. Write an equation that relates the number of trees of a garden (x) to the number of flowers of the garden (y).

18. Draw diagrams to show three more gardens in which the relationship between the number of trees and the number of flowers is the same as in the gardens shown at the right.

19. Create a function table that shows the values for the number of trees (x) and the number of flowers (y) for the gardens shown at the right. Then extend the function table to show the next five gardens in the pattern.

20. Suppose Julio's grandfather creates another garden that fits this pattern. The number of flowers is 84. What is the number of trees?

Aftershock Studios Rental Rates

Number of Hours (x)	Total Costs (y)
1	$250
2	$300
3	$350
4	$400

Use the function table to solve Problems 21–23.

21. Cindy records a CD at Aftershock Studios. She rents a studio for 8 hours. How much does Cindy pay?

22. **Write About It** Write an equation that represents the function in the function table. Explain why the equation represents the function.

23. **You Decide** Echo Studios charges a flat fee of $100 plus a charge of $75 per hour. Describe a situation in which you would record at Echo Studios, and one in which you would record at Aftershock Studios. Explain your examples.

Extra Practice See page 583, Set C.

Mixed Review and Test Prep

Open Response

Divide. (Ch. 4, Lesson 5)

24. 15,567 ÷ 5

25. 3,766 ÷ 3

26. 34,245 ÷ 6

27. 708,066 ÷ 9

28. Greg works 35 hours and earns \$525. How much does Greg earn each hour? Write an equation and solve. (Ch. 21, Lesson 5)

Science Connection

Nutrition Facts

Nutritionists study the way a body uses the nutrients that are in food. Three of the main kinds of nutrients are:

- **Carbohydrates** come from starch and sugar in food.
- **Fats** are contained in eggs, fish, meat, nuts, butter, and shortening.
- **Proteins** come from cheese, eggs, meat, fish, milk, beans, grains, nuts, and vegetables.

You might see the information about nutrients at the right on a yogurt container.

Amount per serving	
Total Fat	2 g
Total Carbohydrate	40 g
Protein	9 g

Use the label and an equation to solve.

1. How many times more carbohydrates are there than fats?
2. About how many times more proteins are there than fats?
3. How many times more carbohydrates are there than proteins?
4. How many grams of carbohydrates are in 6 servings of yogurt?
5. There are 4 calories in 1 gram of carbohydrate. How many calories of the yogurt are from carbohydrate?

WEEKLY WR READER eduplace.com/map

Chapter Review/Test

VOCABULARY

1. A letter that stands for a number in an algebraic expression is called a(n) ____ .

2. ____ are two operations that have opposite effects.

Vocabulary

- equation
- function
- inverse operations
- variable

CONCEPTS AND SKILLS

Solve using inverse operations. (Lessons 1–2, pp. 566–571)

3. $w - 95 = 890$ 4. $231 = x + 67$ 5. $9y = 135$

Copy and complete each function table. (Lesson 4, pp. 576–577)

6. $y = 9 - x$

x	y
4	■
5	■
6	■

7. $y = 8 + x$

x	y
10	■
12	■
14	■

8. $y = 36 \div x$

x	y
3	■
6	■
9	■

Use the function table. Find the value of *y* for the given value of *x*. (Lesson 5, pp. 578–579)

9. If $x = 9$, $y =$ ■.

x	y
3	7
4	9
5	11

PROBLEM SOLVING

Solve. (Lesson 3, pp. 572–573)

10. Last week, each of 5 students spent the same amount of time on homework. They spent a total of 68 hours on homework. How many hours did each student spend on homework?

Show You Understand

Write an equation and then make a function table for the equation. Explain how a function table works.

Extra Practice

Set A (Lesson 2, pp. 568–571)

Solve using inverse operations.

1. $15 + d = 27$ **2.** $e - 118 = 110$ **3.** $6f = 48$ **4.** $12 = g \div 9$

5. $h + 76 = 201$ **6.** $12 \cdot j = 132$ **7.** $145 = k - 423$ **8.** $m \div 8 = 23$

9. $15n = 1{,}275$ **10.** $p + 167 = 903$ **11.** $q \div 13 = 9$ **12.** $r - 619 = 586$

Set B (Lesson 4, pp. 576–577)

Copy and complete each function table.

1. $y = 2 + x$

x	y
6	■
8	■
10	■
12	■

2. $y = 8 - x$

x	y
0	■
1	■
2	■
3	■

3. $y = 5x$

x	y
2	■
4	■
6	■
8	■

4. $y = 24 \div x$

x	y
1	■
2	■
3	■
4	■

Set C (Lesson 5, pp. 578–581)

Copy and complete each function table.

1. $y = 3x + 4$

x	y
0	■
2	■
4	■
6	■

2. $y = 7x - 5$

x	y
2	■
3	■
4	■
5	■

3. $y = (x \div 2) + 6$

x	y
4	■
6	■
8	■
10	■

4. $y = 10x - 8$

x	y
3	■
6	■
■	82
■	112

Use the function table. Find the value of *y* for the given value of *x*. Then give the equation for the function.

5. If $x = 6$, $y = n$.

x	y
1	7
2	8
3	9
4	10

6. If $x = 8$, $y = n$.

x	y
0	2
1	5
2	8
3	11

7. If $x = 10$, $y = n$.

x	y
0	10
2	30
4	50
6	70

8. If $x = 12$, $y = n$.

x	y
2	4
4	16
6	36
8	64

CHAPTER 22

Integers

INVESTIGATION

Use Data

The lowest elevation in the United States is in the Badwater Basin in Death Valley National Park. Elevation is based upon sea level, so $^{-}282$ feet means 282 feet below sea level. Look at the diagram below. What is the difference in elevation between Telescope Peak and Badwater Basin?

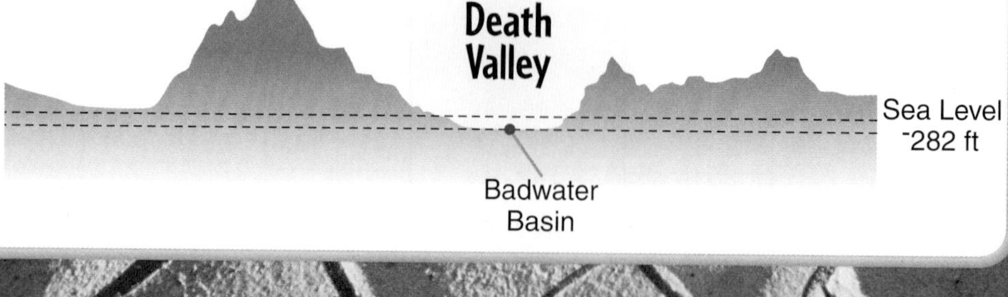

Telescope Peak

11,049 ft

Death Valley

Sea Level

$^{-}282$ ft

Badwater Basin

Use What You Know

Use this page to review and remember what you need to know for this chapter.

VOCABULARY

Choose the best word to complete each sentence.

Vocabulary
above
below
number line
thermometer

1. Use a ____ to measure temperature.
2. On a ____, numbers are assigned to equally spaced points.
3. The temperature $^{-}5$°C is read as "five degrees ____ zero Celsius."

CONCEPTS AND SKILLS

Compare. Write >, <, or = for each ⬮.

4. 357 ⬮ 375
5. 89 ⬮ 98
6. 0.7 ⬮ 0.70
7. 2 ⬮ 0.2

Add or subtract.

8. 156 + 10
9. 459 − 250
10. 348 + 121
11. 627 − 227

Write each missing number.

12.
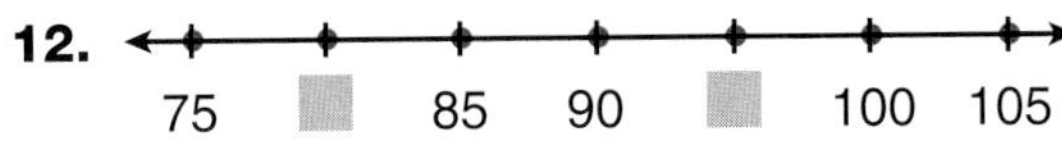

13.
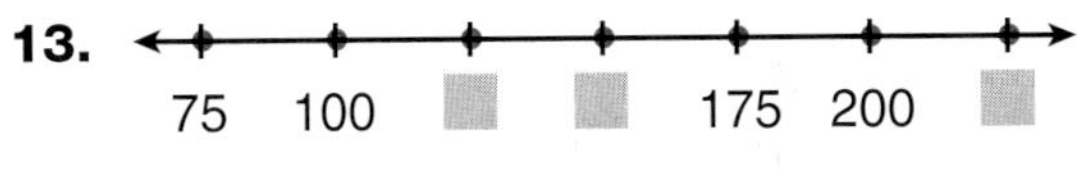

14.
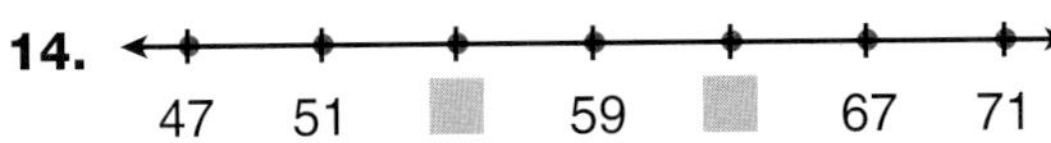

15.
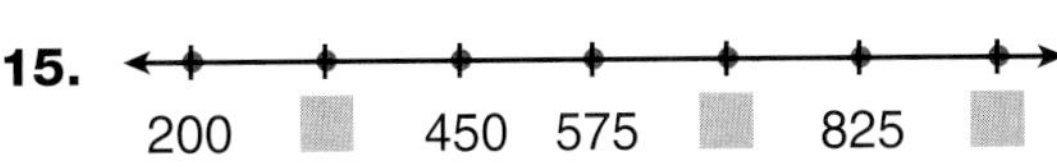

Write each temperature in °F.

16.
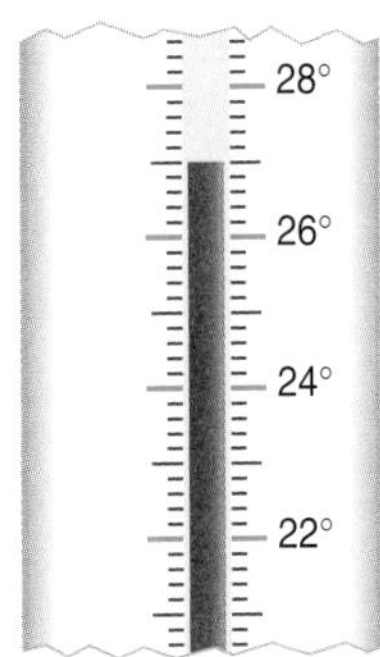

17.
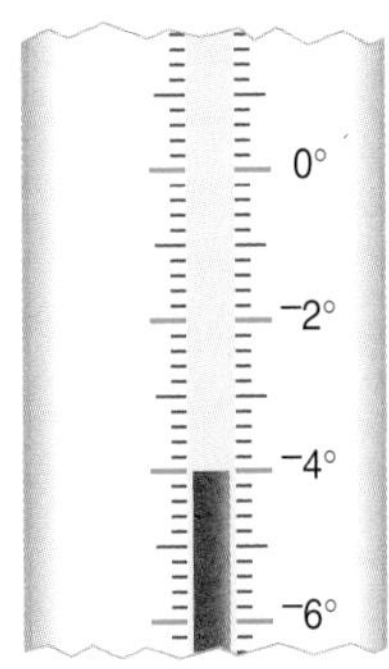

18.
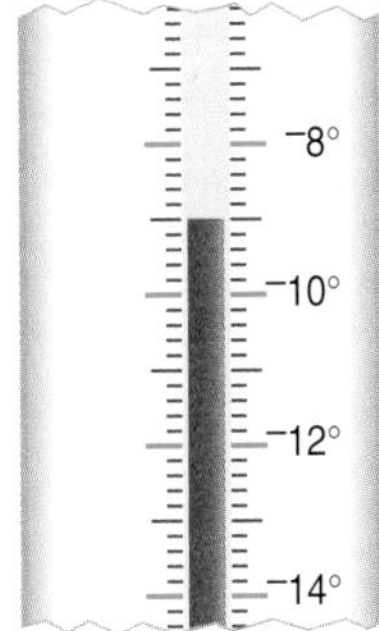

19.
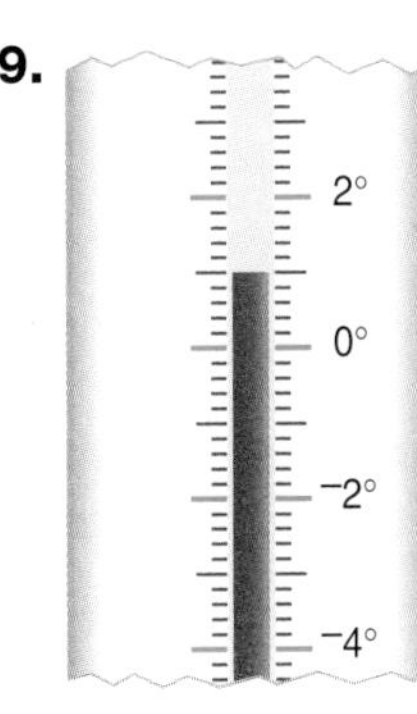

Write About It

20. Suppose the temperature at 8:00 A.M. is 6°F and at 8:00 P.M. is $^{-}2$°F. How many degrees did the temperature drop? Use pictures or words to explain your answer.

Facts Practice, See page 664.

Lesson 1

Audio Tutor 2/32 Listen and Understand

Integers and Absolute Value

Objective Identify integers and find the absolute value of an integer.

Vocabulary
- positive numbers
- negative numbers
- opposite
- integers
- absolute value

Learn About It

The number zero and the numbers greater than zero, called the **positive numbers**, can be shown on a number line. You can extend the number line from zero to show numbers less than zero, called the **negative numbers**.

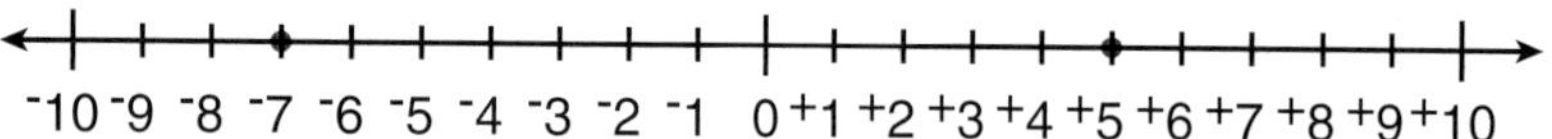

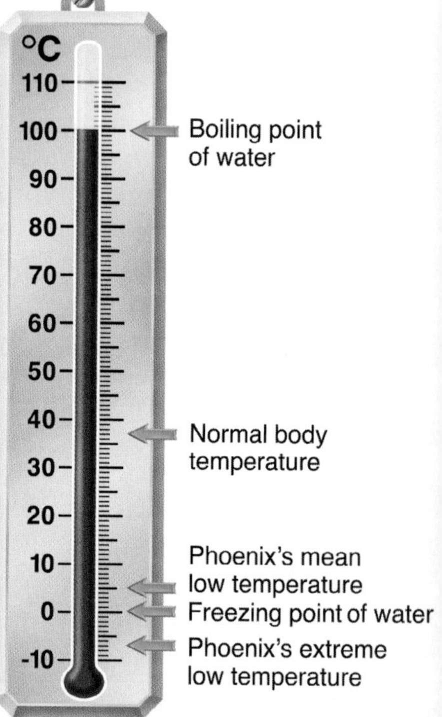

Negative 7, or $^-7$, is the **opposite** of positive 7, or $^+7$. The set of **integers** includes zero, the counting numbers, and their opposites.

To write the opposite of an integer, change its sign.

The opposite of $^+8$ is $^-8$. The opposite of $^-15$ is $^+15$.

Opposite numbers are the same distance from zero on the number line. A number's distance from zero is called its **absolute value.** The absolute value of $^-3$ and $^+3$ is 3 because both are 3 units from zero.

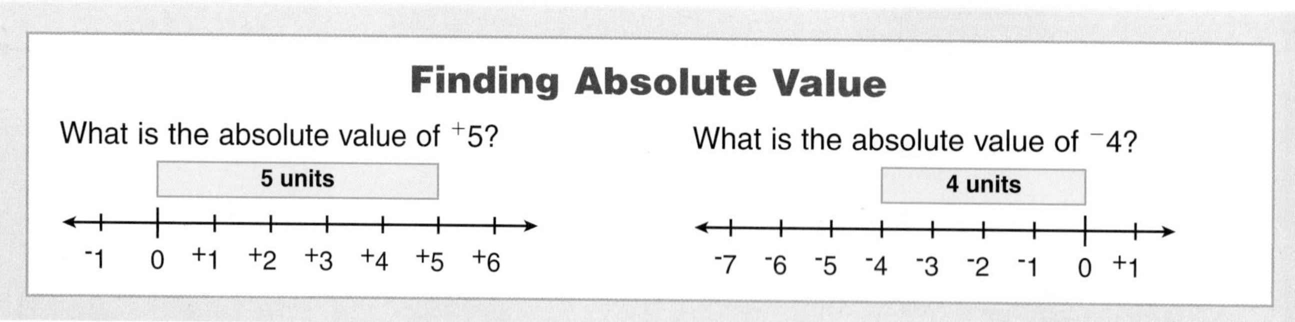

Solution: The absolute value of $^+5$ is 5. The absolute value of $^-4$ is 4.

Guided Practice

Write the opposite of each integer.

1. $^-9$ **2.** $^+6$ **3.** $^-4$ **4.** $^-45$ **5.** $^+134$ **6.** $^+87$

Write the absolute value of each integer.

7. $^+3$ **8.** $^-1$ **9.** $^-8$ **10.** 0 **11.** $^+11$ **12.** $^-23$

Explain Your Thinking ▶ Is the absolute value of an integer the same as the opposite of that integer? Explain.

Extra Help at eduplace.com/map

Practice and Problem Solving

Write the opposite of each integer.

13. $^-17$ **14.** $^-30$ **15.** $^+6$ **16.** $^-12$ **17.** $^+28$ **18.** $^+106$

19. $^+82$ **20.** $^+184$ **21.** $^+19$ **22.** $^-44$ **23.** $^+102$ **24.** $^-59$

Write the absolute value of each integer.

25. $^+7$ **26.** $^-6$ **27.** $^+1$ **28.** $^-7$ **29.** $^-16$ **30.** $^-9$

31. $^-10$ **32.** $^+15$ **33.** $^+6$ **34.** $^-3$ **35.** $^+8$ **36.** $^+10$

Data **Use the graph to solve Problems 37–40.**

37. Which city had an extreme low temperature of $^-16$°C?

38. Which two temperatures shown on the graph are opposites?

39. Which city does not have about a 20°C difference between its mean and extreme low temperatures?

40. Charleston, South Carolina, has an extreme low temperature of $^-14$°C. Which city from the graph has that same extreme low temperature?

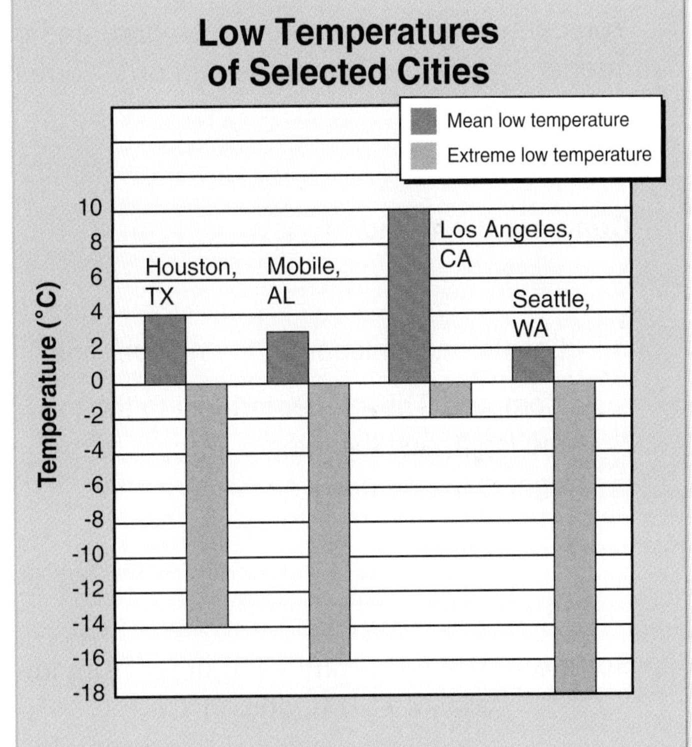

41. Mobile, Alabama, is about 8 feet above sea level. New Orleans, Louisiana, is about 5 feet below sea level. Draw a graph to show the elevations of these two cities.

42. Zero is not positive or negative. What is the opposite of 0?

Mixed Review and Test Prep

Open Response

Solve each equation. (Ch. 21, Lesson 2)

43. $55 = 11y$

44. $n \div 6 = 5$

45. $x \div 8 = 2$

46. $6c = 18$

47. $c \div 9 = 45$

48. $3x = 33$

Multiple Choice

49. The lowest point in the United States is in Death Valley, California. Its elevation is $^-282$ feet. What is the absolute value of this elevation? (Ch. 22, Lesson 1)

A $^-2$ **B** $^-282$ **C** 2 **D** 282

Extra Practice See page 607, Set A.

Lesson 2

Compare and Order Integers

Objective Use a number line to compare integers.

Learn About It

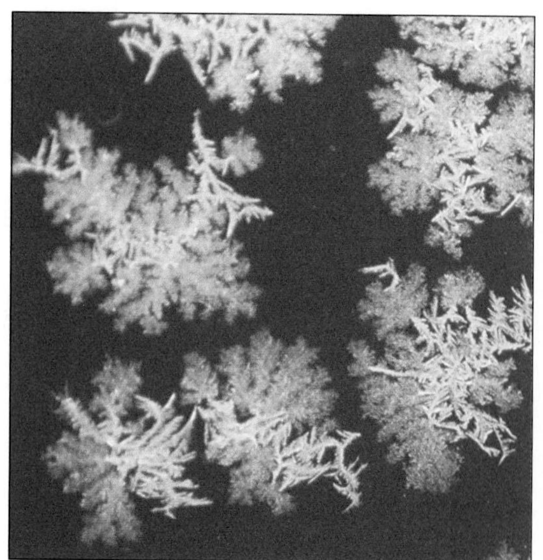

People in northern climates expect snow in the winter. Snow crystals have different shapes depending on the temperature at which they are formed.

At 0°C, water begins to freeze, and ice crystals shaped like thin plates begin to form. At $^{-}4$°C, the crystals look like needles. At $^{+}1$°C, the ice crystals begin to melt. Order the temperatures from lowest to highest.

You can use a number line to compare and order integers, just as you compare and order other numbers.

Compare 0, $^{-}4$, and $^{+}1$.

Locate each integer on the number line.

Compare. The integer farthest to the left is the least, and the integer farthest to the right is the greatest.

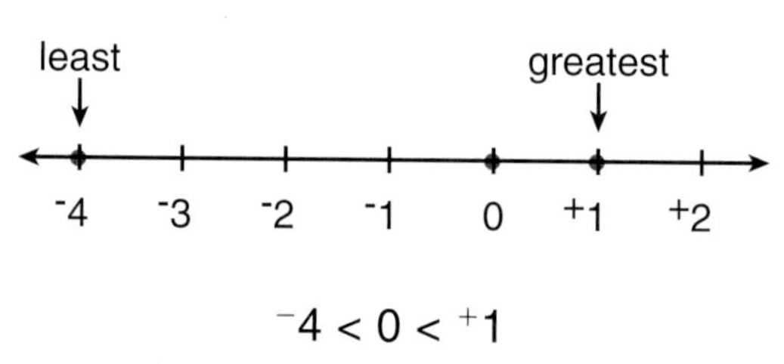

Solution: The temperatures in order from lowest to highest are $^{-}4$°C, 0°C, and $^{+}1$°C.

Guided Practice

Compare. Draw a number line from $^{-}4$ to $^{+}4$ and label each integer. Write $>$, $<$, or $=$ for each ●.

1. $^{+}1$ ● $^{+}2$

2. $^{+}1$ ● $^{-}1$

3. $^{-}3$ ● 0

4. $^{-}3$ ● $^{-}1$

5. $^{-}3$ ● $^{+}2$

6. $^{-}3$ ● $^{-}4$

Ask Yourself

- Did I check on the number line that the integer to the left is less than the integer to the right?

Explain Your Thinking ▶ If you are comparing two negative integers, how can you tell which one is greater?

Practice and Problem Solving

Compare. Draw a number line from $^{-}5$ to $^{+}5$ and label each integer. Write >, <, or = for each ⬤.

7. $^{+}2$ ⬤ $^{-}1$	**8.** $^{-}5$ ⬤ $^{-}2$	**9.** $^{+}5$ ⬤ $^{-}3$	**10.** $^{+}1$ ⬤ 0
11. $^{-}5$ ⬤ $^{+}3$	**12.** $^{-}5$ ⬤ $^{+}5$	**13.** $^{-}1$ ⬤ $^{+}1$	**14.** 0 ⬤ $^{+}2$
15. $^{-}4$ ⬤ $^{-}2$	**16.** 0 ⬤ $^{-}1$	**17.** $^{-}3$ ⬤ $^{-}4$	**18.** $^{-}2$ ⬤ $^{+}1$

Use your number line from Exercises 7–18. Write an integer to make the statement true.

19. $\blacksquare < {}^{-}1$	**20.** $\blacksquare > 0$	**21.** ${}^{-}2 > \blacksquare$	**22.** ${}^{-}5 < \blacksquare$
23. ${}^{-}1 > \blacksquare$	**24.** $\blacksquare < {}^{-}3$	**25.** ${}^{-}4 > \blacksquare$	**26.** $\blacksquare < {}^{+}2$

Write the integer that belongs at each point.

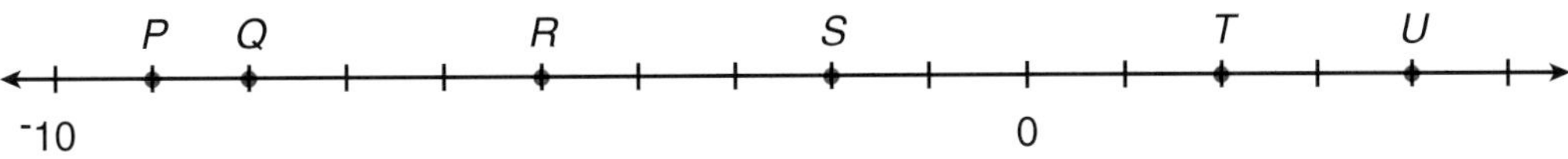

27. point *P*	**28.** point *Q*	**29.** point *R*
30. point *S*	**31.** point *T*	**32.** point *U*

Use the number line below. Write *true* or *false* to describe each statement.

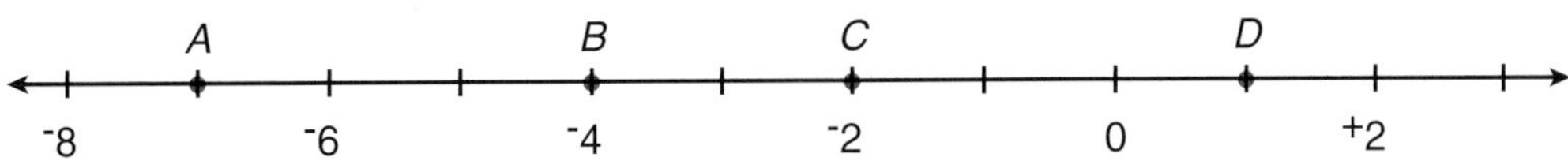

33. $D > C$	**34.** $C < B$	**35.** $D < A$
36. $A > B$	**37.** $C > A$	**38.** $B > D$

Write the integers in order from least to greatest. Draw a number line if you wish.

39. 0, $^{-}4$, $^{-}2$, $^{+}3$	**40.** $^{+}2$, $^{-}2$, $^{+}4$, $^{-}5$	**41.** $^{-}7$, $^{-}10$, $^{-}6$, $^{-}4$
42. $^{-}9$, 0, $^{-}10$, $^{-}5$	**43.** $^{-}3$, $^{-}8$, $^{-}7$, $^{-}2$	**44.** $^{+}5$, $^{-}2$, $^{-}6$, $^{+}6$

Go On

Solve. Draw number lines if you wish.

45. Ice crystals that look like hollow columns first form at $^{-}6$°C. Ice crystals called sector plates look like flowers. Sector plates begin to form at $^{-}10$°C. Which kind of ice crystal forms at the lower temperature?

46. Hollow column ice crystals first form between $^{-}6$°C and $^{-}10$°C. They also form at temperatures lower than $^{-}22$°C. Name three temperatures lower than $^{-}22$°C at which hollow column crystals form.

47. Ice crystals called dendrites look like tree branches. This kind of ice crystal forms between $^{-}12$°C and $^{-}16$°C. Write the integers that are in this temperature range.

48. Use the information in Problems 45–47 to draw and label a number line showing the temperatures at which different kinds of ice crystals begin to form.

49. Create and Solve Use the data given in Problems 45–47 to create your own problem. Solve your problem. Give your problem to a classmate to solve.

50. In January in Barrow, Alaska, normal temperatures range from $^{-}22$°C to $^{-}28$°C. Which is the higher temperature?

51. What's Wrong? Debra drew and labeled the number line at the right. Why is it incorrect? How should she have labeled the number line?

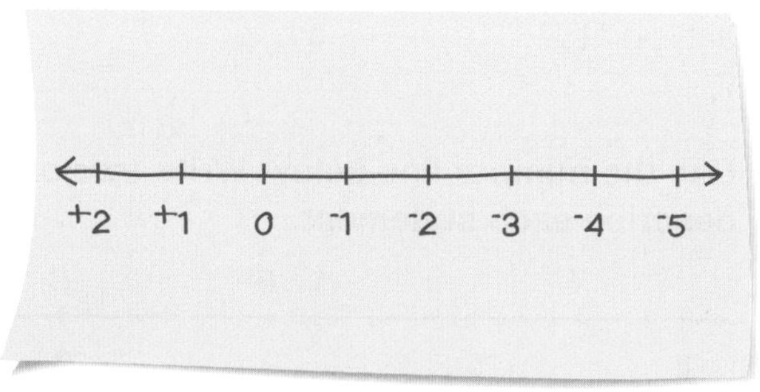

52. Write About It How can drawing a number line help you compare and order integers?

Mixed Review and Test Prep

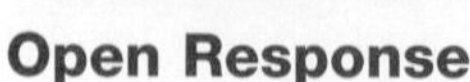

Open Response

Find the percent of the number. Use mental math if you can. (Ch. 19, Lessons 4–5)

53. 10% of 50

54. 5% of \$10

55. 50% of 60

56. 20% of 200

57. 15% of 20

58. 35% of \$60

59. 24% of 90

60. 18% of 7

61. At $^{-}15$°C, water molecules form snowflakes. From $^{-}6$°C to $^{-}4$°C, water molecules make hollow columns. Is the water temperature lower when they form snowflakes or when they form hollow columns? Explain. (Ch. 22, Lesson 2)

Extra Practice See page 607, Set B

Number Sense

Compare and Order Rational Numbers

Rational numbers are numbers that can be expressed in the form $\frac{a}{b}$, where a and b are integers, and b is not zero. Integers, fractions, improper fractions, mixed numbers, and repeating or terminating decimals are all rational numbers.

A number line can be used to order rational numbers just as it is used to order and compare integers and other numbers.

$-\frac{6}{2}$ $-\frac{5}{2}$ $-\frac{4}{2}$ $-\frac{3}{2}$ $-\frac{2}{2}$ $-\frac{1}{2}$ 0 $+\frac{1}{2}$ $+\frac{2}{2}$ $+\frac{3}{2}$ $+\frac{4}{2}$ $+\frac{5}{2}$ $+\frac{6}{2}$

$^{-}3$ $^{-}2.5$ $^{-}2$ $^{-}1.5$ $^{-}1$ $^{-}0.5$ 0 $^{+}0.5$ $^{+}1$ $^{+}1.5$ $^{+}2$ $^{+}2.5$ $^{+}3$

$^{-}2\frac{1}{2} = \frac{^{-}5}{2}$

Order $^{-}1.5$, $\frac{^{+}1}{2}$, and $^{-}2\frac{1}{2}$ from least to greatest.

Locate each number on a number line.

$-\frac{5}{2}$ $-\frac{4}{2}$ $-\frac{3}{2}$ $-\frac{2}{2}$ $-\frac{1}{2}$ 0 $+\frac{1}{2}$ $+\frac{2}{2}$

$^{-}2.5$ $^{-}2$ $^{-}1.5$ $^{-}1$ $^{-}0.5$ 0 $^{+}0.5$ $^{+}1$

Compare the numbers. Use > and <.

- Since $\frac{^{-}5}{2}$ is farthest to the left, $\frac{^{-}5}{2}$ is the least number.
- Since $\frac{^{+}1}{2}$ is farthest to the right, $\frac{^{+}1}{2}$ is the greatest number.

$$\frac{^{-}5}{2} < {^{-}1.5} < \frac{^{+}1}{2}$$

STEP 3

Write the numbers in order from least to greatest.

$$^{-}2\frac{1}{2},\ ^{-}1.5,\ \frac{^{+}1}{2}$$

Order the rational numbers from least to greatest.

1. $\frac{^{-}3}{2}$, $^{+}0.5$, $^{-}1$

2. $\frac{^{+}4}{2}$, $\frac{^{-}4}{2}$, 0

3. $\frac{^{-}2}{2}$, $^{+}1\frac{1}{2}$, $\frac{^{-}1}{2}$

4. $\frac{^{+}1}{2}$, $\frac{^{-}6}{2}$, $^{-}2.5$

5. $^{+}1.5$, $^{-}3$, $^{-}0.5$

6. $\frac{^{-}4}{2}$, $^{-}1$, $^{-}1\frac{1}{2}$

Model Addition of Integers

Materials
For each group:
10 yellow counters
10 red counters

Objective Use counters to model addition of integers.

Work Together

You can use two-color counters to model the addition of integers.

Find $^{-}3 + {}^{+}5$.

STEP 1 Use red counters to represent negative integers.

- Let 3 red counters represent $^{-}3$.

STEP 2 Use yellow counters to represent positive integers.

- Let 5 yellow counters represent $^{+}5$.

STEP 3 Match each red counter to a yellow counter.

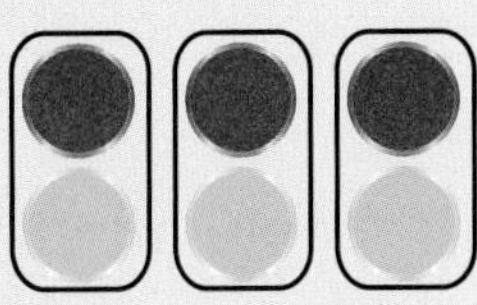

Think
A red (negative) counter and a yellow (positive) counter are a pair of opposite counters. Each pair of opposite counters has a sum of 0.

- How many pairs are there?

STEP 4 The counters that remain represent the sum $^{-}3 + {}^{+}5$.

- How many counters remain?

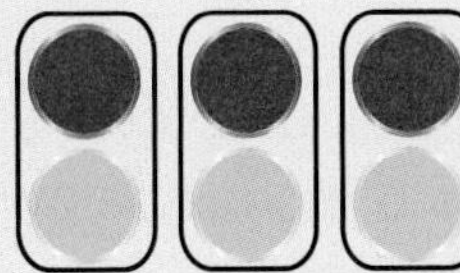

- What color are the remaining counters?

Since 2 yellow counters remain, the sum is positive 2.

$^{-}3 + {}^{+}5 = {}^{+}2$

On Your Own

Write the addition expression shown by the counters and then find the sum.

1.  

2.   

3. 

4. 

5. 

6. 

7. 

8. 

9. 

10. 

Go On

Use two-color counters to find each sum.

11. $^{+}7 + {}^{+}3$ **12.** $^{-}6 + {}^{-}2$ **13.** $^{-}9 + {}^{-}1$ **14.** $^{-}4 + {}^{-}9$

15. $^{-}7 + {}^{+}4$ **16.** $^{-}2 + {}^{+}5$ **17.** $^{+}3 + {}^{-}8$ **18.** $^{-}5 + {}^{+}10$

19. $^{-}5 + {}^{+}3$ **20.** $^{+}7 + {}^{-}6$ **21.** $^{+}8 + {}^{-}8$ **22.** $^{-}4 + {}^{+}5$

Use two-color counters to find each sum. Then compare. Write >, <, or =.

23. $^{-}5 + {}^{+}5 \bigcirc {}^{-}4 + {}^{+}2$ **24.** $^{-}6 + {}^{+}5 \bigcirc {}^{+}3 + {}^{-}4$ **25.** $^{+}9 + {}^{-}3 \bigcirc {}^{-}2 + {}^{+}4$

26. $^{-}6 + {}^{-}1 \bigcirc {}^{+}3 + {}^{-}4$ **27.** $^{-}5 + {}^{-}5 \bigcirc {}^{-}8 + {}^{+}2$ **28.** $^{-}4 + {}^{+}6 \bigcirc {}^{+}4 + {}^{-}6$

Solve.

29. A farmer plants 8 fewer acres of corn than normal. He plants 3 more acres of soybeans instead. Write an integer to represent the change in the number of acres the farmer typically plants.

30. In May, the level of a town's water supply drops 6 inches below normal. In June, it rises 2 inches. At the end of June, how much above or below normal is the water level?

31. **What If?** Suppose in Problem 30 the water level drops 2 inches in July. What integer would represent the number of inches above or below normal the water level is at the end of July?

32. For 6 months, rainfall in an area was 5 inches below normal. During the next 6 months, rainfall was another 3 inches below normal. How many inches below normal is the rainfall in that year?

Talk About It • Write About It

You learned how to use counters to model addition of integers.

33. If you were to combine two sets of yellow counters, what color counter would represent the answer? What does that tell you about the sum of two positive integers?

34. If you were to combine two sets of red counters, what color counter represents the answer? What does that tell you about the sum of two negative integers?

35. When you combine a set of yellow counters and a set of red counters, how can you tell what color counters will represent the answer? What does that tell you about the sum of a positive and a negative integer?

Activity

Math Challenge

Target Practice

Choose one beanbag from each basket so the sum of the three numbers is equal to one of the numbers on the targets.

Use counters to help you.
Do this for all three targets.

Quick Check

Check your understanding for Lessons 1–3.

Write the absolute value of each integer. (Lesson 1)

1. $^{-}5$ **2.** $^{+}4$ **3.** $^{-}6$

Compare. Write >, <, or = for each ●. (Lesson 2)

4. $^{-}3$ ● $^{+}3$ **5.** 0 ● $^{-}1$ **6.** $^{-}4$ ● $^{+}5$

Use red and yellow counters to add. (Lesson 3)

7. $^{+}4 + ^{-}6$ **8.** $^{-}8 + ^{-}1$ **9.** $^{-}5 + ^{+}8$

Solve. (Lesson 3)

10. The water level in a well fell 3 inches from last year to the beginning of this year. Now the water level is up 5 inches from the beginning of the year. Write an integer to represent the water level now as compared to the beginning of last year.

Model Subtraction of Integers

Materials
For each group:
10 yellow counters
10 red counters

Objective Use counters to model subtraction of integers.

Work Together

You can use two-color counters to model the subtraction of integers.

Find $^-6 - {}^-4$.

Use red counters to represent $^-6$.

- What does each counter represent?
- How many counters will you use?

Take away counters to subtract $^-4$.

- How many red counters will you take away?
- What is $^-6 - {}^-4$? How do you know?

Sometimes you may not have enough counters to subtract.

Find $^-5 - {}^+2$.

Use red counters to represent $^-5$.

- How many counters will you place down?

You need to subtract $^+2$ but there are no yellow counters to take away.

STEP 2

Add pairs of red and yellow counters. Each pair represents 0. Adding zero does not change the answer.

- How many pairs do you need to add in order to be able to remove 2 yellow counters?

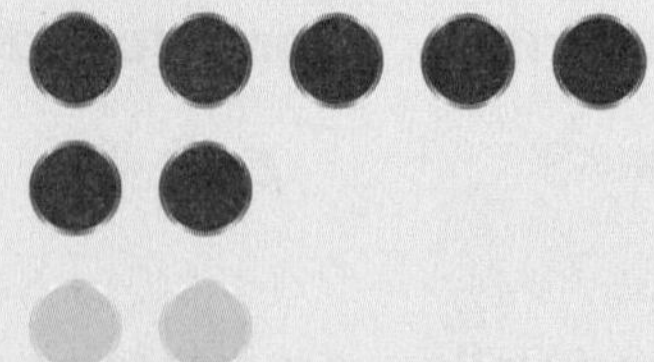

Take away counters to subtract $^+2$.

- How many counters will you take away? What color will they be?

The counters that remain represent the answer.

- How many counters are left?
- What color are they?
- What is $^-5 - {}^+2$?

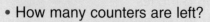

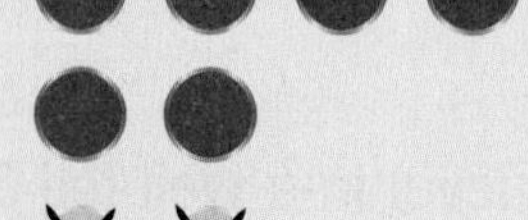
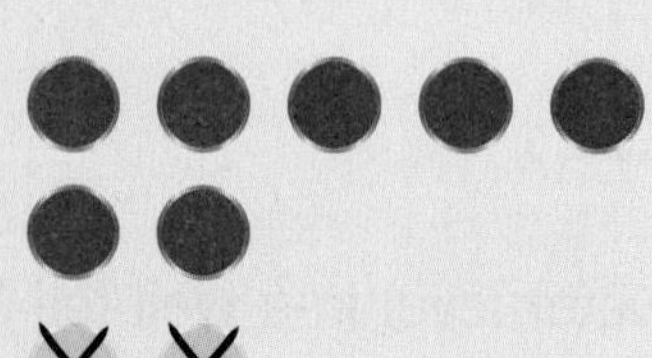

On Your Own

Write a subtraction expression for each. Then find the difference.

1. ● ● ● ● ● ●

   Take away 4 reds.

2. ● ● ● ● ●

   Take away 3 yellows.

3. ● ● ● ●

   Take away 5 reds.

4. ● ● ● ●

   Take away 6 yellows.

5. ● ● ●

   Take away 2 yellows.

6. ● ● ● ● ● ●

   Take away 3 reds.

7. ● ● ● ● ●

   Take away 5 reds.

8. ● ● ●

   Take away 3 yellows.

9. ●

   Take away 3 yellows.

10. ● ●

    Take away 5 reds.

Use two-color counters to find each difference.

11. $^{+}3 - {}^{-}6$
12. $^{+}2 - {}^{-}8$
13. $^{-}2 - {}^{-}6$
14. $^{-}8 - {}^{-}3$
15. $^{-}8 - {}^{-}8$
16. $^{+}8 - {}^{+}4$
17. $^{+}8 - {}^{+}8$
18. $^{-}8 - {}^{+}8$
19. $^{-}4 - {}^{-}4$
20. $^{-}3 - {}^{-}7$
21. $^{+}5 - {}^{-}4$
22. $^{+}2 - {}^{+}7$

Talk About It • Write About It

Use counter models to answer these questions.

23. Find $^{-}3 - {}^{+}4$ and $^{-}3 + {}^{-}4$. Did you get the same result adding the opposite of an integer instead of subtracting?
24. How can you tell if one integer is greater than another integer?
25. If a greater integer is being subtracted from a lesser integer, is the answer positive or is it negative?
26. If a lesser integer is being subtracted from a greater integer, is the answer positive or is it negative?

Lesson 5

Audio Tutor 2/33 Listen and Understand

Add and Subtract Integers

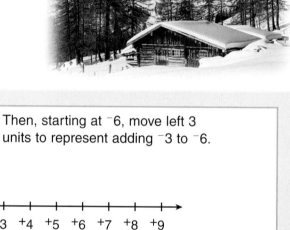

Objective Use a number line to add and subtract integers.

Vocabulary
integers
opposite

Learn About It

Two winters with above-average temperatures caused a decrease in snow cover on a mountain. The snow cover was down 6 inches from normal in one year and down another 3 inches the next year. By how much did the snow cover change during those two years?

You can use a number line to add **integers**.

Find $^{-}6 + {}^{-}3$.

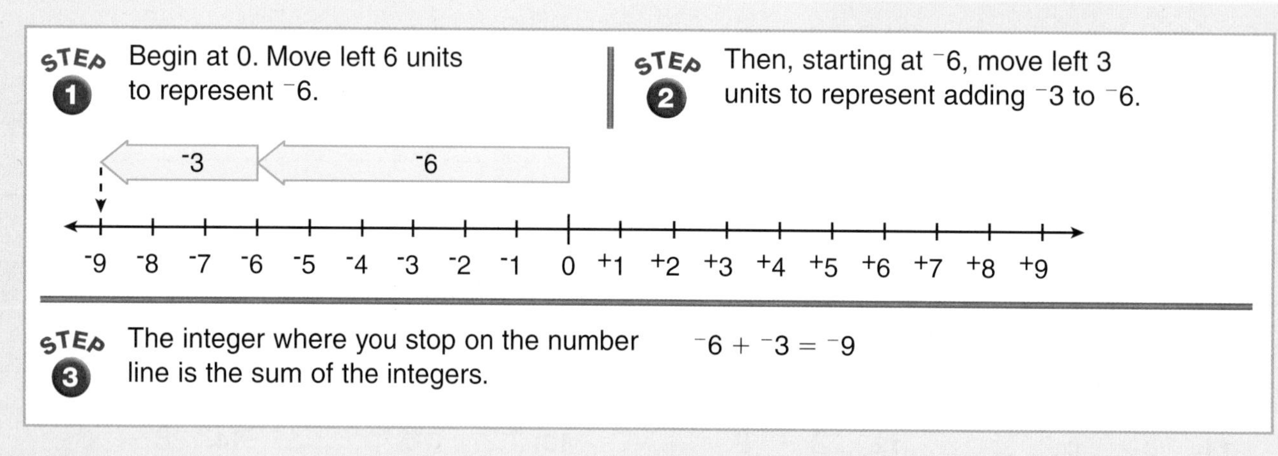

STEP 1 Begin at 0. Move left 6 units to represent $^{-}6$.
STEP 2 Then, starting at $^{-}6$, move left 3 units to represent adding $^{-}3$ to $^{-}6$.
$^{-}3$
$^{-}6$
$^{-}9$ $^{-}8$ $^{-}7$ $^{-}6$ $^{-}5$ $^{-}4$ $^{-}3$ $^{-}2$ $^{-}1$ 0 $^{+}1$ $^{+}2$ $^{+}3$ $^{+}4$ $^{+}5$ $^{+}6$ $^{+}7$ $^{+}8$ $^{+}9$
STEP 3 The integer where you stop on the number line is the sum of the integers.
$^{-}6 + {}^{-}3 = {}^{-}9$

Solution: The snow cover was down 9 inches in the two years.

You can also use a number line to subtract integers.

Find $^{-}7 - {}^{-}5$.

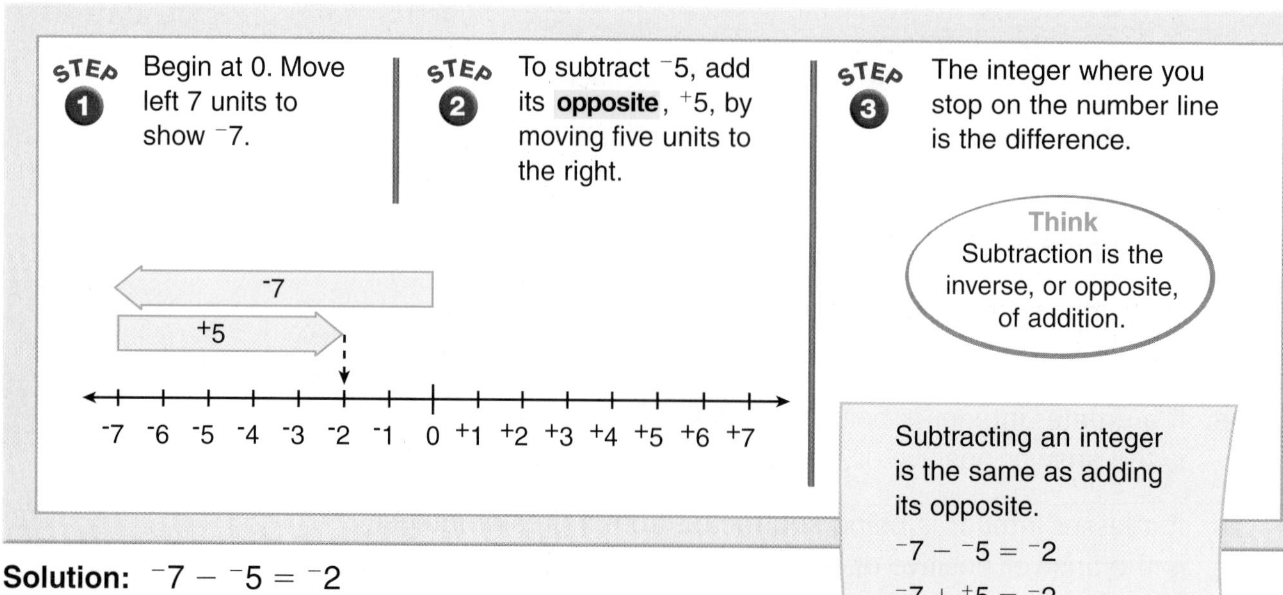

STEP 1 Begin at 0. Move left 7 units to show $^{-}7$.
STEP 2 To subtract $^{-}5$, add its **opposite**, $^{+}5$, by moving five units to the right.
STEP 3 The integer where you stop on the number line is the difference.
Think
Subtraction is the inverse, or opposite, of addition.
$^{-}7$
$^{+}5$
$^{-}7$ $^{-}6$ $^{-}5$ $^{-}4$ $^{-}3$ $^{-}2$ $^{-}1$ 0 $^{+}1$ $^{+}2$ $^{+}3$ $^{+}4$ $^{+}5$ $^{+}6$ $^{+}7$
Subtracting an integer is the same as adding its opposite.
$^{-}7 - {}^{-}5 = {}^{-}2$
$^{-}7 + {}^{+}5 = {}^{-}2$

Solution: $^{-}7 - {}^{-}5 = {}^{-}2$

Before adding or subtracting, you can use these rules to decide whether the sum of two integers will be positive or negative.

The sum of two positive integers is positive.	$^{+}3 - {}^{-}5 = {}^{+}8$ $\mathbf{^{+}3 + {}^{+}5 = {}^{+}8}$
The sum of two negative numbers is negative.	$^{-}3 - {}^{+}5 = {}^{-}8$ $\mathbf{^{-}3 + {}^{-}5 = {}^{-}8}$
The sum of a positive integer and a negative integer will have the same sign as the integer with the greater absolute value.	$^{+}3 - {}^{+}5 = {}^{-}2$ $\mathbf{^{+}3 + {}^{-}5 = {}^{-}2}$ $^{-}3 - {}^{-}5 = {}^{+}2$ $\mathbf{^{-}3 + {}^{+}5 = {}^{+}2}$

Remember
You can change any subtraction expression to addition by adding the opposite.

Other Examples

A. Sum of a Positive and a Negative Integer

Find $^{-}5 + {}^{+}2$.

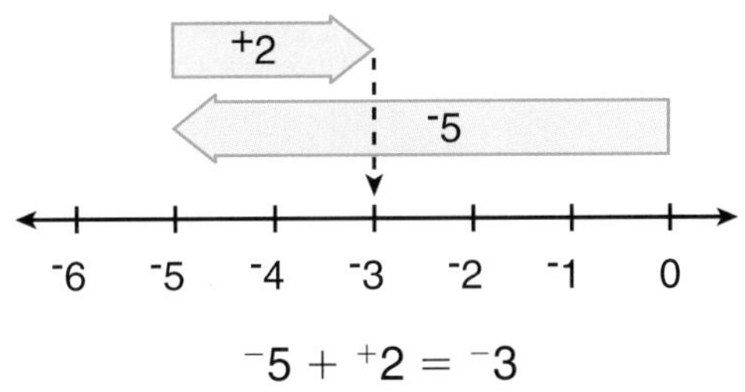

$^{-}5 + {}^{+}2 = {}^{-}3$

B. Sum of Two Negative Integers

Find $^{-}3 + {}^{-}1$.

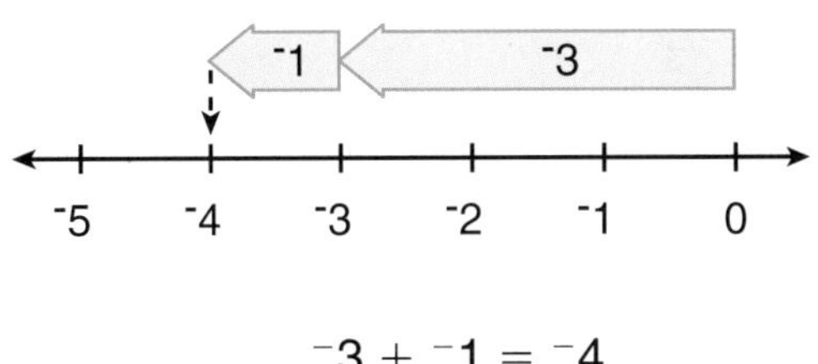

$^{-}3 + {}^{-}1 = {}^{-}4$

C. Difference of Two Negative Integers

Find $^{-}4 - {}^{-}5$.
Write a related addition expression: $^{-}4 + {}^{+}5$.

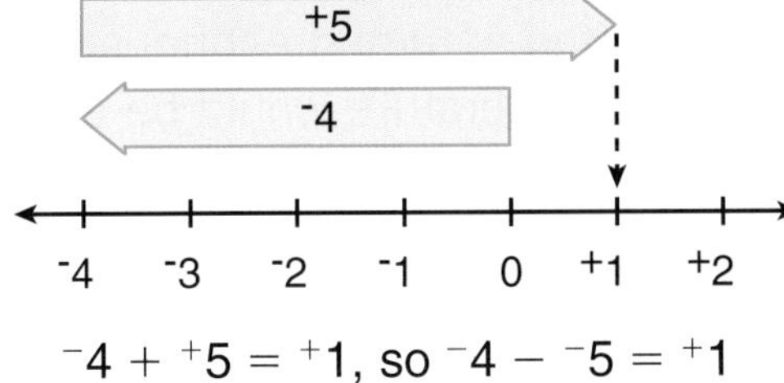

$^{-}4 + {}^{+}5 = {}^{+}1$, so $^{-}4 - {}^{-}5 = {}^{+}1$

D. Difference of Two Positive Integers

Find $^{+}3 - {}^{+}5$.
Write a related addition expression: $^{+}3 + {}^{-}5$.

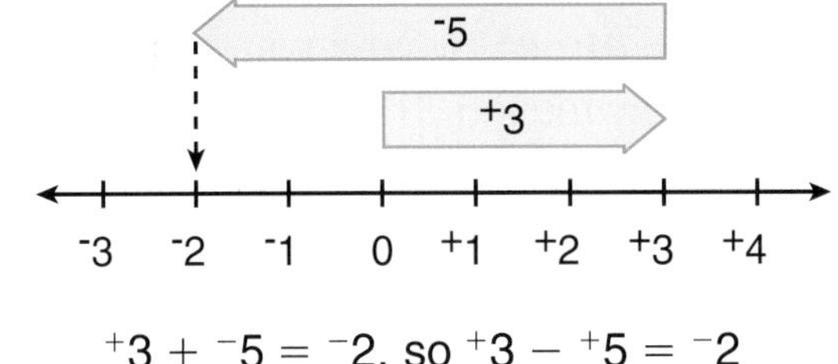

$^{+}3 + {}^{-}5 = {}^{-}2$, so $^{+}3 - {}^{+}5 = {}^{-}2$

Guided Practice

Decide whether the answer will be positive or negative. Then use a number line to add or subtract.

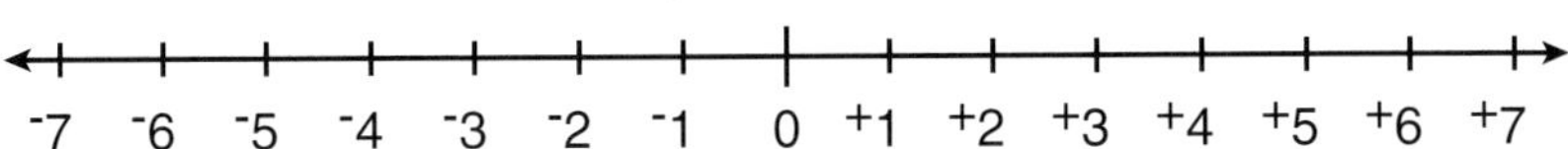

1. $^{+}1 + {}^{+}3$
2. $^{-}4 + {}^{+}2$
3. $^{-}2 + {}^{-}5$
4. $^{-}2 - {}^{-}5$
5. $^{+}3 - {}^{-}4$
6. $^{-}7 - {}^{-}5$

Ask Yourself

- Do I move left or right from 0 for the first integer?
- Can I add the opposite?
- What is the sign of the integer with the greater absolute value?

Explain Your Thinking ▶ Why is subtracting an integer the same as adding its opposite?

Go On

Practice and Problem Solving

Decide whether the answer will be positive or negative. Then use the number line to add or subtract.

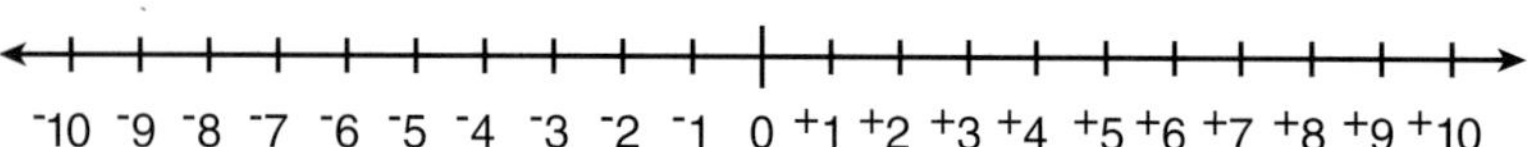

7. $^{+}9 + {}^{-}2$ **8.** $^{+}5 + {}^{+}1$ **9.** $^{-}3 + {}^{+}4$ **10.** $^{+}6 + {}^{-}10$

11. $^{-}1 + 3$ **12.** $^{+}6 - {}^{+}6$ **13.** $^{-}7 + {}^{+}9$ **14.** $^{+}2 - {}^{-}5$

15. $^{-}7 - {}^{-}2$ **16.** $^{-}10 - {}^{-}6$ **17.** $^{-}1 - 0$ **18.** $^{-}9 - {}^{-}9$

Algebra • Equations Solve each equation. Use a number line to help you.

19. $^{-}4 - {}^{-}4 = \blacksquare$
$^{-}4 + {}^{+}4 = \blacksquare$

20. $^{+}8 - {}^{+}3 = \blacksquare$
$^{+}8 + {}^{-}3 = \blacksquare$

21. $^{+}7 - {}^{-}2 = \blacksquare$
$^{+}7 + {}^{+}2 = \blacksquare$

22. $^{+}10 - {}^{-}3 = \blacksquare$
$^{+}10 + {}^{+}3 = \blacksquare$

23. $^{-}9 - {}^{+}4 = \blacksquare$
$^{-}9 + {}^{-}4 = \blacksquare$

24. $^{-}12 - {}^{-}5 = \blacksquare$
$^{-}12 + {}^{+}5 = \blacksquare$

25. $^{-}11 + x = {}^{-}13$ **26.** $x + {}^{+}4 = {}^{-}8$ **27.** $^{+}8 + x = {}^{+}14$

28. $x + {}^{-}2 = {}^{-}4$ **29.** $x + {}^{-}2 = {}^{+}4$ **30.** $x - {}^{-}2 = {}^{-}4$

Solve.

31. Write About It On a warm day, 5 inches of snow melted. That night a storm brought 10 inches of snow. If there is now 20 inches of snow, how much snow was there in the beginning? Explain.

32. Without the natural greenhouse effect, Earth's temperature would be a frigid $^{-}18$°C. Instead, the global temperature is 33°C higher than $^{-}18$°C. What is Earth's temperature?

Mixed Review and Test Prep

Open Response

Use the GCF to write each ratio in simplest form. (Ch. 18, Lesson 2)

33. $\frac{16}{48}$ **34.** 20:30

35. 15 to 5 **36.** $\frac{19}{26}$

37. 7:31 **38.** $\frac{81}{9}$

39. 60:6 **40.** 3:300

Multiple Choice

41. You earn \$6 and spend \$5. Then you earn \$4 more and spend \$5. Which of these does NOT tell you how much you have? (Ch. 22, Lesson 5)

A $({}^{+}6 - {}^{+}5) + ({}^{+}4 - {}^{+}5)$

B $({}^{+}6 - {}^{-}5) + ({}^{+}4 - {}^{-}5)$

C $({}^{+}6 + {}^{-}5) + ({}^{+}4 + {}^{-}5)$

D $({}^{+}6 + {}^{+}4) - ({}^{+}5 + {}^{+}5)$

Extra Practice See page 607, Set C.

Activity

Number Sense

Back Track

Start with $^{+}1$. Add as you move to each number. Find a path that leads to each sum. Can you find different solutions?

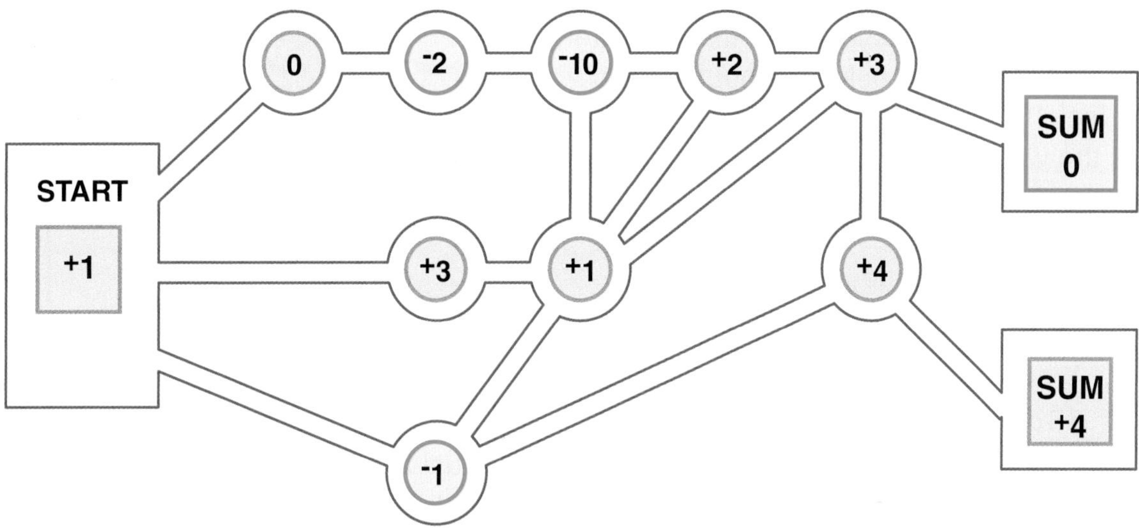

Logical Thinking

Funny Forecast

"This is the hottest day of the year, folks! It's nine degrees warmer than on the same day last year, which was fifteen degrees warmer than yesterday. Get out your swimsuits and sunscreen! This isn't going to last long. Rain is moving in tomorrow, bringing the temperature down about five degrees to 85°F."

What was the temperature yesterday?

Write your own funny forecast for a partner to solve.

Brain Teaser

Find the missing signs to make the number sentence true.

$$\square 1 - \square 2 + \square 3 < {}^{-}4$$

Ask Yourself

- How can I find all the possible choices?

Education Place

Check out **eduplace.com/map** for more Brain Teasers.

Lesson 6

Problem-Solving Application

Use Integers

Objective Solve problems that include integers.

*The wind cools your skin and you feel colder than the actual temperature. This is called **wind chill.***

You can use integers to solve problems.

Problem When Alma stepped outside, the wind was blowing at 5 miles per hour, which made the actual temperature of 10°F feel 9° colder. Ten minutes later, the wind was blowing at 20 miles per hour, which made Alma feel 10° colder than when she first stepped out. What is the wind chill temperature now?

UNDERSTAND

What is the question?

What is the wind chill temperature that Alma feels now?

What do you know?

- The actual temperature is 10°F.
- At first, the wind chill was 9° less than the actual temperature.
- Now the wind chill is 10° less than when Alma first went outside.

PLAN

Record actual temperatures above 0°F as positive integers. Record temperature drops as negative integers. Then find the total change in temperature.

SOLVE

- Find the temperature after the first change of $^{-}9°$.

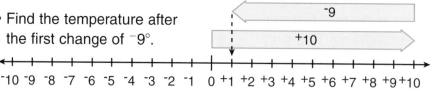

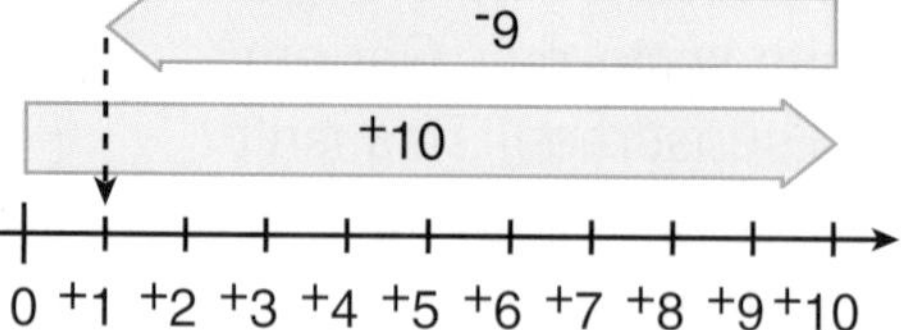

$$^{+}10 + {}^{-}9 = {}^{+}1$$

- Find the wind chill now.

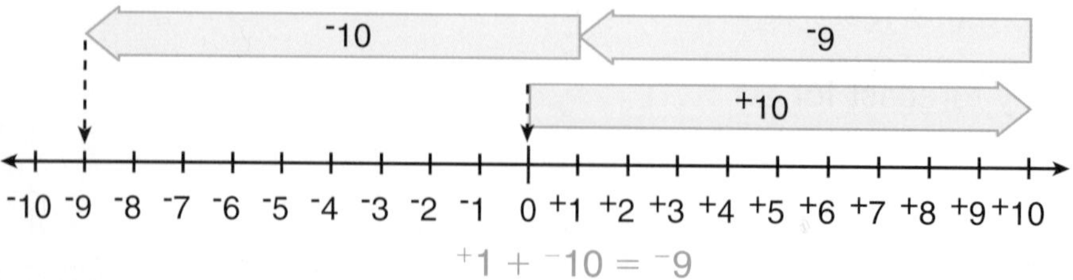

$$^{+}1 + {}^{-}10 = {}^{-}9$$

Solution: The wind chill temperature now is $^{-}9$°F.

LOOK BACK

Look back at the problem. How can you check your answer?

Guided Practice

Use the Ask Yourself questions to help you solve each problem.

1. Use an integer to describe the rise and fall of temperatures, in degrees Fahrenheit, represented by the integers $^{-}3$, $^{+}4$, 0.

2. One day the temperature went up 8° and then down 12°. If the final temperature is $^{-}31$°F, what was the temperature at first?

   Hint How do you record temperatures that go up and those that go down?

Ask Yourself

UNDERSTAND **What does the question ask me to find?**

PLAN **Did I record the correct information?**

SOLVE

- **Did I use positive and negative integers?**
- **Did I use a number line or counters to solve?**

Did I check my answer by working through the problem?

Independent Practice

Solve. Use a number line to help you.

3. At halftime, the temperature was 17° lower than at the start of the game. By the end, the temperature was 6° higher than at halftime. The temperature at the end was $^{-}16$°F. Find the temperature at the start of the game.

4. At a certain temperature, unprotected skin will get frostbitten in 30 minutes. If the temperature drops 26° to $^{-}48$°F, that will cause frostbite in 5 minutes. At what temperature will unprotected skin get frostbitten in 30 minutes?

5. At 6:00 A.M., the temperature was $^{-}5$°F. By noon of the same day, the temperature was 6°F. How many degrees did the temperature change in 6 hours?

6. At the beginning of the day, the temperature was $^{+}2$°F. During the day, the temperature rose 4° and then dropped 10°. What was the temperature at the end of the day?

7. **What's Wrong?** Roberta left the note below for her father. What did Roberta do wrong? What should she have written?

Dad,
Temperature now: $^{-}3$°
Going down to $^{-}12$° tonight.
That's 15° colder than now.
Roberta

Mixed Problem Solving

Solve. Show your work. Tell what strategy you used.

8. Antarctica's climate is the harshest on Earth. The record low temperature there was about 70°F lower than the mean temperature of ⁻58°F. Is ⁻130°F a reasonable estimate for the record temperature? Explain.

9. A liquid lake lies miles below Antarctica's ice sheet. Lake Vostok is 250 kilometers long, 40 kilometers wide, and 0.4 kilometers deep. What is the lake's volume?

10. Jacqui, Ajay, Terri, and Mason are having a race. Jacqui is not riding a bike or roller-skating. Terri is on a skateboard. Mason will not roller-skate or use a scooter. Match each person with the correct mode of transportation.

You Choose

Strategy
- Make a Table
- Solve a Simpler Problem
- Use Logical Reasoning
- Work Backward
- Write an Equation

Computation Method
- Mental Math
- Estimation
- Paper and Pencil
- Calculator

Data The table below shows wind chill temperatures for actual temperatures from ⁺15 to ⁻10°F. Use the table to solve Problems 11–14. Then explain which method you chose.

11. At which actual temperature does the wind chill temperature drop 11°F, then drops 5°, 3°, 3°, and 2° as the winds change from 0 miles per hour to 25 miles per hour?

12. Predict What would be a reasonable prediction for the wind chill temperature at 10°F if the wind speed is 60 miles per hour?

13. An old wind chill formula gave a wind chill index for ⁺5°F and a 5 mi/h wind that was about 5° higher than in this table. What was that wind chill index?

Wind Chill Index

Wind (mi/h)	Temperature (°F)					
0	+15	+10	+5	0	⁻5	⁻10
5	7	1	⁻5	⁻11	⁻16	⁻22
10	3	⁻4	⁻10	⁻16	⁻22	⁻28
15	0	⁻7	⁻13	⁻19	⁻26	⁻32
20	⁻2	⁻9	⁻15	⁻22	⁻29	⁻35
25	⁻4	⁻11	⁻17	⁻24	⁻31	⁻37
30	⁻5	⁻12	⁻19	⁻26	⁻33	⁻39
35	⁻7	⁻14	⁻21	⁻27	⁻34	⁻41
40	⁻8	⁻15	⁻22	⁻29	⁻36	⁻43

Number Sense
Patterns With Integers

You can find and use patterns with integers.

Find the rule and the missing term for this pattern: $^{-}19$, $^{-}15$, $^{-}11$, $^{-}7$, $^{-}3$, ■

Way 1: Use computation.

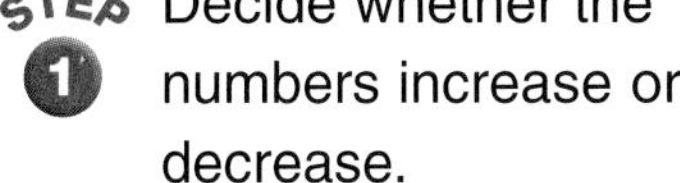

STEP 1 Decide whether the numbers increase or decrease.

The integers in this pattern increase.

STEP 2 Find a rule for the pattern.

$^{-}19 + \text{what integer} = {}^{-}15$?

$^{-}19 + {}^{+}4 = {}^{-}15$

Try adding $^{+}4$ to each term.

$^{-}15 + {}^{+}4 = {}^{-}11$

$^{-}11 + {}^{+}4 = {}^{-}7$

$^{-}7 + {}^{+}4 = {}^{-}3$

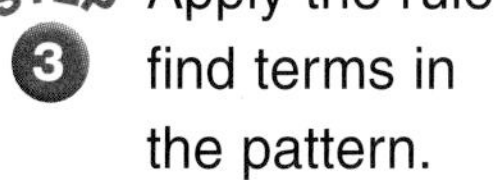

STEP 3 Apply the rule to find terms in the pattern.

$^{-}3 + {}^{+}4 = {}^{+}1$

Solution: The rule is to add $^{+}4$. The missing term is $^{+}1$.

Way 2: Use a Number Line.

STEP 1 Circle all the numbers in the pattern along the number line.

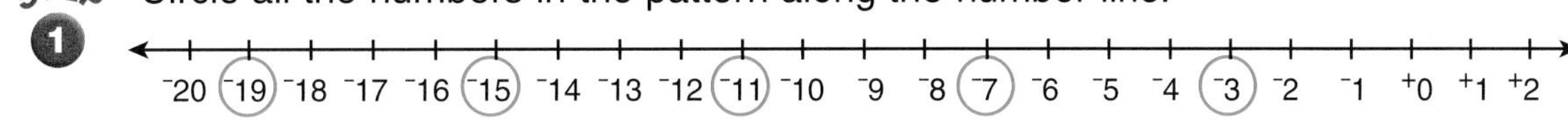

STEP 2 Draw line segments between the numbers in the pattern starting with the first number in the pattern and find the distance between the numbers. Use that distance to find the next number in the pattern.

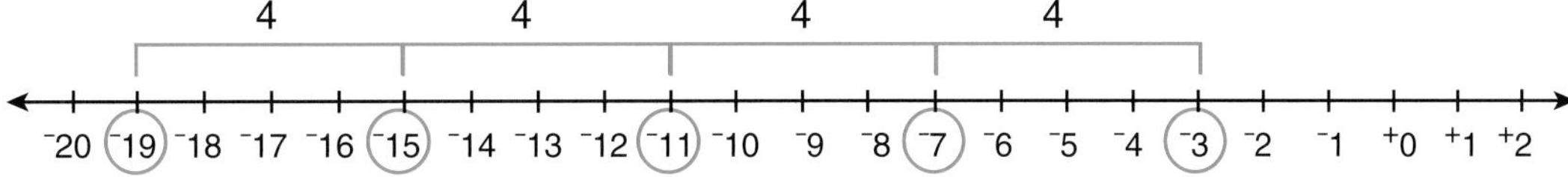

Solution: The distance is 4. The missing term is $^{+}1$.

Write the rule and name the missing term in the pattern.

1. 0, ■, $^{-}10$, $^{-}15$, $^{-}20$, $^{-}25$

2. $^{+}12$, $^{+}8$, $^{+}4$, 0, $^{-}4$, $^{-}8$, $^{-}12$, ■

3. $\frac{11}{2}$, $\frac{9}{2}$, $\frac{7}{2}$, $\frac{5}{2}$, $\frac{3}{2}$, $\frac{1}{2}$, ■

4. $^{-}4.5$, $^{-}3$, $^{-}1.5$, ■, $^{+}1.5$, $^{+}3$

 Chapter Review/Test

VOCABULARY

1. Counting numbers, their opposites, and zero are called _____.

2. Numbers to the left of 0 on a number line are called _____.

3. The distance of a number from 0 on a number line is the _____ of that number.

Vocabulary

absolute value

integers

negative numbers

opposite

positive numbers

CONCEPTS AND SKILLS

Write the opposite of each integer. Then write the absolute value of each integer. (Lesson 1, pp. 586–587)

4. $^{-}98$	**5.** $^{+}75$	**6.** $^{+}629$	**7.** $^{-}52$
8. $^{-}31$	**9.** $^{-}163$	**10.** $^{+}312$	**11.** $^{+}98$

Draw a number line from $^{-}10$ to $^{+}10$ and label each integer. Write >, <, or = for each ●. (Lesson 2, pp. 588–591)

12. $^{-}9$ ● $^{-}4$	**13.** $^{+}3$ ● $^{-}1$	**14.** $^{-}6$ ● $^{+}4$	**15.** $^{+}2$ ● $^{-}10$

Decide whether the answer will be positive or negative. Then use the number line to add or subtract. (Lessons 3–5, pp. 592–601)

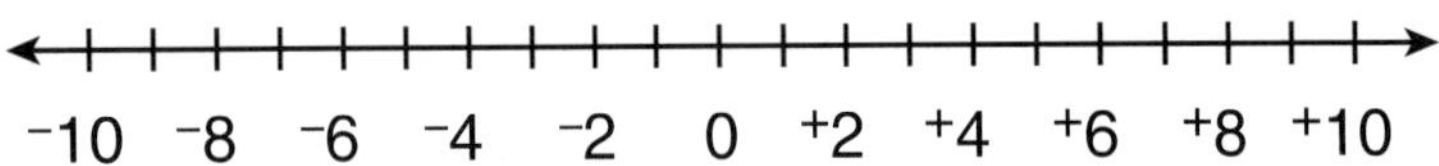

16. $^{-}9 + {}^{+}6$	**17.** $^{+}7 - {}^{-}2$	**18.** $^{-}8 - {}^{+}1$	**19.** $^{-}3 - {}^{-}1$

PROBLEM SOLVING

Solve. Use a number line to help you.
(Lesson 6, pp. 602–605)

20. At noon on Monday, the temperature was $^{-}2$°F. By 6:00 P.M., the temperature had risen 10°. By midnight, the temperature had fallen 8°. What was the temperature at midnight?

Show You Understand

From looking at the absolute value of an integer, can you tell whether that integer is positive or negative? Explain.

Extra Practice

Set A (Lesson 1, pp. 586–587)

Write the opposite of each integer. Then write the absolute value of each integer.

1. $^{+}5$ 2. $^{-}7$ 3. $^{+}17$ 4. $^{+}89$ 5. $^{-}45$

6. $^{-}72$ 7. $^{+}100$ 8. $^{-}36$ 9. $^{-}29$ 10. $^{+}55$

11. $^{-}10$ 12. $^{+}31$ 13. $^{-}127$ 14. $^{+}66$ 15. $^{-}64$

Set B (Lesson 2, pp. 588–591)

Draw a number line from $^{-}8$ to $^{+}8$ and label each integer. Write $>$, $<$, or $=$ for each ●.

1. $^{+}4$ ● 0 2. $^{+}3$ ● $^{+}5$ 3. $^{-}2$ ● $^{-}5$ 4. $^{-}6$ ● 0

5. $^{-}8$ ● $^{+}8$ 6. $^{-}5$ ● $^{-}4$ 7. $^{+}1$ ● $^{-}2$ 8. $^{+}6$ ● $^{+}7$

Write the integers in order from least to greatest.

9. 0, $^{+}7$, $^{-}5$, $^{-}3$ 10. $^{+}5$, $^{+}8$, $^{-}4$, $^{-}5$ 11. $^{-}2$, 0, $^{+}6$, $^{-}1$

12. $^{-}4$, $^{-}8$, $^{+}5$, $^{+}2$ 13. $^{-}5$, 0, $^{+}5$, $^{-}7$ 14. $^{+}3$, $^{-}1$, $^{-}3$, $^{+}1$

Set C (Lesson 5, pp. 598–601)

Decide whether the answer will be positive or negative. Then use the number line to add or subtract.

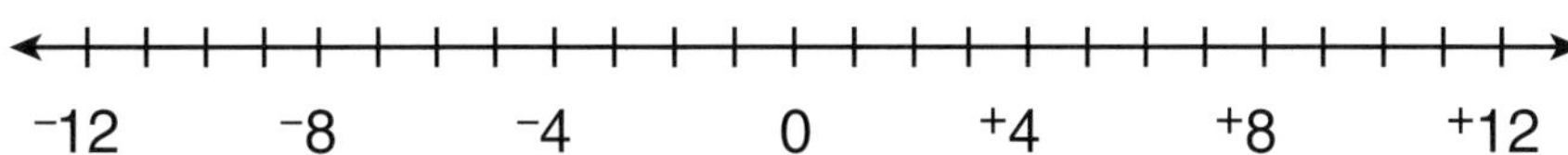

1. $^{+}4 + ^{+}5$ 2. $^{+}6 + ^{-}8$ 3. $^{-}11 + ^{+}7$ 4. $^{-}6 + ^{-}2$

5. $^{+}9 - ^{+}6$ 6. $^{-}4 - ^{-}2$ 7. $^{+}5 - ^{-}3$ 8. $^{-}7 - ^{+}5$

9. $^{+}10 - ^{-}2$ 10. $^{-}8 + ^{+}3$ 11. $^{+}6 + ^{-}5$ 12. $^{-}4 - ^{+}4$

13. $^{+}9 + ^{-}9$ 14. $^{+}2 - ^{+}8$ 15. $^{-}7 - ^{-}5$ 16. $^{-}8 + ^{+}9$

Extra Practice at **eduplace.com/map**

Coordinate Graphing

INVESTIGATION

Use Data

The constellation Cassiopeia looks like a giant "W" or "M". The coordinate graph shows the locations of the major stars in Cassiopeia. Which star is located at ($^{+}2$, $^{-}1$)? Describe a path from Caph to the point closest to Epsilon, moving only horizontally or vertically on the coordinate plane.

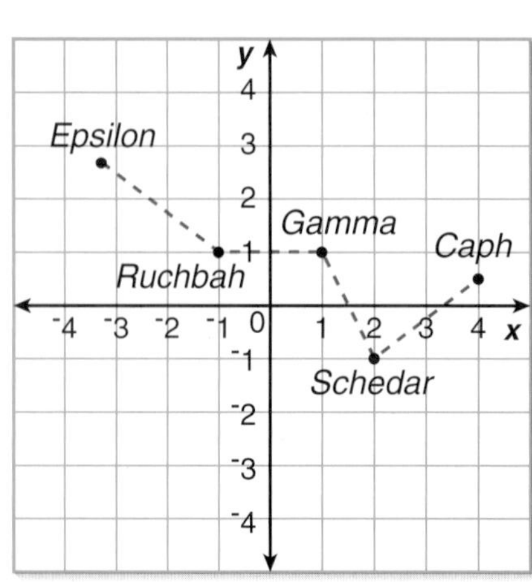

Use What You Know

Use this page to review and remember what you need to know for this chapter.

VOCABULARY

Choose the best word to complete each sentence.

1. The number $^{+}5$ is a ____ number.
2. A(n) ____ is a rule that gives exactly one value of y for each value of x.

Vocabulary
- function
- ordered pair
- opposite
- positive

CONCEPTS AND SKILLS

Compare. Use the number line. Write >, <, or = for each ●.

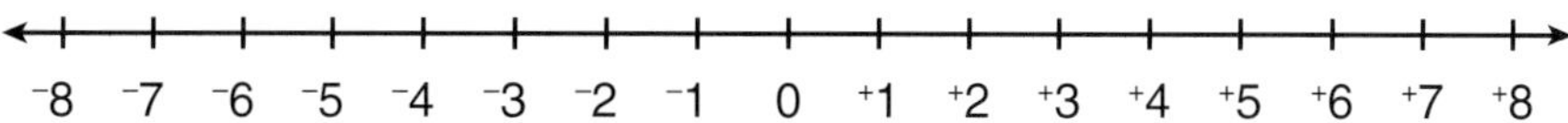

3. $^{-}8$ ● $^{-}6$
4. 0 ● $^{-}5$
5. $^{+}3$ ● $^{-}7$

Add or subtract. You may use the number line above if you wish.

6. $^{+}4 + {}^{-}8$
7. $^{+}1 - {}^{-}3$
8. $^{-}5 + {}^{+}5$
9. $^{-}2 - {}^{+}6$

Write About It

10. Describe the pattern in the values of x and y in the function table below.

x	y
4	18
5	15
6	12
7	9

Facts Practice, See page 659.

Audio Tutor 2/34 Listen and Understand

Integers and the Coordinate Plane

Objective Graph ordered pairs in the four quadrants of the coordinate plane.

Vocabulary
- coordinate plane
- *x*-axis
- *y*-axis
- quadrant
- ordered pair
- origin
- coordinates

Materials
grid paper

Learn About It

Constellations are groups of stars that appear together in the sky. You can portray constellations on a **coordinate plane**.

A coordinate plane is formed by two perpendicular lines called axes, that lie in the plane. The horizontal axis is called the ***x*-axis**. The vertical axis is called the ***y*-axis**. These axes divide the plane into 4 **quadrants**, numbered I, II, III, and IV.

Some of the stars for the constellation Hercules are mapped on the coordinate plane at the right.

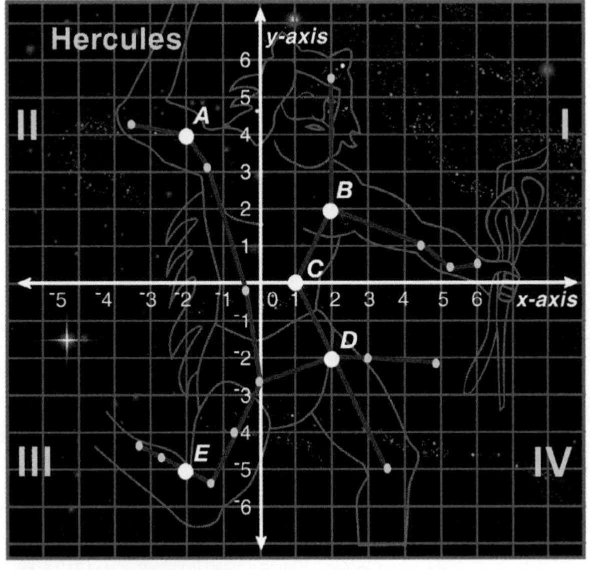

Constellation Hercules

What is another way to describe the location of the star at point *A*?

You can describe any location on the plane by using an **ordered pair** (x, y). The point named by the ordered pair (0, 0) is the **origin**.

- To reach point *A*, move left from the origin to $^-2$ and up to $^+4$.
- The numbers $^-2$ and $^+4$ are the **coordinates** of point *A*.

Solution: The location of the star at *A* is given as $(^-2, ^+4)$ in Quadrant II.

Other Examples

A. Point in Quadrant IV

- Point *D* is in Quadrant IV.
- To reach point *D*, start at the origin. Move right 2 units and down 2 units.
- Point *D* is at $(^+2, ^-2)$.

B. Distance Between Points

- Point *A* is at $(^-2, 4)$ and point *E* is at $(^-2, ^-5)$.
- For two points, if the *x*-coordinates or the *y*-coordinates are the same, you can count to find the distance between those two points.
- The distance between *A* and *E* is 9 units.

Here is how to use ordered pairs to represent the major stars in the constellation Volans, or the Flying Fish.

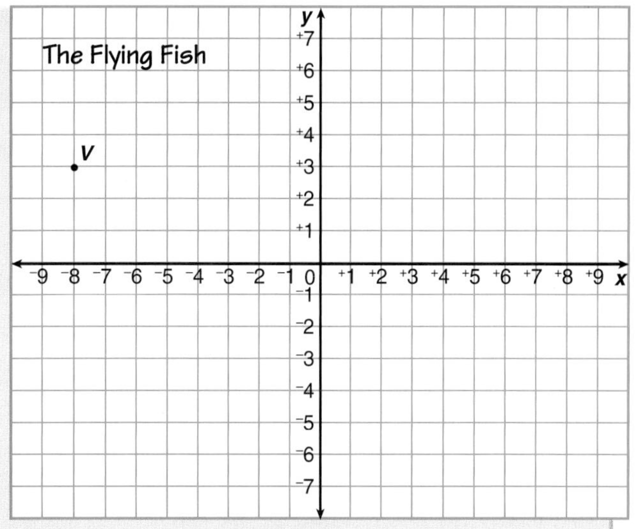

Plot the star located at point $V\,(^-8, ^+3)$.

- Start at the origin (0, 0).
- Go left to $^-8$ and up to $^+3$.
- Mark a point at $(^-8, ^+3)$. Label it V.

To plot the other stars in Volans, copy the graph and use these ordered pairs.

$(^+3, ^-3)$ → (right 3, down 3) → point A
$(^+6, ^+3)$ → (right 6, up 3) → point N
$(0, ^+2)$ → (no move, up 2) → point L
$(^-3, ^+4)$ → (left 3, up 4) → point O
$(^+7, ^-1)$ → (right 7, down 1) → point S

Remember
Always start at the origin. Move left or right along the x-axis first, then up or down along the y-axis.

Guided Practice

Ask Yourself

- Do I move left or right from 0 to find the x-coordinate?

Use the coordinate plane below for Exercises 1–6.

Write the ordered pair for each point.

1. L **2.** M **3.** N

Write the letter name of each point.

4. $(^+4, ^+5)$ **5.** $(^-3, 0)$ **6.** $(^-4, ^-2)$

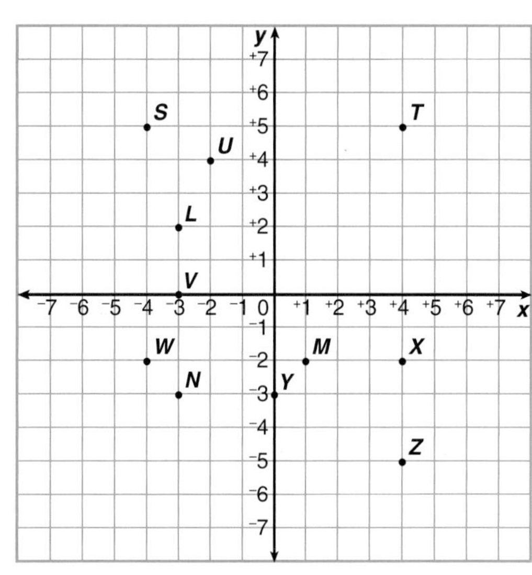

Use the coordinates to plot each point. Label each point with its letter.

7. $A\,(^-2, ^+3)$ **8.** $B\,(^+2, ^+2)$

9. $C\,(^-1, ^+1)$ **10.** $D\,(^-4, ^-1)$

Find the distance between each pair of points.

11. X and Z **12.** W and M

Explain Your Thinking ▶ Is the location $(^-2, ^+3)$ the same as $(^+3, ^-2)$? Why or why not?

Practice and Problem Solving

Use the graph of the Big Dipper and Little Dipper asterisms for Exercises 13–24. Write the ordered pair for each point.

13. *B* **14.** *D*

15. *F* **16.** *I*

17. *K* **18.** *L*

The Little Dipper

North Star

The Big Dipper

Write the letter name of each point.

19. $(^-8, ^-1)$ **20.** $(^-3, ^-4)$

21. $(^-2, ^-7)$ **22.** $(^+3, ^-6)$

Find the distance between each pair of points.

23. *G* and *H* **24.** *Z* and *F*

Use grid paper. Plot points using the coordinates for stars in the constellation called the Whale, or the Sea Monster. Label each point with its letter.

25. $A\ (^-12, ^+5)$ **26.** $B\ (^-11, ^+8)$ **27.** $C\ (^-9, ^+8)$ **28.** $D\ (^-9, ^+4)$ **29.** $E\ (^-8, ^+2)$

30. $F\ (^-4, 0)$ **31.** $G\ (0, ^-4)$ **32.** $H\ (^+4, ^-4)$ **33.** $I\ (^+10, ^-5)$ **34.** $J\ (^+7, ^-9)$

35. $K\ (^-2, ^-10)$ **36.** $L\ (^-11, ^-4)$ **37.** $M\ (^+1, ^-7)$ **38.** $N\ (^+6, ^-5)$

39. Connect points *A*–*L* in order. Then connect *L* to *E* and *M* to *J*. Can you see the whale? Which point represents the eye of the whale?

Algebra • Expressions **Use grid paper. Plot each point when $m = 2$ and $n = 3$.**

40. $P\ (m + 1, n - 2)$ **41.** $Q\ (m - 5, n + 6)$ **42.** $R\ (m - 8, n - 3)$ **43.** $S\ (m + 7, n + 5)$

Solve.

44. Write About It Draw your own constellation on grid paper. List the ordered pairs. Write instructions for drawing your constellation.

46. The constellations Taurus, Cygnus, and Draco look like a swan, a dragon, and a bull. Cygnus is not a bull or a dragon. Taurus is not a dragon. Match each constellation to its animal.

45. What pattern can you find in this group of ordered pairs: $(0, 0)$, $(^+1, ^+2)$, $(^+2, ^+4)$, $(^+3, ^+6)$, $(^+4, ^+8)$, $(^+5, ^+10)$?

47. The coordinates of each point in Quadrant I are always positive: $(+, +)$. Write rules for the coordinates in Quadrants II, III, and IV. Explain why your rules work.

Extra Practice See page 627, Set A.

Mixed Review and Test Prep 

Open Response

Evaluate each expression, when $a = 2$, $b = 4$, and $c = 3$. Write >, <, or = to compare. (Ch. 5, Lesson 6)

48. $2 \times (b - a)$ ● $(a + b) \div c$

49. $(b \times c) \div a$ ● $(10 \div a) + a$

Multiple Choice

50. In which quadrant would the ordered pair ($^{-}3$, $^{+}2$) appear? (Ch. 23, Lesson 1)

A I

B III

C II

D IV

Game

Activity

Where's the Spaceship?

2 Players

What You'll Need • grid paper • colored pencils

How to Play

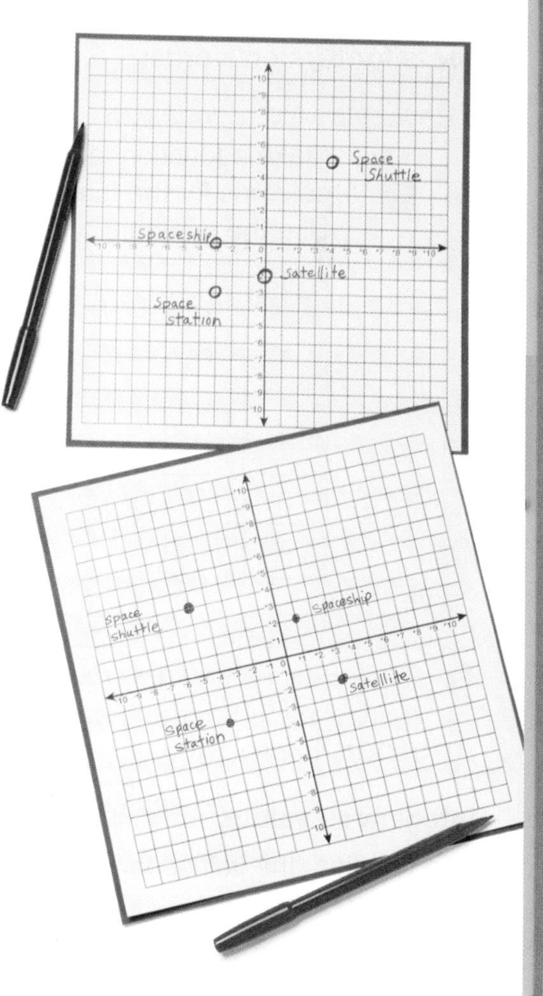

1. Each player draws a coordinate plane on a sheet of grid paper and labels the *x*-axis from $^{-}10$ to $^{+}10$ and the *y*-axis from $^{-}10$ to $^{+}10$.

2. Each player marks the location of 4 spacecraft on the graph without showing the other player. Each spacecraft should be located at a different pair of coordinates.
   - Satellite
   - Spaceship
   - Space shuttle
   - Space station

3. The object of the game is to find each other's spacecraft. Players take turns naming coordinates to try to locate the other player's spacecraft.

4. After each attempt, tell the player if the spacecraft was located or give a hint by telling whether the spacecraft is above, below, to the left of, or to the right of the named point.

The first player to find all the other player's spacecraft wins the game.

Lesson 2

Audio Tutor 2/35 Listen and Understand

Integers and Functions

Vocabulary
function

Objective Use a function rule to find the value of ordered pairs.

Learn About It

You learned that a **function** relates the value of two variables, such as x and y. For each value of x, there is exactly one related value of y.

Kirsten ordered some space posters. Each poster cost \$2, and there was a shipping charge of \$3 per order.

The total cost of Kirsten's order is a function of the number of posters she orders. She can use the equation $y = 2x + 3$, where x is the number of posters ordered.

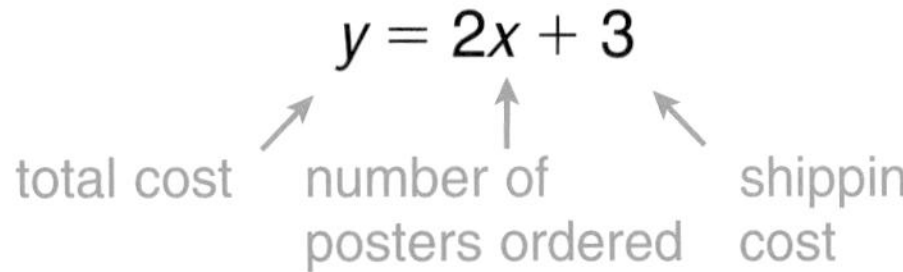

Make a function table to show the possible total costs for Kirsten's order.

STEP 1 Make a function table with x and y columns for the function $y = 2x + 3$. Use the numbers 1 through 4 for x.

$y = 2x + 3$	
x	y
1	
2	
3	
4	

STEP 2 Substitute each value of x into the function to find the value of y.

$y = 2x + 3$		
x	y	
1	5	$(2 \times 1) + 3 = 2 + 3$
2	7	$(2 \times 2) + 3 = 4 + 3$
3	9	$(2 \times 3) + 3 = 6 + 3$
4	11	$(2 \times 4) + 3 = 8 + 3$

Positive 5 can be written as $^{+}5$ or 5

Another Example

Integers as values

In a function, the values for x and y also can be negative.

Substitute to find y.

$y = x - 6$		
x	y	
10	4	$10 - 6$
6	0	$6 - 6$
2	$^{-}4$	$2 - 6$
$^{-}2$	$^{-}8$	$^{-}2 - 6$

Think
$2 + {}^{-}6$
${}^{-}2 + {}^{-}6$

Extra Help at **eduplace.com/map**

Guided Practice

Complete the function table.

1. Function: $y = 3 - x$

x	y
$^{-}2$	5
$^{-}1$	■
0	■

2. Function: $y = 2x$

x	y
3	6
5	■
10	■

Ask Yourself

- Did I substitute the correct value for the variable?
- Can I see a pattern that will help me find the rule?

Explain Your Thinking ▶ Why is it helpful to organize the x- and y-values in a function table?

Practice and Problem Solving

Complete the function table.

3. $y = x + 5$

x	y
$^{-}2$	■
$^{-}1$	■
0	■
1	■

4. $y = x - 5$

x	y
3	■
4	■
5	■
6	■

5. $y = 5x$

x	y
3	■
2	■
1	■
0	■

Solve.

6. The cost for souvenir star charts is $12 each plus $5 shipping per order. Make a table to show the total cost for ordering 1, 2, 3, 4, or 5 charts.

7. Together Bob and Deb scored 28 points. Bob scored 4 more points than Deb. How many points did each person score?

8. Kirk puts money in his savings account each month and his father then adds $5. Write a function to describe how much money is put in the account each month.

9. Who will win the game? Jodi started with 17 points, lost 6, and gained 4. Sara started with 11 points, gained 8, and lost 2.

Mixed Review and Test Prep

Open Response

Multiply or divide. (Ch. 12, Lessons 2–3, 5–6)

10. $\frac{2}{3} \times \frac{1}{2}$

11. $10\frac{4}{5} \times \frac{3}{4}$

12. $6 \div \frac{2}{3}$

13. $2\frac{1}{4} \div \frac{3}{4}$

14. The function $a = e + {}^{-}4$ expresses Anne's age (a) in terms of Earl's age (e). How old will Anne be when Earl is 27? Explain how you found your answer. (Ch. 23, Lesson 2)

Extra Practice See page 627, Set B.

Lesson 3

Use Functions and Graphs

Objective Graph an equation on a coordinate plane.

Learn About It

You can use both a function table and a graph to show the corresponding *x*- and *y*-values of a function rule.

In the last lesson, you saw that $y = 2x + 3$ shows the total cost (y) for the number of posters (x) that Kirsten ordered.

You can graph $y = 2x + 3$ to show the possible total costs for different orders.

$y = 2x + 3$		**Ordered Pair**
x	**y**	
1	5	(1, 5)
2	7	(2, 7)
3	9	(3, 9)

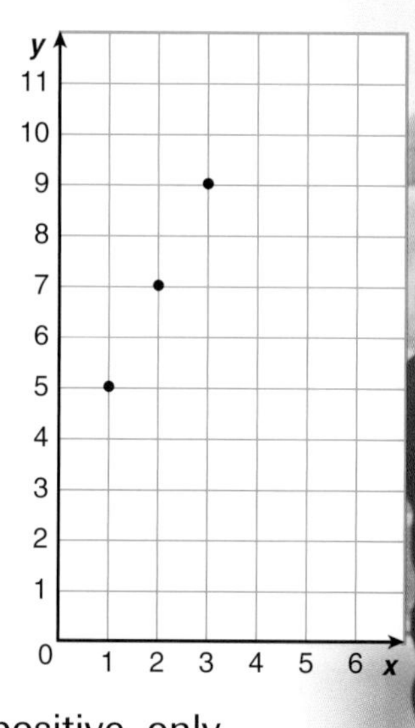

Notice that since all values for *x* and *y* are positive, only the first quadrant of the coordinate plane is shown.

Since you can only buy a whole number of posters, *x* must be a whole number. So only points are graphed.

You can also graph functions that involve negative numbers. To do that, you need to show all quadrants of the coordinate plane.

Graph the equation $y = x - 2$ on a coordinate plane.

STEP 1 Make a function table.

Rule: $y = x - 2$	
x	**y**
$^{-}3$	$^{-}5$
$^{-}2$	$^{-}4$
$^{-}1$	$^{-}3$
0	$^{-}2$
1	$^{-}1$

STEP 2 Graph each ordered pair.

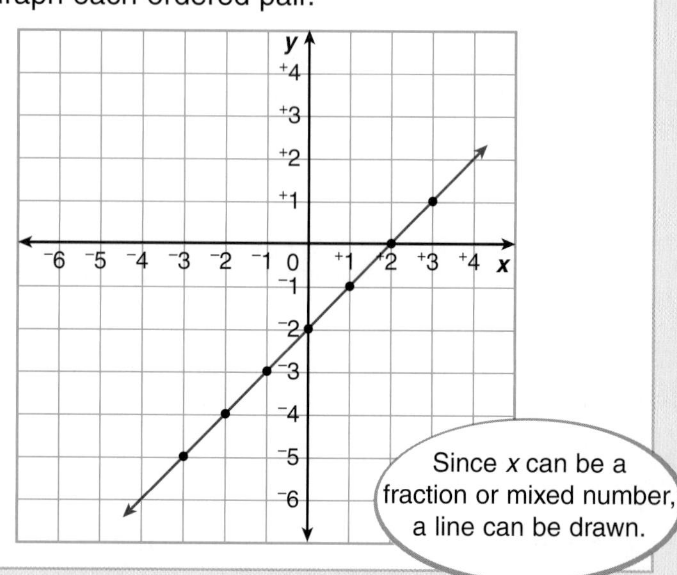

You can also use the graph of a function to predict what other pairs may be included in the function.

Graph the equation $y = x - 2$ on a coordinate plane, using the values $^{-}2$ to 2 for x. Use the graph to predict the value of y when $x = 5$.

STEP 1 Make a function table.

Rule: $y = x - 2$	
x	y
$^{-}2$	$^{-}4$
$^{-}1$	$^{-}3$
0	$^{-}2$
1	$^{-}1$
2	0

STEP 2 Graph each ordered pair.

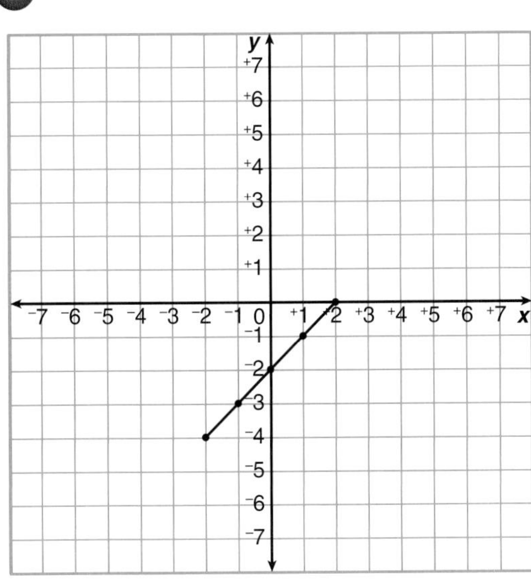

STEP 3 Extend the line. Read the y value where the line crosses the x value 5.

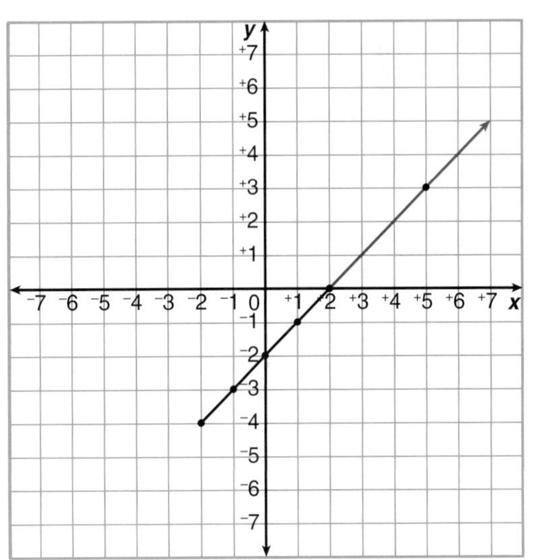

Solution: For $y = x - 2$, when x is 5, y is 3.

Guided Practice

Find values of y to complete each function table. Then graph each function on grid paper.

1. $y = x - 2$

x	y
$^{-}1$	■
0	■
3	■

2. $y = x + 3$

x	y
$^{-}1$	■
0	■
1	■

3. $y = 2x - 1$

x	y
0	■
1	■
2	■

Ask Yourself

- Did I substitute each value for x in the equation to find y?
- Did I graph the equation as a straight line?

Explain Your Thinking ▶ How could extending the graph in Exercise 3 help you find the value for y when $x = {^{-}2}$?

Practice and Problem Solving

Find values of *y* to complete each function table. Then graph each equation as a straight line on grid paper.

4. $y = x - 1$

x	y
$^{-}2$	■
$^{-}1$	■
0	■
1	■

5. $y = x + 4$

x	y
$^{-}3$	■
$^{-}2$	■
$^{-}1$	■
0	■

6. $y = 3x - 2$

x	y
0	■
1	■
2	■
3	■

7. $y = 3x + 1$

x	y
0	■
1	■
2	■
3	■

Find three ordered pairs for each function. Then use them to graph the function as a straight line.

8. $y = x + 1$ **9.** $y = x - 4$ **10.** $y = x + 6$ **11.** $x - 5 = y$

12. $y = 2x$ **13.** $y = 4x$ **14.** $y = 3x - 1$ **15.** $y = 2x + 2$

Solve.

16. Graph $y = 2x$ and $y = 4x$ as straight lines on the same coordinate plane. How are the graphs alike? How are they different?

17. Write About It Graph $y = x - 2$ and $y = x + 2$ as straight lines on the same coordinate plane. How are the graphs alike? How are they different?

18. Explain how you can use the graph at the beginning of this lesson to find how much it would cost Kirsten for 8 posters.

19. Plot 3 or more points in a straight line on a coordinate plane. Find an equation for the line. Ask a partner to check the equation.

Mixed Review and Test Prep

Open Response

Multiply or divide. (Ch. 13, Lessons 2–5; Ch. 14, Lessons 4–7)

20. 8×0.8 **21.** 0.4×0.05

22. $4 \div 0.8$ **23.** $2.8 \div 0.07$

Multiple Choice

24. Which of these ordered pairs is not a solution for $y = 4x + 2$? (Ch. 23, Lesson 3)

A (1, 4) **C** (0, 2)

B ($^{-}1$, $^{-}2$) **D** (1, 6)

Extra Practice See page 627, Set C.

Problem Solving

Social Studies Connection

Where in the U.S.A.?

Mapmakers use a system very similar to a coordinate grid to identify positions of places on Earth. Latitude 0° is at the equator. Latitudes are North (N) or South (S) of the equator.

Longitude 0° passes through Greenwich, England. Longitudes are either West (W) or East (E) of 0°.

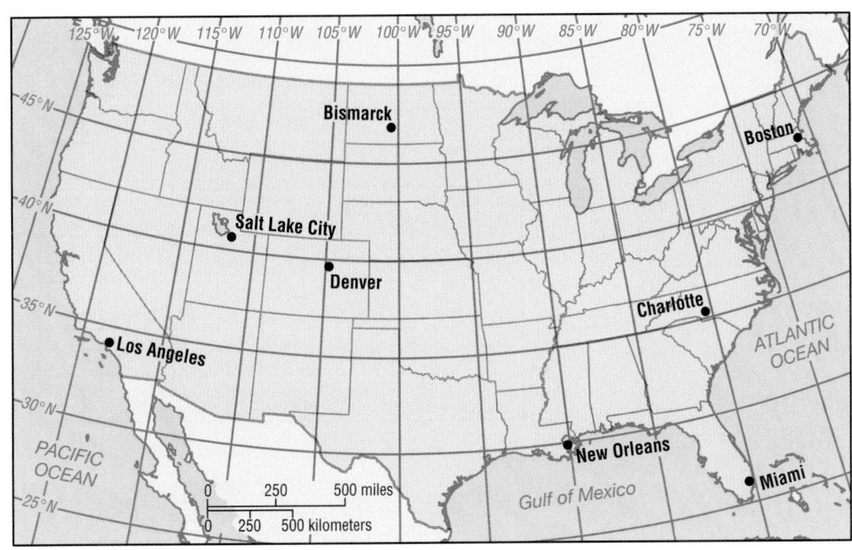

Estimate the latitude and longitude for each city.

1. Boston, MA
2. New Orleans, LA
3. Denver, CO
4. Los Angeles, CA
5. Use a map or an atlas. Find the latitude and longitude for where you live.

Find what city is nearest each location.

6. 25°N, 80°W
7. 45°N, 100°W
8. 40°N, 110°W
9. 35°N, 80°W

10. Explain the differences and similarities of locating and labeling a point on the coordinate plane and locating and labeling a city on a map.

WEEKLY WR READER eduplace.com/map

Quick Check

Check your understanding of Lessons 1–3.

Write the ordered pair for each point. (Lesson 1)

1. *W*
2. *X*
3. *Y*

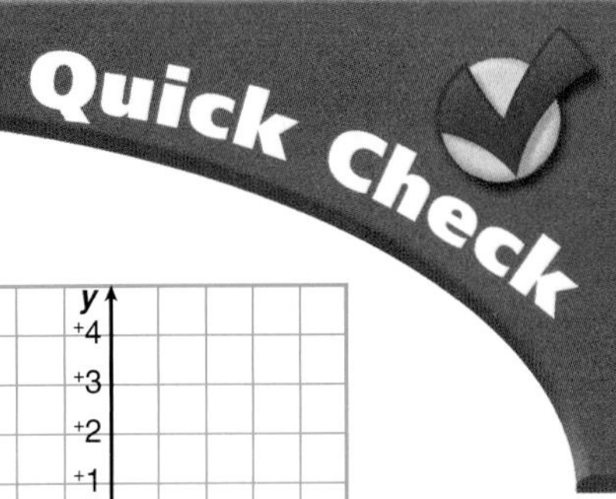

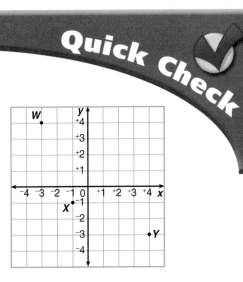

Make a table for each function. Use $x = 0, 1, 2,$ and 3. Write the ordered pairs and then graph the function. (Lessons 2 and 3)

4. $y = x - 4$
5. $y = 2x$
6. $y = 2x + 1$

Lesson 4

Problem-Solving Application

Use a Graph

Objective Use graphs to solve problems.

Sometimes you need to read the data in a graph to solve a problem.

How long does it take light to travel the mean distance of 93,000,000 miles from the Sun to Earth?

The original graph is shown in black. Since 93,000,000 miles is not shown on the graph, the graph was extended as shown in red.

Think: 93 million miles is between 90 million and 100 million miles.

A line is drawn horizontally from about 93,000,000 miles until it meets the graph. Then a vertical line is drawn to find the time.

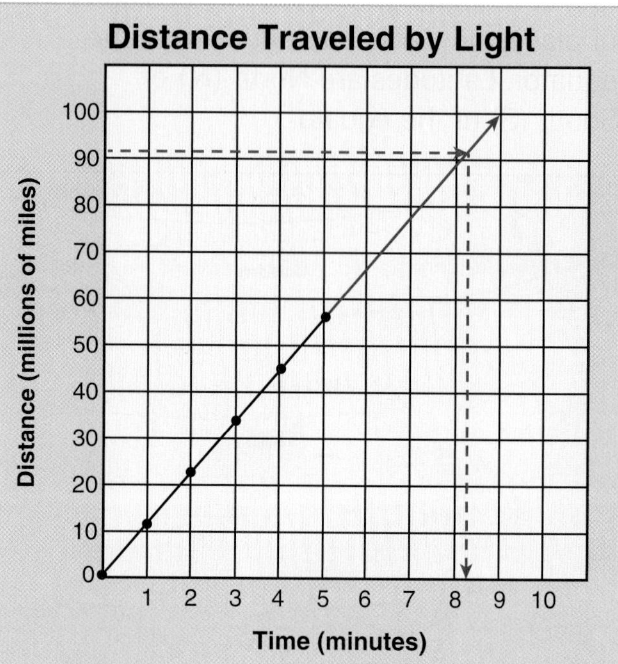

Solution: It takes about $8\frac{1}{2}$ minutes for light to travel from the Sun to Earth.

Sometimes you need to display data in a graph to help you solve a problem.

One planetarium uses the table at the right to determine the cost for a group to see a show. How much would it cost for a group of 9 people?

Number of People (*x*)	Cost (*y*)
2	$7
3	$9
4	$11

STEP 1 Use the table to write ordered pairs. (2, 7); (3, 9); (4, 11)

STEP 2 Graph the given coordinates.

STEP 3 Extend the graph with coordinates for 5 through 9 people, as shown in red.

Solution: The cost for 9 people is $21.

Since you cannot have part of a person, only the points are graphed for counting numbers 2 through 9.

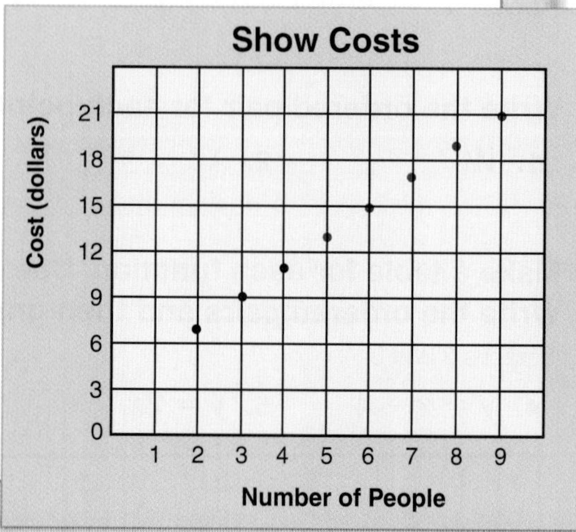

Guided Practice

Use the graphs and the table on page 620 for Problems 1–2.

1. It takes light about 6 minutes to reach Venus from the Sun. About how far from the Sun is Venus?

2. Using the data from the table and its graph, write an equation that relates the number of people to the total cost of admission for the group.

   Hint The equation is $y = (\blacksquare \cdot x) + \blacksquare$. Look at the graph. If you extend the graph to the y-axis, what is the value of y for $x = 0$?

Ask Yourself

- What do I need to find?
- What patterns do I see?

Independent Practice

Solve.

3. The gift shop at the planetarium marks up the cost of model solar systems as shown in the table. Write an equation to show how to find the store price (y) of any model solar system at cost x.

4. Solve the equation you wrote in Problem 3 to find the store price for a model that costs $120.

Cost	Store Price
$20	$40
$25	$50
$30	$60
$35	$70

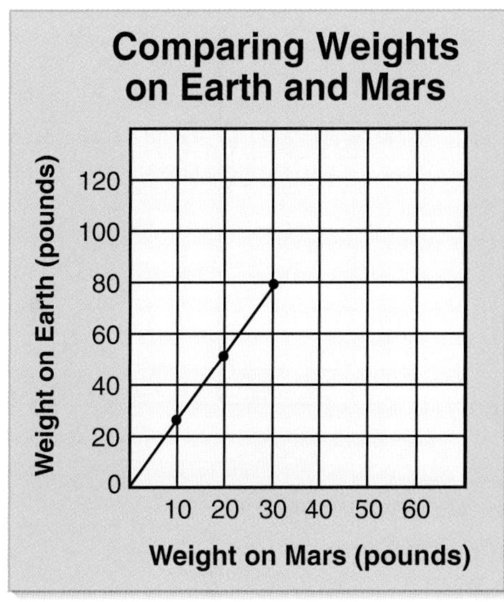

5. The graph at the left shows the relationship between an object's weight on Earth and its weight on Mars. Suppose a rock weighs 15 pounds on Mars. About how much would that same rock weigh on Earth?

6. On Earth an astronaut weighs 118 pounds. About how much would that astronaut weigh if she landed on Mars?

7. Martha says that the equation representing the data in the graph is $y = 4x$. If y is the weight on Earth and x is the weight on Mars, is Martha correct? Explain your reasoning.

Transformations in the Coordinate Plane

Objective Identify and describe transformations in the coordinate plane.

Vocabulary
translation
transformation
reflection
rotation

Materials
coordinate grid
scissors

Learn About It

On Miranda's map, her home is at point (0, 0). She leaves home and walks west 3 blocks and north 5 blocks. Where is she? What **translations** take her to this point? Remember that a translation slides a point or figure a given distance in a given direction.

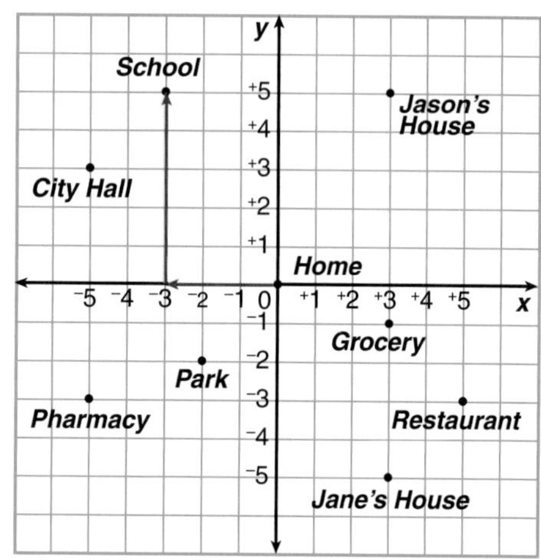

Find Miranda's location after moving 3 blocks west and 5 blocks north.

After walking 3 blocks west, Miranda is at point $(^-3, 0)$. Walking 5 blocks north puts her at $(^-3, ^+5)$.

Solution: Miranda is at her school.

Try this activity to translate figures and points on a coordinate plane.

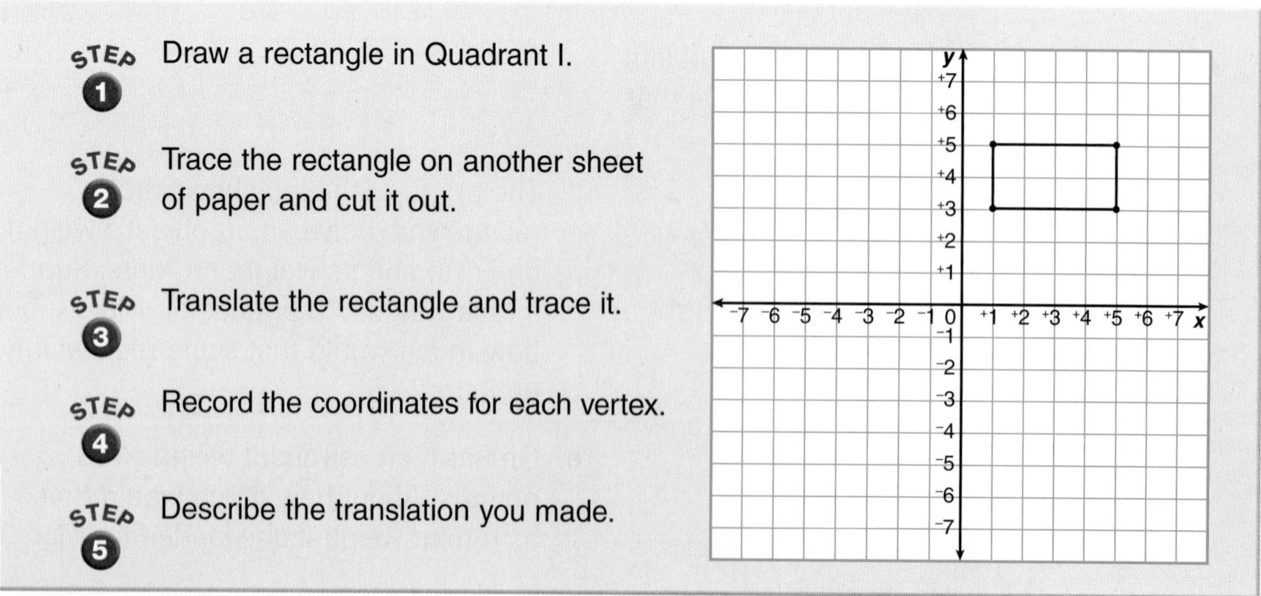

STEP 1 Draw a rectangle in Quadrant I.

STEP 2 Trace the rectangle on another sheet of paper and cut it out.

STEP 3 Translate the rectangle and trace it.

STEP 4 Record the coordinates for each vertex.

STEP 5 Describe the translation you made.

A **transformation** is a change in the position of a figure on a graph. Transformations include translations, **reflections**, and **rotations**.

Reflections and Line Symmetry

▶ A **reflection** is a flip of a figure that results in a mirror image.

Name the coordinates of points *A* and *B* after a reflection across the *y*-axis.

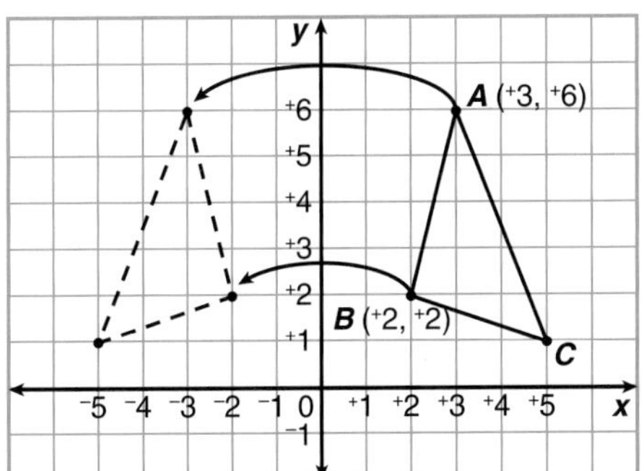

Reflect each vertex across the *y*-axis. The new points will be the same distance to the left of the *y*-axis as *A* and *B* are to its right.

The new points will be (⁻3, 6) and (⁻2, 2).

Use a reflection to decide whether the figure has line symmetry.

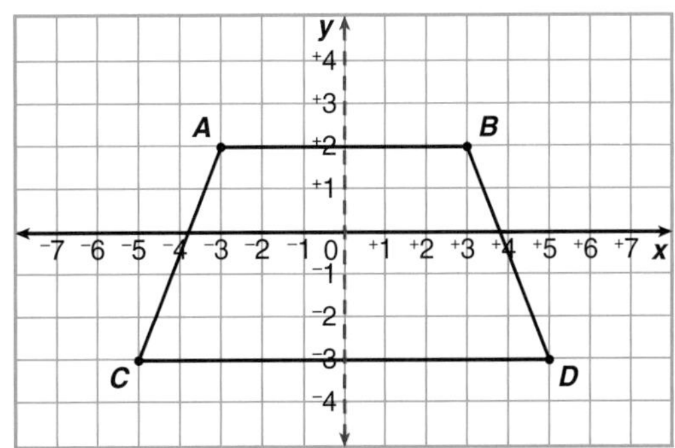

If an axis is a line of symmetry, then either its *x*- or *y*- coordinates will be opposites.

Point *A* (⁻**3**, 2) is opposite Point *B* (**3**, 2).

Point *C* (⁻**5**, ⁻3) is opposite Point *D* (**5**, ⁻3).

Rotations and Rotational Symmetry

▶ A **rotation** is a turn around a given point.

Name the coordinates of point *A* after a half-turn around the origin.

$\frac{1}{4}$ turn = 90° $\frac{1}{2}$ turn = 180°

$\frac{3}{4}$ turn = 270°   1 turn = 360°

Trace the axes, mark point *A,* and turn the tracing 180°.

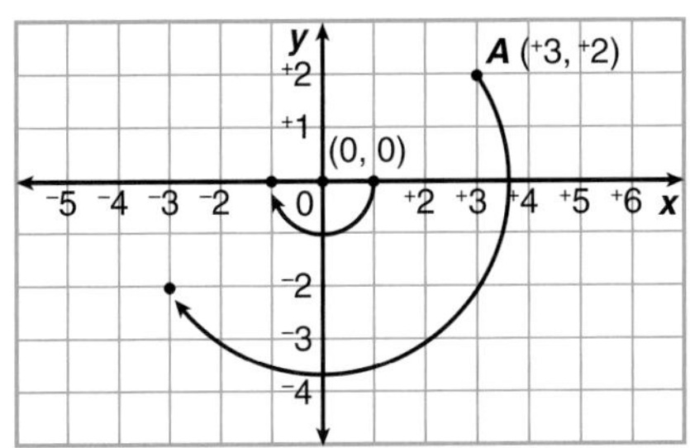

After the rotation, the new point is (⁻3, ⁻2.)

A figure has rotational symmetry if it looks exactly the same after being rotated less than 360° around a center point. When the figure turns 90°, it looks the same. The figure has rotational symmetry.

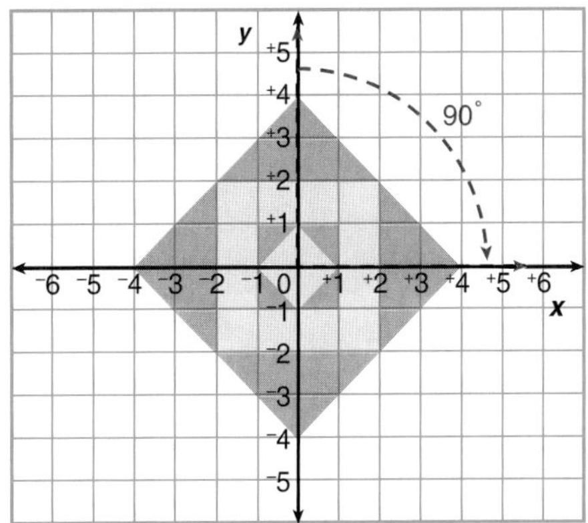

Go On

Guided Practice

Ask Yourself

- Did I move each point in the correct direction?

Use the diagram. Name the coordinates of triangle *LMN* after the transformations.

1. Translate the triangle left 3 units, then down 1 unit.

2. Reflect the triangle over the *x*-axis.

3. Rotate the triangle a $\frac{3}{4}$ turn about (0, 0).

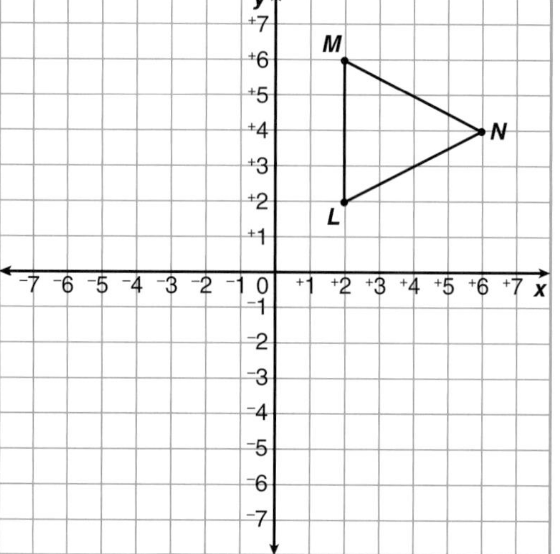

Write *line, rotational,* or *both* to describe the symmetry of the figure.

4. 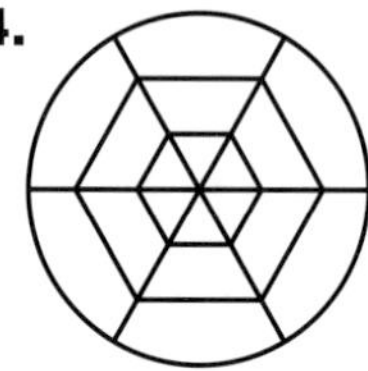

5. 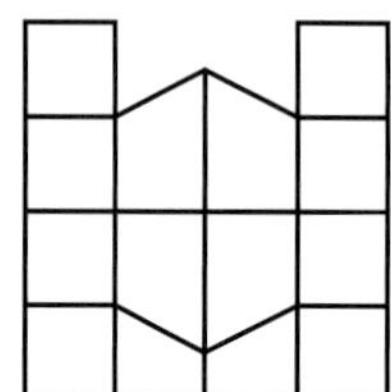

Explain Your Thinking ▶ Does a transformation change the shape of the original figure? Explain.

Practice and Problem Solving

Use the diagram. Name the coordinates of triangle *RST* after each transformation.

6. Translate right 4, then down 1.

7. Reflect over the *y*-axis.

8. Rotate a $\frac{1}{4}$ turn clockwise about (0, 0).

9. Reflect over the *y*-axis. Then rotate counterclockwise a quarter turn around (0, 0).

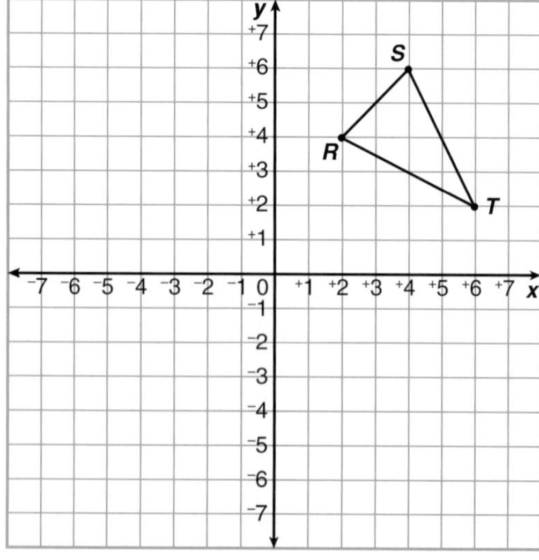

Write *line, rotational,* or *both* to describe the symmetry of each figure.

10. 

11. 

12. 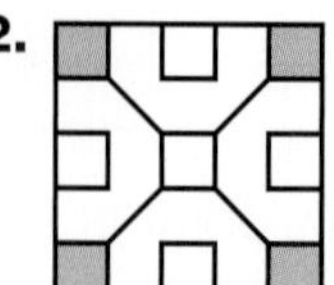

13. Triangle *ABC* was translated left 3 units and up 1 unit. It ended up at *A*(2, 4), *B*(2, 6), and *C* (6, 6). What were the original coordinates?

Extra Practice See page 627, Set D.

Mixed Review and Test Prep 

Open Response

Simplify. (Ch. 5, Lesson 6)

14. $(7 + 19) - 3^2$

15. $20 + 8^2 - (15 + 10)$

16. $4 + 3 \times 6 - 12$

17. $(15 - 8) \times (24 \div 6)$

18. $5 \times 3 + 6^3$

19. $18 + 2 \times 5 - 3$

20. $15 - 2^2 + 6$

21. $(10 + 8) \times 2 \div 12$

22. $9 \times (10 - 2) + 3$

23. $30 - 5 \times 4 - 2$

24. $(19 - 9) \times 3^2$

25. $7^2 - 2 \times 8 + 27$

26. If you rotate trapezoid *MNOP* 180° counterclockwise, what would be its new coordinates? (Ch. 23, Lesson 5)

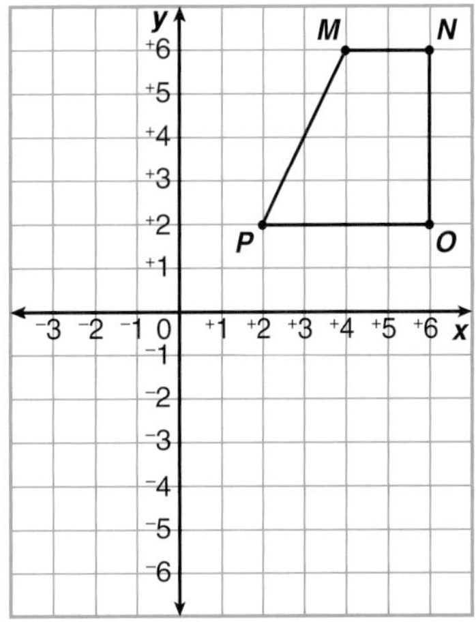

Problem Solving

Visual Thinking

Trans Sym Club

Can you discover the names of the members of Trans Sym Club?

How do you think the members decided on a name for their club?

Chapter Review/Test

Vocabulary

origin
quadrant
reflection
rotation
translation

VOCABULARY

1. One of the four regions in a coordinate plane formed by the coordinate axes is called a(n) ____.
2. A figure that is flipped over a line shows a(n) ____.
3. The ____ is the point at which the x-axis and y-axis of a coordinate plane intersect.
4. A(n) ____ is a figure that is turned about a given point.

CONCEPTS AND SKILLS

Use the coordinates to plot and label each point on grid paper. (Lesson 1, pp. 610–613)

5. $R\,(^-3, ^+3)$
6. $M\,(^+2, ^-2)$
7. $P\,(^-2, ^-4)$
8. $N\,(^-5, 0)$
9. $O\,(^+4, ^+4)$
10. $Q\,(0, ^+3)$
11. $T\,(^+4, ^-3)$
12. $S\,(^-3, ^-2)$

Find 4 ordered pairs for each function. Then use them to graph each function. (Lessons 2–3, pp. 614–619)

13. $y = x + 4$
14. $y = x - 5$
15. $y = 2x + 1$
16. $y = 2x - 6$

Use the diagram. Name the coordinates of triangle *DEF* after the transformations. (Lesson 5, pp. 622–625)

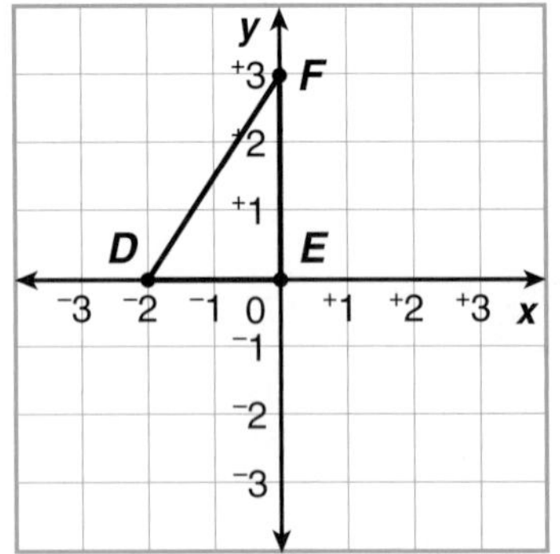

17. Translate right 4 units.
18. Rotate a $\frac{1}{4}$ turn clockwise about (0, 0).
19. Reflect over the y-axis.

PROBLEM SOLVING

Use the table to solve. (Lesson 4, pp. 620–621)

20. Write an equation to show how to find the retail price of an item.

Wholesale Cost (x)	Retail Price (y)
$2	$5
$4	$9
$6	$13
$8	$17

Show You Understand

Does a parallelogram have rotational symmetry? Explain.

Extra Practice

Set A (Lesson 1, pp. 610–613)

Use the coordinate plane at the right for Exercises 1–7. Write the ordered pair for each point.

1. *J* **2.** *E* **3.** *M* **4.** *B*

Write the letter name of each point.

5. $(^{+}1, ^{+}1)$ **6.** $(^{-}3, ^{-}2)$ **7.** $(^{-}2, 0)$

Use grid paper. Use the coordinates to plot and label each point.

8. $W(^{+}3, ^{+}5)$ **9.** $X(^{-}2, ^{-}4)$ **10.** $Y(^{+}4, ^{-}4)$ **11.** $Z(^{-}5, ^{+}1)$

Set B (Lesson 2, pp. 614–615)

Make a function table for each of the following using 0, 4, 8, 12 for *x*.

1. $y = x + 4$ **2.** $y = 4x$ **3.** $y = x - 4$ **4.** $y = 10 - x$

Set C (Lesson 3, pp. 616–619)

Find 4 sets of coordinates for each function. Then graph the functions on grid paper.

1. $y = x - 6$ **2.** $y = x + 5$ **3.** $y = 2x + 2$ **4.** $y = 3x - 5$

Set D (Lesson 5, pp. 622–625)

Use the diagram. Name the coordinates of triangle *ABC* after the transformations.

1. Translate left 5 units.

2. Reflect over the *x*-axis.

3. Rotate a half turn about (0, 0).

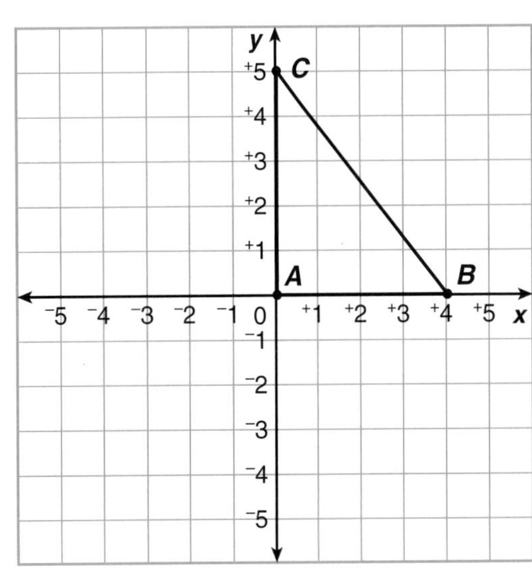

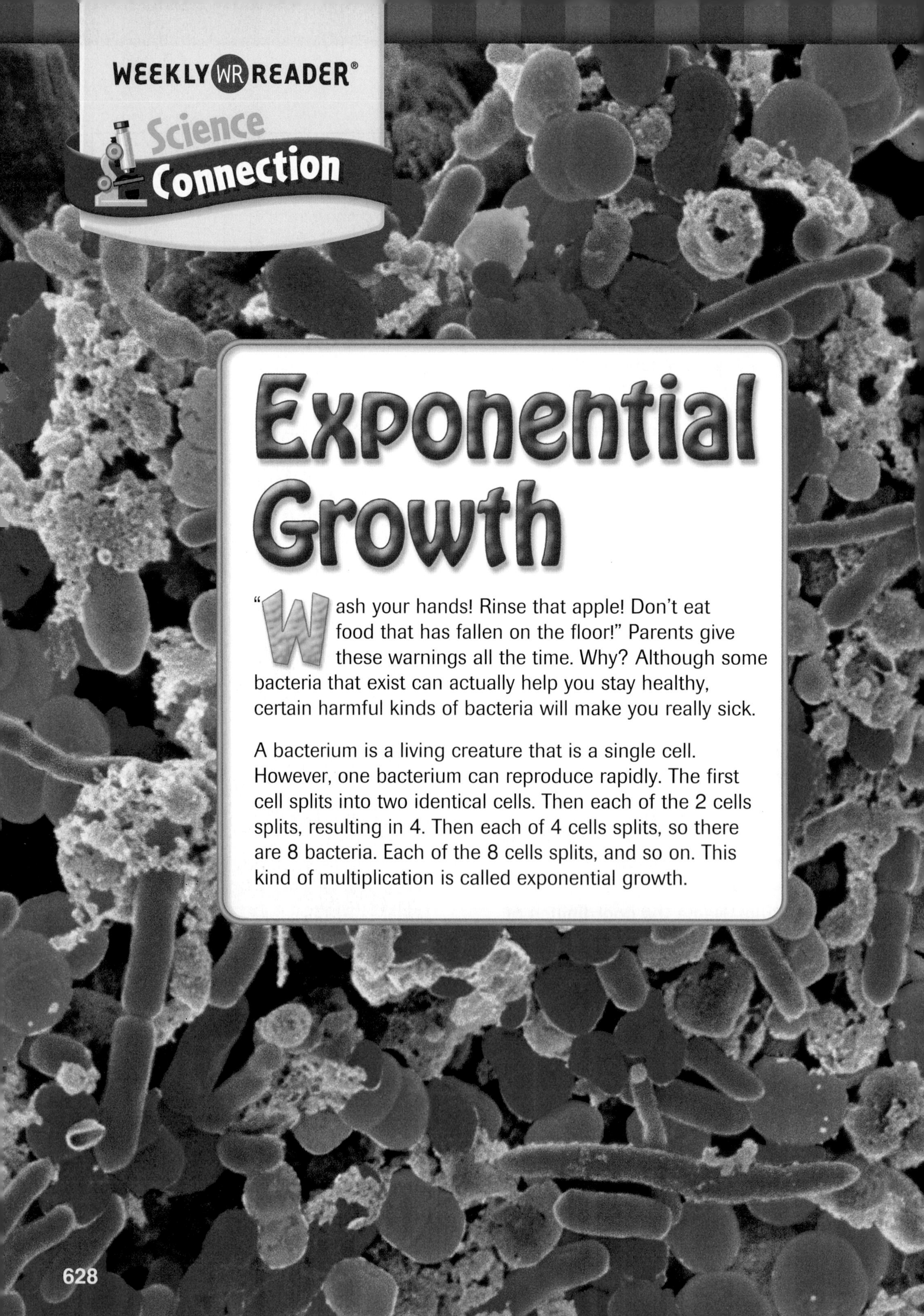

Exponential Growth

"Wash your hands! Rinse that apple! Don't eat food that has fallen on the floor!" Parents give these warnings all the time. Why? Although some bacteria that exist can actually help you stay healthy, certain harmful kinds of bacteria will make you really sick.

A bacterium is a living creature that is a single cell. However, one bacterium can reproduce rapidly. The first cell splits into two identical cells. Then each of the 2 cells splits, resulting in 4. Then each of 4 cells splits, so there are 8 bacteria. Each of the 8 cells splits, and so on. This kind of multiplication is called exponential growth.

Problem Solving

Each bacterium in the table divides into 2 cells every 20 minutes. Use these data to solve Problems 1–6.

Bacterial Growth	
Time	**Number of Bacteria**
0:00	1
0:20	2
0:40	4

1. Create a function table to show the exponential growth of the bacteria in 2 hours.

2. Use your function table from Problem 1 to graph the function of the bacteria's growth. Graph only points. Why should you not connect the points?

3. Describe the shape of your graph. Why do you think the graph has this shape?

4. A school day lasts 6 hours. You start with 1 bacterium at the beginning of the day. How many bacteria are there by the end of the day?

5. How many 20-minute intervals are needed for one bacterium to become at least one million bacteria?

6. If you start with one bacterium, how many bacteria will there be at the beginning of the tenth hour?

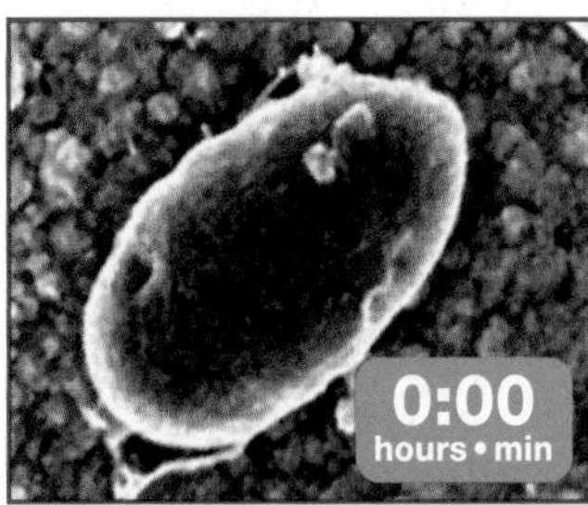

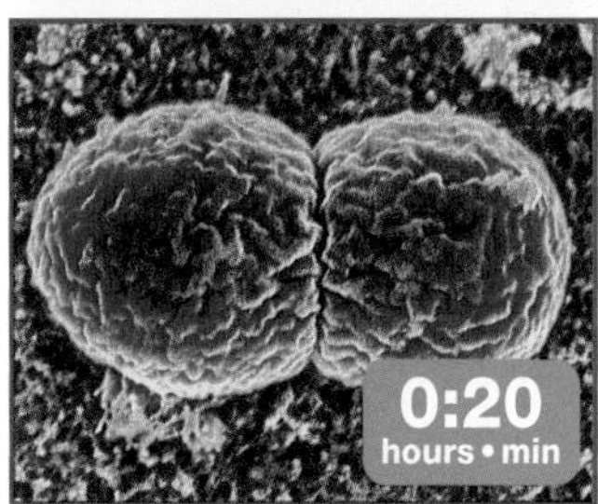

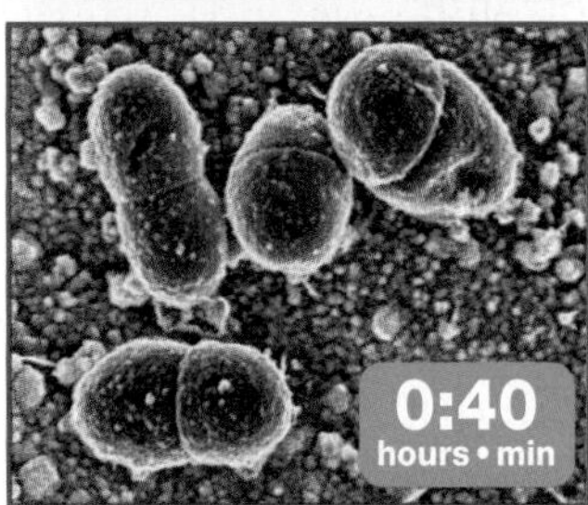

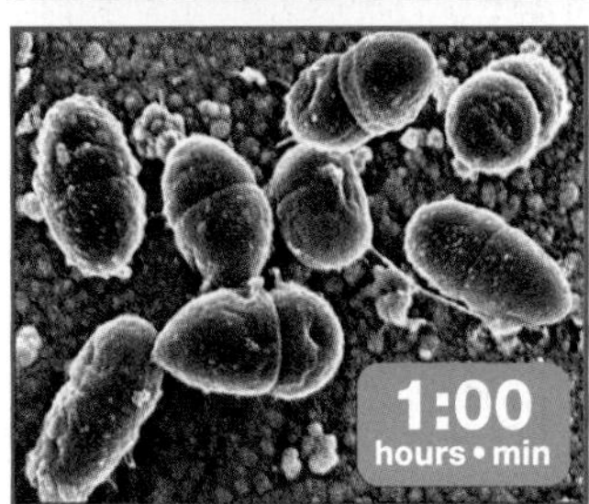

Education Place

Visit Weekly Reader Connections at **eduplace.com/map** for more on this topic.

Enrichment: Picture Graphing

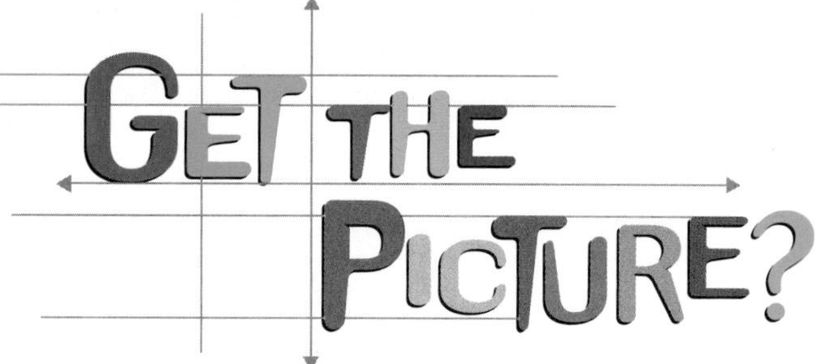

Computer programmers and designers use a grid system to draw the shapes that appear on your monitor's screen. You can use a similar process to create pictures on a coordinate grid.

Follow these steps to draw the rectangular prism on a coordinate grid.

STEP 1 Draw a square whose bottom left corner is at (1, 2) and whose top right corner is at (3, 4).

STEP 2 Draw a square whose bottom left corner is at ($^-3$, $^-1$) and whose top right corner is at ($^-1$, 1).

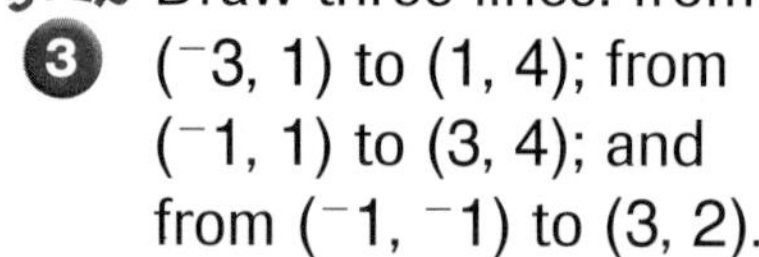

STEP 3 Draw three lines: from ($^-3$, 1) to (1, 4); from ($^-1$, 1) to (3, 4); and from ($^-1$, $^-1$) to (3, 2).

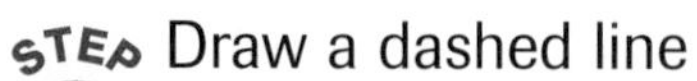

STEP 4 Draw a dashed line from ($^-3$, $^-1$) to (1, 2).

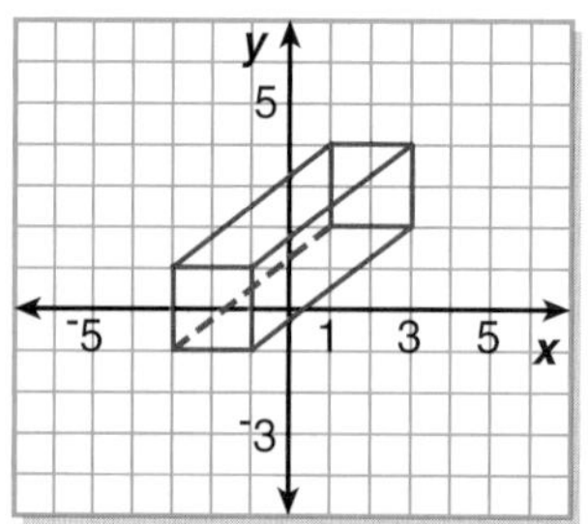

Try These!

1. On a coordinate grid, connect the following points in the order given. Name the object you drew.

(1, $^-6$)	(1, 0)	(2, 0)	(3, 1)	(3, 4)
(2, 4)	(2, 2)	(1, 2)	(1, 5)	(0, 6)
($^-1$, 6)	($^-2$, 5)	($^-2$, 0)	($^-3$, 0)	($^-3$, 2)
($^-4$, 2)	($^-4$, $^-1$)	($^-3$, $^-2$)	($^-2$, $^-2$)	($^-2$, $^-6$)
(1, $^-6$)				

2. **Create Your Own** Write your own set of directions for drawing a picture on a coordinate grid. Give your directions to a partner to follow.

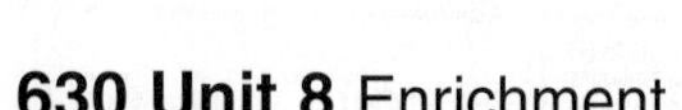

Graph It

You can use a graphing program to create and compare the graphs of equations in Quadrant I.

- Enter and complete the table shown at the right, starting in cell A1.
- Click on cell A1 and drag to cell C6.
- Click on [chart icon].

	A	B	C
1	x	y = x + 1	y = x + 2
2	1	2	
3	2		
4	3		
5	4		
6	5		

Use Easy Sheet to answer the questions below.

1. How is the graph transformed each time you increase x by 1?
2. Predict what the graph for $y = x + 3$ will look like. Enter the values in column D and graph the line.
3. Based on the graphs you made above, predict what the lines will look like for the equations $y = 2x$ and $y = \frac{1}{2}x$.
4. Enter and complete the table shown at the right, starting in cell E1. Make a graph of the data in cells A1 to F6.
5. How is the graph transformed when you multiply by 2? by $\frac{1}{2}$? How do the graphs compare to your predictions?
6. **Challenge** Predict what the graphs of $y = 2x + 1$ and $y = 2x + 2$ will look like based on the lines you have already graphed. Enter the equations and the first 5 values for each, in columns H and I. Make a new graph of the data in cells H1 to I6.

	E	F
	$y = 2x$	$y = \frac{1}{2}x$
	2	0.5

Unit 8 Test

VOCABULARY Open Response

1. Opposite numbers have the same ■, or distance from zero.
2. A(n) ■ is a flip of a figure that results in a mirror image.
3. The point named by the ordered pair (0, 0) is the ■ .

Vocabulary
- origin
- rotation
- integers
- reflection
- translation
- coordinates
- absolute value

CONCEPTS AND SKILLS Open Response

Solve using inverse operations. (Chapter 21)

4. $9n = 495$
5. $m \div 8 = 43$
6. $372 = k - 138$
7. $68 + a = 172$

Copy and complete each function table. (Chapter 21)

8. $y = 36 \div x$

x	y
1	■
2	■
3	■
4	■

9. $y = 21 - x$

x	y
0	■
1	■
2	■
3	■

10. $y = 7x - 3$

x	y
0	■
2	■
■	32
■	53

11. $y = 32 - 5x$

x	y
0	■
■	17
■	12
6	■

Write the opposite of each integer. (Chapter 22)

12. $^{+}37$
13. $^{-}3$
14. $^{-}19$

Write the absolute value of each integer. (Chapter 22)

15. $^{-}22$
16. 0
17. $^{+}19$

Write these integers in order from least to greatest. (Chapter 22)

18. $0, {}^{-}5, {}^{-}3, {}^{+}4$
19. ${}^{-}8, {}^{-}11, {}^{-}7, {}^{+}7$
20. ${}^{-}6, {}^{+}7, {}^{-}8, {}^{+}9$

Add or subtract. (Chapter 22)

21. ${}^{+}8 + {}^{-}3$
22. ${}^{-}7 + {}^{-}8$
23. ${}^{+}7 - {}^{-}5$
24. ${}^{-}9 - {}^{-}5$

Use the coordinate plane for Exercises 25–29. Name the coordinates for each. (Chapter 23)

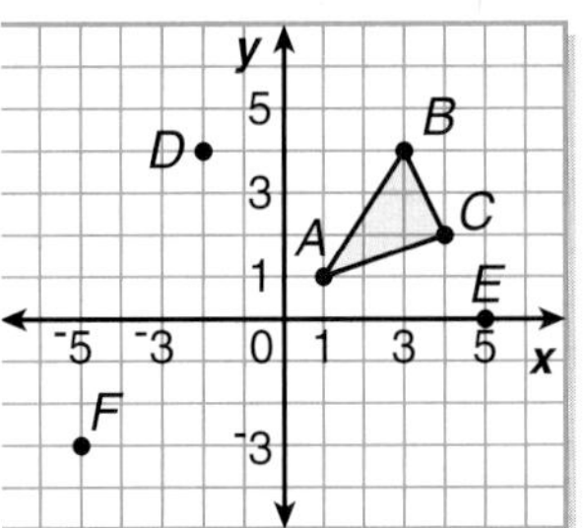

25. point D 26. point C 27. point E

28. triangle ABC after a translation 3 units left

29. triangle ABC after a reflection over the x-axis

PROBLEM SOLVING Open Response

30. At sunrise, the temperature outdoors was $^-4$°C. By the time school started, the temperature had risen 6°. What was the temperature when school started?

31. A carpenter made \$124 for building a bookcase. She paid $\frac{1}{4}$ of that amount to her assistant. Write and solve an equation to find how much she paid her helper.

Use the graph for Problems 32–33. Alice charges a fee of \$30 plus \$5 per hour. Beth charges \$10 per hour.

32. How many hours must Alice work to make \$70?

33. After how many hours will they make the same amount of money? After that, who will make more?

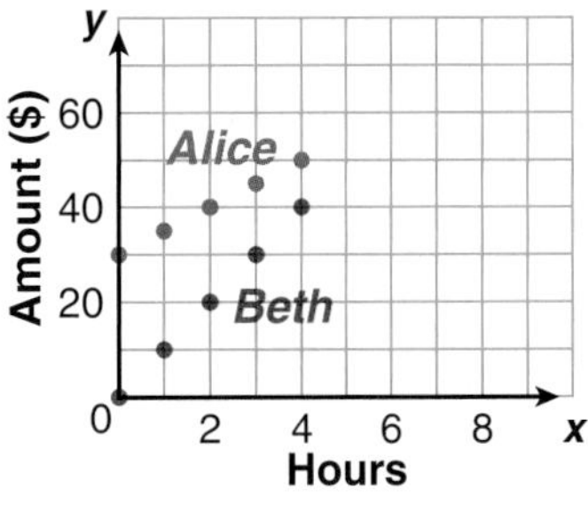

Performance Assessment

Constructed Response

Task Laura, Mitch, and Natalie played a game using the spinner base shown. Each student spun a different set of numbers, but each got a score of 0. What numbers did each student spin? Is it more likely that a person playing this game would get a positive score or a negative score? Explain your thinking.

Information You Need

- Each student got three spins.
- Each student's score was the sum of his or her three spins.
- One of the numbers Laura spun was $^-8$.
- One of the numbers Mitch spun was $^+5$.

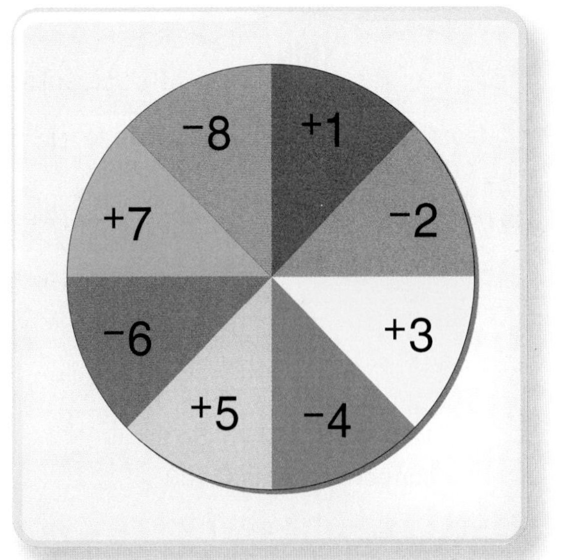

Cumulative Test Prep

Solve Problems 1–10.

Test-Taking Tip

Sometimes when you take a test, you can circle important words that will help you understand what the question is asking.

Look at the example below.

Yuri collected these data on the weights, in pounds, of members of the basketball team:

$122.8, 129\frac{1}{2}, 122.75, 129\frac{1}{4}, 128$

He decided to list the weights from greatest to least. Which weight will be second on his list?

A 122.75 **C** $129\frac{1}{4}$

B 122.8 **D** $129\frac{1}{2}$

THINK

First circle the words "greatest to least," which mean that you have to order the given numbers. Another important word is "second," which indicates that you are looking for the second greatest weight, not the greatest.

The correct order is $129\frac{1}{2}$, $129\frac{1}{4}$, 128, 122.8, 122.75. So the correct answer is **C** $129\frac{1}{4}$.

Multiple Choice

1. Which numbers for n make this inequality true? $n > {}^{-}5$

A $^{-}5, {}^{-}6, {}^{-}7$ **C** $^{-}5, {}^{-}4, {}^{-}3$

B $^{-}6, {}^{-}7, {}^{-}8$ **D** $^{-}4, {}^{-}3, {}^{-}2$

(Chapter 22, Lesson 2)

2. The average temperature for January in Fairbanks, Alaska, is $^{-}10$°F. The average temperature for June is 60°F. What is the difference between these temperatures?

F 50° **H** 70°

G 60° **J** 80°

(Chapter 22, Lesson 5)

3. A hallway measures 3 feet by 9 feet. How many square yards of carpeting are needed to cover the floor of this hallway?

A 3 **C** 12

B 9 **D** 27

(Chapter 16, Lesson 3)

4. In a class of 30 fifth-graders, 20% of the students participated in the science fair. How many of the fifth-graders did not participate in the science fair?

F 6 **H** 14

G 10 **J** 24

(Chapter 19, Lesson 5)

For Test-Taking Tips, see page 652

Open Response

5. A car service uses this formula to determine the cost of a ride. The variable n represents the number of miles.

Cost $= \$8 + \$3 \times (n - 1)$

What is the cost of a 5-mile trip?

(Chapter 5, Lesson 6)

6. Use the stem-and-leaf plot to identify the median of this set of data.

Hours Spent Training for Track Meet

Stem	Leaf
1	2 3 4 5 5 9
2	0 1 6 6 6 9
3	0

Key: 3 | 0 means 30.

(Chapter 8, Lesson 3)

7. In a survey of 36 students, $\frac{1}{3}$ of the students said that their one favorite subject was math and $\frac{1}{4}$ said that their favorite subject was history. How many students in all reported that their favorite subject was either math or history?

(Chapter 12, Lesson 2)

8. A scale drawing has the scale $\frac{1}{4}$ inch: 1 foot. What is the actual length of a room that is $2\frac{3}{4}$ inches long in the drawing?

(Chapter 18, Lesson 5)

9. Ethan bought a sweater that had a price of \$25. The sales tax was an additional 8% of the price of the sweater. How much did Ethan pay in all?

(Chapter 19, Lesson 5)

Extended Response

10. The rectangular prism in the drawing above represents the box design for a new breakfast cereal.

A What is the least number of square inches of cardboard needed to build the box? Explain.

B The cereal company plans to produce a jumbo-sized box with dimensions that are twice those shown. Would twice as much cardboard be needed? Explain.

C Find the volume of the original cereal box and the volume of the jumbo-sized box.

D Suppose you are hired to design a new cereal box in the shape of a rectangular prism. The box must have a volume that is greater than 600 cubic inches but less than 700 cubic inches. What dimensions can you use? Explain how you decided.

(Chapter 17, Lessons 4 and 6)

Education Place

Look for Cumulative Test Prep at **eduplace.com/map** for more practice.

Vocabulary Wrap-Up for Unit 8

Look back at the big ideas and vocabulary in this unit.

Big Ideas

You can use inverse operations to solve equations.

A function written in the form of an equation relates two variables, such as x and y.

You can add and subtract integers using counters or a number line.

Key Vocabulary

inverse operations

function

integer

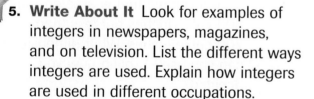

Math Conversations

Use your new vocabulary to discuss these big ideas.

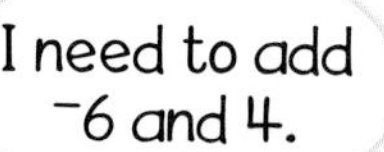

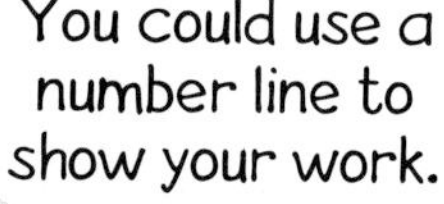

You could use a number line to show your work.

1. Explain how to solve this equation:
   $a - 47 = 47$
2. Explain how to find values for y for the function $y = x - 9$.
3. Explain how to find this difference:
   $^{-}18 - 7$
4. Explain how to locate the point $(5, {}^{-}3)$ on a coordinate plane.

5. **Write About It** Look for examples of integers in newspapers, magazines, and on television. List the different ways integers are used. Explain how integers are used in different occupations.

Student Resources

THE MOST AMAZING Sights in Nature

SOURCE OF INFORMATION: THE WORLD ALMANAC AND BOOK OF FACTS

Topping the list of amazing natural sights is Mt. Everest. It sits on the border between Tibet and Nepal in Asia. Mt. Everest is the highest mountain in the world. However, nobody agrees about just how high it is. Edmund Hillary and Tenzing Norgay first climbed the mountain in 1953. They believed it was 29,002 feet high. Later, the Indian government measured it at 29,028 feet. Satellites have been used to measure the mountain. They suggest that Mount Everest could be more than 29,800 feet high.

Victoria Falls in Africa is no small wonder, either. It is the world's largest waterfall. At its widest point, Victoria Falls is more than a mile across. Its height ranges from 256 feet to about 400 feet at its center.

Arizona's Grand Canyon was slowly carved out of the earth by the Colorado River over the past million years. This wonder is both steep and deep — more than a mile deep, in fact. It runs some 217 miles long and up to 18 miles wide. It is one of the most popular places to visit in the United States.

The length of the Grand Canyon is small compared to the length of the Great Barrier Reef. It is the world's largest coral reef. It stretches 1,250 miles along the northeastern coast of Australia. What is a coral reef? It is formed by the bodies of tiny sea creatures called corals. The Great Barrier Reef is home to 1,500 kinds of fish and 215 types of birds. It also has 500 kinds of seaweed. Whales visit in the winter. You won't find many sharks, however, because they prefer the open sea.

1. The selection tells how high Edmund Hillary believed Mt. Everest to be. What is the difference between his measurement and the Indian government's? What is the difference between Hillary's measurement and the satellite measurements?
2. What is the difference in height between Victoria Falls' lowest point and highest point?
3. How much longer than the Grand Canyon is the Great Barrier Reef?
4. What is the total number of types of fish and birds that live in the Great Barrier Reef?

Ready for Anything

Ryan Shaw

My name is Jedediah, but people call me Jed. My story begins on March 5, 1849. That day, my family and I set out from St. Louis for California.

Our covered wagon, pulled by five yoke of oxen, was loaded with supplies. For you city folk, a yoke is a wood frame that fastens together two animals to pull a wagon or plow. We joined a train of 20 other wagons.

We thought we were ready for anything — huge deserts, fast rivers, and even bandits. Little did we know what was really in store for us.

It started one morning in May. The early sun gave way to dark skies, then a dead calm. Suddenly, a twister was spotted about 10 miles off. It looked like a long, dirty finger. And it was heading straight for us.

As luck would have it, the twister changed direction. We lost most of our belongings but we were alive. Some weren't as lucky. Two families had unknowingly headed right in the path of the twister.

1. In all, how many oxen pulled Jed's family's covered wagon? Write a multiplication sentence to solve.
2. Why, do you think, did Jed explain the meaning of the word *yoke* for "city folk"?

Ships OF the Desert

Source of Information: The Information Please Almanac

Camels are made for the desert. They have broad, flat, leathery pads on each foot. As the camel walks, the pads spread, keeping the foot from sinking into the sand. Camels move both feet on one side of their body and then the feet on the other side. This makes them look as if they are rolling, the way a ship does in the ocean, and explains the nickname "ship of the desert."

How Fast Can Animals Run?

Animals	Speed (in Miles per Hour)
Cheetah	70
Zebra	40
Elephant	25
Grizzly bear	30
Lion	50
Camel	12

Camels can go from 5 to 7 days on little or no food and water. They can also travel great distances, carrying loads ranging from 400 to almost 1,000 pounds. Their usual speed is about 3 miles per hour. However, when they gallop, they can go as fast as 12 miles per hour. Depending on their load, camels can travel between 25 and 50 miles a day.

1. What's the mean, median, and range of the speed of the animals listed in the table?
2. How does the camel's speed affect the mean of the speeds shown in the table?

The Fruitomatic

HELEN STAKENICH

Darcy Devine was bored. Her parents had left for a day trip to Mars to celebrate her dad's birthday. Cousin Mindy was "babysitting" 12-year-old Darcy, as if Darcy wasn't old enough to take care of herself. Sixteen-year-old Mindy was no fun. All she wanted to do was talk on the disto-phone with her friends from the Andromeda Galaxy.

Darcy decided to check out Dad's latest kitchen invention, the Fruitomatic. Dad was always inventing cool, new gadgets for the kitchen — or at least Darcy thought they were cool.

The Fruitomatic could zap any fruit — well, just about any fruit. Watermelons and pineapples were too big to fit into the machine, and raspberries and blueberries were too small. Darcy pulled the Fruitomatic from under the sink, where Mom kept it. The Fruitomatic had two side-by-side chambers. You put the fruit into the chamber on the left, and you could get ice cream, juice, sliced fruit, fruit salad, and even cooked fruit in the chamber on the right.

"That's it," thought Darcy. "I'll make fruit salad." Watching her dad fiddle with the Fruitomatic always eased her boredom. Now she would try the machine herself. But there was a problem; the fruit bowl was empty.

Darcy was about to give up all hope of improving her boring day when she spied lemons on the kitchen counter. She decided to make lemonade instead. She slipped the lemons into the left chamber of the Fruitomatic. Then she entered the number 4 and pressed the Enter button. Darcy looked into the right chamber. It was empty! She entered the number 6 and pressed Enter again. Still nothing. Then she remembered that Dad had said the machine could only make juice using prime numbers. She knew that 3 was a prime number. She entered three and — bingo! Out came more juice than she had ever seen. She entered 5, 7, and 9. Two of the three numbers worked!

By now, the lemon juice was pouring from the machine and Darcy was filling all the pitchers she could find. But she was having too much fun to stop. Darcy entered the number 12 and something strange happened. Out came a lemon cut into two halves. Then she entered 14 and got a lemon sliced into quarters. For some reason, the number 15 created a lemon cut into fifths. Darcy wasn't sure what was going on, but she was having a real blast. Before long, she had every pitcher in the kitchen filled with juice, and every bowl filled with lemon slices.

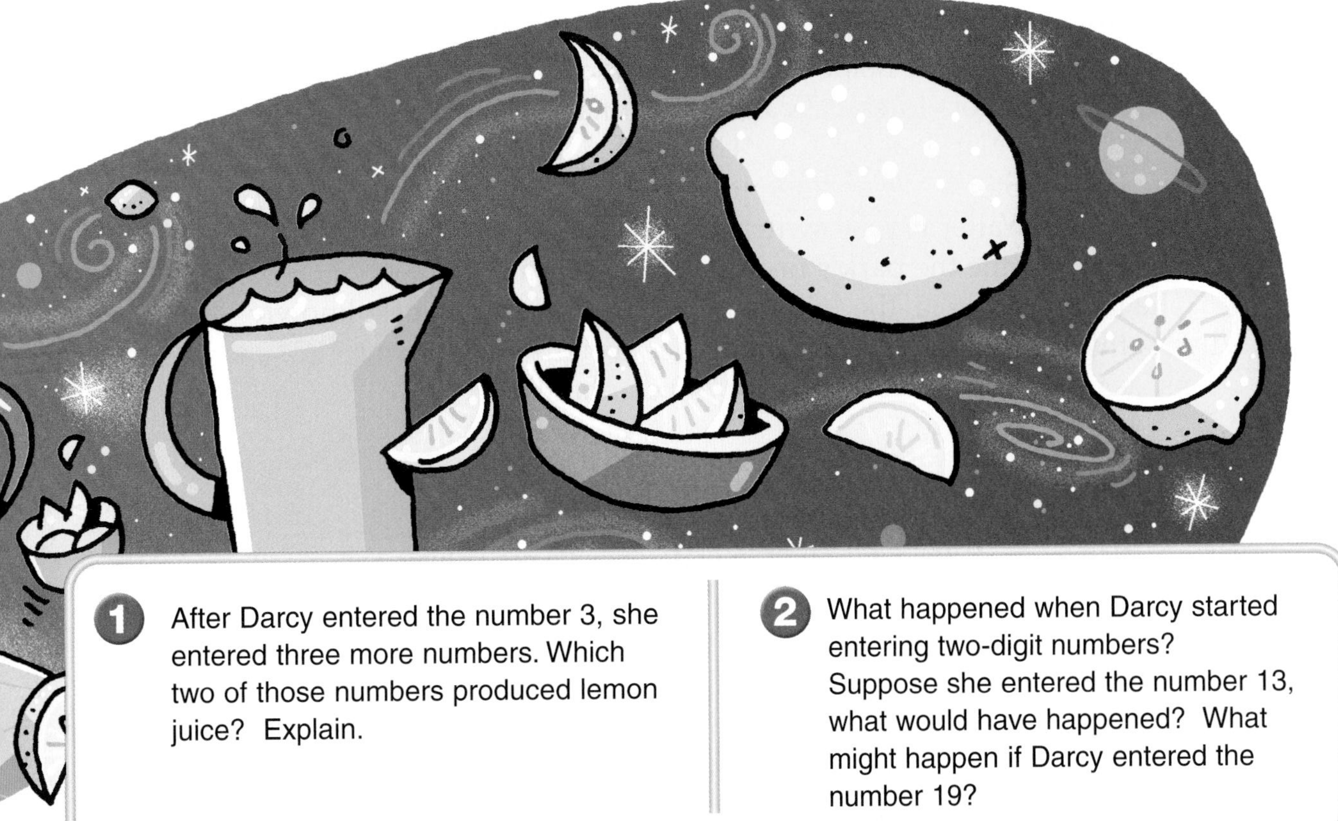

1. After Darcy entered the number 3, she entered three more numbers. Which two of those numbers produced lemon juice? Explain.

2. What happened when Darcy started entering two-digit numbers? Suppose she entered the number 13, what would have happened? What might happen if Darcy entered the number 19?

READING MATH

The World's Largest Trees

Source of Information: The National Park Service

The largest trees in the world are the giant sequoias. They grow on the western side of the Sierra Nevada Mountains in California. The tallest sequoias are as large as a 26-story building. At their base, they are wider than a city street. Sequoias are very old trees. Experts believe the largest of these trees may be as much as 2,700 years old.

In 1888, six loggers spent five days cutting down a giant sequoia. Walter Fry, one of the loggers, counted the growth rings on the tree stump. He knew that most trees add a ring to their circumference about once a year. When Fry finished counting, he was shocked and saddened. The tree they had just cut down was more than 3,000 years old!

Fry quit his job. He helped start a petition to save the sequoias. In 1890, the sequoia forests became a national park. It was named General Grant National Park, for Ulysses S. Grant, the 18th President of the United States. Years later, it was renamed Sequoia National Park. As for Walter Fry, he switched jobs and became a park ranger. Later, Fry became the park's first civilian superintendent.

The largest sequoia, the "General Sherman," is the largest known living thing on earth. The Sherman Tree weighs more than 6,167 tons, as much as 41 blue whales or 740 elephants.

The Five Largest Sequoias

Name	**Height** (feet)	**Circumference** (feet)	**Volume** (cubic feet)
General Sherman	274.9	102.6	52,508
Washington	254.7	101.1	47,850
General Grant	268.1	107.6	46,608
Lincoln	255.8	98.3	45,148
President	240.9	93.0	44,471

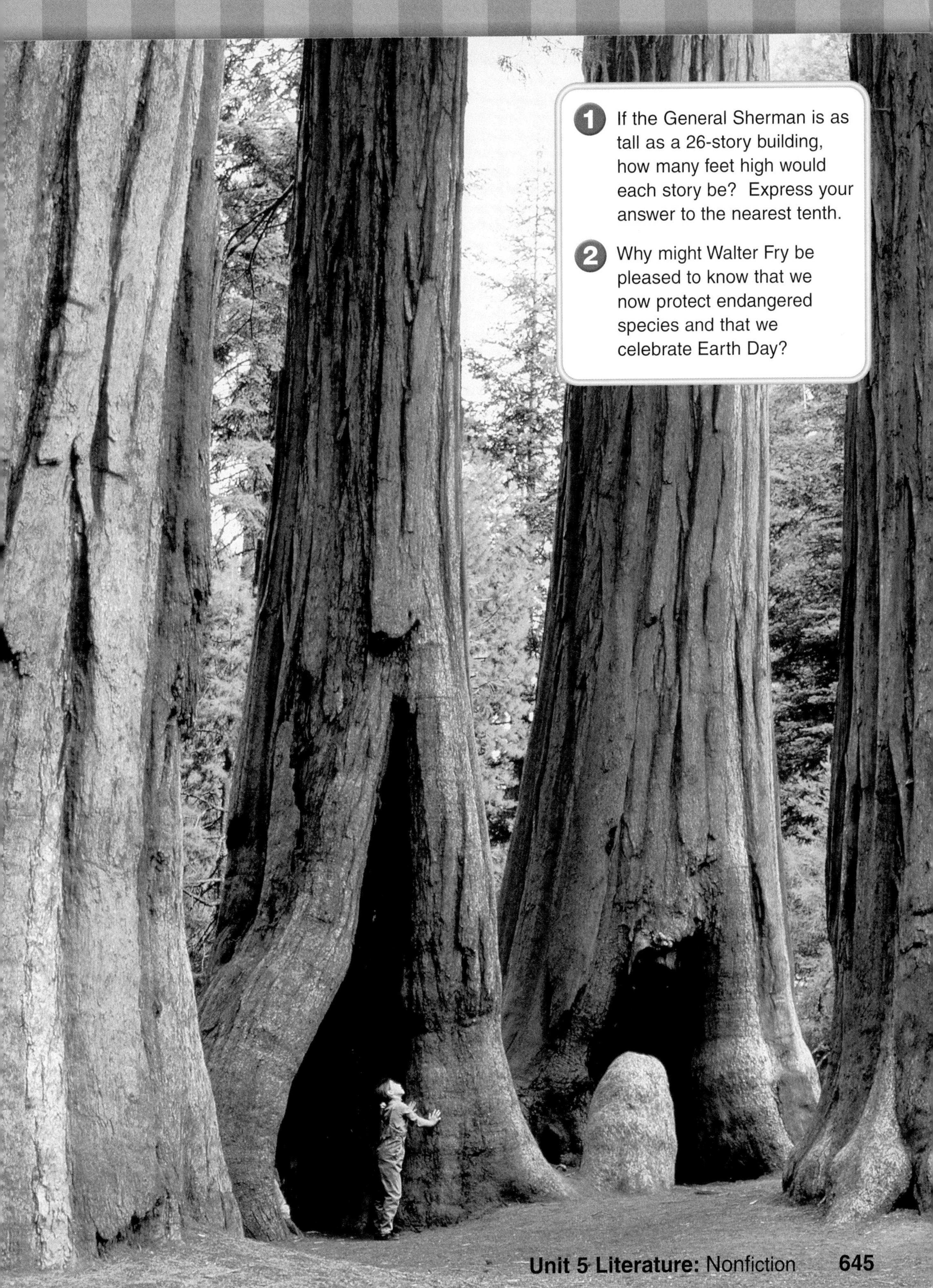

1. If the General Sherman is as tall as a 26-story building, how many feet high would each story be? Express your answer to the nearest tenth.
2. Why might Walter Fry be pleased to know that we now protect endangered species and that we celebrate Earth Day?

No Place to Go

HELENA SERPA

Vanessa, Jen, Megan, and Natasha were 11 years old and friends. They had been looking forward to a summer of fun. Now their vacation was only a week old, and they were already bored.

"We need a place to play," Vanessa said.

"What, like a clubhouse?" Natasha asked.

Suddenly, the same idea struck the four girls. "The shed!" they shouted.

A wooden shed sat unused in the farthest corner of Natasha's back yard. With its triangle-shaped roof, it looked like a real cabin, only lots smaller. Was it too small for a clubhouse? Vanessa ran home and grabbed the tape measure from the toolbox. Minutes later, she was holding one end as Megan pulled the tape and measured the shed's outside dimensions. It was 10 feet long, and much to their surprise, 12 feet wide. And its walls were 7 feet tall.

The shed needed to be patched up and painted. But it was nothing the girls couldn't handle. That night, Natasha's parents quickly agreed to the deal.

Five days later, Natasha held open the freshly-painted door of the new clubhouse.

"Ladies first," she joked, as she waved her friends in.

1. Make a drawing of the clubhouse. Label the measurements of each dimension.

2. Calculate the area of a longer wall of the clubhouse. Then find the area of the clubhouse floor.

NUMBERS

BY MARY CORNISH

from Sing a Song of Popcorn

I like the generosity of numbers.
The way, for example,
they are willing to count
anything or anyone:
two pickles, one door to the room,
eight dancers dressed as swans.

I like the domesticity of addition —
add two cups of milk and stir —
the sense of plenty: six plums
on the ground, three more
falling from the tree.

And multiplication's school
of fish times fish,
whose silver bodies breed
beneath the shadow
of a boat.

Even subtraction is never loss,
just addition somewhere else:
five sparrows take away two,
the two in someone else's
garden now.

There's an amplitude to long division,
as it opens Chinese take-out
box by paper box,
inside every folded cookie
a new fortune.

And I never fail to be surprised
by the gift of an odd remainder,
footloose at the end:
forty-seven divided by eleven equals four,
with three remaining.

Three boys beyond their mothers' call,
two Italians off to the sea,
one sock that isn't anywhere you look.

1. What does the poem say about numbers and what they do?
2. Why is counting important for working with ratio and probability?
3. Which verse describes an inverse relationship?

READING MATH

Treasure Hunt

DOUGLAS COBLEIGH

The treasure hunt was Jack's bright idea. He and I had grown up near Boston. We went to different colleges but stayed close friends. After college, we decided to have some fun. So in December, we joined a company that was digging for treasure. Our destination: Oak Island, off the eastern coast of Nova Scotia, Canada.

Oak Island is 350 nautical miles northeast of Boston. Now, Boston winters can get pretty cold. But we soon discovered they were nothing compared to the damp cold of Nova Scotia. At first, we didn't mind it too much. After all, we were here to search for buried treasure.

We learned this search had been going on since 1795, when a Nova Scotia teenager had come across a sunken spot shaped like a circle. The boy had heard plenty of tales about pirates who had used the islands off Nova Scotia as secret hideouts. Legend had it that Captain Kidd and his crew had buried their treasure on one of these islands.

The next day, the boy returned to the spot with some friends. They started digging. And they continued to dig over the next year until they found a rather large stone with mysterious writing on it. By that time the hole was about 90 feet deep. When they returned the

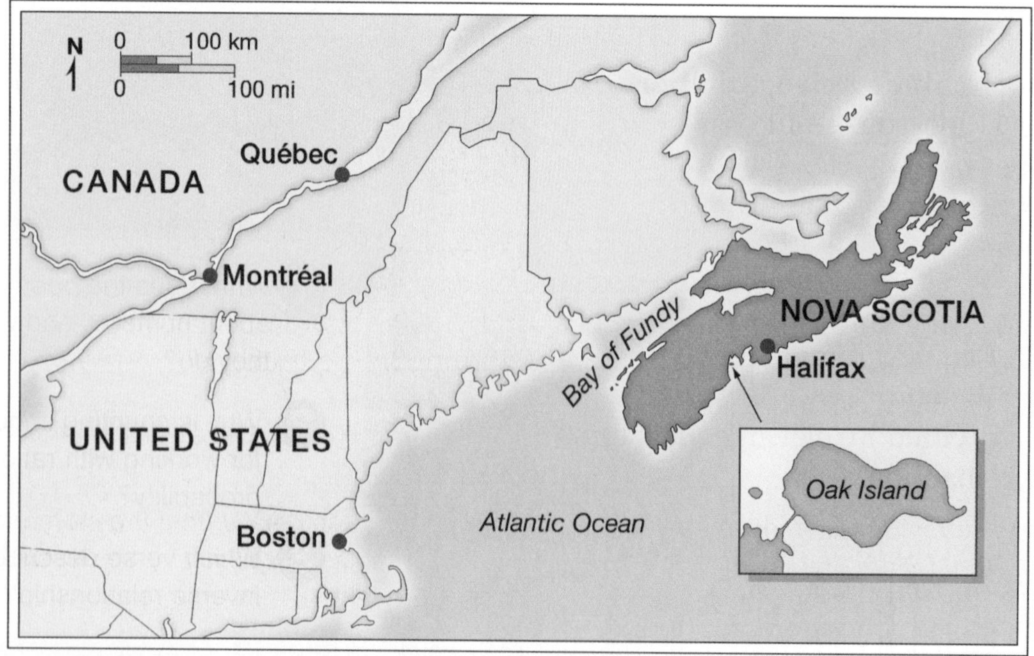

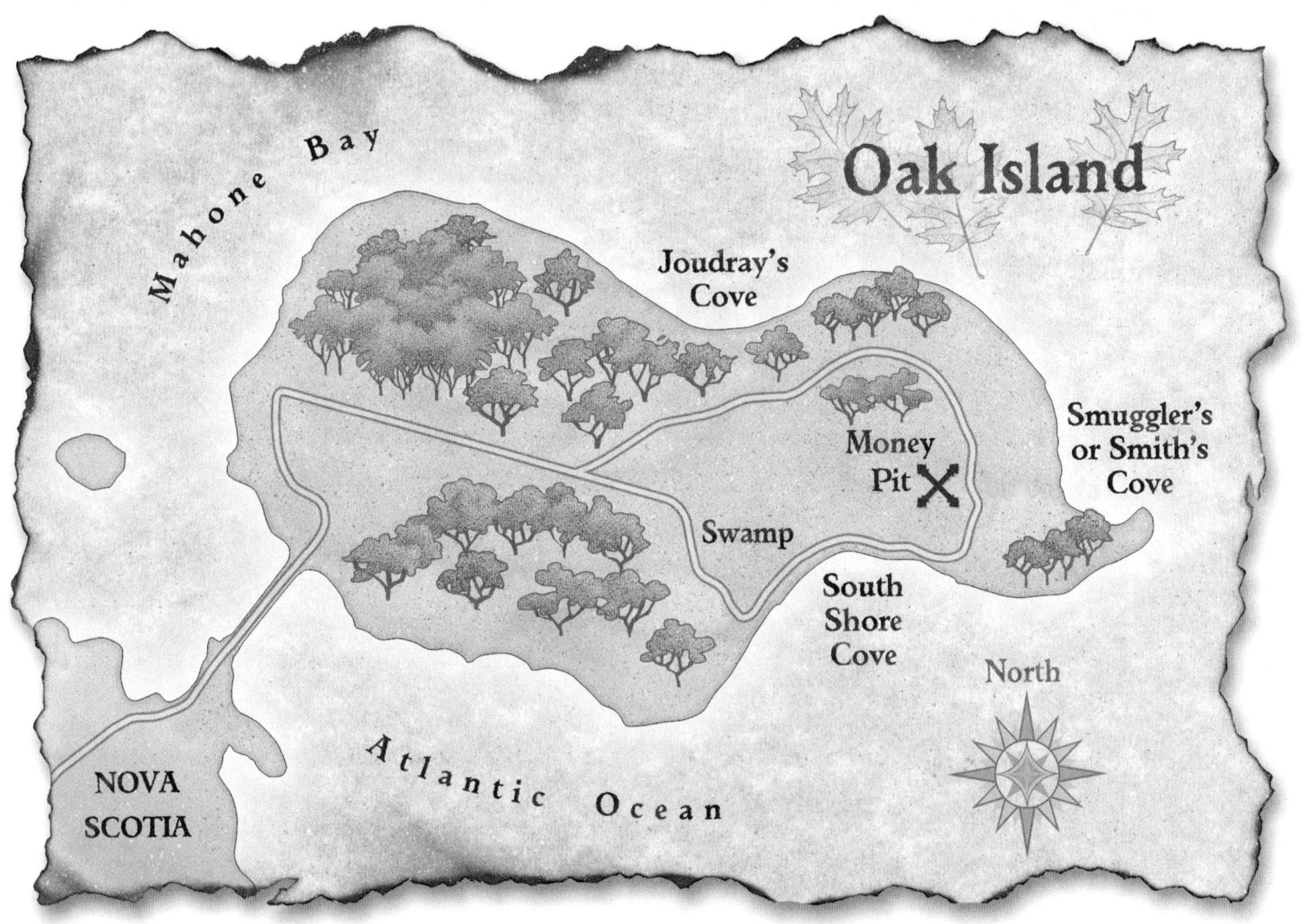

following day, the hole was filled with water. When they removed the stone, they accidentally set off a trap that flooded the hole.

Over the years, various people have taken turns digging out the Money Pit, as the spot came to be called. Several were killed. But treasure hunters continued digging. Eventually, they dug down almost 190 feet. But they failed to find any treasure.

The company Jack and I worked for had a new idea. About 180 feet northeast of the Money Pit, engineers sank a steel tube more than 230 feet into the ground. Then they lowered a specially-made video camera. We could see what looked like three treasure chests and various tools.

The company decided to sink a second shaft close to where the cameras showed the three chests and tools. When we raised the chests, we found old china and glass in one, old bottles in another, and the remnants of what had been clothing in the third.

So much for the Money Pit!

1 What story information does each of the following integers stand for?
A. $^{-}190$; B. $^{+}350$; C. $^{-}230$

2 List three details from the story that are facts. Explain why you think they are facts.

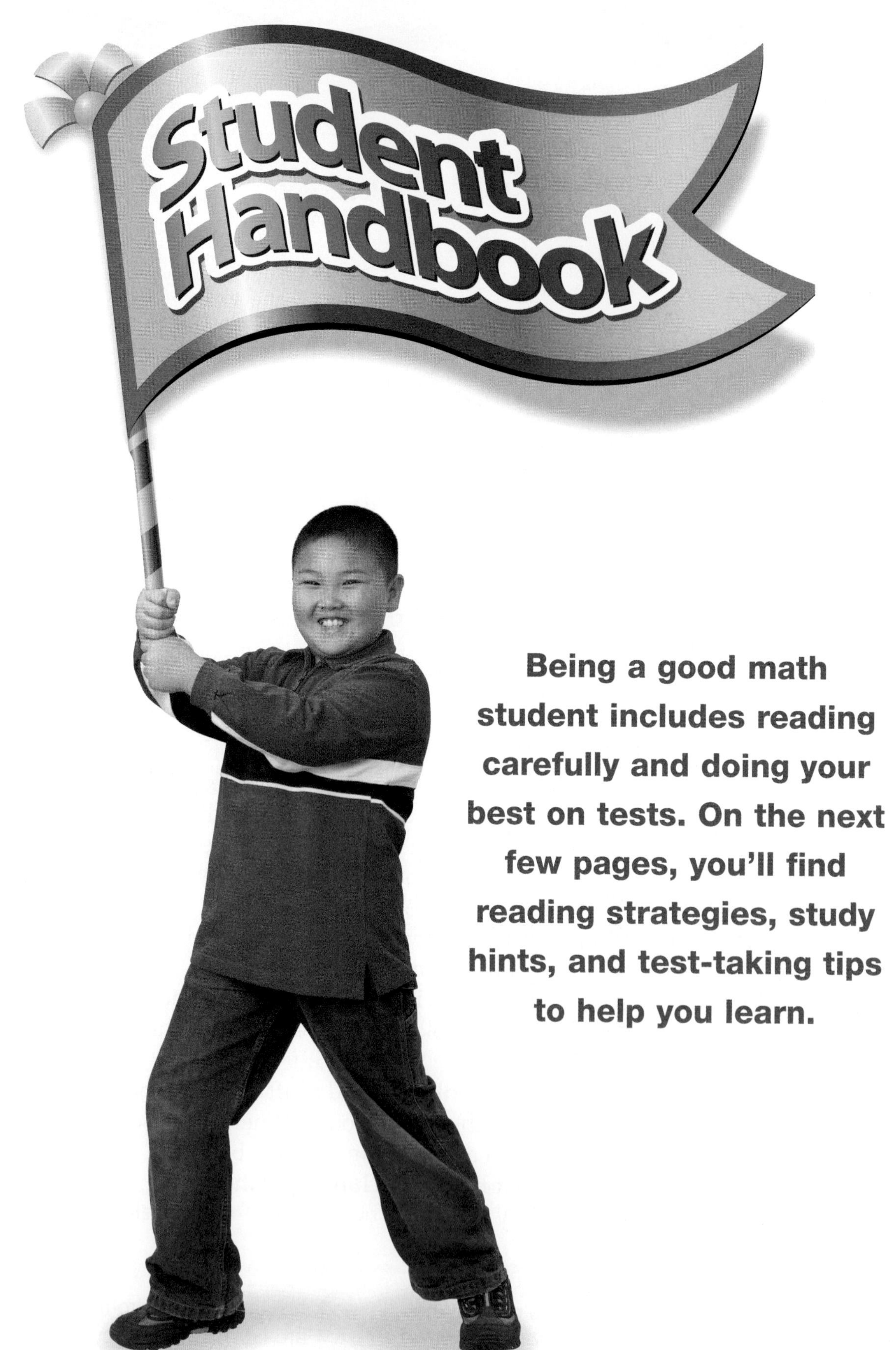

Being a good math student includes reading carefully and doing your best on tests. On the next few pages, you'll find reading strategies, study hints, and test-taking tips to help you learn.

Use Reading Strategies to Think About Math

What you learn during reading class can help you understand how to solve word problems.

Understand What the Question Is

Read the problem once to be sure it makes sense to you. Ask yourself the question in your own words. Picture the situation and make a drawing if it helps.

Think About the Words

As you read, pay attention to the mathematical terms. If you don't understand a word, try to decide what it means by looking at the words around it.

Be Sure You Have Enough Information

Identify the information. Look at tables or graphs as well as the words. Think about what you already know that may help.

Plan What You Will Do

Think about the problem-solving plan and strategies. Decide what computation method is needed. Then make a plan and follow it.

Evaluate Your Work

Look back at what the question asked, and check that your answer really answers that question. Be sure you have labeled your answer.

Strategies for Taking Tests

You need to think differently about how to answer various kinds of questions.

All Questions

If you can't answer a question, go on to the next question. You can return to it if there is time.

Always check your computation.

Multiple-Choice Questions

Estimate the answer. This can help eliminate any unreasonable choices.

On bubble sheets, be sure you mark the bubble for the right question and for the right letter.

Short-Answer Questions

Follow the directions carefully. You may need to show your work, write an explanation, or make a drawing.

If you can't give a complete answer, show what you do know. You may get credit for part of an answer.

Long-Answer Questions

Take time to think about these questions because you often need to explain your answer.

When you finish, reread the question and answer to be sure you have answered the question correctly.

Student Scoring Rubric

Your teacher may use a scoring rubric to evaluate your work. An example is on the next page. Not all rubrics are the same, so your teacher may use a different one.

Scoring Rubric

Rating	My work on this problem
Exemplary **(full credit)**	• has no errors, has the correct answer, and shows that I checked my answer. • is explained carefully and completely. • shows all needed diagrams, tables, or graphs.
Proficient **(some credit)**	• has small errors, has a close answer, and shows that I checked only the math. • is explained but may have missing parts. • shows most needed diagrams, tables, or graphs.
Acceptable **(little credit)**	• has some errors, has an answer, and shows that I did not check my answer. • is not explained carefully and completely. • shows few needed diagrams, tables, or graphs.
Limited **(very little credit)**	• has many errors and may not have an answer. • is not explained at all. • shows no needed diagrams, tables, or graphs.

Two Important Things You Can Do Before a Test

- Get plenty of sleep the night before.
- Eat a good breakfast in the morning.

Your Plan For Problem Solving!

Follow this four-part plan and you'll become a problem-solving superstar!

Remember!

Always START at the "Understand" step and move on. But if you can't get an answer, don't give up. Just go back and start again.

UNDERSTAND

Always be sure you know what the question means! Here are some hints to help you:

- Read the problem and imagine the situation. Draw a picture if it helps.
- Replace any hard names you can't read with easier ones.
- Identify what the question is asking and say it in your own words.
- Look for words that help you decide whether to add, subtract, multiply, or divide.

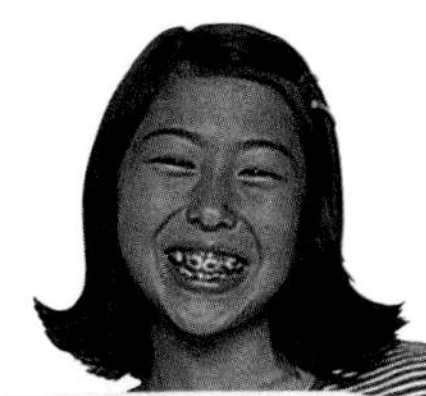

**Start by making a plan!
Ask yourself:**

- What strategy should I use?
- Do I have too much or too little information?
- Should I do more than one step?
- Which operation should I use?
- Should I use paper and pencil, mental math, or a calculator?

You Choose

Strategy
- Act It Out
- Draw a Picture
- Find a Pattern
- Guess and Check
- Make an Organized List
- Make a Table
- Solve a Simpler Problem
- Use Logical Reasoning
- Work Backward
- Write an Equation

Finally! Now you're ready to solve the problem!

- Carry out your plan.
- Adjust your plan if needed.
- Check your calculations.

Congratulations! You've solved the problem. But is it correct? Once you have an answer, ask:

- Is my answer reasonable?
- Is my answer labeled correctly?
- Did I answer the question that was asked?
- Do I need to explain how I found the answer?

Study Skills

Knowing how to study math will help you do well in math class.

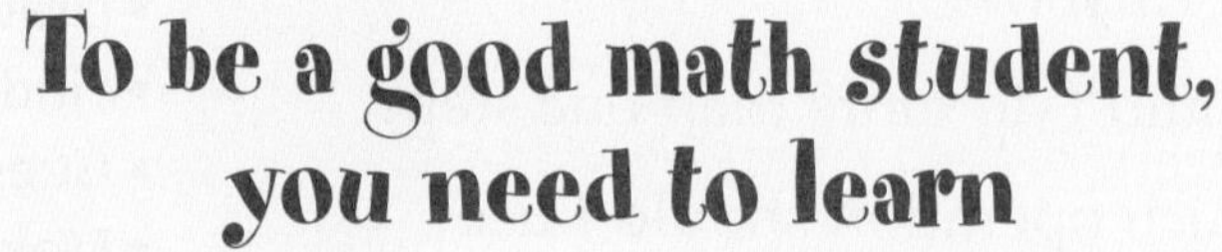
To be a good math student,
you need to learn

- ★ **how to listen when your teacher is teaching.**
- ★ **how to work alone and with others.**
- ★ **how to plan your time.**

Listening Skills

Listen carefully when your teacher is showing the class how to do something new. Try to understand what is being taught as well as how to do each step.

If you don't understand what your teacher is showing the class, ask a question. Try to let your teacher know what you don't understand.

Listening carefully will also help you be ready to answer any questions your teacher may ask. You may be able to help another student by explaining how you understand what your teacher is saying.

Working Alone and with Others

When you work alone, try to connect the math you are learning to math you already know. Knowing how parts of mathematics fit together helps you remember and understand.

When you work with others, help as much as you can. *Cooperating* is another word for working together. When people cooperate, they often learn more because they share ideas.

Planning Your Time

Doing your homework on time is part of being a good math student. Make sure that you take the assignment home with you.

Have a place at home to do your homework—it could be in your room or at the kitchen table or anywhere that works for your family.

Get extra help if you are having trouble. Write questions about what you don't understand. This will help your teacher give you the extra help you need.

Mixed Addition and Subtraction

- To practice adding, do columns A, C, and E of rows 1–5.
- To practice subtracting, do columns B, D, and F of rows 1–5.
- For mixed practice, choose rows to do.

	Column A	Column B	Column C	Column D	Column E	Column F
Row 1.	4 + 4	13 − 7	5 + 6	12 − 6	6 + 8	11 − 2
Row 2.	1 + 1	12 − 9	6 + 6	14 − 9	6 + 4	15 − 6
Row 3.	0 + 3	14 − 8	7 + 8	11 − 7	9 + 6	16 − 9
Row 4.	8 + 4	12 − 4	4 + 5	12 − 5	7 + 7	10 − 5
Row 5.	2 + 2	11 − 3	6 + 7	17 − 8	8 + 9	13 − 9
Row 6.	3 + 3	12 − 7	14 − 6	0 + 0	13 − 8	7 + 5
Row 7.	13 − 4	4 + 7	8 + 6	15 − 9	8 + 7	18 − 9
Row 8.	12 − 8	13 − 6	6 + 9	14 − 7	16 − 8	7 + 6
Row 9.	9 + 4	16 − 7	9 + 9	14 − 5	3 + 8	9 + 8
Row 10.	13 − 5	3 + 9	17 − 9	8 + 5	9 + 2	15 − 8
Row 11.	10 − 8	9 − 9	7 + 4	11 − 6	8 + 8	9 + 7
Row 12.	8 + 3	11 − 9	9 + 5	7 + 8	15 − 7	11 − 4

More Practice

Work with a partner. Make flash cards for the facts that give you trouble. Practice your facts by quizzing each other with the flash cards.

Multiplication

- To practice multiplying by 0, 1, 2, and 3, do columns A and B.
- To practice multiplying by 4, 5, and 6, do columns C and D.
- To practice multiplying by 7, 8, and 9, do columns E and F.
- For mixed practice, choose rows to do.

	Column A	Column B	Column C	Column D	Column E	Column F
Row 1.	1×2	3×5	6×4	4×3	3×7	2×8
Row 2.	4×0	2×1	5×7	4×1	6×8	9×5
Row 3.	2×6	3×4	3×6	6×6	8×0	7×8
Row 4.	7×1	3×3	6×5	4×9	9×8	6×9
Row 5.	1×0	8×3	5×4	6×3	8×4	7×9
Row 6.	9×1	2×9	6×2	4×7	5×9	9×7
Row 7.	2×4	6×0	4×5	4×6	5×8	8×9
Row 8.	0×5	4×2	5×5	5×6	7×2	0×9
Row 9.	1×6	2×2	4×4	5×0	6×7	1×7
Row 10.	0×0	2×7	6×1	2×5	9×3	8×7
Row 11.	3×8	0×7	5×3	6×9	7×7	9×4
Row 12.	8×1	2×6	7×6	4×8	9×9	8×8

More Practice

Work with a partner. Make flash cards for the facts that give you trouble. Practice your facts by quizzing each other with the flash cards.

Mixed Multiplication

- For mixed practice, choose columns or rows to do.

	Column A	Column B	Column C	Column D	Column E	Column F
Row 1.	3 × 2	8 × 5	6 × 3	4 × 3	9 × 7	0 × 8
Row 2.	1 × 4	2 × 6	7 × 7	1 × 1	6 × 5	4 × 5
Row 3.	8 × 6	7 × 4	1 × 8	9 × 5	2 × 0	7 × 1
Row 4.	7 × 5	3 × 9	6 × 4	7 × 3	8 × 8	5 × 1
Row 5.	0 × 0	8 × 1	5 × 6	3 × 3	3 × 4	7 × 6
Row 6.	7 × 2	7 × 9	3 × 8	1 × 5	9 × 8	8 × 0
Row 7.	5 × 3	8 × 9	0 × 6	4 × 9	5 × 7	9 × 3
Row 8.	6 × 8	3 × 7	4 × 4	9 × 2	4 × 8	9 × 9
Row 9.	9 × 6	5 × 9	2 × 9	7 × 8	5 × 4	9 × 0
Row 10.	8 × 4	6 × 7	3 × 5	4 × 9	1 × 7	8 × 3
Row 11.	5 × 5	4 × 6	6 × 9	3 × 6	8 × 2	0 × 7
Row 12.	8 × 7	9 × 1	0 × 3	5 × 8	6 × 6	4 × 7

More Practice

Make triangular flash cards for multiplication and division fact families. Place all cards face down. Without looking at the numbers, pick up a card by a corner so that one number is covered up. Use the numbers you can see to decide what the unknown number is.

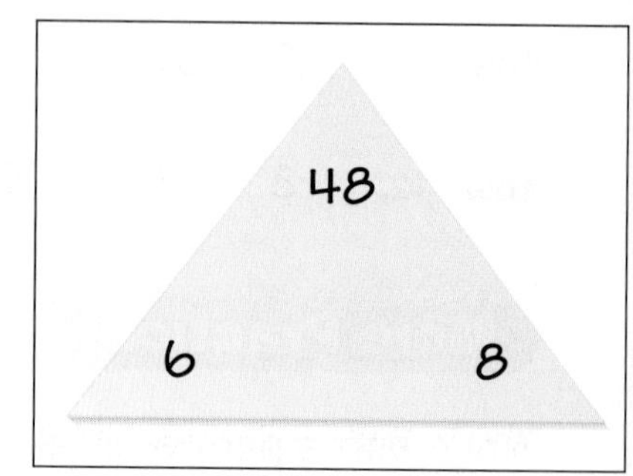

Division

- To practice dividing by 1, 2, and 3, do columns A and B.
- To practice dividing by 4, 5, and 6, do columns C and D.
- To practice dividing by 7, 8, and 9, do columns E and F.
- For mixed practice, choose rows to do.

	Column A	Column B	Column C	Column D	Column E	Column F
Row 1.	3 ÷ 3	16 ÷ 2	35 ÷ 5	54 ÷ 6	21 ÷ 7	35 ÷ 7
Row 2.	14 ÷ 2	6 ÷ 1	24 ÷ 4	5 ÷ 5	72 ÷ 8	9 ÷ 9
Row 3.	12 ÷ 3	15 ÷ 3	36 ÷ 6	45 ÷ 5	18 ÷ 9	56 ÷ 8
Row 4.	8 ÷ 2	2 ÷ 1	42 ÷ 6	28 ÷ 4	81 ÷ 9	24 ÷ 8
Row 5.	21 ÷ 3	9 ÷ 3	0 ÷ 4	15 ÷ 5	54 ÷ 9	42 ÷ 7
Row 6.	3 ÷ 1	2 ÷ 2	30 ÷ 5	48 ÷ 6	49 ÷ 7	0 ÷ 8
Row 7.	6 ÷ 2	6 ÷ 3	24 ÷ 6	18 ÷ 6	14 ÷ 7	64 ÷ 8
Row 8.	27 ÷ 3	0 ÷ 2	12 ÷ 6	5 ÷ 5	63 ÷ 9	36 ÷ 9
Row 9.	18 ÷ 3	4 ÷ 2	40 ÷ 5	20 ÷ 4	48 ÷ 8	45 ÷ 9
Row 10.	0 ÷ 3	18 ÷ 2	16 ÷ 4	25 ÷ 5	27 ÷ 9	40 ÷ 8
Row 11.	12 ÷ 2	9 ÷ 1	30 ÷ 6	36 ÷ 4	63 ÷ 7	72 ÷ 9
Row 12.	24 ÷ 3	10 ÷ 2	0 ÷ 5	32 ÷ 4	54 ÷ 9	32 ÷ 8

More Practice

Work with a partner. Make flash cards for the facts that give you trouble. Practice your facts by quizzing each other with the flash cards.

Mixed Division

- **For mixed practice, choose columns or rows to do.**

	Column A	Column B	Column C	Column D	Column E	Column F
Row 1.	18 ÷ 9	16 ÷ 4	30 ÷ 5	42 ÷ 6	72 ÷ 8	14 ÷ 7
Row 2.	20 ÷ 5	48 ÷ 6	8 ÷ 8	63 ÷ 9	12 ÷ 3	27 ÷ 9
Row 3.	18 ÷ 3	35 ÷ 7	36 ÷ 9	25 ÷ 5	18 ÷ 6	40 ÷ 8
Row 4.	56 ÷ 8	0 ÷ 5	30 ÷ 6	28 ÷ 7	0 ÷ 9	24 ÷ 4
Row 5.	4 ÷ 4	54 ÷ 9	64 ÷ 8	15 ÷ 3	15 ÷ 5	0 ÷ 8
Row 6.	54 ÷ 6	16 ÷ 2	27 ÷ 3	63 ÷ 9	8 ÷ 4	42 ÷ 7
Row 7.	28 ÷ 4	48 ÷ 8	24 ÷ 6	18 ÷ 2	21 ÷ 7	72 ÷ 9
Row 8.	9 ÷ 9	35 ÷ 5	8 ÷ 1	56 ÷ 7	20 ÷ 4	12 ÷ 6
Row 9.	0 ÷ 7	36 ÷ 4	32 ÷ 8	24 ÷ 3	81 ÷ 9	45 ÷ 5
Row 10.	0 ÷ 4	10 ÷ 2	6 ÷ 6	16 ÷ 8	40 ÷ 5	12 ÷ 4
Row 11.	14 ÷ 7	10 ÷ 5	9 ÷ 3	36 ÷ 6	24 ÷ 8	0 ÷ 6
Row 12.	5 ÷ 5	63 ÷ 7	12 ÷ 2	32 ÷ 4	21 ÷ 3	49 ÷ 7

More Practice

Make triangular flash cards for multiplication and division fact families. Place all cards face down. Without looking at the numbers, pick up a card by a corner so that one number is covered up. Use the numbers you can see to decide what the unknown number is.

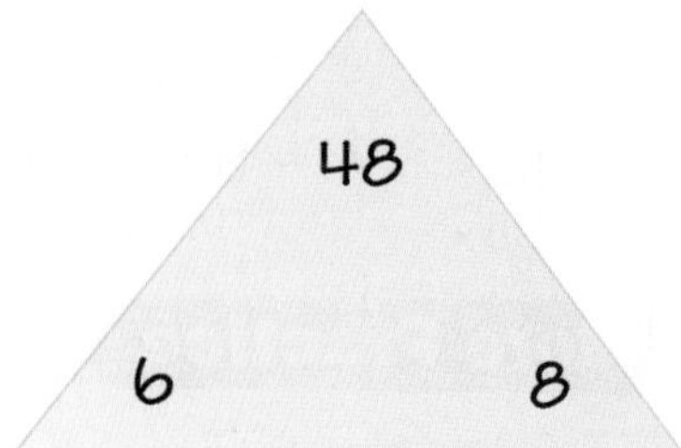

Multiplication and Division

- For mixed practice, choose rows or columns to do.

	Column A	Column B	Column C	Column D	Column E	Column F
Row 1.	$8 \div 2$	4×8	9×3	$40 \div 5$	9×6	$49 \div 7$
Row 2.	5×5	7×9	$24 \div 6$	$36 \div 4$	$12 \div 3$	5×6
Row 3.	$45 \div 9$	$20 \div 4$	4×4	6×6	$48 \div 6$	8×9
Row 4.	4×7	$64 \div 8$	9×9	8×5	0×3	$24 \div 3$
Row 5.	$35 \div 5$	6×7	$18 \div 3$	2×9	$56 \div 8$	4×9
Row 6.	$27 \div 3$	$16 \div 4$	2×1	3×6	1×1	$42 \div 6$
Row 7.	0×0	5×8	$54 \div 6$	$32 \div 4$	$21 \div 3$	7×5
Row 8.	7×8	$4 \div 4$	3×3	$25 \div 5$	7×7	$81 \div 9$
Row 9.	8×3	$72 \div 9$	$30 \div 5$	8×8	9×5	$28 \div 7$
Row 10.	$36 \div 6$	6×8	$18 \div 9$	4×6	$63 \div 7$	4×5
Row 11.	9×4	$36 \div 9$	7×4	$42 \div 7$	6×9	5×7
Row 12.	$48 \div 6$	8×7	$32 \div 8$	9×8	$45 \div 5$	$63 \div 9$

More Practice

Work with a partner. Make flash cards for the facts that give you trouble. Practice your facts by quizzing each other with the flash cards.

Adding Fractions

- To practice adding fractions with like denominators, do columns A and B.
- To practice adding fractions with unlike denominators, do columns C and D.
- To practice adding mixed numbers, do columns E and F.
- For mixed practice, choose rows to do.

Write each answer in simplest form.

	Column A	Column B	Column C	Column D	Column E	Column F
Row 1.	$\frac{1}{4} + \frac{3}{4}$	$\frac{4}{8} + \frac{2}{8}$	$\frac{5}{6} + \frac{1}{5}$	$\frac{1}{3} + \frac{5}{7}$	$2\frac{5}{9} + \frac{5}{7}$	$3\frac{2}{5} + \frac{2}{5}$
Row 2.	$\frac{3}{4} + \frac{2}{4}$	$\frac{6}{7} + \frac{2}{7}$	$\frac{1}{9} + \frac{3}{7}$	$\frac{5}{9} + \frac{2}{5}$	$2\frac{3}{8} + \frac{1}{9}$	$4\frac{3}{8} + \frac{8}{9}$
Row 3.	$\frac{7}{9} + \frac{5}{9}$	$\frac{8}{10} + \frac{1}{10}$	$\frac{1}{3} + \frac{1}{8}$	$\frac{5}{6} + \frac{6}{8}$	$3\frac{1}{6} + \frac{5}{9}$	$5\frac{2}{5} + \frac{5}{6}$
Row 4.	$\frac{3}{7} + \frac{2}{7}$	$\frac{1}{4} + \frac{2}{4}$	$\frac{5}{12} + \frac{1}{11}$	$\frac{9}{12} + \frac{3}{4}$	$2\frac{3}{5} + 1\frac{3}{4}$	$3\frac{1}{7} + \frac{4}{7}$
Row 5.	$\frac{7}{12} + \frac{2}{12}$	$\frac{10}{12} + \frac{10}{12}$	$\frac{7}{8} + \frac{1}{4}$	$\frac{3}{8} + \frac{1}{4}$	$3\frac{2}{3} + 2\frac{1}{4}$	$4\frac{3}{10} + \frac{1}{6}$
Row 6.	$\frac{4}{7} + \frac{1}{7}$	$\frac{2}{6} + \frac{5}{6}$	$\frac{3}{5} + \frac{1}{8}$	$\frac{4}{5} + \frac{6}{7}$	$4\frac{2}{8} + \frac{2}{5}$	$6\frac{5}{8} + \frac{1}{4}$
Row 7.	$\frac{3}{10} + \frac{5}{10}$	$\frac{6}{7} + \frac{1}{7}$	$\frac{1}{3} + \frac{4}{5}$	$\frac{6}{16} + \frac{1}{4}$	$3\frac{2}{6} + \frac{5}{8}$	$6\frac{4}{7} + \frac{4}{6}$
Row 8.	$\frac{2}{8} + \frac{3}{8}$	$\frac{5}{9} + \frac{1}{9}$	$\frac{2}{3} + \frac{3}{6}$	$\frac{1}{3} + \frac{3}{7}$	$1\frac{5}{9} + \frac{3}{5}$	$\frac{3}{8} + 1\frac{1}{2}$

More Practice

Work with a partner. Make flash cards for the problems. Practice by quizzing each other with the flash cards.

Subtracting Fractions

- To practice subtracting fractions with like denominators, do columns A and B.
- To practice subtracting fractions with unlike denominators, do columns C and D.
- To practice subtracting mixed numbers, do columns E and F.
- For mixed practice, choose rows to do.

Write each answer in simplest form.

	Column A	Column B	Column C	Column D	Column E	Column F
Row 1.	$\frac{2}{3} - \frac{1}{3}$	$\frac{2}{4} - \frac{1}{4}$	$\frac{8}{12} - \frac{5}{9}$	$\frac{2}{3} - \frac{1}{7}$	$4\frac{2}{5} - \frac{6}{7}$	$4\frac{5}{7} - 2\frac{3}{8}$
Row 2.	$\frac{4}{5} - \frac{3}{5}$	$\frac{5}{8} - \frac{2}{8}$	$\frac{2}{6} - \frac{1}{5}$	$\frac{5}{6} - \frac{1}{4}$	$2\frac{3}{12} - \frac{3}{6}$	$5\frac{1}{5} - \frac{3}{7}$
Row 3.	$\frac{3}{8} - \frac{1}{8}$	$\frac{3}{4} - \frac{1}{4}$	$\frac{6}{12} - \frac{1}{4}$	$\frac{4}{5} - \frac{1}{10}$	$2\frac{1}{5} - \frac{2}{6}$	$4\frac{1}{8} - 1\frac{3}{6}$
Row 4.	$\frac{3}{6} - \frac{1}{6}$	$\frac{7}{8} - \frac{1}{8}$	$\frac{1}{9} - \frac{1}{10}$	$\frac{1}{6} - \frac{1}{12}$	$5\frac{3}{12} - \frac{1}{2}$	$2\frac{5}{8} - \frac{1}{6}$
Row 5.	$\frac{3}{8} - \frac{2}{8}$	$\frac{7}{9} - \frac{4}{9}$	$\frac{11}{12} - \frac{5}{8}$	$\frac{5}{7} - \frac{1}{4}$	$3\frac{2}{4} - 2\frac{1}{8}$	$2\frac{3}{6} - 1\frac{4}{5}$
Row 6.	$\frac{2}{7} - \frac{2}{7}$	$\frac{3}{7} - \frac{2}{7}$	$\frac{3}{6} - \frac{1}{3}$	$\frac{7}{9} - \frac{2}{5}$	$2\frac{1}{3} - \frac{4}{8}$	$7\frac{1}{5} - 2\frac{3}{5}$
Row 7.	$\frac{2}{6} - \frac{1}{6}$	$\frac{5}{9} - \frac{4}{9}$	$\frac{1}{2} - \frac{1}{5}$	$\frac{5}{8} - \frac{3}{5}$	$2\frac{2}{5} - \frac{3}{8}$	$1\frac{2}{9} - \frac{5}{9}$
Row 8.	$\frac{9}{12} - \frac{3}{12}$	$\frac{9}{12} - \frac{2}{12}$	$\frac{3}{6} - \frac{1}{4}$	$\frac{2}{6} - \frac{3}{9}$	$1\frac{1}{5} - \frac{1}{4}$	$9\frac{1}{5} - 3\frac{1}{3}$

More Practice

Work with a partner. Take turns making up subtraction problems and solving them.

Table Of Measures

Customary Units of Measure / Metric Units of Measure

Length

Customary			Metric		
1 foot (ft)	=	12 inches (in.)	1 centimeter (cm)	=	10 millimeters (mm)
1 yard (yd)	=	36 inches	1 decimeter (dm)	=	10 centimeters
1 yard	=	3 feet	1 meter (m)	=	1,000 millimeters
1 mile (mi)	=	5,280 feet	1 meter	=	100 centimeters
1 mile	=	1,760 yards	1 meter	=	10 decimeters
			1 kilometer (km)	=	1,000 meters

Area

Customary			Metric		
144 square inches (in.^{2})	=	1 square foot (ft^2)	1 square centimeter (cm^2)	=	100 square millimeters (mm^2)
9 square feet	=	1 square yard (yd^2)	1 square decimeter (dm^2)	=	100 square centimeters
			1 square meter (m^2)	=	100 square decimeters

Volume

Customary			Metric		
1,728 cubic inches (in.^{3})	=	1 cubic foot (ft^3)	1 cubic centimeter (cm^3)	=	1,000 cubic millimeters (mm^3)
27 cubic feet	=	1 cubic yard (yd^3)	1 cubic decimeter (dm^3)	=	1,000 cubic centimeters
			1 cubic meter (m^3)	=	1,000 cubic decimeters

Capacity

Customary			Metric		
1 tablespoon (tbsp)	=	3 teaspoons (tsp)	1 liter (L)	=	1,000 milliliters (mL)
1 fluid ounce (fl oz)	=	2 tablespoons	1 liter	=	10 deciliters (dL)
1 cup (c)	=	8 fluid ounces	1 liter	=	1 cubic decimeter (dm^3)
1 pint (pt)	=	2 cups	1,000 liters	=	1 cubic meter (m^3)
1 quart (qt)	=	2 pints	1 milliliter (mL)	=	1 cubic centimeter (cm^3)
1 quart	=	4 cups			
1 gallon (gal)	=	4 quarts			
1 gallon	=	8 pints			

Weight/Mass

Customary			Metric		
1 pound (lb)	=	16 ounces (oz)	1 gram (g)	=	1,000 milligrams (mg)
1 ton (T)	=	2,000 pounds (lb)	1 kilogram (kg)	=	1,000 grams
			1 metric ton (t)	=	1,000 kilograms

Units of Time

1 minute (min)	=	60 seconds (s)	1 year	=	365 days
1 hour (h)	=	60 minutes	1 leap year	=	366 days
1 day	=	24 hours	1 decade	=	10 years
1 week (wk)	=	7 days	1 century	=	100 years
1 year (yr)	=	12 months (mo)	1 millennium	=	1,000 years

Glossary

absolute value The distance a number is from zero on a number line.

acute angle An angle with a measure less than 90°.

acute triangle A triangle in which each of the three angles is acute.

addend A number to be added in an addition expression. In 7 + 4 + 8, the numbers 7, 4, and 8 are addends.

algebraic expression An expression that consists of one or more variables. It could contain some constants and some operations.

Example: $2x + 3y + 6$.

angle An angle is formed by two rays with a common endpoint.

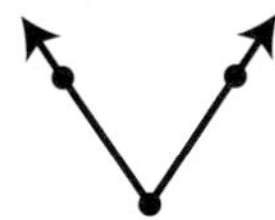

area The number of square units that cover a surface with no overlap.

array An arrangement of objects, pictures, or numbers in columns and rows.

Associative Property of Addition Changing the grouping of addends does not change their sum. It is also called the *Grouping Property of Addition.*

Example: For all numbers *a, b* and *c*, $a + (b + c) = (a + b) + c$.

Associative Property of Multiplication Changing the grouping of factors does not change their product. It is also called the *Grouping Property of Multiplication.*

Example: For all numbers *a, b* and *c*, $a \times (b \times c) = (a \times b) \times c$.

average The number found by dividing the sum of a group of numbers by the number of addends. Also known as the *mean.*

bar graph A graph in which information is shown by means of rectangular bars.

base of a geometric figure A bottom side or face of a geometric figure.

base of a power A number used as a repeated factor in a product. *Example:* 10^3. 10 is the base of the power.

capacity The amount a container can hold.

Celsius The metric temperature scale with the freezing point of water set to 0 degrees, and the boiling point set to 100 degrees.

center of a circle A point that is the same distance from all points on a circle.

central angle An angle with a vertex at the center of a circle.

certain event An event that has a probability of 1.

chord Any segment that connects two points on a circle.

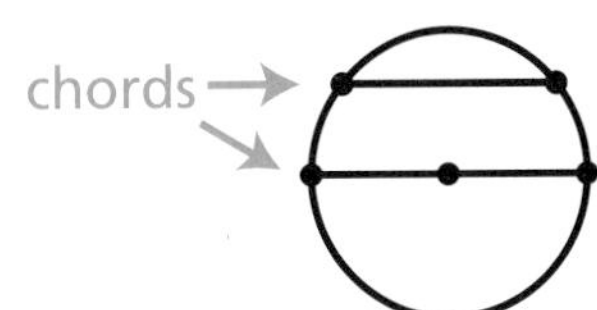

circle A closed figure in which every point is the same distance from a given point called the center of the circle.

circle graph A graph used for data that are parts of a whole.

circumference The distance around a circle.

cluster In a data display, a group of data points that are close to each other.

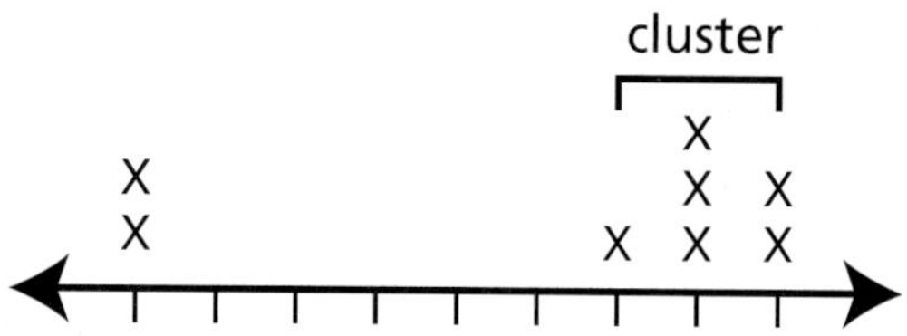

common denominator Any common multiple of the denominators of two or more fractions.

common factor A number that is a factor of two or more numbers.

common multiple A number that is shared as a multiple of two or more numbers.

Commutative Property of Addition Changing the order of addends does not change their sum. It is also called the *Order Property of Addition.*

Example: For all numbers a and b, $a + b = b + a$.

Commutative Property of Multiplication Changing the order of factors does not change their product. It is also called the *Order Property of Multiplication.*

Example: For all numbers a and b, $a \times b = b \times a$.

compatible numbers Numbers that are close to the original numbers and are easy to divide.

composite number A whole number that has more than two factors.

compound event In probability, a combination of two or more events.

cone A solid that has a circular base and a surface from a boundary of the base to the vertex.

congruent figures Figures that have the same size and shape.

coordinate plane A plane formed by two perpendicular number lines in which every point is assigned an ordered pair of numbers.

coordinates An ordered pair of numbers that locates a point in the coordinate plane with reference to the x-axis and y-axis.

cross product A product obtained by multiplying the second term of one ratio by the first term of another.

cube A solid figure that has six square faces of equal size.

cubic unit A unit for measuring volume. A cube with sides one unit long.

customary system The measurement system that uses foot, quart, pound, and degrees Fahrenheit.

cylinder A solid with two circular faces that are congruent and parallel.

data A set of numbers or pieces of information.

data set A collection of numbers or pieces of information.

decimal A number with one or more digits to the right of a decimal point.

decimal point A symbol used to separate the ones and tenths places in a decimal.

degrees A unit used to describe angle measures and also temperature. Its symbol is °.

denominator The number below the bar in a fraction.

diagonal A segment that joins two vertices of a polygon but is not a side.

diameter A chord that connects two points on the circle and passes through the center.

difference The result of subtraction.

discount A decrease in the price of an item.

Distributive Property When two addends are multiplied by a factor, the product is the same as if each addend was multiplied by the factor and those products were added.

Example: $a \times (b + c) = (a \times b) + (a \times c)$

dividend The number that is divided in a division problem.

divisible One number is divisible by another if the quotient is a whole number and there is a remainder of 0.

divisor The number by which a number is being divided.

double bar graph A graph in which data are compared by means of pairs of rectangular bars drawn next to each other.

double line graph A graph that is used to compare two or more sets of data over time.

edge The segment where two faces of a solid figure meet.

endpoint The point at either end of a line segment. The beginning point of a ray.

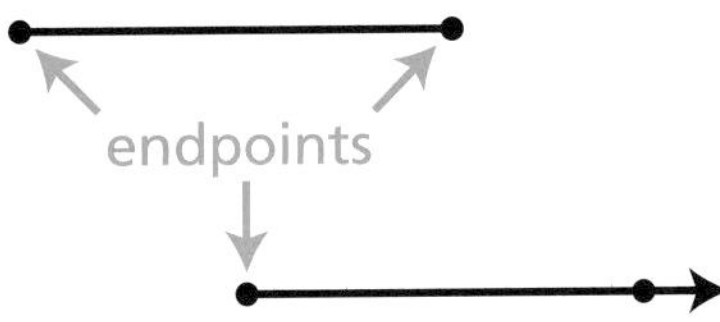

equally likely Events which have the same chance of occurring.

equation A mathematical sentence that shows that two expressions have the same value.

equilateral triangle A triangle that has three congruent sides.

equivalent fractions Fractions that show different numbers with the same value.

equivalent ratios Ratios that show the same comparison.

estimate A number close to an exact amount. An estimate tells about how much or about how many.

evaluate To substitute the values given for the variables and perform the operations to find the value of the expression.

evaluating an expression For a numerical expression, performing the operations to find the value of the expression. For an algebraic expression, substituting number(s) for the variable(s) and then performing the operations to find the value of the expression.

even number A whole number that is a multiple of 2. The ones digit in an even number is 0, 2, 4, 6, or 8. The numbers 56 and 48 are examples of even numbers.

event In probability, a result of an experiment that can be classified as certain, likely, unlikely, or impossible.

expanded form A way of writing a number as the sum of the values of its digits.

experimental probability The number of favorable outcomes in an event divided by the total number of completed trials of an experiment.

exponent The number in a power that tells the number of times the base is used as a factor.

base → 5^3 ← exponent

expression A number, variable, or any combination of numbers, variables, and operation signs.

face A flat surface of a solid figure.

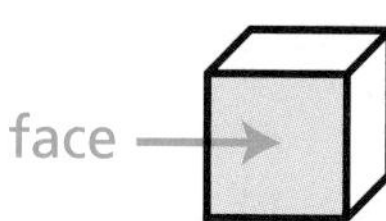

fact family Facts that are related, using the same numbers.

Examples: $1 + 4 = 5$ $4 + 1 = 5$
$5 - 1 = 4$ $5 - 4 = 1$

$3 \times 5 = 15$ $5 \times 3 = 15$
$15 \div 3 = 5$ $15 \div 5 = 3$

factor One of two or more numbers that are multiplied to give a product.

factor tree A diagram that is used to obtain the prime factorization of a number.

Fahrenheit The customary temperature scale.

fraction A number that names a part of a whole, a part of a collection, or a part of a region.

frequency In surveys, the number of times a response is chosen.

frequency table A table used to record the number of times a response is chosen.

front-end estimation Estimation by looking at the digits in the greatest place of each number.

function A rule that gives exactly one value of y for every value of x.

function table A table that matches each input value with one output value.

gap In a data display, a large space between data points.

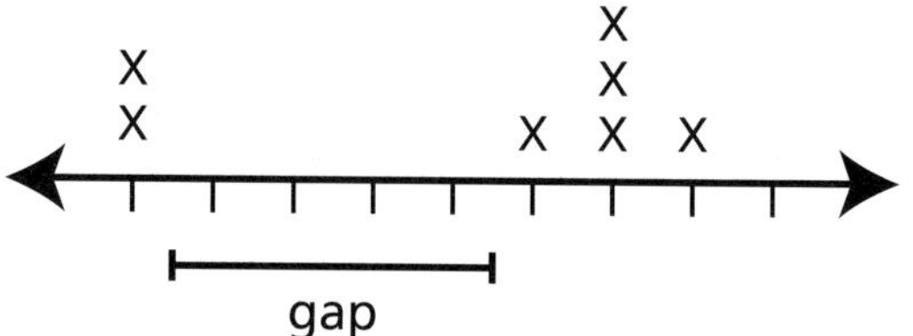

greatest common divisor (GCD) The greatest whole number that is a common factor of two or more numbers. It is also called the *greatest common factor.*

greatest common factor (GCF) The greatest whole number that is a common factor of two or more numbers. It is also called the *greatest common divisor.*

histogram A graph in which bars are used to display how frequently data occurs within equal intervals.

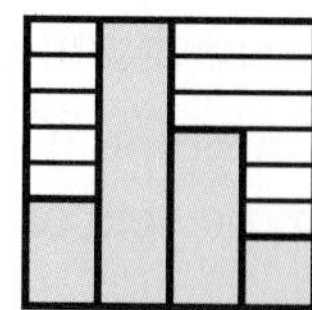

horizontal axis The x-axis in a coordinate system. It is a number line that is used to locate points to the left or to the right of the origin.

Identity Property of Addition The property which states that the sum of any number and 0 is that number.

Example: $x + 0 = x$

Identity Property of Multiplication The property which states that the product of any number and 1 is that number.

Example: $a \times 1 = a$

impossible event An event that has a probability of 0.

improper fraction A fraction that has a numerator that is greater than or equal to its denominator.

inequality A relation that is expressed by placing an inequality symbol between two expressions.

Examples: $8 > 2$, $2 < 8$, $5 + 7 \neq 6 + 4$

integers The set of whole numbers and their opposites.

intersecting lines Lines that meet or cross at a common point.

interval A measure of space between two or more numbers.

inverse operations Operations that have opposite effects. Subtraction is the inverse operation of addition. Division is the inverse operation of multiplication.

invert To interchange the numerator and the denominator.

irregular polygon A polygon with at least one side or angle that is not congruent to the others.

isosceles triangle A triangle that has at least two congruent sides.

leaf The last digit of a number in a stem-and-leaf plot.

least common denominator (LCD) The least common multiple of two or more denominators.

least common multiple (LCM) The least number that is a multiple of two or more numbers.

line A straight, continuous, and unending set of points in a plane.

line graph A graph that is used to show changes in data over time.

line of symmetry The line along which a figure can be folded so that the two halves match exactly.

line plot A diagram that organizes data using a number line.

line segment A part of a line that has two endpoints.

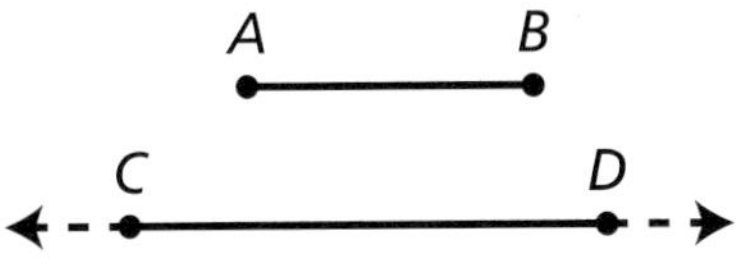

line segments *AB* and *CD*

line symmetry A figure has line symmetry if it can be folded in half and the two halves are congruent.

mass The amount of matter in an object.

mean The number found by dividing the sum of the numbers in a group by the number of addends. Also known as the *average*.

measures of central tendency The mean, median, and mode.

median The middle number when data are arranged in order.

metric system A system of measurement in which the basic units of length, mass, and capacity are the meter, gram, and liter.

midpoint The point that divides a segment into two congruent parts.

mixed number A number made up of a whole number and a fraction.

whole number → $5\frac{2}{3}$ ← fraction

↑

mixed number

mode The number or numbers that occur most often in a set of data.

multiple A number that is the product of the given number and a counting number.

negative numbers Numbers that are less than 0.

net A flat pattern that can be folded to make a solid figure.

number line A line on which numbers are assigned points.

numerator The number above the bar in a fraction.

obtuse angle An angle with a measure greater than 90° and less than 180°.

obtuse triangle A triangle that has one obtuse angle.

odd number A whole number that is not a multiple of 2. The ones digit in an odd number is 1, 3, 5, 7, or 9.

Examples: 67 and 493 are odd numbers.

opposite of a number The same number but of opposite sign. Also called the *additive inverse*.

order of operations Rules for performing operations in order to simplify expressions.

ordered pair A pair of numbers (*x*, *y*) indicating the *x*-coordinate and *y*-coordinate of a point on a graph.

origin The point where the *x*- and *y*-axis intersect in a coordinate plane.

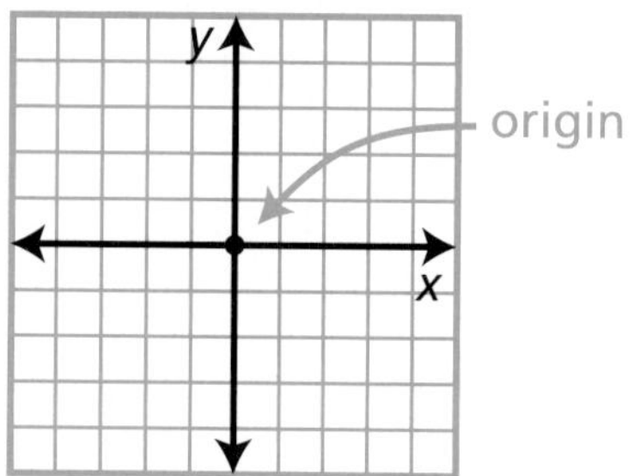

outcome A single result in a probability experiment.

outlier A number or numbers whose values are much less or much greater than the other numbers in the data set.

parallel lines Lines that lie in the same plane and do not intersect. They are everywhere the same distance apart.

parallelogram A quadrilateral in which both pairs of opposite sides are parallel.

partial product In multiplication of numbers with two or more digits, the product of each digit in one factor and the other number.

$$\begin{array}{r} 48 \\ \times\ 23 \\ \hline 144 \\ +\ 960 \\ \hline 1{,}104 \end{array}$$

← partial products (144 and 960)

per Used in talking about rates. *Per* means "to each" or "for each."

percent Per hundred. A ratio of a number to 100. The symbol for percent is %.

period In a number, each group of three digits separated by a comma.

perimeter The distance around a plane figure.

perpendicular Two lines or line segments that cross or meet to form right angles.

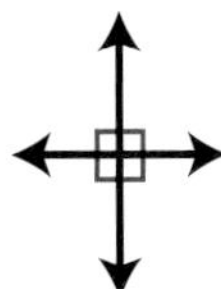

pi (π) A number defined by the ratio of the circumference of any circle to its diameter. Two common approximations used for pi are $\frac{22}{7}$ and 3.14.

pictograph A graph that uses pictures or symbols to represent data.

place value The value of a digit determined by its place in a number.

plane A flat surface made up of a continuous and unending collection of points that are not all in the same line.

point An exact location in space, represented by a dot.

polygon A simple closed plane figure made up of three or more line segments.

positive number A number that is greater than 0.

power of ten A power with a base of 10.

precision A term used to refer to the accuracy of a measurement. A smaller unit produces a more precise measurement than a larger unit.

prime factorization Writing a number as the product of its prime factors.

prime number A whole number greater than 1 that has exactly two factors.

prism A solid figure that has two parallel congruent bases and parallelograms for faces.

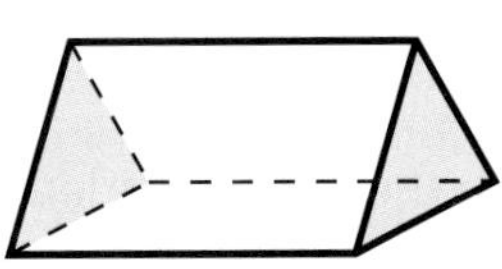

probability The chance of an event occurring. A probability can be any number from 0 through 1.

product The result in multiplication.

proper fraction A fraction in which the numerator is less than the denominator.

Example: $\frac{4}{7}$

proportion A statement that two ratios are equivalent.

pyramid A solid figure whose base can be any polygon and whose faces are triangles.

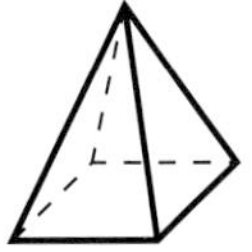

quadrant Each of the four parts into which a plane is separated by the x-axis and the y-axis. The axes are not parts of the quadrant.

quadrilateral A polygon with four sides.

quotient The result in division.

radius A segment that connects the center of a circle to any point on the circle.

range The difference between the greatest and least numbers in a set of data.

rate A ratio of two quantities using different units.

ratio A comparison of two numbers by division.

ray Part of a line that starts at an endpoint and goes on infinitely in one direction.

reciprocal The product of a number and its reciprocal is 1.

rectangle A polygon with opposite sides parallel and four right angles.

rectangular prism A solid figure with six faces that are rectangles.

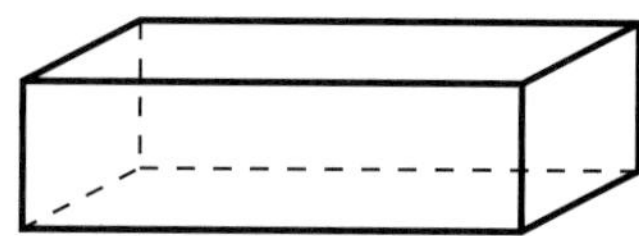

rectangular pyramid A solid figure whose base is a rectangle and whose faces are triangles.

reflection A transformation that flips a figure over a line.

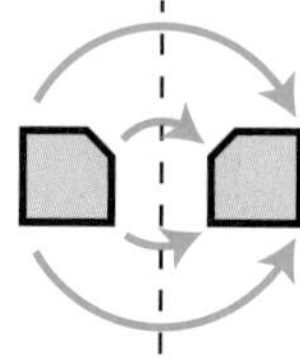

regular polygon A polygon with all sides congruent and all angles congruent.

remainder The number that is left over after one whole number is divided by another.

repeating decimal A decimal quotient that contains a repeating block of digits.

rhombus A parallelogram with all four sides congruent.

right angle An angle that measures 90°.

right triangle A triangle that has one right angle.

rotation A transformation that turns a figure about a given point.

rotational symmetry If a figure can be turned less than a full turn about a given point and the figure looks exactly the way it did before the turn, that figure has rotational symmetry.

sale price The price of an item after the discount is subtracted.

sample space A list of all possible outcomes.

scale A ratio of the measurements in a drawing to actual measurements.

scale drawing A drawing created using a scale.

scalene triangle A triangle with no congruent sides.

sequence An ordered set of numbers.

side One of the line segments that make up a polygon.

similar figures Figures that have the same shape but not necessarily the same size.

simplest form A fraction is in simplest form when the GCF of the numerator and denominator is 1.

simplify To write an expression in simplest form.

solid figure A three-dimensional figure in space.

speed A rate that shows distance per unit of time.

sphere A solid figure that is shaped like a round ball.

square A polygon with four right angles and four congruent sides.

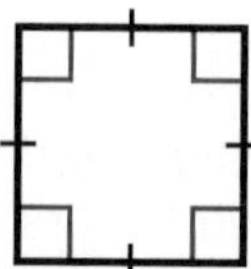

square unit A square with sides one unit long.

standard form A way of writing a number using only digits.

stem The digit or digits to the left of the leaves in a stem-and-leaf plot.

stem-and-leaf plot A frequency distribution that arranges data in order of place value.

straight angle An angle that measures 180°.

sum The result in addition.

surface area The total area of the surfaces of a solid.

survey A method of collecting information about a group of people.

symmetric figure A figure that has line or rotational symmetry.

terms of a ratio The numerator and denominator of a ratio expressed as a fraction. The numerator is the first term, and the denominator is the second term.

tessellation or tiling A repeating pattern that covers a plane without gaps or overlaps.

theoretical probability For a single event, the probability calculated by dividing the number of favorable outcomes in the event by the total number of possible outcomes.

tiling *See* tessellation.

tip A percentage portion of a total bill, customarily left after service.

transformation A transformation changes the position of a plane figure.

translation A transformation that slides a figure a given distance in a given direction.

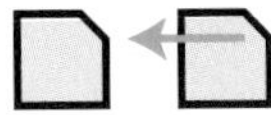

trapezoid A quadrilateral with exactly one pair of parallel sides.

tree diagram A diagram that shows combinations of outcomes of an event.

triangle A polygon with three sides.

triangular prism A prism whose bases are triangles.

triangular pyramid A pyramid whose base is a triangle.

unit cost The cost of a single item.

unit cube A cube with an edge length of 1.

unit fraction A fraction in which the numerator is 1.

unit lengths Standard lengths in the customary and metric systems of measurement.

unit rate A rate in which the second term is 1.

variable A letter that represents a number in an algebraic expression.

variable

$6 + (r \div 2)$

vertex of an angle A point common to the two sides of an angle.

vertical axis The *y*-axis in the coordinate system. It is a number line used to locate points above or below the origin.

volume The number of cubic units that make up a solid figure.

weight The measure of how heavy an object is.

***x*-axis** The horizontal number line in a coordinate plane.

***y*-axis** The vertical number line in a coordinate plane.

Zero Property of Multiplication The property which states that the product of any number and 0 is 0.

Example: $a \times 0 = 0$

Index

Credits

PERMISSIONS ACKNOWLEDGMENTS

Houghton Mifflin Mathematics © 2005, Grade 5 PE/TE

"Numbers," by Mary Cornish. Copyright © 2000 by the Modern Poetry Association. Reprinted by permission of the editor of *Poetry* and the author.

Cover (sunflower) © Photodisc/Getty Images (sunflower stalk) © GK Hart/Vikki Hart/Getty Images.

PHOTOGRAPHY

vi © Leonard de Selva/CORBIS. **vii** © Karl Weatherly/CORBIS. **BG** © Jeremy Woodhouse/Masterfile. **2** © Tom & Dee Ann McCarthy/CORBIS. **4** © Angelo Cavalli/Imagebank /Getty Images. **8** Omni Photo Communications, Inc./Index Stock. **12** © Chabruken/ Getty Images. **16** Courtesy Robert A. Siegel Auction Galleries, Inc. **17** © Leonard de Selva/CORBIS. **22** Spectrum/Robertstock.com. **26** Harold M. Lambert/SuperStock. **28** Camerique/Robertstock.com. **34** © Richard Cummins/CORBIS. **38** SuperStock. **40** Jim Corwin/Stock Boston. **42** Lars Howlett/AURORA. **46-7** © Gallo Images/CORBIS. **47** © Ralph A. Clevenger/CORBIS. **51** (br) Mark Tomalty/ Masterfile. **58** © Morton Beebe, S.F./CORBIS. **60** Guy Spangenberg/Transtock. **66** © Joe Cornish/Stone/Getty Images. **68** © Felix Clouzot/Imagebank/Getty Images. **70** © Frans Lemmens/Imagebank/Getty Images. **72** Robin Hill/Index Stock. **76** Joe Sohm/The Image Works. **79** Danilo Boschung/eStock Photo. **80** Margot Granitsis/The Image Works. **88** © Photomondo/Taxi/Getty Images. **84** Spencer Grant/PhotoEdit. **96** Roger Allyn Lee/SuperStock. **97** Comstock KLIPS. **99** Classic PIO Collection. **108** © Bettman/CORBIS. **110** NASA. **114** © Bettman/CORBIS. **118** Topham/The Image Works. **120** © Otto Herschan/Hulton Archive/Getty Images. **126** Deborah Davis/ PhotoEdit. **128** Marilyn "Angel" Wynn/nativestock.com. **129** Courtesy of The Montana Historical Society. **130** PhotoDisc/Getty Images. **134-5** (b) © Michael & Patricia Fogden/CORBIS. **134** (t) Tom Ulrich/Getty Images. **146** Frans Lanting/Minden Pictures. **147** PhotoDisc/Getty Images. **152** Reinhard/Mauritius/ Robertstock.com. **153** Look GMBH/eStock Photo. **156** Tom Brakefield/SuperStock. **159** IT Stock Int'l/Index Stock. **170** Look GMBH/eStock Photo. **172** Kenneth W. Fink/Photo Researchers, Inc. **176** © Art Wolfe/Stone/Getty Images. **178** Tim Davis/Photo Researchers, Inc. **186** James Urbach/SuperStock. **190** © Lawrence Migdale/Stone/Getty Images. **198** AP/Wide World Photos. **205** © Carl Schneider/Taxi/Getty Images. **210-1** Bob Thomas/Getty Images. **210** (b) Al Bello/Allsport/Getty Images. **211** Ben Radford/Getty Images. **222** The Field Museum, Neg# GN89717, John Weinstein. **224** © Julie Toy/Taxi/Getty Images. **228** Targa/agefotostock. **229** Targa/agefotostock. **230** © Gail Mooney/CORBIS. **231** (t) Ronald Sheridan@Ancient Art & Architecture Collection. **232** courtesy Jeff Koons. **235** Rudi Von Briel/PhotoEdit. **246** Jeff Greenberg/The Image Works. **254** Mark Thayer/Index Stock. **256** Richard Hutchings/PhotoEdit. **260** David Young-Wolff/PhotoEdit. **266** MedioImages/Index Stock. **268** BSIP Agency/Index Stock. **270** Syracuse Newspapers/The Image Works. **272** ComstockKLIPS. **274** Myrleen Cate/PhotoEdit. **280** © Mike Powell/Allsport Concepts/Getty Images. **290** © Neil Rabinowitz/ CORBIS. **292** Fujifotos/The Image Works. **296-7** © Lester Lefkowitz/CORBIS. **308** © Owen Franken/CORBIS. **316** Benelux Press/ Index Stock/Picture Quest. **322** © Bruce Forster/Stone/ Getty Images. **324** © David Hanson/Stone/Getty Images. **328** © Paul A. Souders/CORBIS. **329** Paul Conklin/PhotoEdit. **332** NOVASTOCK/PhotoEdit. **342** © SW Productions/PhotoDisc/Getty Images. **343** Bill Schoening, Vanessa Harvey/REU program/ NOAO/AURA/NSF. **346** David Young-Wolff/PhotoEdit. **350** © Christoph Wilhelm/Taxi/Getty Images. **352** Jose Galvez/PhotoEdit. **354** Scott Barrow/ImageState. **355** Royalty-Free/CORBIS. **356** (l) SuperStock. (r) Stephens B. Myers/ImageState. **357** PROF. P. MOTTA / DEPT. OF ANATOMY / UNIVERSITY, "LA SAPIENZA", ROME / SPI/Custom Medical Stock Photo. **358** Novastock/ PhotoEdit. **360** Tony Freeman/PhotoEdit. **362** Daemmrich/Stock Boston. **364** © Globus,Holway & Lobel/CORBIS. **365** © AFP/ CORBIS. **366** Table Mesa Productions/Index Stock. **368** © Royalty-Free/CORBIS. **372** (t) (l) Comstock KLIPS. **376-7** © H.D. Thoreau/CORBIS. **376** (m) USPS. **377** (r) USPS. **388** © Gunter Marx/CORBIS. **390** Frank Siteman/agefotostock. **398** R.O. Photosure.com/agefotostock. **400** R. Krubner/Robertstock.com. **401** Herb Levart/SuperStock. **408** S. Piumatti/Robertstock.com. **409** © Ralph A. Clevenger/CORBIS. **414** © George Hunter/Stone/ Getty Images. **416** SuperStock. **417** Bill Aron/PhotoEdit. **420** The Newark Museum/Art Resource, NY. **422** Art Resource, NY. **444** © Greg Pease/CORBIS. **464** © Lester Lefkowitz/CORBIS. **470-1** © Lee Snider; Lee Snider/CORBIS. **470** (b) © Bettmann/CORBIS. **471** (b) © Bob Rowan; Progressive Image/CORBIS. **475** (br) PhotoDisc/Getty Images. **482** © Kelley-Mooney Photography/ CORBIS. **488** © Garry Gay/Imagebank/Getty Images. **496** Tony Freeman/PhotoEdit. **501** © Robert Holmes/CORBIS. **504** Tomas del Amo/Index Stock. (b) ComstockKLIPS. **508** Jeff Greenberg/ PhotoEdit. **514** Davis Barber/PhotoEdit. **516** Bob Burch/Index Stock. **518** © Guy Grenier/Masterfile. **526** © Duomo/CORBIS. **537** © Richard Cummins/CORBIS. **552-3** © Blaine Harrington III/CORBIS. **553** (t) RON CHAPPLE/Getty Images. **584** Alan Kearney/agefotostock. **588** © Michael Keller/CORBIS. **590** Barry Runk/Stan/Grant Heilman Photography, Inc. **594** © Bob Krist/CORBIS. **598** Walter Geiesperger/agefotostock. **602** Tom Rosenthal/SuperStock. **603** © Duomo/CORBIS. **608** Tony & Daphne Hallas/Astrophoto.com. **618** © George Hall/CORBIS. **628-9** Gary D. Gaugler/Photo Researchers, Inc. **629** (t) Gary D. Gaugler/Photo Researchers, Inc. **629** (tm)(bm)(b) Gary D. Gaugler/Visuals Unlimited. **636** (tr) Mark Tomalty/Masterfile. **638-9** © Chris Noble/Getty Images. **641** © Ark/Alamy. **645** © Ken Biggs/Getty Images.

ASSIGNMENT PHOTOGRAPHY

xxii, xxviii, xxix © HMCo./Joel Benjamin.

632 (bl) © HMCo./Ray Boudreau.

637 © HMCo./Jade Albert.

650 © HMCo./Ken Karp.

653-657 © HMCo./Joel Benjamin.

2 (t), **56, 144, 220, 306, 386, 480, 562** © HMCo./Dave Bradley.

Credits continued

54, 62, 81, 90, 92, 102, 142, 148, 155, 163, 164, 174, 192, 200, 218, 240, 248, 262, 266, 282, 286, 305, 311, 318, 327, 338, 344, 371, 384, 392, 393, 412, 434, 438, 448, 450, 452, 456, 460, 478, 484, 486, 491, 492, 506, 510, 532, 536, 540, 560, 564, 566, 568, 572, 578, 580, 581, 592, 613, 614, 616, 637 © HMCo./Angela Coppola.

xxiii, xxiv, xxv, © HMCo./Allan Landau.

48, 49, 137 (tr), **299** (tr), **300** (bl), **301** (bc), **478** (tr), **478** (br) © HMCo./Dave Starrett.

2 (cr), **51, 472** (tr), **633** (r) © HMCo./Ron Tanaka.

260 © HMCo./Tony Scarpetta.

ILLUSTRATION

650: (banner) Russell Benfanti

18, 58, 91, 111, 122, 166, 167 (b), **170, 190, 202, 204, 222, 264, 284, 308, 326, 342 , 410, 426, 496, 521, 526, 534** (b), **547, 580** (b), **595, 604,** Argosy. **139, 301** (b), **379, 554** (tr) Steve Attoe. **64, 350, 420, 431** (l), **437, 444, 455** (b), **452, 463, 465** (b) Kenneth Batelman. **136** (tr), **481** (tr) Gary Bullock. **43** Estelle Carol. **417** (r), **432** John Edwards, Inc. **79** Ruth Flanigan. **647** Jim Gordon. **197, 337, 519** Mike Gordan. **215** (tr,) **378** (tr), **473** (br), **557** (b) Jeff Grunewald. **163, 207, 231, 251, 319, 407, 417** Ken Hansen. **150** Robert Hynes. **300** (tr), **304** (r) Kelly Kennedy. **642-43** Dave Klug. **381** (c) Bernadette Lau. **213** (br) **556** (bl) Dave McKay. **539** (tr) Jack McMaster. **154** Martucci Designs. **632** (tr) Dirk Michiels. **112, 648-49** Karen Minot. **10,14, 37,499, 619** Ortelius Design, Inc. **379** (cr), **474** (bl), **562** (br) Jun Park. **158** (t), Precision Graphics. **158** (bl), **158** (br), **162**, **266** Precision Graphics. **26, 65, 66, 94, 108, 182, 194, 206, 239, 254, 276, 288, 340, 409, 457, 458, 466, 500, 520, 529, 533, 534** (t), **548, 550** (t), **573, 574, 586, 610,** Rob Schuster. **218** (tr), **555** (tr) Paul Watson. **640** Rob Wood.

All tech art by Pronk & Associates.